9 Strand Knot © Brian Wyvill

Rope and Tea Pot © Brian Wyvill & Chengfu Yao

R.A. Earnshaw, B. Wyvill (Eds.)

New Advances in Computer Graphics

Proceedings of CG International '89

With 375 Figures Including 126 in Colour

Springer-Verlag

Tokyo Berlin Heidelberg New York London Paris

RAE A. EARNSHAW
Head of Computer Graphics
University of Leeds
Leeds LS2 9JT, UK

BRIAN WYVILL
Department of Computer Science
University of Calgary
Calgary, Alberta
Canada T2N 1N4

About the Cover:
The cover picture shows a scene from the computer animated movie, *The Great Train Rubbery*, Brian Wyvill designed the train made from an iso-surface in a scalar field. Brian Graham made the bridge from an old Canadian Pacific design, Jeff Allan bent the bridge using dynamic simulation techniques and Angus Davis wrote much of the rendering and support software.

The inside cover shows two scenes which demonstrate the results of an algorithm for generating knots and braids. Chengfu Yao developed a generalised cylinder algorithm and draped the rope over the table. Brian Wyvill generated the knot algorithm from some ideas by Larry Bates. Chris Bone and Dave Jevans wrote the ray tracer and selected the material's constants using the Hall Light model.

ISBN-13: 978-4-431-68095-6   e-ISBN-13: 978-4-431-68093-2
DOI: 10.1007/978-4-431-68093-2

Preface

This volume presents the proceedings of the 7th International Conference of the Computer Graphics Society, CG International '89, held at the University of Leeds, UK, June 27-30, 1989. Since 1982 this conference has continued to attract high-quality research papers in all aspects of computer graphics and its applications. Originally the conference was held in Japan (1982-1987), but in 1988 was held in Geneva, Switzerland. Future conferences are planned for Singapore in 1990, USA in 1991, Japan in 1992, and Canada in 1993.

Recent developments in computer graphics have concentrated on the following: greater sophistication of image generation techniques; advances in hardware and emphasis on the exploitation of parallelism, integration of robotics and AI techniques for animation, greater integration of CAD and CAM in CIM, use of powerful computer graphics techniques to represent complex physical processes (visualization), advances in computational geometry and in the representation and modelling of complex physical and mathematical objects, and improved tools and methods for HCI. These trends and advances are reflected in this present volume. A number of papers deal with important research aspects in many of these areas.

From the papers submitted to CG International '89, the International Program Committee selected 44 papers. These have been grouped together into 10 chapters as follows: Algorithms, Computational Geometry, Computer Animation, Computer Art, Theory and Graphics Interface, Hardware, Image Processing, Modelling and CAD, Ray Tracing, Rendering, and Applications. The latter chapter contains a number of contributions in the general area of applications. These were also selected from those submitted. One of the objectives here is to encourage and promote dialogue between computer graphics and its applications areas.

In addition to the reviewed submitted papers, there are also 4 invited papers and one keynote paper. These represent leading-edge research aspects in computer graphics and discuss issues pertinent to the continued advancement of the subject. Countries represented in this volume include USA, UK, Japan, Canada, Australia, People's Republic of China, Finland, Switzerland, Italy, France, Netherlands, and New Zealand. There is thus a wide international coverage.

It is being increasingly recognized that computer graphics is a tool for users and practitioners, not just researchers in computer graphics. This relationship with the real world of scientific investigation has two-way benefits. The application areas benefit by being able to use the latest methods and techniques, and even the latest hardware. In turn, computer graphics benefits by lessons learned in the general areas of useablity, HCI, application interfaces, and the metrics of performance. Visualization in science and engineering is one such area of keen interest: scientisits and engineers are realizing that computer graphics and animation is an important tool for research.

The fields of graphics and image processing are moving closer together through the important developments on the hardware front, and each are benefiting greatly from this mutual association. This volume brings together many of the leading key researchers in these fields. This symbiosis will be important for all those having a serious interest in evaluating current research work and profiling future developments and applications.

Thanks are expressed to the following cosponsors of the Conference: Computer Graphics Society, British Computer Society, University of Leeds, Japan Systems Company Ltd, Graphica Computer Corporation, and the University of Calgary. We are also grateful to all those who assisted with the reviewing of papers and the organization of the Conference. A list of the Committees of the Conference and the reviewers appears at the end of this volume.

R.A. Earnshaw
B. Wyvill

Table of Contents

Chapter 8: Modelling and CAD

Chapter 9: Ray Tracing

Chapter 10: Rendering

Chapter 11: Applications

Chapter 1
Invited and Keynote Papers

An Interactive Display for the 21st Century: Beyond the Desktop Metaphor

H. Fuchs

KEYWORDS: interactive three dimensional computer graphics, head-mounted display, 3D interaction, real-time graphics.

Vannevar Bush's 1945 vision of a personal desk-sized machine (the *memex*) containing a massive library of information and powerful search and recall mechanisms remains an inspired view of a useful personal computer. By 1970 Alan Kay at Xerox Palo Alto (California) Research Center was proposing a dynamic book-sized computer, a *dynabook*, that would satisfy most of the needs of users of all ages. By 1973 a group of his colleagues had built a small desk-sized computer, the Alto, that was starting to satisfy Kay's vision. By the mid-1980's the Apple Macintosh, and similar machines, were having the same effect on users worldwide. Common to all these visions was the computer interaction mechanism consisting of a 2D computer display that appeared like stylized version of the user's desktop: papers strewn about, ones on top obscuring ones below; various objects of interest, such as trash cans and clocks, serving their obvious and useful functions. The user moved objects about the screen and took them in and out of file folders by direct manipulation. In certain situations, the user could "zoom in" to certain papers for a closer look.

This is a fine model for 2D applications and is properly on its way toward universal adoption.   Applying it to 3D applications is more troublesome: it is difficult to visualize 3D objects and scenes on a 2D screen and even more difficult to manipulate them.   To understand the additional burden of 3D over 2D, consider the comprehension of a 3D design of a small house versus the comprehension of a 2D example of schematic layout -- current graphic workstation well adapted to the schematic layout, not well adapted for understanding the 3D spacial structure of the house. Just moving through the house, constantly changing viewing position and looking about would be very awkward. Modifying even a simple portion of the design, such as moving the location of a door, would indeed be difficult.

Sutherland's 1965 vision of the "ultimate display" and his 1968 demonstration of head-mounted display as the first approximation remain the most promising user devises for truly interactive 3D display of the 21st century. Unfortunately Sutherland's 1968 display was so far ahead of its time that little of the enabling technology was then (or even now is) available. A few researchers [Fisher 86] have been developing this vision, but most experts have relegated the head-mounted display to a mere paragraph in each textbook. The military applications have been attractive enough, however, that there is sufficient long-standing interest to support a two-day conference ("Helmet-Mounted Displays", SPIE conference Number 1116, March 28-29, 1989, Orlando, Florida).

Several difficult problems need to be solved before a widely useful system can enlarge the user's computer space from the virtual desk to the virtual office. The image generation needs to be at least 30 frames per second and very likely 60 frames per second. The head gear needs to be reduced from its current helmet size to one that's closer to the size of a pair of clip-on sunglasses. The head-tracking should allow the user to roam within an office-sized environment without constraints.

Fortunately several new technologies based on microelectronics developments might provide solutions to the above problems. The solutions may be as far away as today's "walkman" is from crystal radios, so predictions of success are premature at best. Many would recommend that we abandon these systems for several decades to allow technology to develop. One can only hope that there are some developers who are not content to wait so passively.

ACKNOWLEDGMENTS

The author is grateful for a decade of discussions and work on head-mounted displays and related topics with colleagues Fred Brooks and Steve Pizer. Many graduate research assistants have worked on the project. Particularly appreciated are discussions in recent semesters with James Chung and Michael T. Kelley, and help in the last few weeks from Randy Brown.

The UNC research on head-mounted displays is supported in part by National Institutes of Health grant RR 02170-05 and Office of Naval Research contract N00014-86-0680.

REFERENCES

Bush, Vannevar (1945) As we may think. *Atlantic Monthly*. July 1945.

Chung, J C, M R Harris, F P Brooks, H Fuchs, M T Kelley, J Hughes, M Ouh-young, C Cheung, R L Holloway, M Pique (1989) Exploring virtual worlds with head-mounted displays. to appear in *SPIE Proceedings: Non-Holographic True 3-Dimensional Display Technologies*, vol. 1083.

Fisher, S S, M McGreevy, J Humphries, W Robinett (1986) Virtual environment display system. *Proceedings 1986 Chapel Hill Workshop on Interactive 3D Graphics*, ACM, pp. 77-87.

Sutherland, I E (1965) The ultimate display. *Proceedings of the 1965 IFIP Congress*, vol. 2, pp. 506-508.

Sutherland, I E. (1968) A head-mounted three-dimensional display. *Proceedings of the 1968 Fall Joint Computer Conference*, vol. 33, pp. 757-764.

Biography

Henry Fuchs is Federico Gil professor of computer science and adjunct professor of radiation oncology at the University of North Carolina at Chapel Hill. He received a BA in Information and Computer Science from the University of California at Santa Cruz in 1970 and a PhD in computer science from the University of Utah in 1975. He has been an associate editor of *ACM Transactions on Graphics* (1983-1988) and the guest editor of its first issue. He was the technical program chair for ACM Siggraph'81 Conference, chairman of the 1985 Chapel Hill Conference on Advanced Research in VLSI, and chairman of the 1986 Chapel Hill Workshop on Interactive 3D Graphics. He serves on various advisory committees, including that of NSF's Division of Microelectronic Information Processing Systems and Stellar Computer's Technical Advisory Board.

Address: Department of Computer Science, Sitterson Hall, University of North Carolina, Chapel Hill, NC 27599-3175 USA. Telephone: (919) 962-1911.

Cellular Self-Reproducing Automata As a Parallel Processing Model for Botanical Colony Growth Pattern Simulation

T.L. Kunii and Y. Takai

ABSTRACT

A cellular automaton is a model of natural systems composed of many identical components with local interactions. Particularly, self-reproduction property inherent in the cellular automaton is essential for modeling the biological and ecological growth pattern formation. In simulating such behaviour of cellular self-reproducing automata, interactive visual computing allows us to get intuition from the model more easily and quickly. In this paper, we try to visualize the growth of a botanical colony based on Langton's two-dimensional self-reproducing cellular automaton. The colony consists of a reproducible fringe surrounding a growing core of empty shells. Realistic images of simulated life and death are shown vividly through an interactive visual simulation technique. We also discuss a parallel processing approach as an efficient method for high-speed visual simulation of large-scale cellular automata.

Keywords: cellular automata, self-reproduction, visual simulation, landscape design, parallel processing.

1. INTRODUCTION

A cellular automaton is a mathematical model of complex natural systems composed of a large number of identical components with limited local interactions. Particularly, self-reproductivity inherent in the cellular automaton is essential for modeling biological and ecological growth patterns generation. Cellular automata were originally conceived by John von Neumann as formal structures for modeling self-reproducing machines [Neumann 1966]. Research on cellular automata was very popular in the 1960's, however, it was considered almost disreputable by the 1970's.

A renaissance in cellular automaton research began a few years ago when interactive computer graphics techniques made it feasible to visualize the complex behaviour of cellular automata [Wolfram 1986]. Visual computing is straightforward and intuitive in simulating cellular self-reproducing automata. It can be said that the visual computing has established a new research area: "experimental mathematics" [Brown 1987].

Besides contribution to theoretical fields, the visual computation extended applications of cellular automata to include image generation of botanical specimens and, further, computer-aided natural landscape design. Visualization based on a geometric interpretation of L-system [Prusinkiewicz 1988] which can produce truly realistic plants images, however, seems still limited in essence, attacking only the surface structures of plants and not concerned with the internal principles of life to form shapes. Morphological approach is no longer sufficient. Consideration of cause and effect in a life cycle is indispensable to more realistic visualization of plants including environmental factors. Visualization based on cellular automata allows us to represent the developmental process of living organisms following a central dogma in biochemistry: "transcription and translation".

In this paper, we try to visualize the growth of a botanical colony based on Langton's 2-dimensional self-reproducing cellular automaton. Firstly, we will review Langton's automaton which gives necessary conditions of self-reproduction while satisfying the significant criteria of transcription and translation. Taking an environmental factor into consideration, we explain that the model is powerful enough to simulate botanical colony growth patterns. Secondly, realistic images of simulated life and death are shown through interactive visual simulation. The method used is based on a visualization technique composed of concrete and abstract steps. We also discuss a parallel processing approach as the efficient way to visually simulate the behaviour of large-scale cellular automata at a high speed.

2. SELF-REPRODUCTION IN CELLULAR AUTOMATA

Von Neumann's automaton

The study on cellular automata owes much to the pioneering work of von Neumann [Neumann 1966]. His approach to the problem of self-reproduction was mathematical. He could exhibit a universal Turing machine embedded in a two-dimensional cellular array using 29 states per cell and the 5-cell (left, right, top, bottom, and itself) neighbourhood.

In a formal manner, a two-dimensional cellular automaton is defined by a four-tuple:

$$(Z \times Z, Q, X, F)$$

where Z is a set of integers, Q is a finite set of states, X gives the shape of the neighbourhood, and F is a state transition function. An element of $Z \times Z$ is called a cell. Mapping from a set of cells to a set of states is referred to as the configuration of a cellular space. The state transition function F is defined over an n-Cartesian product of the state set Q:

$$F: Q^n \rightarrow Q.$$

On the other hand, a set of the neighbours is defined as an m-tuple of a two-dimensional vectors:

$$X = (z1, z2, ..., zm).$$

For example, von Neumann's 5-cell neighbourhood, which is very common in two-dimensional cellular automata, is represented as:

Neumann's neighbourhood = ((0, 0), (-1, 0), (1, 0), (0, -1), (0, 1)).

The behavior of a cellular automaton is determined by the state transition function which fixes the next state of each cell based on the current states of the neighbours. According to the state transition rule, all the cells update their current states in a lock step. That is, when we denote the current state of a cell z as $C(z)$, the next state $C'(z)$ is obtained through the state transition function together with its neighbourhood as follows:

$$C'(z) = F(C(z+z1), C(z+z2), C(z+z3), C(z+z4), C(z+z5)).$$

Von Neumann's machine can construct in the array any configuration of cell states described on its input "tape" which is a part of configuration of the machine. Such a machine is called a universal constructor. Self-reproduction follows as a special case where the machine described on the tape is the universal constructor itself.

From the practical point of view, on the other hand, von Neumann's machine was too complex to implement and simulate the whole behaviour of self-reproduction. Even by using the supercomputers of today, we will not obtain any vivid images of simulated life and death on a screen. His machine is so powerful in the sense of computational universality that it includes too many functions not necessary for imitating life.

Von Neumann's work, however, suggests a significant criterion of what is self-reproduction. That is, a self-reproducible machine has to treat its stored information in the two crucially different ways: (1) translation (as instructions to be executed), and (2) transcription (as data to be copied). A machine may be called self-reproducible iff the machine contains the mechanism for the translation and transcription. Actually, the mechanism constitutes a central dogma in real life: genetic information embedded in DNA strands is copied to messenger RNA (transcription stage), then all the proteins building up a cell are synthesized by transfer RNA and ribosomes reading the strand of messenger RNA (translation stage). Hence, according to the criterion, trivial cellular automata such as a well-known "Life Game" [Gardner 1971] are not recognized as self-reproducible.

Langton's automaton

How simple can a machine become while still retaining the capability of reproducing itself? In other words, what kind of logical organization is necessary for an automaton to be able to reproduce itself? Langton answered the question by presenting a very elegant and beautiful self-reproducible cellular automaton [Langton 1984]. His machine was based on a functional element used in Codd's universal constructor [Codd 1968].

Codd demonstrated a universal machine in a 2-dimensional cellular array using 8 states (from "0" through "7") per cell and von Neumann's 5-cell neighbourhood. The most fundamental structure of Codd's automaton is a data-path. The data-path is composed of a sequence of cells in state "1" surrounded by cells in state "2" (sheath cells). The data-paths are used to transmit data in a form of signals. A signal consists of packets of two co-traveling states: a signal state itself followed by a state "0".

As a basic timing element, Codd uses a periodic emitter, which consists of a data-path folding back on itself to form a loop. This simple structure is very important, because it constitutes a dynamic storage element to store a program! Note that both von Neumann and Codd used moving arms back and forth over the stationary program (tape) to read. Hence, the idea of dynamic storage is of tremendous help in the design of a self-reproducible machine since it can eliminate the complicated structures associated with the moving arms.

To construct a structure identical in size to itself, Langton made the storage loop a perfect square, and stored the instructions necessary to build one side and one corner of the loop. Hence, the initial shape of the reproducible configuration is similar to that of a letter of "P". The reproducible loop is 10 cells high and 15 cells wide, and a data-path of 28 cells long is possible to store cycling instructions. Where the transcription and translation will be done? The transcription is carried out at a T-junction of the data-path, then at the tip of the data-path stretched from another end of the T-junction (construction arm), the translation of instructions arrived is achieved.

The whole instruction sequence (program) necessary for self-reproduction is 70-70-70-70-70-70-40-40, where "-" means state "1". The six "70" signals will extend the construction arm by six cells, while the two "40" signals will build the left hand corner at the end of the arm. When these instructions cycle around the loop four times, they will repeat the process of building a side and a corner four times. This process continues until the arm has closed back on and fused with itself. Then, an offspring is born after 151 unit time. From an analogical viewpoint, the instructions sequence cycling in a loop plays the role of a DNA strand in a real cell, and the instructions traveling the construction arm behaves like messenger RNA, which will be a new DNA strand for the offspring loop.

To achieve the self-reproduction above, Langton modified Codd's transition function, and defined the 119 independent rules over a cellular space with an 8-state and von Neumann's 5-cell neighbourhood [Langton 1984]. The transition function satisfies a kind of conservation law:

$$F(0, 0, 0, 0, 0) = 0$$

which means that the ground state "0" remains invariant under time evolution. Moreover, we note that Langton's transition function is symmetrical in rotation:

$$F(C, T, R, B, L) = F(C, R, B, L, T) = F(C, B, L, T, R) = F(C, L, T, R, B)$$

where C, T, R, B, and L stand for a center, top, right, bottom, and left cell state, respectively. This symmetrical property is very essential for the two-dimensionally expanding colony of reproducible loops.

Colony growth patterns generation

As an offspring loop is a perfect duplicate of the parent loop, it will act in the same manner as its parent. After each offspring was born, the construction arm of the parent loop is turned 90 degrees counterclockwise. Hence, the first loop will produce four child loops around it. After the production of the fourth offspring, what happens to the original loop? When the tip of the construction arm of a loop hits another loop residing in a potential offspring site, the loop retracts its arm back into the body. Then the retracted arm blocks its own data-path, which is the beginning of killing itself. That is, when the cycling instructions run into a blockade inside the data-path, they are erased one by one until the loop is left empty of signal states. This is the end of life cycle of the loop.

Each of the four children takes almost the same life cycle as that of the parent. Hence, over a period of time, there will emerge an expanding colony of loops growing out into the cellular space. The colony obtained consists of a reproducible fringe surrounding a growing core of the dead loops.

Here, we must emphasize the fact that the loops will behave differently in different environments in spite of their identical structures. Each loop does not always reproduce its four children. How many offsprings will be produced is determined dynamically by an environmental condition of the parent loop. The determinate environmental factor is the concentration of loops in the immediate neighbourhood.

Parallel processing approach

The primary objective of cellular automata is to abstract the world composed of identical elements with local interactions. Parallelism among the components is essential. Hence, cellular automata may also be able to provide good models for parallel processing. Since possible states to be assigned to each cell are limited to some, however, it is not very useful to apply them directly to asynchronous MIMD machines such as multicomputer networks [Reed 1987]. On the contrary, in the case of VLSI algorithms such as systolic arrays [Kung 1988], cellular automaton models are still available.

From the viewpoint of simulating cellular automata, on the other hand, an MIMD parallel processing approach is very effective. For simulating a cellular automaton by using a conventional sequential machine, one prepares two sets of arrays for the cellular space and a state transition table. Then, a pair of the arrays works as a double buffer for updating all the cell states according to the transition rule. If we have as many processors as cells to be simulated, all the state transition can be done at the same time. It can be safely said that further research on a cellular automaton and its potential applications will be driven only by the parallel processing technique.

So far, many special-purpose parallel machines have been proposed and built for simulating the cellular automaton algorithms efficiently [Preston 1984]. Large-scale and fine-grained SIMD machines such as a Connection Machine [Hillis 1985] are very adequate to simulate the behaviour of a very large cellular space. The potential bottle-neck in updating the cellular space lies in the computation of the state transition function. In such a case, associative memory can be used for fast looking up the transition table.

3. VISUAL SIMULATION OF GROWING COLONY

Methodology

A cellular automaton is a purely formal model for discrete dynamical systems. Therefore, it is not easy to extract some essence from the complex evolution of cellular automata with higher dimensions. This was one of the reasons of disreputation of cellular automaton research in the 1970's.

When recognizing certain complex physical phenomenon, we usually think in two steps: a concrete step and an abstract step. In the concrete step, we assign a different shape to each conceptual state or action within a system in mind. In the abstract step, on the other hand, new concepts are constructed over a set of entities. We usually alternate these two steps almost unconsciously.

To get better intuition from the chaotic behaviour of a cellular space, we also have to take the same steps as those of recognition. In addition, in the case of simulating the growth of patterns on the cellular space, a factor of processing speed should be emphasized. Visual pattern development at a moderate speed is very impressive to human eyes, which may create new ideas with higher level abstraction.

For visualizing the botanical colony growth patterns based on Langton's cellular automaton, we take the following three steps:

(1) The 1st concrete step
Bind a different visual material to each cell state. Since Langton's automaton is defined on an 8-state cellular space, we prepare 7 visually different materials except the ground state.

(2) The 1st abstract step
Identify the stages in the life cycle of each loop. According to the number of 1's contained in a tape cycling around a loop, we divide the life cycle into three stages: alive (12), dying (13-26), and dead (27). This abstract step seems to be a kind of simple 1-dimensional pattern recognition.

(3) The 2nd concrete step
Based on the results of the last step, modify some attributes of visual materials bound to the cells.

Although our first approach described above may appear rather too naive interpretation of configurations on a two-dimensional cellular space, it is not so difficult to continue the alternative steps of visualization toward more realistic images of a botanical colony. For example, by modifying a stretch of trees generated by A-system [Aono 1984], a landscape including ecological effects of forests can be easily obtained.

Implementation and results

According to the above concept for visualization, we have implemented the visual simulator of botanical colony growth patterns on Silicon Graphics IRIS 4D/70GT. As Langton's cellular automaton is mathematically two-dimensional, the cellular space can be represented in a flat plane. In our first implementation, each cell is assigned to a different rectangular solid of which visual attributes are determined by the cell state. All the solids are regularly set on a flat background plane.

Simulated growth patterns of colony are presented in Fig.1 (a)-(h). Here, the cellular space is bounded to 200 x 200 cells. Therefore, we assume a two-dimensionally periodic boundary condition on the cellular space:

$$C(x1, y1) = C(x2, y2) \text{ where } x1 = x2, y1 = y2, \text{ mod } 200.$$

It took just a few seconds to update the whole cell states, and then to render images of the cellular space by using IRIS 4D/70GT. Fig.2 (a)-(f) are the three-dimensional images of a growing colony. Here, the life cycle determines the height of each rectangular solid.

On the other hand, Fig.3 (a)-(d) show the collision process of three growing colonies. It is very interesting phenomenon that a collision of two active loops belonging to different colonies brings about partial destruction of the loops. This fact means that colonies originated from different roots never cooperate with each other in this model. All loops within a colony are growing according to their own timing signal governing the whole colony. When a construction arm touches a sheath cell of another colony, an illegal state not listed in a state transition table are generated. The illegal state brings another illegal state, then the destruction of loops takes place. Hence, by defining new transition rules which cover all the situations of the collision process, we are able to visualize cooperative colony growth patterns too.

4. CONCLUDING REMARKS

A cellular automaton is a formal model for discrete dynamical systems, known to be able to simulate natural phenomena including self-reproduction in biological organizations. Langton's cellular automaton is a good example of satisfying necessary conditions of self-reproduction. It is also capable of taking a simple environmental factor into consideration.

We presented the visually simulated growth patterns of a botanical colony based on the Langton's cellular automaton. Realistic images of simulated life and death were shown through a visualizing procedure consisting of the abstract and concrete steps. This technique can be easily applied to simulating of other kinds of biological and ecological colony formation. Landscape design applications seem also available. In addition, quantitative characterization of colony growth patterns seems to be one of the most interesting open research problems. We are preparing to consider mutations and other environmental factors such as temperature, sunlight, and nourishment.

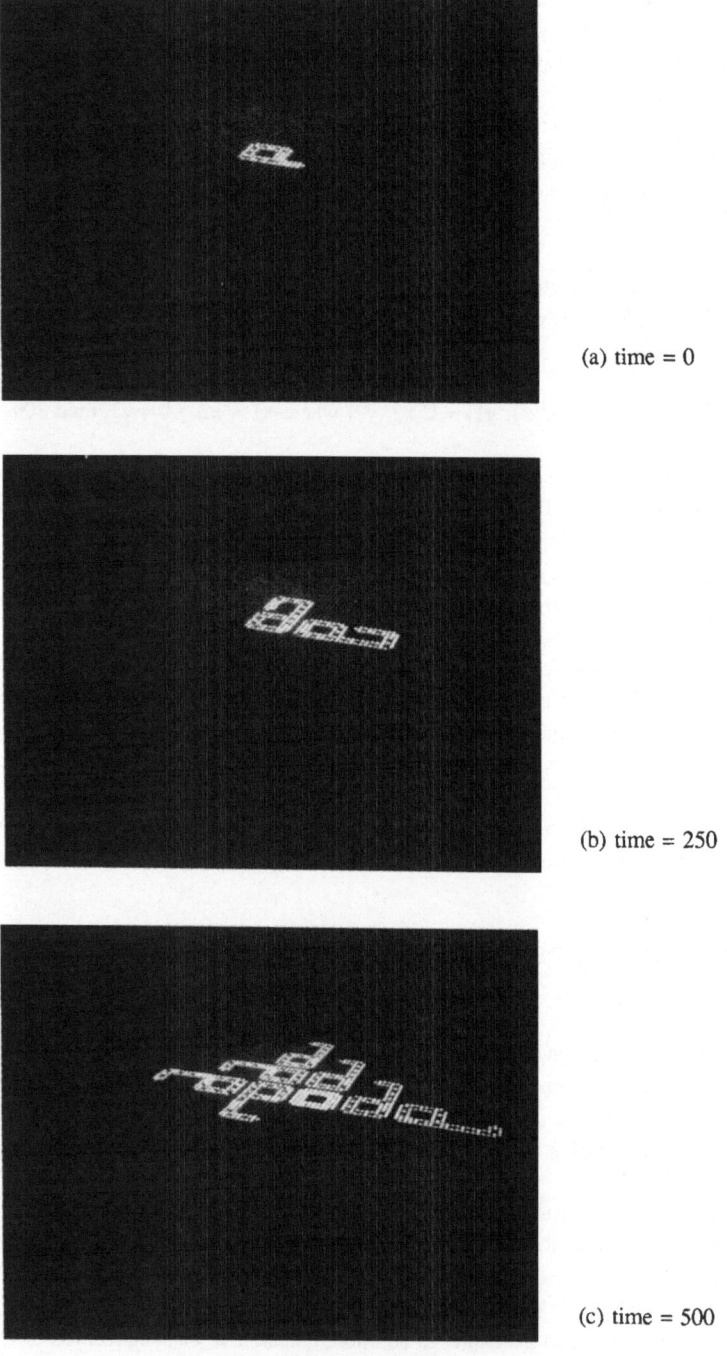

(a) time = 0

(b) time = 250

(c) time = 500

Fig.1 (a)-(c). Evolution of colony growth patterns.

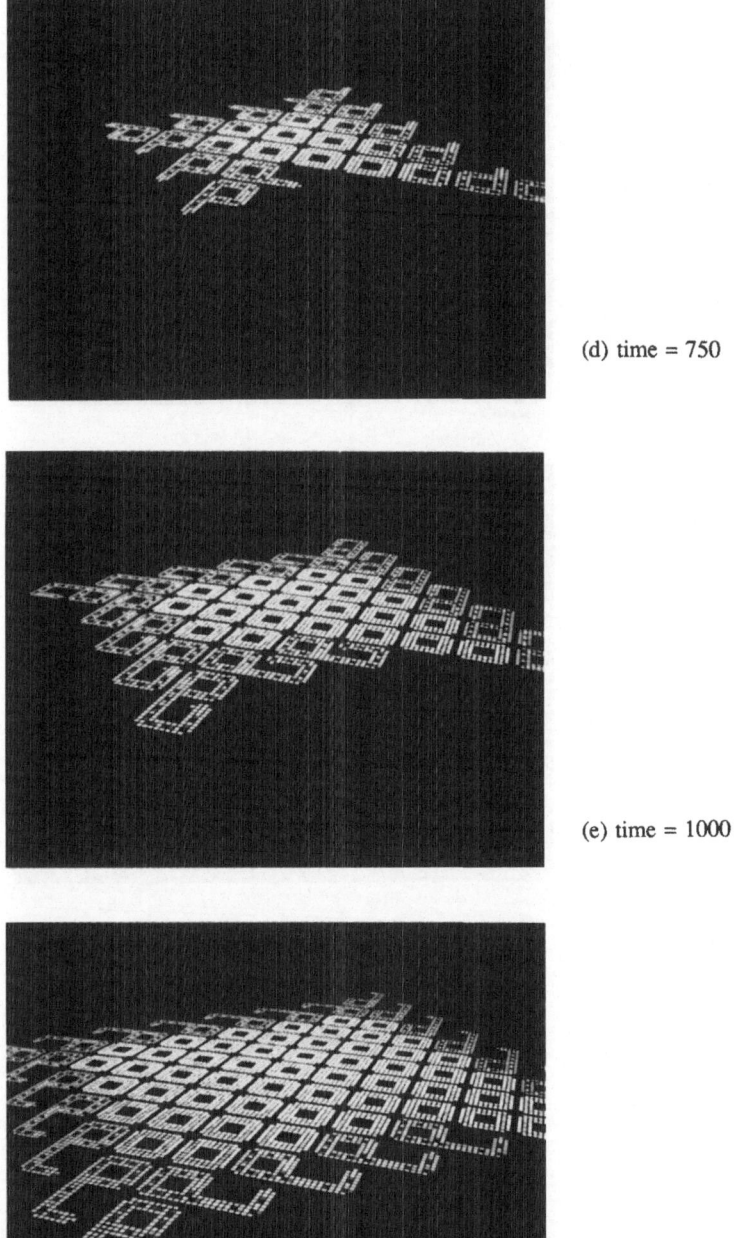

(d) time = 750

(e) time = 1000

(f) time = 1250

Fig.1 (d)-(f). Evolution of colony growth patterns.

(g) time = 1500

(h) time = 1750

Fig.1 (g)-(h). Evolution of colony growth patterns.

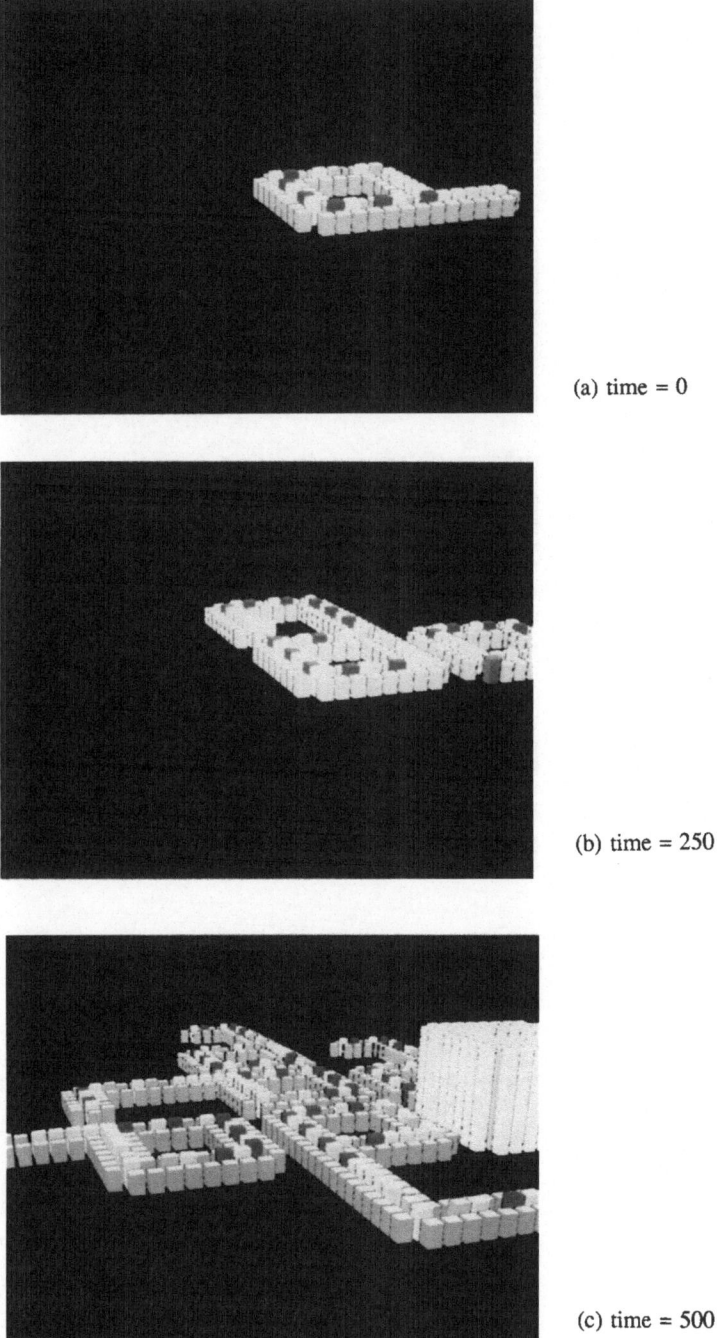

(a) time = 0

(b) time = 250

(c) time = 500

Fig.2 (a)-(c). Three-dimensional view of a growing colony.

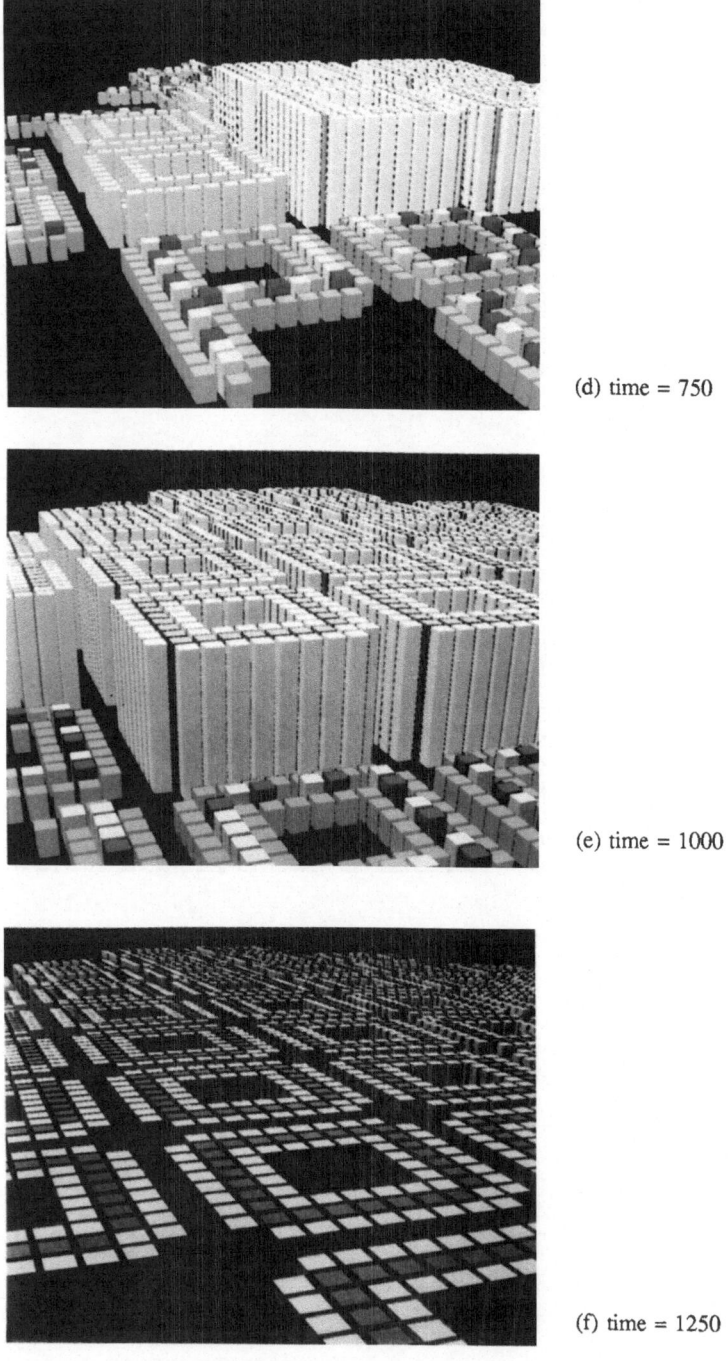

(d) time = 750

(e) time = 1000

(f) time = 1250

Fig.2 (d)-(f). Three-dimensional view of a growing colony.

(a) time = 0

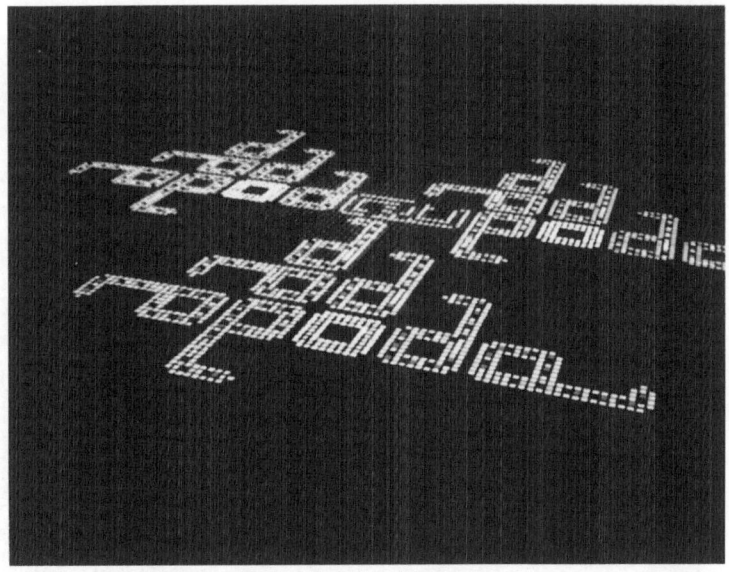

(b) time = 500

Fig.3 (a)-(b). Collision process of three growing colonies.

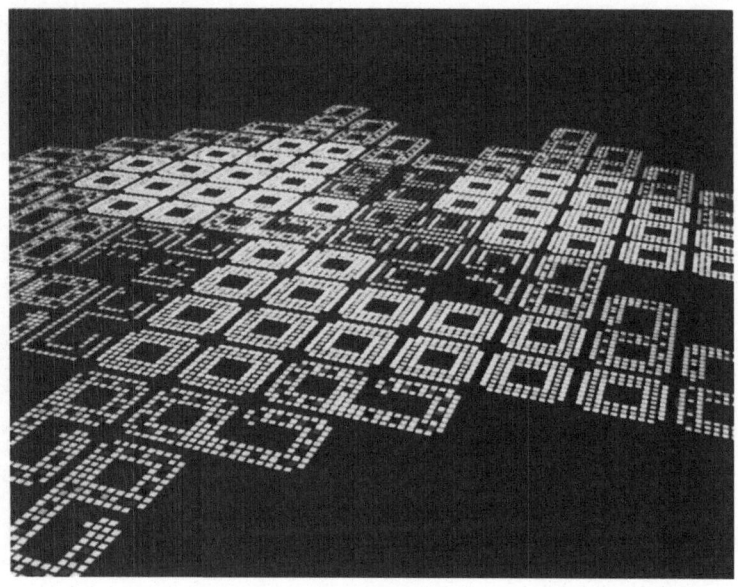

(c) time = 1000

(d) time = 1500

Fig.3 (c)-(d). Collision process of three growing colonies.

ACKNOWLEDGEMENTS

We would like to thank Satoshi Nishimura and Yoshihiko Ichikawa, for their many helpful suggestions. We are grateful to Ricoh Co., Ltd. for financial support and to Japan Silicon Graphics Co., Ltd. for offering IRIS 4D/70GT.

REFERENCES

Aono, M. and Kunii, T.L. (1984) Botanical Tree Image Generation. IEEE CG&A, Vol. 4, No. 5, pp. 10-34

Brown, M.H. (1987) Algorithm Animation. MIT Press, Massachusetts

Codd, E.F. (1968) Cellular Automata. Academic Press, New York

Gardner, M. (1971) Mathematical Games. Scientific American, No. 2-4

Hillis, D. (1985) The Connection Machine. MIT Press, Massachusetts

Kung, S.Y. (1988) VLSI Array Processors. Prentice Hall, Englewood Cliffs

Langton, G. (1984) Self-Reproduction in Cellular Automata. Physica, Vol. 10D, pp. 135-144

Von Neumann, J. (1966) The Theory of Self-Reproducing Automata. University of Illinois Press, Illinois

Preston, K. and Duff, M. (1984) Modern Cellular Automata: Theory and Applications. Plenum Press, New York

Prusinkiewicz, P., Lindenmayer, A. and Hanan, J. (1988) Developmental Models of Herbaceous Plants for Computer Imagery Purposes. Proc. of SIGGRAPH '88, Atlanta

Reed, D.A. and Fujimoto, R.M. (1987) Multicomputer Networks: Message-Based Parallel Processing. MIT Press, Massachusetts

Wolfram, S. (1986) Theory and Applications of Cellular Automata. World Scientific, Singapore

Tosiyasu L. Kunii is currently a Professor and Chairman of the Department of Information Science of the University of Tokyo. He started to work there in raster graphics in 1968, which led to the Tokyo Raster Technology Project. His research interests include computer graphics, database systems, and software engineering. He has authored and edited over 30 computer science related books and published more than 100 refereed academic papers in computer science and applications areas. He is Founding President of the Computer Graphics Society, Editor-in-Chief of the Visual Computer Journal, and a member of the Editorial Board of IEEE CG&A. He is active in IFIP, has organized and is Ex-Chair of the Technical Committee on Software Engineering of the Information Processing Society of Japan, and has organized and is Ex-President of the Japan Computer Graphics Association. He served as General Chairman of the Third International Conference on Very Large Data Bases in 1977, Program Chairman of Intergraphics 83, Computer Graphics Tokyo 84, 85, and 86, and CG International 87, and Honorary Chairman of CG International 88. He received his Bc.Sc., Ms.Sc., and Dr.Sc. in chemistry from the University of Tokyo in 1962, 1964, and 1967.

Yoshiaki Takai is currently a Research Associate of the Department of Information Science of the University of Tokyo. His major research interests include parallel processing, functional programming, computer architectures, cellular automata, visual computation, neuro-computation, and computer graphics applications. He has published 25 academic papers and technical reports in computer science and engineering. He received Bc.Eng. in electronic engineering in 1983, and Ms.Eng. and Dr.Eng. in information engineering in 1985 and 1988 from Tohoku University in Sendai. His doctoral dissertation was "A General-Purpose Pipeline System for the Function-Level Programming Language", which established a novel approach for parallel processing of functional programs based on an MISD architecture. He is a member of IPSJ, IEICE, and IEEE Computer Society.

Authors' address: Department of Information Science, Faculty of Science, the University of Tokyo, 7-3-1 Hongo, Bunkyo-ku, Tokyo 113, Japan.

Computational Geometry: Recent Developments

G.T. Toussaint

ABSTRACT

Recent developments in the field of *computational geometry* are discussed with emphasis on those problems most relevant to *computer graphics*. In particular we consider convex hulls, triangulations of polygons and point sets, finding the CSG representation of a simple polygon, polygonal approximations of a curve, computing geodesic and visibility properties of polygons and sets of points inside polygons, movable separability of polygons and local spatial planning, visibility questions concerning polyhedral terrains, finding minimal spanning covers of sets and various problems that arize in computational morphology including polygon decomposition and detecting symmetry.

1. Introduction

Computational geometry continues to flourish and make its presence felt in new areas. Several books have already appeared on the subject. An introductory text by Preparata & Shamos [PS85] covers most of the early work in this area. Mehlhorn [Me84] contains a subset of the material found in Preparata & Shamos and a few different results. The combinatorial aspects of computational geometry are treated in depth in the book by Edelsbrunner [Ed88]. The questions of visibility, of great interest to graphics specialists, is notoriously absent from the three texts mentioned above. However visibility is given a clear, excellent, and comprehensive treatment in the recent book by O'Rourke [O'R87]. There have also appeared three books which are collections of papers covering almost all aspects of computational geometry. The book edited by Preparata [Pr83] contains twelve papers on early material. More recent results can be found in the two books edited by Toussaint [To85], [To88a] and in the robotics-oriented collections edited by Schwartz et al., [SSH87] and Schwartz & Yap [SY87]. Finally we mention a book which, although may not contain much on the *computational* aspects of geometry, certainly covers much material of direct interest to graphics researchers. This is the book edited by Senechal & Fleck [SF88].

In this paper we survey some of the recent developments in the field of *computational geometry* with emphasis on those problems most relevant to *computer graphics*. In particular we concentrate on convex hulls, triangulations and other tessellations, finding the CSG representation of a simple polygon, polygonal approximations of a curve, computing geodesic and visibility properties of polygons and sets of points inside polygons, movable separability of polygons, visibility questions concerning polyhedral terrains, finding minimal spanning covers of sets and various problems that arize in computational morphology.

2. Convex Hulls of Point Sets

The convex hull is one of the most basic structures in computational geometry and finds application in many areas. It comes as no surprise then that the problem of computing the convex hull for diffenet types of input has received a great deal of attention as far back as the 1960s. For an historical account of the early work on the convex hull problem the reader is referred to Toussaint [To85a].

2.1 Two-dimensional hulls

Given a set of points $S = \{p_1, p_2,..., p_n\}$ in the plane the problem here is to compute the minimum-area convex polygon that contains S. A variety of algorithms have been proposed in the past [To85a] for solving this problem in O(n log n) time in the worst case. Furthermore Shamos [Sh78] established that these algorithms are worst-case optimal by proving an Ω(n log n) lower bound for this problem. The relevant question for the graphics practicioner is which of these O(n log n) time algorithms is the best in practice. Not surprizingly there is a trade-off, among different implementations of even the "same" algorithm, between time and storage. The code published by Bhattacharya and Toussaint [BT83] appears to be the fastest while using only 5n storage space.

2.2 Linear-expected-time algorithms

In 1978 Akl & Toussaint [AT78a] proposed a new approach they dubbed *"the throw-away principle"* to computing convex hulls that led to linear-expected-time algorithms. The idea was to first throw away a "large" subset of the points with a very fast and simple O(n) time procedure and subsequently use any standard convex hull algorithm on the remaining set. This was accomplished by chosing an appropriate fixed number (say four or eight) of directions, searching for the extreme points in those directions, constructing the convex polygon determined by connecting those extreme points in, say, a clockwise order, and finally discarding the points of S that fall in the interior of the resulting convex polygon. Akl & Toussaint [AT78a] showed that for n points uniformly distributed in the unit square a variant of Graham's [To85a] algorithm could be made to run in O(n) expected time. Devroye & Toussaint [DT81] extended these results showing that for n points randomly distributed in *any* non-degenerate rectangle R in the plane, according to *any* density function f whatsoever, as long as f is zero outside R and bounded away from zero and infinity inside R, applying such a throw-away step to any algorithm will result in an overall expected complexity of O(n), even if the convex hull algorithm used after the throw-away step has a worst-case complexity of O(n^2). For a survey of the early work on the expected complexity of geometric algorithms the reader is referred to Devroye [De85]. Very recently there has been renewed interest in fast expected time algorithms [GS88], [Dw88a], [Dw88b]. In fact the *"throw-away principle"* for computing convex hulls has been most recently rediscovered by Golin and Sedgewick [GS88] who provide a different analysis from that in [DT81] to prove the restricted version of the result in [DT81] that an O(n log n) time algorithm can be made to run in O(n) expected time if f is *uniform* in the unit square. It should be noted that the generality allowed on f in the analysis in [DT81] necessarily led to constants as large as 2,000,000. By assuming f to be *uniform* on the other hand Golin & Sedgewick were able to show that the constant is less than 8, thus showing theoretically that the algorithm is practical as well, and lending theoretical support to the empirical evidence that such an algorithm appears to run faster than any other in practice when f is uniform in the unit square [BT83]. Rex Dwyer [Dw88a], [Dw88b] extends the results of Devroye [De85] giving further conditions on probability density functions in high dimensions which are sufficient to yield convex hull algorithms with linear expected running time behaviour.

2.3 Output-size sensitive algorithms

A theoretical breakthrough was made on the convex hull problem by Kirkpatrick & Seidel [KS86] who discovered an adaptive algorithm that for a given set of points in time faster than O(n log n). Their algorithm has worst-case complexity O(n log h) where n is the size of the input set and h is the size of the output, i.e., the number of vertices on the resulting convex hull. Their ingenious algorithm relies on a variation of the well known *divide-and-comquer* paradigm which they call the *marriage-before-conquest* principle. Although this algorithm may be the best in theory it is not clear that it is so in practice. Experiments comparing this algorithm to several others including the one in

[BT83] suggested that the O(n log *h*) algorithm is in fact the slowest [MT85]. On the other hand the experiments in [MT85] suggested that the O(n log *h*) algorithm was the most accurate from the numerical point of view. Given one thousand points randomly generated on a circle, an ideal convex hull algorithm should find a convex polygon of one thousand vertices, barring numerical inaccuracies in the generation process. In practice this is not so. In the experiments in [MT85] the O(n log *h*) algorithm had more convex hull vertices than any other algorithm coded. This "numerical" aspect of computational geometry of considerable practical importance is not yet well understood and is receiving increased attention in the literature today [DS88], [Mi88], [SI89].

2.4   Rectilinear convex hulls

There has also been increasing interest lately in generalizing the notion of convex hull in various ways. In particular, largely because of VLSI, isothetic polygons have received much attention. A polygon or polygonal path is *isothetic* (or *rectilinear*) if its sides are parallel to the coordinate axes. The rectilinear convex hull of a set of points S is the smallest rectilinear polygon such that each pair of points in the polygon has a shortest rectilinear path contained in the polygon [OSW84]. Chhajed and Chandru [CC88] discuss relationships between rectilinear convex hulls and the notion of efficient points in operations research.

2.5   Hulls in higher dimensions

The problem of computing the convex hull in higher dimensions is considerably more complex even in 3-dimensions. A detailed treatment of the 3-dimensional (and higher) problem can be found in Edelsbrunner's book [Ed87]. A short survey of higher dimensional convex hull research can also be found in the recent survey paper by O'Rourke [O'R88].

3.   Polygons

For any integer $n \geq 3$, we define a *polygon* in the Euclidean plane E^2 as the figure $P = [x_1, x_2, ..., x_n]$ formed by n points $x_1, x_2, ..., x_n$ in E^2 and n line segments $[x_i, x_{i+1}]$, i=1,2,...,n-1, and $[x_n, x_1]$. The points x_i are called the *vertices* of the *polygon* and the line segments are termed its *edges*. We normally assume the vertices of P are in *general position*, i.e., no three vertices are collinear and that the polygon is in *standard* form, i.e., the vertices appear in counterclockwise order as their index increases.

Definition: A polygon P is called a *simple* polygon provided that no point of the plane belongs to more than two edges of P and the only points of the plane that belong to precisely two edges are the vertices of P.

A simple polygon has a well defined interior (denoted by *int*(P)) and exterior (denoted by *ext*(P)). We will follow the convention of including the interior of a polygon when referring to P. The vertices of a simple polygon are of two types: *convex* and *concave*.

3.1   Finding the Convex Hull of a Simple Polygon

The $\Omega(n \log n)$ lower bound to computing the convex hull of a set of n points in the plane does not hold when the points are the vertices of a simple polygon. Indeed, during the past two decades a score of linear time algorithms for solving this problem has been published. Unfortunately, half of these algorithms have been discovered to be incorrect in the sense that they are not guaranteed to work for all simple polygons. The first correct linear-time algorithm was discovered by McCallum & Avis [MA79]. This algorithm was fairly involved and used three stacks. Subsequently simpler algorithms were found that needed only one stack. Most notable in this class were the algorithms of Bhattacharya & ElGindy [BE84], D. T. Lee [Le83], and Graham & Yao [GY83]. Probably the simplest algorithm designed to date is that of Melkman [Me87]. Unlike the previous algorithms, Melkman's does not need to start on a convex hull vertex and uses a *deque* as a data structure rather than the usual *stack*.

In graphics and solid modelling objects are often represented not as polygons but as piece-wise smooth curves of low-order degree. Computational geometry researchers are only beginning to address themselves to computational issues concerning these more general classes of input. For convex hulls of piece-wise smooth Jordan curves a step in this direction was taken by Schaffer & Van Wyk [SV87]. Chee Yap considers the related problem of computing the Voronoi diagram of a set of simple curved segments [Ya84].

3.2   Triangulating a Simple Polygon

3.2.1   Introduction

Our problem is that of constructing a *triangulation* of P, i.e., decomposing P into a set of non-overlapping triangles (their interiors do not intersect) without adding new vertices. Mathematicians have been interested in constructive proofs (algorithms) of the existence of triangulations for simple polygons as early as 1911 [Le11]. The "algorithm" of Lennes [Le11] works by recursively inserting diagonals between pairs of vertices of P and runs in $O(n^2)$ time. Since the 1911 paper variations on this type of "algorithm" have reappeared in a score of papers and text books during the past seventy years, and surprisingly, quite frequently containing fundamental errors. See the paper by Chung-Wu Ho [Ho75] for a series of counterexamples to published triangulation "proofs." A rather novel inductive proof was offered more recently by Meisters [Me75]. He proposed a method based on searching for "ears" and "cutting" them off. We call a vertex x_i of polygon P a *principal* vertex provided that no vertex of P lies in the interior of the triangle $[x_{i-1}, x_i, x_{i+1}]$ or in the interior of the diagonal $[x_{i-1}, x_{i+1}]$. A *principal* vertex x_i of a simple polygon P is called an *ear* if the diagonal $[x_{i-1}, x_{i+1}]$ that bridges x_i lies entirely in P. We say that two ears x_i and x_j are *non-overlapping* if $int[x_{i-1}, x_i, x_{i+1}] \cap int[x_{j-1}, x_j, x_{j+1}] = \varnothing$. The following *Two-Ears* Theorem was proved by Meisters [Me75].

Theorem: (the *Two-Ears* Theorem, Meisters [Me75]) Except for triangles every simple polygon P has at least two *non-overlapping ears*.

This theorem suggests the idea of triangulating a polygon by repeatedly finding an ear and "cutting it off" until the remaining polygon of one less vertex is itself an ear. A straighforward implementation of this idea leads to an algorithm for triangulating a simple polygon with a worst-case complexity of $O(n^3)$.

The first algorithm to break the $O(n^2)$ upper bound was that of Garey, Johnson, Preparata & Tarjan [GJPT]. Their algorithm runs in time $O(n \log n)$ which is the time required by the first step to decompose the polygon into monotone pieces. They then apply an algorithm for triangulating the resulting monotone polygons in linear time. We should note here that a simpler linear-time algorithm for the latter problem is now available [To84]. An alternate decomposition method with the same complexity appears in [FM84]. An entirely different *approach via divide-and-conquer* due to Chazelle [Ch82] also achieves an $O(n \log n)$ upper bound. Very recently this upper bound was reduced even further by Tarjan & Van Wyk [TV88]. With complicated and sophisticated data structures they are able to triangulate a simple polygon in $O(n \log \log n)$ time.

It remains one of the most outstanding problems in computational geometry to determine if a simple polygon can be triangulated in O(n) time. In the mean time some researchers are looking for and have found large useful classes of polygons that can be triangulated in linear time. Such classes include *monotone* polygons [GJPT],[To84], *star-shaped* polygons [SV80], [WS85], *edge-visible* polygons [TA82], *spiral* polygons [FP75], [To86], *L-convex* polygons [EAT83], *intersection-free* polygons [LC87], *weakly-externally-visible* polygons [El85], *palm* polygons [ET88], and *anthropomorphic* polygons [To89]. Alternately researchers are looking for adaptive algorithms that will run fast in many situations. Recently Hertel & Mehlhorn [HeMe] have described a sweep-line based algorithm that performs better the fewer reflex vertices it has. The running time of their method is O(n + r log r) where r denotes the number of concave vertices of P. Hertel & Mehlhorn's algorithm takes the first step towards obtaining an adaptive algorithm sensitive to the *shape* of the polygon. Unfortunately r is not a truly relevant measure of the shape complexity. To see this it is sufficient to realize that given any polygon of no matter what shape it is a trivial matter to insert n vertices (one between every original pair) and pull them an infinitessimal amount towards the interior of the polygon. Such a transformation will make r proportional to n without changing the basic shape of the polygon.

Chazelle and Incerpi [CI84] took a further step to achieve a time complexity that more faithfully reflects the *shape complexity* of the polygon. They describe a triangulation algorithm that runs in time O(n log s) with s < n. The quantity s measures the *sinuosity* of the polygon, i.e., the number of times the polygon's boundary alternates between complete spirals of opposite orientation. Unlike r, s has the advantage that in many practical situations it is very small or a constant even for very winding polygons. Consider the motion of a directed straight line $L[x_i,x_{i+1}]$ passing through edge $[x_i,x_{i+1}]$ as i goes from 1 to n-1. Every time $L[x_i,x_{i+1}]$ reaches the vertical position in a clockwise (respectively counter-clockwise) manner we increment (respectively decrement) a *winding-counter* by one. $L[x_i,x_{i+1}]$ is said to be *spiraling* (respectively *anti-spiraling*) if the winding counter is never decremented (respectively incremented) twice in succession. In this way the polygon may be decomposed easily in O(n) time into spiraling and anti-spiraling polygonal chains. An example of a polygon with a sinuosity of five is shown in Fig. 3.2.1. Note that a new polygonal chain is restarted only when the previous chain ceases to be spiraling or anti-spiraling. The *sinuosity* s of P is defined as the number of polygonal chains thus obtained.

The Chazelle-Incerpi algorithm is much more interesting theoretically than the algorithm of Hertel & Mehlhorn because of the implications it has on the complexity of triangulating different known classes of polygons. Since r, the number of concave vertices, is independent of whether a polygons is *monotonic, star-shaped, edge-visible* or whatever, Hertel & Mehlhorn's algorithm can run in O(n log n) time even for these classes of polygons for which linear time algorithms are known. On the other hand *star-shaped* polygons have a sinuosity of one and thus the Chazelle-Incerpi algorithm runs in linear time for these polygons. Furthermore the algorithm makes no use of the *kernel* of P. In [SV80] and [WS85] a point in the *kernel* is required and this implies a non-trivial (although linear time) effort. For a radically diffrent and extremely simple algorithm for triangulating a *star-shaped* polygon without making use of the *kernel* of P see [ET88].

The sinuosity of a polygon is not very satisfactory as a measure of its shape complexity. It has the disconcerting property that it can vary by an order of magnitude depending on the orientation of the input polygon. Consider the *edge-visible* polygon illustrated in Fig. 3.2.2. Recall that a polygon P is edge visible if there exists an edge [u,v] of P such that for each point x in P there exists a point y in [u,v] such that the line segment [x,y] lies in P. The sinuosity for the polygon in Fig. 3.2.2 is O(n) and thus the Chazelle-Incerpi algorithm runs in O(n log n) time on this polygon whereas a linear-time algorithm exists [TA82]. Furthermore by rotating the polygon through an angle of 90 degrees the sinuosity reduces to O(1). This represents an order of magnitude change in the *sinuosity* of P for no change in the *shape* of P (naturally we assume that any interesting measure of shape is invariant under translation and rotation).

3.2.2 An output-complexity-sensitive polygon triangulation algorithm

Toussaint [To88d] describes a new algorithm for triangulating a simple n-sided polygon. The algorithm runs in time $O(n(1+t_0))$, with $t_0 < n$. The quantity t_0 measures the topological complexity of the triangulation delivered by the algorithm. More precisely t_0 is the number of triangles in the output triangulation obtained that share zero edges with the input polygon and is loosely related to the *shape-complexity* of the polygon. Although the worst-case complexity of the algorithm is $O(n^2)$, for several classes of polygons it runs in linear time. The practical advantage of the algorithm is that it is extremely simple and does not require sorting or the use of balanced tree structures. On the theoretical side it is of interest because it is the first polygon triangulation algorithm whose *computational* complexity is a function of the *output* complexity.

The dual of every polygon triangulation is a tree (see Fig. 3.2.3). A tree suggests a natural measure of its shape complexity, namely, its *arborescence* or "branchyness." Is a tree like a *palm* tree

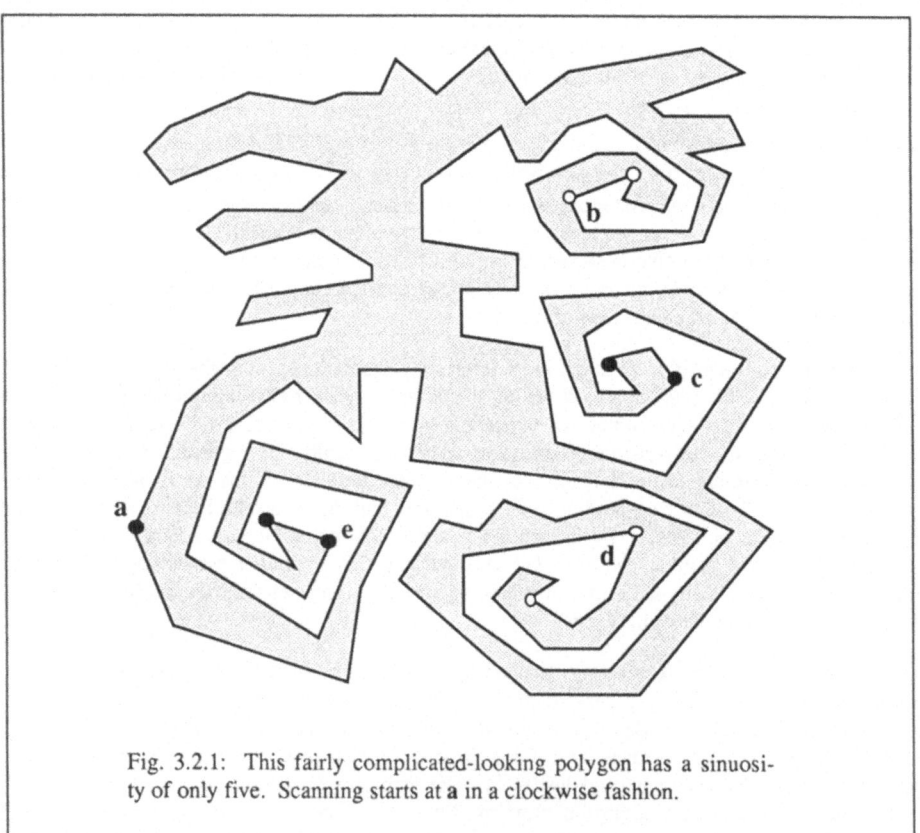

Fig. 3.2.1: This fairly complicated-looking polygon has a sinuosity of only five. Scanning starts at a in a clockwise fashion.

or more like an *oak* ? The perfect measure of the amount of branching in a tree is its number of nodes of degree three. Let t_i denote the number of triangles in a triangulated polygon $T(P)$ that share i edges with P. It is clear that t_0, which we also refer to as the number of "free" triangles in $T(P)$, corresponds to the number of nodes of degree three in the dual tree of $T(P)$. Thus t_0 is a very natural measure of the complexity of a triangulation. This is not to say that it is a good measure of the *shape-complexity* of P. Although there may be a relationship between the complexity of a triangulation of P and the shape complexity of P, it is as yet poorly understood. Consider *triangulated convex* and *anthropomorphic* polygons. A simple polygon P is called *anthropomorphic* provided it contains precisely two ears and one *mouth* [To89]. A *principal* vertex x_i of a simple polygon P is called a *mouth* if the diagonal $[x_{i-1}, x_{i+1}]$ is an *external* diagonal, i.e., the interior of $[x_{i-1}, x_{i+1}]$ lies in the exterior of P. Most people would agree that the shape of the convex polygon is much simpler than the shape of the *anthropomorphic* polygon and yet for the former $t_0 = 5$ whereas for the latter $t_0 = 0$. In fact for a convex n-gon t_0 may be as large as $O(n)$ but for an *anthropomorphic* polygon $t_0 = 0$ for *all* its triangulations. This is so because the *dual-tree* of every triangulation of a two-ear polygon is a *chain*. This suggests that the extreme values of t_0 over all triangulations of a given polygon are more appropriate as a measures of the shape of a polygon.

3.2.3 Bushy and thin triangulations

Given a triangulation of a polygon P, let t_0 be defined as above, let t_1 be the number of triangles that share one edge with the polygon, and t_2 be the number of triangles that share two edges with the polygon. It is also interesting to view t_0, t_1, and t_2 as the numver of vertices of degree 3,2 and 1, respectively, in the dual tree of the triangulation. These three quantities and the number of vertices of P, i.e., n, share the following relationships:

$$t_0 = t_2 - 2$$

$$t_1 = n - 2t_2$$

Therefore, if we know the value of n, computing one of the three quantities is computationally equivalent to computing all three. Now consider the problem of finding, among all possible triangulations of P, those that maximize and minimize the value of t_2. Let the corresponding values of t_2 be $t_{max}(P)$ and $t_{min}(P)$. A triangulation with $t_2 = t_{max}(P)$ is called *bushy*. A triangulation with $t_2 = t_{min}(P)$ is called *thin*.

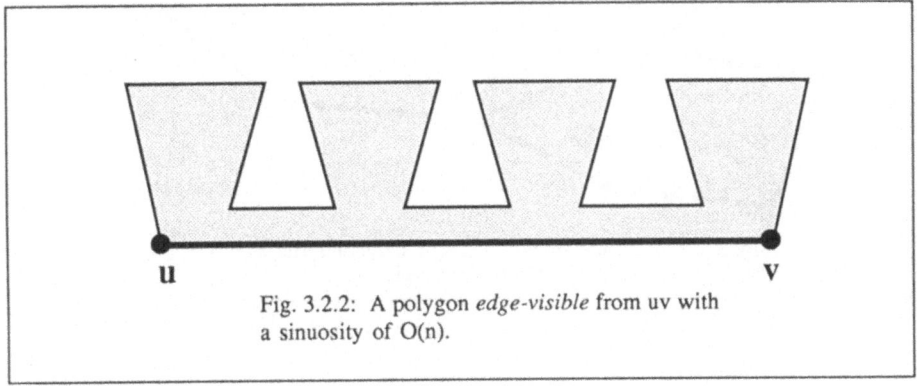

Fig. 3.2.2: A polygon *edge-visible* from uv with a sinuosity of O(n).

Thin triangulations are of interest in pattern recognition and computational morphology [To88a], where minimal representations of polygons are of interest. Bushy triangulations on the other hand are of interest for implementing efficient algorithms for answering geodesic distance queries where the time taken to compute the distance between two points is proportional to the distance of their containing triangles in the dual tree of the triangulation [GHLST], [To88b].

The quantities $t_{max}(P)$ and $t_{min}(P)$ are also of interest because there exists a polygon triangulation algorithm which has a time complexity that depends on $t_{max}(P)$ [To88d], and there are classes of polygons for which $t_{max}(P)$ is a constant [ST88a], [To89], or $t_{min}(P)$ is a constant (e.g. convex, spiral).

3.3   Finding the CSG Representation of a Simple Polygon

A fundamental problem in *solid modelling* is the formal representation of solid objects. The two most popular forms of representation are the *boundary* representation and the *CSG* (standing for Constructive Solid Geometry) representation. In the *boundary* representation an object is described by the collection of surface elements that make up its boundary. In the *CSG* representation an object is described by boolean operations on a set of *primitive* objects. Each representation has its advantages and drawbacks depending on the types of operations one is interested in performing [Re80].

Peterson [Pe84] showed that every simple polygon P in the plane may be expressed by a boolean formula, based on the half-planes supporting its edges, such that the formula is monotone (complementation is not required) and each of the supporting half-planes appears in the formula precisely once. Such a formula is referred to as a *Peterson-style formula*. Dobkin et al., [DGHS] give a simple proof of Peterson's theorem and propose an O(n log n) time algorithm for converting a simple n-gon from a *boundary* to a *CSG* representation.

It is easy to verify that the *boundary-to-CSG conversion* can be performed in O(n) time if P is a

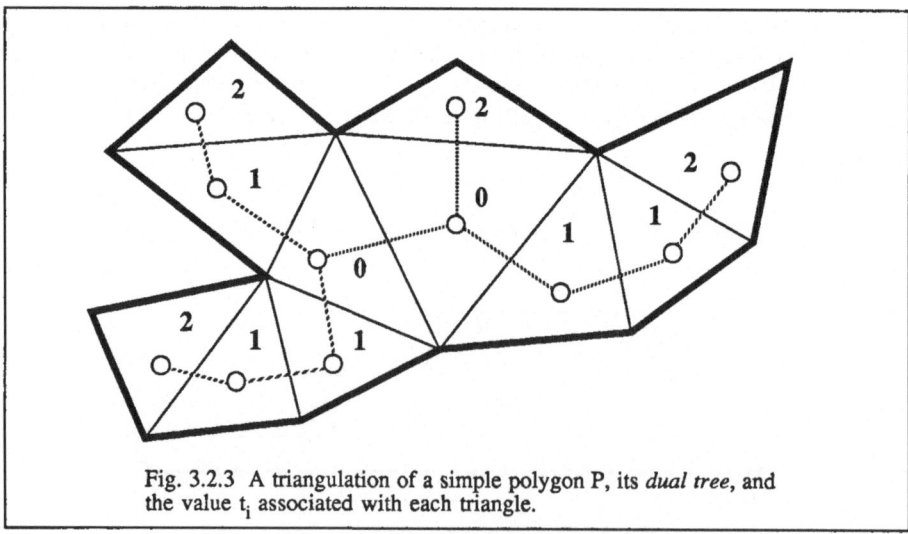

Fig. 3.2.3 A triangulation of a simple polygon P, its *dual tree*, and the value t_i associated with each triangle.

monotone polygon. Several fundamental problems concerning this topic remain open. In particular we make the following conjectures.

Conjecture 3.5.1: Given a triangulated simple polygon of n edges, the *boundary-to-CSG conversion* can be performed in O(n) time.

Conjecture 3.5.2: Given a *Peterson-style formula* for a simple polygon P of n edges, P can be triangulated in O(n) time.

3.4   Polygonal Approximations of a Curve

One of the most fundamental problems in areas such as automated cartography, geographic information systems, computer graphics, pattern recognition and image processing is the problem of approximating complex boundaries of figures by simpler piecewise linear polygonal curves. Although polygonal approximation problems have been studied for almost two decades only recently, with the injection of computational geometry, has the problem been treated in an elegant and rigorous manner. The first such computational geometric treatment was provided by Iri & Imai [II86].

Let $C=P_1, P_2,..., P_n$ denote a possibly self-crossing polygonal chain in $\Re^2$. Imai & Iri [II86] considered the problem of finding the best approximating subchain $P_{i(1)}, P_{i(2)},..., P_{i(m)}$, where i(1) = 1 < i(2) < ... < i(m) = n, and m is minimal such that C never deviates more than a given tolerance w from the subchain. Their algorithm constructs a directed graph G, the nodes of which correspond to the vertices of C, and such that the nodes for vertices P_i and P_j are connected by an arc in G if, and only if, C remains within w of L_{ij} from P_i to P_j, where L_{ij} is the line segment whose endpoints are P_i and P_j. If each edge is assigned a unit weight it is easy to see that the shortest path in the graph from 1 to n yields the approximating chain with the minimum number of segments. Furthermore, since G is acyclic it follows that this path can be found in time linear in the number of edges of G, i.e., $O(n^2)$. The total time complexity of the Imai-Iri algorithm is $O(n^3)$. Melkman & O'Rourke [MO88] reduce this complexity to $O(n^2 \log n)$. Toussaint [To85b] also improved the complexity of the Imai-Iri algorithm to $O(n^2 \log n)$ but for a different error criterion. For a recent survey of the latest results in this area for four different error criteria see Imai & Iri [II88].

3.5   Computing Geodesic Properties in Simple Polygons

3.5.1   Introduction

This section is concerned with the calculation of shortest internal distances and paths between points in the interior of a simple polygon. Figure 3.5.1 illustrates the shortest internal path between two points inside a simple polygon. Such distances and paths are also often qualified as *geodesic* and represent a special case of the problem of computing the shortest path between two points on a surface of an object such as a sphere, polyhedron, or more general surface [SGB83]. However, in general the terms *geodesic* and *shortest* path are not equivalent. The term *shortest* is intuitively quite clear but *geodesic* warrants a definition

The first paper on the shortest path between two points on a general surface was published by Leonhard Euler in 1728. Euler reduced the problem to the solution of a differential equation equivalent to the following geometric theorem derived earlier by Johann Bernoulli in 1698.

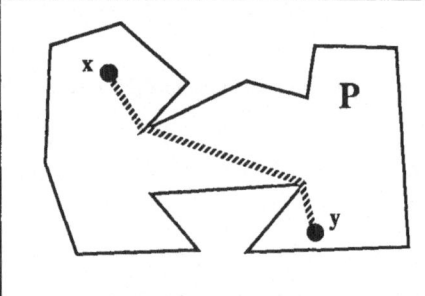

Fig. 3.5.1: Illustrating the sort-
est internal path between two
points x and y in a simple polygon P.

Theorem: (Bernoulli, 1698) The *shortest* path between two points on a surface is a *geodesic* path.

Definition: Let C be a path on a surface Σ. Let a be a point on C and let b and c be any two other points on C close to and on each side of a. In general the three points a,b,c will determine a plane dependent on b and c. The limiting position of this plane as b and c both move on C toward a is called the *osculating plane* to C at point a.

Definition: Let C be a path on a surface Σ. If at each point a of C the *osculating plane* to C and the *tangent plane* to Σ are *perpendicular* to each other, then C is a *geodesic* path.

Clearly, the converse of Bernoulli's theorem is not true in general. Consider two non-diametral points on the surface of a sphere. These two points partition the great circle passing through them into two arcs of different lengths. Both arcs are *geodesic* paths between the pair of points but obviously only one of them is a *shortest* path. More interesting examples on cones and cylinders may be constructed by the reader.

Recently there has been considerable interest in the complexity of computing the shortest path between two points lying on the surface of a convex polyhedron. Mount [Mo84] presents an algorithm for computing the shortest path in $O(n^2 \log n)$ time, where n is the number of faces of the polyhedron (see also Sharir and Schorr [SS84] for an algorithm that solves the same problem in $O(n^3 \log n)$ time). Finally, Franklin and Akman [FA84] consider the situation in which the convex polyhedron is preprocessed in order that shortest-path queries between pairs of query points may be answered efficiently.

A *polygonal path* is a simple path consisting of a sequence of line segments. If p is a polygonal path, then the *length* of p is the sum of the Euclidean lengths of all the line segments comprising p. Given two points x and x' in P the geodesic path between x and x' denoted by GP(x,x'/P) is the minimum-length polygonal path $(x=x_1,x_2,...,x_k=x')$. It is convenient to consider the geodesic path as having a direction and GP(x,x'/P) will imply that the direction is from x to x'. The length of the geodesic path is called the *geodesic distance* and is denoted by $d_G(x,x')$. Two fundamental properties of the geodesic path GP(x,x'/P) are that the path is unique and its vertices x_i, i=2,3,...,k-1 are a subset of the concave vertices of P [Ch82],[LP84]. Chazelle [Ch82] and Lee and Preparata [LP84] independently obtained an elegant algorithm for computing GP(x,x'/P) in linear time provided that P has already been triangulated.

As we saw earlier the dual graph of a polygon triangulation is a tree and both the algorithms of Chazelle, and Lee and Preparata depend strongly on the use of this tree. A *sleeve* is a triangulated polygon the dual tree of which is a chain. The first key result which they use is a linear-time algorithm for finding the shortest path between two points in a sleeve. The second is a lemma which states that the shortest path between two points x and y in a simple polygon P must lie in the sleeve determined by the triangles in T(P) that correspond to the nodes in the dual tree of T(P) that determine the graph-theoretic shortest path between the nodes x',y' in the dual tree of T(P), where x' and y' are the duals of the triangles that contain x and y, respectively. Since the dual tree of a polygon triangulation and the graph-theoretic shortest path in a tree can both be easily computed in linear time it follows that their algorithm performs in linear time on a triangulated polygon. Furthermore, since a polygon can be triangulated in O(n log log n) time [TV87] it follows that the shortest path can be computed within the same time bound. A caveat should be added, however, concerning the use of the algorithm of Tarjan and Van Wyk in a graphics environment where a polygon may not have a large number of vertices. Their algorithm involves rather complicated data structures resulting in a large overhead which may render the algorithm very slow. In practice an algorithm such as that in [To88c] described earlier may be preferred.

Some work has also been done concerning geodesic distance and path *queries*. In particular, Guibas and Hershberger [GH87] show how to preprocess a triangulated polygon in linear time so that, given two query points x and y in P, $d_G(x,y)$ can be computed in time O(log n). Furthermore the geodesic path itself, GP(x,y/P) can be generated in an additional time proportional to the number of turns it makes.

Geodesic paths find application in a variety of areas. In *image processing* they are used for representing, approximating, and smoothing digitized shapes[SCH72]. In *robotics* they are used for motion planning, grasping, and collision avoidance [PRS88b], [PeSa], [To88d], [To88f]. In *graphics* applications concerned with *visibility* and *strong hidden line* elimination they yield elegant and efficient algorithms to solve a variety of related problems [GHLST], [To86a], [To86b]. In *pattern recognition* and *mathematical morphology* they provide new descriptors of shape [LM84], [To88a]. In *computational geometry* they are useful for solving a variety of problems as well as characterizing large families of polygons that admit linear-time triangulation algorithms [ET88], [ET89]. Finally, in *mathematics* geodesic paths can be used to obtain a new proof of Krasnoselskii's theorem concerning star-shaped sets [ST88b], [To88b].

3.5.2 The geodesic diameter of a polygon

The diameter of a set is the maximal Euclidean distance between any two elements of the set. The problem of computing the Euclidean diameter of a set efficiently is more difficult than appears at first glance and has received considerable attention in the computational geometry literature. Several published algorithms have been found to be incorrect . The diameter of a set of n points can be computed in O(n log n) time. However, for a convex polygon O(n) time suffices. Since the diameter of a set is determined by a pair of vertices of the convex hull of the set and since the convex hull of a simple polygon P can be found in O(n) time [MA79], it follows that the diameter of P can be found in O(n) time also. The *geodesic* diameter considered here is a generalization of the Euclidean diameter.

Definition: The *geodesic diameter* of a simple polygon P, denoted by $D_G(P)$, is the maximal geodesic distance between any pair of points in P, i.e.,

$$D_G(P) = \max \{ d_G(x,y) \}$$

where maximization is carried out over all points x and y of P.

Chazelle [Ch82] as well as Reif and Storer [RS85] give $O(n^2)$ time algorithms for computing the geodesic diameter of a simple n-gon. It is known that a geodesic furthest neighbour of a point in a polygon is always a convex vertex of P (see Asano and Toussaint [AT85]). This immediately leads to an algorithm with complexity $O(c^2n + T(n))$ where c is the number of convex vertices of P and T(n) is the time required to triangulate P. Suri [Su87] on the other hand has shown that O(n log n) time is sufficient to compute the geodesic furthest neighbours of all the vertices of P and, hence, to compute the geodesic diameter of P.

3.5.3 The geodesic center of a polygon

The geodesic center of a polygon is a generalization of the Euclidean facility location problem. Given a set of points in the plane called *sites* that represent customers, the Euclidean facility location problem asks for the location of a facility to be used by the customers such that the maximum Euclidean distance that any customer has to travel to get to the facilty is minimized. The center of the *minimal spanning circle* of the sites, i.e., the smallest circle enclosing the sites, is the solution to this problem.

Definition: The *geodesic center* of a simple polygon P, denoted by $C_G(P)$, is a point in P which minimizes the maximum geodesic distance to any point in P. Such a distance is called the *geodesic radius* of P and denoted by $R_G(P)$. More precisely, for any point x in P define the *covering radius* of P from x as:

$$C_r(P/x) = \max_{y} \{ d_G(x,y) \},$$

where y varies over all points in P. Then the geodesic center of P is the point in P for which

$$R_G(P) = \min_{x} \{ C_r(P/x) \},$$

where x varies over all points in P.

It is now well known that the standard Euclidean facility problem can be solved in linear time [Me83], [Dy86], but its generalization to the geodesic metric appears to be more difficult. The problem of computing the geodesic center of a simple polygon was first investigated by Asano and Toussaint [AT85] who showed that it was unique and could be computed in $O(n^4 \log n)$ time. This result was later improved to $O(n^3 \log \log n)$ time in [AT86], to $O(n \log^2 n)$ time in [PS86], and finally to $O(n \log n)$ time in [PSR88a].

3.5.4 Geodesic properties of points in a polygon

Rather than consider geodesic properties of polygons one may be interested in geodesic properties of sets of points inside polygons. Such points may represent cities in a country or pick-and-place locations in the workspace of a robot. In this section we introduce the notion of the *geodesic* (also known in the literature as *relative) convex hull* of a set of points $S = \{s_1, s_2, ..., s_n\}$ called *sites* lying in a simple n-gon P. Note that the cardinalities of S and P need not be equal but this assumption will simplify the complexity formulas. The *geodesic convex hull* of S given P, denoted by $CH_G(S/P)$, turns out to be a fundamental tool for computing many geodesic properties efficiently.

Definition: Let Q be a subset of P. Q is called *geodesically convex* provided that for every pair of points $x, y \in Q$, the geodesic path between x and y constrained to lie in P also lies in Q, i.e., GP(x,y/P) = GP(x,y/Q). Refer to Fig. 3.5.2 for an illustration.

Definition: Let S be a set of sites in P. The *geodesic convex hull*, $CH_G(S/P)$, is the intersection of all *geodesically-convex* sets containing S. Refer to Fig. 3.5.3 for an illustration. Alternately we may also define the *geodesic convex hull* as the *minimum-perimeter weakly-simple* polygon that contains S and is constrained to lie in P.

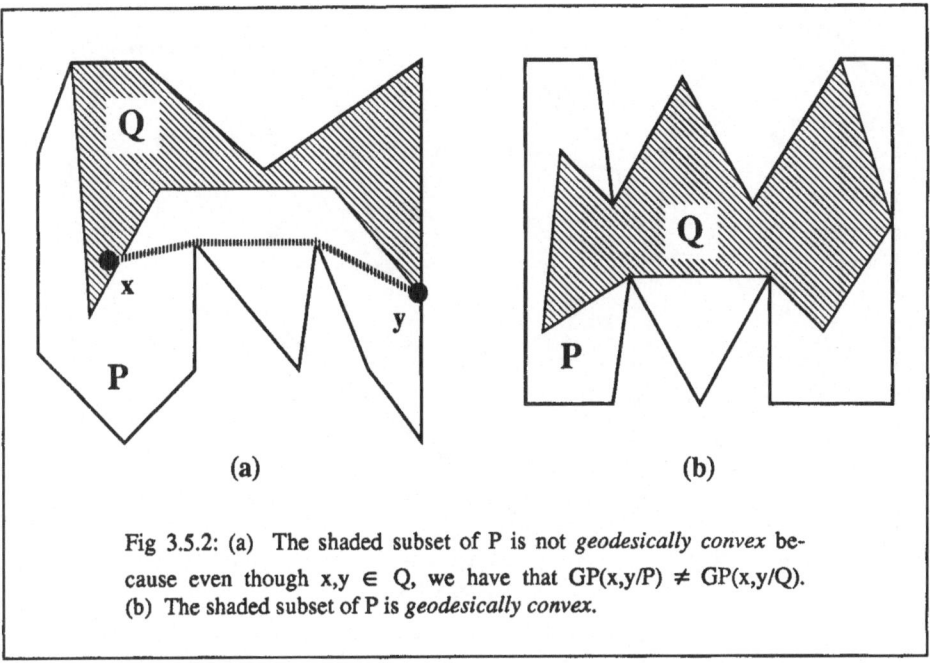

Fig 3.5.2: (a) The shaded subset of P is not *geodesically convex* because even though x,y ∈ Q, we have that GP(x,y/P) ≠ GP(x,y/Q). (b) The shaded subset of P is *geodesically convex*.

Toussaint [To88b] proposes efficient algorithms for solving a variety of geodesic-distance problems on S. The key result and tool used in the design of these algorithms is an $O(n \log n)$-time algorithm for computing the *geodesic convex-hull* of S with respect to P. He illustrates the use of this structure on the following problems:

1) the *geodesic-diameter* of S in P, i.e., the maximal geodesic-distance between   any two sites in S.

2) the *geodesic-center* of S in P, i.e., the point z in P whose maximal geodesic-dis   tance to any site x in S is the smallest possible.

3) the *geodesic-median* of S in P, i.e., the site in S whose maximal geodesic-distance to any other site in S is the smallest possible.

4) the *maximum geodesic distance* between two sets S_1 and S_2 in P.

3.6 Computing Link Distance Properties of Simple Polygons

The notion of a *link-distance* between two points x, y inside P was introduced as early as 1949 by Horn and Valentine [HV49]. The link-distance is defined as the smallest number of links (i.e., straight line segments) in a polygonal path connecting x and y within P, and turns out to be a useful metric for path planning within P when straight motion is easy to accomplish but turns are expensive. Alternately, it is the ideal metric for modelling robots that use telescopic-joint manipulators to pick and place objects in a work-space represented by a simple polygon. Subhash Suri [Su87a] presents a linear-time algorithm for calculating the link-distance between any two given points within

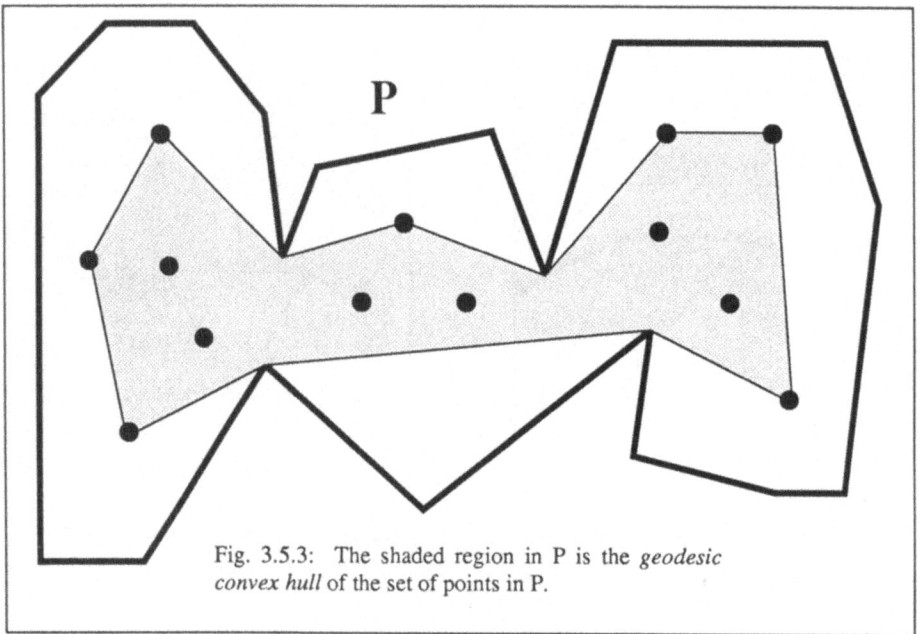

Fig. 3.5.3: The shaded region in P is the *geodesic convex hull* of the set of points in P.

P, provided a triangulation of P is given. Crucial to Suri's technique is a linear-time algorithm for decomposing (a triangulated polygon) P into, so-called, *k-visibility regions* for a fixed source point x, where the i-th visibility region consists of all points within P whose link-distance from x is precisely i. Several link-distance properties of the polygon P itself have already received attention. Suri [Su1] has considered the problem of calculating the *link-diameter* of P, which is defined as the maximal link-distance between any two points in P, and presents a divide-and-conquer algorithm for calculating this diameter in time O(n log n). Bill Lenhart, Ricky Pollack, Jorg Sack, Raimund Seidel, Micha Sharir, Subhash Suri, Godfried Toussaint, Sue Whitesides, and Chee Yap [LPSSSSTWY] have considered the somewhat more difficult problem of calculating the *link-center* of P, defined to be the set of all points x within P whose maximal link-distance to any point of P is the smallest possible. They prove several geometric properties of the link-center and present an algorithm that calculates this set in time O(n^2). They also give an O(n log n) time algorithm for finding a point x in an approximate link-center, namely the maximal link-distance from x to any point in P is at most one more than the value attained from the link-center. Djidjev, Lingas, & Sack [DLS88a] show that a point in the link center can be reported in O(n log n) time. Yan Ke [Ke88] has since shown on the other hand that the entire link center can be computed in O(n log n) time.

From the point of view of geometric location theory, any point in the link-center can serve as a location for a mobile unit that has to reach any point within P so that the maximum number of turns it needs to perform is minimized. From the point of view of manipulator-reachability theory any point in the link center can serve as a position in which to install a robot so that any point in P can be reached with a manipulator having the minimum number of telescopic-joints. Alternatively, a point in the link-center can serve as a location for a transmitter that can broadcast to any point within P (along a path fully contained in P) such that the maximum number of relay-stations necessary to reach any point in P is minimized.

We may also be interested in computing link distance properties of sets of points inside a polygon. ElGindy and Toussaint [ET89a] propose efficient algorithms for solving a variety of link-distance problems. In particular they consider the following:

1) the *link-diameter* of S in P, i.e., the maximal link-distance between any two sites in S.

2) the *link-center* of S in P, i.e., the set of all points z in P whose maximal link-distance to any site x in S is the smallest possible.

3) the *link-median* of S in P, i.e., those sites in S whose maximal link-distance to any other site in S is the smallest possible.

4) the *link-separation* of S in P, i.e., the minimal link-distance between any two sites in S.

5) the *link-hideout* of S in P, i.e., the set of all points z in P whose minimal link-distance to any site x in S is the largest possible.

6) the *link-maverick* of S in P, i.e., those sites in S whose minimal link-distance to any other site in S is the largest possible.

7) the *link-Voronoi-diagrams* of S in P, i.e., the partition of P into regions which are loci of points of P either closer to (the *nearest-link-diagram*), or further from (the *furthest-link-diagram*) one site in S than to any other.

3.7 Computing Visibility Properties of Simple Polygons

3.7.1 Strong visibility

Definition: Two points x and y are said to be *visible* provided that either the line segment [x,y] lies in P or *int*[x,y] lies in *ext*(P). In the first case we have *internal* visibility and in the second *external* visibility.

Definition: A set T is *strongly visible* from a set S provided that for every point x in S all points y in T are such that x and y are visible. We say also that in such a case T is star-shaped from x.

Most of the early work in computational geometry dealing with visibility (the *hidden line* problem) dealt with strong visibility. In recent years however increasing interest has vbeen devoted to so-called *weak visibility* or the *strong hidden-line* problem [To86b].

3.7.2 Weak visibility

Definition: A set T is *weakly visible* from a set S provided that for every point x in T there exists a point y in S such that x and y are visible.

Definition: A polygon P is called *edge-visible* provided that P contains an edge from which P is weakly internally visible.

The notion of weak *internal* visibility has received attention in both the mathematics and computer science literatures. Horn and Valentine [HV49] have characterized L-sets in terms of their weak visibility properties while such characterizations for convex and star-shaped sets have been presented by Shermer and Toussaint [ST88]. Avis and Toussaint [AT81] showed that given a simple polygon P and a specified edge e of P, whether P is edge-visible from e can be determined in O(n) time. A more difficult problem is to determine whether there exists an edge of P from which P is edge-visible. Clearly by applying the algorithm in [AT81] to each edge in turn the latter problem can be solved in $O(n^2)$ time. Sack and Suri [SS88] discovered a linear-time algorithm for determining all (if any) such edges of a given polygon. Recently Yan Ke [Ke88] considered the problem of detecting the weak visibility of a simple polygon from an internal line segment. He presents an O(n log n) time algorithm that tests if a polygon is weakly visible from some internal line segment and reports such a line segment if it exists. He also shows that the shortest such segment can be found in O(n log n) time. Finally he addresses the query version of this problem: given a query line segment in P, is P weakly visible from it? He shows that this question can be answered in O(log n) time after the polygon is preprocessed in O(n log n) time using O(n) space.

We can also focus on weak *external* visibility of a simple polygon. This topic is as yet quite unexplored compared to its *internal* counterpart. Toussaint and Avis [TA82] considered the problem of determining if a polygon is weakly externally visible. In their definition P is *weakly externally visible* if for every point x ∈ *bd*(P) there exists a ray starting at x that does not intersect *int*(P). With the results of [AT81] they show that this problem can be solved in O(n) time. The concept of *monotonicity* on the other hand has received considerable attention in the past. Here we note that monotonicity of P can be viewed as a type of external visibility from a point by an appropriate normalization.

Definition: Given a simple polygon P and a line L not intersecting P, we say that P is *weakly externally visible* from L if for every point x on the boundary of P there exists a point y in L such that the *interior* of the line segment [x,y] does not intersect the *interior* of P.

These problems have the following interpretation: P may represent some region whose exterior boundary it is desired to be guarded, perhaps by a robot travelling in another region or on a straight track represented by line. The above three notions of external visibility can be unified under the following definition of visibility.

Definition: A polygon P is σ-*sector-visible* if the smallest sector of sight lines for which P is externally visible spans an angle σ.

As a consequence of this definition we have that *weak-external-visibility* [TA82] is σ-*sector-visibility* for σ=2π, *weak external visibility from a line* is σ-*sector-visibility* for σ=π, and *monotonicity* is σ-*sector-visibility* for σ=0 (i.e., a point). Bhattacharya, Kirkpatrick and Toussaint [BKT89] shown that, given a simple polygon P, and an angle ψ, whether there exists a ψ-*sector-of-visibility* for P can be determined in Θ(n) time when ψ ≤ π and Θ(n log n) when π < ψ < 2π. Actually the algorithm for the detection problem also computes a succinct description of all such sectors of visibility as well as the shortest sector. They also show that with O(n) preprocessing and O(n) storage space, queries of the form "is polygon P weakly externally visible from query line L?" can be answered in O(log n) time per query. The problem is solved by reducing it first, to one of determining if a set of unbounded convex regions in the plane admits a *transversal* L (or *stabbing* line) with the constraint that L ∈ *ext*(P), secondly, to the problem of determining if a set of arcs on the unit circle C admit a placement of a semicircle on C that intersects every such arc, and finally to the problem of determining if a transformed set of arcs on C actually cover all of C.

Bhattacharya and Toussaint [BT88] consider the question of computing the shortest line segment from which a given convex polygon is weakly externally visible. It is shown that, given a *convex* polygon P, the *minimal length* line segment from which P is *weakly externally visible* can be found in O(n) time. The algorithm is based on the solution to a fundamental geometric minimization problem that is of independent interest and should find application in several different contexts.

3.7.3 How to spy

In 1985 Toussaint [To85b] proposed a new class of polygons, useful in the context of separating polygons in robotics, which he termed *radially monotone*. We say that a polygon P is radially monotone if there exists a point r in the plane such that every infinite half-line emanating from r that intersects P does so only in a single line segment. Clearly *star-shaped* polygons are radially monotone with r a point in the interior *kernel* of P but radially monotone polygons need not be star-shaped. More recently Dean, Lingas, and Sack [DLS88] independently rediscovered this class of polygons in a radically different context (that of spying with "X-ray visibility") and named these polygons *pseudo-star-shaped*. A polygon P is *pseudo-star-shaped* if there exists a point from which the whole interior of P can be seen, provided it is possible to see through single edges of P. Clearly both definitions are equivalent. The maximal set of points for which a polygon P is pseudo-star-shaped is called the *pseudo-kernel* of P. Dean, Lingas, and Sack [DLS88] show that the *pseudo-kernel* of an n-gon P can be computed in $O(n^2)$ time. Furthermore, and surprisingly, Mark Keil has found polygons whose pseudo-kernel consists of as many as $O(n^2)$ pairwise disconnected components. Therefore their algorithm is optimal in the worst case. Toussaint [To85b], and later Dean, Lingas, and Sack [DLS88] show how radially monotone polygons can be triangulated in linear time if it is known that the polygon is radially monotonic from a specified point. Hossam ElGindy has since shown that even if no such point is known a radially monotonic polygon can still be triangulated in linear time. A tantalizing open question remains: can radially monotone polygons be recognized in linear time? A related problem to that of spying is that of hiding. Thomas Shermer considers a variety of problems concerned with hidden sets in polygons [Sh89]. Yet another related problem is that of guarding. Shermer has recently developed a very elegant theory that unifies and extends almost all results known on guarding problems [Sh88a].

3.7.4 The *Superman* problem

In the X-ray model of visibility considered above it is assumed that an agent or detection mechanism can "see through one wall." A rather different visibility model obtains when we use the *Superman* metaphor for visibility. In this scenario we consider the problem that arizes when we have *Superman* standing on a point s outside of a building represented by a polygon P, and we have an object represented by another polygon K in the interior of P that we wish to hide from him. Of course the only way to hide something from *Superman* is to shield it with *kryptonite*. In other words, in this context the spying mechanism can see through not just one wall, but as many walls as desired, unless they are somehow shielded. Mouawad and Shermer [MS88] present an $O(T(n))$ time algorithm that determines the minimum number of edges of P that must be shielded in order to hide K from s, where $T(n)$ is the time required to triangulate a simple polygon.

3.8 Movable Separability of Polygons

The problem of movable separability of polygons is concerned with questions about moving polygons away from other polygons without incurring collisions and is of central concern to graphics, assembly, disassembly, and local spatial planning in robotics. For work on this problem before 1985 the reader is referred to [To85d] for a tutorial survey. More recently Toussaint [To89a] has shown that whether two simple n-gons P and Q can be separated with a single translation can be determined in $O(T(n))$ time, where $T(n)$ is the time needed to triangulate a simple polygon. A more difficult problem is that of determining whether Q can be moved by a *sequence* of translations to a position sufficiently far from P without colliding with P, and produce such a motion if it exists. Pollack, Sharir and Sifrony [PSS88] present an algorithm for solving this problem in time $O(n^2 \, a(n^2) \, \log^2 n)$ where $a(k)$ is the extremely slowly growing inverse Ackermann's function. Some results are also known for special classes of polygons. For example Pujari [Pu88] shows that three *unimodal* polygons can interlock, i.e., they can be placed such that no single polygon can be moved without disturbing the others. Some interesting connections have been made between these problems and partial orders of sets as well as lattice theory by Rival and Urrutia [RU88]. Work on these problems in three dimensions is only now starting [NS88], [NS89] and [RU89].

3.9 Moving Furniture Around the House

Related to the separability problems are other local spatial planning problems concerned with compliant motion. Such problems include the well known *sofa problem* and its variations [Ya84a]. Maddila and Yap [MY86] studied the problem of moving (translating and rotating) an n-sided simple polygon around a corner in a right-angled corridor. In particular they showed that they could construct a motion if one exists in $O(n^2)$ time. For convex polygons they solve the problem in O(n log n) time. Agarwal and Sharir [AS88] show that to determine whether a simple polygon can be moved around such a corner it takes time $O(\lambda_s(n) \log^2 n)$, where $\lambda_s(n)$ is the (almost-linear) maximum length of (n,s) Davenport-Schinzel sequences and s is a small positive constant. Furthermore, they show that if P is either star-shaped or monotone, then the complexity can be further reduced to $O(\lambda_s(n) \log n)$. Marek Teichman shows how to shove a table into a corner as tightly as possible in linear time [Te88]. Related problems are concerned with finding straight-line paths through sets of simple obstacles. For example Houle and Maciel [HM88] find the widest empty empty corridor through a set of n points in the plane in $O(n^2)$ time.

4. Polyhedral Terrains

4.1 Introduction

A polyhedral terrain $S = \{f_1, f_2, ..., f_n\}$, where the f_i denote planar faces, in a region of 3-space is a polyhedral surface with the property that every vertical line in the region intersects the surface exactly at one point. Terrains are frequently used to represent real-life topographical data and are of interest in geographic information systems[Bu86]. There are many computational problems that arize in processing terrains and visibility problems are amongst the most notorious [CS89], [DFPAN].

4.2 Strong Visibility

Strong visibility of a region refers to visibility of the region from a fixed point v. Alternately we may say that the region is star-shaped with respect to v. A polyhedral terrain S is always star-shaped with respect to some point v for v high enough above S. Thus two questions that immediately arize are concerned with computing (1) all points that can see S and (2) the point of minimum elevation that can see S. Let $\pi_1, \pi_2,...,\pi_n$ denote the planes containing the faces $f_1, f_2, ..., f_n$ respectively. Clearly a point v can see S if, and only if, v lies above each and every plane π_i. Let $U_1, U_2,..., U_n$ denote the upper half-spaces determined by $\pi_1, \pi_2,..., \pi_n$ respectively. It is then easy to see that the maximal set of points that can see S consists simply of the intersection $U = U_1 \cap U_2 \cap ,..., \cap U_n$. Furthermore, U can be computed in O(n log n) time with the algorithm of Preparata & Muller [PM79]. It is now also easy to see that the point of minimum elevation that can see S is the lowest point of U. A more interesting problem is the so-called *watchtower problem*. What is the minimum height watchtower that must be constructed on S such that a guard sitting on top of the watchtower can see all of S? Clearly the solution is the minimum perpendicular distance between U and S. Sharir has shown that this distance can be computed in $O(n \log^2 n)$ time. It is an open question whether $O(n \log n)$ suffices.

5.   Updating Triangulations

Triangulations of sets of points are popular methods of representing and storing terrain models in geographic information systems [Bu86]. One common operation that is often required is that of updating such triangulations. In particular one is interested in adding or deleting from a triangulation either vertices or edges that represent new or incorrect data. ElGindy and Toussaint [ET85] recently developed efficient algorithms for this purpose.

6.   Minimal Spanning Covers of Sets and Transversals

Given a family of n sets $F = \{F_1, F_2,..., F_n\}$ and a covering object C, we say that C is a *spanning cover* of F if there exists a placement of C such that for all i=1,2,...,n we have $F_i \cap C \neq \emptyset$. The smallest covering object that is a spanning cover of F is called the *minimal spanning cover* of F. The *spanning cover* problem generalizes and unifies several well known classes of problems previously considered in computational geometry such as determining *common transversals* and computing *reachability* regions in robotics. The *minimal spanning cover* problem on the other hand has been previously unexplored in almost all settings. Bhattacharya and Toussaint [BT89] provide solutions to several instances of this problem.

Common transversals for families of convex sets have been investigated for some time in both the mathematics and computer science literatures. In the latter the more aggressive term *stabber* is more often used for *transversal*. Transversals in the plane find application in several areas including line-fitting and updating triangulations. For recent work in this area the reader is referred to the work by Robert [RO88] and Avis and Wenger [AW87], [AW88], [We88].

7.   Computational Morphology

7.1   Polygon decomposition

The problems of decomposing polygons into various types of simpler polygons have a number of important practical applications and have received considerable attention recently from the theoretical perspective. See [To88a] for several papers discussing recent issues. One exciting result in this area concerns covering a simple polygon with the minimum number of convex polygons. Culberson and Reckhow [CR88] have recently proved that this problem is NP-hard. Independently, Thomas Shermer obtained a simpler proof of the same result [Sh88c].

7.2   The Shape of a Set of Points

One of the central problems in shape analysis is extracting the shape of a set of points. In [To88e] a new graph termed the *sphere-of-influence* graph is proposed as a primal sketch intended to capture the low-level perceptual structure of visual scenes consisting of dot-patterns (point-sets). The graph suffers from none of the drawbacks of previous methods and for a dot pattern consisting of n dots can be computed efficiently in $O(n \log n)$ time. For a survey of the most recent results in this area see the paper by Radke [Ra88].

7.3   Detecting Symmetry

Symmetry is an important feature in the analysis and synthesis of shape and form [LT87]. As such it is not surprising that it has received cosiderable attention in the pattern recognition, image processing, and computer graphics literatures. One of the earliest applications of computational geometry to symmetry detection was the algorithm of Akl & Toussaint [AT78b] to check for polygon similarity. Since then attention has been given to other aspects of symmetry and for objects other than polygons. For example, Sugihara [Su84] shows how a modification of the planar graph-isomorphism algorithm of Hopcroft and Tarjan [HT73] can be used to find all symmetries of a wide class of polyhedra in O(n log n) time.

Given a convex polygon P, associate with each point p in P the minimum area of the polygon to the left of any *chord* through p. The maximum over all points in P is known as *Winternitz's Measure of Symmetry* and the point p* that achieves this maximum is called the *center of area*. Diaz and O'Rourke [DO88] show that p* is unique and propose an algorithm for computing p* in time $O(n^6 \log^2 n)$. For a survey of the most recent work on detecting symmetry see [Ea88].

8.   Numerical Computational Geometry

As was mentioned in section 2.3 there is increasing interest in the design of numerically robust algorithms for solving geometric problems [DS88], [Mi88], [SI89]. Several different approaches to this problem are emerging. Edelsbrunner and Mucke [EM88] describe a technique which they call *simulation of simplicity* that simplifies correctness proofs of geometric algorithms by suggesting a uniform framework with which to deal with degeneracies. For alternate approaches see also [GY86], [HHK88] and [OTU87]. Of particular relevance to computer graphics is the work of Karasick [Ka88] and Sugihara [Su87] who consider numerical computational geometry in the context of *solid modelling*.

9.   References

[AS88]   Agarwal, P. and Sharir, S., "Red-blue intersection detection algorithms, with applications to motion planning and collision detection," *Proc. 4th ACM Symposium on Computational Geometry*, 1988, pp. 70-80.

[AT78a]   Akl, S. G. and Toussaint, G. T., "Efficient convex hull algorithms for pattern recognition applications," *Proc. Fourth International Joint Conf. on Pattern Recognition*, Kyoto, Japan, 1978.

[AT78b]   Akl, S. G. and Toussaint, G. T., "An improved algorithm to check for polygon similarity," *Information Processing Letters*, vol. 7, 1978, pp. 127-128.

[AT85]   Asano, T. and Toussaint, G. T., "Computing the geodesic center of a simple polygon," Technical Report SOCS-85.32, McGill University, 1985.

[AT86]   Asano, T. and Toussaint, G. T., "Computing the geodesic center of a simple polygon," in *Perspectives in Computing: Discrete Algorithms and Complexity, Proc. of Japan-US Joint Seminar*, D. S. Johnson, A. Nozaki, T. Nishizeki, H. Willis, *eds.*, June 1986, pp. 65-79.

[AT81]   Avis, A. and Toussaint, G. T., "An optimal algorithm for determining the visibility of a polygon from an edge," *IEEE Transactions on Computers*, vol. C-30, No. 12, December 1981, pp.910-914.

[AW87]   Avis, D. and Wenger, R., "Algorithms for line stabbers in space," *Proc. 3rd ACM Symposium on Computational Geometry*, 1987, pp.300-307.

[AW88]   Avis, D. and Wenger, R., "Polyhedral line transversals in space," *Discrete and Computational Geometry*, 1989.

[BE84]   Bhattacharya, B. K. and ElGindy, H., "A new linear convex hull algorithm for simple polygons," *IEEE Transactions on Information Theory*, vol. IT-30, No. 1, January 1984, pp. 85-88.

[BKT89] Bhattacharya, B. K., Kirkpatrick, D. G., and Toussaint, G. T., "Determining sector visibility of a polygon," manuscript in preparation.

[BT83]   Bhattacharya, B. K. and Toussaint, G. T., "Time-and-storage-efficient implementation of an optimal planar convex hull algorithm," *Image and Vision Computing*, vol. 1, no. 3, August 1983, pp. 140-144.

[BT88]   Bhattacharya, B. K. and Toussaint, G. T., "Computing minimal sets of external visibility," Tech. Rept. CCS/LCCR TR 88-29, Simon Fraser University, Burnaby, B.C., Canada.

[BT89]   Bhattacharya, B. K. and Toussaint, G. T., "Computing minimal spanning covers of sets," manuscript in preparation.

[Bu86]   Burrough, P. A., *Principles of Geographical Information Systems for Land Resources Assessment*, Clarendon Press, Oxford, 1986.

[CC88]   Chhajed, D. and Chandru, V., "Rectilinear hull, efficient sets, and convex hull: relationship and algorithms," RM. 88-23, School of Industrial Engineering, Purdue University, 1988.

[Ch82]   Chazelle, B., "A theorem on polygon cutting with applications," *Proc. 23rd IEEE Symposium on Foundations of Computer Science, Chicago*, November 1982.

[CI84]   Chazelle, B. and Incerpi, J., "Triangulation and shape complexity," *ACM Transactions on Graphics*, vol. 3, 1984, pp.135-152.

[CR88]   Culberson, J. C. and Reckhow, R. A., "Covering polygons is hard," *Proc. 29th Symposium on Foundations of Computer Science*, October 1988.

[CS89]   Cole, R. and Sharir, M., "Visibility problems for polyhedral terrains," *Journal of Symbolic Computation*, in press.

[De85]   Devroye, L., "Expected time analysis of algorithms in computational geometry," in *Computational Geometry*, ed., G. T. Toussaint, North-Holland, 1985, pp. 135-151.

[DFPAN] DeFloriani, L., Falcidieno, B., Pienovi, C., Allen, D., and Nagy, G., "A visibility-based model for terrain features," *Proc. Int. Symp. on Spatial Data Handling*, Seattle, July 1986.

[DGHS]   Dobkin, D., Guibas, L., Hershberger, J., and Snoeyink, J., "An efficient algorithm for finding the CSG representation of a simple polygon," *Proc. SIGGRAPH'88*, Atlanta, August 1-5, 1988, pp. 31-40.

[DLS88] Dean, J. A., Lingas, A., and Sack, J.-R., "Recognizing polygons, or how to spy," *The Visual Computer*, vol. 3, 1988, pp. 344-355.

[DLS88a] Djidjev, H. N., Lingas, A., and Sack, J.-R., "An O(n log n) algorithm for computing a link center in a simple polygon," Tech. Rept. SCS-TR-148, July 1988.

[DO88] Diaz, M. and O'Rourke, J., "Algorithms for computing the center of area of a convex polygon," Tech. Rept. 88-26, Johns Hopkins University.

[DS88] Dobkin, D. and Silver, D., "Recipes for geometry & numerical analysis - Part I: An empirical study," *Proc. 4th Annual Symposium on Computational Geometry*, Urbana, June 1988, pp. 93-105.

[DT81] Devroye, L. and Toussaint, G. T., "A note on linear expected time algorithms for finding convex hulls," *Computing*, vol. 26, pp. 361-366.

[Dw88a] Dwyer, R. A., "Average-case analysis of algorithms for convex hulls and Voronoi diagrams," Ph.D. thesis, Carnegie-Mellon University, 1988.

[Dw88b] Dwyer, R. A., "On the convex hull of random points in a polygon," *Journal of Applied Probability*, vol. 25, No. 4, 1988.

[Dy86] Dyer, M. E., "On a multidimensional search technique and its applications to the Euclidean one-center problem," *SIAM Journal of Computing*, Vol. 15, 1986, pp. 725-738.

[Ea88] Eades, P., "Symmetry finding algorithms," in *Computational Morphology*, ed., G. T. Toussaint, North-Holland, 1988, pp. 41-51.

[EAT83] ElGindy, H., Avis, D. and Toussaint, G. T., "Applications of a two-dimensional hidden-line algorithm to other geometric problems," *Computing*, vol. 31, 1983, pp.191-202.

[Ed87] Edelsbrunner, H., *Algorithms in Combinatorial Geometry*, Springer-Verlag, 1987.

[El85] ElGindy, H. A., "A linear algorithm for triangulating weakly externally visible polygons," Tech. Report MS-CIS-86-75, University of Pennsylvania, September 1985.

[EM88] Edelsbrunner, H. and Mucke, E., "Simulation of simplicity: a technique to cope with degenerate cases in geometric algorithms," *Proc. 4th Annual Symposium on Computational Geometry*, Urbana, Illinois, June 1988, pp. 118-133.

[ET85] ElGindy, H. A. and Toussaint, G. T., "Efficient algorithms for inserting and deleting edges from triangulations," *Proc. International Conference on Foundations of Data Organization*, Kyoto, Japan, May 22-24, 1985.

[ET88] ElGindy, H. and Toussaint, G. T., "On triangulating palm polygons in linear time," *Proc. Computer Graphics International '88*, Geneva, May 24-27, 1988.

[ET89] ElGindy, H. and Toussaint, G. T., "On geodesic properties of polygons relevant to linear time triangulation," *The Visual Computer*, in press.

[ET89a] ElGindy, H. and Toussaint, G. T., "Computing link-distance properties inside a simple polygon," manuscript in preparation.

[FA84] Franklin, W. Randolph and Akman, Varol, "Shortest paths between source and goal points located on/around a convex polyhedron," *Proc. Twenty-Second Annual Allerton Conference*, Monticello, Illinois, October 1984, pp. 103-112.

[FM84]   Fournier, A. and Montuno, D. Y., "Triangulating simple polygons and equivalent prob-
          lems," *ACM Transactions on Graphics*, vol. 3, April 1984, pp.153-174.

[FP75]   Feng, H-Y. F. and Pavlidis, T., "Decomposition of polygons into simpler components:
          feature generation for syntactic pattern recognition," *IEEE Transactions on Computers*,
          vol. C-24, June 1975, pp.636-650.

[Gh87]   Ghosh, S. K., "A few applications of the set-visibility algorithm," Tech. Rept. CS-TR-
          1797, University of Maryland, March 1987.

[GH87]   Guibas, L., and Herschberger, J., "Optimal shortest path queries in a simple polygon,"
          Proc. Third Annual ACM Symposium on Computational Geometry, University of Water-
          loo, June 1987, pp. 50-63.

[GHLST]   Guibas, L., Hershberger, J., Leven, D., Sharir, M., and Tarjan, R. E., "Linear-time algo-
          rithms for visibility and shortest path problems inside triangulated simple polygons," *Al-
          gorithmica*, vol. 2, 1987, pp. 209-234.

[GJPT]   Garey, M. R., Johnson, D. S., Preparata, F. P. and Tarjan, R. E., "Triangulating a simple
          polygon," *Information Processing Letters*, vol. 7, 1978, pp.175-179.

[GS88]   Golin, M. and Sedgewick, R., "Analysis of a simple yet efficient convex hull algorithm,"
          Proc. 4th Annual Symposium on Computational Geometry, Urbana, Illinois, June 1988,
          pp.153-163.

[GY83]   Graham, R. L. and Yao, F. F., "Finding the convex hull of a simple polygon," *Journal of Al-
          gorithms*, vol. 4, 1983, pp. 324-331.

[GY86]   Greene, D. H. and Yao, F. F., "Finite-resolution computational geometry," *Proc. 27th
          IEEE Symposium on Foundations of Computer Science*, Toronto, October 1986, pp. 143-
          152.

[HeMe]   Hertel, S. and Mehlhorn, K., "Fast triangulation of simple polygons," *Proc. FCT, LNCS*
          158, 1983, pp.207-215.

[HHK88]   Hoffmann, C. M., Hopcroft, J. E., and Karasick, M. S., "Towards implementing robust geo-
          metric computations," *Proc. 4th Annual Symposium on Computational Geometry*, Urbana,
          Illinois, June 1988, pp. 106-117.

[HM88]   Houle, M. and Maciel, A., "Finding the widest empty corridor through a set of points," in
          Snapshots of Computational and Discrete Geometry, G. T. Toussaint, ed., Tech. Report
          SOCS-88.11, Computational Geometry Laboratory, McGill University, June 1988, pp.
          201-214.

[Ho75]   Ho, W.-C., "Decomposition of a polygon into triangles," *The Mathematical Gazette*, vol.
          59, 1975, pp.132-134.

[HT73]   Hopcroft, J. E. and Tarjan, R. E., "A V log V algorithm for isomorphism of triconnected
          planar graphs, *Journal of Computer and System Sciences*, vol. 7, 1973, pp. 323-331.

[HV49]   Horn, A. and Valentine, F. A., "Some properties of L-sets in the plane," *Duke Mathemat-
          ics Journal*, vol. 16, 1949, pp.131-140.

[II86]   Imai, H. and Iri, M., "Computational geometric methods for polygonal approximations of a
          curve," *Computer Vision, Graphics, and Image Processing*, vol. 36, 1986, pp. 31-41.

[II86]   Imai, H. and Iri, M., "Polygonal approximations of a curve - Formulations and algorithms," in *Computational Morphology*, ed., G. T. Toussaint, North-Holland, 1988, pp.71-86.

[Ka88]   Karasick, M., "On the representation and manipulation of rigid solids," Ph.D. thesis, School of Computer Science, McGill University, Montreal, 1988.

[Ke88]   Ke, Y., "Detecting the weak visibility of a simple polygon and related problems," The Johns Hopkins University, manuscript, March 1988.

[Ke88a]   Ke, Y., "An efficient algorithm for link distance problems inside a simple polygon," Johns Hopkins Tech. Rept. 87/27, June 1988.

[KS86]   Kirkpatrick, D. G. and Seidel, R., "The ultimate planar convex hull algorithm?" *SIAM Journal on Computing*, vol. 15, No. 1, February 1986, pp. 287-299.

[LC87]   Lee, S. H. and Chwa, K. Y., "A new triangulation linear class of simple polygons," *International Journal of Computer Mathematics*, vol. 22, 1987, pp.135-147

[Le83]   Lee, D. T., "On finding the convex hull of a simple polygon," *International Journal of Computer & Information Science*, vol. 12, 1983, pp. 87-98.

[Le11]   Lennes, N. J., "Theorems on the simple finite polygon and polyhedron," *American Journal of Mathematics*, vol. 33, 1911, pp.37-62.

[LM84]   Lantuejoul, C., and Maisonneuve, F., "Geodesic methods in quantitative image analysis," *Pattern Recognition*, Vol. 17, 1984, pp. 177-187.

[LT87]   Leou, J.-J. and Tsai, W.-H., "Automatic rotational symmetry determination for shape analysis," *Pattern Recognition*, vol. 20, No. 6, 1987, pp. 571-582.

[LP84]   Lee, D. T., and Preparata, F. P., "Euclidean shortest paths in the presence of rectilinear barriers," *Networks*, Vol. 14, No. 3., 1984, pp. 393-410.

[LPSSSSTWY] Lenhart, W., Pollack, R., Sack, J., Seidel, R., Sharir, M., Suri, S., Toussaint, G., Whitesides, S., and Yap, C., "Computing the link center of a simple polygon," *Proceedings of the Third Annual Symposium on Computational Geometry*, Waterloo, Ontario, Canada, June 8-10, 1987, pp.1-10.

[MA79]   McCallum, D. and Avis, D., "A linear algorithm for finding the convex hull of a simple polygon," *Information Processing Letters*, vol. 9, 1979, pp. 201-206.

[Me75]   Meisters, G. H., "Polygons have ears," *American Mathematical Monthly*, June/July 1975, pp.648-651

[Me83]   Megiddo, N., "Linear-time algorithms for linear programming in R^3 and related problems," *SIAM Journal of Computing*, Vol. 12, 1983, pp. 759-776.

[Meh84]   Mehlhorn, K., *Multidimensional Searching and Computational Geometry*, Springer-Verlag, 1984.

[Mel87]   Melkman, A. A., "On-line construction of the convex hull of a simple polyline," *Information Processing Letters*, vol. 25, April 1987, pp. 11-12.

[Mi88]   Milenkovic, V., "Verifiable implementations of geometric algorithms using finite precision arithmetic," Tech. Rept. CMU-CS-88-168, Carnegie Mellon University, July 1988.

[Mo84]   Mount, D. M., "On finding shortest paths on convex polyhedra," Technical Report, Computer Science Dept., University of Maryland, October 1984.

[MO88]   Melkman, A. A. and O'Rourke, J., "On polygonal chain approximation," in *Computational Morphology*, ed., G. T. Toussaint, North-Holland, 1988, pp.87-95.

[MS88]   Mouawad, N. and Shermer, T., "The *Superman* problem," in *Snapshots of Computational and Discrete Geometry*, G. T. Toussaint, ed., Tech. Report SOCS-88.11, Computational Geometry Laboratory, McGill University, June 1988, pp. 215-232.

[MT85]   McQueen, M. M. and Toussaint, G. T., "On the ultimate convex hull algorithm in practice," *Pattern Recognition Letters*, vol. 3, January 1985, pp. 29-34.

[MY86]   Maddila, S, and Yap, C., "Moving a polygon around a corner in a polygon," *Proc. 2nd ACM Symposium on Computational Geometry*, 1986, pp. 187-192.

[NS88]   Nurmi, O. and Sack, J.-R., "Separating a polyhedron by one translation from a set of obstacles," *Proc. Workshop on Graph Theory*, Amsterdam, 1988.

[NS89]   Nussbaum, D. and Sack, J.-R., "Translation separability of polyhedra," *First Canadian Conference on Computational Geometry*, Montreal, August 1989.

[O'R87]   O'Rourke, J., *Art Gallery Theorems and Algorithms*, Oxford University Press, 1987.

[O'R88]   O'Rourke, J., "Computational geometry," in *Annual Review of Computer Science*, ed., J. F. Traub, vol. 3, 1988, pp. 389-411.

[OSW84]   Ottmann, T., Soisalon-Soininen, E., and Wood, D., "On the definition and computation of rectilinear convex hulls," *Information Sciences*, vol. 33, 1984, pp. 167-171.

[OTU87]   Ottmann, T., Thiemt, G., and Ulrich, C., "Numerical stability of geometric algorithms," *Proc. 3rd Symposium on Computational Geometry*, Waterloo, June 1987, pp. 119-125.

[Pe88]   Pesant, G., "Galleries require more sleepy watchmen: K-guarding simple polygons," in *Snapshots of Computational and Discrete Geometry*, G. T. Toussaint, ed., Tech. Report SOCS-88.11, Computational Geometry Laboratory, McGill University, June 1988, pp. 145-166.

[PeSa]   Peshkin, M. A., and Sanderson, A. C., "Reachable grasps on a polygon: the convex rope algorithm," Teck. Rept. CMU-RI-TR-85-6, Carnegie-Mellon University, 1985, also *IEEE Transactions on Robotics and Automation*, in press.

[PM79]   Preparata, F. and Muller, D., "Finding the intersection of n halfspaces in time $O(n \log n)$ time," *Journal of Theoretical Computer Science*, vol. 8., 1979, pp. 44-55.

[Pr83]   Preparata, F., ed., *Computational Geometry*, JAI Press, 1983.

[PSS88]   Pollack, R., Sharir, M., and Sifrony, S., "Separating two simple polygons by a sequence of translations," *Journal of Discrete and Computational Geometry*, Vol. 3, 1988, pp. 123-136.

[Pu88]   Pujari, A. K., "Separability of unimodal polygons," *Pattern Recognition Letters*, vol. 7, 1988, pp. 163-165.

[Ra88] Radke, J. D., "On the shape of a set of points," *Computational Morphology*, Toussaint, G. T., ed., North-Holland, 1988, pp. 105-136.

[Re80] Requicha, A., "Representations for rigid solids: theory, methods, and systems," *ACM Computing Surveys*, vol. 12, 1980, pp. 437-464.

[Ro88] Robert, J.-M., "Stabbing hyperspheres by a hyperplane," in *Snapshots of Computational and Discrete Geometry*, G. T. Toussaint, ed., Tech. Rep. SOCS-88.11, Computational Geometry Lab., McGill University, June 1988, pp. 181-188.

[RS85] Reif, J. and Storer, J., "minimizing turns for discrete movement in the interior of a polygon," Tech. Rept., Harvard University, December 1985.

[RS88] Reif, J. and Sen, S., "An efficient output-sensitive hidden-surface removal algorithm and its parallelization," *Proc. 4th ACM Symposium on Computational Geometry*, 1988, pp. 193-200.

[RU88] Rival, I. and Urrutia, J., "Representing orders on the plane by translating convex figures," *Order*, vol. 4, 1988, pp. 319-339.

[RU89] Rival, I. and Urrutia, J., "Order models for motion in three-space," *First Canadian Conference on Computational Geometry*, Montreal, August 1989.

[SCH72] Sklansky, J., Chazin, R. L., and Hansen, B. J., "Minimum perimeter polygons of digitized silhouettes," *IEEE Transactions on Computers*, Vol. C-21, March 1972, pp. 260-268.

[SF88] Senechal, M. and Fleck, G., eds., *Shaping Space: A Polyhedral Approach*, Birkhauser, 1988.

[SGB83] Suss, W., Gercke, H., and Berger, K. H., "Differential geometry of curves and surfaces," in *Fundamentals of Mathematics: Vol. II, Geometry*, H. Behnke, et al., eds., MIT Press, 1983, pp. 534-571.

[Sh78] Shamos, M. I., *Computational Geometry*, Ph. D. thesis, Yale University, 1978.

[Sha89] Sharir, M., "The shortest watchtower and related problems for polyhedral terrains," *Information Processing Letters*, in press.

[Sh88a] Shermer, T., "Link guarding simple polygons," in *Snapshots of Computational and Discrete Geometry*, G. T. Toussaint, ed., Tech. Report SOCS-88.11, Computational Geometry Laboratory, McGill University, June 1988, pp. 79-88.

[Sh88b] Shermer, T., "Computing bushy and thin triangulations," in *Snapshots of Computational and Discrete Geometry*, G. T. Toussaint, ed., Tech. Report SOCS-88.11, Computational Geometry Laboratory, McGill University, June 1988, pp. 119-134.

[Sh88c] Shermer, T., "Convex cover is NP-hard," Technical Note, School of Computer Science, McGill University, October 1988.

[Sh89] Shermer, T., "Hiding people in polygons," *Computing*, in press.

[SI89] Sugihara, K. and Iri, M., "Construction of the Voronoi diagram for over 10^5 generators in single-precision arithmetic," *First Canadian Conference on Computational Geometry*, Montreal, August 21-25, 1989.

[SS84] Sharir, M., and Schorr, A., "On shortest paths in polyhedral spaces," *Proc. Sixteenth Annual ACM Symposium in the Theory of Computing,* Washington, 1984, pp. 144-153.

[SS86] Sack, J.-R. and Suri, S., "An optimal algorithm for detecting weak visibility of a polygon," Tech. Rept. SCS-TR-114, Carleton University, Ottawa, Canada, Dec. 1986.

[SSH87] Schwartz, J. T., Sharir, M., and Hopcroft, J., *Planning, Geometry, and the Complexity of Robot Motion,* Norwood, 1987.

[ST88] Shermer, T. and Toussaint, G. T., "Characterizations of convex and star-shaped polygons," in *Snapshots of Computational and Discrete Geometry,* G. Toussaint, editor, Tech. Rept. SOCS-88.11, School of Computer Science, McGill University, June 1988.

[ST88a] Shermer, T. and Toussaint, G. T., "Anthropomorphic polygons can be recognized in linear time," in *Snapshots of Computational and Discrete Geometry,* G. T. Toussaint, ed., Tech. Report SOCS-88.11, Computational Geometry Laboratory, McGill University, June 1988, pp. 7-14.

[ST88b] Shermer, T. and Toussaint, G. T., "Characterizations of star-shaped polygonal sets," manuscript in preparation.

[Su84] Sugihara, K., "An O(n log n) algorithm for determining the congruity of polyhedra," *Journal of Computer and Systems Sciences,* vol. 29., 1984, pp. 36-47.

[Su87] Sugihara, K., "An approach to error-free solid modelling," Notes, *Institute for Mathematics and its Applications,* University of Minnesota, 1987.

[Su87a] Suri, S., "Minimum link paths in polygons and related problems," Ph.D. thesis, The Johns Hopkins University, August 1987.

[Su87b] Suri, S., "The all-geodesic-furthest neighbors problem for simple polygons,"*Proc. Third Annual ACM Symposium on Computational Geometry,* University of Waterloo, June 1987, pp. 64-75.

[SV80] Schoone, A. A. and van Leeuwen, J., "Triangulating a star-shaped polygon," Tech. Report, RUV-CS-80-3, University of Utrecht, April 1980.

[SV87] Schaffer, A. A. and Van Wyk, C. J., "Convex hulls of piece-wise smooth Jordan curves," *Journal of Algorithms,* vol. 8, 1987, pp. 66-94.

[SY87] Schwartz, J. T. and Yap, C. K., *Algorithmic and Geometric Aspects of Robotics,* Erlbaum, 1987.

[TA82] Toussaint, G. T. and Avis, D., "On a convex hull algorithm for polygons and its application to triangulation problems," *Pattern Recognition,* vol. 15, No. 1, 1982, pp.23-29.

[Te88] Teichman, M., "Shoving a table into a corner," in *Snapshots of Computational and Discrete Geometry,* G. T. Toussaint, ed., Tech. Report SOCS-88.11, Computational Geometry Laboratory, McGill University, June 1988, pp. 99-118.

[To84] Toussaint, G. T., "A new linear algorithm for triangulating monotone polygons," *Pattern Recognition Letters,* vol. 2, March 1984, pp.

[To85] Toussaint, G. T., ed., *Computational Geometry,* North-Holland, 1985.

[To85a]   Toussaint, G. T., "A historical note on convex hull finding algorithms," *Pattern Recognition Letters*, vol. 3, January 1985, pp. 21-28.

[To85b]   Toussaint, G. T., "On the complexity of approximating polygonal curves in the plane," *Proc. IASTED International Symposium on Robotics and Automation*, Lugano, Switzerland, 1985.

[To85c]   Toussaint, G. T., "Shortest path solves translation separability of polygons," Tech. Rept. SOCS-85.27, School of Computer Science, McGill University, 1985.

[To85d]   Toussaint, G. T., "Movable separability of sets," in *Computational Geometry*, Toussaint, G. T., ed., North-Holland, 1985.

[To86]   Toussaint, G. T., "New results in computational geometry relevant to pattern recognition in practice," in *Pattern Recognition in Practice II*, E. S. Gelsema and L. N. Kanal, Editors, North-Holland, 1986, pp.135-146.

[To86a]   Toussaint, G. T., "Shortest path solves edge-to-edge visibility in a polygon," *Pattern Recognition Letters*, Vol. 4, July 1986, pp. 165-170.

[To86b]   Toussaint, G. T., "A linear-time algorithm for solving the strong hidden-line problem in a simple polygon," *Pattern Recognition Letters*,1987.

[To88a]   Toussaint, G. T., ed., *Computational Morphology*, North-Holland, 1988.

[To88b]   Toussaint, G. T., "Computing geodesic properties inside a simple polygon," Technical Report CSS/LCCR TR 88-23, Centre for Systems Science, Simon Fraser University, Burnaby, B.C. Canada, October 1988.

[To88c]   Toussaint, G. T., ed., *Snapshots of Computational and Discrete Geometry*, Tech. Report SOCS-88.11, Computational Geometry Laboratory, McGill University, June 1988.

[To88d]   Toussaint, G. T., "An output-complexity-sensitive polygon triangulation algorithm," in *Snapshots of Computational and Discrete Geometry*, G. T. Toussaint, ed., Tech. Report SOCS-88.11, Computational Geometry Laboratory, McGill University, June 1988, pp. 55-68.

[To88e]   Toussaint, G. T., "A graph-theoretical primal sketch," in *Computational Morphology*, Toussaint, G. T., ed., North-Holland, 1988.

[To88f]   Toussaint, G. T., "Detecting weak external visibility of a polygon from a line," in *Snapshots of Computational and Discrete Geometry*, G. T. Toussaint, ed., Tech. Report SOCS-88.11, Computational Geometry Laboratory, McGill University, June 1988, pp. 189-200.

[To89]   Toussaint, G. T., "Anthropomorphic polygons," *American Mathematical Monthly*, in press.

[To89a]   Toussaint, G. T., "On separating two simple polygons by a single translation," *Discrete and Computational Geometry*, 1989.

[TV88]   Tarjan, R. E. and Van Wyk, C. J., "An O(n log log n)-time algorithm for triangulating simple polygons," *SIAM Journal on Computing*, 1988.

[We88]   Wenger, R., "Stabbing and separation," Ph.D. thesis, School of Computer Science, McGill University, February 1988.

[WS85]   Woo, T. C. and Shin, S. Y., "A linear time algorithm for triangulating a point-visible polygon," *ACM Transactions on Graphics*, vol. 4, January 1985, pp.60-70.

[Ya84]   Yap, C. K., "An O(n log n) algorithm for the Voronoi diagram of a set of simple curve segments," Tech. Rept. 161, Courant Institute of Mathematical Sciences, New York University, 1984.

[Ya84a] Yap, C. K., "How to move a chair through a door," Tech. Rept., Courant Institute of Mathematical Sciences, New York University, 1984

Godfried T. Toussaint received the B.Sc. degree from the University of Tulsa, Tulsa, OK., and the M.A.Sc. and Ph.D. degrees from the University of British Columbia, Vancouver, B.C., Canada in 1968, 1970, and 1972, respectively, all in Electrical Engineering.
Since 1972 he has been with the School of Computer Science at McGill University teaching and doing research in the areas of information theory, pattern recognition, and computational geometry. During the summers of 1975 and 1977 he was a Visiting Scholar at the Information Systems Laboratory, Stanford University. The sabbatical year 1980-81 he spent as a Visiting Scientist at the Applied Mathematics Research Center of the University of Montreal. During the spring of 1986 he was a Visiting Scholar at the Courant Institute of Mathematical Sciences, NYU and during the fall of 1988 he was a British Columbia Advanced Systems Institute Fellow at Simon Fraser University.
Dr. Toussaint is past council-member of the North American Branch of the *Classification Society*, and past Associate Editor of the *IEEE Transactions on Information Theory*. Presently, he is Associate Editor of the *Plenum Press Series on Advanced Applications in Pattern Recognition*, Associate Editor of *Pattern Recognition*, and Associate Editor of the *IEEE Transactions on Pattern Analysis and Machine Intelligence*. He is also on the editorial boards of of the journals *Discrete & Computational Geometry* and *Science on Form*. He is a member of several learned societies including the *IEEE*, the *Pattern Recognition Society* and the *New York Academy of Sciences*. He recently edited two books published by North Holland, *Computational Geometry* in 1985 and *Computational Morphology* in 1988. In 1978 he was the recipient of the Pattern Recognition Society's Best Paper of the Year Award and in 1985 he was awarded a *Killam Senior Research Fellowship* by the Canada Council to carry out a two-year research project on movable separability of sets.

Address: Computational Geometry Laboratory, School of Computer Science, McGill University, 3480 University Street, Montreal, Quebec, CANADA H3A 2A7 (e-mail)godfried@opus.cs.mcgill.ca

Tools for the Formal Development of Rasterisation Algorithms

S.M. Eker* and J.V. Tucker**

ABSTRACT

We consider the mathematical foundations of the stepwise refinement of rasterisation algorithms. We describe tools taken from the theory of abstract data types and apply them to the formal derivation of line drawing algorithms. Methods include the refinement of data types and the transformation of functions defined by equations.

Keywords: rasterisation algorithms, line drawing, abstract data types, equational specifications, stepwise refinement of algorithms, transformation of functional programs, formal verification.

0. INTRODUCTION

We present mathematical tools for the formal specification, derivation and verification of rasterisation algorithms (such as Bresenham's line and circle drawing algorithms) based on the mathematical theory of abstract data types. We are particularly concerned with the problem of establishing a general theoretical framework that can analyse and unify the methods for the stepwise refinement of these algorithms.

Expressed generally, a rasterisation algorithm is an algorithm for generating sets of points in a discrete space D, coordinatised by the integers $\mathbf{Z}$, that approximates 'geometric' sets of points in a space S, coordinatised by the real numbers $\mathbf{R}$. Normally attention is restricted to the case $D = \mathbf{Z}^n$ and $S = \mathbf{R}^n$ for $n = 2$ or 3, and in which approximations to algebraic curves and surfaces are drawn. Efficient algorithms are developed that use simple operations on $\mathbf{Z}$ and are incremental in some sense, for example calculating the i th point in an enumeration in terms of the $i-1$th point.

We will examine these two constraints and their influence on algorithm development using the mathematical theory of abstract data types. The derivation of algorithms that use simple operations involves the elimination of sets of complex data and operations on them, such as the set $\mathbf{R}$ of real numbers and the square root function on $\mathbf{R}$, from the specifications and algorithms. The derivation of incremental algorithms involves the introduction of simple recursions into specifications and algorithms.

---

*S. M. Eker acknowledges the financial support of Mullards Ltd.

**J. V. Tucker acknowledges the financial support of the SERC through grant GR/D/90345.

In Section 1 we summerise ideas in the theory of abstract data types that we apply in later sections. In particular, we describe the concept of a *many sorted algebra* and illustrate it with examples relevant to curve drawing. A many sorted algebra models formally a *module* containing the sets of data and primitive functions for the definition of an algorithm. A basic tool in any form of algorithm development is a set of transformations that replace complex basic operations in algorithms by simpler basic operations. These transformations are transformations between algebras and algorithms. We formulate concepts to classify the relative strength or equivalence of computation on two data types.

In Section 2 we present the *primitive recursive equations* in order to specify algorithms by means of functions on many sorted algebras. If an algorithm over an algebra is defined by functions then they may be combined to make a new algebra, modelling a new module. The primitive recursive functions, defined by these equations, are suited to incremental algorithms for rasterisation. Furthermore, their equational definition may be easily converted into algebraic specifications for algebras that present the algorithm in the form of a module. Or the equations can be converted into horn clauses and treated by logic programming methods. The primitive recursive functions were first formulated on the natural numbers by Richard Dedekind in 1888.

In Section 3 we examine a completely formal derivation of Bresenham's line drawing algorithm using the above tools. The problem is to develop the algorithm from a specification by transformations that

(1) introduce an incremental form, and

(2) eliminate the rational numbers and their operations, such as multiplication, in favour of integers with addition only.

A similar transformation process for the formal derivation of Bresenham's circle drawing algorithm is possible wherein the transformations

(1) introduce an incremental form,

(2) eliminate the constructible numbers and the square root operation in favour of the integers with addition and multiplication, and

(3) eliminate integer multiplication by a technique called strength reduction.

However we shall not give this latter derivation.

We will describe the transformation process in considerable detail and pay particular attention to the role of proofs that show that the transformations preserve correctness with respect to the specification. These proofs are given in order to show the ingredients necessary for a computer verification of the transformations. The stepwise derivation of algorithms is guided by the methodological model of the design process described in Eker and Tucker [1988], and the mathematical model of the stepwise refinement process described in Back [1981]. However we are not able to explain the connection on this occasion.

More importantly, there seems to be a particular need for a detailed analysis of the scope and limits of systematic algorithm development techniques in graphics. Consider for example, the problems that arise in our understanding of complicated algorithms such as those in Castle and Pitteway [1985] and Castle and Pitteway [1987]. Or consider the smooth and contrasting derivations of specific algorithms such as those in Sproull [1982], Corthout and Jonkers [1986], and Swenker [1987] which raise interesting questions as to the existence of generally applicable principles.

The general framework under development here is a mathematical theory, based upon algebraic concepts and methods, for the design and analysis of algorithms. As a mathematical theory it is a tool that is independent of any particular specification and programming language. Once an algorithm has been established and studied using the theory it is straight forward to translate the equational descriptions into both functional and logic programming languages, and into algebraic specification languages, for execution and further empirical analysis. It is also straight forward to employ theorem provers and proof checkers for machine supported proofs of correctness.

This paper is third in a series examining the theoretical foundations for the design of algorithms and architectures for rasterisation. In Eker and Tucker [1988] we studied the problem of formalising the design process, and the derivation of line drawing algorithms and concurrent architectures. In Eker and Tucker [1989] we studied the formal verification of a key part of the Pixel Planes architecture.

The prerequisites for the paper are an acquaintance with algebra, algorithm design, and rasterisation algorithms and, of course, interest in foundational problems.

Appropriate basic reference material is Ehrig and Mahr [1985] for abstract data type theory; Back [1980] and Mili, Desharnais and Gagne [1986] for algorithm development; and Rogers [1985] for rasterisation.

We wish to thank R. J. R. Back (Abo Academy, Turku) for useful discussions on the material of this paper.

1. ABSTRACT DATA TYPES FOR RASTERISATION

1.1. Abstract data types

A *many sorted algebra A* consists of sets of data $A_1, \ldots, A_m$ which are called *carriers* or *domains*; distinguished elements $c_1, \ldots, c_p$ drawn from those sets and which are called *constants*; and functions $f_1, \ldots, f_q$ from cartesian products over the domains into domains and which are called *basic* or *primitive operations*. We write

$$A = <A_1, \ldots, A_m \mid c_1, \ldots, c_p, f_1, \ldots, f_q>.$$

The syntactic counterpart to a many sorted algebra is a *many sorted signature* Σ which consists of names $s_1, \ldots, s_m$ for domains which are usually called *sorts*; names $\alpha_1, \ldots, \alpha_p$ for constants; and names $\sigma_1, \ldots, \sigma_q$ for operations. We write

$$\Sigma = <s_1, \ldots, s_m \mid \alpha_1, \ldots, \alpha_p, \sigma_1, \ldots, \sigma_q>.$$

A many sorted algebra models or specifies the data and basic functions involved in an implementation of an abstract data type. However a further property is usually necessary.

An algebra A is said to be *minimal* if each element in any of the domains of A can be generated by the application of a finite sequence of operations to the constants. In consequence, the same sequence of applications applied to the names of the operations and constants, taken from the signature, determines an expression that is a name for each element of any domain of a minimal algebra A.

A minimal algebra A models a *concrete implementation* of an abstract data type, and a class **K** of such algebras models a class of concrete implementations.

Two algebras A and B are equivalent implementations of an abstract data type if they are isomorphic; we write $A \approx B$. Thus we can frame the following general definition of an abstract data type.

An *abstract data type* is a class **K** of minimal algebras closed under isomorphism, i.e. $A \in \mathbf{K}, B \approx A$ implies $B \in \mathbf{K}$.

Often we define such an abstract data type by setting **K** to be the class of all structures satisfying a set E of axioms concerning the operations in Σ. The pair (Σ, E) is called an *axiomatic specification*. If the axioms in E are equations then (Σ, E) is called an *algebraic specification*.

1.2. Standard algebras

The algebras we shall use for our specifications, verifications and transformations of rasterisation algorithms will be so called *standard algebras* in that they contain the following domains and operations:

Counters: $T = <\{0, 1, \cdots\} \mid 0, t+1>$. This is the standard model of the natural numbers but without addition or multiplication. It is used to formulate enumeration algorithms and to support the mechanism of induction or primitive recursion.

Booleans: $B = <\{tt, ff\} \mid tt, ff, \wedge, \rightarrow>$. This is the standard model of the booleans. It is required to support functions like definition by cases, and relations such as equality on carriers.

Given an algebra A we may make a standard algebra by adding the above domains of counters and booleans to the domains $A_1, \ldots, A_m$ of A, together with their many sorted operations, if necessary.

In this paper we will always assume that the booleans are present and have a convention that the equality relation $=_i : A_i \times A_i \rightarrow B$ will always be included for each carrier A_i. Later in Sections 2 and 3, when we formulate enumeration algorithms, we will need to add the counters.

1.3. Examples of data types

We now give some examples of data types. We write down the data type by giving only its characteristic domains, constants and operations; the existence of the booleans and the equality relation on all carriers is assumed but not mentioned.

For simple graphics, the domains we are interested in include various formulations of the integers, rational numbers and constructible numbers, and various abstract ring-like structures.

1.3.1. Integers   A standard formulation of the algebra of the set $Z = \{ \cdots, -1, 0, 1, 2, \cdots \}$ of integers is the algebra

$$Z = <Z|0, 1, +, -, \times>.$$

wherein the operations have their usual interpretation. One alternative we might consider is to remove the multiplication operation, which can be computationally costly, leaving

$$Z_0 = <Z|0, 1, +, ->.$$

We can also add operations to Z; for example *magnitude comparison, absolute magnitude* and *sign*:

$$Z_1 = <Z|0, 1, +, -, \times, \leq>$$

$$Z_2 = <Z|0, 1, +, -, \times, |z|>$$

$$Z_3 = <Z|0, 1, +, -, \times, sign(z)>$$

where $\leq$ is the usual ordering and

$$|x| = \begin{cases} x & \text{if } x \geq 0 \\ -x & \text{if } x < 0 \end{cases}$$

$$sign(x) = \begin{cases} -1 & \text{if } x < 0 \\ 0 & \text{if } x = 0 \\ +1 & \text{if } x > 0. \end{cases}$$

All the algebras are minimal. Strictly speaking, the algebras are algebras of integers *in decimal notation*. Given a signature, say Σ_1, the abstract data type of the integers Z_1, of that signature can be defined to be the class of all Σ_1 algebras isomorphic to Z_1. This class includes the representation of integers in binary and other notation systems for example.

What is the computational power of these data types? Can we compute more with a programming language L based on Z_1 than with L based on Z_2? We will answer these questions in §1.7.

1.3.2. Rational numbers   A standard formulation of the rationals is

$$Q = <Q \mid 0, 1, +, -, \times, \div>.$$

The *magnitude comparison, absolute magnitude,* and *sign* operations may be added as before. We can also add the floor and ceiling operations:

$$Q_1 = <Q \mid 0, 1, +, -, \times, \div, \lfloor x \rfloor >$$

$$Q_2 = <Q \mid 0, 1, +, -, \times, \div, \lceil x \rceil >$$

where $\lfloor \; \rfloor, \lceil \; \rceil : Q \to Z$

$\lfloor x \rfloor$ = greatest $z \in Z$ such that $z \leq x$

$\lceil x \rceil$ = least $z \in Z$ such that $z \geq x$

1.3.3. Constructible numbers   The constructible numbers **C** are the set of lengths in the plane $\mathbf{R}^2$ that can be constructed with a unit ruler and compass. The constructible numbers **C** contain **Q** and are a subfield of the field **R** of reals. This means that if x, y are constructible numbers then so are $x + y$, $x - y$, $x \times y$ and, if $y \neq 0$, then so is $x \div y$. Furthermore, if x is constructible and $x \geq 0$ then $\sqrt{x}$ is constructible. For proofs of these facts see Chapter 25 of Adamson [1964]. A natural formulation of the algebra of the constructible numbers is

$$\mathbf{C} = <\mathbf{C} | 0, 1, +, -, \times, \div, \sqrt{x}>$$

where $\sqrt{x}$ is only defined when x is positive.

1.3.4. Ring with 1   A *ring with 1* is an algebra R with operations $+$, $\times$, $-$ and constants 0, 1 which satisfies the following properties:

(1)	$(a + b) + c = a + (b + c)$	(5)	$(a \times b) \times c = a \times (b \times c)$
(2)	$a + 0 = 0 + a = a$	(6)	$a \times 1 = 1 \times a = a$
(3)	$a + (-a) = (-a) + a = 0$	(7)	$a \times (b + c) = (a \times b) + (a \times c)$
(4)	$a + b = b + a$	(8)	$(a + b) \times c = (a \times c) + (b \times c)$

In computing with a ring R it is useful to add further constructs, such as constants and an ordering, and to assume R is minimal. We employ the abbreviation $a - b$ for $a + (-b)$

The class of all structures satisfying these axioms is called the class of all *rings with identity*. The set of axioms record the basic properties of structures such as **Z** in §1.3 and constitute an *axiomatic specification* of the abstract data type of rings. Since these axioms are equations they also constitute an *algebraic specification*. (Recall 1.1.)

1.3.5. Ordered commutative ring with 1   An *ordered commutative ring with 1* is an algebra R with operations $+$, $\times$, $-$, $>$ and constants 0, 1 which satisfies the properties of a ring with 1 given above, and three additional properties:

(9) $a > a' \wedge b > b' \Rightarrow a + b > a' + b'$

(10) $a > 0, b > 0 \Rightarrow a \times b > 0$

(11) $a \times b = b \times a$

A commutative ordered ring is *archimedian* if is satisfies the following axiom (12) in addition to (1) - (11).

For any $r \in R$ there is some n such that $r < 1 + \cdots + 1$ (n times).

See Cohn [1977] for an excellent account of ordered rings and fields.

1.4. Evaluating polynomials

Often in a graphics algorithm, we need to evaluate a polynomial within a loop (for instance to obtain an error measure in a pixel tracking algorithm) where the argument increases or decreases by 1 at each iteration (as the current position moves from pixel to pixel). We now give a well known optimisation technique for this task which is usually called *strength reduction* when referring to compiler optimisations.

Let $R = <R \mid 0, 1, +, -, \times>$ be a ring with 1. For $n \in T$ and $r \in R$ we define the following notations:

$r + n = r + 1 + 1 + \cdots + 1$ (n times) or r if $n = 0$

$n \times r \ (=nr) = r + r + \cdots + r$ (n times) or 0 if $n = 0$

$r^n = r \times r \times \cdots \times r$ (n times) or 1 if $n = 0$

A polynomial $p_k(x)$ over R of degree k has the form

$$p_k(x) = A_k x^k + A_{k-1}x^{k-1} + \cdots + A_1 x + A_0 \quad \text{where } A_i \in R$$

Given such a polynomial we can derive a polynomial p_{k-1} of degree $k - 1$ as follows

$$p_{k-1}(x) = \left[\binom{k}{k-1} A_k x^{k-1} + \left[\binom{k}{k-2} A_k + \binom{k-1}{k-2} A_{k-1} \right] x^{k-2} + \cdots + \right.$$

$$\left[\binom{k}{k-j} A_k + \binom{k-1}{k-j} A_{k-1} + \cdots + \binom{k-(j-1)}{k-j} A_{k-(j-1)} \right] x^{k-j} + \cdots +$$

$$\left[\binom{k}{1} A_k + \binom{k-1}{1} A_{k-1} + \cdots + \binom{2}{1} A_2 \right] x + \left[A_k + A_{k-1} + \cdots + A_1 \right]$$

1.4.1. Theorem $p_k(x + 1) = p_k(x) + p_{k-1}(x)$

Proof: On expanding $p_k(x + 1)$ using the binomial theorem, and subtracting out $p_k(x)$ and rearranging, we obtain the expression for $p_{k-1}(x)$ given above.

1.4.2. Application Suppose we want to evaluate $p_k(x)$ at m points,

$$x = a, a + 1, a + 2, \ldots, a + (m - 1)$$

This is an example of an enumeration problem in that we want to compute the function $f: T \times R \to R$ defined by $f(t, a) = p_k(a + t)$ at a range of points $t = 0, \ldots, m$. We can avoid using multiplications within the loop defined by incrementing t as follows:

First we determine polynomial p_{k-1} using the above definition, and then repeat the method using p_{k-1} to obtain p_{k-2}, until we reach p_0 which is in fact a constant. We then use the following algorithm:

$t_k = p_k(a); t_{k-1} = p_{k-1}(a); t_{k-2} = p_{k-2}(a); \cdots; t_0 = p_0(a);$
do m **times**
    output (t_k);
    $t_k = t_k + t_{k-1}$;
    $t_{k-1} = t_{k-1} + t_{k-2}$;
    $t_{k-2} = t_{k-2} + t_{k-3}$;
    $\vdots$
    $\vdots$
    $t_1 = t_1 + t_0$
od

Notice that to formulate this application and program we have need of the counters T.

To evaluate a polynomial of degree k on m arguments using Horner's scheme requires mk multiplications and mk additions. In the above algorithm we may consider the cost of deriving the polynomials $p_{k-1}, \ldots, p_0$ as part of the cost of deriving the algorithm rather than part of the cost of executing the algorithm if we consider the polynomials' coefficients to be 'hard-wired'. That is we may apply the technique of *partial evaluation* to a particular application. The initial cost of evaluating the polynomials is

$$k + (k - 1) + \cdots + 2 + 1 = \frac{k(k + 1)}{2} \text{ multiplications}$$

$$k + (k - 1) + \cdots + 2 + 1 = \frac{k(k + 1)}{2} \text{ additions}$$

Thereafter we need $(m - 1)k$ additions. For example, to evaluate $2x^2 - 3x + 4$ at 20 consecutive values of x requires 40 multiplications and 40 additions. Using the above method we require 3 multiplications and 41 additions.

This method can be adapted to cope with polynomials in several variables and for certain non-linear sequences of arguments that are common in rasterisation (such as sequences that change direction and count down after counting up for part of the way; or sequences given by a polynomial of small degree) however the number of program variables required to cope with these cases soon becomes unreasonable.

1.5. Computation over algebras

In order to study and compare the computational power of various algebras we require some sort of programming notation. Let us define three classes of programs over the algebra A together with the sets of functions that are computable by them. A complete treatment of the syntax and semantics of the programming languages is routine using the methods of Tucker and Zucker [1988], for instance.

1.5.1. Straight line programs: We define the set $SPROG(\Sigma)$ of *straight line programs* over Σ informally using a BNF-like notation, where the constructs have their obvious semantics and the technical niceties of typing and initialisation of variables are ignored for the sake of brevity:

$$S ::= (\textbf{skip} \mid v_1, \ldots, v_n := e_1, \ldots, e_n \mid S_1; S_2 \mid \textbf{if } b \textbf{ then } S_1 \textbf{ else } S_2 \textbf{ fi})$$

where $v_1, \ldots, v_n$ are variables, $b, e_1, \ldots, e_n$ are expressions over A and b returns elements of type **B**. $SPROG(\Sigma)$ is the set of all such statements S.

This language construction applies to any algebra with booleans. The next two languages also require counters **T**.

1.5.2. One loop programs The set $OPROG(\Sigma)$ of *one loop programs* over A, is defined in terms of $SPROG(\Sigma)$ above:

$$S ::= P_1; \textbf{do } t \textbf{ times } P_2 \textbf{ od}; P_3$$

where $P_1, P_2, P_3 \in SPROG(\Sigma)$ and t is an expression returning elements of **T**. $OPROG(\Sigma)$ is the set of all such statements S.

1.5.3. Bounded loop programs   The set $BPROG(\Sigma)$ of *bounded loop programs* over A, is defined in a similar manner to $SPROG(\Sigma)$ above:

$$S ::= (\textbf{skip} \mid v_1, \ldots, v_n := e_1, \ldots, e_n \mid S_1; S_2$$

$$\mid \textbf{if } b \textbf{ then } S_1 \textbf{ else } S_2 \textbf{ fi} \mid \textbf{do } t \textbf{ times } S_1 \textbf{ od})$$

where $v_1, \ldots, v_n$ are variables, $b, t, e_1, \ldots, e_n$ are expressions over A, t returns an element of type **T** and b returns elements of type **B**. $BPROG(\Sigma)$ is the set of all such statements S.

1.5.4. Functions computed by programs   Given some program formalism L over signature Σ, such as one of the three described above, we denote the set of programs that can be written in L over Σ by $L(\Sigma)$. An *i/o program* is a triple $p = <S,v,w>$ where $S \in L(\Sigma)$, v is an enumerated set of program variables $v_1, \ldots, v_n$ and w is a program variable.

Let A be an algebra of signature Σ. For each such p we define the function $f_p : A^n \rightarrow A$ computed by p as follows: To compute $f(a_1, \ldots, a_n)$ we initialise program variables v_i to a_i for $i = 1, \ldots, n$, run the program S and if it terminates we return the value contained in program variable w as the result. We define $IO_L(\Sigma)$ to be the set of all i/o programs p written in L over Σ and $FUNC_L(A)$ to be the set of all functions on A computed by members of $IO_L(\Sigma)$.

1.6. Implementation and equivalence

Let L be some programming formalism and A and B be algebras.

1.6.1. Definition   Algebra A is to be *computationally equivalent or stronger* than algebra B under programming formalism L if and only if $FUNC_L(A) \supseteq FUNC_L(B)$. Furthermore if $FUNC_L(A) = FUNC_L(B)$ then we say that algebras A and B are *computationally equivalent* under programming formalism L; we denote this $A \equiv_L B$. Note that the first of these relations can only hold if the domains of B are subsets of domains of A; and the second can hold only if A and B have the same domains.

1.6.2. Definition   Algebra A is said to *implement* algebra B under programming formalism L if and only if for every operation f of B, $f \in FUNC_L(A)$. We say that algebras A and B are *implementationally equivalent* under programming formalism L if A implements B and B implements A.

1.6.3. Definition   A programming formalism L is said to be *transitive* if and only if for any algebras A, B, C we have that if A implements B and B implements C then A implements C.

Example   The straight line and bounded loop programming formalisms given above are transitive, but the one loop programming formalism is not.

1.6.4. Lemma If L includes assignment and is transitive then

$$A \text{ implements } B \iff FUNC_L(A) \supseteq FUNC_L(B)$$

Proof: The backwards implication is trivially true regardless of whether or not *PROG* is transitive because the condition that L includes assignment ensures that all operations of B are be members of $FUNC_L(B)$. We now prove the forward implication. Suppose A implements B and let f be any function in $FUNC_L(B)$ then we have to show that $f \in FUNC_L(A)$. Consider the algebra B' which consists of algebra B with the additional operation f. Clearly B implements B' and as A implements B we have A implements B' by the transitivity of L. Hence $f \in FUNC_L(A)$ by the definition of implementation.

1.6.5. Corollary Let L be transitive and include assignment. Then A is implementationally equivalent to B under programming formalism L if and only if A is computationally equivalent to B under programming formalism L.

1.7. A comparison of integer and rational data types

We now use the definitions of §1.6 to examine and compare the relative power of the data types given in §1.3. We begin with some simple observations.

1.7.1. Lemma Z_1, Z_2, Z_3 are computationally equivalent w.r.t. straight line programs.

Proof: Because the straight line programming formalism is transitive and includes assignment it is sufficient to show that Z_1 implements Z_2, Z_2 implements Z_3 and Z_3 implements Z_1 and appeal to the corollary of lemma 1.6.4. Since these three data types differ only by one operation we only need to show how this extra operation is implemented in each case.

Z_1 implements Z_2:

We compute $b = |a|$ using the operation $\leq$ by the following straight line program:

> **if** $a \leq 0$ **then**
> > $b := -a$
> **else**
> > $b := a$
> **fi**

Z_2 implements Z_3:

We compute $b = sign(a)$ using the operation $|z|$ by the following straight line program:

> **if** $a = 0$ **then**
> > $b := 0$
> **else**
> > **if** $|a| = a$ **then**
> > > $b := 1$
> > **else**

$$b := -1$$

fi

fi

Z_3 implements Z_1:

We compute $b = (x \le y)$ using the operation $sign(z)$ by the following straight line program

$$b := \neg(sign(x - y) = 1)$$

1.7.2. Lemma Z_1, Z_2, Z_3 are computationally equivalent w.r.t. one loop programs and bounded loop programs.

Proof: We notice that any one loop or bounded loop program over one of these three data types may be rewritten over any other of the three data types by replacing each use of an operation not available in the new data type by a program over the new data type that implements it (possibly using some extra variables). By the previous lemma a straight line program to do the job always exists. A one loop program with a straight line program replacing a mention of an operation remains a one loop program and similarly with a bounded loop program.

Next we look at multiplication.

1.7.3. Lemma Z is computationally stronger than Z_0 w.r.t. straight line programs.

Proof: This is a direct consequence of the next lemma.

1.7.4. Lemma Z can not be implemented by straight line programs over Z_0.

Proof: Suppose we have a program $P \in SPROG(\Sigma_0)$ which computes the multiplication operation. Let n be the total number of addition and subtraction operations in P. Now clearly each addition or subtraction operation can be executed at most once in any run of P. Also the absolute magnitude of any result produced by an addition or subtraction operation cannot be larger than twice the absolute magnitude of any value computed or stored in the programs variables previously. Since the initial values available to the first addition or subtraction operation are the input values, say a and b, and the constants of the data type, 0 and 1, the absolute value of the result of this first addition or subtraction operation cannot be greater than $2\max(|a|, |b|, 1)$. A simple inductive argument suffices to show that the absolute magnitude of any value computed by the n addition and subtraction operations in the program is bounded by $2^n \max(|a|, |b|, 1)$.

Now consider the action of P where the input is $a = b = 2^{n+1}$. The result computed by the program is bounded by

$$2^n \max(2^{n+1}, 2^{n+1}, 1) = 2^n 2^{n+1} = 2^{2n+1}.$$

However the multiplication requires the program to return

$$2^{n+1} 2^{n+1} = 2^{2n+2}.$$

Thus we have a contradiction and so P cannot implement the multiplication function.

1.7.5. Lemma Z_1 is computationally stronger than Z w.r.t. straight line programs.

Proof: This is a direct consequence of the next lemma.

1.7.6. Lemma Z_1 can not be implemented by straight line programs over Z.

In order to prove this we want to dispense with the straight line programming formalism and replace it with something with is equivalent but more manageable. Consider expressions in variables v_i over the signature of the following algebra which adds definition by cases as an operation to Z:

$$Z_{DC} = <Z, B|\ 0,\ 1,\ +,\ -,\ \times,\ =,\ tt,\ ff,\ \neg, \wedge, DC>$$

where

$$DC: B \times Z \times Z \rightarrow Z$$

$$DC(b, z_1, z_2) = \begin{cases} z_1 & \text{if } b = tt \\ z_2 & \text{otherwise} \end{cases}$$

1.7.7. Basic lemma No expression $\alpha(v_1, v_2)$ over Z_{DC} with free variables v_1 and v_2 can implement the function $\le: Z \times Z \rightarrow B$.

We build up to a proof of this theorem through the following lemmas.

Lemma Let $Iexp(v)$ be the set of all expressions over Z_{DC} containing the single integer variable v and returning integers. Let $Bexp(v)$ be the set of all expressions over Z_{DC} containing the single integer variable v and returning booleans. Then

(1)   If $i(v) \in Iexp(v)$ then there exists some cofinite subset $S \subset Z$ and some polynomial $p(v)$ over Z in v such that $i(a) = p(a)\ \forall a \in S$

(2)   If $b(v) \in Bexp(v)$ then there exists some cofinite subset $S \subseteq Z$ such that either $b(a) = tt\ \forall a \in S$ or $b(a) = ff\ \forall a \in S$

Proof: By induction on the structure of expressions over Z_{DC}.

Basis: The basis consists of expressions which have no function applications, i.e. constants and variables.

Integer expressions Clearly 0, 1 and v are all polynomials over v so S can be any cofinite subset of Z such as all of Z and the lemma holds.

Boolean expressions Clearly if $b(v) = tt$ then S can be any cofinite set of Z and the lemma holds. Similarly if $b(v) = ff$ then S can be any cofinite set of Z and the lemma holds.

Induction We now take a pair of integer expressions $i(v)$, $j(v)$ where

$$i(a) = p(a)\ \forall a \in S\ \ (p(v) \text{ is a polynomial, } S \text{ is cofinite})$$

$$j(a) = q(a)\ \forall a \in T\ \ (q(v) \text{ is a polynomial, } T \text{ is cofinite})$$

and a pair of boolean expressions $b(v)$, $c(v)$ where

$$b(a) = tt \quad \forall a \in U \quad \text{or} \quad b(a) = ff \quad \forall a \in U \quad (U \text{ is cofinite})$$

$$c(a) = tt \quad \forall a \in V \quad \text{or} \quad c(a) = ff \quad \forall a \in V \quad (V \text{ is cofinite})$$

and show that any new expression constructed from them by a single function application satisfies the lemma. We now consider all the operations in Z_{DC} in turn

Addition   Clearly

$$i(a) + j(a) = p(a) + q(a) \quad \forall a \in S \cap T$$

Now $p(v) + q(v)$ must be a polynomial and $S \cap T$ must be cofinite so the lemma holds.

Subtraction and multiplication   A similar argument to that for addition holds as the difference of two polynomials and the product of two polynomials are still polynomials.

Definition by cases   If $b(a) = tt \quad \forall a \in U$ then

$$DC(b(a), i(a), j(a)) = i(a) \quad \forall a \in U$$

$$= p(a) \quad \forall \ a \in U \cap S$$

Otherwise if $b(a) = ff \quad \forall a \in U$ then

$$DC(b(a), i(a), j(a)) = j(a) \quad \forall a \in U$$

$$= q(a) \quad \forall \ a \in U \cap T$$

Either way, since $U \cap S$ and $U \cap T$ are cofinite the lemma holds.

Equality on integers   Suppose $p(v) = q(v)$, then

$$(i(a) = j(a)) = tt \quad \forall a \in S \cap T$$

and $S \cap T$ must be cofinite so the lemma holds. Now suppose $p(v) \neq q(v)$ then $p(v) - q(v)$ is a non-zero polynomial and by a well known theorem can only be zero for finitely many values of v. Let N be the set of all $a \in Z$ such that $p(a) - q(a) \neq 0$; N is cofinite. Then

$$(i(a) = j(a)) = ff \quad \forall a \in S \cap T \cap N$$

and $S \cap T \cap N$ must be cofinite so the lemma holds.

Boolean negation   Clearly if $b(a) = tt \quad \forall a \in U$ then

$$\neg b(a) = ff \quad \forall a \in U$$

and vice versa so the lemma holds.

Boolean conjunction   Clearly if $b(a) = ff \quad \forall a \in U$ or $c(a) = ff \quad \forall a \in V$ then

$$b(a) \wedge c(a) = ff \quad \forall a \in U \cup V$$

otherwise

$$b(a) \wedge c(a) = tt \quad \forall a \in U \cap V$$

Either way $U \cap V$ and $U \cup V$ are cofinite and the lemma holds. This completes the proof of the lemma.

Lemma The function

$$pos(a) = \begin{cases} tt & \text{if } a \geq 0 \\ ff & \text{otherwise} \end{cases}$$

can not be implemented by an expression $\alpha(v)$ over Z_{DC}.

Proof: Suppose $\alpha(v)$ did implement pos. Then

$$pos(1) = tt, \, pos(2) = tt, \, pos(3) = tt, \, \cdots$$

and

$$pos(-1) = ff, \, pos(-2) = ff, \, pos(-3) = ff, \, \cdots$$

i.e. pos can return tt on infinitely values of v and also ff on infinitely many values of v. But this contradicts the cofiniteness property for boolean expressions proved in the above lemma.

Proof of basic lemma: Suppose we have an expression $\alpha(v_1, v_2)$ over Z_{DC} which implements the function $\leq$. Then we can derive a new expression that implements pos by substituting the constant 0 for occurrences of v_1 in $\alpha(v_1, v_2)$, but this contradicts the previous lemma.

Finally to obtain a proof of lemma 1.7.6, and hence of lemma 1.7.5 we need to show that any function with a scalar range implementable by a straight line program over Z can also be implemented by an expression over Z_{DC} and thus the existence of a straight line program over Z implementing $\leq$ would give rise to a contradiction. The details of this are straight forward (the definition by cases operation effectively replaces the **if then else fi** statement) and we omit them for brevity.

2. PRIMITIVE RECURSIVE FUNCTIONS

In order to facilitate correctness proofs and transformations on programs we express algorithms by means of functions. The particular functions we are interested in are *enumeration functions*. We use a language *PR* that is based on simultaneous primitive recursive equations over an abstract data type. In this section we give a brief description of this notation and give two examples of its use in describing graphics algorithms.

2.1. Algorithms, functions and relations

In simple case studies, we are interested in computing a function f on a set A. Furthermore, the function is an *enumeration function* of the form

$$f : T \times A^p \to A^q$$

with coordinate functions

$$f_1, \ldots, f_q : \mathbf{T} \times A^p \to A$$

such that

$$f(t, a) = (f_1(t, a), \ldots, f_q(t, a)).$$

For example, we want to see Bresenham's algorithm as implementing an enumeration function

$$OL_B : \mathbf{T} \times \mathbf{Z}^2 \to \mathbf{Z}^2$$

where $OL_B(t, a, b)$ is the t-th element in the sequence of grid points approximating the line from $(0, 0)$ to (a, b). We will define this properly in §2.3.

A function f of interest, is in turn specified by a relation R on the set A as follows. We suppose that the relation $R \subset A^p \times A^q$ and function $f : A^p \to A^q$ has the property that for any $a \in A^p$

$$(a, f(a)) \in R.$$

We say that f is some *selection function* for R.

In particular, in the case of an enumeration function, we suppose that $R \subset \mathbf{T} \times A^p \times A^q$ and $f : \mathbf{T} \times A^p \to A^q$, and for $a \in A^p$ and $t \in \mathbf{T}$

$$(t, a, f(t, a)) \in R$$

Later we will give a relation that specifies OL_B.

2.2. PR notation

The *PR* language is defined in order to specify functions on many sorted algebras. The general form of a *PR* specification or program over a signature Σ is

$$f_1(0, a) = g_1(a)$$

$$f_1(t+1, a) = h_1(a, f_1(t, a), \ldots, f_i(t, a), \ldots, f_n(t, a))$$

$$\vdots$$

$$f_i(0, a) = g_i(a)$$

$$f_i(t+1, a) = h_i(a, f_1(t, a), \ldots, f_i(t, a), \ldots, f_n(t, a))$$

$$\vdots$$

$$f_n(0, a) = g_n(a)$$

$$f_n(t+1, a) = h_n(a, f_1(t, a), \ldots, f_i(t, a), \ldots, f_n(t, a))$$

On interpretation in a standard algebra A of signature Σ each pair of equations defines a function by simultaneous induction on the counters $\mathbf{T}$. The first m pairs of equations define functions $f_1, \ldots, f_m$ called *output functions*, while the remaining equations define functions $f_{m+1}, \ldots, f_n$ called *auxiliary* or *hidden functions*.

The symbols $g_1, \ldots, g_n$ represent expressions formed from the argument a, constants and functions from the algebra and definition by cases by the application of composition and other primitive recursive equations. The symbols $h_1, \ldots, h_n$ represent similar expressions but these, as indicated by the argument list, may also depend on the values of any or all of the other functions.

If an expression h_i makes use of the value of function f_j we say function f_i is *dependent* on function f_i otherwise we say that f_i is *independent* of f_j. For a formal treatment of the syntax and semantics of these functions see Tucker and Zucker [1988] and Thompson [1987].

2.3. The optimal line drawing problem

We consider drawing on the lattice $\mathbf{Z}^2$ and refer to members of $\mathbf{Z}^2$ as points. Given two points $P, Q \in \mathbf{Z}^2$, the *optimal line drawing* problem is to find the set $L \subset \mathbf{Z}^2$ which 'best represents' the true line from P to Q in $\mathbf{R}^2$. Without loss of generality, we will consider lines where one endpoint P is the origin, and the other Q lies in the first octant, i.e. $P = (0, 0)$ and $Q = (a, b)$ where $a \geq b \geq 0$. (All other lines may be obtained by reflecting about the axes, translating and interchanging the coordinates.)

An optimal approximation to the true line from $(0, 0)$ to (a, b), hereafter called an *optimal line* from $(0, 0)$ to (a, b), is any sequence $(x_0, y_0), \ldots, (x_a, y_a)$ where for $i = 0, 1, \ldots, a$

(1) $(x_i, y_i) \in \mathbf{Z}^2$

(2) $x_i = i$

(3) $2|bx_i - ay_i| \leq a$

These constraints have the following intuitive interpretation: condition (1) constrains points to lie in the lattice $\mathbf{Z}^2$; condition (2) ensures that there is one and only one point in each horizontal position; condition (3) ensures that the vertical position of each point should be the closest to the true line. This last condition is formulated as an inequality on the integers $\mathbf{Z}$ but in the case where the line is non trivial, i.e. $a > 0$, it may be written more intuitively as the following condition on the rationals $\mathbf{Q}$

$$\left| x_i \frac{b}{a} - y_i \right| \leq \frac{1}{2}$$

where $\left| x_i \dfrac{b}{a} - y_i \right|$ represents the vertical deviation from the true line.

An optimal line drawing algorithm implements an enumeration function

$$OL : \mathbf{T} \times \mathbf{Z}^2 \to \mathbf{Z}^2$$

specified in the first octant by the relation

$$R \subset \mathbf{T} \times \mathbf{Z}^2 \times \mathbf{Z}^2$$

defined by

$$(t, a, b, x, y) \in R \quad \text{iff} \quad x = a \text{ and } 2|ax - by| < a$$

Notice that there are a number of distinct functions that are selection functions for the relation R.

We will ignore the degenerate case where $a = 0$ (a single point) and consider the particular optimal line defined by

$$x_i = i, \, y_i = \left\lfloor i\frac{b}{a} + \frac{1}{2} \right\rfloor \quad \text{for } a \geq 1, \, i = 0, \ldots, a$$

and we now give two algorithms to solve this problem.

2.3.1. Naive algorithm Here we generate the x co-ordinate by starting at 0 and incrementing by 1, and we generate the y coordinate from the x coordinate using the specification of the particular optimal line above. The data type must therefore include the rationals and is given by:

$$A = (\mathbf{B}, \mathbf{T}, \mathbf{Z}, \mathbf{Q} \mid tt, \, ff, \, 0_\mathbf{T}, \, 0_\mathbf{Z}, \, 1_\mathbf{Z}, \, 0_\mathbf{Q}, \, \tfrac{1}{2}_\mathbf{Q},$$

$$t + 1, \, +_\mathbf{Z}, \, -_\mathbf{Z}, \, +_\mathbf{Q}, \, -_\mathbf{Q}, \, \times_\mathbf{Q}, \, /_\mathbf{Q}, \lfloor \, \rfloor, \, q).$$

Here $\mathbf{B}$ is the booleans, $\mathbf{T}$ is a set of the natural numbers, $\mathbf{Z}$ is the set of integers and $\mathbf{Q}$ is the set of rationals. The operation $\lfloor \, \rfloor : \mathbf{Q} \to \mathbf{Z}$ is the floor operation and the operation $q : \mathbf{Z} \to \mathbf{Q}$ converts integers into rationals. Note that the booleans and integer and rational subtraction operations are only included for technical reasons. By an abuse of notation, we will drop the carrier subscripts on constants and functions and also omit the type conversion operation q. The naive algorithm is:

$$OL_A : \mathbf{T} \times \mathbf{Z}^2 \to \mathbf{Z}^2$$

$$OL_A(t, a, b) = \langle x_A(t, a, b), y_A(t, a, b) \rangle$$

where

$$x_A, y_A : T \times \mathbf{Z}^2 \to \mathbf{Z}$$

$$x_A(0, a, b) = 0$$

$$x_A(t + 1, a, b) = x_A(t, a, b) + 1$$

$$y_A(0, a, b) = 0$$

$$y_A(t + 1, a, b) = \lfloor (x_A(t, a, b) + 1) \times (b/a) + \tfrac{1}{2} \rfloor$$

2.3.2. Bresenham's algorithm This algorithm is less intuitive but does not require the rationals and may be defined over a simpler data type:

$$B = (\mathbf{B}, \mathbf{T}, \mathbf{Z} \mid tt, \, ff, \, 0_\mathbf{T}, \, 0_\mathbf{Z}, \, 1_\mathbf{Z}, \, t + 1, \, +_\mathbf{Z}, \, -_\mathbf{Z}, \, <_\mathbf{Z})$$

Here $\mathbf{B}$, $\mathbf{T}$ and $\mathbf{Z}$ and their respective constants and operations have the same meaning as before. We will use the notation $2e$ where e is a variable or expression as an abbreviation for $e + e$. The algorithm is:

$$OL_B : \mathbf{T} \times \mathbf{Z}^2 \to \mathbf{Z}^2$$

$$OL_B(t, a, b) = \langle x_B(t, a, b), y_B(t, a, b) \rangle$$

where

$$x_B, y_B, r_B : T \times \mathbf{Z}^2 \to \mathbf{Z}$$

$$x_B(0, a, b) = 0$$

$$x_B(t+1, a, b) = x_B(t, a, b) + 1$$

$$y_B(0, a, b) = 0$$

$$y_B(t+1, a, b) = \begin{cases} y_B(t, a, b) & \text{if } r_B(t, a, b) < 0 \\ y_B(t, a, b) + 1 & \text{otherwise} \end{cases}$$

$$r_B(0, a, b) = 2 \times b - a$$

$$r_B(t+1, a, b) = \begin{cases} r_B(t, a, b) + 2b & \text{if } r_B(t, a, b) < 0 \\ r_B(t, a, b) + 2b - 2a & \text{otherwise} \end{cases}$$

Notice the use of a hidden function r_B. This corresponds to the decision variable in the more familiar iterative version of Bresenham's algorithm (see Bresenham [1965]).

2.4. The optimal circle drawing problem

We again consider drawing on the lattice $\mathbf{Z}^2$. Given a point $P \in \mathbf{Z}^2$ and a integer length $r \in \mathbf{Z}$, the optimal circle drawing problem is to find the set $C \subset \mathbf{Z}^2$ which 'best represents' the true circle of radius r centred on P. Without loss of generality we will consider circles where P is the origin. (All other circles may be obtained by translation.) There are three standard measures of a point's distance from a true circle, namely, *radial error*, *axial error* and *residue error*; each gives rise to a definition of the optimal approximation to a true circle. The first two of these error measures are shown as e_1 and e_2 on Fig 2.1, while the third has no simple geometric interpretation. However it can be proved that in the integer case all three definitions give rise to a single unique set of points (see McIlroy [1983]). Thus we may use whichever definition is most convenient.

Following the definitions of McIlroy [1983] we will define optimal circles in terms of *transects*. A transect is a closed half grid line extending from either the horizontal or vertical diameter of the circle to intersect the circle (see Fig2.1). We classify transects as horizontal or vertical according to their orientation.

An optimal approximation to a circle or *optimal circle* is the smallest set of grid points containing a point on each transect that minimises the error criterion. The error criterion we choose is that of axial error.

Axial error or *displacement* is the distance from the grid point to the intersection of the circle with the transect. There are two formulae for computing this: vax_err for vertical transects and hax_err for horizontal ones:

Vertical transects

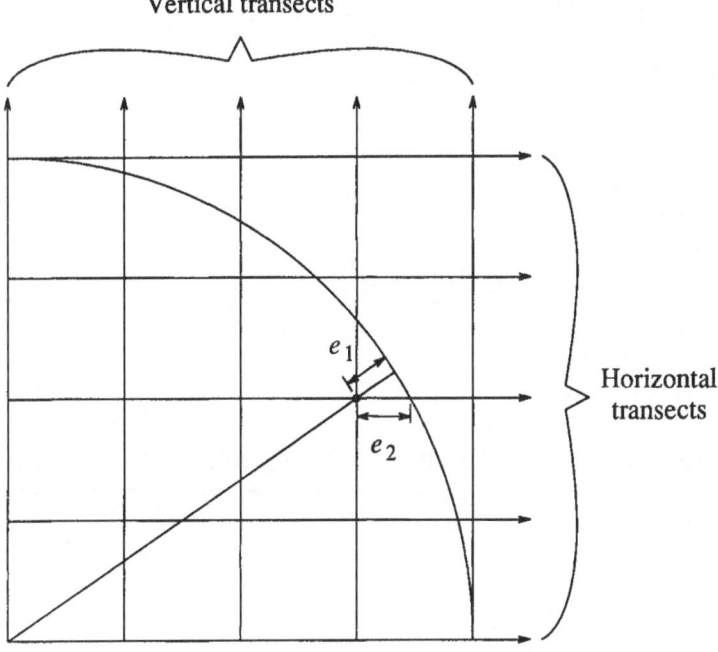

Horizontal transects

Fig 2.1

$$\text{vax\_err}(x, y) = \left| \, |y| - \sqrt{r^2 - x^2} \, \right|$$

$$\text{hax\_err}(x, y) = \left| \, |x| - \sqrt{r^2 - y^2} \, \right|$$

Thus the optimal circle of radius r is a set $OPTCIRC(r) \subset \mathbf{Z}^2$ defined by

$$OPTCIRC(r) = \{(x, y): (|x| \le r \wedge \forall y' [\text{vax\_err}(x, y) \le \text{vax\_err}(x, y')]) \vee$$

$$(|y| \le r \wedge \forall x' [\text{hax\_err}(x, y) \le \text{hax\_err}(x', y)])\}$$

2.4.1. Naive circle algorithm We now give a naive algorithm to solve the optimal circle problem restricted to the first octant; grid points lying in other octants can be obtained by reflection about the axes and diagonals. Because we use square roots the data type must include the constructible numbers **C**.

$$A = (\mathbf{B}, \mathbf{T}, \mathbf{Z}, \mathbf{C} \mid \textit{tt}, \textit{ff}, 0_{\mathbf{T}}, 0_{\mathbf{Z}}, 1_{\mathbf{Z}}, >_{\mathbf{Z}}, 0_{\mathbf{C}}, \tfrac{1}{2}_{\mathbf{C}},$$

$$t + 1, +_{\mathbf{Z}}, -_{\mathbf{Z}}, +_{\mathbf{C}}, -_{\mathbf{C}}, \times_{\mathbf{C}}, /_{\mathbf{C}}, \sqrt{x}, \lfloor \, \rfloor, c)$$

Here the floor operation is a map $\lfloor \, \rfloor : \mathbf{C} \to \mathbf{Z}$ and $c: \mathbf{Z} \to \mathbf{C}$ maps converts integers into constructible numbers. As before we will drop the sort subscripts on constants and functions and omit the sort conversion operation c. The naive algorithm is:

$OC_A: \mathbf{T} \times \mathbf{Z} \to \mathbf{Z}^2$

$OC_A(t, r) = {<}x_A(t, r), y_A(t, r){>}$

where

$x_A, y_A: \mathbf{T} \times \mathbf{Z} \to \mathbf{Z}$

$x_A(0, r) = r$

$x_A(t+1, r) = \lfloor \sqrt{(r^2 - (y_A(t, r) + 1)^2)} + \tfrac{1}{2} \rfloor$

$y_A(0, r) = 0$

$y_A(t+1, r) = y_A(t, r) + 1$

2.4.2. Bresenham's circle algorithm This algorithm is less intuitive but does not require the constructible numbers and may be defined over the simpler data type B of §2.3.2 as before. The algorithm is

$OC_B: \mathbf{T} \times \mathbf{Z} \to \mathbf{Z}^2$

$OC_B(t, r) = {<}x_B(t, r), y_B(t, r){>}$

where

$x_B, y_B: \mathbf{T} \times \mathbf{Z} \to \mathbf{Z}$

$x_B(0, r) = r$

$$x_B(t+1, r) = \begin{cases} x_B(t, r) & \text{if } d_B(t, r) > 0 \text{ and} \\ & 2d_B(t, r) - 2x_B(t, r) + 1 \geq 0 \\ x_B(t, r) - 1 & \text{otherwise} \end{cases}$$

$y_B(0, r) = 0$

$y_B(t+1, r) = y_B(t, r) + 1$

$d_B(0, r) = 2r - 2$

$$d_B(t+1, r) = \begin{cases} d_B(t, r) - 2y_B(t, r) - 3 & \text{if } d_B(t, r) > 0 \text{ and} \\ & 2d_B(t, r) - 2x_B(t, r) + 1 \geq 0 \\ d_B(t, r) + 2x_B(t, r) & \\ \quad - 2y_B(t, r) - 6 & \text{otherwise} \end{cases}$$

Here the hidden function d_B plays the role of the decision variable in the original (see Bresenham [1977]).

2.5. Modules and algebras

We may use modules, as modelled by many sorted algebras, to organise program construction as follows. First, consider the informal idea that *programming creates a program module P from a component module C in order to obtain a task module T*. A module involves sets and functions on those sets; that is, a many sorted algebra.

Suppose we want to compute some functions $f_1, \ldots, f_m$ on a set A using functions $\sigma_1, \ldots, \sigma_p$. Then we have a *task algebra*

$$A_{Task} = (A \mid f_1, \ldots, f_m)$$

and a *component algebra*

$$A_{Comp} = (A \mid \sigma_1, \ldots, \sigma_p)$$

and we want to create a *program algebra*

$$A_{Prog} = (A, B \mid f_1, \ldots, f_m, f_{m+1}, \ldots, f_n, \sigma_1, \ldots, \sigma_p)$$

involving auxiliary sets, such as B, and functions such as $f_{m+1}, \ldots, f_n$.

Clearly the main aim of the *PR* notation is now seen to be to define program algebras over given component algebras. The use of *PR* for creating algebraic specifications of program algebras from algebraic specifications of component algebras is explained in detail in Thompson and Tucker [1989].

3. FORMAL PROGRAM TRANSFORMATIONS

In this section we first look at general transformations on systems of primitive recursive equations and then apply them to perform a Sproull-like development of Bresenham's algorithm.

3.1. General transformations

All transformations on systems of *PR* equations of interest to us may be written as a sequence of instances of the following three general types of correctness preserving transformation.

3.1.1. Add equations   Given a correct (relative to some relation on the output functions) set P of equations or program and a set S of equation pairs defining functions with the same arguments as those in P, the program denoted $P + S$ consisted of P with the addition of the equations in S is correct.

3.1.2. Delete equations   Given a correct program P and a subset of equation pairs $S \subset P$ such that all functions in S are hidden functions and no function in $P - S$ (the set difference of P and S) is dependent on any member of S then the program denoted $P - S$ consisting of P with all members of S deleted is correct.

3.1.3. Substitute in a right hand side   Suppose P is a correct program and $\alpha = \beta(\gamma)$ is an equation in P with γ as subexpression. Let δ be a expression involving only constants and functions from the algebra and expressions of the form $f(t, a)$ for some f defined in P. If it is provable that

$$\forall t \geq 0 \ [\gamma = \delta]$$

then the program denoted $P[\alpha = \beta(\delta)/\alpha = \beta(\gamma)]$ consisting of P with δ replacing γ in the equation $\alpha = \beta(\gamma)$ is correct.

3.2. Transformational development of Bresenham's algorithm

We now take an obvious naive line drawing algorithm and by using a sequence consisting of low level transformation steps of the kind described above we derive Bresenham's algorithm. The sequence has a pattern and can be seen as a sequence of larger steps. Each large step is called a *cycle*, and consists of

(1)   adding a function,

(2)   using it in a substitution, and then, possibly,

(3)   deleting a function that has been made redundant by the substitution.

We use four such cycles; each cycle corresponds approximately to one or two transformations in Sproull's informal derivation of Bresenham's algorithm.

In principle we could get directly to Bresenham's algorithm by just one cycle (consisting of two low level transformation steps):

Add the r function (see 3.2.11).

Make the substitution for the right hand side of y (see 3.2.12).

Intuitively however, this is not an obvious thing to do (where does r come from?) and the proof required for the substitution in the right hand side of y becomes the entire proof needed for the the correctness of Bresenham's algorithm (see Eker and Tucker [1988]).

3.2.1. Data type

The derivation of Bresenham's algorithm involves the familiar types of the rationals and the integers, of course. However we must be careful about what properties we use in the proofs of correctness for transformations in order to formulate a strategy for machine assisted proof checking and development. We use an abstract data type where the main carrier is the field of fractions F over an ordered archimedian commutative ring R with 1; all the properties of data we need can be deduced from the axioms in §1.3.5.

In order to define the floor operation we define a subring Z of R which is isomorphic to the integers:

$$Z = \{ \cdots, -1-1, -1, 0, 1, 1+1, 1+1+1, \cdots \}.$$

We will denote elements of Z by the symbols normally used to denote the corresponding elements of $\mathbf{Z}$; for example 2 denotes $1 + 1$. The floor operation may now be defined by

$$\lfloor a \rfloor = \text{greatest } z \in Z \text{ such that } z \leq a.$$

The floor operation can be shown to have the following properties which we shall need.

(P1) $a \geq 0 \wedge a < 1 \Rightarrow \lfloor a \rfloor = 0$

(P2) $a \geq 1 \wedge a < 2 \Rightarrow \lfloor a \rfloor = 1$

(P3) $a \in Z \Rightarrow \lfloor a + b \rfloor = a + \lfloor b \rfloor$

To avoid confusion with equality on the field we will use the symbol $\leftrightarrow$ to denote equality on booleans. Also, since all non-relational operators in the algebra are associative, we will omit brackets where it make expressions easier to read and omit explicit mention of the associativity property in the proofs.

3.2.2. Derivation

The initial algorithm is:

Draft 0

$$x(0, a, b) = 0$$

$$x(t + 1, a, b) = x(t, a, b) + 1$$

$$y(0, a, b) = 0$$

$$y(t + 1, a, b) = \left\lfloor (x(t, a, b) + 1) \times \frac{b}{a} + \frac{1}{2} \right\rfloor$$

We notice that the expression $(x(t, a, b) + 1) \times (b/a) + \frac{1}{2}$ can be computed incrementally (this can be seen as an application of the technique described in §1.4 to a polynomial of degree 1). To this end the next two steps introduce a new function f to compute the successive value of the expression and substitute a reference to this function in place of the expression.

3.2.3. Add a function: Let x, y be as before

$$f(0, a, b) = \frac{b}{a} + \frac{1}{2}$$

$$f(t + 1, a, b) = f(t, a, b) + \frac{b}{a}$$

3.2.4. Substitution for rhs sub-expression: Claim

$$\forall t \geq 0 \left[f(t, a, b) = (x(t, a, b) + 1) \times \frac{b}{a} + \frac{1}{2} \right]$$

Proof: By induction on t.

Basis:

$$(x(0, a, b) + 1) \times \frac{b}{a} + \frac{1}{2} = (0 + 1) \times \frac{b}{a} + \frac{1}{2} \qquad \text{(def)}$$

$$= 1 \times \frac{b}{a} + \frac{1}{2} \qquad \text{(add id)}$$

$$= \frac{b}{a} + \frac{1}{2} \qquad \text{(mult id)}$$

$$= f(0, a, b) \qquad \text{(def)}$$

Induction:

$$(x(t+1, a, b) + 1) \times \frac{b}{a} + \frac{1}{2} = x(t+1, a, b) \times \frac{b}{a} + 1 \times \frac{b}{a} + \frac{1}{2} \qquad \text{(dist)}$$

$$= x(t+1, a, b) \times \frac{b}{a} + \frac{b}{a} + \frac{1}{2} \qquad \text{(mult id)}$$

$$= (x(t, a, b) + 1) \times \frac{b}{a} + \frac{b}{a} + \frac{1}{2} \qquad \text{(def)}$$

$$= (x(t, a, b) + 1) \times \frac{b}{a} + \frac{1}{2} + \frac{b}{a} \qquad \text{(add com)}$$

$$= f(t, a, b) + \frac{b}{a} \qquad \text{(ind hyp)}$$

$$= f(t+1, a, b) \qquad \text{(def)}$$

We now complete the first cycle by making the substitution in the right hand side of y, yielding

Draft 1

$$x(0, a, b) = 0$$

$$x(t+1, a, b) = x(t, a, b) + 1$$

$$y(0, a, b) = 0$$

$$y(t+1, a, b) = \lfloor f(t, a, b) \rfloor$$

$$f(0, a, b) = \frac{b}{a} + \frac{1}{2}$$

$$f(t+1, a, b) = f(t, a, b) + \frac{b}{a}$$

We now use the idea from Sproull of splitting the value of f into integer and fractional parts, the integer part already being computed by function y. The next three steps introduce a new function g to compute the fractional part, substitute it in to the new scheme for computing the integer part (i.e. the right hand side of y), and delete the function f which has now been made redundant.

3.2.5. Add a function: x, y, f as before.

$$g(0, a, b) = \tfrac{1}{2}$$

$$g(t+1, a, b) = \begin{cases} g(t, a, b) + \dfrac{b}{a} & \text{if } g(t, a, b) + \dfrac{b}{a} < 1 \\[2ex] g(t, a, b) + \dfrac{b}{a} - 1 & \text{otherwise} \end{cases}$$

3.2.6. Substitution for rhs sub-expression: Claim

$$\forall t \geq 0 \left[\lfloor f(t, a, b) \rfloor = \begin{cases} y(t, a, b) & \text{if } g(t, a, b) + \dfrac{b}{a} < 1 \\[2ex] y(t, a, b) + 1 & \text{otherwise} \end{cases} \right]$$

To prove this we first need the following lemma which makes the relation between the y, f and g functions explicit.

Lemma

$$\forall t \geq 0 \, [f(t, a, b) = y(t+1, a, b) + g(t+1, a, b)]$$

Proof: By induction on t.

Basis:

$$y(1, a, b) + g(1, a, b)$$

$$= \lfloor f(0, a, b) \rfloor + \begin{cases} g(0, a, b) + \dfrac{b}{a} & \text{if } g(0, a, b) + \dfrac{b}{a} < 1 \\[2ex] g(0, a, b) + \dfrac{b}{a} - 1 & \text{otherwise} \end{cases} \qquad \text{(def)}$$

$$= \left\lfloor \dfrac{b}{a} + \dfrac{1}{2} \right\rfloor + \begin{cases} \dfrac{1}{2} + \dfrac{b}{a} & \text{if } \dfrac{1}{2} + \dfrac{b}{a} < 1 \\[2ex] \dfrac{1}{2} + \dfrac{b}{a} - 1 & \text{otherwise} \end{cases} \qquad \text{(def)}$$

We now consider two cases.

Case 1: $\dfrac{1}{2} + \dfrac{b}{a} < 1$

$$y(1, a, b) + g(1, a, b) = \left\lfloor \dfrac{b}{a} + \dfrac{1}{2} \right\rfloor + \dfrac{1}{2} + \dfrac{b}{a} \qquad \text{(from above)}$$

$$= \left\lfloor \dfrac{1}{2} + \dfrac{b}{a} \right\rfloor + \dfrac{b}{a} + \dfrac{1}{2} \qquad \text{(add com)}$$

$$= 0 + \dfrac{b}{a} + \dfrac{1}{2} \qquad \text{(P1)}$$

$$= \frac{b}{a} + \frac{1}{2} \qquad \text{(add id)}$$

$$= f(0, a, b) \qquad \text{(def)}$$

Case 2: $\dfrac{1}{2} + \dfrac{b}{a} \geq 1$

$$y(1, a, b) + g(1, a, b) = \left\lfloor \frac{b}{a} + \frac{1}{2} \right\rfloor + \frac{1}{2} + \frac{b}{a} - 1 \qquad \text{(from above)}$$

$$= \left\lfloor \frac{1}{2} + \frac{b}{a} \right\rfloor + \frac{b}{a} + \frac{1}{2} - 1 \qquad \text{(add com)}$$

$$= 1 + \frac{b}{a} + \frac{1}{2} - 1 \qquad \text{(P2)}$$

$$= 1 - 1 + \frac{b}{a} + \frac{1}{2} \qquad \text{(add com)}$$

$$= 0 + \frac{b}{a} + \frac{1}{2} \qquad \text{(add inv)}$$

$$= \frac{b}{a} + \frac{1}{2} \qquad \text{(add id)}$$

$$= f(0, a, b) \qquad \text{(def)}$$

Induction   We consider two cases

Case 1: $g(t+1, a, b) + \dfrac{b}{a} < 1$

$$y(t+2, a, b) + g(t+2, a, b)$$

$$= \lfloor f(t+1, a, b) \rfloor + g(t+1, a, b) + \frac{b}{a} \qquad \text{(def)}$$

$$= \left\lfloor f(t, a, b) + \frac{b}{a} \right\rfloor + g(t+1, a, b) + \frac{b}{a} \qquad \text{(def)}$$

$$= \left\lfloor y(t+1, a, b) + g(t+1, a, b) + \frac{b}{a} \right\rfloor + g(t+1, a, b) + \frac{b}{a}$$

$$\text{(ind hyp)}$$

$$= y(t+1, a, b) + \left\lfloor g(t+1, a, b) + \frac{b}{a} \right\rfloor + g(t+1, a, b) + \frac{b}{a} \qquad \text{(P3)}$$

$$= y(t+1, a, b) + 0 + g(t+1, a, b) + \frac{b}{a} \qquad \text{(P1)}$$

$$= y(t+1, a, b) + g(t+1, a, b) + \frac{b}{a} \qquad \text{(add id)}$$

$$= f(t, a, b) + \frac{b}{a} \qquad \text{(ind hyp)}$$

$$= f(t+1, a, b) \qquad \text{(def)}$$

Case 2: $g(t+1, a, b) + \dfrac{b}{a} \geq 1$

$y(t+2, a, b) + g(t+2, a, b)$

$$= \lfloor f(t+1, a, b) \rfloor + g(t+1, a, b) + \frac{b}{a} - 1 \qquad \text{(def)}$$

$$= \left\lfloor f(t, a, b) + \frac{b}{a} \right\rfloor + g(t+1, a, b) + \frac{b}{a} - 1 \qquad \text{(def)}$$

$$= \left\lfloor y(t+1, a, b) + g(t+1, a, b) + \frac{b}{a} \right\rfloor + g(t+1, a, b) + \frac{b}{a} - 1$$

$$\text{(ind hyp)}$$

$$= y(t+1, a, b) + \left\lfloor g(t+1, a, b) + \frac{b}{a} \right\rfloor + g(t+1, a, b) + \frac{b}{a} - 1$$

$$\text{(P3)}$$

$$= y(t+1, a, b) + 1 + g(t+1, a, b) + \frac{b}{a} - 1$$

$$= y(t+1, a, b) + g(t+1, a, b) + \frac{b}{a} + 1 - 1 \qquad \text{(add com)}$$

$$= y(t+1, a, b) + g(t+1, a, b) + \frac{b}{a} + 0 \qquad \text{(add inv)}$$

$$= y(t+1, a, b) + g(t+1, a, b) + \frac{b}{a} \qquad \text{(add id)}$$

$$= f(t, a, b) + \frac{b}{a} \qquad \text{(ind hyp)}$$

$$= f(t+1, a, b) \qquad \text{(def)}$$

We now proceed with the main proof by induction over t.

Basis: We consider two cases.

Case 1: $\dfrac{b}{a} + \dfrac{1}{2} < 0$

Since

$$g(0, a, b) + \frac{b}{a} = \frac{1}{2} + \frac{b}{a}$$

we only need to consider the first case in the definition by cases in the original claim.

$$\lfloor f(0, a, b) \rfloor = \left| \frac{b}{a} + \frac{1}{2} \right| \qquad \text{(def)}$$

$$= 0 \qquad \text{(P1)}$$

$$= y(0, a, b) \qquad \text{(def)}$$

Case 2: $\dfrac{b}{a} + \dfrac{1}{2} \geq 0$

Since

$$g(0, a, b) + \frac{b}{a} = \frac{1}{2} + \frac{b}{a}$$

we only need to consider the second case in the definition by cases in the original claim.

$$\lfloor f(0, a, b) = \left| \frac{b}{a} + \frac{1}{2} \right| \qquad \text{(def)}$$

$$= 1 \qquad \text{(P2)}$$

$$= 0 + 1 \qquad \text{(add id)}$$

$$= y(0, a, b) + 1 \qquad \text{(def)}$$

Induction: We consider two cases.

Case 1: $g(t+1, a, b) + \dfrac{b}{a} < 1$

$$\lfloor f(t+1, a, b) \rfloor = \left\lfloor f(t, a, b) + \frac{b}{a} \right\rfloor \qquad \text{(def)}$$

$$= \left\lfloor y(t+1, a, b) + g(t+1, a, b) + \frac{b}{a} \right\rfloor \qquad \text{(above lemma)}$$

$$= y(t+1, a, b) + \left\lfloor g(t+1, a, b) + \frac{b}{a} \right\rfloor \qquad \text{(P3)}$$

$$= y(t+1, a, b) + 0 \qquad \text{(P1)}$$

$$= y(t+1, a, b) \qquad \text{(add id)}$$

Case 2: $g(t+1, a, b) + \dfrac{b}{a} \geq 1$

$$\lfloor f(t+1, a, b) \rfloor = \left\lfloor f(t, a, b) + \frac{b}{a} \right\rfloor \qquad \text{(def)}$$

$$= \left\lfloor y(t+1, a, b) + g(t+1, a, b) + \frac{b}{a} \right\rfloor \qquad \text{(above lemma)}$$

$$= y(t+1, a, b) + \left\lfloor g(t+1, a, b) + \frac{b}{a} \right\rfloor \qquad \text{(P3)}$$

$$= y(t+1, a, b) + 1 \qquad \text{(P2)}$$

This completes the proof of the original claim. The equations for x, f and g are as before.

$$y(0, a, b) = 0$$

$$y(t+1, a, b) = \begin{cases} y(t, a, b) & \text{if } g(t, a, b) + \dfrac{b}{a} < 1 \\ y(t, a, b) + 1 & \text{otherwise} \end{cases}$$

3.2.7. Delete a function: Function f deleted.

This completes the second cycle of the derivation, yielding

Draft 2

$x(0, a, b) = 0$

$x(t+1, a, b) = x(t, a, b) + 1$

$y(0, a, b) = 0$

$$y(t+1, a, b) = \begin{cases} y(t, a, b) & \text{if } g(t, a, b) + \dfrac{b}{a} < 1 \\ y(t, a, b) + 1 & \text{otherwise} \end{cases}$$

$g(0, a, b) = \frac{1}{2}$

$$g(t+1, a, b) = \begin{cases} g(t, a, b) + \dfrac{b}{a} & \text{if } g(t, a, b) + \dfrac{b}{a} < 1 \\ g(t, a, b) + \dfrac{b}{a} - 1 & \text{otherwise} \end{cases}$$

Notice now that the values computed by the g function are used only in tests and to compute inductively the next value of the g function. Multiplying the tests and the inductive computation through by $2a$ removes fractions and allows the algorithm to be written over a simpler data type (that of the original ordered ring with 1). The next three steps accomplish this by adding a new function h which is effectively g multiplied by $2a$, substituting the new tests in the right hand side of function f and deleting the now redundant g function.

3.2.8. Add a function x, y, g as before.

$h(0, a, b) = a$

$$h(t+1, a, b) = \begin{cases} h(t, a, b) + 2b & \text{if } h(t, a, b) + 2b < 2a \\ h(t, a, b) + 2b - 2a & \text{otherwise} \end{cases}$$

3.2.9. Substitution for rhs sub-expression: Claim

$$\forall t \geq 0 \left[\left[g(t, a, b) + \frac{b}{a} < 1 \right] \leftrightarrow (h(t, a, b) + 2b < 2a) \right]$$

To prove this we first need to prove two lemmas.

Lemma

$$\forall t \geq 0 \left[h(t, a, b) = 2a \times g(t, a, b) \Rightarrow \right.$$

$$\left. (h(t, a, b) + 2b < 2a) \leftrightarrow \left[g(t, a, b) + \frac{b}{a} < 1 \right] \right]$$

Proof:

$$h(t, a, b) = 2a \times g(t, a, b)$$

$$\Rightarrow (h(t, a, b) + 2b < 2a) \leftrightarrow (2a \times g(t, a, b) + 2b < 2a) \qquad \text{(subst)}$$

$$\Rightarrow (h(t, a, b) + 2b < 2a) \leftrightarrow \left[\frac{1}{2a} \times (2a \times g(t, a, b) + 2b) < \frac{1}{2a} \times 2a \right]$$

$$\text{(order)}$$

$$\Rightarrow (h(t, a, b) + 2b < 2a) \leftrightarrow$$

$$\left[\frac{1}{2a} \times 2a \times g(t, a, b) + \frac{1}{2a} \times 2b < \frac{1}{2a} \times 2a \right] \qquad \text{(dist)}$$

$$\Rightarrow (h(t, a, b) + 2b < 2a) \leftrightarrow \left[g(t, a, b) + \frac{b}{a} < 1 \right] \qquad \text{(mult inv)}$$

Lemma

$$\forall t \geq 0 \ [h(t, a, b) = 2a \times g(t, a, b)]$$

Proof: By induction on t.

Basis:

$$2a \times g(0, a, b) = 2a \times \tfrac{1}{2} \qquad \text{(def)}$$

$$= a \qquad \text{(mult inv)}$$

$$= h(0, a, b) \qquad \text{(def)}$$

Induction: We consider two cases.

Case 1 $h(t, a, b) + 2b < 2a$

From the induction hypothesis and the previous lemma we have

$$g(t, a, b) + \frac{b}{a} < 1$$

so

$$2a \times g(t+1, a, b) = 2a \times \left[g(t, a, b) + \frac{b}{a} \right] \qquad \text{(def)}$$

$$= 2a \times g(t, a, b) + 2a \times \frac{b}{a} \qquad \text{(dist)}$$

$$= 2a \times g(t, a, b) + 2b \qquad \text{(mult inv)}$$

$$= h(t, a, b) + 2b \qquad\qquad \text{(ind hyp)}$$

$$= h(t + 1, a, b) \qquad\qquad \text{(def)}$$

Case 2 $h(t, a, b) + 2b \geq 2a$

From the induction hypothesis and the previous lemma we have

$$g(t, a, b) + \frac{b}{a} \geq 1$$

so

$$2a \times g(t + 1, a, b) = 2a \times \left[g(t, a, b) + \frac{b}{a} - 1 \right] \qquad\qquad \text{(def)}$$

$$= 2a \times g(t, a, b) + 2a \times \frac{b}{a} - 2a \times 1 \qquad\qquad \text{(dist)}$$

$$= 2a \times g(t, a, b) + 2b - 2a \qquad\qquad \text{(mult inv)}$$

$$= h(t, a, b) + 2b - 2a \qquad\qquad \text{(ind hyp)}$$

$$= h(t + 1, a, b) \qquad\qquad \text{(def)}$$

The proof of the original claim follows directly from the above two lemmas by the rules for universal quantification and modus ponens. The equations for x, g and h are as before.

$$y(0, a, b) = 0$$

$$y(t + 1, a, b) = \begin{cases} y(t, a, b) & \text{if } h(t, a, b) + 2b < 2a \\ y(t, a, b) + 1 & \text{otherwise} \end{cases}$$

3.2.10. Delete function: Function g deleted.

This completes the third cycle of the derivation, yielding:

Draft 3

$$x(0, a, b) = 0$$

$$x(t + 1, a, b) = x(t, a, b) + 1$$

$$y(0, a, b) = 0$$

$$y(t+1, a, b) = \begin{cases} y(t, a, b) & \text{if } h(t, a, b) + 2b < 2a \\ y(t, a, b) + 1 & \text{otherwise} \end{cases}$$

$$h(0, a, b) = a$$

$$h(t+1, a, b) = \begin{cases} h(t, a, b) + 2b & \text{if } h(t, a, b) + 2b < 2a \\ h(t, a, b) + 2b - 2a & \text{otherwise} \end{cases}$$

The final cycle is to simplify the tests by translating the h function by $2(b - a)$. This is accomplished is a similar manner to that before by creating a new function, r, substituting it into the right hand side of function y and deleting the redundant function h.

3.2.11. Add a function x, y, h as before.

$$r(0, a, b) = 2b - a$$

$$r(t+1, a, b) = \begin{cases} r(t, a, b) + 2b & \text{if } r(t, a, b) < 0 \\ r(t, a, b) + 2b - 2a & \text{otherwise} \end{cases}$$

3.2.12. Substitution for rhs sub-expression: Claim

$$\forall t \geq 0 \ [(h(t, a, b) + 2b < 2a) \leftrightarrow (r(t, a, b) < 0)]$$

To prove this we first need to prove two lemmas.

Lemma

$$\forall t \geq 0 \ [r(t, a, b) = h(t, a, b) + 2b - 2a$$
$$\Rightarrow (r(t, a, b) < 0) \leftrightarrow (h(t, a, b) + 2b < 2a)]$$

Proof:

$$r(t, a, b) = h(t, a, b) + 2b - 2a$$
$$\Rightarrow (r(t, a, b) < 0) \leftrightarrow (h(t, a, b) + 2b - 2a < 0) \qquad \text{(subst)}$$
$$\Rightarrow (r(t, a, b) < 0) \leftrightarrow (h(t, a, b) + 2b - 2a + 2a < 2a) \qquad \text{(order)}$$
$$\Rightarrow (r(t, a, b) < 0) \leftrightarrow (h(t, a, b) + 2b < 2a) \qquad \text{(add inv)}$$

Lemma

$$\forall t \geq 0 \ [r(t, a, b) = h(t, a, b) + 2b - 2a]$$

Proof: By induction on t.

Basis:

$$h(0, a, b) + 2b - 2a = a + 2b - 2a \qquad \text{(def)}$$
$$= 2b + a - 2a \qquad \text{(add com)}$$

$$= 2b - a \qquad \text{(add inv)}$$

$$= r(0, a, b) \qquad \text{(def)}$$

Induction: We consider two cases.

Case 1 $r(t, a, b) < 0$

From the induction hypothesis and previous lemma, $h(t, a, b) + 2b < 2a$, so

$$h(t+1, a, b) + 2b - 2a = h(t, a, b) + 2b + 2b - 2a \qquad \text{(def)}$$

$$= h(t, a, b) + 2b - 2a + 2b \qquad \text{(add com)}$$

$$= r(t, a, b) + 2b \qquad \text{(ind hyp)}$$

$$= r(t+1, a, b) \qquad \text{(def)}$$

Case 2 $r(t, a, b) \geq 0$

From the induction hypothesis and previous lemma, $h(t, a, b) + 2b \geq 2a$, so

$$h(t+1, a, b) + 2b - 2a = h(t, a, b) + 2b - 2a + 2b - 2a \qquad \text{(def)}$$

$$= r(t, a, b) - 2a + 2b \qquad \text{(ind hyp)}$$

$$= r(t+1, a, b) \qquad \text{(def)}$$

The proof of the original claim follows directly from the above two lemmas by the rules for universal quantification and modus ponens. The equations for x, h and r are as before.

$$y(0, a, b) = 0$$

$$y(t+1, a, b) = \begin{cases} y(t, a, b) & \text{if } r(t, a, b) < 0 \\ y(t, a, b) + 1 & \text{otherwise} \end{cases}$$

3.2.13. Delete function: Function h deleted.

This completes the fourth cycle and the derivation, yielding:

Draft 4: Bresenham's algorithm.

$$x(0, a, b) = 0$$

$$x(t+1, a, b) = x(t, a, b) + 1$$

$$y(0, a, b) = 0$$

$$y(t+1, a, b) = \begin{cases} y(t, a, b) & \text{if } r(t, a, b) < 0 \\ y(t, a, b) + 1 & \text{otherwise} \end{cases}$$

$$r(0, a, b) = 2b - a$$

$$r(t+1, a, b) = \begin{cases} r(t, a, b) + 2b & \text{if } r(t, a, b) < 0 \\ r(t, a, b) + 2b - 2a & \text{otherwise} \end{cases}$$

3.2.14. Note on logical principles   In addition to the properties of ordered archimedian rings and fields, the above proofs are based upon elementary logical principles such as substitution of equalities and induction over counters.

References

Adamson [1964].
>   I. T. Adamson, *Introduction to field theory,* Oliver and Boyd (1964).

Back [1980].
>   R. J. R. Back, *Correctness preserving program refinements: proof theory and applications,* Mathematical Centre Tracts 131, Amsterdam (1980).

Back [1981].
>   R. J. R. Back, "On correct refinement of programs", *Journal of computer and system sciences* **23** pp. 49-68 (1981).

Bresenham [1965].
>   J. E. Bresenham, "Algorithm for computer control of a digital plotter", *IBM Systems Journal* **IV**(1) pp. 106-111 (1965).

Bresenham [1977].
>   J. E. Bresenham, "A Linear Algorithm for Incremental Digital Display of Circular Arcs", *Communications of the ACM* **20**(2) pp. 100-106 (February 1977).

Castle and Pitteway [1985].
>   C. M. A. Castle and M. L. V. Pitteway, "An application of Euclid's algorithm to drawing straight lines", pp. 135-139 in *Fundamental algorithms for computer graphics,* ed. R. A. Earnshaw,Springer-Verlag (1985).

Castle and Pitteway [1987].
>   C. M. A. Castle and M. L. V. Pitteway, "An Efficient Structural Technique for Encoding 'Best-fit' Straight Lines", *Computer Journal* **30**(2) pp. 168-175 (1987).

Cohn [1977].
>   P. M. Cohn, *Algebra Volume 2,* John Wiley and Sons (1977).

Corthout and Jonkers [1986].
>   M. E. A. Corthout and H. B. M. Jonkers, "The transformational development of a new point containment algorithm", *Philips Journal of Research* **41**(2) pp. 83-174 (1986).

Ehrig and Mahr [1985].
>   H. Ehrig and B. Mahr, *Fundamentals of algebraic specifications 1 - Equations and initial semantics,* EATCS Monograph Series Vol 6, Springer-Verlag (1985).

Eker and Tucker [1988].
> S. M. Eker and J. V. Tucker, "Specification, Derivation and Verification of Concurrent Line Drawing Algorithms and Architectures", pp. 449-516 in *Theoretical foundations of computer graphics and CAD*, ed. R. A. Earnshaw,Springer-Verlag (1988).

Eker and Tucker [1989].
> S. M. Eker and J. V. Tucker, "Specification and Verfication of Synchronous Concurrent Algorithms: A Case Study of the Pixel Planes Architecture", in *Parallel processing for computer vision and display*, ed. P. M. Dew, R. A. Earnshaw and T. R. Heywood,Addison-Wesley, Reading (1989).

McIlroy [1983].
> M. D. McIlroy, "Best Approximate Circles on Integer Grids", *ACM Transations on Graphics* **2**(4) pp. 237-263 (October 1983).

Mili, Desharnais and Gagne [1986].
> A. Mili, J. Desharnais, and J. R. Gagne, "Formal Models of Stepwise Refinement of Programs", *ACM Computing Surveys* **18**(3) pp. 231-276 (1986).

Rogers [1985].
> D. F. Rogers, *Procedural elements for computer graphics,* McGraw-Hill (1985).

Sproull [1982].
> R. F. Sproull, "Using program transformations to derive line drawing algorithms", *ACM Transactions on Graphics* **1**(4) pp. 259-273 (October 1982).

Swenker [1987].
> J. B. Swenker, *Development of a line drawing algorithm,* University of Groningen, Report CS8701 (1987).

Thompson [1987].
> B. C. Thompson, *A mathematical theory of synchronous concurrent algorithms,* PhD Thesis, Department of Computer Studies, The University of Leeds (1987).

Thompson and Tucker [1989].
> B. C. Thompson and J. V. Tucker, *Synchronous Concurrent Algorithms,* Centre for Theoretical Computer Science, University of Leeds (in preparation) (1989).

Tucker and Zucker [1988].
> J. V. Tucker and J. I. Zucker, *Program correctness over abstract data types, with error state semantics,* North-Holland, Amsterdam (1988).

Steven M. Eker received the Bsc. degree in computational science from the University of Leeds in 1986. He is currently a final year research student at that institution. His research interests include pixel level graphics algorithms and the formal specification and verification of algorithms and architectures.

John Tucker is Director of the Centre for Theiretical Computer Science at the University of Leeds. His research interests include the theory of programming languages, program specification and verfication, and data abstrctions, where he has published many papers. He is currently leading a team involved in theoretical and experimental work on constructs for synchronous parallel algorithms.

Visualization in Scientific Computing: Achievements and Prospects

M.J. Wozny

ABSTRACT

Scientific visualization requires not only computer graphics, but more fundamentally, a total modeling environment. Graphical representation of data derived from inadequate mathematical models is meaningless. Future graphics environments with specialized modeling engines will be needed to infer behavior about the world around us.

KEYWORDS: scientific visualization, mathematical models, workstations, computer graphics.

The term "scientific visualization: is used to describe the process of extracting meaningful information, in an interactive manner, from a graphics representation of a physical phenomenon. The purpose is to enhance our understanding of the underlying phenomenon. Generally, the phenomenon is so complex, or not amenable to experimental observation, that relationships are not directly evident. The graphical environment gives us a virtual world in which to model phenomena and search interactively for intuitive insight about possible dependencies.

Since graphics interpretation is so pervasive and applicable to essentially all scientific disciplines, we have seen a serge of activity in many scientific areas [VIS 87, CROMIE 88, HABER 88, CRAY 88]. This surge is due primarily to the availability of supercomputers for modeling aspects and high performance graphics workstations for interactive interpretation.

In some cases, graphical representations in one discipline have facilitated the interpretation of a phenomena from the viewpoint of another discipline, prompting the notion that visualization is a "universal language" which ties together the various scientific disciplines. Is there really something here? Is there a language of pictures, interactions and shapes that allows disparate scientific disciplines to meaningfully communicate? We are still a long way from answering this question.

To extract understanding one can represent phenomena graphically either by (1) displaying data generated from a physical experiment, or by (2) first developing an underlying mathematical (computer) model that generates the graphical data. Typically in engineering, we postulate a mathematical model designed to address a specific class of questions about our limited understanding; and then infer answers by observing the graphical (and possibly dymanical) output in response the "asking of those questions".

For a given physical phenomena we must first create an appropriate model, suitable for "answering" questions. Thus, the model is inextricably tied to our anticipated responses. Even the best graphics environment will reveal little if the models are not appropriate (of course flexibility is needed to allow for the unanticipated!). Consequently, we need both the appropriate modeling environment and the appropriate graphics environment in order to extract maximum information about underlying dependencies in complex information.

Graphics environments today provide excellent interactive graphics capabilities (albeit, we always want more!), but existing environments stop short of providing a total modeling environment. We have taken the first step by incorporating geometry (i.e., non-uniform rational B-splines) into the graphical pipeline [PHIGS+ 88, SHANTZ 88, ABI-EZZI 88]. We have also seen the growth of accelerating engines such as the SUN TAAC1 board [VLIW Application Accelerator]. However, it is still premature to speculate about symbolic math engines, or a Maxwell law engine.

On the other hand, we have seen rapid growth over the past few years of "physically based graphics" [CG 88]. In effect, we are seeing the early stages of an evolution where computer graphics (animation) is driven by physical laws in a general way.

It will be in specific scientific-focused research areas where new computer graphics requirements, paradigms and architectures will evolve and provide the desired visualization environment.

REFERENCES

[VIS 87]
"Visualization in Scientific Computing," Computer Graphics, Volume 21, Number 6, Edited by Bruce H. McCormick, Thomas A. DeFanti, Maxine D. Brown, ACM SIGGRAPH, 1987.

[CROMIE 88]
Cromie, W.J., "Computer Images in Five Dimensions," MOSAIC, Volume 19, Number 2, Summer 1988.

[HABER 88]
Haber, R.B., "Visualization in Engineering Mechanics: Techniques, Systems and Issues," Visualization Techniques in the Physical Sciences, SIGGRAPH '88, August 1988.

[CRAY 88]
Cary Channels, A Cray Research, Inc., Publication, Summer 1988.

[PHIGS+ 88]
PHIGS+ Committee, "PHIGS+ Functional Description Revision 3.0," Edited by Andries van Dam, Computer Graphics, Volume 22, Number 3, July 1988.

[SHANTZ 88]
Shantz, M. and Lien, S.L., "Rendering Trimmed NURBs with Adaptive Forward Differencing," Computer Graphics, 22(4), August 1988, pp. 189-196.

[ABI-EZZI 88]
Abi-Ezzi, S., "The Graphical Processing of B-Splines," PhD Thesis, TR-88051, Rensselaer Design Research Center, Rensselaer Polytechnic Institute, Troy, NY, 12180, 1988.

[CG 88]
Computer Graphics, ACM SIGGRAPH '88 Conference Proceeding, Volume 22, Number 4, August 1-5, 1988.

MICHAEL J. WOZNY took a leave, from September 1986 to September 1988, from the Rensselaer Polytechnic Institute (RPI), Troy, NY, to the National Science Foundation where he was Division Director, for the Design, Manufacturing, and Computer-Integrated Division. At RPI, Dr. Wozny is Professor of Electrical, Computer and Systems Engineering; Professor of Computer Science; and Director of the Rensselaer Design Research Center.

Dr. Wozny received his PhD degree from the University of Arizona in 1965. His previous appointments include Purdue University, Oakland University, GM Research Labs, NASA Electronics Research Center and NSF. His research interests are in CAD/CAM, engineering design, computer graphics, and dynamics systems.

He serves on the editorial boards of Visual Computer, CAD/CIM Alert, Workstation Alert, and Marquis Who's Who in Computer Graphics; he was the founding Editor-in-Chief of IEEE Computer Graphics and Applications (1981-85) and is on the editorial board of IEEE Proceedings (1985-88).

Dr. Wozny is the recipient of the IEEE Centennial Medal (1984), the IEEE Computer Society Outstanding Contribution Award (1985), and the National Computer Graphics Association Academic Award (1988).

Address: mwozny@rdrc.rpi.edu, Rensselaer Design Research Center, CII 7015, Rensselaer Polytechnic Institute, Troy, NY, 12180-3590, USA.

Chapter 2
Algorithms

Conic Rescue of Bezier Founts

F. Hussain

ABSTRACT

Attractive and aesthetically satisfying founts are now widely conceivable when using high resolution laser printers. The outline of these founts have frequently been defined by Bezier splines. Pratt (1985) has developed a means of defining fount outline by using conic sections. Furthermore, he has shown how conic sections can adequately be used to represent curves that were previously thought to require cubic splines. This paper presents an algorithm which takes a given Bezier cubic spline and efficiently outputs its equivalent conic representation. The approximation always results in conic sections that best describe, in terms of least-squares error values, founts that were constructed using Bezier cubic splines.

Keywords and Phrases: Bezier, Conic, Fount

1. INTRODUCTION

In Computer Graphics, it is often necessary to represent a hand-drawn shape accurately. Generating such shapes manually is both cumbersome and commercially expensive. Most Computer-Aided-Design (CAD) systems have a spline routine to assist the designer in this respect. The designer uses several parametric cubic segments to construct the given hand-drawn shape. An effective method to achieve this has been developed by Bjorkenstein and Westberg (1987).

One of the most accepted and elegant techniques used to represent input shape information has been developed by Bezier (1972). In particular, splines defined by Bezier (1972) have increasingly been used to capture outline shapes of founts for laser printer packages. The captured founts produced by high-resolution laser printers are of high quality in terms of their representation and appearance.

Pratt (1985) has shown that attractive founts can also be produced using conic splines. In addition to showing how conic splines could be used to approximate some of the properties of cubic curves, Pratt (1985) has developed a means of generating conic splines using an all-integer version of Pitteway's algorithm (1967). This also ensures that the specified arcs always join exactly, thus avoiding any 'bleeding' problems that may occur when seedfilling the interior of a character outline.

In this paper a comparison is made between founts defined using Bezier cubic splines with those defined using conic splines. In particular, an algorithm is presented which converts any Bezier cubic spline (in this case, a fount) to its conic form. The algorithm uses a linear least-squares technique to always return the best-fit conic description of a given Bezier cubic fount.

2. SPLINES: CUBICS VERSUS CONICS

A four-point (cubic) Bezier curve consists of two control points and two endpoints. The positioning of the control points governs both the overall shape of the curve segment and the respective endpoint tangents. As highlighted by Forrest (1971), an additional parameter u is used to fully describe the curve segment. This parameter is normalised to range from 0 (startpoint) to 1 (endpoint). Examples of Bezier cubic curves are depicted in Fig 1.

An inherent property of Bezier cubic splines, as pointed out by Pratt (1985) and Pavlidis (1983), is that they allow curvature (C_2) continuity between curve segments. This, and the fact that cubic splines have zero curvature at inflection points, form two important reasons for using Bezier cubic splines to represent an input shape such as a fount outline.

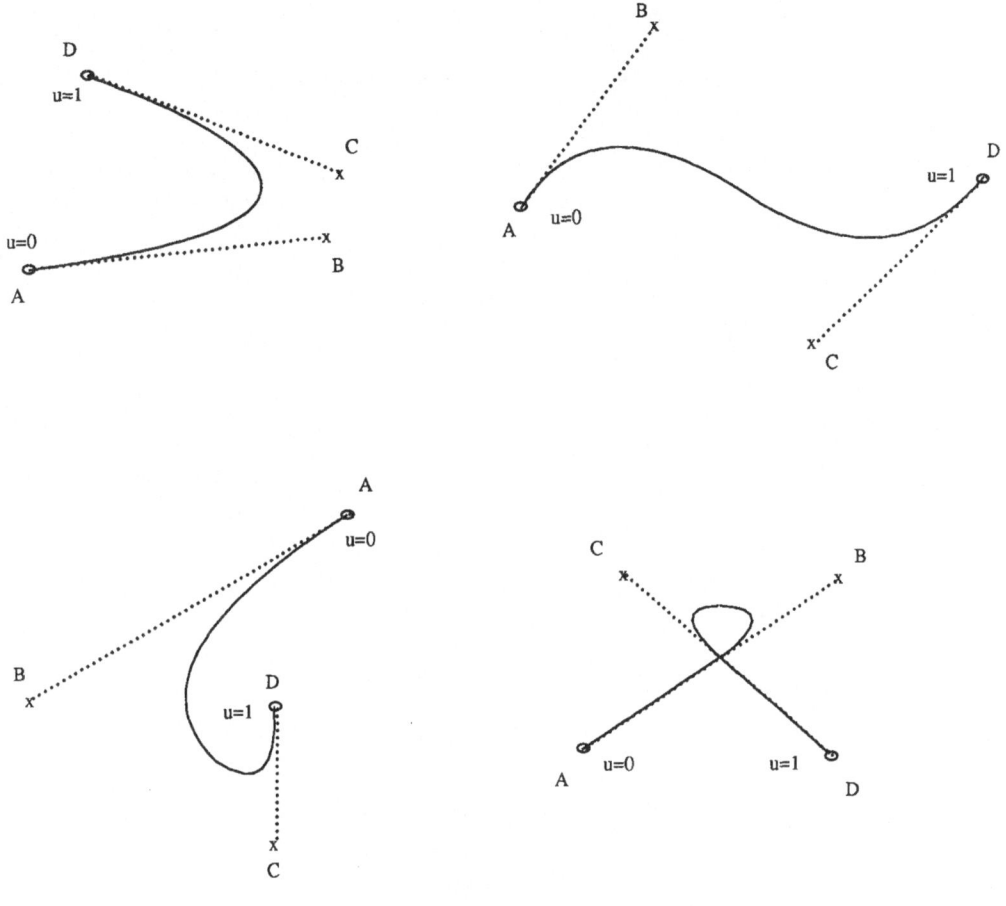

Fig 1 Examples of Bezier Curves,
where A & D are endpoints, and
B & C are control points.

Conic (ie quadratic) curve segments can also be used to produce a required shape. The method developed by Pratt (1985) forms a clean and simple way of representing conic sections. The mechanism used for defining conic sections is based on earlier work carried out by both Forrest (1968) and Pavlidis (1983). As shown in Fig 2, the type (and thus shape) of a conic section is determined by a parameter termed sharpness. According to Pratt (1985), this parameter will need to have the following values in order to yield the respective conic arc:

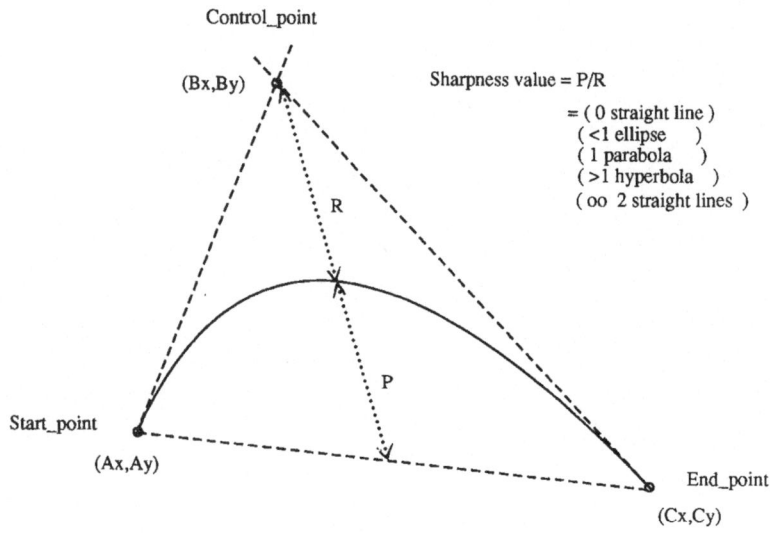

Fig 2 Pratt's Conic Definition

Sharpness	Conic shape
0	straight line
<1	ellipse
1	parabola
>1	hyperbola
∞	2 straight lines

As any conic section can be achieved by a combination of a single control point (where the two endpoint tangents intersect) and a 'curve weighted' parameter (ie sharpness value), it gives added value for using conics rather than cubic splines. In fact, since in the case of Bezier cubic curves only the positioning of the control points governs the shape of a curve segment, advanced techniques such as those developed by Plass and Stone (1983) are required to automate the use of Bezier cubic splines to yield a desired input shape.

To prefer conics for generating outline of founts, the inherent properties of cubic splines have to be sought. Pratt (1985) has looked particularly at developing a mechanism for approximating, using conics, the two main properties (curvature continuity and zero curvature at inflection points) offered by cubics. His findings can be summarised as follows:

a) Curvature continuity using conics.

A formula for evaluating curvature at the endpoints of a conic curve is derived by using the fact that, as the sharpness value goes from zero to infinity, the corresponding curvature at the endpoints goes from infinity to zero. The formula can then be used to match endpoint curvatures between conic segments.

b) Zero curvature at inflection points.

As points of inflection (zero curvature) are non-existent in conics, except for lines, a method to represent such points using conics was developed. This involved using the formula, mentioned in a), to make the curvature at the inflection point much smaller than any prevailing curvature at some distance away from the inflection point, thus enabling piecewise conic segments to approximate zero curvature at inflection points.

Another feature of Bezier cubic curves is that they offer eight degrees of freedom compared to the seven (including the sharpness parameter) offered by conics. This does not seriously hinder the value of conics. The extra degree of freedom leads to the production of shapes such as cusps and loops, which can (as the next section will show) be approximated by two or more conic segments.

Pavlidis (1983), apart from highlighting the fact that conics have a longer and solid historical background, has noted one of the main benefits of using conics, namely that it is much easier to find the intersection of a line with a conic than with a cubic. The solution for this problem is required in many applications of computer graphics (eg hidden surface removal), and its demand has led to the development of recursive subdivision techniques (Cohen 1980) for cubic splines.

In summary, it can be seen that most of the advantages offered by Bezier cubic splines can equally be matched by quadratic splines. Indeed, Pratt (1985) has shown that the main features of cubic curves, to provide curvature continuity between curve segments and zero curvature at inflection points, can to a good degree be approximated by conics. Furthermore, conic splines offer a simple and feasible way of representing fount outline, with added shape control via a sharpness parameter.

3. CONCEPT OF RESCUE

When deciding how to recover the outline of founts, described by Bezier cubic curve segments, two possibilities (as illustrated in Fig 3a and 3b) have to be considered. The first possibility occurs when the two endpoint tangents do not intersect. In this case, as depicted in Fig 3a, the Bezier curve needs to be subdivided into two halves, with two different conics representing each half. Although in most cases (excluding Bezier curves with inflection points) the Bezier curve could be subdivided at $u = 0.5$, there is no guarantee that splitting at this point will always result in conic sections that best-fit the original Bezier curve. Thus to efficiently recover Bezier cubic curves a measure of the quality of the conic-fit needs to be made at different splitting points along the Bezier curve (see Fig 4a). This would then result in a graph similar to that shown in Fig 4b being realised. The 'error' term indicates the goodness-of-fit, with its minimum value being chosen as the best point to split.

The second possibility occurs, as shown in Fig 3b, when the two endpoint tangents do intersect. Although this Bezier curve could be subdivided and approximated by two best-fitting conic sections, the need to do so will depend on whether a single conic approximation is within a desired best-fit criterion. That is, since an equivalent conic representation can be gained by choosing the intersection point (of the two endpoint tangents) as a control point and then using the x and y positions at $u=0.5$ (mid-point of Bezier curve) to evaluate the required sharpness value, the need to split such a Bezier curve only becomes necessary if and when a single conic approximation is both numerically and aesthetically unacceptable.

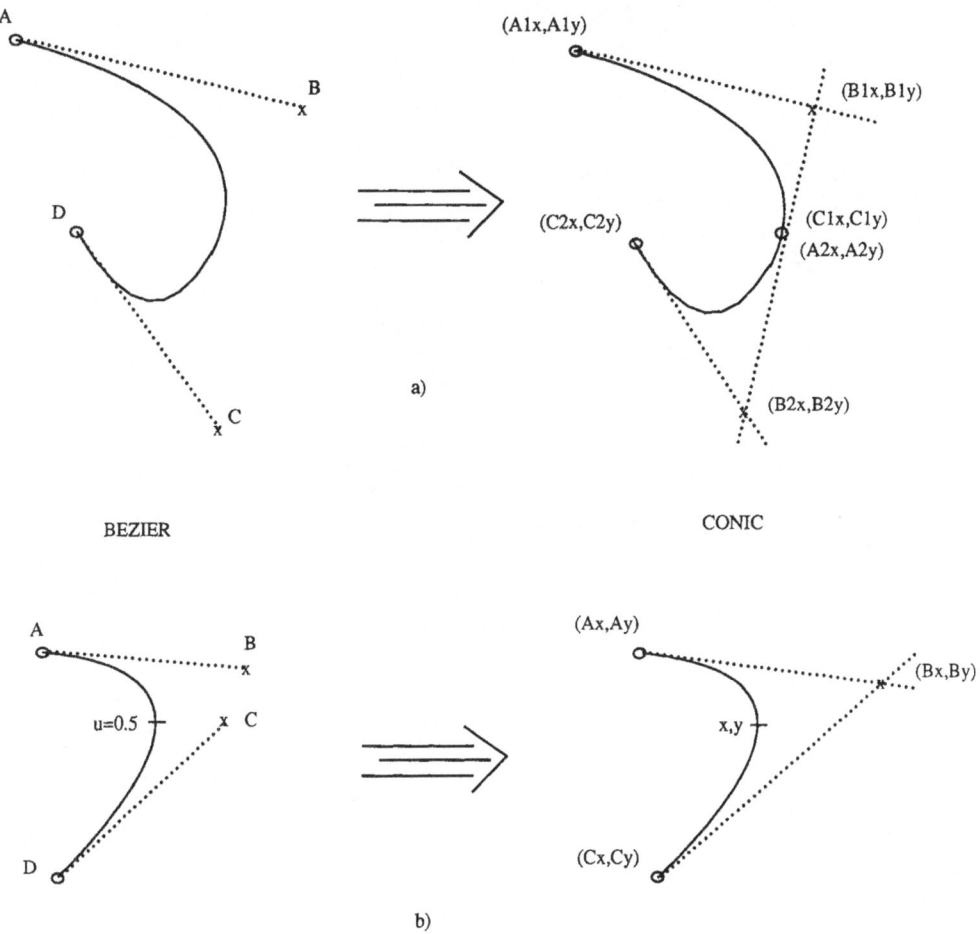

Fig 3 Shows two possibilities of conic rescue of Bezier curves,
a) where the endpoint tangents do not intersect and the Bezier
curve needs to be subdivided to form two conics, and
b) where the Bezier endpoint tangents do intersect.

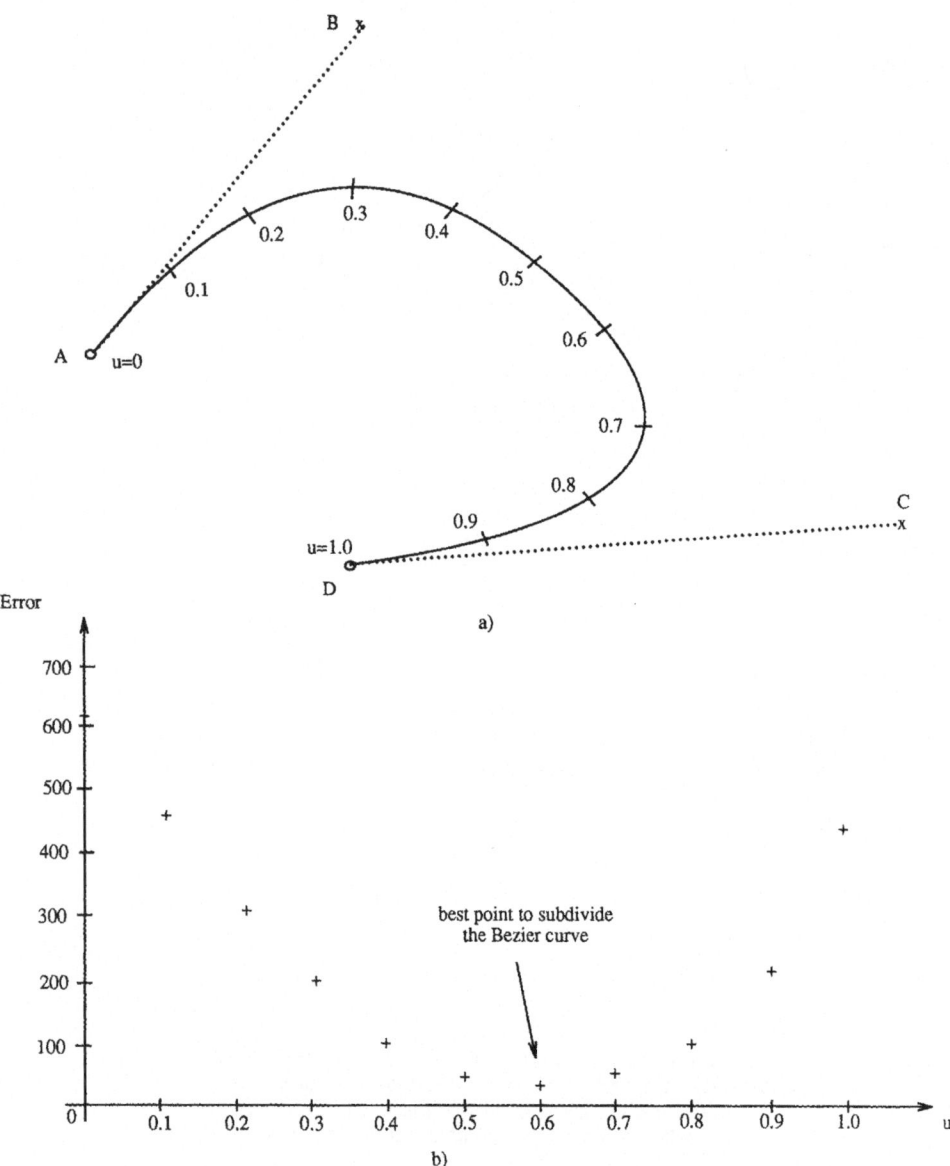

Fig 4   Shows the concept of attaining the best
point to split the Bezier curve,
a) Bezier curve with its split points, and
b) corresponding best-fit graph.

4. REALISATION OF RESCUE

The problem of fitting the best conic(s) to a given Bezier cubic curve can be considered as a general problem of fitting the best curve to a given set of data points. The solution to these type of problems is normally achieved by using some form of least-squares method, wherein a measure of the deviation of a curve from its desired shape is made.

Albano (1974), Bookstein (1979), Sampson (1982) and Forbes (1987) have all used least-square techniques to fit conic sections to a required data shape. The approach used here, however, differs in that the least-squares method is of a linear type and that, more importantly, it encompasses the basic definition of conics presented by Pratt (1985). Furthermore, the technique is algorithmically simple and computationally efficient.

The basis of the technique starts with the fundamental quadratic equation that describes all conic sections (ie ellipses, circles, parabolas and hyperbolas), which takes the form $d = 0$, where

$$d(x,y) \equiv 2vx - 2uy - \alpha y^2 - \beta x^2 - 2\gamma xy + c \quad \ldots (1)$$

If, for convenience, the starting point (point A in Fig 2) for the conic curve $d(x,y) = 0$ is set at the origin, then the constant c will equal zero. The conic curve will also need to pass through the endpoint C, so that setting $x=C_x$ and $y=C_y$ satisfies $d(x,y) = 0$. The control point B is used to define the initial gradient $\frac{v}{u}$, so, by taking advantage of the arbitrary scale, the control positions u and v are set equal to B_x and B_y respectively. The gradient at any point on the conic curve can be expressed as:

$$\frac{dy}{dx} = \frac{v - \beta x - \gamma y}{u + \gamma x + \alpha y} \quad \ldots (2)$$

Since the control point B also defines the gradient at the endpoint C, the corresponding gradient at this endpoint will take the form:

$$\frac{v - \beta C_x - \gamma C_y}{u + \gamma C_x + \alpha C_y} = \frac{C_y - v}{C_x - u} \quad \text{.... (3)}$$

By using the conic equation $d(C_x, C_y) = 0$ and the respective gradient equation at the endpoint (ie equations (1) and (3)), an expression for u and v can be realised in terms of α, β, γ, C_x and C_y as follows:

$$u = \frac{C_x - \gamma C_x - \alpha C_y}{2}$$

$$v = \frac{C_y + \beta C_x + \gamma C_y}{2} \quad \text{.... (4)}$$

Substituting these findings in equation (1), the general conic form becomes:

$$d(x,y) \equiv \alpha (yC_y - y^2) + \beta (xC_x - x^2) + \gamma (xC_y + yC_x - 2xy) + (xC_y - yC_x) \quad \text{.... (5}$$

The quantity $d(x,y)$, in equation (5), will equal zero when a conic data point matches exactly a given Bezier point; otherwise, $d(x,y)$ will take on a small non-zero value to indicate a slight deviation in the conic approximation from its required Bezier point.

For each Bezier cubic curve segment, described in terms of its endpoints and two control points, the following parametric form is used to obtained the x and y positions:

$$x(u) = x_0 (1-u)^3 + 3 x_1 u (1-u)^2 + 3 x_2 u^2 (1-u) + x_3 u^3$$

$$y(u) = y_0 (1-u)^3 + 3 y_1 u (1-u)^2 + 3 y_2 u^2 (1-u) + y_3 u^3 \quad \text{.... (6)}$$

where u ranges from 0 to 1,
        x_0, y_0 and x_1, y_1 denote the start and end points respectively, and
        x_2, y_2 and x_3, y_3 are the respective control points.

To generate, therefore, a Bezier curve consisting of say 1001 data points (ie x and y values), the parameter u has to be incremented at each point by

0.001, so that the 1001 positions are produced within the parameter's normalised range of 0 to 1. Each data point, in turn, is then substituted into equation (5) to gain a corresponding residue value $d(x_i, y_i)$.

With this realisation, equation (5) is used to set-up 1001 simultaneous equations (one for each data point) to solve (in a least-squares sense) for the three unknowns, α, β and γ. The solution of these unknowns is such that it minimises the summation of the squared residue at each data point, that is:

$$\frac{\partial}{\partial \alpha} \sum_{i=0}^{1000} d^2(x_i, y_i) = 0 \ ,$$

$$\frac{\partial}{\partial \beta} \sum_{i=0}^{1000} d^2(x_i, y_i) = 0 \ ,$$

$$\frac{\partial}{\partial \gamma} \sum_{i=0}^{1000} d^2(x_i, y_i) = 0 \quad \dots (7) \ ,$$

so that the "best" possible conic section is used to approximate the given Bezier spline. A computationally fast subroutine developed by Lewis (1986) is then used to process the 1001 data points. This outputs both the values for the 3 unknowns and also the total value of the squared residue.

Once the values for α, β and γ are gained, the corresponding control positions (u and v) are evaluated by using equation (4). The sharpness value (S) for this conic section is acquired by utilising the expression

$$\alpha\beta - \gamma^2 = \frac{1}{S^2} - 1 \ ,$$

so that

$$S = \frac{1}{\sqrt{1 + \alpha\beta - \gamma^2}} \quad \dots (8)$$

Since, at each Bezier splitting point, two conic sections are fitted, the total residue from both conics is used to assess which is the best point to split. This ensures that conics fitted to both sides of the splitting point are those that return the overall minimum residue value.

5. CURVATURE AND INFLECTION POINTS

The method for obtaining best conic approximations, as described in the previous section, does not encompass the curvature matching mechanism (of conic segments) developed by Pratt (1985). The mechanism can, however, be included if this becomes necessary, although the algorithm does inherently take note of all Bezier curve data points, including the endpoints where the matching will take place. The results (see later section) show that the exclusion of the 'curvature matcher' does not seriously hinder the performance, or reduce the quality, of output obtained from the algorithm. In fact, the quality of conic segment matching suggests that the algorithm, to a good degree, preserves the curvature features of Bezier cubic splines.

As noted earlier, Bezier splines can possess (within their curve segments) points of zero curvature (ie inflection points). This property of Bezier splines cannot be recaptured directly by using a single conic section, as the latter representation does not exhibit inflection points.

One method of representing Bezier curves with inflection points is to apply the described conic recapturing technique. This method, as demonstrated for the curve in Fig 5, will return the best place to split the Bezier curve to be at the inflection point itself. The technique is thus being used indirectly to locate the point where the curvature of a Bezier cubic spline goes to zero. Although this method can be used, it is neither the most elegant nor the fastest way of acheiving the desired result.

A better approach could be to use the 2nd derivative of the Bezier curve (ie $\frac{d^2y(u)}{dx(u)^2}$) at each splitting point to test for the inflection point. As manifested in Fig 6a, this would result in the 2nd derivative being positive for a curve that is concave upwards, negative for a curve that is concave downwards and zero where the curve has zero curvature. This, along with the 1st derivative (ie $\frac{dy(u)}{dx(u)}$), could be used to detect inflection points. The problem with this approach, however, is that it is only sufficient for Bezier curves that do not have multiple data points within each curve segment; otherwise, as illustrated in Fig 6b, additional points could be taken as being points of inflection.

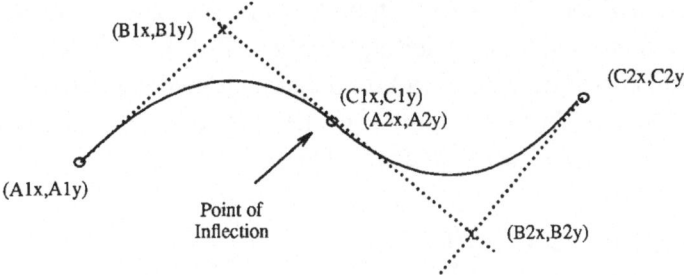

Fig 5   Shows that the best point to split a Bezier
curve, containing an inflection point, is at the
inflection point.

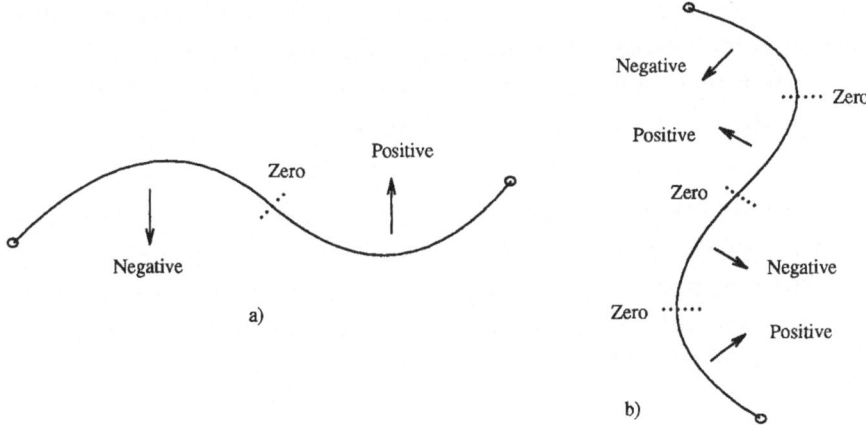

Fig 6 Shows the sign of the 2nd derivative along
a Bezier curve containing an inflection point:

a) an example where the 2nd derivative returns
a 'true' inflection point when it becomes zero,

b) an example of a multiple point Bezier curve
where the 2nd derivative would return three
possible inflection points,although the
middle zero value is the actual point
of inflection.

A much better and ideally suited method to attain curvature information has been used by many authors, including Roulier (1987). The method returns the appropriate curvature value $k(u)$ for a curve defined parametrically by u. The expression for $k(u)$ in terms of the 1st and 2nd derivatives (ie $x'(u), y'(u)$ and $x''(u), y''(u)$ respectively) takes the form:

$$k(u) = \frac{x'(u)y''(u) - y'(u)x''(u)}{(x'(u)^2 - y'(u)^2)^{3/2}} \quad \dots (9)$$

The way equation (9) is used to detect inflection points is by checking if the sign of the curvature value $k(u)$ changes within a Bezier curve segment. If there is no change of sign then the curve does not contain an inflection point. If, on the other hand, a change of sign in $k(u)$ is detected then there exists an inflection point between the points where the sign change has taken place. Once an inflection point is detected, the Bezier cubic curve is split at this point to yield the two appropriate conic sections.

Pratt's method (1985) for matching conic segments with zero curvature at inflection points could again be used once the appropriate conic approximations have been evaluated. However, as in the case of matching curvature continuity, the results obtained show that the aesthetic characteristic of zero curvature matching is of acceptable levels.

6. THE ALGORITHM

The basic outline of the algorithm is given in Fig 7. It includes, in addition to the Bezier curve-splitting mechanism, subroutines that are used for initialising, checking and evaluating various types (and thus shapes) of Bezier cubic curves. In essence, the algorithm is made robust to cater for any Bezier cubic curve that is being used to define a fount outline.

The algorithm is invariant with respect to translation, rotation and change of scale: Thus, if a given Bezier fount outline is translated, rotated or rescaled, the best-fitting conics to the transformed fount are the same as those that would have resulted by appropriately translating, rotating and rescaling the best-fitting conics to the original fount.

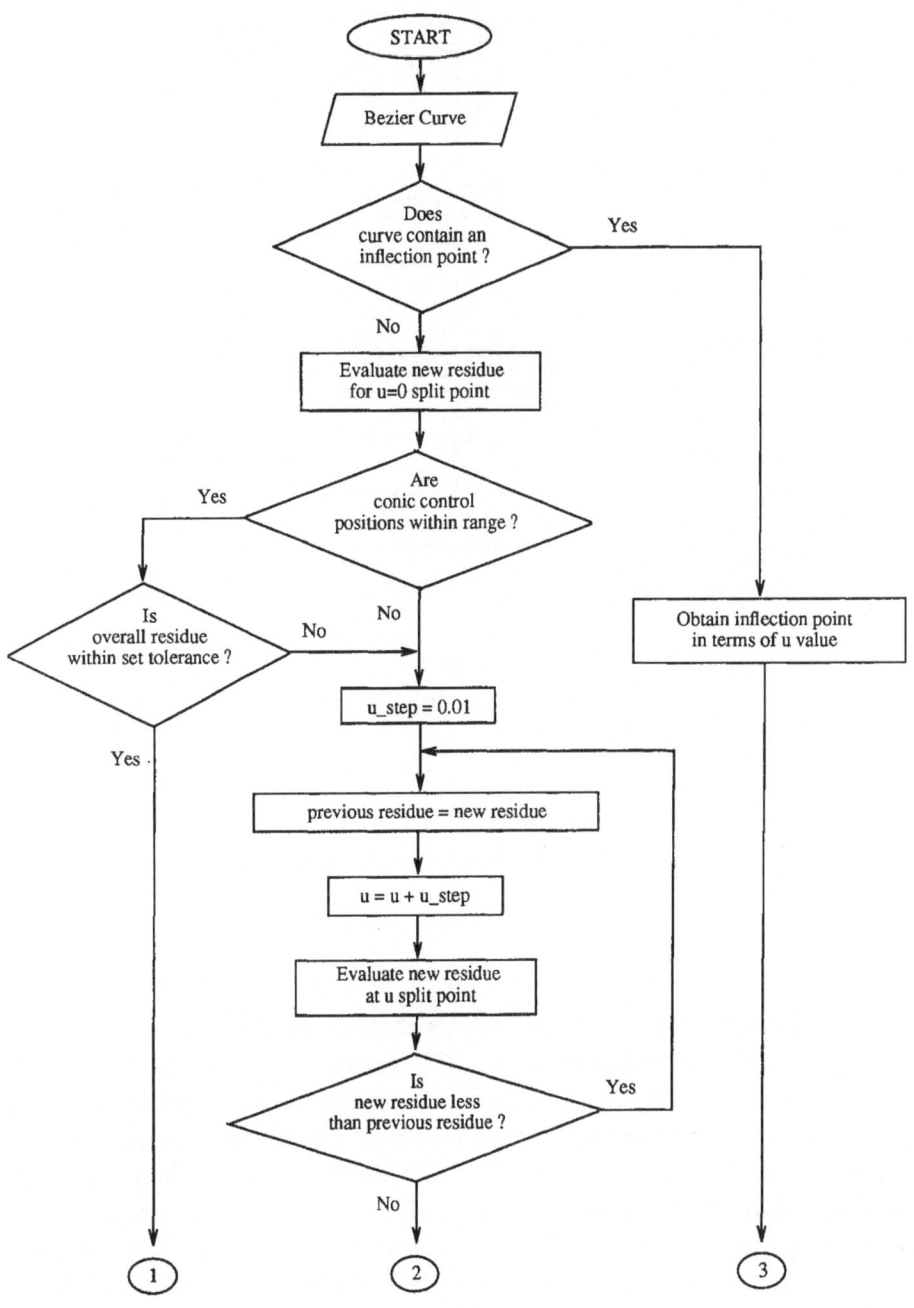

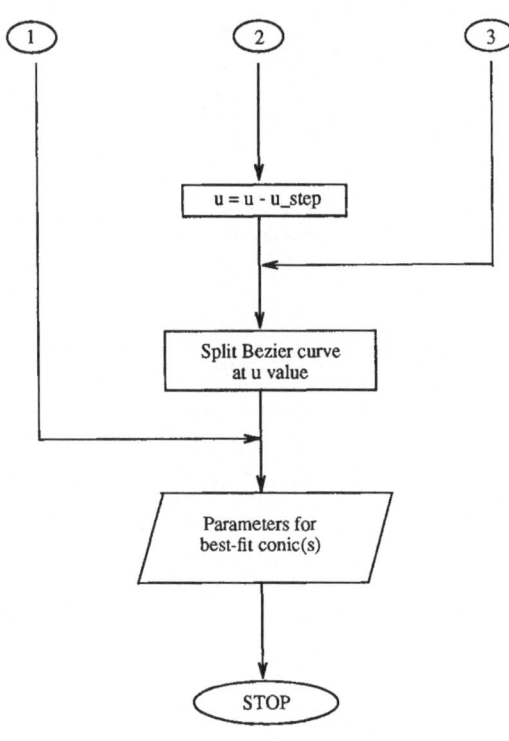

Fig 7   The conic rescue algorithm

The algorithm accepts all Bezier founts that are represented in the format used by Osland (1986). On reception of a Bezier curve, a check to see if the curve contains an inflection point is initially made. This is done by checking if there is a change in the sign of the curvature expression $k(u)$, at $u=0.001$ and at $u=0.999$ respectively. If this check proves positive, then the Bezier curve is split at the inflection point. Otherwise, the curve does not contain an inflection point and the procedure to obtain best-fit conic approximations is then activated. As shown in Fig 7, a check is then made to evaluate whether the Bezier curve needs to be subdivided. The subdivision procedure will be initiated if, when the Bezier curve is 'split' at $u=0$, either of the following two conditions prove positive:

a) The overall residue value is above a required goodness-of-fit value. In this situation the two endpoint tangents do intersect; however, as

Fig 8a shows, the single conic approximation returns a goodness-of-fit value that is not within a required acceptable tolerance; implying that the Bezier curve needs to be subdivided.

b) The corresponding control positions yield the wrong conic section. This occurs when the two endpoint tangents do not intersect; however, the algorithm outputs a conic section which would represent, as depicted in Fig 8b, the other half of an ellipse. Although the overall residue value will be a good indicater if this happens, this check is made to further increase the robustness of the algorithm, with little increase in the computation.

If the subdivision procedure is activated then the Bezier curve is subdivided, in a manner similar to that presented in the earlier sections, to yield two conic sections that best-fit the curve. At each split evaluation the validity of the control positions is checked by using the same subroutine as in b) above.

This way, the algorithm shown in Fig 7 is used to process each Bezier curve segment to construct a corresponding conic data structure that fully describes a given Bezier icon outline. The processing of straight lines, however, is not shown in Fig 7, as conic representation of these can simply be attained by setting the sharpness value equal to zero and the corresponding conic control positions equal to the mid-positions of the line.

7. INTEGER POSITIONS

Before presenting the results, one of the most important aspects of the algorithm is its usage of integer positions. The assumption has been made, thus far, that the algorithm returns best splitting points and control points to be in terms of integer values. However, the only guaranteed integer positions that the best-fit conics will inherently encompass are the two Bezier endpoint positions, leaving the split positions and the control positions as real values.

The solution developed was to round the real split positions to the nearest integer mesh-points before evaluating the best-fit conic. This ensured that the endpoint positions of the two conics at the split point were piecewise-segmented using integer positions. The side-effect of using integer split positions is that the error graph, as depicted in Fig 4b, loses its smoothness.

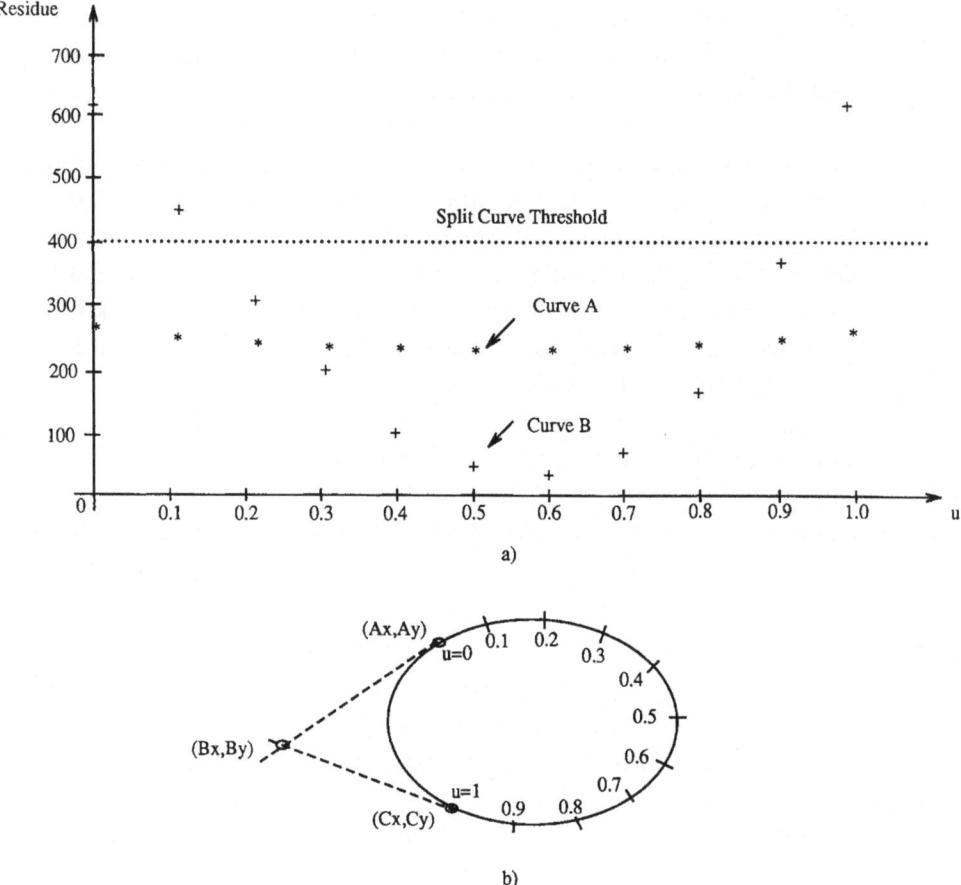

Fig 8 Illustrates two reasons for
subdividing a Bezier curve:

a) when the residue value at u=0
is above a set threshold
(eg Curve B requires to be split,
whilst curve A does not), and

b) when the algorithm returns
the wrong conic section.

This results in the algorithm needing to process (for Bezier curves that do not possess points of inflection) a set range of split points,eg from u =0.35 to 0.65, to establish the best point to split. Although it appears that more split points would be examined than necessary, the inclusion of an additional subroutine (to make certain that those split points that have a high probability of returning large values of overall residue are filtered out) somewhat compensates for the full coverage of the split range. The filtering is performed by avoiding all those split points that are above a set tolerance from an integer mesh-point. In addition, the usage of integer split points means that there are fewer new positions to subdivide the Bezier curve, which further enhances the algorithms performance.

As far as the control positions are concerned, these too are rounded to yield the nearest integer mesh-points. The difference in this case, however, is that since the algorithm returns the best control positions in terms of real values, changing these positions to integer values would theoretically imply that both the overall residue value and also the sharpness value will require recalculation. The process of recalculating the overall residue can be done without much difficulty by using equation (5); recalculating the sharpness value, however, does become rather complex. In fact, since expressions for α, β and γ (see appendix 1) would need to be substituted in equation (5) to evaluate the 'compensated' sharpness value, additional computation would be required which would seriously reduce the overall performance of the algorithm with little benefit. Thus, the need to recalculate any parameter was not computationally justified as the quality of conic fit, produced by integer endpoints and control points, was found to be numerically and aesthetically of an acceptable level.

8. THE RESULTS

Before discussing the results, it should be noted that these were produced using a SUN workstation, with a screen resolution of 900 x 1152 pixels, and the corresponding hard-copies were obtained on a APPLE laser printer, with a resolution about three times greater than the screen. Furthermore, the 'S' icon has been chosen as an example to highlight the efficiency of the algorithm, although the algorithm could equally be used on other Bezier defined icons.

The Bezier-described icon is generated using the parametric form expressed in equation (6). The corresponding output, shown in Fig 9a, is produced by using rounded x and y integer positions. The icon consists of four curves and eight straight lines. The curves are represented by six Bezier cubic curves, two of which contain a point of inflection. The straight lines are drawn using the parametric form of the conic representation (Pratt 1985), with the sharpness value set to zero, as this is the most economical way of drawing lines.

The Bezier-defined icon is then processed by the algorithm to produce the respective conic version. This describes the outline of the icon in terms of endpoints, control points and sharpness values. As discussed by Pratt (1985), the sharpness values can be rationalised so that the conic representation is described fully by integer arithmetic.

Once the complete recovery of the Bezier icon has been made and a corresponding data structure set-up, the conic version of the icon's outline is drawn by one of two methods. The first output, depicted in Fig 9b, is generated by using Pitteway's conic generation algorithm (1985), which returns the best integer positions for the given conic data structure. For comparative purposes, the second output is generated using the parametric form of the conic definition (Pratt 1985), so that the icon's x and y outline positions are rounded to yield corresponding integer mesh-points. This produces the desired output shown in Fig 9c.

If a visual comparison is made between the given Bezier icon and the two generated conic approximations (ie Fig 9a, 9b and 9c respectively), it can be seen that most of the distinct features of the original Bezier cubic version have, to a good degree, been recovered. Indeed, since all of the Bezier curves (used to define the icon) needed to be split, so that two best-fitting conic sections were used for each Bezier curve segment, the quality of conic approximations can be further appreciated.

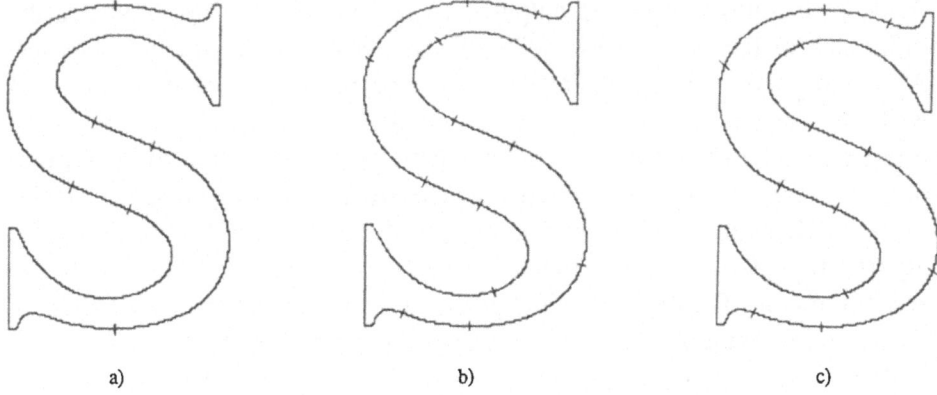

a)   b)   c)

Fig 9 Highlights the various outputs that were obtained:

a) The Bezier 'S' icon, with rounded x & y positions,

b) the corresponding best-fit conic approximation,
drawn using Pitteway's algorithm, and

c) the best-fit conic approximation, drawn
using rounded x & y positions.

a)   b)   c)

Fig 10 Shows the differences between various icon
outputs being exclusively OR-ed,

a) Bezier & Pitteway conic version,

b) Bezier & rounded x,y conic version, and

c) Pitteway & rounded x,y conic versions.

A closer examination of the output is shown in Fig10. This illustrates the difference in terms of an exclusive-OR of the respective integer versions. Although, theoretically (ie if real x and y positions were being used to both evaluate and represent the best-fit conics) there would be no such differences, the output in Fig 10a and 10b demonstrates that the algorithm does yield a few integer positions which are out of step with the Bezier version. These differences are due both to the integer working used by the algorithm and also to the method used to generate the outline for the recovered icon. The difference in representation occurs when one method (eg Bezier representation) chooses its next output position to be at (x_i, y_{i+1}), whilst the other method (eg the Pitteway conic version) chooses (x_{i+1}, y_i). This fact is highlighted in Fig 10c, where the differences in integer positions between the two conic sections is shown.

The two Bezier curve segments containing an inflection point have been mostly recaptured by the conic versions. Although it might appear from Fig 10a and 10b, that splitting at the inflection points (with rounded x and y split positions) could have led to unsatisfactory conic approximations, the numeric evaluations indicated otherwise. Indeed, evaluations of the overall residue made at integer split positions surrounding the inflection points verified the fact that the minimum residue (ie best splitting point) occured where the Bezier curve segments exhibited zero curvature.

9. SUMMARY

This paper has presented a detailed comparison of conic and cubic splines. Although cubic splines have been found to have many advantages, the simplicity and high degree of approximation offered by conic splines, has resulted in the latter being a realistic alternative for generating fount outline.

An algorithm is presented which, by means of a linear least-squares method, converts any fount outline, described by Bezier cubic splines (including those that contain points of inflection), to its conic form. The algorithm, in addition, incorporates integer arithmetic to match Pratt's description of conics (1985). The recovered fount has been found to be numerically and aesthetically acceptable.

REFERENCES

Albano A (1974) Representation of Digitised Contours in Terms of Conic Arcs and Straight-Line Segments. Computer Graphics & Image Processing 3:23-33.

Bezier P (1972) Numerical Control: Mathematics and Applications. John Wiley & Sons.

Bjorkenstam U, Westberg S (1987) General Cubic Curve Fitting Algorithm using Stiffness Coefficients. Computer-Aided-Design 19:58-64.

Bookstein FL (1979) Fitting Conic Sections to Scattered Data. Computer Graphics & Image Processing 9:56-71.

Cohen T, Lyche T, Riesenfeld R (1980) Discrete Beta-Splines and Subdivision Techniques in Computer-Aided Geometric Design and Computer Graphics. Computer Graphics & Image Processing 14:87-111.

Forbes AB (1987) Fitting an Ellipse to Data. National Physical Laboratory report DITC 95/87.

Forrest AR (1968) Curves and Surfaces for Computer-Aided-Design. Cambridge University CAD Group Ph.D. Thesis.

Forrest AR (1971) Interactive Interpolation and Approximation by Bezier. Polynomials. The Computer Journal 15:71-79.

Lewis D (1986) Gaussian Elimination Subroutine. NOAA Research Laboratory, Baulder, Colarado, USA.

Osland CD (1986) Bezier Font. Rutherford Appleton Research Laboratory, Private Communication.

Pavlidis T (1983) Curve Fitting with Conic Splines. ACM Transactions on Graphics 2:1-31.

Pitteway MLV (1967) Algorithm for Drawing Ellipses or Hyperbolae with a Digital Plotter. Computer Journal 10:282-289.

Pitteway MLV (1985) Algorithms of Conic Generation. Fundamental Algorithms for Computer Graphics (Springer-Verlag NATO ASI series F) 17:219-237.

Plass M, Stone M (1983) Curve-Fitting with Piecewise Parametric Cubics. Computer Graphics 17:229-239.

Pratt V (1985) Techniques for Conic Splines. Computer Graphics (ACM SIGGRAPH) 1985:151-159.

Roulier JA (1988) Bezier Curves of Positive Curvature. Computer Aided Geometric Design 5:59-70.

Sampson PD (1982) Fitting Conic Sections to ' Very Scattered Data': An Iterative Refinement of the Bookstein Algorithm. Computer Graphics & Image Processing 18:97-108.

APPENDIX 1

For a conic section described by the general quadratic equation and incorporating Pratt's sharpness parameter, the coefficients α, β and γ are expressed as follows:

$$\alpha = \frac{(Cx-2u)^2 + C_x^2(\frac{1}{S^2}-1)}{4\Delta}$$

$$\beta = \frac{(Cy-2v)^2 + C_y^2(\frac{1}{S^2}-1)}{4\Delta}$$

$$\gamma = \frac{-[\,(Cy-2v)(Cx-2u) + CxCy\,(\frac{1}{S^2}-1)]}{4\Delta}.sp$$

where:

Δ is area of the conic triangle ABC, and is given by:

$$\Delta = \frac{vCx-uCy}{2}.$$

ACKNOWLEDGEMENTS

I would like to thank Professor Pitteway, of Brunel University, for his helpful suggestions and also the staff of the Computer Science Department, Brunel University, for their assistance throughout the development of this work.

I am currently doing research (leading to a PhD) in the field of Computer Graphics. In particular, my research considers the representation of 'curvy' shapes (such as outline of founts) on modern digital displays. My research interests, therefore, evolve around the methods used to digitally represent hand-drawn shapes; concentrating both on their aesthetic value, as well as, on their simplicity in terms of computation.

My qualifications include a BSc (Honours) degree from Hatfield Polytechnic in Electrical and Electronics Engineering, and a MSc degree from the University of Nottingham in Modern Electronics. I am also an Associate Member of the Institution of Electrical Engineers (AMIEE).

Address: Computer Science Department, Brunel University, Uxbridge, Middlesex UB8 3PH, England, U.K.

Algorithms for 2D Line Clipping

V. Skala

ABSTRACT

New algorithms for 2D line clipping against convex and non-convex windows are being presented. Algorithms were derived from the Cohen-Sutherland´s and Liang-Barsky´s algorithms. Algorithms are easy to modify in order to deal with holes too. The presented algorithms have been verified in TURBO-PASCAL. Because of unifying approach to the clipping problem solution algorithms are simple, easy to understand and implement.

Keywords: line clipping, convex polygon, non-convex polygon, algorithms

1. INTRODUCTION

Clipping is a very important part of all graphics packages. Generally it is the evaluation of a line intersection against a window boundary. Many efficient algorithms are known, as the Cohen-Sutherland´s (Newman, Sproull 1979), Liang-Barsky´s (1983) , Cyrus-Beck´s (1978) ones. All these algorithms have some presumptions, e.g. the windows must be orthogonal or convex with oriented edges, etc.

In the following new algorithms will be described for convex-polygon and non-convex polygon clipping without need to orient edges in any order. Particular care was devoted to handle all special situations properly. Algorithms are based on the only basic idea that is gradually widened for more general cases.

As far as the author is concerned none of these algorithms have been published in the accessible literature.

2. CONVEX POLYGON CLIPPING

The bellow given convex polygon clipping algorithm is based on the principle of Liang-Barsky´s algorithm and is simpler than the Cyrus-Beck algorithm and does not need an anticlockwise orientation of the polygon edges as Liang-Barsky´s algorithm does.

Provided a convex polygon is given by its vertices in the clockwise or in the anticlockwise order arbitralily and none pair of edges lies on the same line (it is not a principle restriction). Let us consider some situations that might occur if a line segment with end points P_r and P_s ought to be clipped, see fig.2.1.

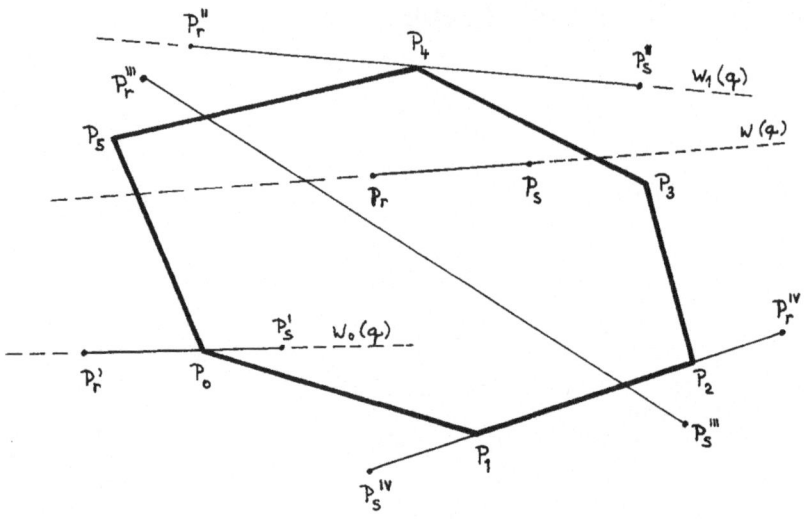

Fig.2.1.

All intersections of the line w with edges of the convex polygon are obtained by solving the following linear equations:

$$x(q) = x_r + (x_s - x_r) \cdot q \qquad q \in \langle 0 , 1 \rangle$$

$$x(p) = x_i + (x_{i \oplus 1} - x_i) \cdot p \qquad p \in \langle 0 , 1) \quad i=0,1,\ldots,n-1$$

where $\oplus$ means addition modulo n and point P_k has coordinates x_k

The interval for parameter p is not closed in order to get rid of all ambiguities in case that the line segment is "passing" (line $w_0(q)$) or "touching" (line $w_1(q)$). a polygon vertex. The bellow given algorithm is based on the fact that a line segment can intersect a convex polygon only in two points. The algorithm finds the q values for all intersection points of a line on which the given line segment lies with the edges of the convex polygon and then the proper part of the line segment that is inside the convex polygon can be found. The algorithm is shown in fig.2.2. It is necessary, of course, to solve special cases when a line segment touches or passes a vertex or when it lies on a polygon edge.

The algorithm given in fig.2.2. is faster than the Cyrus-Beck's algorithm (it doesn't need an inner normal computation) and for a rectangle polygon is equivalent to the Liang-Barsky algorithm in case that computation of all intersections is simplified for polygon edges parallel to the axes. The algorithm can be easily generalized or modified for a case when two edges of the given polygon lie on the same line Skala (1988).

```
VAR i,k: INTEGER; (* end points of the polygon edges *)
    j: INTEGER; (* counter *)
    t: ARRAY [1..2] OF REAL;
BEGIN
    j:=0;i:=0;k:=n-1; (* set end points for the first edge *)
    REPEAT
        IF an intesection point exists for the edge x_k x_i
        AND the line w(q) so that p ∈ ⟨0,1) THEN
        BEGIN j:=j+1; t[j]:=q (* save the q value *) END
        ELSE
        IF the edge x_k x_i lies on the line w(q) THEN
        BEGIN t[1]:= a value q that corresponds to the
                        vertex x_k;
              t[2]:= a value q that corresponds to the
                        vertex x_i;
              j:=2
        END;
        k:=i; i:=i+1; (* take the next polygon edge *)
    UNTIL ( j = 2 ) OR ( i > n );
    IF j <> 0 THEN
    BEGIN
        IF j = 1 THEN t[2]:=t[1] (* the line w(q) "touches"
                                    a vertex *)
                ELSE IF t[1] > t[2] THEN t[1] SWAP t[2];
        t[1]:= max ( 0.0 , t[1] ); (* maximal value *)
        t[2]:= min ( 1.0 , t[2] ); (* minimal value *)
        LINE ( x (t[1]) , x (t[2]) )
    END
END;
```

Fig.2.2.

3. NON-CONVEX POLYGON CLIPPING

An algorithm for non-convex polygon clipping is based on the
parametric equations that express linear segments. In this case the
algorithm must be more complex, because the line w(q) can intersects
the polygon in many points. Assume that a non-convex polygon is given
by its vertices in clockwise or anticlockwise order. Further that two
successive edges do not lie on the same line, that all vertices have
different coordinates, that not a single vertex lies on any edge of
the given polygon and that two edges might have only a vertex as a
common point.

Let us consider again some situations that might occur if a line
segment with end points P. and P. ought to be clipped, see fig.3.1.
The given line segment that ought to be clipped can be expressed by:

$$x(q) = x_r + (x_s - x_r) . q \qquad q \in \langle 0 , 1 \rangle$$

and the edges of the non-convex polygon can be expressed by:

$$x(p) = x_i + (x_{i \oplus 1} - x_i) . p \qquad p \in \langle 0 , 1) \quad i=0,1,\ldots,n-1$$

Then we will look for all intersection points of the line w(q) and
non-convex polygon. The parametric equation:

$$x(q) = x_r + (x_s - x_r) . q \qquad q \in (-\infty ,+\infty)$$

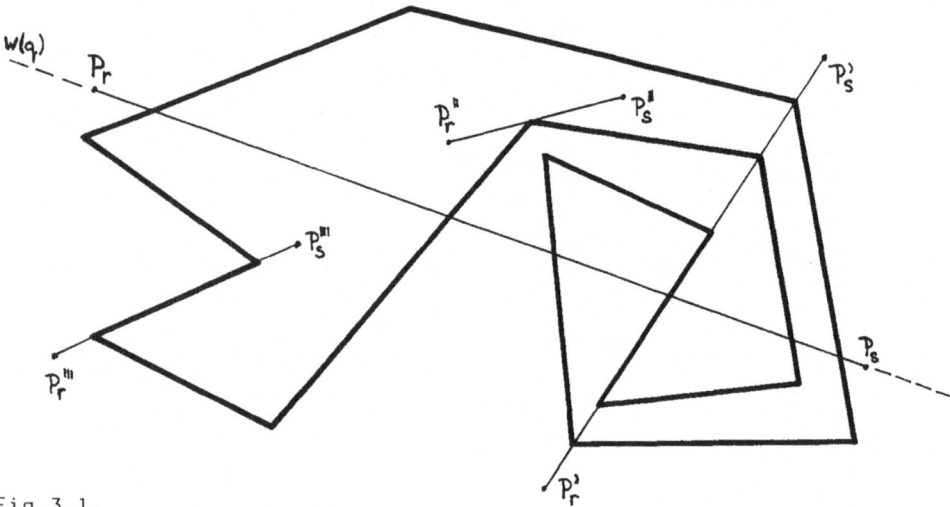

Fig.3.1.

expresses the line w(q). Coordinates of all intersection points will be determined by the value of the parameter q. But it is necessary to take into consideration the following special cases when the line w(q) passes or touches a vertex of the polygon. There are two possibilities, see fig.3.2.:

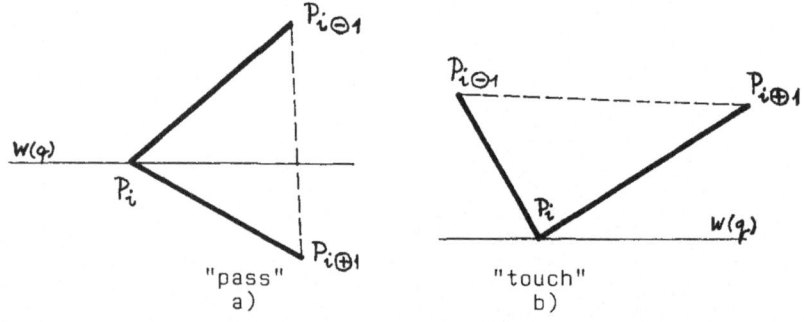

where $\oplus$ means addition modulo n, $\ominus$ means subtraction modulo n

Fig.3.2.

In fig.3.2.a. is generated only one intersection point, while in fig.3.2.b. double intersection point is generated. In both cases these points are processed as an ordinary intersection point.

A quite different situation is when the line w(q) lies on an edge of the polygon. There are two possible situations, see fig.3.3.

The values of q parameters that correspond to the points P_i and $P_{i\oplus 1}$ in these cases must be generated. But it is necessary to distinguish between the type by attributes ++ or -- for these q values. If points $P_{i\oplus 2}$, $P_{i\ominus 1}$ are the same, then it is necessary to generate only q value which corresponds to the point P_i, see fig.3.3.c. (a special case when the given polygon is a triangle). Therefore the intersection point will be determined not only by value q but also by a type of the intersection as follows:

```
⌣    intersection with edge, intersection of the  type  pass
     or touch
+    line w(q) lies on edge - case ad a)
-    line w(q) lies on edge - case ad b)
```

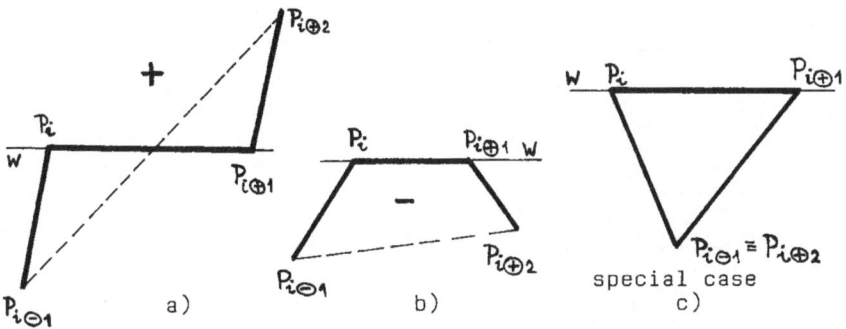

Fig.3.3.

When all intersection points are found together with their types, the
given set of q values is sorted together with their attributes so that
couples with attributes ++ or -- should not be split, e.g. sequencies:

$$q_1 \quad q_1 \quad q_2 \qquad \text{or} \qquad q_1 \quad q_2 \quad q_2$$
$$+ \quad ⌣ \quad + \qquad\qquad\qquad + \quad ⌣ \quad +$$

must be transferred to sequencies:

$$q_1 \quad q_1 \quad q_2 \qquad \text{or} \qquad q_1 \quad q_2 \quad q_2$$
$$⌣ \quad + \quad + \qquad\qquad\qquad + \quad + \quad ⌣$$

Similarly for attributes --.

The set of q values will be processed according to table 3.1. Results
that determine these parts of the line w(q) which are inside the given
polygon are couples of q values.

Now it is necessary to determine which parts of the line segment $P_r P_s$
are inside the given polygon, e.g. to determine those parts of the
line w(q) that are inside and that are part of the line segment $P_r P_s$.
According to the process of getting parts of the line w(q) it is
necessary to make intersection of all couples of the q values with the
interval $\langle 0 , 1 \rangle$, see fig.3.4.

```
i:=1;
WHILE i <= No of intersection -1 DO
BEGIN IF max ( 0.0 , q_i ) = min ( 1.0 , q_{i+1})
      THEN save ( max ( 0.0 , q_i ) , min ( 1.0 , q_{i+1} ) );
      i:=i+2
END;
```

Fig.3.4.

Table 3.1. Possible situations

attributes		situation	action
q_i	q_{i+1}		
⌣	⌣	q_i q_{i+1} w	save (q_i , q_{i+1}) i:=i+2
⌣	+	q_i q_{i+3} w q_{i+1} q_{i+2}	save (q_i , q_{i+3}) i:=i+4
⌣	−	q_{i+3} w q_i q_{i+1} q_{i+2} q_{i+4}	save (q_i , q_{i+2}) i:=i+3
−	−	q_{i-1} w q_{i-2} q_i q_{i+1} q_{i+2}	save (q_i , q_{i+2}) i:=i+3
−	⌣	q_i q_{i+3} w q_{i+1} q_{i+2}	vertex touches an edge
+	+	q_i q_{i+1} q_{i+3} q_{i+2} w	save (q_i , q_{i+1}) i:=i+2
+	⌣	w	improper polygon
−	+		impossible situation
+	−		impossible situation

The coordinates of the resulted points determined by their q values
can be obtained from the equation for the line w(q)

$$x(q) = x_r + (x_s - x_r) \cdot q$$

The whole algorithm can be described as follows in fig.3.5. The
presented algorithm enables to clip a given line segment against
non-convex polygon. The assumptions stated above are not substantial
with the only exception that edges may not intersect one another and
algorithm can be easily modified for these assumption. The algorithm
is based on the similar idea as the previous one and because the
polygon in non-convex some additional operations must be employed.

```
j:=0; (* counter of q values *)
k:=n-1;
FOR i:=0 TO n-1 DO
BEGIN IF the edge $x_k x_i$ lies on the line w(q) THEN
      BEGIN determine the type;
            IF $x_k$ <> $x_{k\oplus2}$ (* not a triangle *)
              THEN IF type = '+' THEN generate ( $q_{1+}$ , $q_{2+}$ )

                              ELSE generate ( $q_{1-}$ , $q_{2-}$ )

            ELSE generate ( $q_{1\sqcup}$ )
      END
      ELSE IF the line w(q) passes or touches the vertex $x_k$
            THEN IF type is touch THEN generate ( $q_{1\sqcup}$ , $q_{1\sqcup}$ )

                              ELSE generate ( $q_{1\sqcup}$ )

          ELSE IF the line w(q) intersects edge $x_k x_i$
               THEN generate ( $q_{1\sqcup}$ );
      k:=i
END;
SORT ( values q );
REDUCE ( set of q values );
SELECT ( subintervals as $\langle q_k , q_{k\oplus1}\rangle \cap \langle 0 , 1\rangle$ );
COMPUTE ( the end points );
```

Fig.3.5.

4. CONCLUSION

The presented algorithms are based on the principle of the
Liang-Barsky´s algorithm. It is shown how the algorithms become more
complicated if the requirements are more general. The presented
algorithms were verified in TURBO-PASCAL on IBM-PC. The algorithm for
the clipping line against a convex polygon is simpler than the
Liang-Barsky´s, if it is simplified for a rectangle clipping window,
and in general it doesn´t need oriented half-planes of the clipping
window. The second algorithm solves the situation when the clipping
polygon is non-convex. The increase of complexity is expressed in the
need to distinquish between different cases and to sort the final set
of intersection points. The algorithms are fast and all special cases
are handled properly. Both algorithms might be used for hatching, too.
Of course, in that case it is convenient to rotate the clipping area
so that the hatching lines are horizontal, find intersection points
and then rotate their coordinates back. In this case all algorithms
can be significantely simplified. The presented algorithms can be
generalized for non-convex areas when the clipping area is formed by
line segments and arcs (Skala 1988).

5. ACKNOWLEDGMENT

The author would like to express his thanks to Prof.L.M.V. Pitteway,
Dr. J.P.A. Race (Brunel Univ., U.K.), Dr. J.E. Bresenham (Winthrop
College, U.S.A.) and Dr.R.A. Earnshaw (Univ. of Leeds, U.K.) for
their helpfull discussions during his stay in U.K., to Miss I.
Kolingerova (Inst. of Technology, Plzen) her interest, comments and
the final implementation on IBM-PC, who enabled to find unspecified
special cases and errors, and to students of Computer Graphics course
that stimulated this work.

6. LITERATURE

Cyrus M, Beck J (1978) Generalized Two- and Three Dimensional
Clipping, Computers and Graphics, Vol.3, No.1., pp.23-28.
Foley JD, van Dam A (1982) Fundamentals of Interactive Computer
Graphics, Addison-Wesley, Reading, Mass.
Liang YD, Barsky BA. (1983) An Analysis and Algorithms for Polygon
Clipping, CACM 26, No.11 (November), pp.868-876.
Liang YD, Barsky BA (1984) A New Concept and Method for Line Clipping,
ACM Transaction on Graphics, Vol.3., No.1., pp.1-22.
Newman WM, Sproull RF (1979) Principles of Interactive Computer
Graphics, 2nd ed., McGraw Hill, New York.
Nicholl TM, Lee DT, Nicholl RA (1987) An Efficient New Algorithm for
2D Line Clipping: Its Development and Analysis, ACM Computer
Graphics, Vol.21, No.4., July, pp.253-262.
Skala V (1988) Line Clipping by Polygons and Areas with Arcs.
TR-209-11-88 Computer Science Dept., Inst.of Technology, Plzen.

Vaclav Skala is a associate professor of
computer science at the Institute of Technology.
He studied Technical Cybernetics and Computer
Science at the Institute of Technology in Plzen.
In 1975 he took a master degree in Computer
Science followed by a PhD degree specialising in
Database Systems at the Technical University in
Prague. From 1975 to 1981 he worked as a
researcher. In 1978 he studied Computer Science
at MEI in Moscow and in the academic year
1983-84 Computer Graphics at Brunel University
in London. In 1981 he took up position as senior lecturer at the
Cybernetics Department teaching programming languages, database
systems and Computer Graphics. He is a member of Czechoslovak
Scientific and Technical Society and a member of the Society of
Cybernetics, chairman of Computer Graphics and CAD Systems Group
within the Czechoslovak Academy of Sciencies.

Generating n-Sided Patches with Partial Differential Equations

M.I.G. Bloor and M.J. Wilson

ABSTRACT

In design processes involving free form surfaces, the problem often arises of having to find a surface to cover a polygonal region having three or more than four distinct edges. We present a method where this problem is solved by regarding the generation of such a surface as a boundary value problem, where the surface is represented by a <u>single</u> parametric patch which is the solution of an elliptic partial differential equation.

Keywords: computer-aided-design, computational geometry, surface design, parametric surfaces, polygonal holes, partial differential equations.

1. THE RELEVANCE OF N-SIDED PATCHES TO SCULPTURED SURFACES

1.1 Sculptured Surface Technologies

Sculptured surface technologies usually aim to represent an object by constructing its surface from a 'quilt' of parametric patches. Such methods are based upon the fact that we may represent a surface as an explicit function of two parameters, u & v say, thus $\underline{X} = \underline{X}(u,v)$. It is usual to consider rectangular regions in a (u,v) parameter space so that the corresponding patch of surface in E^3 will also be (topologically) rectangular; and furthermore it is usual for most sculptured surface technologies to produce surface patches by using polynomial functions of u & v of varying degree (Barnhill 1985). The solid can then be constructed by piecing together such surface patches to form a boundary representation of its surface. There is a problem, however, since the surface of many solid objects cannot be covered by a regular array of rectangular patches, and this usually manifests itself in the appearance, somewhere in the 'quilt' of rectangular patches covering the object, of a polygonal hole with n edges, where n is an integer not equal to 4 e.g. 3, 5 or more (Varady 1987, Woodwark 1987). Furthermore, this feature of such objects is a fundamental property of the topology of their surface rather than their specific geometry.

1.2 Topological Considerations

Topologically, the surfaces of all objects in the world of everyday experience, are homeomorphic to either a sphere (S) or the connected sum of n Tori (nT). Expressed more simply, this means that if we were able to distort their surfaces as we would a rubber sheet, that is without tearing or cutting, we could manipulate them until we ended up with either a sphere, a torus, or n tori 'glued together'; see for example Firby & Gardner (1982). Now although topological considerations may apparently tell us very little about the specific geometry of a particular object, they can, never-the-less,

tell us important things about some of the properties that equivalent surfaces
have in common. For instance, over the surface of a given object we may
define a vector field so that at each point p of the surface of the object we
associate a vector $v(p)$ whose direction and magnitude are specified by some
rule. Now it turns out that for all surfaces, except those that are
'torus-like', it is not possible to define a vector field for which the
direction and magnitude of the vectors $v(p)$ change continuously at all points
of the surface. At the very least there must be a finite set of points, the
critical points of the vector field, where the field direction changes
discontinuously; and by considering the Euler number for a surface it is
possible to deduce the minimum number of critical points a surface must
possess, as well as something of their character. Furthermore, since the
Euler number is the same for all surfaces that are topologically equivalent,
the minimum number and nature of the critical points on a surface is the same
for surfaces of the same topological type (Firby & Gardner 1974). An example
from everyday experience which illustrates this is the fact that there is
usually a 'crown' in the hair on a human head, baldness excepted ! This is a
consequence of the fact that it is not possible to brush the hair on a hairy
ball so that at no point does the hair direction suddenly reverse.

From these considerations it follows that many surfaces cannot be covered by a
parameter mesh having no singular points; at some point on such surfaces a
complete reparametrization is necessary if every portion of the surface is to
be covered with a 'good' set of coordinates. An example of this is the
parametrization of the surface of a sphere by the spherical polar
coordinates (ϑ, ϕ): at the poles the azimuthal isoparametric lines meet at a
point. The only surfaces which can be parametrized by a single non-singular
coordinate net are those which are topologically equivalent to a single torus.
  Now, since we can regard a mesh of good coordinates as being made up of a
collection of topologicaly rectangular parametric patches, it follows that
many objects cannot be covered entirely with a regular array of rectangular
patches; this is true, for example, of those objects that are homeomorphic to
a sphere. Now one might object that the surfaces of bodies such as cuboids
are exceptions to this, in the sense that their surfaces are constructed from
a regular array of rectangular facets. However, such objects posses singular
points and singular lines where the direction of any tangent field defined on
their surface changes discontinuously i.e. on their edges and vertices. So,
while it is true that such objects can be made from a rectangular quilt-work
of patches, there is no continuity higher than C^o between adjacent patches.
As soon as we wish for a smooth surface e.g. we round the corners and edges of
these cuboids, triangular regions appear at the corners.

1.3 Methods for filling Polygonal Holes

A number of different methods for circumventing this problem have already been
devised. Since the 'holes' that appear in patched surfaces are most
conveniently treated if they are centred on some corner or vertex in the
object, much attention has been devoted to constructing special corner
patches.[1] The first effort to create corner patches is generally attributed
to Barnhill (1974) who considered smooth interpolation over triangles and in
particular triangular Coons' patches. Gregory (1974) also considered this
problem at about the same time and he has more recently consider triangular
and pentagonal Coon's patches (Gregory 1983). Triangular Bezier patches have
also been investigated; for instance, Farin (1982) and Hosaka & Kimura (1984)
have considered 3, 5 and 6-sided Bezier patches. Also, Sabin (1986) has
created triangular B-spline surfaces. A rather different approach has been

---

[1]There is no intrinsic reason why a single bi-parametric patch cannot cover a
corner. However, to achieve a reasonably smooth and accurate surface would
require a large number of control points and, furthermore, a 'singular' hole
would appear elsewhere on the surface of the object, albeit in the middle of
a smooth region of surface perhaps.

taken by Chiyokura & Kimura (1983) and also by Fjällström (1986) who fill the non-four-sided regions that occur in their surface representation models with rectangular patches which do not meet orthogonally in parameter space. More recently Hahn (1988) has used a similar approach and considered filling n-sided holes, for arbitary $n \geq 3$, with n rectangular patches. For a survey of the field of n-sided patch generation, the interested reader should consult Varady (1987).

It is not our purpose in this paper to consider the specific merits of these different approaches, or to provide an exhaustive review of them either. As we have seen, the basic problem is common to all boundary representation schemes, and we would like to consider how the method of Bloor and Wilson (1989a) can tackle the same problem. This method was introduced as a means of generating blending surfaces by regarding the problem of blending two (or more) primary surfaces together as a boundary value problem. It involves solving elliptic partial differential equations (PDEs) over a region of the (u,v) parameter plane subject to certain boundary conditions on the dependent variable $\underline{X}$ and its derivatives with respect to u & v. The solution $\underline{X}(u,v)$ so generated represents the blend surface as a parametric function of the two parameters u & v. The required degree of continuity between the blend surface and the 'primary' surfaces to which it adjoins is ensured by an appropriate choice of boundary conditions and also of differential equation. As important point to make about this method is that by making an appropriate choice of parametrization, it is possible to cover an n-sided region, where n is (in prinicipal) any number ≥ 3, with a single patch of surface.

In Section 2 we give a brief description of the method, while in Section 3 we outline the problem of filling a n-sided hole; we consider in particular an example of a six-sided patch. Section 4 contains some necessary analysis of the boundary conditions. Section 5 is concerned with the numerical generation of surface and gives some results for patches that fill the polygonal region described in Section 3. In section 6 we draw some brief conclusions.

2. GENERATING SURFACES WITH A PARTIAL DIFFERENTIAL EQUATION

2.1 A Blend as a Solution to a Boundary Value Problem

Mathematically we view the calculation of a blending surface as an answer to the following question: given a finite domain Ω in a (u,v) parameter plane, with boundary $\partial\Omega$, can we find a function $\underline{X}$ (the blend surface) over that domain that satisfies specified boundary data? The boundary data will typically be in the form of $\underline{X}$ and a number of its derivatives on $\partial\Omega$. The number of derivatives specified will depend on the required degree of continuity between the blend and the surfaces to which it adjoins. We may also require of the blending surface that it be, in some specified sense, 'well-behaved'. For example, a blend may be wanted that is smooth and non-oscillatory.

Since we are essentially seeking to define a surface in Euclidean 3-space E^3, $\underline{X}$ ($=(x,y,z)$) will be a function of two parameters, u & v say, such that $\underline{X}=\underline{X}(u,v)$. We can view u & v as the coordinates of a point in Ω ($\subset R^2$) and $\underline{X}$ as a mapping from that point in Ω to a point in 3-space: R^2 (Ω) $\rightarrow R^3$ (E^3). The lines of constant u and v (the isoparametric lines) will define a coordinate system within the surface.

Our method for satisfying these requirements is to regard $\underline{X}$ as the solution of a partial differential equation

$$L^m_{u,v}(\underline{X}) = 0$$

here $L^m_{u,v}(\ )$ is a partial differential operator of order m in the independent variables u & v. Since we are interested in boundary-value problems and smooth solution functions, it was natural to consider the class of elliptic partial differential equations.

2.2 Blend Design

In Bloor & Wilson (1989a) we concentrated on illustrating the type of surfaces that could be generated by this method by means of a few examples of practical significance.   We continued this theme in Bloor & Wilson (1989b) where we indicated how, by varying certain free parameters that occur within the chosen PDE and its boundary conditions, this method allows for the manipulation of the surfaces so generated. In this way we indicated how the actual process of design can be incorporated into the generation of the surface.

3. A POLYGONAL HOLE

As mentioned above, in this paper we now want to discuss how this method can generate patches to fill polygonal regions, for instance those that appear at some point on the surface of an object that is being designed using free-form surface methods.   This is best illustrated by means of an example in which we use our method to generate a surface to cover a 6-sided region.

3.1 Boundary Conditions on $\underline{X}(u,v)$

Consider the closed curve shown in Fig. 1 which is formed at the junction of four cylinders and two planes.

We may describe it in terms of six line segments together with the associated normal vectors of the surfaces that terminate at these line segments:

Curve C1: $\underline{X}(0,v) = (-1,\ 1 - \sin v,\ 1 + \cos v)$; $\pi/2 \leq v \leq \pi$

$\qquad \underline{n}_1 = (0, -\sin v, \cos v)$

Curve C2: $\underline{X}(0,v) = (1,\ 1 - \sin v,\ -1 - \cos v)$; $\pi/2 \leq v \leq \pi$

$\qquad \underline{n}_2 = (0, -\sin v, -\cos v)$

Curve C3: $\underline{X}(1,v) = (1 - \cos v,\ -1 + \sin v,\ -1)$; $0 \leq v \leq \pi/2$

$\qquad \underline{n}_3 = (-\cos v, \sin v, 0)$

Curve C4: $\underline{X}(1,v) = (-1 + \cos v,\ -1 + \sin v,\ 1)$; $0 \leq v \leq \pi/2$ $\hfill (1)$

$\qquad \underline{n}_4 = (\cos v, \sin v, 0)$

Curve C5: $\underline{X}(u,0) = (0, -1,\ 1 - 2u)$; $0 \leq u \leq 1$

$\qquad \underline{n}_5 = (1, 0, 0)$

Curve C6: $\underline{X}(u,\pi) = (-1 + 2u, 1\ ,\ 0)$; $0 \leq u \leq 1$

$\qquad \underline{n}_6 = (0, 0, 1)$

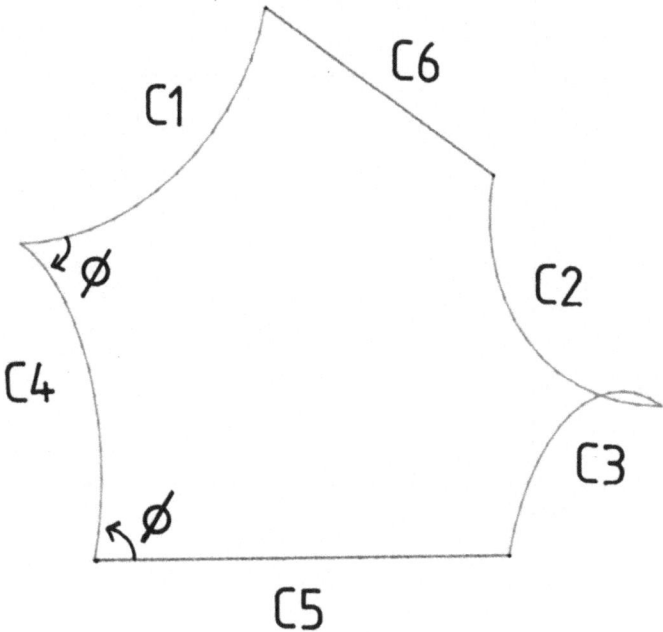

Fig. 1: The boundary of the polygonal region over which a surface is to be generated.

We will assume that this curve forms a hole, in the boundary representation of some object, which we wish to cover with a new patch of surface. The mapping of these curves onto a rectangular domain in the (u,v) parameter plane (specifically the region $0 \leq u \leq 1$, $0 \leq v \leq \pi$) is shown in Fig. 2. From this it should be clear that we are attempting to cover the entire region with this single surface patch. Our problem is to find a surface with boundary $\partial\Omega$: C1 $\cup$ C2 $\cup$ C3 $\cup$ C3 $\cup$ C4 $\cup$ C5 $\cup$ C6.

3.2 Boundary Conditions on $\underline{X}_u$ and $\underline{X}_v$

To ensure tangent continuity between the patch and the surfaces lying outside the curve to which it blends, the derivatives with respect to u & v of the coordinate functions $x(u,v), y(u,v)$ & $z(u,v)$ for the surface $\underline{X}(u,v)$ and their derivatives must satisfy appropriate boundary conditions. Note that by tangent continuity we mean that there is no discontinuity in the limiting directions of the surface normals to the patch and to the adjacent region of surface at the boundary curve. Further note that the first derivatives of x, y & z essentially determine the direction of the surface tangent vectors $\underline{X}_u$ & $\underline{X}_v$ at the edge of the patch.

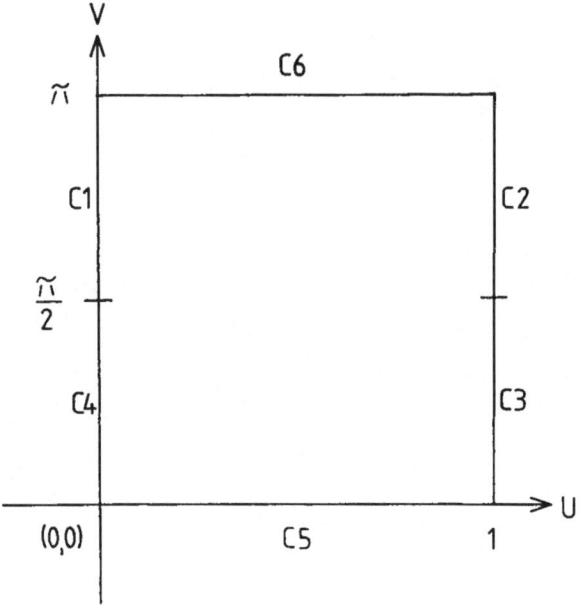

Fig. 2: The mapping of the curves C1,C2,C3,C4,C5,C6 from E^3 onto the (u,v) parameter plane.

3.3 A Suitable Partial Differential Equation

Since we have boundary conditions on the function $\underline{X}$ and its first derivatives, the equation we must solve in order to satisfy all these requirements is fourth order. The equation we shall consider is the elliptic system

$$\left[\frac{\partial^2}{\partial u^2} + a_x^2 \frac{\partial^2}{\partial v^2}\right]^2 x = 0$$

$$\left[\frac{\partial^2}{\partial u^2} + a_y^2 \frac{\partial^2}{\partial v^2}\right]^2 y = 0 \qquad (2)$$

$$\left[\frac{\partial^2}{\partial u^2} + a_z^2 \frac{\partial^2}{\partial v^2}\right]^2 z = 0$$

where a_x, a_y, a_z are constants which we shall refer to as smoothing parameters after Bloor & Wilson (1989b). In previous papers we have often been able to solve such equations analytically by the method of separation of variables. Such an approach is not possible here because of the exotic nature of the boundary curves, therefore we use numerical solution techniques to solve the equation, and of this we shall say more later.

3.4 Free Parameters and Singularities in the Problem

There are a number of free parameters in the problem. These are the three smoothing parameters a_x, a_y, a_z, and the components of the tangent vectors $\underline{X}_u$ & $\underline{X}_v$ on the boundaries of the patch. In specifying the variation in the tangent magnitudes along the boundaries we must be careful, for although we are free to specify what variation we wish (within the constraints of tangent continuity), we must realise what consequences this might have for the solution surface. In particular, it is possible to choose boundary conditions in which there are discontinuities in the derivatives of the coordinate functions at various points on the patch boundary. For instance, consider the following set of derivative boundary conditions:

Curve C1: $x_u = x_o$; $y_u = 0$; $z_u = 0$ (3a)

Curve C2: $x_u = x_1$; $y_u = 0$; $z_u = 0$ (3b)

Curve C3: $x_u = 0$; $y_u = 0$; $z_u = -z_1$ (3c)

Curve C4: $x_u = 0$; $y_u = 0$; $z_u = -z_o$ (3d)

Curve C5: $x_u = 0$; $y_u = y_o$; $z_u = 0$ (3e)

Curve C6: $x_u = 0$; $y_u = y_1$; $z_u = 0$ (3f)

The tangent magnitudes $(x_o, x_1, y_o, y_1, z_o, z_1)$ on the boundary curves are taken to be non-zero constants, as this will give rise to the highest order singularities at the corners (see below). Note that for this choice of boundary conditions, although the requirements of tangent continuity are met (cf equation (1)), there are discontinuities in some of the components of the tangent vectors $\underline{X}_u$ and $\underline{X}_v$ at the points where the six curve segments join. For example, consider the point where curves C_1 and C_4 meet. The composite curve $C_1 \cup C_4$ is the isoparametric line u=0 and along it y_u remains continuous. However, x_u and z_u do not. Now, consider the limits of these quantities as we approach the singular point from either direction along u=0.

$$\lim_{\substack{v \to \pi/2- \\ u=0}} (x_u) = x_u^- \; ; \; \lim_{\substack{v \to \pi/2+ \\ u=0}} (x_u) = x_u^+ \; ; \; \lim_{\substack{v \to \pi/2- \\ u=0}} (z_u) = z_u^- \; ; \; \lim_{\substack{v \to \pi/2+ \\ u=0}} (z_u) = z_u^+ \quad (4)$$

Let us write the 'jump-conditions' in the derivatives as follows

$$x_u^+ - x_u^- \equiv [x_u] \; ; \; z_u^+ - z_u^- \equiv [z_u] \quad\quad\quad (5)$$

For our choice of boundary conditions, at the meeting point of C_1 and C_4,

$$[x_u] = x_o \; ; \; [z_u] = z_o \; . \quad\quad\quad\quad\quad\quad (6)$$

The consequence of these non-zero jump-conditions is that the surface $\underline{X}$ that results is likely to be self-intersecting in certain circumstances. Furthermore, it is sometimes impossible to exactly apply these boundary conditions numerically, at least without further analysis. However, we can analyse the nature of the singularity and determine under what circumstances our choice of boundary conditions is likely to cause trouble.

4. SINGULARITY ANALYSIS.

For the choice of boundary conditions we have made in equations (1) & (3), the six vertices of the polygon are all singular points, but they are of only two types. The singularities at the four vertices of the (u,v) rectangle being of one type (type **A** say) while the remaining two, which lie at the mid-points of the isoparametric lines u=0 and u=1, are of another type (**B**). The difference between these two types should become clear in the following discussion.

4.1 Type A Singularities

First, we will consider all type **A** points by reference to the point (0,0) in the (u,v) plane, which corresponds to the point (0,-1,1) in real space. Furthermore, we will simplify the analysis by choosing the smoothing parameters a_x, a_y and a_z to be unity. The extension to other constant values for the scaling parameters simply represents a rescaling of the coordinate v.

Choosing polar coordinates (r, ϑ) defined by

$$r \cos\vartheta = u$$
$$r \sin\vartheta = v \tag{7}$$

the equation satisfied by $\underline{X}$ is

$$\left[\frac{\partial^2}{\partial r^2} + \frac{1}{r} \frac{\partial}{\partial r} + \frac{1}{r^2} \frac{\partial^2}{\partial \vartheta^2} \right]^2 \underline{X} = 0 \tag{8}$$

while the boundary conditions, obtained from equations (1) and (3), can be written in the following form:

On $\vartheta = 0$: $\underline{X} = (0,-1,1-2r)$; $\underline{X}_\vartheta = (0, ry_o, 0)$ $\tag{9}$

where terms of $O(r^3)$ have been neglected.

On $\vartheta = \pi/2$: $\underline{X} = (-r^2/2, -1+r, 1)$; $\underline{X}_\vartheta = (0,0, rz_o)$. $\tag{10}$

where, again, only leading order terms in r have been retained.

The form of the boundary conditions suggests that we look for a local solution of the form

$$\underline{X} = (r^2 F_1(\vartheta), -1 + rF_2(\vartheta), 1 + rF_3(\vartheta)) \tag{11}$$

Substitution of equation (11) in equation (8) yields ordinary differential equations for F_1, F_2, F_3 which we can solve, the arbitary constants of integration being determined by the boundary conditions. The solutions are

$$F_1(\vartheta) = \frac{1}{4}(\cos 2\vartheta - 1)$$

$$F_2(\vartheta) = \{(y_o - 1)\vartheta\cos\vartheta + (1 - \frac{\pi^2 y_o}{4} + \pi\vartheta \frac{(y_o - 1)}{2}) \sin\vartheta\}/(1-\pi^2/4) \tag{12}$$

$$F_3(\vartheta) = \{[\frac{\pi^2}{2} - 2 + (\frac{\pi z_o}{2} - 1)\vartheta]\cos\vartheta + [1 - \frac{\pi z_o}{2} + (z_o - 2)\vartheta]\sin\vartheta\}/(1-\pi^2/4)$$

Note that the solution in the vicinity of the singularity is entirely determined by the nature of the singularity itself, not the boundary conditions on distant parts of the patch. We also notice that each of these is a single-valued function of ϑ. However, for sufficiently large values of y_o and z_o, the angle defined by

$$\phi = \tan^{-1}\left[\frac{y+1}{z-1}\right] = \tan^{-1}\left[\frac{F_2(\vartheta)}{F_3(\vartheta)}\right] \tag{13}$$

is multivalued for $0 \leq \vartheta \leq \pi/2$. Note that ϕ is a 'physical' polar coordinate in E^3 centred on the singularity (refer to Figure 1). In other words, under these circumstances, the surface can have self-intersecting loops in it. This is understandable if one thinks of the tangent gradients z_u $(= -z_o)$ on C_4 and $y_v (= y_o)$ on C_5 becoming so large that the surface crosses 'through' itself under the influence of these gradients.

Rather than become involved in tedious algebraic manipulation, we shall illustrate this effect by showing the surface in the neighbourhood of the singular point for various values of y_o and z_o. Fig. 3(a,b,c,d) shows this part of the surface for y_o and z_o = 2,4,6,8 respectively. The self-intersecting nature of the surface is clearly shown for the larger values of y_o and z_o.

4.2 Type B Singularities

Let us now consider the singularities of type B, typified by the point with parametric coordinates u=0, v=π/2 which corresponds to the point (-1,0,1) in E^3. We define a new set of coordinates (r,ϑ) by

$$r\sin\vartheta = u$$
$$\pi/2 + r\cos\vartheta = v \tag{14}$$

The equation satisfied by $\underline{X}$ is again equation (8), with boundary conditions:

On $\vartheta = 0$: $\underline{X} = (-1, r^2/2, 1-r)$; $\underline{X}_\vartheta = (rx_o, 0, 0)$. $\tag{15}$
On $\vartheta = \pi$: $\underline{X} = (-1+r, -r^2/2, 1)$; $\underline{X}_\vartheta = (0, 0, rz_o)$. $\tag{16}$

We find a local solution in the way outlined previously by looking for a solution of the form

$$\underline{X} = (-1 + r^2 F_1(\vartheta), r^2 F_2(\vartheta), 1 + rF_3(\vartheta)) \tag{17}$$

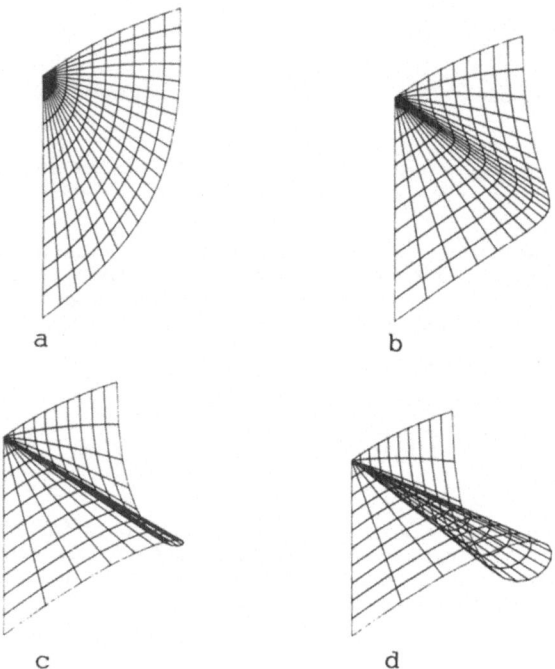

a

b

c

d

Fig. 3: Details of the surface near the type A singularity at (0,-1,1) for various values of the slope parameters z_o & y_o. The parameter values are $z_o = y_o = 2,4,6,8$ in Fig. 3a, 3b, 3c & 3d respectively.

where

$$F_1(\vartheta) = -\frac{\vartheta}{\pi}\cos\vartheta + (x_o + \frac{1}{\pi} - \frac{x_o\vartheta}{\pi})\sin\vartheta$$

$$F_2(\vartheta) = A_y - \frac{\vartheta}{\pi} (\frac{1}{2} - A_y)\cos 2\vartheta + \frac{1}{2\pi}\sin 2\vartheta \qquad (18)$$

$$F_3(\vartheta) = (-1 + \frac{\vartheta}{\pi})\cos\vartheta - (\frac{1}{\pi} + \frac{z_o\vartheta}{\pi})\sin\vartheta$$

Note that the constant A_y is dependent on conditions remote from the singular point; in the case of symmetry, $A_y = 1/2$. Again, F_1, F_2 & F_3 are single-valued functions of ϑ, but ϕ, having the same physical interpretation as in the previous discussion, and defined by

$$\phi = \tan^{-1}\left[\frac{x+1}{z-1}\right] = \tan^{-1}\left[\frac{F_1(\vartheta)}{F_3(\vartheta)}\right] \qquad (19)$$

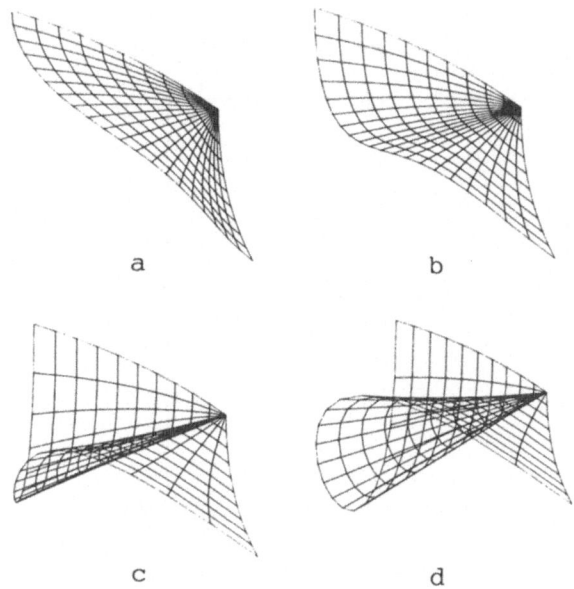

Fig. 4:   Details of the surface near the type B singularity at (-1,0,1) for various values of the slope parameters z_o & x_o. The parameter values are $z_o = x_o = 0.5, 1, 2, 3$ in Figure 4a, 4b, 4c & 4d respectively.

is multivalued for sufficiently large x_o and z_o.

Fig. 4(a,b,c,d) illustrates the surface in the neighbourhood of (-1,0,1) for various values of $x_o = z_o = 0.5, 1, 2, 3$ respectively.   The multivalued nature of the surface for the larger values of x_o and z_o is evident and of course understandable for the reasons given earlier.

This type of singularity analysis allows us to determine the bounds which must be imposed on x_o, y_o and z_o in order to obtain a single-valued and physically acceptable blending surface.   However, the analysis could also be used to provide local solutions so that regular methods might be used for surface generation over a modified patch which had no singularities.

5. NUMERICALLY GENERATED PATCHES

Now let us consider the numerical solution of the system of PDE's given in equation (2) subject to the boundary conditions of equations (1) and   (3).

5.1 Discretization and Numerical Method

The approach we employed was to discretize the relevant portion of the (u,v) plane,   as   shown   schematically   in   Figure   5,   and   to   use   central finite-differences to approximate to the differential operators in equation

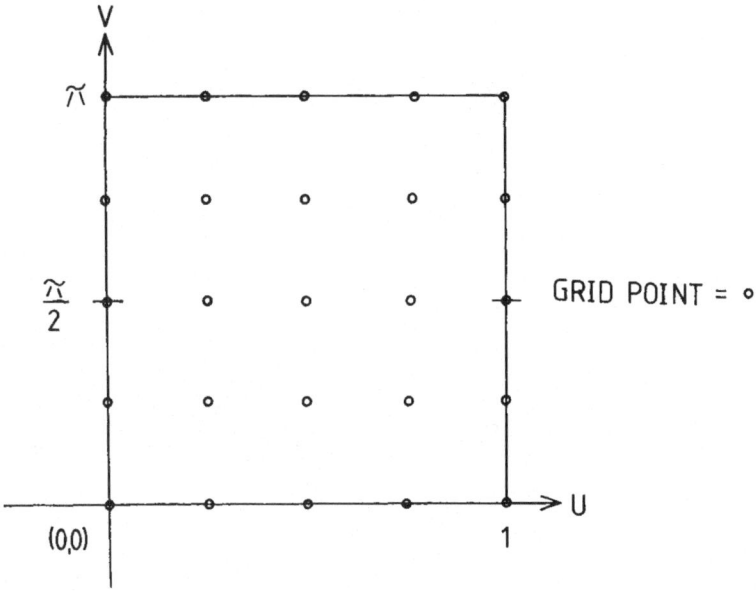

Figure 5: Schematic illustration of the distribution of grid points on the discretized (u,v) parameter plane. Note that there is a grid point at all type A and type B singularities. For the sake of clarity only 25 grid points are shown, whereas the actual mesh used to calculate the numerical surfaces shown in Figure 6 consisted of 31 x 31 grid points.

(1). The resulting set of algebraic difference equations were then solved using Successive-Over-Relaxation, although there are a variety of other techniques we could have chosen for the purpose. The solution is obtained in the form of the (x,y,z) Cartesian Coordinates of points on the blend surface which are the 'image' points in E^3 of the grid points in the discretized (u,v) plane.

To obtain a converged solution took approximately 10 CPU seconds on the University of Leeds Amdahl 580 mainframe. We note that the numerical solution technique we adopted is by no means the most efficient way of numerically solving the difference equations. However, in this paper we have opted for a discussion of the analytic properties of the surface, rather than the ways in which a numerical approximation to it can best be obtained. Even so, we will just mention one way whereby the convergence properties of the numerical scheme might be enhanced, and this is by using Multigrid Methods. The use of these methods and the considerable savings in computational work that are possible by using them are well documented (see for example Brandt 1977).

5.2 Boundary Conditions

As far as numerically imposing the boundary conditions given by equation (1) is concerned, there is no problem anywhere on the boundary of the patch since the function $\underline{X}$ is everywhere at least C^0 continuous. The same is also true of the numerical derivative boundary conditions given by equation (3) with the

exception of the two type **B** singular points found at the junction of curves
C_1 & C_4 and C_2 & C_3, the point being that the jump in the derivatives $[X_u]$
is non-zero in at least some of the components, and therefore there is no
unique value for the derivative boundary conditions that should be imposed at
the mesh points coincident with the singularities. To obtain a numerical
solution, however, the difference scheme needs a value for the derivative to
be specified at all mesh points points along the boundary (excepting the
points at the corner of the mesh). As a 'solution' to the problem, we used a
numerical algorithm that imposed the value of the lower limit of X_u at these
points. This had of effect of allowing the scheme to converge; but, of
course, the question is, to what solution ? Note that this problem does not
arise for the four singular points of type **A**, since the numerical scheme does
not actually require a derivative boundary condition at these points, lying as
they do at the corners of the (u,v) patch.

5.3 Numerical Results

In this section are shown various surfaces, each of which is a numerical
approximation of a surface that covers the polygonal hole described in Section
3. The surfaces have been rendered by plotting out the isoparametric lines on
their surface using a hidden-line algorithm. Fig. 6(a,b,c) shows numerically
generated patches corresponding to the case where $x_o = x_1 = y_o = y_1 = z_o = z_1 =$
constant, where constant = 1,2,3 respectively. The significance of this choice
of tangent magnitudes is as follows.

5.3.1 Figure 6a: constant = 1
Fig. 6a shows a case where, theoretically, we would expect no 'roll-up' to
occur at any of the six singular points on the patch (type **A** or **B**) since the
tangent magnitudes on either side of the singular points are sufficiently
small. As one can see from Fig.6a, there is a smooth surface filling the
polygonal region.

5.3.2 Figure 6b: constant = 2
In Fig. 6b the tangent magnitudes have increased, not sufficiently for
'roll-up' to occur at type **A** singular points, but sufficiently for 'roll-up'
to take place at the type **B** singularities. As one can see by inspecting the
figure, however, there is no sign of 'roll-up' at the **B** points; and so the
question of why this should be arises. The answer is to be found in the
actual details of how the derivative boundary conditions have been imposed
near the singular points. Consider the type **B** singular points where we have
discretized the (u,v) in such a way that a mesh point on the discretized
(u,v) plane is mapped directly onto the singular point. As mentioned above,
since the value of this derivative is not defined at the singular point,
during the actual process of numerical solution some value of X_v must be
specified and, as mentioned above, in this case we have actually chosen to
impose the 'lower' limit at these points. The resulting numerically generated
surface is perfectly well behaved in the sense that it doesn't begin a roll-up
starting from these points, even though one would expect an analytic solution
which correctly satisfied the boundary conditions to do so. What in effect
has been done is to smooth the discontuity in the first derivative. It is as
though there is now a linear variation of x_v^- and z_v^- to the values x_v^+ and z_v^+
over the space of one grid point, and we have 'pushed' the discontuity at the
singular point to the second derivatives. We could also have achieved this
effect by choosing our discretization so that the singular point fell between
two mesh points in the discretized (u,v) parameter mesh.

5.3.3 Figure 6c: constant = 3
In Figure 6c, even though the tangent magnitudes have been increased still
farther there is still no sign of roll-up from the singular points.

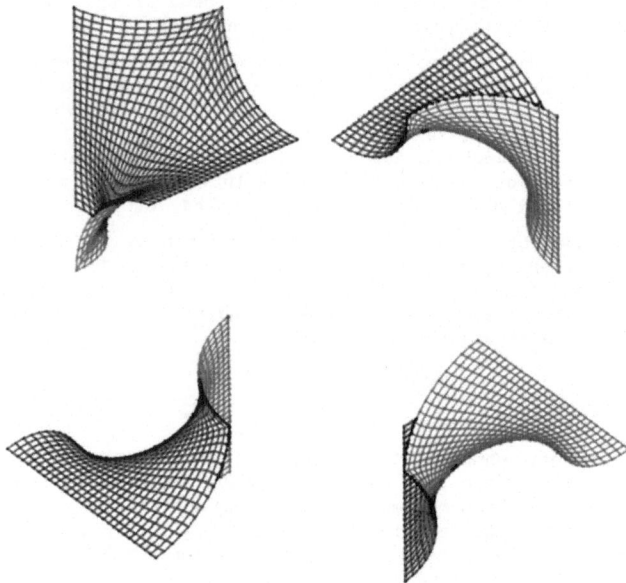

Fig. 6a: The numerically generated surface that covers the region of space bounded by the space curve shown in Fig. 1.   The tangent magnitudes $(x_0, x_1, y_0, y_1, z_0, z_1)$, specified in the derivative boundary conditions, are all 1. The smoothing parameters is unity.

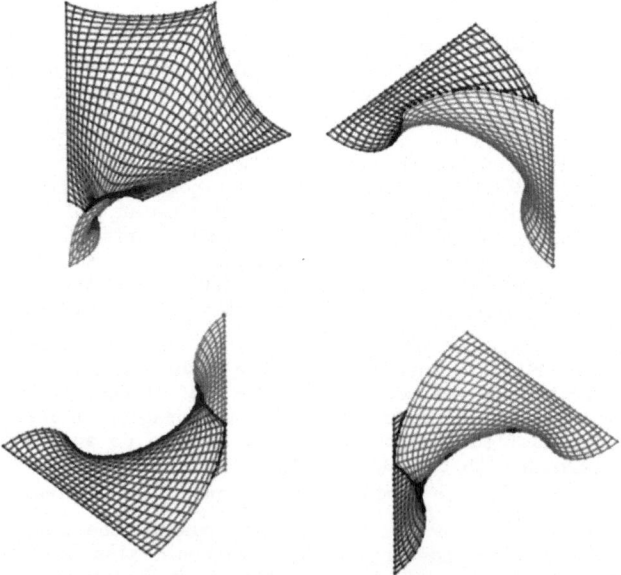

Fig. 6b: The numerically generated surface that covers the region of space bounded by the space curve shown in Fig. 1.   The tangent magnitudes $(x_0, x_1, y_0, y_1, z_0, z_1)$, specified in the derivative boundary conditions, are all 2. The smoothing parameters is unity.

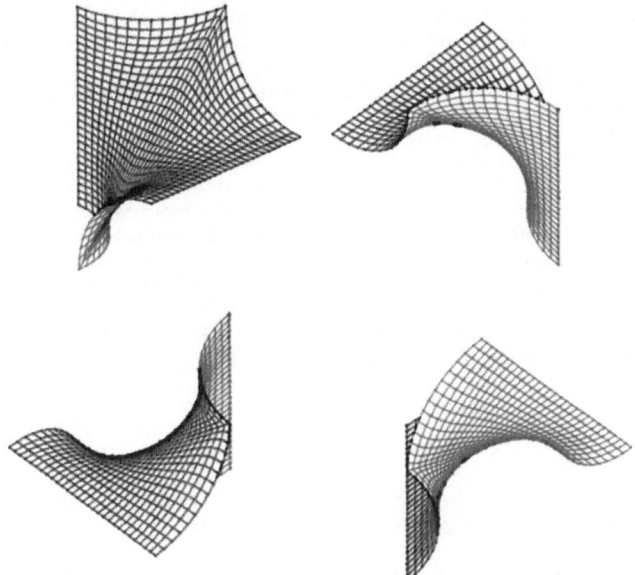

Fig. 6c: The numerically generated surface that covers the region of space bounded by the space curve shown in Fig. 1. The tangent magnitudes $(x_o, x_1, y_o, y_1, z_o, z_1)$, specified in the derivative boundary conditions, are all 3. The smoothing parameters is unity.

Thus, besides that fact that the method is suitable for generating the required blend surfaces, we see that we also have a way of circumventing the problems that are caused by derivative discontinuities at the boundaries. We can generate a numerical solution and 'ignore' the discontinuity in the sense that we allow the discretization effectively to remove the discontinuity. The surface we get is then perfectly well behaved, and by reducing the mesh size we can ensure that the numerical boundary curve approximates the actual boundary curve to the desired degree of accuracy. If such a 'brute-force' approach is not favoured, the presence of a singularity in the desired boundary conditions can be detected by a suitable analysis (such as that above); and then a solution can be obtained over the patch by combining a numerical solution, used for most of the patch, with a local analytic solution, used in the vicinity of the singularity. Or else, one can simply make sure that one does not impose singular boundary conditions, if this is possible.

6. CONCLUSIONS

In this paper we have hoped to indicate how it is possible to generate surface patches with an arbitary number of sides using the PDE approach of Bloor & Wilson. In our opinion, a significant feature of the method is that the surface is given in terms of a single parametric patch. Since the surface patch is the solution of an elliptic partial differential equation it is as smooth as the boundaries will allow, and can blend to the surrounding surfaces with the desired degree of continuity. Because of space, we have only considered the generation of a single patch. The example we have chosen is a polygonal patch having six sides, but the generalisation of the method to an arbitary n-sided patch (where n≥3) should be clear. The set of isolated singular points that may occur on the edges of patch as a result of the boundary conditions can either be analysed so that the singular behaviour of the surface near those points can either be avoided by a suitable modification of the boundary conditions, or be circumvented numerically. Furthermore, we wish to emphasise that the occurence of these singularities is due to their presence in the boundary conditions , and so they are not a feature of the PDE method. Any surface generation system that produces a surface satisfying such boundary conditions will give a surface with singular points on its boundary. However, it is a feature of the PDE method that a quantative analysis of the behaviour of the surface near these points is possible.

REFERENCES

Barnhill RE (1974), Smooth interpolation over triangles, In: Barnhill RE & Riesenfeld RF(eds) Computer Aided Geometric Design, Academic Press, New York London ,1974.

Barnhill RE (1985), Surfaces in CAGD: A survey, In: Barnhill RE & Boehm W (eds) Surfaces in Computer Aided Geometric Design '84, North-Holland, Amsterdam, pp 1-17.

Bloor MIGB, Wilson MJ (1989a), Generating Blending Surfaces with Partial Differential Equations, Computer Aided Design, to appear April.

Bloor MIGB, Wilson MJ (1989b), Blend Design as a Boundary Value Problem, submitted to Staßer (ed) Theory and Practise of Geometric Modelling, Springer, New York Berlin Heidelberg Tokyo.

Brandt A (1977), Multi-level adpative solutions to boundary-value problems, Mathematics of Computation 31 No 138: 333-390.

Chikura H, Kimura F (1983), Design of solids with free-form surfaces, Computer Graphics 17(Proceedings of SIGGRAPH 83, Detroit):25-29.

Farin G (1982), Describing a C1 surface consisting of triangular cubic patches, Computer-Aided Deisgn 14:253-256.

Fjällström PO (1986), Smoothing of polyhedral models, Proceedings of the 2nd ACM Symposium on Computational Geometry, Yorktown Heights, pp226-235.

Gregory JA (1974), Smooth interpolation without twist constraints In:Barnhill RE & Riesenfeld RF Computer Aided Design, Academic Press, New York, pp71-87.

Gregory JA (1983), C1 rectangular and non-rectangular surface patches, In: Barnhill RE & Boehm W Surfaces in Computer Aided Geometric Design, North-Holland, Amsterdam, pp 25-33.

Hahn J (1989), Filling Polygonal Holes with Rectangular Patches, submitted to Straßer (ed) Theory and Practise of Geometric Modelling, Springer, New York Berlin Heidelberg Tokyo.

Hosaka M, Kimura F (1984), Non-four-sided patch expressions with control points, Computer Aided Geometric Design 1:75-86.

Sabin MA (1986), Some negative results in N sided patches, Computer-Aided Design 18: 38-44.

Woodwark JR (1987), Blends in Geometric Modelling, In: Martin RR The Mathematics of Surfaces II, Clarendon Press, Oxford, pp255-287.

Varady T (1987), Survey and Results in N-Sided Patch Generation, In: Martin RR The Mathematics of Surfaces II, Clarendon Press, Oxford, pp203-235.

Malcolm Ian Gibbons Bloor received a BSc in Mathematics from the University of Manchester in 1962, after two years research in Applied Mathematics at Manchester he took up a lectureship at the University of Leeds, completing his Phd for the University of Manchester in 1966. He was made a senior lecturer in 1976, and is currently Director of Mathematics for Applied Sciences in the University of Leeds. He has spent two summer visits, one to Stanford and the other to Caltech. His research interests throughout this period have been in various areas of Fluid Mechanics and more recently in Computer Aided Geometric Design.

Address: Department of Applied Mathematics, The University of Leeds, Leeds LS2 9JT, UK.

Michael John Wilson received his first degree, in Natural Science, from the University of Cambridge in 1981. From 1981 until 1983 he was a research student with the Radio Astonomy Group in the University of Cambridge Physics Department. He received his Phd in 1984. He then moved to the Applied Mathematics Department of the University of Leeds, first as a research assistant and then as a Lecturer in Applied Mathematics. His research interests have been in the fields of Astrophysics and Computational Fluid Dynamics, and more recently in Computer Aided Geometric Design.

Address: Department of Applied Mathematics, The University of Leeds, Leeds LS2 9JT, UK.

Reconstructing Smooth Surfaces from a Series of Contour Lines Using a Homotopy

Y. Shinagawa, T.L. Kunii, Y. Nomura, T. Okuno, and M. Hara

Abstract

A new method is presented to reconstruct surfaces from a series of contour lines. The method can be applied to contour lines represented by parametric curves as well as linear line segments. It is shown that the method includes the triangulation as a special case and generates smooth parametric surfaces from contour line definitions using a homotopy. First, a heuristic method is presented that finds the optimal path on the toroidal graph. Then the toroidal graph is expanded to a continuous version. Finally the homotopy is used for reconstructing parametric surfaces from the toroidal graph representation. When a straight-line homotopy is used, the resulting surface is a loft surface. A homotopy that corresponds to the cardinal spline surface is also introduced. 3-D surface reconstruction of human auditory ossicles illustrates the capability of the above method.

Key Words and Phrases: surface reconstruction, contour data, serial sections, continuous toroidal graph representation, homotopy

INTRODUCTION

There is often a need for reconstructing a three-dimensional object from its cross-sectional data. Particularly in the medical field, to construct the entire shape of the organ from a set of sections is of great significance. As classified by Tam et al (1988), there are four main classes of approaches for generating 3-D medical datasets. The first two methods are based on surface models and the rest are based on solid models. These methods are as given below.

(1) The triangular tile techniques: triangular patches are generated between adjacent contour lines that are approximated by linear line segments (Fuchs et al 1977; Christiansen et al 1978; Boissonat 1988).

(2) Spline approximation: surfaces are reconstructed with a spline approximation (Wu et al 1977).

(3) The cuberille method: 3D surfaces are represented by means of a cuberille, which is a partitioning of space into equal cubes (Herman et al 1979).

(4) Octree-encoding: the original image is compressed in a octree (Meagher 1982; Mao et al 1982).

Surface modeling is advantageous when modification of contour data is necessary. Actually, thin slices of organs are easy to be deformed and hence modification of the contour data to get the accurate location of points is indispensable. This paper presents a new method which uses a homotopy to aggregate and generalize the two surface models given by (1) and (2). The surface is reconstructed using a homotopy from digitized outline curves of objects.

As for the method (1), Fuchs et al (1977) used the toroidal graph representation and based on graph theory, illustrated an example which minimizes surface area. This approach requires a great deal of computation to get the optimal solution. Christiansen et al (1978) provided a simpler triangulation scheme based upon the shortest diagonal algorithm, which can be regarded as a kind of greedy algorithm. Their approach also included handling branches, which is adopted in this paper. While this scheme works well when adjacent loops are similar in shape, it produces defective triangles if the consecutive contours vary widely. Kaneda, Harada, and Nakamae et al (1987) proposed the addition of another condition to the shortest diagonal algorithm to remedy this problem. This condition, however, cannot be always satisfied and the algorithm is still greedy. This paper proposes a heuristic and global algorithm that avoids defective triangles. The toroidal graph is expanded to a continuous version to provide a new method that uses a homotopy to generate smooth parametric surfaces. Although triangulated surfaces with smooth shading seem smooth, the surface normals are ambiguous and it is hard to understand the exact shape of the objects when the shape is complicated. It is necessary to obtain absolutely smooth surfaces when observation of the exact shape is required. This is realized by applying the the homotopy. The resulting surface is a generalization of classical parametric surfaces, and includes the method given by (2). Two examples are shown, one corresponding to the refinement of loft surfaces by using a straight-line homotopy and and another a cardinal spline surface.

A HEURISTIC APPROACH TO FIND THE OPTIMAL PATH

First, assume that a contour line is to be approximated by a string of linear line segments. Let one contour be defined by a sequence of m distinct contour points $P_0,...,P_{m-1}$, and let the other contour be defined by $Q_0,...,Q_{n-1}$. Let us assume that the orientation of both loops are the same. As Christiansen et al (1978) pointed out, triangulation must satisfy two conditions: if two nodes of the same contour are to be defined as the nodes of the same triangle, they must neighbor each other on the contour line. Also no more than two vertices of any triangle may be recruited from the same contour line. Fuchs et al (1977) reduced this rule to one in graph theory. They represented mutual topological relations of triangles in a toroidal graph, which is adopted as the basic representation in this paper. In this graph, vertices correspond to the set of all possible spans between the points $P_0,...,P_{m-1}$ and the points $Q_0,...,Q_{n-1}$ and the arcs correspond to the set of all the possible triangles (see Fig. 1). The graph of an acceptable surface has exactly one vertical arc in every row and exactly one horizontal arc in every column. There are two kinds of acceptable surfaces: one is homeomorphic to a cylinder and the other homeomorphic to two cones. In this paper, the discussion is limited to the former case unless otherwise noted. Fuchs et al proved that the graph of an acceptable surface homeomorphic to a cylinder is connected and is in the form: for every vertex of the graph, one arc is incident to it and one arc is incident from it. Based upon this theorem, they provided an algorithm to find the minimum cost acceptable trail. This is a massive search, while the shortest diagonal algorithm given by Christiansen is a simple and greedy one. First, the adjacent contour lines are mapped onto a unit square. Let us assume that P_0 and Q_0 are proximate. The shortest diagonal algorithm commences triangulation by connecting P_0 and Q_0. After P_i and Q_j are connected, the shorter of the two candidate P_i-Q_{j+1} and $P_{i+1}-Q_j$ is selected as the next one. This method produces defective triangles when two consecutive contour lines differ widely in shape. In Fig. 2, for example, defective triangles are formed around P_{41} and P_{67}. To remedy this, Kaneda, Harada, Nakamae et al (1987) added another condition: for each triangle edge, the shortest of the possible candidates is selected. It cannot, however, be always satisfied. This is obvious when one plots on the toroidal graph every pair of P_i-Q_j that are mutually the closest. For convenience, these vertices are defined as the closest pair vertices.

DEFINITION 1. A vertex (P_i,Q_j) is a **closest pair vertex** if

$$d(P_i,Q_j) = \min_{0 \leq k < n} d(P_i,Q_k)$$
$$d(P_i,Q_j) = \min_{0 \leq k < m} d(P_k,Q_j)$$

hold. Here, d(P,Q) is the distance between the point P and Q.

Finding a closest pair vertex is a special case of the all nearest-neighbors problem (Preparata, Shamos 1985).

REMARK 1. At most one closest pair vertex exists on each row and on each column of the toroidal graph.

Acceptable paths that connects all the closest pair vertices do not exist when those vertices are distributed as shown in Fig. 2. Therefore, connecting as many closest pair vertices as possible is examined next. First, vertices are weighted 1 when they are the closest pair vertices and 0 otherwise. $\Psi(S)$ is defined as the total weight of the vertices that S passes through. In other words, $\Psi(S)$ is the number of the closest pair vertices that an acceptable path S passes through. Then the problem can be reduced to finding the maximum cost acceptable path. However, a simpler approach which groups closest pair vertices is explored in this paper. Careful observation of Fig. 2 leads to the fact that closest pair vertices can be grouped. A group consists of a set of closest pair vertices $(P_i,Q_j),(P_{i+1},Q_{j+1}),...,(P_{i+k},Q_{i+k})$, which is referred to as the run R of the closest pair vertices whose length L(R) is k+1, and when a vertex p is the constituent of a run R, it is noted as p $\in$ R. Then the following proposition holds.

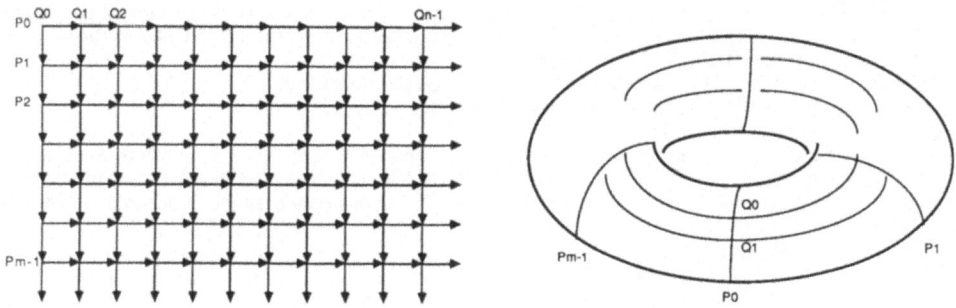

Fig. 1. Toroidal Graph Representation (Fuchs et al 1977)

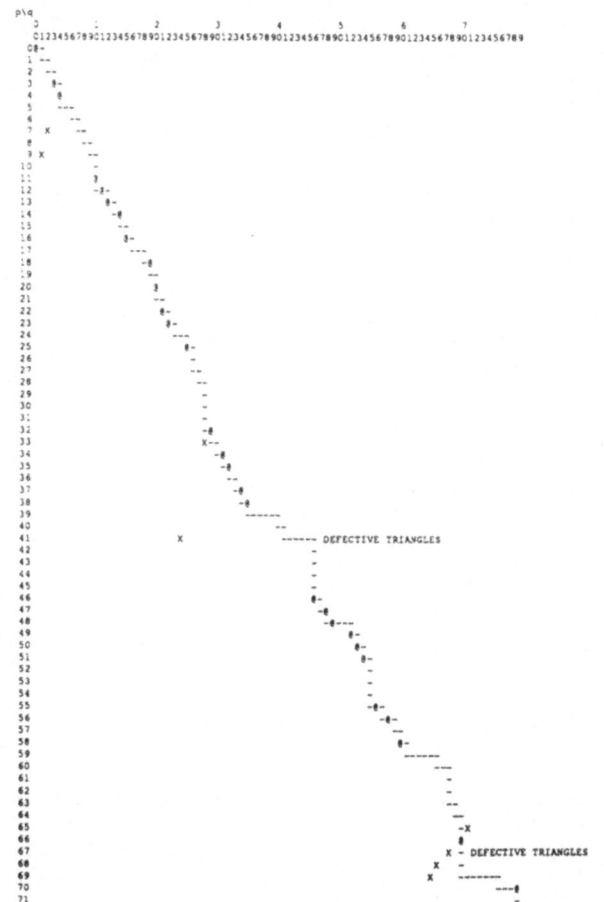

X at (p,q) -> proximate pair vertex
- at (p,q) -> the path chosen by the shortest diagonal algorithm goes through here
@ stands for X with -

Fig. 2. Distribution of Closest Pair Vertices and
the Path Chosen by the Shortest Diagonal Algorithm

PROPOSITION 1. When there exists an acceptable path S_1 that passes through a closest pair vertex (P_i,Q_j), there exists another acceptable path S_2 that passes through all the closest pair vertices of the run R where $(P_i,Q_j) \in R$ and $\Psi(S_1) \leq \Psi(S_2)$.

PROOF. Without loss of generality, it can be assumed that $L(R) \geq 2$.

Case 1; $(P_{i+1},Q_{j+1}) \in R$ and S_1 does not pass through this vertex.

Case 1-a; S_1 passes through (P_{i+1},Q_j).

Let (P_k,Q_{j+1}) be the last vertex at which S_1 leaves the row $j+1$. Let $S_1 = S_3 S_4 S_5$ where S_4 is a path from (P_{i+1},Q_j) to (P_k,Q_{j+1}). $\Psi(S_4) = 0$ holds by REMARK 1. Obviously there is a path S_6 from (P_{i+1},Q_{j+1}) to (P_k,Q_{j+1}) and $\Psi(S_6) = 1$. Therefore when S_2 is constructed as the concatenation of S_3, S_6 and S_5, $\Psi(S_2) = \Psi(S_1) + 1$.

Case 1-b; S_1 passes through (P_i,Q_{j+1}).

The discussion is the same as in Case 1-a.

Case 2; $(P_{i-1},Q_{j-1}) \in R$ and S_1 does not pass through this vertex.

The discussion is the same as in Case 1.

Applying this construction method recursively, the path S_2 of PROPOSITION 1 is obtained. □

By PROPOSITION 1, only runs have to be taken into consideration to maximize Ψ. Thus the objective stated previously is reduced to the following one: to choose an acceptable set of runs that maximizes Ψ. Here, a set of runs that an acceptable path passes through is defined as an acceptable set of runs. Obviously, any set of runs that consists of two runs is acceptable. A set of three runs $\{R_1, R_2, R_3\}$ that are not acceptable is as follows: suppose $R_1 = (P_{i1},Q_{j1}),...,$ $R_2 = (P_{i2},Q_{j2}),...,$ $R_3 = (P_{i3},Q_{j3}),...,$ and $i_1 < i_2 < i_3$ (mod m). If $j_1 < j_3 < j_2$ (mod m) or $j_2 < j_1 < j_3$ (mod m) or $j_3 < j_2 < j_1$ (mod m), this set is not acceptable. A set of more than three runs are acceptable if and only if any three element constitutes an acceptable set. Therefore, the objective stated above needs an exhaustive search like the knapsack problem.

Confronted with this complexity, we decided to explore a heuristic scheme. As one cause of the complexity lies in the use of modulo m, it is abandoned. This corresponds to cutting a torus to a plane. By this simplification, acceptability becomes a binary relation of runs instead of the ternary relation. A set of two runs $(P_{i1},Q_{j1}),...,$ and $(P_{i2},Q_{j2}),...,$ is acceptable if $i_1 < i_2$ and $j_1 < j_2$ or $i_1 > i_2$ and $j_1 > j_2$. When a set $\{R_1, R_2\}$ is not acceptable, R_1 is said to be inconsistent with R_2. This is much easier to test while strictness is lost. Finally, to choose the runs that maximize Ψ, a heuristic algorithm which makes use of a stack is adopted as follows.

ALGORITHM. Assume there are N runs and for each run $R_k = (P_{i_k},Q_{j_k}),..., i_1 < i_2 <,...,<i_k <,...,<i_N$ holds. At first, the stack is empty.

Step 1. Push R_1 onto the stack.

Step 2. $k = 2$.

Step 3. Let R be the run at the top of the stack.

Step 4. If R_k and R is consistent, R_k is pushed onto the stack.
　　　　Else if $L(R_k) \leq L(R)$ R_k is removed and $k = k+1$.
　　　　Otherwise R is removed from the stack.

Step 5. If $k \leq N$, go to step 3.

As for R_k, less than k iterations are needed. Therefore, the time complexity of this algorithm is $O(N^2)$. By this algorithm, an acceptable set of runs that makes Ψ close to the maximum is obtained.

CONTINUOUS VERSION OF THE TOROIDAL GRAPH

Next, it is necessary to decide the trail of the path in detail. Although the path must pass through the vertices of the runs chosen by the previous algorithm, other vertices still remain arbitrary. In this paper, "linear interpolation" of closest pair vertices is proposed to decide the trail. Before discussing it in detail, an introduction to a continuous version of the discrete toroidal graph is necessary.

First of all, the lower and the upper contours must be represented by parameters: points on the contours is designated by a function f, g: $I \rightarrow \mathbf{R}^3$ where $I \subset \mathbf{R}$ is an interval [0, 1] and $f(0) = f(1)$ and $g(0) = g(1)$. In the continuous toroidal graph, horizontal and vertical distance between two vertices represents the difference of the parameter values between the two.

EXAMPLE 1. Arc-length is used as the parameter. Let l_1 and l_2 be the length of the lower and the upper loop. For example, the horizontal distance between (P_{i1}, Q_{j1}) and (P_{i2}, Q_{j2}) represents the arc-length between P_{i1} and P_{i2} over l_1 and the vertical length represents the arc-length between Q_{j1} and Q_{j2} over l_2. The point (x,y) on the graph represents the pair of P and Q where P is the point whose arc-length from P_0 is xl_1, and Q is the point whose arc-length from Q_0 is yl_2. O

There are various ways to choose the parameter.

EXAMPLE 2. When the shape of contour lines are close to circles, the argument can be used as the parameter. In this case, it is essentially same as with the cylindrical coordinate system.   O

The contour lines need not be approximated by linear segments. Parametric curves such as the Bezier curve, the B-spline curve or the cardinal spline curve can be used instead.

EXAMPLE 3. The parameter of the spline basis function is used as the parameter of the graph. To use the linear interpolation discussed later, arc-length representation is desirable. However, the conversion from the curve parameter to the arc-length is not easy to compute. One remedy is to approximate the spline curves by linear line segments and use its length instead of actual arc-length. Display examples presented later use this approximation.   O

When a path passes through (x,y) where f(x) is P and g(y) is Q, it means that P and Q is "connected" by a homotopy discussed in detail later.

As long as the parameter monotonously increases as the point on the contour line goes farther from the initial node, it does not matter essentially what parameter is used in the following discussion. The continuous version of an acceptable path is represented on this graph as a monotonously increasing (or decreasing) "multi-valued function." Strictly speaking, the path is represented as the concatenation of the graph $y = U_i(x)$ and $x = V_i(y)$ $(i = 0,...,nn-1)$ where $U_i: [x_{2i}, x_{2i+1}] \rightarrow I$ and $V_i: [y_{2i}, y_{2i+1}] \rightarrow I$ $(0 = x_0 \le x_1 \le,...,\le x_{2nn-1} < 1, 0 = y_0 \le y_1 \le,...,\le y_{2nn-1} < 1)$ are monotonously increasing (decreasing) functions and on each joint (x_{2i+1}, y_{2i+1}) of U_i and V_i, $U_i(x_{2i+1}) = V_i(y_{2i+1})$ and $U_1(0) = V_{nn-1}(1)$ hold and on each joint (x_{2i+2}, y_{2i+2}) of V_i and U_{i+1}, $V_i(y_{2i+2}) = U_{i+1}(x_{2i+2})$ hold. This representation is the generalization of a monotonously increasing function. Fig. 3 shows an example where $nn = 2$. The discrete toroidal graph is the special case of this continuous version and the conversion is straightforward (see Fig. 4): its graph is the concatenation of that of $y = q_i$ and $x = p_i$. The surface represented by this path is as in Fig. 6. As for the connection, straight-line connection is used as an example. It represents triangles, all the points on the base being connected with the opposite vertex.

Finally, the details of the path is determined on this graph. Suppose the closest pair vertices are (x_i, y_i) $(i = 0,1,...,k-1)$ and $0 = x_0 <,...,< x_{k-1}$. The path is to be represented as a function U(x): I →I such that

$$U(x) = (y_{i+1} - y_i) \frac{(x - x_i)}{(x_{i+1} - x_i)} + y_i \quad (x_i \le x < x_{i+1}).$$

As stated previously, this is the linear interpolation of (x_i, y_i) and (x_{i+1}, y_{i+1}) (see Fig. 5). The surface represented by this path is as in Fig. 7. This example shows a loft surface. Comparing Fig. 6 and Fig. 7, it is obvious that the surface in Fig. 7 is smoother than that in Fig. 6. Fig. 8 shows an example corresponding to EXAMPLE 3.

The concept of a closest pair vertex can be also expanded to a continuous version, i.e., closest pair points can be defined as the pair of points on the contour lines that are mutually closest. In this paper, however, this has not yet been used. As the number of the closest pair points can be infinity, sampling them and choosing finite number of points among them will be appropriate for implementation purposes. Generation of surfaces between contour lines from the toroidal graph representation using U(x) is discussed later.

GENERATION OF PARAMETRIC SURFACES USING HOMOTOPY

It has been previously stated that a vertex on the continuous toroidal graph represents the correspondence between the point of the upper contour line and that of lower and that corresponding points are connected by a homotopy. This chapter discusses in detail the connection by a homotopy. When the homotopy is a straight-line homotopy, it simply means that they are connected by a straight line segment.

Let the lower and the upper contour line be expressed by maps $f,g:X \rightarrow \mathbf{R}^3$ where $X = [x_0, x_1] \subset \mathbf{R}$. Then f is homotopic to g if there exists a map $F:X \times I \rightarrow \mathbf{R}^3$ such that $F(x,0) = f(x)$ and $F(x,1) = g(x)$ for all points $x \in X$. This map F is called a homotopy from f to g. When F is defined by $F(x,t) = (1-t)f(x) + tg(x)$, it is called a straight-line homotopy (Armstrong 1983).

For simplicity, let the lower contour line be on the plane $z = 0$ and the upper $z = 1$ and $X = I$. In

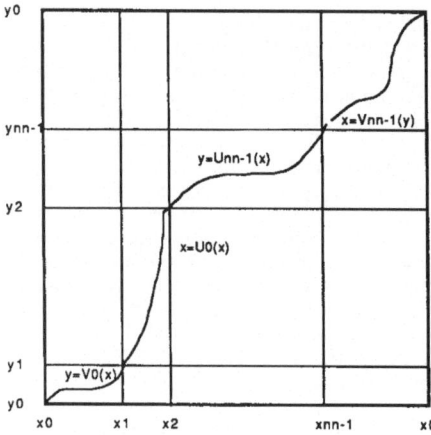

Fig. 3. Acceptable Path on
Continuous Toroidal Graph

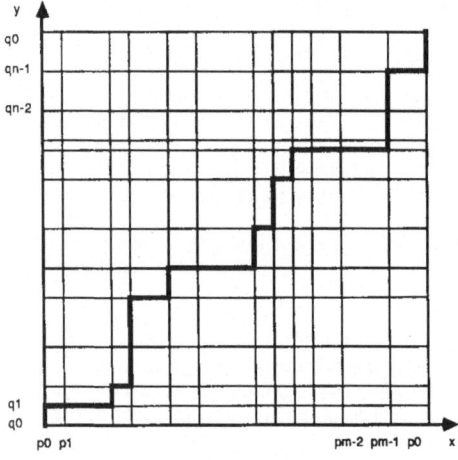

Fig. 4. Natural Expansion of
Discrete Toroidal Graph
to the Continuous Version

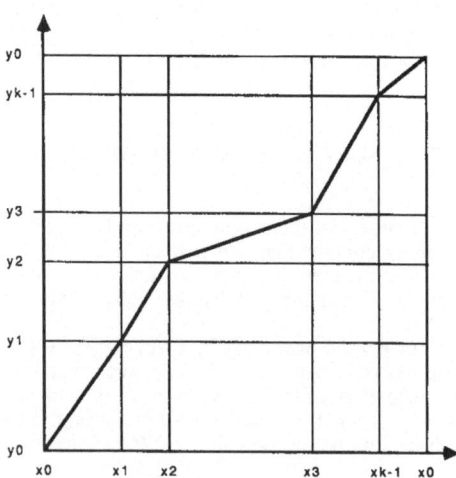

Fig. 5. Linear Interpolation
of Closest Pair Vertices

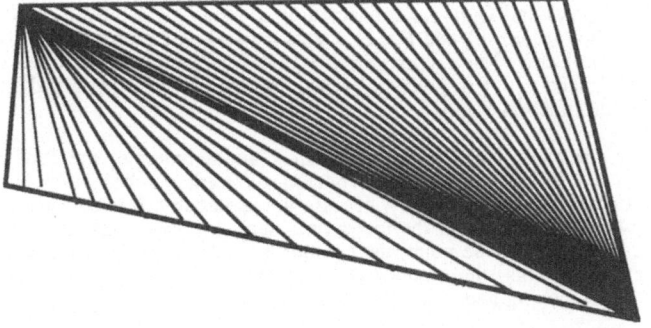

Fig. 6. Correspondence Between Two Adjacent Contours of Triangular Mesh

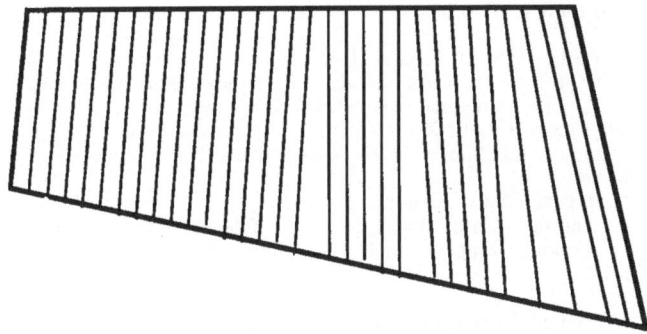

Fig. 7. Correspondence Between Two Contours of a Loft Surface

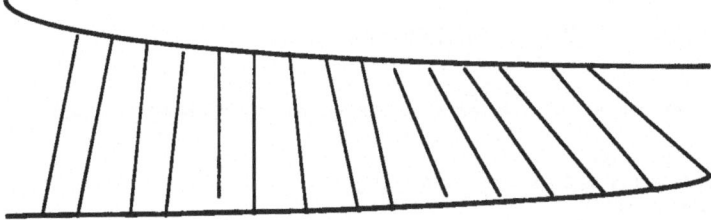

Fig. 8. Correspondence between Smoothly Curved Contour Lines

this paper, "two points $P(p_x, p_y)$ and $Q(q_x, q_y)$ connected by a homotopy F" means that there exists x $\in$ I such that $F(x,0) = f(x) = (p_x, p_y, 0)$ and $F(x,1) = g(x) = (q_x, q_y, d)$ hold. In this paper, a homotopy is used to represent surfaces. Namely, the cross section of the surface between the lower and the upper contour on the plane $z = t$ is given by $F(x,t)$ for $x \in X$. In other words, the surface is represented by the bivariate function $F(x,t)$.

When the two contour lines are both single loops, they are homotopic, the fundamental group (Armstrong 1983) being Z. When two contours contains different number of loops, they are not homeomorphic. In that case, branch handling is necessary. Essentially, it is solved by introducing a virtual contour line between the upper and the lower ones such that two rings joined together at one point; when this joint is regarded as one point, the contour consists of two loops, and when this joint is regarded as two separate points, the contour consists of a single loop. Christiansen's method (1987) is one case of this branching and is used in this paper.

REMOVAL OF THE PARAMETER ARBITRARINESS OF VALUES

In the formalization stated above, different $F(x,t)$'s produce the same surface. For example, for two straight-line homotopies F_1 and F_2, let

$F_1(x, 0) = F_2(x / 2, 0)$ for $x \in [0, 0.5]$

and

$F_1(x, 0) = F_2(0.25 + 1.5 (x - 0.5), 0)$ for $x \in [0.5, 1.0]$.

Then $F_1(x, t)$ and $F_2(x, t)$ produce the same surface. To remove this arbitrariness of parameter x, "quotient" function is used. First, a relation ~ is defined as follows.

DEFINITION 2. As for $F_1(x,t)$, $F_2(x,t)$: $X \times I \rightarrow \mathbf{R}^3$, $F_1 \sim F_2$ holds if and only if there exists monotonously increasing continuous function c: $X \rightarrow X$ such that $c(x_0) = x_0$, $c(x_1) = x_1$ and $F_1(x,t) = F_2(c(x),t)$ for all $x \in X$ and $t \in I$.

PROPOSITION 2. ~ is an equivalence relation.

PROOF. F ~ F holds using the identity map i_d:$X \rightarrow X$. When F ~ G holds using c, G ~ F holds by using c^{-1}. When F ~ G holds using c_1 and G ~ H holds using c_2, F ~ H holds using composite function $c = c_2 \cdot c_1$. □

Using this equivalence relation, $\overline{F}$ is defined as follows. Let $\mathbf{F} = \{ F: X \times I \rightarrow \mathbf{R}^2 \}$. Then $\overline{F}$ is defined as $\mathbf{F} / \sim$. $F \in \mathbf{F}$ is also described as $[F](x,t)$ where [ ] expresses its equivalence class. Using $\overline{F}$ instead of F, arbitrariness in the parameter value is removed. The major benefit of the "quotient" homotopy representation is that the resulting surface does not depend on how contour lines are expressed by parameters. After the division by ~, it depends only on the shape of the contour lines. Therefore, it is easy to construct the surface based on the correspondence designated by the continuous toroidal graph. Programming is done by fixing the choice of the parameter and using it as the representative of its equivalence class. One way is to use the arc-length as the parameter as in EXAMPLE 1.

RELATION WITH OTHER PARAMETRIC SURFACES

A homotopic representation of a surface is the generalization of parametric surfaces. For example, a loft surface

$F(x,t) = (1-t)f(x) + tg(x)$

can be regarded naturally as a straight-line homotopy

$F(x,t) = [(1-t)f(x) + tg(x)]$.

A Boolean sum surface

$$F(x,t) = (h_0(x), h_1(x)) \cdot (r(t), s(t)) + (h_0(t),h_1(t)) \cdot (f(x), g(x)) + (h_1(x),h_1(x)) \begin{bmatrix} f(0) & g(0) \\ f(1) & g(1) \end{bmatrix} \begin{bmatrix} h_0(t) \\ h_1(t) \end{bmatrix}$$

where $F(0, t) = r(t)$, $F(1, t) = s(t)$ and h_i: $I \rightarrow I$ ($i = 0, 1$) are blending functions is another example of a homotopy. Triangular mesh generated by Fuchs' or Christiansen's method can also be expressed by a straight-line homotopy. For simplicity, it is assumed that $f(x)$ and $g(x)$ represent single line segments and that between them, triangles $(f(0), f(1), g(0))$ and $(f(0), g(1), g(0))$ are formed. Then the triangular mesh is expressed as follows.

$$\overline{F}(x,t) = \begin{cases} [(1-t)f(x)+tg(0)] & \text{if } x \leq t \\ [(1-t)f(0)+tg(x)] & \text{if } x > t \end{cases}$$

$\frac{\partial F}{\partial x}$ is not defined on the line x = t and the generated surface is not smooth. There is another way of connecting the line segments to produce the triangular mesh. That is, the point $f(0)$ is expanded to the whole lower line segment and then the whole upper line segments other than $f(0)$ retracts to the point $g(1)$. This is the correspondence that the continuous toroidal graph designates. Although this cannot be expressed by a homotopy because it is impossible to formalize this by maps, it is not difficult to understand this intuitively as the natural expansion of the concept of the homotopy.

The homotopic representation has one more degree of freedom. In a boolean sum surface, for example, when x is fixed, the curve F(x, t) is on the plane that contains the points f(x) and g(x), while in the case of homotopy representation, the curve F(x, t) is not limited to that plane. In the implementation, however, this degree of freedom has not yet been used.

GENERATION OF SURFACES FROM THE TOROIDAL GRAPH REPRESENTATION

Let f, g: $I \rightarrow R^3$ be the function representing the lower and the upper contour line. For the homotopy representation, the acceptable path to be considered must be represented on the toroidal graph by a monotonously increasing continuous function U: $I \rightarrow I$ that has its inverse function U^{-1}. Then the surface to be generated is expressed by the homotopy between f(x) and g(U(x)). When straight-line homotopy is used, it is expressed as follows:

$F(x,t) = [(1-t)f(x) + tg(U(x))]$

Cardinal splines (Clark 1981) can be also used. Let the function representing a series of four contour lines be f_{-1}, f_0, f_1, f_2 and the respective acceptable paths be U_{-1}, U_0, U_1. Then the surface between f_0 and f_1 is

$F(x,t) = w_{-1}(t)f_{-1}(U_{-1}^{-1}(x)) + w_0(t)f_0(x) + w_1(t)f_1(U_0(x)) + w_2(t)f_2(U_1(U_0(x)))$

where

$$[w_{-1}(t) \ w_0(t) \ w_1(t) \ w_2(t)] = [t^3 \ t^2 \ t \ 1] \begin{bmatrix} -a & 2-a & -2+a & a \\ 2a & -3+a & 3-2a & -a \\ -a & 0 & a & 0 \\ 0 & 1 & 0 & 0 \end{bmatrix}.$$

When f_i are represented by cardinal spline function, the surface is referred to as the cardinal spline surface and a display example is presented later. When f_i are represented by B-spline, this equation is similar to that of Wu et al (1977). However, the major difference is in the use of U_i, which makes it possible to handle the parameter values more precisely. This is useful for reconstructing complicated objects. Wu's can be considered to be the special case where U_i's are the identity maps.

AREA OF THE RECONSTRUCTED SURFACE

Let the two adjacent contours be represented by f_1, f_2 ($\in C^1$) : $I \rightarrow R^3$ such that the third component of f_1 is 0 and that of f_2 is d $\in$ R. Let the acceptable path be represented by y = U(x) on the continuous toroidal graph. Then the surface area generated by a straight-line homotopy between the contours is given by

$$\int dS_1 + \int dS_2$$
$$= \frac{1}{2} \int F(x,y,y') \, dx.$$
$$= \frac{1}{2} \int |(f_1(x) - f_2(y)) \times f_2'(y)dy| + |(f_2(y) - f_1(x)) \times f_1'(x)dx|$$
$$= \frac{1}{2} \int |(f_1(x) - f_2(U(x))) \times f_2'(U(x))U'(x)| + |(f_2(U(x)) - f_1(x)) \times f_1'(x)|dx$$

(see Fig. 9).
For simple cases such as

$f_1(x) = (p_1 + a_1x, q_1 + b_1x, 0)$
$f_2(y) = (p_2 + a_2y, q_2 + b_2y, d)$,

F(x,y,y') is in the form of

$$F(x,y,y') = \sqrt{D_2^2 + (\alpha x - \gamma_2)^2} + \sqrt{D_1^2 + (\alpha y - \gamma_1)^2}$$

where

$$\alpha = \begin{vmatrix} a_1 & a_2 \\ b_1 & b_2 \end{vmatrix}$$

$$\gamma_1 = \begin{vmatrix} a_1 & \Delta p \\ b_1 & \Delta q \end{vmatrix}$$

$$\gamma_2 = \begin{vmatrix} a_2 & \Delta p \\ b_2 & \Delta q \end{vmatrix}$$

$$\Delta p = p_1 - p_2$$
$$\Delta q = q_1 - q_2$$
$$D_1^2 = d^2 (a_1^2 + b_1^2)$$
$$D_2^2 = d^2 (a_2^2 + b_2^2).$$

To compute $y = U(x)$ that gives the minimal surface area, a variational method is used. Solving Euler equation $\frac{\partial F}{\partial y} - \frac{d}{dx}(\frac{\partial F}{\partial y'}) = 0$,

$$|D_2| |\alpha x - \gamma_1| = |D_1| |\alpha y - \gamma_2|$$

is obtained. This solution, however, does not satisfy the boundary condition. Therefore, it is not easy to compute the acceptable path that minimizes the surface area on the continuous toroidal graph. Therefore, simple "linear interpolation" of the closest pair vertices is an appropriate method.

HUMAN EAR DATA

A human temporal bone with the ear lobe was obtained from a cadaver and subjected to the conventional celloidin processing. A motor-driven drill was used to place reference marks in a celloidin block (Nomura et al). A larger celloidin section may be unevenly distended when mounted on a slide, causing movement of reference marks and distortion of parts of the ear structure. The celloidin block was serially sectioned into slices 20 μm thick. All slices were stained with hematoxylin and eosin (H-E) and mounted in glass slides. A color photograph was taken of each of the H-E stained specimens.

The photographs were converted to image data by a drum scanner G-225C (Graphica Co., Japan) and outline curves of the objects to be reconstructed were plotted with a stylus pen. The computer used here was HP9000 series model 550 (Hewlet-Packard Co., USA). The coordinate values of each selected nodes were modified using six reference marks (see Fig. 10) as follows.

(1) Let the true location of the reference marks be t_i ($i = 1,...6$) $\in \mathbf{R}^2$.

(2) Let the location of the reference marks of the slice j be $r_{j,i}$ ($i = 1,...6$) $\in \mathbf{R}^2$.

(3) For $i = 1,...,5$, compute the geometric transformation that moves $r_{j,i}$ to t_i and $r_{j,i+1}$ to t_{i+1}. i.e. Compute a_i, d_i and $R(\theta_i)$ such that

$$a_i R(\theta_i) r_{j,i} + d_i = t_i$$
$$a_i R(\theta_i) r_{j,i+1} + d_i = t_{i+1}$$

where $a_i \in \mathbf{R}$, d_i is a two dimensional vector and $R(\theta_i)$ is a two-dimensional rotation matrix. Solving these simultaneous equations,

$$a_i = \frac{|t_{i+1} - t_i|}{|r_{j,i+1} - r_{j,i}|}$$

$$\cos \theta_i = \frac{(t_{i+1} - t_i) \cdot (r_{j,i+1} - r_{j,i})}{|t_{i+1} - t_i| |r_{j,i+1} - r_{j,i}|}$$

$$d_i = t_i - a_i R(\theta_i) r_{j,i}$$

are obtained and the sign of $\sin \theta_i$ coincides with the sign of $(r_{j,i+1} - r_{j,i}) \times (t_{i+1} - t_i)$. Therefore, the form of $R(\theta_i)$ is completely decided. Here, $\cdot$ expresses the inner product and $\times$ expresses the outer product.

(4) For each selected vertex P_k, compute

$$V_{k,i} = a_i R(\theta_i) P_k + d_i \quad (i = 1,...,5)$$

If there is no deformation in the slices when mounted on the slides, $V_{k,i}$ has the same value for $i = 1,...,5$.

(5) Compute the weight w_i for each $V_{k,i}$ ($i = 1,...,5$). There are several ways to decide the weight values. One way is to define w_i as follows:

$$w_i = \frac{|r_{j,i} - r_{j,i+1}|}{|P_k - r_{j,i}| + |P_k - r_{j,i+1}|}$$

In the implementation,

$$w_i = \frac{|r_{j,i} - r_{j,i+1}|}{|P_k - r_{j,i}| + |P_k - r_{j,i+1}| - |r_{j,i} - r_{j,i+1}|}$$

was used. When the denominator is 0, w_i is set to ∞. Smooth weighting results in the smooth contour line.

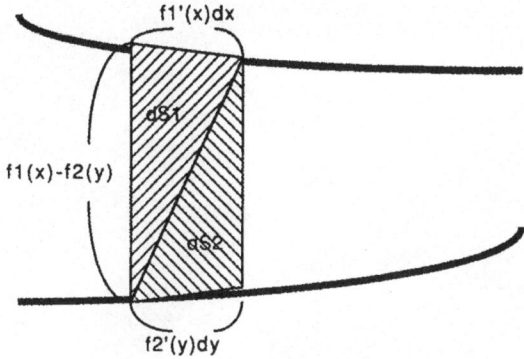

Fig. 9. Area of the Reconstructed Surface

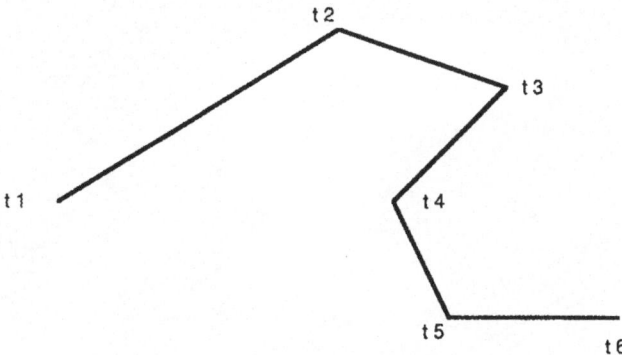

Fig. 10. The Location of the Reference Marks

(6) Let $W = \sum_{i=1}^{i=5} w_i$. Then modified location of the vertex P_k is given by

$$p_k = \sum_{i=1}^{i=5} \frac{w_i}{W} V_{k,i}$$

Finally the modified contour data were fed into IRIS 4D/70GT (Silicon Graphics Co., USA), where the three dimensional reconstruction is performed.

DISPLAY EXAMPLES

This section presents examples of the finished product. Fig. 11 shows the three auditory ossicles (malleus, incus, stapes). The outline curves are approximated by the cardinal spline and a straight-line homotopy is used for surface reconstruction. As noted in EXAMPLE 3, the arc-length of the cardinal spline curve is approximated by the length of linear line segments. Fig. 12 shows the same objects reconstructed by using a homotopy that corresponds to the cardinal spline surface. The outline curves are approximated by the cardinal spline. Fig. 13 shows the same objects reconstructed by Christiansen's triangulation method with Gouraud shading. As was mentioned earlier, the shape seems ambiguous.

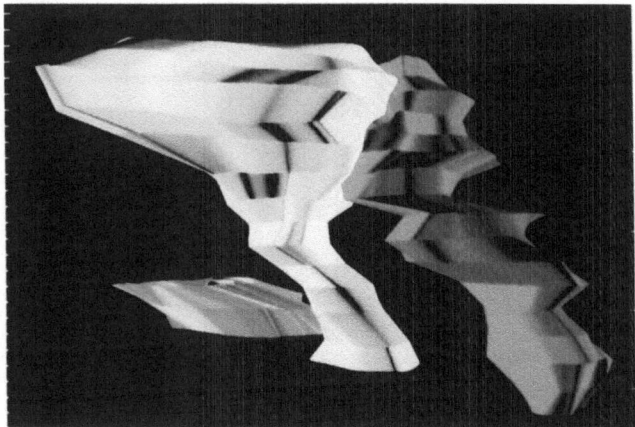

Fig. 11 Three Auditory Ossicles Reconstructed by a Straight-Line Homotopy

Fig. 12 Three Auditory Ossicles Reconstructed by a Homotopy Corresponding to a Cardinal Spline Surface

Fig. 13 Three Auditory Ossicles Reconstructed Using the Triangulation Method with Gouraud Shading (Nomura et al)

CONCLUSIONS

A new method for reconstructing surface from a series of contour lines has been presented. It includes both the triangulation method and parametric surfaces as special cases. A heuristic method has been used for finding the optimal acceptable path. The toroidal graph representation is extended to the continuous version. The homotopy is used for reconstructing surfaces from the toroidal graph representation. When a straight-line homotopy is used, the resulting surface is a loft surface, and also the homotopy that corresponds to the cardinal spline surface has been presented. 3-D surface reconstruction of human auditory ossicles have been shown as display examples.

ACKNOWLEDGMENTS

We wish to express our gratitude to Mr. Kansei Iwata, the president of Graphica Co., Ltd. and Mr. Norimasa Koyama, the executive director of Cadtech Inc. for offering the drum scanner, G-225C, Yokogawa Hewlet Packard Co., Ltd. for HP900 model 550 and Silicon Graphics Co., Ltd. for IRIS 4D/70GT.
Special thanks are extended to Dr. Issei Fujishiro of the Ikebe Laboratory of the Institute of Information Sciences and Electronics, University of Tsukuba, Mr. Yasuto Shirai, Ms. Deepa Krishnan, Ms. Xiaoyang Mao, Mr. Satoshi Nishimura and Mr. Martin Duerst of the Kunii Laboratory of Computer Science, the University of Tokyo.

REFERENCES

Armstrong MA (1983) *Basic Topology*. Springer, New York Berlin Heidelberg Tokyo, p.92

Boissonnat JD (1988) Shape Reconstruction from Planar Cross Sections. *Computer Vision, Graphics, and Image Processing*, Vol.41, No.1, pp.1-29

Christiansen HN, Sederberg TW (1978) Conversion of Complex Contour Line Definitions into Polygonal Element Mosaics. *Proc. ACM SIGGRAPH'78*, pp.187-192

Clark JH (Nov. 1981) Parametric Curves, Surfaces and Volumes in Computer Graphics and Computer-Aided Geometric Design. *Computer Systems Laboratory, Technical Report No.221*, Stanford University.

Fuchs H, Kedem ZM, and Uselton SP (Oct. 1977) Optimal Surface Reconstruction from Planar Contours. *Comm. ACM Vol.20, No.10*, pp.693-702

Herman GT, Liu HK (1979) Three-Dimensional Display of Human Organs from Computer Tomograms. *Computer Graphics and Image Processing*, Vol.9, pp.1-21

Kaneda K, Harada K, Nakamae E, Yasuda M, and Sato AG (1987) Reconstruction and Semi-Transparent Display Method for Observing Inner Structure of an Object Consisting of Multiple Surfaces. In: Kunii TL (ed) *Computer Graphics 1987*. Springer, New York Berlin Heidelberg Tokyo, pp. 367-380

Mao X, Kunii TL, Fujishiro I, Noma T (Dec. 1987) Hierarchical Representations of 2D/3D Gray-Scale Images and Their 2D/3D Two-Way Conversion. *IEEE Computer Graphics & Applications*, pp.37-44

Meagher DJ (1982) Geometric Modeling Using Octree-Encoding. *Computer Graphics and Image Processing*, Vol.19, pp.129-147.

Nomura Y, Okuno T, Hara M, Shinagawa Y, Kunii TL, Walking through a Human Ear. To appear in *Acta Otolaryngol* (Stockh).

Preparata FP, Shamos MI (1985) *Computational geometry: an introduction*. Springer, New York Berlin Heidelberg Tokyo

Tam Y, Davis WA (1988) Display of 3D Medical Images. *Graphics Interface '88*, pp.78-86

Wu S, Abel JF, Greenberg DP (Oct. 1977) An Interactive Computer Graphics Approach to Surface Representation. *Comm. ACM Vol.20, No.10*, pp.187-192

Yoshihisa Shinagawa is currently a master course graduate student of information science at the University of Tokyo. His research interests include computer graphics and its applications. He received the B.Sc. degree in information science from the University of Tokyo in 1987. He is a student member of the IEEE Computer Society and the Information Processing Society of Japan.
Address: Department of Information Science, Faculty of Science, the University of Tokyo, 7-3-1 Hongo, Bunkyo-Ku, Tokyo, 113 Japan

Yasuya Nomura is currently Professor and Chairman of the Department of Otolaryngology, the University of Tokyo. He received his M.D. in 1956 and Dr.Med.Sci. in 1975 from the University of Tokyo.
Address: Department of Otolaryngology, Faculty of Medicine, the University of Tokyo, 7-3-1 Hongo, Bunkyo-Ku, Tokyo, 113 Japan

Taeko Okuno is currently Instructor of the Department of Otolaryngology, the University of Tokyo. She received her M.D. in 1977 from Chiba University Medical School and Dr.Med.Sci. in 1984 from the University of Tokyo.
Address: Department of Otolaryngology, Faculty of Medicine, the University of Tokyo, 7-3-1 Hongo, Bunkyo-Ku, Tokyo, 113 Japan

Makoto Hara is currently Assistant of the Department of Otolaryngology, the University of Tokyo and Research Fellow of the Massachusetts Eye & Ear Infirmary, Harvard Medical School. He received his M.D. in 1981 and Dr.Med.Sci. in 1988 from the University of Tokyo.
Address: Department of Otolaryngology, Faculty of Medicine, the University of Tokyo, 7-3-1 Hongo, Bunkyo-Ku, Tokyo, 113 Japan

161

Tosiyasu L. Kunii is currently Professor of Information and Computer Science, the University of Tokyo. At the University of Tokyo, he started his work in raster computer graphics in 1968 which was let to the Tokyo Raster Technology Project. His research interests include computer graphics, database systems, and software engineering. He authored and edited more than 20 computer science books, and published more than 100 refereed academic/technical papers in computer science and applications areas.

Dr. Kunii is Former President and Founder of the Computer Graphics Society, Chairman of the Board of the Handheld Computer Society, Editor-in-Chief of *The Visual Computer: An International Journal of Computer Graphics* and on the Editorial Board of *IEEE Computer Graphics and Applications*. He is on the IFIP Data Base Working Group and the IFIP Computer Graphics Working Group. He organized and was chairing the Technical Committee on Software Engineering of the Information Processing Society of Japan from 1976 to 1981. He also organized and was President of the Japan Computer Graphics Association(JCGA) from 1981 to 1983. He served as General Chairman of the 3rd International Conference on Very Large Data Bases(VLDB) in 1977, Program Chairman of InterGraphics '83 in 1983, Organizing Committee Chairman and Program Chairman of Computer Graphics Tokyo in 1984, Program Chairman of Computer Graphics Tokyo in 1985 and 1986, Organizing Committee Chairperson and Program Chairperson of CG International '87 in 1987, Program Co-Chairman of COMPSAC 87 in 1987, and Honorary Committee Chairperson of CG International '88 in 1988. He is serving as Organizing Committee Chairperson and Program Chairperson of IFIP TC-2 Working Conference on Visual Database Systems to be held in 1989.

He received the B.Sc., M.Sc., and D.Sc. degrees in chemistry all from the University of Tokyo in 1962, 1964, and 1967, respectively.
Address: Department of Information Science, Faculty of Science, the University of Tokyo, 7-3-1 Hongo, Bunkyo-Ku, Tokyo, 113 Japan

Chapter 3
Computational Geometry

A Localized Method for Intersecting Plane Algebraic Curve Segments

J.K. Johnstone and M.T. Goodrich[1]

ABSTRACT

In this paper, we present a local method for the computation of the intersections of plane algebraic curve segments. The conventional method of intersection is global, because it must first find all of the intersections between two curves before it can restrict to the segments in question; hence, it cannot take advantage of situations in which one is dealing with the intersection of short curve segments on complex curves. Our local method, on the other hand, will directly find only those intersections that lie on the segments, as it is based upon an extension of methods for tracing along a curve.

Keywords: intersection, algebraic curves, curve tracing, plane sweep, resultants, theory of elimination, geometric modeling

1 INTRODUCTION

Intersection is one of the most universal and basic problems in geometric modeling. Although all of the boolean operations are axiomatic to geometric modeling, intersection is particularly important and particularly challenging. It is usually required for the definition of a geometric model (e.g., CSG (Requicha 1980)) and it is fundamental to applications of the model such as interference detection or hidden-surface elimination (Mortenson 1985; McKenna 1986; Sechrest and Greenberg 1982). The classical view of the intersection of algebraic curves and surfaces is that it is equivalent to the solution of a simultaneous system of equations, such as $\{f(x,y) = 0, g(x,y) = 0\}$ for two plane algebraic curves. (Since the representation of the curves is the implicit representation, methods of intersection that rely on the parametric representation (Mortenson 1985) are not applicable.) Canonically, the system of equations is reduced to a single univariate equation, the univariate equation is solved, and full solutions are built from these partial solutions. An artifact of this approach is that all of the intersections are found. But in geometric modeling one is usually interested only in the intersections between two short segments of the curves. Thus, if one follows this approach, then one must first compute all of the intersections between the entire curves and then decide which of these intersections actually lie on the segments (a decision that is decidedly nontrivial, involving the sorting of points along a curve (Johnstone 1987)). Therefore, segment intersection is clearly more complex than curve intersection when one uses the traditional approach.

One would hope, then, for a method that makes segment intersection simpler than curve intersection, especially if the segments are short. This is especially urgent because, as geometric

---

[1]This author's research was supported by the National Science Foundation under Grant CCR-8810568.

models become more complex with the natural maturation of the field, intersection of higher-degree curves with the global system of equations method is becoming prohibitively expensive, while the curve segments involved remain short. In this paper, we shall present a new method for the intersection of plane algebraic curve segments. The method is input-sensitive: the simpler and shorter the segment, the more efficient the intersection computation.

Our method is based upon crawling, a method for moving along a curve that has received much attention of late (Bajaj et. al. 1987; Dobkin et. al. 1986; Hoffmann 1987; Hoffmann and Lynch 1987; Owen and Rockwood 1987; Timmer 1977). We find intersections by crawling along the two segments in a coordinated fashion. Since crawling is a method for moving along a single curve, we must adapt it to two curves (Section 3). This crawling is easiest if both segments are *xy-monotone* (monotone with respect to both coordinate axes), so the curve segments are first decomposed into xy-monotone segments (Section 7). Two methods of coordinated crawling along xy-monotone segments are presented: the simultaneous and the staircase crawl (Sections 4 and 5). Several optimizations are also suggested, including a way of recognizing when two xy-monotone segments cannot intersect and two ways of eliminating long crawls within a coordinated crawl (Section 8). A variant of the plane sweep method (familiar from computational geometry: Bentley and Ottmann 1979; Edelsbrunner 1987; Preparata and Shamos 1985) is used to find the intersections of the collection of xy-monotone segments that comprise the two segments that we are intersecting, using several calls to coordinated crawling (Section 9). We end with some conclusions.

2   THE SYSTEM-OF-EQUATIONS (SOE) METHOD OF INTERSECTION

In this section we review the global method of intersection that we are trying to replace, which we refer to as the *system of equations (SOE) method of intersection*. An example will clarify the details of the SOE method.

Example 2.1 *Suppose that we wish to find the intersection of the two plane algebraic curves $f(x, y) = 0$ and $g(x, y) = 0$. The two equations are reduced to a single equation and a variable is eliminated by taking the (Sylvester or Bezout/Cayley) resultant $h(x)$ of f and g with respect to y (Sederberg et. al. 1984; van der Waerden 1953; Walker 1950). Even if there are more than two equations, techniques from the theory of elimination can be used to reduce the system to a single univariate equation, perhaps by using several rounds of Sylvester resultants or a multivariate resultant. Next, the univariate equation (which encodes the common roots) is solved, perhaps by Newton's method, yielding one coordinate of each solution of the original system. For example, if x_0 is a root of $h(x)$, then there exists y_0 such that $f(x_0, y_0) = 0 = g(x_0, y_0)$. Finally, the full solutions are built up from these partial solutions by solving more univariate equations. For example, $f(x_0, y)$ is solved, yielding $y_1, \ldots, y_k$, and y_i's such that $g(x_0, y_i) \neq 0$ are discarded. The remaining y_j's form full solutions or intersections (x_0, y_j).*

Notice that all of the intersections between the curves are found. In particular, it is impossible to find only the intersections on a given segment of each curve with the SOE method. (There is no way of predicting where the intersection will be until it is fully computed, and the method deals with the equation of the entire curve.) Segment intersection would require expensive postprocessing. (The intersections would be sorted along each curve and those that are not between the endpoints of the appropriate segment would be discarded.) Thus, with the SOE method, segment intersection is noticeably more complex than curve intersection.

Another problem with the SOE method is that it requires the solution of a univariate equation of high degree. In particular, the degree of the resultant polynomial $h(x)$ is potentially the product of the degree of $f(x, y)$ and the degree of $g(x, y)$.

3 COORDINATED CRAWLING

In this section we give a short introduction to crawling and a general overview of coordinated crawling. The reader is referred to Bajaj et. al. (1987), Hoffmann (1987), and Hoffmann and Lynch (1987) for the details of crawling. Crawling is a method of traversing a curve. Progress is made by repeatedly making short steps away from the curve and relaxing back onto the curve (Fig. 1). There are various ways of stepping away from the curve, such as stepping along the tangent or in a direction parallel to the axes. The relaxation back onto the curve can be achieved with Newton's method. One of the useful properties of crawling is its locality: it relies only on the behavior of the curve in a restricted neighborhood of the current position.

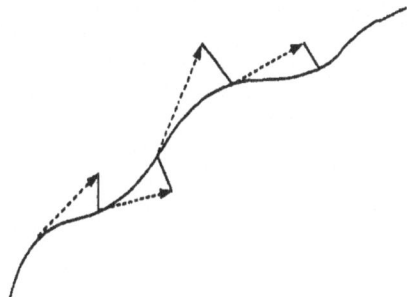

Figure 1: Crawling along a curve

The size of each step of a crawl can be adjusted. It cannot be too large, since it might lose the curve, and it must be particularly small near singularities and other places where confusion is likely. However, within the bounds of these restrictions, it is possible to talk of coarse crawls with large steps and fine crawls with small steps. We shall be intent upon keeping the crawl as coarse as possible, since the larger the steps, the faster the crawl.

One of the contributions of this paper is to show that crawling can also be used to discover the intersections between two xy-monotone curve segments. Let $\overparen{AB}$ and $\overparen{CD}$ be two xy-monotone curve segments. Starting at the beginning of each segment, we shall crawl along the two segments in tandem, alternating the crawl along $\overparen{AB}$ with the crawl along $\overparen{CD}$ so that, at any given time, progress is being made along only one of the segments (Fig. 2). The crawl along a segment continues until a *switching condition* becomes true. The alternation between segments continues until an *end condition* becomes true, signalling that an intersection has been found or that the two segments do not intersect. The segment along which one is presently crawling (resp., not crawling) is called the *active* (resp., *dormant*) segment. A crawl along an active segment between switching conditions will often be referred to simply as a crawl (of the coordinated crawl).

Example 3.1 *Consider the coordinated crawl of Fig. 2(a). Horizontal and vertical lines have been added to the picture to reveal the structure of the crawls. The first crawl is along $\overparen{Aa_1}$ of $\overparen{AB}$. $\overparen{AB}$ then becomes dormant and the second crawl is made along $\overparen{Cc_1}$ of $\overparen{CD}$, and so on. Eventually, the crawls get progressively smaller and converge to an intersection x. If no intersection exists, then the coordinated crawl reaches the end of one of the segments (Fig. 2(b)).*

The coordinated crawl as we have presented it will only find the first intersection. The second intersection is found by starting another coordinated crawl from the first intersection. A new

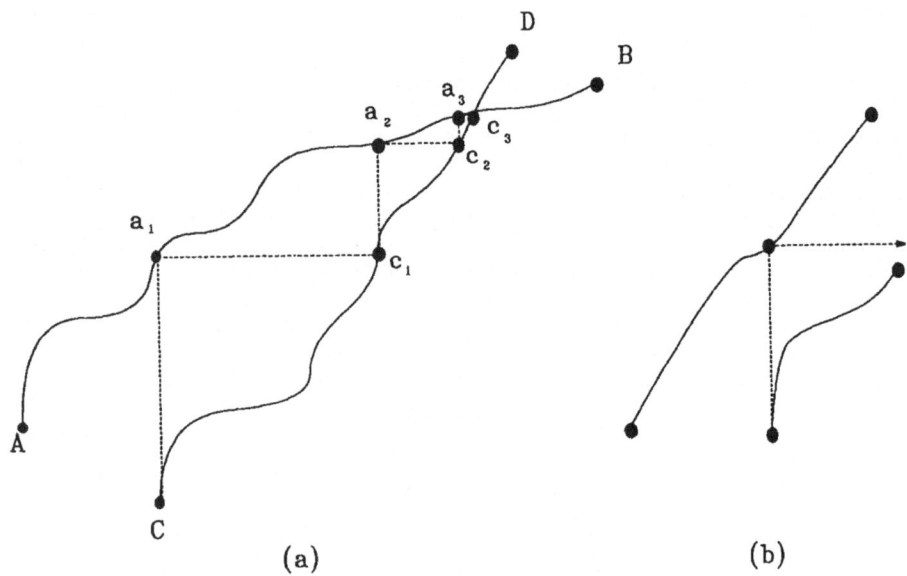

Figure 2: (a-b) Two staircase crawls

coordinated crawl should be begun from each intersection until it is determined by the end condition that the segments do not intersect any further.

We shall present two variants of coordinated crawling, because there are two types of xy-monotone segment. A *rising* xy-monotone segment increases in y as it increases in x, while a *falling* xy-monotone segment decreases in y as it increases in x. The first method of coordinated crawling, which we call the *simultaneous crawl*, can be used to crawl along any pair of xy-monotone segments; however it is best suited to crawling along one rising and one falling segment. The second method, which we call the *staircase crawl*, will only apply to two rising or two falling segments.

We need to define some notation and assumptions. Our notation for a curve segment will not only specify the endpoints, but also the order of the endpoints, in the sense that it is assumed that $x(A) \leq x(B)$ is always true of the segment $\widehat{AB}$, where $x(A)$ denotes the x-coordinate of the point A. P_{active} (resp., P_{dormant}) is our notation for the present point on the active (resp., dormant) segment during a coordinated crawl. Finally, in the remainder of this paper, we assume that all curves are nonlinear, irreducible, plane algebraic curves.

3.1 No Intersection Method is Exact

It is usually impossible to be exact in geometric computations. The reason for this is twofold: (i) because of the use of numerical methods that converge rather than compute exactly, and (ii) because of finite machine precision. This is certainly the case with the system-of-equations method of intersection, which uses numerical methods such as Newton's method. Coordinated crawling is no different, and so we make the following natural assumptions:

1. Two intersections that are less than ϵ distance apart are considered to be the same, where $\epsilon > 0$ is very small and must be part of the input of an intersection problem.

2. If the distance between the two segments decreases below ϵ, then we are free to decide that there is an intersection near this point. In other words, if there is an intersection, then we will always recognize it; but if there is no intersection, then we may sometimes make a mistake and diagnose an intersection.

ϵ may be chosen as small as desired without affecting the efficiency of the coordinated crawl (see Lemma 3 below).

These two assumptions simplify the presentation of coordinated crawling considerably. Moreover, for the purposes of applications such as graphics, the two assumptions are valid not only because of inherent error in computations but because of the inherent crudeness of algorithms, e.g., two segments may as well intersect if they get closer than a pixel. However, if necessary, it is possible to do without them. For a coordinated crawl along a rising and a falling segment, neither of the assumptions is necessary. (That is, a near-intersection will never be mistaken for an intersection, and intersections will always be found within the accuracy of the crawling method that is being used.)

The first assumption can always be removed by the choice of a proper ϵ. For example, one can use Canny's 'gap theorem' (Theorem 1), which reveals that the intersections of two algebraic curves are never too close together.

Lemma 1 (Canny's gap theorem (Canny 1987)) *Let $\wp(d,c)$ be the class of polynomials of degree d and coefficient magnitude c. Let $f_1(x_1,\ldots,x_n),\ldots,f_n(x_1,\ldots,x_n) \in \wp(d,c)$ be a collection of n polynomials in n variables which has only finitely-many solutions when projectivized. Then if $(\alpha_1,\ldots,\alpha_n)$ is a solution of the system, then for any j either $\alpha_j = 0$ or $\ |\alpha_j| > (3dc)^{-nd^n}$.*
∎

Corollary 1 *Let $f_1(x,y) = 0$, $f_2(x,y) = 0$ be two irreducible plane algebraic curves of degree d and coefficient magnitude c. If $\epsilon < (3dc)^{-nd^n}$, then no two intersections will be within an ϵ-distance of each other.*

Proof: In order to apply the lemma, one of the two intersections must be translated to the origin.
∎

The second assumption may be controversial, because the presence of an intersection, or lack thereof, might be important. Therefore, in Section 8, we show how to remove it by checking whether the segments do actually intersect in the neighbourhood in which the distance between the segments is very small.

3.2 Coarse vs. Fine Crawls

In coordinated crawling, we shall distinguish between coarse and fine crawls, depending on the size of each crawl step. A fine crawl will be used to find something accurately and to avoid skipping over an intersection. Thus, fine crawl steps are of length less than ϵ. Coarse crawl steps are as long as possible without losing the curve. Obviously, for reasons of efficiency, it is important that coarse crawls be used as much as possible. The desired paradigm is to use coarse crawls to get close to the intersection and fine crawls only at the end to accurately find the intersection.

For any pair of xy-monotone segments, we shall present a coordinated crawling method such that fine crawls are always short-lived and coarse crawls dominate. Later sections (Section 8.2 and 8.3) will investigate the use of even coarser traversals of the curve, where one skips over a large subsegment of the curve with a single bound (using a line-curve intersection).

4 THE SIMULTANEOUS CRAWL

In order to fully define a coordinated crawl, the switching and end conditions must be defined. In this section, we present the first of our two coordinated crawling methods, the *simultaneous crawl*. With the simultaneous crawl, one simulates crawling along both segments at the same time while maintaining the same velocity with respect to the x-axis, hence its name (Fig. 3(a)). The associated switching condition is $x(P_{\text{active}}) > x(P_{\text{dormant}})$.

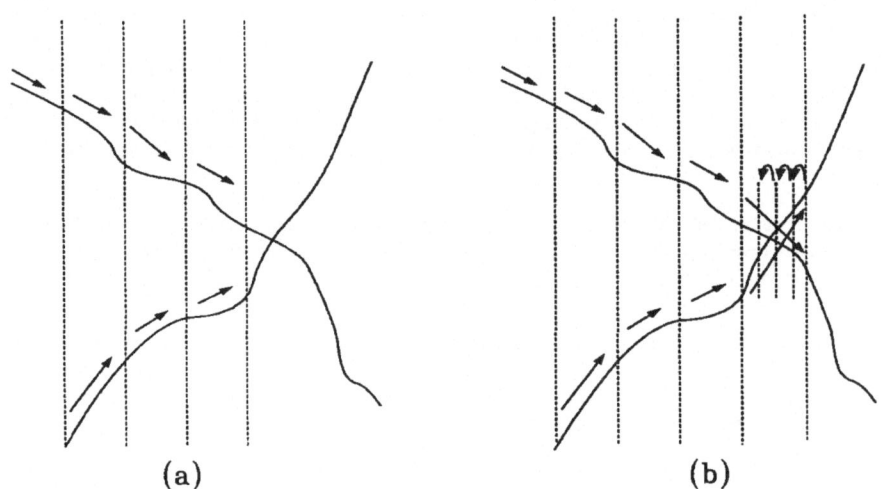

Figure 3: (a) a simultaneous crawl (b) at the end, it must back up finely

The end condition must signal an intersection or the end of a segment. In the neighbourhood of an intersection between a rising segment and a falling segment, the relative vertical order of the segments is reversed. Therefore, a simultaneous crawl along a rising and falling segment can proceed with coarse steps until the relative vertical order of the segments is reversed, and then crawl backwards with finer steps to accurately find the intersection (Fig. 3(b)). (The backwards crawl should continue until the relative vertical order switches once more, which is where the intersection is placed.) There is no danger of skipping over two intersections with the coarse crawl, because a rising and a falling segment can have only one intersection.

Because of x-monotonicity, it is simple to recognize the end of a segment $\widehat{AB}$: the condition is $x(P_{\text{active}}) \geq \min\{x(B), x(D)\}$. Thus, for a simultaneous crawl along a rising segment $\widehat{AB}$ and a falling segment $\widehat{CD}$, the entire end condition is

$$((y(A') < y(C')) \neq (y(A) < y(C))) \;\vee\; x(P_{\text{active}}) \geq \min\{x(B), x(D)\}$$

where A' (resp., C') is the present point on $\widehat{AB}$ (resp., $\widehat{CD}$) during the crawl. The end condition that signals an intersection actually signals only the passing of an intersection: i.e., one must retrace steps back to the intersection before outputting it.

Theoretically, the simultaneous crawl can also be used for two rising (or two falling) segments. A simultaneous crawl along two rising segments is dangerous, because it is possible to skip over a pair of intersections without noticing (Fig. 4). By Lemma 1, this danger could be avoided if the crawl is fine enough. That is, the crawl steps must be finer than 2ϵ where $\epsilon < \sqrt{2(3dc)^{-2nd^n}}$.

(The switch and end conditions would be the same as above, except that there is no need to back up to the intersection after the end condition is signalled since steps are already fine.) Because a simultaneous crawl along two rising segments would require fine steps at all times, the staircase crawl of the next section is preferred for these segments.

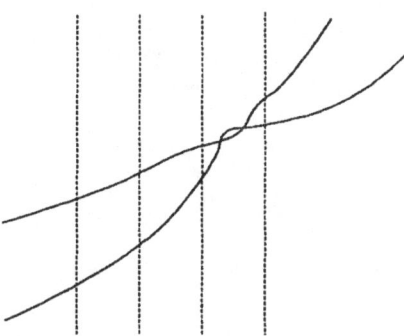

Figure 4: The danger of a simultaneous crawl along two rising segments

5   THE STAIRCASE CRAWL

In this section we present our second method of coordinated crawling, namely for crawling along two rising segments. (Two falling segments are dealt with analogously.) Rather than switching segments as soon as the x-coordinate of the active segment exceeds the x-coordinate of the dormant segment, in the staircase crawl one waits until both the x-coordinate and the y-coordinate of the active segment exceed those of the dormant segment before switching. We call this a *staircase crawl* because if the endpoints of the crawls are joined by straight lines, a staircase leading towards an intersection will result (Fig. 2 and Lemma 2). The associated switching condition is

$$x(P_{\text{active}}) > x(P_{\text{dormant}}) \ \wedge \ y(P_{\text{active}}) > y(P_{\text{dormant}})$$

Because of the granularity of the crawl, an intersection might be overlooked with this switch condition (Fig. 5). To correct this, before switching segments one should back up one step so that the active segment remains behind the staircase. (This is similar to backing up in the simultaneous crawl to find the intersection accurately.)

An intersection is signalled when a stair of height less than ϵ is encountered. (This is the only place that the second assumption about ϵ from Section 3.1 is used.) Every intersection will be found with this end condition, because the staircase converges to an intersection (see Lemma 2) and we do not jump past the staircase. Thus, the end condition for a staircase crawl is simply:

$$\mid y(P_{\text{active}}) - y(P_{\text{dormant}}) \mid < \epsilon \ \vee \ x(P_{\text{active}}) > \min\{x(B), x(D)\}$$

Coarse crawls are used until the coordinated crawl approaches near an intersection. At this point, each crawl then becomes very short and fine crawls should be used. If a coarse crawl is used near an intersection, it is possible to enter an infinite loop: continually going forward one step (at which point both x and y coordinates of the active segment exceed those of the dormant) and then back one step (to stay behind the staircase). With a fine crawl, however, this will not happen, because if only one fine step (of length less than ϵ) separates the x and y-coordinates, the height of the present stair must be less than ϵ and an intersection will be signalled. Since an

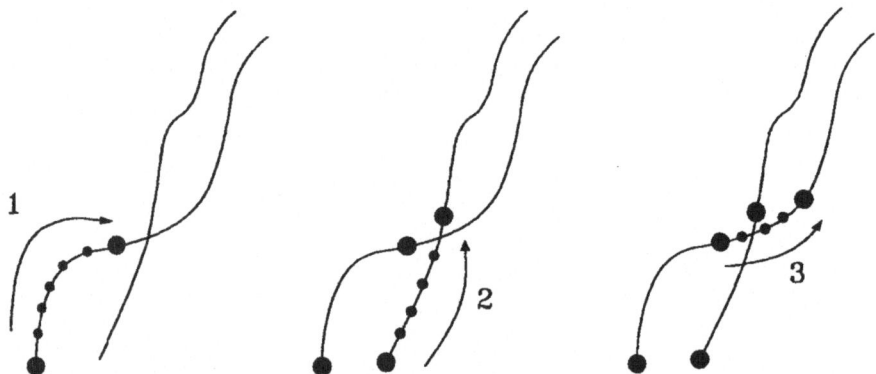

Figure 5: The danger of a staircase crawl that does not back up one step after each crawl

infinite loop is only possible when the length of a stair of the staircase becomes as short as a step of a coarse crawl, fine crawls are only necessary near the intersection. (In an intermediate phase when strictly coarse crawls are too crude but strictly fine crawls are too slow, one might use a coarse crawl to crawl forward and a fine crawl to back up.)

We must show that the staircase crawl converges to the first intersection of the segments, if one exists.

Lemma 2 *Let $\widehat{AB}$ and $\widehat{CD}$ be two rising segments. The staircase crawl along $\widehat{AB}$ and $\widehat{CD}$ will converge to the first intersection of $\widehat{AB}$ and $\widehat{CD}$, if such an intersection exists. Otherwise, it will reach the endpoint (B or D) of one of the segments.*

Proof: Firstly, one does not jump over an intersection. This is best seen by considering the perfect staircase: the staircase consisting of true horizontal and vertical line segments. (The stairs of the staircase connecting the endpoints of the actual staircase crawl would not be perfectly horizontal or vertical.) It is easy to see that the perfect staircase converges to an intersection. The staircase crawl is guided by the perfect staircase. Because the staircase crawl backs up before switching segments, it is indeed constrained by the perfect staircase.

Secondly, progress is made with each crawl. If there is no progress, then the stair must be of height less than ϵ and we say that an intersection has been found. In particular, progress of at least ϵ (usually much more) is made with each crawl. Thus, the staircase crawl must eventually find the first intersection, if one exists. ∎

A staircase crawl diagnoses an intersection when the stairs become shorter than ϵ. Two questions arise: where should the intersection be placed and where should the crawl start over to look for the next intersection? The crawl cannot place the intersection where it stopped and continue from there, because it will immediately stop and diagnose another intersection. We introduce the concept of an ϵ-zone to provide the answer to these questions. The *ϵ-zone* is a pair of subsegments of the curves that stay within a vertical distance of ϵ. We enter an ϵ-zone when the vertical distance between the segments becomes less than ϵ (in practice, the ϵ-zone actually begins when a stair of height $< \epsilon$ is found) and exit it when the vertical distance becomes greater than ϵ (Fig. 6).

Now the two questions can be answered. When a stair of a staircase crawl becomes shorter than ϵ, we skip over the associated ϵ-zone, and restart the staircase crawl there. The intersection is placed in the middle of the ϵ-zone (or it can be found exactly with the method outlined in Section 8.4).

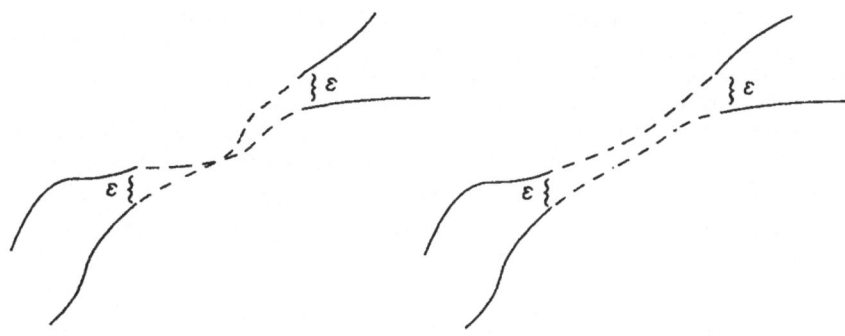

Figure 6: ϵ-zones

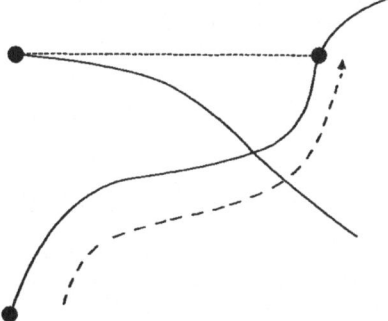

Figure 7: A staircase crawl cannot be used for a rising and a falling segment

A simultaneous crawl is used to cross the ϵ-zone. (As mentioned at the end of Section 4, this will use fine crawls so it is perfect for crossing the ϵ-zone.)

The first crawl after an intersection must be treated as a special case, because neither segment dominates. In order to get things started, one should make an ϵ-crawl along one of the segments. It might seem that this crawl is dangerous because it may skip over an intersection, being blind and unconstrained by any staircase. However, recall that any two intersections that are within ϵ of each other are considered equivalent; thus, it is impossible to skip over a relevant intersection.

We end this section and our discussion of methods for coordinated crawling by noting that the staircase crawl cannot be used to find the intersection of a rising and a falling segment. This is shown by Fig. 7. Since we have already noted that the simultaneous crawl is not well suited for the intersection of two rising segments (because fine crawls are always necessary), one can see that both types of coordinated crawling are necessary. With the ability to do a simultaneous crawl and a staircase crawl, one can find the intersection(s) of any pair of xy-monotone segments by crawling, and moreover most of the crawling uses coarse steps.

6   EFFICIENCY

A simultaneous crawl is continually switching from one segment to the other. Indeed, of the two segments between any two adjacent vertical lines in Fig. 3(a), one will be a single crawl step long. It might appear that this large number of switches will make the crawl expensive. The following lemma shows that this is not the case, because switches are essentially free.

Lemma 3 *The number of switches in a coordinated crawl is irrelevant.*

Proof: A coordinated crawl along two segments is slightly less efficient than crawling independently along the entire first segment and then crawling independently along the entire second segment, because one must test the switching and end conditions at each step. However, the number of switches does not matter because stopping and starting a crawl takes no time. This can be seen as follows. Let $\widehat{AB}$ and $\widehat{CD}$ be xy-monotone segments. We can keep two separate regions in memory, one set up for crawling along $\widehat{AB}$, the other for crawling along $\widehat{CD}$. Switching crawls merely involves jumping to the other part of memory. (In Section 8 we shall show that a coordinated crawl need not crawl along all of the two segments, so that the complexity of a coordinated crawl is actually less than the complexity of making two 'independent crawls with condition testing'.) ■

It might seem that if the segments remain very close for a long time, then a staircase crawl will be slow because the staircase is very fine with very short stairs. Similarly, it might appear that a staircase crawl will slow down as its stairs get very short during convergence to an intersection. Lemma 3 shows that these intuitions are also wrong.

7   XY-MONOTONE DECOMPOSITION

Since our coordinated crawling methods work upon xy-monotone segments, the first step in intersecting two segments with the coordinated crawling method is to partition each curve segment into xy-monotone curve segments. Observe that a curve segment is xy-monotone if and only if it contains no local extrema (no changes in direction with respect to the x-axis or y-axis). An xy-monotone decomposition of a segment can be computed by crawling along the segment. One simply marks points at which $x(P)$ or $y(P)$ changes direction, where $P = (x(P), y(P))$ is the present point on the crawl. The nature of crawling guarantees that one will not miss any direction changes during a crawl. Therefore, the complexity of the xy-monotone decomposition of a segment is the complexity of crawling along the segment.

An alternative method is to compute the local extrema of the segment algebraically, using the fact that the local extrema of a curve $f(x, y) = 0$ are the solutions of $\{f_x = 0, f = 0\}$ and $\{f_y = 0, f = 0\}$. Indeed, since it is trivial to compute the local extrema of a curve as part of computing the singularities of a curve (since the singularities are the solutions of $\{f_x = 0, f_y = 0, f = 0\}$) and the singularities of an algebraic curve are fundamental to many geometric modeling algorithms (e.g., Abhyankar and Bajaj 1986; Johnstone 1987), the local extrema may already be known. If not, one can use the SOE method to compute the local extrema via $\{f_x = 0, f = 0\}$ and $\{f_y = 0, f = 0\}$. This may seem to lead to a circularity in our method. However, the key is to consider the xy-monotone decomposition as a one-time overhead. That is, the amortization of a total of two curve-curve intersections over many intersections (when coordinated crawling is used) is an improvement over the need for a curve-curve intersection for each intersection. The expense of preprocessing is well warranted for curves in a solid model, because they are relatively permanent and intersection is a common operation. After computing the extrema, they must be sorted along the curve in order to pair the extrema into xy-monotone segment endpoints.

Although we mention the algebraic method for xy-monotone decomposition for completeness, xy-monotone decomposition by crawling is probably the best choice, since we are dealing with segments.

8   IMPROVEMENTS

8.1   Aborting Early

In this section we outline some methods for improving the efficiency of a coordinated crawl. A coordinated crawl can be aborted as soon as it becomes apparent that the two segments cannot intersect. We begin with a set of conditions that guarantee the distinctness of two xy-monotone segments.

Lemma 4 *Let $\widehat{AB}$ and $\widehat{CD}$ be xy-monotone segments. If any of the following conditions is true, then $\widehat{AB}$ and $\widehat{CD}$ do not intersect.*

1. $x(B) < x(C)$

2. $x(D) < x(A)$

3. $\{y(A), y(B)\} < \{y(C), y(D)\}$

4. $\{y(C), y(D)\} < \{y(A), y(B)\}$

5. $\widehat{AB}$ and $\widehat{CD}$ are convex (a segment is convex if no line has more than two distinct intersections with it) and $\triangle AB \cap \triangle CD = \emptyset$ (Fig. 8). $\triangle AB$ is the triangle whose sides are the tangent at A, the tangent at B, and $\overline{AB}$.

Proof: The sufficiency of conditions (1)-(4) is a straightforward consequence of the xy-monotonicity of the segments. (Recall that $x(A) \leq x(B)$ is implicit from the notation $\widehat{AB}$.) The sufficiency of the fifth condition follows from noting that if $\widehat{AB}$ is convex, then $\triangle AB$ contains $\widehat{AB}$. ∎

These conditions should be tested throughout the coordinated crawl. (Of course, the condition involving convex segments would only be tested if we had prior knowledge that the segments were convex as well as xy-monotone.) In order to lighten the computational burden, they might only be tested intermittently, rather than after every step.

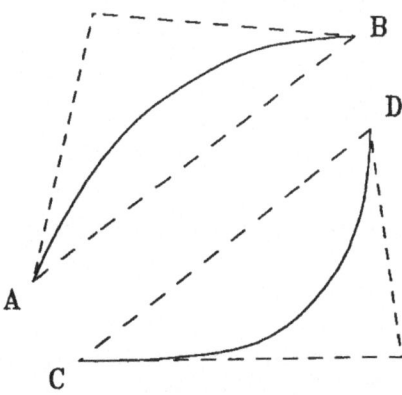

Figure 8: $\widehat{AB}$ and $\widehat{CD}$ cannot intersect

8.2 Eliminating Long Crawls in the Staircase Crawl

We have noted that a coordinated crawl should use coarse crawls whenever possible. In this section, we show how to make even larger jumps in a staircase crawl. In particular, it is possible to replace a crawl (from one stair endpoint to the next) by a single line-curve intersection.

In a staircase crawl, one climbs a staircase towards an intersection. This process can be fully characterized by the series of endpoints of the stairs. For example, the staircase crawl of Fig. 2 can be represented by C, a_1, c_1, a_2, c_2,..., x. The act of climbing a stair (i.e., finding the next endpoint in the series) is equivalent to finding the intersection of a line with one of the curve segments. In particular, the endpoint that follows endpoint E on curve segment 1 is the intersection with curve segment 2 of a horizontal or vertical line through E. This suggests another method for climbing the stair: use the system-of-equations (SOE) method to find the intersection of the line and curve segment.

Since a staircase crawl is being used, supposedly the SOE method is not practical for the intersection of the two curve segments. However, it may be feasible for the simpler intersection of a line and one of the curve segments. The time to climb a stair $E_i E_{i+1}$ of the staircase $E_1, E_2, \ldots, E_n$ by crawling depends upon the length of the segment $\widehat{E_{i-1}E_{i+1}}$, whereas the time to climb a stair with a line-curve intersection depends on the degree of the curve that we are climbing to. Therefore, the taller the stair and the lower the degree of the curve, the more attractive it is to climb the stair with a line-curve intersection.

It may be difficult to decide when the next stair should be climbed with a line-curve intersection rather than a crawl. The following lemma could be used to approximate the cost of climbing it with a crawl.

Lemma 5 *The length of an xy-monotone segment $\widehat{AB}$ is bounded by $\sqrt{2}dist(A,B)$.*

Proof: Consider the right triangle with hypotenuse $\overline{AB}$, whose other sides are horizontal and vertical (Fig. 9). By xy-monotonicity, it is easy to see that the length of $\widehat{AB}$ is bounded by two of the sides of the triangle, $\mid x(B) - x(A) \mid + \mid y(B) - y(A) \mid = a + b$. The result follows by noticing that $a + b = c(\sin\theta + \cos\theta)$ and $\max_\theta(\sin\theta + \cos\theta) = \sqrt{2}$ (at $\theta = \frac{\pi}{4}$). ∎

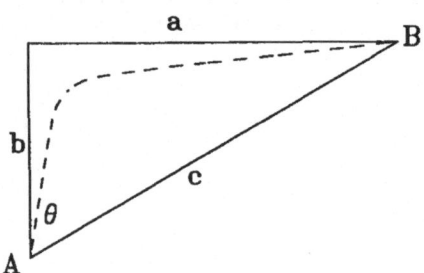

Figure 9: The length of $\widehat{AB}$ is bounded by $a + b$

8.3 Speeding Up the Simultaneous Crawl

The simultaneous crawl can also benefit from the use of line-curve intersections to replace crawls. In this case, the analogy is to root-finding of univariate polynomials, where binary search is used to isolate a region for the root before Newton's method is applied. In finding the unique intersection of a rising and a falling segment, it may be useful to use a binary search for the intersection with line-curve intersections before beginning the actual simultaneous crawl (Fig. 10). (A binary search is not possible for the intersection of two rising segments, since there may be more than one intersection and a binary search only makes sense when searching for a single element.) A probe of this 'binary search' is the intersection of a vertical line with both curve segments to determine their relative vertical order. If the relative vertical order is the same as the beginning of the segments, then the intersection must lie to the right of the probe.

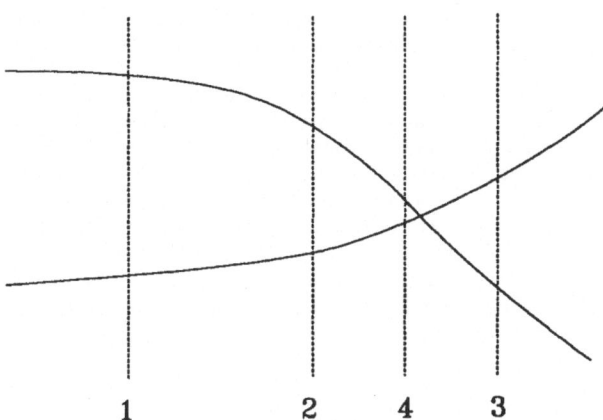

Figure 10: A binary search for the intersection

The binary search may allow the simultaneous crawl to begin closer to the intersection. It is difficult to determine the number of probes that should be made. There is a tradeoff between the number of line-curve intersections that are computed and the amount of crawling that is saved. As a general rule, the binary search would continue longer if the degree of the curves is low (since line-curve intersections will be cheap) or if the curve segments are long (since one can anticipate a lot of crawling).

8.4 Finding an Intersection Exactly

In the staircase crawl, we only approximated the intersection by placing it in the middle of an ϵ-zone. Moreover, we assumed that there actually was an intersection in the ϵ-zone, although there might not have been one. This was justified by the second assumption of Section 3.1. However, it is possible to discover whether or not there is an intersection and, if there is, to find it more exactly. The idea is to use two Newton's method searches for the intersection, restricting the search to the ϵ-zone of the potential intersection.

Suppose that we are intersecting the xy-monotone segments $\widehat{AB}$ and $\widehat{CD}$ on curves $f(x,y)$ and $g(x,y)$, respectively. Suppose that an ϵ-zone begins at $p \in \widehat{AB}$ and ends at $q \in \widehat{AB}$. We shall restrict our search to the rectangle R bounded by $x = x(p)$, $x = x(q)$, $y = y(p)$, and $y = y(q)$. Let $h(x)$ be the resultant of f and g with respect to x (see Section 2), so $h(x_0) = 0$ if and only if f and g have an intersection (x_0, y_0). First, perform a search for a root x_0 of $h(x)$, using Newton's method starting at $\frac{x(p)+x(q)}{2}$ and abandoning the search if it leaves $[x(p),x(q)]$. Second, perform a search for a root y_0 of $f(x_0,y)$, using Newton's method starting at $\frac{y(p)+y(q)}{2}$ and abandoning the search if it leaves $[y(p),y(q)]$. (x_0, y_0) is an intersection in the ϵ-zone. If no (x_0, y_0) is found, then report that the segments do not intersect. Note that both searches take very little time, since we are restricting them to a very small region.

9 INTERSECTING ARBITRARY CURVE SEGMENTS

We have discussed how to intersect two xy-monotone segments. However, the original goal was to intersect two arbitrary segments. Since the two original segments were decomposed into xy-monotone segments, we must show how to find the intersections of a collection of xy-monotone segments. Rather than using the naive $O(n^2)$ algorithm of intersecting every pair, we shall use a variant of plane sweep to reduce this to looking at only $O(n + k)$ pairs, where k is the number of intersections. The advantage of this plane sweep method (based on the familiar plane sweep of Bentley and Ottmann 1979) is that it avoids testing pairs that are never vertically adjacent.

We begin by inserting all of the xy-monotone segment endpoints into a priority queue E (sorted by x-coordinate). We will be sweeping a vertical line L through the plane from left to right. As we sweep we will maintain a data base D, which consists of all curve segments that intersect L, stored in sorted order by their intersections with L. We represent D as a (2,3)-tree (Aho et. al. 1974) (or some equivalent efficient dynamic search structure). Note that since the segments are xy-monotone, each segment will intersect L at most once. As we sweep L to the right we need to stop at various *event* points to maintain the consistency of the data base D. The priority queue E determines the events. An event is either an endpoint or an intersection point. With each curve C we also keep a priority queue E(C), which stores the names of all the curves that we have compared with C already. These lists will prevent us from performing any redundant intersection tests.

A generic step in the plane-sweep algorithm is as follows. Remove the point in E with minimum x-coordinate. Let p be this point. Intuitively, this corresponds to moving L to the right until it hits p. We must then update D depending on the identity of p. We identify each of the possible cases below.

Case 1. The point p is the left endpoint of a curve segment C (Fig. 11). In order to maintain the consistency of our data base, we must insert C in D. To do this we must find the curve segment C_1 in D such that C_1 intersects L in the highest point below p, i.e., C_1 is directly below p. We can do this by making $O(\log n)$ curve comparisons to find a path in the tree D from the root to the place where C belongs. Each such curve comparison determines if a curve C' intersects L above or below p, and is implemented by crawling along C' from the previous event point on C' until you reach L, as in Fig. 11 (or by performing a line-curve intersection). After we have located where C belongs in D, suppose that C_1 (resp., C_2) is C's predecessor (resp., successor) curve in D. We check if C_1 is already in $E(C)$ and, if not, intersect C with C_1 (using coordinated crawling). Similarly, we check if C_2 is already in $E(C)$ and, if not, intersect C with C_2. We add all discovered intersection points p to the priority queue E as long as the two curves cross at p (as opposed to simply 'touching'). We also add C to $E(C_1)$ and $E(C_2)$ and add C_1 and C_2 to $E(C)$. At first glance, one might worry that the crawling involved in the curve comparisons might become prohibitive. However, even in the pathological worst case, the entire time required for inserting C into D is bounded by the time to crawl along $\log n$ segments, which is not a significant expense when compared to the alternative of finding the intersections between all $O(n^2)$ segment-pairs.

The coordinated crawl for intersecting two xy-monotone segments should be started from L, not from the beginning of the segments.

Case 2. The point p is an intersection point. If C_1 and C_2 are the two curves that intersect at p, then we swap them in D. Without loss of generality, assume C_2 now occurs before C_1 in the list D. Let C_0 be the new predecessor of C_2 and let C_3 be the new successor of C_1. Provided C_0 is not in $E(C_2)$, we find the intersections of C_0 and C_2 (and insert them into the event queue E). Similarly, we intersect C_1 and C_3, provided C_3 is not in $E(C_1)$. We then update $E(C_0)$, $E(C_1)$, $E(C_2)$, and $E(C_3)$ as necessary.

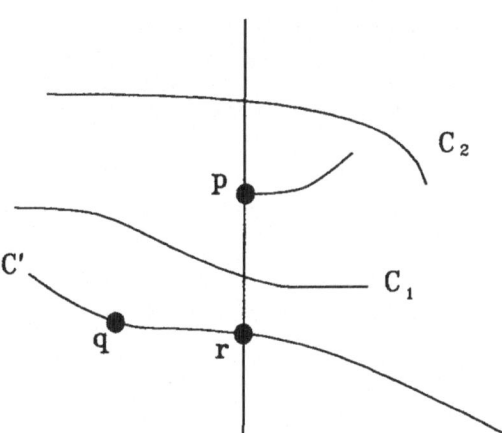

Figure 11: A curve comparison between C' and p: crawl from q to r

Case 3. The point p is a right endpoint of a curve C. In this case, we delete C from D. We then need to intersect the two neighbours C_1 and C_2 of C at p (which are now adjacent), after checking if C_1 is already in $E(C_2)$. Of course, we then update $E(C_1)$ and $E(C_2)$ as necessary.

Since these are all the possible cases, this completes the algorithm. We summarize with the following theorem:

Theorem 1 *Given n xy-monotone curve segments in the plane, one can compute all of their intersection points with $O(n + k)$ segment-segment intersections, where k is the number of intersection points.*

Proof: The only time that segment-segment intersections are made is when inserting or deleting an event from the event queue E. Each (of $2n$) segment endpoints and each (of k intersections) are inserted and deleted from E, and at most two segment-segment intersections are performed with each insertion or deletion. ∎

The benefits of this algorithm will be most strongly felt when the segments S are of a different order of complexity from the curves $C \supset S$. Note that the same plane-sweep algorithm can be applied to the intersection of any collection of algebraic curve segments, just as well as two algebraic curve segments.

10 CONCLUSIONS

By extending the technique of crawling along one segment to a technique of coordinated crawling along two segments, we have introduced a new method for intersecting plane algebraic curve segments. It takes advantage of the locality and simplicity of the segments, unlike the system-of-equations method of intersection. Rather than first finding all of the intersections between the curves (which seems unnatural), our method directly finds only the intersections between the segments.

The coordinated crawling method can be especially useful when combinatorial explosion of degree sets in with the SOE method. That is, among other things, the conventional SOE method entails the solution of a univariate equation (the resultant of the two curves) whose degree is the product of the degrees of the curves, and the solution of an equation of high degree soon becomes prohibitive. The coordinated crawling method only involves the evaluation of equations whose degree is the degree of the curves (for crawling), which is simpler for two reasons: because of the lower degree of the equation and because evaluation is easier than solution. Therefore, the coordinated crawling method may be the only feasible method when the degree of the curves becomes large.

ACKNOWLEDGEMENTS

We would like to thank C. Bajaj and M. S. Kim for helpful conversations.

REFERENCES

Aho A, Hopcroft J, Ullman J (1974) The design and analysis of computer algorithms. Addison-Wesley, Reading, MA.

Abhyankar S, Bajaj C (1986) Automatic parameterization of rational curves and surfaces III: algebraic plane curves. Tech. Rep. CSD-TR-619, Dept. of Computer Science, Purdue University.

Bajaj C, Hoffmann C, Hopcroft J (1987) Tracing planar algebraic curves. Tech. Rep. CSD-TR-637, Dept. of Computer Science, Purdue University.

Bentley JL, Ottmann TA (1979) Algorithms for reporting and counting geometric intersections. IEEE Trans. on Computers C-28(9): 643–647.

Canny JF (1987) The complexity of robot motion planning. Ph.D. Thesis, Dept. of Computer Science, MIT.

Dobkin DP, Thurston WP, Wilks AR (1986) Robust contour tracing. Tech. Rep. CS-TR-054-86, Dept. of Computer Science, Princeton University.

Edelsbrunner H (1987) Algorithms in combinatorial geometry. Springer-Verlag, New York.

Hoffmann CM (1987) Algebraic curves. Tech. Rep. CSD-TR-675, Dept. of Computer Science, Purdue University.

Hoffmann CM, Lynch RE (1987) Following space curves numerically. Tech. Rep. CSD-TR-684, Dept. of Computer Science, Purdue University.

Johnstone JK (1987) The sorting of points along an algebraic curve. Tech. Rep. 87-841, Ph.D. Thesis, Dept. of Computer Science, Cornell University.

McKenna M (1987) Worst-case optimal hidden-surface removal. ACM Trans. on Graphics 6(1): 19–28.

Mortenson ME (1985) Geometric modeling. John Wiley and Sons, New York.

Owen JC, Rockwood AP (1987) Intersection of general implicit surfaces. In: Farin G (ed) Geometric modeling: algorithms and new trends. SIAM, Philadelphia, pp. 335–345.

Preparata FP, Shamos MI (1985) Computational geometry: an introduction. Springer-Verlag, New York.

Requicha AAG (1980) Representations for rigid solids: theory, methods, and systems. Computing Surveys 12(4): 437–464.

Sechrest S, Greenberg DP (1982) A visibility polygon reconstruction algorithm. ACM Trans. on Graphics 1(1): 25–42.

Sederberg TW, Anderson DC, Goldman RN (1984) Implicit representation of parametric curves and surfaces. Computer Vision, Graphics, and Image Processing 28: 72–84.

Timmer HG (1977) Analytical background for computation of surface intersections. Douglas Aircraft Company Technical Memorandum C1-250-CAT-77-036, cited in (Mortenson 1985).

van der Waerden BL (1953) Modern Algebra. Frederick Ungar, New York.

Walker RJ (1950) Algebraic curves. Springer-Verlag, New York.

John K. Johnstone is an assistant professor of computer science at The Johns Hopkins University. He earned a Ph.D. in computer science from Cornell University in 1987, where he was supported by a Canadian NSERC Scholarship and a Cornell Sage Fellowship. Prof. Johnstone conducts research in geometric modeling and robotics. Methods that can be applied to models involving curves and surfaces of high degree are of especial interest.
Address: Dept. of Computer Science, The Johns Hopkins University, Baltimore, MD, USA, 21218.

Michael T. Goodrich is an assistant professor of computer science at The Johns Hopkins University. He earned a Ph.D. in computer science from Purdue University in 1987, where he was a Compere Loveless Fellow. With National Science Foundation support, Prof. Goodrich conducts research in computational geometry and parallel algorithms.
Address: Dept. of Computer Science, The Johns Hopkins University, Baltimore, MD, USA, 21218.

Optimal Linear Octree Construction Algorithm by Sweep Operations

S.N. Yang and B.S. Jong

ABSTRACT

The octree and the sweep are two well known representations in solid modeling. In this paper, we will introduce efficient linear octree construction algorithms from both translational and rotational sweeps. The underlying notion of our algorithms are based on the greedy method to devise an optimal sweeping process. We show the total sweeping time is linear with respect to the number of nodes generated if we leave these nodes unsorted. Then we develop an improved algorithm which can produce well ordered octree nodes in linear time. The extension from translational sweep to rotational sweep is also studied. Examples are given to demonstrate the capability of the sweep operations.

Keywords : algorithm complexity, linear quadtree, linear octree, solid modeling, Sweep representation.

1. INTRODUCTION

A geometric modeling system provides various representations that allow user to create, manipulate and display the described solids. Existing geometrical modelings such as Constructive Solid Geometry(CSG) and the boundary representation have problems with Boolean operations and interference checking, which are essential to CAD/CAM applications. The octree data structure has been found suitable for these operations (Meagher 1982).

The octree data structure can be considered as an approximation of a 3D object by a set of cubes organized hierarchically according to their sizes (Chen and Huang 1988; Hunter and Steiglitz 1979; Jackins and Tanimoto 1980; Meagher 1982). Since the pointer based octree structures require much more computer storage, recently there has been a considerable amount of interest in pointerless tree structures (Gargantini 1983; Samet and Tamminen 1985). The linear structure which stores only the location code of each black node in a sorted array has been shown to be effective in memory saving and practical in many applications (Atkinson, Gargantini, and Walsh 1986; Gargantini 1982a, 1982b, 1983, 1986; Lin and Yang 1987; Samet and Tamminen 1985; Shaffer and Samet 1987).

Using octree data structure to model 3D objects has been studied extensively by many researchers. In (Yau and Srihari 1983), a method for constructing the octree of an object from quadtree encoded cross sections was presented. Chien and Aggarwal (1986) designed an algorithm for constructing an octree from its three face views. A comprehensive survey of various constructions for octrees can be found in (Chen and Huang 1988). Most of these constructions are based on the octree with pointers and in this paper we will focus on the constructions of linear octrees.

For the octree construction, since many solids involve a great amount of octree nodes, it is too verbose for a user to define a solid node by node interactively. Hence most existing constructions are carried out automatically according to certain algorithms. On the other hand the sweep representation which specifies a solid either by sweeping a planar region along a line segment or rotating it about a given axis, provides a rather simple way for user to define certain class of solid objects. Therefore we are motivated by trying to have a modeling method with the sweep representation as its external definition and the linear octree as its internal definition.

In this paper we will introduce automatic conversions from both translational and rotational sweep to the linear octree representation. First we assume the two dimensional region is encoded with a linear quadtree structure, this can be done easily (Gargantini 1982). Then by sweeping each quadtree node properly, we will obtain all octree nodes of the swept object. In order to avoid further condensations, we propose an incremental sweeping scheme to ensure a linear time construction. Since in many applications, tree nodes are required to be sorted, the complexity of this simple sweeping algorithm is bounded by the sorting process.

By carefully examining the spatial relations among tree nodes, we devise a new sweeping procedure which can generate all sorted octcodes in linear time. That is the improved algorithm runs in time $O(B)$ and the previous one runs in time $O(B\log B)$ asymptotically, where B is the number of black nodes in the octree. Empirical tests will be given to compare these two methods. Finally we discuss the extension from the translational sweep to the rotational sweep.

2. DEFINITIONS

The octree data structure is basically an approximation of a three dimensional object by a set of cubes in various sizes. To create hierarchical indices for a octree representation, we begin with a cube, called the universe (Meagher 1982), large enough to accommodate the object which we wish to model. Then the octree is generated by dividing the universe into eight equal cubes called octants. And each octant is repeatedly subdivided into suboctants until each octant has the uniform attribute or reaches the given resolution (Figure 1).

Here we assume the universe is composed of $2^n * 2^n * 2^n$ voxels. The root of an octree corresponds to the object itself and each node in an octree is either a leaf node or a gray node which has out–degree eight. To be more precisely, a leaf node is the node with uniform attribute and can be typed either black or white depending on whether its corresponding octant is entirely inside or entirely outside of the represented object, and a gray node is an octant with non–uniform attribute and subjected to further decomposition.

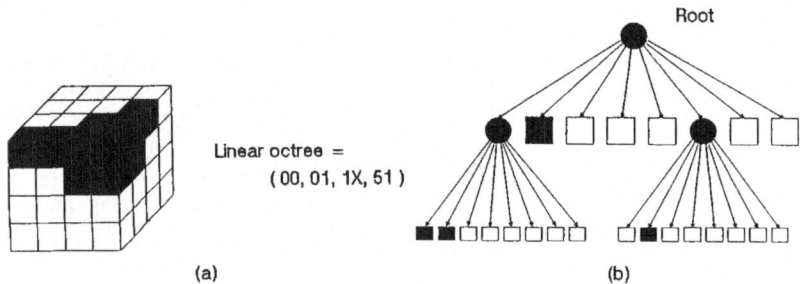

Linear octree =
(00, 01, 1X, 51)

(a)   (b)

Fig. 1.   Octree and linear octree representations of the object

Inevitable in octree structure is the use of pointers which occupy a considerable amount of storage and possibly result in an increase of processing time due to high rate of page faults. Hence the concept of linearization emerges (Gargantini 1982a, 1982b). It can be regarded as an encoding scheme with the following characteristics (Gargantini 1982a, 1982b): (1) Only black nodes are stored. (2) Pointers are eliminated. (3) The code of each node encodes the path from the root to each node implicitly. (4) Octree nodes are arranged in a strictly increasing sequence according to their codes. (5) The sorted sequence of encoded nodes retains the order in the post–order traversal of the octree. (6) The linear octree can be transformed back to a pointer based octree without loss of information. The quadtree and the linear quadtree are two dimensional versions of the octree and the linear octree respectively, therefore they share similar properties.

In this paper we will adapt the encoding scheme and the coordinate system introduced in (Gargantini 1982a, 1982b). Let the universe is a $2^n * 2^n * 2^n$ spatial array, then each voxel D is encoded as $D = (D_{n-1}D_{n-2}...D_0)$, where D_i is an octal number. An octree node is of level i if it represents an octant of size $2^i * 2^i * 2^i$. Condensation can be introduced to encode linear octree, that is, if a black node is of level i (i = 1,2, ... , n−1), then we replace $D_{i-1}D_{i-2}...D_0$ by some kind of marker, here denoted by x. As an example, the object and its corresponding linear octree are shown in Figure 1.

A similar encoding scheme for linear quadtree can be found in (Gargantini 1982a). The terms octcode and quadcode will then refer to the coding schemes just introduced. Since there is a one to one correspondence between a tree node and its code, we will use them interchangeably.

3. TRANSLATIONAL SWEEP

The translational sweep is a way to define a solid by moving a planar region along certain direction. For convenience, we will call that initial plane as the base plane. A sweep is called an orthogonal sweep if the sweeping direction is perpendicular to the base plane. In this paper we will confine ourself to the following sweep.

Definition: Let R be a planar region represented by the linear quadtree encoding. A linear quadtree to a linear octree sweep (LQO) is a triple (R,s,e) which defines a linear octree encoded solid by the following orthogonal sweep along the positive Z axis: (1) The base plane is parallel to the X–Y plane with $(0,0) \in R$ placed at $(0,0,s)$. (2) The coordinate axes on the base plane is the orthogonal projection of X and Y axes. (3) The sweep starts at $(0,0,s)$ and ends at $(0,0,e)$.

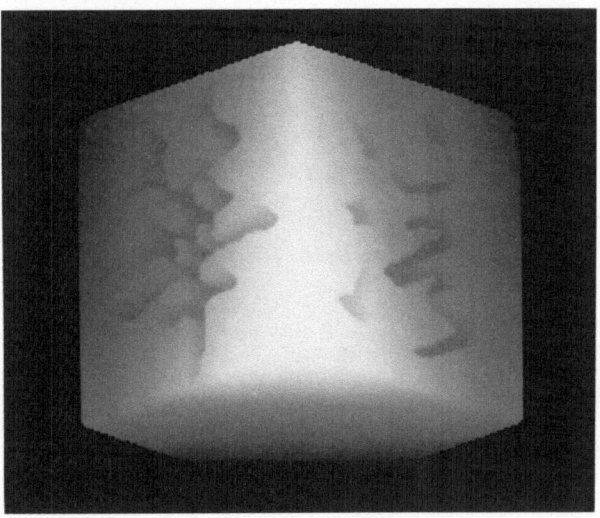

Fig. 2.   Chinese seal modeled by the LQO sweep

Objects which can be described by the variance of cross–sections are best suited to apply LQO sweep even it has holes inside. Figure 2 shows that a negative chinese seal can be modeled by the LQO sweep.

4. LQO SWEEP ALGORITHM

A naive way to construct a swept linear octree can be done by sweeping black pixels and then carry out the bottom up condensations of all voxels. This construction will take time proportional to the number of voxels in the octree. In the following we introduce an algorithm which takes time proportional to the number of black nodes generated. Therefore it is optimal as far as the generation itself is concerned. Extra sorting process is required if we want to keep these nodes in order. The underlying notion of our method is very simple, if we sweep each quadtree node individually to form a 3D column then we can show the whole solid is the union of these columns and there is no further condensation among different columns. Therefore we only have to study how to sweep each column efficiently. The following lemmas state this fact.

Lemma 1 Let $R = \cup q_i$, where q_is are quadtree nodes then $(R,s,e) = \cup (q_i,s,e)$. Furthermore if o is an octree node of (R,s,e) then $o \in (q_i,s,e)$ for some i.

Now let us consider (q_i,s,e) where q_i is a quadtree node. If we sweep too far we may need recursive subdivisions to find all octree nodes in this sweep. If we sweep too near, further condensations will be called. Our goal is to manage the step size so that the octree nodes generated by one step of the sweep can be computed easily and efficiently. In the other words we try to control the sweeping speed so that each step is on the right place without causing any further condensation and subdivision. The following lemmas provide upper bounds for the step size.

Lemma 2 Let q_0 be a quadtree node of level i, then all octree nodes in (q_0,s,e) are of level less than or equal to i.

Lemma 3 An octant of level l must have its front face on the plane $Z = k2^l$ ($0 \le k < 2^{n-l}$). Conversely if the front face of an octant is on the plane $Z = k2^l$ ($k \neq 0$) then its level is no less than l. Furthermore if k is odd then its level is bounded by l.

For computational purpose, we give another version of lemma 3. Suppose $(b_{n-1}b_{n-2}...b_0)$ is the binary representation of $0 \le s < 2^n$. We define $LSB(s) = \min \{ j, b_j \neq 0 \}$, if $s \neq 0$; $LSB(0) = n$ if $s = 0$. Then we have the following.

Lemma 4 Let an octree node $o \in (q_0,s,e)$ with its front face at $Z = s$. Let $l = LSB(s)$, then the level of o is bounded by l.

Our sweeping algorithm is based on the greedy strategy, that is for each step we have to sweep a largest possible size of a cube to avoid further condensation. But the upper bounds in lemma 2 and lemma 4 will prevent us from too greedy. Therefore we can choose the minimum of these two bounds as our step size. Then by exploiting the neighbor index computing scheme, we can compute all octcodes within this step of sweep. This process can be continued incrementally as long as the step size is within the range. Now we will investigate the sweeping process when it approaches to the end. Consider the sweep (q_0,s,e). Suppose the level of q_0 is i and $LSB(s)=l$. Let $d = e - s$ and $(d_{n-1}d_{n-2}...d_0)$ be the binary representation of d. Let $m = MSB(d) = \max \{ j, d_j \neq 0 \}$, that is the most significant bit position where $d_j \neq 0$.

Lemma 5 If $s + 2^k > e$. where $k = \min (i,l)$, then the largest octree node in $(q_0,s,e,)$ is of level m, where $m < k$.

Lemma 5 shows if the step size is beyond the end position, the binary representation of d will provide the proper stopping scheme of the sweep. According to our greedy principle, we first choose 2^m as a step size and update s then apply lemma 5 again to find next step size and so on. In general, we will decrease our step size according to positions of nonzero bits of d. Therefore the number of ending sweeps equal to the number of nonzero bits of d. For example d = (0011010), then we will sweep three times with each step size 2^4, 2^3, and 2^1 respectively. The algorithm given below describes the detail process of the LQO sweep.

Algorithm LQO:
For each linear quadtree node q do
     1.1 Find the level i of q.
     1.2 Set starting position s.
     1.3 Compute k = min(i,l), where l = LSB(s).
     1.4 While $s + 2^k \le e$, do
          1.4.1 Generate octree node in $(q,s,s+2^k)$.
          1.4.2 Let $s = s + 2^k$.
          1.4.3 Compute k = min(i,l), where l = LSB(s).
     1.5 Process the ending procedure according to the binary representation of MSB(e−s). (see lemma 5)

Theorem 1   The time complexity of LQO algorithm is O(B), where B is the number of nodes in (R,s,e).
proof: According to the choice of each increment from lemma 2, lemma 4, and lemma 5 the result follows.

The LQO algorithm generates an unsorted octcode list, an extra sorting process is required to keep octree nodes in order, therefore the LQO algorithm is dominated by the sorting process, which requires O(BlogB) time.

5. IMPROVED LQO ALGORITHM

In this section we will introduce a new translational sweep algorithm which takes only linear time to generate an ordered linear octree array. To achieve this goal, a proper control scheme will be developed to keep these nodes in order. For explanatory purpose, we first introduce the constrained translational sweep which limits the starting position at Z = 0 and allows the ending position to be arbitrary. Then a more general sweep with no constraint on the starting position will be given.

First, let us take a close look at the ordering relation between a given quadtree R and its swept octree O = (R,s,e). Let q_i and q_{i+1} be two consecutive quadcodes in R with $q_i <$ q_{i+1}. Then we have the following observations: (1) Node q_i has to grow before q_{i+1}, this is because the octcode of the initial sweep of q equals to q itself. (2) Before growing q_{i+1}, the furthest position q_i can be grown is bounded by q_{i+1}. For example, q_i = 00x, q_{i+1} = 100, and e = 6, then $(q_i,0,6)$ = { 00x, 04x, 40x }, and $(q_{i+1},0,6)$ = { 100, 104, 140, 144, 500, 504 }. That is, q_i can only grow two steps before q_{i+1}'s term without violating the required order. (3) The growth of q_{i+1} is also related to the growth of q_i. In general we find if q_{i+1} has grown to the same level as q_i, then any further growth of q_{i+1} will cause q_i to grow first. To illustrate this property, consider the previous example, as q_{i+1} has grown four steps, we have to generate node 40x before nodes 500 and 504 can be generated. The underlying notation of our algorithm is based on these observations to devise a control scheme which will grow octree node one by one according to the octcode sequence. A more details discussions of these observations will be given in the following.

Let q and q' be two quadtree nodes, we define the sibling function SB(q,q') to be the level h such that in this level the ancestor of q and the ancestor of q' are siblings. For example, $q = 00x$, $q' = 100$, then $2 = SB(q,q')$. It can be shown that $SB(q,q')$ equals to the index of the most significant quaternary digit where their quadcodes are different. The following lemma shows how the notion of SB function can be used to control the growth of each quadtree node.

Lemma 6 Let q_i and q_{i+1} be two consecutive quadtree nodes such that $q_i < q_{i+1}$. If $SB(q_i,q_{i+1}) = h$, then the nodes in $(q_i,0,2^h)$ will have their octcodes less than those swept by q_{i+1}.

From the previous discussion, we give our new algorithm as following.

Algorithm Improved LQO:
step1   Read the first node from linear quadtree, then calculate its level.
step2   Let stop parameter $s = \lceil \log(\text{end position}) \rceil$.
step3   For $i = 2$ to $m+1$ do { where m is the number of quadtree nodes }
    3.1 If not end–of–file then
        Read the quadtree node q_i then calculate its level.

    3.2 If not end–of–file then
        Calculate $h = \min (SB (q_{i-1},q_i),s)$.

    else
        Let $h = s$.
    3.3 Let current growth index $g =$ the level of q_{i-1}.

    3.4 Grow q_{i-1} one step forward and store the $o(q_{i-1},0,2^g)$ to the output list, then set the growth index of $o(q_{i-1},0,2^g)$ to g.

    3.5 While $g < h$ do
        3.5.1 In the output list, find $S(g)$ { $S(g)$ is the set of octcodes whose growth index equal to g}.
        3.5.2 Grow each element in $S(g)$ one step forward. If the grown node is beyond the end position then process end procedure.
        3.5.3 Update the growth index of every element in $S(g)$ to $g+1$.
        3.5.4 Store these nodes to the output list and mark its growth index to $g+1$.
        3.5.5 Let $g = g+1$.

Now, let's give an example to explain our algorithm.

Example 1:   Give a linear quadtree pattern 0xx, 10x, 110, 221, 31x, 320, 321, and we sweep it from 0 to 4.
SOL:

node	size	SB function	output list
0xx	4	x	
10x	2	2	0xx
110	1	1	0xx, 10x
221	1	2	0xx, 10x, 110, 114, 14x, 150, 154
31x	2	2	0xx, 10x, 110, 114, 14x, 150, 154, 221, 225, 261, 265
320	1	1	0xx, 10x, 110, 114, 14x, 150, 154, 221, 225, 261, 265, 31x
321	1	0	0xx, 10x, 110, 114, 14x, 150, 154, 221, 225, 261, 265, 31x, 320
step 3.4			0xx, 10x, 110, 114, 14x, 150, 154, 221, 225, 261, 265, 31x, 320, 321
repeat step 3.5			0xx, 10x, 110, 114, 14x, 150, 154, 221, 225, 261, 265, 31x, 320. 321, 324, 325
repeat step 3.5			0xx, 10x, 110, 114, 14x, 150, 154, 221, 225, 261, 265, 31x, 320, 321, 324, 325, 35x, 360, 361, 364, 365

As for the translational sweep with arbitrary starting and ending position, we may divide the sweep process into two subprocesses, namely, the forward sweep and the backward sweep. This is because the best position to apply the greedy algorithm may fall in the middle of the range [s,e]. In general the point $Z = k2^l$, where $l = \max \{ i, s \le k2^i < e$ and k is odd $\}$ is the most greedy location to start the sweep. The algorithm of backward sweep can easily be derived from the forward sweep, then the final result is obtained by merging two sorted sequences.

6. ROTATIONAL SWEEP

In this section we discuss the possible extension of translational sweep to the rotational sweep.

Definition: Let R be a linear quadtree encoded region in the base plane. A rotational linear quadtree to the linear octree sweep (RLQO) of R is a linear octree encoded solid generated by rotating R around certain axis.

For convenience, we will assume the base plane is parallel to the X–Y plane and placed at $Z = 2^{n-1}$. The rotational axis is the line $X = Z = 2^{n-1}$.

Definition: A region is called x–convex if and only if each horizontal line intersects the region at most one line segment.

The orthogonal projection of rotational sweep of R on the base plane is R itself if R is x–convex. Therefore if we perform the translational sweep of R, each generated octree node will be the candidate of the rotational sweep. The x–convex property will not reduce the descriptive power of rotational sweep since the difference operator is available.

By the symmetry of the rotational sweep, it suffices to consider the sweep in octants four and six of the universe. As we sweep node by node, we have to use the set membership classification (Tilove 1980) to ensure the generated node is legally inside the swept domain. If the node is classified as gray, subdivide the node and repeat the classification process. The following lemma shows the sweep is stopped when it is classified as a white node.

Lemma 7 In octants four and six during the sweeping process, the backward neighbor of a black node is also black and the forward neighbor of a white node is also white.

The algorithm of rotational sweep is shown in the following. (We assume that the region to be swept is symmetric to the y–axis and the base plane is embedded on the plane $Z = 2^{n-1}$.)

Algorithm RLQO:
step1   For each linear quadtree node q do
     1.1 Sweep one step forward according to the LQO sweep.
     1.2 Perform membership classification
        1.2.1 Check the type of the swept node.
        1.2.2 If the swept octree node is black then
            1.2.2.1 Output the octcode to the output list.
            1.2.2.2 Grown the forward neighbor node.
            1.2.2.3 Repeat step 1.2 until ending position.
        1.2.3 If the swept octree node is gray then
            1.2.3.1 Split the swept octree node to the next level.
            1.2.3.2 For each subnode repeat step 1.2 until ending position.
step2   Generate octcodes in octants five and seven via reflection operation with respect to the plane $X = 2^{n-1}$.
step3   Generate octcodes in octants zero, one, two, three via reflection operation with respect to the plane $Z = 2^{n-1}$.
step4   Sort all octcodes.

The algorithm is also based on the greedy principle, and both classification and reflection operations can be done in constant time, therefore its time complexity is $O(B)$, where B is the number of linear octree nodes. Since a sorting process is required to reorder octree nodes, the total time complexity is $O(B\log B)$.

7. EXPERIMENT RESULTS

We have implement a solid modeler with LQO and RLQO functions on a VAX 11/750 using workstation COMTAL 1/10 as I/O device. The resolution parameter is 8. Moreover Boolean operations on octrees are also supported to increase the descriptive power of our solid modeler. Figure 2 and Figure 3 show objects modeled by the system.

Table 1 shows cpu time of two different translational sweep algorithms. The experiment results shown that LQO takes less time to sweep but will cost a deal if sorting is required. The improved translational sweep algorithm takes little more time to sweep but its merge cost is much cheaper than sorting. When swept nodes increase the LQO algorithm is dominated by sorting routine, however the improved translational sweep algorithm runs in linear time.

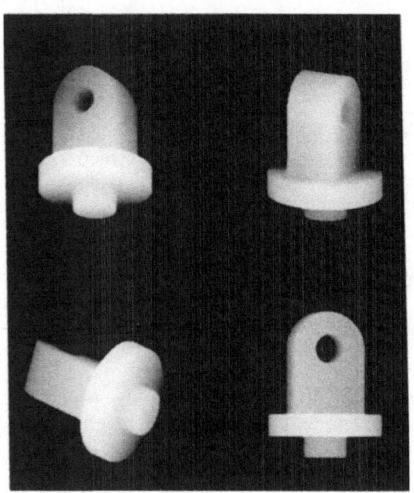

Fig. 3.   Modeled objects

Table 1.   Cpu time of different translational algorithms

LQO Algorithm: unit: ms

Picture	Start Point	End Point	Quadtree Nodes	Octree Nodes	Sweep Time	Sort Time	Total Time
1	0	50	256	10223	21920	76060	97980
2	180	200	256	4050	8790	25300	34090
3	100	200	419	32246	68830	240670	309500
4	15	55	419	16082	28600	116270	144870
5	125	238	284	26434	54430	197120	251550
6	26	61	284	8764	17020	63370	80390
7	12	199	209	31471	65360	241120	306480
8	0	255	209	42551	89010	334610	423620

Improved LQO Algorithm:

Picture	Start Point	End Point	Quadtree Nodes	Octree Nodes	Sweep Time	Merge Time	Total Time
1	0	50	256	10223	25930	1460	27390
2	180	200	256	4050	10610	510	11120
3	100	200	419	32246	78940	2310	81250
4	15	55	419	16082	33820	2130	35950
5	125	238	284	26434	58560	1470	60030
6	26	61	284	8764	18280	1210	19490
7	12	199	209	31471	74400	2880	77280
8	0	255	209	42551	91820	3610	95430

8. CONCLUDING REMARK

In this paper we have shown both translational and rotational sweep to construct an octree encoded solid. The given algorithms are optimal in the sense that they are bounded by the number of output nodes. We think our methods are simple and easy to be implemented. Experimental results are given. It shows our methods are about proportional to the number of output nodes. The comparison between two translational sweeps is discussed from the points of view of theoretical analysis and empirical data.

There are some further improvements can be made for our sweep algorithms. For example, a fast neighbor finding scheme (Yang and Jong 1988) will speed up the computation of octree nodes if the step size is given. In some cases we can have more sophisticated control scheme to enlarge the step size. Furthermore, an improved rotational sweep can also be derived from improved LQO algorithm.

REFERENCES

Atkinson HH, Gargantini I, Walsh TRS (1986) Filling by quadrants or octants. CVGIP 33(2):138--155

Chen HH, Huang TS (1988) A survey of construction and manipulation of octrees. CVGIP 43:409--431

Chien CH, Aggarwal JK (1986) Volume/surface octrees for the representation of three dimensional objects. CVGIP 36:100--113

Gargantini I (1982) An effective way to represent quadtrees. CACM 25(12):905--910

Gargantini I (1982) Linear octrees for fast processing of three--dimensional objects. CGIP 20(4):365--374

Gargantini I (1983) Translation, rotation and superposition of linear quadtrees. Int. J. Man--Machine Studies 18:253--263

Gargantini I, Walsh TR, Wu OL (1986) Viewing transformations of voxel--based objects via linear octrees. IEEE CG&A pp.12--21

Hunter GM, Steiglitz K (1979) Linear transformations of pictures represented by quadtrees. CGIP 10(3):289--296

Jackins CL, Tanimoto SL (1980) Oct--trees and their use in representing three--dimensional objects. CGIP 14(3):249--270

Lin TW, Yang SN (1987) An improved border algorithm for octree representation. Proceedings of National Computer Symposium pp.355--359

Martin WN, Aggarwal JK (1983) Volumetric descriptions of objects from multiple views. IEEE PAMI 5(2):150--158

Meagher D (1982) Geometric modelling using octree encoding. CGIP 19(2):129--147

Requicha AAG (1980) Representations for rigid solids: theory, methods, and systems. Computing Surveys 12(4):437--465

Samet H, Tamminen M (1985) Computing geometric properties of images represented by linear quadtrees. IEEE PAMI 7(2):229--240

Shaffer CA, Samet H (1987) Optimal quadtree construction algorithms. CVGIP 37:402--419

Tilove RB (1980) Set membership classification: an unified approach to geometric intersection problems. IEEE Transactions on Computers C29(10):874--883

Yang SN, Jong BS (1988) Optimal algorithms on linear quadtree and linear octree construction. Technical Report, Institute of Computer Science, Tsing Hua University

Yau MM, Srihari SN (1983) A hierarchical data structure for multidimensional digital images. CACM 26:504--515

Shi Nine Yang received the B.S. degree from National Normal University Taiwan in 1967 and the PH.D. degree from SUNY at Buffulo, Buffulo, N.Y. in 1976. During 1976 – 1985 he joined the faculty of Chung Yuan University, Chung–Li, Taiwan. From 1978 – 1984 he was the chairman of the Department of Information Engineering, Chung Yuan University. Currently, he is a professor in the Institue of Computer Science, National Tsing Hua University, Hsin–Chu, Taiwan. His research interests include computer graphics, computer aided design and computational geometry. Dr. Yang is a member of the Computer Socity of the Republic of China, the Association for Computing Machinery and the IEEE Computer Society.

Bin Shyan Jong received the B.S. degree in Computer Science from Chung Yuan University in 1978 and the M.S. degree from Institute of Computer Science in 1983. During 1980 – 1985 he was a project manager at CAPITAL Computer CO., Taipei, Taiwan. Currently, he is a PH.D. candidate in the Institute of Computer Science, National Tsing Hua University and he also lecture in the Department of Information Engineering, Chung Yuan University. His research interests include computer graphics, Computer aided design, data base management, and computer network.

MAILING ADDRESS: Institute of Computer Science, National Tsing Hua University, Hsin–Chu, Taiwan, 30043, R.O.C.

PictureEditor: A 2D Picture Editing System Based on Geometric Constructions and Constraints

N. Kin, T. Noma, and T.L. Kunii

ABSTRACT

PictureEditor is proposed as a new constraint-based picture drawing system. Most constraint-based systems are based on numerical methods, that exhibit numerical instability. Our system, however, satisfies constraints by converting them to construction operations. This is a stable technique and it enables us to check consistency among constraints in a straightforward manner.

Keywords: constraint, direct manipulation, geometric construction, picture description, 2-forest propagation

1. INTRODUCTION

"What is the best user interface?" — a number of researchers have been trying to answer this question. The most common answer to this question is an interface based on direct manipulation.

The principle of direct manipulation is to simulate human activities. A number of picture drawing systems based on direct manipulation use an approach similar to geometric construction with a ruler and a pair of compasses. Although this approach is simple and clear, it restricts human ability to draw pictures intuitively.

As a method of intuitive picture description, constraints, which represent the relationships among geometrical objects, are getting popular. Constraints are a very powerful method to draw pictures intuitively, but satisfying constraints is a very difficult problem. Most of the current constraint-based systems rely on numerical methods to satisfy the constraints. Such methods, however, are numerically unstable and time-consuming.

In this paper, we describe a 2D picture editing system combining direct manipulation and intuitive picture drawing with constraints and exact picture description. In addition, a quick and stable constraint solver in the form of a conversion system from constraints to construction operations is described.

2. BASIC CONCEPTS OF PictureEditor

The purpose of developing PictureEditor is to construct a picture drawing system which provides an exact and unambiguous picture description for professionals and provisions for novices. Thus, our PictureEditor is based on direct manipulation, geometric constructions, and constraints.

2.1. Direct Manipulation

"Direct manipulation" is a familiar phrase. In particular, visual interfaces with a mouse tend to be called direct manipulation interfaces. Since we aim at such an interface, we especially pay attention to the principle of direct manipulation. Although the term "direct manipulation" is very popular, its meaning or principles are not very clear. "Direct manipulation" means to directly manipulate the object of interest.

Several principles of direct manipulation have been formulated (Shneiderman 1983; Apple 1987). But they do not define what is "direct". They are rather the explanations of the principles of interactive systems. Indeed, interfaces based on direct manipulation are interactive. However, we feel that direct manipulation is different from interaction itself. The essence of direct manipulation has something to do with the word "direct". Then, what is direct manipulation?

The answer to the above question, according to us, is that the principle of direct manipulation is the simulation of human activities. It tries to "directly" imitate the user in the real world. A deletion operation of "vi", a screen editor in UNIX(TM) operating system, is a good example. To delete a character, we stroke an "x" key. This imitates our activity of typing "x" across the characters to be deleted, in a real life situation.

Interfaces simulating human activities enable new users to handle the system easily. Expert system programs are not necessary any more. They can quickly acquire enough knowledge to use the system from learning by analogy, and the small gap between using computers and doing the work manually, causes less frustration. Not only novices but also experts gain largely since they can work rapidly and intuitively. Intuition enables smooth execution of their work, and extends the range of their creation.

Due to the reasons mentioned above, interfaces based on direct manipulation are thought to be the best user interfaces. Such interfaces cater to both novices and experts. Thus, the interface of PictureEditor is based on direct manipulation.

2.2. Geometric Constructions

When people draw geometrical objects, they use a ruler and a pair of compasses. From the viewpoint of direct manipulation, picture drawing systems should take an approach similar to geometric constructions with a ruler and a pair of compasses. We call this a construction-based approach. The simulation of the ruler and compass technique does not require the solution of more than two quadratic equations simultaneously for positioning of geometrical objects. This means that a construction-based approach need not solve a large system of equations. And the equations, that fix the positions of points, are solved very quickly.

2.2.1. Related Work

Gargoyle (Bier and Stone 1986) and L.E.G.O. (Fuller and Prusinkiewicz 1988) are systems that adopt a construction-based approach. Both of them provide a visual interactive interface.

The main concept of Gargoyle is called snap-dragging. It is based on snapping the cursor to points and curves using a gravity function. For precise positioning of points, the user simulates the function of a ruler, a pair of compasses, a protractor, and a T-square. The process of simulation is forgotten as soon as it is finished, rather than becoming a part of the data storage. Hence in this system, no consideration is given to textual picture description.

L.E.G.O. imitates the function of a ruler and a pair of compasses faithfully, and extends two-dimensional constructions to three-dimensional cases. Since L.E.G.O. has command language similar to LISP, textual picture description is available. The visual interface of L.E.G.O. might be rather the tool for creating command sequences without typing. But L.E.G.O. does not concern itself with ambiguity in picture description. If the description is ambiguous, different systems produce different pictures from the same description. This is not acceptable to the user. For a description to be exact and usable in various applications, it must be unambiguous.

2.2.2. Constructive Picture Description

As an easy, intuitive, and unambiguous picture description, we have proposed constructive picture description (Noma et al. 1988, 1989). As the name indicates, this approach is construction-based. Similar to the process of drawing with a ruler and a pair of compasses, the points which specify pictures are defined through repetitive geometric constructions. The operations or commands, however, are not limited to those of direct interpretation of Euclidean constructions with a ruler and a pair of compasses. There is no standard style, and application-oriented commands can be prepared in our approach. Table 1 shows an example operation set based on Euclidean constructions.

In addition, our method of constructive picture definition is unambiguous. For example, the intersections of a circle and a line are usually two points. Which point shall we choose? The other kinds of construction-based picture description do not consider this problem. Our method allows the user to select a suitable point by introducing direction. In this example, a line is supposed to be directed, and the two intersection points are defined in turn according to the direction of the line (Fig. 1). The intersection of two circles is determined as in Figure 2.

2.2.3. A Problem of a Construction-Based Approach

Since constructive picture description is unambiguous, it can be utilized in various applications. We have already developed a preprocessor (Kin et al. 1988) and other specific systems (Noma et al. 1986, 1988, 1989). These systems perform textually-oriented editing only. Thus, we have attempted to build

Table 1. An Example Operation Set of Constructive Picture Description

Operation	Meaning
LINE l p1 p2	draw line l through points p1 and p2
CIRC c p r	draw circle c with center p and radius r
P1LL p l1 l2	define point p where lines l1 and l2 intersect
P1PL p1 p2 l d	define point p1 at a distance of d from point p2 along line l
P2CL p1 p2 c l	define points p1 and p2 where circle c and line l intersect
P2CC p1 p2 c1 c2	define points p1 and p2 where circles c1 and c2 intersect
LTTK p1 p2	put the length from points p1 to p2 into the queue

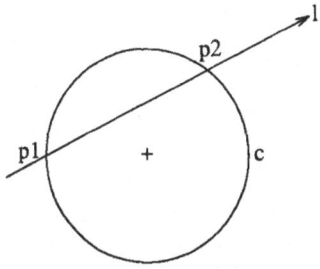

Fig. 1. Operation P2CL

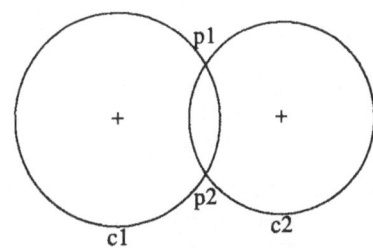

Fig. 2. Operation P2CC

an interactive picture drawing system based on direct manipulation, as an improvement of the initial system.

Since our picture description is construction-based, it is suitable for direct manipulation. In designing the system, however, we have been confronted with a problem. Certainly, direct manipulation, which is the simulation of human activities, is easy to use up to some degree. Since the ruler and compass technique is familiar to most of people from an early age, a construction-based approach may be sufficiently intuitive. But, for example, a user drawing an equilateral triangle ABC, has to specify a condition in the form of "AB = BC = CA". This does not describe the construction process. It merely declares a feature or condition to be satisfied while drawing the geometrical object. As long as a construction-based approach is adopted, the user must first think in terms of geometrical construction processes. Thus, his/her thinking process is required to take a circuitous route. Direct manipulation combined with a construction-based approach restricts human ability to draw pictures according to their intuition.

We therefore feel the necessity of improving upon the original definition of direct manipulation. The burden of conversion has to be diminished. The system must offer an environment where the user can act intuitively. For this purpose, the principle of direct manipulation should involve the simulation of human intuition rather than that of human activities. From this viewpoint, we also take into account constraints which represent the relationships among geometrical objects.

2.3. Constraints

Recently constraints have become popular as a new method of programming (Leler 1988). "Constraints" are used to express the relationships among objects.

In the previous section, we stated that direct manipulation should be based on human intuition. How is the geometrical intuition represented? As mentioned above, when we try to draw an equilateral triangle, we first think of the condition "AB = BC = CA". This describes the relationships between geometrical objects, that is the equality of the length of three line segments AB, BC, and CA. Therefore, constraints are thought to be appropriate for the simulation of human intuition.

2.3.1. Problems of a Constraint-Based Approach

A construction-based approach takes the form of imperative commands, while a constraint-based approach takes the form of declarative commands. The users of constraint-based systems needs not convert their constraints represented as a set of commands to the corresponding procedural imperatives. This is done by the system. Satisfying constraints, however, is a very difficult matter. It is because a number of constraints are described in the form of nonlinear equations. For example, the equality of the length of two line segments AB and CD is represented as a quadratic equation:

$$(x_A - x_B)^2 + (y_A - y_B)^2 = (x_C - x_D)^2 + (y_C - y_D)^2$$

$$A:(x_A, y_A) \quad B:(x_B, y_B) \quad C:(x_C, y_C) \quad D:(x_D, y_D)$$

Thus, to simplify the problem, most of the constraint-based systems resort to numerical methods.

Several constraint-based picture drawing systems have been developed. The first one is Sketchpad (Sutherland 1963). To solve constraints, this system first employs the "one path method," which utilizes propagation of degrees of freedom. If this method fails, relaxation is used.

ThingLab (Borning 1981) is based on Smalltalk. This system incorporates the basic concepts of Smalltalk, such as object-oriented programming techniques and inheritance. Besides propagation of degrees of freedom, this system employs propagation of known states for constraint satisfaction. In this system also, the failure of these techniques leads to the use of relaxation.

For simple constraints, relaxation may be fast enough. When there are many, or complicated constraints, the method is too slow. In any case, relaxation is not guaranteed to converge.

To improve the efficiency of a constraint solver, Juno (Nelson 1985) employs the Newton-Raphson iteration, which is faster than relaxation. In spite of this, the time taken is still roughly proportional to the cube of the number of variables.

The given constraints may not always be sufficient (exactly-determined). They might be incomplete (under-determined) or redundant (over-determined). If the constraints are under-determined, there are infinitely many solutions, and if over-determined, a consistent solution might not exist. We call this problem the exact-determination problem. In addition, exactly-determined constraints might merely guarantee that the number of the solutions is finite. In a case where a constraint has more than one solution, which does the system choose? This reintroduces the problem of ambiguity as described in section 2.2. Let us consider the construction of an equilateral triangle ABC again. "AB = BC = CA" is the only condition that most people can think of. But it is not sufficient to determine the triangle uniquely. There are still four degrees of freedom. The triangle can change size, position, and rotation. If one vertex is fixed, infinitely many solutions exist. Even if one vertex and the length of the sides are given, there are still infinitely many solutions. The inclination of the base cannot be determined uniquely. When two vertices, such as A and B, are fixed, the number of the solutions is finite. But C can be on either side of the line AB (Fig. 3). Like this, it is difficult for the user to understand what constraints are sufficient to determine the object uniquely.

In Juno, for example, the system does nothing in an over-determined case, and if constraints are under-determined, the command is non-deterministic. In other words, the system allows any solution that satisfies the constraints. This may not be the solution you expect. As for the problem of ambiguity, Juno overcomes it by allowing the user to help the system decide on the solution. This means that the user cannot hope for a unique solution if he specified only the constraints. Other information is also needed.

As a solution of the exact-determination problem, White (1988) has developed a prototype system named HILS. He adopts only a least squares adjustment, which can be realized as relaxation, to satisfy constraints even in the under-determined and over-determined cases. Like Juno, his approach relies only on a numerical method.

Numerical methods, however, can be unstable. As mentioned above, such methods may fail to solve constraints even when a solution exists. Even if a solution could be obtained, there still may be other solutions. The time needed to solve constraints may be large for interactive applications. Hence, the

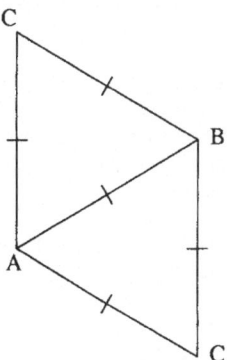

Fig. 3. Equilateral Triangle ABC

action of a constraint solver based on numerical methods is unpredictable by the user. This is troublesome especially for users unfamiliar with computers, and is not suitable for unambiguous and exact picture description.

2.3.2. The Treatment of Constraints in PictureEditor

The main problem of the constraint solvers described above is that they employ numerical methods, which can be unstable by nature. Hence, a new technique of constraint solving, which does not rely on numerical methods, is required.

Beynon and Yung (1988) proposed a definitive notation for interactive graphics. This notation essentially consists of a sequence of variable definitions and evaluations. Although their prototype system as of now gives very limited support for constraints, there would not be many problems encountered while handling constraints (Beynon and Yung 1988). Their definitive notation can easily be translated into an incremental or constructive notation.

Our PictureEditor uses a similar technique. It adopts a conversion system from constraints to construction operations, and does not resort to numerical methods. These construction operations can be represented by constructive picture description. Additional constraints can be defined on objects already present on the display. When a construction operation has several solutions, the system outputs the solution which is nearest to the position of the displayed objects. Thus, PictureEditor makes unambiguous and exact picture description possible. In the next section, we describe the mechanism of this conversion.

3. CONSTRAINT SOLVING IN PictureEditor

This section explains how constraints are solved in our PictureEditor. The main idea is to limit the acceptable set of constraints on points so that they can be translated into a geometrical construction operation. The translation is performed by the 2-tree propagation technique (Todd 1986).

3.1. Constraint Solving

As discussed in the previous section, the defects of current constraint solvers are (1) the speed and stability of the constraint solving mechanism, and (2) the difficulty in specifying an unambiguous picture. In this subsection, we focus on the first problem.

Since a system of general constraint is hard to solve, a constraint solving problem is usually treated for a specific application. In the case of picture description, a set of constraints is usually transformed into a system of equations, whose variables are coordinate values of points. To solve the simultaneous equations, many techniques have been proposed, including propagation, redundant views, transformation, relaxation, and Newton-Raphson iteration (Leler 1988).

Propagation is the simplest method for constraint solving. Its principle is "If you can deduce something immediately, then do so." Constraints can be represented in the form of a constraint net (also called a constraint graph). Figure 4 is an example representing the constraint "A + B = C". The squares such as A, B, and C are called cells. If cells A and B are known, then C can be deduced. Similarly, B can be determined from A and C, and A is from B and C.

To apply propagation efficiently, propagating degrees of freedom is often utilized. In this technique, a cell with few enough constraints is looked for so that its value can be changed to satisfy its constraints.

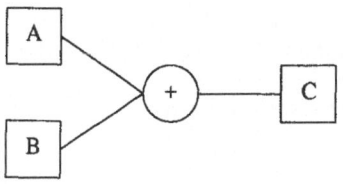

Fig. 4. Constraint Net representing "A + B = C"

In most cases, cells are scalars, and a cell has enough freedom if it has only one constraint on it (Leler 1988).

In addition, propagation planning is performed by precompilation. This technique prunes cells with only one constraint and the constraints themselves step by step. The order of cell removal is the reverse of the order of propagation.

In constraint solving, it is an accepted method to use propagation as much as possible. For example, in Sketchpad (Sutherland 1963) and ThingLab (Borning 1981), precompilation is tried first, and relaxation is utilized for the rest of the constraint net. In MAGRITTE (Gosling 1983), to expand the usefulness of propagation, the transformation technique is introduced.

Propagation, however, does not have a wide range of application, as it is restricted to cells with one degree of freedom. In other words, propagation is effective only for a tree-structured constraint net. The rest of the net where propagation cannot be applied has to be solved with a much slower and numerically unstable constraint solving method such as relaxation or Newton-Raphson iteration.

3.2. 2-Forest Propagation

As discussed in the previous subsection, with propagation, only one equation can be solved at a time. In constructive picture description, two equations and/or constraints are solved at a time, and thus its applicability is wider than that of propagation. In practice, it turns out that constructive picture description is able to handle most of the realistic cases without difficulty. We therefore extend propagation to handle the cases which can be represented by constructive picture description.

The narrowness of the applicability of propagation results not from propagation itself but from the granularity of the objects where propagation occurs. Hence we select a point as the object.

With two degrees of freedom, a point can be propagated from two constraints simultaneously. Suppose that point A is constrained so that (1) the distance between points A and B is 2, and (2) the distance between points A and C is 3. If the positions of B and C are given, then A is determined as an intersection point of two circles: one with center B and radius 2 and one with center C and radius 3.

Before going further, let us classify constraints among points from the viewpoint of construction. A constraint "the distance between points A and B is 2" means two constructions: one is that B is restricted on the circle with center A and radius 2, and the other is that A is on the circle with center B and radius 2. The former occurs when A is determined before B and the latter does when B precedes. In both case, however, the number of the predetermined points necessary for construction is one. The number of newly constrained points is one. In addition, the lost degrees of freedom per point is one. In our classification, each constraint is labeled as p-q-r constraints, if the number of predefined points is p, the number of newly constrained points is q, and the lost degrees of freedom is r. For example, the above distance constraint is a 1-1-1 constraint. Similarly, the midpoint constraint is 2-1-2, the trisection point constraint is 2-2-2, and the fixation of a point to (x,y) is a 0-1-2 constraint.

Now the algorithm of 2-forest[1] propagation is described:

Algorithm (2-forest propagation)

(1) Remove a point if the sum of the lost degrees of freedom of the constraints connected with the point, is less than or equal two.

(2) Remove the constraints connected with the above point if the number of newly constrained points is 1. Otherwise, transform the constraint so that the number decreases by one.

(3) Repeat (1) and (2) until (a) all the points are removed, or (b) no points can be removed further. Obviously, in case (a), precompilation succeeded, and (b) is not.

(4) After that, determine the positions of points in a constructive manner in the reverse order of the removed points.

The essence of this algorithm lies in that the point which can be determined with other points should be removed first. In other words, our 2-forest propagation algorithm makes the reverse list of constructive picture description, and this is why the algorithm can construct a picture unambiguously.

Todd (1986) proposes an algorithm for determining consistency and manufacturability of dimensioned drawings with the notion of a 2-tree. In his algorithm, a dimensioned drawing is represented by a graph where geometrical objects such as points and lines are nodes and there exists an arc between the nodes if there exists a dimensional specification between the geometrical objects represented by the nodes. If we can remove a node connected to two arcs, and the arcs themselves, step by step, the drawing is consistent, and otherwise not.

Our 2-forest propagation is an extension of Todd's algorithm. The major difference between Todd's algorithm and our 2-forest propagation resides in two points:

(1) Todd deals with points and lines, while we treat points only.

(2) Todd deals only with dimensioning, while we treat more general constraints.

Figure 5(a) shows an example of points and the constraints between the points. The points are A, B, C, and D. The constraints are:

- A is fixed at (0, 0) ----- 0-1-2 constraint
- D is fixed at (2, 1) ----- 0-1-2 constraint
- The distance between A and B is 1.8 ----- 1-1-1 constraint
- The distance between A and C is 1.5 ----- 1-1-1 constraint
- The distance between C and D is 1.1 ----- 1-1-1 constraint
- B and C are horizontal ----- 1-1-1 constraint

2-forest propagation is performed as follows:

(1) Point B is constrained by two 1-1-1 constraints. Then B and the two constraints concerning B is removed (Figure 5(b)).

(2) Point C is constrained by two 1-1-1 constraints. Then C and the two constraints concerning C is removed (Figure 5(c)).

(3) Points A and D are constrained by one 0-1-2 constraint, respectively. Then the two points and the fixation constraints are removed

(4) There left no points and constraints. 2-forest propagation succeeded.

---

[1] The name of a 2-forest is inappropriate from the graph theoretical viewpoint. It is an analogy of Todd's (1986) 2-tree.

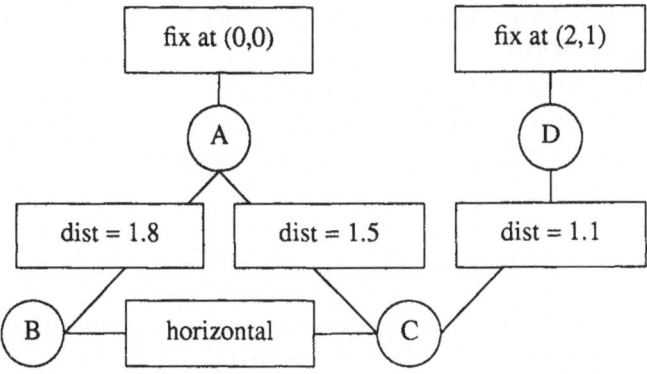

(a) The Start of 2-Forest Propagation

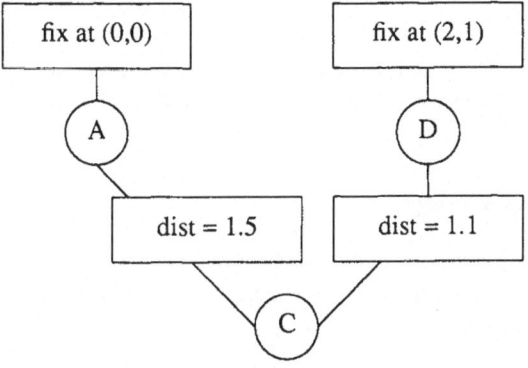

(b) Removing Point B and the Constraints Concerning B

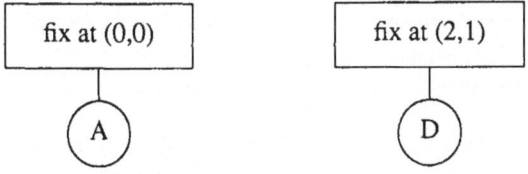

(c) Removing Point C and the Constraints Concerning C

Fig. 5. An Example of 2-Forest Propagation

The positions of the points are determined in the reversed order.

(1)   Points A and D are fixed.

(2)   A circle with center A and radius 1.5 is drawn.

(3)   A circle with center D and radius 1.1 is drawn.

(4)   Point C is determined as the intersection point of the two circles.[2]

(5)   A circle with center A and radius 1.8 is drawn.

(6)   A horizontal line through point C is drawn.

(7)   Point B is determined as the intersection point of the circle and the horizontal line.

As discussed in (Gosling 1983), propagation is sensitive to the equations that represent the constraints. Even if two sets of constraints have the same meaning, it is possible that one succeeds and the other fails. To prevent this, in our system, we adopt a slightly modified 2-forest propagation with simple geometric reasoning. A detailed discussion of the 2-forest propagation is given in (Noma 1989).

4. DESIGN AND IMPLEMENTATION OF PictureEditor

PictureEditor has been developed on a SONY NEWS workstation (under the UNIX[TM] operating system) using the X window system, the Xrlib library, and the C programming language.

4.1. Principles of Design

The main design principles of PictureEditor are as follows:

(1)   A useful interface based on the simulation of human intuition.

(2)   Production of exact picture description.

(1) is the aim of our direct manipulation. (2) is realized using constructive picture description.

4.1.1. The Simulation of Human Intuition

PictureEditor uses a visual interactive interface based on direct manipulation. Besides constraints, it takes into account the following aspects for simulating human intuition:

- The form of operations should be noun-then-verb.
- Operations should be modeless as far as possible.

In several drawing systems, such as L.E.G.O., the user first chooses an action (the verb) in the menu, and then selects the objects (the nouns) to be manipulated. Although this form (verb-then-noun) is suitable to the picture description language, this order is not appropriate for human thinking and language (Apple 1987). Generally, people say "Hey, you - do this". This is the form noun-then-verb. Object-oriented languages such as Smalltalk thus take this form.

The form verb-then-noun also introduces modes. When the user selects a command in the menu, the following actions are restricted by the command context. On the contrary, the noun-then-verb form is more modeless. When the user chooses objects, the command syntax can be ignored. He/she only pays

---

[2] We do not discuss which point is to be selected between alternative intersection points.

attention to the objects that need to be handled. This helps him/her to follow the command syntax naturally, and if objects that are not suitable for the command are chosen, the system will do nothing except to indicate the error.

But several commands require modes. For example, a move operation cannot be fulfilled only by selecting an object and then a command. It also needs to indicate how the object is moved. In such cases, the system should clearly indicate to the user the current mode, and offer an easy method to escape from the mode.

4.1.2. Production of Exact Picture Description

In PictureEditor, not only the picture itself but also its textual description is produced. There is no reason to restrict picture availability to only a specific system. A picture edited in one system should be usable in various applications. To represent pictures exactly, PictureEditor adopts constructive picture description.

If the user directly types statements of constructive picture description, no consideration is necessary any more. In PictureEditor, the user does not change the description itself, but edits a picture interactively through trial and error. Hence other operations which do not appear in text editing are required. Examples of such operations are moving or deletion of geometrical objects. They require care to maintain the consistency between a picture and its description.

4.2. Consistency of a Picture and Its Description

Most of the operations in PictureEditor are directly converted to the corresponding picture description statement. But MOVE and DELETE operations do not have such statements. Hence more consideration is needed for consistent picture description. Only brief comment is given here. A detailed discussion is given in (Kin 1989).

Since constructive picture description defines new objects using already defined objects, it introduces dependency between objects. If one object is moved or deleted, other objects which depend on this one are also influenced. This is preferable in some cases, but not in other cases. Then, when the user carries out these operations, the system asks him whether the operation is restricted to the selected object or influences the related objects.

Let us suppose that the user wants to operate only on a selected object, say P. If P is changed, an object Q defined using P will also change. Thus, when the user likes to delete only P, the system merely does not display P, but does not delete P internally. Consequently, a new constructive picture description statement, UNDW (undraw), is needed. When the statement "UNDW P" is executed, P is cleaned from the display. If the user wants to move only P, the system undraws P and creates a new object P' at the position where P is moved to.

When the user wants to manipulate the related objects together P, the system looks for the statement S which defines P. If P is deleted, this statement and all the following statements that are based on S are removed. As a result, all objects related to P are deleted, too. If P is moved, a statement which defines P at the new position is inserted just after S. The following statements are carried out once more. Since the position of P has changed, the objects related to it move.

In this way, we make operations like MOVE and DELETE consistent with constructive picture description.

4.3. Description of Use

The screen is partitioned into three windows (Fig. 6). The top window contains pushbuttons representing operations. Table 2 shows the operations which are available now. The left window is used for picture construction. In the right one, the corresponding statements of constructive picture description are listed.

In principle, the user first selects objects by picking it up with the mouse, then chooses a pushbutton which designates the intended operation. If the user selects more than the required number of objects, the operation is applied to those selected first. If fewer objects are selected, the most recent objects

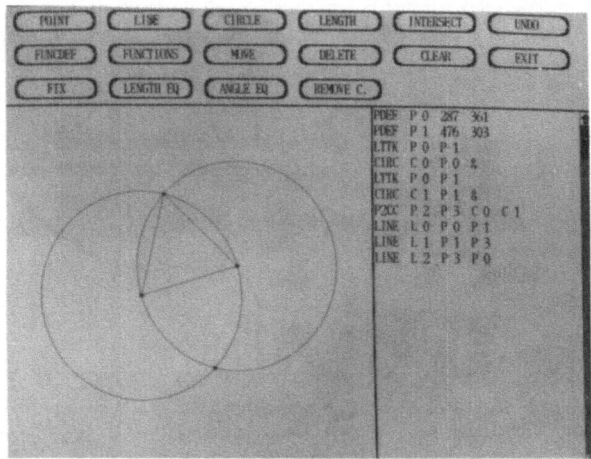

Fig. 6. The Example of PictureEditor Screen

Table 2. Operations in PictureEditor

Operation		Meaning
Construction-Based	POINT	draw a point
	LINE	draw a line segment between two points
	CIRCLE	draw a circle
	LENGTH	put the length between two points into the queue
	INTERSECT	define the intersection of two objects
Constraint-Based	FIX	fix a point
	LENGTH EQ	add a constraint to the length between two points
	ANGLE EQ	add a constraint to the angle from horizontal line or the angle between two lines
	REMOVE C.	remove a constraint
Utilities	FUNCDEF	define a macro function
	FUNCTIONS	execute a macro function
	MOVE	move an object
	DELETE	delete an object
	UNDO	undo the operation executed just before
	CLEAR	clear the displayed picture and its description
	EXIT	exit from PictureEditor

including some selected for earlier commands are used. These makes the system flexible, and no error message is required. If the result is not desirable, the user can use the UNDO operation. LINE, LENGTH, and INTERSECT follow this principle faithfully. MOVE and DELETE additionally ask whether they should influence dependent objects. POINT has two usages. One is to click on the place where a point is to be positioned, and to select the POINT button next. The other is to select the POINT button first. A dialogue box then appears, allowing the user to enter the coordinate values of a point exactly. In the case of the operation CIRCLE, after picking a point as the center of the circle and pressing the CIRCLE button, a dialogue box for the circle radius appears. The user types a number or an ampersand (&) to select the value of the last LENGTH operation.

PictureEditor also supports function definition. The user defining a macro function selects the objects as the arguments, and the FUNCDEF button. He/she then executes the operations defining the function. When the required operations are finished, the FUNCDEF button is pressed again. Then the user is asked for the name of the function. In this case, the function defining mode becomes the current mode. This mode is indicated by displaying created objects in a distinct color, and the mode can be exited by choosing the FUNCDEF button again. A function defined in this way can be executed by selecting objects and the FUNCTIONS button. When the FUNCTIONS button is selected, a menu containing macro functions appears.

The way of adding constraints is also similar. The user fixing a point picks that point and then selects the FIX button. If two points are picked and the LENGTH EQ button is pressed, the length between the two points can be set at a specified value or equated with another length. In the former case, any key can be pressed, and a dialogue box asking for the length value emerges. In the latter case, two other points defining the desirable length are picked. This method is very natural for the user, because it takes the form of "AB = n" or "AB = CD". The ANGLE EQ button is used similarly, except that in this case, the user specifies two lines (by means of four points), and the angle between them. When these constraints are added, the system returns their identification numbers. In the left side of a constraint statement, its identification number is also displayed. If the user wants to remove a constraint, the REMOVE C. button may be chosen and its number typed in a dialogue box.

To enable the user to decide his next action, many dialogue boxes are employed in PictureEditor. This introduces modes, but is necessary for the user to use PictureEditor smoothly and diminishes the burden of memorizing the usage correctly. However, it is possible that the user may sometimes get annoyed while looking at a dialogue box and want to escape its mode (want to stop the operation). Hence, PictureEditor offers a simple method of escaping. The user only clicks on the dialogue box. Then the state before starting the operation is regained.

5. CONCLUSIONS

PictureEditor is an interactive picture drawing system based on geometric constructions and constraints. The user interface is designed to simulate human intuition. As a new method of satisfying constraints, it adopts a conversion system from constraints to constructions. This method is quicker and more stable than traditional numerical ones. PictureEditor also allows us to produce an unambiguous and exact picture description. Hence, a picture drawn using the PictureEditor can be utilized in other systems or applications.

PictureEditor is still under development. In particular, the user interface needs more consideration. For example, there may be other ways of dealing with the case in which the user selects more or fewer objects. It might be better to restrict applicable operations by the number of selected objects. We intend to improve the interface and make it more elegant.

ACKNOWLEDGEMENTS

We are grateful to Dr. Geoff Wyvill, University of Otago, New Zealand, for his careful review and valuable comments on this manuscript. We are also grateful to Mr. Martin J. Dürst and Ms. Deepa Krishnan for their thoughtful comments.

REFERENCES

Apple Computer Inc. (1987) Human interface guidelines: the Apple Desktop Interface. Addison-Wesley, Reading, Massachusetts

Beynon M, Yung E (1988) Implementing a definitive notation for interactive graphics. In: Magnenat-Thalmann N, Thalmann D (eds) New trends in computer graphics, Proc CG International '88. Springer, Berlin Heidelberg New York London Paris Tokyo, pp 456-468

Bier EA, Stone MC (1986) Snap-dragging. ACM SIGGRAPH Comput Graph 20(4):233-240

Borning A (1981) The programming language aspects of ThingLab, a constraint-oriented simulation laboratory. ACM Trans Program Lang Syst 3(4):353-387

Fuller N, Prusinkiewicz P (1988) Geometric modeling with Euclidean constructions. In: Magnenat-Thalmann N, Thalmann D (eds) New trends in computer graphics, Proc CG International '88. Springer, Berlin Heidelberg New York London Paris Tokyo, pp 379-391

Gosling J (1983) Algebraic constraints. CMU Tech Rep CMU-CS-83-132, Department of Computer Science, Carnegie-Mellon University, Pittsburgh, Pennsylvania

Kin N, Noma T, Kunii TL, Enomoto H (1988) A drawing input method and its implementation using a preprocessor. In: Proc 36th Annual Conf. Information Processing Society of Japan, Tokyo, pp 2109-2110

Kin N (1989) PictureEditor: a 2D picture editing system based on geometric constructions and constraints. Master's Thesis, Department of Information Science, Faculty of Science, The University of Tokyo, in preparation

Leler W (1988) Constraint programming languages: their specification and generation. Addison-Wesley, Reading, Massachusetts

Nelson G (1985) Juno, a constraint-based graphics system. ACM SIGGRAPH Comput Graph 19(3):235-243

Noma T, Terai K, Kunii TL (1986) VIRGO: a computer-aided apparel pattern-making system. In: Kunii TL (ed) Advanced computer graphics, Proc Computer Graphics Tokyo '86. Springer-Verlag, Tokyo Berlin Heidelberg New York, pp 379-401

Noma T, Kunii TL, Kin N, Enomoto H, Aso E, Yamamoto T (1988) Drawing input through geometrical constructions: specification and applications. In: Magnenat-Thalmann N, Thalmann D (eds) New trends in computer graphics, Proc CG International '88. Springer, Berlin Heidelberg New York London Paris Tokyo, pp 403-415

Noma T, Kunii TL, Kin N, Enomoto H, Aso E, Yamamoto T (1989) Constructive picture description with Euclidean geometry. The Visual Computer, to appear

Noma T (1989) Geometric construction, constraints, and propagation. Doctoral Dissertation, Department of Information Science, Faculty of Science, The University of Tokyo, in preparation

Shneiderman B (1983) Direct manipulation: a step beyond programming languages. IEEE Computer 16(8):57-69

Sutherland IE (1963) Sketchpad: a man-machine graphical communication system. In: Proc Spring Joint Comput Conf. pp 329-346

Todd P (1986) An algorithm for determining consistency and manufacturability of dimensioned drawings. In: Smith A (ed) Knowledge engineering and computer modelling in CAD, Proc CAD86. pp 36-41

White RM (1988) Applying direct manipulation to geometric construction systems. In: Magnenat-Thalmann N, Thalmann D (eds) New trends in computer graphics, Proc CG International '88. Springer, Berlin Heidelberg New York London Paris Tokyo, pp 446-455

Nami Kin is currently a master course graduate student of information science at the University of Tokyo. Her research interests include computer graphics and its applications. She received the B.Sc. degree in information science in 1987 from the University of Tokyo. She is a student member of IEEE and the Information Processing Society of Japan.

Tsukasa Noma is currently a doctoral graduate student of information science at the University of Tokyo. His research interests include computer graphics and computer aided design. He received the B.Sc. degree in mathematics in 1984 from Waseda University, and the M.Sc. degree in information science in 1986 from the University of Tokyo. He is a student member of ACM and IEEE, and also a member of the Information Processing Society of Japan and the Computer Graphics Society.

Tosiyasu L. Kunii is currently a professor of information and computer science at the University of Tokyo. He started work there in raster graphics in 1968, which led to the Tokyo Raster Technology Project. His research interests include computer graphics, database systems, and software engineering. He has authored and edited 29 computer science books and published more than 100 refereed academic/technical papers in computer science and application areas.

Prof. Kunii is the Past President of the Computer Graphics Society, the Chairman of the Board of the Handheld Computer Society, and a member of the Editorial Board of IEEE Computer Graphics and Applications. He is active in IFIP, has organized and is ex-chair of the Technical Committee on Software Engineering of the Information Processing Society of Japan, and has organized and is ex-president of the Japan Computer Graphics Association. He served as general chairman of the Third International Conference on Very Large Data Bases in 1977, and program chairman of Intergraphics 83, Computer Graphics Tokyo 84, 85, and 86, and CG International 87.

Prof. Kunii received his B.Sc., M.Sc., and D.Sc. in chemistry from the University of Tokyo in 1962, 1964, and 1967.

Address: Department of Information Science, Faculty of Science, the University of Tokyo, 7-3-1 Hongo, Bunkyo-ku, Tokyo 113, JAPAN.

A Note on Improving the Performance of Delaunay Triangulation

J.R. Davy and P.M. Dew

ABSTRACT

The purpose of this paper is to report on recent work aimed at improving the performance of the Delaunay triangulation algorithms for reconstructing a surface from range data. Two main improvements are considered. The first is the design of a coarse grain parallel algorithm for processor network architectures typified by the Meiko Computing Surface, and the second is a technique for reducing the amount of data needed to represent the surface. Experimental results are given to illustrate the improvement that can be achieved in each case. Finally the paper outlines a new coarse grain parallel algorithm that combines these improvements.

Keywords: Delaunay triangulation, coarse grain parallel algorithms, surface reconstruction from range data, processor network architecture.

1. INTRODUCTION

This paper reports work in progress to develop efficient parallel algorithms for constructing surface representations from range data. Such techniques have a wide applicability: including automated inspection - Cardew-Hall et al (1988), computer vision - Boissonat and Germain (1981), terrain modelling - De Floriani et al (1985), and medical imaging - Arridge et al (1985).

Our current work is restricted to surfaces of the form

$$S = \{ f(x, y) : (x, y) \in D \subseteq \mathbf{R}^2 \}$$

where $f : \mathbf{R}^2 \rightarrow \mathbf{R}$ is a single-valued C^0 function defined on domain D. Hence there is a unique value of z corresponding to each (x, y) pair. The input to our algorithm is a range image

$$I = \{ (x_i, y_i, z_i) : 1 \leq i \leq n, (x_i, y_i) \in D, z_i \in \mathbf{R} \}$$

where D is the rectangular domain

$$\{ (x, y) : x_{min} \leq x \leq x_{max}, y_{min} \leq y \leq y_{max} \}$$

This represents a single view of the object, with measurements taken parallel to the z-axis. Although such depth measurements are typically sampled at a rectangular grid of points from D we allow for a more general pattern of measurement, including random distribution of points.

For engineering applications such data would commonly be obtained from a coordinate measuring machine (CMM), Cardew-Hall et al (1985), or a laser range-finder , Boissonal and Germain (1981). We do not, however, restrict ourselves to a specific acquisition method and simply assume that appropriate range data is available. By matching the representations obtained from two opposite views it is possible to obtain a complete representation of the surface for a wide range of objects .

Strategies for implementing such object reconstruction are dependent on the application in hand. Inspection, for instance, may use a database holding a model generated at an earlier design stage and such *a priori* knowledge may influence both the measurement patterns and the reconstruction methods, Cardew-Hall et al (1988). By contrast, the digitisation of an object for input to robot vision or CAD systems may need no existing computer model. Our own work was influenced in its early stages by such initial model-building requirements, hence we assume no previous knowledge of the object.

The output from our algorithms is a representation of the surface S. In the absence of prior knowledge of the digitised object, it is plausible that the range image may include significant numbers of redundant points, in large planar or near-planar areas for instance. We anticipate that the representation produced may be subject to a range of postprocessing steps, dependent on the application in hand, such as graphical display, finite element analysis, contour extraction or object recognition. In each case the inclusion of redundant points will needlessly increase the size of the representation and significantly affect the efficiency of the postprocessing step(s). Hence an important aim is to implement an appropriate data reduction strategy in which redundant points can be discarded in areas where a coarser grid is acceptable, while still retaining a high point density in high-curvature regions where this is required for an accurate representation.

Many surface reconstruction techniques have been documented. A wide ranging survey is given by Lancaster and Salkauskas (1986). We have chosen to implement methods based on *Delaunay triangulation*. This gives a C^0 representation based on optimally "well-shaped" triangular patches, De Floriani (1987), which are suitable for numerical postprocessing. If the demands of the application require a C^1 representation, further interpolants can be built upon the triangles (eg Klucewicz (1978)). Furthermore the Delaunay triangulation can be constructed to any desired accuracy using only a subset of the sampled points, thereby implementing effective data reduction, De Floriani (1985). The mathematical properties of the triangulation are well documented and it can be extended to three or more dimensions. Hence it also provides a basis for solid model-building techniques which are derived from less restricted sampling patterns, Boissonat (1984).

The experimental testbed for our work has been the Meiko Computing Surface, an extensible system based on the Inmos Transputer. This supports coarse grain MIMD parallelism based on powerful microprocessors. It is a distributed memory architecture in which inter-process communication is by message-passing.

The structure of the paper is as follows. Section 2 surveys the principles of Delaunay triangulation and outlines the main serial algorithm which is the basis of our work. In section 3 we describe a general approach to parallelising the Delaunay triangulation followed in section 4 by details of its implementation and some practical results. The main data reduction strategy is described in section 5 and its efficacy is demonstrated. In section 6 we propose an alternative parallel implementation strategy for the data reduction algorithm, aimed at better processor utilisation, and finish with a brief summary in section 7.

2. TRIANGULATION: PRINCIPLES AND ALGORITHMS

We approximate the surface S as a collection of triangular patches by generating a set of triangles with vertices at the projections of the sampled points in the $x-y$ plane. Inclusion of the sampled z-coordinates then gives the desired surface representation. Hence we need only consider the problem of building a triangulation in 2 dimensions.

Formally, let $V = \{ P_i : P_i = (x_i, y_i), 1 \le i \le n \}$ be the set of projections on the $x-y$ plane and let $E = \{ (P_i, P_j) : P_i, P_j \in V, i \ne j \}$ be the set of edges joining pairs of points in V. A *triangulation* of V is a graph $T(V) = (V, E_T)$ where E_T is a maximal subset of E such that no two edges of E_T intersect except at their common vertex. A *face* of $T(V)$ is a region bounded by a cycle with no edge of E_T inside it. $T(V)$ is a planar connected graph and the maximality of E_T guarantees that each face is a triangle. There are many possible triangulations of V, all with exactly $3(n-1) - n_b$ edges and $2(n-1) - n_b$ triangles, where n_b is the number of points on the convex hull of V, Shamos (1977).

The *Delaunay* triangulation can be further characterised by three additional properties, the *IN-CIRCLE* criterion, the *MAX-MIN ANGLE* criterion and the *Voronoi neighbourhood* property. These have been proved by Lawson (1977) to be equivalent, hence any one of them can be taken as a definition. We use the *IN-CIRCLE* criterion to specify Delaunay triangulation, since it is the basis of our computational method. The *MAX-MIN ANGLE* criterion is also described because it clarifies the nature of the optimality of the triangulation. A definition of Voronoi neighbourhood can be found in De Floriani (1987).

A triangulation $T(V)$ satisfies the *IN-CIRCLE* criterion if and only if no point of V is interior to the circumcircle of any triangle of $T(V)$. This principle gives a method for constructing the Delaunay triangulation. For every convex quadrilateral, the choice of diagonal which forms the triangulation is determined by the *IN-CIRCLE* rule, as illustrated in Fig. 1. If P_4 is inside the circumcircle of $P_1P_2P_3$ the diagonal of the quadrilateral must be swapped. An arbitrary triangulation $T(V)$ can be transformed into a Delaunay triangulation by the repeated application of the *IN-CIRCLE* criterion to each edge. When no more edges need to be swapped (i.e. each edge is *locally optimal*), $T(V)$ is a Delaunay triangulation Sibson (1978).

Equivalently, the Delaunay triangulation satisfies the *MAX-MIN ANGLE* criterion: if the diagonal of any strictly convex quadrilateral is replaced by the opposite one, the minimum of the six internal angles is not increased. By locally maximising the minimum interior angle of such quadrilaterals, this criterion gives a triangulation which is "optimally equiangular".

The Delaunay triangulation of a set of points is unique except for *degeneracies* caused by four or more concyclic points, Green and Sibson (1978). If four points form a cyclic quadrilateral the triangulation may be formed by joining either of the prospective diagonals, without violating the *IN-CIRCLE* criterion. Such ambiguities do not affect the essential equiangularity of the triangulation.

Many algorithms have been devised for constructing the Delaunay triangulation, as surveyed by de Floriani (1987). Serial algorithms may be classified as *divide-and-conquer* or *incremental*. The former approach builds the triangulation one point at a time, starting from an interior point or the boundary of the region. The latter recursively

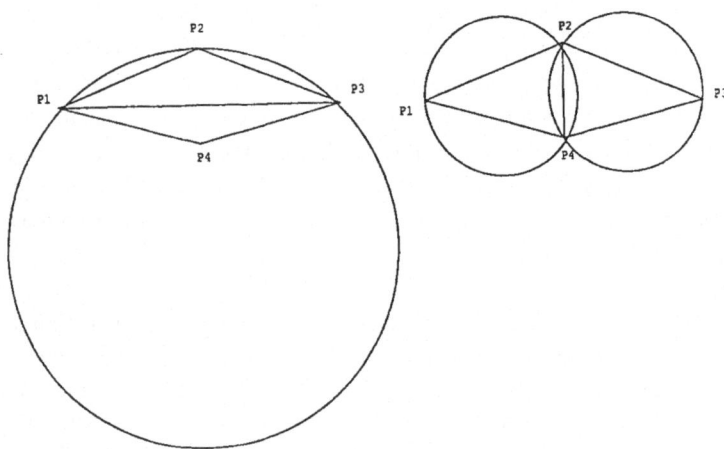

Fig. 1 The IN-CIRCLE Criterion

partitions the set of data points into equally-sized subsets until trivial triangulations can be obtained. The resulting triangulations are then merged pairwise. Incremental algorithms typically have $O(n^{3/2})$ or $O(n^{4/3})$ average time complexity. Lee and Schachter

(1980) give an example which shows that the worst case complexity for such algorithms is $O(n^2)$. Divide-and-conquer algorithms typically have worst case complexity $O(n \log n)$, which Shamos has shown to be optimal Shamos (1977).

An alternative classification distinguishes between *static* and *dynamic* methods. In the former, the complete set of data points must be available before building the triangulation, typically because some preprocessing is required. Divide-and-conquer algorithms are necessarily static, since pre-sorting is required to carry out the partitioning. Many incremental algorithms are also static: once the triangulation is complete the insertion of a new point requires the whole triangulation to be rebuilt. By contrast, dynamic algorithms permit efficient updating of existing triangulations, allowing triangulations to be built as points are received, without preprocessing.

There are few published parallel algorithms for Delaunay triangulation. Yap (1987) quotes an unreferenced paper by Saxena, Bhatt and Prasad (1986) showing a spectrum of processor-time tradeoffs, varying from $O(n)$ parallel time with $O(\log n)$ processors to $O(1)$ parallel time with $O(n^4)$ processors. Aggarwal *et al* give an algorithm requiring $O(\log^2 n)$ parallel time with $O(n^2)$ processors for computing the closely related Voronoi diagram, Aggarwal et al (1987). Yap also quotes results for various generalisations of the Voronoi diagram. All these methods are based on the CREW PRAM or CRCW PRAM models of synchronous parallelism, Schwartz (1980), for a shared memory multiprocessor. The number of processors must be scalable with the input size and a rather fine grain of parallelism is involved. These algorithms are not well suited to coarse grain, processor networks such as the a transputer-based machine which is the target architecture for this paper. It is well known, see for example Barton(1988), that the most effective way to program these machines is replicate existing serial algorithms across a number of processors and distributing the data between them. For this reason, in the work reported here, we have chosen to exploit existing serial methods rather than invent novel parallel algorithms.

The choice of a specific algorithm to be the basis of our work was influenced by the desire for construction and display of the model ultimately to proceed as quickly as the fastest data acquisition techniques, thus opening up the prospect of real time applications such as graphical monitoring of machining processes. Hence static algorithms were not considered. There are relatively few truly dynamic algorithms and we have chosen to implement, with minor modifications, an algorithm due to Guibas and Stolfi. This has the required property of allowing the reconstruction to proceed on an incremental basis as the points are received. Since this algorithm (which we call *DT)* is the basis of most of our work we briefly describe it.

The first stage of the algorithm creates a *supertriangle* which surrounds the complete set of points in the plane. One point at a time is then read and inserted to create an updated Delaunay triangulation, the presence of the supertriangle guaranteeing that each new point is interior to the previous triangulation. When all the points have been inserted the vertices of the supertriangle are deleted, together with any edges incident upon them.

The major work of the algorithm comes in the process for point-insertion. This has two main stages, a search of the existing triangulation to locate the triangle enclosing the new point followed by updating the data structure to include the new point. The search strategy involves a walk through the triangulation starting from some specified triangle until the enclosing triangle for the new point is located. Variants of this walk have been described by several writers: Lawson (1977), Green and Sibson (1978), and Guibas and Stolfi (1985). Its average time complexity (for location of the nth point) has been estimated as $O(n^{1/2})$.

The insertion of a new point P into the triangulation occurs in two stages. Firstly three new triangles are created by joining P to the edges of its enclosing triangle, which is then deleted. Any of these edges which are not on the boundary of the triangulation are now 'suspect', since their adjoining triangles may no longer satisfy the *IN-CIRCLE* criterion. They are therefore stacked, in clockwise order, along with their adjoining triangles. The original enclosing triangle is then deleted. In the second phase the edges are unstacked in turn and tested by the *IN-CIRCLE* criterion. Where this is not satisfied the diagonal of the offending quadrilateral is swapped, thereby deleting two triangles and creating two new ones with a common vertex at P. The edges of the new triangles not incident on P are now suspect and are also stacked in clockwise order. This process continues until there are no more edges on the stack. Guibas and Stolfi have shown that the stacking procedure always terminates and correctly produces the Delaunay triangulation. An outline description of the procedure *UPDATE-TRIANGULATION* is shown as algorithm 1 below.

The result of inserting a point is the creation of several new edges, all connected to P. Boissonat and Tellaud (1986) have shown that the mean number of new edges is asymptotically less than 6, and the mean numbers of triangles created and deleted are therefore asymptotically less than 6 and 4 respectively. Hence point insertion has $O(1)$ average complexity giving $O(n^{1/2})$ complexity for the total locate-and-insert process. The average-case complexity for algorithm DT is therefore $O(n^{3/2})$.

A serial version has been implemented in C and executed on a range of machines, including a Sun 3/60 workstation, an IBM PC and a single node of a Meiko Computing Surface. It has been used succesfully for deriving a terrain model for archeological sites and for discretising regions for solution of particle conservation equations.

For the parallel version described in section 3 it is necessary to merge two disjoint Delaunay triangulations. Continuing our policy of exploiting existing serial software, we make use of the merge procedure from Guibas and Stolfi's divide-and -conquer algorithm, referred to as *MERGE* Guibas and Stolfi (1985). Assume the two triangulations are called *T1* and *T2*, and are separated by a line *l*. Starting from the points of *T1* and *T2* closest to *l* a search is made to find the end points of the lower common tangent of *T1* and *T2*. These points are joined to form an edge of the merged triangulation and other new cross edges between *T1* and *T2* are created in the order in which they cross *l*, until the upper common tangent is reached. In general, a number of edges in the original triangulations *T1* and *T2* are deleted in the process. Further details can be found in Guibas and Stolfi (1985).

procedure *UPDATE_TRIANGULATION* (p, t)
{ *p is new point, t is triangle in which it is located* }
begin
   for each edge e of t (in clockwise order) **do**
     create new triangle t' from e, p ;
      if e is not on the boundary of the triangulation **then** { *e is suspect* }
       stack e, t' and the triangle adjoining t' across e ;
      endif
   endfor
   delete triangle t ;
   while stack is not empty **do**
     remove an edge e and associated triangles from stack;
     consider quadrilateral Q whose diagonal is e ;
     if e fails the *IN-CIRCLE* test **then**
      swap diagonals of Q ;
      stack edges of Q not adjacent to new point (in clockwise
       order), together with adjoining triangles;
     endif
   endwhile
end { *UPDATE_TRIANGULATION* }

Algorithm 1 : procedure *UPDATE-TRIANGULATION*

3. PARALLELISING THE DELAUNAY TRIANGULATION

A natural means of obtaining coarse-grain parallelism is to replicate the algorithm in a number of identical processes, and distribute the data between them. In the case of the algorithm *DT* we can partition the input image I into a number of equally-sized disjoint *stripes* and allocate one stripe to each process. This produces a number of disjoint triangulations which can then be merged pairwise, as in divide-and-conquer

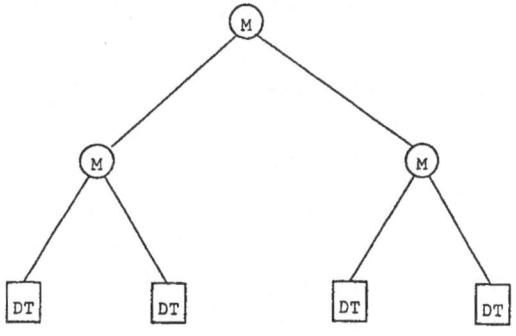

Fig. 2 Task Graph for Four Stripes

Delaunay algorithms. The resulting *task graph* is then a simple binary tree, with *DT* at the leaves and *MERGE* at all other nodes, as shown in Fig. 2 for an initial partition into 4 stripes. All leaf processes may be executed concurrently. Any non-leaf process may begin execution when its children have completed.

The approach has been used with 10 processors on the Warp computer for the computation of Voronoi diagrams, as a benchmarking exercise, Deutch (1988). We generalise the method and consider alternative approaches to its implementation.

The computational model used to derive the parallel algorithm is based on data partitioning and is widely used for image processing operations. Proceeding more formally, consider a partition of the rectangular domain into N equal-width disjoint stripes $\{ I_i : 0 \le i \le N-1 \}$ parallel to the x-axis, so that

$$\bigcup_{i=0}^{N-1} I_i = I$$

and

$$I_i \cap I_j = \varnothing \quad \text{if } i \ne j.$$

For clarity, we initially assume $N = 2^M$ for some integer M.

Let Δ be the function, defined by algorithm DT, which transforms a range image I into its corresponding Delaunay triangulation T. Let M be the function, defined by algorithm $MERGE$, which merges two disjoint Delaunay triangulation into a single Delaunay triangulation. Although the Delaunay triangulation is not unique (because of degeneracies), Δ and M are single-valued since they are defined by deterministic algorithms.

We now introduce the *partial triangulation* function PT for stripe i at *merge-level* l. If $l = 0$,

$$PT(i, l) = \Delta(I_i)$$

so the initial triangulations occur at merge-level 0. If $1 \le l \le \log_2 N$,

$$PT(i, l) = M(PT(i, l-1), PT(i + 2^{l-1}, l-1))$$
$$\text{for } i = 0, 2^l, 2.2^l, \cdots, (N/2^l - 1).2^l$$

Each *MERGE* operation increases the merge-level by 1. $PT(i, l)$ is the triangulation which includes the stripes $I_i, I_{i+1}, \cdots, I_{i+2^l-1}$ after the application of l merges. Hence, where no ambiguity occurs, we also use PT as an abbreviation for the triangulation structure produced by the function PT.

The *PT* function completely defines the task graph, the final result being given by

$$PT(0, \log_2 N)$$

Fig. 3 illustrates the merging processes in terms of *PT*, with $N = 4$.

It is desirable that N should not be limited to a power of 2, especially if the size of the initial partition is to be matched to specific number of processors. The difficulty then is that at some levels there will be a *PT* which has no partner to merge with, so must be merged at a higher level. We ensure merges are carried out in a consistent order by pairing off *PTs* from the lowest stripe number upwards, as illustrated in Fig. 4, with seven stripes. If the rightmost stripe at any level is left unmerged it is considered for merging at the next level up. When two *PTs* at different levels are merged, the merge-level of the resulting *PT* is one more than the higher level. Pairing from the left guarantees that all but the rightmost tree at any level will be be *complete* (ie perfectly balanced).

Let *subtrees*(l) be the number of disjoint trees when level l merges are complete. The function *subtrees* is defined by

$$subtrees(0) = N$$

$$subtrees(l) = subtrees(l-1) \text{ div } 2 + subtrees(l-1) \text{ mod } 2 \quad \text{for } 1 \leq l \leq \lceil \log_2 N \rceil$$

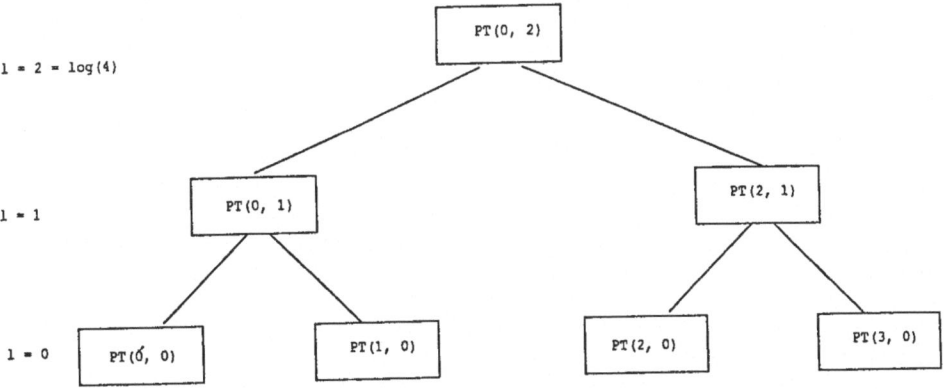

Fig. 3 Partial Triangulation Function

When merges at level l are carried out there will be *subtrees*($l-1$) trees at lower levels to be merged. Let *merges*(l) be the number of merge operations required. Then

$$merges(l) = subtrees(l-1) \text{ div } 2$$

If *subtrees*($l-1$) is odd, all the trees to merged will be complete (since the only incomplete tree is omitted), hence will be at level $l-1$. If *subtrees*($l-1$) is even, the rightmost subtree may not be complete. Its merge level, *end_level*(l), will be the height of its root above its leaves, ie

$$end\_level\ (l) = \lceil \log_2(\ number\ of\ its\ leaves\ )\rceil$$

The other trees at level $l-1$ all have 2^{l-1} leaves, since they are complete. Hence the number of leaves of all these other subtrees is

$$2^{l-1} * (\ subtrees\ (l-1)-1\ )$$

so

$$end\_level\ (l) = \lceil \log_2(N - 2^{l-1} * (\ subtrees\ (l-1)-1))\rceil$$

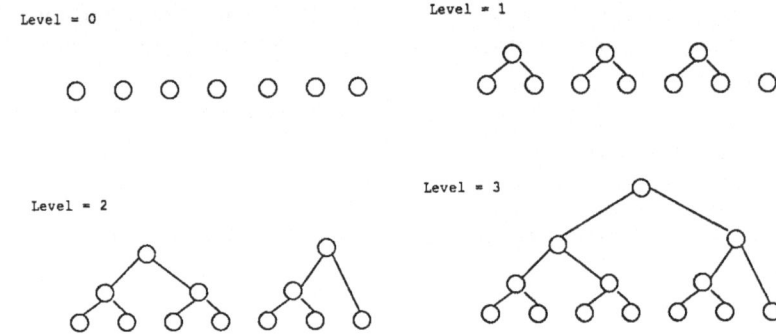

Fig. 4 Merging Pairwise from the Left

We are now in a position to define the PT function precisely in the general case. As before, if $l = 0$,

$$PT(i, l) = \Delta(I_i)$$

but now, if $1 \le l \le \lceil \log_2 N \rceil$,

$$PT(i, l) = M(PT(i, l-1), PT(i + 2^{l-1}, partner\_level\ (i, l))$$
$$\text{for } i = k* 2^l, \quad 0 \le k < merges\ (l)$$

where

$$partner\_level\ (i, l) = \quad \text{if } odd\ (subtrees\ (l-1))\ \text{ or } i < 2l * (merges\ (l) - 1)$$
$$\text{then } l-1 \quad \text{else } end\_level\ (l)$$

The computational time for the function PT is proportional to the size of the data set, I_i, which means that the parallel algorithm is extensible for sufficiently large data sets. Thus it is suitable for any size processor network, independent of topology, providing the problem size, N, is sufficiently large.

4. PRACTICAL IMPLEMENTATION

The simplest way to implement the above parallel algorithm on a coarse grain processor network is to match the number of stripes to the available processors. For example, consider a processor network configured as a one-dimensional array with bi-directional communication, as shown in Fig 5. The root processor is dedicated to a *front end* process and all other processor execute *worker* processes. Input of the range image, distribution of the stripes and saving the final triangulation are all handled by the front end process. The worker processes hold both *DT* and *MERGE*, as well as code for copying triangulations between processors and for control of the merging. Each stripe is triangulated on the processor to which it is initially sent. When a merge is to take place the *PT* with the higher-numbered stripe(s) is copied to the processor holding the *PT* with which it is to be merged. Hence both *DT* and *MERGE* utilise only data stored in the processor's local memory. The processors are numbered as shown in Fig. 5 and the final triangulation is always obtained on processor 1. When a processor has copied its triangulation it remains idle except for routing data between other processors.

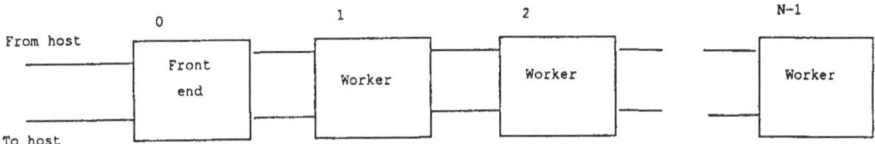

Fig. 5 One-Dimensional Array with N Processors

DT and *MERGE* are implemented using the modified winged-edge data structure described by de Floriani. This maintains the lists of edges, vertices and triangles. Since these lists are required by more than one processor, a static array-based structure is used so that pointers to elements within the lists have no address-space dependencies. Copying is implemented by appending a copied list to the corresponding list on the receiving processor and offsetting all indices within the copied elements. The two lists can then be treated as a single uniform structure by *MERGE*.

The above algorithm has been implemented on a transputer array using C code embedded within an Occam2 communication harness. The functions *DT* and *MERGE* are implemented entirely in C, as is the front end process. The communications software is built in two layers. It is necessary to be able to route messages between any two processors. A set of high level functions enables a range of message types to be built up in buffers and dispatched from the sending process. Similar functions receive messages in buffers and enable their contents to be easily extracted. All these functions are implemented in C with extensions for message passing. Routing the messages to the appropriate process is accomplished by a set of Occam2 procedures which run concurrently with the worker or front end process on each processor.

Table 1 : Parallel Delaunay triangulation timings

1024 points			
no. of nodes	time (secs)	speed-up	processor utilisation (%)
1	9.4		
2	4.8	1.96	98
3	3.3	2.85	95
4	2.5	3.76	94
5	2.4	3.92	78
6	2.3	4.09	68
7	2.3	4.09	58

2500 points			
no. of nodes	time (secs)	speed-up	processor utilisation (%)
1	29.2		
2	14.4	2.03	101
3	9.5	3.07	102
4	7.6	3.84	96
5	6.0	4.87	97
6	5.8	5.03	84
7	5.6	5.21	74

4096 points			
no. of nodes	time (secs)	speed-up	processor utilisation (%)
1	54.5		
2	26.8	2.03	102
3	18.0	3.03	101
4	12.9	4.22	106
5	10.9	5.00	100
6	9.9	5.51	92
7	9.5	5.73	82

Practical results have been obtained on a Meiko Computing Surface with eight processors. Table 1 shows timings for parallel versions using between two and seven workers, as well as for a serial version on a single processor. Results for data sets of size 1024, 2500 and 4096 are given. The timings exclude the initial time to read the points into the front end process and to save the triangulation. It should be noted that these results give a slight overestimate of the speedup obtained by the parallel version, since the triangulation finishes on processor 1. Exact comparison with the serial version would require the triangulation to be copied in entirety to root processor before saving, adding the time to copy the final triangulation between processors. This accounts for the apparently better than ideal speedup shown by some of the experimental results.

The figures indicate good speedups for a small number of processors, but for small data sets processor utilisation degrades rapidly as the number of processors increases. For the largest data set tested, processor utilisation is well maintained as the number of processor increases. We have been unable as yet to test the program on a larger array of processors but the evidence of these results suggests that significantly more processors could be effectively utilised with larger data sets.

5. DATA REDUCTION

Algorithm *DT* is the basis of a data reduction strategy described by de Floriani, giving a Delaunay triangulation at a predefined error tolerance. The boundary of the region (or in our case a bounding triangle) is first triangulated. An error value is then computed for each remaining point P_j.

$$Err_j = |\ measured\ z_j - interpolated\ z_j\ |$$

where linear interpolation from the vertices of the enclosing triangle is used. If all the values of Err_j are less than some specified threshold *Eps*, the surface approximation is said to be complete *at level Eps of accuracy* and any points not included in the surface can be discarded. Otherwise, the point with the greatest error is added to the triangulation and the errors are recomputed. The process continues until all remaining error values are less than *Eps*. De Floriani indicates that the value of $max(Err_j)$ will eventually converge to less than *Eps*, though not necessarily monotonically. Details of this algorithm, which we call *APPROX_DT* can be found in Floriani et al (1985).

De Floriani suggests that need to recompute errors and select the maximum error at each stage potentially increases the complexity of the algorithm by a factor of n. This, however, is partly offset by the smaller number of points actually inserted and in practice the amount of recomputation can be minimised at the cost of some extra storage. The main additional implementation details of *APPROX_DT* are as follows:

(a) All the image coordinates are read into an array of vertex nodes, which holds two separate linked lists (triangulated vertices and unused points). Initially all the points are in the latter; the former contains only the supertriangle. When a point is inserted into the triangulation its node is linked into the triangulated vertex list.

(b) Each unused point node contains an index to the triangle which encloses it, avoiding needless repetition of the point-in-triangle search. It also holds the most recently computed error value for the point.

(c) Insertion of a new point creates and deletes some triangles. Each triangle node therefore has a flag which shows whether it has been altered by the most recent insertion. Together (b) and (c) mean that it is only necessary to search for the enclosing triangle and recompute the error for points whose enclosing triangle has been altered by the last insertion.

(d) Each triangle node stores the coefficients a, b, c and d of the equation $ax + by + cz + d = 0$ of the plane passing through its vertices. These are computed once when the triangle is created and avoid needless repetition in the computation of error values when multiple unused points are enclosed within a triangle. Although this adds significantly to the size of a triangle node there is the benefit that triangle normal values are there 'for free' if subsequently required for shading. Moreover none of the additional information in (a), (b) and (c) is part of the essential topological and geometric description of the triangulation, so it may be discarded when the triangulation is saved, unless needed by the application.

The serial algorithm has been implemented in C on a single transputer. Results for two different simulated objects are shown in table 2. The first is a hemisphere on a horizontal plane, the second is a quadric surface. In each case the compute and save times are given are given at three different error tolerances (Eps = 1, 0.1 and 0.01) and the number of vertices unused. For comparison purposes we also show the results for the same data with algorithm DT.

We make the following observations about the results:

- The percentage of data reduction (measured as the proportion of unused points) is high (frequently over 80%), except with the smallest images at a high level of accuracy. The benefits for postprocessing are demonstrated by the much-improved save times.

Table 2 : Results for DT_APPROX compared with DT

Hemisphere on plane										
	APPROX_DT									DT
	Eps = 1.0			Eps = 0.1			Eps = 0.01				
n	c	s	u	c	s	u	c	s	u	c	s
256	1.3	0.2	220	1.4	0.3	212	1.4	0.3	212	1.6	1.7
1024	5.9	0.5	956	7.3	0.9	888	7.3	0.9	888	9.4	7.3
1600	11.2	0.7	1496	14.5	1.7	1379	15.0	1.6	1376	16.5	11.8
2500	19.7	0.8	2387	29.0	2.3	2166	29.6	2.3	2165	29.2	18.7
3600	28.0	0.9	3470	45.3	3.0	3180	45.8	3.4	3122	46.4	27.1

Quadric surface										
	APPROX_DT									DT
	Eps = 1.0			Eps = 0.1			Eps = 0.01				
n	c	s	u	c	s	u	c	s	u	c	s
256	1.3	0.3	211	3.2	1.7	1	3.2	1.7	0	1.6	1.7
1024	7.1	0.4	973	15.5	3.0	627	21.8	8.1	0	9.4	7.3
1600	10.3	0.4	1553	24.3	2.8	1186	42.2	12.1	0	16.5	11.8
2500	17.2	0.4	2450	39.1	2.8	2097	87.4	19.7	7	29.2	18.7
3600	21.5	0.3	3557	54.1	3.4	3185	156.3	27.6	97	46.4	27.1

n = number of points in range image
c = time to compute triangulation (secs)
s = time to save triangulation (secs)
u = number of unused points

- Actual timings are data-dependent. The hemisphere on a plane is faster because it has a substantial planar area whereas the quadric surface has none. These surfaces may be viewed as representing extremes of realistic data.

- The *APPROX_DT* timings have typically the same order of magnitude as the *DT* timings. This may be attributed to both the smaller number of iterations of the main point-insertion loop and gains through trading space for time. Only with the highest level of accuracy on the more complex data set is the *APPROX_DT* time significantly greater.

We conclude that the *APPROX_DT* algorithm gives a practical approach to obtaining large data reductions without significant processing cost. Experimental results have not yet been obtained for a parallel version of *APPROX_DT*. Its implementation is, however, straightforward, since the function *APPROX_DT* simply replaces *DT* in the parallel formulation of section 3.

6. AN ADAPTIVE PARALLEL ALGORITHM USING DATA REDUCTION

In attempting to make the most efficient use of a processor array it is necessary to consider the issue of load-balancing. The parallel Delaunay triangulation algorithm of sections 3 and 4 is naturally load-balanced, since the computation time for the *DT* function is proportional to the size of the data set and this time dominants the total computational time of the algorithm for sufficiently large data sets. Although some processors are idle during the merge stages the effect on performance is relatively slight as merging occupies only a small part of the total computation.

The situation is rather different with the *APPROX_DT* algorithm, because the computation time for a stripe depends on the geometric complexity of that part of the surface. Since this complexity may vary significantly between different parts of the domain, load balancing will no longer be automatic. In the worst case all the non-trivial geometry of the surface may be concentrated in a single stripe when performance will degrade to that of the serial algorithm (or worse). A similar situation occurs in parallel graphics applications where different sub-images may require significantly different rendering times. This has led to the development of dynamic scheduling techniques where an image is partitioned into a number of sub-images greater than the number of processors. Load balancing may then be obtained by sending sub-image rendering tasks to processors on demand, Morris (1987). This appraoch is an example of the *processor farm* model, May and Shephard (1986), which has provided a framework for a range of parallel applications. An extended form of the processor farm model is described below.

The root processor farms out the image strips to the worker processors on demand. This time we partition the image into more strips than we have processors. In order to combine the benefits of dynamic scheduling with a workable static storage mangement system each *PT* remains at processor which generates it until it is time for its next merge. If it is on the receiving processor, it then receives the *PT* from the sender and merges exactly as in the static case. The sender, on the other hand, copies its *PT* to the receiver and is then free to receive another initial stripe from the root processor. This can be implemented by means of a simple task controller in the front end which maintains a *task table* with an entry for each worker. If the worker's most recent task is *PT(stripe_no, level)* the entries are *stripe_no, level* and a flag which indicates whether the node has completed the task. On completion of a task the workers send a *TASK_COMPLETE* message to the controller which then initiates the appropriate action and updates the task table.

The optimium partition of the range image requires further investigation. In addition the use of a two-dimensional partition into squares is also worthy of consideration. In this case the *PTs* within a row can be combined followed by the merging of complete rows. The serial divide-and-conquer algorithm by Dwyer demonstrates the feasibility of this approach, which offers more flexibility than the one-dimensional partition in handling variable geometric complexity, at the cost of more complex control. There seems no benefit, however, in using the hybrid techniques for the straightforward Delaunay triangulation, since the extra complexity of control brings no benefit in load-balancing.

7. SUMMARY AND FUTURE WORK

We have implemented a data reduction strategy for Delaunay triangulation and shown that, contrary to earlier opinion, it can make large reductions in the output data structure without significant increase in execution time. A general approach to parallelising the Delaunay triangulation by using existing serial algorithms has been presented. Using a static implementation this has been shown to give significant speedups with up to seven transputers, and the experimental evidence suggests that larger networks can profitably be utilised for substantial data sets. The same parallel approach is also applicable to the data reduction algorithm and an alternative load-balancing implementation has been outlined in this case.

8. ACKNOWLEDGEMENTS

We wish to thank Derek Capper, whose proposal for data reduction in the context of surface reconstruction was the starting point of this work. David Morris and Nick Holliman have been involved in helpful discussions at various stages. The first author's research has been supported by a Studentship from the Science and Enginering Research Council, UK.

9. REFERENCES

Aggarwal, A., Chazelle, B., Guibas, L., O'Dunlaing, C., and Yap, C. (July 1987) *Parallel Computational Geometry*, Courant Institute of Mathematical Sciences, New York University.

Arridge, S., Moss, J. P., Linney, A. D., and James, D. R. (June 1985) "Three-dimensional Digitization of the Face and Skull," *Journal of Maxillofacial Surgery*, vol. 13, no. 3, pp. 136-143.

Barton, E. (January 1988) "Data Concurrency on the Meiko Computing Surface," in *Proc. BCS Conf. on Parallel processing for Computer Vision and Display*, Leeds, UK.

Boissonat, J-D. and Germain, F. (1981) "A New Approach to the Problem of Acquiring Randomly Oriented Workpieces out of a Bin," in *Proc. 7th Int. Joint Conf. on Art. Int., Vancouver*, vol. 2, pp. 796-802.

Boissonat, J-D. (October 1984) "Geometric Structures for Three-Dimensional Shape Representation," *ACM Trans. Graphics*, vol. 3, no. 4, pp. 266-286.

Boissonat, J. D. and Tellaud, M. (1986) "A Hierarchical Representation of Objects: the Delaunay Tree," in *Proc Second ACM Symposium on Computational Geometry, Yorktown Heights*, pp. 260-268.

Cardew-Hall, M., Cosmas, J., and Ristic, M. (1988) "Automated Proof Inspection of Turbine Blades," *Int. Journ. of Adv. Manufacturing Technology*, vol. 3, no. 2, pp. 67-88.

Deutch, J., Maulik, P. C., Mosur, R., Printz, H., Ribas, H., Senko, J., Teng, P. S., Webb, J. A., and Wu, I-Chen (January 1988) "Performance of WARP on the DARPA Architecture Benchmarks.," in *Proc. BCS Conf. on Parallel Processing for Computer Vision and Display*, Leeds, UK.

Dwyer, R. A. (1987) "A Faster Divide-and-Conquer Algorithm for Constructimg Delaunay Triangulations.," *Algorithmica*, vol. 2, no. 2, pp. 137-151.

Floriani, L. De, Falcidieno, B., and Pienovi, C. (1985) "A Delaunay-based Representation of Surfaces defined over Arbitrarily-shaped Domains.," *Comp. Vision, Graphics and Image Proc.*, vol. 32, pp. 127-140.

Floriani, L. De (1987) "Surface Representations based on Triangular Grids," *The Visual Computer*, vol. 3, pp. 27-50, Springer-Verlag.

Green, P. J. and Sibson, R. (1978) "Computing Dirichlet tesselations in the plane," *Comput. J.*, vol. 21, no. 2, pp. 168-173.

Guibas, L. and Stolfi, J. (April 1985) "Primitives for the Manipulation of General Subdivisions and the Computation of Voronoi Diagrams," *ACM Trans. Graphics*, vol. 4, no. 2, pp. 74-123.

Klucewicz, I. M. (1978) "A Piecewise C1 Interpolant to Arbitrarily Spaced Data," *Comp. Graphics and Image Proc.*, vol. 8, pp. 92-112.

Lancaster, P. and Salkauskas, K. (1986) *Curve and Surface Fitting*, Acadamic Press.

Lawson, C. L. (1977) "Software for C1 Surface Interpolation," in *Mathematical Software III*, ed. J. R. Rice, pp. 161-194, Academic Press.

226

Lee, D. T. and Shachter, B. J. (1980) "Two algorithms for constructing a Delaunay Triangulation," *Int. Journ. Computer and Inf. Sciences*, vol. 9, no. 3, pp. 219-242.

May, D. and Shephard, R. (1986) *Communicating Process Computers*, Oxford programming Research Group.

Morris, D. T., 1987, *Parallel Algorithms and Architectures for the Display of Constructive Solid Geometry*. Ph.D. Thesis Leeds University

Saxena, S., Bhatt, P. C. P., and Prasad, V. C., 1986, *Fast Parallel Algorithms for Delaunay Triangulation.*, Extended Abstract.

Schwartz, J. T. (1980) "Ultracomputers," *ACM Trans. on Programming Languages and Systems*, vol. 2, pp. 484-521.

Shamos, M. I. (1977) "Computational Geometry," Ph. D. Thesis, Yale University.

Sibson, R. (August 1978) "Locally Equiangular Triangulations," *Comput. J.*, vol. 21, no. 3, pp. 243-245.

Yap, C-Y. (May 1987) "What can be parallelised in Computational Geometry?," in *Proc. Int. Workshop on Parallel Algorithms and Architectures*, pp. 184-195.

John R. Davy is currently a second year research student in the School of Computer Studies and the Department of Mechanical Engineering at Leeds University. He has spent 15 years as a school teacher in mathematics, and will take up a lectureship in the School of Computer Studies in October 1989. Davy received his BA in Mathematics from Oxford (1970), and M.Sc in Computer Science from Manchester (1987).

Address: School of Computer Studies, The University, Leeds LS2 9JT, UK.

Peter M. Dew is currently professor of computer science at Leeds University. His research interests lie in the application of computer science techniques to problems in computer aided engineering. These include: parallel program design, visualisation techniques, and mathematical software for differential equations. He was program co-chair for the International Conference in Parallel Processing for Computer Vision and Display, held at Leeds University in January 1988. Dew received his B.Tech and Ph.D in Mathematics from the University of Bradford in 1970 and 1973.

Address: School of Computer Studies, The University, Leeds LS2 9JT, UK.

Chapter 4
Computer Animation

Quaternions and Motion Interpolation: A Tutorial

R. Heise and B.A. MacDonald

ABSTRACT

This paper provides a tutorial for straight–line interpolation of solid object motion, such as robot end effector translation and rotation. Smoothly changing orientation is accomplished using quaternions — a way of representing every orientation as four numbers (an angle and an axis of rotation). The first portion of the paper clarifies quaternions to provide an intuitive understanding of their role in rotation. Interpolation is then discussed, concluding with some problems encountered during real manipulator implementation. The interpolation method has been tested on an Excalibur robot.

Keywords: Quaternions, interpolation, robotics.

INTRODUCTION

This paper addresses the problem of planning a smooth trajectory for moving an object along a linear path. Such controlled motion is required, for example, in robotics, during obstacle avoidance and object approach. Often the position of an object is expressed with respect to world coordinates as

1. a location, (x, y, z), and
2. an orientation, $(roll, pitch, yaw)$, indicating a rotation of $roll$ about the x-axis, followed by a rotation of $pitch$ around the y-axis, and finally a rotation of yaw about the z-axis.

As will be shown, it is trivial to interpolate location. The difficulty lies in interpolating the orientation. It is not enough to smoothly change each of the angles $(roll, pitch, yaw)$, since this results in an uneven overall motion. The orientation change must be converted into rotation of a single angle, which is interpolated, about one axis. Quaternions aid this interpolation process by providing an explicit representation and efficient path control.

Recently several publications have appeared (Brady 1986; Canny 1988; Pletincks 1988; Shoemake 1985, 1987; Taylor 1986) promoting quaternions for rotation in graphics and robotics. Many formulae are given indicating the ease with which this is done: how quaternions cause rotations and how to optimize the calculations to outperform standard matrix techniques. As yet it is difficult to gain a clear, intuitive understanding of quaternions, and, as one author comments " <one> may stumble a bit over quaternions" (Shoemake 1985). This paper de–mystifies quaternions and their role in rotation. Section 1 provides motivation for quaternions, along with their definitions and operations. The next section describes how quaternion multiplication causes vector rotation. Straight–line interpolation, using quaternions for orientation change, follows in section 3. Finally, the implementation on an actual robot is discussed. This includes a section indicating the conversion process between robot joint angles and quaternions.

1   WHAT IS A QUATERNION?

Quaternions were invented by Sir William R. Hamilton (Hamilton 1969; Kelland 1904), as he sought an easy way to change one vector into another. Given any two vectors, u and v, there must be some simple quantity[1] q which transforms u into v:

$$qu = v.$$

In one dimension, determining q is easy: $q = \frac{v}{u}$. Generally, q expresses a relative length and direction between two vectors; it is the quotient of two vectors. A vector has direction and magnitude, hence specifying the change in each of these is the minimum information required for q. Figure 1 shows this in three–space:

a. Change the length of u to correspond to the length of v. This requires one number (1).

b. Rotate u through an angle in a plane until it is parallel to v. This requires three numbers — the angle of rotation (2) and the plane in which the rotation is to occur (the offset (3 and 4) from two known axes).

From this requirement of four numbers comes the name *quaternion*. Quaternions are an extension of the complex numbers to four–space, and are represented as algebraic quantities with three orthonormal "imaginary" axes ($\mathbf{i}, \mathbf{j}, \mathbf{k}$), as shown table 1. A quaternion is simply a four–vector: it inherits all vector properties and operations, including dot product, scalar multiplication, addition and norm. Where quaternions are special is in the definition of multiplication, which is traditional algebraic multiplication with the property that $\mathbf{i}^2 = \mathbf{j}^2 = \mathbf{k}^2 = \mathbf{ijk} = -1$. Quaternions are a non–abelian division ring (Herstein 1975), whose common operations are summarized in table 1.

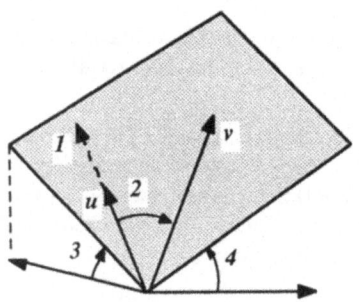

Fig. 1: Changing u into v

---

[1] Matrices are one such quantity, but they are more complex than necessary.

Table 1: Quaternion operations

A Quaternion
$$q = S + X\mathbf{i} + Y\mathbf{j} + Z\mathbf{k} = [S, \bar{w}]$$
where
$$\mathbf{i}^2 = \mathbf{j}^2 = \mathbf{k}^2 = \mathbf{ijk} = -1$$

---

addition
$$q_1 + q_2 = [S_1, \bar{w}_1] + [S_2, \bar{w}_2]$$
$$= [S_1 + S_2, \bar{w}_1 + \bar{w}_2]$$

---

additive identity
$$0 = [0, \bar{0}]$$

---

scalar multiplication
$$\kappa q = [\kappa S, \kappa \bar{w}]$$

---

multiplication
$$q_1 q_2 = [S_1, \bar{w}_1][S_2, \bar{w}_2]$$
$$= [S_1 S_2 - \bar{w}_1 \cdot \bar{w}_2, S_1\bar{w}_1 + S_2\bar{w}_2 + \bar{w}_1 \times \bar{w}_2]$$

---

multiplicative identity
$$1 = [1, \bar{0}]$$

---

multiplicative inverse
$$q^{-1} = [\tfrac{S}{\zeta}, \tfrac{-\bar{w}}{\zeta}]$$
where $\zeta = \| q \| = \sqrt{S^2 + X^2 + Y^2 + Z^2}$

---

2 QUATERNION MULTIPLICATION AND THREE–SPACE

An important use for quaternions is vector rotation. Any three–vector[2] $\bar{v}$ can be mapped into four space as $v = [0, \bar{v}]$ and treated as a quaternion. When such vectors are multiplied by quaternions, rotation and scaling may occur. This section limits this to rotation by considering a special subset of quaternions, namely, the unit quaternions, which preserve the vector norm. A rotation of $\bar{v}$ by θ around the unit axis $\bar{u}$ is given by qvq^{-1} where

$$q = [\cos\frac{\theta}{2}, \ (\sin\frac{\theta}{2})\bar{u}].$$

An explanation justifying this expression proceeds below and gives intuitive insight into quaternion rotation. Any vector $\bar{v}$ can be decomposed into vectors perpendicular and parallel to any other vector $\bar{w}$. It is informative to determine the effect of quaternion multiplication on a three–vector by examining rotation about a perpendicular axis and about a parallel axis. Combining the two cases results in an understanding of general quaternion rotation.

---

[2]The remainder of this paper uses bar notation to indicate that the vector comes from three–space, italic capitals to distinguish scalars, and italic lower case for quaternions.

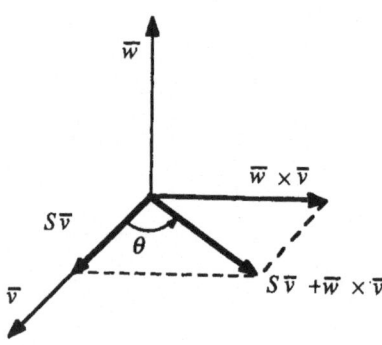

Fig. 2: Effect of a quaternion on a perpendicular vector

2.1   Case I: Perpendicular

Suppose that the vector $\bar{v}$ is perpendicular to the vector portion of a unit quaternion $q = [S, \bar{w}]$, i.e. $\bar{v} \perp \bar{w}$. Multiplying on the left by q yields

$$
\begin{aligned}
qv &= [S, \bar{w}][0, \bar{v}] \\
&= [-\bar{w} \cdot \bar{v}, \; S\bar{v} + \bar{w} \times \bar{v}] \\
&= [0, \; S\bar{v} + \bar{w} \times \bar{v}].
\end{aligned}
$$

As the scalar portion is zero, the result represents another three–vector which is the original $\bar{v}$ rotated about $\bar{w}$, as illustrated in fig. 2. To ascertain what this new vector is, it is necessary to determine its length and the angle through which it has rotated.

Using Pythagorus' Theorem, the squared length of the new vector is:

$$
\begin{aligned}
\| S\bar{v} + \bar{w} \times \bar{v} \|^2 &= \| S\bar{v} \|^2 + \| \bar{w} \times \bar{v} \|^2 \\
&= S^2 \| \bar{v} \|^2 + \| \bar{w} \|^2 \| \bar{v} \|^2 \\
&\qquad \text{from Lagrange's Identity} \\
&= (S^2 + \| \bar{w} \|^2) \| \bar{v} \|^2 \\
&= \| \bar{v} \|^2 \qquad \text{since } S^2 + \| \bar{w} \|^2 = \| q \| = 1.
\end{aligned}
$$

The length of the resulting vector is the same as the length of the original vector. It has, however, been rotated through an angle, θ, about the axis $\bar{w}$. This angle arises from the right triangle formed between $S\bar{v}$ and $S\bar{v} + \bar{w} \times \bar{v}$:

$$
\cos \theta = \frac{\| S\bar{v} \|}{\| \bar{v} \|} = S.
$$

The angle of rotation determines the first element or scalar portion of the quaternion, while the axis of rotation determines the vector portion. This vector portion must be chosen to ensure that the norm of the quaternion is one.

$$
S^2 + \| \bar{w} \|^2 = 1
$$

$$\cos^2 \theta + \| \bar{w} \|^2 = 1$$
$$\| \bar{w} \| = \sin \theta.$$

Thus, $\bar{w} = (\sin \theta) \cdot$(unit axis of the rotation). Multiplying by a unit quaternion causes rotation of a vector that is perpendicular to the vector portion of the quaternion. The parallel case must now be considered, after which it shall be necessary to return to this perpendicular case.

2.2 Case II: Parallel

Now assume that the vector $\bar{v}$ is a scalar multiple of the vector portion of q, i.e. $A\bar{v} = \bar{w}$ for some scalar A. Rotation of a vector, which lies on the axis of rotation, should leave that vector unaltered. To determine if this happens with quaternions, multiply by q:

$$\begin{aligned}
qv &= [S, \bar{w}][0, \bar{v}] \\
&= [-\bar{w} \cdot \bar{v}, \ S\bar{v} + \bar{w} \times \bar{v}] \\
&= [-\bar{w} \cdot \bar{v}, \ S\bar{v}].
\end{aligned}$$

As the scalar portion of this result is not zero, qv does not represent purely a rotation of v and the quantity has no intuitive meaning. To obtain a quaternion with a null scalar, one must examine qvq^{-1}.

$$\begin{aligned}
qvq^{-1} &= [-\bar{w} \cdot \bar{v}, \ S\bar{v}][S, \ -\bar{w}] \\
&= [-S\bar{w} \cdot \bar{v} + S\bar{v} \cdot \bar{w}, \ (\bar{w} \cdot \bar{v})\bar{w} + S^2\bar{v} - S\bar{v} \times \bar{w}] \\
&= [0, \ S^2\bar{v} + (\bar{w} \cdot \bar{v})\bar{w}].
\end{aligned}$$

Further simplification of the vector portion confirms the expected identity.

$$\begin{aligned}
S^2\bar{v} + (\bar{w} \cdot \bar{v})\bar{w} &= S^2\bar{v} + (A\bar{v} \cdot \bar{v})A\bar{v} \\
&= S^2\bar{v} + (A\bar{v} \cdot A\bar{v})\bar{v} \\
&= (S^2 + \| \bar{w} \|^2)\bar{v} \\
&= \bar{v}.
\end{aligned}$$

It is essential to return to case I and determine how qvq^{-1} fares in the perpendicular case. Look at vq^{-1}:

$$\begin{aligned}
vq^{-1} &= [0, \bar{v}][S, -\bar{w}] \\
&= [\bar{v} \cdot \bar{w}, S\bar{v} - \bar{v} \times \bar{w}] \\
&= [0, S\bar{v} + \bar{w} \times \bar{v}] \\
&= qv.
\end{aligned}$$

In the perpendicular case, qvq^{-1} rotates the vector $\bar{v}$ twice as far about the same axis as qv. Thus qvq^{-1} is a general method for quaternion rotation. The next section summarizes this discussion, yielding a general formula for quaternion rotation.

2.3 General Quaternion Rotations

Suppose that $q = [S, \bar{w}]$ is a unit quaternion, where $S = \cos \alpha$ and $\bar{w} = (\sin \alpha) \cdot$(unit axis of rotation). Any vector $\bar{v}$ can be written as the sum of two vectors:

> Rotation of vector $\bar{v}$ by θ about the unit axis $\bar{u}$ is given by the vector portion of
>
> $$qvq^{-1} = [0, \bar{v} + 2S(\bar{w} \times \bar{v}) + 2\bar{w} \times (\bar{w} \times \bar{v})]$$
>
> where
>
> $$q = [S, \bar{w}] = [\cos\frac{\theta}{2}, (\sin\frac{\theta}{2})\bar{u}]$$

Fig. 3: Quaternion rotation [See (Funda 1988) for this simplified formula.]

1. a part perpendicular to $\bar{w}$ and

2. a part parallel to $\bar{w}$.[3]

Combining cases I and II indicates that qvq^{-1} is a rotation which leaves the portion of $\bar{v}$ parallel to the axis alone and rotates the perpendicular part by 2α. This is summarized in fig. 3.

It is possible to formulate quaternion rotation of a vector $\bar{v}$ as

$$
\begin{aligned}
qv_\perp + v_\| &= [S, \bar{w}][0, \bar{v} - \frac{\bar{v}\cdot\bar{w}}{\|\bar{w}\|^2}\bar{w}] + [0, \frac{\bar{v}\cdot\bar{w}}{\|\bar{w}\|^2}] \\
&= [0, \; S\bar{v} + (1-S)\frac{\bar{v}\cdot\bar{w}}{\|\bar{w}\|^2}\bar{w} + \bar{v}\times\bar{w}] \\
&= [0, \; \bar{v} - \bar{w}\times\bar{v} + \frac{1}{S+1}\bar{w}\times(\bar{w}\times\bar{v})]
\end{aligned}
$$

where $q = [S, \bar{w}] = [\cos\theta, (\sin\theta)\bar{u}]$ and $\bar{v}_\perp$ is the part of $\bar{v}$ which is perpendicular to the axis of rotation $\bar{u}$ while $\bar{v}_\|$ is parallel to $\bar{u}$. This method of representing rotations should not be used since it results in problems when θ is an odd multiple of π, i.e. $q = [-1, \bar{0}]$. In this case, the representation has lost the axis of rotation, making it impossible to manipulate orientation using quaternions alone. For rotations of π the axis of rotation must be known in order to perform the transformation. When $q = [1, \bar{0}]$, θ is an even multiple of π and the absence of the axis has no effect since a vector rotated by zero degrees will always remain the same, independent of this axis. Another problem faced by this formulation arises during the composition of rotations. This is unmanagable as the quaternions cannot simply be multiplied. Each rotation must be kept separate and applied sequentially so that new perpendicular and parallel vectors can be calculated.

Using qvq^{-1} for rotations, as shown in fig. 3, alleviates the aforementioned uncertainties. The axis of rotation is explicitly present, except when θ is an even multiple of π. Here no problem arises, since these rotations do not depend on the axis — the orientation of the object remains the same regardless of this axis. Composition of rotations is now well–defined as quaternion multiplication since

$$q_2(q_1 v q_1^{-1})q_2^{-1} = (q_2 q_1)v(q_2 q_1)^{-1}.$$

Multiplying by the degenerate quaternions, $[1, \bar{0}]$ and $[-1, \bar{0}]$, creates no problems since they either have no effect or change the sign on the final result. But changing the sign on a quaternion preserves the rotation, as is observed from

$$(-q)v(-q^{-1}) = -- qvq^{-1} = qvq^{-1}.$$

---

[3]See any first year algebra textbook, e.g. (Anton 1981).

Every orientation can be uniquely expressed as a quaternion lying on one hemisphere of the 4-D unit sphere. In representing orientation, quaternions are preferred to matrices since the (cosine of the) angle and axis of rotation are explicitly represented, while consuming less space.

3   INTERPOLATION

Often when using a manipulator it is necessary to move the end effector on a controlled path, the simplest of which is a linear path. Moving the "hot spot"[4] of a robot smoothly on a straight line is simple linear interpolation of Cartesian three–space, as shown first in this section. Thought must also be given to the change in the orientation of the gripper. In some cases, this may not be an issue since orientation can be changed once — at the end of the move. Other times, such drastic motions are intolerable anywhere along the path. In such situations, it is essential that orientation changes evenly throughout the motion. Any general linear interpolation would combine both location and orientation interpolation.

3.1   Location (Linear) Interpolation

Moving from a location p_1 to a new location p_2, as t goes from one to zero, is given by taking a fraction of the difference between the two points.

$$new\_location(t) = t(p_1) + (1 - t)p_2 = p_2 - t(p_2 - p_1).$$

3.2   Orientation (Spherical) Interpolation

If orientation is specified as roll, pitch, and yaw, it may seem that smooth motion over time can be accomplished by interpolating each of these angles, changing $roll_1$ into $roll_2$, and so forth. When this is done, the orientation changes radically since the object is revolving about three different axes at the same time. It is essential to find a single angle which changes the first orientation into the second. This angle is interpolated for a smooth orientation change.

A natural way to handle orientation is through unit quaternions, since each orientation is represented as (the cosine of) an angle and an axis. Just as in three–space smooth motion occurs on a straight line — the shortest path between two vectors — the four space interpolation path must travel the shortest path between two quaternions. Since orientations lie on the unit 4-D sphere, interpolation involves traversing the "arc" joining two unit quaternions. Interpolating roll, pitch, and yaw does not work because it results in an erratic path over the unit 4-D sphere, as suggested in the 3-D interpretation of fig. 4(a). Shown in part (b) of the figure is the desired, shortest path. The equation for this arc, the interpolation path, for moving from q_1 to q_2 as t goes from one down to zero is:

$$new\_orientation(t) = \frac{\sin(t\theta)}{\sin \theta}q_1 + \frac{\sin[(1 - t)\theta]}{\sin \theta}q_2 \tag{1}$$

where $\cos \theta = q_1 \cdot q_2$.[5]

To remove any doubts about the validity of this formula, fig. 5 shows that the orientation path always lies on the unit 4-D sphere. Figure 6 then shows that at any t the angle travelled is $(1-t)\theta$, indicating that the arc is being followed. The equation does what is required — except when $\sin \theta = 0$, i.e.

$\theta = 0, \pi, -\pi$. When θ is close to zero, the arc between the two quaternions looks much like a straight line. Linear interpolation of four–space should be done, using the formula of the previous section. If

---

[4]The middle point between the two fingers.
[5]Suggested in (Shoemake 1985) and proven here.

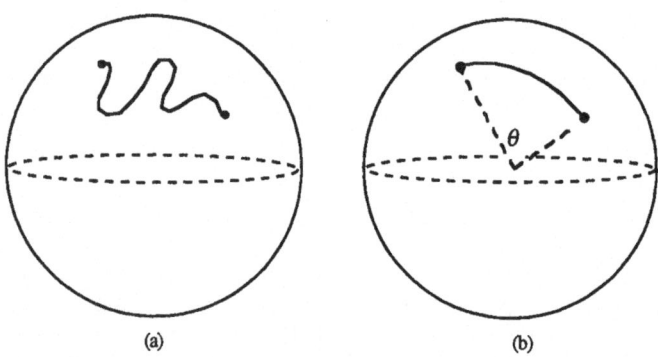

Fig. 4: Interpolating on the sphere.

$\theta = \pm\pi$, then $q_1 = -q_2$ and both quaternions represent the same orientation. Should it be necessary to move between two equivalent orientations, the path is divided into two rotations, each of $\frac{\pi}{2}$ radians: from q_1 to a midpoint quaternion q_{mid} and from q_{mid} to q_2. There are many choices for q_{mid}, provided that $q_1 \cdot q_{mid} = 0$. For example, if $q = [S, X, Y, Z]$, then a simple choice for q_{mid} is $[X, -S, Z, -Y]$. The same interpolation formula (somewhat reduced since $\sin\theta = 1$) is used on both parts of the path.

[Taylor 1986] provides a brief description of an alternate formulation for quaternion interpolation. He determines a quaternion q_{int} which transforms q_1 into q_2 through composition, i.e. $q_{int} = q_1^{-1}q_2$. From q_{int} the angle θ and axis of rotation $\bar{u}$ are determined, so that quaternion interpolation from q_1 to q_2 as t goes from one to zero is

$$q_1[\cos \frac{(1-t)\theta}{2}, \ \sin \frac{(1-t)\theta}{2}\bar{u}].$$

The computational requirements of this algorithm exceeds that of the great arc formula in equation 1.

Comparisons between quaternions and matrices in rotational tasks are given in table 2. Notice that the complexity involved in using quaternions is lower than in using matrices for all tasks except vector rotation. Even here, quaternions are generally the preferred representation since setting up the matrix is more complex than determining the quaternion for rotation.

4 IMPLEMENTATION ON A ROBOT ARM

Manipulator positions are measured in joint coordinates where the position of each link is an angle relative to the previous link. The motion interpolation described in this paper assumes that position is a location and a quaternion, hence joint coordinates must be converted into this form. Software packages controlling a robot generally contain forward kinematics allowing transformation between joint coordinates and world coordinates, which are a Cartesian location and an orientation. This orientation is conventionally specified as:

1. three vectors ($\bar{n}$, $\bar{o}$, and $\bar{a}$) which form an orientation matrix, or

2. a sequence of angles such as *roll*, *pitch*, and *yaw*.

Details of the conversion between joint angles and these forms of orientation are well-known (Paul 1981), yet expressing orientation as a quaternion is rare. This section bridges the gap, showing

Check that the length of the quaternion *new_orientation*(t) is one for any $t \in [0, 1]$.

$$
\begin{aligned}
\| \text{new\_orientation} \|^2 &= \text{new\_orientation} \cdot \text{new\_orientation} \\
&= \sin^2 t\theta \sin^2 \theta \, q_1 \cdot q_1 + \frac{2 \sin t\theta \sin(1-t)\theta}{\sin^2 \theta} q_1 \cdot q_2 \\
&\quad + \frac{\sin^2(1-t)\theta}{\sin^2 \theta} q_2 \cdot q_2 \\
&= \frac{\sin^2 t\theta + 2 \sin t\theta \sin(\theta - t\theta) \cos \theta + \sin^2(\theta - t\theta)}{\sin^2 \theta}
\end{aligned}
$$

Expand this using the identity
$$\sin(\alpha - \beta) = \sin \alpha \cos \beta - \sin \beta \cos \alpha$$

$$
\begin{aligned}
&= \frac{1}{\sin^2 \theta} \big(\sin^2 t\theta + 2 \sin t\theta \sin \theta \cos t\theta \cos \theta - 2 \sin^2 t\theta \cos^2 t\theta \\
&\qquad\qquad + \sin^2 \theta \cos^2 t\theta - 2 \sin \theta \cos t\theta \sin t\theta \cos \theta + \sin^2 t\theta \cos^2 \theta \big) \\
&= \frac{\sin^2 t\theta \, (1 - \cos^2 \theta) + \sin^2 \theta \cos^2 t\theta}{\sin^2 \theta} \\
&= \frac{\sin^2 \theta \, (\sin^2 t\theta + \cos^2 t\theta)}{\sin^2 \theta} \\
&= 1.
\end{aligned}
$$

Fig. 5: Ensuring that the orientation path lies on unit sphere.

Showing that the angle travelled at any t is $(1 - t)\theta$, thus the orientation path is an arc. If α is this angle, then

$$
\begin{aligned}
\cos \alpha &= q_1 \cdot \left(\frac{\sin(t\theta)}{\sin \theta} q_1 + \frac{\sin[(l - t)\theta]}{\sin \theta} q_2 \right) \\
&= \frac{\sin t\theta}{\sin \theta} q_1 \cdot q_1 + \frac{\sin(\theta - t\theta)}{\sin \theta} q_1 \cdot q_2 \\
&= \frac{\sin t\theta}{\sin \theta} + \frac{\sin(\theta - t\theta) \cos \theta}{\sin \theta} \\
&= \frac{\sin t\theta + \sin \theta \cos t\theta \cos \theta - \sin t\theta \cos^2 \theta}{\sin \theta} \\
&= \frac{\sin t\theta(1 - \cos^2 \theta) + \sin \theta \cos t\theta \cos \theta}{\sin \theta} \\
&= \frac{\sin \theta(\sin \theta \sin t\theta + \cos \theta \cos t\theta)}{\sin \theta} \\
&= \cos(\theta - t\theta).
\end{aligned}
$$

As $\alpha = 0$ when $t = 1$ and $\alpha = \theta$ when $t = 0$, the above equation indicates that $\alpha = (1 - t)\theta$ for arbitrary $t \in [0, 1]$.

Fig. 6: Interpolation path traces out arc.

Table 2: Operation counts for rotation tasks.

Operation[a]	Quaternions	Matrices
Rotating a Vector	15 M, 12 A	9 M, 6 A
Composition of Rotations	16 M, 12 A	24 M, 15 A
Setting up the rotation from an angle and a unit axis	4 M, 1 A, 1 Sqrt, 1 Trig	22 M, 11 A, 1 Sqrt, 1 Trig
Extracting angle and axis from rotation	4 M, 1 A, 1 Trig, 1 Sqrt	10 M, 16 A, 2 Sqrt, 1 Trig
Interpolation — finding the next rotational knot point	8 M, 4 A, 2 Trig	30 M, 15 A

[a]References to the formulae used in calculating the operation counts appear in appendix A

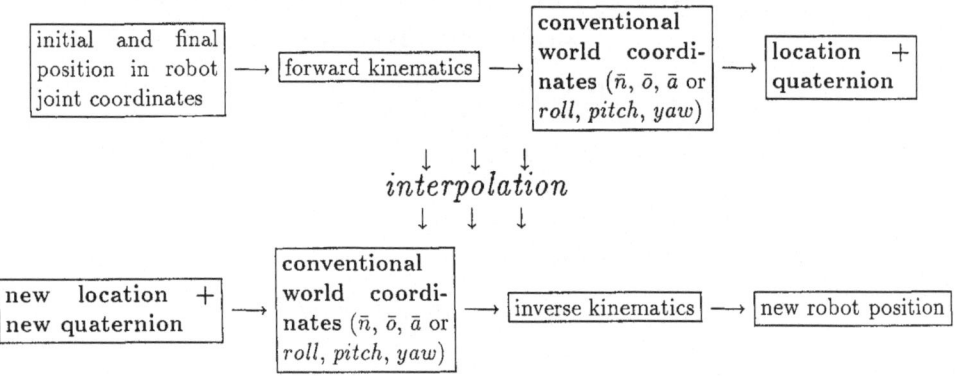

Fig. 7: Robot motion interpolation

the relation from matrices and sequences of angles to quaternions. Figure 7 diagrams the steps involved in robot straight–line motion — starting with joint angles, converting to a location and a quaternion, performing the interpolation, and finally, converting back to joint angles to move the robot. Ideally, the two extra steps necessary to convert between conventional orientation and quaternions would be alleviated, resulting in a direct path between joint angles and quaternions. More research in quaternion kinematics of general manipulators is necessary, but Funda (1988) provides a good example in the application of quaternions to solve the inverse kinematics of a Puma robot arm. Following the conversion between the three equivalent forms of orientation, considerations for implementing straight–line motion on a robot are presented. A quaternion based interpolation method, following fig. 7, has been implemented on the Excalibur robot.

4.1 Quaternion to Matrix ($\bar{n}, \bar{o}, \bar{a}$)

The quickest way to determine the corresponding matrix, M, for any transformation is to investigate its effects on the standard basis.[6] Applying $q = [S, X, Y, Z]$ to element m in the standard basis yields the mth column of the matrix:

---

[6]In R^3 this is $\{(1, 0, 0), (0, 1, 0), (0, 0, 1)\} = \{\mathbf{i}, \mathbf{j}, \mathbf{k}\}$.

$$M = \begin{pmatrix} | & | & | \\ n & o & a \\ | & | & | \end{pmatrix} = \begin{pmatrix} 1 - 2Y^2 - 2Z^2 & 2XY - 2SZ & 2XZ + 2SY \\ 2XY + 2SZ & 1 - 2X^2 - 2Z^2 & 2YZ - 2SX \\ 2XZ - 2SY & 2YZ + 2SX & 1 - 2X^2 - 2Y^2 \end{pmatrix}. \tag{2}$$

4.2 Matrix ($\bar{n}$, $\bar{o}$, $\bar{a}$) to Quaternion

To convert from an orthonormal matrix to a unit quaternion, assume that the matrix has the form of equation 2 and find $q = [S, X, Y, Z]$. This is accomplished by investigating linear combinations of the matrix components. First, examine the trace

$$\begin{aligned} trace + 1 &= 1 - 2Y^2 - 2Z^2 + 1 - 2X^2 - 2Z^2 + 1 - 2X^2 - 2Y^2 + 1 \\ &= 4 - 4(X^2 + Y^2 + Z^2) \\ &= 4 - 4(1 - S^2) \quad \text{since } \| q \| = 1 \\ &= 4S^2. \end{aligned}$$

Thus, $S = \frac{1}{2}\sqrt{trace + 1}$. Combining the M_{ij} element with the M_{ji} element yields the axis of rotation, which is easily normalized if necessary:

$$\begin{aligned} X &= \frac{M_{32} - M_{23}}{4S} \\ Y &= \frac{M_{13} - M_{31}}{4S} \\ X &= \frac{M_{21} - M_{12}}{4S}. \end{aligned}$$

When $S = 0$, these equations are undefined and other combinations of the simplified matrix components along with the identity $X^2 + Y^2 + Z^2 = 1$ are used to determine the axis of rotation. A full description appears in (Shoemake 1985).

4.3 Roll, Pitch, and Yaw to Quaternion

A series of rotations is converted into a quaternion by converting each individual rotation into a quaternion and multiplying them together in the proper order. Expressing each of *roll*, *pitch*, and *yaw* as a quaternion yields:

$$\begin{aligned} q_{roll} &= [\cos\frac{roll}{2}, \, (0, 0, \sin\frac{roll}{2})] \\ q_{pitch} &= [\cos\frac{pitch}{2}, \, (0, \sin\frac{pitch}{2}, 0)] \\ q_{yaw} &= [\cos\frac{yaw}{2}, \, (\sin\frac{yaw}{2}, 0, 0)]. \end{aligned}$$

Multiplying these together as $q_{yaw}q_{pitch}q_{roll} = [S, X, Y, Z]$ gives the desired quaternion with

$$\begin{aligned} S &= \cos\frac{yaw}{2}\cos\frac{pitch}{2}\cos\frac{roll}{2} - \sin\frac{yaw}{2}\sin\frac{pitch}{2}\sin\frac{roll}{2} \\ X &= \cos\frac{yaw}{2}\sin\frac{pitch}{2}\sin\frac{roll}{2} + \sin\frac{yaw}{2}\cos\frac{pitch}{2}\cos\frac{roll}{2} \\ Y &= \cos\frac{yaw}{2}\sin\frac{pitch}{2}\cos\frac{roll}{2} - \sin\frac{yaw}{2}\cos\frac{pitch}{2}\sin\frac{roll}{2} \\ Z &= \cos\frac{yaw}{2}\cos\frac{pitch}{2}\sin\frac{roll}{2} + \sin\frac{yaw}{2}\sin\frac{pitch}{2}\cos\frac{roll}{2}. \end{aligned}$$

These formulae[7] specify the quaternion uniquely, though $-q$ induces the same rotation on a vector as q.

4.3.1 Quaternion to Roll, Pitch, and Yaw

Conversion in the other direction is much more difficult, since roll, pitch, and yaw angles are not unique. Inverting the previous equations to solve for roll, pitch, and yaw is practically impossible, so another method must be sought. If a transformation is represented in matrix form it is easy to determine the corresponding angles (Paul 1981).

To determine roll, pitch, and yaw, only seven of the matrix elements of equation 2 are required. If M_{ij} is the element occurring in the ith row and jth column of the matrix, then using the formulae given in (Paul 1981) yields:

$$roll = \begin{cases} 0 & \text{if both } M_{11} \text{ and } M_{21} \text{ are } 0 \\ atan(M_{21}, M_{11}) & \text{otherwise} \end{cases}$$

$$pitch = atan(-M_{31}, M_{11}(\cos roll) + M_{21}(\sin roll)))$$

$$yaw = atan(M_{13}(\sin roll) - M_{23}(\cos roll), \ M_{22}(\cos roll) - M_{12}(\sin roll)).$$

4.3.2 Choosing the Knot Points

The formulae given in the last two sections assumed t went continuously from 1 down to 0. When applying these to a machine discrete points from within this interval will have to be used as knot points. These knot points may need to be chosen in an application specific manner so that any error made on the path between the points is tolerable. Brady (1986) suggests a control rate falling in the range of $20Hz$ to $200Hz$ so that the motion is smooth. He further suggests using joint interpolation, which is computationally less expensive, in between knot points so that the points are much closer in time than the natural period of the arm. Taylor (1986) presents a method for bounding the deviation from interpolated paths, by recursively halving the distance between knot points until a satisfactory deviation is obtained half–way between the points. The method reasonably assumes the mid–point deviation to be approximately the worst error over the segment.

4.3.3 Problems in Application to a Robot

In an implementation of straight line motion on a manipulator many problems arise. These difficulties are primarily due to the geometry of each robot arm. Three such issues, whose solutions are often manipulator and task dependent, or non–existent, are now described.

Although the manipulator can reach both endpoints, the straight line joining them may contain points which cannot be attained (because it would cause the robot to move "through itself" or it requires a joint position beyond the limits of the robot). It is difficult to predict such conditions without calculating the line and checking that no points are out of reach. This is computationally expensive. A better solution may be to start the linear path, stopping the manipulator when the unreachable point occurs. Verifying attainable positions must be done at each step of the path. This problem can be solved by pre–motion planning, so long as obstacles are known. See, for example, the recent and excellent work of Canny (1988).

---

[7] Different from Shoemake (1985), since he treats quaternion rotation as $q^{-1}vq$ and uses a left–handed coordinate system.

Degenerate manipulator configurations and redundant configurations reaching the same position are another source of problems in any controlled motion, and Cartesian interpolation breaks down under degeneracy (Paul 1981). Is it possible to calculate all manipulator configurations which attain the required position? If so, it will be computationally expensive. Furthermore, how does one know which joint arrangement should be used?

Finally, small transitions in Cartesian position may cause huge changes in joint positions. This results in the manipulator moving irregularly. Even though the end effector travels linearly, delays in the motion may occur. The effects are difficult to predict (Paul 1981). No solution to this problem exists. However, when there are more than six degrees of freedom the extra joints might be used to smooth out these irregularities.

5 CONCLUSION

This paper describes straight line motion of objects, interpolating both location and orientation. Linear interpolation in Cartesian three–space is well–known, hence orientation was the focus of concentration. The recently revived method of quaternions is used. Rather than just presenting the formulae, an intuitive understanding of quaternions is encouraged by our careful explanation, showing how they relate to vectors, matrices, and roll, pitch, and yaw. Quaternion multiplication plays the main role in rotation, providing an alternative to the usual matrix multiplication. A quaternion contains four components — the cosine of half the angle of rotation and the three–vector axis of rotation. It was shown that the quaternion method is superior to standard matrix techniques in representation and in most standard tasks involved in vector rotation. Quaternion interpolation was successfully used in the implementation of straight–line motion for a robot. Uses for quaternions, however, extend far beyond robotics.

Acknowledgements

This work is supported by the Natural Sciences and Engineering Research Council of Canada and by a Province of Alberta Scholarship. Thanks to Jon Rokne for help at an important moment during the development of this paper and to David Pauli for commenting on a draft of it.

REFERENCES

Anton H (1981) Elementary linear algebra. John Wiley & Sons, Toronto
Brady M (1986) Trajectory planning. In: Brady *et al* (ed) Robot motion: planning and control. The MIT Press, Cambridge, pp 221–243
Canny JF (1988) The complexity of robot motion planning. The MIT Press, Cambridge
Funda J (1988) Quaternions and homogeneous transforms in robotics. Master's Thesis, Department of Computer and Information Science, The University of Pennsylvania, Philadelphia
Hamilton Sir WR (1969) Elements of quaternions, Third Ed. Chelsea Publishing, New York
Herstein IN (1975) Topics in Algebra, 2nd ed. Wiley and Sons, Toronto
Kelland P, Tait PG (1904) Introduction to quaternions. The MacMillan Company, New York
Paul RP (1981) Robot manipulators: mathematics, programming, and control, The MIT Press, Cambridge
Pletincks D (1988) The use of quaternions for animation, modelling and rendering. In: Magnenat N, Thalmann D (eds) New trends in computer graphics, Proceedings of CG International '88. Springer–Verlag, New York, pp 44–53

Shoemake K (1985) Animating rotation with quaternion curves. Computer Graphics 19(3):245–254

Shoemake K (1987) Quaternion calculus and fast animation. In: Siggraph 87 Course 10: "computer animation: 3D motion specification and control"

Taylor RH (1986) Planning and execution of straight–line manipulator trajectories. In: Brady *et al* (ed) Robot motion: planning and control. The MIT Press, Cambridge, pp 265–286

A   NOTES ON FORMULAE USED IN OPERATIONS COUNTS

This appendix provides extra reference to the formulae used in calculating operation complexity for table 2.

Rotating a Vector

> Quaternion: Using the formula given in fig. 3.
>
> Matrices: Pre–multiplying a three–vector by a 3×3 matrix.

Composition of Rotations

> Quaternion: Using the formula from table 1.
>
> Matrices: The first two columns obtained by matrix multiplication and the last column as the cross product of the first two.

Setting up the rotation from an angle and a unit axis

> Quaternion: Specification of q as in fig. 3.
>
> Matrices: Formula on page 28 of (Paul 1981).

Extracting angle and axis from rotation

> Quaternion: Inverting specification of q in fig. 3.
>
> Matrices: Method on page 19 of (Funda 1988).

Interpolation — finding the next rotational knot point

> Quaternion: The calculation assumes that the endpoint quaternions have already been scaled by $\sin\theta$. An extra 6 M and 1 Trig are necessary for this once at the beginning of interpolation.
>
> Matrices: It is unclear what the most efficient formulation of matrix–based orientation interpolation is. If the two endpoints are expressed as the matrices M_1 and M_2 then $M_{int} = M_1^T M_2$ is the matrix which changes M_1 into M_2. As t goes from zero to one the interpolated orientation is
>
> $$M_1[f(t)M_{int}]$$
>
> where $f(t)$ is a continuous function with $f(1) = 1$ and $f(0) = 0$. This formula is used for the operations counts, which may be higher depending on $f(t)$.

Rosanna Heise was born in Edson, Alberta, Canada. She graduated with a B.Sc.(Honors) in Mathematics from the University of Alberta in 1986. Currently, she is studying for her master's degree at the University of Calgary in the area of machine learning with applications to robotics.
Address: Department of Computer Science, The University of Calgary, 2500 University Drive NW, Calgary, Alberta, Canada, T2N 1N4
UUCP: ihnp4!alberta!calgary!heise **CDNet**: heise@calgary.cdn

Bruce MacDonald was born in Taupo, New Zealand. He received a 1st class Bachelors (1978) then a Ph.D in robotics and artificial intelligence (1984) both in the Electrical Engineering department of the University of Canterbury, Christchurch, New Zealand. He worked for two years with New Zealand Electricity, and one year for the Automation section of the Department of Scientific and Industrial Research, before joining the Computer Science department of the University of Calgary as an assistant professor. His research is focussed on instructable systems; how casual non–expert users can communicate tasks to robots and other computer controlled systems. Other interests are machine learning, neural net architectures for learning systems, and robotics.
Address: Department of Computer Science, The University of Calgary, 2500 University Drive NW, Calgary, Alberta, Canada, T2N 1N4
UUCP: ihnp4!alberta!calgary!bruce **CDNet**: bruce@calgary.cdn

Composition of Multiple Figure Sequences for Dance and Animation

T.W. Calvert, C. Welman, S. Gaudet, and C. Lee

Abstract

Insights gained from an interdisciplinary study of the creative processes involved in dance composition are the basis for the development of computer based tools to support dance composition and animation. The system which has been developed (COMPOSE) provides an interactive hierarchical environment where the user can reduce the complexity of the task by flexibly switching between spatial and temporal views of the composition. Realistic animation of the final result is also available. COMPOSE, which is implemented on IRIS and Macintosh workstations, has proven itself to be of real value in dance composition. It is now being tested as the front-end of a conventional animation system for use in the animation of multiple articulated figures.

Keywords: Human animation, composition, complexity, design, human interface, creative design, aesthetic design, dance.

Acknowledgement: This work was supported in part by grants from the Social Sciences and Humanities Research Council of Canada and the Natural Sciences and Engineering Research Council of Canada.

1. COMPOSITION IN DANCE AND ANIMATION

There are many similarities and many differences between the ways in which a choreographer composes a dance and an animator composes a sequence of human animation. After conceiving the original theme and possibly roughing out the ideas with a few notes or sketches, the choreographer usually works with a group of dancers in a studio to develop the outline of the movement sequences and to define the detailed choreography. This process is extremely time consuming, frequently taking many multi-hour sessions spread over weeks or months. It is expensive in its use of space and of the time of the dancers. After the complete dance has been refined to the satisfaction of the choreographer, it is ready for performance. Although some companies record their dances with a notation system such as Labanotation (Hutchinson, 1960), Benesh notation (Benesh and Benesh, 1956) or Eshkol-Wachman notation (Eshkol and Wachman, 1958), this is not standard practice. Also the notation is not used to compose, only to record. More commonly, a record of the performance is made on videotape.

The composition of a sequence of human animation starts similarly. The theme is conceived and some rough sketches are made. However, borrowing from film and video production, the animator will usually develop a detailed storyboard showing the important scenes in the sequence. This has traditionally been done with pen and paper, but graphic tools on a 3-d workstation provide an obvious way to support this planning. After completing the storyboard, the animator goes to work, but unlike the choreographer the animator must first model the figures to be used. State of the art animation systems (e.g. Cubicomp/Vertigo, Wavefront, etc) provide the tools for the animator to "work-out" the detailed movements on an interactive 3-d workstation in a way very similar to that in which the choreographer develops a dance with live dancers. The animator must specify the position and posture of each figure for each step in time. Some simple interpolation may be possible, but there is no direct support for complex articulated figures. Just as with the live dance, a complicated animation of articulated figures can take months to complete.

For the past 3 years an interdisciplinary team of choreographers and computer scientists at Simon Fraser University has been studying the creative process involved in dance composition and developing computer based tools to support this composition process. Although the primary goal for the work has been to better understand the processes involved in creative composition, an important secondary goal has been to develop tools which will allow choreographers to plan and develop their work more efficiently. It should be emphasized that there is no intent to replace the creativity of the choreographer, but rather to provide planning tools which allow the choreographer to explore many more possibilities than would be feasible in working with live dancers. With the tools we have developed the choreographer should be able to alternate between composition sessions on the computer and work with live dancers. It should be possible to arrive at the final composition much more quickly.

Having produced a tool which has proven itself to be of some value in dance composition (Calvert, 1988; Lee, 1988), we are now proposing a to combine the composition system with a conventional animation system for use in the animation of multiple articulated figures. This paper describes the COMPOSE system, how it can be used in dance composition and how it can be used as a front-end for a general purpose 3-d animation system.

2. CHARACTERISTICS OF A COMPOSITION SYSTEM

2.1 The Creative Process

The creative composition process is poorly understood - not only is the process different for each individual but it changes from time to time for a given individual. However, some generalizations are possible (Simon, 1969):

> • The process is hierarchical;
>
> • A knowledge base is required;
>
> •Complexity can be reduced if there are alternative ways to view intermediate results;
>
> • Realistic visualization of the final result is desirable.

These characteristics will be discussed in turn and the implications for a composition system will be described.

2.2 Hierarchy of abstraction.

Initially there is a general outline of the composition; this can be a simple sketch or merely an idea in the mind of the artist. This is the highest level conceptualization of the shape, energy flows and timing of the composition. Because it is inherently an abstraction, this highest level is the most difficult to represent. The composition then becomes successively more concrete as details are added and the process moves to lower and lower levels of abstraction. The lowest level in the abstraction hierarchy is a complete physical realization of the composition. An important element of the creative process is the need to move flexibly back and forth between levels. Successive refinement of the low level details may reveal the need to change the high level theme (Calvert, 1986).

Implementation: 1. High Level. There is a need to specify a high level general outline to allow the composer to quickly sketch the essence of the composition. It is fairly easy to see how the movement patterns of a dancer or a group of dancers can be indicated, but it is not at all obvious how such imprecise parameters as "energy flow", "emotional flow", "essence", or "aesthetic shape" can be captured. A start will be to allow some high level specification of the dynamics and the effort/shape notation of Laban provides some guidance (Badler, 1986; Laban and Lawrence, 1974). Another problem is to find a way to propogate the high level description to a lower level, fully fleshed-out representation. The ideal system will take the high level description and generate from this at least a feasible implementation of the final result.

Implementation: 2. Low Level. Conventional animation systems provide a basis for specifying the detailed movements of each dancer. However, as in all animation, this is extremely tedious and the system should make it easy to build up libraries of standard body positions and standard sequences. Other methods of generating movement sequences are also possible. One approach involves capturing movement from a live demonstration; for example, a ccd camera system such as SELSPOT or WATSMART can be used to digitize the movement of a dancer or instrumentation systems such as goniometers (Calvert et al, 1980) or a Data Suit can give direct input to a computer. Although these approaches work, they tend to be cumbersome and difficult to set up, and consequently they are rarely used. Another approach involves simulation. For example, dynamic models of human biomechanics can be used to generate sequences of walking, running, etc, with a variety of different parameters (Bruderlin and Calvert, 1989). Other simulation techniques are being developed to automatically generate the natural body movements which all individuals carry out when they interact with each other. Except for dynamic simulation, none of these advanced approaches are being implemented for our composition system at this time.

2.3 Use of Knowledge

Any composition takes place in the context of a given environment and its constraints. This includes the physical setting, and more importantly, the cultural setting. For example, in dance composition this could be ballet, a particular kind of folk dance or modern dance. Each set of constraints defines the kinds of movements to be expected. Another element is the use by the composer of prior knowledge and experience. Every architect has a style and tends to reuse not only stylistic mechanisms, but also actual sub-components of a larger design. The same applies to choreography where the composer tends to make use of components from previous work.

Implementation: The libraries of stances and movement sequences which the composer builds up provide a data base for the system. An obvious addition would be to build in knowledge about different dance styles (ballet, ballroom, folk, modern, etc) so that the composer would be relieved of detailed specification. However, a more fundamental approach requires that the system have knowledge about how the dancers should interact with each other. In this way movement patterns for a dance can be specified in a very general way and the result can evolve more naturally (Ridsdale, 1987).

2.4 Handling Complexity with Alternate Views

Since the human mind can only handle a limited number of independent variables at one time, it is important to be able to reduce the complexity of the task by to studying the composition from different points of view (Simon, 1969). For example, in composing a dance, at any point in time the spatial inter-relationships of the dancers can be studied and refined. Alternatively, the composer can review developments over time. Yet another view would be the paths of the dancers on a plan view of the stage. All of these are components of the final physical realization. It is important for the composer to have flexible access to these alternate views and to be able to move back and forth between them.

Implementation: For dance composition it seems clear that the major alternatives are between space and time. At any given time, a view of the spatial inter-relationships of the dancers can be given for review and editing. Alternatively, a display analogous to a music score can summarize the patterns in time, and again this can be edited. Yet another view is a floor plan of the stage on which the paths of the individual dancers can be plotted with some indication of the time scale on each path. It is important to be able to switch flexibly between these alternative representations. It should also be possible to move easily between levels, i.e. between the high level general description, the alternative representations in space and time and the complete animation of the final result.

2.5 Visualization of the Final Result.

Normally the only true evaluation of a composition is to view the physical realization of the final result, i.e. a live performance. However, if the representation is good enough, a composition viewed in simulation or viewed from different abstractions may allow the composer and others to evaluate the work.

Implementation: The composition process should result in an animation which is as realistic as possible. In composition, an evaluation of the movement and the use of space is probably most important, and since even the most powerful workstations will limit performance, the quality and complexity of the bodies will have to be compromised. It is also important for the composer to be able to interact with the animation and view it from any angle.

3. THE COMPONENTS OF COMPOSE

3.1 General

The composition system is built around a Silicon Graphics IRIS 2400 Turbo workstation. It is important to note that the system makes full use of the inherent multi-dimensionality of the interactive graphics workstation environment, as opposed to a one-dimensional script based approach using dance notation (Calvert et al, 1982; Herbison-Evans, 1979).

Initially, the user visually composes the key scenes for the piece. A scene consists of a number of figures placed appropriately on a stage, each having a posture chosen from a menu. These are stored as they are composed and additional, intermediate key scenes are put in as the composition is fleshed out. This process is analogous to the development of a storyboard for a movie. After the key scenes have been set out, the detailed choreography can be planned using one or more of several approaches described below and an animation of the final result can be prepared and reviewed.

3.2 Composition in Space - The Stage

The composer first sees a screen which is divided into a number of display areas or windows (Figure 1). Down the right-hand side there is a menu of figures in standard dance positions; up to 18 figures in standing, lunging, sitting, kneeling or lying positions can be displayed at any one time (additional figures are available in other named menus - our current library has a total of about 300 stances). To the left of this there is a large display area providing a view of the stage which the choreographer can continuously adjust by using the mouse (rotate, translate, zoom in or zoom out). There is also a smaller plan view of the stage and a number of menus and potentiometers for the various controls.

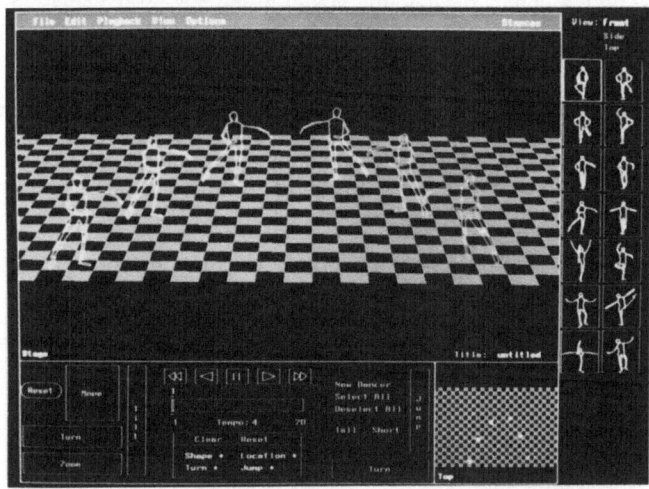

Figure 1. The stage display for spatial planning.

The composer starts by setting up an initial scene. Dancers are chosen from the menu of positions and are placed on the floorplan using the mouse. The directions which they face are then individually adjusted. Different dancers are identified with different colours (a closeup is shown in Figure 2). When the initial scene is satisfactory, it is stored, and a second scene is created; this is repeated for as many scenes as are needed to define this segment of the dance. As noted above, these scenes are similar to the series of storyboard sketches used in planning a film, but the interactive 3-d workstation allows the choreographer to zoom-in or zoom-out from the stage and to view it from all angles.

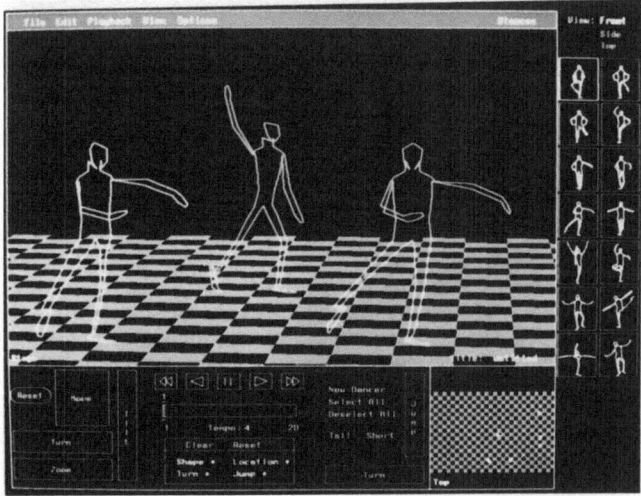

Figure 2. A close-up view of figures on the stage.

3.3 Composition in Time - The Timeline

The timeline (Figure 3) provides the composer with a score-like display showing how the stance of each dancer changes from beat to beat. Each figure on the timeline display corresponds to the equivalent figure in one frame of the stage display. Composition can be carried out either on the spatial display (the stage) or the temporal display (the timeline). However, whereas it is easy to change spatial configurations on the stage, temporal patterns are best adjusted on the timeline.

The timeline provides editing functions analogous to those available in a wordprocessor (e.g. *cut* , *paste* , etc). This allows the user to define one movement sequence and copy it to the score line for another dancers at any point in time by using an *append* or *insert*.. Also, timing can be squeezed or stretched. However, this raises questions about how the sequences in time should be mapped in space.

In the spatial (stage) display, the composer is provided with menus of dancers in different stances. In the timeline, the analogous menus are being extended to provide movement sequences which can be selected and inserted at appropriate positions on the timeline. The variety and richness of these menus is only limited by the sequences available. The next section describes how these menus are created.

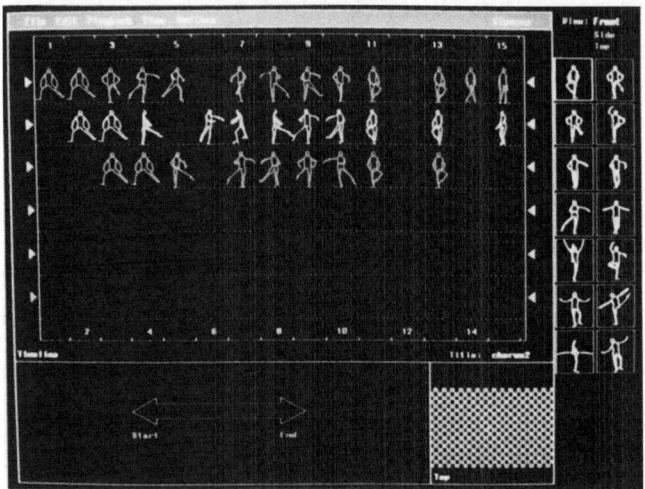

Figure 3. The timeline display for temporal planning.

3.4 Choreography of Stances and Sequences - The Body Screen.

Body stances are specified on a third display - the body screen. In this display (Figure 4), a three dimensional human body is first shown in a default position. The limb segments are selected in turn with the mouse and their positions are adjusted interactively until the desired stance is achieved. The body itself is a fairly complex structure - definition of a stance can require the specification of 44 individual joint angles. Complexity has been reduced by (a) treating the neck and back as single entities even though they consist of multiple joints; a spline assures a smooth distribution of bend across these joints; (b) the mirror image of any stance can be produced by selecting a button; (c) existing stances can be copied fully or in part from the menus. The spheres which display the movement ranges about the selected joint provide a particularly convenient way to select a 3-d orientation on a 2-d display. When the stance is satisfactory to the composer, it can be added to a specified stance menu or copied directly onto the spatial display. More details of this approach are described by Ridsdale et al (1986) .

patterns are fully specified. Alternatively, as discussed above, the sequence can be generated by demonstration or simulation; we are currently using simulation of the dynamics of locomotion to generate walk sequences (Bruderlin and Calvert, 1989). The completed sequence is added to the menu of sequences on the timeline display.

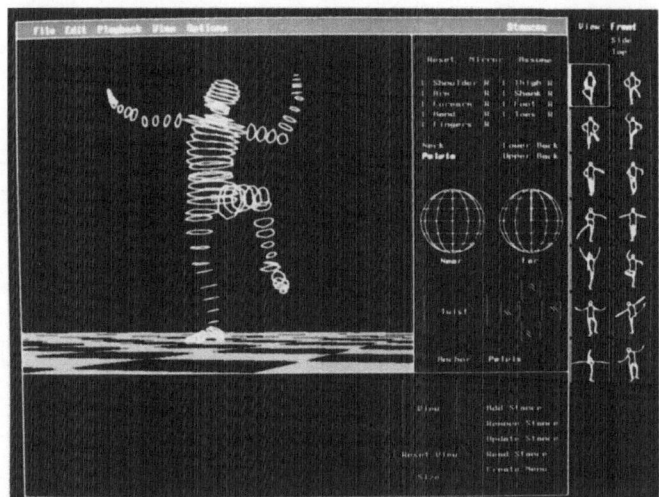

Figure 4. The body display for the design of stances and sequences.

3.5 The Design of Movement Paths

We intend to separate the specification of a path through space from the time at which things occur on that path. The path is laid out on a plan view of the stage. The initial path is specified in a piece-wise manner with the mouse. A numerical routine automatically fits a spline to the path and displays the smooth result. The path is edited by moving the control points for the spline.

Initially, the timing is linear, i.e. dots are uniformly spaced along the path length to indicate the beats. This initial spacing can then be adjusted with the mouse to achieve the timing required.

When a movement sequence is copied and pasted in the time-line display, the path for the inserted segment may be either the path of the segment which was copied or it may be pasted onto a path which has already been specified. In both cases, further editing is possible. These techniques are currently still being implemented and are expected to evolve with experience.

3.6 The Printout

Both for archival reasons and in order to have a medium to communicate with live dancers, a summary printout has been developed. As shown in Figure 5, this is essentially the timeline display, but it also includes the path to be followed by each dancer. We expect that this will be modified as we gain experience. The printout is produced from a Postscript representation and should be produced on a laserprinter if possible.

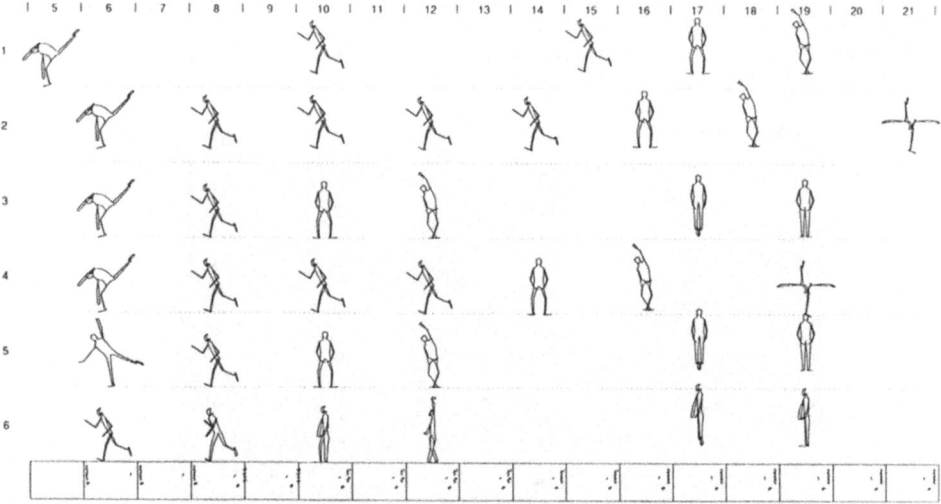

Figure 5. The hardcopy printout.

3.6 Visualizing the Final Result

As each scene is composed, earlier scenes can be reviewed in the stage display. The simplest and fastest display is a crude "stutter" animation - this is crude and uneven since the individual scenes may be quite far apart in time and in addition, they may not be equally spaced in time.

A better notion of how the figures move around the stage is obtained if intermediate frames are interpolated between the keyframes. In order to fully interpolate between keyframes with specific movement patterns (such as a walk, a prance, or a jump) it is necessary to interpolate joint angles and in our implementation these are represented as quaternions (Shoemake, 1985). Linear interpolation is fastest but a spline based interpolation, although slower, gives smoother movement. Users prefer the the smooth animation but frequently are willing to compromise to get better interaction.

3.7 Assessment of the Implementation of COMPOSE

Choreographers and dance students who have been exposed to the COMPOSE system have found it to be a useful and very interesting tool. A simplified version is currently being reimplemented on the Macintosh to make the system more widely available. When the Macintosh system is available we plan a comprehensive evaluation with the assistance of students in a dance composition class.

4. COMPOSE AS AN ANIMATION FRONT-END

In our laboratory COMPOSE has been interfaced to the Cubicomp/Vertigo V2000 animation system. The output of COMPOSE is data specifying the spatial co-ordinates and orientation of each limb segment of each figure for each frame of the animation. The

V2000 system is used to build the 3-d body models for each limb segment and to specify the surface characteristics. Then the animation production proceeds in the normal way with specification of other physical objects in the scene, lighting, camera positions etc. Rendering is then carried out together with any compositing necessary to complete the production. While it would be possible to specify the body movement sequences using the tools available in the V2000 system this would be extremely time-consuming. A video tape of an animation produced using COMPOSE as a front-end to the V2000 is available to illustrate this paper.

5. DISCUSSION AND CONCLUSIONS

The major components which still have to be implemented in the IRIS 2400 version are path specification and some method for high level planning. The former has been designed and was described above - no serious implementation difficulties are foreseen. High level planning is less straightforward. Since the highest levels are inherently abstract they are the most difficult to represent. How, for example, should the *shape* or the *energy flows* of a movement sequence be represented? Some ideas for this have been discussed by Bradford and Coté-Laurence (1988).

Another issue is the need to make the system more "intelligent". As noted above, it should be quite feasible to build in knowledge about different dance styles and both the movement paths and detailed movement patterns which should be associated with them. A more difficult issue is to provide for interaction between the dancers (Ridsdale, 1987). This involves many of the same issues as in robot path planning (Xie et al, 1986).

The particular representations we have implemented - the spatial view, the timeline, the path specification and the body specification - have evolved as a result of several years of work with choreographers. Obviously there are many other ways in which this could have been done. Since more flexible windowing software is now available for the IRIS we expect to reimplement the system to allow individual users to customize the layout of displays to meet their needs and individual preferences.

The IRIS 2400 version of COMPOSE is available from the authors. It is expected that by the time this paper is presented an IRIS 4D version will also be available. The Macintosh version is still experimental but a pre-release version is available from the authors. This version runs best on a Mac II with a colour display, but will also run on a Mac Plus or Mac SE.

6. REFERENCES

Badler, NI (1986) Animating Human Figures: Perspectives and Directions, in Proc. Graphics Interface 86 Conference, pp. 115-120, Vancouver.

Benesh R and Benesh J (1956) An Introduction to Benesh Dance Notation. A.C.Black, London.

Bradford JH and Coté-Laurence P (1988) Animate Tokens, Tech. Report CS-88-01, Department of Computer Science, Brock University, St. Catherines, Ont.

Bruderlin A, Goal Directed, Dynamic Animation of Bipedal Locomotion, M.Sc. Thesis, School of Computing Science, Simon Fraser University. (Also available as a Technical Report).

Calvert T (1988), The Challenge of Human Figure Animation, invited paper, Proc. Graphics Interface 88, pp. 203-210.

Calvert TW, Lee C, Welman C, Gaudet S and Dill JC (1988), Interacting with Complexity in Composition and Design, submitted to Computers and Graphics.

Calvert TW (1986), Towards a language for human movement. Computers and the Humanities, 20:2, pp. 35-43.

Calvert TW, Chapman J and Patla A (1982), Aspects of the Kinematic Simulation of Human Movement. IEEE Computer Graphics and Applications, vol. 2, pp. 41- 50.

Calvert TW, Chapman J and Patla A (1980), The integration of subjective and objective data in animation of human movement. Computer Graphics, vol. 14, pp. 198- 203.

Eshkol N and Wachmann A (1958), Movement Notation. London: Weidenfeld and Nicholson.

Herbison-Evans D (1979), A human movement language for computer animation, in Language Design and Programming Methodology, Tobias J (ed), New York: Springer-Verlag, pp. 117-128.

Hutchinson A (1960), Labanotation, New York: Theatre Arts Books, second edition.

Laban R and F. C. Lawrence FC (1974), Effort, Plymouth, UK: MacDonald and Evans.

Lee C (1988), A New Way to Make Dances, Dance in/au Canada, vol. 55, pp. 16-23.

Ridsdale G (1987), Knowledge representation for figure animation, Ph.D. Thesis, School of Computing Science, Simon Fraser University, Burnaby, BC Canada.

Ridsdale G, Hewitt S and Calvert T (1986), The interactive specification of human animation, in Proc. Graphics Interface 86 Conference, pp. 121-130, Vancouver.

Shoemake K (1985), Animating Rotation with Quaternion Curves, SIGGRAPH 85 Proceedings, pp. 245-254.

Simon HA (1969), The Sciences of the Artificial, Cambridge, MA.: MIT Press.

Xie SE, Calvert TW and Bhattacharya BK (1986), Planning viewpoints and the navigation route of a patrol robot in a known 2-d environment, Proc. SPIE Mobile Robots Conference, vol. 727, pp. 206-212.

Thomas W. Calvert is currently a professor of computing science, engineering science and kinesiology at Simon Fraser University, where he is also vice-president for research and information systems. His research interests include computer animation, computer vision and simulation of physiological systems. Before joining Simon Fraser University in 1972 he was on the faculty of Carnegie-Mellon University. He also held positions at Canadair Ltd. and Imperial Chemical Industries Ltd.
Calvert received his BSc(Eng) degree from University College, London in 1957, his MSEE from Wayne State University in 1964 and his PhD from Carnegie-Mellon University in 1967.

Christopher Welman is currently a graduate student in the School of Computing Science at Simon Fraser University. He previously worked for Vertigo Systems International in Vancouver. His research interests include motion specification and control.
Welman received his BSc degree at Simon Fraser University in 1987.

Severin Gaudet is currently a Research Associate in the Graphics Research Group at Simon Fraser University. His research interests include computer animation and hardware architecture.
Gaudet received his BSc degree from University of Victoria in 1978 and his MSc from Simon Fraser University in 1985.

Catherine Lee is currently a Research Associate in the Graphics Research Group at Simon Fraser University, as well as being an independent choreographer and dancer. Her research interests include dance composition and computer applications in dance.
Lee received her Hons. BA from Queen's University in 1971 and her Hons. BA from York University in 1973.
Address: Graphics Research Group, Centre for Systems Science, Simon Fraser University, Burnaby, BC, V5A 1S6, Canada.

A Software Architecture for Integrated Modelling and Animation

M. Chmilar and B. Wyvill

Abstract

A software architecture is presented which integrates the data structures for 3D modelling and animation. The benefits are: the ability to describe time-based models for animation which can change their geometric shapes; efficiency gained by exploiting temporal coherence; and the ability to create a unified interface to modelling and animation. The system is based on an extensible kernel implemented in C++; it allows new modelling primitives and motion control experiments to be added easily into a powerful, integrated environment. A versatile graphics language for scene and animation description, CHARLI, accompanies the kernel.

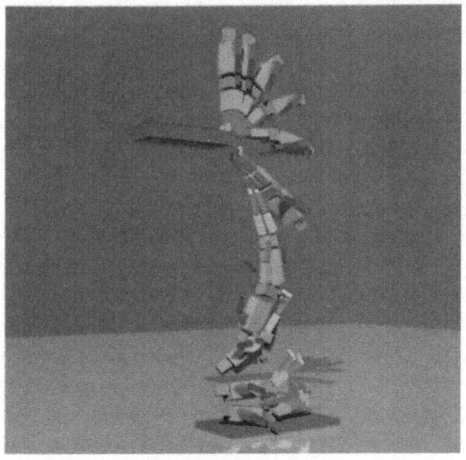

Keywords: animation, modelling, object oriented, recursion.

1   Introduction

While a current trend in the design of computer graphics systems is to break down the process of specifying and generating images into a number of separate parts, we are exploring the possibilities of a system which closely couples these parts, allowing intense interaction between them. The system integrates the specification of model geometry, model and scene structure, and animation. We believe that this "holistic" approach provides benefits not available from the "reductionist" approach.

We have created a software architecture which unifies the data structures used in modelling and animation. It allows us to animate all parts of a scene, including the shapes of models. This is because we do not introduce a false division between models and animation, preferring to mix them together into an orthogonal system. The merits of this approach will be discussed. To maintain modularity in the system while allowing free animation of the parameters to modelling primitives, attributes, and transforms, we have used an object-oriented programming language to implement an interfacing data structure between motion control and modelling.

Because we are involved in research, we also required a system which provides a good testbed for experimenting with new primitives and motion control techniques. We have, therefore, devised a *kernel* which can be extended, and incorporated into programs which will drive graphical animation, without requiring modifications. The new techniques can be used in a general, powerful environment, rather than being segregated from our production system, with little hope of being integrated with various renderers and with other modelling and motion control methods.

2   A Comparison of Two Design Philosophies

2.1   The "reductionist" approach

An example of a "compartmentalised," or "reductionist" approach is FRAMES[Potmesil 87]. In the FRAMES system, a set of "graphics tools" analogous to Kernighan and Plauger's "software tools"[Kernighan 81] is used to generate images. The process of creating graphics can be seen as a pipeline of tasks to be performed on a set of data[Foley 82]; each FRAMES "tool" implements one of these tasks, and the Unix pipe facilities are used to connect them. The programs typically read their input, which is in a standard format, modify or add to it, and output it to the next tool. Tools are provided to create geometric bodies, animate them, shade them, texture them, and so on. Instructions, from a script, are mixed into the data, and each tool executes the instructions meant for it, passing the rest along.

The FRAMES system has advantages: the order of operations (programs) can be changed around for different results; new modules may be coded independently and added to the system; modules may have duplicates that perform the same task at different "quality" levels, and different speeds; and bugs can be isolated. However, disadvantages also exist: the authors developed a "binary" data format for intertool communication because too much system time was spent passing data; the communication is unidirectional—intertool feedback is prohibited; and it would be difficult to develop an interactive user interface to sit atop this system. The authors state that they are working on a more flexible communication scheme which would solve some of these problems.

FRAMES is an extreme case of modularisation, but most systems do isolate three major components of the graphics process: *modelling, animation,* and *rendering.* They also tend to separate the specification of three types of information:

Geometry: the shapes of models, or model components.

Structure: the way geometric bodies are built up into complex models.

Animation: the changes that occur in a scene over time.

Geometric bodies are built, and then structured, hierarchically, into complex models, which are then animated. Three contexts are thrust upon the user; he may use two or three different interactive programs to build his models and animation, or write two or three separate script files.

Rendering information, such as object *attributes* (colours, textures, *etc.*) and light sources, must also be given. This may be mixed in with the other specifications (attributes with geometry, lights with structure) or given in yet another separate script.

The disadvantages of the "reductionist" approach are these:

- Because the models' geometry and structure has been given before motion control is specified, animation is limited to using the three basic transformations (*translation, rotation,* and *scaling*), and changing attributes. It is difficult to animate changes in geometry, because the geometry of models has been committed at a previous stage, and there is no feedback from the animation program to the modelling program.

- It is inefficient to pass large amounts of scene description data between programs. This is especially true if a scene is animated, and the entire scene description, with small changes, is retransmitted to the renderer for each frame.

- The user must specify three or four types of data, in three or four contexts. If modelling and animation are done with separate programs, there may be two or more interactive interfaces, as it is difficult to provide one unified interface.

- Integration of external high-level motion control programs, such as for *dynamic simulation,* cannot be done unless they can access information about model geometry.

Haeberli[Haeberli 88] has developed a successful user interface package that works with a "reductionist" approach. He has even turned the modularity of the system into a strength. Users are allowed to "cook up" their own interfaces, although, as he states "if you aren't a good cook, then the sandwich [interface] won't be very tasty." This approach is best suited to interactive viewing, and would not work well for developing and storing complex, animated scenes. While such freedom is appealing, we would rather allow the user to *use* the system than play with the interface; besides, similar flexibility can be achieved without distributing the system over a number of processes.

2.2 The "holistic" approach

Our system is centred on a graphics and animation *kernel,* which combines all processes, contexts, and interfaces in one place. This is not to imply that we are ignoring the advice of Kernighan and Plauger, and forsaking good software engineering. The system remains highly modular. We are merely applying their advice through a more powerful mechanism, object-oriented programming, rather than through the restrictive Unix pipes. Object-oriented languages, and specifically C++[Stroustrup 86], our implementation language, provide the data and function encapsulation that separate programs do, but also provide a multi-directional communication scheme between modules, without the need to copy data. We can still substitute modules (classes) within the system, although we do require an extra linking step—a price we are willing to pay for increased runtime performance.

The current work does not deal heavily with rendering. For experimenting with lighting, shading, texturing, *etc.* the FRAMES approach is ideal, although there is no disadvantage to a "holistic" approach for rendering. The Reyes Image Rendering Architecture[Cook 87] uses a "holistic" approach to speed up rendering, reducing operating system paging by exploiting geometic and texture locality. Rather, we are addressing the areas where a "tools" approach is undeniably weak: modelling and animation.

Our primary goal is the integration of all modelling and animation processes. This guarantees a truly "orthogonal" system, where *anything* can be animated: not only position, orientation, and size, but shape and structure too. As in most cases where orthogonality is achieved, we have discovered other, unexpected benefits:

Temporal coherence: The notion that, between two consecutive frames in a sequence, there is very little change, can be be exploited to speed the time taken in rendering animation. By specifying animation data directly in the models and structure of a scene, we can carefully avoid redoing calculations if their results have not changed since the last frame. The scene is built once, and changed incrementally during animation. This is especially important considering that some high-level modelling primitives are computationally expensive to render.

Recursive animation: This is best illustrated by an example. One is given in section 5.3.

A new specification paradigm: If modelling and animation are separated, an animator first builds a scene, and then causes changes to occur in it over time; but in his mind, the initial scene—the "setup"—is firmly rooted. Our approach encourages the animator to think of the scene as unfixed, changing over time; time becomes a factor in building a model: it looks different at different times. Depending on your bias, you could call this *time-based modelling* or *embedded animation*.

Model orthogonality: We have specifically designed the system to allow multiple modelling primitives to be used in one scene or model. Many systems support only one type of primitive, reducing their functionality. Because different modelling techniques have different strengths and weaknesses, we allow primitives to be *cast*, or "converted" to other forms, where possible. This orthogonality of models provides us with greater flexibility.

Green and Sun[Green 88] point out that for procedural models and motion, traditional key-frame or script techniques do not work well, because of the large numbers of primitives in them, and the complex, pseudorandom nature of the motions, and because the generation and animation of these models is often the same process. They have developed a special language, MML, to generate and animate these types of models. With the ability of models, in our system, to animate themselves, combined with features of our scripting language we will be discussing—variables, expressions, recursion, and extensibility—we can generate similar models, with perhaps a lesser degree of sophistication, but integrated into a rich environment.

3 Design goals

There are two, sometimes conflicting, objectives when designing a graphics system: one is to develop a good "testbed," where experiments with new modelling and motion control techniques can be easily facilitated; the other is to have a system that can produce animation of commercial quality for a wide variety of applications. The first objective requires an "open" software architecture, so programmers can modify or add to it. The second requires stability, speed, and reliability: the results must be consistent, quickly obtained, and guaranteed.

In our case, the kernel is a stable central structure. Experiments are implemented in an "extension layer" outside the kernel, without recourse to internal kernel modifications. The class inheritance mechanism of object-oriented languages makes this simple to do. It is possible to add new modelling primitives, new transforms, and new attributes. Different primitive types may be mixed together in one model, and may be "cast" to different types (see section 5.7). The kernel implements basic parameter interpolation functions for animation, but an interface is provided to allow "external" program code to drive animation. High-level motion control for animation can then be linked into the kernel.

The kernel is implemented as a library of functions. It reads scene description scripts, builds and traverses the modelling hierarchy, coordinates animation and rendering, and provides functions to allow interactive interfaces to modify the hierarchy. The kernel library is compiled into renderers and interactive interfaces; it provides access to the functions and data that these programs will need to use.

Finally, we want to interact with a graphics system at three levels:

Interactive interface: This is good for novice or non-technical users, like artists and animators. It is very productive when designing scenes and animation where the only concern is how it *looks*.

Scripting language: We have designed a powerful graphics language, called CHARLI. The kernel can read and write CHARLI scripts, and they are used to pass information between interactive interfaces and production renderers. Such a scripting language can be used to describe models or motions which are algorithmic in nature, and awkward to describe interactively. Scripts allow command sequences to be incrementally modified and refined. Scripts are also handy when precise data is available describing model dimensions. A discussion of the merging scripts and interaction is available in [Schlag 86].

Direct programming: This is the last resort when a result cannot be obtained with the scripting language. It is also necessary for extending the system's capabilities. As we have implemented the system, and routinely written various useful C++ classes, we have found ourselves extending the language, making it more "graphics specific." This makes it less arduous to do direct programming, although CHARLI and interactive interfaces still provide a more convenient way to use the system.

We forsee users building the basic scene using the script language, and using the interactive interface to check the design, place objects in their final positions, prototype animation, and generally "fine tune" the models and animation. Our experience with using both interactive and scripting systems, separately, has shown us that this is the preferable way to use both types of interface.

4 Animation

There are two styles of motion control: low-level and high-level. Each has its use. We have made it possible to use both within our system.

4.1 Low-level motion control

The most basic type of animation for computer graphics is *key-parameter interpolation*, also known as *track* animation [Gomez 85]. In its simplest form, the parameters to transformations—such as the degree of a rotation—are changed over time. The information needed to create an animation track is the start and end values for the parameter, and the start and end times. A function is chosen to compute the value of the parameter for frames that are between the two times. The function may cause a linear change in the value, or create the effect of *slow-in* (acceleration), *slow-out* (deceleration), or a combination of the three. Bicubic splines are often used to "shape" the interpolation curve[Kochanek 84].

The kernel provides this style of animation as a "basic service."

4.2 High-level motion control

High-level motion control is used to generate motions that look very realistic, or to reduce an animator's effort when he is creating a complex animation. The techniques used are based on algorithms or simulations, and tend to offer an interface that provides the animator with a set of parameters which he can adjust, while the motion control system manipulates a larger set of parameters, or *degrees of freedom*, for a lower-level model. Such motion control techniques include *dynamic simulation, inverse dynamics, inverse kinematics, constraints, goal-direction*, and *stochastic processes*. [Sturman 86] and [Wilhelms 86] provide good overviews of these types of techniques.

The same results could be obtained using low-level parameter interpolation, but when changes in a number of parameters must be subtly linked, they are difficult to achieve. On the other side of the coin, high-level systems often introduce an element of randomness into their results, or changes in the high-level parameters do not generate predictable results: the animator must either "take what he gets," or spend time adjusting the parameters until he is satisfied.

We have provided four ways to allow high-level motion control to be used in our system:

A simulation interface: Many high-level techniques can be implemented as quasi-continuous or discrete event simulations which drive graphical animation. Facilities are provided to allow simulation code, written in C++, to be linked into the kernel, with its outputs tied to parameters in the same fashion that tracks are substituted for ordinary parameters.

Tracks linked through variables: Variables and expressions can be used in CHARLI scripts, and tracks may be assigned to variables and expressions, allowing one track, in modified forms, to affect many parameters. These parameters will all be linked. A simple example is given in sections 5.3 and 5.4.

Operations on modelling primitives: Operations allow modellers to work with primitives at a higher level than merely altering their parameters. A good example is pulling a hill up from a large, flat polygon mesh grid made of triangles. With the right operations [Allan 88], this is easy: a vertex is selected to be the apex of the hill; a range of influence is specified around the vertex; a bell-shaped "decay" function is chosen to determine how far vertices in the range will move, relative to the central one; the central vertex is "pulled" upward. To animate the hill growing, we attach *one* track to pull the central vertex. Without operations, we would have to attach tracks to many of the vertices in the mesh, and it would be cumbersome to calculate how far to pull each one.

Self-animating primitives: Section 6 will describe how new modelling primitives may be added to the system. These primitives may be arbitrarily complex, even being able to animate themselves. A model such as Parke's face model [Parke 82] could be implemented as a primitive; it is made up of many lower-level primitives, but is implemented as a single primitive; an animator is restricted to using the parameters it presents. Procedural models would be included in our system as this type of primitive; the program code generated from a language like MML[Green 88] could be linked into our system at this level.

5   The Charli Graphics Language

The CHARLI graphics language and the kernel's design are very closely tied: CHARLI embodies our decision to combine the specification of geometry, structure, and animation. Therefore, it will be illustrative of our design philosophy, and the kernel's structure, to first examine CHARLI through a set of examples. These examples also demonstrate many of the capabilities of the kernel. The implementation details of the features will be presented in the next section.

There are many examples of scripting languages that have been developed and used for modelling and animation. One approach has been to create a new language, which is designed specifically for describing models or animation, and which is interpreted or compiled; they may be simple or complex; examples are ARTIC[Blinn 87], Polygon Groper[Wyvill 86], and Em (NYIT). Another approach is to use an existing, general-purpose language, but implement a large library of data types and functions that allow scenes and animation to be described at a high level [Thalmann 83][Reynolds 82], add classes to an object-oriented language such as Simula[Haugen 82], Smalltalk-80[Goldberg 85], or C++[Grant 86] to add graphics to its basic functionality, or extend the syntax of a language and write a "preprocessor" to translate the new code into the target language [Green 88].

CHARLI takes the first approach mentioned above, and retains the vital characteristics of Polygon Groper (PG), our earlier language. CHARLI drops the interactive editing features of PG and adds variables, scoping, operations, casting, and animation. It retains PG's basic hierarchical data structure, a directed acyclic graph, which enables models to be recursively defined. We previously used a separate, simple animation program which produced PG commands for each frame.

5.1 Geometry, structure, and recursion

First, we will show how structure and geometry can be combined with recursion to create a compact description of a cube:

```
# Comments begin with '#' and continue to end of line
def cube
    def square
        # square contains a polygon primitive. The
        # parameters are vertex triplets in x,y,z order.
        polygon( 0,0,0, 1,0,0, 1,1,0, 0,1,0 );
    end;

    def tube     # A cube with no ends.
        # Use a square for the sides.
        square;

        # tube references itself. The transforms following
        # will be applied to the reference.
        tube rotatex( 90 ) translatey( 1 );

        limit 4;     # Recursion limit.
    end;

    colour( 0.7, 0.1, 0 );   # Give the cube a colour.

    # cube is a tube with ends capped off.
    tube;
    square rotatey( 90 );
    square rotatey( -90 ) translatex( 1 );
end;
# Add a cube to the world.
cube;
```

The recursive portion of the script is the **tube** definition. The **tube** is made from one reference to the **square**, and then a copy of itself rotated to be perpendicular to the **square**, and translated to meet the **square**'s end. The self-reference to the **tube** will be "executed" again, so another square will be made (rotated and translated from the last **square**'s position). This happens twice more. The **limit** value is what prevents the recursion from continuing infinitely—the **tube** definition can only be "executed" four consecutive times.

5.2 Adding animation

Animation specification is also integrated into CHARLI. If the final line of the **cube** script is changed to

```
cube rotatey( { 0 at 0 sec linear 360 at 1 sec } );
```

the cube will spin 360 degrees over one second at a constant rate. The statement encased in the braces ({}) is a track specification. These, and our way of using them, is equivalent to Reynolds' "newtons" in ASAS[Reynolds 82].

The power of combining the specification of animation with geometry can be seen when we animate the shape, or geometry, of a triangular polygon:

```
def triangle
    polygon( 0,0,0, 1,0,0, 0.5,{ 0.6667 at 0 sec linear 2 at 1 sec },0 );
end;
```

5.3 The "coup d'etat"

Of course, the examples given so far should be reasonably easy to duplicate with any powerful system. However, we can make the final combination of geometry, structure, and animation to create *recursive animation*!

```
var theta, t, lim;        # Floating point variables.

theta = { 90 at 0 sec linear 450 at 1 sec };
t = 0.5;
lim = 5;

def H
    line( -t, 0, 0, t, 0, 0 );
    H scale( 0.7 ) rotatey( theta ) translatex( -t );
    H scale( 0.7 ) rotatey( -theta ) translatex( t );
    limit lim;
end;
H;
```

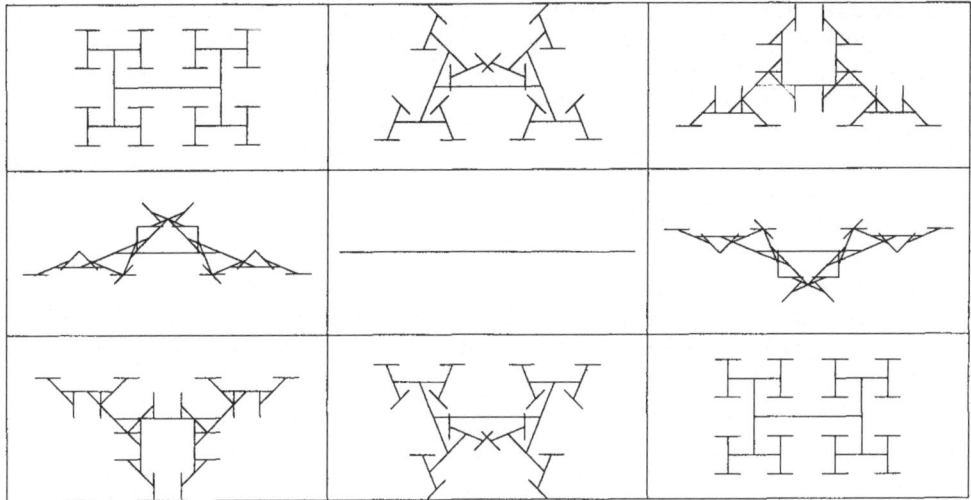

Fig. 1: Recursive animation.

The classic recursive 'H' [Wyvill 75] is modelled, and then animated, as demonstrated in figure 1. The 'H' is made from a line for the centre bar, and two instances of itself rotated and translated to make the ends. The track causes the two ends to rotate, but, of course, their two ends rotate, and their two ends rotate, and so on. The product of this script would be very tedious to create using another animation system.

5.4 Variables

The 'H' example demonstrates the use of variables and expressions in CHARLI. Variables theta, t, and lim are declared; variables are always floating-point numbers. They can be assigned values from expressions, and expressions may contain tracks, which means that their results can be time-dependent. For instance, theta is used twice as a parameter to rotatey transforms, and one is negated. The motion resulting from these animated rotations, although slightly different, is linked. The script may now be quickly and conveniently modified, while maintaining the correct relationships between parameters. By carefully using tracks in expressions, and assigning their values to variables, it is possible to build elaborate animated models with complex motions, which are controlled from a small set of tracks. This is a type of high-level motion control.

Variables are also a convenient way to communicate with the kernel, sending or receiving information from CHARLI scripts. There are predefined variables that can be used to communicate with the kernel:

Parameter controls: These are used to set parameters in the kernel. They have default values if they are not set in the script. Examples would be seqlength (sequence length) and fps (frames per second). To change fps from its default value of 30 to 24, a statement in the script would say "fps = 24".

Global information: Scripts can access the current frame number (curframe) or current time (curtime) through special variables. These are really system constants whose values change with time, and are updated by the kernel. They cannot be assigned to.

Import/export: These variables are used to set up communication between the kernel and high-level motion simulation programs. Import variables are tied to outputs from simulations; they may be used in expressions. Export variables are used to set parameters for the simulations by assigning values to them: these variables are declared as **export** or **import** in the CHARLI scripts, and the simulations "attach" to them at initialisation so they can read or change their values.

5.5 Scoping

Although CHARLI is not a general purpose programming language, there are similarities: A model definition in CHARLI corresponds to a procedure in Pascal[Jensen 74] (and most other scoped, procedural languages). Model names and variables declared within definitions obey the same lexical scoping rules as procedures and variables do in Pascal.

5.6 Operations

Operations are defined in section 4.2. To apply them to a primitive, a list of operations is given after a primitive is instanced in a script. The CHARLI statement for the example given in section 4.2 is

```
polymesh( ... ) select( 3.4, 0, 23.87 )
                range( 3 )
                decay( "bell" )
                pull( { 0 at 0 sec slowinout 1.8 at 2 sec } );
```

5.7 Casts

To maintain compact descriptions of models, and allow the different modelling primitives to be exploited fully, we have introduced a "type conversion" or *casting* operation to be used in scripts to change one type of modelling primitive to another.

The parameters to the polygon mesh grid in the last example would be very messy, consisting of a list of vertices in the mesh, and then a description of how they are interconnected; a large set of numbers is given, and if there are any errors, they will be difficult to find and correct. However, it is easy to generate a similar model using single polygons and recursion:

```
def grid
    def square
        # square is made of two triangles.
        polygon( 0,0,0, 0,0,1, 1,0,0 );
        polygon( 0,0,1, 1,0,1, 1,0,0 );
    end;
    def row
        square;
        row translatex( 1 );
        limit 40;
    end;

    row;
    grid translatez( 1 );
    limit 40;
end;
```

We cannot use the polygon mesh operations to make hills from these discrete polygons. In the script, we can say

```
grid cast to polymesh select( 3.4, ... ;
```

to eliminate this problem. The kernel will cause the discrete polygons to be converted into the data structure of a polygon mesh.

Many renderers deal solely with polygons. If other modelling primitives are used in a scene, they are converted to polygons before they are rendered. This conversion is done implicitly, and every primitive in the system provides a conversion routine. We have merely allowed script writers to convert explicitly between primitives if they find it useful to do so, and we have extended the idea beyond having only polygons as the target type: casting between any two primitives types is allowed if it is reasonable, and an algorithm is available, to do so.

5.8 Flow Control

Simple flow control is done in model definitions with an **if-else** construct. The **if** statement can evaluate arithmetic comparison statements (ie. **curframe + 3 >= 22**).

if statements can be used in an interesting way with recursion. A simple recursive tree can be defined like this:

```
def tree
    def leaves   ...  end;
    def trunck   ...  end;

    if( limit == 0 )
        leaves;
    else
        trunk;
    end;

    tree scale( 0.5, 0.7, 0.5 ) rotatez( 30 ) rotatey( 60 ) translatey( 5 );
    tree scale( 0.5, 0.7, 0.5 ) rotatez( 45 ) rotatey( -60 ) translatey( 5 );
    tree scale( 0.5, 0.7, 0.5 ) rotatez( 45 ) rotatey( 180 ) translatey( 5 );
    tree scale( 0.4, 0.5, 0.4 ) rotatez( 60 ) translatey( 3.5 );
    limit 6;
end;
```

The branches of the tree are smaller trees. The **limit** value, a global information variable, counts down during recursion; on the last pass, rather than including another trunk, for a dead-looking tree, leaves are put on the ends of the branches.

There is no **for** statement: it can be simulated using recursion. Combined with expressions, we can even create arithmetic progressions with recursive scaling; otherwise, we would only be able to create geometric scaling progressions[Wyvill 75].

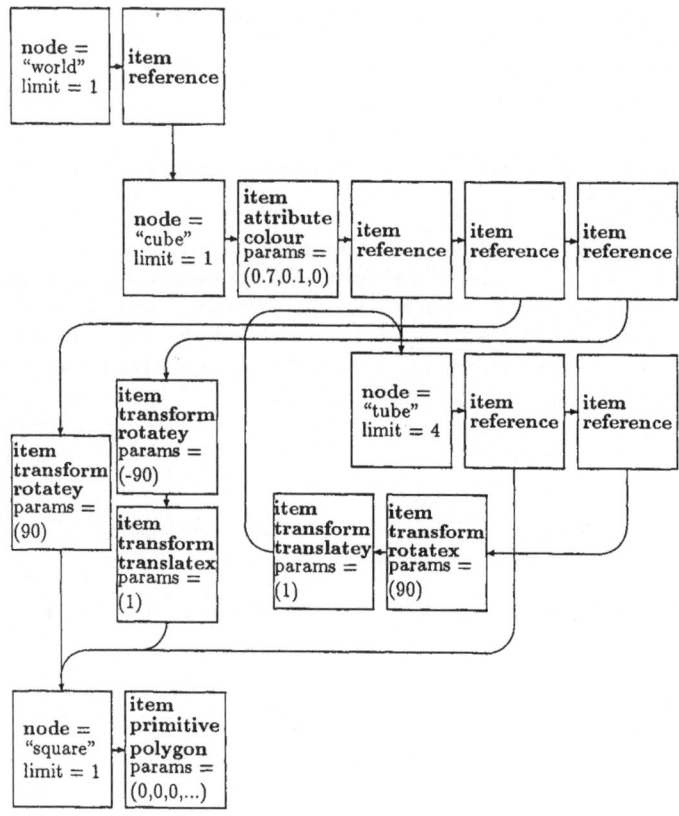

Fig. 2: The cube script.

6 The Kernel Data Structures

6.1 The modelling hierarchy

The primary data structure that the kernel manages is the modelling hierarchy. The hierarchy is reflected closely in the CHARLI language. It is a directed acyclic graph.

The structure built from the cube script is shown in figure 2. Each defined model in the script has a *node* with a list of *items*. Each item corresponds to a script statement. References to models are represented by a *reference* item, which keeps a pointer to the model's node, with some optional transforms on the way.

Traversal To produce an image, the hierarchy is traversed to output a scene description, where primitives are placed in their final positions, with attributes set. For each item in a node's list, an appropriate action is taken. When a reference item is found, the current transformation matrix and attribute list are pushed, and the referenced node is traversed; when the subgraph traversal is finished, the old matrix and attributes are restored, and the item list traversal is continued.

When a node is passed through, its limit value is checked. If it is zero, the node is not traversed; otherwise, its limit is decremented, and it is traversed. This is how recursion in controlled, as in [Wyvill 75].

There is some flow control that controls the traversal of the lists: the `if-then` construct makes it possible for the list of `items` to fork into two possible paths, depending on the value of the conditional expression in the `if` statement.

Implementation When a CHARLI script is read by the kernel, the hierarchy data structure is built. The hierarchy is built from two basic C++ classes, `node` and `item`. When a model definition is encountered, a `node` object is created, which will contain the name of the model, its limit, and the number of local variables it has. A `node` heads a list of `items`. For most statements in a definition body, an `item` is made and put into the list.

Class `item` does not really have many capabilities, because it is intended that subclasses be derived from it. It does contain some functions and data that its derivatives will find useful, and it defines some virtual functions that they must implement. It looks like this:

```
class item : public listitem
            // listitem base class lets these objects be
            // placed in lists
{
protected:
    param_list*   plist;
public:
                  item( param_list* p ) { plist = p; }
    virtual void  render_action();
    virtual void  touch();
    // useful functions ...
};
```

`item` is next specialised into classes `primitive`, `attribute`, and `transform`, as well as classes to implement assignment statements, flow control, and references. We will look at class `primitive`, but `attribute` and `transform` are essentially similar.

```
class primitive : public item
{
public:
                  primitive( param_list* p ) : (p) {}
    // functions useful to primitives ...
};
```

`primitive`, again, does not really do anything but provide a base for further class derivation. `primitive` is made available to programmers who wish to implement new primitive classes for the system. One such class is `polygon`:

```
class polygon : public primitive
{
        // store vertices for internal representation
    vertex          v[ MAXVERTICES ];
public:
                    polygon( param_list* p ) : (p);
    void            render_action();
    void            touch();
};
```

Class `polygon` is fully functioning primitive. It implements the functions and stores the data values that are specific to polygons. Other classes are `bicubic_patch`, `soft_object`, `particle_system`, `face`, *etc.*

When traversing the hierarchy, the kernel does not need to know what a polygon is, or even a primitive. It treats all `items` generically, and simply calls the `render_action` function for each one. If it is a `transform`, it will concatenate its matrix onto the current transformation matrix; an `attribute` will change its value in the attribute list; a `primitive` will describe itself to the renderer; and a `reference` will tell the kernel to push the current matrix and attributes, and traverse the node it points to.

Full class derivation histories are given in boldface font for each object in the hierarchy of the cube script, in figure 2.

[Grant 86] suggests a class derivation tree that could be built atop class `primitive`.

Extensibility The subclass derivation and virtual function features of C++ are what allow the kernel to be easily extended. The definitions of the base classes are made available to programmers, and they may then implement new features. To incorporate a new primitive, for instance, all that is required is to add its name, and a pointer to a creation function, into the kernel's table of active primitives, and recompile the file containing the table. The kernel also has tables for active attributes and transforms.

6.2 Parameters

As the CHARLI examples show, most items in the hierarchy have a set of parameters passed to them The script parser gathers the parameters into an array, or *parameter vector*. When a new `item` object is created, the kernel passes it a pointer to its parameter vector. C++ programmers implementing classes for the system can access the parameters in the vector, and use their values. In the `polygon` class example, the parameter vector is read, and the numbers in it are interpreted to be vertex triplets. These are stored in the `vertex` array as the object's internal representation.

There are three types of parameters, from a hierarchy item's point of view: floating-point numbers, character strings, and pointers to models. The most important of these are numeric parameters. They appear as C++ `doubles` to the item, but their values may be gathered from expressions or tracks. They are actually objects of a class called `superdouble`, which will be described in detail in section 6.7.

6.3   Tracks

The tracks shown in the example scripts are of the simplest kind, with only a start and end value, and one interpolation function. We are presently developing a more sophisticated style of track, which contains multiple *cues*. A *cue* is a time/value pair. Between two cues, there is an interpolation function. Splines, with various bases, can be run through the cues.

The time values in the cues can be absolute, given in frames or seconds, or relative to other cues, offset by frames or seconds. This is similar to the cue structure of S-Dynamics on the Symbolics Lisp Machines[Symbolics].

Tracks maintain lists of pointers to the parameters and expressions they are used in. When the track changes value, the kernel knows what items in the hierarchy are affected. It calls their touch function; "touching" an item is a signal to it that its parameters have changed, and that it should rebuild its internal representation.

6.4   Expressions

Expressions in a CHARLI script are converted into postfix form, and saved. During traversal, a stack is maintained to store the values of variables, and to evaluate expressions. When a node is entered, space is allocated on the stack for its variables, and static and dynamic links are set up. References to variables are translated into the number of static links to chain back through, and the offset into the stack block. Expressions are evaluated by pushing values onto the stack, and applying operators to them.

6.5   Casts

Casting can be performed explicitly, in a script, or implicitly, by the current renderer. The converted form of the model is stored as a "secret" node in the hierarchy. If the model does not change between any two frames in an animation, then the cast is computed once for the first frame, and reused in the second.

Converting between two representations for a model may be computationally expensive. We wish to avoid doing this whenever possible.

When a cast is requested, the model definition being cast is traversed, but, rather than sending its representation to the renderer, it is evaluated in its local coordinates, and the representation is saved. The function that implements the specific cast is called and given this representation; it builds the new one, using the target primitive type.

6.6   Display list

We want to avoid traversing the hierarchy for every frame in an animation. Instead, we traverse it once to produce a "flat" display list for the first frame. For subsequent frames, we retraverse the entire hierarchy quickly, to ensure that all variables are updated correctly, but at each node and item, unless they have been "touched," we do nothing. When we consider this, along with casting, we can avoid many calculations. It may be possible to decide, for each frame, what paths in the hierarchy *must* be traversed, and ignore the others, further reducing the time taken.

The display list format can be traversed much more quickly than the hierarchy, so it is preferable for working interactively on a graphics workstation. The display list is editable, so the kernel can modify and replace parts of it.

The "internal representation" of items mentioned in the section on parameters is really a set of pointers to the representation the item built of itself in the display list. The polygon class would not have an array of vertices, but a pointer to where its vertices are stored in the display list. When an item is touched, it deletes its old representation from the list, and replaces it with a new one.

6.7 "Superdoubles"

A C++ class called superdouble is the nexus through which the animation and modelling data structures are linked. As the introduction states, it is the key component of the kernel's architecture which allows models and motion controllers to interact. Here is a skeleton of the class:

```
enum doubtype { S_DOUBLE, S_TRACK, S_VALUATOR, S_EXPR, S_SIM };

class superdouble
{
    doubtype    type;
    union       {
                double    d;
                track*    t;
                valuator* v;
                expr*     e;
                simvar*   s;
                };
public:
    operator    double();
    superdouble& operator=( superdouble& s );
    superdouble& operator=( double dd );
    superdouble& operator=( track& tt );
    superdouble& operator=( valuator& vv );
    superdouble& operator=( expr& ee );
    superdouble& operator=( simvar& ss );
};

superdouble::operator double()
{
    switch( type )
    {
    case S_DOUBLE:    return d;
    case S_TRACK:     return t->getval();
    case S_VALUATOR:  return v->getval();
    case S_EXPR:      return e->evaluate();
    case S_SIM:       return s->getval();
    }
}
```

A superdouble may contain an ordinary double, or a pointer to a track object, a valuator object, an expression, or an imported simulation variable. The `operator double()` function decides what to do when a `superdouble` is accessed, depending on what it actually contains. `valuators` are interaction devices, such as mice or knobs. `simvars` are gateways to simulation results.

All numeric parameters to `items` in the modelling hierarchy, and literals in expressions, are stored by the kernel as `superdoubles`. They are in the parameter lists that C++ objects of classes derived from `primitive`, `attribute`, *etc.* access when they build their internal representations; but these objects do not "know," when they are reading one of their parameters, that they are accessing a track, or causing an expression to be evaluated: C++ makes `superdoubles` look and behave like ordinary doubles to these objects. The internal representation and machinations of superdoubles are protected from mischief by unruly programmers.

All animation information, all changes to parameters, gets filtered through `superdoubles`, whether it comes from a track or a simulation program. (Valuators can be considered as "interactive tracks.") This has advantages:

- New motion controllers can be added to the system as new internal types inside of class `superdouble`, and no other program code is changed.

- The kernel can find which parameters have changed for which objects, and "touch" them.

- If a high-level motion control technique is computationally expensive, the streams of values it generates for its outputs can be saved by the `superdoubles` they are filtered through. Rerunning the animation can be done without rerunning the simulation. The simulation is only rerun if *its* parameters have changed.

- In conjunction with the previous advantage, an animator can "tweak" the values in the saved stream if they do not quite produce the desired motion, and avoid rerunning the simulation. The streams could possibly be analysed and converted into equivalent tracks.

6.8 The event queue, animation, and simulation

We need a mechanism to synchronise high-level motion simulations with each other, and with the sampling of frames for animation. This is accomplished by allowing the kernel to manage an *event queue* in the style of discrete-event simulation[Birtwistle 79]. Most simulations are discrete-event or quasi-continuous. They are allowed to schedule their events in the queue. The kernel schedules an event for each frame that will be captured, at the beginning of the animation. The queue is processed, and the simulations run in step, making calculations and changing the parameters they are tied to. Whenever a *frame event* arrives, the kernel renders a "snapshot" of the current graphical state.

Currently, *event notices* in the queue are implemented using objects with virtual functions. We are considering using C++ coroutine classes[Stroustrup 87] to implement full process-based simulation.

7 Further Work

The enhancements to track specification that are being developed have already been discussed. Other enhancements to the system that are in development or being implemented are:

Labels: If models are labelled, then it becomes easy to place models relative to each other: "`apple at table translatey( 2 )`" would place an apple on a table. Animation can be made by moving an object between two others in the same way [Wvyill 75].

Temporal changes to the hierarchy: It is useful to be able to rearrange the structure of the hierarchy during animation. For example, this would allow a figure to carry a cup in its hand, place it on a table, and release it [Kroyer 86].

Closely integrated dynamic simulation: We are working on integrating dynamic simulation with the kernel in a more powerful fashion than the current simulation interface allows. We wish to link dynamically simulated motion with the kinematic type of motion that parameter interpolation provides, and allow information for dynamics to be specified directly in CHARLI scripts.

Parameters to models: Seeing the Pascal-like scoping mechanisms in CHARLI, a logical extension is to allow instances of models to have parameters passed to them. This allows instances of models to vary from one another.

Mathematical functions: Another simple extension of CHARLI as a programming language. We can provide a library of functions, such as sine, cosine, and random, to be used in expressions.

Using temporal coherence in rendering: The kernel can provide the information necessary to a renderer that will allow it to use temporal coherence to avoid redoing calculations for clipping, shading, hidden surface, *etc.* We are considering a ray-tracing method that will make use of this information.

Implementing more primitives and motion control: The extant body of primitives and motion control techniques is large. We will incorporate as many of these into our system as possible. We have currently only implemented a small set, in order to test our design ideas.

8   Conclusions

This paper has shown the usefulness of unifying the data structures for modelling and animation, and described the skeleton of a software architecture which implements it. The architecture also provides a good, stable testbed for research purposes.

Our experience with the system has been positive, and we feel that it advances the state of the art in computer animation. This is a field where research is concentrating on making the specification of animation faster, easier, and more powerful, and making the generation of images, photorealistic or otherwise, faster as well. The system described here provides us with a platform on which to perform this research, and upon which we can build to achieve higher goals.

9   Acknowledgements

We would like to thank the students, researchers, and associates of the *Graphicsland* project who have contributed code or ideas to the system, and the diversity of whose work has forced us to take a wider view in our design: Dave Jevans, Dave Hankinson, Chip Herr, Anja Haman, Jeff Allan, Bill Jones, Chris Bone, Angus Davis, Trevor Paquette, Perry Kundert, and Cheng-Fu Yao. We would also like to thank the Natural Sciences and Engineering Research Council of Canada. Mike thanks the band.

References

[Allan 88]   Jeffrey B. Allan. Polygon Mesh Modelling for Computer Graphics. Master's thesis, University of Calgary, Dept. of Computer Science, September 1988.

[Birtwistle 79] G.M. Birtwistle. *Discrete event modelling on Simula*. Macmillan, London, England, 1979.

[Blinn 87]   James F. Blinn. Siggraph '87, course #6, the mechanical universe: An integrated view of a large scale animation project, 1987.

[Cook 87]   Robert L. Cook, Loren Carpenter, and Edwin Catmull. The Reyes Image Rendering Architecture. In *Computer Graphics*, volume 21. ACM SIGGRAPH, July 1987.

[Foley 82]   James D. Foley and Andries van Dam. *Fundamentals of Interactive Computer Graphics*. Addison-Wesley, 1982.

[Goldberg 85]   Adele Goldberg and David Robson. *Smalltalk-80: The Language and its Implementation*. Addison-Wesley, 1985.

[Gomez 85]   Julian E. Gomez. Twixt: A 3D Animation System. *Computers and Graphics*, 9(3):291–298, 1985.

[Grant 86]   Eric Grant, Phil Auburn, and Turner Whitted. Exploiting Classes in Modelling and Display Software. *IEEE Computer Graphics and Applications*, 6(11), November 1986.

[Green 88]   Mark Green and Nanqiu Sun. A Language and System for Procedural Modeling and Motion. *IEEE Computer Graphics and Applications*, 8(6), November 1988.

[Haeberli 88]   Paul E. Haeberli. ConMan: A Visual Programming Language for Interactive Graphics. In *Computer Graphics*, volume 22, pages 103–111. ACM SIGGRAPH, August 1988.

[Haugen 82]   O. Haugen and K. Skijfeld. Class Graphics - A Powerful Tool in Interactive Computer Graphics. *Proc. X Association of Simula Users Conference, Oslo,Norway*, June 1982.

[Jensen 74]   K. Jensen and Niklaus Wirth. *Pascal User Manual and Report*. Springer-Verlag, 1974.

[Kernighan 81] Brian W. Kernighan and P. J. Plauger. *Software Tools in Pascal*. Addison-Wesley, 1981.

[Kochanek 84] . D. Kochanek. Interpolating Splines with Local Tension, Continuity and Bias Control. In *Computer Graphics*, volume 18, pages 33–41. ACM SIGGRAPH, 1984.

[Kroyer 86]   Bill Kroyer. Animating with a hierarchy. *SIGGRAPH '86, Course #22, Advanced Computer Animation*, 1986.

[Parke 82]   Fred Parke. Parameterized Models for Facial Animation. *IEEE Computer Graphics and Applications*, 2(9):61–68, 1982.

[Potmesil 87]   Michael Potmesil and Eric M. Hoffert. FRAMES: Software Tools for Modeling, Rendering and Animation of 3D Scenes. In *Computer Graphics*, volume 21, pages 85–93, July 1987.

[Reynolds 82]   Craig W. Reynolds. Computer animation with scripts and actors. In *Computer Graphics*, volume 16, July 1982.

[Schlag 86]   John F. Schlag. Eliminating the Dichotomy Between Scripting and Interaction. In *Proceedings Graphics Interface '86 Vision Interface '86*, pages 202–206, May 1986.

[Stroustrup 86]   Bjarne Stroustrup. *The C++ Programming Language*. Addison-Wesley, 1986.

[Stroustrup 87]   Bjarne Stroustrup and Jonathan E. Shapiro. A Set of C++ Classes for Co-routine Style Programming. In *C++ Workshop Proceedings*, pages 417–439. USENIX Association, 1987.

[Sturman 86]   David Sturman. A Discussion on the Development of Motion Control Systems. *SIGGRAPH '86, Course #23, Computer Animation: 3-D Motion Specification and Control*, 1986.

[Symbolics]   Symbolics. S-Dynamics. Computer Program.

[Thalmann 83]   Daniel Thalmann and Nadia Magnenat-Thalmann. Actor and Camera Data Types in Computer Animation. In *Proceedings Graphics Interface '83*, pages 203–209, 1983.

[Wilhelms 86]   Jane Wilhelms. Towards automatic motion control. *SIGGRAPH '86, Course #23, Computer Animation: 3-D Motion Specification and Control*, 1986.

[Wvyill 75]   Geoff Wvyill. Pictorial Description Language II. *Proc. ONLINE 75, Brunel University, Uxbridge, UK*, 1975.

[Wyvill 75]   Brian Wyvill. *An Interactive Graphics Language*. PhD thesis, University of Bradford, December 1975.

[Wyvill 86]   B. Wyvill, C. McPheeters, and R. Garbutt. The University of Calgary 3D Computer Animation System. *Journal of the Society of Motion Picture and Television Engineers*, 95(6), 1986.

Michael Chmilar is currently taking a graduate degree in computer graphics, specialising in animation and modelling systems and techniques, at the University of Calgary. He received a B.Sc (Honours) in Computer Science from Calgary in 1985. He spends his spare time performing with a local, independent band.
Address: Department of Computer Science, The University of Calgary, 2500 University Drive N.W., Calgary, Alberta, Canada, T2N 1N4.

Brian Wyvill received his Ph.D. from University of Bradford in 1975 and continued his interest in computer animation as a research fellow at the Royal College of Art, where he worked on such projects as animation sequences for the film *Alien*. Wyvill is now a Professor at the University of Calgary, where he leads the GRAPHICSLAND animation research team. His current interests are in "soft" objects, motion control, and recursive data structures for computer animation. He is a member of ACM, CGS, and SIGGRAPH, and the editorial board of The Visual Computer.
Address: Department of Computer Science, The University of Calgary, 2500 University Drive N.W., Calgary, Alberta, Canada, T2N 1N4.

An Integrated Control View of Synthetic Actors

D. Boisvert, N. Magnenat-Thalmann, and D. Thalmann

Abstract

This paper presents the global design of a system for synthetic actor animation. We discuss the concepts that must be part of an ideal animation system: positional constraints, adaptive motion control, trajectory planning and task planning. A complete diagram of the components of such a system is presented together with the relations between these components. An example of constraint-based animation sequence is also presented: the synthetic actress Marilyn getting up from her chair.

keywords: synthetic actor, task planning, kinematics, dynamics, constraints

The synthetic actor approach

Three-dimensional human modeling and animation have existed for more than 15 years[1][2]. However emphasis has been placed on separate aspects of this animation. For example, a great deal of research has been done on the modeling and animation of the body [3][4][5], on facial animation[6][7][8][9][10][11][12][13] and hand animation [14][15][16]. More recently, researchers have incorporated mechanical aspects factors into the animation of articulated bodies[17][18][19][20][21][22]. Also task level factors have been studied by several researchers [23][24][25][26]. Other authors have tried to animate more realistic characters, from an image synthesis point of view, but using primitive methods like rotoscopy or image-based keyframe animation. The synthetic approach corresponds to an integration of all methods, allowing the creation of 3D characters, with the appearance of real human characters.

Ideal synthetic actors should satisfy the following criteria:

. they should have the appearance of real persons
. their behavior should be similar to that of real persons
. they should have their own personality: two different actors should have different personalties, i.e. different reactions to the same situation
. they should be directed by task level commands
. they should be conscious of their environment
. they should at least be able to walk, speak, have emotions, and grasp objects
. their body and face should be naturally deformed during motions

Existing people, dead or alive can be recreated as synthetic actors or synthetic actresses. But fictitious people may also be created in this way.

Research in this area implies the development of techniques:

. for improving the physical aspects of the actors: shapes, colors, textures, reflectances
. for improving the motion of limbs and their deformation during motion
. for improving facial expressions and their animation
. for specifying the tasks to be performed
. for implementing tools for automatic motion control

Fig.1 shows complete diagram of the components of the Human Factory system presented together with the relations between these components.

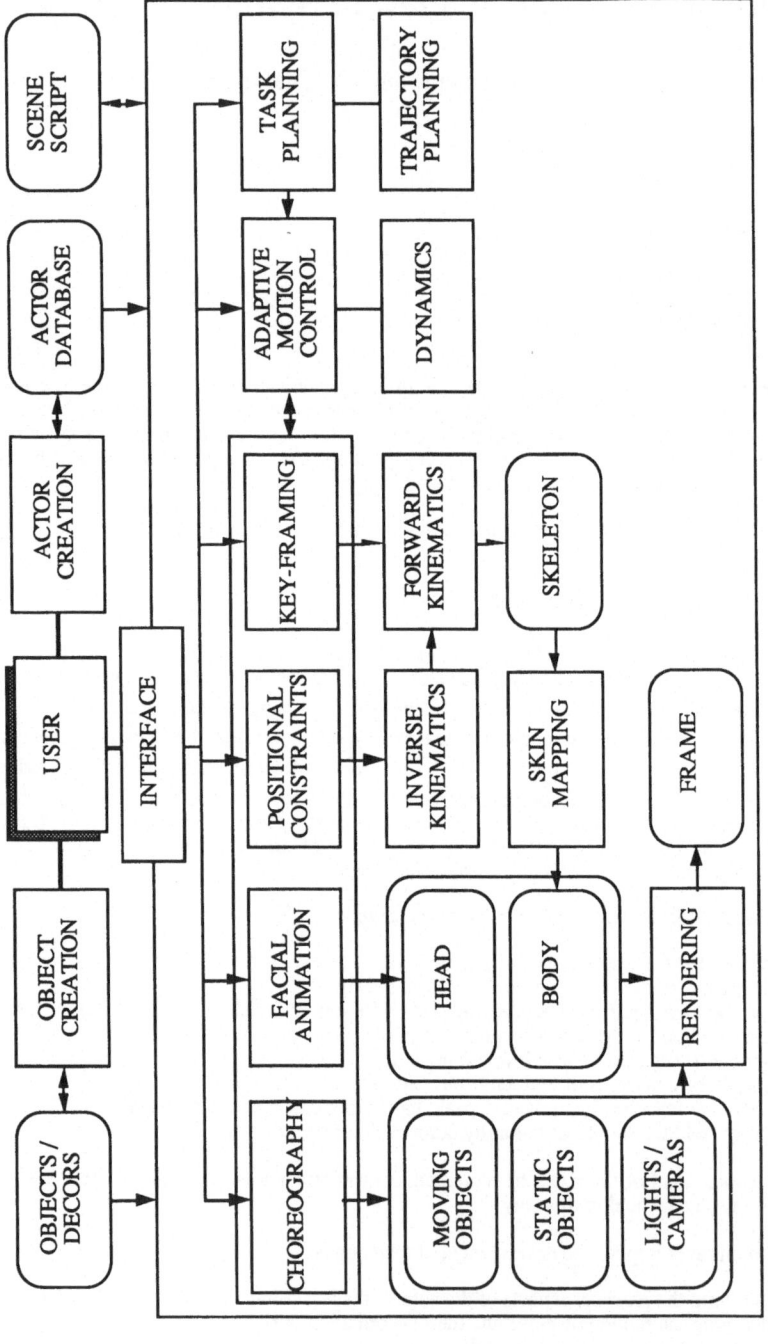

Fig.1 An integrated system

Traditional computer animation

Most authors [2] [24] [27] [28] [29] distinguish between two types of three-dimensional computer animation: key-frame animation and algorithmic animation.

Keyframe animation consists of the automatic generation of intermediate frames, called inbetweens, based on a set of key-frames supplied by the animator. There are two fundamental approaches to keyframe animation:

1. The inbetweens are obtained by interpolating the keyframe images themselves. This technique is called **image-based keyframe animation**. This is an old technique, introduced by Burtnyk and Wein [30].

2. A way of producing better images is to interpolate parameters of the model of the object itself. This technique is called **parametric keyframe animation** [24] [28] [29]. In a parameter model, the animator creates keyframes by specifying the appropriate set of parameter values, parameters are then interpolated and images are finally individually constructed from the interpolated parameters.

In algorithmic animation, motion is algorithmically described. Physical laws are applied to parameters of the human figures (e.g. joint angles).

Positional constraints

In this section, we address the important problem of limb positioning, e.g.: what are the angle values for the shoulder, elbow and wrist if the hand has to reach a certain position and orientation in space. This is a well-known problem in robotics, called the **inverse-kinematics problem**. It involves the determination of the joint variables from the given position and orientation of the end of the manipulator with respect to the reference coordinate system. The limb positioning is the key problem, because the independent variables in a robot as well as in a synthetic actor are joint variables. Unfortunately, the transformation problem from Cartesian coordinates has no closed-form solution in general. However, there are a number of special arrangements of the joint axes for which closed-form solutions do exist. An example is given by manipulators with 6 joints, where the three joints nearest the end effector are all revolve and their axes intersect at one point (he wrist). Several solutions to the latter have been suggested in the context of animation [31] [32] [33] [34] [35]. Forsey and Wilhelms [36], in their dynamics-based system, solve one constraint to a limb by linking it together with a pseudo-segment having a large mass value.

In order to make a synthetic actor sit down on a chair, for example, it is necessary to specify the relevant constraints on the feet, on the pelvis and on the hands. A system which allows to specify only one constraint at a time is not a very efficient way to solve this problem. Badler et al. [2] have introduced an iterative algorithm for solving multiple constraints using inverse kinematics. In their system, the user has to specify also the precedence of each constraint in the event case they cannot all be simultaneously

The orientation of the hand or the foot should also be specified by the user. The orientation may be defined with respect to the limb, the actor or the world. For example, to ensure that the feet are flat on the floor, the user defines the foot orientation relatively to the world, whatever the position and orientation of the pelvis may be. The physical limitations of the joints have to be taken into account by the system. The interactivity of the system may be improved using input devices with multiple degrees of freedom.

A simple algorithm solving the positional constraint problem has been implemented in the Human Factory System. The animator may impose constraints at the hands, the feet and the pelvis levels. The position and orientation of the hand or the feet may be specified in the local coordinate system attached to the limb (arm or leg), or in the actor system or the world system. A constraint may be a fixed position/orientation or a 6D trajectory. Tools are available for constructing constraints as functions of the actor environment and his envelop (e.g. contact of the foot and the floor).

In order to solve the constraints, the system makes use of the position and orientation of the pelvis and the trunk angles (vertebrae and clavicles) for finding the origin of the hips and the shoulders. it then calculates the limb angles required to reach the intended position. In the case where no solution exists, the intended position is projected on the volume of moving of the arm (leg).

A complete example is shown in the Appendix.

The skeleton has seven degrees of freedom at the arm (leg) level and the constraint has six degrees (position/orientation). Since the model is redundant from a kinematics point-of-view, this implies the existence of an infinity of solutions to reach the intended position, . This is a well-known situation; as an example, when an actor is sitting down with a foot resting on the floor, he may rotate his knee around a hip-ankle axis. The variation of the rotation angle is constrained by the physical limitations of the joints. It may also be pointed out that the comfortable position for the knee (elbow) depends on the orientation of the foot (hand).

One solution consists of minimizing the angle variation of the angle between the leg (arm) and the foot (hand). It is also possible to have the user select the solution by giving an opening parameter. The position/orientation/opening constraint allows to select a unique solution from the arm's (or the leg's) seven degrees of freedom. Other criteria such as the collision of the limb with an object may play a role in the selection of the solution.

The key framing technique and the positional constraints may be considered as the low level commands of an animation system. The higher level commands may produce keyframes and joint constraints. The animator must have access to the various levels of the hierarchy in order to be able to do the fine-tuning of the actor motion.

Adaptive motion control

Adaptive motion control of an actor means that the environment has an impact on the actor motion and conversely. Informations about the environment and the actor must be available during the control process. Traditional animation techniques like rotoscopy or key framing cannot be considered as adaptive control techniques, because the animator has to explicitly control by hand the relation between the environment and the actors.

The purpose of adaptive control motion is to decrease the amount of information entered into the computer by the animator. This is done by using existing informations about the scene and the actor. The system should also have an efficient representation of the geometry of the objects in order to automatically plan tasks as well as prevent collisions.

Girard [4] gives a good example of this type of control applied to the motion of humans and animals on a flat terrain. At the low level, the animation is performed on a sequence of key positions of the limbs which define angle trajectories (direct kinematics) or Cartesian positions (inverse kinematics). These trajectories are calculated using optimizing criteria with kinematics or dynamics constraints.

The model should also produce realistic motion. In order to take into account internal and external forces acting on the actor, the system has to use a dynamics-based model. Techniques based on dynamics have already been used in computer animation [17] [18] [19] [20] [21] [22], but only for simplified and rigid articulated bodies with few joints, geometrical bodies (cylinders) and without any deformation. The use of the dynamics in an animation system of articulated bodies like the human body, provide several important disadvantages.

First, the animator does not think in terms of forces or torques to apply to a limb or the body in order to perform a motion. The design of a specific user interface is essential.

Another problem of the dynamics is the amount of CPU time required to solve the motion equations of a complex articulated body using numerical methods. It considerably reduces the possibility of interaction of the system with the user. Only very short sequences have been produced, because of the lack of complete specification for complex motions and because of the CPU time required for certain methods.

Moreover, although dynamics-based motions are more realistic, they are too regular, because they do not take into account the personality of the characters. It is unrealistic to think that only the physical characteristics of two people carrying out doing the same actions make these characters different for any observer. Behavior and personality of the human beings are also an essential cause of the observable differences.

To animate a body using kinematics (direct or inverse), the animator should specify the trajectories of the joint angles or the trajectories of the limb extremities. The trajectory must include time information (velocities and accelerations). Kochanek-Bartels[37] splines may be used for example; however, the realism of the motion is not guaranteed. A good compromise is an integration of both models as suggested by Girard [21], who obtained very good results using his system.

In the Human Factory system, we have decided to build a library of basic parametric motions (like walk and grasp) and each type of motion uses the kinematics when possible and only the dynamics when it is required for the realism of the motion. Each command produces a sequence of keyframes and positional constraints. A user which is not satisfied with the generated motion may then edit it.

Trajectory planning

The trajectory planning problem is classical and was extensively studied in robotics and Artificial Intelligence. For example, given the starting position of the actor hand and objects on a table, the problem is to find the trajectory to follow in order to avoid obstacles. For a synthetic actor, the problem is more complex due to the non-rigidity of the actor. In the Human Factory system, any joint motion may be defined in three ways corresponding to the above classification:

1. Key values are selected at fixed times; spline interpolation is performed using the Kochanek-Bartels [37] approach.

2. The variation of angle is defined by a procedural law (parametric curve with evolution)

3. The trajectory may be generated using an automatic trajectory-planning algorithm. In our case, we use an anti-collision algorithm in a polytopic environment (n-dimension) with creation of a graph from hyperplane bundle. This method developed in our team seems more appropriate than the robotics methods [38]

Task planning

Task planning is a major problem in robotics and artificial intelligence. The problem complexity is directly dependent on the generality of the actor micro world. Given a task description, the problem consists in decomposing the task in a sequence of elementary movements (see Fig.2).

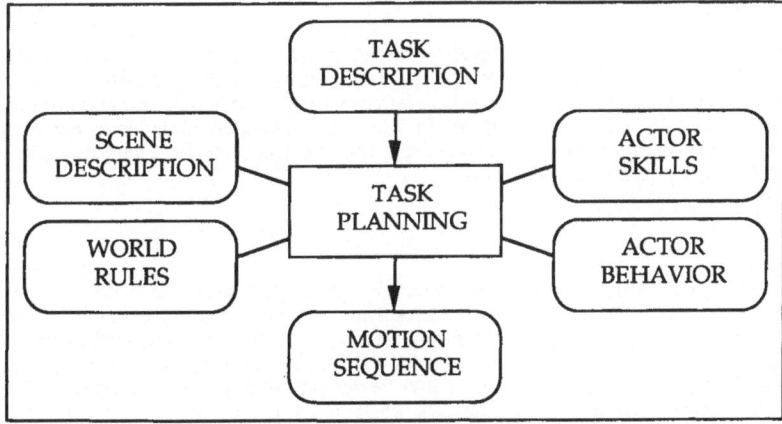

Fig.2 Task planning

In order to generate these movements, the system should possess the following informations:

. description of the scene (topology, position and orientation of the objects)
. database of the rules governing the micro world (e.g. it is necessary to stand up before walking)
. actor behavior (which shall modify the way of doing the movement; it corresponds to style parameters)
. library of elementary movements which may be done by the actor (actor skills)

For example, the task "answer to the phone" may be decomposed in the following sequence of elementary actions:

. stand up from his chair
. determine a trajectory that avoids obstacles in the actor motion
. walk according to the trajectory
. determine a trajectory that avoids obstacles for object grasping
. grasp the telephone
. answer

There are three ways of specifying tasks in a task-level system:

1. by example
2. by a sequence of model states
3. by a sequence of commands

The specification by example means for the operator "to perform the task at least once in order to explain it to the system." This is suitable in robotics, because the task may be physically specified by manually guiding the robot. This is of course impracticable in animation.

In the second type of method, the task is considered as a sequence of model states; each state is given by the configuration of all the objects in the environment. The configuration may be described by a set of spatial relationships. But what is the level of these relationships ? High-level relationships correspond for example to indicating that at a given time an object A must be at a certain height and in front of another object B. The problem in this case is that the set of relationships should be converted into a set of equations and inequations which may be very difficult to solve. Moreover, a set of configurations may overspecify a state. Low-level relationships may correspond to the coordinates of the objects at a certain time, which is a simple keyframe description. Several methods for obtaining configuration constraints from symbolic spatial relationships have been proposed [39] [40] [41].

The specification by a sequence of commands is the most suitable and popular. As stated by Zeltzer [24], the animator can only specify the broad outlines of a particular movement and the animation system fills in the details. A non-expert user may be satisfied with the default movements, as generated by a task specification like WALK FROM A TO B. However, a high-end user may want nearly total control over every nuance of an actor's movement to make a sequence as expressive as possible. This means that the animator does need to access different levels of the control hierarchy in order to generate new motor skills and to tweak the existing skills.

Note that the transformation from a high level specification to a sequence of elementary motions is very similar to the problem of compiling. As in the processing of programming languages, three cases are possible: translation into a low-level code (classical compilers), translation into another programming language (preprocessor) and interpretation. In each case, the correspondence between the task specification and the motion to be generated is very complex. Consider three very essential tasks for a synthetic actor: walking, grasping and talking.

walking

To generate the motion corresponding to the task "WALK from A to B", it is necessary to take into account the possible obstacles, the nature of the terrain and then evaluate the trajectories which consist of a sequence positions, velocities and accelerations. Given such a trajectory, as well as the forces to be exerted at end effectors, it is possible to determine the torques to be exerted at the joints by inverse dynamics and finally the values of joint angles may be derived for any time. In summary, the task-level system should integrate the following elements: obstacle avoidance, locomotion on rough terrains, trajectory planning, kinematics and dynamics.

grasping

To generate the motion corresponding to the task "PICK UP the object A and PUT it on the object B", the planner must choose where to grasp A so that no collisions will result when grasping or moving them. Then grasp configurations should be chosen so that the grasped object is stable in the hand (or at least seems to be stable); moreover contact between the hand and the object should be as natural as possible. Once the object is grasped, the system should generate the motions that will achieve the desired goal of the operation. A free motion should be synthesized; during this motion the principal goal is to reach the destination without collision, which implies obstacle avoidance. In this complex process, joint evolution is determined by kinematics and dynamics equations. In summary, the task-level system should integrate the following elements: path planning, obstacle avoidance, stability and contact determination, kinematics and dynamics.

talking

To generate the motion corresponding to the task "SAY THE SENTENCE How are you? ", the system must analyze the sentence and separate it into phonemes, and then facial expressions corresponding to these phonemes must be selected. These expressions are themselves expressed as face deformations caused by muscles: jaw opening, eye opening, face folds etc. Once the expressions have been selected, the system should indicate to the computer at which times the expressions must be activated and generate the frames according to a law (spline for example). In summary, the task-level system should integrate the following elements: phonemes detection, selection of facial expression selections, handling of facial parameters, animation generation.

We have implemented in our animation system the Winograd [42] blocks world. Although this blocks world was created for natural language understanding, it is especially interesting for human animation, because it corresponds to planning motion sequences. To generate the motion sequence, we use a notation from compiling theory. This notation is similar to the syntactic diagrams used to define the syntax of a programming language. We assume terminal and non-terminal symbols. Terminal symbols in our case are generating commands: **GRASP B, MOVE B TO P, UNGRASP** B. Non-terminal symbols correspond to meta-commands such as: "places a block B1 at 3D location P on block B2" or "clears the top of the block B". We use the method of recursive descent popular in compiler construction. A procedure (which may be recursive) is written for each non-terminal symbol in order to construct a goal tree. Each node of the goal tree is a goal, which is only satisfied when their immediate subgoals are satisfied.

References

[1] Badler NI (1982) (Ed.) Special issue on "Modeling the Human Body for Animation", IEEE Computer Graphics and Applications, Vol.2, No9

[2] Magnenat-Thalmann and Thalmann D (1985) Computer Animation: Theory and Practice, Springer, Tokyo

[3] Badler NI and Smoliar SW (1979) Digital Representation of Human Movement, ACM Computing Surveys, March issue, pp.19-38.

[4] Kroyer B (1986) Animating with a Hierarchy, Seminar on Advanced Computer Animation SIGGRAPH '86.

[5] Forest L, Magnenat-Thalmann N, Thalmann D (1986) An Integration of Keyframe and algorithmic animation, Proc. Computer Graphics Tokyo '86.

[6] Parke F.I. (1972) Animation of Faces, Proc. ACM Annual Conf., Vol.1

[7] Parke F.I. (1974) A Parametric Model for Human Faces, PhD dissertation, University of Utah, department of Computer Science

[8] Platt S, Badler N (1981) Animating Facial Expressions, Proc. SIGGRAPH '81, pp.245-252.

[9] Pearce A, Wyvill B, Wyvill G and Hill D (1986) Speech and expression: a Computer Solution to Face Animation, Proc. Graphics Interface '86, pp.136-140.

[10] Hill DR, Pearce A and Wyvill B (1988) Animating Speech: an Automated Approach Using Speech Synthesised by Rules, The Visual Computer, Vol.3, No5

11 Lewis JP, Parke FI (1987) Automated Lip-synch and Speech Synthesis for Character Animation, Proc. CHI '87 and Graphics Interface '87, Toronto, pp.143-147.

12 Magnenat-Thalmann N, Primeau E, Thalmann D (1988c) Abstract Muscle Action Procedures for Human Face Animation, The Visual Computer, Vol.3, No5

13 Nahas M, Huitric H and Saintourens M (1988) Animation of a B-spline Figure, The Visual Computer, Vol.3, No5

14 Catmull E (1972) A System for Computed-generated movies, Proc. ACM Annual Conference, pp.422-431.

15 Badler NI and Morris MA (1982) Modelling Flexible Articulated Objects, Proc. Computer Graphics '82, Online Conf., pp.305-314.

16 Magnenat-Thalmann N, Laperrière R and Thalmann D (1988b) Joint-dependent Local Deformations for Hand Animation and Object Grasping, Proc. Graphics Interface '88

17 Armstrong WW and Green MW (1985) Dynamics for Animation of Characters with Deformable Surfaces in: N.Magnenat-Thalmann and D.Thalmann (Eds) Computer-generated Images, Springer, pp.209-229.

18 Armstrong WW and Green M (1985b) The Dynamics of Articulated Rigid Bodies for Purposes of Animation, The Visual Computer, Vol.1, No4, pp.231-240.

19 Wilhelms J and Barsky B (1985) Using Dynamic Analysis to Animate Articulated Bodies such as Humans and Robots, in: N.Magnenat-Thalmann and D.Thalmann (Eds) Computer-generated Images, Springer, pp.209-229.

20 Wilhelms J (1987) Towards Automatic Motion Control, IEEE Computer Graphics and Applications, Vol.7, No 4, pp.11-22

21 Girard M (1987) Interactive Design of 3D Computer-animated Legged Animal Motion, IEEE Computer Graphics and Applications, Vol.7, No 6, pp.39-51

22 Isaacs PM and Cohen MF (1987) Controlling Dynamic Simulation with Kinematic Constraints, Bahvior Functions and Inverse Dynamics, Proc. SIGGRAPH'87, Computer Graphics, Vol.21, No4, pp.215-224

23 Zeltzer D (1982) Motor Control Techniques for Figure Animation, IEEE Computer Graphics and Applications, Vol.2, No9, pp.53-59.

24 Zeltzer D (1985) Towards an Integrated View of 3D Computer Animation, The Visual Computer, Vol.1, No4, pp.249-259.

25 Badler NI, Korein JD, Korein JU, Radack GM and Brotman LS (1985) Positioning and Animating Figures in a Task-oriented Environment, The Visual Computer, Vol.1, No4, pp.212-220.

26 Badler NI, Manoochehri KH and Walters G (1987) Articulated Figure Positioning by Multiple Constraints, IEEE Computer Graphics and Applications, Vol.7, No 6, pp.39-51

27 Hanrahan P and Sturman D (1985) Interactive Animation of Parametric Models, The Visual Computer, Vol.1, No4, pp.260-266.

28 Steketee SN, Badler NI (1985) Parametric Keyframe Interpolation Incorporating Kinetic Adjustment and Phrasing Control, Proc. SIGGRAPH '85, pp. 255-262.

29 Parke FI (1982) Parameterized Models for Facial Animation, IEEE Computer Graphics and Applications, Vol.2, No 9, pp.61-68

30 Burtnyk N, Wein M (1971) Computer-generated Key-frame Animation, Journal of SMPTE, 80, pp.149-153.

31 Badler NI, Korein JD, Korein JU, Radack GM and Brotman LS, Positioning and Animating Human Figures in a Task-Oriented Environment, The Visual Computer, Dec. 1985, pp.212-220.

32 Badler NI, Manoochehri KH and Walters G, Articulated Figure Positioning by Multiple Constraints, IEEE CG&A, June 1987, pp.28-38

33 Girard M and Maciejewski AA, Computational Modeling for the Computer animation of Legged Figures, Proc. SIGGRAPH '85, pp.263-270

34 Girard M, Interactive Design of 3D Computer-Animated Legged Animal Motion, IEEE CG&A, June 1987, pp.39-51

35 Korein JU, Badler NI, Techniques for Generating the Goal-directed Motion of Articulated Structures, IEEE CG&A, Nov.1982, pp.71-81

36 Forsey D and Wilhelms J, techniques for Interactive Manipulation of Articulated Bodies Using Dynamics Analysis, Proc. Graphics Interface '88, pp.8-15

3 7 Kochanek D and Bartels R (1984) Interpolating Splines with Local Tension, Continuity and Bias Tension, Proc. SIGGRAPH '84, pp.33-41.

3 8 Lozano-Perez (1982) Task Planning in: Brady M (Ed.) Robot Motion: Planning and Control, MIT Press, Cambridge, Mass.

3 9 Popplestone RJ, Ambler AP and Bellos IM (1980) An Interpreter for a Language for Describing Assemblies, Artificial Intelligence, Vol.14, pp.79-107

4 0 Taylor RH (1976) The Synthesis of Manipulator Control Programs from Task-Level Specifications, Artificial Intelligence Laboratory, Stanford University, AIM-282

4 1 Lozano-Perez (1976) The Design of a Mechanical Assembly System, Artificial Intelligence Laboratory, MIT, AI TR 397

4 2 Winograd T (1972) Understanding Natural Language, Academic Press, NY

Appendix: an example of constraint-based animation

48-frame animation with Marilyn getting up from her chair:

- Two fixed constraints at the feet (frames 1 to 48):

Position
right foot: <-20,-380,-90>
left foot: < 20,-380,-90>
System: world

Orientation
both feet: <0,0,0> (flat on the floor)
System: world

- One fixed constraint at the pelvis (frames 1 to 24):

Position: <0,-300,0>

Orientation: from 0 to 40 around the X-axis
System: world for the pelvis

- One trajectory-based constraint at the pelvis (frames 24 to 48):

Trajectory: right (Catmull law acceleration-deceleration)
start: <0,-300,0>
end: <0,-210,-103>

Orientation: from 40 to 0 (X)
System: world

Constraints are shown in Plate 1, skeleton with constraints are displayed on Plates 2-3 and a two-second animation is presented in Plates 4-9.

286

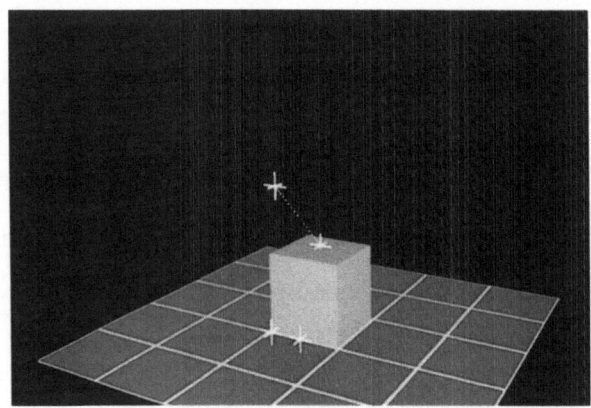

Plate 1 constraints

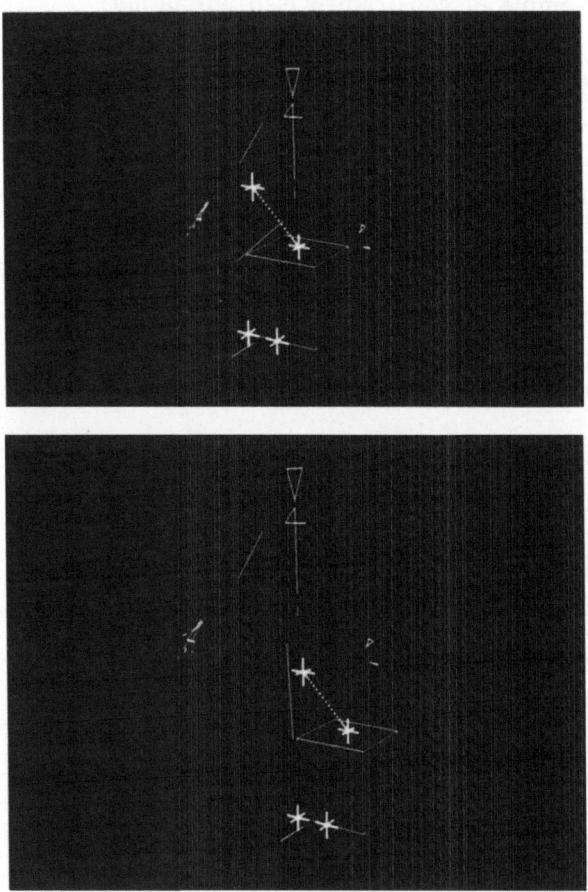

Plate 2-3 skeleton with constraints (in wire-frame)

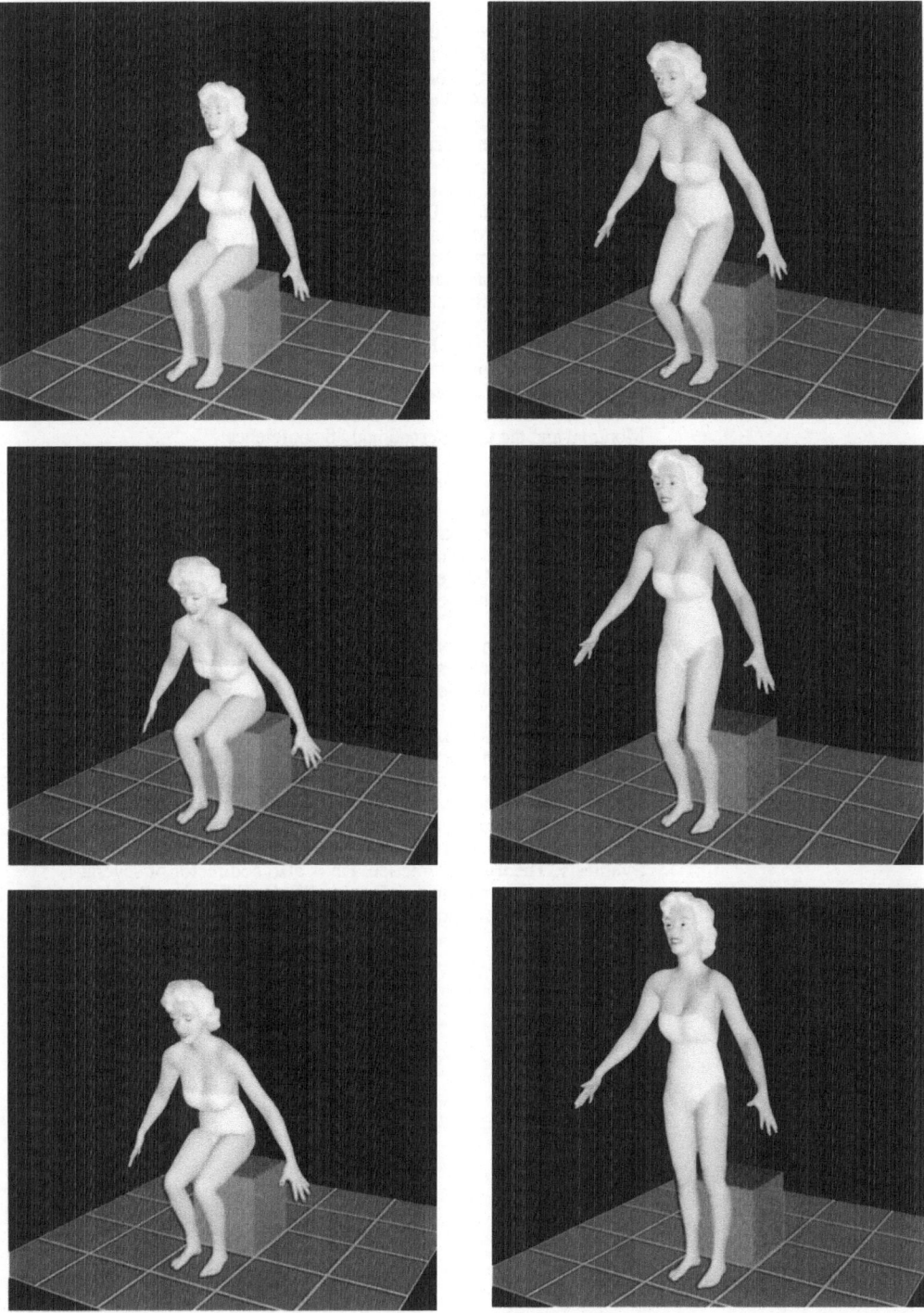

Plate 4-6 three frames of a two-second animation
sequence

Plate 7-9 three frames of a two-second animation
sequence

Nadia Magnenat Thalmann is currently full Professor of Computer Science at the University of Geneva, Switzerland. A former member of the Council of Science and Technology of the Government of Quebec and of the Council of Science and Technology of the Canadian Broadcasting Corporation, she also has served on a variety of government advisory boards and program committees. She has received several awards, including the 1985 Communications Award from the Government of Quebec. In May 1987, she was nominated woman of the year in sciences by the Montreal community. Dr. Magnenat Thalmann received a BS in psychology, an MS in biochemistry, and a Ph.D in quantum chemistry and computer graphics from the University of Geneva. Her previous appointments include the University Laval in Quebec, the Graduate Business school of the University of Montreal in Canada. She has written and edited several books and research papers in image synthesis and computer animation and was codirector of the computer-generated films *Dream Flight, Eglantine, Rendez-vous à Montréal* and *Galaxy Sweetheart*. She served as chairperson of the Canadian Graphics Interface 85 Conference in Montreal and the CG International 88 conference.

Daniel Thalmann is currently full Professor and Director of the Computer Graphics Laboratory at the Swiss Federal Institute of Technology in Lausanne, Switzerland. Since 1977, he was Professor at the University of Montreal and codirector of the MIRALab research laboratory. He received his diploma in nuclear physics and Ph.D in Computer Science from the University of Geneva. He is member of the editorial board of the Visual Computer and cochairs the EUROGRAPHICS Working Group on Computer Simulation and Animation. He was director of the Canadian Man-Machine Communications Society and is a member of the Computer Society of the IEEE, ACM, SIGGRAPH, and the Computer Graphics Society. Daniel Thalmann's research interests include 3D computer animation, image synthesis, and scientific visualization. He has published more than 60 papers in this areas and is coauthor of several books including: Computer Animation: Theory and Practice and Image Synthesis: Theory and Practice. He is also codirector of several computer-generated films: *Dream Flight, Eglantine, Rendez-vous à Montréal, Galaxy Sweetheart*.

Chapter 5
Graphics Interface and Theory

Evaluating Definitive Principles for Interaction in Graphics

M. Beynon

ABSTRACT

This paper is an appraisal of current progress towards supporting interactive graphics within the framework of a general-purpose programming paradigm based upon definitions. It considers how the use of definitive principles relates to other work, why it appears promising, and what progress has been made towards the resolution of technical difficulties. As a sequel to [2], it re-examines potential for applications of definitive principles in interactive graphics in the light of more recently developed ideas about dealing with control issues and dynamically changing relationships in a definitive programming framework. It also takes account of new research into notations for graphics that makes use of geometrical constructions. As a subsidiary theme, the paper contrasts the support for reference and representation of geometric relationships in various kinds of interactive graphics systems.

Key words: interactive graphics, spreadsheets, geometric constructions, constraint-based graphics systems, functional programming, reference, animation

1.   INTRODUCTION

Most existing interactive graphics systems focus on providing the user with a toolkit that makes it possible to draw complex diagrams; they reflect a view that is oriented towards tools rather than frameworks. The emphasis is upon programming as a "means to an end", viz the depiction of a complex diagram. Though graphical interfaces are fashionable, and user-computer interaction concerns are deemed important, the underlying idiom often resembles batch programming. The user is an unequal partner who makes use of an interactive interface for convenience, but is not thereby enabled to intervene more significantly and directly in the computational process.

Modern applications for graphics demand a broader perspective. It has become necessary to think of "interaction in the large": to consider the issues of managing many thousands of drawings, perhaps over many years of development, within the broader semantic context of such applications as engineering design and manufacture. In developing interactive graphics systems that can support large applications, it is surely important to first identify simple and powerful principles for their design. More sophisticated tools *per se* are no panacea. Experience has shown that developing tools based upon ostensibly less powerful techniques can enhance the range of application: c.f. [7]

> " ... the use of geometric constructions eliminates the need for solving large systems of non-linear equations inherent in declarative constraint-based systems. Consequently, L.E.G.O. can be used to model comparatively more complex objects."

A framework within which existing approaches to interactive graphics can be interpreted and integrated must depend upon generic techniques with wide - if not universal - applicability.

Unification of principles in interactive graphics appears hard to attain. The methods used are notoriously diverse; there is a conspicuous lack of formalisation and standardisation, and *ad hoc* techniques are prevalent. The problem of formulating an abstract view is compounded by the very different functions that graphical images can serve: as in computer-generated art, medical image analysis, symbolic representations in architecture or circuit design, or technical drawing. The many different types of hardware and software support for graphics pose complementary problems. Nor are existing techniques for formal specification necessarily well-suited for interactive applications.

This paper aims to appraise current progress towards supporting interactive graphics within the framework of a general-purpose programming paradigm based upon definitions: "definitive programming". Previous papers dealing with related work include [1,2,3]. Though many of the issues addressed were considered in [2], there have been several subsequent developments that motivate a re-examination. As described in [4,5], the concept of definitive programming has itself been enriched through the identification of an abstract machine model that can support far more sophisticated computation than the "pure definitive notations" of [1]. This significantly enhances the scope for representing dynamic data relationships, and dealing with concerns - such as animation - where control structures are required. Of additional interest is the parallel development of interactive graphics systems based upon geometric constructions [7,13]: work that can be directly related to the definitive programming approach - with mutual benefit. For instance, definitive programming provides a much broader perspective within which to consider the use of "imperative constraints", whilst research on construction-based modelling suggests new and better solutions to the technical problems of dealing with complex operators raised in [2].

2.   FUNDAMENTAL ISSUES FOR INTERACTIVE GRAPHICS

The focus in this paper is upon graphics systems that involve interaction in a significant sense. A system that supports "visual programming" is not necessarily such a system: the main function of a graphical interface may be to permit convenient editing of a program that routinely generates graphical images in an autonomous way. To invoke the concept of "significant interaction" is itself to beg a question: "Is it possible to make an objective claim that one system supports richer interaction between the user and the computer than another?" This paper argues that it is - provided that the reader will accept the thesis that a spreadsheet gives better support for interactive calculation than a pocket calculator.

To appreciate the context in which "interaction" is being interpreted, the user may think of a major design project involving the abstract description and evaluation of a complex artefact such as a building. A very large number of drawings may be developed in the design process, and the timescale may be such that drawings have to be revised many months after they are first drawn. Naively, the user will need to be able to specify relationships between objects and components of objects that are to be stored and maintained by the computer. Several key issues arise: How are the relationships to be established? When is the maintenance of relationships carried out? To what extent are relationships maintained through autonomous action on the part of the computer? How is the current status of the design to be represented to the user? How can data relationships be represented in such a way that semantic analysis or simulation can be conveniently performed?

The demands that a user would ideally wish to make upon a design system are very great:

- relationships should be easily perceptible, and conveniently modified

- it should be possible to record partial information about relationships conveniently

- relationships should be expressible at many levels of abstraction

- it should be possible to accommodate a temporary failure to meet constraints, to compensate at a later stage, and conveniently make consequent changes retrospectively.

For the user, a transaction with the system will typically be an incremental change - a single addition to the sequence of perhaps many thousands of previous transactions. The architect who moves a wash-basin a metre nearer to the door will not expect the plans for the entire building to be reprocessed, but might reasonably expect to be advised that the waste pipe is obstructed by a balcony on the floor below. Many existing programming paradigms for interactive graphics are better suited for the complete reappraisal of a design after every trivial amendment than to modest and selective processing proportionate to a minor transaction. To some extent, this is a symptom of a more profound difficulty: how to represent relationships between objects so subtly that a trivial action has some impact, but not too much. Such problems of maintaining relationships that are both consistent and admit a multitude of very minor modifications have promoted the development of systems that avoid the embarrassment of user-intervention wherever possible. Thus a sophisticated design system might invoke a computational scheme of enormous ingenuity that involved reconfiguring all the waste pipes and balconies on an entire wall, at considerable computational cost, and perhaps in violation of the user's aesthetic preferences.

3.   CURRENT APPROACHES

The above discussion indicates that the effective representation of geometrical relationships is essential for significant interaction in a graphics system. Many existing approaches fail to address this issue adequately. When the emphasis is on supporting a repertoire of drawing operations (as in say MacDraw), the graphical image is described by the cumulative effect of procedural actions, and the geometric relationships that can be established are limited to the independent manipulation of explicitly defined groups of points and lines. Within such a framework it is not possible to support   relationships between geometric entities at an appropriate level of abstraction.

It is clear that an interactive graphics system that gives effective support for abstract relationships must be based upon higher-level primitives. Construction-based modelling recognises this by adopting fundamental geometric constructions as the primitive operations, and describing structural relationships in terms of these. The formulation of data relationships over an appropriate system of data types and operators at a reasonable level of abstraction is common to many approaches: their difference lies in the way that this "underlying algebra" is exploited. Four interrelated approaches to modelling geometric relationships are particularly relevant to this paper:

- functional programming principles (c.f. [9] p255),

- equational / constraint-based principles (c.f. [6]),

- construction-based modelling [7,13],

- definitive programming principles [2,3].

Systems to represent planar line-drawings within these paradigms would typically be based upon an underlying algebra consisting of scalars, **points**, **lines**, and **shapes** comprising multisets of points and lines, together with elementary geometric operators e.g. specifying the line joining a pair of points, the angle between two lines, or the union of two shapes. A brief outline of the different superstructures that can be built upon this foundation within these paradigms will be useful.

Following [9], a functional programmer might represent an abstract **shape** by a function

$$\textbf{point} \times \textbf{point} \rightarrow \textbf{shape}$$

(i.e. as the set of **points** and **lines** determined by a choosing a particular coordinate system as represented by a pair of **points**), and define complex **shapes** by applying higher-order functions to basic **shapes**. During interaction, the current status of the functional programming system will be determined by what functions have been defined, and the image currently depicted will be determined by what function evaluations have been performed. Geometric relationships are specified and modified by editing a script that defines appropriate higher-order functions, and redisplay is effected through function re-evaluation.

In a constraint-based system, geometric entites are represented by variables, and geometric relationships are expressed as equational constraints between variables over the underlying algebra e.g. insisting that four points lie on a circle, or that two lines are parallel. Ideally, these constraints are considered to be purely declarative in nature: they prescribe the relationships that must hold without burdening the user with details of how they are maintained. Interaction involves editing the current set of constraints, invoking a constraint-satisfaction process that first attempts to reconfigure the geometric entities appropriately, and subsequently leads to their redisplay.

In a construction-based modelling system, the relationships between data are formulated through a sequence of "imperative constraints". In effect, the locations of geometric entities are specified relative to each other through explicit prescriptions that are directly or indirectly expressed in terms of the operators of the underlying algebra. The constraints established in this way are conceived and stored as procedural fragments that encapsulate the description of a graphical image, and can be edited for purposes of reconfiguration or re-display.

In a definitive programming idiom [2], the **points**, **lines** and **shapes** that make up the graphical image are represented by a system of variables of the appropriate type. The value of a variable can either be specified explicitly, or implicitly by an algebraic expression in terms of the values of other variables and constants. The system of variable definitions is free of cyclic reference, so that the variables can be partially ordered by a data dependency relation:

$v \leq w$ if the value of w is defined - directly or indirectly - in terms of the value of v.

Every part of the image is associated in this way with a variable, and the interrelationship between parts is expressed through the defining formulae. Interaction is effected through editing the current system of definitions, re-evaluation of those variables whose values may be affected, and redisplay of the associated entities.

4. LIMITATIONS OF CURRENT INTERACTIVE SYSTEMS

The different programming paradigms for interactive graphics briefly sketched above are often ostensibly evaluated and compared on performance considerations. For instance, construction-based modelling is primarily seen as avoiding the technical problems posed by complex constraint satisfaction in constraint-processing systems (c.f. [7] §3.1). It will be argued in this paper that *performance considerations apart* neither a functional nor an equational programming idiom is an appropriate basis for interactive systems for major applications, and that the merits of construction-based modelling are in part related to a separate concern: the coincidental advantages that result from formulating geometric relationships in a way that *de facto* exploits systems of variable definitions. To dispel any impression that this links definitive programming more closely to construction-based modelling than to the other paradigms, it should be added that definitive programming is in certain respects more akin to functional and equational programming; it merely introduces one significant abstract concept (viz variable definition) that can be very directly linked to the use of geometric constructions.

The evaluation of interactive systems proposed here is based upon the criteria for significant interaction outlined in §2 above. The questions that are most relevant to the user's concern in interacting with a graphics system may be formulated as: "What are the current relationships between entities? How can I reference entities? How can I modify the relationships?" The architect who moves the wash-basin may not appreciate the implications of this simple action. In a well-conceived system, it is to be expected that some effects of actions consequent upon moving the basin - such as moving an associated mirror - are performed automatically, but such automatic responses have their limitations, and may need to be activated at the user's discretion. In a badly conceived system, moving the basin might involve changing the dimensions of the building to accommodate a dislocated balcony at the corner of an external wall. Such an illustration highlights the very significant part played by data dependencies in an interactive system: it may be exceeedingly hard to anticipate what entities can be referenced in isolation, and what the implications of modification might be.

How can issues of reference of this nature be handled in existing paradigms? Irrespective of which paradigm is used, it seems clear that a solution must involve making the program code that generates an image transparent to the user. For instance, to give informal support to the architect who wishes to understand the consequences of moving the basin, it would be necessary to highlight those parts of the code pertaining to the basin, to indicate in some way how modifying this code would affect the rest of the program, and - to ensure a truly interactive rather than batch processing environment - equip the compiler to interpret a local change to the code without complete recompilation. The effectiveness of a programming paradigm for interaction may be better gauged by how easily these processes can be performed than by traditional criteria. Paradoxically, the fundamental principles that are represented as special virtues of good programming idioms, viz referential transparency in declarative systems, and modularity and information hiding in sophisticated procedural systems, do not assist the recognition of implicit data dependencies.

The notion of "moving the basin" is itself rooted in a procedural computational framework. Conceptually, there is a specific variable **wash_basin** whose value is an image of a basin on the architectural plan, and whose value is changed when the basin is moved. In the L.E.G.O. idiom, the basin might itself be represented by a procedure including a parameter specifying its position. By editing this procedure definition, it would certainly be possible to relocate the basin in isolation, but to model the relationship between the basin and the mirror would require some data dependency between the procedures drawing the mirror and the basin. From an implementation perspective, an object-oriented paradigm may clarify this model, making it possible to represent the basin by an object rather than a family of primitive procedural variables, and the geometric relationship between the basin and the mirror through a message passing protocol, but the data dependencies established in this way will nonetheless be difficult to ascertain.

Within a purely declarative programming paradigm, there is - ideally - no direct way to model procedural variables such as **wash_basin**: a program is a set of functions, or a system of equations, that defines a set of values through evaluation, or solution. In this respect, the philosophical foundations of declarative paradigms militate against rich support for reference. To modify the graphical image the user must edit the set of functions or equations, so that in principle a totally new program has to be interpreted. Though some special provision for modularisation could be made by elaborating the specification (c.f. [10]), these are unlikely to enable the user to view the specification flexibly as incorporating references to parts of the image that are subject to change.

In a constraint-based framework, there are variables to represent geometric entities, though it may not be easy to choose these at an appropriate level of abstraction. Even if the problem of identifying the constraints that pertain to the wash-basin can be solved, formidable difficulties remain. Determining whether the simplest new constraint leads to inconsistency is presumably algorithmically undecidable in general, so that its impact can neither be conveniently represented to the user, nor acknowledged by the compiler.

Within the definitive programming paradigm, it is still necessary to determine data dependencies through examination of the program code. The difference is that the use of definitions makes these dependencies transparent, in that they can be precisely identified syntactically, and readily interpreted. These virtues are epitomised in numeric rather than geometric applications by the spreadsheet, which allows relationships and values to be defined and modified in an easily comprehensible manner. This has important ramifications, to be investigated below.

5.   GEOMETRIC CONSTRUCTIONS AND DEFINITIONS

To explore the significance of using definitions to formulate geometric relationships, it will be helpful to recast a construction-based specification in definitive terms. This is easily done for the simple example of a geometric construction "bisection of a line", as formulated in L.E.G.O in [7]:

(point 400 370 A)	**point** a = {400,370}
(point 600 470 B)	**point** b = {600,470}
(line A B L)	**line** l = [a,b]
(circle A L C1)	**circle** c1 = circle of radius l with centre a
(circle B L C2)	**circle** c2 = circle of radius l with centre b
(intersection C1 C2 X1 X2)	**pointset** {x1,x2} = intersection (c1,c2)
(line X1 X2 P)	**line** p = [x1,x2]

The left-hand column is the original L.E.G.O specification; the right-hand an equivalent formulation using a fictional variant of the definitive notation DoNaLD [2,3]. Note that the "operators of the underlying algebra" required for this definitive notation correspond precisely to the primitive constructions of L.E.G.O. The strong syntactic resemblance between the two specifications should not detract from very fundamental semantic distinctions. The order of the definitions on the right is not significant: the data relationships that they express is intrinsic in the variable references. The definitions are not to be interpreted as a sequence of constructions to be carried out, but as an explicit description of the data dependencies between geometric entities. Such systems of definitions can form a component of a larger definitive specification irrespective of whether the variables to which they refer are currently well-defined. The effect of redefining a variable is to update that part of the specification that is linked through data dependency to the variable, and to lead - through re-evaluation - to selective redisplay.

The above illustration may suggest that the distinction between the L.E.G.O. and DoNaLD approaches is cosmetic. After all, the difference between the two code fragments above is small enough for easy re-interpretation in either direction. It can be argued - for instance - that storing a set of definitions that describes the bisector of the line AB when A and B denote the same point, is essentially the same as storing a procedural file of instructions that happens at present not to be executable. The data dependencies between variables in the L.E.G.O. specification are in this case easy to identify, and incremental recompilation of the procedural specification after any single statement were to be modified (as in "redefining a variable") is well within the scope of current compiler technology [14].

The virtues of the new perspective afforded by definitive programming cannot be fully appreciated from such a small example. To justify the L.E.G.O. specification as a system of "imperative constraints" requires an interpretation of the variables different from that used in a traditional procedural approach, lest they exist only whilst the drawing procedure is being executed. The reinterpretation of construction steps as definitions captures this distinction, and exposes the characteristics of a small-scale L.E.G.O. specification that make it conceptually simple for the *user* to interpret. As the history of procedural programming testifies, a procedural fragment can become very hard to interpret in the context of a large specification. On these grounds, a definitive reformulation seems to be a promising way to express the particular qualities of specifications in the L.E.G.O. idiom, provided that it can be shown that definitive programming in principle has the expressive power to support major applications.

6. TOWARDS DEFINITIVE PROGRAMMING IN THE LARGE: DATA REPRESENTATION

How do definitive programming principles scale up? There are two aspects to be considered: the representation of data, and the specification of control. The issue of treating complex data types within a definitive framework has received much attention in previous papers [1,2]. The principle is clear: defining the value of a variable of a complex data type should be possible at many different levels of abstraction, so that *either* a recipe for the entire value of a variable is supplied *or* the variable is composed of a family of independently defined variables whose values describe its constituent parts. Two methods of dealing with this issue have been developed: the use of "moding" as in the definitive notation ARCA, and the use of **openshape** variables that permit a hierarchical definition of sets of **points** and **lines** as in DoNaLD [3,4]. The principal outstanding problem is describing a formal framework in which to treat the specification of operators of a complex type: a topic that provides a natural context for the further consideration and comparison of functional, construction-based and definitive methods.

The issues are well illustrated by considering the design of user-defined operators of type **shape** within DoNaLD. The naive view is that a user-defined operator of type **shape** is an extension to the underlying algebra, and should be described by a pure function returning a value of type **shape**. The idea of using a definitive notation to specify the function itself is superficially unattractive - within the function body, there seems to be no purpose in having variables whose values are specified by definitions. In the original DoNaLD design [3], this was the position adopted: a new **shape** operator should be a function without side-effects to be specified using a simple procedural or functional notation.

Such a convention is not wholly satisfactory. A typical use of the **shape** operator f(a,b,c,...) would involve a **shape** variable declaration followed by a definition:

shape S; S=f(A,B,C,...).

The problem then arises: in making use of the implicitly defined variable S, what references to the constituents of S are valid? For instance, if f returns a set of points and lines that defines a square, how is it possible to reference its edges and vertices? Oddly enough, though functional programming might appear to be the obvious paradigm to choose for the specification of a pure function, it is unhelpful in this respect. It seems that the problems associated with interactive revision of a functional specification referred to in connection with interaction in §4 above also impinge where only *reference* to a specification rather than revision is involved.

A trivial illustration will clarify the issues, and indicate why the present proposal for the specification of DoNaLD **shape** operators is as much influenced by the ostensibly procedural treatment of function definition in L.E.G.O. as by functional programming ideas. Following [9], a system of lines resembling the rungs of a ladder might have the following functional specification:

ladder: N×V×V → P

ladder(n,a,b) ≡ **if** n=1 **then** line(a,b) **else** picture(line(n.a,b),ladder(n-1,a,b)).

In this specification, a and b are parameters representing vectors, n is an integer to specify the number of rungs, and P designates the data type "picture". It is an elegant and concise description, but is many ways inappropriate in an interactive graphics setting. To depict the rungs of a ladder, a function evaluation such as

ladder(n,<1,2>,<2,1>)

must be performed. To reference a particular rung of the ladder, as might be required in simulating "climbing the ladder", is impossible without embellishment of the original specification. To model a real ladder, that might consist of two congruent hinged sections that could be locked into a V-shaped or linear relation, it would not be enough to use such a functional specification - even in conjunction with a DoNaLD **shape** variable. Of course, it is not infeasible to elaborate functional methods to partially redeem the situation (c.f. [10]), but there appear to be fundamental limitations associated with the strictures of referential transparency.

By contrast, a procedural approach to the specification of the ladder() function makes the problems of attaching references to the individual rungs of the ladder less acute. In effect, it is relatively to easy to formulate a procedural description of a function that returns not only a value of type **shape** to represent the ladder, but a family of variables of type **line** to represent the rungs. To illustrate the form that such a specification might take, consider the two following specifications - the one written in the construction-based L.E.G.O. idiom, the other in the definitive DoNaLD style:

```
(define_function ladder(n a b))          openshape ladder(int n, point a,b)
(line n.a n.a+(b-a) l)                    within ladder {
(write_function)                              line L = [n.a, n.a+(b-a)]
(if (n>1) then                                if n>1 then {
      (ladder n-1 a b)                              shape Ladder = ladder(n-1,a,b)
(end_function)                                }
                                          }
```

The same considerations that applied to the comparison of the "bisection of the line" construction discussed above again apply. The dual semantics that makes it possible to view a L.E.G.O. specification from a procedural and a definitive perspective is helpful here in interpreting the specification on the right as defining an operator together with a system of references to the value it returns. By introducing such operator specifications it is possible to formulate a DoNaLD definition:

shape Ladder; Ladder = ladder(7, {1,2},{2,1})

so that Ladder/L refers to the top rung, Ladder/Ladder to the remaining set of rungs, of which Ladder/Ladder/L is the topmost etc. This is the kind of referencing facility that is required when establishing relationships between complex objects that cannot conveniently be explicitly defined.

6.   DEFINITIVE PROGRAMMING IN THE LARGE: CONTROL

In this paper, the case for "programming with definitions" has so far been made on technical grounds. The primary argument has been that conventional interactive graphics involves editing functional, procedural or constraint-based specifications that typically correspond only in a very obscure way to the cognitive models the user requires. Particular attention has been focussed on the limited way in which conventional paradigms for interactive graphics support references to objects and their constituent parts. Some of the problems can be attributed to the vague semantics of variables, and the dichotomy between declarative frameworks in which references are too inflexibly established, and procedural environments in which they are too impermanent. The result is that interactive systems are frequently ill-equipped for significant user intervention.

In what respects does definitive programming potentially offer better prospects? To an extent, the ideas introduced above meet the need for better support for the abstract description and referencing of graphical images, and allow incremental changes to relationships to be subtly and efficiently represented. The representation of dependencies between data using definitions is a particularly significant concept, since it enables the user to prescribe, and to anticipate, the effects of amending a specification.

The significance of using definitions to support interaction goes beyond technical considerations alone, however. A central thesis of current work on definitive programming is that a definitive system is a useful cognitive model not merely for user-computer interaction, but for the actions of an agent in a concurrent system [4,5]. In effect, a single system of definitions is best conceived as articulating the effects of a particular action or intended action. Only by such a generalisation of the concept of "definitive notations for interaction" does it become possible to express the fact that an architect's expectations on moving the wash-basin might or might not encompass an automatic compensating movement of the mirror, and could lead to the invocation of an automatic process to reconfigure the external balconies.

As this illustration suggests, though it may not be possible for the user to predict the outcome of an automatic computation initiated during an interaction, it is necessary to give the user both a degree of control over such computation, and a good appreciation of its effects. The perspective taken in this paper is that the description and manipulation of geometrical relationships throughout the entire user-computer interaction should be seen as one consistent (non-terminating) computation comprising many simple transactions. In this interactive process, the user and the computer participate via sequences of homogeneous actions, and the effect of each individual action is transparent to the user. This means, in particular, that the user knows the effective geometric relationships throughout the entire interaction, even to the extent that it is possible for the user to suspend and intervene during an automatic computation.

The appropriate abstract machine model adopted for this purpose is the abstract definitive machine (ADM), as described in [4,3,5]. A full discussion of the ADM is beyond the scope of this paper, but a brief sketch of its use in the animation of a simple concurrent system will be used to illustrate the key ideas. In many respects, this ADM simulation resembles examples developed using the NoPumpG software [12].

Suppose that two blocks b1 and b2 are connected by a string of length d, and that the blocks are independently controlled by two handlers. The behaviour of the pair of blocks can be described by the ADM program in Figure 1. The handlers are represented by entities: each entity comprises a set of variable declarations and definitions, and a set of guarded actions. In this context, each action consists of a sequence of redefinitions. The operation of the ADM is such that in each machine cycle the guards of all actions within currently instantiated entities are evaluated, and the actions associated with true guards are performed in parallel (subject to non-interference). The entity handler1() for instance, may at any stage be holding b1 - as defined by the variable h1, and when holding the block may be pushing left (pl1) or right (pr1). The movement of the blocks is determined by the bmover() entity, and depends upon the directions in which the blocks are currently being driven (dr1, dl1, dr2, dl2).

The ADM control program in Figure 1 is taken from [5], where a fuller discussion may be found. For brevity and convenience, some simplifications have been made: the use of parametrised entities has been avoided, and only the specification of one of the block handlers (handler1()) is given. The use of the colon (:) to separate actions indicates that precisely one of these actions is to be performed when the associated guard is true.

The specification of bmover() illustrates how the context within which variables are redefined must be altered to reflect conditions such as whether the blocks are touching (t12), and whether the string is taut (st). For instance, if b1 is being driven to the left, and the string is taut, the action

$$\text{"dl1 and st -> p2=p1+d; p1=|p1|-1"}$$

is enabled, indicating that the movement of b1 to the left must necessarily drag b2 to the left also. As it stands, the specification does not include any method for resolving interference between actions, as for instance would arise if b2 were simultaneously being driven to the right (c.f. [5]).

The entity bstate() records the current position and status of the blocks: their positions (p1, p2) and whether the string either should snap or has been snapped (nostr).

The simulation is very simply animated by complementing the ADM specification with a file of DoNaLD definitions to describe the required display. The DoNaLD definitions of the **openshapes** b1 and b2 that represent the blocks, and the **line** str that represents the string can be abstractly viewed as an additional entity within the ADM specification. The block display registers the location of the blocks (as specified by the variables p1 and p2), and the handler-block relationship (as specified by h1, dl1, dr1 etc). The simulation snapshot depicts a situation in which b1 is being driven to the right, and the block b2 is being held, for instance.

CONCLUDING REMARKS

This paper has argued the case for giving serious consideration to the development of definitive programming as a medium for describing interactive systems, and perhaps indicated something of its potential. There are many issues still to be explored, and work is in progress on a variety of related topics, including applications to CAD, and to the simulation of concurrent systems.

Good semantic models for graphics and interaction deserve closer consideration. There are many indications in this paper of the apparent inadequacy of our present theoretical foundations for programming in respect of data representation and manipulation (c.f. [11]). An intriguing historical sidelight on this issue is the demise of the concept of a mathematical variable as "representing a variable quantity" during the arithmetisation of analysis in the 19th century [8]. Perhaps the development of better methods of programming for interactive graphics can stimulate reconsideration of the formal status of the rich - if obscure - concept of *variable* that geometrical intuition formerly inspired.

```
entity handler1()
{
    definition
        d1 = dl1 or dr1,
        dl1 = h1 and pl1, dr1 = h1 and pr1,
        pl1 = 0, pr1 = 0, h1 =0
    action
        not h1 -> h1=1,
        h1 and not d1 -> h1=0: pl1 =1: pr1=1,
        dl1 -> pl1 = 0, dr1 -> pr1 = 0
}

entity bstate()
{
    definition
        p1, p2, d,
        st = not nostr and (p2-p1)==d,
        t12 = (p2-p1)==1,
        nostr = 0
    action
        not nostr and (p2-p1)>d -> nostr=1
}

entity bmover()
{
    action
        dl1 and not st -> p1=|p1|-1,
        dl1 and st -> p2=p1+d; p1=|p1|-1,
        dr2 and not st -> p2=|p2|+1,
        dr2 and st -> p1=p2-d; p2=|p2|+1,
        dr1 and not t12 -> p1=|p1|+1,
        dr1 and t12 -> p2=p1+1; p1=|p1|+1,
        dl2 and not t12 -> p2=|p2|-1,
        dl2 and t12 -> p1=p2-1; p2=|p2|-1,
}

bstate(); bmover(), handler1(); handler2()
```

```
openshape b1
within b1 {
    point O
        O = {500+~/p1*100, 500}
    point NE,NW, SW,SE
    NE = O + {50,50}
    NW = O + {50,-50}
    ...........
    line n,s,e,w
    n = [NW,NE]
    s = [SW,SE]
    ...........
    point N, E, S, W, X
    N = if ~/h1 then (NE+NW) div 2 else O
    S = if ~/h1 then (SE+SW) div 2 else O
    E = if ~/h1 then (NE+SE) div 2 else O
    W = if ~/h1 then (NW+SW) div 2 else O
    X = if ~/dr1 then E else
                 if ~/dl1 then W else O
    line WE, NX, SX = [W,E], [N,X], [S,X]
}
int  p1,h1,dr1,dl1,p2,h2,dr2,dl2,nostr
line str
str = [b1/E, if nostr then b1/E else b2/W]
```

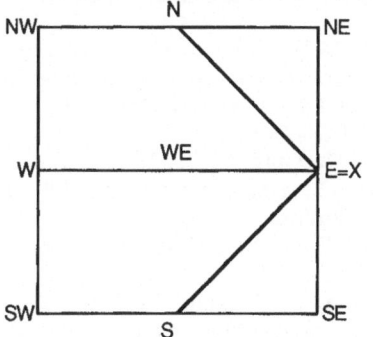

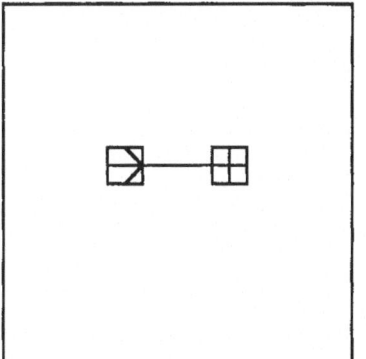

Above: The ADM control program

Bottom right: Simulation snapshot

Middle right: Detail of the block1 display

Top right: DoNaLD display specification

Figure 1: A block moving simulation using definitive principles

ACKNOWLEDGEMENTS

I am indebted to Mike Slade and to Edward Yung for their support in designing and implementing software prototypes for DoNaLD and the ADM, and to Steve Russ for many helpful discussions on the subject of reference and interaction.

REFERENCES

1. W M Beynon *Definitive notations for interaction*, Proc hci'85 CUP 1985, 23-34
2. W M Beynon *Definitive principles for interactive graphics*, NATO ASI series F:40, 1987, 1083-1097
3. W M Beynon, D Angier, T Bissell, S Hunt *DoNaLD: a line drawing system based on definitive principles*, Univ of Warwick RR#86, 1986
3. W M Beynon, Y W Yung, *Implementing a definitive notation for interactive graphics*, New Trends in Computer Graphics, ed N Magnenat-Thalman, D Thalman Springer-Verlag 1988, 456-68
4. W M Beynon, M D Slade, Y W Yung *Parallel computation in definitive models*, in Proc Conpar'88 (to appear)
5. W M Beynon *Definitive programming for parallelism*, CS RR#132, Warwick Univ, 1988
6. A Borning *The programming language aspects of ThingLab, a constraint-oriented simulation laboratory*, ACM Transactions on Programming Languages 3(4), 1981, 353-387
7. N Fuller, P Prusinkiewicz *Geometric Modelling with Euclidean Constructions*, New Trends in Computer Graphics ed N Magnenat-Thalmann, D Thalmann, Springer-Verlag 1988, 379-391
8. P Geach, M Black *Philosophical Writings of Gottlob Frege*.
9. P Henderson *Functional Programming*, Prentice-Hall International 1980
10. J Hughes *Why Functional Programming Matters*, PMG Report #16, Chalmers Univ of Tech & Univ of Goteborg, 1984
11. W Kent *Data and Reality*, North-Holland 1978
12. C Lewis *Using the NoPumpG primitive*, Dept of Computer Science and Inst of Cog Sci, Univ of Boulder
13. T Noma, T L Kunii, N Kin, Henomoto, E Aso, T Yamamoto *Drawing Input Through Geometrical Constructions: Specification and Applications*, New Trends in Computer Graphics, ed N Magnenat-Thalman, D Thalman, Springer-Verlag 1988, 403-415
14. T W Reps *Generating Language-Based Environments* MIT Press 1984

Meurig Beynon is currently a lecturer in computer science at the University of Warwick. His research interests have included geometric aspects of partially-ordered algebras, mathematical algorithms, and the algebraic theory of boolean circuits. His most recent research has been concerned with the development of a programming paradigm based upon definitions ("definitive programming") that has been applied to the design of prototype software for interactive graphics and CAD applications, and for modelling and simulating concurrent systems. The current focus of this research is on exploiting definitive principles as a method for software specification, and as the basis of a general-purpose model for parallel programming.

Beynon is the author of 22 refereed papers on mathematics and computer science. He was an SRC Postdoctoral Research Fellow at University College Swansea from 1973-5, and a visiting Research Fellow at British Telecom Research Laboratories in 1986. He was the principal organiser of the 2nd British Colloquium for Theoretical Computer Science in 1986, and the secretary of the colloquium committee from 1986-8.

Beynon received his BSc and PhD in mathematics from King's College, London in 1969 and 1973.

Department of Computer Science, University of Warwick, Coventry CV4 7AL, UK.

Constraint-Solving in Interactive Graphics:
A User-Friendly Approach

D.L. Maulsby, K.A. Kittlitz, and I.H. Witten

ABSTRACT

Solving constraints is an important part of interactive graphics, and many constraint solvers that operate in this domain have been created. However, most are deficient in two respects: the method of specifying constraints is unnatural, and the class of possible constraints is restricted. After describing these problems, we propose a simple constraint solver and its user interface, Metamouse. The user specifies constraints by examples in the form of execution traces, from which a generalized procedure is induced. Specification is natural — the user simply performs his task as usual — and representable constraints include anything the user could accomplish manually.

KEYWORDS
  AI and graphics; machine learning; intelligent user interfaces; constraints

1 INTRODUCTION

A drawing has an implicit specification in terms of spatial constraints. When drawing, people often execute procedures to satisfy the constraints they have in mind. Although interactive graphics editors provide some facilities to help with constraints, by and large the users do the work. This often requires precision or tedious repetition and should therefore be automated. Over the past three decades much research has been done on constraint solvers and methods of specification. The approaches taken to date have on the whole been unsuitable for people who want to draw rather than program. With the introduction of direct-manipulation graphics, the opportunity and the necessity to induce constraints from examples has become clear. This paper describes a system for inducing graphical procedures, which serves as an interface to a simple constraint solver.

The system is based on studies of users and of the drawing process. A graphical apprentice, Metamouse, observes the user at work, induces patterns of activity, and makes conjectures about subsequent actions. Metamouse learns procedures with constants, variables, branches and loops. Each step expresses a constraint to be satisfied by translating a single point or by rotating about it. Thus the constraint solver is relatively simple. Domain knowledge enables the system to isolate constraints from the spatial relations established by each step of the user's teaching trace. Examples of tasks taught to the system are shown in Figures 1–3.

The paper begins with an overview of previous work on specifying graphical constraints, describes the domain model, constraint solver and user interface, and concludes by evaluating the pilot system.

2 CONSTRAINT SYSTEMS IN GRAPHICS

There have been two major lines of development in systems for interactive drawing. The first seeks to improve either the naturalness or the power of declaratively-specified constraints. The second takes a procedural approach and lets the user construct programs that express his intention in geometric terms.

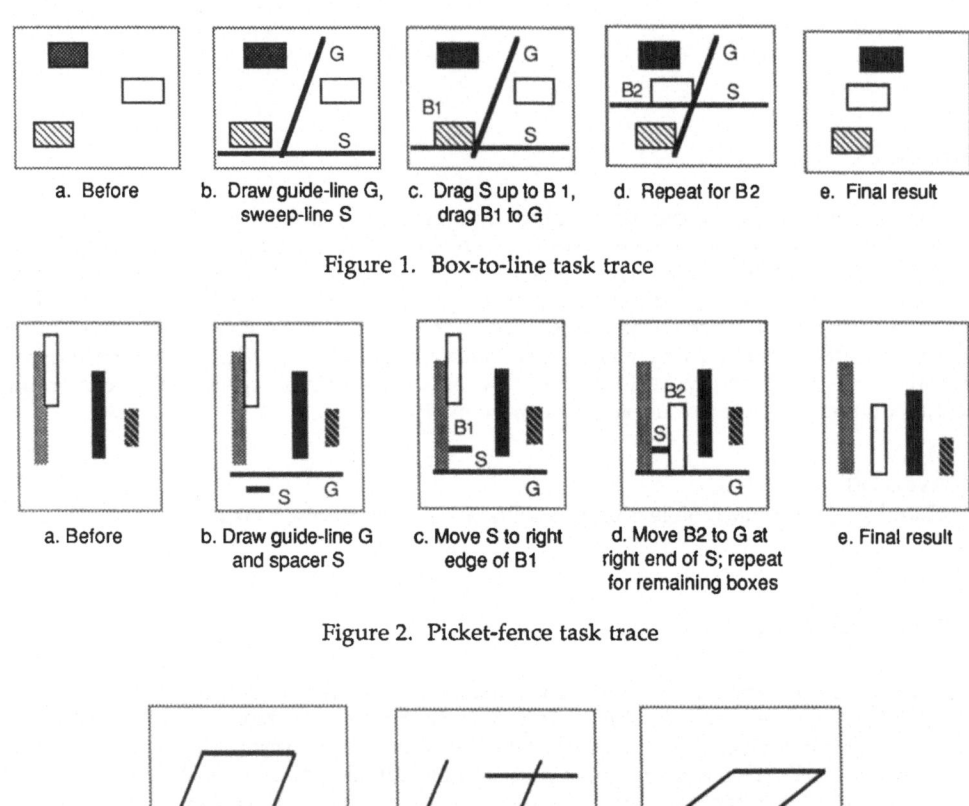

a. Before	b. Draw guide-line G, sweep-line S	c. Drag S up to B 1, drag B1 to G	d. Repeat for B2	e. Final result

Figure 1. Box-to-line task trace

a. Before	b. Draw guide-line G and spacer S	c. Move S to right edge of B1	d. Move B2 to G at right end of S; repeat for remaining boxes	e. Final result

Figure 2. Picket-fence task trace

a. Before	b. Input: user moves one edge	c. Final result

Figure 3. Connectivity task

2.1 The Declarative Approach

The widespread use of various forms of "gravity field" in interactive graphics exemplifies the first approach by providing a very natural way to constrain the placement of objects (Foley and Van Dam, 1982). Sutherland (1963) equipped SKETCHPAD with constraints to make lines vertical, horizontal, parallel or perpendicular; to make points lie on lines or circles; to align symbols in vertical rows; and to relate symbols to other drawing parts such as points or lines. An interactive editing sequence typically involved new object definitions interleaved with constraint specifications. These early ideas are reincarnated in contemporary interactive drafting systems.

Bier and Stone (1986) note that two principal methods are used to facilitate high-precision interactive positioning: grids and constraints. The former are limited in expressive power, offering only a small fraction of the desired types of precision, while the latter require the user to specify additional structures that are often difficult to understand and time-consuming to manipulate. To combine the convenience of grids and the power of constraints, the SNAP-DRAGGING technique equips the user with a variety of alignment objects — such as circles of specified sizes, horizontal and vertical lines — and "snaps" points of the drawing onto them. However, the constraints are forgotten as soon as points are placed, so that subsequent manipulations do not respect the original positioning operations.

A more traditional use of constraints is exemplified by White's (1988) "human interface to least squares" scheme. This lets users place constraints on distances and angles and then, on request through an *adjust* command, applies a least-squares relaxation method to solve them. Constraints are remembered, so users can add points, lines, and constraints in any order and *adjust* them at any time, but there is no way to store or manipulate a *sequence* of constraint-satisfaction problems.

One striking drawback to most constraint-satisfaction drawing aids is the inability to define new constraints. For example, to add new kinds of constraints to Borning's (1981) THINGLAB, one had to write code in SmallTalk. However, Borning (1986) has recently addressed this deficiency by allowing graphical definition of constraints. The user draws an equational network, with icons that represent variables, constants, arithmetic operators and function calls (to other constraint routines). To define the variables, the user draws an example and labels points accordingly. The important limitation of THINGLAB with respect to graphics applications is the declarative method used to specify the program. Drawing is naturally procedural (Van Sommers, 1984), yet THINGLAB'S equational network requires the user to have an algebraic model of his problem.

2.2 The Procedural Approach

The second, procedural, approach to expressing constraint in graphical systems has a long and noble history. Descartes' conceptual breakthrough of making geometry algebraic provided the theoretical basis for early graphics programs — although the supporting technology was a long time coming. In the beginning, computer drawing was very much like programming, and images intended for production on a graphics plotter were typically expressed as FORTRAN programs. Sutherland's SKETCHPAD was an innovation which freed the user from hated algebra and substituted incremental interaction for the Cartesian representation.

From the point of view of the user interface, Descartes' invention was a *faux pas*. Procedural graphics was well-known to the ancient Greeks — indeed, as Preparata (1985) points out, geometry inspired the first investigations into the very notion of a formal procedure. In the last two decades, constructive computer graphics have bounded back a couple of millennia towards purely geometric specification of graphical procedures.

For example, L.E.G.O. specifies constraints using the traditional ruler and compass methods of geometric construction (Fuller and Prusinkiewicz 1988). An extension of LISP, it provides the primitive objects *point, line* and *circle*, and an operator that returns one or two points of *intersection* between objects. It allows one to automate constructions by procedural programming. Variables are identified by naming points — in this case those returned by the *intersection* function. Although it has a graphical programming interface, it requires the user to explicitly identify input and output variables and control structures.

Noma *et al* (1988) also use a language based on Euclidean primitives. The user creates a geometric construction by writing a small program in this language. Concrete objects are named. Abstractions (like the length of a line) are not, because the concept of a "variable" was held to be too difficult for ordinary users. Instead, the language provides a limited stacking facility to allow each primitive in the program to communicate parameters to the next.

Procedural Euclidean geometry is a viable alternative to constraint systems for specifying figures to high precision. Kin *et al* (1989) argue that it is superior in that a) constraint systems require considerable computation for large problems while constructive geometry is linear in the number of objects, and b) specifying consistent and sufficient constraints for a desired picture is a difficult task. However, the small set of primitives may lack appeal to lesser mathematicians than Euclid — popular drafting programs have found it expedient to offer a rich set of pragmatically-motivated objects and operations. More important, the need to deal explicitly with procedural abstractions, expressed textually, negates the advantages of direct-manipulation environments.

3 DOMAIN MODEL

Users of drawing programs carry out procedures that implicitly express constraints. Specifications can be inferred from such procedures by distinguishing the relevant features of actions and generalizing them. Garnering specifications from examples has the obvious advantage of keeping the user in his accustomed work paradigm — he continues drawing as usual, with minimal interruption from the system.

In order to isolate relevant features the system needs a model of the user's task behavior. A rich model might include traits of the individual user. Ours restricts itself to generalities about computer drawing. Its main components are the primitives and operators of a drawing program, the structure of procedures, a notion of program variables, and a classification of spatial constraints.

3.1 Graphics Primitives and Operators

The constraint solver must be able to reproduce any of the user's actions. Moreover, it must accept descriptions of spatial relations between named parts of objects. Thus it needs to model the operators of the drawing program and the user's perception of objects. The operators may be adopted outright or decomposed into a functionally complete set. The user's perceptual capabilities can only be modeled to a crude approximation, but this is sufficient for a useful system and is easily explained to the user.

Consider the following graphics system $G = (P, A, O)$, of primitive objects P, auxiliary objects A, and operators O. In contrast to that proposed by Noma *et al* (1988), it is based on the elements of a simple MacDraw-style drawing package (Cutter *et al*, 1987), rather than the requirements of geometric construction.

$P = $ [box (bottom-left, top-right),
line (endpt$_1$, endpt$_2$),
point (x, y)]

$A = $ [CurrentPoint : point,
CurrentObject : {box, line},
DisplayList : list of {box, line}]

O = [create-object (CurrentObject, CurrentPoint, type),
set-pick (CurrentPoint, CurrentObject, DisplayList, x, y),
translate-handle-of-object-to-point (hndl, CurrentObject, CurrentPoint),
delete-object (CurrentObject),
undo-previous-operation (CurrentObject, CurrentPoint, DisplayList)]

With the exception of *point*, the primitives are just the types of objects the user may select from the drawing palette. *Point* is the type of a hidden auxiliary object, *CurrentPoint*, which is the screen location most recently selected by the mouse. Drawing and transformation operations begin at one value of *CurrentPoint* and terminate at the next. Only one object may be selected for transformation and is distinguished as *CurrentObject*. The operators are independent of each other but have side-effects, updating the auxiliary objects. *Set-pick* places *CurrentPoint* and updates *CurrentObject* if *CurrentPoint* is placed within the gravity field of some primitive. The only transformation operator is *translate-handle-of-object-to-point()*, which moves some key-point handle of *CurrentObject* and updates *CurrentPoint*. It translates or scales the object, depending upon the choice of handle, as in MacDraw.

Obviously, the fundamental primitives and operators have a great impact on the user's expression of constraints. The pilot system given above has some notable omissions, such as circles, rotation, and the grouping of objects in hierarchies. These features are certainly desirable (either circles or rotation would be necessary for Euclidean construction), but would complicate the constraint solver's implementation and thus have been left for future work.

3.2 Constraint Problems as Procedures

In drawing, users meet complex constraints by sequences of simple operations. Analysis of drawing task performance by Van Sommers (1984) showed that people organize their work systematically. This bodes well for the procedural approach taken by Fuller and Prusinkiewicz (1988) and Noma *et al* (1988). The system presented here tests Van Sommers' hypothesis by *inducing* such procedures from example execution traces. Each example action is assumed to be governed by constraints. Branches and loops can be induced by matching or failing to match such generalized actions.

An example program graph, for the Box-to-line task (Figure 1), is illustrated in Figure 4. Each node describes one statement in the program, and the conditions on its performance. Formally, it is an *action-step* tuple: *(node-id, predecessors, successors, preconditions, operator, postconditions)*. The *action-step's* locality is given by the lists of its *predecessors* and *successors* in the graph. The *pre-* and *postconditions* are lists of constraints that must apply before and after executing the *operator*. Specific parameter values for the *operator* are derived by solving for the *postcondition* constraints. Since all operations are based on translating *CurrentPoint*, the only parameter is a 2-dimensional vector.

As mentioned above, a set of conditions is represented as a list of *constraint (Data, Class, Used)* tuples. *Data* is a touch relation, path, position or distance descriptor. *Class* is the constraint classification, described in Section 3.4 below. *Used* is a flag indicating whether the constraint is enforced or ignored. Some constraints may be ignored because others are sufficient, or because they do not apply in all situations that have been matched to each other. *Precondition* constraints are always ignored unless needed to distinguish situations that would otherwise match against the user's wishes.

For example, in Figure 4, step S_5 has steps S_4 and S_8 as predecessors, and S_6 as a successor. Its preconditions (derived by disjoining the postconditions of S_4 and S_8) are ignored, since the user has accepted predictions of S_5 in all situations encountered so far. Its operator is

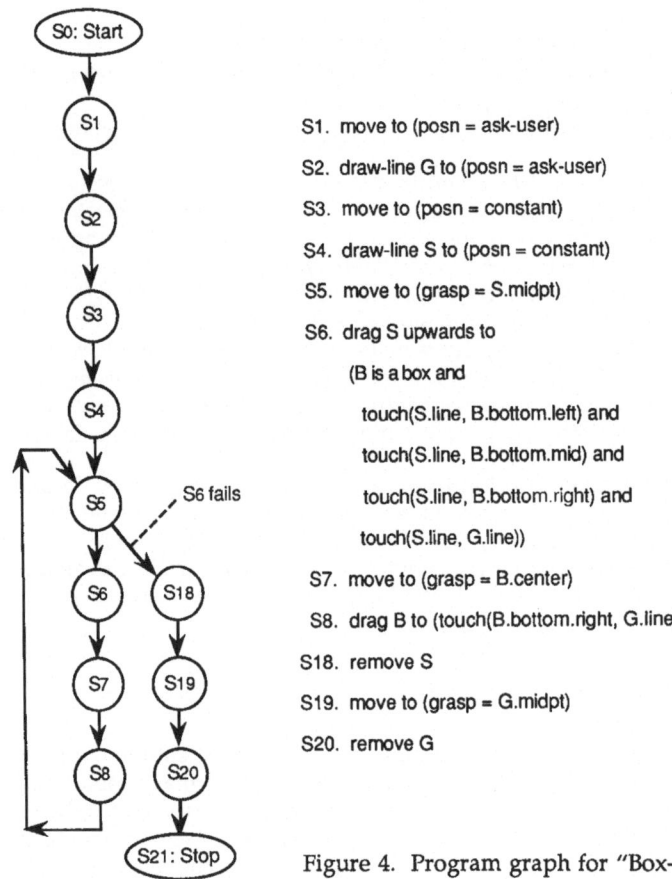

S1. move to (posn = ask-user)

S2. draw-line G to (posn = ask-user)

S3. move to (posn = constant)

S4. draw-line S to (posn = constant)

S5. move to (grasp = S.midpt)

S6. drag S upwards to

    (B is a box and

      touch(S.line, B.bottom.left) and

      touch(S.line, B.bottom.mid) and

      touch(S.line, B.bottom.right) and

      touch(S.line, G.line))

S7. move to (grasp = B.center)

S8. drag B to (touch(B.bottom.right, G.line))

S18. remove S

S19. move to (grasp = G.midpt)

S20. remove G

Figure 4. Program graph for "Box-to-line"

set-pick, and its postcondition is that the mid-point of line S is in grasp. Thus, set-pick moves *CurrentPoint* to the center of the S.midpt handle and sets *CurrentObject* to S.

3.3 Representing Spatial Relations

In Euclidean construction, spatial constraints are expressed as touch relations between distinguished parts of objects. This notion is readily extended from formal proofs to drawing tasks. For example, a vertical distance can be represented by a vertical line; contact with its end-points expresses the distance constraint. Touch relations occur between distinguished parts of objects and thus are expressed as a correspondence of object parts, *touch* (*object₁.part₁* : *object₂.part₂*), where *partᵢ* indicates some part of *objectᵢ*. Typically, an action's pre- and postconditions are sets of touch relations.

The drawing program's user interface distinguishes certain parts of boxes and lines, namely the vertex and mid-point handles and the line segments between them. The former are especially important, for many steps in a user's execution trace involve placing *CurrentPoint* at a handle. Moreover, Van Sommers (1984) notes that constraints often occur between extremal points of objects. Although line segments are distinguished as parts, they are not subdivided, since no division points are visible to the user. Such divisions are easily constructed by the end-points of other lines.

Touch relations are distinguished according to the degree of constraint they express. Three types of constraint are especially useful: point-to-point, point-on-line, and line-crosses-line. The first is the most restrictive, the third is the least. An object's handles are treated as points.

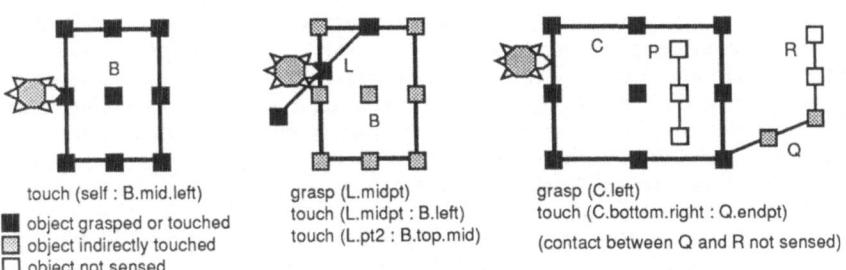

touch (self : B.mid.left)

■ object grasped or touched
▨ object indirectly touched
□ object not sensed

grasp (L.midpt)
touch (L.midpt : B.left)
touch (L.pt2 : B.top.mid)

grasp (C.left)
touch (C.bottom.right : Q.endpt)

(contact between Q and R not sensed)

Figure 5. Examples of touch relations observed

Touch relations are also described in terms of their role in the user's current action. A direct touch occurs between *CurrentPoint* and some object. A grasp relation is a direct touch of *CurrentObject*. An indirect touch occurs between *CurrentObject* and some other object. These types of touch are sufficient when observing the steps of a formal construction. Higher degrees of indirect touch may in fact be useful when modeling drawing tasks. Examples of touch relations are shown in Figure 5. (The turtle icon, whose snout is at *CurrentPoint*, is described in §4.) Direct touch is shown as a one-element touch relation.

Touch relations observed during an execution trace must be generalized by substituting variables for references to specific objects. The system induces variables by searching a limited number of recent steps for previous occurrences of objects in current touch relations. Each reference to a variable is also marked with a flag indicating whether the action has changed its value. Thus, a variable is defined as *variable-definition (name, value)*, and a reference to it as *variable-reference (name, valuation-flag)*.

3.4 Ordering the Constraints

Not all constraints observed are equally useful. Some, such as the grasping of a line's endpoint as it is drawn, are trivial consequences of actions. Others are overdetermined but may be needed to distinguish one situation from another. In order to get at the user's intentions the system isolates useful constraints by classifying and ordering observed touch relations. This analysis also reveals whether the action is sufficiently constrained to be an automated step in the program.

A touch relation between two objects A and B involves several degrees of freedom: the selection of A and B; the selection of named parts of A and of B; and the location of specific points within those parts. A generalized relation, such as *touch (S.line, B.bottom.?)*, may fix some of these and leave others variable. The *valuation-flag* (see §3.3) indicates whether an the value of an object variable (*eg. S*) is fixed or may be changed. The selection of a part is free if the name has been generalized, as in *B.bottom.?*, where "?" can be replaced with one of {*left, mid, right*}. Position is variable only within line segments. Given this information, a touch relation's degree of constraint can be calculated. For example, the case above has three degrees of freedom: the choice of box assigned to *B*; the specification of a handle for *B.bottom.?*; and the selection of a point along the line segment *S.line*. All degrees of freedom are not equal, however. When matching situations, the choices of object and part are far more important than position.

The role a constraint plays in an action is also important. A touch relation may result from an action, occur as a trivial consequence, or remain unchanged. Role and degree form the basis for classifying constraints in our system. Constraints achieved by an action are called *resultant*; they help determine an operation's parameters, and are further classified as *determining, strong,* or *weak.* A *determining* constraint leaves zero degrees of freedom. A *strong* constraint leaves only the selection of one object free, and thus can determine exact position when combined with a path constraint: for example, *touch (S.endpt, B.bottom.left),* where *B* is found by scanning upwards. Other *resultant* constraints are *weak.* In the presence of a determining constraint, others are reclassified as *overdetermined.* In the absence of a determining constraint, the direction (path) along which *CurrentPoint* has been translated is included as a constraint. Paths can be generalized to quadrants (*eg.* upward, rightward) or axes (*eg.* horizontal, vertical) as required.

Unchanged conditions persist through an operation and thus appear in both pre- and postconditions. The *trivial* ones, such as maintaining the grasp of a handle while dragging it, are given by the definitions of operators. Discarding them makes no difference to a postcondition's generality. *Sustained* constraints are *touch* relations that do not change, as when moving along a line.

If touch predicates fail to constrain an action's parameters sufficiently, then either position or distance moved may be important. In this case, the system asks the user whether the action is determined by a constant or a run-time input position or distance. If none of these, then the action is governed by a spatial constraint that the user has neglected to express by construction.

Having classified a postcondition's constraints, the system generalizes it by marking some as ignored, as in (Michalski 1983). The generalization heuristic is a list of classes that may be ignored. Overdetermined, unchanged and trivial constraints are safely ignored in solving most problems. Nonetheless, the system should prepare for those occasions when the user intends that a constraint be preserved, by remembering it.

> *Generalize-Postcondition* (PostCond, PreCond, Operator, Path, Heuristics)
>> **Set-Class** of PostCond *position, distance* and *path* as Trivial
>> **Classify** PostCond *touch* predicates into subclasses of Resultant or Unchanged
>>> using knowledge about Operator and PreCond - to - PostCond transitions
>> if any item is in class Determining then
>>> **Reclassify** items in Resultant or Unchanged to Overdetermined
>> if **Sufficient-justification** of Operator,
>>> based on classification of PostCond touch predicates, then
>>> if no item is Determining, **Reclassify** *path* as Weak
>>> **Discard** some Overdetermined predicates according to Heuristics
>> else if **Reclassify** *position or distance* to class User-given succeeds
>>> **Discard** all other PostCond predicates
>> otherwise
>>> signal failure to justify action

The algorithm for isolating constraints in a postcondition is given above. Since a precondition is just the previous action's postcondition, its elements need not be re-classified. All touch relations and other feedback such as position and path are initially classified according to the rules outlined above. If a determining constraint is found, the rest are reclassified as overdetermined. The algorithm then checks for sufficient constraint and suggests a path constraint or consults the user if need be.

3.5 Constraint Solver

In order to perform an action, the system must be able to solve the set of constraints that describe its postcondition. The constraint solver must search for objects to instantiate variables, select parts of objects to match generalized part-names, and assign numerical values to the translation vector to be applied to CurrentPoint. The first two of these constraint-solving operations are amenable to combinatorial search, where solutions are simply *(object, part)* pairs. The third operates in a continuous 2-dimensional space (or at least a high resolution sampling thereof), in which search is not practical. The solver should generate a range of solutions, which could be represented by the hull of the solution set. Multiple "competing" constraints would require the solver to find the intersection of several such hulls, as illustrated in Figure 6, where CurrentPoint must be moved so that line A is in contact with both lines B and C.

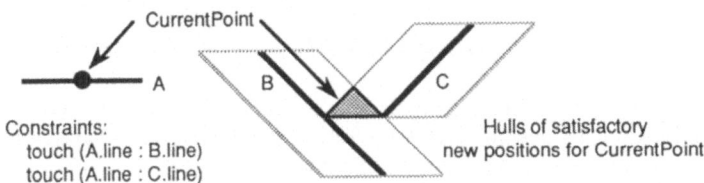

Figure 6. Intersection of solution sets for competing constraints.

The solver implemented for the first version of our system adopts the combinatorial approach only. It tackles continuous constraints by sampling the range of solutions at a small number of subdivisions. Thus, in Figure 6, the solver would try moving CurrentPoint to either end of B, to its mid-point, and to similar points on the left and right edges of the solution hull for *touch (A.line : B.line)*, until either *touch (A.line : C.line)* was found to hold simultaneously or the sample points were exhausted. The solution hull is not computed directly; rather, the solver tries extremal and medial cases easily derived from the hierarchical representation of object parts and touch relations. If path has been classified as a useful constraint, the solver checks for a solution on its axis before sampling cases.

> *Solve-constraints (Constraints, Operator, CurrentPoint)*
> **Sort** (Constraints)
> if Constraints empty then return Success
> else
>> Path ← **Get-path-descriptor** (Constraints)
>> Solutions ← empty list
>> repeat until Success or Failure signalled
>>> if **Satisfy** (first-of (Constraints), Path, Operator, CurrentPoint, Solutions)
>>> fails then signal Failure
>>> else if **Check** (rest-of (Constraints), Operator, CurrentPoint) succeeds
>>>> signal Success
>> return signal

Constraints are sorted in order of strength. The solver generates a solution to the first constraint and then checks that the rest hold. If not, it backtracks to the first and tries an alternative solution. This process repeats until all the constraints hold or no more solutions exist. The constraint solver's algorithm is given below:

Sort. The list of constraints is initially sorted by class and ignored constraints are discarded. The sorting order is [Determining, Strong, Weak, Sustained].

Get-path-descriptor. This routine returns a path constraint if one exists in the Constraints list. If the constraint involves variable position (ie. touching a line segment), Path is used to generate the first solution.

Satisfy. This routine instantiates the translation vector to achieve the first constraint in the list. Each instantiation tried is added to the Solutions list and is used only if it did not already appear there. The routine fails if no new instantiation can be found. If the constraint is determining, there is only one solution — the vector that moves *CurrentPoint* to the specified handle of the specified object. Otherwise, the solver scans in the direction of Path for the first object that satisfies the constraint.

Check. This routine examines each of the remaining Constraints to see if it holds after the translation vector has been applied to *CurrentPoint* and any object in grasp.

4   USER INTERFACE TO CONSTRAINT SYSTEM

The constraint system described above is too complex for users to work with directly. Rather than understand its design, the user is encouraged to adopt what Dennett (1987) calls an "intentional stance" — to do what seems reasonable and learn about the system by observing its responses. The user sees his interaction with the constraint system as a matter of teaching it a task. The system in turn demonstrates what it has learned (right or wrong) by predicting actions. It indicates its limited perception of spatial relations by highlighting those objects it believes to be participants in relevant constraints and by asking questions when it observes insufficient constraint.

Maulsby's (1988) study of potential users unearthed a great deal of extraneous activity in action traces, and showed that users vary greatly in their ability to express constraints by constructive methods. To counteract these problems, the system enforces a teaching protocol inspired by Van Lehn's (1983) "felicity conditions." Traces should contain no erroneous or extraneous actions, but must include every necessary action and construction object. The interface helps the user meet these rather stringent conditions.

First, as MacDonald and Witten (1987) point out, extra care and expressiveness are encouraged by adopting a teaching metaphor. This is embodied in an iconic turtle called Basil (the graphics expert in the Metamouse family). Basil tracks CurrentPoint, indicating the system's (and the user's) focus of attention. In a brief description given to potential users, Basil is described as near-sighted but having a discriminating sense of touch (hence the reliance on geometric construction).

Second, the system gives the user immediate feedback regarding constraints it has observed. Objects that touch are specially highlighted. If an action seems insufficiently constrained, then Basil queries the user as described in §3.4.

Third, the system tries to prevent mistakes and extraneous actions by predicting steps as soon as possible. It induces program graphs and conjectures a loop or return from a subprogram (branch) whenever it observes a user action that matches one already in the graph. Basil carries out predicted actions but can be told to undo them, in which case he asks the user to perform the right action. In this way the system can identify steps that have been overgeneralized and learn correct specialized alternatives. Moreover, the user is not committed to accept solutions produced by the constraint solver, and may make fine adjustments.

5 EVALUATION

The pilot system has been evaluated in two respects: its ability to induce programs, and the ease with which potential users understand the Metamouse metaphor.

The system induced procedures for the tasks illustrated in Figures 1–3. For each task it was presented with several teaching traces. Its efficiency as a pupil was measured in terms of its ability to predict actions correctly during each trace and to reduce erroneous (rejected) predictions. The quality of procedures induced is reflected both in the number of rejected predictions and the complexity of program graphs, measured as the number of edges. The results, given in Table 1, indicate that the system learns quickly and that the graphs are correct and simple.

Table 1. Learning system performance

Task	Trace #	Steps Performed in Task				Edges in Program Graph	
		Total	by Basil	Ratio	Rejected	Total	Growth
Box-to-Line	1	20	8	0.4	0	13	13
	2	24	24	1	0	13	0
	3	20	20	1	0	13	0
Picket-Fence	1	35	12	0.34	5	22	22
	2	27	27	1	0	22	0
Connectivity	1	6	0	0	0	7	7
	2	6	6	1	0	7	0
	3	6	6	1	0	7	0
	4	6	6	1	0	7	0
	5*	4	1	0.25	2	11	4
	6	4	4	1	0	11	0
	7	6	6	1	0	11	0
	8	6	6	1	0	11	0

* variant of task: move one end-point rather than entire line

The system was given three traces of the Box-to-Line task, having different initial arrangements of boxes and orientations of the guide-line. In the first trace Basil predicted 8 out of the total of 24 action steps performed. It began predicting after the user commenced the second iteration of the main loop (see Figure 4). Basil correctly predicted all actions in subsequent traces. The program graph contains 13 edges.

The Picket-Fence task was more difficult; in fact the system made 5 erroneous predictions during the first trace because it falsely conjectured loops resulting from similar action sequences (these mistakes were retracted and hence did not affect the program graph).

The Connectivity task was varied significantly on the fifth trace; instead of moving the entire edge, the user moved only one end-point. The system learned this variant and afterwards was able to correctly perform either version of the task in response to the user's transformation of the line.

The teaching metaphor was tested using a questionnaire given to potential teachers. Maulsby and Witten (1989) found that users quickly learn to predict and understand the system's behavior as expressed through the Metamouse.

6   CONCLUSION

Metamouse enables users to specify constraints without leaving their normal direct-manipulation paradigm.   The system takes a procedural view of drawing (which is supported by experiments on human performance) by considering a picture as a sequence of constraint-satisfaction problems.   Some of these involve constructors drawn explicitly for the purpose of elucidating constraints.   In order to turn unannotated direct manipulations into constraint procedures, some inference is needed since purely fortuitous coincidences of points and lines must not be treated as important constraints.   Consequently techniques from machine learning must be used to infer intended constraints from observed relationships.   These inferences can be checked and overruled by the user when Basil predicts actions.

The procedural model enables the specification of complex constraints as sequences of much simpler ones.   In fact, the constraint solver need only find a 2-dimensional translation vector that, when used as the parameter of a drawing operation, produces a set of touch relations amongst objects.

The pilot implementation provides a graphics package, a simple constraint solver, a Metamouse interface, inference mechanisms for inducing variables and isolating constraints, and an algorithm for constructing procedures.   It can be developed into a more useful drawing and constraint-specification system by adding circle and polygon primitives, and operators for rotation and grouping.   Although these introduce some interesting new problems, such as how to distinguish vertices of a polygon from each other, we believe that the constraint mechanism described here will accommodate these enhancements with little or no modification.   Performance on line intersection problems can be improved by using a constraint solver that produces numerical solution ranges.

The system is intended particularly for use by the casual user, who has enjoyed the ease of use of direct-manipulation interfaces but until now has had difficulty creating precise drawings, suffered the tedium of repetitive operations, and been unable to solve these problems by programming without abandoning the direct-manipulation paradigm.   The system's success will hinge on the extent to which users can adopt a teaching role and comprehend Basil's capabilities and shortcomings.   Tests have in fact shown that the metaphor is easily understood.   Consequently we believe that it is feasible for a system to induce procedures interactively from casual users.   This significantly broadens the application of machine learning techniques, facilitates the investigation of intelligent user interfaces, and, last but not least, benefits the many users of interactive graphics systems.

ACKNOWLEDGEMENTS

This research is supported by the Natural Sciences and Engineering Research Council of Canada. We gratefully acknowledge the key role Bruce MacDonald has played in helping us to develop these ideas, and the stimulating research environment provided by the Department of Computer Science at the University of Calgary.

REFERENCES

Bier EA, Stone MC (1986) Snap-dragging. *Proc. ACM SIGGRAPH '86*, pp 233–240

Borning A (1981) The programming language aspects of ThingLab, a constraint-oriented simulation laboratory. *ACM Trans Programming Languages and Systems*, 3 (4): 353–387

Borning A (1986) Defining constraints graphically. *Proc. ACM SIGCHI '86*, pp 137–143

Cutter M, Halpern B, Spiegel J (1987) MacDraw. Apple Computer Inc.

Dennett DC (1987) *The Intentional Stance.* MIT Press, Cambridge MA

Foley J, Van Dam A (1982) *Fundamentals of interactive computer graphics.* Addison-Wesley. Reading MA

Fuller N, Prusinkiewicz P (1988) Geometric modeling with Euclidean constructions. In: Magnenat-Thalmann and Thalmann (1988), pp 379–391

Kin N, Noma T, Kunii TL (1989) PictureEditor: a 2D picture editing system based on geometric constructions and constraints. In: Wyvill BLM (1989) (ed) *Proc. CG International '89.* Springer-Verlag (in press)

MacDonald BA, Witten IH (1987) Programming computer controlled systems by non-experts. *Proc. IEEE Systems, Man and Cybernetics Annual Conference,* pp 442–437

Magnenat-Thalmann N, Thalmann D (eds) *New Trends in Computer Graphics: Proc CG Int'l '88.* Springer-Verlag, Berlin Heidelberg New York London Paris Tokyo

Maulsby DL (1988) Inducing procedures interactively. Masters thesis. Dept. of Computer Science, University of Calgary

Maulsby DL, Witten IH (1989) Inducing programs in a direct-manipulation environment. *Proc. ACM SIGCHI '89* (in press)

Michalski RS (1983) A theory and methodology of inductive learning. In: Michalski RS, Carbonell JG, Mitchell TM (eds) *Machine Learning.* Tioga, Palo Alto CA, pp 83–134

Noma T, Kunii TL, Kin N, Enomoto H, Aso E, Yamamoto TY (1988) Drawing input through geometrical constructions: specification and applications. In: Magnenat-Thalmann and Thalmann (1988), pp 403–415

Preparata FP, Shamos MI. *Computational Geometry: an introduction.* Springer-Verlag. New York Berlin Heidelberg Tokyo. 1985.

Sutherland IE (1963) Sketchpad: a man-machine graphical communication system. *Proc. AFIPS Spring Joint Computer Conference,* vol. 23: 329–246

Van Lehn K (1983) Felicity conditions for human skill acquisition: validating an AI-based theory. Research Report CIS-21. Xerox PARC, Palo Alto CA

Van Sommers P (1984) *Drawing and Cognition.* Cambridge Univ. Press, Cambridge UK

White RM (1988) Applying direct manipulation to geometric construction systems. In: Magnenat-Thalmann and Thalmann (1988), pp 446–455

David Maulsby recently completed his MSc in Computer Science at the University of Calgary and is proceeding with his research on "apprenticeship" learning systems.

Dept. of Computer Science, University of Calgary,
Calgary T2N 1N4 Canada.
E-mail: maulsby@cpsc.UCalgary.CA.

Kenneth Kittlitz is a Computer Science undergraduate at the University of Calgary, and plans to begin graduate studies in September. His research interests include programming-by-example, concept-learning and human-computer interaction. In his spare time, he plays lead chainsaw in a local independent band.

E-mail: kittlitz@cpsc.UCalgary.CA.

Ian H. Witten received degrees in Mathematics from Cambridge University, Computer Science from the University of Calgary, and Electrical Engineering from Essex University, England. His research interests span the field of man-machine systems, and currently include prediction and modeling, programming by example, and autonomous systems.

Dept. of Computer Science, University of Calgary,
Calgary T2N 1N4 Canada.
E-mail: ian@cpsc.UCalgary.CA.

Chapter 6
Hardware

MIGS: A Multiprocessor Image Generation System Using RISC-like Microprocessors

M.L. Anido, D.J. Allerton, and E.J. Zaluska

ABSTRACT

This paper describes a Multiprocessor Image Generation System termed MIGS based upon RISC-like engines for Image Generation - RIG's. The internal RIG architecture is also discussed, focusing on its characteristics to achieve high processing power for the very demanding Geometric Computations required in Real-Time Image Generation (RTIG). RIG is a 16 MIPS processor that executes the Geometric Procedures fifteen times faster than a MC68000-12Mhz microprocessor due to the following innovations and characteristics:

A novel *Data Ready* technique, in which data is available without waiting for external memory. Data is transferred in Direct Memory Access (DMA) burst mode directly into processor internal registers in parallel with processing.

Indices to the General-Purpose Registers instead of *Register Windows* schemes, as a fast and efficient parameter passing mechanism in procedure calls.

Fast multiplication and division instructions together with a three-staged pipeline architecture with *data forwarding*.

Keywords : Computer Architecture, Computer Image Generation, Real-Time Image Generation, Parallel Processing, Reduced Instruction Set Computers.

1. INTRODUCTION

The field of Computer Image Generation (CIG) is very large and contains specialist topics such as Real-Time Image Generation (RTIG). The emphasis in RTIG is to produce good quality images at a sufficient rate (an update rate of at least 17 times per second) to convey smooth motion, in response to control inputs from the user, to the detriment of some degree of realism. Other sub-areas of CIG emphasize realism, with less regard for real-time operation.

The demand for systems capable of producing high quality images in real-time (25 to 60 frames per second) has increased considerably and the areas in which RTIG can be applied are growing rapidly. Up to now these systems have been mostly used in flight simulation applications but other fields like motion pictures, computer aided design, motion analysis, traffic simulation and arcade games have become feasible.

Commercially available microprocessors have a limited performance when employed to accomplish complex geometric computations and the development of a specialized processor is attractive because of the existing gap between personal computers with limited graphics capability and the extremely expensive equipment used in commercial CIG systems.

2. BACKGROUND

Real-Time Image Generation can be subdivided into four main areas: Data-Base Access, Geometric Computations, Scan Conversion and Image Enhancements [1][2]. The geometric computations of interest are well covered in the literature [1][2] and consist of back-facing surface removal, clipping, transformations (translation, rotation, scaling) and perspective operations.

If back-facing faces are to be eliminated, face normals are computed. If the angle between the face normal and the line of sight is obtuse, that face is discarded. This operation involves computing the scalar product of two vectors.

The clipping operation eliminates objects that are behind the observer or that exceed the limits of the screen. After clipping, vertex points must have their intensity of illumination recalculated. This operation comprises two sub-tasks: edge position comparison and intersection calculation. Edge position comparison involves the comparison of polygon vertices against pre-defined limits (viewing pyramid limits). Intersection calculation comprises the determination of the cross-point of two straight lines, requiring addition, subtraction, multiplication and division instructions.

Transformations can be synthesized by means of a matrix (3x3 or 4x4 elements) which when multiplied by a vector(a point in 3D) transforms this point from the world co-ordinate system into the viewed co-ordinate system.

Perspective operation performs the projection of 3D points onto 2D points on the screen and the calculation of the proximity value for hidden surface removal. It demands multiplication, addition and division arithmetic instructions.

3. PROBLEM ISSUES

If we consider a medium range performance system capable of rendering 1,000 polygons (quadrilaterals) in real-time, the amount of instructions required per second exceeds 40 million [17]. This figure increases proportionally when high-performance RTIG systems capable of rendering 1,000 to 10,000 polygons per second are considered. Clearly, this processing demand is far beyond the processing capability of current microprocessor systems. Fortunately, the workload can be distributed and parallel processing/pipelining techniques can be easily employed.

Another key issue to perform geometric computations efficiently is to effect data transfer in parallel with processing. The data transfer time is of the same order of magnitude that processing time and can not be neglected. For example, a geometric computations engine can perform the geometric computations of one polygon in 60 us (or less), with today's technology, but each polygon may require up to 50 Input and Output data values to be transferred during that time. If a data transfer time of 300ns per polygon co-ordinate is considered, it can be concluded that 15 us are required for I/O, which can not be neglected when compared to the processing time. Henceforth, concurrent processing and I/O data transfer are mandatory.

Geometric Computations involve large number of arithmetic instructions, including multiplications and divisions which are normally absent of most commercial RISC instruction-sets, or which are very slow. Thus, fast arithmetic operations is another fundamental topic to perform geometric computations efficiently.

The workload partition method and the vertical parallelism employed in the MIGS system consider the execution of one polygon at a time. Dealing with one polygon at a time provides data storage simplifications that contribute to enhance system performance. In order to estimate the register file to be used, the polygon vertice's data structure is

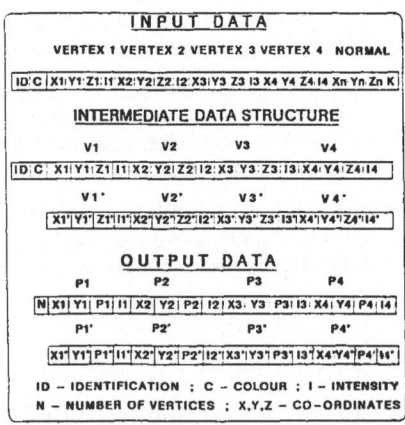

Fig. 1 - Polygon Information and Data Structure

presented in figure 2. It consists of vectors storing polygon characteristics, such as: polygon identification, color, vertex co-ordinates, intensity, depth information and surface normal. The quantity of information associated with each polygon depends on the requirements of the aplication.

The additional information required to perform geometric computations consists of the transformation matrix (nine or sixteen values) and the viewpoint co-ordinates (three co-ordinates).

4. EXISTING SOLUTIONS

Description of commercial RTIG system architectures are not usually published in the open literature. Most existing systems are highly expensive (1M dollars) and usually consist of high-speed general-purpose computers coupled to parallel/pipelined specialised processors using floating-point arithmetic[5].

The GE C-130 Visual Simulator [5] is an example of a commercial RTIG system. It was introduced into the market in 1979 and is still in use. The system employs a 32-bit general-purpose computer to realize the system modelling and data base access tasks. To accomplish geometric computations, programmable pipelined processors running in parallel are used.

One of the earliest chips designed to perform geometric calculations was the Geometry Engine [7][8]. The Geometry Engine uses twelve chips in a pipelined organization to perform Geometric Computations using floating-point arithmetic.

Following a similar approach to the Geometry Engine, but providing more processing power and flexibility, the MAGIC II chip set is under development at the university of Sussex[6]. The Sussex group had already designed the MAGIC I system, which employed a floating-point co-processor.

Another approach to produce a low-cost RTIG system has been used in the Southampton University(S.U.) Flight Simulator, employing up to thirty MC68000 microprocessors running concurrently [4][9]. The S.U. system differs from the Geometry Engine and MAGIC II approaches in terms of the flexibility attainable by using programmable microprocessors. For example, it is possible to program additional tasks such as scan conversion.

The project presented in this paper is an evolution of this idea, using application-specific RISC-like engines to achieve higher performance with fewer packages.

5. MIGS - A Multiprocessor Image Generation System

In order to achieve high polygon throughput, the workload is partitioned among several RIG processors working in parallel. This task is performed by a Host Processor that associates one subregion of the potentially visible polygons per processor. In the presented MIGS architecture several RIG processors are organized in a loosely-coupled MIMD array [18], as indicated in figure 2.

By programming the DMA controller addresses, the Host Computer can easily partition the workload and provide fast data transfer between the visible data-base memory (Vector Memory) and the sepecialized processors. The Host Computer can also perform load-balancing by monitoring the DMA counters, and, accordingly, redistribute the workload among all RIG processors.

Input synchronization is performed by means of a DMA controller that receives requests from RIG processors, reads data from the Vector Memory and writes it into each RIG processor General-Purpose Registers. The output synchronization/transfer task is performed by another DMA controller that reads 2D co-ordinates from RIG processors and transfers them to the Scan-Conversion System. The processing time of each RIG processor is long enough to allow the transfer of input and output co-ordinates and to cover the contention time that exists due to the common input and output buses. DMA controllers can serve RIG processors on a *First-Come-First-Served* basis or using *Round-Robin* schemes.

In order to provide the high performance required in real-time, and taking into account that each stage depends on the result of the previous stage, the Geometric Computations System, the Scan-Conversion System and the Image Enhancements System are organized in pipeline, as indicated in figure 2. This pipelined organization allows these tasks to be executed in parallel and consequently enhance the performance of the overall CIG system.

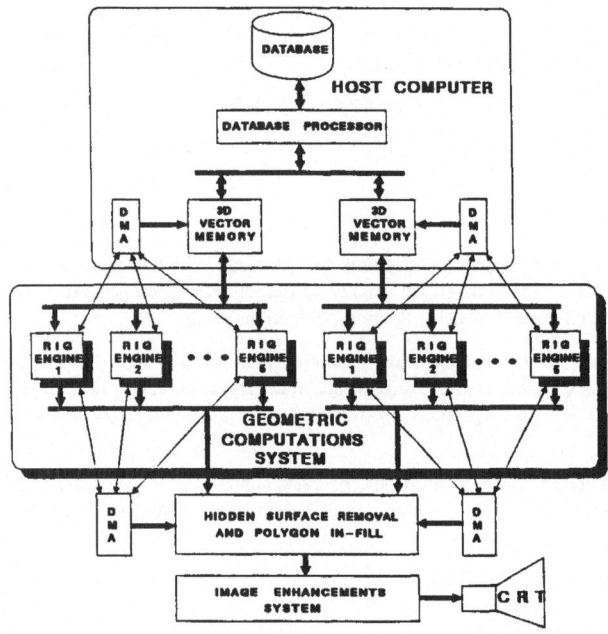

Fig. 2 - MIGS - A Multiprocessor Image Generation System

6. THE ARCHITECTURE OF RIG: A RISC for Image Generation

Differing from general-purpose RISC architectures, this is an *application-specific* RISC and is characterized by an emphasis on: fast input/output communication, fast multiplication/division instructions and the use of the General-Purpose Registers as the main data storage area. Another important guideline towards the design of a suitable processor was its integration in the overall RTIG architecture. RIG interface with the MIGS architecture should be fast and simple with minimum external circuit.

Below we state the most important characteristics of the RIG processor synthesized by the architecture of figure 3.

RIG instruction specification is biased towards the application. While fast arithmetic/shift instructions are essential, the usual bit/byte/longword instructions are not necessary, neither are complex addressing modes.

RIG performs the processing of one polygon at a time. By using an adequate number of internal registers (128), no external RAM is required for most applications, thus avoiding data delays in the pipeline and improving processor performance. Nevertheless, *Load based* and *Store based* instructions are provided to cater for applications requiring more data area.

RIG provides an extremely fast mechanism to transfer polygon co-ordinates. Data is transferred (in DMA burst mode) directly between the external world and the internal registers, in parallel with processing. This mechanism is termed *Data Ready* because it provides the processor with information ready to be processed.

A program space of 4K instructions (16 Kbytes) is compatible with the application, which allows the specification of embedded address in the instruction field for Jump/Call instructions and hence avoids double delayed jumps in the three-staged pipeline.

The targeted application does not require a large stack, nevertheless a very fast call/return mechanism is demanded. A small internal stack is used.

Special attention is given to the improvement of multiplication and division instructions. A Booth-encoded combinational multiplier is employed.

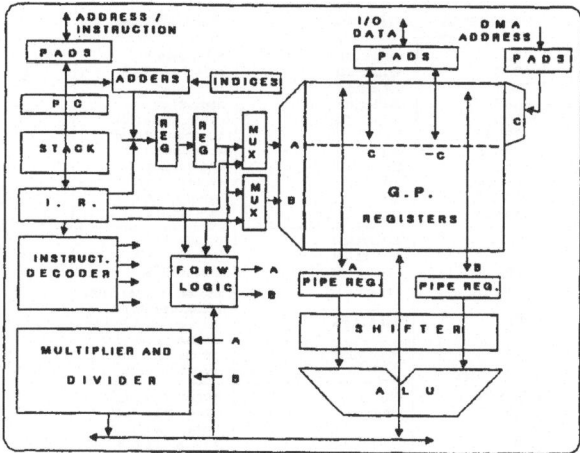

Fig. 3 - RIG Internal Architecture

6.1 RIG Instruction Format

The architecture of the RIG processor is register oriented because fast operand access and efficient use of the register file is extremely important to achieve high performance and also minimise area. Henceforth, three-address instructions are employed to achieve maximum register usage flexibility. All RIG instructions have a fixed width of one word for simplicity of the fetch unit, with operand address fields at fixed locations, for direct and fast instruction decoding.

The addressing range of RIG does not have to be very large, because the targeted software size is small and 12 bits suffice for the application. This allows the direct specification of the branch address in the instruction word. Another positive aspect of the instruction width is the ability to embed constants into the instruction field. Figure 4 depicts RIG instruction format.

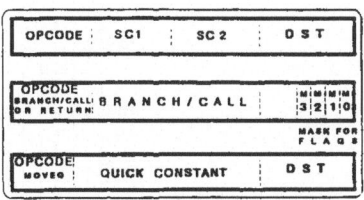

Fig. 4 - RIG Instruction Format

6.2 RIG Instruction Set

In order to assess the most used and time-demanding instructions employed in a Geometric Computations application, qualitative and quantitative analyses of the S.U. Flight Simulator (which employs MC68000 microprocessors) were carried out[11]. The results of these analyses showed that multiplication consumed 19 % of the processor time and division 17 %. Next came Branches with 12 % and procedure calls with 8 %.

Taking into account the results of the previous analyses and also other issues, the RIG instruction set (which is depicted on figure 5) was delineated and a hardware emulation was accomplished. A dynamic analysis of RIG instruction set indicates that a better instruction balance was achieved (when compared with the MC68000), as indicated on figure 6a. Figure 6b indicates the number of instructions executed during such analysis and by comparing figures 6a and 6b it can be seen that Division is the most time-consuming instruction and its optimisation is under way.

OPERATION	OPERANDS	DESCRIPTION
ADD	sc1,sc2,dst	dst:=sc1+sc2
ADDC	sc1,sc2,dst	dst:=sc1+sc2+cy
SUB	sc1,sc2,dst	dst:=sc1-sc2
SUBC	sc1,sc2,dst	dst:=sc1-sc2-cy
MULS	sc1,sc2,dst	dst:=low(sc1*sc2)
STPROH	dst	dst:=product high
DIVSTEP	sc2	sc2:=divisor
LDDIVL	sc1	dividlow:=sc1
LDDIVH	sc1	dividhigh:=sc1
STQUOT	dst	dst:=quotient
STREM	dst	dst:=remainder
AND	sc1,sc2,dst	dst:=sc1&sc2
OR	sc1,sc2,dst	dst:=sc1 v sc2
XOR	sc1,sc2,dst	dst:=sc1$\oplus$sc2
SLA	sc1,sc2,dst	dst:=sc1 s.l. sc2 posit. lsb=0;cy=msb; msb=x
SRA	sc1,sc2,dst	dst:=sc1 s.r. sc2 posit. msb=msb ; cy:=lsb
SRL	sc1,sc2,dst	dst:=sc1 sr sc2 pos msb=0 ; cy:=lsb
BRAcc	addr	if cc= 1 PC:= addr
CALLcc	addr	if cc= 1 PC:= addr stack:= old PC + 3
RETcc		if cc= 1 PC:= stack
LOAD	n(sc1),dst	dst := (sc1+n)
STORE	sc2,n(sc1)	(sc1+n) := sc2
PRIOR	sc1,dst	finds no. shifts to have msb=1;dst=no. shifts
NOP		
LDSCAF	sc1	sc1:= no. shifts
SCALE	sc1,sc2,dst	dst=(sc1 & sc2) >> n positions; msb=msb
MOVEQ	n,dst	dst := n
RDSTAT	dst	dst := status reg
WRCMD	sc1	cmdreg := sc1

Fig. 5 - RIG Instruction Set

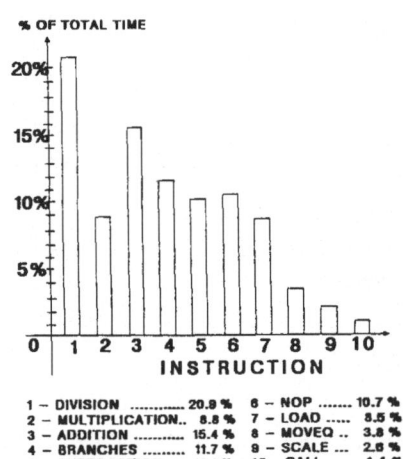

1 – DIVISION .... 20.9 %
2 – MULTIPLICATION.. 8.8 %
3 – ADDITION .... 15.4 %
4 – BRANCHES .... 11.7 %
5 – SUBTRACTION .... 10.1 %
6 – NOP .... 10.7 %
7 – LOAD ..... 8.5 %
8 – MOVEQ .. 3.8 %
9 – SCALE ... 2.6 %
10 –CALL ..... 1.4 %

Fig.6a-Dynamic Analysis of Geometric Procedures for the RIG processor (percentage of the total time)

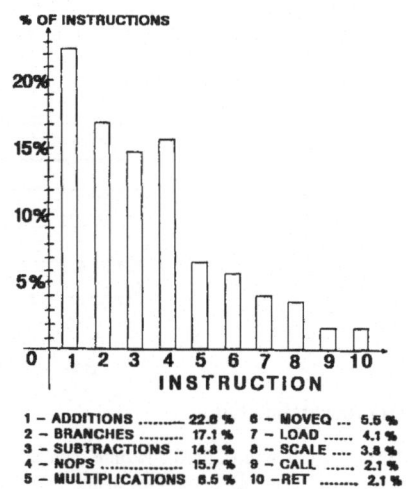

1 – ADDITIONS .... 22.6 %
2 – BRANCHES .... 17.1 %
3 – SUBTRACTIONS .. 14.8 %
4 – NOPS .... 15.7 %
5 – MULTIPLICATIONS 8.5 %
6 – MOVEQ ... 5.5 %
7 – LOAD .... 4.1 %
8 – SCALE ..... 3.8 %
9 – CALL .... 2.1 %
10 –RET .... 2.1 %

Fig.6b-Dynamic Analysis of Geometric Procedures for the RIG processor (percentage of instructions)

6.3 RIG Registers

Many parallel/pipelined systems use FIFOs or memory banks for communication between processors or between processors and the external world. The method presented here has the following advantages when compared with the above mechanisms: it uses a smaller and more regular silicon area, requires less buses, uses a simpler control and relieves the processor from the task of fetching data into its internal registers.

RIG Register File is composed of two-port / two-access and three-port / three-access cells, as indicated in figure 7a. Figure 7b ilustrates the concurrence between processing and I/O. Three-port cells are used for both processing and I/O and two port cells only for processing. The *A* and *B* decoders decode addresses provided by the *sc1, sc2* or *dst* Instruction Register Fields. The *C* decoder decodes addresses provided by the external DMA controller.

The CPU reads (writes) operands (results) via the *A* and *B* buses that cross the register file and both buses are connected to all the cells. The *C* and *NC* buses connect the three-port cells to the external world, via the data bus.

The three-port cell is a modified version of the two-port cell used by Horowitz *et al* [19] in the design of the MIPS-X microprocessor. A self-timed precharge circuit is employed to speed-up bit line precharging and improve processor speed.

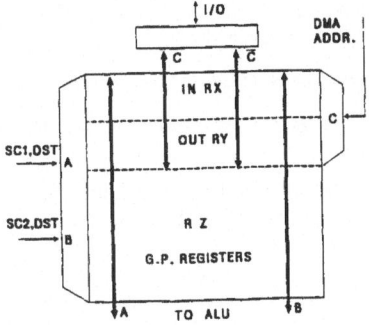

Fig. 7a - Combined Two-port/Three-port Register File

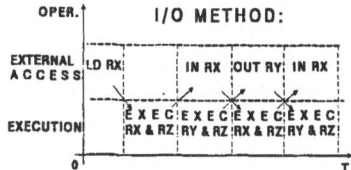

Fig. 7b - Concurrence between processing and I/O

6.4 Indices to Registers

The RIG RISC has a totally different requirement concerning general-purpose registers than that found in general-purpose RISCs, like the Berkeley RISC [10] or the Stanford MIPS [16]. General-purpose RISCs deal with procedure calls with considerable nesting depth levels and, normally, few parameters are passed in procedures[10]. This is tackled in RISC II by using overlapped *register windows*, where the overlapping registers specify the input and output parameters. MIPS relies on the compiler using the *Graph coloring* algorithm to allocate/deallocate registers[15][16].

Neither *overlapping register windows* nor the *Graph coloring* approach are suitable for this application. The nesting depth level is usually very small (two levels on average); the number of parameters passed is normally large (more than 12) and most important of all the data structure is regular (figure 1), thus making the use of indices attractive.

To pass parameters to a procedure, only the indices have to be changed which can be done in one instruction. This is performed by adding constants(indices) to the source1, source2 and destination fields of the instruction. In order not to increase the processor cycle time caused by the addition that has to be realized, such a task is performed in series with the memory access operation. The memory is faster than the processor, thus the extra delay required to accomplish the addition does not impact the processor cycle time. Only part of the general-purpose registers can be indexed, the remaining registers are used for locals, globals and for I/O.

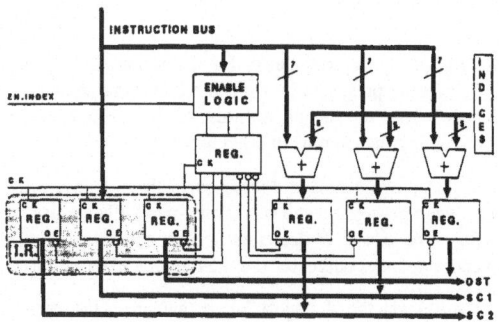

Fig. 8 - Register Indexing Mechanism

6.5 Three-Staged Pipeline

Pipelining has been an essential technique to improve processor performance [10][16]. RIG uses a three-stage pipeline as indicated in Figure 9 and, using this approach, it keeps all its function units (fetch, decode, execute) 100 % busy. It greatly benefits from its streamlined architecture to make its pipelining very efficient, due to:

No data delays are required in the pipeline. Data is normally ready to be processed in its internal registers.

Neither several levels of interrupt nor exceptions are required and therefore there is no need to save several levels of Program Counter.

All addresses used in branch or call instructions are absolute and are part of the instruction word. Thus, even with a three-stage pipeline only one NOP instruction has to be inserted after Call or Branch instructions.

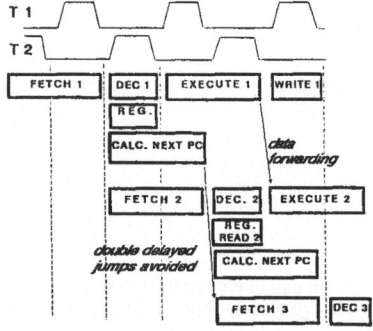

Fig. 9 - RIG Three-Staged Pipeline

6.6 Fast Fixed-Point Arithmetic

Another key-point in RIG characteristics is the use of scaled fixed-point arithmetic in contrast with the traditional floating-point method. Floating-Point arithmetic is essential when the magnitude or the precision of the number to be represented does not fit into the computer word. Normally, the applications covered by Real-Time Image Generation do not demand large magnitude nor precision and fixed-point number representation together with fast scaling can also be used.

To achieve high speed in arithmetic operations some instructions are performed by fast hardware. This is the case with multiplication and multiple-bit shifts.

Multiplication (16 bit x 16 bit) is performed by a fast Booth-encoded combinational multiplier[12], which is regular, iterative and uses a smaller area than an array multiplier. To perform the multiplication operation and store the result takes only two processor cycles (125 ns).

Multiple-bit shifts and scaling are performed by a barrel shifter [13] in a single processor cycle (62 ns). Scaling is required to cope with overflow and underflow problems and the wide range of variables that can arise [9]. The scaling (normalization) process consists of previously multiplying or dividing a number by a constant, so that extreme values that could cause errors are avoided. This operation does not affect results because it is cancelled during Perspective Projection.

Division (32-bit by 16-bit) is accomplished in instruction steps ,using the ALU. Addition and Subtraction are performed in a single processor cycle.

7. PERFORMANCE

Table 1 depicts a time comparison between some MC68000-12Mhz instructions and the equivalent RIG-16Mhz instructions.

Measured performance indicates that a 16Mhz RIG processor executes the Geometric Procedures at 15 times faster than a MC68000-12Mhz microprocessor.

Table 2 illustrates some time measurements realized on RIG Geometric Procedures. They indicate that, on average, RIG is capable of delivering a transformed polygon every 66 us, which corresponds to 15,000 polygons per second or 880 polygons in real-time (17 times per second update rate). However, the geometric procedures shown do not include either back-facing surface removal, or depth calculation. A 20 % increase in time is estimated for these additional procedures. Using a more conservative evaluation, we can consider that one RIG processor can process 600 polygons in real-time.

Using five RIG engines, the MIGS system can perform the geometric computations of at least 3000 polygons (on average) in real-time. This performance is compatible with commercially-available systems, but at a significantly lower cost.

Table 1
Comparison between MC68000-12Mhz
and RIG-16Mhz for some instructions

INSTRUCTION	MC68000	RIG	IMPROVEM.
Add	166 ns	62.5 ns	2.6 x
Shift	1.66 us	62.5 ns	26.6 x
Call (Bsr)	1.33 us	62.5 ns	21.3 x
Multiply	4 us	125 ns	32.0 x
Divide	10 us	2 us	5.0 x
Branch	666 ns	62.5 ns	10.6 x

Table 2
Time Measurements on RIG
Geometric Procedures

PROCEDURE	BEST CASE	AVERAGE	W.CASE
Scaling	2.8 us	7.8 us	11.2 us
Transform.	13.5 us	13.5 us	13.5 us
Clipping	15.6 us	26.2 us	94.0 us
Perspective	4.4 us	18.4 us	50.0 us
Total Time Per Polygon	36.3 us	65.9 us	168.7 us

8. STATE OF THE WORK AND NEXT STEPS

The RIG processor has been designed and implemented using proprietary MSI and LSI chips. The hardware emulation provided an accurate performance evaluation and instruction set correctness demonstration. The architecture has been devised from the outset with a VLSI implementation in mind and the corresponding CMOS-2um chip design is under development. The transistor count is estimated around 25,000.

9. CONCLUSIONS

The architecture of a Multiprocessor Image Generation System and a RISC-like *application-specific* processor tailored to perform geometric computations have been shown. RIG includes a novel, extremely-fast technique to transfer data to a processor by using a three-port / three-access register file and DMA data transfers to it.

A solution to the problem of passing a large number of parameters to procedures that manipulate regular data structures inside the general-purpose registers has been given. While the indexed-register argument passing mechanism proved to be efficient for this application, in general-purpose RISCs, schemes such as *Overlaped Register Windows* or *Graph Coloring* will usually be preferable.

Finally, this project shows that the use of parallel processing together with *application-specific* processors makes it possible to provide very efficient solutions for computational-demanding RTIG problems at economic cost.

Acknowledgements

We acknowledge the financial support provided by the Brazilian organisation CNPQ, the Federal University of Rio de Janeiro and the ORS Award Scheme (U.K.) for the research of M.L. Anido at the University of Southampton.

References

[01] Newman, W.W. and Sproull, R.F., "Principles of Interactive Computer Graphics", Addison Wesley, Reading, Mass., 1980.

[02] Foley, J.D. and Van Dam, A., "Fundamentals of Interactive Computer Graphics", Addison Wesley, Reading, Mass., 1984.

[03] Katevenis, M.G.H., "Reduced Instruction Set Computer Architectures for VLSI", MIT Press, 1985, pp. 9-41.

[04] Allerton, D.J. and Zaluska, E.J., "A multi-processor Approach to Image Generation", IEE Int. Conf. Simulators, Warwick, England, 1986.

[05] Schachter, B. J., "Computer Image Generation For Flight Simulation", IEEE CG&A, October, 1981, pp. 29-68.

[06] Finch, H.R., Agate, M., Garel, A.A., Lister, P.F., Grimsdale, R.L., "A Multiple Application Graphics Integrated Circuit-MAGIC II" - Advances In Computer Graphics Hardware II, Springer-Verlag 1988.

[07] Clark, J.H., "Structuring a VLSI system architecture", Lambda, Vol.1, No.2, Second Quarter 1980, pp. 25-30.

[08] Clark, J. H., "The Geometry Engine: A VLSI Geometry System for Graphics", Proc. of SIGGRAPH 82, ACM, 1982, pp.127-133.

[09] Allerton, D.J. and Zaluska, E.J., "Computer Image Generation in Real Time", Electronic Displays, London, England, 1985, pp. 17-31.

[10] Patterson, D.A. and Sequin, C.H., "A VLSI RISC", Computer, September 1982, pp. 8-22.

[11] Anido, M. L., "A RISC-like Processor for Real-Time Image Generation Geometric Computations", internal report, Dept. of Electronics, Univ. of Southampton, U.K., June 1987, pp. 1-155.

[12] Henlin, D.A., Mazin, M., Fertsch, M.T., Lewis, E.T., "A 16x16 Pipelined Multiplier Macrocell" - IEEE Journal on Solid-State Circuits, April, 1985, pp. 542-547.

[13] Sherburne, R.W., Katevenis, M.G.H., et al,"Datapath Design for RISC", Conf. on Advanced Research in VLSI, M.I.T., 1982, pp. 53-63.

[14] Chow, F.C. and Hennessy, J.L., "Register Allocation by Priority Based Coloring", in Proc. 1984 Compiler Construct. Conf., ACM, Montreal, P.Q., Canada, June 1984.

[15] Hennessy, J. L., "VLSI Processor Architecture", IEEE Trans. on Computers, c-33(12), Dec., 1984, pp. 1221-1246.

[16] Hennessy, J.L., Jouppi, N., et al, "Design of a High Performance VLSI Processor", 3rd. Very Large Scale Integration Conf. Caltech, Pasadena, 1983, pp. 33-54.

[17] Ohr, S., "How Silicon ICs are Reshaping the Graphics Picture", Electronic Design, June 26, 1986, pp. 72-79.

[18] Flynn, M.J., Proc. IEEE, 54, 1966, pp. 1901-1909.

[19] Horowitz, M., Chow, P., Stark, D. et al., "MIPS-X: a 20 MIPS Peak, 32-bit microprocessor with On-Chip Cache", IEEE Journal of Solid-State Circuits, Vol. sc-22, no. 5, October 1987, pp. 790-799.

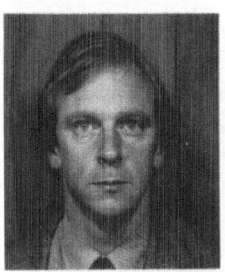

David J. Allerton is currently a Senior Lecturer in Computer Science in the Department of Electronics and Computer Science at the University of Southampton. He joined this Department in 1981 after working as a Principal Engineer for Marconi Space and Defence Systems. His research interests include real-time computer graphics, computer architectures, silicon compilation, flight simulation and operating systems. He has published over twenty papers in Computer Science and applications areas.

He received his Bsc form Rugby College of Engineering Technology in 1972, a post-graduate Certificate in Education from Loughborough of Education in 1973 and a PhD from the University of Cambridge in 1977. He is a member of the Institute of Electrical Engineers.

Address: Department of Electronics and Computer Science, University of Southampton, Highfield, Southampton SO9 5NH, UK.

Ed Zaluska is a senior lecturer in the Department of Electronics and Computer Science at the University of Southampton. His principal research interests include advanced computer systems, real-time computer graphics and design automation for VLSI. He has written a textbook on microprocessors as well as a number of refereed academic papers.

He received the B.Sc. in Electronic Engineering from the University of Southampton in 1971. He is a chartered engineer and a member of the IEE and the IEEE.

Address: Electronics & Computer Science, University of Southampton, Southampton SO9 5NH, UK.

Manuel L. Anido was born in Spain and received the B. Sc. and M. Sc. degrees from the Federal University of Rio de Janeiro (UFRJ)(Brazil) in 1976 and 1980, respectively. He has been working with the Computing Center of UFRJ (NCE/UFRJ), since 1976, where he is a lecturer and a senior design engineer. Presently his is doing his Ph. D. in computer architecture / computer graphics at the University of Southampton, England.

At NCE/UFRJ he jointly developed a supermicrocomputer (PEGASUS-32X project), which employs multiple MC68020 microprocessors, each with CACHE and MMU units. This system runs PLURIX - a UNIX-like multiprocessed operating system also developed at NCE/UFRJ. Both systems have been successfully transferred to industry.

Address (Brazil): NCE/UFRJ, Caixa Postal 2324, CEP 20 001, Rio de Janeiro, Brasil.

Address (U.K.): Dept. of Electronics and Comput. Sc., University of Southampton, Highfield, SO9 5NH, U.K.

On a DAP Based Data Parallel Graphics Output Pipeline

T. Theoharis

ABSTRACT

We consider how the stages of a polygon-based graphics output pipeline can be implemented in data parallel mode on a Single Instruction Multiple Data stream machine like the DAP. The polygon per processor assignment is increasingly attractive as the number of polygons in images gets larger and their sizes smaller. However it appears that the routing operations necessary in the shading calculation and rendering stages may be a significant drawback of the polygon per processor assignment.

Key words and Phrases: graphics output pipeline, Single Instruction Multiple Data stream processor, DAP.

1 INTRODUCTION

General Purpose Parallel Processors (GPPP's) are increasingly being used by scientists to solve large numerical problems which frequently produce massive amounts of data; this data can often be presented most conveniently in pictorial form. When this is coupled with the flexibility that GPPP's offer over special purpose graphics machines one can see why there is a growing demand for graphics software on GPPP's.

This paper is concerned with a Single Instruction Multiple Data Stream (SIMD) GPPP called Distributed Array Processor (DAP) (Parkinson 1983). SIMD machines are used most efficiently when the same operation must be performed on different data i.e. when the application exhibits *data parallelism*. The stages of the graphics output pipeline offer a large degree of data parallelism as there are a large number of objects (polygons, vertices) and a large number of pixels which require similar processing; the processing is not identical however and a certain amount of flexibility on the part of the SIMD machine is necessary. We discuss how well the DAP provides this flexibility in the context of the implementation of a 3D polygon-based graphics output pipeline. Crow (1988) discusses the issues involved in the implementation of a graphics output pipeline on another GPPP, the Connection Machine.

The DAP is an $N \times N$ array of bit-serial Processing Elements (PE's). Each PE has its own, local, bit-wide memory and is connected to its four nearest neighbours. A full adder and 3 registers are the main components of a PE (all are bit-wide). One of the registers, the activity register, has special significance; an instruction is only executed by those PE's whose activity registers are set. It is thus possible to control which PE's execute any one instruction by setting the activity registers as necessary, a process called masking. The DAP we use is located at Queen Mary College (London University), was manufactured by ICL in the late 1970's (it has a cycle time of 200ns) and consists of 64x64 PE's. The recent AMT DAP 510's have 32x32 PE's and a cycle time of 100ns.

2 MAPPING DATA ONTO THE PE'S

There are two basic types of data that must be distributed among the memories of the PE's. Polygon data i.e. information about polygons (e.g. coordinates, normal, colour) and pixel data i.e. information about each pixel which includes its colour (the frame buffer) and the depth of the nearest polygon (z-buffer).

There are two ways of distributing the pixel data among the memories of the DAP PE's (Reddaway 1988). In *sheet* mapping the frame buffer is interlaced between the memories of the PE's as originally proposed by Fuchs (1977). In other words each PE stores the colour of pixels that are N pixels apart (in both directions). Conversely in *crinkled* mapping the frame buffer is divided into contiguous blocks and each block is assigned to the memory of a single PE. The z-buffer is distributed in the same way as the frame buffer.

The polygon data can also be distributed in two ways: polygon per PE or vertex per PE. Assuming that there are at least as many polygons as PE's and that polygons have (approximately) the same number of vertices, then the polygon per PE approach is preferable because it does not necessitate inter-PE communication for accessing the polygon data.

We shall next calculate the memory requirements for the storage of the polygon and pixel data in a manner similar to Crow (1988). Assuming a very simple shading model (no textures or antialiasing), the data necessary for a vertex is:

- World space coordinates (3*32 bits)

- Integer screen space coordinates (10+10+32 bits)

- Normal vector (3*32 bits)

- Surface RGB colour (3*32 bits)

- Vertex RGB colour for interpolation (3*8 bits)

Thus about 364 bits are required for the data of a single polygon assuming 4 vertices per polygon. If the pixel data consists of 24 bits for RGB (frame buffer) and 32 bits for depth (z-buffer) that makes 56 bits per pixel. The 64x64 ICL DAP had 4Kbits of memory per PE while the recent 32x32 AMT DAP 510 has 32Kbits of memory per PE. Unfortunately neither of these is sufficient to store the pixel data of a high resolution image (1024x1024 pixels). A medium resolution image (512x512) plus the data of about 50,000 polygons can be stored in the memory of the DAP 510. The discussion in this paper will not be concerned with these memory limitations. After all, with decreasing memory prices and increasing capacities, future generations of the DAP and similar machines are likely to offer significant increases in memory capacity.

3   THE DATA PARALLEL GRAPHICS OUTPUT PIPE-LINE

A number of approaches have been taken for the introduction of parallelism in the graphics pipeline. One is the assignment of physical processors to the stages of the pipeline thus constructing a physical pipeline (Schumaker 1980; Theoharis 1985); the amount of parallelism that can be introduced by this method is limited by the number of stages in the pipeline. Another approach is the assignment of a processor to every pixel (or group of pixels) in order to process the pixels covered by a polygon in parallel (in the execution of the rendering operations which are the performance bottleneck of the pipeline). Fuchs's system, Pixel-Planes (Fuchs 1985), and Sproull's 8x8 Display (Sproull 1983) are examples of this approach. However as scenes get more complicated polygons tend to get smaller and the amount of parallelism that can be exploited by this approach is falling. The obvious way of exploiting highly parallel architectures, with growing numbers of small polygons, is therefore to assign a polygon to each processor. This is the approach considered in this paper.

The stages of the graphics pipeline we shall consider, in order of data flow, are mod-elling and viewing transformations, clipping, perspective transformation, smooth shading calculations and rendering. The last stage includes the operations that are performed at the pixel level i.e. filling, hidden surface elimination using the z-buffer method and smooth shading.

3.1 Coordinate Transformations

Applying the viewing and perspective transformations is simple when the polygons are distributed among the PE's. For the viewing transformation, the 4x4 transformation matrix is multiplied in parallel by the coordinates of N^2 polygon vertices and, for the perspective transformation, the division of the x, y and z coordinates of each vertex by the w coordinate is also performed in parallel for N^2 polygon vertices (assuming homogeneous coordinates). On the 64x64 ICL DAP, a viewing transformation on 64^2 32-bit real vertices (one vertex per PE) takes about 7ms. It consists of 16 multiplications and 12 additions performed on the coordinates of 64^2 vertices in parallel.

In the case of the modelling transformations, which precede the viewing transformation in the pipeline, it is not easy to take advantage of the available parallelism if there are many independently moving objects. This is because each of those objects will require the application of a different modelling transformation matrix to the polygons that constitute it. Using the host of the DAP for the modelling transformations is also difficult because, although both the host and the DAP can access the DAP memory, it is necessary to convert the data format (converting a 64x64 matrix of 32-bit reals takes about 1ms). However, with increasing object complexity (more polygons per object) it is becoming more attractive to perform the modelling transformations on the DAP (imagine the situation where an object consists of N^2 polygons, all requiring the same modelling transformation).

An interesting point is made by Crow (1988) for the case of hierarchical modelling transformations. On a serial machine, the transformation matrices are first concatenated and then applied. However, since matrix application is done in parallel for N^2 vertices on a SIMD machine like the DAP, it is more efficient to apply the matrices in turn rather than concatenating them first if the number of vertices per PE is less than 4. A 4x4 matrix application costs 16 multiplications and 12 additions while the concatenation of two 4x4 matrices costs 64 multiplications and 48 additions.

3.2 Clipping

The Sutherland-Hodgman polygon clipping algorithm (Sutherland 1974) can be efficiently implemented in data parallel mode on the DAP. A detailed account of the implementation can be found in (Theoharis 1989); we summarise it here.

The polygon per PE mapping turns out to be very convenient. The implementation consists of 2 nested loops. The outer loop steps through the 6 clipping planes (3D clipping) while the inner one runs through the polygon vertices; the ith vertex of all N^2 polygons is thus processed in parallel. The number of steps in the inner loop is equal to the number of vertices in the polygon with the largest number of vertices. The ith vertex of all N^2 polygons is compared in parallel to the current clipping plane in order to determine its state (inside / outside). The combined states of the last two vertices processed give one of the four states that an edge can have in the Sutherland-Hodgman algorithm. Masking is then used to take appropriate action for each of the four different groups of edges; the most expensive action is the calculation of the intersection of the edge with the clipping plane. Deleted vertices are marked and new vertices (due to intersection calculations) are temporarily stored in overflow arrays. Between the processing of subsequent clipping planes some data shifting is performed in order to close the gaps of deleted vertices and create space for the new vertices where necessary; of course this is done in parallel for N^2 polygons and the number of steps involved is again proportional to the largest number of vertices that any of the polygons has.

Two points are worth noting about the above data parallel clipper. First, the number of steps involved in the inner clipping loop as well as in the data shifting is proportional to the number of vertices in the polygon which has the largest number of vertices. Processing will therefore be more efficient if there are no polygons with many more vertices than the average. Second, the trivial acceptance / rejection tests that are used in order to improve the efficiency of sequential clipping algorithms are not usable in the data parallel clipper; it makes no difference to performance whether the intersection calculation is performed for 1 or for N^2 edges.

Our 64x64 ICL DAP implementation of the data parallel clipper (Theoharis 1989) took 25ms to clip 64^2 polygons against a single clipping plane (or 150ms for the 6 clipping planes); we assumed that the maximum number of vertices per polygon was 10. Account must be taken of the age of the ICL DAP (built in the late 1970's, cycle time of 200ns) and the fact that we coded the algorithm in DAP Fortran rather than DAP assembler.

3.3   Smooth Shading Calculations

By smooth shading calculations we mean the computation of vertex normals by averaging the normals of the polygons that share a vertex. Vertex normals are then used for Gouraud or Phong shading in the rendering stage.

The calculation of the polygon normals can easily take place data parallel for N^2 polygons. However averaging the normals of polygons that share a vertex requires the routing of these normals to a single PE (the PE that holds the vertex). Normals will actually be *exchanged* between PE's. An alternative which avoids routing at the expense of extra computation, is to store in each PE enough adjacent polygon vertices to allow the calculation of neighbouring polygon normals to be performed locally (3 vertices of each adjacent polygon need be stored). It is then necessary to carry these extra vertices through all the transformation stages and then calculate normals from them. Wide variance in the number of polygons sharing a vertex will lead to low processor utilisation.

Experiment can show which of the two methods is the quickest. However, in the case of routing, the number of data items (normals) that will have to be transmitted to each PE and the distance they will have to travel will not be regular because there are no rules about the number of neighbours that a polygon can have in a model. The DAP is not good at performing irregular routing operations; more on this in a later section.

3.4 Rendering

It is possible to perform polygon rendering on an SIMD processor like the DAP by sheet mapping the pixel data onto the PE's and processing the polygons one at a time as described in (Theoharis 1987; Theoharis 1988). All such polygon-serial pixel-parallel techniques (others are described in (Fuchs 1977; Clark 1980; Sproull 1983; Fuchs 1985)) have a basic problem. With decreasing polygon sizes the processor utilisation diminishes because there are not enough pixels in the polygons to take advantage of the parallelism; polygons with only a few tens of pixels are common place in todays images. At the same time however the number of polygons is increasing and it becomes more attractive to render them in polygon-parallel mode.

The major difficulty of polygon-parallel rendering is that it involves a change of mapping; the PE that hosts a polygon does not necessarily host the pixels that the polygon covers. There are two main ways of dealing with this problem.

The first possibility is to scan-convert the polygon in its host PE (that is create the <pixel, shade, depth> triplets for each of the pixels covered by the polygon) and then distribute the resulting pixel data to the appropriate PE's. The PE's receiving the pixel data perform the z-buffer algorithm. This approach involves a major routing operation; the pixel data is a much less compact representation of a polygon than its original vertex form. Furthermore the routing operation will be irregular and, as mentioned earlier, the DAP cannot perform irregular routing operations efficiently; more on this in a later section. The z-buffer operation can be load-balanced by sheet mapping the frame buffer onto the PE's.

The second approach attempts to reduce the amount of data that has to be shifted in the routing operation by moving the polygons to the PE's that host the pixels they cover and only then scan-converting the polygons. This can be achieved by crinkle mapping the frame buffer onto the PE's and sorting the polygons in both the x and y directions so that they end up in the appropriate PE's. Polygons spanning the frame buffer partitions of several PE's must be transmitted to all relevant PE's. Notice that an irregular routing operation is also required here but the amount of data that it has to handle is greatly reduced. The disadvantage of this approach is the risk of uneven load-balancing in the scan-conversion operation if the polygons are not evenly distributed in image space. This is a disadvantage inherent in crinkled mapping.

The large variety of polygon shapes and sizes means there will be many different cases to be considered in the scan-conversion process; this will result in low processor utilisation. One way of load-balancing scan-conversion is to restrict the range of polygons to a simple standard form like the triangle or trapezium. Crow (1988) presents an outline of a data parallel triangle scan-conversion algorithm. Essentially the incremental descriptions of each of the three sides are precomputed and two loops perform incremental scan-conversion down the polygon sides and across scan-lines. The algorithm is very similar to sequential scan-conversion and can take advantage of the incremental techniques that have been developed for scan-conversion (in contrast to polygon-serial pixel-parallel systems). Polygons which have different areas will also give rise to load-balancing problems in the scan-conversion process. The area of a polygon in image space is dependent on the viewpoint and direction. Any solution that attempts to subdivide polygons with large areas can therefore only operate after the perspective transformation (there is no way of preconditioning the model so that all image space polygons have the same area).

3.5 Display Refresh

Assuming that a frame has been created in the frame buffer, which is divided between the memories of the DAP PE's, how do we extract it for display? On the ICL DAP this was a slow process. However the AMT DAP 510 offers a "fast data channel" which is essentially a "planar" (32x32) register that can be loaded from any memory "plane" in one 100ns cycle and then be asynchronously clocked out at a rate of 50MBytes/s. A single 32x32 memory "plane" (128 bytes) can thus be output in about 2.7μs. A frame buffer of 1Mbyte will take 22ms.

4 THE PROBLEM OF IRREGULAR ROUTING

We saw in the previous two subsections that irregular routing operations are necessary for the implementation of the smooth shading and rendering operations. They are irregular in two ways; first the number of items destined for each PE is not fixed and second the distance and direction that items have to travel (between PE's) are also not fixed.

The first irregularity poses a problem because the DAP does not provide separate addressing capability in each PE, in other words all PE's must access the same memory address in any one cycle. Thus it is not possible to build up or access data arrays which are of variable length without creating gaps of unused storage within them. The second irregularity is a problem because DAP routing operations are performed synchronously by all PE's in the same direction. Thus it is not possible to cater efficiently for simultaneous data transfers in different directions or across varying distances.

5 CONCLUSIONS

We conclude with a number of remarks that should be useful to anyone considering the implementation of a graphics pipeline on an SIMD processor like the DAP. We divide our observations into two groups; those concerning the DAP hardware and those relating to the structure of the graphics algorithms and data structures.

The DAP provides hardware support for bit-serial word-parallel arithmetic in the form of a single bit full adder and carry register in each PE; this is essential for all stages of the pipeline (some SIMD machines only provide support for Boolean operations in each PE). The fast data channel of the latest DAP is indispensible to the display refresh operation. The memory provided with the current version of the DAP 510 is insufficient for high resolution (1024x1024) frame and z-buffers but adequate for medium resolution (512x512). An address modifier in each PE would make irregular routing operations (necessary in some stages of the pipeline) cheaper both in terms of time and memory.

As image complexities increase, the polygon per PE mapping becomes more attractive. This mapping however poses the following implementation problems:

1. Irregular routing operations are necessary in the smooth shading calculation and rendering stages.

2. Load-balancing may be difficult in the rendering stage due to the diversity of polygon shapes and sizes.

3. It may be hard to achieve good processor utilisation in the application of the modelling transformations because the relevant matrices can be varied; particularly if many small objects are moving independently.

By restricting the types of allowable polygons we can improve the load-balancing in all the stages of the pipeline.

ACKNOWLEDGEMENTS

I would like to thank the Queen Mary College Centre for Parallel Computing for the use of their DAP and Coreen for her quick typing.

REFERENCES

Clark JH, Hannah MR (1980) *Distributed Processing in a High-Performance Smart Image Memory.* Lambda 4th quarter 1980: 40-45

Crow F (1988) *3D Image Synthesis on the Connection Machine.* In: Proc. Parallel Processing for Computer Vision and Display, Leeds, U.K., Jan. 1988 (to appear)

Fuchs H (1977) *Distributing a Visible Surface Algorithm Over Multiple Processors.* In: Proc. 1977 Annual ACM Conference, pp. 449-451

Fuchs H, Goldfeather J, Hultquist JP, Spach S, Austin JD, Brookes FP, Eyles JG, Poulton J, (1985) *Fast Spheres, Shadows, Textures, Transparencies and Image Enhancements in Pixel-Planes.* ACM Computer Graphics 19(3): 111-120

Parkinson D (1983) *The Distributed Array Processor (DAP).* Computer Physics Communications 28: 325-336

Reddaway SF (1988) *Mapping Images Onto Processor Array Hardware.* In: Page I (ed) Parallel Architectures and Computer Vision. Oxford University Press

Schumaker RA (1980) *A New Visual System Architecture.* In: Proc. 2nd Interservice / Industry Training Equipment Conference, pp. 94-101

Sproull RF, Sutherland IE, Thompson A, Gupta S, Minter C (1983) *The 8x8 Display.* ACM Transactions on Graphics 2(1): 32-56

Sutherland IE, Hodgman GW (1974) *Reentrant Polygon Clipping.* Comm. ACM 17(1): 32-42

Theoharis T (1985) *Exploiting Parallelism in the Graphics Pipeline.* Technical Monograph PRG-54, Oxford University Computing Laboratory

Theoharis T, Page I (1987) *Parallel Polygon Rendering With Precomputed Surface Patches.* In: Eurographics 1987, published by North-Holland, pp.85-99

Theoharis T, Page I (1988) *Incremental Polygon Rendering on a SIMD Processor Array.* To appear in Computer Graphics Forum 7(4)

Theoharis T, Page I (1989) *Two Parallel Methods for Polygon Clipping.* To appear in Computer Graphics Forum

Theoharis Theoharis has been a research fellow of St Catharine's College, Cambridge since October 1987. His research interests lie in the areas of parallel processing, computer graphics and the applications of parallel processing in computer graphics and linear algebra. His work so far has involved the Transputer and the DAP. Theoharis received his B.Sc. from Queen Mary College (London University) in 1984 and his M.Sc. and D.Phil. from Oxford University in 1985 and 1988 respectively.

Address: St Catharine's College, Cambridge CB2 1RL, U.K.

Effective Parallel Processing for Synthesizing Continuous Images

H. Kobayashi, H. Kubota, S. Horiguchi, and T. Nakamura

ABSTRACT

One of the biggest problems in computer animation is the enormous amount of computations necessary to synthesize an animation sequence. In this paper, effective parallel processing for synthesizing continuous images is presented. Our parallel architecture is based on object-oriented parallel processing a ray-tracing algorithm. A task allocation strategy using **load coherence of each subspaces** *between continuous images is proposed for balancing computational loads among processing elements. For the performance evaluation of our parallel architecture, we examine, in detail, the effect of load balancing by computer simulation.*

Keywords and phrases: image synthesis, parallel processing systems, ray tracing, space subdivision, performance evaluation, animation

INTRODUCTION

Ray tracing is an efficient tool to synthesize very realistic images (Whitted 1980). However, ray tracing is very time-consuming since ray-object intersection calculations exponentially increase as the complexity of scenes increase. Especially, fast image synthesis for animation is one of the most important topics in computer graphics.

Several multiprocessor systems have been proposed to reduce computation time of ray tracing (Nishimura et al. 1983; Dippe and Swensen 1984; Kobayashi et al. 1987; Bouatouch and Priol 1988; Gaudet et al 1988). Theses parallel processing systems are classified into two categories: ***pixel-oriented parallel processing and object-oriented parallel processing***. The pixel-oriented parallel processing is based on only pixel parallelism of a screen. Processing elements (PEs) of a parallel system create subimages of a screen. PEs require pixels of subimages and the related object description to a host computer to calculate given pixel intensity. This approach is very simple and effective in small systems. However, as the number of PEs increases, this control scheme causes a large amount of communications overhead between PEs and the host computer. Increase in communications overhead makes PEs ineffective.

On the other hand, the object-oriented parallel processing is based on object space parallelism as well as pixel parallelism. Only a small part of object description of a space is stored in each PE of a parallel system. Intersection calculations and intensity calculations on intersecting objects for given rays are carried out by the PE having the description of the intersecting objects. Ray information is transferred between PEs as if rays are propagated through an object space. Therefore, there are much locality in the object-oriented parallel processing. If locally communicating tasks (subspaces) are mapped into neighbouring PEs, the communications overhead can be reduced to a minimum. Under the above condition, there is no global communications within the system even though large systems are constructed (Kobayashi et al. 1988).

In order to achieve highly effective parallel processing of ray tracing, the above parallel processing systems have employed static and dynamic load balancing schemes. However, they consider load balancing among PEs for only one scene. When an animation sequence is synthesized, there is much room for improvement of load balancing, especially in the object-oriented parallel processing.

In this paper, we present the object-oriented parallel processing system for ray tracing based on space subdivision, and propose the task mapping strategy using **load coherence** of each subspace between continuous images.

PARALLEL ARCHITECTURE FOR RAY TRACING BASED ON SPACE SUBDIVISION

In image synthesis using ray tracing, calculations of local intensity, reflection and refraction are carried out on each object in a space. Thus, computational efforts for image synthesis occur on each object, and can be localized. Therefore, it is natural to define objects as parallel tasks in ray tracing, and the object-oriented parallel processing is best suited for parallel ray tracing than the conventional pixel-oriented parallel processing (Kobayashi et al. 1987, 1988) In the object-oriented parallel processing system, objects description of an object space is distributed among PEs. Rays travel within the parallel system by inter-PE communications. Thus, the PE space as a geometrical configuration of the parallel system corresponds to the object space. PEs determine the intersecting objects for given rays, and calculates the local intensity of the intersecting objects. If a ray does not intersect with an object, or rays are newly generated after reflection/refraction process, PEs transfer these rays to the neighbouring PEs according to their directions.

Figure 1 illustrates the organization of the parallel processing system. PEs are interconnected by the torus network. Each PE has some subspaces of an object space, and determines whether or not given rays intersect with objects in the subspace. If a ray intersects with an object, the PE calculates the local intensity

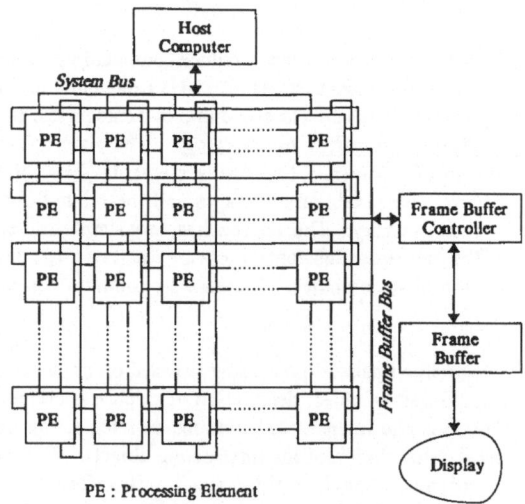

PE : Processing Element

Fig. 1 System organization.

on the intersecting object, and sends the intensity to the frame buffer controller via the frame buffer bus when the intersecting point is not in a shadow. For ray propagation in a space, PEs transfer rays to the next PEs including the appropriate subspaces according to the direction of the rays. In the system, a term of a 'ray' means a ray information packet.

In our system, we regularly divide an object space into subspaces of appropriate sizes and allocate these subspaces to the respective PEs. This is because subspaces to be traversed by given rays are easily determined by using a three-dimensional digital differential analyzer (3DDDA) (Fujimoto et al. 1986). We implement the 3DDDA in each PE.

The result obtained in each PE for a given ray is either a local intensity or a shadow on an intersecting object. If the intersecting point on the object is not in a shadow, the frame buffer controller accumulates a intensity in the frame buffer to calculate global intensities of pixels on a screen.

The host computer controls the system, defines objects description and the related parameters for the scene to be rendered, allocates subspaces to PEs, generates primary rays, and allocates these rays to the appropriate PEs. Communications between the host computer and PEs are carried out via the system bus.

TASK MAPPING STRATEGY FOR SYNTHESIZING CONTINUOUS IMAGES

A. Mapping for only one scene

In object-oriented parallel processing, tasks correspond to the subdivided object spaces. Therefore, the system performance is dominated by the strategy for mapping subspaces to PEs. In order to achieve highly effective parallel processing, the load balancing among PEs is indispensable. Since the computational loads of ray tracing tend to concentrate in a local space, it is necessary to distribute loads concentrated in several neighbouring subspaces to PEs uniformly. To realize static load balancing among PEs, the distributed allocation for object-oriented parallel processing has been proposed (Kobayashi et al. 1988). Figure 2 illustrates the distributed allocation for a 4x4 torus-connected system. The numbers in Fig. 2 refer to PE numbers to be allocated. The distributed allocation algorithm assigns subspaces at certain interval apart to one PE so that neighbouring subspaces are allocated to the different PEs. Since each object occupies several neighbouring subspaces due to spatial coherence, the distributed allocation is able to distribute much heavier loads existing in a local space to PEs approximately uniformly. The static load balancing by the distributed allocation is effective for tens-PE systems (Kobayashi et al. 1988).

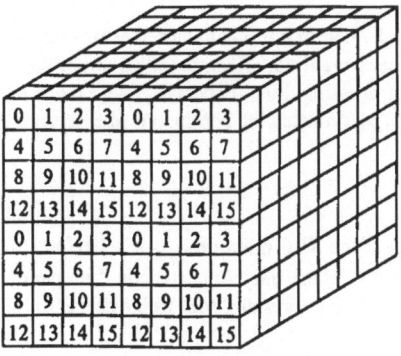

Fig. 2 Distributed allocation.

B. Mapping for continuous images

When we create only one image, it is impossible to predict the loads of each subspace strictly. Therefore, there are limitations of static load balancing by the distributed allocation. However, for synthesizing continuous images, we can estimate the loads of subspaces by using the loads of the preceding image, since difference between the loads for synthesizing continuous images is very small. We call it **load coherence**. This is applicable to load balancing for the object-oriented parallel processing. Thus, for the first frame of animation, we allocate subspaces by the distributed allocation. Then, for the next continuous frames, we allocate subspaces so as to balance loads of the preceding frame among PEs. Here, we define the amount of computational loads of a subspace as processing time for given rays in the subspace. Our mapping strategy is to map subspaces to PEs in order that each PE may have nearly equal processing time. The mapping algorithm is described as follows:

Algorithm

1) The host computer calculates the threshold of loads by dividing the total of computation times in all subspaces by the number of PEs.

2) Each PE sorts subspaces in descending order according to computation times in the subspaces. The subspaces in which computation times are larger than the threshold or are equal to zero are allocated to the same PEs. The subspaces in which computation times are less than the threshold are candidates of re-allocation.

3) The host computer sorts subspaces to be re-allocated in descending order according to their computation times, and re-allocates subspaces, having the heaviest loads, to the PE having the lightest loads in the system, according to the total computation times of subspaces which each PE has. This process is continued until all the candidates of re-allocation subspaces are completely assigned to PEs.

Especially, in the case where objects moves or changes shape with time, the subspaces which enclose moving objects may change. Therefore, it is necessary to allocate moving objects to the appropriate subspaces frame by frame. However, since dynamic information of each object can be encapsulated in the respective objects in the object-oriented environment, each PE can independently control objects in the subspaces. Thus, the object description of a space is locally modified by each PE in parallel. Here, we assume that the paths of all moving objects have been previously specified. When moving objects move beyond the boundaries of the subspaces, PEs transfer the moving objects to the appropriate PE, having the subspaces which enclose them, via the inter-PE network. After the positions of all moving objects are determined, the subspace re-allocation is carried out according to the previously presented algorithm.

PERFORMANCE ANALYSIS

We consider the performance evaluation of our parallel architecture by computer simulation. The mapping strategy is examined by total processing time, effective utilization of the PEs, and the relation between the ray transmission time and total processing time. Especially, we examine *the subspace re-allocation* , described in the previous section, by synthesizing continuous images with changing view angle.

A. Simulation Model

We assume that each PE consists of the NEC microprocessor V30 (Intel 8086 compatible) and the floating-point co-processor 8087. The $n \times n$ PEs are interconnected via 8-bit parallel lines in the torus fashion. For more detailed simulation parameters of the system, see (Kobayashi et al. 1988).

Figure 3 shows the test images used for the performance evaluation. Figure 3-(a) (Image 1) is composed of 369 spheres, whose surfaces cause diffuse reflections and whose positions are determined by a certain recurrence formula. Figure 3-(b) (Image 2) contains one transparent sphere and one specular reflective sphere in front, and 121 diffuse reflective spheres in a plane fashion as the background. The object space has been divided into 24x24x24 subspaces, and then 144x144 pixels are traced.

B. Experimental results and discussion

Number of PEs vs. Total Processing Time

Figure 4 shows total processing times of Image 1 and Image 2 as a function of the number of PEs. In the figures, ○ shows the total processing time in the case of "*subspace re-allocation* ," which uses already calculated loads of each subspaces. For comparison with *the subspace re-allocation* , we show the total processing time in the case of the distributed allocation by ☐ . In both figures, it is found that the total processing time using *the subspace re-allocation* is two to three times shorter than that using the distributed allocation. When the number of PEs is less than 256 for the Image 1 and 64 for the Image 2, the total processing times linearly decrease as the number of PEs increases. Therefore, we conclude that *the subspace re-allocation* is excellent in view of static load balancing.

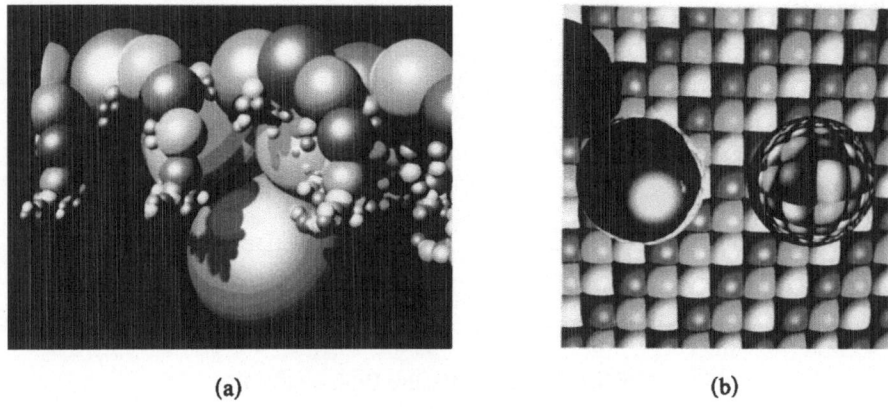

(a)   (b)

Fig. 3 (a) Test image 1. (b) Test image 2.

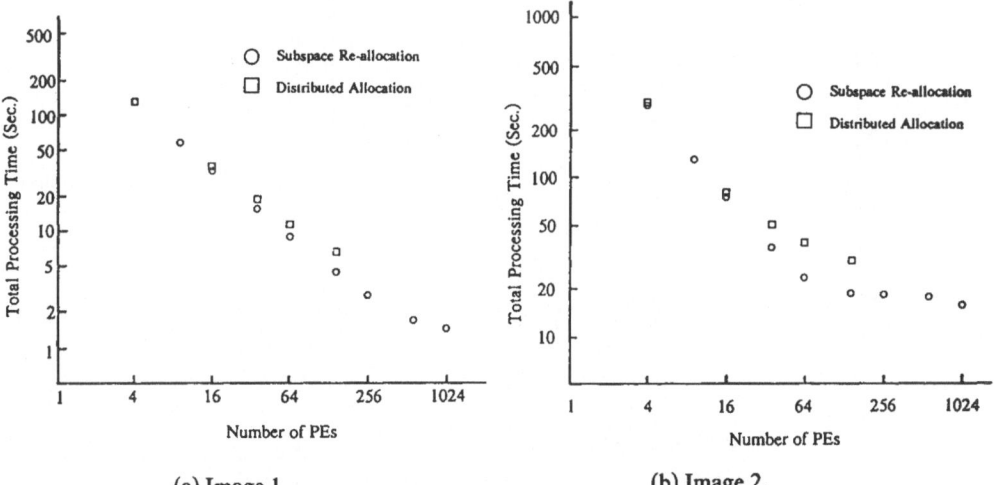

(a) Image 1.   (b) Image 2.

Fig. 4 Number of PEs vs. Total Processing Time.

Figure 5 shows the effective utilization of PEs as a function of the number of PEs. Here, let the effective utilization of PEs be defined by the following equation:

$$\underline{\text{Effective utilization}} = T_{UP} / T_{MP} / N * 100 \ (\%)$$

Where,
T_{UP} is the uni-PE processing time,
T_{MP} is the multi-PE processing time, and
N is the number of PEs.

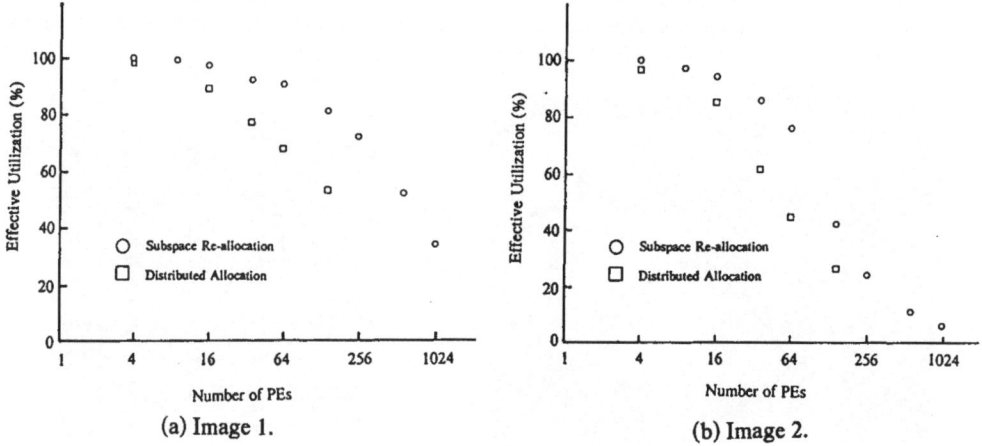

(a) Image 1.   (b) Image 2.

Fig. 5 Number of PEs vs. Effective Utilization of PEs.

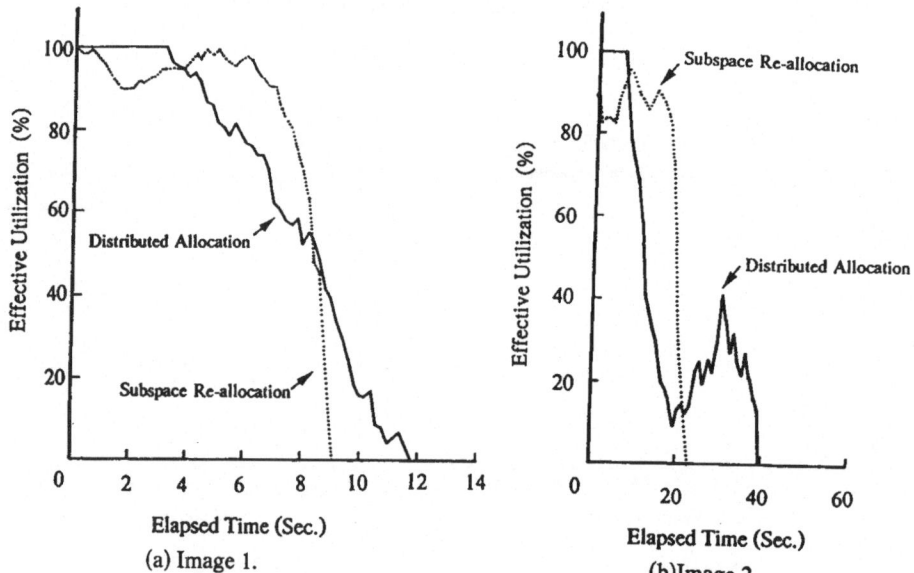

(a) Image 1.   (b)Image 2.

Fig. 6 Transition of effective utilization as a function of elapsed time.

From Fig. 5, it is found that the system with *the subspace re-allocation* shows higher effective utilization than the system with the distributed allocation. In order to examine system behavior in more detail, we measure time transition of the effective utilization as shown in Fig. 6. A solid and dotted lines show the results of the distributed allocation and *the subspace re-allocation* , respectively. The ideal load balancing should give the time transition like a step function. In the distributed allocation, all the PEs are active in the first few seconds. However, after that, the effective utilization gradually decreases as time elapses. In the Image 2, the second peak of the effective utilization is due to the secondary rays caused by specular and transparent spheres.

On the other hand, though not all the PEs are active in *the subspace re-allocation* , most PEs are active for a long time as with step function-like utilization, compared with the distributed allocation. After that situation, the effective utilization rapidly decreases, and processing is completed. Therefore, in the case of *the subspace re-allocation* , there are many active PEs, and effective load balancing is achieved during processing.

As simple examples, we examine the effectiveness of *the subspace re-allocation* to continuous images by changing view angle. Figure 7 shows effective utilization as a function of view angle measured by degrees. The performance is evaluated in the case of a 6x6 torus-connected (36 PEs) system. In the figures, marks ●, ○, and □ are the result of *the subspace re-allocation* which re-allocates subspaces to PEs every ten degrees, the result of *the subspace re-allocation* which is applied to the first frame only, and the result of the distributed allocation, respectively. Figure 7 shows that it is not necessary to apply *the subspace re-allocation* to every continuous images and to re-allocate subspaces to PEs. The estimation of load balancing is effective for the following several frames. In this example, the average number of subspaces which are re-allocated to the different PEs by *the subspace re-allocation* is 2040 out of 13824 in the Image 1 and 1986 out of 13824 in the Image 2, and approximately 85 percent of entire subspaces are not re-allocated to the different PEs. Thus, the overhead of *the subspace re-allocation* scheme is relatively small. As for the case of the continuous scenes including moving objects, we are currently analyzing the system performance.

As the number of PEs become more than a thousand, the system performance does not improve. Especially, the performance in the case of the Image 2 is saturated. This is because the number of subspaces allocated to the PEs becomes small as the number of PEs increases, and the total processing time is governed by the PE with the heaviest load. The subspaces in the Image 2 have much heavier loads than

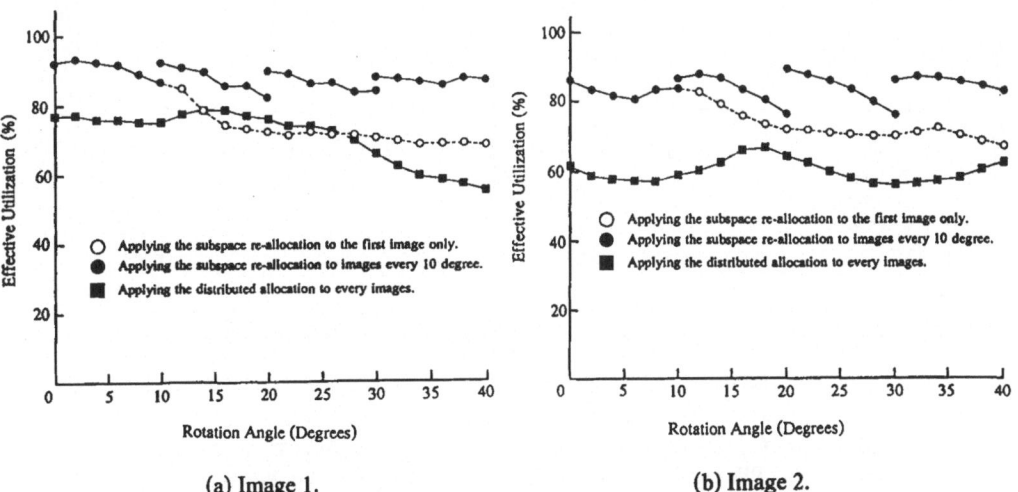

(a) Image 1.   (b) Image 2.

Fig. 7 View Angle vs. Effective Utilization of PEs.

the subspaces in the Image 1, since there are transparent and specular spheres in a space. In this situation, there is no room for static load balancing. Therefore, the static scheme is not effective for load balancing when the degree of space subdivision is not sufficient compared with the number of PEs. In this case, *the subspace re-allocation* is effective for hundreds-PE systems.

Total Processing Time vs. Ray Transmission Time

In object-oriented parallel processing, there are so many communications between PEs caused by ray propagation in a space. In the distributed allocation, neighbouring subspaces are completely allocated to the neighbouring PEs. However, in *the subspace re-allocation,* the neighbouring relationship between subspaces is destroyed in a PE-space since neighbouring subspaces cannot perfectly be allocated to the neighbouring PEs. Therefore, for transferring rays from one subspace to another neighbouring subspace, the ray may travel several intermediate PEs.

To examine the effect of communications overhead on total processing time, we show the total processing time as a function of transmission time of a ray between the neighbouring PEs in Fig. 8. Total processing time is sensitive to transmission time, because the diameter of the torus network is large as the number of PEs increases. However, even though the number of PEs is 1024, transmission time which is less than 100 (μs/ray) does not affect total processing time. As a ray information packet is about 28 bytes long, our estimate of transmission time is 50 (μs/ray). Therefore, it is clear that the communications overhead is not severe for *the subspace re-allocation* scheme.

For comparison with the torus network, Figure 9 depicts the performance of the system whose PEs are interconnected by the Hypercube network. The Hypercube (Saad and Schultz 1985) has short diameter which is *log* N, where N is the number of PEs. On the other hand, that of the torus network is $N^{1/2}$. Figure 9 shows that transmission time which affects the total processing time is more than 5000 (μs/ray) and we can use low speed communication lines for the Hypercube network. However, since the cost of the Hypercube is proportional to N*log* N and processing speed of PEs, i.e. NEC V30, is relatively slow compared with network speed, the torus seems to be excellent in view of performance/cost. When we use high performance 32-bit microprocessors as building elements of PEs, the Hypercube network is the best inter-PE network.

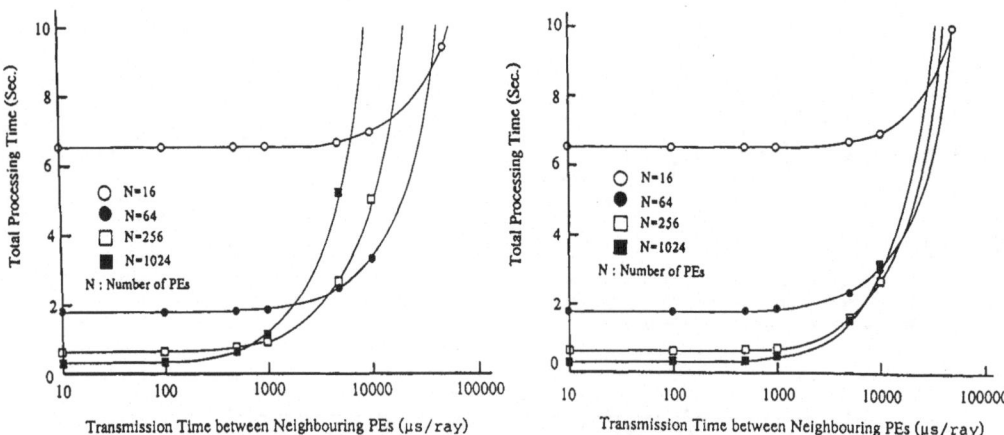

Fig. 8 Transmission Time of a Ray between Neighbouring PEs vs. Total Processing Time (torus network).

Fig. 9 Transmission Time of a Ray between Neighbouring PEs vs. Total Processing Time (Hypercube network).

CONCLUSIONS

In this paper, we have presented efficient parallel processing for synthesizing continuous images like computer animation. Our system is based on object-oriented parallel processing of ray tracing. In order to balance loads among processing elements of a parallel system and to achieve highly effective parallel processing for synthesizing continuous images, we have proposed the strategy for mapping subspaces to processing elements in the system, which is based on **load coherence** of each subspace between continuous images. For synthesizing one frame image in an animation sequence, subspaces are re-allocated to processing elements by using the already calculated loads of each subspace for the preceding frame. As a result of performance evaluation of our system by computer simulation, we have concluded that the mapping strategy is very effective as a static load balancing scheme and suited for hundreds-PE systems. In order to realize large scale parallel systems consisting of more than a thousand PEs, the hierarchical parallel system employing dynamic load balancing as well as static one is one good solution (Kobayashi et al. 1988). The mapping strategy discussed in this paper is applicable to the hierarchical parallel system.

ACKNOWLEDGEMENTS

The authors are grateful to Professor Tosiyasu L. Kunii of the University of Tokyo for motivating them to do this research and helpful conversations.

REFERENCES

Bouatouch K, Priol T (1988) An Experience on an iPSC Hypercube. (N.Thalmann & D.Thalmann Eds.) New Trends in Computer Graphics (Proc. of CG International '88) 170-187

Dippe M, Swensen J (1984) An Adaptive Subdivision Algorithm and Parallel Architecture for Realistic Image Synthesis. Computer Graphics 18:3:149-158

Fujimoto A, Tanaka T, Iwata K (1986) ARTS: Accelerated Ray-Tracing System. IEEE CG & Applications 6:4:16-26

Gaudet S, Hobson R, Chilka P, Calvert T (1988) Multiprocessor Experiments for High-Speed Ray Tracing. ACM Trans. on Graphics 7:3:151-179

Kobayashi H, Nakamura T, Shigei Y (1987) Parallel Processing of an Object Space for Image Synthesis using ray tracing. The Visual Computer 3:13-22

Kobayashi H, Nishimura S, Kubota H, Nakamura T, Shigei Y (1988) Load Balancing Strategies for a Parallel Ray-Tracing System based on Constant Subdivision. The Visual Computer 4:197-209

Nishimura H, Ohno H, Shirakawa I, Omura K (1983) LINKS-1: A Parallel Pipelined Multimicrocomputer System for Image Creation. Proc. of 10th Ann Int Symp Comput Archi :387-394

Saad Y, Schultz MH (1985) Topological Properties of Hypercubes. Dept. of Comput. Sci., Yale Univ., Yale Univ., New Haven, CT, Res. Rep. 389

Whitted T (1980) An improved Illumination Model for Shaded Display. CACM 23:343-394

Hiroaki Kobayashi is currently a Research Associate in the Department of Mechanical Engineering at Tohoku University, Sendai, Japan. His research interests include computer architecture, parallel processing systems and applications, and computer graphics. He received the B.E. degree in Communication Engineering, and the M.E. and D.E. degrees in Information Engineering from Tohoku University in 1983, 1985, and 1988, respectively. He is a member of the IEEE Computer Society, the ACM, the IEICE of Japan and the IPS of Japan.

Hideyuki Kubota is currently a researcher in the Yamato Research Laboratory at IBM Japan, Ltd. His research interests include computer architecture and computer graphics. He received the B.E. degree in Communication Engineering and the M.E. degree in Information Engineering from Tohoku University in 1986 and 1988, respectively. He is a member of the IEICE of Japan.

Susumu Horiguchi is currently an associate professor of Department of Information Science, Tohoku University. He graduated from Department of Communication Engineering, Tohoku University in 1976, and received the M.S. and DR. degrees both from the same university in 1978 and 1981, respectively. From 1981 to 1982 he was a Research Associate in the Department of Communication Engineering at Tohoku University, and since 1982 he has been a faculty of Department of Information Science at Tohoku University. He is also with Education Center for Information Processing, Tohoku University. His research interest has been mainly concerned with parallel computing for computer graphics, parallel computing algorithm, parallel computer architecture, and VLSI architecture. Dr. Horiguchi received the first prize of student paper from IEEE in 1979. He was a visiting scientist of IBM Thomas J. Watson Research Center from 1986 to 1987 to study on parallel computing algorithm. He is a member of IEEE, IEICE, and IPS of Japan.

Tadao Nakamura was born in Ube, Japan, on January 25, 1944. He received the Dr. of Eng. degree from Tohoku university in 1972. His major was on Computer Aided Design in semiconductor electronics. Since 1972 he has been a faculty member of the Faculty of Engineering of Tohoku University. He is currently a Professor of Computer Science in the Department of Mechanical Engineering, Tohoku University. He has been studying computer architecture frequently at the Computer System Laboratory, Stanford University since 1983. His present research interests include computer architecture, supercomputer architecture, computer graphics, and distributed processing systems. He is an Editorial Board Member of The Visual Computer. He is also a Senior Member of the IEEE and a member of the IEICE of Japan, the IEEE COMSOC Communications Software Committee and the IEEE COMSOC Computer Communications Committee.

Address: Department of Mechanical Engineering, Faculty of Engineering, Tohoku University, Sendai 980, JAPAN.

Chapter 7
Image Processing

Image Pattern Recognition
Using Configurable Logic Cell Arrays

J. Viitanen and T. Kean

ABSTRACT

A new approach to the solution of computation intensive problems using programmable logic cell array devices as dynamically run-time reconfigurable processors is introduced. The applicability of the approach for real problems is demonstrated in the case of two time-critical parts of image pattern recognition using the hierarchical chamfer matching method. The execution times of the programs performing certain computation intensive parts of the recognition process on a normal sequential computer and the new architecture are compared. Significant speedups are achieved over the sequential approach by exploiting optimisation and parallel processing at the gate level. The potential role of the approach in future computers is discussed, the application development process and the required development tools are described.

Keywords: *Image pattern recognition, VLSI design, computer architecture, template matching, parallel processing*

INTRODUCTION

The availability of logic cell array devices that can be programmed dynamically at run-time has made it possible to utilise a new approach for computation of data-intensive tasks. These devices are primarily intended for applications where traditional two-level Field Programmable Logic Array (FPLA) and the closely related PAL and PROM devices have been used extensively but are significantly more general in that arbitrary connections of gates and latches are supported allowing much more complex systems to be implemented. The run-time programmable/ reconfigurable logic cell array consists of a volatile block of static memory that defines the state of a switching matrix which connects the logic cell elements in the desired configuration, just like the fusible links configure the cells in an FPLA. The logic function of each cell is also defined by volatile memory. Hereafter, this kind of device is termed CLCA (Configurable Logic Cell Array) to emphasise the differences between it, the fuse-programmable and UV-erasable PAL devices and the fixed- logic gate array devices. In this paper we will consider two families of these devices: commercial Logic Cell Array (LCA) chips (Xilinx 1986) and a newer architecture called Configurable Array Logic (CAL) designed at the University of Edinburgh.

Even though the commercially available devices are not designed to be used in computer-type applications, their dynamic programmability makes it possible to load different 'programs' (the configuration data) into them for executing various types of computational tasks. Thus they can be used as coprocessors within a general purpose computer for speeding up specific tasks, where large amounts of data are processed using relatively simple algorithms. The Edinburgh system has been specifically designed with computational tasks in mind. The typical configuration of either CLCA for computational tasks is as a gate-level pipelined processor: but naturally any forms of parallelism which fit the device structure can be used. The examples that are presented in this paper deal with image pattern recognition using a template matching technique.

1. CHARACTERISTICS OF CONFIGURABLE LOGIC CELL ARRAYS

1.1. Background

The recently introduced CLCA is a descendant of the Field Programmable Logic Array (FPLA) devices that have been used for years for replacing various SSI or MSI logic chips on a typical digital circuit board. A traditional FPLA consists of logic cells that can be programmed to perform desired logic functions by opening the fusible links at proper positions inside the circuit. These devices are limited to implementing one or more two level AND/OR logic functions of input variables. Erasable Programmable Logic Devices (EPLD's) which can be reprogrammed after erasure by UV light were introduced later.

There are two main differences between the new CLCA devices and these architectures.

1. The programming is done using transistor switches controlled by static RAM cells. This has several important consequences:

    (i) The device is reprogrammable an arbitrary number of times.

    (ii) The store is volatile and must be restored every time power is applied, and

    (iii) The size of RAM cells limits the number of programmable connections in the device.

2. These architectures allow much more general interconnection structures than earlier devices. There are fundamental reasons which imply that higher generality arrays rather than simply larger two level arrays are necessary to implement large systems on a configurable architecture (Kean 1989).

1.2. The Commercial LCA Devices

The commercial LCA device is modelled after the gate-array architecture common in Application Specific Integrated Circuit (ASIC) designs. It consists of a relatively small number of complex logic cells separated by a wiring area. There are two families of these devices: the 2000 family contains 64 cells in an 8x8 grid and has been available for about two years and the 3000 family which supplies up to 320 cells and has just come into production. The 2000 family logic cells are capable of computing any function of 4 variables or any two functions of 3 variables and a complex flip-flop. The 3000 family cells can compute functions of 5 variables or two functions of 4 and have two flip-flops: the inter-cell routing structure is also slightly more complex. Note that the amount of control store required to implement any function of n variables increases as 2^n (since there are 2^{2^n} possible functions) so with constant processing technology one could have around twice as many 4 variable cells as 5 variable cells. Cell delays are of the order of 10ns. These devices are primarily intended as stand alone chips to replace random logic within target systems. Complex programmable I/O blocks are provided which are very useful in EPLD applications, but mean that regular arbitrary sized multi-chip arrays cannot be built since the interconnection structure is broken up at chip boundaries.

1.3. The Structure of the University of Edinburgh CAL.

The Configurable Array Logic (CAL) devices developed in the University of Edinburgh are radically different from the LCA's. The basic architecture is a cellular array with only nearest neighbour connections: thus longer connections must run through intermediate cells. This makes the switching structures on long interconnections more apparent but does not necessarily imply that there will be more intervening switches than in an LCA type architecture with separate routing facilities. Each cell within the array can realise two-variable logic functions or simple latches as well as providing routing support for pass through connections.

The architecture of the CAL device is motivated by three main design goals: simplicity, regularity and efficiency. We will consider the implications of each of these in turn.

- Simplicity. Architectural simplicity means that users and, more importantly, Design Automation tools have a clean model of the structure. Since CAL is intended to implement large systems most resource allocation decisions will be made by computer programs. This makes the provision of large irregular function units much less attractive, such units can often be used effectively in hand-crafted designs but cannot be used as effectively by design automation software. The situation is similar to the CISC/RISC debate in Von-Neumann computers: compiler writers prefer a small well defined set of fast instructions. This goal also applies to the routing system where only a single kind of routing resource is provided. This allows channel-routing algorithms instead of the much slower and less efficient maze routing algorithms to be used.

- Regularity. It is important that a system to support high generality designs provides a completely symmetrical routing structure. This allows sub-designs from a library to be rotated and reflected to meet global floorplanning goals.

Similarly, the system has only one resource: the cell (instead of several resources e.g. logic cells, wiring channels and long lines). In a system with many resources a design can fail in several different ways (not enough logic blocks, not enough wiring tracks etc.) whereas in a system with a single resource it is only a question of how many cells are required. This property simplifies the design of Design Automation tools. Regularity is extended to arrays containing many CAL chips: the architecture makes the individual chip boundaries transparent at the cellular level. This allows single subunits to be split over multiple chips and greatly simplifies the placement problem. This transparency is possible because routing delays in cellular structures are significantly higher than those in silicon designs (because of intervening multiplexers). Input/Output pads have also been getting significantly faster and delays are smaller than normal in array structures where pads drive only a single input on an adjacent chip. Thus I/O pads are not necessarily a bottleneck in cellular designs (incurring a delay equivalent to around 3 routing multiplexers for a chip boundary crossing) and, with carefully designed circuitry, can even be shared between several signals at an array edge without excessive performance penalties.

- Efficiency. Efficiency in the use of silicon area is central to the CAL design. It falls out naturally from the previous two considerations. Since we have a large array of very simple cells it is possible to put a large amount of effort into finding an efficient layout for the repeating unit (c.f. commercial RAM designs).

The array structure of the CAL device is apparent from the example design in figure 5. Apart from the nearest neighbour signals there are three global signals routed to all cells in the array. Two are inputs (G1 and G2) which can be used as a two-phase non-overlapping clock in user designs; the third (FTEST) is a test signal which can monitor the function unit output of any cell in the array. This simplifies access to internal signals for debugging purposes. Each cell can implement any of the 16 functions of two Boolean variables or one of 4 types of D latch (D,Clk),(D',Clk),(D,Clk'),(D',Clk'). The routing structure within each cell is shown in figure 1: it approximates a full crossbar switch with unnecessary connections (e.g. South In to South Out) removed. The cell is controlled by 20 bits of RAM. Use of a multiplexer based routing structure makes very efficient use of the control store. The present prototype device contains a 16x16 array of cells in a core symbol of just under 4817x4596um in 2um CMOS. Much larger arrays are possible: a 32x32 array in 1.5um tecnology is currently under development (Algotronix 1988) and a 64x64 array would be possible with the advanced processing technology used in commercial SRAM's. The architecture of the CAL chip is described in detail by Kean (1989).

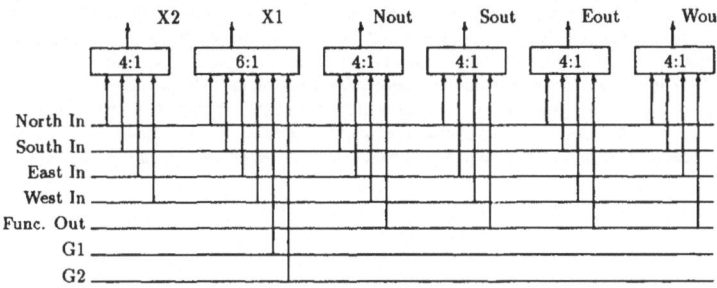

Fig. 1: The CAL cell routing.

2. THE APPLICABILITY OF CLCA's TO IMAGE PROCESSING

Image processing and image pattern recognition are fields where reconfigurable special processors could be useful. Early image processors like the Cytocomputer (Sternberg 1985) were fast pipelined processors performing a limited set of operations using a fixed neighborhood size. Typical functions were performed over a period of one complete image frame (several milliseconds); during this time the function of the neighborhood logic remained fixed. Many SIMD-processors have similar characteristics: performing fixed operations over many data items is very fast but changing programs is fairly slow (because code must be propagated to each processor). In systems without a dedicated broadcast channel for code transfer programs commonly remain fixed over the time period of one image frame or window (although the programs stored in each PE may be quite long). Examples of such SIMD-processors are CLIP (Fountain 1983) and the NCR GAPP (Davis 1984). Some more general purpose processors, like the Connection Machine (Hillis 1985), have similar features. All these computers typically are coprocessors controlled by a general purpose computer which takes care of program and data traffic.

Image processing is an application area where a fast processor with a small 'program store' and slow 'instruction fetch' could be successful because algorithms often have loops with high repetition counts and relatively simple operations inside the loop body. Other potential target areas include statistical simulation, and traditional vector processor applications such as ray tracing, and finite element methods. In this paper we shall consider one possible system architecture using CLCA's consisting of a master CPU with a connected slave CLCA (or several of them). The master processor controls the configuration of the CLCA, sends data to it, and reads back the results. This architecture provides an attractive development environment but the need to channel data going to and from the CLCA array through the microprocessor can be a bottleneck in many applications. Architectures with high-bandwidth connections and fast memories are necessary to take advantage of the raw power of large CLCA arrays in highly parallel applications such as cellular automata algorithms (Kean 1989).

The principal difference between the CLCA and previous cellular array computers is its gate-level programming. This may appear to be a limitation in that each 'processor' can only execute very simple operations: however the reverse is true. Using behavioural compilation techniques developed for silicon compilers we can configure the array to implement almost any operation we desire (it is easy to show that CLCA arrays are general computing structures in the sense of Turing machines). We could even implement a complete Von Neumann processor on the CLCA if that kind of operation was required. Traditional cellular computers with their small function units are much more limited in this sense. The number of available cells in the CLCA and propagation delays on long wires within it provide a practical limit on the size of the functional units implemented.

There are several types of image processing operations that could be considered for implementation on a CLCA. Some obvious ones are preprocessing tasks, like image smoothing with simple masks, edge detection, median filtering, and thresholding. Other possibilities are histogram calculation, searching for maximum or minimum, and similar tasks. However, in the coprocessor architecture we are considering the speedup for these operations may be quite low compared to a program run on a high performance signal processor or a RISC (reduced instruction set computer). This is because these operations are so simple that data I/O overhead will be a major part of the execution time and the host CPU may be able to calculate the function itself almost as quickly as it can transfer the data to and from the coprocessor. Special processors are already available with real-time execution speeds for many of these basic image preprocessing functions.

Operations with intermediate complexity, where the I/O overhead percentage is lower, but large image data sets are processed are better suited to the external coprocessor architecture. Examples of such tasks in the field of image pattern recognition are pattern matching, distance calculation using different metrics, coordinate transforms and Hough transforms. This paper will describe the use of a CLCA in two important steps of pattern recognition, the distance image calculation and hierarchical matching. The original implementation was done using commercial LCA devices but we will also describe a CAL implementation of the distance transform unit to allow comparison. A system with a single LCA is assumed, with logic array reconfiguration at the beginning of each task. The execution speed of the new approach, based on simulations of the designed configurations of the LCA, is compared with a previously tested program on a standard sequential signal processor.

3. THE SAMPLE PROBLEM

Our example application, the Hierarchical Chamfer Matching Algorithm (HCMA), was first described by Borgefors (1988) and fast algorithms for its calculation were presented by Viitanen et al. (1987, 1988) for the three-parametric translation-rotation problem. The advantage of HCMA is its robustness but in previous implementations it had the disadvantage of relatively long execution times.

HCMA is a model based, template matching operation. It uses simple operations, like additions, searching for a minimum, and offset addressing into small tables. The main phases in the recognition are image capture, feature detection (typically simple edge detection and thresholding to a binary image), calculation of a distance image (an image where the pixel values are proportional to the distance, or approximated distance, of the pixel from the closest detected feature), hierarchical pyramid creation from the distance image (quadtree, octree, or even pentatree rules can be used), and finally, the actual matching. Coarse matching is done at the lowest resolution pyramid, trying every third or fourth translational position in both directions; rotation is estimated at the same time. Finer matching is done at higher resolution levels for a few best candidate positions.

The matching process involves transforming the model coordinates to different geometrically distorted positions with respect to the distance image. The practical case with three parameters, rotation and X-Y translation, is analysed in the references. Those values of the distance image that are addressed by the distorted model coordinates are picked up and accumulated. The accumulated sum is proportional to the 'average' distance of the model from the 'correct' position under the metrics used in the distance transform. This is a classical multidimensional optimisation problem where the distance image values form the cost function. The reduction in computational load over the traditional template matching method (where the cross-correlation function is calculated between the model and the scene) is obvious since only additions are needed. Viitanen (1987, 1988) shows how the explicit polar coordinate transforms can be avoided in the geometric transforms. Furthermore, the local convergence properties of the distance image are good allowing several levels of the hierarchical representation of the image data to be used. This reduces the amount of data and the processing time considerably.

Here we will improve the speed of the time consuming distance image calculation and matching parts of the algorithm using CLCA acceleration. In (Viitanen 1988) the measured execution times on a sequential processor were 1.7 seconds for calculating the distance image, and 10 to 20 seconds/model for matching against a 256 by 256 image, with a maximum of

48 coordinate points in the model. For practical use in robotics, the processing times should be a few hundred milliseconds. We will show how to achieve this performance using CLCA's. The next section describes the calculations which must be performed in detail.

3.1. The Distance Transform Calculation

The 3-4 integer distance approximation is applied in the calculation of the distance transform (DT) used for creating the distance image. The approximation has small errors compared to the true Euclidean distance but is sufficiently accurate for practical use. The calculation of the distance transform involves two passes over the binary edge image, using the method of Borgefors (1986). The calculation in the first iteration is done as follows. Let F(x,y) be the two-dimensional discrete image array with row index x and column index y, where F(x,y) = 0 at valid feature points and maximum otherwise, then the corresponding distance image value for each array position in the first iteration is:

$$G(x,y) = \min\{ b(x,y), G(x-1,y)+3, G(x,y-1)+3, G(x-1,y-1)+4, G(x+1,y-1)+4 \} \quad (1)$$

where processing is done row-by-row, in increasing x and y values. The second iteration is similar, expect that now the input image F(x,y) is the result of the first iteration, decreasing index values are used, and the signs of the index offsets above are negated. Because of the addition, a new search for the minimum has to be done among all the five pixels every time the mask is moved in the image. This makes the distance transform calculation fairly slow on a sequential computer.

A block diagram of the hardware to compute the 3-4 DT is shown in figure 2. It contains five registers in two groups corresponding to the two mask rows. The outputs of the registers are fed to adders which add the correct offsets. The most important part of the circuit is the parallel comparitor section which selects the minimum of the five elements in one asynchronous, ripple-through process.

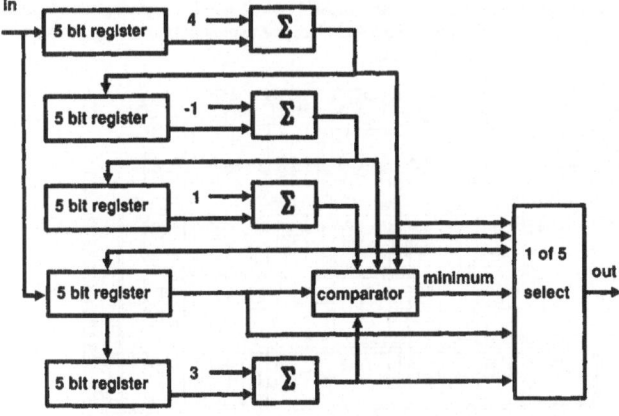

Fig. 2: The CLCA configuration for calculating the distance image.

3.1.1 The LCA Implementation.

The structure of the comparitor part of the circuit in figure 2 is shown in figure 3. It compares in parallel corresponding bits of the five pixels (marked by A ... E) with five bit accuracy. The result of the comparison ripples down from the MSB to the LSB, and the result is used to select the first pixel with the smallest value (several pixels may have this value). The circuit gives approximately constant time for the comparison from a certain bit significance level regardless of the difference. We could also have used faster lookahead to get a lower time for those comparisons where the minimum value could be determined at a high bit position but, since the host processor reads the results synchronously, the constant time approach was chosen. This unit consists of 84 gates, or the equivalent functional parts, in the LCA.

360

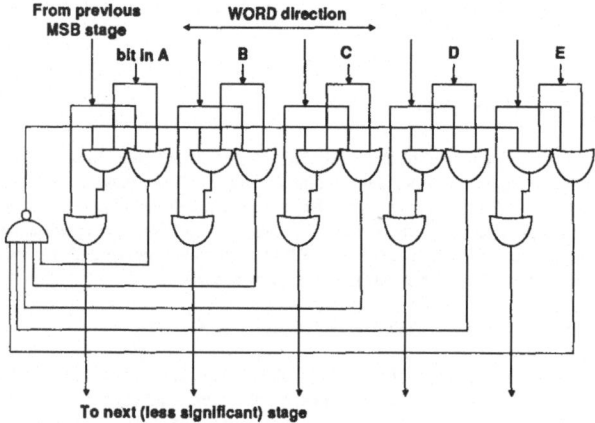

Fig. 3: One bit-slice of the parallel comparitor logic configuration.

Figure 4 shows the placement and the routing of the different functional parts on the LCA in this configuration. The smallest available LCA with 64 configurable logic cells was used: as we can see, only three cells were left unused and the routing capacity of the device was fully used at many positions. The smaller cells at the edges of the layout are programmable I/O blocks; a0...a4 and c0...c1 are the input terminals, and S0...SE4 output terminals, giving the selected minimum pixel value. Each logic cell has the inputs at the left, upper, and lower side, and two outputs at the right side. Clock is marked by 'ck'. Switching units are located in between the logic cells.

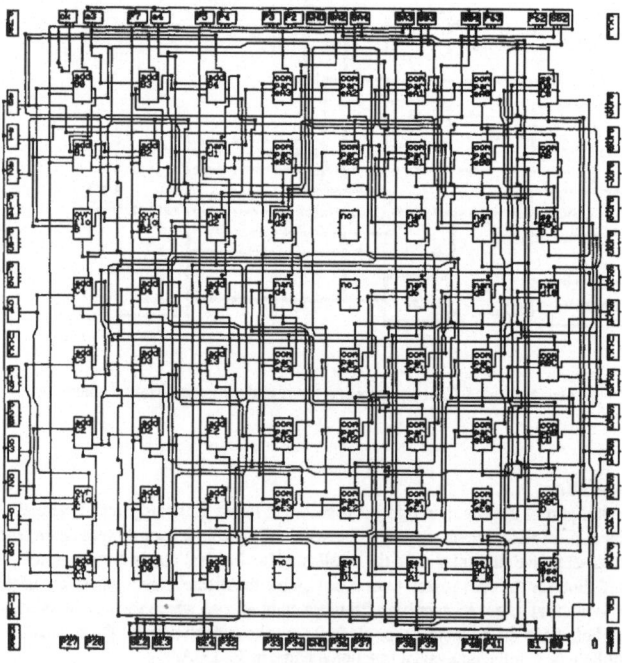

Fig. 4: The routing and placement of the LCA's logic cells of the configuration in Fig. 2.

The total delay through the comparitor is not a linear function of the equivalent gate delays along the signal path, because the LCA evaluates all Boolean functions up to four variables at the same speed; the performance of the circuit was estimated using the simulator supplied by the manufacturer. It gave a maximum value of 250 ns for the selection of the minimum from the worst case MSB transition. The maximum delay for one configurable logic block was 10 ns for the model used.

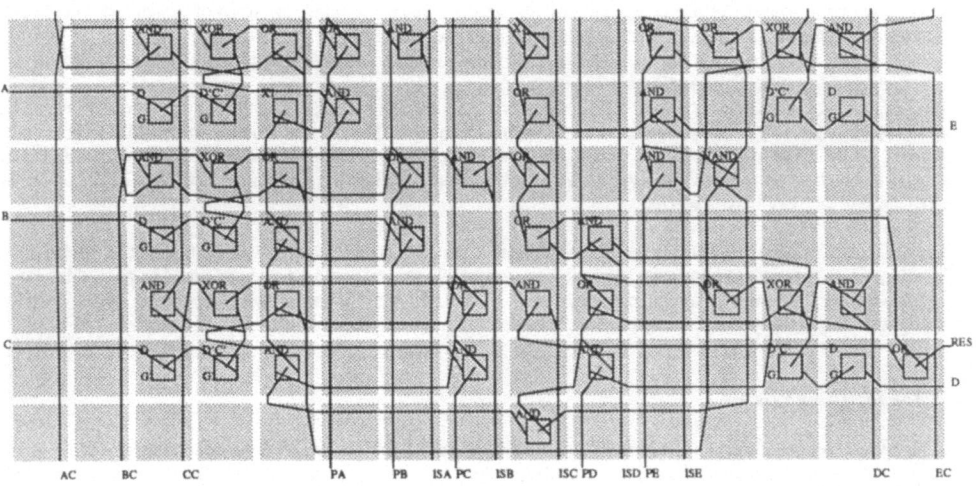

Fig. 5: The CAL design for the Distance Transform Unit.

3.1.2. The CAL Implementation.

Figure 5 shows a 'typical' bit slice through the CAL implementation of the comparitor. This design is different from the LCA one in that all the major units are integrated into a single regular structure. The adders are at the far left and right of the central logic. Half adders are used since we only need to add constants - when we want to add 1 at the current bit position we would use XNOR and OR instead of XOR and AND to generate SUM and CARRY to the next stage. Each adder looks like a 2x2 square with a master/slave register on the bottom and the SUM (XOR) and CARRY (AND) gates on the top. The registers are clocked by one of the global signals (G1). Carry routing goes from bottom to top on the left and right.

The selectors and mimimum detectors are implemented in the central area, 5 signals pA...pE go down the unit, and another 5 isA...isE up, pA...pE correspond to 'possibly' A through E and 'isA..isE' to definitely A through E (after all bit positions have been compared). The 'iSA...isE' signals are AND'ed with A...E and OR'ed (in the centre and far right of the design) to form a 5:1 selector and produce the result at this bit position (marked (RES)). The right hand side of the central area is less regular since it takes advantage of extra vertical space arising from only having two adders to save an extra column of cells.

The design is 14x7=98 cells, a complete comparitor would require 5 of these units. At the base (LSB) of the unit an extra row of cells is used to invert the 'pA...pE' signals and connect them directly to the 'isA...isE' signals. Potentially more than one 'is' signal can be high - this does not matter because the numbers corresponding to the high 'is' signals are equal so the selector will still give the correct result. At the top of the unit 3 rows of cells are used to connect the overflow signals from the adders to the corresponding 'p' signals in the MSB: this prevents pixels where the addition has overflowed from being selected as the minimum. The case in which all the additions overflow is also detected and the 'ovf' signal set which forces all result outputs to 1 (corresponding to the maximum legal value). The extra routing area could be avoided if special layouts were done for the MSB and LSB slices but this method produces a more regular design. The whole unit requires 546 cells.

The best way to compare this figure with the LCA is in terms of control store required since this will cancel out differences in processing technology and die size. The LCA array has 12038 bits of configuration RAM. At 20 bits of RAM per CAL cell this represents 601 CAL cells. This shows that the implementations are almost equivalent in terms of 'area' efficiency despite the large numbers of relatively high fan-in gates in the design. It must be noted that the LCA design has been fitted into a single chip where the CAL design is an arbitrary shaped rectangle of cells. This is representative of the different ways the two systems are intended to be used. CAL designs will normally be done in a large array built up from several chips and the comparitor would represent only a small part of the total system whereas LCA arrays are intended for relatively small designs which fit on a single chip. At present there are no facilities for accurately simulating the delays in a CAL design, however, rough calculations based on circuit simulations and measurements on the prototype chip suggest that the speed in this example would be of the same order.

The CAL design is much more regular than the LCA design and was produced faster (about 2 days versus 1 week) despite the fact that it was done as a hand layout whereas the LCA design used automatic routing tools and a good graphical editor. Most of the time in the LCA design was spent in manual editing of the routing since the autorouter quickly exhausts the routing resources in a design of this complexity leaving signals unrouted. Overall, the speed of design and its regularity coupled with the slight area advantage vindicate the 'keep-it-simple' philosophy of the CAL system.

3.1.3. Comparison with Conventional Processor

The corresponding operations on a TMS 32010 signal processor take from 29 to 37 instruction cycles of 200 ns, so the speedup factor is from 23 to 30, compared to the LCA implementation. The I/O overhead has to be added to both cases, depending on the actual implementation, so the total time for building the complete 256 by 256 distance image can be estimated to be about 64 milliseconds using a fast host CPU with a 120 ns I/O cycle time. The TMS 32010 sequential implementation took more than a second.

There are about 239 gate equivalents in the CLCA implementation, this number of additional gates would be needed in the ALU of a general processor to implement the same 'instruction'. No general purpose processor would be given this amount of additional gates for such a special purpose - even without the trend towards RISC computers! With 'reusable' reconfigurable arrays the special circuitry becomes feasible.

3.2. The Matching Process

The matching process utilises knowledge from both the model and the distance image. A window of the size of the model (or a part of it) is processed each time at every candidate position x,y of the distance image. In (Viitanen 1988) an algorithm is described that gives an estimate for the best matching rotational angle, as well as a measure of the fidelity of the match at that translational position using the best matching angle.

The matching is based on the following formulation: we denote by $F(\alpha, r, x, y)$ the distance image, and by $G(\beta, h)$ the model to be matched, both in polar coordinates. α and β are the angles with respect to the x axis, and r and h are the distances from the origin of the window where the calculation is carried out; x and y are the rectangular coordinates of the origin of the window on the scene. Both are discrete two- dimensional arrays. G( ) is a binary image with ONE's at the valid model feature points and zeros otherwise.

The estimation involves calculation of the following summation:

$$A(\alpha, x, y) = \sum_{n=1}^{N} \sum_{m=1}^{2} F(\alpha - \beta(n, m), h(n), x, y) G(\beta(n, m), h(n)) \qquad (2)$$

where N steps are taken over the valid (discrete) radial distance, and 2 model points are used in the calculation at distance n. The angle α that corresponds to the minimum value of A is taken as the best orientation of the model at position (x,y) and the minimum value itself is proportional to the average distance from the estimated correct position.

Figure 6 shows the block diagram of the CLCA in the configuration for calculating (2). Besides the logic cell array, two memories are needed. The first is used for storing the angle difference values of the steps along the 3-4 equal distance circle for every distance value of the polar coordinate representation. The second memory is used for storing the accumulated distance image values A( ) with the angle value as an address. The 'angle offset' register holds the model angle value at that distance. The minimum of A( ) and the corresponding angle are continuously updated and output as results of the calculation. As we can see from this example a computer design using CLCA's would benefit from some dual-port memory addressable by both the CLCA and the host for fast exchange of scalars, vectors, and tables.

A carefully optimised assembly language loop for this calculation took 30 cycles of 200ns on a TMS32010 signal processor giving a total time of 6000 ns. The critical part of the CLCA implementation which determines the speed of the matching is the loop that is formed by the 8 bit address counter, the RAM, the 5 bit adder, and the 5 bit latch. The 70 MHz version of the 64 cell LCA was used. The adder speed suffered from the slow carry lookahead possible on the LCA, so the worst case propagation delay from LSB in to sum out was 41 ns. We must also include the RAM update time of about 25 ns maximum from an address change using a fast device, the I/O latch and direct input delays of 20 ns maximum, and the address counter output delay at 10 ns. Adding a small safety margin, the total update time would be 100 ns. This gives a total speedup factor for this example of about 60.

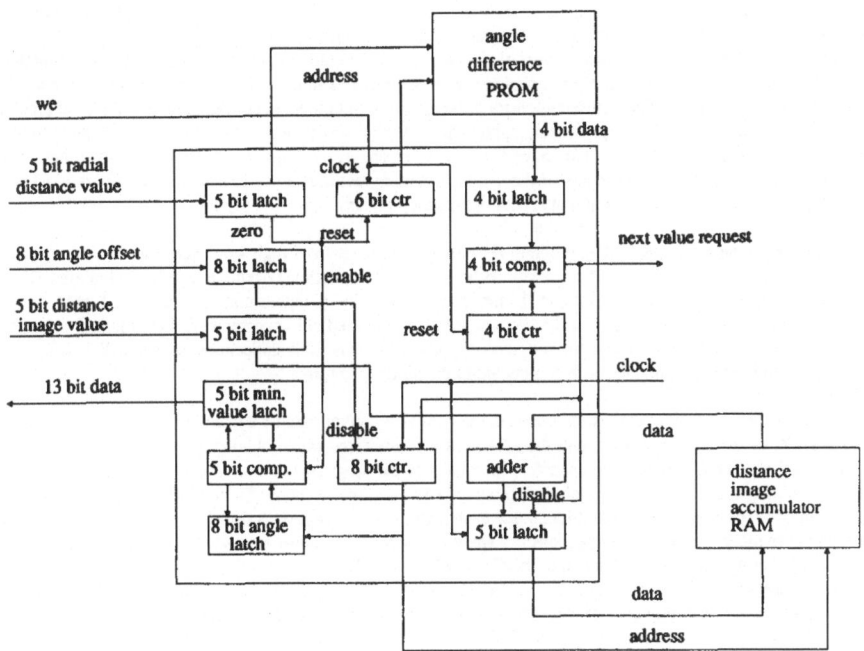

Fig. 6: The CLCA Configuration for the Matching Operation.

3.3. The Complete HCMA Calculation

We will now consider the total time for the whole operation rather than just the inner loop computation. In a typical case we might have the following time for performing a complete matching operation on one model, eg. for finding the best fitting location and the angle of rotation for the model in the image. We would use a three level pyramid, with dimensions 256 by 256, 128 by 128, and 64 by 64 at each level. The model has a size 63 by 63, with 40 valid model points, maximum of two points at each radial distance, and 24 radial steps at the lowest level, 12 at the next, and 6 at the highest pyramid level. At the highest pyramid level we would examine every third translational location, for a total trial count of 256. At the next lower levels we examine a maximum of 16 best candidate positions, and their 8 closest neighbors, and at the lowest level 4 candidates and the neighbors. So the total time at the highest level would be 100*256*2*6*256 ns = 78.6 ms. At the next level the corresponding figures are: 100*256*2*12*16*9 ns = 88.5 ms, and at the lowest level: 100*256*2*20*4*9 ns = 36.9 ms. The total time would thus be 204 milliseconds for one model. These times for the HCMA calculation are quite sufficient for use in robotics.

4. THE CLCA APPLICATION DEVELOPMENT PROCESS

In this section we will discuss the feasibility of implementing 'active' compilers for conventional high level languages which generate configuration data for CLCA's rather than normal machine instructions. These compilers are termed active because the computation is done by active computing elements (logic gates) rather than by a separate unit interpreting a passive byte stream.

Historically, many research projects have been carried out into behavioural compilation for catalogue part and silicon designs, notably the work at Carnegie Mellon University on the CMU-DA system and related projects (Thomas 1983). Recently, a highly developed system has been produced at IBM Yorktown Heights (Brayton 1986). This system features novel multi-level logic synthesis techniques and is probably the most fully engineered behavioural system available. We will model our discussion after the IBM compiler and another interesting system reported by Peng (1987). This uses Pascal as the behavioural description language and an asynchronous control strategy. The integrated development system is called CAMAD. CAMAD includes a data flow analyser that extracts the parts of the program executable in parallel.

The asynchronous control is realised as an ETPN (Extended Timed Petri Net) structure and the implementation merges the data manipulation and the control structure in the final realisation on silicon. CAMAD synthesises the control structure as centralised microprogram storage that monitors the guards of the operations and has control over the functional units (although Peng does not explicitly limit the model to consist of only one microcode engine and refers to other methods of control realisation). This kind of centralised microprogram control is not the most efficient way to realise the pipeline parallelism that is present in many image processing applications. A more distributed control strategy is dictated by the simple structure of the present CLCA models: they have logic cells that are easily usable for distributed control, but a centralised microprogram store would spend too many of the available routing facilities going to and from the operational units. Propagation delay on long control lines would also be a significant problem.

Figure 7 illustrates the proposed CLCA program development process from high level language source to configuration information. This diagram is typical of most silicon behavioural compilation systems and is modelled after Peng (1987). The process is normally split into two parts: in the first part the behavioural representation is converted into a structural one (e.g. a hierarchical netlist of gates) and in the second (sometimes termed silicon assembly) the structural representation is converted into physical layout. Tools for the second phase are fairly well understood so we will concentrate on the behavioural compilation step and take each component of the diagram in turn.

The use of a standard HLL as source is important in the hardware configuration we have in mind of a fast general purpose CPU (e.g. RISC or bit slice processor) and the CLCA as a coprocessor which obtains its configuration data via the host CPU. The 'active' compiler would then decide which parts of the program to run on the CLCA and which to run on the host by considering the execution times of both processors (taking into account CLCA configuration loading time). With present technology, only loops or parts of loops that have high enough repetition counts (say over a few hundred) would be considered for running on the CLCA coprocessor. There are many tradeoffs to be made in this part of the process: while fully automatic compilation from a language like C or PASCAL is desirable from the point of view of ease of use it can never take advantage of the full power of the CLCA. This is because the specification of the computation to be performed using a language like C is overly constrained. An obvious example of this is that a problem which only requires 5 bit precision may be coded to work on 32 bit integers in C: the 'active' compiler has no way of telling from the source code that the extra 27 bits are redundant. This problem occurs in more subtle forms as well: for example, a C programmer might specify a quicksort algorithm where a hardware implementation would be faster using a distributed bubblesort. It is sometimes impossible for the programmer to write efficient code without knowing which processor it will run on. For these reasons some degree of manual control over what parts of the program get implemented on the CLCA and more hardware oriented specification languages may be desirable.

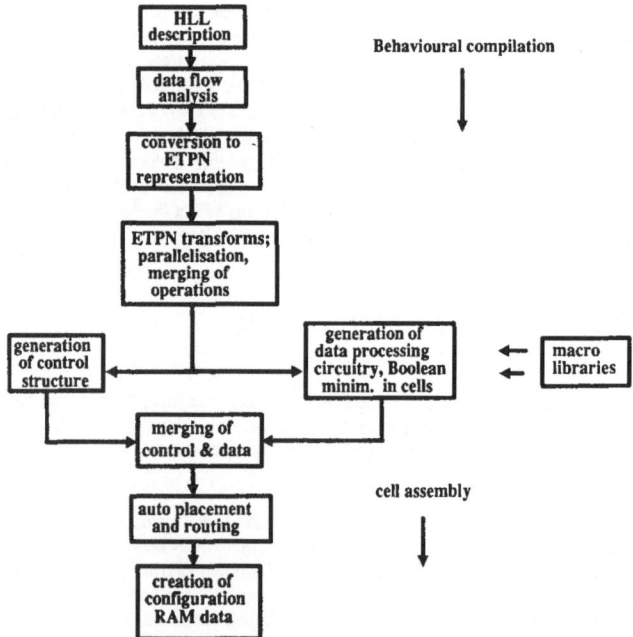

Fig. 7: The proposed CLCA development process

In order to obtain reasonably efficient hardware realisations it is often necessary that many operations in the data-flow graph be performed by a single physical unit. There are two steps in figure 7, where this merging of operation can be done. The first comes, when the sequential program is transformed to the ETPN description. This utilises the control structure of the Petri net and compresses the straight line sections of the program with no external data dependencies to single operational units. The second merging step comes with the Boolean minimisation. Here, additions by a constant and similar ALU-only operations can be merged with the following operation. Programmable logic circuitry handles several variables at a time providing another useful speedup over traditional processors. A third merging phase may also be desirable where multiple units with data-dependancies are merged. Naturally, this reduces the amount of parallelism present and potentially reduces speed but it can also drastically cut down the amount of hardware in the implementation and the more compact unit could well be faster because of reduced routing delay. This merging phase can be done by manual intervention (perhaps using graphical tools to manipulate the ETPN)) or automatically using 'expert' systems or other heuristic techniques.

Our example of searching for the minimum of five words after adding a constant to each one is a good illustration of these optimisations. Several comparison operations can be formed into a single Boolean expression over all the five input words. The expression can be optimised at compilation time and the resulting logic function can be assigned to CLCA cells. The efficient automatic realisation of such Boolean expressions has only recently become feasible with advances in multi-level logic synthesis techniques (Brayton 1986). A sequential program for this operation would take at most two words at a time for processing, and consume several cycles for each suboperation. A parallel processor implementation would distribute partial comparisons to different processors and thus introduce a major communication overhead.

After the optimisation of the Boolean expression, we have a complete structural description of the design in terms of a net-list of logical units capable of being implemented by the primitive cells in the target array. The next steps in the process could be termed cell-assembly and consist of floorplanning, global routing and local placement and routing of functional cells. Floorplanning and global routing are high level processes applied to large hierachical structures (e.g. our five way comparitor) within the structural description. Given this high level plan detailed placement and routing within the large sub-structures and channel routing to connect them up into the final design is also required. Usually, heavy computation is needed in automatic placement and routing - techniques such as simulated annealing are often used in the floorplanning step to ensure good results. Good placement of the computational units is very important since excessive delays will result from long wires. Minimising the computation involved is important in a system like ours where frequent recompilations will occur as the program is developed. It is at this point that the advantages of the CAL architecture become apparent:

1. The architecture scales transparently over chip boundaries. Realistic size systems will never fit on a single programmable chip given the overhead of the configuration memory thus it is essential that multi-chip systems be supported. Architectures which use 'special-purpose' input-output blocks are unsuitable for large systems since single units (for example large logic blocks) in user designs will be hard to split over multiple chips.

2. The architecture is completely symmetrical: this is important when floorplanning large systems since it allows large subunits to be rotated and reflected to obtain a dense packing. Algorithms for floorplanning silicon designs take advantage of this flexibility.

3. There is a single resource in the system. Large units are built up by composing small resources rather than breaking up large ones. One area where this is particularly important is channel routing. In a large design channels with as many as 20 tracks are likely to occur: in the CAL architecture there is potentially no limit to the number of tracks in a channel, although each additional track may require an additional line of cells (often two tracks can be fitted in a single line of cells). In an architecture such as the LCA with special fixed width wiring channel resources problems occur when that width is exhausted; possibly resulting in routing failure or grossly inefficient use of resources.

4. The routing model is simple and safe. Routing in a CAL design is easy, although potentially quite slow: there is only one class of routing resource so there is no question about which is the most suitable for a given signal. All paths are fully buffered so there is no need to worry about logic levels. These factors are important because they allow the use of standard 'channel routing' algorithms which can produce high quality routing relatively quickly.

More complex architectures can still be routed automatically using 'maze' routers but the results are likely to be worse and computation time significantly longer.

At its present stage of development the CAD tools for the CAL system are fairly primitive because of the limited manpower available for their development: channel routing, logic synthesis and tools to support manual design have been written. It is intended that support for CAL should eventually be integrated into an existing silicon compiler since many existing programs for functions like floorplanning, global routing and structural language input could be used unchanged. Thus designs could proceed from a single source format into either a silicon or a configurable logic implementation. This capability is important since one of the target application areas for CAL's is in Application Specific IC prototyping (Kean 1989).

The tools that are available for application development with the commercial LCA families consist of a logic cell editor, a macro library, a simulator, an autorouter and an autoplacement utility. At present design using these tools normally requires manual intervention to solve routing problems so they are not really suitable for use as a 'cell assembler' back end to an active compiler.

5. DISCUSSION: FUTURE GATE-LEVEL DYNAMICALLY RECONFIGURABLE PROCESSORS

The techniques discussed in the last section can provide significant speedups in many operations, however, to take advantage of them significant work will be required on both the active compiler system and the architecture of the CLCA's. New programming languages closer to current hardware description languages may also be required to make full use of the configurable structure. In the context of self-timed control structures use of an extended form of OCCAM with word length specification for operations is worth considering, especially if a transputer is used as the host computer.

The CLCA has four main speed advantages over normal processors:

1. There is no instruction fetch or instruction decode. In a CLCA the 'instruction' is the configuration information and it is fixed before processing starts. This provides a considerable speed advantage at the expense of requiring much more processing hardware - if two operations need to be performed then in effect we have two ALU's rather than time sharing the same one. Naturally, this poses a severe limitation on the complexity of the code which can be implemented on CLCA's. Small sequences of 'inner-loop' instructions extracted from HLL programs or simple calculations performed in systolic algorithms are attractive for CLCA implementation.

2. The hardware performs exactly the calculation required. In most processors computation cycles are synchronised to a clock set for a 'worst-case' instruction (e.g. carry propagation in a 32 bit adder), in a CLCA simple computations take only a few gate delays. This flexibility extends to the width of the operation and the number of operands used. Often several 'ALU' operations can be merged into one complex Boolean expression and implemented directly in the CLCA. In a systolic algorithm implemented on a fixed size CLCA all the silicon can be used effectively - if the computation requires relatively few cells then more Processing Elements (PE's) can be implemented on the array. Compare this with a conventional parallel computer where the number of PE's is fixed in advance.

3. Pipelining. In many of the inner-loop and systolic computations performed by CLCA's pipelining can be implemented very naturally. This is especially effective on the CAL architecture where pipeline registers use only a single small cell and can often make use of function units in cells which would otherwise be used just for routing. Pipelining can often make up for the slow propagation delays along the programmable interconnect. Reconfigurable pipelines have difficulty in making efficient use of fixed operational units, because the different tasks implemented may require different resources along the pipeline. Solutions like sharing of operational units or adding non-compute delays have not been found to be effective (Hwang 1984). CLCA's can solve these problems by building the resources on demand.

4. Routing Flexibility. Many calculations involve manipulations which can be accomplished by wiring rather than active circuitry. Examples are swapping registers, extracting bit fields and manipulating masks. Most conventional processors perform these operations extremely inefficiently because of their long word lengths. Often a problem specific routing structure can eliminate a large amount of redundant computation.

5. The advantages of asynchronous processing have been pointed out in recent works on VLSI design, for instance by Peng (1987), emphasising that the problems in large synchronous VLSI designs with large clock skews that limit the maximum clock frequency can be solved using asynchronous structures. A research computer designed for asynchronous processing is described by Nowak (1987), showing significant speed increases with only a few processing units. Asynchronous, self timed structures could be a potential choice to the control structure of a CLCA computer.

The examples given in this paper give hints of the potential of CLCA's to speedup inner loop code. We could program sections of 29 to 37 instructions on the smallest 64-cell device with 5 bit data obtaining a speedup factor of 23 to 30 in one case and a speedup factor of 60 in the another over a reasonably powerful microprocessor.

For wider use, at least 16 bit processing, and loops with more operations will be needed. The largest available LCA has roughly ten times the capacity of the device used in this paper so the extension in the wordlength can be achieved although use of bit-serial arithmetic may be preferable to having wide arithmetic units because of routing delays in carry chains. CAL can take this even further by allowing a board full of configurable devices to be used allowing implementation of large systems. Slow programming will always be a problem although the bottleneck can be expected to move from the CLCA's themselves to the rate at which the host processor can supply the configuration data. CLCA acceleration will always be most suitable for programs which require large numbers of repetitive operations so that the configuration data can stay constant for long periods.

Two other examples of the application of CAL to carefully chosen problems in (Kean 1989, Gray 1989) are also worth mentioning. In the first a DES encryptor is built from a large (about 8000 cells) CAL array, this computation is inherently bit level and very amenable to pipelining. Using a ten stage pipeline within the critical f-box section of the DES algorithm a performance of 500,000 encryptions per second can be obtained. This is as fast as the best DES custom chips (Verbauwhede 1988): optimised DES software running on conventional processors is about 1000 times slower (mainly because the bit scrambling done using wiring channels in the hardware versions is very hard to implement efficiently on a conventional processor). In the second example CAL is used to provide the computation in a cellular-automaton model for fluid flow simulation (Salem 1986). Using a system with 26 large 64x64 cell CAL arrays providing 128 pipelined update processors supported by a large dynamic RAM memory to keep the computation unit supplied with data performance of the same order as a Connection Machine multiprocessor, reported by Wayner (1988), is predicted. These figures give an indication of the raw power of the configurable logic approach in appropriate problem domains. The DES design required careful manual layout and the fluid-flow design requires a special purpose memory system to supply the data quickly enough so this kind of performance is not to be expected from the system described here.

6. CONCLUSIONS AND FUTURE WORK

The application areas of CLCA's are obviously those, where relatively simple operations are performed over large data sets. These kinds of task are found in image processing, computer graphics, statistical simulation and finite element methods. With appropriate compiler technology we would hope to obtain speed-up factors of roughly 20 times using fairly small CLCA arrays with normal procedural programming languages. With a large manual design effort on a particular problem much greater speedups are achievable.

More work is needed in future on the development of better tools for automatic configuration program generation and new and better structures for the configurable logic cell arrays. Better methods of expressing the newly available forms of parallelism are also needed in the source languages.

7. REFERENCES

Algotronix (1988) CAL1024 Preliminary Data Sheet, Edinburgh UK, 1988.

Borgefors G (1986) On Hierarchical Edge Matching in Digital Images Using Distance Transformations, dissertation TRITA-NA-8602, The Royal Institute of Technology, Stockholm, Sweden 1986. (To appear in IEEE PAMI)

Brayton RK, Camposano R, DeMicheli G, Otten RHJM, van Eijndhoven J (1986) The Yorktown Silicon Compiler System, Technical Report RC12500, IBM T.J. Watson Research Centre, Yorktown Heights.

Davis R, Thomas D (1984) Systolic array chip matches the pace of high-speed processing. Electronic Design, October 31, 1984, pp. 207 - 218.

Fountain TJ (1983) The development of the CLIP7 image processing system, Pattern Recognition Letters 1 pp. 331 - 339, North-Holland.

Gray JP, and Kean TA (1989), Configurable Hardware: A New Paradigm for Computation, to appear in Proc. Decennial Caltech Conference on VLSI, (1989).

Hillis WD (1985) The Connection Machine, MIT Press, Cambridge, Mass., U.S.A.

Hwang K, and Briggs FA (1984) Computer architecture and parallel processing, McGraw-Hill, New York, U.S.A. pp. 208...212.

Kean T (1989) Configurable Logic: A Dynamically Programmable Cellular Architecture and its VLSI Implementation, PhD Thesis, University of Edinburgh, Dept. of Computer Science.

Nowak L (1987) SAMP: A General Purpose Processor Based on a self-Timed VLIW Structure, Proc. 1987 Conference on Architectural Support for Programming Languages, pp. 32-39.

Peng Z (1987) A Formal Methodology for Automated Synthesis of VLSI Systems, Linkoping Studies in Science and Technology, Dissertation No 170, Dept. of Computer and Information Science, Linkoping University, S-58183 Linkoping, Sweden.

Salem JB, Wolfram S (1986) Thermodynamics and Hydrodynamics with Cellular Automata. Theory and Applications of Cellular Automata, Paper 3.10, pp 362--365. World Scientific Publishing Co., Singapore.

Sternberg SR (1985) Computer architectures specialised for mathematical morphology, in "Algorithmically Specialized Parallel Computers", ed. by L.Snyder et al. Academic Press, pp. 169 - 176.

Thomas D, Hitchcock III C, Kowalski T, Rajan J, Walker R (1983) Automatic Data Path Synthesis, IEEE Computer, December, pp. 59 - 79.

Verbauwhede I, Hoornaert F, Vandewalle J (1988) Security and Performance Optimisation of a new DES Data Encryption Chip. IEEE Journal of Solid State Circuits, Vol 23, pp 647--656, June 1988.

Viitanen J, Hanninen P, Saarela R, Saarinen J (1987) Hierarchical pattern matching with an efficient method for estimating rotations. Proc. of the IEEE Industrial Electronics Society conference IECON'87, Cambridge, Massachusetts, U.S.A. 3-6 November.

Viitanen J, Hanninen P, Saarela R, Saarinen J (1988) An Efficient Method for Image Pattern Matching, Proc. of The International Conference on Parallel Processing for Computer Vision And Display, Leeds, U.K. 12-15 January 1988.

Wayner P (1988) Modelling Chaos, Byte, May 1988, pp. 253 - 258.

Xilinx (1986) The Programmable Gate Array Design Handbook, Xilinx Inc. U.S.A. 1986.

Jouko O. Viitanen
Was born in Orivesi, Finland, on October 13, 1954. He received the M.S. degree in electronics in 1978, and the Lic.Tech. degree in computer science in 1984 from Tampere University of Technology. He is currently a Senior Researcher at the Research Institute for Information Technology, Tampere University of Technology. His research interests are image processing, image processor and computer architecture.

Tom Kean has recently completed his Doctoral thesis within the Computer Science Department of Edinburgh University. His research interests are in dynamically programmable logic arrays, VLSI design and silicon compilation. He received the BSc degree in computer science with first class honours from Edinburgh University in 1985.

Present address:
   SARI Project,
   Department of Electrical Enginnering,
   University of Edinburgh,
   The King's Buildings,
   Mayfield Road,
   Edinburgh, UK.

Satellite Images in Raster Graphics: A New Methodology

S. Pham

ABSTRACT: We introduce a new methodology: **line-to-line-conformal mapping**, which applies raster graphics to reproduce digitized satellite images. We discuss five different phases: 1) receiving images, 2) clipping images in the area of interest, 3) correcting distortions, 4) projecting images into different geometries, and 5) transmitting images to screen. We present an algorithm to map a satellite image scanline to a curve which is represented as a chain code of directions; provide a complete solution for reconstructing multiple images in real-time; and pose some new problems.

Categories and Subject Descriptors: I.3.3 [Computer Graphics]: Picture/Image Generation; F.2.2 [Analysis of Algorithm and Problem Complexity]: Geometric Problems and Computations.

Key words: secant polar stereographic, resolution perspective, pixel of angle size, distortion, control point, clipping, forward and backward bilinear interpolation, scanline, line to line conformal mapping, pitch, roll, yaw, skew, digital straight lines, chain codes of directions.

1. INTRODUCTION

The Geostationary Operational Environmental Satellite (GOES) is equipped with a camera which rotates on an axis parallel to the axis of the earth. The coverage of the satellite is fixed and has a window which faces the earth. This window is about 20 degrees by 20 degrees, allowing the camera to view the earth. On each rotation, the camera scans a 15000 km x 1km strip of the earth from west to east and registers the 15000 intensities of 1km² areas. One km on the earth subtends 20 micro-radians at the camera; 15000 times 20 micro-radians is about 20 degrees, the size of the window. After each scan, it shifts downward 20 micro-radians for the next rotation. It takes about 6400 scanlines to cover a hemisphere. (See Figure 1).

Images produced after correction for distortion, are used to chart the movement of clouds and hence to predict weather (Smith and Phillips, 1972). Many research papers have studied GOES images, such as Suomi and Parent (1968), Hubert (1969), Doolittle et al(1970), and Leese et al (1971). Satellite images need to be displayed in real time for navigators and air plane pilots to see atmospheric conditions in their areas, especially during storms. Images produced by different sensors at different frequencies provide different information; e. g., infrared scans show heat patterns on earth and can be interpreted to reveal population patterns, which can be compared with those of prior years to identify changes. Consecutive images can be superimposed and compared to identify new features or objects that have moved, after correction for distortion by the satellite.

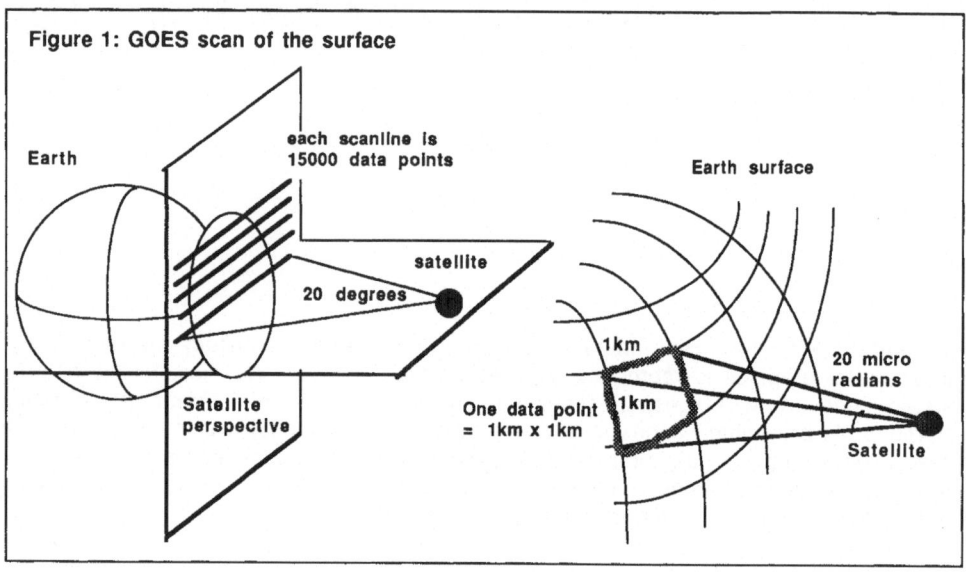

Figure 1: GOES scan of the surface

Our goal is to build a system that receives satellite data and constructs the images. The system should be built to satisfy time constraints, e.g., that the image should be constructed within 60 seconds after the last bit is received. Our system also aims to correct the distortions caused by imperfections in the orientation of the satellite. Various types of these first-degree distortions are discussed later. Moreover, we may wish to view partial areas of a complete image, and view these areas using different projection geometries and resolutions. The number of images to be produced for each raw satellite image, along with the projection geometries, terrestrial areas of interest, must be given in advance. Two suggested projection geometries are 1) satellite perspective(SP) and 2) secant polar stereographic perspective(SPSP). (See Figure 2).

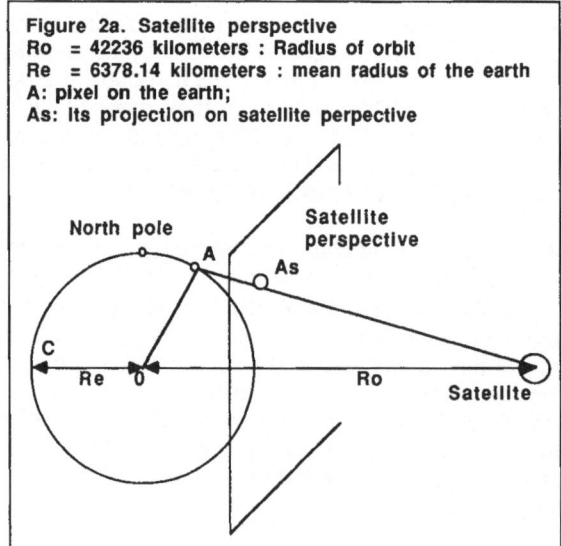

Figure 2a. Satellite perspective
Ro = 42236 kilometers : Radius of orbit
Re = 6378.14 kilometers : mean radius of the earth
A: pixel on the earth;
As: Its projection on satellite perpective

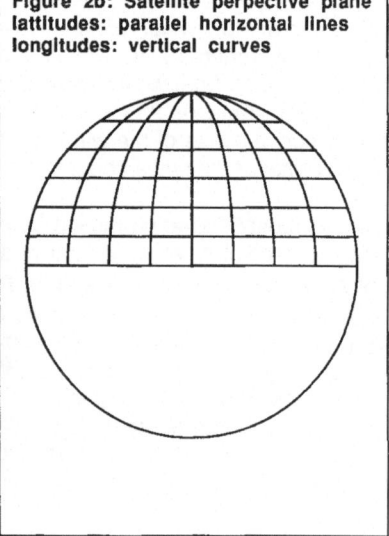

Figure 2b: Satellite perpective plane
lattitudes: parallel horizontal lines
longitudes: vertical curves

In the rest of this section, we define the term *pixel*, introduce the two above-mentioned projection geometries, discuss all possible types of first degree distortion and explain how they arise, relate raster graphics to satellite images, and finally provide the organization of the rest of this paper.

Figure 2c :Secant polar stereographic perspective A: a pixel on the earth; Ap: its projection on SPSP N: North pole; S: South pole	Figure 2d: SPSP plane Lattitudes as the concentric circles Longitudes as the concentric lines ABCD is the area viewed by satellite
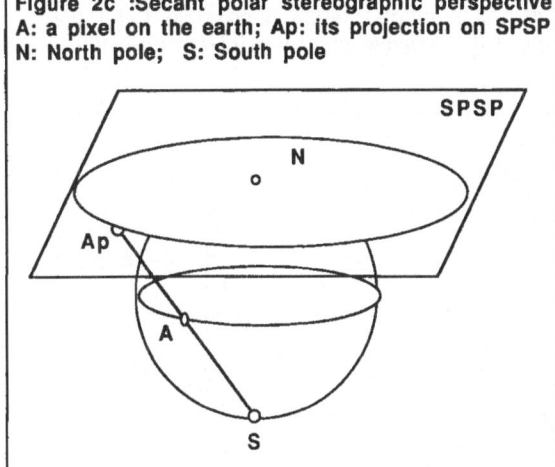	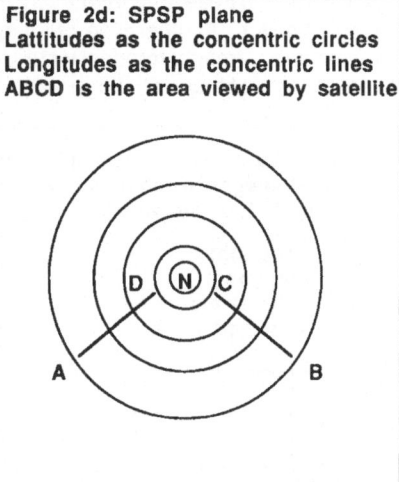

1.1 Definition of Pixel:

A pixel is defined as the smallest unit of area distinguishable by the camera. In this case the size is approximately of 1 km x 1 km. We can look at the size of a pixel by angles which are the horizontal rotation angle and the vertical rotation angle of the camera, which is 20 microradians x 20 microradians. These angles are derived from the satellite spin rate to assure that the angle widths are held at a constant value. Therefore the linear size of a pixel may vary due to the curvature of the earth. For example if the camera points orthogonal to the midwest of the USA, then the pixel size is about 0.9 km x 0.9 km, while the pixel size at the east and west coasts is about 1.1 km x 1.1 km. Throughout the paper, what call we pixel size refers to the constant angle size.

1.2. Definitions of two Perspectives

a) Satellite perspective(SP): Consider the satellite as a projection point. SP is the projection of the earth on the plane which is tangent to the earth's sphere at the orthogonal point of the satellite to the earth. In other word, SP is the image which is viewed from the satellite. (Figures 2a and 2b).

b) Secant polar stereographic perspective(SPSP): In this perspective the projection point is the south pole, the projection plane is the plane parallel to the equator and tangent at the north pole. The SPSP is the projection of the surface of the northern hemisphere on the projection plane. In this case the longitudes and latitudes are projected to be radial lines and concentric circles respectively. Since the satellite can only view one side of the earth, the SPSP image is pie-shaped.   Because we choose one pole as the projection point, only a hemisphere is projected. To project the whole earth, we need two images, one for the northern hemisphere as mentioned above and the other for the southern hemisphere with the north pole as projection point, and the plane tangent at the south pole as projection plane. (Figures 2c and 2d). Notices that a pixel from the equator is "stretched" to fit the projection, while one near the pole is compressed.

1.3 Types of Distortions:

Imperfections in the orientation of the satellite are responsible for three types of first-degree image distortions: 1) vertical displacement, 2) horizontal displacement, and 3) skew displacement. These distortions are correctable if the actual orientation of the vehicle is precisely known. Another type of image distortion, image rotation, is possible, but in practice never occurs. Image rotation would occur if the satellite spin axis is rotated in the plane normal to the sighting axis. (Figure 3)

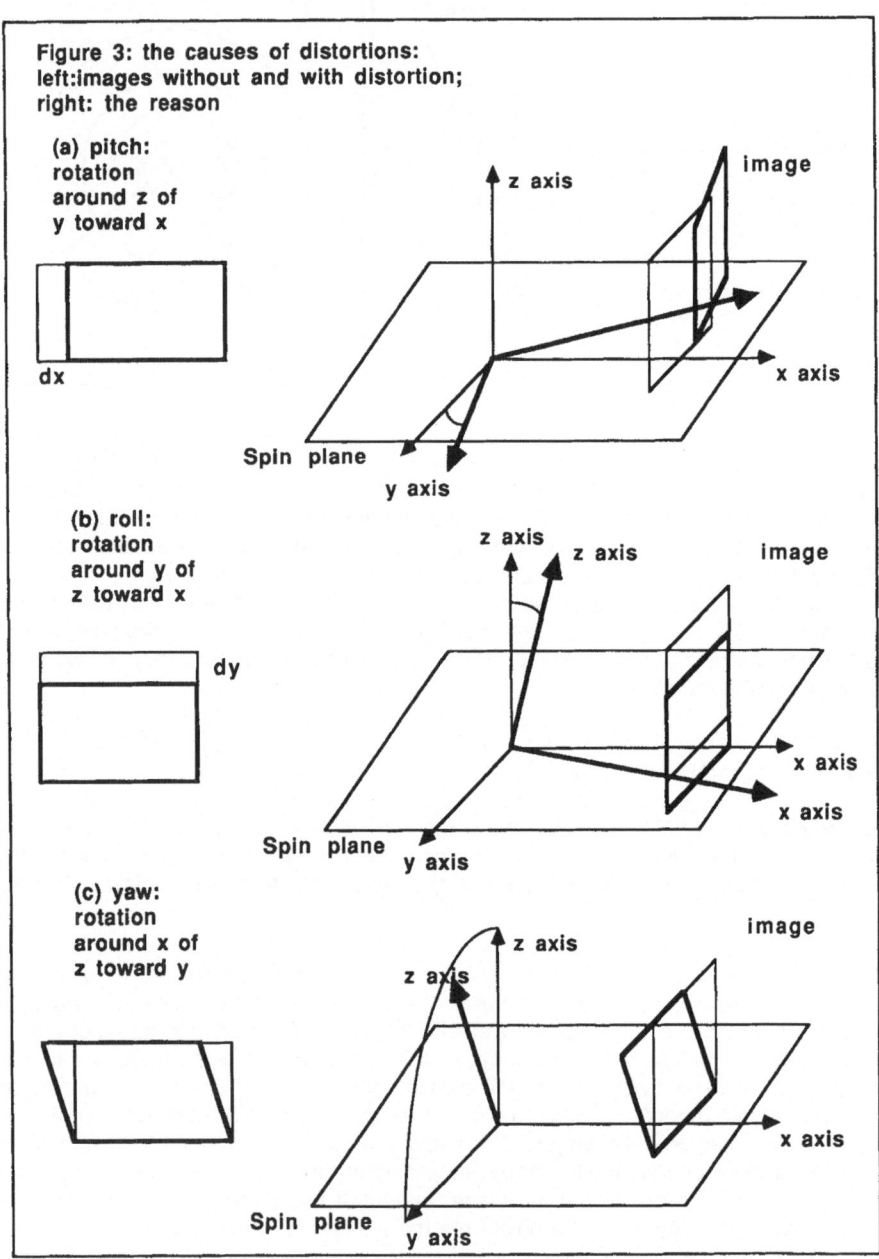

Figure 3: the causes of distortions:
left:images without and with distortion;
right: the reason

(a) pitch: rotation around z of y toward x

(b) roll: rotation around y of z toward x

(c) yaw: rotation around x of z toward y

1.4 Why we Have these Distortions:

We choose a system of xyz coordinates for the satellite as follows: The x axis passes through the center of the earth and the satellite, the z axis parallels the axis of the earth (south pole to the north pole), and the y axis is orthogonal to the xz plane. Three types of distortion can be classified:

(a)pitch: In this case the distortion is caused by a rotation around the z axis of the y axis toward the x axis. The spin plane which is the one containing the equator is fixed, but it is rotated around the z axis; therefore the image is moved to the left if the y axis is tilted to the x axis counterclockwise and to the right if clockwise. The displacement is horizontal and measured by dx.

(b)roll: In this case the distortion is caused by a rotation around the y axis of the z axis toward the x axis. The spin plane is tilted around the y axis. Therefore the image is moved down if the z axis is rotated toward the x axis counterclockwise and up if clockwise. The displacement is vertical and measured by dy.

(c)yaw: In this case the distortion is caused by a rotation around the x axis of the z axis toward the y axis. The spin plane is fixed and the camera is stepped down along the tilted z axis, therefore the shape of the image is distorted to be an parallelogram. The displacement is skew and measured by ds.

1.5. Raster Graphics and Satellite Images:

In raster graphics, a pixel is defined as a point where a beam strikes a screen. The size of a pixel is never considered. Resolution is the number of pixels on the screen. A line on the screen is digitally represented as a sequence of pixels. A line can be defined as straight if its pixels satisfy either Freeman's criteria or Rosenfeld's chord property. In general the straight digital lines can be obtained by any method of digitization of real straight lines. Much research has investigated the properties, the characteristics, and the classes of digital lines. Curves sometimes are called lines, not necessarily straight, and circles have also been investigated in the past decade.
In satellite images, pixels are also defined as points on a screen as mentioned above. The size of pixel can be viewed as angles for the width and the length of the rectangular area seen from a point of view (e.g., the satellite). Each area viewed by the sensor is represented as a pixel on the screen. Variations in the intensities of the areas read by a sensor can be represented by variations in the brightness or color of pixels on the screen. For the satellite perspective, longitudes are the parallel nearly straight digital lines on the screen and latitudes are digital curves. For the SPSP, longitudes are digital circles concentric around the north pole pixel, and longitudes are digital straight lines which converge at the north pole pixel. With the above comparison, raster graphics theory can be applied to construct satellite images.

1.6. Organization of this Paper.

In the remainder of this paper we will
    Section 2: survey the existing methodologies for reconstructing satellite images,
    Section 3: introduce a new methodology which applies raster graphics to satellite image problems,

Section 4: create a logical solution of a system to receive satellite image, clip it, transform it, and then transmit it,

Section 5: extend the solution for multiple images, and

Section 6: pose new problems.

New results are included in Sections 3-6.

2. SURVEY OF EXISTING METHODOLOGIES:

In this section , we discuss three approaches: Brute-force, forward bilinear interpolation, and reverse bilinear interpolation. The first approach is a clear and obvious approach but it requires large memory and excessive CPU time to process the satellite image in the course of image construction, and the two later ones provide an approximation of the images to avoid the memory and CPU problems of the first one, but they end up with poor image quality and open some unsolved problems of missing pixels and estimating errors. In the last two approaches, the concept of control points and pixels are introduced. (See Figure 4 for the forward and reverse bilinear interpolation approaches).

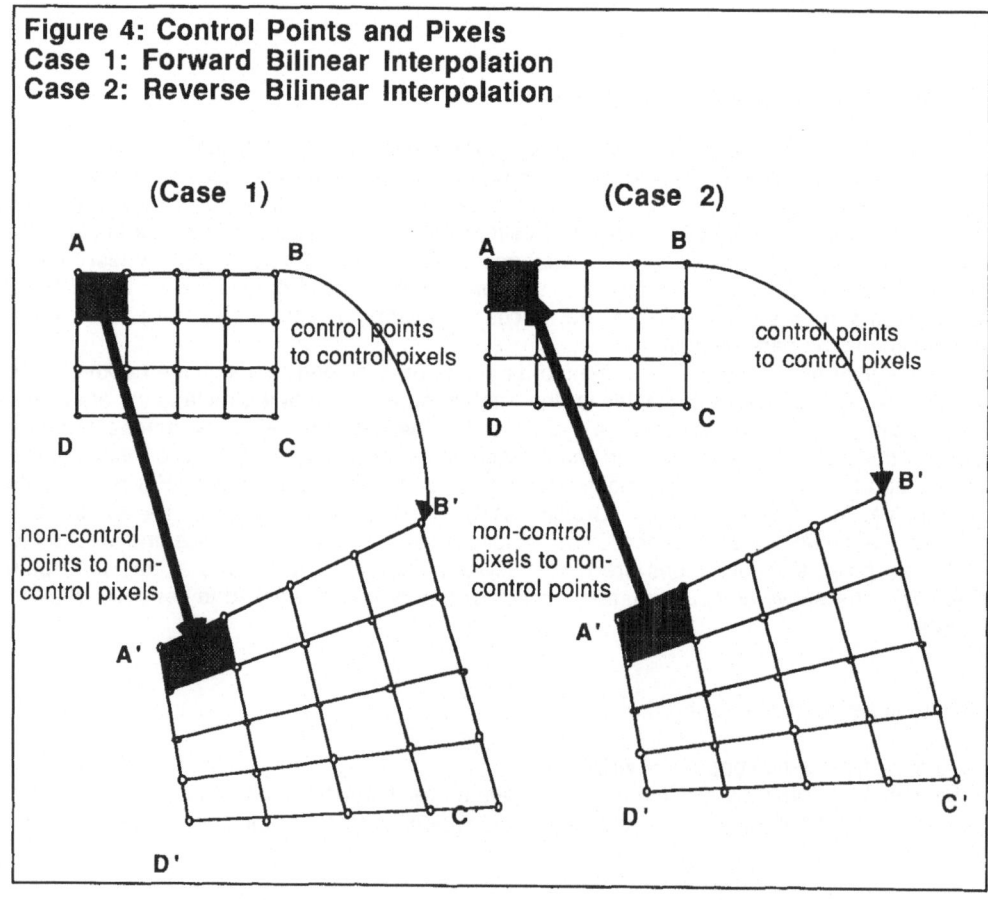

Figure 4: Control Points and Pixels
Case 1: Forward Bilinear Interpolation
Case 2: Reverse Bilinear Interpolation

2.1. Brute-force Approach:

This approach can be forward or reverse. In the forward case, each satellite-generated intensity reading datum is mapped to a pixel in the output image by a coordinate transformation. In the reverse case, for each pixel in the output image, we find the satellite datum that produced it. Initially, it was felt that image warping (also known as rubber sheeting), pixel selection, and coordinate transformation should be performed on a pixel by pixel basis from the input or stretched satellite data. An analysis of the processing requirements for this approach indicates that approximately 700 high level instructions, including a number of floating point trigonometric operations, are required for each processed pixel. As a result, an array processor is required to perform the task. This brute force approach provides error-free output products, but it requires high costs for software development and complex hardware. So this approach is rejected.

2.2. Bilinear Interpolation Approach.

To reduce the high costs of the brute force approach, we consider the bilinear interpolation approach, which is a modification of the brute force approach. First, only a subset of satellite data is selected to be processed in a manner similar to that of the forward brute-force approach. We call these *control points*. In other words, the forward brute-force approach determines the pixels in the output image corresponding to the selected control points. After the control points are assigned and their corresponding control pixels are found, the points between control points and the pixels between control pixels are interpolated linearly in one of two different ways:

a) Forward bilinear interpolation: In this case, each point is positioned linearly, based on the surrounding control points. As a result, a set of parameters is found. These parameters are used to locate the pixels for the non-control points. Consequently this method might create vacant pixels that no points map into.

b) Reverse bilinear interpolation: In this case, each pixel is positioned first, based on the surrounding control pixels. As a result, a set of parameters is found. These parameters are used to locate the points corresponding to the non-control pixels. By its nature, this method will not create any vacant pixels.

In both cases the density of control points is typically selected so that the linear interpolation errors do not adversely affect the image pixel position accuracy. This means that there is a trade-off between control point density and pixel position accuracy.

Time and memory requirement problem:
Bilinear interpolation is currently in used by the National Oceanalgraphic and Atmospheric Administration at Boulder, Colorado, and it produces images of acceptable quality. However, it suffers some problems. If forward bilinear interpolation is used, output images will have some vacant pixels, and locating the vacant pixels is still an open problem. Therefore the forward bilinear interpolation has been rejected. If reverse bilinear interpolation is used, either very large random access memories or rapid disk accesses are required. This is because most of the raw satellite data must be buffered for processing. Analysis of the core algorithm revealed that approximately 44 Pascal-like instructions, including some floating point, are required to process each pixel, and approximately 20 minutes to produce the output image. In summary, both methods of bilinear interpolation do not meet the requirements. The forward one faces us with a difficult open problem and the reverse one requires a large memory and cannot meet the real-time requirement for product generation.

3. RASTER GRAPHIC AND SATELLITE IMAGES: A NEW METHODOLOGY:

In this section we introduce a new methodology which uses the concepts of raster graphics to construct images. First, some terms are defined; second, a name for the methodology is selected; third, types of distortions and methods of correcting them by this methodology are introduced; fourth, an algorithm for the core part is discussed; and finally, a comparison with other methodologies is presented.

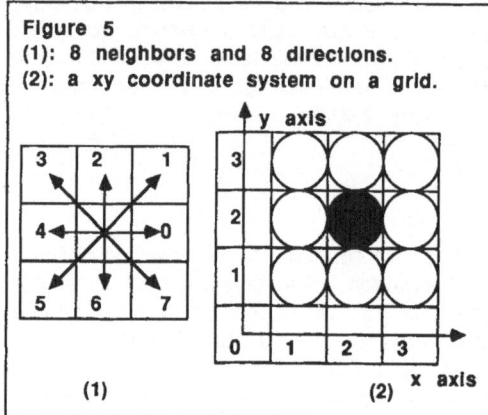

Figure 5
(1): 8 neighbors and 8 directions.
(2): a xy coordinate system on a grid.

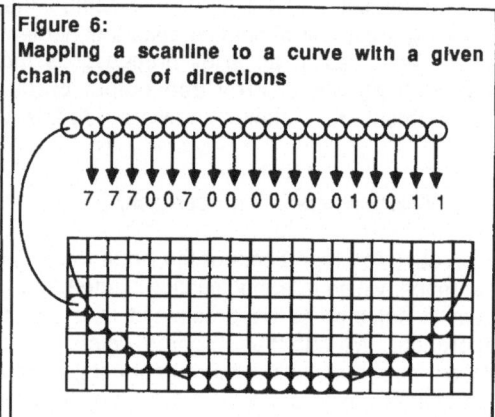

Figure 6:
Mapping a scanline to a curve with a given chain code of directions

3.1 Definitions.

In raster graphics a system of integer xy coordinates is called a *grid*, and a point with integer coordinates is called a *pixel* or *digital point*. Let (i, j) be a pixel. The eight pixels (i+1, j), (i+1, j+1), (i, j+1), (i-1, j+1), (i-1, j), (i-1, j-1), (i, j-1), and (i+1, j-1) are called the eight *neighbors* of (i, j). They are labeled counterclockwise 0, 1, 2, 3, 4, 5, 6, and 7, respectively. (Figure 5). These same numbers can be used to name the *directions* that, say, a beam or plotter must move from one pixel to one of the eight neighbors.

A set of pixels is called a *digital curve* or *digital arc* if for every pixel except two (the first and last) in the set, has exactly two of its neighbors in the set. The first and last pixels have only one of its neighbors in the set.

A digital curve or arc can be represented as a sequence of directions as follows: select the starting pixel which is one of the two pixels having only one neighbor. Identify the neighbor of the starting pixel and record the relative direction number 0-7. From this neighboring pixel, identify its unselected neighbor and record its direction number. (We note that one of its two neighbors is the starting pixel.) From this new neighbor, identify its unselected neighbor and so on until the ending pixel is found. The process is similar to tracing the links of a chain until one reaches the last link. Therefore, the sequence of directions of a digital curve or arc is called a *chain code*. Given the starting pixel, a chain code is an equivalent representation of digital curve or arc.

Digital straight lines:
Suppose a real straight line is drawn by pencil and ruler on a grid. To digitize this real straight line is to find a set of closest pixels to the real straight line, that forms a digital arc; this arc is called a digital straight line.

The importance of straightness has been studied extensively by Kim (1982) and Kim and Rosenfeld (1982), and numerous authors have studied the equivalent characterizations for straightness and related properties (Arcelli and Massaroti, 1975; Bresenham, 1965; Pfaltz and Rosenfeld, 1967; and Rosenfeld, 1974, 1969.) Algorithms for these characterizations have also been studied (Brons, 1974; Chang, 1971; Wu, 1982). In general, there are two main topics in raster graphics: one is to generate the digital objects and the other is to recognize or characterize them. For objects such as digital straight lines, the generation can be approached algebraically by the linear property of the lines (Pham, 1986), analytically (Dorst and Smeulders, 1984), or approximately by the method of rounding-off (Bresenham, 1965). Recognizing a line to be straight is to verify that its chain code satisfies the Freman's criteria or the Chord properties. Hence, it leads to complex algorithms (Brons, 1974; Chang, 1971; Wu, 1982). To reduce the complexity of the algorithms, a relaxation of the straigtness criteria is introduced (Pham, 1986). The idea is to determine the position of the chain code in the area bounded by two digital straight lines. Because generating digital straight lines is quite simple, the determination of their chain codes is straightforward, but an arbitrary chain code's being in the area does not guarantee its straightness.

Digital circles:
Digital circles are the digital images of real circles. Each digital circle can be represented by a chain code of directions. A necessary and sufficient condition for a given chain code to be a digital circle provided that the center is given was investigated by Nakamura and Aizawa (1984). Many algorithms to generate circles were studied by Suenaga *et al* (1979), Bresenham (1977), Kulpa (1979), Doros(1979), Danielson(1978), Kulpla and Doros (1981), Horn (1976). The chain codes of circles can have all 8 possible directions. If the circle is divided into 8 different equal arcs, then each segment contains at most two different directions. For example, the segment in the region of 0-45 degree has the directions 2 and 3. Moreover the circle is symmetric around any line passing through its center (in particular to the vertical, horizontal and ±45⁰ diagonal lines. So the circle can be generated from any one of the eight segments mentioned above.

3.2 Naming the New Methodology: Line-to-Line Conformal Mapping (LLCM).

A satellite camera sweeps from west to east when rotating clockwise, a sequence of intensities of areas of 1 kilometer square are collected, and the satellite transmits it to a station down on earth. This sequence produces one *scanline*. A system in the receiving station corrects it if necessary, transforms it to the appropriate geometry(SPSP), and transmits it to a display system. Each scanline is transformed to either a digital straight line for SP or a digital circle for SPSP. Because the transforming step preserves the topology of the image and all steps are processed in units of a scanline, we call this method line to line conformal mapping. Other methods mentioned earlier have the same steps of receiving, correcting, transforming, and transmitting, but these steps process different units. For example, the brute force approach processes pixels, and the bilinear interpolation approach processes control pixels and approximates other pixels from surrounding control pixels. The brute-force approach can process a pixel immediately after receiving it while the bilinear interpolation approach can only be used after the surrounding control points are received, so that it can only work after a number of scanlines are received. This number is increased if there are only a few are control pixels and decreased if there are more; the case that all pixels are control pixels is just the brute-force approach. Our LLCM approach can begin processing after receiving one scanline.

Here we summarize all approaches in the following table:

TABLE: **Comparison of four different approaches**

Approach	Mapping unit	Method of correction/Error
LLCM	scanline to digital arc	dx, dy, ds; and error-free

Forward Bilinear Interpolation	control points to control pixels; areas between control points to areas between control pixels	geometric transformation; error on non-control pixels due to the approximation
Reverse Bilinear Interpolation	control points to control pixels; areas between control pixels to areas between control points	geometric transformation; error on non-control pixels due to the approximation
Brute-force	data point to pixel	geometric transformation; error-free

3.3 Correcting Distortions Using LLCM

As we mentioned above, there are three types of first-degree distortions: vertical displacement, horizontal displacement, and skew displacement. The brute-force and bilinear interpolation approaches do not require us to investigate the different types of distortions because the transformation for mapping point data to pixels already carries the coefficients for correct these types of error. For both forward and reverse bilinear interpolation, the distortions are corrected only at the control points and pixels. Other non-control points and pixels are estimated from control points and pixels; therefore these non-control pixels carry some error due to the approximation of the earth's curved areas by the flat areas. The error in this approximation varies on the selection of control points and it has no relationship to the satellite distortions.

We observe that every pixel of one scanline has the same error, which may be different than that for other scanlines. Therefore one correction can be made for every pixel in one scanline.

a) Vertical displacement distortion. For this distortion, we can correct the error by offsetting the scanline number. That is the kth scanline is mapped to the (k+dy)th chain code of directions, where dy is the vertical displacement. The vertical displacement need to be corrected only one time for the whole image at the beginning of the process.

b) Horizontal displacement distortion. For this distortion, we can correct each scanline by offsetting the chain code. The kth scanline is mapped into the kth chain code of direction, but the starting points and pixels are offset by dx directions, where dx is the measurement of horizontal displacement in pixels.

c) Skew displacement distortion. For this distortion, we also correct scanline-by-scanline as for horizontal displacement, but the displacement will be a multiple of the scanline number. That means the kth scanline is mapped to the kth chain code with displacement $k*ds$ where ds is the skew displacement measurement.

For the case of combined distortions, we can correct the image scanline-by-scanline with a combination of the displacements. For example, if we have dx, dy, and ds displacements, the kth scan line is mapped to the (k+dy)th chain code of directions with a displacement on the chain code of $dx+k*ds$ directions.

3.4 Algorithm.

In this section we introduce an algorithm to map a scanline to a curve which is represented by a chain code of directions. This curve can be a straight line or a portion of a circle. Data points in the scanline might not be mapped one-to-one to its chain code due to a different resolution. In other words, we map from a high to a low resolution, and we select data points in the scanline to map to the chain code. The data points to be selected can be represented by a sequence of the number of points to skip over. For example, if the selection is to extract every 3rd data point and every 2nd data point alternately, then the sequence is 2, 1, 2, 1,... Moreover instead of mapping data points from left to right in the scanline, we map from the center out because of the symmetry of the image product. That means the first selected data point is in the middle of scanline and is mapped to the center of the curve. This way will be very convenient in correcting for horizontal displacement and will reduce the size of the table of chain codes as well as the sequences of skipping intervals.

Scope: Map the scanline of intensities to a curve in the image product. The curve is represented by the first pixel and a chain code of directions. Because of the symmetry of the curve, we discuss only the right half of the scanline and the right half of the curve. We present successive algorithms to accomplish this task, each an improvement or refinement of its predecessor.

Pseudo code 1: (See Figure 6 for an example to map a scanline to a curve).

Step 1: Map the first intensity to the first pixel.

Step 2: Use the sequence of the skip intervals to locate the next intensity in the scanline to select.

Step 3: Look up the chain code of directions to locate the next pixel in the image product.

Step 4: Map the new intensity in Step 2 to the new pixel in Step3, then go to Step 2. The process is terminated when the last direction in the chain code is used.

Meaning of variables:
Scanline is an array of data points and the index of the first selected data point is *CenterPointIndex*. The pixel for this first selected data point has the coordinates (*xCenterpixel, yCenterPixel*). The sequence *ChainCode* is an array of directions of the curve. It contains only the directions of the half curve from the center to the right. The other half curve on the left can be determined from the right because of symmetry. Corresponding to this sequence, a sequence of skip intervals is used to extract the proper data points. We name this sequence *SkipIntervalSequence*. The two dimensional array *Image* is the image output product.

Here are the local variables:
Counter: is an index into the array ChainCode,
PointIndex: is an index into the array Scanline.
x, y : are x-coordinate and y-coordinate of a pixel in *Image*.
(See Figure 7 for a mapping a scanline with a sequence of skip intervals and a chain code of directions).

Pseudo-code 2:

```
x := xCenterPixel;   y := yCenterPixel;
PointIndex := CenterPointIndex;

For Counter from 1 to length(Chaincode)  do
```

Step 1: Image(x, y) := Scanline(PointIndex);
Step 2: Increment the PointIndex by a SkipInterval
   PointIndex := PointIndex + SkipIntervalSequence(Counter)
Step 3: Look up the chain code to update the pixel (x, y)
    Case ChainCode(Counter) of
      0 : x := x+1;   y := y;
      1 : x := x+1;   y := y+1;
      2 : x := x;   y := y+1;
      3 : x := x-1;   y := y+1;
      4 : x := x-1;   y := y;
      5 : x := x-1;   y := y-1;
      6 : x := x;   y := y-1;
      7 : x := x+1;   y := y-1;
    EndCase
EndFor

Notes: 1) The steps in the for loop correspond to the steps in Pseudo-code 1. 2) The case statement in Step 3 contains 8 different cases depending on the 8 different directions. As mentioned in Section 3.1, for an eighth of a circle there are only two possible directions: 0 and 1 in the case of the 0-45 degree region.

Pseudo-code 3: Map a scanline to both right and left sides of the curve:

Pseudo-code 3 is a modification of pseudo code 2 to include the left part of the curve. The pixel (x,y) in pseudo code 2 is substituted by two pixels (xR, yR) and (xL, yL) for the right and the left curve respectively. Similarly for the variable PointIndex of the array Scanline is replaced by PointIndexR and PointIndexL. These two indices are updated by only one skip interval. PointIndexR is updated forward to the right, while PointIndexL is updated backward to the left. The pixels (xR, yR) and (xL, yL) are updated depending on the directions, and are symmetric around the y-axis.

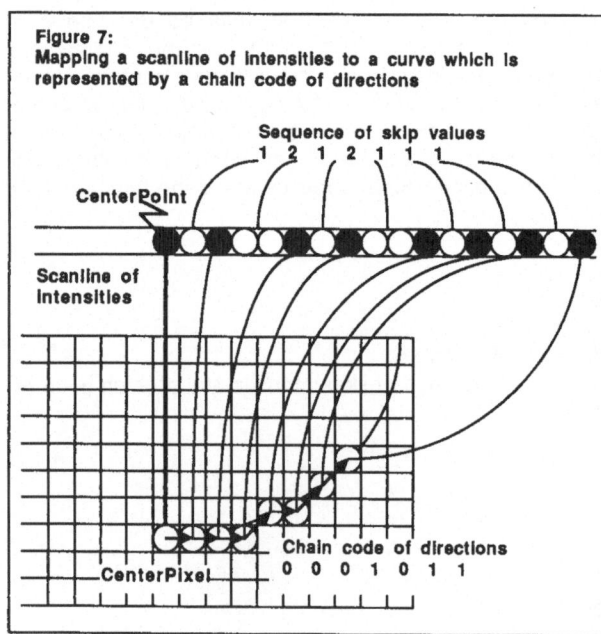

Figure 7:
Mapping a scanline of intensities to a curve which is represented by a chain code of directions

Sequence of skip values
1 2 1 2 1 1 1

CenterPoint

Scanline of intensities

Chain code of directions
0 0 0 1 0 1 1

CenterPixel

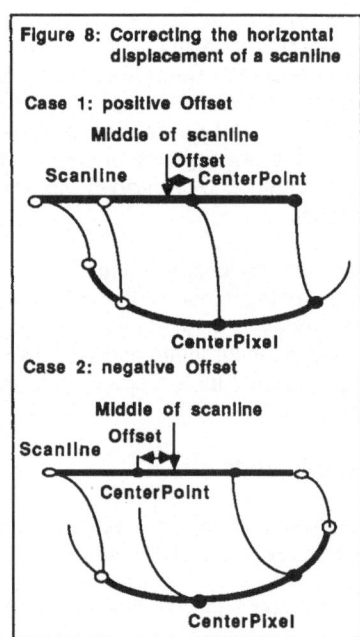

Figure 8: Correcting the horizontal displacement of a scanline

Case 1: positive Offset

Middle of scanline

Scanline
Offset
CenterPoint

CenterPixel

Case 2: negative Offset

Middle of scanline

Scanline
Offset
CenterPoint

CenterPixel

```
xR, xL := xCenterPixel;  yR, yL := yCenterPixel;
PointIndexR, PointIndexL := CenterPointIndex;

For Counter from 1 to length(Chaincode)  do
     Step 1:   Image(xR, yR) := Scanline(PointIndexR);
               Image(xL, yL) := Scanline(PointIndexL);
     Step 2: Increment the PointIndex by a SkipInterval
      PointIndexR := PointIndexR + SkipIntervalSequence(Counter)
      PointIndexL := PointIndexL - SkipIntervalSequence(Counter)
     Step 3: Look up the chain code to update the pixels (xR, yR) and (xL, yL)
          Case ChainCode(Counter) of
          0 : xR := xR+1;  yR := yR;     xL := xL-1;  yL := yL;
          1 : xR := xR+1;  yR := yR+1;  xL := xL-1;  yL := yL+1;
          EndCase
EndFor
```

Pseudocode 4: Correct for horizontal distortion. (See Figure 8 for correcting the horizontal displacement on a scanline, and see Figure 9 for a clipped scanline).

In the following, we will discuss the case of the scanline having a distortion that offsets it due to horizontal displacement and skew displacement. For convenience, let *Offset* be a value of displacement. It can be calculated in terms of pixels.

$$\text{Offset} := dx + k * ds,$$

where dx is the horizontal displacement, ds the skew displacement, and k is the kth scanline. We assume that Offset is an integer value. Non-integer values of Offset can be rounded off. Pseudocode 3 will be modified to correct this type of distortion. First the CenterPointIndex is corrected by the offset; i.e,

$$\text{CenterPointIndex} := \text{roundoff}(1/2 \text{ size of Scanline} + \text{Offset}).$$

The rest of Pseudocode 3 remains the same, except for the data points at the two ends of Scanline. For example, if the Offset is positive, then the length of the right side of Scanline from CenterPointIndex will be less than the left one by Offset, so the mapping process for the right and the left sides of Scanline will terminate when it reaches the right end, then will continue only for the remaining data points on the left side. The remaining data points are 2 * Offset in length. (See Figure 9 for a demonstration).

In pseudocode 3, the loop is a for-loop with *length*(ChainCode) ass the number of repetitions. This for-loop is not convenient in the case of displacement because the symmetry property no longer remains at one end of the scanline. This end of Scanline is the left for positive Offset and right for the negative Offset. Therefore we will use a while-loop for the repetition and the number of repetitions is the number of the extracted data points, which is

$$\text{Length(scanline)} \underline{\text{div}} 2 - \text{Offset},$$

In order to save the CPU time, the scanline can be reduced to the area of interest, so the scanline should be clipped at both ends to the area of interest. The number of repetitions would be

$$\text{Length(ClippedScanline)} \underline{\text{div}} 2 - \text{Offset}.$$

The while-loop control variables are PointIndexR and PointIndexL. PointIndexR (PointIndexL) should be less than (greater than) the maximum (minimum) index of the array ClippedScanLine. We name these two bounds *MaxIndex* and *MinIndex* respectively.

$$\text{CenterPointIndex} := \text{roundoff}(1/2 \text{ size of scanline} + \text{Offset});$$

(* The main part to map the middle points of scanline to the middle pixels of the target curve *)

xR, xL := xCenterPixel;   yR, yL := yCenterPixel;
PointIndexR, PointIndexL := CenterPointIndex;

Counter := 1;
While (PointIndexR < MaxIndex of ClippedScanLine &
        PointIndexL < MinIndex of ClippedScanLine) do

     Step 1: Image(xR, yR) := ClippedScanline(PointIndexR);
          Image(xL, yL) := ClippedScanline(PointIndexL);
     Step 2: Increment the PointIndex by a SkipInterval
      PointIndexR := PointIndexR + SkipIntervalSequence(Counter)
      PointIndexL := PointIndexL - SkipIntervalSequence(Counter)
     Step 3: Look up the chain code to update the pixels (xR, yR) and (xL, yL)
          Case ChainCode(Counter) of
          0 : xR := xR+1; yR := yR;   xL := xL-1; yL := yL;
          1 : xR := xR+1; yR := yR+1; xL := xL-1; yL := yL+1;
          EndCase
     Additional Step: Counter := Counter + 1;
EndWhile
(** end of the main loop**)

(* The following code includes the mapping of the remaining scanline to the remaining left curve (then-block with Offset>0) or to the remaining right curve (else-block with Offset<0) ****)

If Offset is positive
then map the remaining data points on the left side:
  While PointIndexL > MinIndex do
     Step 1: Image(xL, yL) := Scanline(PointIndexL);
     Step 2: Increment the PointIndex by a SkipInterval
      PointIndexL := PointIndexL - SkipIntervalSequence(Counter)
     Step 3: Look up the chain code to update the pixels (xL, yL)
          Case ChainCode(Counter) of
          0 : xL := xL-1; yL := yL;
          1 : xL := xL-1; yL := yL+1;
          EndCase
     Additional step: Counter := Counter + 1;
  EndWhile

else map the remaining data points on the right side:
  While PointIndexR < MaxIndex do
     Step 1: Image(xR, yR) := Scanline(PointIndexR);
     Step 2: Increment the PointIndex by a SkipInterval
      PointIndexR := PointIndexR + SkipIntervalSequence(Counter)
     Step 3: Look up the chain code to update the pixels (xR, yR)
          Case ChainCode(Counter) of
          0 : xR := xR+1; yR := yR;
          1 : xR := xR+1; yR := yR+1;
          EndCase
     Additional step: Counter := Counter + 1;
  EndWhile

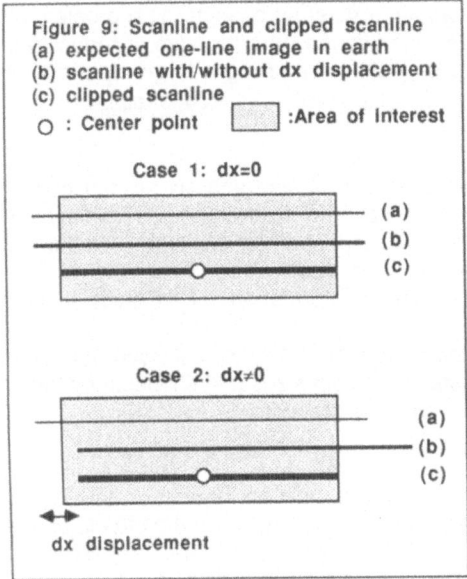

Figure 9: Scanline and clipped scanline
(a) expected one-line image in earth
(b) scanline with/without dx displacement
(c) clipped scanline
○ : Center point   ▢ :Area of Interest

Case 1: dx=0

(a)
(b)
(c)

Case 2: dx≠0

(a)
(b)
(c)

◄►
dx displacement

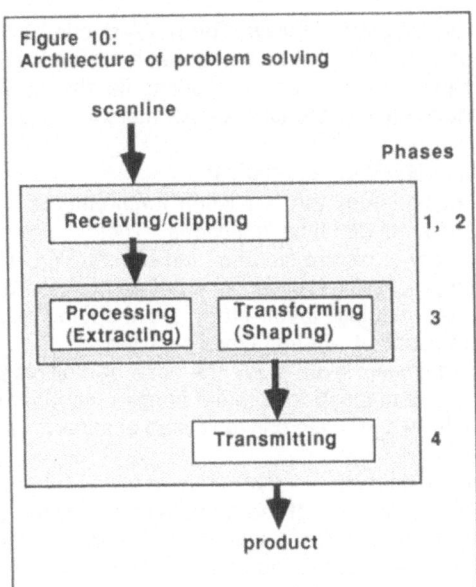

Figure 10:
Architecture of problem solving

scanline

Phases

Receiving/clipping   1, 2

Processing   Transforming   3
(Extracting)   (Shaping)

Transmitting   4

product

Analysis of running time:
For each pixel in the image product, it requires a total of 4 arithmetic operations to do mapping: They are:
- One operation to move the intensity to the pixel   Image(x, y) := Scanline(Index)
- One operation to update the index for the next data point Index := Index + SkipInterval
- Two operations to update the pixel coordinates by a direction.
   For example x := x; y := y+1, for direction 0, and x := x+1; y := y+1, for the direction 1.

Therefore the running time for a scanline is 4 arithmetic operations x length (ClippedScanline), and hence for the whole image product, it is the sum of the above number overall extracted ClippedScanlines. As a result the running time for a image product is 4 x (# of pixels in the area of interest).

4. A COMPLETE LOGICAL SOLUTION: AN ARCHITECTURE

In this section a complete analysis and solution of reconstructing satellite images is introduced. First the problem is analyzed in different points of views, then 4 phases of the solution are introduced with their goals of minimizing memory and processing time. Finally an architecture is introduced in diagrams. Figure 10 shows the architecture for solving the problem and Figure 11 shows its data flow diagram.

4.1 Analysis of Problem:

Definition of problem: The satellite problem can be considered as a problem of mapping a high resolution image to multiple, low-resolution images so that
   a) its shape is preserved(SP) or
   b) its shape is transformed conformally(SPSP).

Different points of view: The problem can be viewed in 4 different aspects: 1) a problem of a high resolution image being mapped to a low resolution image, 2) a problem of reducing the size of an image and preserving its shape, 3) a problem of reducing a large input memory requirement to a smaller output memory usage, 4) a problem with a time constraint.

Three levels of the problem:
1) basic: study the resolution requirements, the correlation of size and shape, the memory constraints and time limitations. These studies should have the following goals: minimize the memory or picture storage, and separate processing into real and non-real time. The non-real time processing can be done before the data image is transmitted.
2) intermediate level: study the mapping and shape transformation. This study includes corrections of different types of distortions.
3) advanced level: study the case of multiple output products. That means each data set of image is mapped to different image output products of different sizes and shapes. Our goal at this level is to have only one read of satellite raw data for all products.

Area of interest:
All scanlines are of the same length. Within each scanline, only an interval of data is valid where the image of the earth is. The first scanlines contain less image data than the later ones which are closer to the equator. Data should be clipped within the valid data. Moreover each product will specify the focus area on earth; therefore we should clip data within the area of interest where the image will be reconstructed. We define a valid pixel as a pixel in the area of interest. Our goal is to do processing on the valid pixels.

Phases: There are 4 phases to reproducing images. They are 1) receiving satellite data, 2) clipping scanlines to the area of interest based on resolution, 3) processing scanlines or data reduction of scanlines, which is based on the resolution, and shaping scanlines in the case of SPSP, and 4) transmitting data. (See Figure 11 for a data flow diagram of these 4 phases).

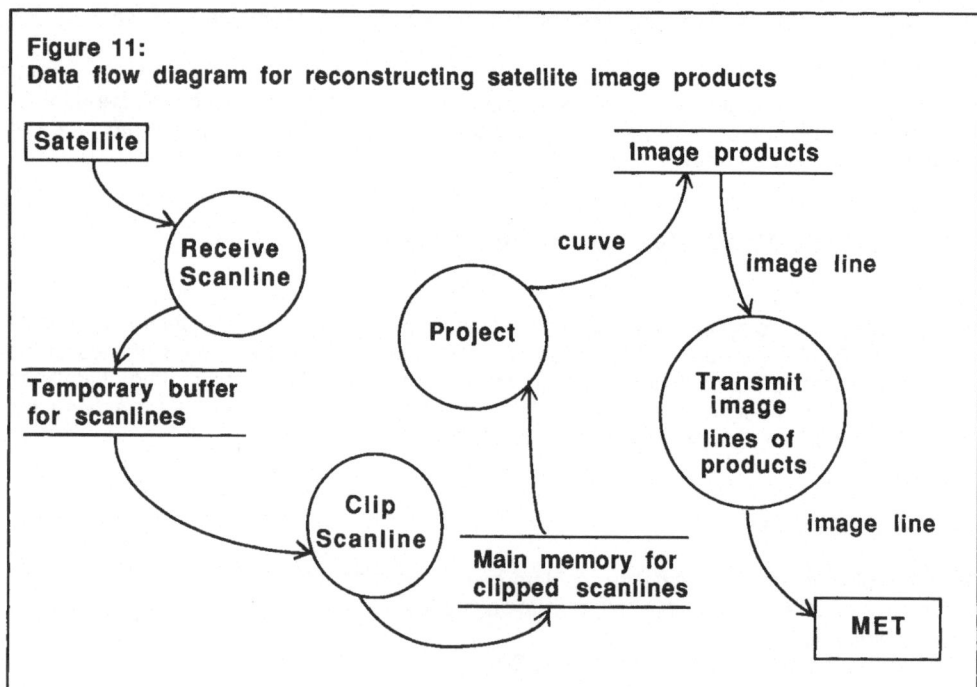

Figure 11:
Data flow diagram for reconstructing satellite image products

Receiving scanlines. The satellite transmits scanlines and their identifications. The system should have as highest priority the storing of scanlines in real time. Temporary memory for all scanlines can be organized into drum or circular of scanline size in order to avoid cleaning memory and extended use of memory. Memory should be large enough to contain the unprocessed scanlines during the time of processing.

Clipping and selecting scanlines. Not all scanlines are selected because of the low resolution we have to produce. Therefore selecting proper scanlines can be done systematically by a method of raster graphics which is introduced later. Before storing these selected scanlines, they are clipped according to the are of interest. The information about the area of interest is non-real time and is given in advance before receiving satellite data.

Processing scanlines. Each selected and clipped scanline is registered on the screen display memory with the guide of a chain code of directions. The chain code is calculated in advance and saved in a table. Each product will have its own table of chain codes. The size of the table will be discussed later. This step is responsible for distortions also. Types of projection geometries are included in the tables. For the case of satellite perspective, the processing includes uniformly extracting data from the scanline to the register in a digital straight line, while for the case of SPSS, the extracting is non-uniform because of the circles in register data. Data will be compressed in the latitudes near the north pole and expanded in the latitudes near the equator. The problem of overlapping or vacant pixels arises here.

Transmitting. The final product are not usually transmitted as scanlines but as horizontal lines in the image-screen display memory. This means for the satellite perspective, the transmitting can occur throughout the processing of a scanline, while in SPSP it can only be done at the ends of scanlines due to the curvature of the projection in SPSP. (See Figure 12 for transmitted lines).

4.2 Architecture (see Figure 10):

Satellite data are treated as scanlines each of which is one-line image of the earth. The first two phases 1 and 2 are combined into a process named *Receiving/Clipping*. The third and fourth phases are combined to *Extracting/Shaping*, and the last one is *Transmitting*.

Phase 1. Phase 1 requires a driver program in real time. Here is a driver program:

    if interrupt occurs
    then increment the InterruptNumber by 1

    if InterruptNumber+dy is a requested scanline number
    then save scanline in the location (InterruptNumber modulo n) where n is the
        size of the buffer in scanlines.
    else resume other phases as 2, 3, 4.

Note: InterruptNumber is initialized to 1, and dy is the vertical displacement which is calculated before any data transmission.

Phase 2. In this phase the data in the scanline is clipped and moved to main memory to be processed by phases 3 and 4. Clipping a full length scanline to its area of interest is based on the information on the image product. Associated with a ClippedScanline is
    1) scanline number: s
    2) length of clipped scanline: h
    3) position of the center point: c

Note: The center point index can be calculated by c = h/2 + dx + ds * (s - dy). (See Fig 9).

Phases 3. In this phase the clipped scanline is processed by the algorithm of section 3.4. Data points in the clipped scanline are extracted and projected according to the chain code of directions on the screen display.

Phase 4. The screen display is transmitted line by line. A line can only be transmitted when all pixels are filled up in the area of interest. (See Figure 12).

4.3 Topics in the Satellite Problem.

Topic: Selecting proper scanlines.
Scanlines are mapped to lines or curves in an image product. Since the raw data is high resolution (e.g., 15000 data points in each scanline, and 6400 scanlines in the northern hemisphere) and the image product has a low resolution (e.g., 400 x 640), selecting scanlines should be done. Let m be the number of scanlines, n the number of data points in each scanline, p the number of rows, and q the number of pixels in each rows in the image product. Reducing resolution mxn to pxq can be done in several ways.
(1) rescale the raw data by p/m in rows and q/n in columns to fit the image product. In this case each pixel will be the average of m/p x n/q data points if m/p and n/q are integers. In the case of non-integer m/p and n/q, they can be rounded to integers. This way is CPU time-intensive and requires a large memory to keep the scanlines before averaging them. Besides, the problem of correcting distortions makes it more complex. Therefore, we propose another way.
(2) extract p out of m scanlines. Assume that m/p = k is an integer, so one scanline can be extracted for every k scanlines. In the case m/p is not an integer, the extracting can be done as follows: (a) factorize m to be m = k*p + m1, (b) find the chain code of directions representing the straight line of slope m1/p. Since m1< p, the directions can only be 0 or 1. Bresenham's algorithm can be used to find this chain code (Bresenham, 1965). Other algorithms to find the chain codes of lines can also be used. This chain code will be a cycle of length p. Let denote this chain code by d1, d2,...,dp. (c) the extracted scanlines are at positions (k+d1), (k+d2),...(k+dq), (k+d1), (k+d2),... Therefore we extract the kth or (k+1)th scanlines depending on the values of the d's.

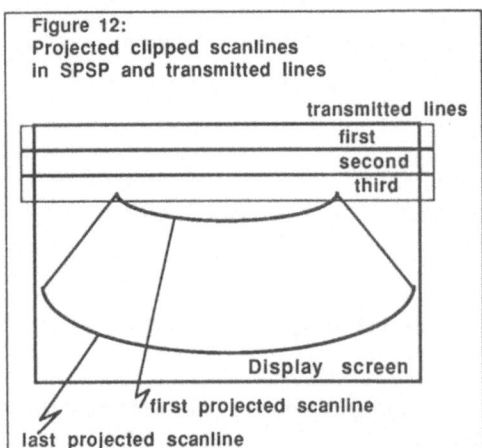

Figure 12:
Projected clipped scanlines
in SPSP and transmitted lines

transmitted lines
first
second
third

Display screen
first projected scanline
last projected scanline

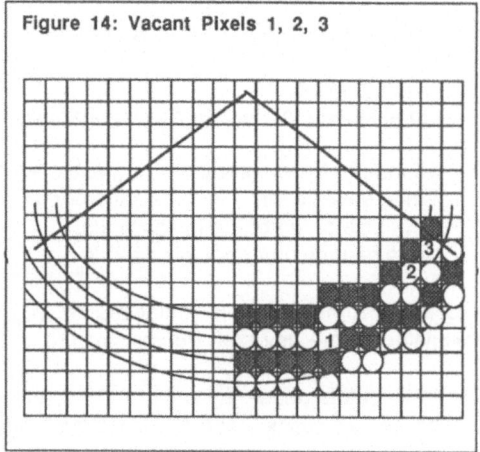

Figure 14: Vacant Pixels 1, 2, 3

Topic: Size of the table of chain codes.

Each extracted scanline is mapped to the image product to be a straight line or a portion of a circle whose representations can be chain codes. For the straight lines, the chain codes can have at most two directions. If they are horizontal lines then their chain codes have only 0 as a direction. For a portion of the circle, the directions can be reduced to at most two directions as follows: The eighth of the circle in the region quadrant (270 -315 degree range) has only two directions 0 and 1 and the eighth of circle in the region (225 - 270 degree range) is symmetric. Therefore for each scanline to be mapped to a chain code, the chain code can be reduced by a half. In other words, the mapping can be done from the center of the scanline toward both ends and the chain code is for only the right half because the left is symmetric to the right. Let pxq be the resolution of image product. A half of the circle of radius q/2 has length of pi*q/2 pixels. Therefore the chain code will have length pi*q/4 directions. Each direction can be encoded by 1 bit, so each chain code needs at most pi*q/4 bits. For each image product, the scanlines might have different length, but all of them form the area of interest; therefore the table size for each image product is pi * (# of pixels in the area of interest) bits.

Topic: Correct the vertical displacement.

One type of distortion is a vertical displacement. In this case the satellite raw data image is moved up or down by a vertical displacement. Let dy be the displacement. Then the kth scanline should be mapped to the (k+dy)th chain code of directions. We assume the value dy is an integer which represents the number of scanlines to be offset. We can round if dy is non-integral. Therefore, correcting the vertical displacement can be done just before receiving the raw data from satellite.

5. MULTIPLE IMAGE PRODUCTS: AN ARCHITECTURE

In this section we will discuss a raw input data satellite image with multiple output products. Each output product is characterized by the following three categories:
- resolution: the numbers of rows and columns,
- area of interest: the area specified by two bounded longitudes and two bounded latitudes, and
- type of projections: either satellite perspective or secant polar stereographic perspective.

There are 24 different predefined output products, but for each raw input image, our system should be capable of producing only 4 different output products. In other words, for one input image, a set of 4 output products is constructed, and for the next input image, another set of 4 different outputs products is constructed. These two sets are subsets of the set of all 24 possible predefined output products.

Our satellite is capable of taking pictures every 15 minutes. It is planned in normal condition to take pictures every 2 hours. i.e, 12 raw satellite images will be taken in a day. During critical events such as storm and hurricanes, the satellite will run at full speed, taking a picture every 15 minutes. The restriction of 4 output products out of a possible 24 for each raw input image will help us to speed up the process. Moreover, these possible 24 are predetermined; hence many calculations can be done in advance before transmitting the satellite data, such as area of interest, resolution, chain codes of directions for scanlines in a specific perspective; as well as the chain code of skip intervals for data reduction for scanlines and points within a scanline. However, all 4 output products must be complete after the last raw data bit is received. This limitation is very critical. To meet this time requirement, an array processor or multiple processor is used to perform the task. The multiple processor is preferable, and will be discussed in this section. Our goal is to provide an architecture with a receiver to receive raw data from satellite, and a multiple processor to map scanlines to curves in multiple output products. Figure 13 provides details of the general architecture for multiple image products.

A system memory is required to store the selected scanlines within the area of interest. The selected scanlines numbers and the area of interest are predetermined and are calculated in non real time. Due to the significant reduction of the raw data image to the 4 output products, not every scanline is selected; therefore, while receiving data from the satellite, the long periods between consecutive selected scanlines can be used to process something else. Moreover selected scanlines are clipped within the area of interest, so the memory will be minimized.

A block control is the part of the architecture that distributes the selected scanline numbers into queues, one queue for each product, and each queue will be linked to a table of the chain codes which contain the directions and skip intervals.

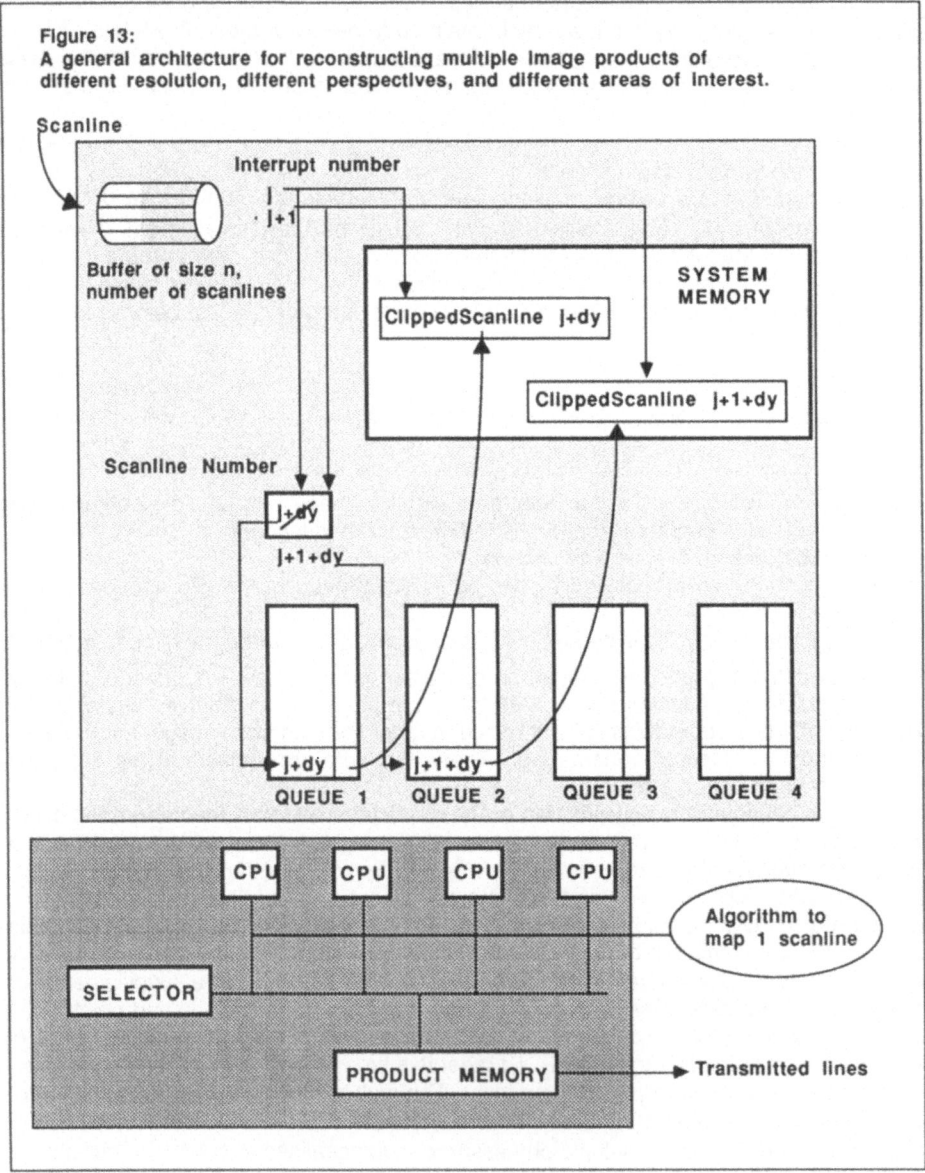

Figure 13:
A general architecture for reconstructing multiple image products of different resolution, different perspectives, and different areas of interest.

A CPU scheduling block determines the availability of queues, and a selector selects the fullest queue to process. This processing pops a selected scanline number out of the queue and designates the next available CPU to map the corresponding scanline to the output product with the help of two chain codes: a chain code of directions and a chain code of skip intervals.

A block of identical processors run identical algorithms to map scanlines to curves in output products. When a processor finishes a scanline, it receives a new scanline, two chain codes of directions and skip intervals, and the target output product.

Comments:
(1) The selector balances the availability of the queues.
(2) The scanline in memory will be discarded when it is used in all queues. That means the scanline number will be less than the numbers in the queues. Of course, numbers in each queue are in increasing order.
(3) This architecture will guarantee that there is no duplication of a scanline even it is mapped into many output products.
(4) This architecture can have arbitrary many CPU's in the processor block. The more CPU's we have, the faster processing we get, and hence less memory for the queues is required.
(5) The number of output products need not be restricted to four. The more output products to be produced, the more CPUs are required so that the time limitation can be met.

6. OPEN PROBLEMS

Problem 1: Mapping a curve from high to low resolution.
Given a curve in a screen of resolution m x n, the problem is to find the curve of the same shape in a screen of lower resolution, e.g., p x q, where $p < m$ and $q < n$. This is a problem of data reduction. One of the intermediate solutions is to find a transformation between two screen systems. Place a xy system on the screen of resolution m x n, and a x'y' system on the screen of resolution p x q. The transformation to map (x, y) to (x', y') is calculated by the following formula:

$$x' = (p/m) \cdot x, \qquad y' = (q/n) \cdot y$$

Therefore the pixels in one system can be mapped to other system by these formulas. The function round-off is used to find the integer coordinates of the new system. Hence there are multiple pixels in the xy system which are mapped to one pixel in the x' y' system. We call this pixel in the x'y' system an overlapping pixel. Similarly, we will have a vacant pixel if the transformation from a low resolution to a higher one. We also can say that the reverse transformation will cause vacant pixels. (See Figure 14 for an example of vacant pixels).

The problem is more difficult if the curve is represented by a chain code of directions. That means that the problem is to transform a chain code of directions from one system to another one. This is an open problem. Let examine a simple case, the case of digital straight lines. Overlapping pixels and vacant pixels will occur respectively from a mapping from high to low and from low to high resolution. Let consider the case of overlapping pixels (the other case is similar because it is the reversed case). The problem is rephrased as follows: Given a curve C which is represented by a chain code of directions in a system of resolution m x n. Find a chain code of directions of the same curve in another system of resolution p x q, where $p < m$ and $q < n$. Moreover if a pixel in the target system is given, determine all the pixels in the source system. The curve in the source system is decomposed into a sequence of consecutive sub-curves which are mapped one-to-one to the pixels of the target curve. Since the source curve is a chain code of directions, the sequence of the lengths of sub-curves should be investigated and it might turn out to be a chain code, called a chain code of the skip intervals. Henceforth the mapping becomes complete if we know two chain codes: the chain code of directions in the target system and the chain code of skip intervals of the source curve. The special case that should be investigated first is the case of the digital straight lines.

Problem 2: Mapping parallel curves from a high resolution to a lower one.
Given a set of the parallel curves in the source system, the problem is to find the corresponding curves in the target system. This is a continuation of problem 1. We assume that the source parallel curves have no blank pixels between any two of them, so two consecutive curves have their pixels adjacent to each other. The corresponding target curves are expected to be parallel and have no blank pixels between any two consecutive curves. Initial investigation indicates that there are some blank pixels which are pixels having no source pixels to be mapped from. Moreover, going from a high resolution to a lower one, we expect several source curves could be mapped to one target curve. The problem of grouping the sources curves having the same target curve as well as the problem of identifying the blank pixels among the target curves are open. As a special case, these parallel curves are digital straight lines, and hence the above problem will be a problem of selecting digital straight lines (select one line in each group) to map to the target system. This selection will reduce the number of rows in the source system to the target one, and the chain code of skip intervals in Problem 1 will map each line to the target system and hence reduces the number of columns from the source system to the target one.

Problem 3:   Satellite and two perspectives.
Satellite image can be considered as an image of the parallel digital straight lines in a source system of a very high resolution (e.g. 6400x15000), and the output image products are considered the mapping to a target system of low resolution (e.g. 400x640). Mapping the parallel lines from the source system to the other parallel lines of the same shape of the target system involves the open problems 1 and 2. The image output products might contain vacant pixels, and several source lines might map to a target line, and several pixels in each source line might map to one pixel in the target system. The mapping in SPSP will increase the complexity of the problems. In this case parallel lines are mapped to portions of circles. Theoretically, these circles are concentric, and hence the circles near the north pole center have smaller circumferences than the ones near the equator circle. The mapping of the parallel lines to these concentric circles will have a double problem of overlapping and vacant pixels. Overlapping occurs in the circles of smaller radius, and vacant pixels occurs in the circles of larger radius. We should distinguish that the overlapped/vacant problem can occur in the pixels within each line and between lines. Within each line, a chain code of skip intervals is used to extract the source points to map to the pixels in a smaller circle in the target system; and the chain code of enlargement values is used to map each source data point to several consecutive pixels in the target circle of a large radius. Since the problems of enlarging and reducing sizes in the target curves can happen in the same image product, finding a method to determine the longitude and latitude of a given pixel in the target system become an open problem.

Problem 4: Control points and error.
The bilinear interpolation approximates the image output products by the control points, and hence it opens a problem of determining the number of control points and positioning them. Certainly the positions as well as the number of control points will influence the error. In the output product the edges of the image will need more control points in order to reduce the error value due to the curvature of the earth. Methods of estimating the error are still an open problem. The quality of each output product is characterized by its error of approximation.

Acknowledgments. I would like to thank KimThu and BeTra for their encouragement, David and Lien for their help, and referees for many suggestive comments.

REFERENCES

C. Arcelli and A. Massarotti, Regular arcs in digital contours, Comput. Graphics Images Process. **4**, 1975, 339-360; Erratum, Comput. Graphics Images Process. **5**, 1976, 280.

N. Badler, Disk generators for rater display device, Computer Graphics and Image Processing, 6, 1977, pp. 589-593.

J. Bresenham, Algorithm for computer control of a digital plotter. IBM Systems J. **4**, 1965, 25-30.

J. Bresenham, A linear algorithm for incremental digital display of circular arcs, Communication of ACM, Vol. 20, No 2, Feb. 1977, pp. 100-106.

R. Brons, Linguistic methods for the description of a straight line on a grid. Comput. Graphics Image Process. **3**, 1974, 48-62.

S. K. Chang, Picture processing grammar and its applications, Inform. Sci. **3**, 1971. 121-148.

P. Danielson, Comments on circle generator for display devices, Computer Graphics and Image Processing, 7, 1978, pp.300-301.

R.C. Doolittle. C.L. Bristor, and L. Lauritson, Mapping of geostationary satellite pictures: an operational experiment, ESSA Tech. Memo NESO TM-20, Mar. 1970.

M. Doros, Algorithms for generation of discrete circles, rings, and disks, Computer Graphics and Image Processing, 10, 1979, pp.366-371.

L. Dorst and R. P. W. Duin, Spirograph theory: a framework for calculations on digitized straight lines. IEEE Trans. Pattern Anal. Mach. Intell **PAMI-6**, No. 5, 1984. 632-639.

L. Dorst and A. W. M. Smeulders, Discrete representation of straight lines. IEEE Trans. Pattern Anal. Mach. Intell **PAMI-6**, No. 4, 1984. 450-463.

B. K. P. Horn, Circle generators for display devices, Computer Graphics and Image Processing, 5,1976, pp. 280-288.

L. F. Hubert, Accuracy of wind estimatesfrom geostationary satellites, Meteorol. satellite lab., N.O.A.A. , Suitland, Md., Memo, 1969.

S. H. Y. Hung, On the straightness of digital arcs, IEEE Trans. Pattern Anal. Mach. Intell **PAMI-7**, No. 2, 1985. 203-215.

C. E. Kim and A. Rosenfeld, Digital straight lines and convexity of digital regions, IEEE Trans. Pattern Anal. Mach. Intell. PAMI, 1982, 149-153.

C. E. Kim, On cellular straight line segments, Comput. Graphics Image Process. **18**, 1982, 369-381.

J. Kulpa, On the properties of discrete circles, rings, and disks, Computer Graphics and Image Processing, 10, 1979, pp348-365.

J. Kulpa, and M. Doros, Freeman digitization of integer circles minimizes the radial error, Computer Graphics and Image Processing, 17, 1981, pp. 181-184.

J. A. Leese, C.S. Novak, and B. B. Clark, An automated technique for obtaining cloud motion from geosynchronous satellite data using cross correlation, J. Appl. Meteorol., Vol 10, Feb. 1971, pp. 118-132.

M. D. McIlroy, Best approximation circles on integer grids, ACM Transactions on Graphics, Vol. 2, No. 4, October 1983, pp 237-263.

N. Nakamura and K. Aizawa, Digital circles, Computer Vision, Graphics, and Image processing, 26, 1984, pp. 242-255.

J. L. Pfaltz and A. Rosenfeld, Computer representation of planar regions by their skeletons. Comm. Asso. Comput. Mach. **10**, 1967, 119-125.

S. Pham, Digital straight segments, Comput. Vision, Graphics, and Image Processing, **36**, 1986, 10-30.

S. Pham, On the Boundary of Digital Straight Line Segments, International Computer Graphics Conference, Tokyo, April 22-25, 1986

A. Rosenfeld, Digital straight line segments, IEEE Trans. Comput. **C-23**, 1974, 1264-1269.

A. Rosenfeld, Picture Processing by Computer, Academic Press, New York, 1969.

E. A. Smith and D. R. Phillips, Automated cloud tracking using precisely aligned ATS pictures, IEEE Transactions on Computers, Vol. C-21, No. 7 July 1972, pp.715-729.

Y. Suenaga, T. Kamae, and T. Kobayashi, A high-speed algorithm for the generation of straight lines and circular arcs, IEEE Transactions on Computers, Vol. c-28, No 10, Oct. 1979 pp. 728-736.

V. E. Suomi and R. J. Parent, A color view of planet earth, Bull. Amer. Meteorol. Soc. , Vol. 49, Feb. 1968, pp. 74-75.

L. D. Wu, On the chain code of a line, IEEE Trans. Pattern Anal. Mach. Intell. **PAMI-4**, NO. 3, 1982, 347-353.

Son Pham is currently an associate professor of computer science, College of Engineering at the California State University at Northridge. His research interests include computer graphics and software engineering. He has published a dozen refereed academic/technical papers in computer science. He is a member of ACM and IEEE-CS.

Pham received his BA in mathematics from the University of Saigon, Viet Nam in 1973; MA in mathematics from the University of Louisville, Kentucky in 1975; PhD in statistics from the University of Cincinnati, Ohio in 1978; and PostDoc in Computer Science from the University of California, Berkeley in 1980.

Address: Department of Computer Science, School of Engineering and Computer Science, California State University at Northridge, 18111 Nordhoff Ave., Northridge, CA 91330, USA.

Some Problems in Overlaying 3D Graphics onto 2D Image

J. Wu, M. Zhu, and Z. He

ABSTRACT

One of the crucial problems in overlaying 3D graphics onto 3D image
is that 3D information can not be easily extracted from 2D image. So
space relation between 3D graphics and existing scenes in image is
unavailable. Another problem is how to render 3D graphics having the
same illumination as existing scenes. In this paper we study some
key problems in this subject and also propose some practical methods
to solve them.

Keyword: composition, graphics rendering, illumination, image taking,
extracting scene, recognizing scene, overlaying graphics, perspective
concordance.

1. INTRODUCTION

There are four types of composition of graphics and image:
image-to-graphics, graphics-to-graphics, graphics-to-image, and
image-to-image. Here we do not concern the image-to-image, because it
is studied in image processing.

The image-to-graphics or texture mapping is a technique mapping
2D image onto the surfaces of 3D graphics to generate more realistic
graphics. The mapping is carried out during rendering graphics. The
graphics-to-graphics speeds up graphics rendering, and now used in
animation and complex graphics rendering. It composites more than one
graphics together to generate a perfect graphics.

The common trait above two types is that the 3D information is
available, so the composition can be executed exactly. But it is unavailable in graphics-to-image. In order to overlaying 3D graphics
onto 2D image naturally, the graphics should be rendered to fit existing scenes in both perspective and illumination. One of the crucial
problems is we can not extract 3D information from 2D image easily.
Another is how to render qualified graphics.

As a more and more interested subject in computer graphics, we
think to study the problems exposed in it is helpful to obtain better
results.

This paper discuss what we should notice in this subject on taking image, rendering graphics, and overlaying graphics. At last, a
Computer Assisted City Planning System (CACPS) is briefly introduced.
The CACPS overlays architecture graphics onto the photographic image
of planned area and help designers to investigate and analyze the
designed result.

2. PROBLEMS IN OVERLAYING 3D GRAPHICS ONTO 2D IMAGE

The problems exposed in this field can be listed as three aspects: image taking, graphics rendering, and graphics overlaying.

A. Image taking
.Building object space and image space
.Measuring climate condition
.Measuring visibility

B. Graphics Rendering
.Determining illumination conditions
.Determining resolution

C. Graphics overlaying
.Perspective concordance
.Obstructing and obstructed
.Image editing

3. IMAGE TAKING

An image is a photograph taken from landscape with a camera. In order to put 3D graphics on it naturally, some information recorded on the spot of image taking is useful in guilding graphics rendering. This section discuss what information is needed and how to collect it. The following discussion assumes that the graphics located the presumed position.

3.1. Building Object Space and Image Space

Object space or world coordinates puts all existing scenes under a unified reference system. It is the base of investigating the space relation between existing scenes and 3D graphics.

A direct way to build object space is to take the sea level as X-Z plan and vertical line which the camera is on as Y axis, at the same time make X axis indicate to the east and Z to the north. But the more convenient model is to move X-Z plan to the place where camera is on. Thus the camera, the viewpoint, is at the origin. We denote the object space XYZ coordinates.

The image space must be also built to show location of existing scenes in photographic image. We denote it UVW coordinates. Where W is the direction of visual line. It is the direction of the line emit-ting from the center of lens. The U, V directions are the two edges of rectangle image. The origin of UVW is on the visual line (See Fig. 1). The UVW is determined according to the camera plane in XYZ. If the focus is known and the rate of image size to film size is also known, the viewpoint direction of any location in image can be computed easily (See Fig.2). Another advantage using image space is that the window in which scene is appear on the image is known. This window can guide us to render graphics economically.

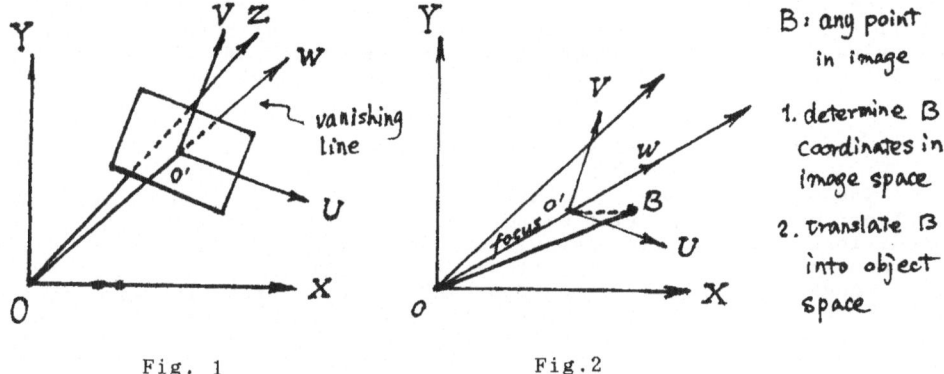

Fig. 1   Fig.2

3.2. Measuring Climate Condition

The climate condition is one of the important factors influencing illumination of existing scenes in almost every aspects, and also it is the resource data guiding to render qualified graphics. Generally it is enough to judge what climate is by measuring the light intensity in shaded area and unshaded area respectively, because the atmosphere divides light reaching the earth into the direct light which is part of the sunshine passing through the atmosphere and the indirect light which is the reflection and refraction of the sunshine by the atmospheric moleculars and water vapor. In clear day, as the atmosphere become thiner, more sunshine can reach the earth, and less is reflected or refracted, therefore direct light becomes stronger and indirect light becomes weeker. In cloud day, the atmosphere becomes thicker, less direct light reaches the earth but more indirect light does. So the rate of direct light to indirect light reflect the change of the climate conditions. In accuracy, to measure light intensity should be taken in the brightest areas and the blackest areas. One thing we should notice is that the intensity measured in the brightest area is the sum of intensity of direct light and indirect light.

Measuring light direction is simple. It can be computed by erecting a staff and then measuring its projecting length and direction in the XYZ coordinates.

3.3. Measuring Visibility

Visibility or transparence varies with the climate. It shows as the changes of illumination and color saturation. The visibility can be controlled by the absorptivity and distance between viewpoint and scenes [Willis (1987)][Blinn (1982)]. But to determine absorptivity correctly is difficult. The absorptivity concerns not only the distribution and size of water vapor but also the district condition, such as industrial city or countryside, and geographic conditions. Further more, the absorptivity is various with different light spectrum. A little precise way to measure absorptivity is to put several sample objects along with the visual line direction, to record their intensities and color saturations at different location, and then to construct a polynomial to compute absorptivity. In not very precise situation, we can only adjust the distance under some presumed absorptivity to control visibility.

4. GRAPHICS RENDERING

Because the rendered graphics will be overlaied onto image, it should fit existing scenes in illumination, light direction, and perspective. This section we discuss the problems of illumination of graphics. The perspective will be concerned in next section.

4.1. Determining Illumination Condition

The outdoor scene is taken under certain climate condition: weather conditions, light direction, and light intensity. The weather conditions include what weather is, clear or cloud, and which season is when the image is taken. It heavily affects illumination of existing scenes. The light direction and light intensity are factors affecting illuminations. They also affect each other. For example, the intensity is stronger at noon than in the morning. The light direction also affects the light color. We have experience that the light is redder in the morning or dusk than that at noon. So when rendering qualified graphics, we must know these data and their relation each other. However measuring these data usually need special skills and also concerns the problem how to convert it so that it can be used appropriately in rendering graphics. In many cases, these data can be looked up in literates under ideal conditions.

It is necessary to stimulate natural light. The worthy literates have provided many effective methods [Brotman (1984)][Nishita (1986)][Cohen (1985)]. But there is a common shortcoming that almost all of them did not considered the relation between direct light and indirect light. As discussed above section, this relation is very important in determining different illumination, so we set up a light source model based on adjusting the rate of direct light to indirect light. relation. It can stimulate different illumination under different weather conditions and at different time in a day flexiblily and effectively. This model is used in CACPS and will be simply introduced in section 6.

For the indoor scene, there usually contains one or more artificial light sources such as lamp and fluorescent lamp. If there are both sources, they should be considered together. In this case, the rendering method plays an important role.

4.2. Determining Resolution

We should also consider the illumination affected by distance. The atmospheric moleculars and water vapor make illumination and color saturation of scene vary with its location in object space. Speaking roughly, it results in different resolution. The factor affecting visibility contains distance and absorptivity. The reference [Willis (1987)] showed a simple relation between two factors. In many cases, different visibility is obtained by changing distance under a prior absorptivity.

A more feasible and simple way is to use a low-pass filter to smooth graphics. It can be added in graphics scaling to get different visibility under different distance as doing in CACPS.

5. GRAPHICS OVERLAYING

Once a proper 3D graphics is rendered, next step is to overlay it on 2D image. In this procedure, some image processing must be done. It is unlackable in melting graphics with image. In fact, many processings in this step are the most difficult because they concern 3D information extraction. But interactive technique can simplify many processings.

5.1. Perspective Concordance

The perspective concordance of 3D graphics and 2D image gives a direct result whether two parts have a good match. The key step for obtaining perspective concordance is to find accurate position of new scene in object space. If the data mentioned in section 3.1 are known, the viewpoint direction can be computed and proper graphics scaling can be gotten by moving it along this direction. Although the computation can not give its depth in object space, it is a good compromise between measurement and flexibility. Another way is to draw the vanishing lines on image, and then adjust a sample object which has the same volume as the new scene in object space so that its edges match the vanishing lines. This way is successfully used in CACPS. Generally speaking, it is impossible to accurately computer perspective relation, each method merely guides to obtain more precise perspective relation fast.

5.2. Obstructing and Obstructed

When a new scene is added to an environment, it may obstruct existing scene and also may be obstructed by existing scene. If new scene obstructs an existing scene, we overlay it onto image directly. If the shadow of new scene obstructs an existing scene, we can construct a pseudo-environment which the shadow may cast on. Although the environment can not be accurately constructed, especially for complex scenes, the shadow has almost monotonous grey, so the result is still ideal.

In the case of new scene be obstructed, processing is more complex. When existing scene obstructs an new scene, if the existing scene has a simple contour, we only need to clip the new scene according to this contour; if the existing scene, such as a tree, has a complex contour, this way is not applicable. In this case, we hope to extract the precise contour of tree by method of scene recognization applied in computer vision. The recognization here is simpler than that in computer vision because we can indicate what and where we want to recognize

When the shadow of existing scene casts on new scene, the contour of shadow should be changed so that it fits new scene. It also needed to extract the contour, and then deform it according to the shape of new scene.

In order to overlay graphics and its shadow onto the image, the shaded part and unshaded part of graphics should be rendered respectively. It is beneficial to cast the shadow of new scene on existing scene.

5.3. Image Editing

Image editing is necessary in obtaining good match. For example, we want to plant a rank of tree in desired place where there is not formerly. It is obvious that not only rendering tree costs a lot but also the generated tree is not very true, so digging some trees from one place in image and then move them to another is a good idea.

The image editing should include extracting, deforming, and moving for an identified scene. The extracting is the most radical and also the most intractable. This function recognizes a scene, takes it out from the image, and further extracts its characteristics. The deforming translate the extracted scene into required shape. The moving function copys a scene from one area to another. It is can be completed by first indicating the source area with a polygon and then pointing a goal area with a homogeneous polygon. These two polygons are triangles, and then the copying is carried out between each corresponding triangle of two polygons. One advantage is that it move one area to another area with different shapes.

6. OUTLINE OF CACPS

CACPS is a composition tool for helping designers to investigate and analyze the result of putting a new building on planned area. It is developed in AI Institute, Zhejiang University, P.R.China. It runs in MICRO-VAX/II system under UNIX environment. CACPS is composted of 3D realistic graphics rendering and computer montage. Fig.3 shows its flowchart.

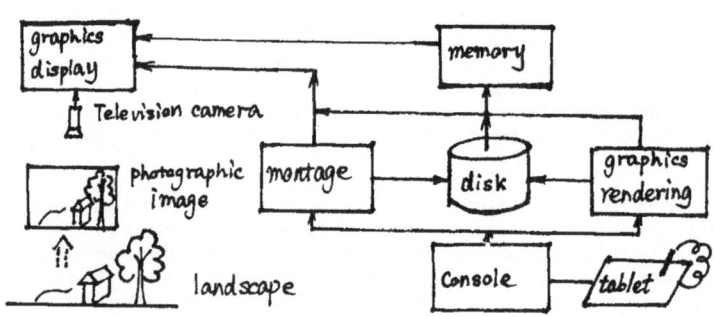

Fig. 3

In order to stimulate natural light, we developed a sphere cap light source model. The model contains a series of point light sources distributed on a sphere cap in a lattice at some resolution. Every point light source contains direct and indirect light. Its intensity depends on climate conditions and the position of the sun. The weather condition is controlled by a brightness factor b. It changes the rate of direct light and indirect light and the total intensity. The position of the sun is determined by the light direction, and it is used to get different illumination at different time in a day.

The computer montage provides a set of powerful utilities for overlaying graphics onto the background photograph. The montage is an interactive environment. It consists of image and graphics processing utilities. It also can be expanded easily by adding other utilities. At present, the montage in CACPS mainly provides functions of clipping, shifting, and scaling for graphics, functions of moving, filtering for image.

The perspective concordance is fitted through finding the vanishing lines in image and then translate new scene in object space to match the vanishing line.

The console program allows planner to see all designing processes on the screen. Generally, using CACPS for photomontage, planner can take the following steps:

1. Taking background photograph from planned area.

2. Generating 3D new building graphics

3. Overlaying the new building graphics onto the photograph.

The Fig. 4 and 5 show the results of CACPS. The first photograph is a planned area before constructed, the second is the scene after new building has been built on the planned area. It used moving function to change field in Fig4. into grass in Fig.5. Because of low resolution and monochromaticity of camera, the color photograph is taken through three color filters, so the quality of photograph is not very satisfactory.

Fig. 4   Fig.5

7. CONCLUTION

To overlay 3D graphics onto 2D image is a subject of combination of computer graphics and computer vision. The radical solution for this subject is to reconstruct 3D image from 2D image. But the research result in computer vision has proved that it is impossible to take out 3D information from one 2D image. With the development of artificial intelligence we can recognize scene from 2D image under certain prior knowledge. Another difficult problem exposed in graphics overlaying is that the processing shadow of both new scene and existing scene. The reshaping the shadow plays an important role in keeping concordance. At last, extract illumination condition from 2D image is another interested subject.

From the discussion above, we can see that only combining computer graphics and computer vision closely can we obtain satisfactory overlaying.

8. ACKNOWLEDGE

The first author sincerely thanks his college Xuejun Tong for helpness and encouragement in his research. The first author also want to thank Libin Shao, an assistant in China Textile University, to help author in preparing this paper.

9. REFERENCE

Balland DH and Brown CM (1982) Computer vision. Prentice-Hall, Inc.

Blinn JF and Newell ME (1976) Texture and reflection in computer generated image. ACM Comm., Vol.19, No.10.

Blinn JF (1982) Light reflection for simulation of clouds and dusty surface. Computer Graphics, Vol.16, No.3.

Brotman LS and Badler NI (1984) Generating soft shadows with a depth buffer algorithm. IEEE Computer Graphics and Application, Oct.

Cohen MF and Greenberg DP (1985) The hemicube a radiosity solution for complex environment. Computer Graphics, Vol.19, No.3.

Duff T (1985) Compositing 3D rendered image. Computer Graphics, Vol.19, No.3.

Gardner GY (1984) Simulation of natural scenes using texture quadric surface. Computer Graphics, Vol.18, Vol.3.

Lorig G (1986) Advanced image synthesis --- shading. in Advance in Computer Graphics, Ed. by Enderle and etc, Springer-Verlag.

Max NL (1986) Atmospheric illumination and shadows. Computer Graphics, Vol.20, No.4.

Nakamae E, Harafa K, Ishizaki T and Nishita T (1986) A montage method: overlaying of computer generated image onto a background photograph. Computer Graphics, Vol.20, No.4.

Nishita T and Nakamae W (1986) Continuous tone representation of 3D objects illumination by sky light. Computer Graphics, Vol.20, No.4.

Porter T and Duff T (1984) Compositing digital image. Computer Graphics, Vol.18, No.3.

Shuzhen Z (1982) Atmospheric light phenomenon. Science publishing House, Shanghai, P.R.China.

Turnbell WF and Gourlay I (1987) Visual impact analysis: A case study of computer-aided system. CAD, vol.19, No.4.

Warn DP (1983) Light control for synthetic image. Computer Graphics, Vol.17, No.3.

Willis PJ (1987) Visual simulation of atmospheric haze. Computer Graphics Forum, No.6.

Wu J (1988) Display of 3D object illumination by natural light and computer montage. Master Thesis, Zhejiang University, Hangzhou, P.R.China, May.

Jintong Wu is an assistant of computer science at Zhejiang University. His research interests include CV and CG. He received BS and MS in computer science from Zhejiang University in 1983, and 1988.
ADDRESS: AI institute, Zhejiang University,
        Hangzhou, P.R.China

Miaoliang Zhu is an associate professor of computer science at Zhejiang University. His research interests include CV and AI. He is the director of AI laboratory. In 1985 he was a visiting scholar at University of Maryland for one year. He received BS in automation from Nanjing Institute of Technology and MS in computer science science from Zhejinag University in 1968, and 1982.
ADDRESS: AI institute, Zhejiang University, Hangzhou,
        P.R.China

Zhijun He is a professor of computer science at Zhejiang University. His research intersets include AI, CG, and CV. He responses of several projects on expert systems and CG. Prof. He is currently the president of the AI Institute of Zhejinag University. He received BS in electric engineering from Zhejiang University in 1945.
ADDRESS: AI institute, Zhejiang University, Hangzhou,
P.R.China

Chapter 8
Modelling and CAD

Boolean Operations of Solids with Free-From Surfarces Through Polyhedral Approximation

H. Toriya, T. Takamura, T. Satoh, and H. Chiyokura

ABSTRACT

The paper describes a new implementation method for Boolean operations between solids with free-form surfaces. Boolean operations consist of two processes, topological modification and geometric modification which are performed separately in our method. This separation makes the Boolean operation process simple and robust. Surfaces contained in the final solid are interpolated by the repatching facility using Gregory patches.

Keywords: free-form surface, polyhedral approximation, Boolean operation, repatching, Gregory patch

1   INTRODUCTION

A significant number of industrial parts possess free-form surfaces which play an important role, both functionally and aesthetically, in today's CAD systems. Surface Modeling systems have a high degree of free-form surface coverage which has not been equaled in solid modelers. Consequently few facilities exist in solid modelers to modify these free-form surfaces. One of the most important facilities of solid modelers is Boolean operations between solids with free-form surfaces. For practical use in an engineering environment, these Boolean operations should be accurate and robust. In appearance design the results need not be as accurate, since the shape is an approximation, suitable only for aesthetic purposes. On the other hand, many industrial parts that require accuracy are often represented in terms of quadric surfaces. In these cases, intersections between quadric surfaces must be accurately calculated and represented.

Although CAD systems that support Boolean operations between solids with free-form surfaces have been developed, problems still remain in robustness, accuracy and speed. In conventional Boolean operations, the topological structure of solids is modified according to the result of geometric calculations such as surface to surface intersection. These intersection calculations are still a major problem in computer geometric design (Pratt 1986). Ill-conditioned cases frequently appear in surface to surface intersections, which are quite difficult to solve. The Boolean operations based on such intersections are not considered to be robustly or accurately performed in many cases.

We therefore propose a new Boolean operations algorithm between solids with free-form surfaces. In this method, preprocessing and postprocessing of polyhedral Boolean operations have been implemented as separate processes. In preprocessing, the intersection curves between two solids are calculated and the solids are approximated by polyhedrons. To generate the topological structure of the resultant solid, polyhedral Boolean operations are applied to the solids. The created polyhedron is modified according to the result of the intersection data calculated during preprocessing. The topological and geometric modification of the final solid is performed in different modules, adding to the simplicity and reliability of the Boolean operations algorithm. Even if the intersection calculation fails, a final solid that approximates the correct one can be generated. This method has been implemented in the solid modeler DESIGNBASE (Chiyokura 1988).

2 BACKGROUND

Down through the history of solid modeling, several methods for Boolean operations for solids have been proposed. Although they depend on data representation of solids such as CSG or boundary representations (B-reps), most of them are based on the boundary evaluation/merging methods in which edges are classified by faces and then combined. Requicha and Voelcker (1985) described the boundary evaluation method used in PADL based on CSG. Many Boolean operation methods for solids represented by B-reps are proposed by several authors (Mäntylä 1982; Yamaguchi 1984), though their methods must treat many special cases even for polyhedral solids. Complex geometric intersections between faces and edges such as overlap or coplanar must be detected and treated properly. Mäntylä (1986) presented the topologically complete Boolean operations algorithm for planar polyhedral 2-manifold objects, but its disadvantage is that it cannot be extended directly to objects with free-form surfaces.

In conventional Boolean operations algorithms, intersection curves between surfaces are first calculated and then the shapes of the solids are modified using the result. The intersection calculations must be accurate, robust and fast to accomplish Boolean operations for practical use. Many intersection calculation methods such as the algebraic (Sederberg 1985, 1986), marching (Barnhill 1987) and recursive subdivision (Houghton 1985) methods have been proposed, however, none of them satisfy all of the requirements of Boolean operations as described by Pratt (1986). In practical systems, for example, free-form surfaces are often represented by bicubic patches and the intersection curve for two bicubic surface patches is degree 324 (Sederberg 1983). Because it is difficult to calculate such intersections correctly in every case, Boolean operations based on intersection calculations are not robust.

Even if the intersection curves are calculated successfully, how should the curves be approximated as edges on the final solid ? If low degree splines are used for the approximation, the intersection curve may not lie entirely on either original surface as described by Miller (1986). In such a case, trimmed surface patches are used to represent surfaces in the final solid (Casale 1987; Farouki 1987). A trimmed patch is a portion of an entire patch which represents the shape of the surface.

If a surface F shown in Figure 1(a) is divided, F1 and F2 in (b) are treated as if they are on the original surface F. The intersection curves between the surfaces are approximated using edges on the boundary of the trimmed surface patches. Because the intersection curves often play an important role in design, designers often wish to modify the shape of the curves. In some systems this modification is not possible since it destroys the trimmed patch data.

To overcome these problems, we propose a new Boolean operations algorithm. This algorithm consists of preprocessing and postprocessing of the polyhedral Boolean operations. We have implemented the algorithm in the solid modeler DESIGNBASE. In this system, B-reps are used to represent solid shapes, and primitive operations, which include Euler operations, are used to manipulate B-reps. Each primitive operation has a corresponding inverse which can be used to

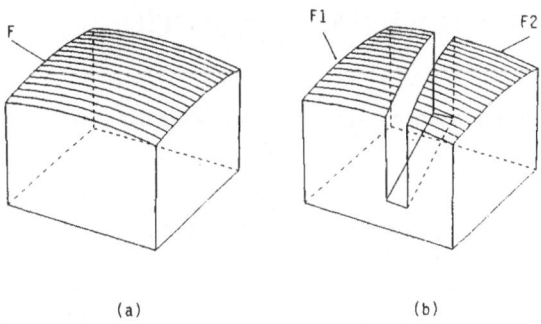

Fig.1. An example of a trimmed surface

undo operations on the solid (Toriya 1986). Curved edges are represented by cubic Bézier curves and free-form surfaces are interpolated by Gregory patches (Chiyokura 1983). Surface patches can be generated using the surface boundary edge data, which makes it possible to re-generate Gregory patches for surfaces in the resultant solid. Such a method is called repatching (Sarraga 1983). The following shows several advantages of our new algorithm:

- Suppose that some solid modeling systems already support Boolean operations between polyhedral solids. The general strategy to enhance them for free-form surfaces is to extend the polyhedral Boolean operations programs. Such an enhancement is difficult because Boolean operations for polyhedrons are themselves very complicated and both topological and geometric data of the original solids must be modified in the same program. In our method, on the other hand, Boolean operations for polyhedral solids are used to generate a topological structure which approximates the resultant solid. We have implemented a pre-processor which calculates intersection curves and converts free-form surfaces to flat faces and a postprocessor which modifies the shape of the resultant solid referring to the inter-section curve data. Because topological structure data and geometric data are generated independently, the algorithm becomes simple and easy to implement.

- The intersections are calculated in the preprocessor and even if the calculations fail, the Boolean operations can be completed. In that case, the intersections appear in the polyhe-dral Boolean operations process as some straight edges and they are modified to adequate curves. The final solid can be obtained as an approximation of the correct one. Therefore the Boolean operations are performed robustly.

- Because surfaces in the resultant solid can be interpolated using the repatching facility, designers can, even after Boolean operations, modify edges which approximate the inter-section curves. In trimmed surface representation, the patch data is partially used, whereas it is entirely used in our method, making the data structure and application programming very simple.

- When designers need accuracy, quadric data can be given to free-form surfaces. This data is utilized to accurately calculate intersection curves. The shapes of surfaces divided through Boolean operations may change if they are generated by repatching. This can be avoided for quadric surfaces because the quadric data is stored during the Boolean operations.

A system which supports polyhedral Boolean operations can be enhanced for free-form surfaces by adding preprocessing and postprocessing without modifying the polyhedral Boolean opera-tions. Although Lichten and Samek (1987) have also tried to integrate free-form surfaces into a polyhedral solid modeling system based on CSG using polyhedral approximation, their method still has problems in accuracy and model size. In our method, such problems do not appear, because polyhedral approximation is only used to generate the topological structure.

3 OVERVIEW OF BOOLEAN OPERATIONS

The Boolean operations algorithm consists of the following five steps:

1. Calculation of intersection curves : To avoid making a complicated surface which can not be repatched, subdivide the free-form surfaces which intersect with edges of the other solid. Curved or straight edges are created on these surfaces. Then the intersection curves between the surfaces are calculated and curved edges are made on them. The curve information of newly created edges is stored. Figure 2(a) shows two solids before the Boolean operation. As shown in figure 2(b) edges are created on the intersection curves to subdivide the surfaces. All edge data created in this step is stored and the edges are deleted.

2. Polyhedral approximation : The free-form surfaces of the solids are approximated by poly-hedrons. Curved edges are converted to straight edges and then the surfaces are approxi-mated by flat faces. The approximated solid is found in figure 2(c).

3. Boolean operation between approximated solids : Apply a polyhedral Boolean operation to the approximated solids. The Boolean operation is implemented using the primitive operations. Because the primitive operations have corresponding inverses, the Boolean operation is invertible. Figure 2(d) shows the resultant solid.

4. Surface generation : Delete unnecessary edges and convert straight edges to curved edges. For each intersection edge, find the corresponding curve data stored in step 1 and modify the shape of the edge. Some new edges are added for repatching. The final solid is drawn in figure 2(e).

5. Repatching : After the Boolean operation, regular or irregular surfaces are generated. These surfaces are interpolated by Gregory patches. Figure 2(f) shows the control points of the Gregory patches.

Among the steps described, step 3 and step 5 are discussed in (Toriya 1985; Chiyokura 1983) respectively. The rest of the paper focuses on steps 1, 2 and 4.

4 DETAILED DESCRIPTION OF THE BOOLEAN OPERATION

4.1 Calculation of intersection curves

The intersection curves between the two solids A and B must be calculated before they are approximated by polyhedrons.

4.1.1 Subdivision of surfaces

The system does not have a facility to generate surface patches for a surface containing holes. The surfaces are subdivided so as to avoid making such a surface during the Boolean operation process. As shown in figure 3(a), a surface Fa of the solid A which intersects an edge Eb of the solid B is subdivided by generating edges on the surface. At first, intersection points between the

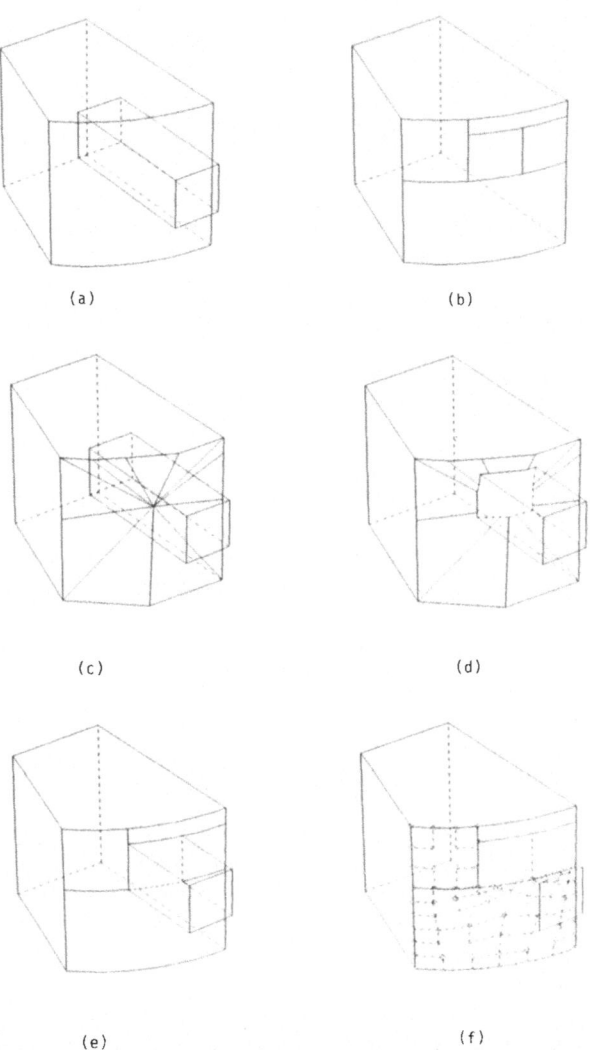

Fig.2. The Boolean operation process by polyhedron approximation.

edge Eb and the surface Fa are calculated. Then a plane which contains one of the intersection points is selected as a cut plane of the surface Fa. For example, if the edge Eb connects two flat faces, a plane which contains one of the faces is selected. In the example, the lower of the two faces is selected.

Intersection curves between the plane and the surface Fa are calculated and curved edges are created on the intersections (figure 3(b)). The edge Ea intersects with the edge Eb at the intersection point V. The two edges are divided at the intersection point by creating a vertex on each edge (figure 3(c)). This process is also applied to surfaces of solid B which intersect with edges of solid A. Edges and vertices created in this step are marked. For marked vertices, the surface IDs on which they lie are stored. In this way, vertices are created on the intersection points between all the edges in one solid and the curved surfaces of the other solid.

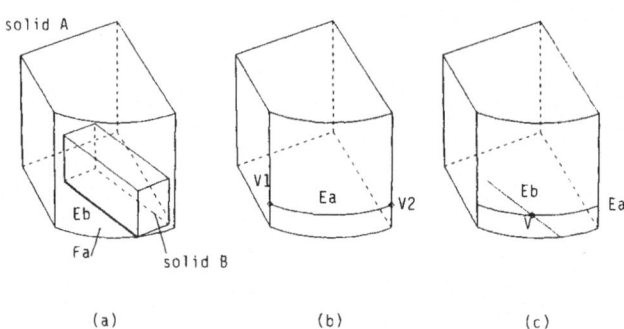

(a) (b) (c)

Fig.3. Division of a free-form surface

4.1.2 Intersection calculation between edges and flat faces

Intersection points between all edges of solid A and flat faces of solid B are calculated and vertices are generated on the edges. In the same way, new vertices are created on the edges of solid B which intersect with the flat faces of solid A. These vertices are marked and the face IDs are stored. After this process, vertices are generated on all intersection points between the edges of one solid and the flat faces of the other solid.

4.1.3 Intersection curve calculation

Next, the intersection curves between two intersecting faces of solid A and B are calculated. For all vertices on the intersecting surface, vertices which were marked in previous steps are found. If these vertices have stored face IDs of the other solid, then the face and surface intersect. The intersection curves between them are calculated and edges are generated on the curves.

If the intersecting faces are quadric surfaces, then their geometric data is utilized to calculate the intersection curves, which increases the speed and accuracy of the calculations. For example, the intersection between a cone and a flat face is a conic curve and it can be easily calculated if the end points of the curve are calculated. Moreover, a conic curve can be well approximated by a parametric cubic curve such as a cubic Bézier curve (Mortenson 1985).

4.1.4 Save the intersection curve data

The edges marked in sections 4.1.1 and 4.1.3 are stored in an intersection curve table. This table contains the coordinates of end vertices and control point data of the curved edges. If faces adjacent to the edge have attributes of quadric data, they are also stored in the table. All the edges are then deleted to obtain a simpler topology for the polyhedral approximation process.

4.1.5 Example

Figure 4 shows the process of these steps. Two intersecting solids A and B are depicted in figure 4(a). Because the edges Eb1 and Eb2 intersect with the surface Fa1, the surface is subdivided and a new surface Fa2 is generated (figure 4(b)). In this case, the flat face Fb2 is selected as a cut plane of the surface Fa1. Four vertices Va1, Vb1, Va2 and Vb2 are generated on each edge at the intersection points and are marked (figure 4(b)).

The intersection points between edges and flat faces are then calculated. In figure 4(c), the edge Ea1 intersects with the faces Fb1 and Fb3. Intersection points between them are calculated and vertices Va3 and Va4 are generated on the points and are marked.

Intersection curves between intersecting faces are calculated. The surface Fa2 has four marked vertices Va1, Va2, Va3 and Va4. Vertices Va1 and Va3 have the face Id Fb1 which indicates that the two faces, Fb1 and Fa2 intersect (figure 4(d)). The intersection curves between the two faces are calculated and an edge Ea2 is generated on the curve (figure 4(e)). In the same way, the intersection curve between Fa2 and Fb3 is calculated and an edge Ea3 is generated on the curve.

All edges created in this step are deleted and their curved data is stored in the intersection table (figure 4(f)). Vertices Va3, Va4, Vb1 and Vb2, etc. which are on the exact intersection points between edges and faces remain. In the polyhedral Boolean operation, edges are generated between vertices Vb1 and Va3, and between Vb2 and Va4. The shape of these edges will be later modified according to the intersection curve data.

4.2 Polyhedral approximation

Before applying polyhedral Boolean operations to solids, the solids must be approximated by polyhedrons. At first, curved edges are converted to straight lines, then curved surfaces are approximated by flat faces.

4.2.1 Approximation of curved edges

Curved edges are approximated by two straight edges. As shown in figure 5, an intersection point C between the tangent lines of the Bézier curve at end vertices A and B is calculated. The Bézier curve is approximated by two straight edges AC and BC. If the Bézier curve is not on a plane, then the curve must be projected on to an adequate plane where the intersection point can be calculated. If the two tangent lines are parallel or the point C is too far from the curve, the curve is subdivided at the middle point. The newly created vertex C keeps control points and end vertex coordinates of the original Bézier curve, and also quadric surface information if the faces adjacent to the original edges were quadric. Figure 6 shows an example of this approximation method. Curved edges in figure 6(a) are approximated by straight edges and the resultant solid is depicted in 6(b).

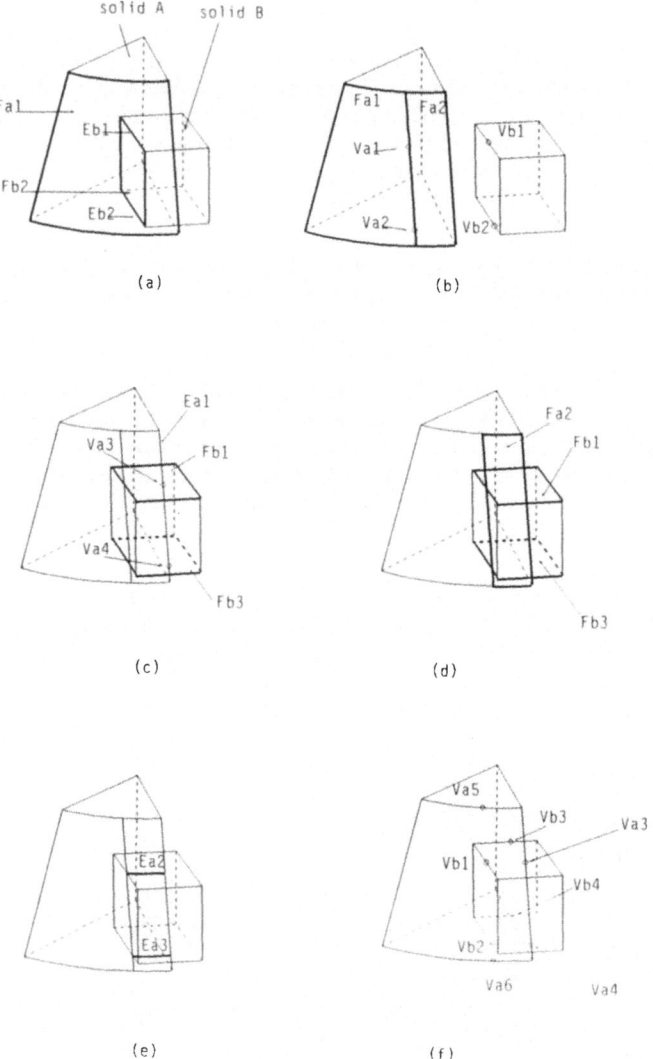

Fig.4. The intersection calculation process

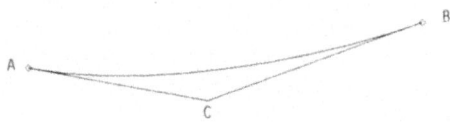

Fig.5. Approximation of a curve

4.2.2   Approximation of curved surfaces

All curved surfaces which consist of straight edges are approximated by several flat faces. The center of gravity of the surface is calculated. Edges between the center point V and vertices on the surface are generated until all the faces around the vertex become flat (figure 6(c)). Edges created in this step are also marked.

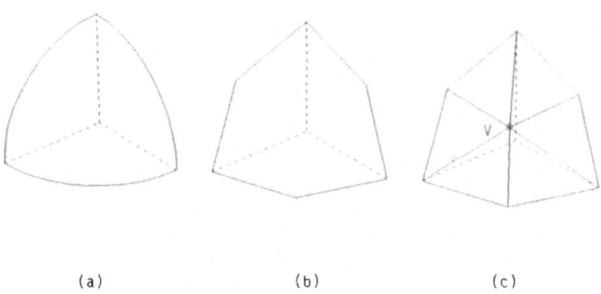

(a)　　　　　　　(b)　　　　　　　(c)

Fig.6. Polyhedral approximation

The two solids A and B are approximated by polyhedrons by the procedure described above. The polyhedral Boolean operation is subsequently applied to these solids. All marked edges and vertices will be utilized in the next step.

4.3   Surface generation

The resultant polyhedral Boolean operation solid is a polyhedral approximation of the desired solid (figure 2(d)). This solid will be modified to the desired solid by applying the following four steps.

4.3.1   Edge deletion

Edges in the polyhedral solid can be categorized by the following three types:

1. Edges generated in the polyhedral approximation step.
2. Edges generated during the polyhedral Boolean operation.
3. Edges which were in the original solid.

Because type 1 edges were used to approximate the curved surfaces and are unnecessary for the desired solid, they must be deleted. These edges were marked in section 4.1.4 and are easy to find and delete. As a result, a solid with surfaces bounded by straight edges is generated as shown in figure 7(a). The type 2 and type 3 edges are modified in the next step according to the curve data stored in the system.

4.3.2 Curved edge generation

As depicted in figure 7(a), vertices which connect two edges like vertices V1 and V2 are rounded to generate curved edges. These vertices fall into one of three categories depending on how they were generated:

1. Vertices generated in the curved edges approximation step.

2. Vertices generated during the polyhedral Boolean operation.

3. Vertices which were in the original solid.

Nothing should be done to the type 3 vertices and they are ignored in this step.

Type 1 vertices were marked when curved edges were approximated by straight edges as described in section 4.2.1. End points or control points coordinates of the original curves were also given to these vertices. The positions of the two vertices connected to the type 1 vertex are not changed, unless the geometric data around the type 1 vertex was modified during the polyhedral Boolean operation. The intersection points between all edges of a solid and the faces of the other solid were calculated, and the edges were divided at the points before the solids were approximated. Therefore, in most cases, edges around type 1 vertices do not intersect with faces of the other solid. If the vertex coordinates data stored at the type 1 vertex coincides with

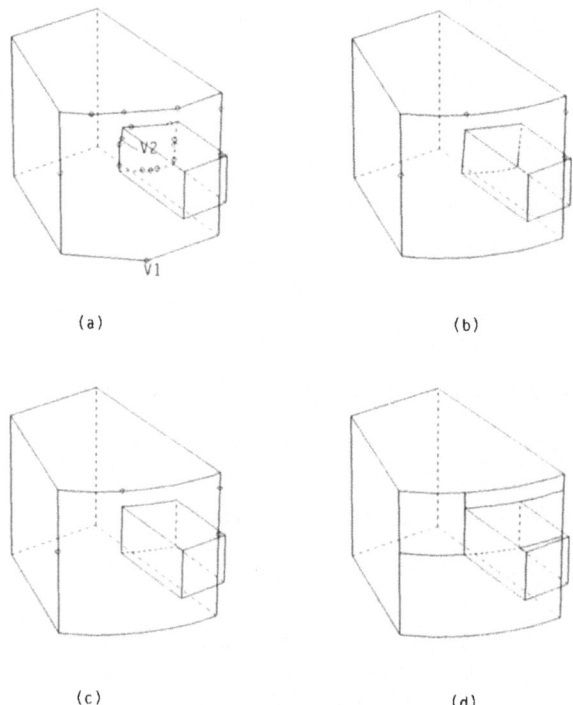

(a)

(b)

(c)

(d)

Fig.7. Rounding of a polyhedral solid

the original vertices connecting to the edge, then the edges around the type 1 vertex can be curved using the stored control points data. The type 1 vertex is deleted and the curved edge is generated which is the same as the original one.

The type 2 vertices are also deleted and curved edges which are tangent to the two edges connecting the type 2 vertex are generated. The curved edges approximate edges of the desired solid. In the next step, the curved edges will be replaced by the exact edges calculated previously. Now, no type 1 nor type 2 vertices should remain and the resultant shape of the solid closely approximates the desired solid(figure 7(b)).

4.3.3 Modification of the curved edges

The approximated curves are modified by consulting with the exact curve data calculated previously. The end point coordinates of approximated edges are compared to the result of the intersection edges calculated in section 4.1.2 and the closest curve data is found for each approximated edge. The shapes of these edges are modified according to the exact curve data (figure 7(c)) and then the exact data in the intersection table is deleted. If quadric data is saved in the intersection table, then quadric attributes are given to the faces adjacent to the curved edge if all vertices on each face are also on the quadric face.

4.3.4 Curved edge addition

Curved edges created in section 4.1.1 were deleted in section 4.1.4 and therefore these edges do not exist in the solid generated by the polyhedral Boolean operation. The corresponding intersection curve data of these edges remains. In such a case, a pair of vertices which are coincident to end points of the intersection data is found. Using the curve information, a new curved edge is created between the two vertices (figure 7(d)). Surface shapes after the Boolean operations become simple and holes are deleted in the free-form surfaces. Repatching of the newly created surfaces is now easier. This curved edge addition step can be omitted if complicated free-form surfaces or surfaces with holes can be repatched.

The Boolean operations between free-form surfaces are now complete. Gregory patches are generated when curved surface data is needed. As for quadric surfaces, the quadric data is maintained after the Boolean operations. All shape modifications are performed by primitive operations, all of which have corresponding inverses. Thus, the Boolean operations for free-form surfaces are invertible.

5   EXAMPLES

An example of a solid generated using Boolean operations is shown in figure 8. Figure 8(a) and (b) show a cone and a polyhedral solid. In this case, quadric surfaces and flat faces are intersecting. The result is shown in figure 8(c) and the shaded image in (d).

Figure 9 depicts the Boolean operations between intersecting solids with free-form surfaces and quadric surfaces. Figure (a) shows a mechanical part and (b) shows a cylinder. The shaded image of the result of the union operation between the solids is shown in (c).

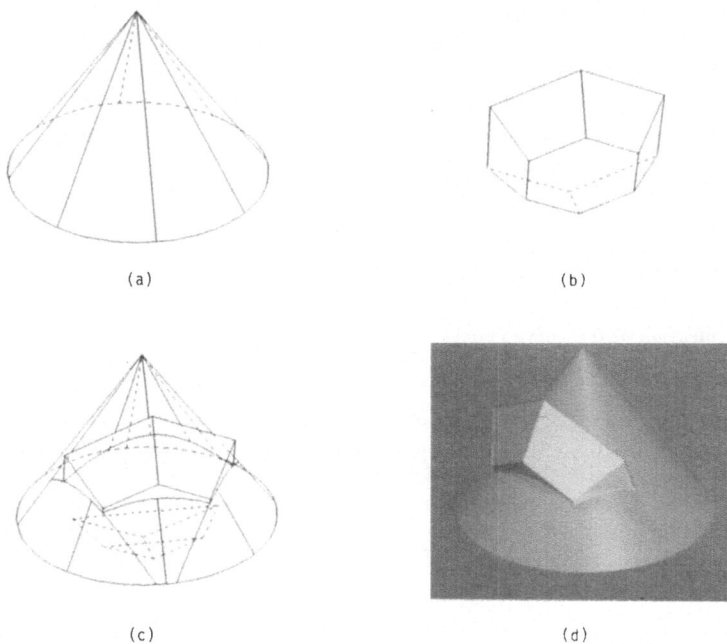

(a)　　　　　　　　　　　　(b)

(c)　　　　　　　　　　　　(d)

Fig.8. Boolean operation between quadric surfaces and flat faces

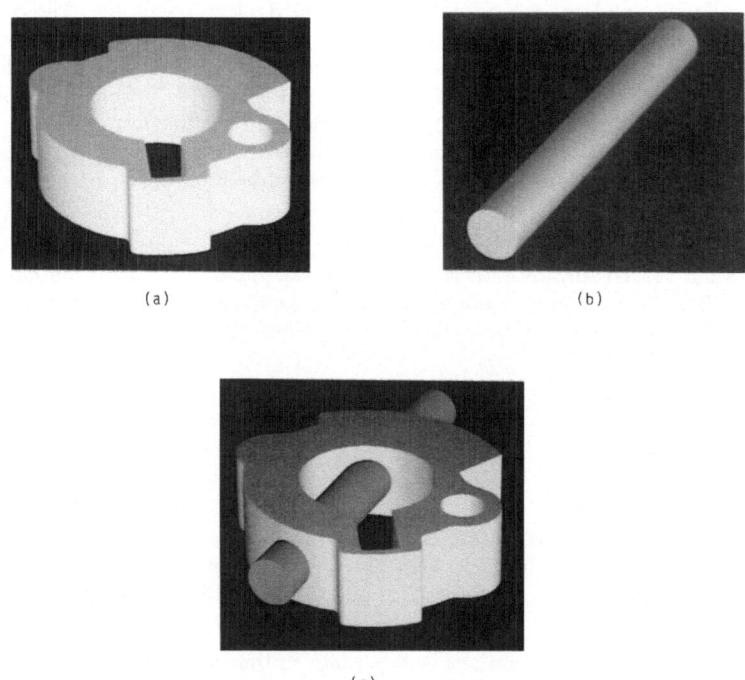

(a)　　　　　　　　　　　　(b)

(c)

Fig.9. Boolean operation between quadric surfaces and free-form surfaces

6   CURRENT PROBLEMS

Although the method we have proposed works well in most cases, the current implementation still has several problems which are listed below:

1. Intersection calculation libraries for free-form surfaces are not yet completed, therefore the intersection curves between surfaces are not accurate. Corresponding edges to these intersection curves approximate the real curves on the final solid.

2. The method works correctly only when edges of one solid intersect surfaces of the other solid. Suppose that two surfaces intersect each other but no edges on the boundary of the surfaces intersect with the other surface. Intersection curves can not be found, because they are calculated when intersection points between edges on the surface boundary and the other surface intersect.

3. When a solid with free-form surfaces is approximated by a polyhedral solid, the geometric relationship between the two solids may change. For example, even if the original surfaces do not intersect with each other, they may intersect after the polyhedral approximation. In such a case, the resultant solid created by polyhedral Boolean operations has a different topological structure compared to the desired result.

Problem 1 can be solved by enhancing intersection libraries for free-form surfaces. The intersection curves could be represented by several Bézier curves. As for problem 2, by subdividing the surface, the intersections could be found. This subdivision of surfaces is currently under research.

To solve problem 3, unnecessary edges created during polyhedral Boolean operations should be deleted. The unnecessary edges are edges which do not have corresponding intersection curves calculated previously. Currently, because some intersection calculation libraries are not fully developed, it is difficult to find unnecessary edges. Turner (1988) proposed a polyhedral approximation method which keeps topological relationships between two solids. It could be utilized in our method.

7   CONCLUSION

We have discussed a new method for Boolean operations between solids with free-form surfaces. To accomplish the Boolean operations, only a preprocessor and a postprocessor are implemented. Compared to conventional methods, this method has several advantages:

- Topological structure data and geometric data of the resultant solid are generated independently, making the algorithm simple.

- Even if intersection calculations fail, a final solid which approximates the correct one can be obtained.

- Because surfaces in the final solid are interpolated by the repatching facility unlike a trimmed surface based system, no partial surfaces appear. Therefore application programs are easy to implement.

- Intersection curves can be calculated accurately for surfaces with quadric attributes and the attributes are inherited in the surfaces of the final solid.

- The shapes of edges on intersection curves generated by the Boolean operations can be modified locally.

This method enhances Boolean operations on free-form surfaces by the use of polyhedral solid approximation. However, further research is necessary to improve the accuracy of intersection curves and to generate a correct solid even in topologically ill-conditioned cases.

8 ACKNOWLEDGMENTS

We would like to thank Tosiyasu L. Kunii and Fumihiko Kimura, professors of the University of Tokyo, for their valuable suggestions; Hideko S. Kunii, general manager of RICOH's Software Research Center and Kenji Ueda of RICOH CO. for their valuable comments and discussion; and Aidan O'Neill of RICOH CO. for assistance with the text.

REFERENCES

Barnhill R.E., Farin G., Jordan M. and Piper B.R. (1987), "Surface/surface intersection", *Computer Aided Geometric Design*, 4(1):3-16

Casale M.S. (1987), "Free-Form Solid Modeling with Trimmed Surface Patches", *IEEE Computer Graphics and Applications*, 7(1):33-43

Chiyokura H. and Kimura F. (1983), "Design of Solids with Free form Surfaces", *Proc. SIGGRAPH 83*, 17(3):289-298

Chiyokura H. (1988), Solid Modeling with DESIGNBASE, Addison-Wesley

Farouki R.T. (1987), "Direct Surface Section Evaluation", *Geometric Modeling: Algorithm and New Trends*, Farin G. ed., SIAM, Philadelphia, pp 319-334

Houghton E.G., Emnett R.F., Factor J.D. and Sabharwal C.L. (1985), "Implementation of a divide-and-conquer method for intersection of parametric surfaces", *Computer Aided Geometric Design*, 2(1):173-183

Lichten L. and Samek M. (1987), "Integrating Sculptured Surfaces into a Polyhedral Solid Modeling System", *Geometric Modeling: Algorithm and New Trends*, Farin G. ed., SIAM, Philadelphia, pp 109-122

Mäntylä M. (1982), "Computational Topology: A Study of Topological Manipulations and Interrogations in Computer Graphics and Geometric Modeling", *Acta Polytechnica Scandinavica, Mathematics and Computer Science Series No. 37*, Helsinki

Mäntylä M. (1986), "Boolean Operations of 2-Manifolds through Vertex Neighborhood Classification", *ACM Transactions on Graphics*, pp 1-29

Miller, J.R. (1986), "Sculptured Surfaces in Solid Models: Issues and Alternative Approaches", *IEEE Computer Graphics and Applications*, 6(12):37-47

Mortenson M.E. (1985), Geometric Modeling, John Wiley & Sons

Pratt M.J. and Geisow A.D. (1986), "Surface/surface intersection problems", *The mathematics of Surfaces*, Oxford Univ. Press, pp 117-142

Requicha A.G. and Voelcker H.B. (1985), "Boolean Operations in Solid Modeling: Boundary Evaluation and Merging Algorithms", *Proc. of the IEEE*, 73(1):30-44

Sarraga R.F. and Waters W.C. (1983), "Free-form Surfaces in GMSOLID: Goals and Issues", *Solid Modeling by Computers: from Theory to Applications*, Pickett M.S. and Boyse J.W. ed., pp 187-204

Sederberg T.W. (1983), "Implicit and parametric curves and surfaces for computer aided geometric design", *Ph.D. thesis, Purdue Univ.*

Sederberg T.W. (1985), "Steiner Surface Patches" *IEEE Computer Graphics and Applications*, 5(5):pp 23-36

Sederberg T.W. (1986), "Algebraic Geometry for Computer-Aided Geometric Design" *IEEE Computer Graphics and Applications*, 6(6):52-59

Toriya H., Satoh T., Ueda K. and Chiyokura H. (1986), "UNDO and REDO Operation for Solid Modeling", *IEEE Computer Graphics and Applications*, 6(4):35-42

Toriya H., Satoh T., Ueda K. and Chiyokura H. (1985), "Invertible Set Operations for Solid Modeling" *Computer Graphics*, Kunii T.L. ed., Springer-Verlag, Tokyo, pp 3-20

Turner J.U. (1988), "Accurate Solid Modeling Using Polyhedral Approximations", *IEEE Computer Graphics and Applications*, 8(3):14-28.

Yamaguchi F. and Tokeida T. (1984), "A unified algorithm for Boolean shape operations", *IEEE Computer Graphics and Applications*, 4(6):24-37

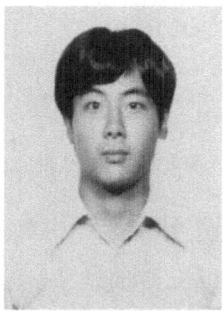

Hiroshi Toriya is a member of the 3D CAD project at RICOH's Software Research Center. His research interests include solid modeling, geometric modeling, computer graphics, and their applications. He received a BS in information science in 1983 from the University of Tokyo where his research included octree data structures and their manipulations. He entered the solid modeling project at RICOH in 1984, which has now developed into the product DESIGNBASE. He is a member of the Information Processing Society of Japan. Several of his papers have been selected by NICOGRAPH.
Address: RICOH COMPANY, LTD. 1-17, Koishikawa-cho 1-Chome Bunkyo-ku, Tokyo, 112, Japan

Teiji Takamura, a member of the 3D CAD project at RICOH's Software Research Center, is interested in solid modeling, free-form surface interpolation and computer graphics. His current research includes general free-form surface intersections and rational parametric surface interpolations by using rational Bézier patches. He received a BS in information science in 1982 from the University of Tokyo. He is a member of ACM SIGGRAPH and the IEEE Computer Society.
Address: RICOH COMPANY, LTD. 1-17, Koishikawa-cho 1-Chome Bunkyo-ku, Tokyo, 112, Japan

Toshiaki Satoh is a member of the 3D CAD project at RICOH's Software Research Center. His areas of research interest include solid modeling, computer graphics and the application of artificial intelligence techniques to computer-aided design. He received BS in information science in 1984 from the University of Tokyo. He is a member of ACM SIGGRAPH, the Information Processing Society of Japan, and the Japan Society of Precision Engineering. His papers have been selected by NICOGRAPH.
Address: RICOH COMPANY, LTD. 1-17, Koishikawa-cho 1-Chome Bunkyo-ku, Tokyo, 112, Japan

Hiroaki Chiyokura is a manager of the 3D CAD project at Software Research Center at RICOH CORPORATION. His research interests are solid modeling, computer graphics, and their applications to computer-aided design and manufacturing. He received his BS and MS in mathematics from Keio University in 1979 and 1980, respectively. He earned his Dr.Eng. in precision machinery engineering from the University of Tokyo in 1984. He has written a book "Solid Modelling with DESIGNBASE: Theory and Implementation", recently published by Addison-Wesley. He is a member of ACM SIGGRAPH.
Address: RICOH CORPORATION, Techmart Suite 455, 5201 Great American Parkway, Santa Clara, CA 95054, U. S. A.

A Flexible, Quantitative Method for NC Machining Verification Using a Space Division Based Solid Model

Y. Kawashima, K. Itoh, T. Ishida, S. Nonaka, and K. Ejiri

ABSTRACT

A geometric modeling method called Graftree and a system configuration technique for Graftree based a NC (numerical control) machining simulator are proposed. Graftree is constructed by combining Oct-tree and CSG so as to simulate machining process precisely in 3-dimensional space. Using Graftree the Boolean operation has no risk to yield topological conflicts which often cause to stop the simulation process abnormally. Founded on the properties of Graftree, a NC machining simulator is constructed which consists of three individual subsystems: (1) data input operations, (2) geometric simulation, and (3) interactive verification. In this system, whole cutter motions are simulated in the batch processing, and the results are stored so as to be available for the verification. In the verification subsystem, the machined shape at any cutter motion is selectively reconstructed and visualized using them. Furthermore, the machined shape is evaluated through the the quantitative information for correcting NC program.

Key words: Numerical control machining, NC, Geometric simulation, Solid modeling, Oct-tree, Space division, Z-buffer, CSG, Interference detection.

1. INTRODUCTION

Numerical control (NC) machining with complicated multiaxis cutter motions for 3-dimensional parts has a high risk in wrong actions caused by cutter interferences, over-cuttings and so on. To avoid them, it is indispensable to verify the NC program and correct it before machining begins. So far, the task of verification was conducted using the machine tool with no workpiece on it, but this was much time-consuming (more than the effective machining) and difficult to do the verification precisely.

Machining simulation using a solid modeling technique was proposed almost ten years ago to verify NC programs rapidly and precisely. A number of studies have obtained successful results. For example, Hook(1986) proposed a method to visualize milling processes very rapidly on a special hardware equipment. Wang & Wang(1986,1987) applied their simulator to a machining process with over 200,000 step cutter motions and they presented an idea to verify the machined shape which included a consideration of the tolerance.

However, the existing studies have almost all been focused only on a step-by-step visualization of the cutting processes. Machining are simulated only on a 2.5-dimensional display space by a visualization procedure such as a Z-buffer method with some extensions. While we accept that the 2.5 dimensional simulation can generate images of the machining scene rapidly, is difficult to obtain effective information from it to detect and correct wrong cutter actions. Such a simulation should be performed on a 3-dimensional space. That is why we began this study.

Our approach consists of two parts, that is, to construct (1) a new geometric modeling suitable for machining simulation which are precise and reliable in a 3-dimensional space, and (2) a machining simulation system where the user can easily get the information needed to verify and correct the NC program.

For the machining simulation, geometric modeling for 3-dimensional objects, such as workpieces, cutter swept volumes etc., is the most fundamental and important subject. Geometric models should have two characteristics, preciseness of geometric expression and robustness for the Boolean operation which simulates cutting process. However, none of the existing solid modelings has both characteristics at the same time, so we built a new method called Graftree which suffices the requirements.

As to the machining simulation system, no methodology has been presented in the past studies. Our fundamental considerations are that verification should be done selectively for cutting motions because machining often has many cutter motion steps and usually all of them work well except for a few motions; and that it should be done quantitatively in order to provide effective information for the NC program correction.

For Graftree, definition, set operation procedure and visualization method are presented in the next section. The system configuration method is described in the third section.

2. GEOMETRIC MODELING

2.1 DEFINITION

Graftree is a geometric modeling method based on a space division technique which is used for Oct-tree (Meagher 1983) and its derivatives (Wyvill 1986) (Duest 1988). In Oct-tree, a cubic space where an object lies, is divided recursively into small spaces (called cells) until each cell is sorted out as belonging to either of the following two classes for a certain degree of accuracy (resolution):
    FULL   homogeneous cell included in the object, and
    EMPTY   homogeneous cell excluded outside of the object.
The result of the space division is described using an octonal tree structure, and an object is expressed as a set of the 'FULL' cell spaces.

In the case of Graftree, the space division procedure is the same as Oct-tree except on two points. The first difference is in the cell classification, that is
    FULL   homogeneous cell included in the object,
    EMPTY   homogeneous cell excluded outside of the object, and
    INTERSECT   a cell containing all or part of the object in a
                    certain restriction (where 'restriction' is defined
                    later in 2.2).

An object is expressed as a set of the 'FULL' cell spaces and the intersecting spaces between the 'INTERSECT' cell spaces and the object itself.

In each 'INTERSECT' cell, the intersecting space is described using an CSG (Constructive Solid Geometry) (Requicha 1982) form with a certain restriction which makes the CSG enough simple so that geometric processing such as the Boolean operation or visualization can be applied easily. In other words, the space division in Graftree works to simplify the object description, but not to encord it like in Oct-tree.

The second differing point is that when the space division reaches a given resolution, each of the smallest cells is kept to hold the description of the object in an unrestricted CSG. This means that the degree of accuracy is dynamically controllable.

2.2 STRUCTURE

Graftree forms the data structure shown in Fig.1, where CSG trees for 'INTERSECT' cells are 'grafted' upon Oct-tree (this is the origin of the name Graftree).

In our implementation, CSG for each 'INTERSECTION' cell is constructed with half-spaces bounded by an infinite surface. In short, a half-space is regarded as primitive. For such CSG form, the restriction in the 'INTERSECT' cell is defined as the the maximum number of surfaces able to exist on the CSG tree. Fig.2 presents examples of Graftree (2-dimensional) generated with different restrictions. In example 1, each 'INTERSECT' cell has at most one surface, and in example 2, within two surfaces. As shown in this figure, the restriction, i.e., the maximum number of surfaces is selective. Practically, it is determined to be three or less by considering the visualization procedure.

2.3 GENERATION

Graftree is generated from CSG through the conversion process shown in Box.1. It should be noted that processes A, B, C, and F-a are performed by a function which judges if each CSG primitive (half-space in our implementation) intersects the Sub_Space or not. Therefore the boundary elements such as edges or vertices of the intersecting space need not be calculated.

2.4 SET OPERATION

The Boolean operation (spatial set operation) between solid objects is the most fundamental process for machining simulation, since cutting is performed in the simulator as a difference operation between the workpiece and the cutter swept volumes.

Box.2 shows the procedure for the difference operation. The other operations are almost the same except for several operation-oriented statements.

It should be noted that the set operations for Graftree have high robustness because they consist of the procedure make_GT mentioned above which does not treat the topological structure of the modeled object. Repetition of the determining topological structure, which is used in set operation of B-rep.(Requicha 1982) for example, probably yields conflicts between topologies and geometries because of properties of numerical computing. Generally such conflicts are very

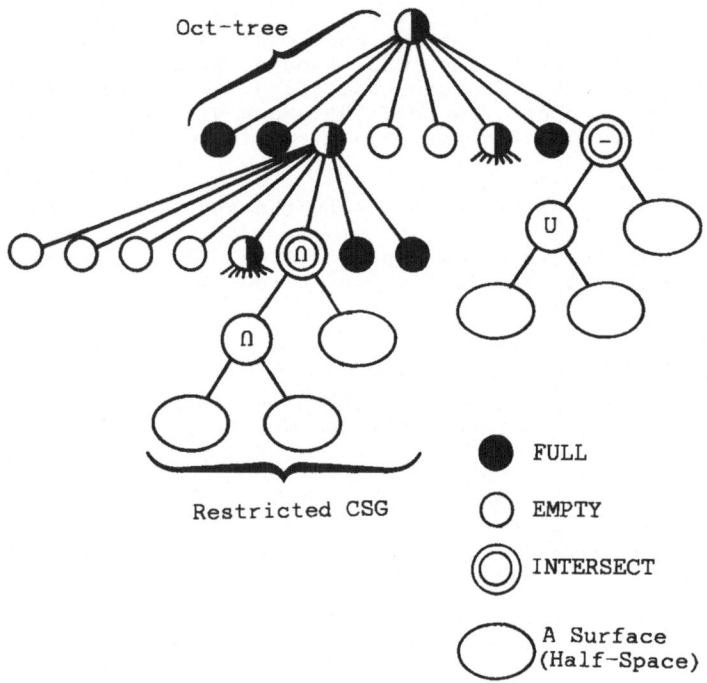

Fig. 1. Data Configuration

```
                    Box 1.   Procedure make_GT

(1)   Preparation
   - model an object in CSG form,
   - set cubic space enclosing the modeled object,
   - set resolution.
(2)   Procedure make_GT( Object, Space )
  A.   if ( Space exists within the Object ) return( FULL );
  B.   if ( Space exists out of the Object ) return( EMPTY );
  C.   if ( CSG for Object satisfys the restriction )
              return( Object );
  D.   if ( Space < resolution ) return( Object );
  E.   get eight Sub_spaces of Space;
  F.   for i-th Sub_space (i=0,7)
              i-th Sub_Object =
                  intersection between Object and i-th Sub_Space,
              i-th Sub_GT =
                  make_GT( i-th Sub_Object, i-th Sub_space );
  G.   return( Oct-tree consists of eight Sub_GTs );
```

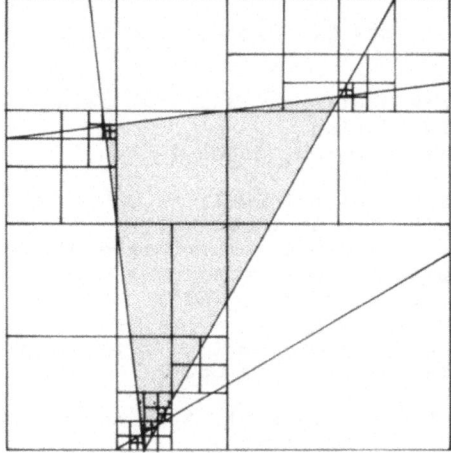

Example 1(restriction= 1)

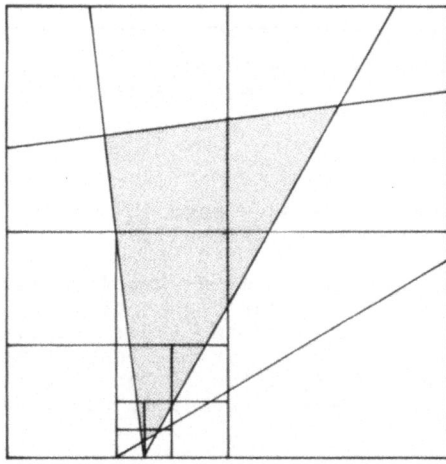

Example 2(restriction= 2)

Fig. 2. Contorl of CSG Restriction

```
                    Box 2.   Procedure diff_GT

(1)   Preparations
      A and B are both Graftrees generated using the same cubic space
      and the same resolution.
(2)   Procedure: diff_GT( A, B, Space )

  A.   if ( B is FULL ) return( EMPTY );
  B.   if ( A is EMPTY ) return( EMPTY );
  C.   if ( A & B is both CSG ) return( make_GT( A-B, Space ) );
  D.   get eight Sub_spaces of Space:
  E.   if ( A is Oct-tree and B is CSG )
          for i-th Sub_space
              i-th Sub_B = make_GT( B, i-th Sub_space );
  F.   if ( B is Oct-tree and A is CSG )
          for i-th Sub_space
              i-th Sub_A = make_GT( A, i-th Sub_space );
  G.   if ( A & B is both Oct-tree )
          for i-th Sub_space
              i-th Sub_A = make_GT( A, i-th Sub_space ),
              i-th Sub_B = make_GT( B, i-th Sub_space );
  H.   for i-th Sub_space ( i=0,7 )
              i-th Sub_GT =
                  diff_GT( i-th Sub_A, i-th Sub_B, i-th Sub_space );
  I.   return( Oct-tree consists of eight Sub_GTs );
```

difficult to remove, and often abnormally stop the simulation process.
Graftree does not have a problem with conflicts.

2.5 VISUALIZATION

For Graftree, two methods are developed for visualization, ray tracing
visualization and polyhedral visualization.

The ray tracing visualization makes highly realistic images. Ray
tracing for Graftree is rather high-speed because the the geometric
elements are sorted out according to their spatial position by the
space division (Wyvill 1986), but a long time is still needed to
generate an image, and recalculation is required to change the viewing
direction. So it is not a method for daily use, and further description
is omitted.

The polyhedral method is used to give Graftree to graphic equipment
with a 3-dimensional displaying facility such as Z-buffer. In this
method, the display quality is not very high, and it is necessary to
calculate boundary elements of the object as polyhedrons. However,
with polyhedral data, the object can be displayed from any viewing
direction.

The general flow of polyhedral visualization is shown in Box.3. The
boundary elements are determined from the infinite surfaces which
consists of the CSG tree in 'INTERSECT' cells through a clipping
process shown in Fig.3. In our implementation, the clipping processor
can deal with three infinite surfaces at the same time, which
determines the restriction for CSG in the 'INTERSECT' cell.

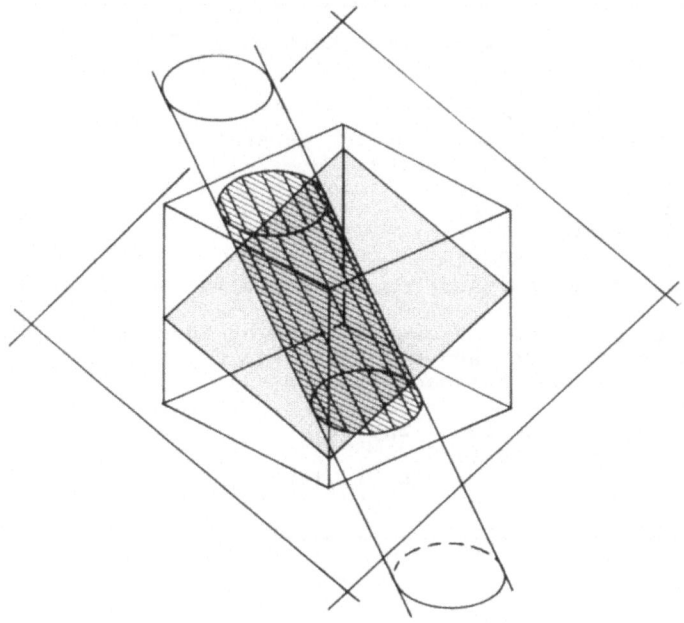

(a)Cell clipping: clip infinite surfaces by a cell space

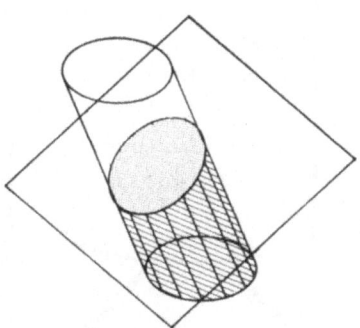

(b)Surface clipping: clip surfaces with each other

Fig. 3. Clipping for Boundary Evaluation

Box 3. Procedure poly_GT

(1) Preparations
  - GT is a Graftree.
  - Space is a cubic space used for generating GT.
(2) Procedure poly_GT(GT, Space)
  A. if (Space < resolution) return;
  B. if (GT is FULL) return;
  C. if (GT is EMPTY) return;
  D. if (GT is INTERSECT)
   a) get a list of polyhedrons approximating to surfaces on the CSG,
   b) clip polyhedrons for each surface by Space(cell clipping),
   c) clip polyhedrons each other(surface clipping),
   d) put the clipped polyhedrons, and
   e) return;
  E. Get eight Sub_spaces of Space;
  F. for i-th Sub_space (i=0,7)
        poly_GT(i-th Sub_GT, i-th Sub_Space);

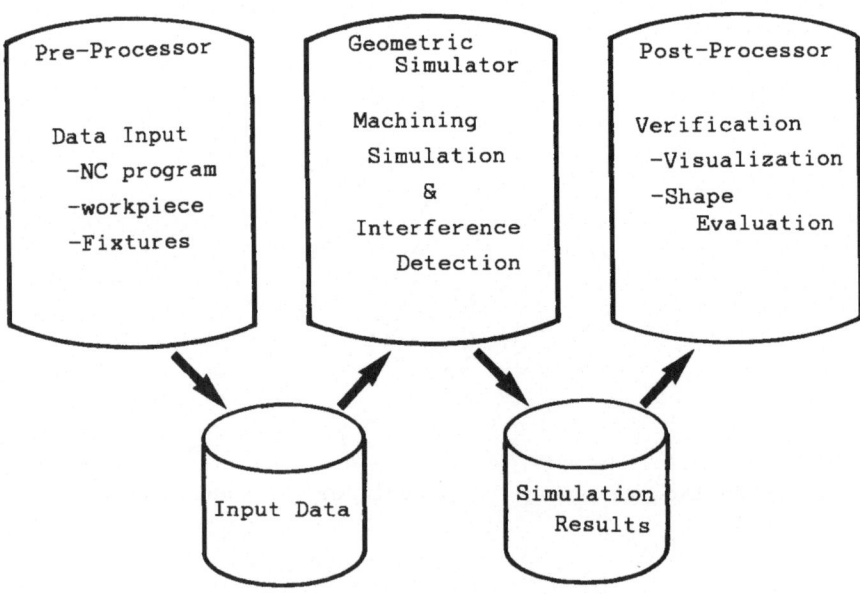

Fig. 4. System Configuration

3. NC MACHINING SIMULATOR

3.1 OVERVIEW

As mentioned in the first section, machining verification should be done selectively with respect to the cutter motions as well as quantitatively. These requirements, especially selectivity, are concerned not only with the elementary functions but also the system configuration method.

Fig.4 shows the configuration scheme of the NC machining simulator.

The basic idea is to assign simulation and verification to the different subsystems, and to apply verification functions to simulation outputs after all of the machining process is simulated (interference detection must be performed at the same time as simulation). Then the user can verify only the important portion of the cutting process, instead of watching the process from the first step to the end of the machining sequence.

Therefore, its implementation, the system should consist of three subsystems, a geometric simulator, and pre- and post-processors.

The pre-processor is an interactive subsystem used for setting up simulation inputs, i.e., NC data, workpiece data, machine tool model, etc. The post-processor is another interactive system where the user gets many sorts of information using the prepared verification functions. The geometric simulator performs machining simulation and interference detection, and stores their results in a certain format (given below in detail). The geometric simulator can be executed in the background, because cutting simulation is rather time-consuming even if Graftree is appropriate for it. Therefore while executing it in the background, the user can do his/her jobs concurrently. This is another advantage of this system scheme.

In the post-processor, the following fundamental functions should be prepared.
1) Cutter motion searching function, which finds a special cutter motion in the simulation results, and reconstructs the workpiece model machined in the motion.
2) Visualization function, which visualizes the machining scene.
3) Interference detecting function, which reports when interferences would occur.
4) Shape evaluation function. This reports what the interferences would be, or how good the machined object would be with respect to the design requirements.

To realize these, we developed two new techniques for reconstruction of the machining scene and machined the shape evaluation. In the next subsection, both are described in detail.

3.2 RECONSTRUCTION AND VISUALIZATION OF MACHINING SCENE

Reconstruction of the machining scene is used to verify a special cutter motion where the interference or over/under cutting might occur. The problems are
1) how to store simulation outputs in as small a storage size as possible, and
2) how to reconstruct the machining scene as rapidly as possible.

To solve these problems, we propose a 'removed volume' method. The removed volume is defined as follows using set operation formula:

$$R(j) = W(j) \& C(j); \qquad \dots\dots (1)$$

where
j: the serial number of a cutting motion, (j=1, N; N is the total motions)
W(j): the workpiece after j-th cutting motion in the machining sequence,
C(j): the cutter swept volume at j-th cutting motion,
R(j): the removed volume at j-th cutting motion,
'&': spatial 'and' operator.

Note that the cutting process itself is represented as the formula

$$W(j) = W(j-1) - C(j); \qquad \dots\dots (2)$$

where '-': spatial 'difference' operator.

In this method, the geometric simulator executes the formulas (1) and (2), then stores the final machined shape W(N) and removed volumes for each cutting motion {R(j) | j=1, N}. The post-processor reconstructs the machined object at the k-th motion W(k) according to the following relation:

$$W(k) = W(N) \bigcup_{j=k+1}^{N} R(j) \qquad \dots\dots (3)$$

where 'U': spatial 'or' operator.

Generally speaking, the workpiece W(j) becomes more complex as the machining proceeds. So a large amount of storage is needed if storing W(j) for all motions is done. Conversely, the complexity of the removed volume R(j) is not concerned with the sequence of machining. Besides, the removed volume is simpler than the machined shape itself, in general. Hence the removed volume method can save on storage for simulation outputs.

On the other hand, reconstruction of the machining scene can be performed rapidly by using the property that W(N) and removed volumes have no intersecting space. The 'or' operation in the formula (3) is equal to the operation which combines two separated spaces into one.

Furthermore, for visualization of the cutting scene, the Z-buffer algorithm works very effectively with this method. In the Z-buffer algorithm, the addition display data can be put in the existing picture. Therefore, the image of the workpiece machined at the k-th motion can be given only by drawing W(N) and { R(j) | j=k+1, N} individually. This also means that it is very easy to generate animation of the machining scene in a reversal sequence by displaying W(N) first, and then putting the removed volume one after another on the image, in reverse of the cutting steps.

3.3 MACHINED SHAPE EVALUATION

The machined shape evaluation is a function to compare the machined shape with the design requirement. In this system, it is realized as a simulation of measuring task(Fig.5), where the user applies measuring instruments to the shape, and compares it with the design requirement interactively.

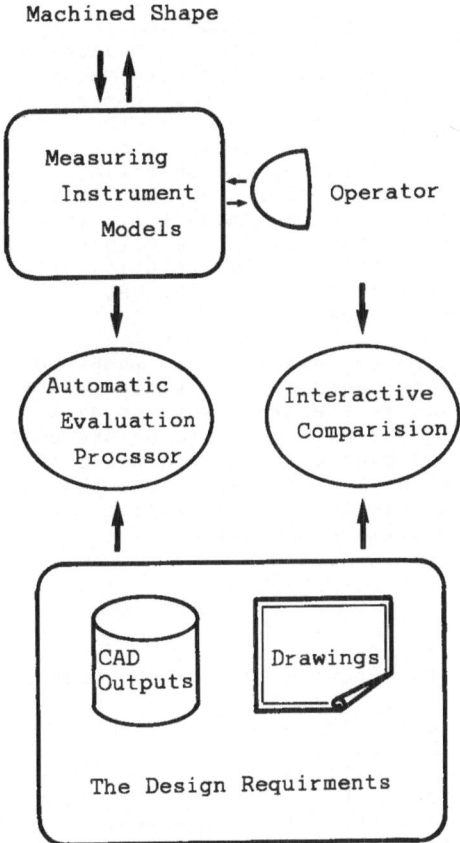

Machined Shape

Fig. 5. Measuring Task Simulation

There are three advantages in this method. First, the comparison can be done quantitatively. Next, it has high adaptability for expression of the design requirements. Though 3-dimensional CAD systems have been becoming more popular, a certain ratio of design requirements are as yet expressed on drawings. Therefore, it is important not to limit their acceptable media or form only to CAD data. Another problem is that the measuring task itself is hard to program because it includes a shape recognition problem. The measuring task simulation overcomes this through interactive operations. If the requirement data exist in CAD data, however, automatic measuring and comparison method can be considered. An example of automatic shape evaluation is presented later in this section. Finally, the measuring task must be familiar to the user, so that he/she can do an operation as almost the same as the actual measuring task.

Fig.6 shows the principle of the measuring instrument model with two typical examples, (a) a dimensional measuring instrument such as a caliper and (b) a 3-dimensional coordinate measuring instrument. Each model of these instruments takes certain inputs and gives a dimension/position. In the model of the dimensional measuring instrument, the actual operation of applying the instrument to the face of the product is substituted by the operation to pick the geometric elements on the display screen. The model gives the distance between the picked elements. In the model of the coordinate measuring instrument, the current position or trajectory of the sensing probes is given to the model, then the spatial relation between the probe and the measured shape or the intersecting point between the trajectory and the shape is obtained respectively.

Fig.6(c) shows a method to evaluate a machined shape automatically using the model of the coordinate measuring instrument when the design requirements are given as free-form surface data. The trajectory of the probe is determined at the sample points on the required surface, and then the amount of over-cutting or under-cutting is calculated as the distance between two surfaces on the trajectory under the consideration of the tolerance. This evaluation method can be used broadly in free-form surface machining.

3.4 IMPLEMENTATION

A system using the proposed methods was implemented on the workstation Hitachi Engineering Workstation 2050G (CPU: Motorola 68020).

Fig.7 is an example of cutter motion searching performed in the post-processor. The picture in (a) is the final machined product and (b) is the workpiece after the cutting motion which generates the surface picked by the cursor in (a). In (c) the cutter interference detected by the geometric simulator is presented. The picture of (b) is generated by the following steps: (1) searching out the cutter motion which generates the pointed surface; (2) reconstructing the machined shape just after the found cutter motion from the final shape and the removed volumes stored by the geometric simulator; (3) visualizing the reconstructed shape. The picture of (c) is generated by almost the same steps as (b), except the cutter motion is searched from among the results of interference detection.

The diagram of Fig.8 shows the execution time to reconstruct a machined shape for each cutter motion where (a) shows reconstruction with the raw workpiece and the cutter swept volumes the as same as the conventional machining simulation, and (b) shows reconstruction from the final shape and the removed volumes. The removed volume storing method is much more effective for reconstructing a machining shape by random sequence. However, its execution time is still long. This problem remains to be improved in the future.

The picture shown in Fig.9 is an example of the output of the machined shape evaluation. The model of a 3-dimensional coordinate measuring instrument and the measuring method shown in Fig.6 are used. The result is expressed by the color and length of the line at sample points on the required surface in this picture. It would be better if the presentation of evaluation results could be made clearer. We would like to use the presentation techniques used for physical simulation in CAE.

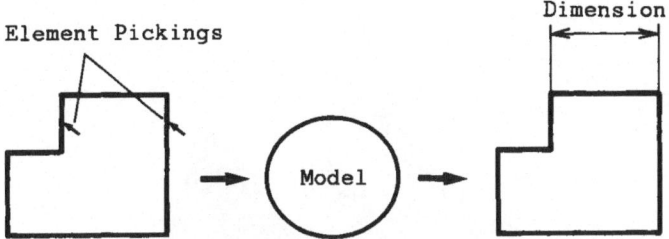

(a) Model of Dimensional Measuring Instrument

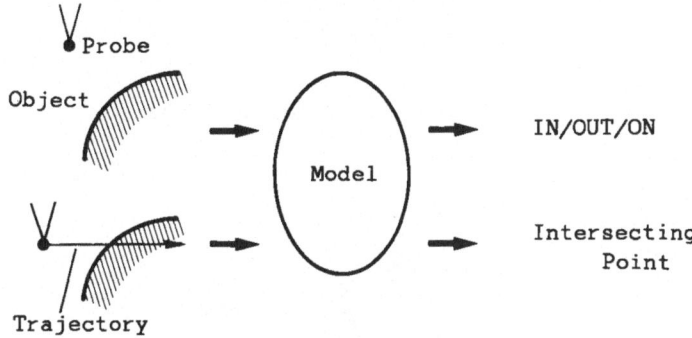

(b) Model of 3-dimensional Coordinate Measuring Instrument

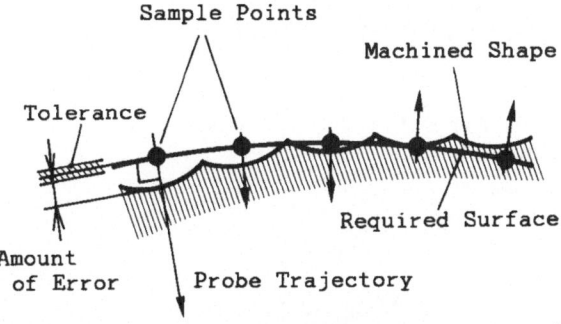

(c) Evaluation of a Free-Form Surface using a Model of
a 3-dimensional Coordinate Measuring Instrument

Fig. 6. Measuring Instrument Models

(a) Picture of Machined Shape

(b) Cutter Motion Searching

(c) Presentation of Interference

Fig. 7. Cutter Motion Searching

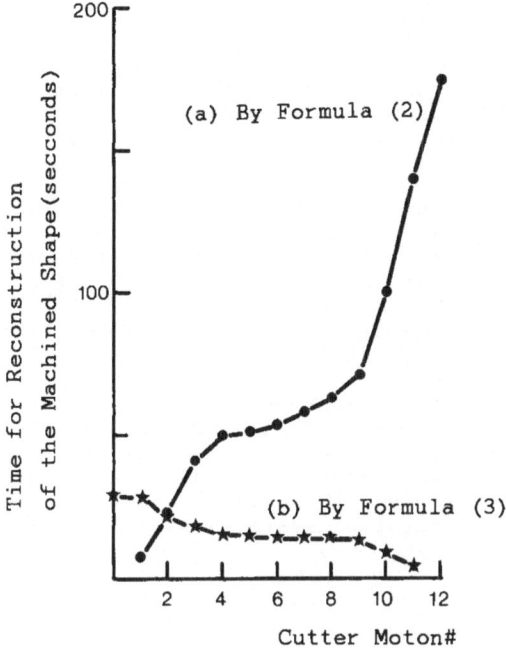

Fig. 8. Time For Machined Shape Reconstruction

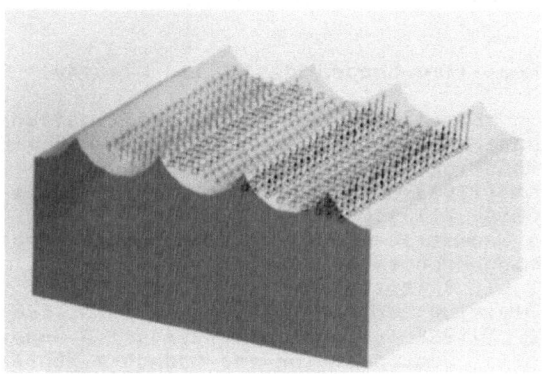

Color : Type of Error
  RED   – Over-Cutting
  BLACK – Under-Cutting
  bLUE – Within Tolerance

length : Amount of Error

Fig. 9. Output of Machined Shape Evaluation

4. CONCLUSION

In this article, new methods for geometric modeling and the system configuration for an NC machining simulator were described. They have been implemented in a workstation system and their efficiency has been confirmed:
- machining simulation is precise and reliable in a 3-dimensional space, so that the user can get the various information effective for correcting the NC program;
- the user is not forced to watch all of the cutting process, but can verify only the important portion selectively without regard to the machining sequence;
- the machined shape is evaluated flexibly and quantitatively through interactive or automatic operations.

The remaining problem is the computing performance, but this is not very big, because in our method machining simulation can be performed in the background, moreover, the role of animation of the machining scene is not critical importance compared to the other functions such as the cutter motion searching. We believe that increased computing performance of the workstation system itself will probably eliminate the problem.

ACKNOWLEDGEMENTS

Special thanks to Messers, Takashi Rokutani, Katsuhiro Kido, Jun-ichi Hirai, and Noriaki Fujushima of Hitachi Works, Hitachi Ltd. for their kind advice and significant discussions on our study. And we would like to thank all members of the 32Group, Hitachi Research Laboratory, Hitachi Ltd. for their various suggestions and encouragement.

REFERENCES

Hook, TV (1986) Real-Time Shaded NC Milling Display. Computer Graphics 20(4):15-20
Wang, WP, Wang, KK (1986) Real-Time Verification of Multiaxis NC Programs with Raster Graphics. Proc. of 1986 IEEE International Conference on Robotics and Automation, pp 166-171
Wang, WP, Wang, KK (1987) Geometric Modeling for Swept Volume of Moving Solids. IEEE CG&A, 7(12):8-17
Meagher, D (1982) Geometric Modeling Using Octree Encording. Computer Graphics and Image Processing 19(2):129-147
Wyvill, G, Kunii, LT, Shirota, Y (1986) Space Division for Ray Tracing in CSG. IEEE CG&A, 6(4):28-34
Duest, MJ, Kunii, LT 1988 Integrated Polytrees: A Generalized Model for Integrating Spatial Decomposition and Boundary Representation. Tech. Report 88-002 Tokyo Univ
Requicha, AAG, Voelcker, HB (1982) Solid Modeling: A Historical Summary and Contemporary Assistant. IEEE CG&A 2(2):9-24.

Yasumasa Kawashima is a researcher working for Hitachi Research Laboratory, Hitachi Ltd. His research interests include the application of geometric modeling, computer graphics and artificial intelligence in mechanical CAD. He recieved his BS and MS in precision engineering from Hokkaido University in 1981 and 1983, respectively. He is a member of Japan Precision Engeneering Society and Information Processing Society of Japan.
Address: Hitachi Research Laboratory, Hitachi, Ltd. Kuji-cho 4096, Hitachi, Ibaraki, 319-12 Japan.

Kumiko Itoh is a researcher working for Hitachi Research Laboratory, Hitachi Ltd. Her research interests include applied mathematics. She recieved her BS in mathematics from Tsukuba University in 1983. She is a member of Japan Precision Engeneering Society and Information Processing Society of Japan.
Address: Hitachi Research Laboratory, Hitachi, Ltd. Kuji-cho 4096, Hitachi, Ibaraki, 319-12 Japan.

Tomotoshi Ishida is a researcher working for Hitachi Research Laboratory, Hitachi Ltd. His research interests include modeling and evaluation of machinery in mechanincal CAD. He recieved his BS, MS and PhD in mechanical engineering from Tokyo University in 1979, 1981 and 1985, respectively. He is a member of Japan Sciety of Mechaninal Engineers, Japan Precision Engeneering Society, Japan Society for Design & Drawing and Information Processing Society of Japan.
Address: Hitachi Research Laboratory, Hitachi, Ltd. Kuji-cho 4096, Hitachi, Ibaraki, 319-12 Japan.

Shiro Nonaka is a researcher working for Hitachi Research Laboratory, Hitachi Ltd. His research interests include advancement of mechanical CAD system. He recieved his BS in mechanical engineering from Tokyo University in 1979. He is a member of Japan Sciety of Mechaninal Engineers and Japan Soiety of Applied Phyics and Information Processing Society of Japan.
Address: Hitachi Research Laboratory, Hitachi, Ltd. Kuji-cho 4096, Hitachi, Ibaraki, 319-12 Japan.

Kazuhiko Ejiri is an industrial engineer working for Hitachi Works, Hitachi Ltd. He has been engaged in development of a CAM system. He recieved his BS in management engineering from Aoyama Gakuin University in 1981.
Address: Hitachi Works, Hitachi, Ltd. Saiwai-cho 3-1-1, Hitachi, Ibaraki, 317 Japan.

Development of a Multi Modeller

N. Futagami, Y. Nagata, K. Ogasawara, K. Otoi, and K. Kobori

ABSTRACT

This paper describes a Multi Modeller which represents a new approach to three dimensional modelling technique. This modeller has several useful features. The first is an automatic mutual conversion among three model types. The second is a reconstructive operation for managing the design process history. These features are described in detail.

Keywords: Multi Modeller, mutual conversion, wireframe problem, winged edge, reconstructive operation

1. INTRODUCTION

In recent years, CAD/CAM systems have been used widely in mechanical industries. Especially three dimensional modelling technique is the main technology for CAD/CAM systems and is used for analysis, manufacturing, simulation and other applications. In general, current modelling types can be classified as follows; wireframe modelling, surface modelling and solid modelling. Recently, non-manifold modelling which is a new approach to define objects is studied.[1] Though it is a good approach to model objects, it takes time to use widely because of immature of its technology. Finally above former model types will be used widely for some time.

This paper shows two kind of contents. One is the synthesis of three model types. Applicatioin programs for CAD systems are almost depend on one of above three model types. Engineers must select appropriate modelling form at any given design situation and input the same object with another modelling form to use various applications. It is not effective operation for engineers. The synthesis of three model types enables engineers to provide comfortable design environment. The other is a design history management. As the design history is displayd on a screen in the system, engineers can realize easy modification of models and regenerate their previous design. Chapter 5 describes the design process management function in detail.

2. CURRENT MODELLING TECHNIQUE

Currently, three types of modelling technique are well known. Each modelling technique's characteristic is summarized as follows.

2.1 Wireframe Model

A wireframe model represents objects by the edge curves. Wireframe modelling technique has several deficiencies. One of them occurs in the representaion of objects including curved surfaces. Fig. 1 an example of an object with curved surfaces. Some "pseudo edges" which aren't physical edges are need to grasp the curved surface shape. Pseudo edges.

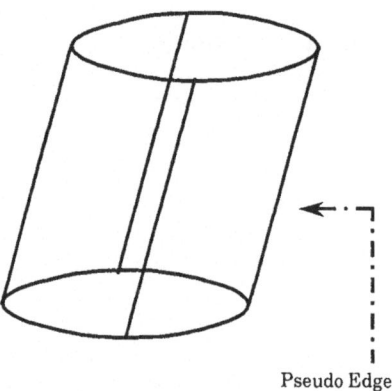

Pseudo Edge

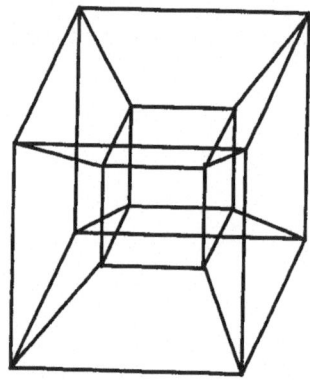

Fig. 1. Pseudo Edges of Wireframe Model

Fig. 2. Wireframe Ambiguity

Fig. 2 shows another deficience. This wireframe model is ambiguous. This may represents any of the three objects. Areas where surfaces exist and the shape of surfaces are decided by users in accordance with defined wireframe edges. It is very difficult to handle wireframe model with complex objects. However, this modelling technique's virtue is a concise internal data structure and better performance.

2.2 Surface Model

Surface model has mathematical descriptions of the surface data of objects. Each surface exists in pieces on 3D space, has no relation the others and can not define volume objects. Users recognize objects by making divided 3D space with surfaces. This modelling technique provides wider application domain than wireframe model: for example, generating 3 Axis NC data, analyzing shell model, various kind of shading model and so on, and is the most popular technique in current commercial CAD/CAM systems.

2.3 Solid Model

The previous two models are simplified for easy processing by computers and have partial data of objects. They do not always satisfy user requirements. Solid modelling technique was developed to represent objects completely. A solid model has both topological and geometrical information about an object. The use of solid models can be made a variety of processes automatically that can not be done by the above two modelling techniques, for example, calculation of mass property and hidden line removal. On the other hand, the computational costs increase because of the larger internal data structure. A variety of representational forms have been developed for solid models.[2) 3)] Each form has its own features, depending on the various applications. We don't focus solid modelling form in this paper. (For further information on solid form, see Computer Graphics and Applications[4].)

3. MULTI MODEL

In the previous chapter, each modelling technique's characteristic was described. Although the solid modelling technique is a most useful method of representing objects, a large internal data structure and the heavy burden on computers are deficiencies. And the popular method of defining the volume objects (such as assembling primitives with Boolean set operations) is advantageous for computer processing but no advantage to engineers. As three model forms have one's characteristic, it is important to use one's modelling type skillfully with making good use of each modelling characteristic.

The Multi Modeller combines above three models closely and doesn't make engineers be conscious of model types. Engineers can choose any model type at any design situation for one's application and can convert one model to another for another application. Fig. 3 shows the concept of the Multi Modeller and an example of application of each model.

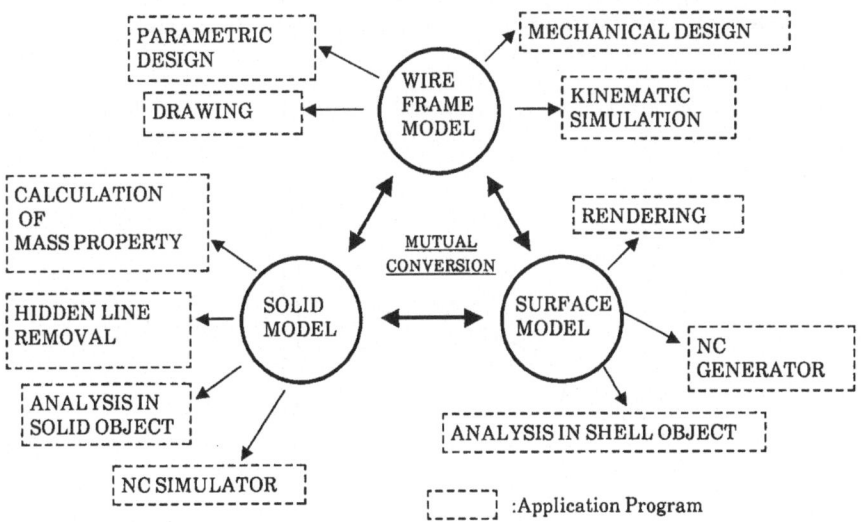

Fig. 3. A concept of Multi Modeller

In the automatic conversion among the three model types, it is very easy to convert from the solid model to the surface or wireframe model, because the solid model has more information than other two model types. While the reverse conversions, conversion from the wireframe model to the solid model what is called wireframe problem, include some difficult problems. This paper describes the conversion method from the wireframe model to the solid model. And the conversion techniques from the wireframe model to the surface model and from the surface model to the solid model are the part of the wireframe problem.

On the next chapter, we describe the detail of the conversion algorithm.

4. AUTOMATED GENERATION OF SOLID OBJECTS FROM WIREFRAME DATA

In this field, some works are practiced. Markowsky and Wesley have published "Fleshing Out Wire Frames"[5]. But geometric information was used to make planar faces in this algorithm and it is very difficult to be applied to curved surfaces. Hanrahan showed linear time algorithm to convert automatically the wireframe to the solid objects.[6] Our basic concept is based on his idea. That is to say that the wireframe problem is equivalent to finding the embedding of a graph on a closed orientable surface. Once a graph has been embedded, we can define faces as circuits that do not contain interior edges. The feature of our algorithm is to find correct circuits effectively(which are equivalent to the faces of an object) using only topological information.

4.1 Data Structure and Graph

Before the detail explanation of the algorithm, we define some graph terms. A node means a point on graph. A branch means a path between two nodes. A circuit is a closed loop on a graph. A node corresponds to a vertex on an object and a branch corresponds to an edge on an object. There are circuits corresponding to surfaces on an object. A cut vertex is a node which divides a graph into several nonseparable components. Other terminology used in this paper is based on fundamental graph theory. (Fig. 4)

A winged edge data structure is a good representation method for wireframe problem. Because it records topological information of an object. Our conversion result is represented by winged edge data structure.

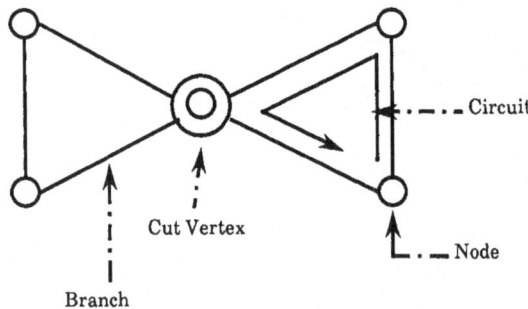

Fig. 4. Graph terminology

4.2 Restriction of Input Data

We have some restrictions for embedding graph on a closed orientable surface. Objects are set of points in three dimensional space, and is compact, connect and regular. A surface is a closed, orientable and a two dimensional manifold. And this algorithm treats simply connected graph.

a) Joining two volumes along a single edge or a single vertex is not acceptable.

b) The edge which has endpoints v1, v2 is defined uniquely and has a finite length.

c) An object which includes a multi loop or a self loop(pseudo graph) is not acceptable. Because it is very difficult problem to find loops using only topological information.

d) As input graph is simply connected, an object including holes is not acceptable.

4.3 Outline of Conversion Algorithm

The conversion algorithm consists of five stages.

Step 1.)   The incidence relationships of vertices and edges given by wireframes are converted to a graph.

Step 2.)   A branch is selected, and a circuit which is candidate surface is found in all the circuits which include the edge. (loop)

Step 3.)   Loop is checked upon whether it is equivalent to actual or pseudo face. Step 2 and 3 are repeated until each branch has two loops which are equivalent to actual faces.

Step 4.)   The front side of all the faces are determined.

Step 5.)   Making winged edge data structure.

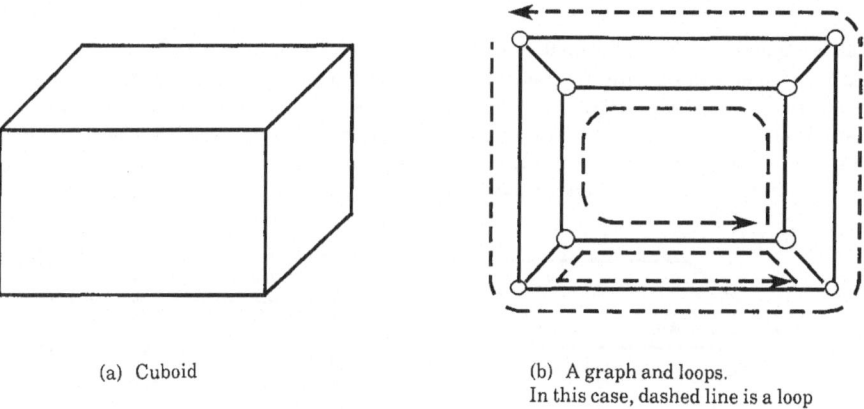

(a) Cuboid

(b) A graph and loops.
In this case, dashed line is a loop

Fig. 5. A solid object and the loops of its graph

4.4 Finding Candidate Surfaces

The candidate surfaces of an object can be found by searching for loops in the graph. Each edge of an object is uniquely defined by two faces. similarly, each branch of a graph has one loop on each side. A loop is found relating to each branch. This loop is a candidate surface on one side of an edge and consists of closed minimum edges. The candidate surface on the other side is found similarly. Fig. 5 shows a cuboid and the loops which are found from the graph. When N, B, L are defined as follows, the Euler formula is valid in a graph.

$$N - B + L = 2 \qquad (1)$$

Where N is the number of nodes. B is the number of branches, and L is the number of loops equivalent to actual faces. As the loops include pseudo faces, this step is repeated more than $(2 - N + B)$ times.

4.5 Finding the Loops Equivalent to Surfaces

It is clear from the winged edge data structure that two loops equivalent to actual faces exist in both sides of each branch. However, in the case of Fig. 6 , the branch b1 equivalent to the edge e1 has three loops(loop A, loop B, loop C). One of these loops is a loop equivalent to a pseudo face. In Fig. 6, loop C is equivalent to a pseudo face because it has nodes and branches in the inner region of the loop. Whether a loop is selected in Step 2, graph operation is done in order to evaluate the selected loop. The nodes of the loop are replaced by one node, and the graph is reconstructed. Then, the branches which make up the loops are removed. If nonseparable components of its modified graph increase after performing these operations, or in other words, if the collected nodes change into the cut vertex, we judge that this loop is equivalent to the pseudo face. If the loop doesn't contain interior edges, the loop is converted to a shrinking node with graph operation and the node isn't a cut vertex. Fig. 6 (c) shows cut vertex D, which is created by shrinking loop C. When we shrink the face f1 in Fig. 7 (a) and make one vertex from v1, v2, v3, v4, the incidence relationship of other faces is not affected. In case of shrinking f2 in Fig. 7 (b), the object is separated by the pseudo face. With the above step all the pseudo face can be removed. As this step is carried out whenever loop is found, it does not need to hold all the candidate surfaces to choose correct faces.

4.6 Determining the Front Side of the Faces

After all actual faces are found, the front sides of the faces are determined. If the vertices of each face can be aligned in a counterclockwise direction from the outer side of the object, it is possible to find the normal vector for the outer sides. Any face is selected and then an ordered set of vertices of the face is selected. The other faces are found similarly. Since the faces of the object are equivalent to two-dimensional manifold, it is possible to create an ordered set of the vertices of all the faces. The volume of the object is calculated. If the volume is positive, its ordered set is correct and it is negative, its ordered set must be revised.

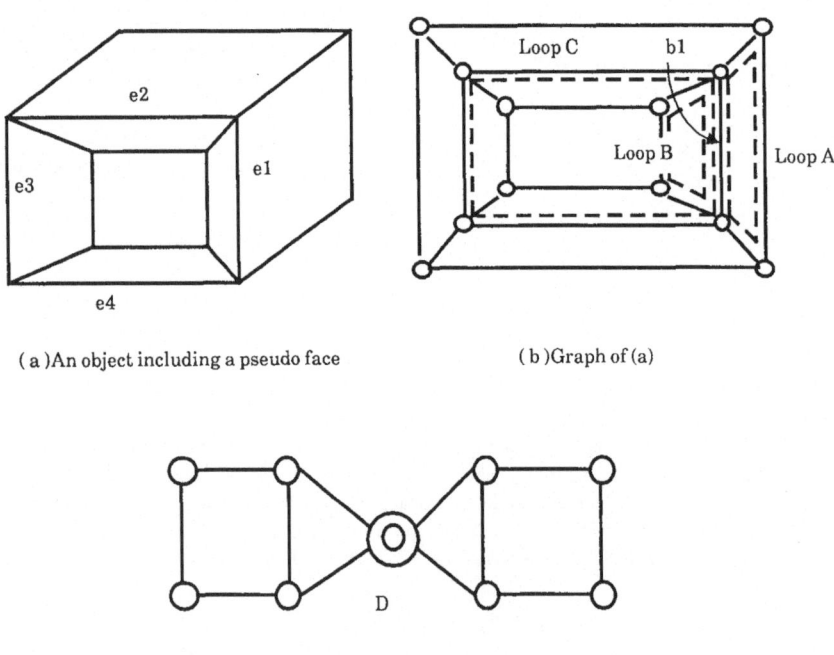

(a)An object including a pseudo face   (b)Graph of (a)

(c)The graph reconstructed by shrinking loop C in (b)

Fig. 6.   A solid object with a pseudo face and the loops of its graph.

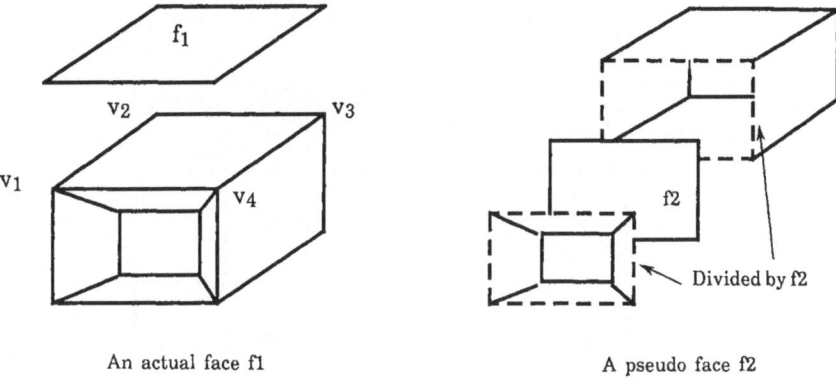

An actual face f1	A pseudo face f2

Fig. 7. Difference between actual face f1 and pseudo face f2

4.7 Result of the Experiment

The above algorithm is implemented in the programming language Fortran 77 on Micro Vax - II. Table 1 shows some experimental results. Object 1 ~ 3 are examples of polyhedral approximated solid objects and 4 is an example of a solid object with curved surfaces.

5. RECONSTRUCTIVE OPERATION
(HISTORY MANAGEMENT OF DESIGN PROCESS)

Another feature of the Multi Modeller is a reconstructive operation. It is a method of representing and manipulating design process history.[7] The structure and the process of the reconstructive operation is shown below.

5.1 Outline of Reconstructive Operation

Fig. 8 shows the structure of the modeller and the reconstructive operation functions. The history management unit controls the other all units. Every time a normal modelling operation has been done, the management unit records the design process and saves the data to history data storage. When engineers request the display of a design history, the management unit controls the display unit to display the design history. When engineers request an operation of the design history, the management unit controls the operation unit and the UNDO and the REDO units reject and regenerate models.

5.2 Record of Design Process History

It is necessary for the operation of design process to record the operation history. Fig. 9 shows the internal data structure of design process history. When a modelling operation has been done, event data (which corresponds to the models generated by the operation) is generated. Each event data has some pointers. In the event data area, first pointer indicates an entity data group which holds geometric data relating to its event data. The next two pointers indicate a group of UNDO and REDO commands which are used when carrying out "undo" and "redo" operations. Reference event means that the event is referenced by one's operation. For example, when n1 and n2 are primitives and n3 is generated by a boolean operation using n1 and n2, event data n3 has two reference event pointers to the reference event n1 and n2.

Table 1 Calculation Time for Generating Solid Objects

Object		Edge/Vertex	Processing Time		(Unit Sec)
			Make Graph	Find Loops and Actual faces	Decide both sides of faces
1)		36/ 24	0.03	0.20	0.06
2)		34/ 16	0.01	0.18	0.06
3)		171/ 113	0.17	2.56	0.23
4)		162/ 106	0.18	3.90	0.26

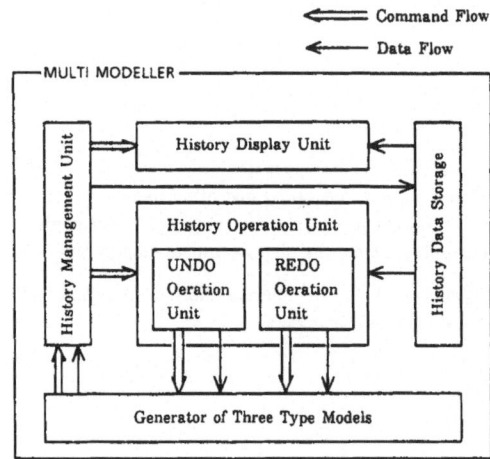

⬅ Command Flow
← Data Flow

Fig. 8. Structure of History Management System

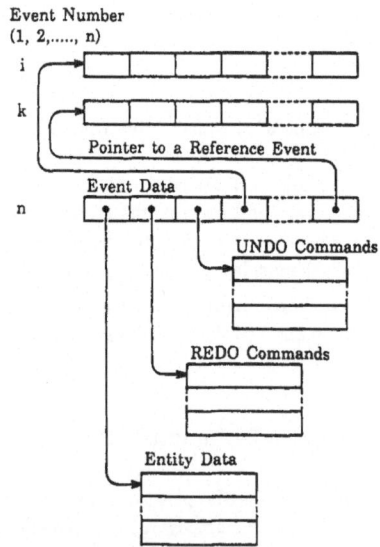

Event Number
(1, 2,....., n)

Pointer to a Reference Event

Event Data

UNDO Commands

REDO Commands

Entity Data

Fig. 9. Internal Data Structure of Design History

5.3 Display of Design Process History

It is very useful for engineers to display design process whie drawing up a design plan. Especially it is effective when engineers modify the design and re-use the past design. Our system can display a directed graph for representing the design process on a graphic display. Fig. 10 shows an example of display of a design process history graph. Each node corresponds to each event and a first letter of each node indicates a kind of operation. (For example, P: generation of primitive, B: boolean operation, etc.) The following number means a serial number of operations.

5.4 Handling of Design Process History

A manipulation of design process history can be done interactively. One example of the UNDO operation is as follows. Assume B11 is a current existing model in Fig. 10. First, a user indicates a target node to go back. If a target node is B8, he hits a node B8 on screen. Then UNDO command is activated and cancel B11, B10 and M9. As a result, P2 and B8 are regenerated automatically. Because existing of P2 and B8 is essential to regenerate B11.

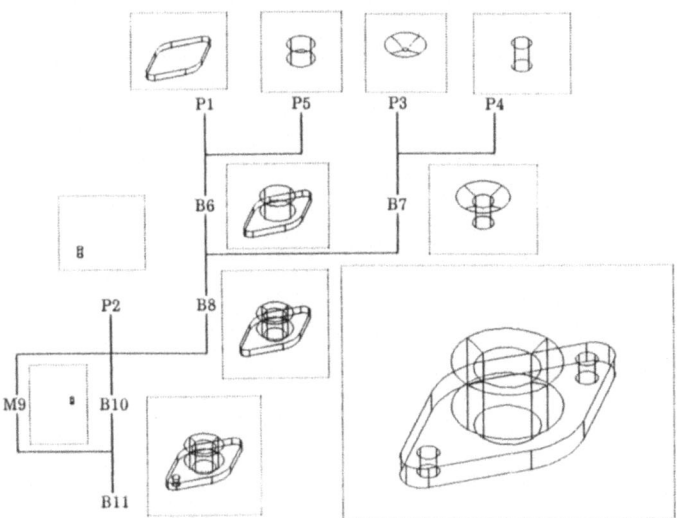

Fig. 10. Example of Displaying Design Histories

6 CONCLUSION

We have described an outline of a Multi Modeller, which supports a wide range of design activities from industrial design to the manufacturing. This system has contributed much to increasing design supports. Development is continuing on more comfortable environment for engineers.

ACKNOWLEDGEMENT

we would like to thank Dr. Toru Kawada, general manager of Computer Systems Laboratories of Sharp Co., and Dr. Nishioka, general manager of Computer Division of Sharp Co. for their valuable suggestions; Keiji Kawasaki and Tetuya Inoue of Sharp Co. for making program.

REFERENCES

1) Kevin Weiler (1986) Non-Manifold Geometric Modelling. Extended Abstruct for IFIP W.G. 5.2 Workshop on Geometric Modelling

2) N.Okino, Y.Kakazu, H.Kubo (1973) Technical Information Processing System for Computer Aided Design, Drawing and Manufacturing, Proc. of PROLAMAT '73

3) B.G.Baumgart (1974) Geometric Modeling for Computer Vision, Report No. AIM-249, STAN-CS-74-463, Stanford Artifical Intelligence Laboratory, Stanford Univ. Oct.

4) A.A.G.Requicha, H.B.Voelcker (1983) Solid Modelling Current Status and Research Directions, IEEE CG&A, Vol. 3, No. 7, Oct., pp 25 - 37

5) G.Markowsky, M.A.Wesley (1980) Fleshing Out Wire Frames, IBM J. RES. Develop., Vol. 24, No. 5, pp 582 - 597

6) P.M.Hanrahan (1982) Creating Volume Models from Edge-Vertex Graphs, SIGGRAPH'82 Conference Proceedings, Vol 16, No. 3, pp 77 - 84

7) Hiroshi Toriya, Toshiaki Satoh, Kenji Ueda, Hiroaki Chiyokura (1986) UNDO and REDO Operations for Solid Modelling, IEEE CG&A, Apr. pp 35 - 42

Noriyuki Futagami works for Computer Systems Laboratories of Sharp Co. , Ltd. His research interests are geometric modelling, computer graphics and knowledge engineering. He received his B.E. degree in mechanical engineering from Kobe University, Hyogo, Japan in 1980. He is a member of Information Processing Society of Japan.
Address: Computer Systems Laboratories, Sharp Co., Ltd., 2613-1, Ichinomoto-cho Tenri-shi, Nara 632, Japan.

Yoshihiro Nagata received the B.S. degree in computer science from the faculty of technology at Hiroshima University, Hiroshima, Japan, in 1982. Since then he has been with Sharp Corporation and is currently an engineer in its Computer Systems Laboratories. His major interests are CAD and computer graphics. Nagata is a member of the Information Processing Society of Japan.
Address: Computer Systems Laboratories, Sharp Co., Ltd., 2613-1, Ichinomoto-cho Tenri-shi, Nara 632, Japan.

Kotaro Ogasawara has worked for Computer Systems Laboratories of Sharp Co., Ltd. since 1984. He is a system software engineer for CAD systems and applications. His current research interests are computer graphics, computer-aided geometric design and applications. He received a B.D.(bachelor of design) degree from Kyushu Institute of Design, Fukuoka, Japan in 1984.
Address: Computer Systems Laboratories, Sharp Co., Ltd., 2613-1, Ichinomoto-cho Tenri-shi, Nara 632, Japan.

Katsuya Otoi works for Computer Systems Laboratories of Sharp Co., Ltd. His research interests are geometric modelling and their applications. He received the B.E. and M.E. degrees in mechanical engineering from Kobe University, Hyogo, Japan, in 1983 and 1985. He is a member of Information Processing Society of Japan and the Japan Society of Precision Engineering.
Address: Computer Systems Laboratories, Sharp Co., Ltd., 2613-1, Ichinomoto-cho Tenri-shi, Nara 632, Japan.

Ken-ich Kobori received the B.S. and M.S. degrees in electronic engineering from Yamanashi University, Yamanashi, Japan, in 1973 and 1975, respectively, and the Ph.D. degree in electronic engineering from University of Osaka Prefecture in 1987. Since 1975 he has been with Sharp Corporation and is currently a manager in its CAD Development Center, Engineering Division. His major interests are mechanical CAD and computer graphics. Kobori is a member of the Information Processing Society of Japan and the Institute of Electronics and Communication Engineers of Japan.
Address: Computer Systems Laboratories, Sharp Co., Ltd., 2613-1, Ichinomoto-cho Tenri-shi, Nara 632, Japan.

A Methodology for Direct Manipulation of Polygon Meshes

J.B. Allan, B. Wyvill, and I.H. Witten

ABSTRACT

While many modelling techniques used in computer graphics produce polygon meshes, few methods have been reported for modifying such meshes interactively. This paper describes how to manipulate polygon meshes directly in a controlled, general, and powerful manner. The scheme is based on a primitive operation which moves one vertex without altering the topology of the mesh. Extending this operation allows the geometry of arbitrary regions to be modified according to generalized "decay functions" that control the shape. The technique has been implemented and tested, and examples are given which show that a rich class of models can be generated. The method has many desirable properties and compares favourably with other modeling techniques.

Key words: Computer graphics, animation, solid modelling, polygon mesh, surface modelling.

1 INTRODUCTION

Many different geometric modelling techniques have been used for computer graphics, each with its advantages and disadvantages. Free-form surfaces are usually expressed as analytic functions, either implicit (eg quadric surfaces (Blinn 1986), soft objects (Wyvill 1988a)), or parametric (eg cubic splines (Bartels 1987)). Constructive methods (Mantyla 1988) account for most solid modelling. Interestingly, though, modelling systems based on these techniques almost invariably produce output in the form of polygons or polygon meshes.

Polygon mesh data structures are popular because they can be drawn quickly as wire frames for interactive previewing, and rendering algorithms can be implemented easily and efficiently when the input is in this form. A second use of polygon meshes is to store data that has been captured by digitizing a physical object. The mesh represents the data exactly, to the precision at which it has been digitized. In both cases, however, a model is not usually modified once it has been represented in polygonal form.

There is very little evidence of direct manipulation of polygon meshes. One exception is a solid modelling technique which manipulates a polyhedral mesh using topology-preserving Euler operations. For example, the system described in (Chiyokura 1983) includes local and global Euler operations, and also "move" and "lift" operations for repositioning a vertex, edge, or face. While these allow the geometry of a polyhedron to be altered in a general way, they are not very powerful since only one element is moved at a time.

This paper presents a methodology that allows polygon meshes to be manipulated directly in a controlled, general, and powerful manner. The basic operation moves one vertex without altering the topology of the mesh. Extending this primitive allows the geometry of arbitrary regions to be modified according to generalized "decay functions." Sequences of such operations can be used to create approximations to free-form surfaces or constructive solids, and to manipulate digitized data in a controlled and flexible way. By abstracting the manipulations, the system can be made "programmable" in the sense that editing sessions can be recorded, modified textually, and replayed in a manner analogous to a computer program operating on data. Indeed, the same editing transformation can be applied to different models. This provides a high-level description that can represent complex objects in an economical and perspicuous fashion.

We also describe an implementation of the technique. Since all polygon meshes in this work are built from triangles, the system is called DELTA.

1.1   Terminology

A modelling technique comprises three components: the *description* supplied by the designer (also called the *representation*), a number of *manipulation methods* for altering the description, and the resulting *model* produced from it. An *object* is the actual (physical or imaginary) entity being modelled. In short, a description specifies a model which represents an object.

A *modelling system* is an implementation of modelling techniques, together with other support systems such as data structures and a user interface. It may embody several modelling techniques. The term *designer* is used to refer to the person building the model. This avoids the confusion of *modeller*, which could denote either designer or modelling system.

2   POLYGON MESH MODELLING

Polygon mesh modelling is a technique that enables the geometry of a mesh to be manipulated in a general and powerful way. Editing meshes directly is a difficult undertaking because of the discrete nature of the data structure. While Euler operations are complete in that they can construct any polyhedral mesh, they are very awkward to use. Designers may wish to modify a sub-mesh of many polygons, or a set of disjoint vertices, in one operation. They may want to move related vertices by different distances, or in different directions, in a controlled manner. Although some of the ideas developed below may have been used previously for computer graphics modelling or CAD, we know of no systematic collection of mesh manipulation operations such as that described here.

2.1   Move-Vertex Operation

The basic operation in polygon mesh modelling is *move vertex*, which specifies a new 3D position for a specific vertex called the *current vertex*. All edges that terminate at this point are stretched or contracted as necessary in order to stay connected to it while remaining straight. In this way, the geometry of a mesh can be arbitrarily rearranged into any form that its topology will allow. Because it is difficult to maintain planarity of polygons with more than three vertices, we force meshes to consist of triangles only.

The move-vertex operation is, by itself, completely general. Despite this generality, or perhaps because of it, the operation is not very convenient to use. Modifying a large object with thousands of vertices would be a tedious and error-prone undertaking for the designer. Several useful extensions to the basic operation are discussed in the following sections.

2.2 Range of Influence

The first extension is the notion of a *range of influence* around the current vertex. This is a connected subset of the mesh centred on the current vertex. When the latter is moved, all vertices in the range—and all of their connected edges—move with it, as illustrated in Figure 1a. (Assume for the moment that each vertex is moved the same distance in the same direction.) In this way, an arbitrarily large portion of the model can be modified by a single move-vertex operation.

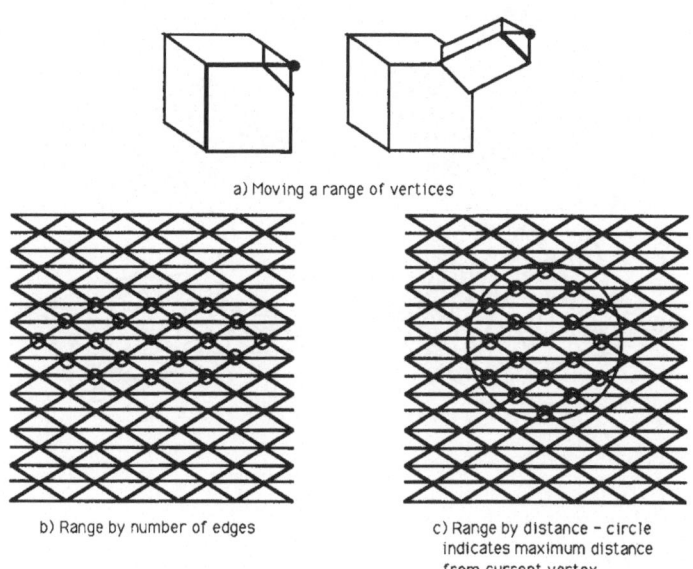

a) Moving a range of vertices

b) Range by number of edges

c) Range by distance – circle
indicates maximum distance
from current vertex

Fig. 1: Range of influence

The range can be specified by any method of defining a connected sub-mesh that includes the current vertex. Figure 1 illustrates two possibilities. The first (Figure 1b) encompasses all vertices that can be reached from the current one by traversing less than a given number of edges, while the second (Figure 1c) includes those within some given Euclidean distance from the current one. The former method is perhaps easier for the designer to understand, but the shape of the range may be less predictable. The latter has the advantage that the shape of the range is independent of the geometry of the mesh.

2.3 Decay Function over the Range of Influence

The mechanism described above moves the entire range of influence, together with the current vertex, by the same distance along what we call the *movement vector*. This is not always the intention of the designer. For example, to produce a cone-shaped protrusion one still must relocate each vertex individually. It would be better to be able to move different vertices in the range by different amounts in a controlled manner.

A *decay function* is used to determine the amount by which each vertex moves. It maps each vertex in the range to a scale factor, which is used to scale the movement vector before being added to the vertex. Figure 2 illustrates several decay functions applied to a flat mesh. Note that the shapes produced will be different if the mesh is not initially flat since the shape of the decay function is added to the mesh's original shape.

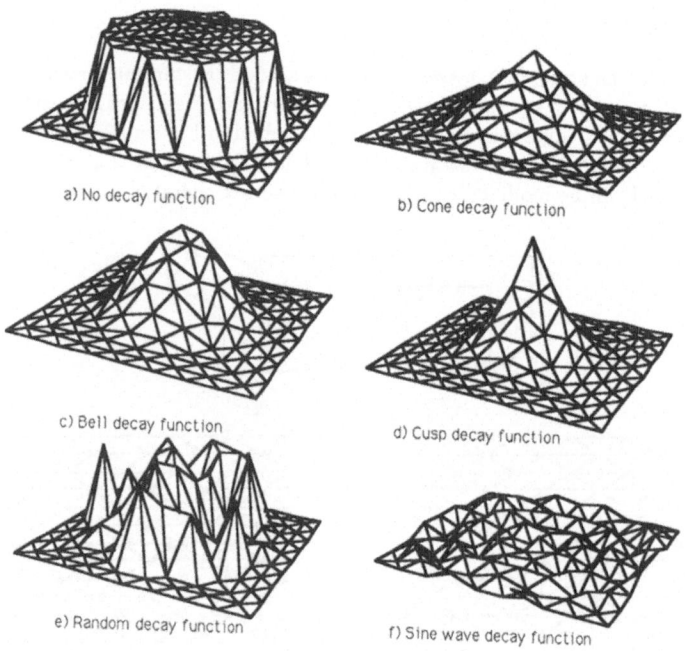

a) No decay function

b) Cone decay function

c) Bell decay function

d) Cusp decay function

e) Random decay function

f) Sine wave decay function

Fig. 2: Decay functions

2.4 Binding Vertices

Together, the range of influence, decay function, and move-vertex operation offer a powerful set of capabilities. However, they have the limitation that only vertices lying in a connected sub-mesh can be moved. Often it is necessary to move some vertices without affecting intervening ones. To this end, individual vertices can be *bound* to the current vertex. When the current vertex is moved, each bound vertex translates by the same amount.

When a range of influence is defined, the same sized region around each bound vertex is also affected (Figure 3a). Vertices in these ranges behave in exactly the same way as those around the current vertex. When two or more ranges overlap, some points are influenced by more than one vertex. This situation can be handled in several ways. For example, the vertex can be moved by each bound or current vertex, producing an interference effect (Figure 3c), or it can be moved by the nearest one alone (Figure 3d).

2.5 Anchoring Vertices

Further control may be obtained by *anchoring* certain vertices to their current positions so that they cannot be moved, even if they lie within the range of a current or bound vertex. The effect of moving the current vertex can be viewed as radiating outward from it toward the boundary of the range, but stopping short if an anchored vertex is encountered. By anchoring a connected path, a designer can create a dyke through which the effect cannot radiate. This can be used to make an abrupt edge on an otherwise smooth shape (Figure 3b).

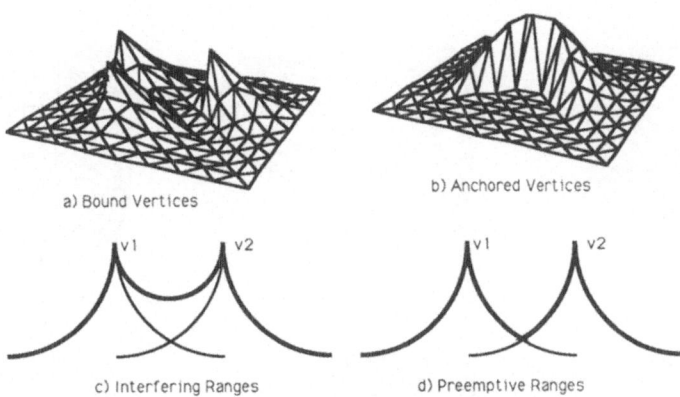

a) Bound Vertices

b) Anchored Vertices

c) Interfering Ranges

d) Preemptive Ranges

Fig. 3: Bound and anchored vertices

2.6 Non-Parallel Move-Vertex Operations

So far, the methodology offers three capabilities: to specify a current vertex and move it in space, to move neighboring vertices with it, and to control the attenuation of the effect with distance. Next we relax the restriction that all vertices follow the direction of the current one. Under this restriction, the move-vertex operation is called the *parallel* operation. Some alternatives are illustrated in Figure 4.

Stretch stretches the mesh as though it were made of elastic. *Grow* causes the object to expand or contract by moving each vertex along its normal vector, calculated as the average of the normals to its incident faces. *Randomise* moves each vertex by a randomly chosen vector whose length is restricted by the length of the movement vector. The effect of fractal geometry (Fournier 1982) can be achieved by controlling the randomness, and recursively subdividing the mesh (see next subsection). *Smooth* reduces sharp discontinuities of slope. This list indicates the rich variety of effects that can be achieved by locally altering the operations performed when moving a vertex.

2.7 Subdividing the Range of Influence

All the editing mechanisms discussed so far have modified the geometry of the object. One topological operation is invaluable in polygon mesh modelling: the ability to sub-divide a polygon into smaller ones. The need for this arises when an area in which detailed work is to be done contains too few polygons. The new polygons occupy the same area, and lie in the same plane, as the old one.

2.8 Saving and Restoring

Any interactive editor must be capable of allowing editing to be resumed after an interruption. Each operation is given a textual equivalent with some qualifying parameters, and a script file is created to keep track of a session. The script may be replayed later on and the work continued. It can be applied to other meshes too, so that a script file can be conceptualized as a procedural abstraction. Section 3.6 discusses script files further.

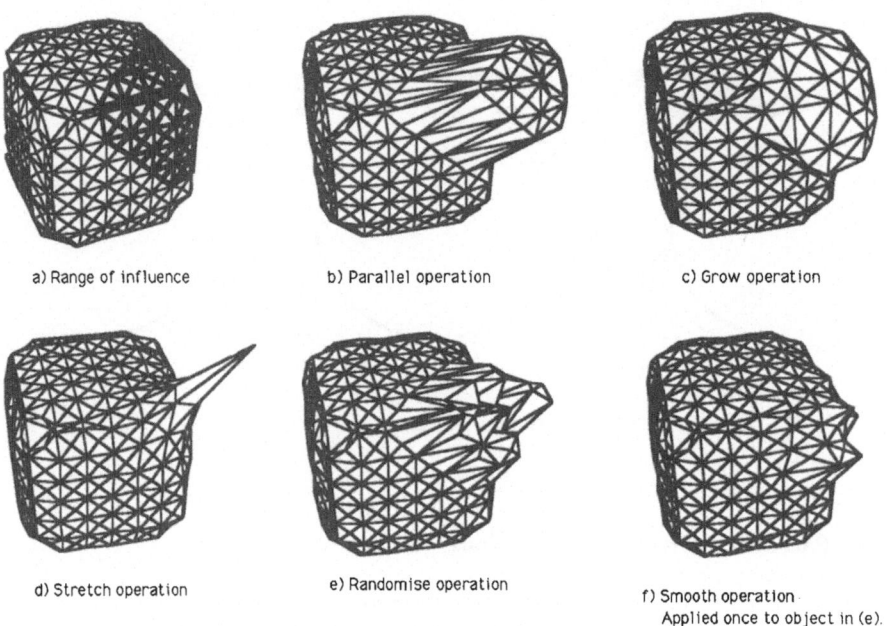

a) Range of influence b) Parallel operation c) Grow operation

d) Stretch operation e) Randomise operation f) Smooth operation
Applied once to object in (e).

Fig. 4: Variations of the move-vertex operation

3 IMPLEMENTING MESH OPERATIONS

DELTA is a system that implements all the capabilities described above. It interacts with other components of the Graphicsland computer animation system at the University of Calgary (Wyvill 1986). The current version runs on Iris 3000 series workstations (Silicon Graphics Inc).

3.1 Polygon Mesh Data Structure

The data structure used to represent the mesh is based on the standard hierarchical polygon list structure (Foley 1982). There are three important differences. First, the polygon list references the vertex list directly (instead of the edge list). This is because it is used only for back-face removal and for writing objects to a data file; and vertices, not edges, are needed for these operations. Second, face structures include exactly three vertex pointers instead of a list of them, since every polygon has just three vertices. Third, each vertex record has pointers to all vertices that share an edge with it. These cross-references are used to traverse the mesh laterally (see Section 3.4).

To save space, the face, edge, and vertex lists are implemented as arrays rather than linked lists. These arrays are extended dynamically when they overflow. If this necessitates relocating the vertex list then all vertex pointers in the data structure must be offset accordingly, but this overhead is negligible compared to the time taken to build the data structure, and has not been noticed for objects as large as 10^5 polygons. Offsetting is unnecessary for the edge and polygon lists since there are no references to them.

Polygon list   This is used to determine which vertices belong to front-facing polygons for the purpose of back-face removal. A "`visible`" flag is set for each vertex of a front-facing polygon. Vertex pointers are stored in anti-clockwise order as seen from the front of the polygon, as required by the front-facing calculation.

Edge list   This list, which contains references to each edge's end vertices, is traversed when drawing the object. For back-face removal, only those edges for which both vertices are marked visible are drawn. If objects were drawn by traversing the polygon list instead, then edges belonging to two front-facing polygons would be drawn twice.

Vertex list   The vertex record is the most complex, and contains most of the specific information needed for polygon mesh modelling. There are several fields for vertex coordinates:

`pnt`	world coordinates of vertex
`new_pnt`	tentative new location during move-vertex operation (so that the designer can cancel the operation)
`old_pnt`	position of vertex before it was last moved (for undo)
`pixel`	device coordinates (2D) where vertex was last drawn (for selecting vertices and back-face removal).

The list is traversed linearly to transform the object into device coordinates.

Pointers are stored to each adjacent vertex, since in polygon mesh modelling the mesh must be traversed laterally from one vertex to the next. These occupy an extendible array since different vertices have different numbers of incident edges. Several other fields are used specifically for mesh editing. The integer field `serial` is used as a time stamp (Section 3.4), and the boolean fields `bound`, `anchored`, and `inrange` are state flags. The `left` and `right` vertex pointers are used to build a binary tree of vertices when reading a polygon file.

3.2   Building the Data Structure

DELTA reads polygon files and constructs corresponding data structures. There is no prescribed order to the polygons in the file. Since shared vertices and edges will appear more than once, as polygons are read their vertices and edges must be checked to see if they already exist in the data structure. For this reason, the vertex list is threaded as an unbalanced binary tree during reading.

As polygons are read, they are triangulated (if not already a triangle) according to the algorithm in (Garey 1978), and each vertex is sought in the binary tree. Those not encountered previously are added. For a mesh with V vertices, building the vertex list takes $O(V log V)$ time. The threading pointers are only used during reading and are not maintained thereafter.

Each edge of a new polygon must also be sought and added if necessary. However, since the vertices are known, and since each contains a pointer to adjacent vertices, searching for an edge is simply a matter of checking to see whether the vertex at one end of it has a pointer to the vertex at the other end. If so, nothing need be done; if not, the new edge is added to the edge list and cross-reference pointers are included in the two vertices. For a polygon mesh with E edges, building this list takes $O(E)$ time.

For closed, triangulated polyhedra, the values of V and E are proportional to the number of triangles F ($V = F/2 + 2$ and $E = 3/2F$). Therefore the overall time required to build a polygon mesh data structure from a polygon file is $O(F \log F)$.

3.3 Moving Vertices in 3D

To move a vertex, the designer specifies a 3D line through it called the *primary axis* of movement (Figure 5b). There are several methods of choosing this.

Vertex Normal	The normal vector passing through the current vertex.
Edge Parallel	The vector parallel to an edge of the current vertex. This edge is selected interactively with the mouse.
Face Normal	The normal vector to a face of the current vertex. This face is selected interactively with the mouse.
Vertical	The vector (0,1,0) which is up in the world coordinate system.
Type Move	The vector typed by the designer in global coordinates.

The first three define the primary axis relative to the object's geometry, while the others define it in the world coordinate system. By itself, the primary axis offers the designer one degree of freedom along which to move the current vertex. In the example of Figure 5, it is vertical.

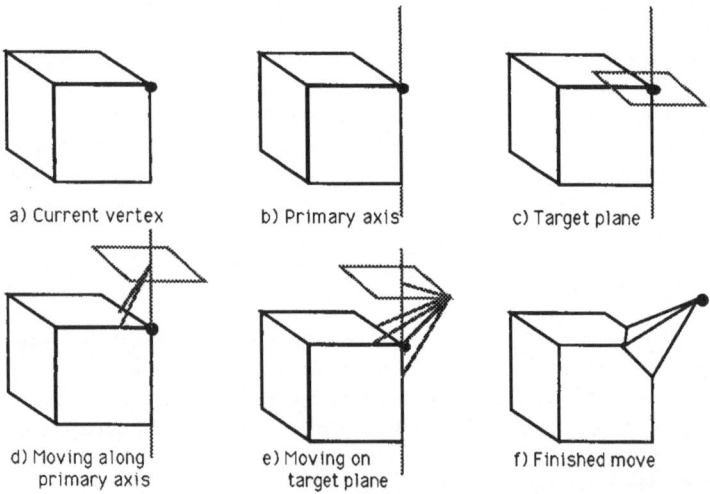

a) Current vertex b) Primary axis c) Target plane

d) Moving along primary axis e) Moving on target plane f) Finished move

Fig. 5: Moving a vertex—primary axis and target plane (for clarity, the cube is not triangulated)

Perpendicular to the primary axis is a plane called the *target plane*. Initially passing through the current vertex (Figure 5c), the designer can move it along the primary axis (Figure 5d). Finally, the current vertex can be placed anywhere on the target plane. This gives the designer two more degrees of freedom, allowing him to site the current vertex anywhere in 3-space.

These aspects are controlled interactively, and the move-vertex operation can be completed or cancelled at any time. One mouse button is used to move the target plane along the primary axis, while another locates a position on the plane. After choosing the primary axis, the designer can repeatedly adjust the new location for the current vertex with both buttons. The primary axis and target plane (represented by a 3D square polygon) are drawn as the vertex is moved, and the updated positions of all vertices in the range are shown too. DELTA allows the designer to change the view, the decay function, and the range without interrupting a move-vertex operation.

Implementation of move-vertex operation For each device coordinate generated by the mouse cursor, the line of projection through that coordinate is transformed into world coordinates using the inverse of the viewing transformation matrix. When movement is specified along the primary axis (via one mouse button), the point on the axis closest to the transformed projector is found (Figure 6a), and the target plane positioned to pass through this point. When movement is specified on the target plane (the other mouse button), the projector is intersected with it to find the new vertex position (Figure 6b), which is stored as a vector relative to the centre of the target plane (where it intersects the primary axis).

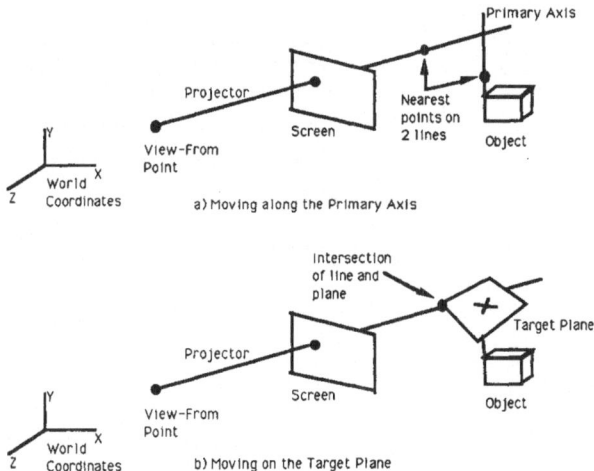

Fig. 6: Geometry of the move-vertex operation (for clarity, the cube is not triangulated)

3.4 Propagation of the Move-Vertex Operation

For efficiency, all vertices in the range of influence are marked with the `inrange` flag, and their distance from the nearest current or bound vertex is recorded in the `position_value` field.[1] The range is marked every time it is changed, whether by selecting a new current vertex, by binding or anchoring vertices, by subdividing it, or by adjusting the range parameter.

The `adjacent` pointers in the vertex list are used to perform a *flood traversal* of the mesh, which processes the current vertex, then recursively visits each neighbour. The traversal floods outward until all vertices in the range have been visited. Before calling the procedure, a global counter is incremented to give a serial number unique to this traversal, and each vertex visited is stamped so that it will only be processed once. The traversal stops when it encounters an anchored vertex or a

---

[1] Actually, the normalised position within the range is stored, $1 - distance/range$.

vertex that is out of range of the current one (for efficiency, the square of the range is compared with the square of the distance, to avoid evaluating square roots for vertices that are out of range). For each bound vertex, the global serial number is incremented again and the traversal procedure called once more. Vertices which are within range of more than one current or bound vertex are processed once for each and retain the lowest position value.

The flood traverse is optimal in that it makes one recursive call for each vertex in the range. It requires only constant time per vertex since it can be shown that the maximum average number of adjacent vertices is six (Allan 1988).

3.5 Decay Functions

On every mouse interrupt during a move-vertex operation, the position value for each vertex is mapped into a scale factor by one of the functions in Table 1. The movement vector is then scaled by this factor, added to the vertex position, and stored in the `new_pnt` field.

Constant	$f(x) = 1.0$	Does not change the shape over the range
Cone	$f(x) = x$	Influence of the move decreases linearly
Cusp	$f(x) = x^2$	Creates a cusp-shaped protrusion
Bell	$f(x) = sin((1 - x)\frac{\pi}{2})$	Produces a bell-shaped curve
Wave	$f(x) = sin(Kxr)$	A rippling wave effect
Random	$f(x) = \text{rand}()$	Perturbs surface randomly and uniformly

Table 1: Decay functions (x is position value; r is range)

3.6 Saving and Restoring Meshes

Script files record all editing operations performed, in the human-readable format illustrated in Figure 7. They can be examined and edited directly, and replayed by DELTA—possibly on a different object. Complex operations such as changing the view or moving a vertex are represented by tokens that summarise their effect. The use of script files bestows several advantages.

Reduced file storage space A large, complex polygon mesh object can be stored efficiently as a small, simple polygon file and a script file, providing an excellent example of *database amplification*— the re-creation of large amounts of low-level information from small amounts of high-level information. For example, the text in Figure 7 transforms a unit cube into the complex polygon mesh object shown.

Programmability Script files can be written and edited like computer programs. For example, if the four legs of the chair in Figure 7 had been made with four separate move-vertex operations, the script file could have been edited to give them the same length.

N-step undo Although DELTA provides a one-step undo facility by storing previous values of vertices when they are moved, an N-step undo would necessitate saving extensive state information since the move-vertex operation is irreversible—the set of vertices in the range of influence changes when the current vertex is moved. Script files provide a crude N-step undo capability by allowing the designer to truncate the script and re-execute it.

```
# TRANSFORM A CUBE INTO A CHAIR

# SQUASH
currentvertex 0.000000 1.000000 0.000000
bindvertex -0.500000 1.000000 0.500000
bindvertex -0.500000 1.000000 -0.500000
bindvertex 0.500000 1.000000 -0.500000
bindvertex 0.500000 1.000000 0.500000
range 1.224745
decayfunction Linear
movevertex 0.000000 -0.468986 0.000000

# DIVIDE RANGE
dividerange
dividerange
unbindall
range 0.000000

# LEGS
currentvertex -0.500000 -0.086061 0.500000
bindvertex -0.250000 -0.086061 0.500000
bindvertex -0.375000 -0.086061 0.375000
bindvertex -0.500000 -0.086061 0.250000
bindvertex -0.500000 -0.086061 -0.500000
bindvertex -0.500000 -0.086061 -0.250000
bindvertex -0.375000 -0.086061 -0.375000
bindvertex -0.250000 -0.086061 -0.500000
bindvertex 0.250000 -0.086061 -0.500000
bindvertex 0.375000 -0.086061 -0.375000
bindvertex 0.500000 -0.086061 -0.250000
bindvertex 0.500000 -0.086061 -0.500000
bindvertex 0.500000 -0.086061 0.500000
bindvertex 0.250000 -0.086061 0.500000
bindvertex 0.375000 -0.086061 0.375000
bindvertex 0.500000 -0.086061 0.250000
movevertex 0.000000 -0.908793 0.000000
unbindall
```

```
# ROUND BACK
currentvertex -0.500000 0.531014 0.000000
range 0.000000
anchorvertex -0.125000 0.473706 -0.500000
anchorvertex -0.125000 0.473706 0.500000
anchorvertex -0.125000 0.531014 -0.375000
anchorvertex -0.125000 0.531014 0.375000
anchorvertex -0.250000 0.531014 -0.250000
anchorvertex -0.250000 0.531014 0.000000
anchorvertex -0.250000 0.531014 0.250000
anchorvertex -0.375000 0.473706 -0.500000
anchorvertex -0.375000 0.473706 0.500000
anchorvertex -0.500000 0.376745 -0.500000
anchorvertex -0.500000 0.376745 0.500000
anchorvertex -0.500000 0.416399 0.000000
anchorvertex -0.500000 0.416399 0.250000
anchorvertex -0.500000 0.473706 -0.125000
anchorvertex -0.500000 0.473706 -0.375000
anchorvertex -0.500000 0.473706 0.125000
anchorvertex -0.500000 0.473706 0.375000
anchorvertex 0.000000 0.531014 -0.500000
anchorvertex 0.000000 0.531014 0.500000
range 1.891632
decayfunction Bell
dividerange
movevertex 0.000000 1.213332 0.000000
```

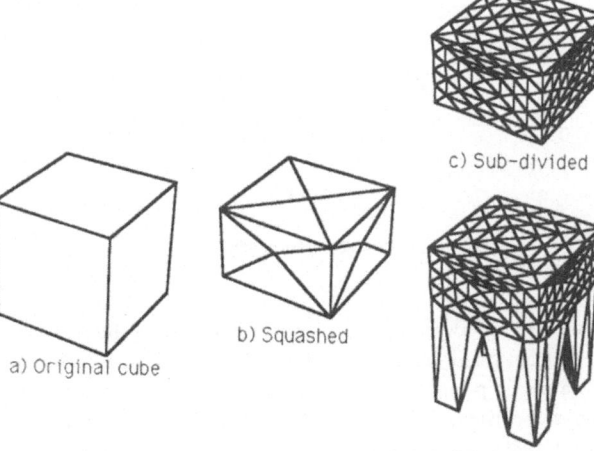
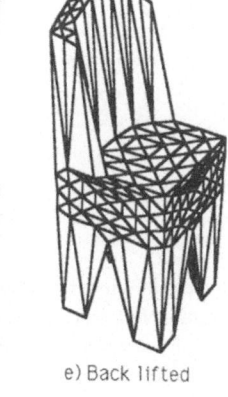

a) Original cube

b) Squashed

c) Sub-divided

d) Legs extracted

e) Back lifted

Fig. 7: Example DELTA script file

Debugging Scripts have been invaluable in correcting bugs during program development. The ability to edit and re-execute scripts expedites the location of errors.

Starting with different meshes A coarse mesh can be used to develop an editing script quickly, then the script can be re-executed on a finer version of the same object. This form of prototyping can save both time and storage space. The finer mesh must contain a vertex at the same location as each vertex identified in the script or the result will be undefined.

Transforming polygon meshes It may be less expensive to transform a small polygon mesh object and change the parameters of the script file before executing it, than to transform the object afterward. This is especially true if the script subdivides the mesh a great deal.

Animation The move-vertex operation can be interpolated parametrically by scaling the movement vector. A sequence of object descriptions can then be used to animate the operation. This capability has been implemented using a simple linear interpolation. More complex animation would be possible by allowing several operations to occur during overlapping time periods, but this has not yet been explored.

3.7   Specifying the View Graphically

DELTA provides three graphically interactive techniques for specifying the view: dolly, pan, and orbit (Figure 8). Only the view-from and view-to points are altered. The *view vector* is the difference between these.

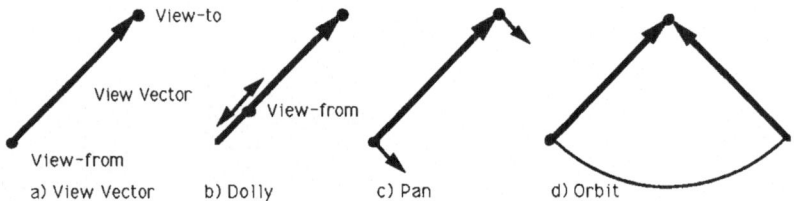

Fig. 8: Interactive viewing techniques

Dolly moves the view-from point toward or away from the view-to point along the view vector. Moving the mouse left causes the view-from point to dolly out and vice versa. *Pan* moves the view-from and view-to points by the same amount perpendicular to the view vector. The offset is controlled by incremental change in the mouse position, so that mousing up and right will move objects in the viewport up and right. The offset vector is found by transforming the device coordinates for two consecutive mouse cursor positions into world coordinates (using the inverse viewing transformation matrix) and subtracting them. *Orbit* moves the view-from point around the view-to point, maintaining the distance between them. Moving the mouse up and right spins objects in the viewport up and right about the view-to point. An offset vector in world coordinates is found as before, but is added to the view-from point only. This point is then moved toward the view-to point to maintain the length of the view vector.

Mapping device space to world space One problem with graphically interactive view specification techniques is mapping the device space offset into an appropriate world space offset. As Figure 9 illustrates, the projectors through the previous and current device coordinates diverge, and the farther they are from the view-from point the farther apart they become. The problem is establishing an appropriate distance from the view-from point to measure the distance between them.

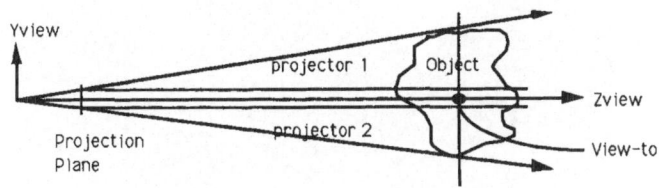

Fig. 9: Diverging projectors

The distance between projectors where they intersect the projection plane seems, at first, a reasonable choice. However, as the Figure shows, the projection window can be dwarfed by the object being viewed. Moving the mouse the full width of the device would produce a tiny world-space offset in comparison with the size of the object—even though it entirely fills the viewport!

The distance at the view-to point is a better choice because the designer can move it toward or away from the view-from point without affecting the view. By positioning it near the object being viewed, the distance between projectors corresponds better to the designer's intention[2]. Therefore the offsets used for Pan, Dolly, and Orbit are scaled by the ratio of the length of the view vector to the distance between view-from point and projection plane.

Singularities Singularities occur with interactive viewing techniques when the view-from and view-to points coincide or become vertically aligned. The Dolly operation can cause the points to converge by moving view-from up to view-to. When this happens, all the graphical techniques fail because they scale by the length of the view vector, and non-graphical methods must be used to separate the two points. The Orbit operation can align the view-from and view-to points, and when this happens the object appears to spin suddenly to one particular view because of the sense of "up" assumed by the viewing transformation (Newman 1979). Both of these conditions could be avoided by detecting when they are about to occur and preventing the points from quite converging or aligning. In order to provide a predictable interface, a history of recent views must be kept to determine the direction in which to repel the view-to point.

4 EXAMPLES

This section presents several examples of objects modelled with DELTA, chosen to illustrate some aspect of the methodology or its application to a modelling problem.

---

[2]For this reason (amongst others), Delta facilitates positioning the view-to point at the centre of the object or at the position of the current vertex.

Fig. 10: Scene from *The Great Train Rubbery* using polygon mesh landforms.

Landscape Figure 10 illustrates the landscape designed for the "Great Train Rubbery" computer animation (Wyvill 1988b). Preemptive, overlapping ranges and bell decay functions were used to create the hills atop the "hoodoo" landforms and on the valley floor. It also demonstrates the integration of DELTA into the Graphicsland animation system; polygon meshes, iso-surfaces, and explicit polygons were all used for the film.

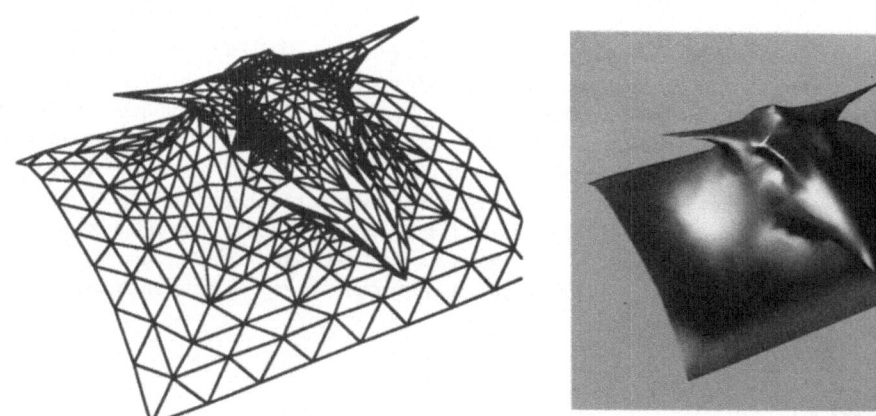

Fig. 11: Animal head

Animal head The head in Figure 11 is based on an example in (Forsey 1988) used to illustrate refinement of B-splines, and was reproduced with DELTA to demonstrate the equivalent capability of polygon mesh modelling. The original mesh was a single square polygon. Divide Range was used to increase the resolution where needed for detail work, without unnecessarily refining the mesh elsewhere. Bilateral symmetry was enforced by the system, but could have been accomplished by modelling the changes to one side, then editing the script to reflect the changes on the other side.

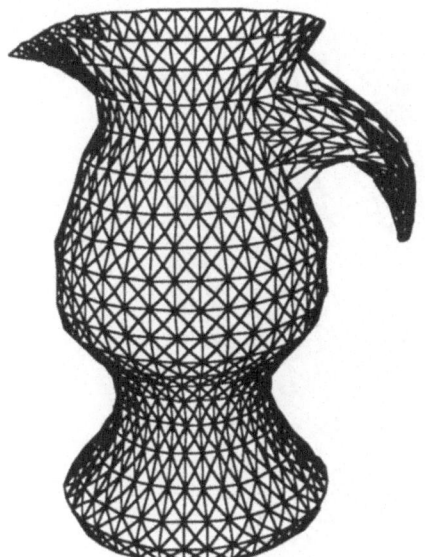 

Fig. 12: Grecian urn with lip and handle

Grecian urn The urn in Figure 12 was modelled as a simple surface of revolution using the Graphicsland modelling system. The lip and handle were added using DELTA with a few move-vertex operations; both features were made by locally increasing the resolution of the mesh. This illustrates the use of DELTA to add finishing touches to a model produced by another technique. Local Euler operations would be infeasible for such a task. A spline surface may suffice; however this could require dozens of patches. The urn does not resemble any of the quadric surfaces, and, since it is open, could not be modelled using constructive solid geometry or iso-surfaces.

Prosthetic medicine application DELTA has been used to help generate prosthetic devices for below-knee amputees. The digitised data of the patient's residual limb are converted to a mesh (Figure 13a) and modified interactively by the prosthetist to create a positive mold (Figure 13b), which is fabricated with a digital milling machine. The physical mold is then used to create the socket of the prosthetic limb for the patient. Sensitive areas of the limb data must be raised to give relief, and weight-bearing areas depressed to provide support. The grow operation and bell decay function are used for this.

The limb data was originally in the form of a cylindrical array of 3D points. An alternative method of representation would be to use these points to control an interpolating spline surface. There are two reasons why a polygon mesh is better suited. First, the resolution of the input is extremely high—there are as many as 512^2 data points in the digitiser input[3]. With such fine resolution, interpolation is not necessary and would be extremely slow. Second, the input for the digital milling machine is the same as the output of the digitiser. A spline surface would have to be converted back into discrete points when output.

---

[3]Figure 13 shows only one point for every 100 in the model.

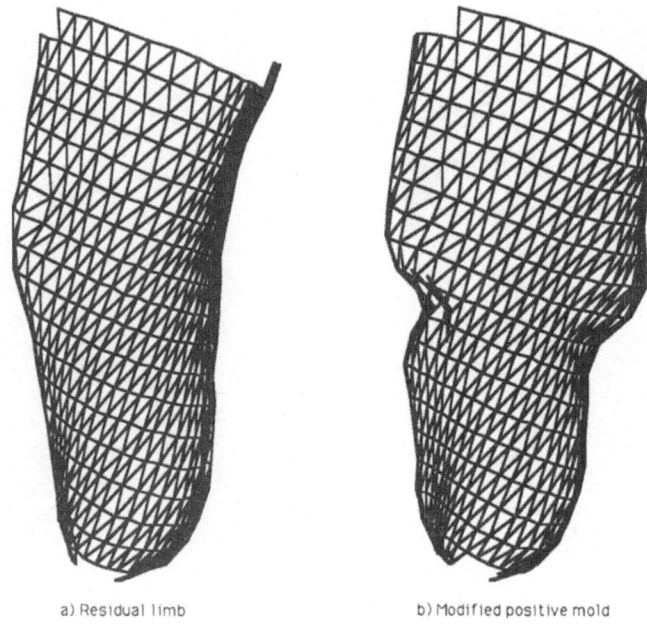

a) Residual limb   b) Modified positive mold

Fig. 13: Residual limb and positive mold

5   EVALUATION OF POLYGON MESH MODELLING

Here we summarize the advantages of the technique, along with some disadvantages which are inherited from the polygon mesh itself.

+ Expressive power   Polygon meshes can represent any surface, whether open or closed, with any topological genus. The technique does not, however, allow the designer to alter the genus.

+ Convertability   Most other representations—including digitized data—can be converted into polygonal approximations. Polygon mesh modelling can then be applied to perform custom alterations not readily accomplished with the other techniques.

+ Controlled resolution   The resolution is increased locally as needed by dividing the range. The designer can use appropriate levels of detail in different parts of the model.

+ Manipulation speed   The delay between an action like moving a vertex or changing the view and the result on the screen is very small because the data structure is convenient for display. Unlike functional and constructive techniques, no conversion into a wire frame or other approximation is needed.

+ **Computational efficiency** Very little computational effort is required to derive certain geometric properties that are not explicitly specified in the model. Extents, intersections, surface normals, and surface area are commonly used by rendering and animation techniques and are very fast to compute.

+ **Possibility of animation** The move-vertex operation offers a high level of control for manipulating the mesh, and objects can be animated by interpolating moves over time.

+ **Convenient rendering** Geometric information is readily available for polygonal models. Scan line coherence can be well utilised due to the planarity of polygons. Sorting can also be used because of their discrete nature.

– **Discreteness** Even a finely divided mesh rendered with a smoothing algorithm will have a faceted silhouette. However, when polygon meshes must be used, due to available data or the nature of a modelling task, polygon mesh modelling offers capabilities which in most cases match, and sometimes surpass, those of other modelling techniques.

– **Space efficiency** Storage requirements are large since all topological and geometric information must be stored explicitly. The disc storage problem can be alleviated by using script files.

– **Geometric consistency** Two forms of geometric inconsistency are generally associated with polygon meshes: self-intersection and non-planar polygons. The former can occur when moving vertices, and the designer must take responsibility for avoiding it. The latter is not a problem since the polygon mesh is triangulated.

6 CONCLUSION

We have presented a method for interactively manipulating polygon meshes in a general way, together with a full, interactive implementation. It is based on the idea of modifying the current vertex by the move-vertex operation (parallel and non-parallel), which has an associated range of influence, decay function, and bound and anchored vertices. The ability to divide all polygons in the range of influence allows the designer to change the mesh resolution as needed. Script files provide several capabilities, such as programmability, N-step undo, and economical storage on disk.

Among several desirable properties the methodology includes the ability to model a large and general class of objects. Easy to use, it puts considerable power in the hands of the designer. Polygon meshes have the added advantage that they can easily approximate most other modelling representations, and can accurately represent digitised data. For many purposes these advantages outweigh the drawbacks of the technique, namely the planar nature of meshes, the large storage requirement, and the possibility of self-intersections.

Acknowledgements

We would like to acknowledge the help of all those who have contributed to Graphicsland over the years. This research is partially supported by grants from the Natural Sciences and Engineering Research Council of Canada.

REFERENCES

Allan JB (1988) Polygon Mesh Modelling for Computer Graphics. Master's thesis, University of Calgary, Dept. of Computer Science

Bartels R, Beatty B, Barsky B (1987) An Introduction to Splines for use in Computer Graphics & Geometric Modeling. Morgan Kaufmann, Los Altos, Calif

Blinn J (1986) The algebraic properties of homogeneous second order surfaces. ACM SIGGRAPH Tutorial Notes

Chiyokura H, Kimura F (1983) Design of solids with free-form surfaces. Computer Graphics (Proc. SIGGRAPH 83), 17(2):289-298

Foley JD, Dam A Van (1982) Fundamentals of Interactive Computer Graphics. Addison-Wesley

Forsey DR, Bartels RH (1988) Hierarchical B-spline refinement. Computer Graphics (Proc. SIGGRAPH 88), 22(4):205-212

Fournier A, Fussel D, Carpenter L (1982) Computer Rendering of Stochastic models. Commun. ACM, 25(6):371-384

Garey MR, Johnson DS, Preparata FP, Tarjan RE (1978) Triangulating a simple polygon. Information Processing Letters, 7(4):175-179

Mantyla M (1988) An Introduction to Solid Modeling. Computer Science Press, Rockville, Maryland

Newman WM, Sproull RF (1979) Principles of Interactive Computer Graphics. McGraw-Hill, New York

Wyvill B, McPheeters C, Garbutt R (1986) The University of Calgary 3D Computer Animation System. Journal of the Society of Motion Picture and Television Engineers, 95(6):629-636

Wyvill B, Wyvill G (1988a) Field functions for iso-surfaces (inpress). The Visual Computer, 1988. Also published in Proc. CG International 88.

Wyvill B (1988b) The Great Train Rubbery. ACM SIGGRAPH '88 Electronic Theatre and Video Review, Issue 26 (inpress)

Jeff Allan received his B.Sc in Computer Science in 1985, followed by his M.Sc in computer graphics in 1988 from the University of Calgary, Canada. His research interests include 3D geometric modelling and user interface design. Currently, he is working in the area of distributed simulation, while consulting in the computer graphics and geometric modelling fields.

Address: Jade Simulations International Corporation, #80, 1833 Crowchild Trail NW, Calgary, Alberta, Canada, T2M 4S7

UUCP: ihnp4!alberta!calgary!jsi-fsa!allan

Brian Wyvill received his PhD from the University of Bradford in 1975 and continued his interest in computer animation as a research fellow at the Royal College of Art. After working as an animation consultant for projects such as some scenes from the film 'Alien', he joined the University Calgary faculty in 1981. He is now a full professor and leads the Graphicsland animation research group. Current interests include deformable objects for computer animation, including iso-surfaces (Soft Objects) and generalised cylinders. He is a member of ACM, CGS, IEEE computer Society and the editorial board of the Visual Computer.

Address: Department of Computer Science, The University of Calgary, 2500 University Drive NW, Calgary, Alberta, Canada, T2N 1N4

UUCP: ihnp4!alberta!calgary!blob **CDNet:** blob@calgary.cdn

Ian H. Witten received degrees in Mathematics from Cambridge University, Computer Science from the University of Calgary, and Electrical Engineering from Essex University, England. A Lecturer and subsequently Senior Lecturer at Essex University from 1970, he returned to Calgary in 1980 where he served as Head of Computer Science from 1982 to 1985.

His research interests span the field of man-machine systems. He has published around 100 papers on machine learning, speech synthesis and signal processing, text compression, hypertext, and computer typography. His current interests include prediction and modeling, machine learning, programming by example, and autonomous systems. He has written three books – Communicating with Microcomputers (Academic Press, 1980), Principles of Computer Speech (Academic Press, 1982), and Talking with Computers (Prentice Hall, 1986) ; with another in press entitled Text compression (Prentice Hall).

Address: Department of Computer Science, The University of Calgary, 2500 University Drive NW, Calgary, Alberta, Canada, T2N 1N4

UUCP: ihnp4!alberta!calgary!ian **CDNet:** ian@calgary.cdn

A Feature-Based Modelling System Built on Top of Euler Operators

L. Casu and B. Falcidieno

ABSTRACT

In this work we propose a system to build the Feature-Based Model of an object by a set of Euler operators and macro-operators.

This system consists of an assembly modeller which uses a data base of objects built by Euler operators and corresponding to unworked material blocks or to form features; it permits the direct costruction of the feature-based model of a part by a set of suitably adapted boolean operators.

The use of the system is simplified by a graphics interface which allows the user to select the starting object, the feature to be added, the result of the composition and the final structure of the feature-based model.

Keywords: Solid modelling, CAD, CAM, Euler operators.

1. Introduction.

The solid modellers used in CAD systems do not usually represent the functionality of a part in its application context, but only the geometric characteristics in terms of low level entities, such as faces, edges and vertices in a boundary representation. On the contrary, the object functionality is better described by pointing out the most significant form features in a model which could represent them explicitly, that is a so-called Feature-Based Model (or FBM) which, together with the form features of the part, also represents their mutual relationships.

Until now, for the feature identification of a part and the relative costruction of its feature-based model, three fundamental approaches have been proposed:

Human-assisted feature recognition, where the user has to identify on the object shape the parts he/she wants to recognize, thus permitting the grouping of relative geometric data as form features and combining them with tolerance relations.

Automatic feature recognition and extraction, where features are recognized and extracted from a solid model and then organized in a hierarchical graph. Obviously, these systems cannot derive information that does not exist, such as tolerances and finish, which are not represented in the geometric model.

The algorithms for automatic recognition of form features are generally complex and modeller-specific; the method used in [Fal 87], for example, consists of an automatic system which recognizes and organizes features in a hierarchical graph; the recognition part is based on syntactical rules proposed by Kyprianou [Kyp

80] which, by classifying edges as concave or convex, allow recognition of features belonging to the classes of protrusions or depressions.

Feature-based modelling: this approach provides a means for building an object model by assembling features stored in libraries. These systems allow the definition of a feature-based model at multiple abstraction levels [Sha 88]. The general method consists of building a data base of objects representing classes of form features, defining functions for the construction of an object with form features and defining a system which allows the creation, manipulation and modification of the FBM. The model obtained can permit, besides form features, definition of tolerances, maximum and minimum dimensions, etc.

Except for the first approach which is neither convenient nor efficient, both automatic recognition and direct creation have been usefully employed according to the context requirements.

The method we propose in this work belongs to the category of feature-based modelling systems and allows to define the representation of an object and its form features, by using a boundary modeller based on Euler operators.

2. Boundary representation schemes.

The range of objects we consider belong to the class of two-manifold objects bounded by compact, closed, oriented two-manifold surfaces. The boundary of an object is divided into a finite number of subsets, called **faces**, every face is described by the edges and vertices bounding it.

A topological description of the boundary of a two-manifold object is a relational model in which the three primitive topological entities defining its boundary, named **face**, **edge** and **vertex**, are explicitly represented together with their mutual relationships.

Besides these primitive entities, compound entities are also defined [Cam 82]: **loop** that is the connected and non self-intersecting set of edges that have a common face; **shell** which corresponds to a connected and closed set of faces and **object** defined as the set of shells composing a complete solid.

A boundary representation B_s of an object S can be defined as a triple (V_s, E_s, F_s), in which the sets E_s of edges and V_s of vertices define two relationships over the set F_s of faces:

1) two faces f_1 and f_2 are called **edge-adjacent** if and only if there exists an edge e in E_s shared by f_1 and f_2;

2) two faces f_1 and f_2 are called **vertex-adjacent** if and only if there exists a vertex v in V_s shared by f_1 and f_2.

Face-edge relation and the partition of F_s into equivalence classes defined by the face-vertex one can be represented in the form of a hypergraph, which can be intuitively defined as a graph in which arcs may connect an arbitrary number of nodes. The hypergraph to which we refer, called **Face Adiacency Hypergraph** (or FAH), is defined as a triple $G=(N, A, H)$ such that every node represents a face, every arc represents an edge and every hyperarc a vertex [Ans 85].

The FAH model does not explicitly represent the information about shape features of objects, thus making necessary the definition of a model which better represents feature information. Therefore the Face Adiacency Hypergraph of an object has been organized into a hierarchical form in order to represent the object at successively finer levels of specification, giving rise to a structured hypergraph called **Structured Face Adjacency Hypergraph** (or SFAH) as defined in [Fal 87].

The SFAH model can be formally defined as a pair $g^*=(H,G)$ where G is the acyclic oriented graph describing its hyerarchical structure and H is a family of hypergraphs, each of which, called component of g^*, is associated with a distinct node in H. There are special nodes, called **roots**, from which all other nodes originate. A component H_i in g^* is a **parent** if it refers other components and, conversely, it is a **child** if it is referred by other components. Any non-root component in g^* is the FAH representation of a feature in its parent graph. The parent-child relation between any pair of components H_i and H_j of g^* is defined by a set of nodes which belong to both H_i and H_j. These nodes are called **connection nodes** in the parent component H_i and **dummy nodes** in the child component H_j. The connection nodes of H_j in H_i correspond to those faces in the object to which the feature is attached, while in H_j the dummy nodes describe the faces added to the feature represented by H_j in order to form an admissible solid object [Fal 87].

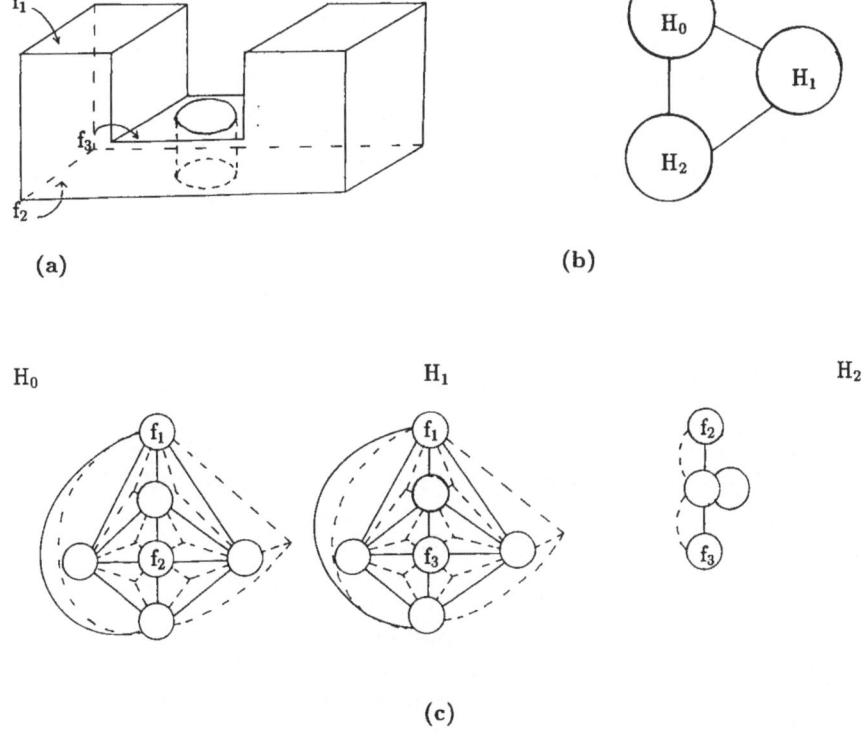

Fig. 1: (a) an object with a slot and a through hole; (b) its SFAH representation and (c) FAH representation of each component.

In this graph, features are explicitly represented by specifying all the faces that compose them.

In figure 1 an object with two features (a slot and a through hole) is shown; its SFAH representation is composed by three graphs: component H_0, which describes the main object shape (the big box), component H_1 which describes the slot on the face f_1 of the box and component H_2 which represents the through hole and is attached to the two faces f_2 and f_3 belonging to the box and the slot respectively.

The relation between H_1 and H_0 is defined by the connection node f_1 in H_0, and the dummy node f_1 in H_1. The relation between H_2 and H_0 is described by the connection node f_2 in H_0 and the dummy node f_2 in H_2, whereas the relation between H_2 and H_1 is defined by the connection node f_3 in H_1 and the dummy node f_3 in H_2.

3. Euler operators.

The FAH representation of an object completely describes its topological and geometric properties. The topological validity of a FAH model can be checked by applying an extension of Euler's rule [Big 86]:

$$v - e + f = 2(s - g) + h$$

where v=number of vertices of the object, e=number of edges, f=number of faces, s=number of shells, g=genus and h=number of holeloops on the faces.

Instead of performing a validity check at each updating, it is convenient to decompose each object modification into a sequence of atomic steps, called **Euler operators**, which ensure that the topological validity requirement expressed by Euler's rule is always satisfied. Hence, any valid object can be constructed by a sequence of these operators, where each operator defines a specific action in solid creation.

In table 1 the five basic constructive Euler operators and their inverses which have been defined in [Ans 85] for the boundary FAH modeller are shown.

Tab. 1: basic Euler operators and their description.

CONSTRUCTIVE OPERATORS	DESCRIPTION	INVERSE OPERATORS
MFVS(f,v,s)	Make Face Vertex Shell	
	Kill Face Vertex Shell	**KFVS**(f,v,s)
MEF(f,e)	Make Edge Face	
	Kill Edge Face	**KEF**(f,e)
MEV(e,v)	Make Edge Vertex	
	Kill Edge Vertex	**KEV**(e,v)
KFSMH(f,s,h)	Kill Face Shell Make Hole	
	Make Face Shell Kill Hole	**MFSKH**(f,s,h)
KFMHG(f,h,g)	Kill Face Make Hole Genus	
	Make Face Kill Hole Genus	**MFKHG**(f,h,g)

4. Euler macro-operators.

The previously indicated Euler operators provide a minimal complete set of basic functions for defining and manipulating three-dimensional solid objects, but they have a low level functionality and their use is often impractical and highly inefficient. Thus, it has been necessary to introduce a set of higher-level operators, called **macro-operators**, which are defined as a sequence of basic operators, and make the manipulation of objects easier, always preserving the topological validity.

The macro-operators defined in [Ans 85] for the FAH boundary modeller are the **sweep** macro-operator which trasforms a two-dimensional face or lamina (L) into a three-dimensional object by sweeping this face along a given direction d; the **glue_face** and **glue_face_make_handle** macro-operators that glue two coincident faces f_1 and f_2, respectively belonging to two separate shells (s_1 and s_2) or to a single shell (s).

Those macro-operators work on the object faces, that is on the object surface, but not on its volume. Thus, it is still difficult for the user to define complex objects as composition of more simple parts. To this aim, the boolean operators **Union**, **Intersection** and **Difference** have been defined in [Cas 88].

In table 2 the complete set of macro-operators defined for the FAH modeller are listed.

Tab. 2: the set of Euler macro-operators defined for the FAH modeller.

EULER MACRO-OPERATORS

SWEEP(L,d)

GLUE_FACE(s_1,s_2,f_1,f_2)

GLUE_FACE_MAKE_HANDLE(s,f_1,f_2)

UNION(obj$_1$,obj$_2$)

INTERSECTION(obj$_1$,obj$_2$)

DIFFERENCE(obj$_1$,obj$_2$)

Boolean operators allow to obtain the result of these operations in a way which is consistent with the boundary representation, since the boundaries of the objects are divided into four parts which, suitably attached, give the result of set operations on the initial objects. To this aim, we have adopted the general idea proposed by Mantyla in [Man 83] and successively extended in [Man 86]. In this work the boundaries of the two initial objects A and B are classified with respect to each other, in order to obtain four parts: the part of A boundary lying in the exterior of B (**AoutB**), the internal one (**AinB**), the part of B boundary lying in the exterior of A (**BoutA**) and the internal one (**BinA**). These four parts, suitably attached by the glue macro-operator, give as result a set operation, since the union of the two objects is obtained by gluing the two external parts, the intersection by gluing the two internal ones and the difference by gluing the external part of the first object and the complement of the internal part of the other object.

We must observe that the glue macro-operator attaches two solid objects having a coincident face, while the four parts obtained by the boundary classification are only sets of faces or parts of faces. Considering that set operations work on volumes, we have adopted a solution that differs from Mantyla's method and builds the complete boundaries of the four parts by the definition of compound faces, called **macrofaces**.

The introduction of macrofaces permits to calculate the results of all set operations by gluing the two solid volumes corresponding to the suitable parts.

In table 3 the four set operations on the objects A and B ($A \cup B$, $A \cap B$, $A \backslash B$, $B \backslash A$) are described as the result of the glue operator applied to two of the four parts just defined; $(BinA)^{-1}$ is the complement of $BinA$.

Tab. 3: description of the four set operations.

$A \cup B = A$*out*B *glue* B*out*A
$A \cap B = A$*in*B *glue* B*in*A
$A \backslash B = A$*out*B *glue* $(B$*in*$A)^{-1}$
$B \backslash A = B$*out*A *glue* $(A$*in*$B)^{-1}$

---

5. Description of the system.

Euler operators and FAH model have been used as the base of a solid modeller defined in [Ans 85] and for the reconstruction of form features in an automatic recognition system [Fal 87]. On the contrary, in this work Euler macro-operators constitute the core of a feature based modelling system.

To this goal, the SFAH structure has been adapted to encode a feature-based model by the addition of a set of attributes which complete the form feature information. The information stored by the SFAH structure besides the geometry of an object also encodes how its components can be assembled. However, it does not give any suggestion about other important characteristics such as material, functionality, etc., which make a model a product model qualified for a process planning activity. By product model we mean a complete model which represent all relevant properties of a product in a consistent and integrated way [Kje 88].

Properties considered relevant concern geometry, topology, composition of the product and the constraints it has to obey.

Specific attributes have been defined for each admissible feature; these attributes have been classified into **simple** and **complex** attributes.

By simple attributes we mean those that have a one-to-one correspondence with the entities they qualify [Bra 88]. The simple attributes considered in this work concern dimensions of the features, angles formed by faces, the number of faces forming the feature and the maximum and minimum values for dimensions.

On the other hand, the complex attributes, that is those having a one-to-many correspondence with the entities they qualify, define topological relations among feature entities and the object entities to which the feature is applied. These relations are constituted by the faces to which the feature is attached and its location (a reference point). In this sense, tolerance and dimension constraints have been considered complex attributes and included in the model [Fal 88].

The diagram of figure 2 shows the types of features considered in this work and the attributes for a pocket.

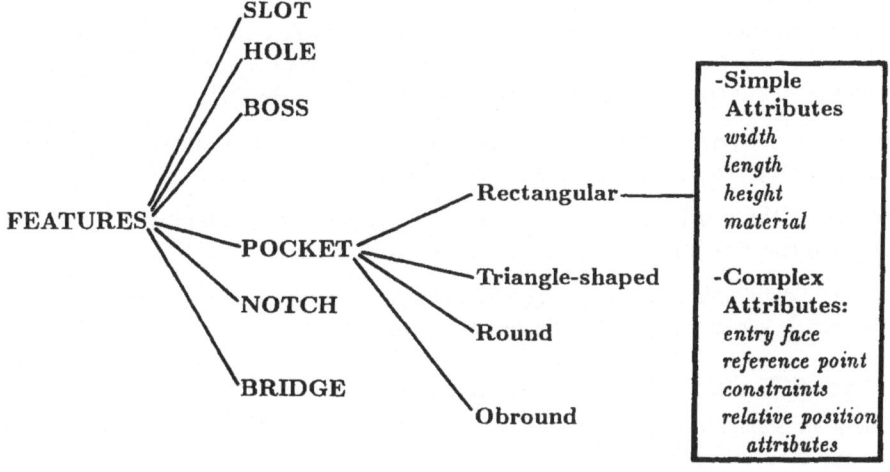

Fig. 2: feature classification.

The system for constructing the Feature-Based Model (FBM) of a solid object by Euler operators and macro-operators is structured in order to allow the user to select an initial object, represented by a FAH model, on which he/she can recursively add features selected from a library. In this way, it is possible to simultaneously obtain the requested FBM and the geometric model of the result of the composition.

For constructing the feature-based model we have used an extended version of the boolean operators which allows the user to work directly on the FBM structure at different levels of representation and produces as result the feature-based representation of an object.

Moreover, by using the extended boolean operators it is possible to obtain the information necessary to build the FBM, and also check the validity of the resulting model in the case of collision of the new feature with previously defined ones.

The method we have adopted for constructing the feature-based model of an object works in three parts: in the first, the volume of the feature is reconstructed depending on the object to which it is applied and on the relative position, that is on the so-called *entry faces* for the feature. In this phase, the feature is defined by the parameters necessary for its construction: feature type (*pocket, hole, boss, notch, slot,* etc. [Cam 85]), dimensions, entry faces (the connection faces for the SFAH description) and finally a reference point on these faces.

Euler operators are then used for constructing the FAH model of the feature object: the construction is dependent on the type of the selected feature and the result is always topologically correct, due to the use of Euler operators. The parameters required for the definition of pockets and bosses, for example, are: dimensions (*width, length and height*) and the entry face; also for a through hole we have to know the entry and exit faces, while its height depends on the object to which the hole is attached. Thus, some parameters are implicit, i. e. they depend on the object on which the feature must be applied, while other ones are explicit, that is they must be given by the user.

In this way, the construction of the object is really object based, because the feature volume is directly calculated on the object; hence the volume is the real volume added to or subtracted from the object by the feature definiton.

In the second part, the volume of the result from the composition of the feature with the object is calculated by the extended boolean operators.

Finally, in the third part, by using the results given by the two previous steps, the hyerarchical structure corresponding to the FBM is built.

In the following algorithm the sequence of steps necessary for constructing the FBM of a part is shown. The following functions and procedures are used as primitives:

SELECT_OBJECT($list\_of\_objects, obj\_name, obj\_model, g^*$): allows to select the model obj_model of the object obj_name in the list of objects stored in a library and to copy it into the current FBM g^*;

SELECT_FEATURE($list\_of\_features, feat\_name, ftype, attr\_list$): allows to select the feature $feat\_name$ of type $ftype$ in the list of features stored in a library; ftype can be protrusion or depression; $attr\_list$ is the list of the attributes necessary for building the FBM; the name of the feature can be: pocket, hole, slot, etc.;

READ_FACES($obj\_name, conn\_face\_list$): returns the list $conn\_face\_list$ of the connection faces of the object obj_name; the connection faces are those to which the selected feature must be applied;

BUILD_FEAT_OBJ($feat\_name, attr\_list, conn\_face\_list, feat\_model$): builds the FAH model $feat\_model$ for the feature $feat\_name$ with the explicit attributes stored in attr_list and the implicit attributes calculated on the basis of the faces in $conn\_face$ _list;

STORE_OBJECT($g^*, new\_obj\_name, list\_of\_objects$): stores with the assigned name, new_obj_name, the model g* corresponding to the created object; the new_obj _name is added to the list of objects.

Algorithm FBM(g^*);

% g^* represents FBM %

(* first step *)

SELECT_OBJECT($list\_of\_objects, obj\_name, obj\_model, g^*$);

while not stop **do**
  SELECT_FEATURE(*list_of_features,feat_name,*
         ftype,attr_list);
  READ_FACES(*obj_name,conn_face_list*);
  BUILD_FEAT_OBJ (*feat_name,attr_list,*
         conn_face_list,feat_model)

(* second step *)

   if ftype = protrusion
    then UNION(*obj_model,feat_model,coplanar_face_*
       list,current_obj_model,intersection_flag)
    else DIFFERENCE(*obj_model,feat_model,coplanar_*
       face_list,current_obj_model,intersection_flag);

(* third step *)

    if intersection_flag
     then BUILD_FBM(*feat_model,conn_face_list,*
        coplanar_face_list,attr_l,g*)
    else ERROR

end while
STORE_OBJECT(g^*,*new_obj_name,list_of_objects*)
end FBM

5.1 The construction of the resulting object.

This phase corresponds to the second step of the system and allows the creation of a complete object with features using the extended boolean operators.
In particular the boolean operators used are the UNION operator, for protrusion features and the DIFFERENCE operator, for the depression ones. Both these operators, such as the intersection operator which is only internally used, are described by a procedure called **bool_operation**, described below.
This procedure verifies if the two objects intersect each other; on the contrary a flag (*intersection_flag*) takes the value false, thus avoiding the construction of a meaningless FBM in the subsequent phase.

The algorithm for the procedure BOOL_OPERATION uses the following primitives:

  TEST_INTERSECTION(A,B): takes the value true if the two boxes containing the objects A and B do not intersect each other, the value false otherwise;

  SEARCH_COPLANAR_FACES($A,B,$*coplanar_face_list*): returns the list of coplanar faces of the two objects A and B, also indicating the coincident and the nested ones;

  FIND_INTER_POINT($A,B,$*list_of_int*): searches the intersection points between the two objects A and B, giving in *list_of_int* the list of intersection points;

TRUE_INTERSECTION(A,B): takes the value true if the two objects A and B properly intersect each other, that is if their intersection is still three-dimensional, the value false otherwise;

BOUNDARY_CLASS($A,B,list\_of\_int,AoutB,AinB,BoutA,BinA,mf_1,mf_2$): classifies the boundaries of the two objects A and B, with respect to each other, in external and internal parts; mf_1 and mf_2 are the two macrofaces obtained by the boundary classification;

NON_BOOL($A,B,coplanar\_face\_list,res\_obj\_model$): deals with the particular cases in which the glue macro-operator cannot be used. For example, when the two objects have more than a coincident face and a generalized glue operator or glue_face_make_handle operator must be used;

GLUE($obj_1\_model,obj_2\_model,f_1,f_2,res\_obj\_model$): is the operator which attaches the objects obj_1_model and obj_2_model by gluing the two coincident faces f_1 and f_2; this macro-operator returns the result in res_obj_model.

Algorithm BOOL_OPERATION ($A,B,operation,res\_obj\_model,$
$coplanar\_face\_list,intersection\_flag$);

% A e B are the two objects

operation is the type of operation to do (union, intersection and difference)

res_obj_model is the resulting model

intersection_flag is false when the two objects do not intersect each other %

intersection_flag:=TRUE;

if TEST_INTERSECTION(A,B)
  then SEARCH_COPLANAR_FACES($A,B,coplanar\_face\_list$);
      FIND_INTER_POINT($A,B,list\_of\_int$);
      if TRUE_INTERSECTION(A,B)
        then BOUNDARY_CLASS($A,B,list\_of\_int,AoutB,AinB,$
                    $BoutA,BinA,mf_1,mf_2$);
            case *operation* **of**
                INTERSECTION:GLUE($AinB,BinA,mf_1,mf_2,$
                        res_obj_model);
                UNION   :GLUE($AoutB,BoutA,mf_1,$
                        mf_2,res_obj_model);
                DIFFERENCE :GLUE($AoutB,(BinA)^{-1},mf_1,$
                        mf_2,res_obj_model)
            end case
        else NON_BOOL($A,B,coplanar\_face\_list,res\_obj\_model$)
  else intersection_flag:=false
end BOOL_OPERATION

5.2 The Feature-Based Model construction.

To build the FBM model it is necessary to know "high level" information about topological relations among the entities of the object; hence it is very important to know the faces of the object on which features are present and the corresponding faces of the feature.

Connection faces are the object faces to which the feature is attached and they have been indicated during the procedure Read_Face; on the contrary, dummy faces are retrieved during the application of extended boolean operators. In fact, the list of coplanar faces between the two objects represents, for the parent object, the list of connection faces, while for the child object, that is the feature, it represents the list of dummy faces.

Thus, every time a feature is built and it is added to the list of the FBM components, the appropriate attributes are added to its component in the FBM and the connections among the nodes are arranged.

For each connection face the correspondent dummy face in the current component is searched in the list of coplanar faces; but, as we can see in figure 1, the connection face can belong to a previously defined feature (i.e. the slot), thus making it necessary to search the name of this parent feature. Then, the correspondence map between the parent and the child object (the current feature) is created by pairs of connection and dummy faces.

The algorithm BUILD_FBM given below formalizes this third step; the primitives used for the construction of the FBM are the following:

ADD_COMPONENT_FBM(g^*,H_k): inserts a new component H_k into the structure g^* representing FBM;

ADD_ARC_FBM($g^*,(H_i,H_j)$): adds a new arc (H_i,H_j) into the structure g^* which describes FBM;

ADD_CORRESPONDENCE($conn\_face,dum\_face,q_k$): defines the mapping q_k of correspondence between the dummy face dum_face and the connection face $conn\_face$;

ADD_DUMMY_FACE(H_k,dum_face): adds the dummy face dum_face to the set of dummy faces of the component H_k in g^*;

UPDATE_CONNECTION_FACE_SET($g^*,(H_i,H_k),(H_i,H_j)$): updates the connection -face set of H_i wrt H_j by deleting all the connection faces of H_i that now belong to H_k;

UPDATE_DUMMY_FACE_SET($g^*,(H_i,H_k),(H_i,H_j)$): updates the dummy-face set of H_i wrt H_j by deleting all the dummy faces of H_i that now belong to H_k;

GET_DUMMY_FACE($feat\_name,coplanar\_list,conn\_face,dum\_face$): , returns in dum_face the name of the dummy face in $feat\_name$ corresponding to the connection face $conn\_face$; dum_face is searched in the list of the faces coplanar with $conn\_face$; this list is a result of boolean operators;

GET_PARENT_COMPONENT(g^*,*conn_face,parent_component_name*): returns in *parent_component_name* the name of the component of g_* containing the connection face *conn_face*;

ADD_COMPONENT_ATTRIBUTES(g^*,H_i,*attr_list*): adds to the component H_i of g^* the attributes present in the list attr_list.

Algorithm BUILD_FBM (*feat_model,conn_face_list,*
coplanar_face_list,attr_list,g^*);

% *feat_model* is the name of the child component

conn_face_list is the list of connection faces in the parent component

coplanar_face_list is the list of coplanar faces

attr_list is the list of attributes of the child component

g^* describes the FBM of the resulting object %

ADD_COMPONENT_FBM(g^*,*feat_model*);
for every conn_face in conn_face_list **do**
    GET_PARENT_COMPONENT(g^*,*conn_face,parent_component_name*);
    ADD_ARC_FBM(g^*,*(parent_component_name,feat_model)*);
    GET_DUMMY_FACE(*feature_name,coplanar_list,conn_*
                face,dum_face);
    ADD_DUMMY_FACE(*feat_model,dum_face*);
    ADD_CORRESPONDENCE(*conn_face,dum_face,q_k*)
    end for

  for every node H_k in g* **do**
    UPDATE_CONNECTION_FACE_SET(g^*,*(H_k,feat_model)*,
                    (parent_component_name,H_k));
    UPDATE_DUMMY_FACE_SET   *(g^*,(H_k,feat_model)*,
                    (parent_component_name,H_k));
    ADD_COMPONENT_ATTRIBUTES(g^*,H_k,*attr_list*)
    end for

end BUILD_FBM

6. The implementation of the user interface.

The use of the feature-based modelling system is simplified by the definition of an interface that allows the user to construct the feature by specifying the values of the explicit parameters, such as dimensions, and directly indicating connection faces on the object.

In the figure from 3 to 8 we can see the sequence for constructing a complex object; in figure 3 the initial object, a square slab is shown. Then, the type of the first feature to build is selected: a rectangular pocket. Dimensional parameters and the entry face on the slab are also assigned.

At this point it is possible to know if the assigned parameters are correct by a pre-view of the result; if not, they can be changed. In figure 4 we can see the pre-view of the addition of the pocket to the slab.

After having fixed the values for parameters and attributes, the resulting object, slab with pocket, and its FBM are constructed.

In figure 5 the object and its FBM are shown.

Then it is possible to add other features to the object just defined: in this example a set of four cylindrical through holes (figure 6) and a set of three cylindrical through holes are added, as shown in figure 7.

In figure 8 the resulting FBM is shown. In this description the final object is represented as subsequent subtractions of volumes, because all the features added belong to the class of depressions.

The pocket, which is attached to the top face of the slab, is subtracted from the root node, corresponding to the initial slab.

The four cylindrical through holes are removed from the current object; these holes have as entry faces the faces on the top and on the bottom of the slab; hence, they do not interfer with the pocket, as indicated also in figure 8.

Finally, the three cylindrical through holes, which have as entry faces the bottom faces of both pocket and slab, are subtracted from the object "pocket with slab with holes"; the faces on the bottom of the pocket and of the slab are the connection faces of all the three holes.

Concluding remarks.

The system described in this work has been implemented in Pascal as a prototype feature-based modeller on an Apollo 4000 workstation.
For the graphics interface GMR3D and Dialogue facilities have been used.

This system constitute an alternative to that based on feature automatic recognition and presented in [Fal 87].
The use of a boundary solid modeller based on Euler operators guarantees the topological validity of the resulting feature-based model.
Moreover, it is important to point out that with this method we can obtain a true feature based description of an object, that is different from a volumetric representation such as a CSG model, since, by Euler operators and extended boolean operators we can use in the description the real boundary of the feature objects in dependence on the object they are applied.

Acknowledgement : this work has been partially supported under the agreement between the I.M.A. - C.N.R. and the Italcad S.p.A.

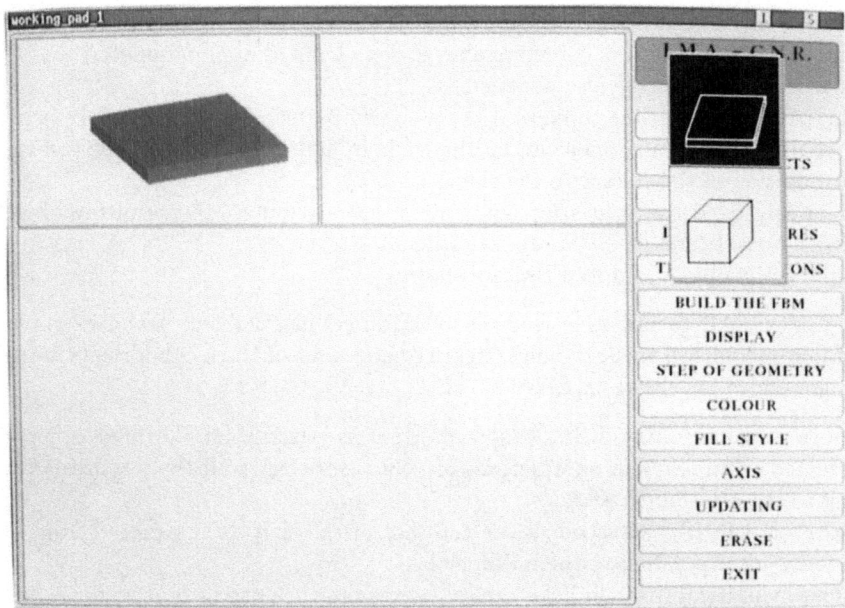

Fig. 3: the initial object, a slab.

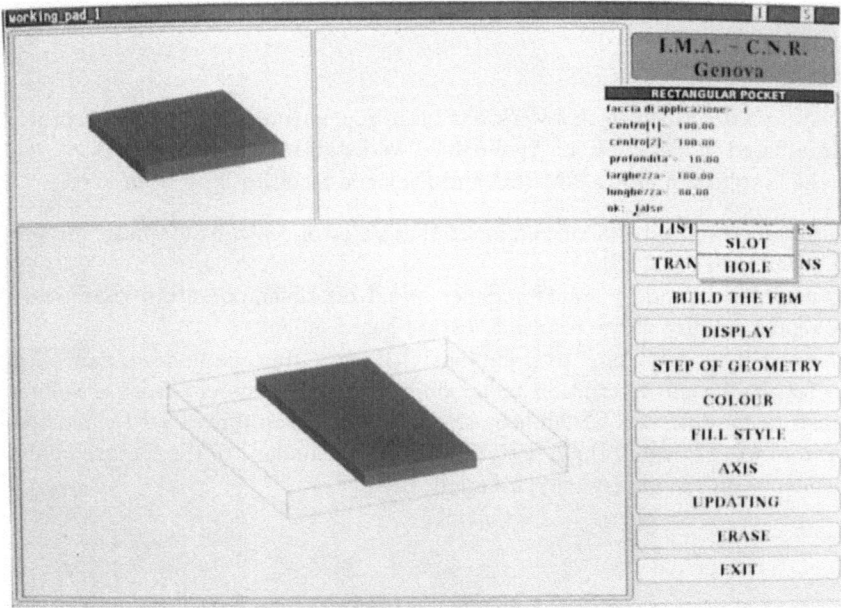

Fig. 4: pre-view of the first composition: the slab with a rectangular pocket.

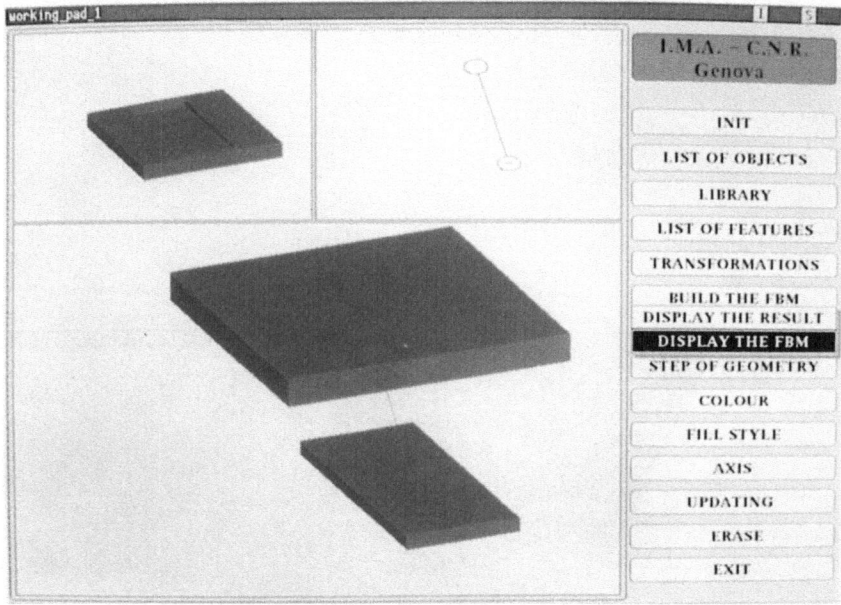

Fig. 5: the result "slab with pocket", and its FBM.

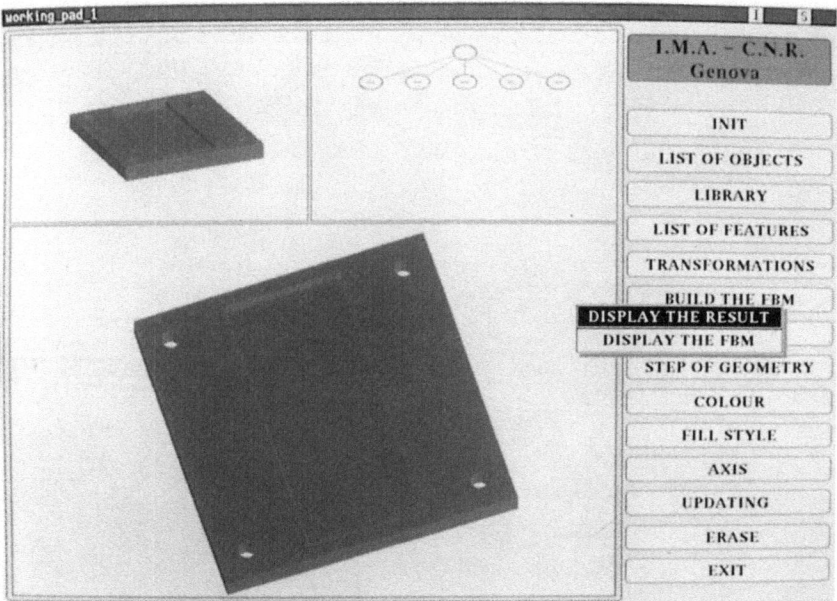

Fig. 6: the object after the addition of the four cylindrical through holes.

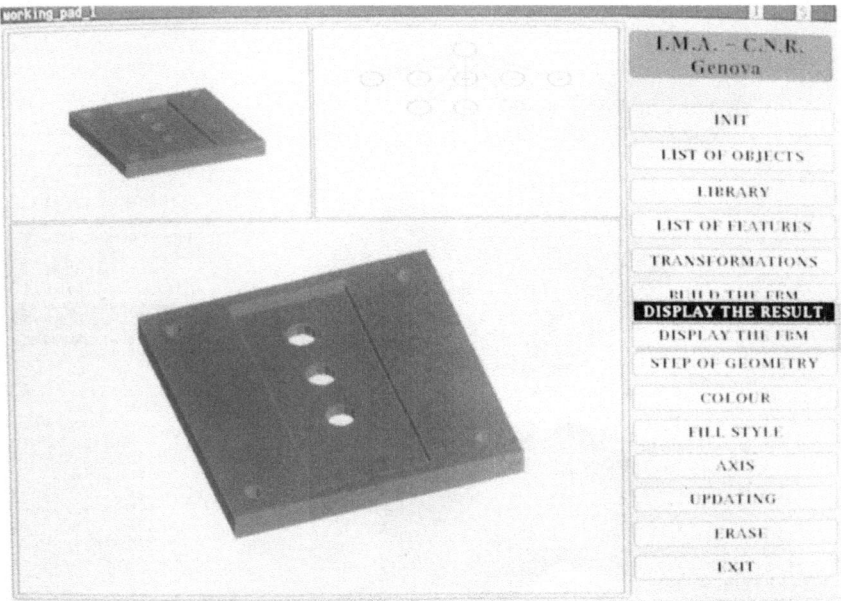

Fig. 7: the final resulting object obtained as recursive subtraction of volumes.

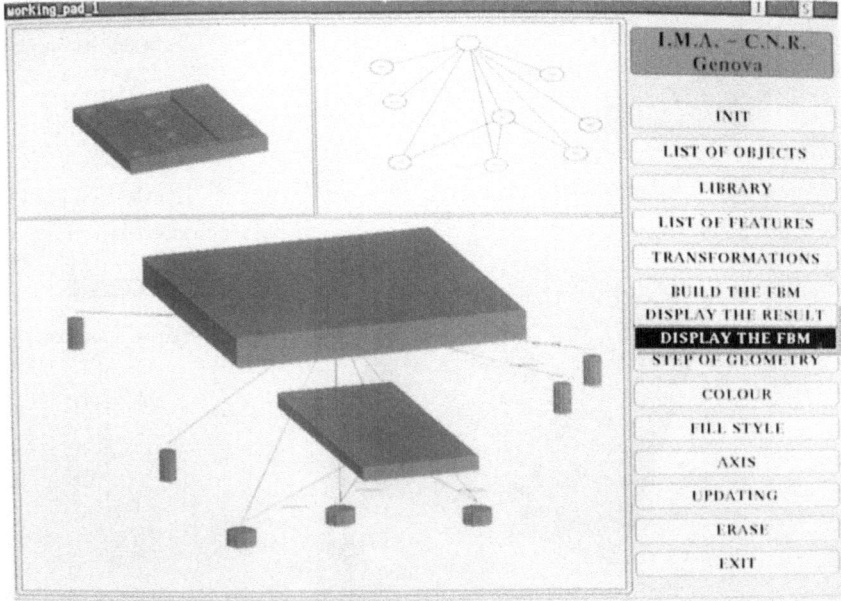

Fig. 8: the final feature-based model and its hierarchical graph representation.

REFERENCES

[Ans 85] Ansaldi, S., DeFloriani, L., Falcidieno, B. "Geometric modeling of solid objects by using a face adjacency graph representation" Computer Graphics, volume 19, n. 3, (SIGGRAPH 1985).

[Big 86] Biggs, N.L., Lloyd, E.K., Wilson, R.J. "Graph Teory" Clarendon Press - OXFORD 1986.

[Bra 88] Braid, I.C. "Improving product models and kernel modellers" Proc. Int. Toyota Conference, Tokyo, October 1988.

[Cam 82] CAM-I Geometric Modeling Project Boundary File Design (XBF-2) R-81-GM-02.1, October 1982.

[Cam 85] Wilson P. W., Pratt M. "Requirements for support form features in a solid modelling system" Tech. Report Geometric Model Project CAM-I 1985.

[Cas 88] Casu L., Falcidieno B. "Definition of a set of boolean macro-operators in a boundary solid modeller" Tech. Report n. 38/1988, IMA-CNR (in italian).

[Fal 87] Falcidieno, B., Giannini, F. " Feature Extraction and Organization into a Structured Boundary Model " Proceedings EUROGRAPHICS '87, Amsterdam, September 1987.

[Fal 88] Falcidieno, B., Fossati, B. " Representing tolerance information in feature-based solid modelling " Proceedings EUROGRAPHICS '89, Hamburg, 1989 (to appear).

[Kje 88] Kjelberg, T. "Tools for intelligent human communication and collaboration for better manufacturing" Proc. Int. Toyota Conference, Tokyo, October 1988.

[Kyp 80] Kyprianou, L.K. "Shape classification in Computer-Aided-Design" Ph. D Dissertation, Computer Laboratory, University of Cambridge, England, July 1980.

[Man 83] Mantyla, M. "Set operation algorithm on GWB" Computer Graphics Forum, vol. 2, 2/3 August 1983.

[Man 86] Mantyla, M. "Boolean operation of 2-manifolds through vertex neighborhood classification" ACM Transaction on Graphics, vol. 5, 1 January 1986.

[Req 80] Requicha, A.A.G. "Representation for rigid solid: theory, methods and systems" ACM Computing Surveys, December 1980.

[Sha 88] Shah, J.J., Roger, M.T. "Functional requirements and conceptual design of the Feature-Based Modelling System" Computer Aided Engineering Journal, February 1988.

Bianca Falcidieno is a Senior Researcher at the Istituto per la Matematica Applicata of the National Research Council in Genova.
In this Research Institute she now acts as a leader of research groups on Computer Graphics. She is the coordinator of the Computer Graphics group activity in the national Computer Science association A.I.C.A. and Italian rapporteur in the ISO SC24 WG2 (Application Programming Interfaces).

As a member of various societies and associations (ACM, IEEE, EUROGRAPH-ICS, AICA, etc.) she has partecipated and contributed to several conferences on Computer Graphics and Computer Aided Design.
Her research interests include Geometric Modelling, Computational Geometry and Graphics Standards.
She has published over 30 papers in these areas and two books on the standardization in Computer Graphics.
Currently she is heading a research team working on the problem of shape feature extraction and representation in Solid Modelling.

Lucia Casu graduated from the Department of Mathematics, University of Genova, in 1988.
She currently holds a Research Fellowship at the Istituto per la Matematica Applicata del C.N.R., Genova.
Her currently research activity concerns the use of boundary modellers for product modelling.

Authors' address: Istituto per la Matematica Applicata del C.N.R., v. L. B. Alberti 4, 16132 Genova - Italy.

Reconstruction of 3-Dimensional Solid Objects Represented by Wire-Frame Descriptions

P. Minardi

ABSTRACT

A widely established CAD technique consists in representing objects by means of wire-frames.
This paper introduces a rigorous method for the reconstruction of <u>all</u> the complex polyhedrons (plane-faced objects) represented by a generic rectilinear-segments wire-frame starting from the wire-frame itself. This method has been formulated within the conceptual framework established by Markowsky & Wesley (1980) and has been implemented into a computer program.
The exact and formally complete definition we gave of our method of solution carries out Markowsky & Wesley's approach. This original effort led us to formulate a renewed algorithm able to reconstruct <u>each</u> <u>kind</u> of pathological complex polyhedron (such as the full range of polyhedrons with vertices or edges contacting faces).
We coded both our algorithm and Markowsky & Wesley's and we compared the resulting programs. Our program performed well on any test while Markowsky & Wesley's was not able to reconstruct some complex interconnected polyhedrons. For example, starting from the wire-frame of Fig. 1(a) as input, our program correctly reconstructed the polyhedron shown in Fig. 1(b) while Markowsky & Wesley's aborted.

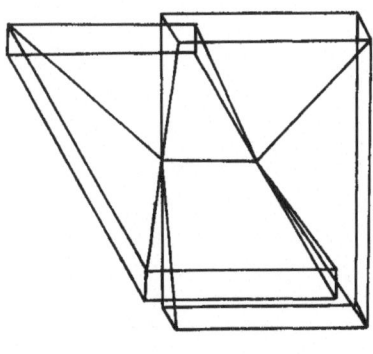

Fig. 1(a)

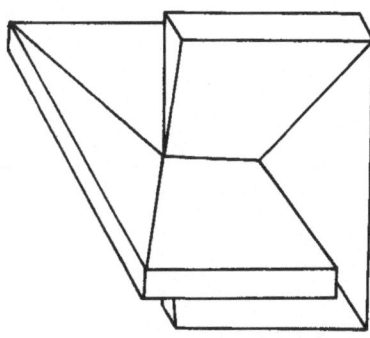

Fig. 1(b)

Keywords: wire-frame, reconstruction problem, polyhedron, triangulation, illegal intersections.

1. INTRODUCTION

The use of digital computers as an aid in designing and simulation of apparatus requires an adequate modelling and the consequent description of 3-dimensional solid objects in a numerical computer-oriented format. A widely established CAD technique for system description consists in representing an object by means of a 1-dimensional wire-like structure (wire-frame) situated on the object's surface. A wire-frame can be defined informally as a collection of segments, curved or rectilinear, which represent the 'edges' of an object (see Fig. 2).

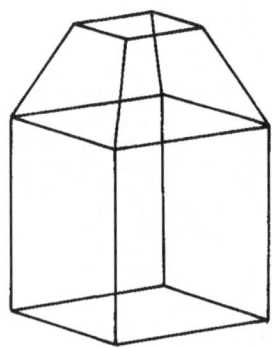

Fig. 2

A wire-frame is easy to be built up and handled but may result ambiguous, giving rise to different interpretations. For example, the wire-frame of Fig. 3(a) can represent any of the three distinct polyhedrons shown in Fig. 3(b).

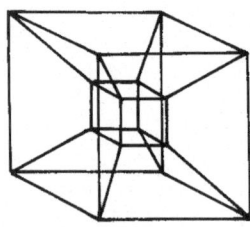

Fig. 3(a)

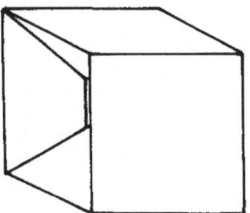 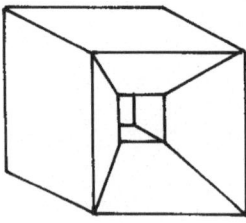 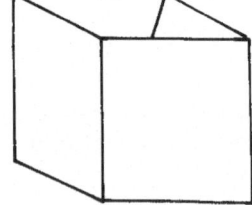

Fig. 3(b)

In this paper we face the reconstruction problem, i.e. the problem of
converting nonsolid structures to solid form, and formulate a rigorous
method for the reconstruction of complex polyhedrons starting from a
generic rectilinear-segments wire-frame. The reconstructed polyhedrons
are all and the only polyhedrons (none, one, more than one) represented
by the given wire-frame. The method has been coded into a computer
program that represents the output polyhedrons by means of sets of
oriented faces ('boundary' representation).
The algorithm has been formulated within the conceptual framework
proposed by Markowsky & Wesley, trying to come up with an exact and
formally complete definition of the method in order to guarantee the
correctness of the algorithm itself.
It is worthwhile pointing out that this is a topological method.
Therefore it can be applied to reconstruct curved polyhedrons (curved-
surface objects). Some authors (Hanrahan 1982; Courter,Brewer 1986)
faced the reconstruction problem by using graph theory. Their approach
is strictly topological and therefore, from a theoretical point of view,
curved polyhedrons can be reconstructed by their algorithms. Yet these
polyhedrons must be without holes and their surfaces must be two-
dimensional manifolds, that is every pathological case is not
considered. Moreover, while Hanrahan's algorithm does not handle
ambiguous wire-frames, Courter & Brewer state that only one object can
be reconstructed by their algorithm starting from an ambiguous wire-
frame. Both these algorithms seem not to detect invalid wire-frames.

2. MATHEMATICAL BACKGROUND AND TERMINOLOGY

In the course of this exposition, we will employ some concepts of
algebraic topology (introduced informally in the appendix A) as well as
some notions (like validity, completeness, etc.) about representations
and representation schemes. For a rigorous definition of these concepts
and for a proof of the algebraic topology theorems enunciated in the
paper, the reader is referred to Alexandrov (1947) or to Spanier (1966)
(see Requicha 1977 for a less deep insight). The definition of
representation and related notions is according to the work of Requicha
(1980, 1981).

In the sequel, homogeneously n-dimensional triangulations will be simply
called n-dimensional triangulations, for brevity. Bearing in mind this
convention and remembering that a homogeneously n-dimensional
triangulation is defined univocally by the collection of its n-
dimensional simplexes, throughout the paper with n-dimensional
triangulation we will refer to both proper triangulation and the
collection of the n-dimensional simplexes of this triangulation, the
meaning being specified by the context.

3. METHOD OF SOLUTION

In this paragraph we will deal formally with the reconstruction problem
and its solution. The definitions 3.1 and 3.2 are taken from Markowsky &
Wesley (1980).

Definition 3.1
A face f is the closure of a nonempty, bounded, connected, coplanar,
open (in the relative topology) subset of R^3 whose boundary is the union
of a finite number of line segments. ∎

Definition 3.2
An object O is the closure of a nonempty, bounded, open subset of R^3 whose boundary is the union of a finite number of faces. ∎

Remark 3.3: An object is a regular 3-dimensional polyhedron. ∎

Definition 3.4
Let O be an object. Consider the set that the bodies of the 1-skeletons of all the 2-dimensional triangulations of the boundary of O have in common. We denote with E(O) the 1-dimensional triangulation of this set such that every other 1-dimensional triangulation of the set is a sub-triangulation of E(O).
The segments of E(O) are called 'edges' of the object O (according to the common sense of the word 'edge'). ∎

Definition 3.5
A wire-frame in R^3 is a 1-dimensional triangulation. ∎

Definition 3.6
Let O be an object. We call 'wire-frame of O' and denote it by WF(O) any 1-dimensional triangulation T^1 such that:
  − $\underline{E(O)} \subseteq \underline{T^1}$ (*)
  − $\underline{T^1}$ is contained in the boundary of O. ∎

(*) Given a collection of sets A = {A_i}, $\underline{A}$ denotes the union $\bigcup_i A_i$. For example if T^n is an n-dimensional triangulation, $\underline{T^n}$ denotes the body of the triangulation.

For example, in Fig. 4 three wire-frames of a cube O are shown. The wire-frame 4(c) is E(O).

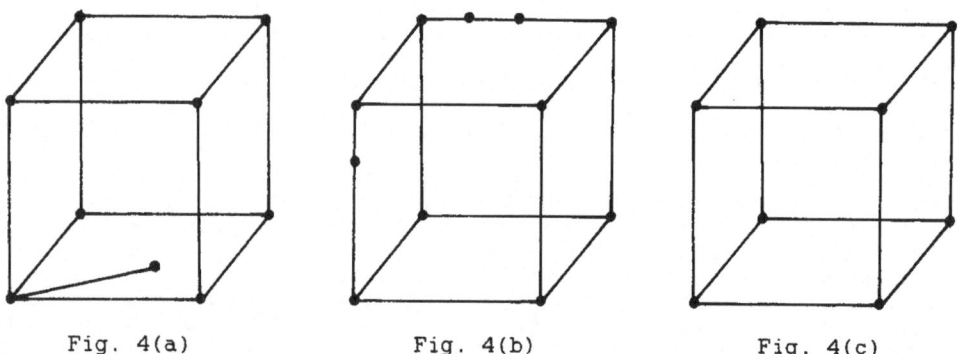

Fig. 4(a)   Fig. 4(b)   Fig. 4(c)

Remark: Given a wire-frame WF, we shall say that an object O 'has WF as a wire-frame' if WF is a wire-frame of O, that is if there exists a set WF(O) that coincides with WF. ∎

Then the reconstruction problem can be formulated in the following terms:
    Given a wire-frame WF, find the objects O_i, i=1,...,m (should they exist) having WF as a wire-frame.

Remark 3.7: Objects may be put in biunivocal correspondence with their boundaries (see remark B.2). A representation scheme that associates to an object a non-ambiguous representation of its boundary is therefore complete. ∎

Remark 3.8: The boundary of an object is the union of a finite number of faces and may be represented without ambiguity by such a collection of faces. By remark 3.7 an object may be therefore represented in a complete way by a collection of faces.   ∎

Remark 3.9: In remark 3.8 we defined, over the domain of the objects, a boundary representation scheme in which the space of representations consists of collections of faces. It is possible to restrict this space of representations by imposing, as a further condition of syntactic correctness, that the collections of faces are 2-dimensional triangulations. The advantage of employing this restricted space of representations consists in the fact that, while maintaining unaltered the descriptive capacity of the scheme – each object may be represented by a 2-dimensional triangulation of its boundary –, it is easy to verify the validity of a representation. In fact (see also appendix B) it may be proved that:

Theorem 3.10

| A 2-dimensional triangulation represents an object | <========= if and only if =========> | Each segment of the triangulation is incident with (*) an even number of triangles of that triangulation [**condition 3.11**]. ∎ |

(*) A segment is said to be incident with a face and vice-versa if the segment is a side of that face.

Remark: A 2-dimensional triangulation that satisfies condition 3.11 is called a 2-cycle.   ∎

We denote by K_{WF} the collection of all the faces whose boundary is made up of segments of the wire-frame (whose boundary is the body of a subtriangulation of the wire-frame, more precisely). The faces of K_{WF} are called 'virtual', as they are candidates for belonging to the boundary of some object having WF as a wire-frame.
For example, the set $\underline{K}_{WF}$ relative to the wire-frame WF in Fig. 5(a) is the union of the boundary of the cube represented by WF with the virtual face shown in Fig. 5(b) (the square top face and the bottom one of the cube contain each two triangular virtual faces and are virtual faces themselves).

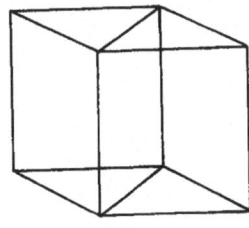   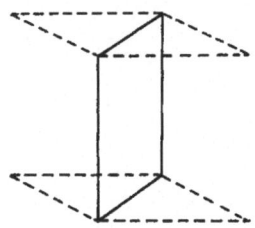

Fig. 5(a)   Fig. 5(b)

The closures of the components of $R^3 - \underline{K}_{WF}$ are referred to as the 'elementary blocks' relative to wire-frame WF and denoted by c_i , i=1,...,p, where p depends on WF (p is finite, see remark B.3) .
Furthermore, let l_{WF} denote the set of only the bounded elementary blocks relative to wire-frame WF. Since p is the number of elementary blocks, l_{WF} consists of p–1 elements.

In Fig. 6 are shown the bounded elementary blocks relative to the wire-frame depicted in Fig. 5(a).

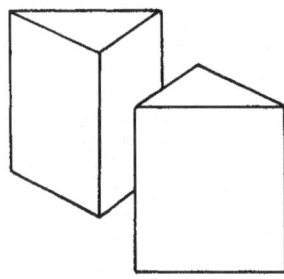

Fig. 6

Corollary 3.12 (*)
If a collection of faces $\{f_i\}$ belongs to $P(K_{WF})$, the closure of each component of $R^3 - \{f_i\}$ is the union of elementary blocks relative to WF. ∎

(*) The author proved this corollary in a fairly straightforward way by using notions of elementary and algebraic topology (see remark B.7).

Let O be an object having WF as a wire-frame. It can be proved that the boundary of O is the union of a collection of faces $\{f_i\}$ contained in K_{WF} (see definition 6 and theorem 7 in Markowsky & Wesley (1980)). O is the union of the closures of the bounded components of $R^3 - \{f_i\}$ and therefore remark 3.12 gives:

Remark 3.13
If O is an object having WF as a wire-frame, O is the union of elementary blocks relative to WF. ∎

Each object O having WF as a wire-frame is therefore in correspondence with the set $\{c_j\}$ of elementary blocks such that $O = \{c_j\}$, where each c_j, O being bounded by definition, is a bounded elementary block. This implies that, if we take the set $P(l_{WF})$ (whose elements are sets of bounded elementary blocks) as a space of representations, the representation scheme which is obtained interpreting each element $\{c_j\}$ of $P(l_{WF})$ as the representation of the object $\{c_j\}$ is sufficiently powerful, from a descriptive point of view, to represent all the objects having WF as a wire-frame.
To find such objects it is sufficient to specify the conditions that an element of $P(l_{WF})$ must satisfy in order that the object it represents have WF as a wire-frame.
Once such conditions have been determined, the elements of $P(l_{WF})$ can be examined one after the other verifying whether each of them satisfies the conditions or not. This operation is significant from a computational point of view because it terminates after a finite number of steps. In fact $P(l_{WF})$ is finite since l_{WF} is finite.

We express now the conditions that must be satisfied by a set of bounded elementary blocks to represent an object having WF as a wire-frame.

Definition 3.14
Consider the set that the bodies of the 1-skeletons of all the 2-dimensional triangulations of $\underline{K}_{WF}$ have in common. Let T^1 be the 1-dimensional triangulation of the set such that every other 1-dimensional

triangulation of the set is a sub-division of T^1. We call 'cutting segments' of WF the segments of T^1 that are not contained in $\underline{WF}$. ∎

Let $\{c_j\}$ be an element of $P(1_{wF})$. The elementary blocks belonging to $\{c_j\}$ are called full, those that do not belong to $\{c_j\}$ are called empty. The object $\underline{\{c_j\}}$ has WF as a wire-frame if:
1) Each segment of WF belongs at least to one full and to one empty elementary block.   [condition 3.15]
2) Each cutting segment of WF is not incident with two noncoplanar faces each of which belonging to one full and to one empty elementary block (Markowsky and Wesley 1980)   [condition 3.16]

4. COMPARISON WITH THE SOLUTION METHOD PROPOSED BY MARKOWSKY AND WESLEY

From a computational point of view, finding the elementary blocks implies, due to remark 3.9, the determination of 2-dimensional triangulations of their boundaries. In particular, if T^2 is a 2-dimensional triangulation of the union of the virtual faces, the boundaries of the elementary blocks may be represented by 2-cycles contained in T^2, that is by valid 2-dimensional sub-triangulations of T^2.
Therefore the computation of the elementary blocks requires the exhibition of a 2-dimensional triangulation of the union of the virtual faces. Actually, for our purposes it is not necessary that the 2-dimensional simplexes are triangles (taken as open): it is sufficient that they are faces (again taken as open). In this case we will not say any more 'triangulation' but 'decomposition'.

Remark: In particular, we shall denote by S^2 and call '2-dimensional decomposition' a finite collection of simplexes of dimension ≤ 2, where:
- the 0-dimensional simplexes are points;
- the 1-dimensional simplexes are open (in the relative topology) rectilinear segments;
- the 2-dimensional simplexes are open (in the relative topology) faces;
and such as to satisfy the following conditions:
- at least one 2-dimensional simplex belongs to the collection;
- the simplexes of the collection are disjointed;
- if a simplex belongs to the collection, also its faces belong to the collection (a point is a face of a 1-dimensional or a 2-dimensional simplex if it is an endpoint or a vertex of the simplex, respectively; a 1-dimensional simplex is a face of a 2-dimensional simplex if it is a side of the simplex; each simplex is a face of itself). ∎

Remark: In the sequel, by 'faces of a decomposition' we will refer to the faces (i.e. to closed sets – see definition 3.1 –) whose insides are the 2-dimensional simplexes of the decomposition. ∎

Once a 2-decomposition of the union of the virtual faces has been exhibited, the elementary blocks may be represented by 2-cycles contained in the decomposition. In order to compute these 2-cycles we have developed a suitable algorithm.

Remark 4.1: It is worthwhile pointing out that both this algorithm and the analogous one described in Markowsy & Wesley (1980) find the elementary blocks correctly, only starting from 2-dimensional decompositions of the union of the virtual faces. ∎

Summarizing, to compute the elementary blocks we need:
1) a program to decompose (or, in particular, to triangulate) unions of faces, that is such that:
   - its input is   n faces $\{f_1^{in}, \ldots, f_n^{in}\}$;
   - its output is   the m faces $\{f_1^{out}, \ldots, f_m^{out}\}$ of a 2-dimensional decomposition of the set $\bigcup_{i=1}^{n} f_i$.
2) a program to compute the components in which the faces of a 2-dimensional decomposition subdivide R^3, that is such that:
   - its input is   the p faces $\{f_1^{in}, \ldots, f_p^{in}\}$ of a 2-dimensional decomposition;
   - its output is   j sets of faces, that represent respectively the boundaries of the j components in which the input faces subdivide R^3 (namely the components of $R^3 - \bigcup_{i=1}^{p} f_i^{in}$). Each of the j sets is a subset of $\{f_1^{in}, \ldots, f_p^{in}\}$, that is the boundary of each component is the union of faces of the input decomposition.

In fact, if we consider the set of the virtual faces as input to the first program, we shall have a 2-dimensional decomposition of the union of the virtual faces as output. If we then consider this decomposition as input to the second program, we shall have just boundary representations of the elementary blocks. Figure 7 illustrates the sequence of these operations.

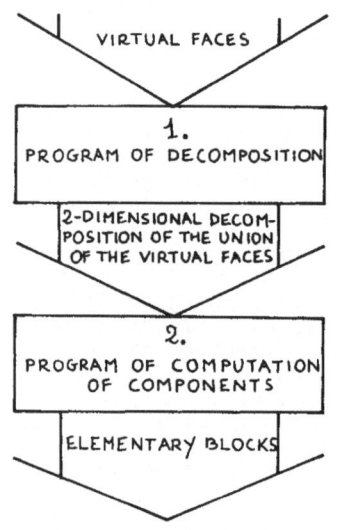

Fig. 7

Now we shall make some remarks, useful to define the decomposition algorithm outlined in the remark 4.5. We shall come to the individuation of some cases that, in our opinion, the decomposition algorithm explained in Markowsky & Wesley (1980) is not able to handle correctly.

The simplexes of a decomposition are two-by-two disjointed by definition. This implies that:

Remark 4.2: The faces of a decomposition intersect each other, if ever they do, in boundary points. ∎

Definition 4.3
We say that two faces intersect illegally if there exists one point of their intersection which is inside at least one of the two faces. ∎

Remark 4.4: By virtue of definition 4.3, remark 4.2 may be restated as follows:
- The faces of a decomposition do not intersect illegally.
Now we are going to prove the inverse proposition:
- Consider a collection $\{f_i\}$ of faces that do not intersect illegally: the faces of the collection are the faces of a decomposition

Proof:
Let T^1 be a 1-dimensional triangulation of the union of the boundaries of the faces of such a collection. Each element of T^1 has a null intersection with the inside of each face of the collection. In fact, if we assume the contrary, there would exist at least one point belonging to the boundary of some face (as belonging to some element of T^1) and inside some other face of the collection, a fact which violates the assumption that the faces of the collection do not intersect illegally. In addition, since by hypothesis the insides of the faces of the collection are two-by-two disjointed, the set consisting both of the elements of T^1 and of the insides of the faces of the collection is a 2-dimensional decomposition S^2 of $\{f_i\}$. ∎

Remark 4.5: In practice, given a collection $\{f_i\}$ of faces, a 2-dimensional decomposition of $\cup f_i$ can be found by detecting the illegal intersections between the faces of the collection and then by subdividing in subfaces the faces having the illegal intersections. This permits to find a collection $\{f_j\}$ of faces, consisting of faces of $\{f_i\}$ and subfaces of faces of $\{f_i\}$, not intersecting illegally and such that $\cup f_i = \cup f_j$. By virtue of remark 4.4, this is equivalent to exhibit a 2-dimensional decomposition of $\cup f_i$, where the faces of $\{f_j\}$ are the faces of the decomposition.
Figure 8(a) shows the set $\{f_1, f_2, f_3\}$. Now we intend to find a 2-dimensional decomposition of $\overset{3}{\underset{i=1}{\cup}} f_i$, namely of the set shown in Fig. 8(b). The two faces f_2 and f_3 intersect illegally; therefore f_2 and f_3 must be suitably subdivided in subfaces. Figure 9(a) shows one of the possible subdivisions: both f_2 and f_3 were subdivided in three subfaces denoted respectively by f_4, f_5, f_6 and by f_7, f_8, f_9. The faces $f_1, f_4, f_5, f_6, f_7, f_8, f_9$ are the faces of a 2-dimensional decomposition of $\overset{3}{\underset{i=1}{\cup}} f_i$; in fact they do not intersect illegally and their union coincides with $\overset{3}{\underset{i=1}{\cup}} f_i$. Figure 9(b) shows this decomposition. ∎

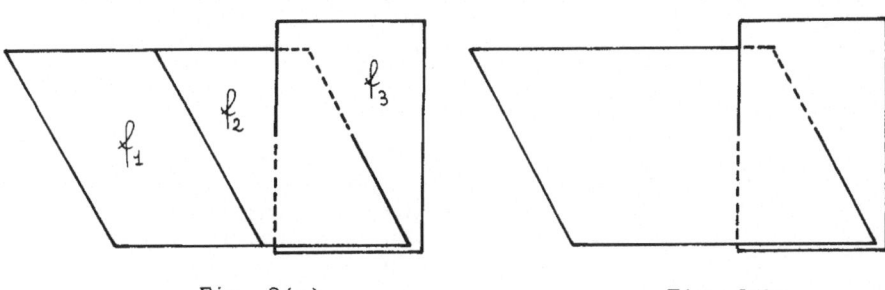

Fig. 8(a)   Fig. 8(b)

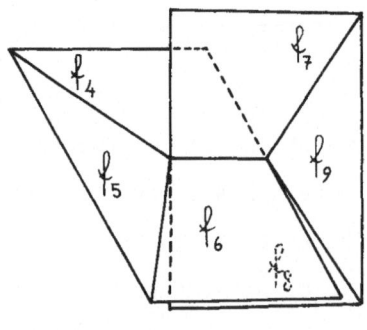

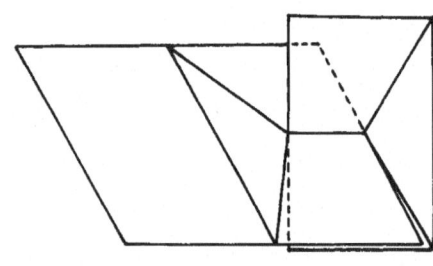

Fig. 9(a)   Fig. 9(b)

We are now going to examine the decomposition algorithm proposed in
Markowsky & Wesley (1980). Also this algorithm starts by detecting
illegal intersections between virtual faces (*). In this respect the
authors state that the illegal intersections can be classified only in
two ways:

type I :   an interior point of an edge of one contains an interior
           point of the other;
type II: the above type of intersection does not occur, yet a vertex
           of one is in the plane of the other, and there exists a point
           that is interior to both faces.

If, from a purely theoretical point of view, this classification is
exhaustive, the algorithm proposed by Markowsky & Wesley (1980) to
detect illegal intersections does not allow the detection of a whole
subclass of type II intersections. We shall call 'type III
intersections' the intersections of this subclass.
Besides, another element lead us to think that type III intersections
passed unnoticed to Markowsky & Wesley; in fact they state that (pg. 589
- stage 4):

     If two virtual faces intersect illegally, they can't be both real
     faces of the object.

On the contrary we shall show later how two virtual faces having a type
III intersection can be both real faces of the object.

(*) According to a definition of virtual face slightly different from
    the one assumed in this article, in Markowsky & Wesley (1980) the
    virtual faces never superpose one on the other, although their union
    is equal to $\underline{K}_{WF}$; in other words an illegal intersection between
    coplanar virtual faces can never occur. Only noncoplanar virtual
    faces can therefore intersect illegally.

Figure 10(a) depicts an example of a type III intersection.

Roughly speaking, one may say that two virtual faces have an illegal
intersection of type III when they intersect in an edge of the object
and there exists a point of this edge that lies inside both two faces.
In other words, a type III intersection is a type II intersection in
which the segment of intersection is an edge of the object. More
precisely:

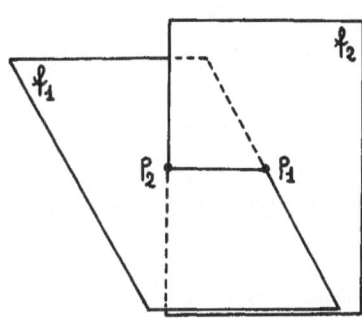

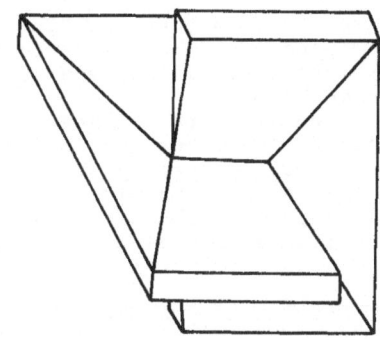

Fig. 10(a)   Fig. 10(b)

Given two virtual faces relative to a wire-frame WF and having a type II intersection, we say that the two faces have a type III intersection if $\underline{T^1 \subseteq WF}$ where T^1 is the finite set of segments in which the two faces intersect.

Two faces having a type III intersection may be both real faces of the object (which doesn't happen for type I and II intersections as they are meant by Markowsky & Wesley). For example, one sees that both virtual faces shown in Fig. 10(a) are real faces of the object in Fig. 10(b).

Let us now analyze the two methods proposed in Markowsky & Wesley (1980) (page 590) to deal practically with type II intersections. We shall see that both methods fail to detect type III intersections.
- The first method consists in picking maximal subsets of virtual faces which lack a type II intersection, to proceed then through the remaining stages of the wire-frame algorithm.
Since type III intersections are particular type II intersections, two virtual faces having a type III intersection can never belong simultaneously to one of these subsets; therefore objects like the one shown in Fig. 10(b), cannot be reconstructed.
This method is not correct since it relies on the aforementioned statement: if two virtual faces intersect illegally, they cannot be both real faces of the object.
The second method is intended to be a quick means for checking for type II intersections. It is based on an observation which is proved using the following assumption:
When two faces f_1 and f_2 have a type II illegal intersection, no boundary point of f_1 is an inside point of f_2 and vice-versa.
On the basis of this assumption, in Markowsky & Wesley (1980) it is then proved that:
When two virtual faces have a type II intersection, the endpoints of the intersection segment are vertexes of the object and boundary points of both faces.
According to this remark, the following method for checking for type II intersections is proposed: to examine sequentially the vertexes of the object and, for each vertex, verify if the faces for which the vertex is a boundary point intersect illegally.
But observing Fig. 10(a), one notices that for both points p_1 and p_2 the previous assumption is not verified. In fact p_1 (p_2) is a boundary point of f_1 (f_2) being also an inside point of f_2 (f_1). That is, both p_1 and p_2 are boundary points of only one face and therefore the

second method precludes the detection of any illegal intersection in correspondance of these vertexes.
Therefore type III illegal intersections cannot be detected by using this method.
But ignoring type III intersections may lead to find a collection of subfaces and faces (see remark 4.5) which does not represent any 2-dimensional decomposition. It may thus occur (see remark 4.1) that, for some elementary block, the 2-cycle that decomposes its boundary is not computed. Therefore the correctness of the results of the wire-frame algorithm will not be guaranteed any longer.

5. TOWARDS THE RECONSTRUCTION OF CURVED-SURFACE OBJECTS

The solution method proposed in this paper is a topological one. This implies that it can be applied to reconstruct curved polyhedrons, namely curved-surface objects homeomorphic to polyhedrons. In fact theorems B.1 and B.3 can be reformulated in terms of r-sets (see Appendix B) and in theorem B.5 no assumption is made on the nature of the two sets A and B. This means that the formal apparatus is still valid for entities homeomorphic to the ones we have dealt with so far. In particular corollary 3.12 is valid even if the virtual faces are curved faces.

CONCLUSION

In this paper we formulated a rigorous method to find all the 3-dimensional polyhedrons represented by a wire-frame. Indeed we reorganized and completed the conceptual framework developed by Markowsky & Wesley (1980). But our work is also a new elaboration aiming, we hope, at providing new contributions both from the point of view of the theory and from that of its application. In particular we provide the definition of a new kind of illegal intersection, whose detection, given a rectilinear-segments wire-frame, permits to rebuild every polyhedron represented by the wire-frame. This should not be assured by handling the only kinds of illegal intersection detected in Markowsky & Wesley.
A clear definition of the solution method in the case of rectilinear-segments wire-frames appears to us to be a necessary step towards the solution of the reconstruction problem in the more general case of curvilinear-segments wire-frames. This is the purpose of our current research.

APPENDIX A

♦ Under the name of 'n-dimensional simplex' (the interest is here limited to the case $n \leq 3$) we denote:
  - for $n = 0$, a point or 'vertex';
  - for $n = 1$, an open (in the relative topology) rectilinear segment, that is a segment without the endpoints;
  - for $n = 2$, an open (in the relative topology) triangle, that is a triangle without vertexes and sides;
  - for $n = 3$, an open (in the relative topology) tetrahedron, that is a tetrahedron without vertexes, edges and faces.　　　■

An n-dimensional simplex may also be seen as the convex hull of $n + 1$ points which are referred to as 'vertexes' of the simplex. Therefore an n-dimensional simplex may be represented by the set $\{ e_0 , \ldots , e_m \}$ of its vertexes. Given an n-dimensional simplex, the subsets of the

set of its vertexes represent as many simplexes of dimension $\leq$ n; these simplexes are said 'faces' of the given n-dimensional simplex. So, for example, a 3-dimensional simplex { e_0 ,e_1 ,e_2 ,e_3} has:
- 1 3-dimensional face : { e_0 ,e_1 ,e_2 ,e_3}, that is the 3-dimensional simplex itself;
- 4 2-dimensional faces : { e_0 ,e_1 ,e_2}, { e_0 ,e_1 ,e_3}, { e_0 ,e_2 ,e_3}, { e_1 ,e_2 ,e_3}, that is the triangles which the common sense singles out as the faces of the tetrahedron;
- 6 1-dimensional faces : { e_0 ,e_1}, { e_0 ,e_2}, { e_0 ,e_3}, { e_1 ,e_2}, { e_1 ,e_3}, { e_2 ,e_3}, that is the segments which the common sense singles out as the edges of the tetrahedron;
- 4 0-dimensional faces : { e_0}, { e_1}, { e_2}, { e_3}, the vertexes of the 3-dimensional simplex, that is the points which the common sense singles out as the vertexes of the tetrahedron.

♦ An 'n-dimensional triangulation' T^n, for $0 \leq n \leq 3$, in a given R^m is a finite collection of simplexes that satisfies the following conditions:
- n is the greatest dimension of the simplexes of the collection;
- the simplexes of the collection are disjointed;
- if a simplex belongs to the collection also its faces belong to the collection. ∎
We shall refer to the 0-dimensional simplexes of the triangulation as 'the vertexes of the triangulation'.

♦ Let T^n be an n-dimensional triangulation. A sub-triangulation is defined as any triangulation contained in T^n. ∎

♦ The r-dimensional skeleton of an n-dimensional triangulation T^n ($r \leq n$) is a sub-triangulation T^r whose simplexes are all and only those simplexes of T^n of dimension $\leq$ r. ∎

♦ The 'body' of an n-dimensional triangulation is the point set union of the elements of the triangulation. ∎

♦ A n-dimensional polyhedron is the body of an n-dimensional triangulation. ∎

♦ A triangulation T^n is said to be homogeneously n-dimensional if every simplex of T^n is a face of some n-dimensional simplex of T^n. ∎

♦ It can be proved that an n-dimensional polyhedron is regular if and only if it is the body of a homogeneously n-dimensional triangulation. ∎

♦ Let T_1^n be a triangulation. A 'subdivision' of T_1^n is any triangulation T_2^n such that:
- the body of T_1^n coincides with that of T_2^n;
- each simplex of T_2^n is contained, as set of points, in some simplex of T_1^n. ∎

APPENDIX B

Theorem 3.10 is a particular case of the following more general theorem (also valid for n > 3):

Theorem B.1 (*)
Let $\underline{T}^{n-1}$ be a (n-1)-dimensional polyhedron and T^{n-1} one of its triangulations.
1) If $\underline{T}^{n-1}$ is the boundary of a regular n-dimensional polyhedron, T^{n-1}
is a (n-1)-cycle.
2) If T^{n-1} is a (n-1)-cycle, $\underline{T}^{n-1}$ is the boundary of a unique regular
n-dimensional polyhedron. ∎

(*) For the concepts, like (n-1)-cycle, and the proof see Alexandrov
(1947).

Theorem B.1 may, in reality, be generalized to a very vast class of
sets, comprising regular n-dimensional polyhedrons: the class of r-sets,
that is semi-analitical compact and regular sets (for the definition of
a semi-analytical set see for example Requicha (1977). As the r-sets are
homeomorphic to regular polyhedrons (for the proof see Hironaka (1974)),
they may be intuitively seen as curved polyhedrons bounded by well-
behaved surfaces. ∎

Remark B.2: Theorem B.1 establishes a biunivocal correspondence betweeen
regular n-dimensional polyhedrons and their boundaries (where the
boundaries are regular (n-1)-dimensional polyhedrons bodies of (n-1)-
cycles). This consideration and remark 3.3 lead immediately to remark
3.7. ∎

Remark B.3: If P is a polyhedron of R^m according to Alexander's duality
law (*) it follows that $R^n- P$ has a number of components equal to the
(n-1)-th number of connectivity of P plus one.
It may be proved that the numbers of connectivity of a triangulation are
finite. Therefore $R^m- P$ has a finite number of components. ∎

(*) Alexander's duality law is a very general theorem valid for compact
subset of R (see p.296 of Spanier 1966).

Now we are going to deal with corollary 3.12. In order to prove it, the
two more general theorems B.5 and B.6 have been formulated and proved by
the author. To be brief we give only the proof of theorem B.6.
Let us introduce before some notations and an additional theorem of
elementary topology:
- let i(A), h(A), c(A) denote the inside, the closure and the
  complement of a set A, respectively.
- let $C_{\underline{d}}^{A}$ denote a component of c(A) and C^{A} the set of the components of
  c(A).
- **Theorem B.4**
  Given the sets A_i, i = 1,...,k:

$$h(A_1 \cup A_2 \cup \ldots \cup A_k) = h(A_1) \cup h(A_2) \cup \ldots \cup h(A_k)$$ ∎

Theorem B.5
Let A and B be two sub-sets of a locally connected space S and such
that $B \subseteq A$, $i(A-B)=0_A$ and let B be closed. Then, for each β, there
exists a sub-set $\{C_{\underline{d}}^{A}\}_{\underline{d}}$ of C^{A} such that:

$$h(C_{\beta}^{B}) = h(\underset{\underline{d}}{\cup} C_{\underline{d}}^{A}).$$ ∎

Theorem B.6
Let P be a polyhedron contained into a (n-1)-dimensional polyhedron
P^{n-1} of R^m. Then the closure of a component of $R^m - P$ is the union of
the closure of components of $R^m - P^{n-1}$.

Proof:
Since every polyhedron of R^m generates in R^m a finite number of components (see remark B.3), from B.5 (P is closed, $i(P^{m-1} - P) = 0$ and R^m locally connected) and from B.4 the thesis follows immediately. ▪

Remark B.7: Corollary 3.12 is a particular case of theorem B.6. In fact, given a collection of faces $\{f_i\}$ belonging to $P(K_{wf})$, $\{f_i\}$ is a 2-dimensional polyhedron contained in the 2-dimensional polyhedron K_{wf}. ▪

ACKNOWLEDGMENTS

Our thanks are due to Prof. A. Lanteri (Mathematical Department of 'Università degli Studi' in Milan) for his advice on some aspects of algebraic topology. Special thanks to Prof. P.L. Quartapelle (Physics Department of 'Politecnico' in Milan) for his advice and moral support in writing this paper.

REFERENCES

Alexandrov PS (1947) Topologia combinatoria. Edizioni Scientifiche Einaudi
Courter SM, Brewer JA (1986) Automated Conversion of Curvilinear Wire-Frame Models to Surface Boundary Models: A Topological Approach. ACM SIGGRAPH '86 20(4):171–178
Hanrahan PM (1982) Creating Volume Models from Edge-Vertex Graphs. ACM Computer Graphics 16(3):77–84
Hironaka H (1974) Triangulations of algebraic sets. Algebraic Geometry, Arcata, Proc. of Symposia in Pure Mathematics
Markowsky G, Wesley MA (1980) Fleshing out wire frames. IBM J. Res. Develop. 24(5):582–594
Requicha AAG (1977) Mathematical Models of Rigid Solids Objects. Production Automation Project, University of Rochester
Requicha AAG (1980) Representations for Rigid Solids: Theory, Methods and Systems. Production Automation Project, University of Rochester
Requicha AAG (1981) An Introduction to Geometric Modelling and its Applications in Mechanical Design and Production. Production Automation Project, University of Rochester
Spanier EH (1966) Algebraic topology. Mcgraw-Hill

Paolo Minardi is currently C.A.D. consultant and teacher of Computer Science at I.T.I.S. Cannizzaro in Rho (Milan). His research interests include computer graphics and artificial intelligence.
He got his degree in Physics (Cybernetic branch) at the University of Milan with a thesis concerning the reconstruction of solid objects starting from wire-frames. He started work at the Politecnico of Milan in representation methods in solid modelling and implemented a prototype of an objects-reconstruction program starting from wire-frames.
He was relator for 'Computer Graphics Course' at Politecnico in Milan (1986-1987) and for 'Course for experts in design by C.A.D networked systems' at 'C.F.P. Vigorelli' in Milan (1987).
Address: I.T.I.S. Cannizzaro, Via Raffaello 2, 20017 Rho (Milan), ITALY.

Chapter 9
Ray Tracing

Chapter 9
Jazz Training

Optimistic Multi-Processor Ray Tracing

D.A.J. Jevans

Abstract

An optimistic method for ray tracing on multi-processors which communicate by message passing is presented. This method exploits more parallelism than previously published algorithms, and makes multi-processor ray tracing of complex scenes practical. An implementation which uses the Time Warp synchronization method is discussed. A second more efficient implementation which makes use of the Virtual Time concept and the Time Warp implementation of cancellation is presented as a more practial solution to the problem of efficient multi-processor ray tracing and load balancing. The algorithm is compared to previous algorithms for message passing multi-processors and shared memory multi-computers.

Key Words: ray tracing, multi-processor, space subdivision, load balancing, optimistic.

1 Previous Work

Ray tracing [Whitted 80] is an elegant solution to realistic image synthesis which is becoming more widely used as a rendering technique as the demand for realistic images increases. Ray tracing is a computationally expensive procedure often requiring hours of rendering time to produce a single frame. Large memory requirements are typical of ray tracing programs as the entire object description of a scene must reside in memory.

1.1 Sequential Algorithms

The speeding up of ray tracing has been an important research issue since its inception. Techniques that have been investigated for speeding up the execution of ray tracing on a single processor are:

- **Bounding Volumes.** Rubin and Whitted [Rubin 80] determined that the majority of time in ray tracing was spent performing ray/object intersections. They proposed the use of bounding rectangular parallelepipeds around objects because rays can be more quickly intersected with bounding volumes than with the objects that they contain. If a ray does not intersect the bounding volume then the more expensive ray/object intersection tests need not be performed.

- **Adaptive Spatial Subdivision.** Glassner [Glassner 84] used octrees to subdivide space in order to reduce the number of ray/object intersection calculations. Rays are traced through sub-volumes of space, represented as leaf nodes of an octree, and only tested for intersection against objects which lie inside the areas through which the rays pass.

- **Object Hierarchies.** Kay and Kajia [Kay 86] developed the idea of bounding object hierarchies to include arbitrarily tight fitting bounding volumes. These volumes are constructed hierarchically around a group of objects so that a ray is not tested for intersection with objects lying inside a bounding volume with which it does not intersect.

- **Regular Spatial Subdivision.** Vatti [Vatti 84], Fujimoto [Fujimoto 86], and more recently Arnaldi et al. [Arnaldi 87], Amanatides [Amanatides 87], Scherson and Caspary [Scherson 87], and Cleary and Wyvill [Cleary 88] have proposed and analysed methods for quickly traversing a ray through a regular voxel grid. These methods provide rapid traversal of rays through empty voxels and perform very well for scenes with objects which are well distributed in 3-space.

- **Combined methods.** Snyder and Barr [Snyder 87] combined regular subdivision and hierarchical bounding volumes in order to attain the benefits of both methods. Jevans and Wyvill [Jevans 88] [Jevans 89] combined adaptive subdivision and regular subdivision to attain similar results.

- **Other Methods.** Numerous other techniques have been developed to speed up ray tracing including Arvo and Kirk's [Arvo 87] use of ray classification to speed up ray tracing, Heckbert and Hanrahan's [Heckbert 84] beam tracing, Kaplan's [Kaplan 85] constant time space tracer, Shinya et al.'s pencil tracing [Shinya 87], and Amanatides' [Amanatides 84] cone tracing.

1.2 Parallel Algorithms

As the complexity of scene description increases and the demand for ray tracing increases, the need for faster image synthesis also increases. With the introduction of large commercially available multiprocessors and vector processors, parallel ray tracing algorithms have become an important research area. Previous research includes:

- **Parallel Rendering of Multiple Frames.** The most common form of parallel ray tracing is to render a complete frame on a single machine, and to render many frames of an animation sequence at once on a network of machines [Leister 88]. This is a valid technique but provides no speedup when rendering a single frame, and in no way allows memory to be shared between processors.

- **Vectorization.** Vectorization of ray tracing provides an immediate and well understood speedup. Vectorization was until recently the domain of super-computers such as the CDC Cyber and Cray machines, although Convex, Floating Point Systems, and others are reducing the price of mini-super-computers [Plunkett 85].

- **Image Space Parallelism.** Another common method of speeding up ray tracing is to duplicate the object space on many machines and allocate pixels to be rendered among the machines. This method can provide almost linear speedup as processors are added, although sharing of object space is not possible since processors only communicate in order to output results and get new tasks [Nishimura 83]. Shared memory machines distribute object space among all processors and can process rays to completion on each processor since object space is stored in shared memory.

- **Object Space Parallelism.** This is the least widely used form of parallelisation for speeding up ray tracing. Object space is divided between processors, allowing much larger scenes to be rendered than with other algorithms. On message passing systems, rays are passed between processors as they traverse the object space [Dippé 84], [Cleary 86].

1.3   Previous Multi-Processor Implementations

Pearce [Pearce 87] and Cleary [Cleary 86] used regular 3D voxel grids to subdivide a scene and allocated cubic blocks of voxels to processors on the University of Calgary Mesh Machine [Cleary 83]. Dippé and Swensen [Dippé 84] used a similar technique with movable voxel corners to support dynamic load balancing. Nemoto [Nemoto 86] and Kobayashi et al. [Kobayashi 87] used adaptive subdivision to distribute object space among processors. Nemoto used sliding boundaries to achieve dynamic load balancing. Kobayashi used two types of processors: ray/object intersection processors and shading/pixel storage processors, in an attempt to increase the parallelism. Scherson and Caspary [Scherson 88] adapt hierarchical bounding volumes to multi-computers.

These methods send rays out into the processor grid from the processor which contains the eye. A ray makes its way through the scene by passing from processor to processor as it leaves the bounds of the sub-space contained on each processor. Load balancing is often difficult with these methods, as sub-spaces must be adjusted in size, requiring the adjustment of the size of adjacent sub-spaces residing on remote processors.

1.4   Motivation

The current trend in modeling and animation is towards complex scenes composed of many objects. Kay and Kajia [Kay 86] and Snyder and Barr [Snyder 87] have ray traced scenes composed of many hundreds of thousands of polygons. These scenes require a great amount of memory and computation. To make ray tracing of such large scenes practical, algorithms which make use of the distributed memory and parallel computation afforded by multi-processor systems must be developed.

Previous multi-processor ray tracing algorithms have relied on 2D or 3D grids of processors to render small numbers of objects, typically a few hundred or a few thousand, and have not presented effective load balancing schemes. This paper proposes an optimistic multi-processor ray tracing algorithm which is suitable for both message passing systems and shared memory machines. The algorithm subdivides space into a regular voxel grid and distributes voxels randomly among the available processors. The optimistic nature of this algorithm can provide more speedup than is possible with any other multi-processor algorithm presented to date, and the process oriented approach that is used allows for a multitude of load balancing techniques. The first implementation proposed uses the Time Warp synchronisation mechanism to obtain speedup, and the second implementation makes use of several concepts from Time Warp in order to more efficiently ray trace scenes.

2   Overview of Virtual Time and Time Warp

Virtual Time [Jefferson 85] defines a process abstraction in which processes are synchronized by a logical clock and communicate by sending and receiving timestamped messages. Processes perceive logical time as monotonically increasing, and receive messages in the order of their timestamps, regardless of the order in which they arrive at the process. *Time Warp* implements Virtual Time by means of an optimistic synchronization mechanism that relies on generalized process *lookahead* and *rollback* [Lomow 88].

Time Warp is a mechanism for synchronizing a system of loosely coupled communicating distributed processes which communicate and are synchronized on the basis of the timestamped messages that they exchange. Each process maintains a local virtual clock, the value of which is called the Local Virtual Time. Messages that are sent by one process to another are marked with a timestamp which indicates the Virtual Time at which the message is to be received. When a process goes to receive a message, only messages greater than or equal to the process's Local Virtual Time may be received. The message with the lowest timestamp that satisfies this condition is returned to the process and the process's Local Virtual Time is set to the value of the message's timestamp.

As long as messages arrive in a process's input queue with timestamps greater than or equal to the process's Local Virtual Time, execution continues normally. If a message arrives for a process with a lower Virtual Time timestamp than the Local Virtual Time of the process a *conflict* occurs. The *straggler* message indicates that the causality of the system has been violated. The conflict is resolved and the processes re-synchronized by:

1. Rolling the receiving process back to a previous non-conflicting state.

2. Cancelling the effects of any messages sent by the receiving process during its erroneous execution.

3. Continuing execution of the receiving process in the rolled back state with the newly sorted input queue.

To allow a process to be rolled back to a previous non-conflicting state, Time Warp maintains a set of timestamped *checkpoints* of old computation states and old message queues. These checkpoints are taken whenever a processes goes to receive a message. When a conflict is detected, the process is rolled back by restoring a checkpoint with a timestamp less than the timestamp of the straggler. The effects of the erroneous execution are cancelled by sending an *anti-message* for each message that was sent during the erroneous execution. Since anti-messages have timestamps, they may cause destination processes to rollback as well. Once the process has been rolled back, execution resumes with the straggler inserted into the input queue in the proper order.

Time Warp is an optimistic synchronization scheme because it allows processes to continue computation until they either complete or must be rolled back to resolve a conflict. Time Warp incurs the cost of rolling back and cancelling the effects of the optimistic execution of processes when they encounter a straggler. The time spent executing optimistically is not wasted, however, because a conservative synchronization mechanism would have had the process blocked waiting for messages. Berry [Berry 86] has shown that Time Warp with *lazy cancellation* (see Section 3.5) can perform better than the theoretical lower bound that can be achieved by any conservative synchronization mechanism [Bryant 77], [Peacock 79], [Chandy 81].

2.1   Jade TimeWarp

Processes on the Jade TimeWarp^{tm} system are rollbackable entities that execute on processors. TimeWarp allows many processes to execute on a single processor through the use of coroutines. Processes are allocated to processors in a configuration file which is read in at run time, facilitating static load balancing without recompilation. Primitives for message sending, receiving, and increasing a process's Local Virtual Time are provided by TimeWarp, which handles all synchronization.

3   Ray Tracing on Time Warp

The algorithm described in this section uses the Time Warp synchronization mechanism. It is designed to run on a multi-processor which communicates through message passing or on a shared memory multi-computer which simulates message passing. A prototype ray tracer is being developed

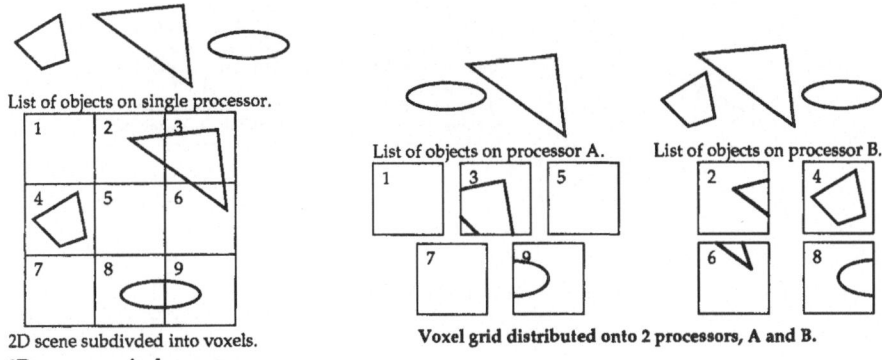

Figure 1: Distributed Voxel Grid

on the Jade Simulations International TimeWarp system which runs on networks of SUN workstations, the Meiko Transputer based Computing Surface, and the BBN Butterfly.

3.1 The Notion of Time in Ray Tracing

In order to take advantage of optimistic computation, the notion of time must be introduced. To do this we assume that a ray takes some amount of Virtual Time to traverse a scene. Object space is subdivided with a regular 3D voxel grid. Each time a ray enters a new non-empty voxel the Local Virtual Time of the process doing the traversal is incremented.

3.2 Subdividing the Scene

To subdivide space, a regular 3D grid of cubes, called voxels, is overlayed on the scene. Each voxel contains a pointer to the objects which lie inside it. Objects may reside in more than one voxel.

When the voxel grid is distributed among processors, each processor must have a copy of only the objects which lie inside the voxels that reside on it. This can allow larger scenes to be rendered on multi-processors than on single processors due to the larger amount of memory that is available on a multi-processor system. If an object resides in many voxels, it is possible that multiple processors require copies of the object (Figure 1). This does not become a problem unless the scene is composed primarily of very large objects which occupy many voxels and may require copies on a large number of the processors.

3.3 Intersection Processes

The new algorithm uses two types of processes: ray/object intersection processes and ray generation processes. Ray/object intersection processes contain a single voxel in the regular subdivision grid, and are responsible for performing the tests and shading calculations for all rays that enter the voxel with all objects inside the voxel. There may be many ray/object intersection processes residing on a processor, and they are allocated in a random fashion across the system in an attempt at static load balancing. Only non-empty voxels are associated with intersection processors, as ray generators handle skipping rays through empty voxels.

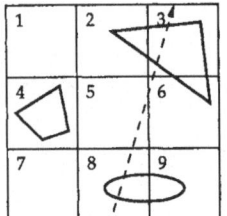

A ray generator determines which voxels the ray passes through. Intersection requests are sent for non-empty voxels to intersection processes. Intersection calculations are performed in parallel for voxels 8 (LVT = 0), 6 (LVT = 1), and 3 (LVT = 2). The intersection processes for voxels 8 and 3 return positive intersection messages to the ray generator. The intersection in voxel 8 is the correct one.

Figure 2: Ray Traversal

Rays are passed to intersection processes as messages. When a message arrives, indicating that a ray has entered the voxel, the intersection process performs the requested intersection tests and shading calculations if required. If an intersection was found, a positive intersection message is returned to the sender. These are timestamped with the same Virtual Time as the request message.

3.4 Ray Generation Processes

Ray generators start rays and traverse them through the voxel grid. They are allocated, one per processor, randomly across the system. Each generator process has a subsection of the frame buffer for the pixels that it is responsible for. Whenever a ray is started, its contribution to the color of the pixel is calculated so that it can be added into the frame buffer without maintaining a ray tree [Dippé 84].

Each generator has a copy of the entire voxel grid. The grid is stored as a 1D hashtable rather than a 3D array in order to reduce memory requirements [Pearce 87]. Each bucket in the hashtable represents a single non-empty voxel, and contains the process id of the ray/object intersection process for that voxel, instead of the objects which reside in the voxel. The Cleary voxel traversal algorithm [Cleary 88] is used to traverse rays quickly through the voxel grid. As a ray enters each voxel the hashtable is consulted. If the hashtable contains an entry for the current voxel, then the voxel is non-empty, and the the ray is sent as a message to the intersection process for that voxel (Figure 2). This intersection request message is timestamped with the Local Virtual Time of the generator process, and the Local Virtual Time of the process is incremented.

The generator does not wait for responses to these messages, but completes the traversal of the ray through the grid assuming, optimistically, that the ray did not intersect with any objects. Since traversal of a ray through a voxel grid is a fast procedure involving very few arithmetic instructions and a hashtable lookup for each voxel traversed, this usually completes before any intersection calculation can be processed and returned.

The ray generator continues firing rays and sending intersection calculation requests until a message arrives informing it that a ray has intersected an object. Since intersection requests are timestamped with the Local Virtual Time of the generator when the intersection request was made, and the messages returned by the intersection processes are similarly timestamped, the generator will be rolled back to when it made the intersection request.

The ray generator rolls back and stores the result of the intersection in the pixel framebuffer. All secondary rays that were optimistically fired by the ray generator are cancelled. All requests for intersection of this ray with voxels later in Virtual Time are cancelled. The generator resumes execution by firing any required secondary rays and advancing to the next ray to be fired.

3.5 Problems

Since rays are independent, the rollback of a ray generator should not cause the rest of the rays (other than erroneous secondary rays) to be cancelled. Unfortunately Time Warp does not handle non-causal events, such as the firing of adjacent primary rays, very well. The optimistic firing of these rays will be rolled back over, cancelled, and then re-executed. Ray/object intersection processes will also suffer from rollback, as an intersection request arriving out of order could cause a rollback and force intersections that have already been calculated to be recomputed. Fortunately, two improvements to Time Warp, *lazy cancellation* [Jefferson 85] and *lazy reevaluation* [West 88], can alleviate this problem.

Lazy cancellation means that the Time Warp system does not immediately send anti-messages to cancel erroneous execution as soon as a process is rolled back. It is possible that, even though a process has executed erroneously, some of the messages that it sent were correct. As the process resumes execution, output messages are compared to those stored in the rolled back output queues. If the messages differ, then the rolled back message is cancelled with an anti-message and the new message is sent. If, however, the messages are identical, nothing is done because the correct message has already been sent.

Lazy reevaluation examines the states that were rolled back over as execution resumes. If the current state identically matches a state that was rolled back over, then the Local Virtual Time of the process is advanced to what it was before rollback, because computation would be the same. It is this fact that allows ray tracing to benefit from Time Warp. After handling a rollback, ray generators can resume execution at the highest Virtual Time to which they have computed, and intersection processes will also advance and avoid recalculating intersections.

3.6 How More Parallelism is Achieved

Previous methods are conservative in that they process a ray sequentially as it traverses the scene. This method introduces a new level of parallelism above that of tracing each ray in parallel; tracing each voxel of each ray in parallel. Time Warp allows it to run optimistically because ray generators optimistically assume that rays do not intersect any objects on their way through the scene. If an intersection message arrives at a ray generator it is rolled back, the new value is stored in the frame buffer, and then lazy reevaluation lets it resume execution where it left off. Figure 3 shows the execution of a ray generator including a rollback.

4 Implementation Without Time Warp

The algorithm just described makes use of the optimistic computation that Time Warp provides. To take full advantage of the optimism in Time Warp, however, lazy cancellation and lazy reevaluation are required. This section describes an implementation that makes use of the Time Warp concepts of optimistic computation and cancellation, does not perform state checkpoint and restore, does not incur much of the overhead of Time Warp, and can be implemented without a Time Warp system.

4.1 Overview

The system operates much the same as does the Time Warp version. There are two types of processes in the system, ray generators and ray/object intersectors. They communicate through timestamped messages, although rays now maintain their own Virtual Time rather than processes maintaining

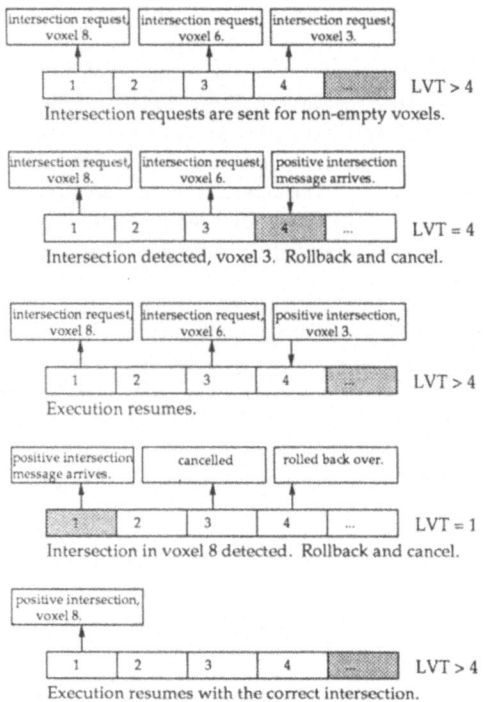

Intersection requests are sent for non-empty voxels.

Intersection detected, voxel 3. Rollback and cancel.

Execution resumes.

Intersection in voxel 8 detected. Rollback and cancel.

Execution resumes with the correct intersection.

Figure 3: Execution of the ray generator from Figure 2

a Local Virtual Time. Rollbacks are eliminated, as are lazy cancellation and lazy reevaluation. A simple coroutine package is used to allow processors to handle multiple processes.

4.2 Separating Virtual Time and Ray Identifiers

It is necessary to maintain the notion of time in ray traversal, although it is undesirable to enforce a causal relationship between adjacent rays that does not exist in the ray tracing abstraction. In order to achieve this, rays have a unique identifier and a timestamp. Timestamps are are incremented as a ray travels from voxel to voxel, as in the Time Warp version, but each ray has its own timestamp which is initialized to 0 when the ray is started.

4.3 Ray Trees

Ray generator processes must maintain a ray tree for each pixel instead of a simple frame buffer. This is necessary to simulate rollback because state checkpoints are not taken in this implementation. The ray tree entries are timestamped so that intersection messages can be checked against stored intersections. Tree nodes represent ray/object intersections. Each node contains information about the intersection, such as color and surface normal, and a branch for each secondary ray. Tree nodes also contain a unique ray identifier, the timestamp of the intersection, and an output queue of intersection request messages that were sent between the start of the ray and the timestamp of the ray, to facilitate cancellation. Figure 4 illustrates a pixel's ray tree.

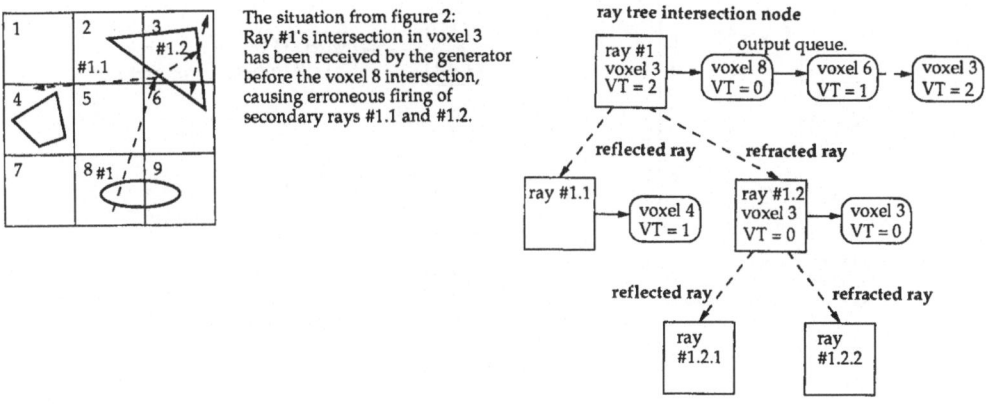

Figure 4: A Ray Tree

4.4 Ray Generators and Intersection Processes

Ray generators fire rays through their voxel grids, sending messages to intersection processes when rays pass through non-empty voxels. A copy of each message is stored in the output queue of the ray's node in the current pixel's ray tree. When a positive intersection message arrives at a ray generator, a rollback is simulated. The originating ray tree and the originating node are identified by the identifier in the message. The timestamp of the intersection message is compared to the timestamp stored in the ray tree node. If the timestamp is greater than the one stored, the message is ignored because the new intersection occurred farther along the ray than the one already stored.

If the timestamp of the intersection message is less than the timestamp stored in the ray tree node, then the new intersection is closer to the ray origin than that which is stored. The new intersection point is stored and the timestamp in the ray tree node is updated. Intersection requests for the ray between the new intersection time and the old intersection time must be cancelled to avoid wasting computation, since it is known that they are all farther from the origin than the new intersection point. To do this, anti-messages are sent for all messages stored in the ray tree's output queue that have a greater timestamp than the new intersection. Cancelled messages are then deleted from the output queue. Anti-messages must also be sent for all secondary rays that may have been fired. This process of cancellation must continue recursively until all erroneous messages have been cancelled (Figure 5). Once the intersection has been handled, the ray generator can resume execution where it left off when the message arrived.

Since the performance of the system will be adversely affected if a large number of erroneous rays are fired, secondary rays are actually fired after all primary rays have been fired. Some optimism is lost with this approach, although it deters the potential propagation of an exponential number of erroneous higher order rays.

Intersection processes do not need to rollback or maintain output queues in this implementation. They do, however, order their input queues based on the timestamps of all intersection requests. This is based on the observation that it is better to detect false intersections as early as possible to reduce the spread of erroneous rays. These techniques encourage, but do not enforce, the system to perform the ray tracing in a breadth first manner.

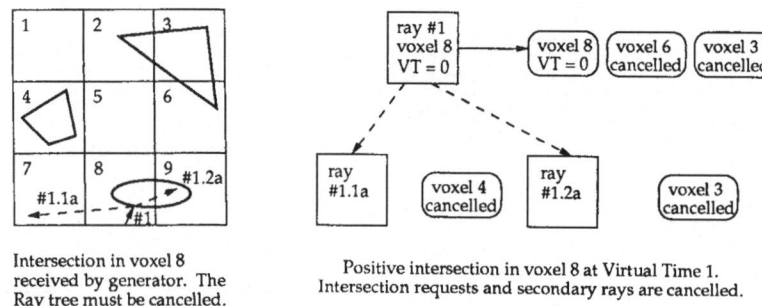

Intersection in voxel 8
received by generator. The
Ray tree must be cancelled.

Positive intersection in voxel 8 at Virtual Time 1.
Intersection requests and secondary rays are cancelled.

Figure 5: Cancellation of a ray tree

4.5 Termination and Garbage Collection

Termination of the system is determined by circulating a termination token among all processors. The token starts circulating with an initial value of 0. When the token arrives at a processor, all processes are checked to see if they are waiting for messages. If this is true then the token is passed on un-modified. If one or more processes have input or output pending then the token's value is set to 1 and the token is passed to the next processor in the system. If the value of the token is 0 when it arrives back at the originating processor then execution is complete and the system can terminate. If, however, the token's value is 1, at least one process in the system has work to perform, and the token must be circulated again at a later time.

Garbage collection, which includes collapsing ray trees and deleting ray tree output queues, is not addressed in this paper. Distributed garbage collection is a complex issue and requires further research. Mechanisms to be investigated involve circulating garbage collection messages among processors to determine the lowest timestamp of an intersection that still needs to be calculated, determining whether intersections for specific rays still need to be calculated, and whether all rays of a specific generation have been calculated.

4.6 Overhead

This new approach to parallel ray tracing incurs some overhead that is not present in conventional algorithms. The largest overhead is that of increased message traffic. Previous algorithms maintain blocks of voxels or branches of octrees on each node. Rays can travel through several voxels or leaf nodes without leaving the processor. The method proposed in this paper distributes each voxel randomly across the system, therefore it is highly possible that many messages will be required to trace a ray through a scene. This is offset somewhat by the fact that ray generators do not send messages if a ray is traversing empty voxels.

Cancellation anti-messages are required when an erroneous execution is detected. If secondary rays have been fired before a conflict is determined, a flood of anti-messages may occur. Future research of this algorithm will determine whether optimisations to reduce the number of messages in the system are required.

Ray generator processes must maintain ray trees for each pixel that they render. Ray trees cannot be reduced to find the color of the pixels until all messages have been handled and the entire image has been rendered. This can be optimised by collapsing ray trees once it is known that the ray has been tested for intersection with all of the non-empty voxels on its path through the scene. This cannot be determined unless ray/object intersection processes always return a message to the ray generators indicating whether or not the ray has intersected any objects. This will greatly increase message traffic in the system, but may be required if memory is limited on the processors.

Some optimisations of regular spatial subdivision methods are not possible with this new approach. Arnaldi's [Arnaldi 87] technique of recording the identifier of the last ray to intersect each object, in order to prevent a ray from being intersected more than once with an object that lies in more than one voxel, is not possible across processors. On a multi-processor system, a single object may reside in many voxels on many processors, requiring enormous numbers of messages to exchange the required information to implement this optimisation.

4.7 Benefits Over the Time Warp Implementation

The second implementation benefits from the fact that it does not have to be implemented on top of a Time Warp system. The many features that make Time Warp suitable for discrete event simulation require more computation and memory than the algorithm presented in this paper. Time Warp assumes a causal relationship between all communicating processes executing in the system, whereas ray tracing does not have such causality between rays. The need for state saving and restoration is eliminated because the pixel ray trees maintain all the data that is necessary for optimistic execution and cancellation. Maintaining these trees requires less computation and memory than maintaining a series of Time Warp checkpoints.

Ray/object intersection processes have no need to be rolled back or to have their states saved. They compute all intersection requests that arrive, sorting their input queues by the rays' timestamps, and return the results to the ray generators. Since ray generators ignore intersection results that are farther along a ray than ones already stored in the ray trees, intersection processes have no need to cancel messages. Time Warp also ensures determinism, the property that messages with the same timestamps always arrive in the same order, which is unnecessary for this application.

Time Warp requires a great deal of development before it can support a ray tracer. The effort that is required to implement a functioning Time Warp system far exceeds that of implementing the entire algorithm described here. The development of a Time Warp system, such as Jade TimeWarp, comprises many man years of research and development.

5 Load Balancing

A problem with all previous multi-processor ray tracing algorithms has been that of load balancing. The approach presented in this paper lends itself to several simple and very effective load balancing schemes.

- **Static Load Balancing.** Since each voxel is associated with its own intersection process, voxels can be allocated evenly among processors. Randomly allocating voxel intersection processes to processors is a simple means of helping to ensure even load balance among processors. This technique has proven effective for multi-processor simulations [Nicol 88]. A similar technique of allocating voxels to processors in a round robin fashion has been simulated and shown to be effective [Kobayashi 88].

- **Balancing Ray Generation.** As there are many ray generators in the system, a simple method of ensuring an even distribution of load on all processors is to have each generator working on a different area of the screen. Since rays fired from pixels on opposite sides of the screen rarely travel through the same voxels (the opposite side of the ray coherence coin) [Kaplan 85] this can help keep all processors busy.

- **Process Migration.** If a processor becomes too highly loaded in relation to its neighbors, determined by examining the sum of the lengths of its and its neighbor's process input queues, it can migrate intersection processes. When a voxel intersection process is migrated, its objects and input queue must be moved with it to the new processor. Messages which arrive for the migrated process are forwarded to the new processor and a message is returned to the sending processor informing it of the migration so that further messages can be sent directly.

- **Process Cloning.** If an intersection process becomes too highly loaded, determined by examining the lengths of the input queues of all processes on a processor, it can clone itself and migrate the clone to another processor. Once this is done it is necessary to inform some processors of the duplicate voxel intersection process in order to split the load. This is accomplished by the original intersection process forwarding some of the ray messages bound for it to the clone. As it does this, it sends a message to the originating processor as to the location of the clone to where its messages have been forwarded.

- **Clone Reaping** When a clone process determines that it is underloaded it can request to be killed. A message is sent to its parent requesting that the clone be allowed to die and re-route all its messages to the parent. If the parent deems this appropriate, by weighing the request against any other death requests, the process is sent a message allowing it to die. The clone sends its input queue to the parent and dies. The processor which hosted the clone must forward all messages for the clone to the parent, and inform all senders of the routing change. Underloaded parents may request that clones kill themselves and return their input queues to the parent. A process may not die if it has clones of its own which are still alive.

These methods are all much simpler and more effective than readjusting the size of a voxel and having to adjust the sizes of all adjacent voxels on other processors, as previous algorithms required. A combination of these methods could provide good load balancing, although experiments will have to be performed to determine the impact of each method.

6 Discussion

The algorithm presented in this paper utilizes optimistic computation methods to speed up ray tracing. This section details some of the problems and benefits of this method as compared to previous multi-processor algorithms.

6.1 Disadvantages

This algorithm suffers from several disadvantages that previous algorithms do not. The main disadvantage is complexity of implementation: the process oriented optimistic algorithm requires multi-process capability on each processor; two different types of processes are required: ray generators and ray/object intersectors; a timestamped ray tree must be maintained for each pixel by the ray generators; input queues must be ordered by timestamp; and message cancellation is required.

Message traffic is increased over previous algorithms when rendering complex scenes, although no messages are required to trace rays through empty voxels. In the worst case it is possible for exponential numbers of erroneous higher order rays to flood the system.

6.2 Advantages

The prime advantage of this algorithm is speedup over previous algorithms. Since the bottleneck of ray tracing is in intersection and shading calculation, this algorithm exploits parallelism in these computations and attempts to optimistically calculate pixel intensities. When traversing empty voxels this algorithm does not pass messages since ray generators only send intersection requests to non-empty voxels. Load balancing is also greatly simplified with this process oriented approach.

6.3 Analysis of the Algorithm

For the purposes of comparison, assume that a single processor implementation of regular subdivision ray tracing has an execution time of 1, and that there is no cost associated with message passing. Let n = the number of rays and m = the number of voxels.

- **Duplication of Object Space.** Methods which duplicate the object space on each processor can make use of a maximum of one processor per ray, since the tracing of a ray is a sequential process, and each processor would trace a single ray. n processors can give a speedup of n over a sequential implementation. Adding more than n processors to the system provides no additional speedup.

- **Distributing Object Space - Conservative Method.** Previous methods of sharing object space distribute voxels among the available processors and pass rays from processor to processor as they travel through the scene. If there are m processors available, the lower bound of speedup is 1 if all rays pass through the same processors. The upper bound is m if no rays pass through the same voxels. These methods can make use of n * m processors providing a lower bound of speedup of n/m * m = n, which is the same as that available when duplicating the object space on all processors, since all rays could pass through the same voxels even though there are n copies of each voxel. The upper bound for speedup with n * m processors is also only n if no rays pass through the same voxels, hence the potential speedup of n * m is not attained. This is true since rays pass from processor to processor in a sequential fashion and do not exploit the extra parallelism inherent in spatial subdivision methods, as illustrated in this paper.

- **Distributing Object Space - Optimistic Method.** The optimistic algorithm presented in this paper *can* efficiently make full use of n * m processors. Even if all rays pass through the same voxels, with n copies of each of the m voxels, the lower and upper bounds for speedup over a sequential implementation are n * m. This is possible because rays are traversed through all of the voxels in their path in parallel.

7 Conclusion

A new method for ray tracing on parallel computers has been presented. The system uses Time Warp concepts to optimistically render scenes and expose new parallelism inherent in spatial subdivision ray tracing. No special machine interconnection configuration is required to take advantage of this method. The process oriented approach allows for simple static and dynamic load balancing to ensure optimal usage of processors.

A prototype version of this algorithm is being developed on the Jade TimeWarp system. Jade TimeWarp runs on networks of SUN workstations, the BBN Butterfly, and is being ported to a Transputer system. A follow up paper will present results and timings comparing the method to uniprocessor and traditional multi-processor algorithms.

Figure 6: Image generated on a single processor.

8 Acknowledgements

I would like to thank Dr. Brian Wyvill for his insight and enthusiasm for this and other projects, Mike Chmilar for his suggestions and patience, Konrad Slind for his editorial assistance, Darrin West for his ideas and encouragement, the Graphicsland Research Group at the University of Calgary, Jade Simulations International, and the band.

References

[Amanatides 84] John Amanatides. Ray tracing with cones. In *Computer Graphics*, volume 18. ACM SIGGRAPH, 1984.

[Amanatides 87] John Amanatides and Andrew Woo. A fast voxel traversal algorithm for ray tracing. *Proc. Eurographics '87*, 1987.

[Arnaldi 87] B. Arnaldi, T. Priol, and K. Bouatouch. A new space subdivision method for ray tracing csg modelled scenes. *The Visual Computer*, 3(2):98–108, 1987.

[Arvo 87] James Arvo and David Kirk. Fast ray tracing by ray classification. In *Computer Graphics*, volume 21. ACM SIGGRAPH, 1987.

[Berry 86] O. Berry. *Performance Evaluation of the Time Warp Distributed Simulation Mechanism*. PhD thesis, University of Southern California, Los Angeles, 1986.

[Bryant 77] R. Bryant. *Simulation of Packet Communication Architecture Computer Systems*. PhD thesis, Massachusetts Institute of Technology, November 1977.

[Chandy 81] K. Chandy and J Misra. Asynchronous distributed simulation via a sequence of parallel computations. *Communications of the ACM*, 24(4), April 1981.

[Cleary 83]   John Cleary, Brian Wyvill, Graham Birtwistle, and Reddy Vatti. Multiprocessor ray tracing. Technical Report 83/128/17, University of Calgary, Dept. of Computer Science, 1983. Revised version published in *Computer Graphics Forum*, 5(1), 1986.

[Cleary 86]   J. Cleary, B. Wyvill, G. Birtwistle, and Vatti R. Multiprocessor ray tracing. *Computer Graphics Forum*, 5(1), 1986.

[Cleary 88]   John Cleary and Geoff Wyvill. Analysis of an algorithm for fast ray tracing using uniform space subdivision. *Visual Computer*, pages 65–83, July 1988.

[Dippé 84]   Mark Dippé and John Swensen. An adaptive subdivision algorithm and parallel architecture for realistic image synthesis. *Computer Graphics*, 18(3), July 1984.

[Fujimoto 86]   A. Fujimoto, T. Tanaka, and K. Iwata. ARTS: Accelerated ray-tracing system. *IEEE Computer Graphics and Applications*, 1986.

[Glassner 84]   Andrew S. Glassner. Space subdivision for fast ray tracing. *IEEE Computer Graphics and Applications*, pages 15–22, October 1984.

[Heckbert 84]   P. Heckbert and P. Hanrahan. Beam tracing polygonal objects. In *Computer Graphics*, volume 18. ACM SIGGRAPH, 1984.

[Jefferson 85]   David Jefferson. Virtual time. *ACM Transactions on Programming Languages and Systems*, 7(3), July 1985.

[Jevans 88]   David Jevans and Brian Wyvill. Ray tracing implicit surfaces. Technical Report 88/292/04, University of Calgary, 1988.

[Jevans 89]   David A. J. Jevans. Adaptive voxel subdivision for ray tracing. In *Proceedings of Graphics Interface '89*, 1989. In Press.

[Kaplan 85]   Michael R. Kaplan. The uses of spatial coherence in ray tracing. *SIGGRAPH '85 Course Notes 11*, 1985.

[Kay 86]   Timothy L. Kay and James T. Kajiya. Ray tracing complex scenes. In *Computer Graphics*, volume 20, pages 269–278. ACM SIGGRAPH, 1986.

[Kobayashi 87]   H. Kobayashi, T. Nakamura, and Y. Shigei. Parallel processing of an object space for image synthesis using ray tracing. *The Visual Computer*, 3(1):13–22, February 1987.

[Kobayashi 88]   H. Kobayashi, S. Nishimura, H. Kubota, T. Nakamura, and Y. Shigei. Load balancing strategies for a parallel ray-tracing system based on constant subdivision. *Visual Computer*, 4(4):197–209, October 1988.

[Leister 88]   W. Leister, T. Maus, H. Muller, B. Neidecker, and A. Stosser. 'occursus cum novo', computer animation by ray tracing in a network. In *New Trends in Computer Graphics*. CG International, 1988.

[Lomow 88]   G. Lomow, J. Cleary, B. Unger, and D West. A performance study of time warp. In *Distributed Simulation*. Society for Computer Simulation, 1988.

[Nemoto 86]   K. Nemoto and T. Omachi. An adaptive subdivision by sliding boundary surfaces for fast ray tracing. Graphics Interface, 1986.

[Nicol 88]   D. Nicol. Mapping a battlefield simulation onto message-passing parallel architectures. In *Distributed Simulation*. Society for Computer Simulation, 1988.

[Nishimura 83] H. Nishimura, H. Ohno, T. Kawata, I. Shirakawa, and K. Omura. Links-1: A parallel pipelined multimicrocomputer system for image creation. *IEEE 1983 Conference Proceedings of the 10th Annual International Symposium on Computer Architecture*, 1983.

[Peacock 79] J. Peacock, J. Wong, and E. Manning. Distributed simulation using a network of processors. *Computer Networks*, 3(1), February 1979.

[Pearce 87] Andrew Pearce. An implementation of ray tracing using multiprocessor and spatial subdivision. Master's thesis, University of Calgary, Dept. of Computer Science, 1987.

[Plunkett 85] D. Plunkett and M. Bailey. The vectorization of a ray-tracing algorithm for improved execution speed. *IEEE CG&A*, 5(8), August 1985.

[Rubin 80] Steve M. Rubin and Turner Whitted. A three-dimensional representation for fast rendering of complex scenes. *Computer Graphics*, 14(3):110–116, July 1980.

[Scherson 87] L. Scherson and E. Caspary. Data structures and the time complexity of ray tracing. *The Visual Computer*, 3(4):201–213, 1987.

[Scherson 88] I. D. Scherson and E. Caspary. Multiprocessing for ray-tracing: A hierarchical self-balancing approach. *Visual Computer*, 4(4):188–196, October 1988.

[Shinya 87] M. Shinya, T. Takahashi, and N. Seiichiro. Principles and applications of pencil tracing. In *Computer Graphics*, volume 21. ACM SIGGRAPH, 1987.

[Snyder 87] John M. Snyder and Alan H. Barr. Ray tracing complex models with surface tessellations. In *Computer Graphics*, volume 21. ACM SIGGRAPH, 1987.

[Vatti 84] Reddy Vatti. Multiprocessor ray tracing. Master's thesis, University of Calgary, Dept. of Computer Science, 1984.

[West 88] Darrin West. Optimising time warp. Master's thesis, University of Calgary, 1988.

[Whitted 80] Turner Whitted. An improved illumination model for shaded display. *Comm. ACM*, 23(6):343–349, June 1980.

David Jevans received his B.Sc in Computer Science from the University of Calgary in 1988. He is currently employed by Jade Simulations International to develop simulation software for parallel computers. David has had papers published in the areas of high quality rendering, ray tracing algorithms, and three dimensional graphics for simulation. His graduate research focuses on multi-processor ray tracing. In his all too scarce spare time, David performs with a local independent band.
Address: Jade Simulations International, #80 1833 Crowchild Trail N.W., Calgary, Alberta, Canada, T2M 4S7.

Rapid Ray Tracing of General Surfaces of Revolution

P. Burger and D. Gillies

ABSTRACT

Previous ray tracing of general surfaces of revolution involved the solution of sixth order algebraic equations by iteration. When the spline curve which generates the surface is expressed in the form: $r^2 = A z^3 + B z^2 + C z + D$, the resulting equations become cubic which can be solved directly. Smooth surfaces can be generated by using any of the well known cubic spline techniques. Further reduction of processing time can be achieved with a hierarchical description of the objects and easily tested bounding volumes. These techniques have been applied to scenes containing a general surface of revolution for which multiple reflections and shadows can be calculated on a personal computer.

Keywords: ray tracing, spline generated surfaces, surfaces of revolution, hierarchical object models, bounding volume tests.

1. INTRODUCTION

Ray tracing is still the generally accepted method by which objects with the most general surface shapes and characteristics can be effectively rendered. With the increasing availability of personal computers and their increasing computing power, it has now become possible to ray trace selected object types on these small processors, a task which was delegated to large and powerful machines in the past. The ray tracing of objects defined by general surfaces of revolution have been treated in the past (Roth (1982), Kajiya (1983), Wijk (1984)). So far, in all reported work, cubic splines were used to define the planar curve that generated the surface and the intersection calculations required the solution of sixth order algebraic equations. The ordinary cubic splines are expressed in the form: $r = Az^3 + Bz^2 + Cz + D$ where the z axis is chosen as the axis of rotation. In our treatment the generating curve is defined by the equation: $r^2 = Az^3 + Bz^2 + Cz + D$, which provides all the possibilities of a cubic spline but the resulting equations for intersecting the ray with the surface is only third order and can be solved directly.

Using this new spline has no disadvantage compared with the other formulation. For both functions the surface and its derivative are both continuous. There is, of course, a singular point at r=0 where the surface gradient is not defined, but this is equally the case for the conventional splines unless the derivative dr/dz is zero at r=0. A practical solution is to represent the surface as a spheroid around r=0 (set A=C=0). Since the surface is usually defined by segments of control points, this would only require placing the last control point near to r=0 beyond which a portion of a sphere can be used. In most practical cases, however, the r=0 region is excluded anyhow.

The advantage of a direct solution involving square and cube roots instead of iterative methods is two-fold. First, the solution is guaranteed and accuracy is automatically controlled by the floating point processor. For completely general surfaces it is quite possible that the iterative methods break down or that the accuracy controls for the iterative method are incorrectly set. Secondly, if the overall processing time is influenced mainly by the solution of the intersection calculations between rays and surfaces of revolution, the square root and cube root functions can be tabulated and table look up used in place of floating point calculations.

With the new formulation of the controlling spline curve, it has been possible, as the colour slides show, to ray trace highly reflective general surfaces of revolution and include shadow calculations as well. In the past most reflective surfaces were calculated only for spheres. Multiple reflections can be found in this picture where the green sphere shows the reflection of the chalice which reflects the floor.

In the remainder of the paper we describe the methods we used in detail. Since we have done all our processing on easily accessable personal computers, we thought that some of our readers would like to try to develop their own ray tracing programs on similar lines and this information would be useful to them. Those not interested in the mathematical details can skip to Section 5.

2. RAY TRACING BASICS

In ray tracing a scene containing several objects, it is convenient to define separate co-ordinate systems for the viewer and for each object.

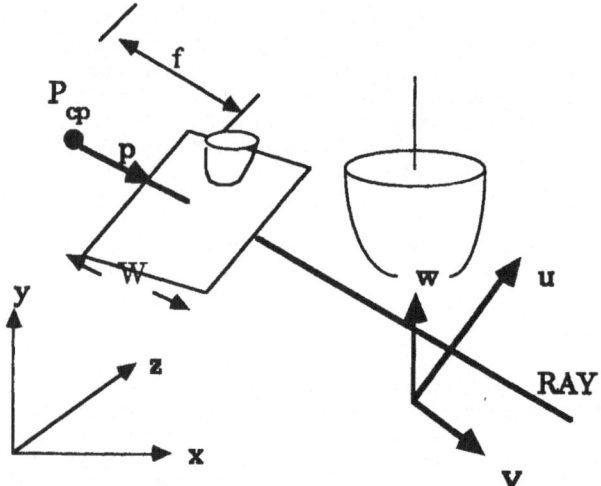

Figure 1 Object and viewer co-ordinate systems for multiple images

As shown in Figure 1, a fixed x-y-z co-ordinate system for the viewer defines the view point (or center of projection) as $P_{cp} = [x_{cp}, y_{cp}, z_{cp}]$ and a direction of view unit vector $p = [x_p, y_p, z_p]$. The projection plane is perpendicular to vector p and is f focal distance away from it. A centered square window with sides W is used to view the scene. Often one uses translation and rotation to move P_{cp} to the origin and to line up the viewing vector p along the positive z axis. This transformation is not necessary for ray tracing but makes the equations easier to handle which pays off in debugging time when the actual code is written. If this transformation is used then we can write:

$$k = [0,0,1] = V p \qquad (1)$$

where the rotation matrix V is used for one particular view point.

The viewing ray equation which passes through the i'th pixel column in the horizontal (x) and the j'th pixel row in the vertical (y) directions is given by the parametric line equation:

$$RAY_{i,j} = \mu\, P_{pixel} = \mu\, [\, W(\, -0.5 + i/(N-1)\,)\, ,\, W(\, -0.5 + j/(M-1)\,)\, ,\, f\,] \qquad (2)$$

where there are "N" columns and "M" rows of pixels numbered from 0 to N-1 and 0 to M-1 respectively. Obviously, when reflections or shadows are calculated we have to use a general ray equation which starts at an arbitrary point (S) having arbitrary direction (d). In this case the parametric equation is simply:

$$\mathbf{RAY} = \mathbf{S} + \mu\, \mathbf{d} = [\, x_s + \mu\, x_d \,,\, y_s + \mu\, y_d \,,\, z_s + \mu\, z_d \,] \tag{3}$$

The position and orientation of each object are defined by a new co-ordinate system fixed to the object. We will use separate u-v-w co-ordinates for these object co-ordinate systems, each characterised by three mutually perpendicular unit vectors $\mathbf{u}$, $\mathbf{v}$, and $\mathbf{w}$. The origin of the u-v-w co-ordinate system is given by point $\mathbf{P_0} = [x_0 \,,\, y_0 \,,\, z_0]$. Since the object co-ordinate systems must be translated in order to move the center of projection to the origin of the x-y-z co-ordinate system and then rotated, the ray parameters expressed in object co-ordinates depend on both the viewpoint and the object co-ordinate parameters. Each ray is expressed in this new co-ordinate system by components:

$$\mathbf{RAY}^* = \mathbf{S}^* + \mu\, \mathbf{d}^* = [\, u_s + \mu\, u_d \,,\, v_s + \mu\, v_d \,,\, w_s + \mu\, w_d \,] \tag{4}$$

where the * indicates that the vector components are now given in the u-v-w system. Combining both viewpoint transformation and rotation, the position vector $\mathbf{S}^*$ and direction vector $\mathbf{d}^*$ are expressed by the following vector-matrix equations:

$$\mathbf{S}^* = \mathbf{B}\,[\,\mathbf{S} - \mathbf{V}\,(\mathbf{P_0} - \mathbf{P_{cp}})\,] \qquad \text{and} \qquad \mathbf{d}^* = \mathbf{B}\,\mathbf{V}\,\mathbf{d} \tag{5}$$

where the matrix $\mathbf{B}$ relates the orientation of the u-v-w object system to the fixed x-y-z sytem and can be expressed by row vectors $\mathbf{u}$, $\mathbf{v}$, and $\mathbf{w}$ as:

$$\mathbf{B} = \begin{vmatrix} \mathbf{u} \\ \mathbf{v} \\ \mathbf{w} \end{vmatrix} = \begin{vmatrix} x_u & y_u & z_u \\ x_v & y_v & z_v \\ x_w & y_w & z_w \end{vmatrix} \tag{6}$$

Once the ray equation is expressed in the object co-ordinate system, the intersection or bounding volume test can be made. For the original viewing rays many of the transformations can be pre-calculated. The constant position vector $\mathbf{S}^*$ is the transformed center of projection, a constant for a given object. The direction vector is a linear function of the i and j indices, thus:

$$\mathbf{d}^*_{i,j} = \mathbf{d_c}^* + i\,\Delta\mathbf{d_1}^* + j\,\Delta\mathbf{d_2}^* \tag{7}$$

where following a scan line, any ray from its neighbour can be calculated by three additions. Since these calcuulations are proportional to the number of pixels times the number of objects, it is worthwhile to do the pre-multiplication of the matrices.

If reflections or refractions are calculated then the starting point and the new direction of the ray will be given in the object, or u-v-w co-ordinate system. Normally, we would have to transform back this ray equation into the x-y-z co-ordinate system using the inverse of the rotation matrix $\mathbf{B}$ or $\mathbf{B}^{-1}$. However, since we need to test this new ray with all the objects, the ray will have to be transformed again according to the origins of all the object co-ordinate systems and rotation matrices. It is again possible to pre-calculate the matrices which transform the ray equation from one object co-ordinate system to another. Hence, from the k'th object co-ordinate system to the l'th we pre-calculate a transformation matrix:

$$\mathbf{T_{k,l}} = \mathbf{B_l}\,\mathbf{B_k}^{-1} \tag{8}$$

and the transformation for a general ray is given by:

$$\mathbf{d_l}^* = \mathbf{T_{k,l}}\,\mathbf{d_k}^* \tag{9}$$

$$\mathbf{S_l}^* = \mathbf{T_{k,l}}\,(\mathbf{S_k}^* + \mathbf{P_{0,k}}) - \mathbf{B_l}\,\mathbf{P_{0,l}} \tag{10}$$

where the last term, a constant, can also be pre-calculated. The indices l and k refer to the object co-ordinate systems and the $*$ indicates, as before, that the vector components are expressed by the respective u-v-w co-ordinates.

At this time we consider only a few complex objects for which the over-all bounding volume tests require a small proportion of the total processing time, therefore, space division methods are not used. Of course, each object which is made up of a number of spline segments is equivalent to a number of sub-objects. For a large number of objects the space division method reduces the number of objects tested for each ray.

3. INTERSECTION OF RAY WITH SURFACE OF REVOLUTION

A general ray is expressed by the parametric line equation given in Equation 4.

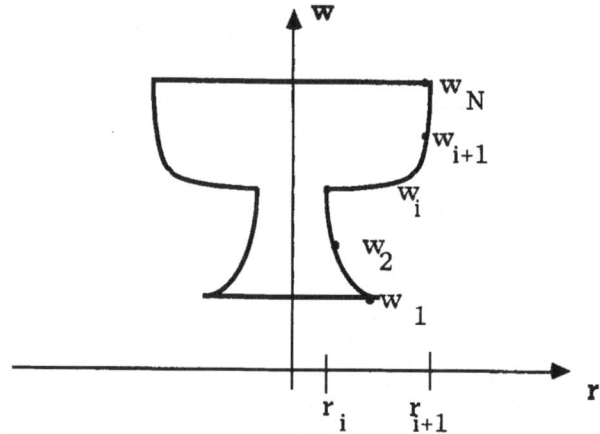

Figure 2 Controlling spline curve for the surface of revolution

The surface of revolution is defined by a curve in the r-w plane as shown in Figure 2. The curve is controlled by interpolating N knots [r_i , w_i] with i numbered from 1 to N and is given by the equations:

$$r^2 = A_i w^3 + B_i w^2 + C_i w + D_i \qquad (w_i <= w < w_{i+1}) \qquad (11)$$

This is an unusual spline in the sense that it is not in a parametric but functional form. If the knot positions w_i are equally spaced then there is a direct correspondance between any of the popular cubic splines one may use and Equation 11. In this case the parameter is simply equal to w. For not equally spaced knots the spline equations require adjustment. The fact that on the right hand side there is a third power of w which grows faster than r^2 is important as it allows the description of general surface shapes.

For a general intersection point for the surface of revolution, the left hand side of Equation 11 is replaced by the radius square or $(u^2 + v^2)$ and the u, v, and w values of the ray are substituted into the equation. We get then:

$$(u_s + \mu u_r)^2 + (v_s + \mu v_r)^2 =$$
$$A_i (w_s + \mu w_r)^3 + B_i (w_s + \mu w_r)^2 + C_i (w_s + \mu w_r) + D_i \qquad (12)$$

which is a third order equation in μ and can be solved directly. Substituting the resulting μ value into Equation 4 gives us the intersection point co-ordinates in the object co-ordinate system:

$$\mathbf{Pint}^* = [\ u_{int}\ ,\ v_{int}\ ,\ w_{int}\ ] \tag{13}$$

The calculation of the normal $\mathbf{n}^*$ is done in two steps. First, the normal is calculated in the plane containing the intersection point and the object origin, where the derivative $d(r^2)/dw$ can also be expressed as $2\ r\ dr/dw$, so we get:

$$(dr/dw)_{int}\ \ =\ \ \frac{3(A_i w_{int})^2 + 2B_i\ w_{int} +\ C_i}{2\ \ r_{int}} \tag{14}$$

where $(dr/dw)_{int}$ is the derivative at the intersection point and:

$$r_{int}\ =\ [\ (u_{int})^2 +\ (v_{int})^2\ ]^{1/2} \tag{15}$$

If the intersection point is in the $v=0$ plane then $dv/dw=0$ and du/dw becomes equal to dr/dw. If the intersection point is in the $u=0$ plane then $du/dw=0$ and $dv/dw = dr/dw$. For the general case we have to rotate the vector:

$$[\ (dr/dw)_{int}\ ,\ 0\ ,\ 1]$$

into the plane of the intersection point which gives us the unit direction vector of the normal to the surface:

$$\mathbf{n}^* = \pm\ [(u_{int}/r_{int})(dr/dw)_{int}\ ,(v_{int}/r_{int})(dr/dw)_{int}\ ,1\ ]\ /\ [1+(dr/dw)^2_{int}\ ]^{1/2} \tag{16}$$

The $\pm$ sign indicates that this vector may be either the inside or the outside normal to the surface, but since the incoming ray direction is known, the dot product between the ray and the outside normal must be negative which selects the correct sign for Equation 16. From the direction of the ray, the normal, and the intersection point, all other variables can be calculated such as diffusive or specular reflection intensities, the refracted ray direction or shadows. Many other calculations may be done in the pre-processing phase. For example, light source positions can be transformed into each object co-ordinate system in advance, since all the ray equations are given in terms of object co-ordinates.

4. HIERARCHICAL OBJECT MODELS

The processing time required for ray tracing of objects defined by surfaces of revolution is decreased by the elimination of intersections using a hierarchical list of bounding volumes. The hierarchical bounding volumes (Weghorst (1984), Scherson (1987)) consist of a small set of primitives which can be very easily tested providing a very efficient algorithm for the ray tracing process. Each sub-object may consist of a number of surface primitives, other sub-objects and one bounding volume.

The list structure is shown in Figure 3. The bounding volume is used to rapidly eliminate the chance of an intersection and it is as efficient as the ratio of sub-object volume to empty space within the bounding volume. Surfaces of revolution provide convenient cylindrical bounding volumes. The most general one is shown in Figure 4 where four constants are defined: r_{min}, r_{max}, w_{min}, and w_{max}.

The easiest way of dividing one object into sub-objects is by the knot positions. Thus, w_{min} and w_{max} become equal to w_i and w_{i+1} respectively for each spline segment. The values for r_{min} and r_{max} are pre-calculated for each segment. They can be found at the point where $dr/dw=0$, or at the boundaries, i.e., the knot positions.

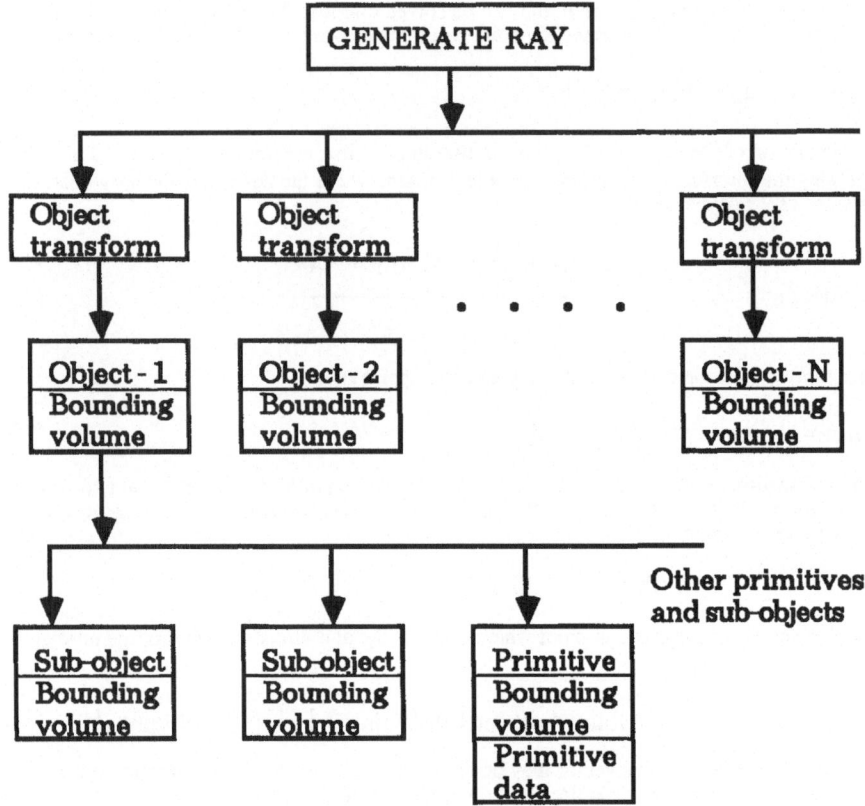

Figure 3 The hierarchical list structure of objects and sub-objects

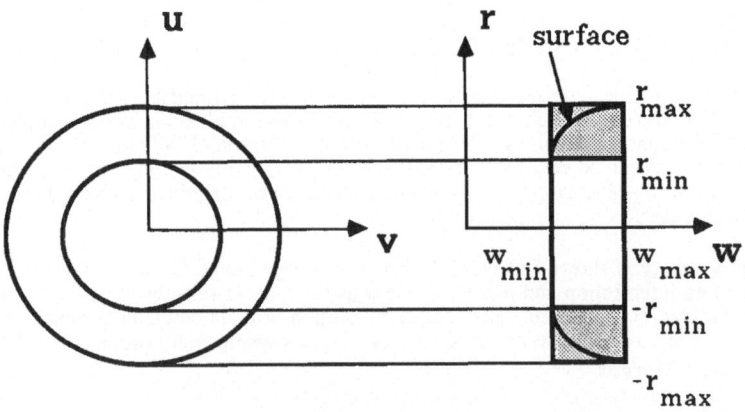

Figure 4 The general bounding volume for each spline section

The bounding volume test can be applied in two orthographic projections. As shown in Figure 5, in the w=0 plane there are two circles and the test for no intersection is:

$$\mathbf{S}^* \bullet \mathbf{q}^* > r_{max} \tag{17}$$

where $\bullet$ indicates dot product and the unit vector $\mathbf{q}^*$ is perpendicular to the direction of $\mathbf{d}^*$, the direction of the ray and is given by:

$$\mathbf{q}^* = (1/r_d)\,[\ v_d\ ,\ -u_d\ ,\ 0\,] \tag{18}$$

where the radius r_d is the magnitude of the two dimensional vector, or:

$$r_d = (\ u_d + v_d\ )^{1/2} \tag{19}$$

In the v=0 plane the bounding volume appears as two rectangles as shown in Figure 4. A modified Sutherland-Cohen test may be made according to the position of the starting point and the direction of the ray. The conditions for no intersection are:

$$(u_s > u_{max})\ \textbf{and}\ (u_d \geq 0\,)$$

$$\textbf{or} \qquad (u_s < -u_{min})\ \textbf{and}\ (u_d \leq 0\,)$$

$$\textbf{or} \qquad (w_s > w_{max})\ \textbf{and}\ (w_d \geq 0\,) \tag{20}$$

$$\textbf{or} \qquad (w_s < w_{max})\ \textbf{and}\ (w_d \leq 0\,)$$

Any one of the tests ensures that the ray does not intersect the object. The order in which these five tests (including the test for the circle) should be applied may not be known at the start because it depends on the location of the center of projection. Coherence may be used to test neighbouring rays and we test the condition first which has been satisfied for the preceeding ray. If all five tests fail then the intersection points between the ray and the bounding rectangles determine whether the spline intersects the ray or not. Only after these tests have shown that intersection is possible, the cubic equation is considered for a possible surface intersection point.

Other rotational surface elements can be described as special cases of the general bounding volume. If $w_{min}=w_{max}$ then we get a plane with a ring, a useful surface element for a thin walled glass, for example. If $r_{min}=0$ then we have a simple cylinder, while both conditions provide a circular disk. Spherical surfaces are included by setting the spline coefficients $A_i=C_i=0$.

5. EXAMPLES

The methods described above have been used to generate ray traced pictures for three scenes. The parabolic blending curve is the simplest and most convenient cubic interpolating spline (Rogers (1976)) which was adopted for our surface generating curves. The four coefficients of the spline segment between knots $[r_i,w_i]$ and $[r_{i+1},w_{i+1}]$ are calculated by four linear equations using the two neighbouring knots to the segment to fix the derivatives $d(r^2)/dw$ at the two end points of the segment. The four equations are:

$$w_i^3\,A_i + w_i^2\,B_i + w_i\,C_i + D_i \qquad = u_i^2 + v_i^2$$

$$(w_{i+1})^3 A_i + (w_{i+1})^2\,B_i + w_{i+1}\,C_i + D_i \qquad = (u_{i+1})^2 + (v_{i+1})^2$$

$$3\,w_i^2\,A_i + 2\,w_i\,B_i + C_i \qquad = (1/2)(u_{i+1} - u_{i-1}) \tag{21}$$

$$3\,(w_{i+1})^2 A_i + 2\,w_{i+1}\,B_i + C_i \qquad = (1/2)(u_{i+2} - u_i)$$

(Courtesy: Addison Wesley Publishers, UK)

The first coloured slide shows a complex scene with a highly specular and reflective general surface of revolution made up of 25 segments, a textured surface and two reflective coloured spheres. Multiple reflections and shadows are calculated. The second slide includes a solid glass shaped object made of refracting material. The third slide includes a thin walled glass made up of two surfaces of revolution. All processing has been done on an IBM AT personal computer using both 80286 and 80287 processors running at 10 MHertz. R-G-B intensities are calculated and rounded to eight bit accuracy for a 300x400 pixel array.

Our first calculations were done by brute-force ray tracing. The maximum processing time for the first slide was 9.3 hours. The second and third slides take considerably less time to calculate. When bounding volume testing was introduced, interesting statistics emerged. The ratio of the number of bounding test successes (meaning, no intersection calculations are required) vs. failures for both spheres was 10:1. The same ratio for the chalice as a whole was 2:1, but the ratio for the individual spline segments were 7:1. This shows the efficiency of the sub-object description and associated bounding volume tests. The total time of processing for the first slide decreased to 2.4 hours.

ACKNOWLEDGEMENT

We would like to acknowledge the hard work and many contributing ideas of Roger Sayle, a second year honours student at Imperial College who has done most of the actual programming and picture generation for this work.

REFERENCES

Kajiya, J. T., New techniques for ray tracing procedurally defined objects.
ACM Trans. Graphics **2** (1983), 3, 161-181.
Rogers D.F. and Adams, J.A., Mathematical Elements for Computer Graphics,
McGraw Hill, New York, 1976.
Roth, S. D., Ray casting for modelling solids. Comput. Gr. Image Process **18** (1982), 2,
109-144.
Scherson, I.D. and Caspary, E. Data structures and the complexity of ray tracing. Visual Comp.
3 (1988), 201-203
van Wijk, J.J. Ray tracing objects defined by sweeping planar cubic splines.
ACM Trans. Graphics **3** (1984), 3, 223-237.
Weghorst, H., Hooper, G. and Greenberg, D.P., Improved computational methods for
ray tracing. ACM Trans. Graphics **3** (1984) , 1, 52-69.

Peter Burger received a BEEE from Vanderbilt Universdity, Nashville, and MSc and PhD degrees from Satnford University, USA in 1966. After two years at Stanford as a Research Associate, he worked for NASA and then joined University of Lowell in Massachusetts where he became a full professor in 1975. He moved to England in 1984 and is currently a Senior Lecturer in the Department of Computing of Imperial College. His current research interests are in computer graphics and vision.

Duncan Gillies graduated from Cambridge University with a degree in Engineering Science in 1971. He subsequently obtained the MSc Degree in Computing and a PhD in the area of artificial intelligence from London University. After teaching for six years at the Polytechnic of the South Bank, he moved to his current position as Lecturer in the Department of Computing in Imperial College in 1983. His research interests are in computer graphics and vision.

Peter Burger and Duncan Gillies are currently working on the final proofs of a text book on Interactive Computer Graphics which is scheduled to be published in February, 1989 by Addison Wesley.

An Illumination Model for Atmospheric Environments

M. Inakage

ABSTRACT

Current three dimensional computer graphics assumes a vacuum space. The inclusion of atmosphere is essential for the modeling and rendering of natural phenomena. This paper presents an illumination model in the presence of atmosphere. The model is built within a framework called the atmospheric cube. The atmospheric cube, or the A-cube, is a finite volume that encloses the three dimensional scene to be modeled. The atmosphere is defined by particles of varying radii that are distributed over the cube. The distribution of particles determines the density of atmosphere. The interaction of light with the atmosphere is divided into four cases to capture the characteristics of the atmospheric illumination by particles of different radii: absorption, Rayleigh scattering, Mie scattering, and geometric optics. The atmospheric equation is a combination of modeling techniques which cover the four cases. To render the interaction of light with the atmosphere, discrete points in the A-cube are volume sampled. Examples of blue sky, sunset, hazy sky, shaft of light beam, and rainbow are given.

Keywords: A-cube, scattering, volume sampling

1. INTRODUCTION

Significant advances in the image syntheses have been made to achieve realism. Most of the techniques have been based on the visible surface algorithms which ignore the existence of invisible matter, the atmosphere. Therefore, the lighting models have only considered the interaction of light between surfaces in a vacuum environment.[10] For years, it has been known in optics, meteorology and visual arts that the presence of the atmosphere makes significant contribution to the realism in visual perception. In computer graphics, the consideration of atmosphere becomes essential to the image syntheses of natural phenomena.

Blinn first introduced the atmospheric scattering of light to computer graphics lighting model[2]. Blinn's technique assumed a thin layer of clouds and chose a relatively low albedo coefficient. These simplifications were suitable for modeling the rings of Saturn, but not suitable for a more general case. Kajiya and Von Herzen [14] modified Blinn's algorithm for thick layer of clouds with high albedo coefficient. Max[16] has presented a model to generate atmospheric haze. Rushmeier and Torrance[22] have introduced the scattering effect in the context of radiosity method. Similarly, Nishita, Miyawaki and Nakamae[18] showed a method for displaying the shaft of light beams. Recently, Klassen[15] has introduced a scattering model which accounts for different size of particles in the atmosphere. This model was adopted for rendering the color of the sky in the presence of fog. These methods are restricted to solve for specific problems of the light-atmosphere interactions.

The goal of this paper is to provide a general illumination model in the presence of atmosphere. The atmosphere can be arbitrarily defined. The addition of atmosphere to the existing illumination models introduces new problems such as:

- the atmospheric volume can become infinitely large in the open air
- the interaction of light with the atmosphere is extremely complex for an arbitrary atmosphere
- a point in space is either occupied by objects or atmosphere (never empty)

Three key ideas are presented in this paper for solutions to these problems in the context of the atmospheric illumination model. First, the atmospheric cube, or the A-cube, is used as the basic framework for the model. The A-cube acts as a bounding volume for the environment to be modeled. The A-cube limits the modeling space to a finite volume, hence excessive calculations can be eliminated. The atmospheric equation is presented as a simplified model to aacount for the interaction of light with the atmosphere. The current model cannot handle reflections by clustered large particles. To solve for the third problem, a volume sampling strategy is adopted. Since all the points in the A-cube make contributions to the final image, points are sampled inside the A-cube. The sampled points are calculated based on the atmospheric equation. In this paper, secondary reflections of diffuse particles are not considered.

The basic concepts and simplified theories are reviewed in Section 2, the atmospheric illumination model is discussed in Section 3, and the implementation results are shown in Section 4. Although the model presented in this paper is based on simplifications of the theories in meteorology and optics, the visual effect is pursued, not strictly the physical effect.

2. BASIC CONCEPTS

A complete theory of the interaction between a light ray and the atmosphere is extremely complex and yet incomplete. Several assumptions are made to make the model more comprehensible and practical. The model assumes that the atmosphere consists of various particles distributed over the volumetric space. A particle is assumed to be spherical, and it is defined by its radius. For larger particles, the reflection and refraction coefficients are also needed. The distribution of particles defines the density of the atmosphere. The model assumes that the density of a miniscule region in the atmosphere consists of particles of similar size.

2.1 The Atmospheric Energy Equilibrium

The thermal radiation theory summarizes the atmospheric energy balance. Figure 1 illustrates the energy interaction between the solar radiant energy, the atmosphere defined by particles, and the ground (Earth). An incoming radiant energy (i.e. solar radiant energy) is either absorbed, reflected, transmitted, or scattered. In Eagleman[9] and Ogura [19], approximately 17% of the solar radiant is absorbed by the atmosphere, and 20% absorbed by the ground. In addition, 12% of the radiant energy is scattered of which 6% reaches the ground. Clouds absorb 3% of the energy, reflecting 20%, and transmitting 24%. The remaining 4% is reflected by the ground.

These interactions of light with atmosphere are divided into four cases to capture the behavioral characteristics of the atmosphere caused by different scales of particles.[4,13,17,25] The first case treats the atmospheric absorption by miniscule molecules such as ozone and carbon dioxide. The radiant energy is converted to heat which raises the temperature in the atmosphere. The second case deals with the molecular scattering. Molecular scattering is caused by particles large enough but smaller than the wavelength of light such as the dust particles. This class of scattering is called Rayleigh scattering. Rayleigh scattering assumes the albedo for single scattering, and further assumes that the incoming radiant energy is simply redirected without being absorbed. For particles greater or equal to the wavelength, the particulate scattering is considered.[11] The particulate scattering is further divided into Mie scattering and geometric optics model. Mie scattering, a scattering by particles equivalent to the

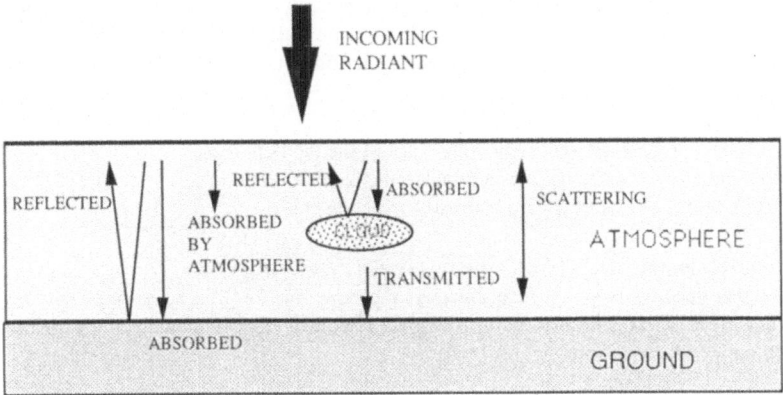

Figure 1 The atmospheric energy balance

wavelength of light, is classified as the third case. Finally, the fourth case involves geometric optics model which simulates the interaction of light and particles much larger than the wavelength. The nature of molecular and particulate scattering is examined in more detail.

2.2 Light Ray Scattering

When the light enters from one medium to another, reflection and refraction occur. However, if the medium which the light enters is composed of miniscule particles, the distinction between reflection and refraction becomes ambiguous. For such case of light and atmosphere interaction, the scattering theory is applied. The characteristics of scattering differ for different size of particles.

For the size of particles smaller than the wavelength of light ray such as smoke of a cigarette, dusts and other miniscule particles in the atmosphere, Rayleigh scattering model is used. Typical examples of Rayleigh scattering are the color of the sky (blue sky and red sky for sunrise and sunset), and the bluish color of the cigarette smoke. The characteristics of Rayleigh scattering are outlined as:

> • the intensity of scattered light ray is inversely proportional to the fourth power of the wavelength
> • the phase function of the scattering is approximated by $k (1 + cos^2\epsilon)$, where k is a constant
> • there is no absorption of light energy (albedo=1)

From these features, the equation for Rayleigh scattering can be derived:

$$I_s = I_o \frac{(n' - n)^2}{n^2} (1 + cos^2\theta) \frac{N \pi V^2}{d^2 \lambda^4}$$

where I_s is the intensity of scattered light, I_o is the intensity of initial incoming light ray, n and n' are the indices of refraction of the medium and particles respectively, N is the number of particles per cubic centimeters, V is the volume of each particle, d is the distance from the scattering region to the viewer, and λ is the wavelength. The angle ϵ is the angle between the direction of the incident ray and the scattered ray.[24] Note that the term $(1 + cos^2\epsilon)$ indicates that the scattering is directional as shown in figure 2a. Rayleigh scattering scatters light in both forward and backward directions.

The scattering of light ray becomes less wavelength dependent as the radius of particles increases. For particles of size up to the wavelength of light such as miniscule water droplets of fog, cloud particles, and particles responsible for the polluted sky, the scattering is modeled by Mie scattering. The features of Mie scattering are:

- the color of the scattered light is the color of the incident light
- the scattering is extremely directional in the forward direction
- some of the incident light is absorbed (0<albedo<1)

The directional characteristics of Mie scattering is illustrated in figure 2b. The directionality increases as the particles become larger. Unfortunately, the equation for Mie scattering involves complex mathematics.[3] Nishita, Miyawaki and Nakamae [18] provide satisfactory approximations for the phase function of Mie scattering:

$k(1+9\cos^{16}\theta/2)$ --- Mie scattering by the haze atmosphere
$k(1+50\cos^{64}\theta/2)$ --- Mie scattering by murky atmosphere

In this paper, these approximations are used to simulate the directional characteristics of Mie scattering, and the scattering function is modified for wavelength independent scattering. For particles much larger than the wavelength, the distinction between reflection and refraction becomes clear. At this point, the geometric optics model can be adopted to the interaction of light and atmosphere.

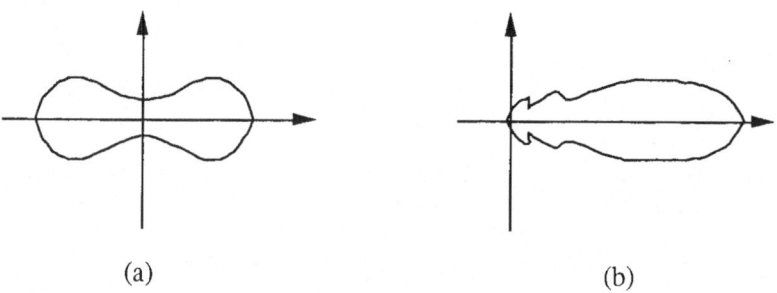

(a)   (b)

Figure 2 The directionality of scattering, (a) Rayleigh scattering (b) Mie scattering

2.3 Geometric Optics

For large particles suspended in the atmosphere, the principle of geometric optics becomes effective. A typical example is a rainbow. The raindrops and small refractive particles in the atmosphere act as refractive prisms. The index of refraction is dependent of the wavelength, creating the dispersive refraction. The dispersive refraction is responsible for the separation of color spectrum. Thomas [23] has modeled the dispersive refraction for ray tracing, but the rainbow effect was not treated. In Cook [6], the rainbow effect was mentioned as part of the atmospheric tree, but the implementation details were not given. In this paper, the formation of a rainbow is examined as a case of geometric optics applied to the atmospheric effect.

The rainbow model assumes that the raindrops are spherical. This leads to a simple optics problem of spherical lenses for a given raindrop. Refraction of light ray by a spherical lens can be treated as an extension of trigonometric ray tracing geometry in optics.[24] Figure 3 shows a ray of light entering a spherical lens at point A. The ray is partially reflected and the rest refracted. To find the angle of refraction at point A, Snell's law is used:

$$sin\ \theta = \frac{n}{n'}\ sin\ \varphi$$

where n and n' are refraction of indices of the medium and the particle respectively. This equation can be rewritten as

$$\theta = sin^{-1}\ (\frac{n}{n'}\ sin\ \varphi)$$

The refracted ray travels inside the lens until it encounters the surface at point B. Here again, the ray is partially reflected and the rest refracted. The refracted ray exits the lens while the reflected ray bounces inside the lens. The ray further travels and hits point C. The ray is once again divided into reflected and refracted rays. The refracted ray exits the lens. The internally reflected ray continues the reflection and refraction process. The energy of the entering light is diminished as it is reflected and refracted. To complete the geometric optics of a raindrop, the dispersive refraction is added. Since the dispersive refraction is a wavelength dependent refraction process, the index of refraction n' is replaced by n'_λ. Snell's Law can be modified as

$$\theta_\lambda = sin^{-1}\ (\frac{n}{n'_\lambda}\ sin\ \varphi)$$

Although the optics of a raindrop can be solved by this process, clusters of raindrops must be considered to generate the rainbow effect. The refraction problem for clustered particles is a complex problem which is still left open to be solved. Similarly, the reflection model for clustered particles is also an unsolved problem, although in many cases Mie scattering may be substituted for approximations.

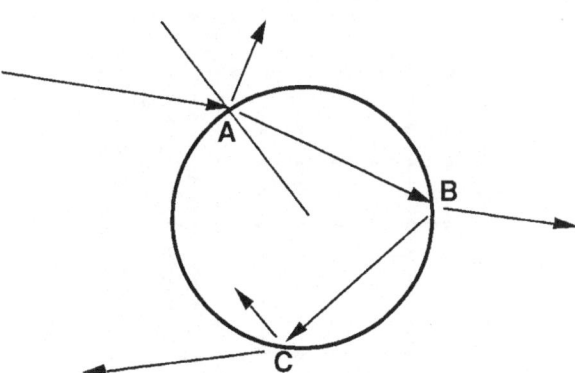

Figure 3 The rainbow optics

3. THE ATMOSPHERIC ILLUMINATION MODEL

3.1 The A-Cube

In this section, a simple model of atmospheric illumination model is presented. The model is built within a framework called the atmospheric cube, or the A-cube. The framework is provided to

- eliminate excessive calculations by limiting the space into a finite volume
- be able to handle pre-computed data of the atmospheric conditions

The A-cube is a finite volume which encloses the three dimensional scene that is to be modeled and rendered. The space where objects do not exist is filled with the atmosphere. The atmosphere is composed of miniscule particles scattered by some distribution function. The distribution of particles defines the density of atmosphere. A point in the A-cube is considered to be a minute fragment of the atmosphere. The basic attributes for this infinitesimal volume are:

- radius of particles
- density of atmosphere
- albedo coefficient
- index of refraction

It is assumed that these attributes are uniform over the fragmented volume. The basic model of the A-cube further assumes that the attributes are defined by functions such as the particle systems [21], the frequency modeluation sysnthesis [12], and stochastic synthesis [26].

For a complex atmospheric description, atmospheric simulation by complex formulae or sources from actual meteorological data may be needed. The A-cube is modified to be able to handle pre-defined atmospheric data. The A-cube is subdivided into sub-cubes (figure 4). Each sub-cube is bounded by vertices which act as a three dimensional array. The pre-defined data are stored at the vertices. During the rendering process, these tabulated values are interpolated to obtain attribute values for an arbitrary point inside the sub-cube. The voxel cube defined by the sub-cubes can be combined with other functionally-defined atmospheric models. Thus, the A-cube is not limited to funtional nor voxel data, but both approached are integrated in the rendering.

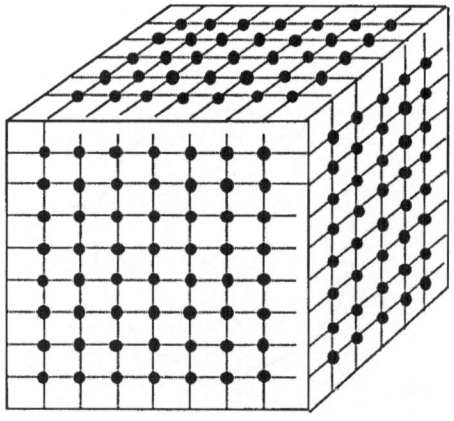

Figure 4 The A-cube with sub-cube subdivision

3.2 The Atmospheric Equation

A method is described for calculating the contributed intensity of light for a given point in the A-cube. The contributed intensity of light is defined as the intensity of light in the direction toward the eye point. Figure 5 shows the geometric terms for the atmospheric equation. The incident light is entering an infinitesimal atmospheric volume, denoted by point P. The atmospheric volume is isotropic, since all particles are assumed to be spherical. The problem is to obtain the contributed light intensity leaving the volume at point P. To simplify the interaction model of light and the atmospheric volume, the atmospheric effects for an incident light are divided into four cases by the size of particles:

- radius much smaller than the wavelength: atmospheric absorption
- radius smaller than the wavelength: Rayleigh scattering
- radius similar to the wavelength: approximated Mie scattering
- radius much larger than the wavelength: geometric optics

The geometric optics is only considered for a special case of dispersive refraction at the current stage of research. Therefore, the equation assumes that the radius of particles are only up to the size of the wavelength of light, with an exception for large refractive particles. Furthermore, secondary scattering which introduces interreflections between particles is not considered.

The problem solving is performed in two steps, the calculation of incident light intensity Ii and the calculation of contributed light intensity Ic. The total atmospheric effects for the path $L1$ must be considered to calculate the incident light intensity arriving at point P. The particles along the path $L1$ may be arbitrarily defined by any of the four cases. The light intensity leaving an atmospheric volume in the direction of the incident angle, denoted as Ii'_λ, can be simplified as:

$$Ii'_\lambda = (ka + krs_\lambda + kms)Ii_\lambda$$

where ka, krs_λ, kms are the coefficients for absorption, Rayleigh scattering, and Mie scattering. In order to calculate the total atmospheric effects for the span of $L1$, Ii'_λ is integrated over the path $L1$. Similarly,

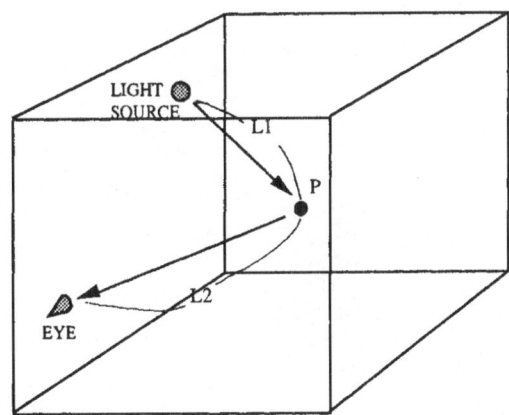

Figure 5 Illustration for the atmospheric equation

the contributing light intensity Ic_λ at point P can be expressed as

$$Ic_\lambda = (ka + krs_\lambda + kms\ )\ TIi'_\lambda$$

where TIi'_λ is the total incident light intensity along the path $L1$. The contributing light intensity which reaches the eye point is the integration of contributing light intensity along the path $L2$.

It is generally difficult to calculate the integration of light intensities because we allow arbitrary distibution of particles of the four cases. The integration calculation is approximated by volume sampling method.

3.3 Volume Sampling

The inclusion of the atmosphere in the modeling environment invalidates the basic assumption made to the existing visible surface algorithms, a vacuum space. All the paths between the surfaces, the light source and the eye point are occupied by atmospheric particles. To be more precise, the entire space is filled with atmospheric particles or objects. All the points in space are contributing to the illumination model regardless of their visibility. The problem is to calculate the total contributed light intensity along the line of sight, the eye vector. The problem can be much simplified if the atmosphere is defined constant or by a linear function. Then, the total intensity can be calculated by simply integrating the intensity over the distance that the eye vector travels. To calculate the total intensity for the atmosphere with arbitarily defined densities and size of particles, a different method is required. The proposed technique is called the volume sampling.

The volume sampling process is a sampling process performed in three dimensions. In addition to the regular spatial sampling based on the viewing screen, the depth direction sampling is performed along the path of each extended eye vector. To calculate the total contributed light intensity arriving the eye point, consider an eye vector $\vec{E}$ with N sample points and an incident light vector $\vec{L}$ with M sample points reaching point P, as shown in figure 6. Point P is both a sample point for the eye vector and the light vector. The calculation process by volume ray tracing is summarized as follows:

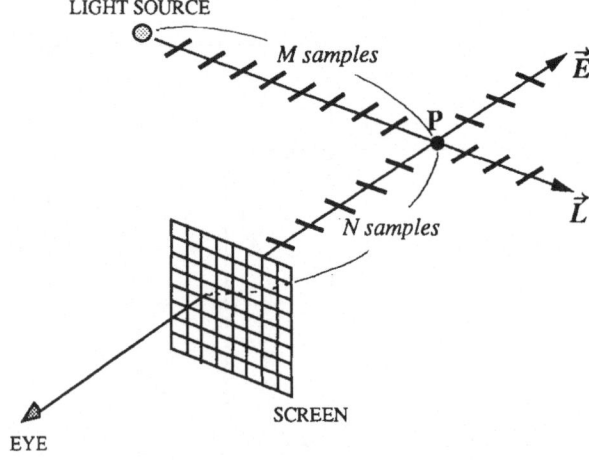

Figure 6 Ray tracing by volume sampling

First Step: Compute the incident light intensity arriving at point P.
This can be obtained by calculating the contributed attenuation effect of the sample points between the light source and point P, sequentially starting from the light source.

Second Step: Calculate the contributed light intensity at point P.

Third Step: Calculate the contributed light intensity reaching the eye point. This can be obtained by computing the attenuation effect for all the sample points in between point P and the eye point, starting from point P.

Fourth Step: Repeat the first three steps N times for all the sample points along the path $\vec{E}$, starting from the eye point. Stop the process if the ray intersects with an object or hits the A-cube surface.

Fifth Step: Sum all the contributed intensities reaching the eye point to obtain the total contributed intensity for an eye vector $\vec{E}$.

Note that shadow testing, shading algorithms for primitive surfaces, and other built-in features of ray tracing can be used.

The advantage of volume sampling is that the atmospheric equation can be used for any point inside the A-cube, which allows incoherent atmosphere. One of the disadvantages is the highly expensive computation cost, which is inherent to the volume sampling method. The computational cost is traded with the quality of the rendered image. The aliasing effect appears as bands of discontinuous intensities, similar to the Mach band effect. The other problem is the approximation error of intersections between the eye vector and the primitives. Because the eye vector is extended incrementally, there is no guarantee that the sampled point hits the surface exactly. These problems may be alleviated by adopting the well accepted anti-aliasing techniques such as the adaptive sampling[27] and stochastic sampling.[7,8] To further improve the algorithm, 2 pass solution to volume ray tracing is used. For each eye ray, first we analytically solve for surface intersections with the standard ray tracing. The second pass is dedicated to calculate the atmospheric effects.

4. IMPLEMENTATION DETAILS

The A-cube model is implemented on a 16-bit CPU, NEC PC-9801 VM2 machine (PC-APC4 in U.S.) with a floating point co-processor. A YDK,Inc. 36-bit frame buffer with 1024x512 resolutions is used for the frame buffer. Each pixel is calculated with 24 bits of colors.

Three color primaries (red, green and blue) are used to approximate the characteristics of the visible color spectrum. The use of three color primaries not only reduces the number of samples to cover the wavelength of light, but it also eliminates the transformation process of wavelength to the CIE trilinear color space.

Figures 7a, 7b and 7c show the blue sky with varying density of atmosphere. The atmosphere is filled with Rayleigh scattering particles, and the sun is assumed to emit white light. Note that the lightness of the sky increases as the density is increased. Figures 7d, 7e and 7f show the same sky with Mie scattering added (i.e. hazy sky). The sky becomes desaturated and the lightness is increased as the haze factor is added.

Figures 8a and 8b demonstrate the sunset (or sunrise) effect with different sun position. As the sun approaches the horizon, the redness is emphasized because the sunlight travels longer distance to reach the eye point.

Figure 9 show an example of the atmospheric effects characterized by Mie scattering. The hazy sky at night scatters the city lights. Stars and the mountain range are painted for visual effect.

Figure 10 is an example of dispersive refraction by water droplets in the atmosphere. Instead of calculating multiples of refraction and reflection process for a sampled point, the angle of eye vector and the incident light vector is compared with the pre-calculated refraction angle. 42 degrees, 41 degrees and 40 degrees of refraction angles are used for red, green and blue components respectively. Only the first bow effect is considered. Other bows may be generated by the same method, simply changing the comparison angles. Detailed informations on refraction angles for rainbows may be found in [4].

Figures 11 and 12 illustrate the shaft of light beam pouring over a suspended sphere. Note that the sphere is casting a shadow onto the atmospheric particles. Figure 11 shows the aliasing artifact of the volume sampling. Figure 12 appears smoother because a higher sampling rate is used. The calculation time for figures 11 and 12 are:

Figure 11: 150x130x16 samples   32min.
Figure 12: 640x480x128 samples   approx. 48hours

Figures 13 and 14 show 2 pass solution to the volume ray tracing. The surface of a sphere is analytically solved while the atmospheric scattering is calculated by volume sampling. Note that the shaft of light and shadow of the sphere are pouring onto the textured plane. Figure 14 uses particals sphere for the primitive.

5. CONCLUSIONS

An illumination model accounting for the atmospheric environment is presented. The model includes three key concepts: the atmospheric cube, the atmospheric equation, and the volume sampling. The atmospheric cube is used to limit the volume of the atmsophere to be considered. The A-cube is subdivided into a number of sub-cubes for storing pre-computed data into voxels. The rendering allows both voxel data and functional models. To model the interaction of light within a defined atmosphere, the atmospheric equation is used. The equation supports atmospheric absorption, Rayleigh scattering, Mie scattering and the rainbow geometry as a special case of dispersive refraction by atmospheric particles. The actual calculation of this illumination model is based on the volume sampling. Volume sampling samples the atmospheric volume in the A-cube. The atmospheric equation is applied to the sampled points in space. To improve the volume ray tracing, 2 pass solution is used: analytical solution to the surface intersection and the volume sampling for atmospheric effects.

There are still many open ended issuses needed to be solved. The atmospheric equation is not fully developed to capture the interaction of light with clustered particles much greater than the wavelength of light. In meteorology, it is known that the atmospheric temperature is also an important element. A mirage effect, for example, is a refraction process caused by the temperature differences in the atmosphere. For the rendering issues, the volume sampling is computationally expensive, and algorithms for efficiency considerations should be included.

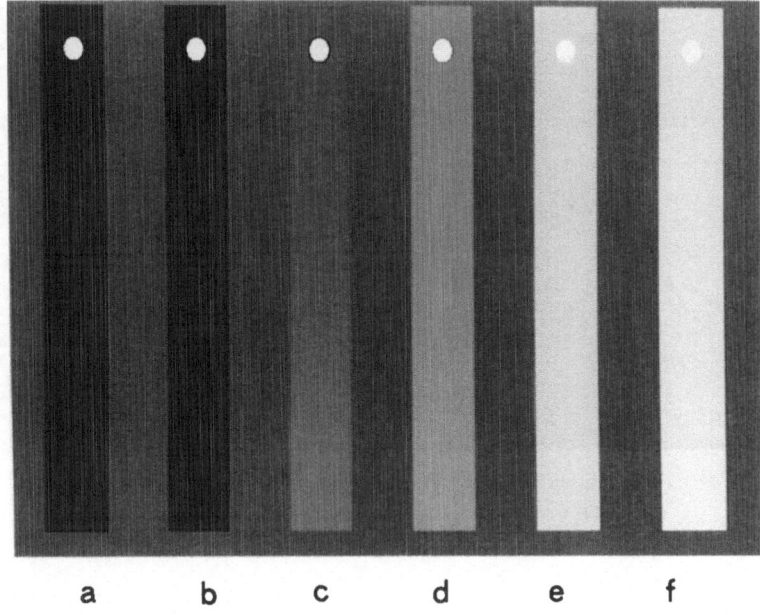

FIGURE 7 Blue sky with white sun: from left, (a),(b),(c) varying densities, (d),(e),(f) Mie scattering added

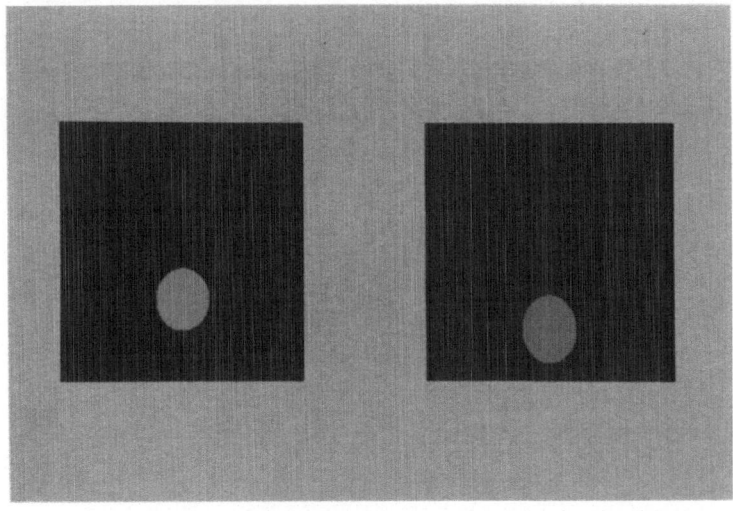

FIGURE 8 Sunset at different elevations: from left; (a) and (b)

FIGURE 9 Night sky scattering the city lights, Mie scattering

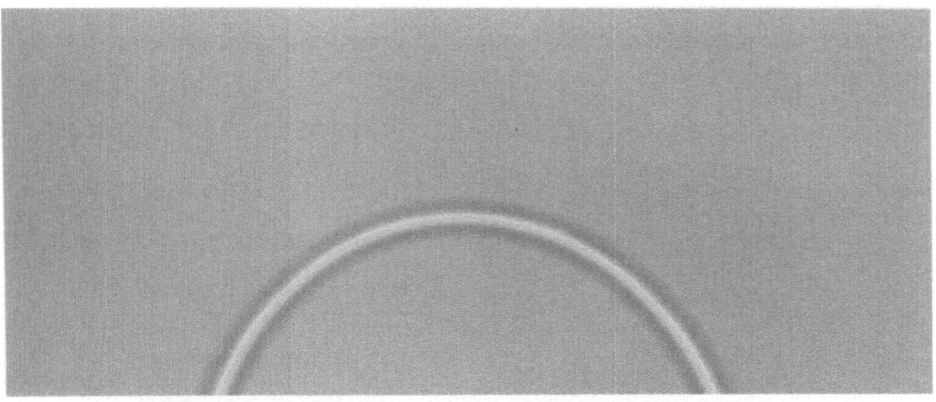

FIGURE 10 Rainbow

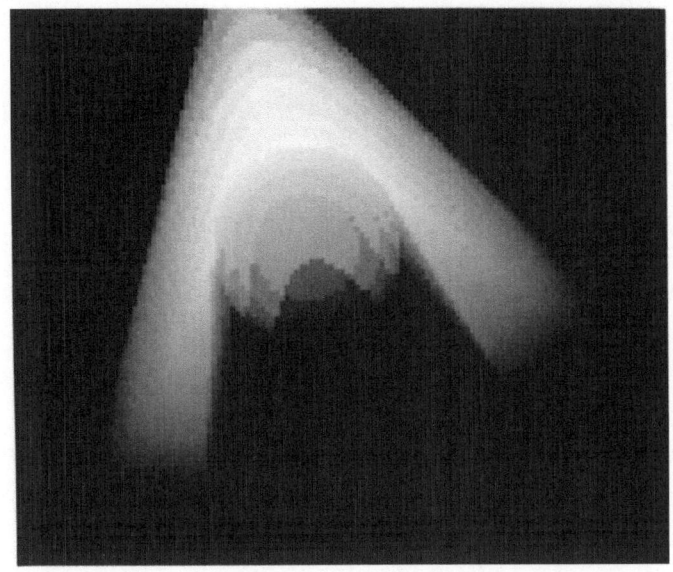

FIGURE 11 Volume sampling at 150 x 130 x 16 resolution

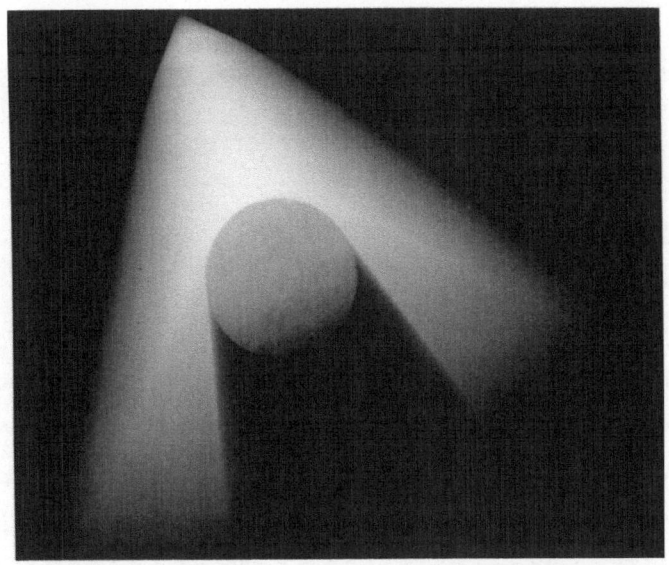

FIGURE 12 Volume sampling at 640 x 480 x 128 resolution

FIGURE 13 2 pass solution to volume ray tracing. Sphere and textured plane.

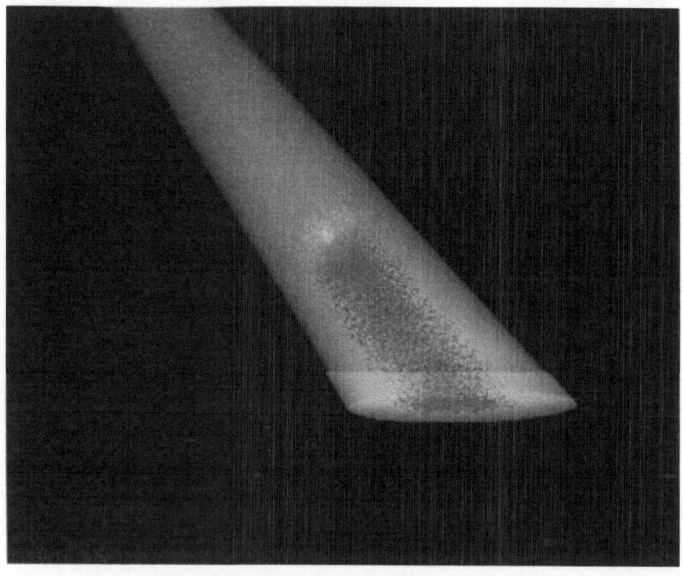

FIGURE 14 2 pass solution to volume ray tracing. Particals and textured plane.

REFERENCES

[1]Aida,M., *The Atmosphere and Radiation Process*, Tokyo-do Pub., Tokyo, 1986 (in Japanese)

[2]Blinn,J.F.,"Light Reflection Functions for Simulation of Clouds and Dusty Surfaces," *Computer Graphics,16*,3,1982,21-29

[3]Born,M. and Wolf,E., *Principles of Optics*, Pergamon Press, Oxford,U.K.,1975

[4]Boyer,C.B., *The Rainbow: From Myth to Mathematics*, Princeton University Press, Princeton, N.J., 1987

[5]Cohen,M.F. and Greenberg,D.P.,"The Hemi-cube: A Radiosity Solution for Complex Environments," *Computer Graphics,19*,3,1985,31-40

[6]Cook,R.L.,"Shade Trees," *Computer Graphics,18*,3,1984,223-231

[7]Cook,R.L.,"Stochastic Sampling in Computer Graphics," *ACM Transactions on Graphics,5*,1,1986,51-72

[8]Dippe,M.A. and Wold,E.H.,"Antialiasing Through Stochastic Sampling," *Computer Graphics,19*,3, 1985,69-78

[9]Eagleman,J.R., *Meteorology*, Wandsworth Pub., Belmont,CA, 1985

[10]Hall,R.,"A Characterization of Illumination Models and Shading Techniques," *The Visual Computer,2*, 5,268-277

[11]Hallman,J.P., *Heat Transfer*, McGraw-Hill Book Co., New York, 1976

[12]Inakage,M.,"Frequency Modulation Synthesis," *Computer Graphics 1987*, Kunii,T.L. ed., Springer-Verlag, Tokyo, 1987, 381-390

[13]Johnson,J.C., *Physical Meteorology*, John Wiley & Sons, Inc., New York, 1954

[14]Kajiya,J.T. and Von Herzen,B.P.,"Ray Tracing Volume Densities," *Computer Graphics,18*,3,1984,165-174

[15]Klassen,R.V.,"Modeling the Effect of the Atmosphere on Light," *ACM Transactions on Graphics, 6*,3,1987,215-237

[16]Max,N.L.,"Atmospheric Illumination and Shadows," *Computer Graphics,20*,4,1986,117-124

[17]Minnaert,M., *The Nature of Light & Colour in the Open Air*, Dover Pub., New York, 1954

[18]Nishita,T., Miyawaki,Y. and Nakamae,E.,"A Shading Model for Atmospheric Scattering Considering Luminous Intensity Distribution of Light Sources," *Computer Graphics,21*,4,1987,303-310

[19]Ogura,Y., *The General Metereology*, Tokyo Univeristy Press, Tokyo, 1987 (in Japanese)

[20]Peachey,D.R.,"Solid Texturing of Complex Surfaces," *Computer Graphics,19*,3,1985,279-286

[21]Reeves,W.T.,"Particle Systems--A Technique for Modeling a Class of Fuzzy Objects," *Computer Graphics,17*,3,1983,359-376

[22]Rushmeier,H.E. and Torrance,K.E.,"The Zonal Method for Calculating Light Intensities in the Presence of a Participating Medium," *Computer Graphics,21*,4,1987, 293-302

[23]Thomas,S.W.,"Dispersive Refraction in Ray Tracing," *The Visual Computer,2*,1,1986,3-8

[24]Valasek,J., *Introduction to Theoretical and Experimental Optics*, John Wiley & Sons,Inc., New York, 1949

[25]Van de Hulst,H.C., *Light Scattering by Small particles*, Dover Pub., New York, 1981

[26]Voss,R.,"Random Fractal Forgeries," SIGGRAPH "85 tutorial notes

[27]Whitted,T.,"An Improved Illumination Model for Shaded Display," *Comm. ACM,23*,6,1980, 343-349

Masa Inakage is a media artist and researcher at the Media Studio, Tokyo, Japan. He obtained his B.A. from Oberlin College, Ohio and M.F.A. from California College of Arts and Crafts. He did research on rendering, animation and user interface issues at the Media Lab., MIT. His current interests include sound and graphics integration, various modeling and rendeing methods, and user interface design.

address: The Media Studio, 3-5-17 Aobadai, #303, Meguro, Tokyo, 153, Japan

Vista Ray-Tracing: High Speed Ray Tracing Using Perspective Projection Image

A. Hashimoto, T. Akimoto, K. Mase, and Y. Suenaga

ABSTRACT

This paper presents a new high speed algorithm of ray-tracing named Vista Ray-tracing. In Vista Ray-tracing, time consuming intensity calculations are done only for "active" pixels which really need precise ray-tracing, while the intensity of "moderate" pixels is calculated by interpolation. The perspective projection image, or Vista, is generated at the first stage to be used as a guide map in active pixel selection. In this paper, a new method for obtaining Vistas for CSG model of quadratic surface ojects is presented as a key technology. A new texture mapping algorithm is also presented. Vista Ray-tracing is actually 16-75 times faster than standard ray-tracing, and can be even faster if other acceleration methods are employed. Consequently, Vista Ray-tracing is very useful for intermediate processes in making various images for TV animation, movies, high definition television, printing, etc.

Keywords : ray-tracing, adaptive sampling, under sampling, perspective projection image, Vista, texture mapping

1. INTRODUCTION

Ray-tracing (Whitted 1980) is a powerful and flexible method for synthesizing realistic images. The realism of ray-tracing results from the fact that it is normally based on point sampling. Consequently, ray-tracing suffers from the defects of point sampling such as high computational cost and aliasing noise. In terms of image quality, the weak points of sampling methods can be reduced by increasing the number of sampling points. For ray-tracing, anti-aliasing (Lee 1985, Cook 1984, 1986) can be achieved by using spatial over-sampling. The effect of motion blur can be represented by temporal over-sampling (Distributed ray-tracing) (Cook 1984). However, over-sampling in spatial or time domain directly increases the computational cost. The computational cost of ray-tracing is so high that it is avoided in many applications (Cook 1987).

Various methods for reducing the number of calculations have been proposed from the beginning of ray-tracing research. Whitted (1980) proposed a fast method using simple primitives ("extents") which surround complex objects. Overall calculation time is reduced by testing the extents first. Glassner (1984) proposed the oct-tree method where the space is hierarchically subdivided into boxes according to objects. Ray-object intersection is tested only in the boxes which include a ray. Fujimoto (1985) proposed a method using uniform size boxes ("voxels"). He showed that the overhead of rays traversing through voxels is smaller than that using Glassner's method. All these methods, while relatively successful, are still too slow for widespread use.

Fast ray-tracing methods based on adaptive sampling have been used for over-sampling to reduce aliasing noises (Lee 1985, Cook 1986, Mitchell 1987). The purpose is the improvement of image quality, not the acceleration of synthesizing speed. Over-sampling is only applied to appropriate areas by using adaptive sampling. The difference in intensities between a sampling point and neighbor points is usually used to determine whether or not to apply over-sampling. Mitchell (1987) proposed using a criterion based on a property of human vision.

Under-sampling is very effective for ray-tracing acceleration, but few reports have been published on this important subject. This seems to be due to the unfavorable properties of under-sampling, i.e, poor image quality. Under-sampling generates images by interpolating between sampling points. Problems such as blurring of structural and spectral details are very common, and are caused by interpolation errors. Shannon (1949) showed that the problems cannot be completely solved by using only sampling point information. These interpolation errors can be classified into the following two types.

(Type-1) Interpolation error between sampling points of the same object
(Type-2) Interpolation error between sampling points of different objects

In under-sampling, Type-1 and Type-2 errors occur more frequently and are more serious. Therefore, in order to develop a practical under-sampling technique, it is very important to investigate methods which can reduce image quality degradation. Type-1 error occurs when a linear interpolation is applied to a non-linear intensity change. Akimoto (1986) succeeded in making Type-1 error negligible by employing hierarchical adaptive sampling. Shinya (1987) proposed an accurate error evaluation method using the information about rays and the curvature of objects. Therefore, Type-1 errors can be overcome, or at least be made negligible by hierarchical adaptive sampling.

On the other hand, Type-2 errors are more serious, since there is no way to check coherency among sampling points. It should be noted that Type-2 errors occur with any sampling technique. Even if a very high sampling frequency f is used, distributions of regions cannot be detected if they have spatial frequencies greater than $f/2$. Low frequency visible moire noise occurs when the frequency is nearly equal to f. According to the sampling theorem (Shannon 1949), the only way to remove aliasing noises completely is to suppress details with high sampling frequencies. However, in computer graphics, it is impossible to do this about modeling data. Neither over-sampling nor jitter-sampling can provide a complete solution in the mathematical sense; they can only reduce image quality degradation caused by aliasing.

Essentially, Type-2 errors cannot be solved by using only sampling point information. In order to solve this problem, we propose a new idea: using data which can be obtained from the perspective projection image (Vista). Vista Ray-tracing is a fast ray-tracing method using the Vista to detect different regions within the sampling area. By using this information, sampling points can be efficiently concentrated in different regions, thus enhancing speed while maintaining good image quality. Since Vista Ray-tracing interpolates efficiently by using a Vista, synthesizing speed is much faster than standard sampling (standard ray-tracing), and even faster than uniform adaptive under-sampling.

This paper consists of two parts. A new flexible method for synthesizing a Vista of CSG model constructed by quadratic surfaces and a method of selecting sampling pixels are presented. In the seconds part (Chapter 3), a new rendering algorithm for Vista Ray-tracing is also presented to render efficiently texture mapped objects. A practical method to calculate partitioned intensity and intersection using interpolated ray is presented.

2. VISTA RAY-TRACING

2.1 Outline

Ray-tracing is a very slow rendering algorithm, since time consuming computations are needed for each pixel. It should be noted that usual images have local area coherency: adjacent pixels have the same ray-object intersection history and very similar pixel intensity. In this paper, it it assumed that only quadratic surfaces and planes are used to express all the objects in a CSG model, although the basic notion of Vista Ray-tracing itself can be generally applied to any kind of model whose Vista can be obtained prior to ray-tracing. It is important that the pixels corresponding to object edges can be identified in advance of ray-tracing, by using the Vista as a guide map, when the object model is expressed by quadratic surfaces and planes, as shown below. The basic notion of Vista Ray-tracing is as follows.

(1) First, the Vista is generated.
(2) Then, using the Vista information, pixels are classified into these categories:
    (a) Category A: "active" pixels near the contours of graphic primitives
    (b) Category B: "moderate" pixels within graphic primitives
(3) Ray-tracing is applied only to the pixels in Category A.
(4) Interpolation is applied to the pixels in Category B.

In the following sections, it will be shown that the Vista for any kind of quadratic primitive can be derived analytically. Moreover, a simple procedure will be shown to derive the Vista from any kind of CSG model defined by quadratic functions. This algorithm generates Vistas only for directly observable objects.

2.2 Generation of Vista

2.2.1 Vista for Objects Defined by Quadratic Surfaces

The first step in Vista Ray-tracing is to generate the Vista, in order to efficiently select proper ray-tracing pixels. In general, the Vista for the quadratic primitive is not generated directly, except for the case of simple objects such as spheres, cones and cylinders (Atherton 1983, Pueyo 1987).

The new Vista generation algorithm, presented here, exploits the fact that perspective projection P_{pers} is equivalent to parallel projection P_{par} after perspective transformation T, as shown in Fig.1. More precisely, it is written as

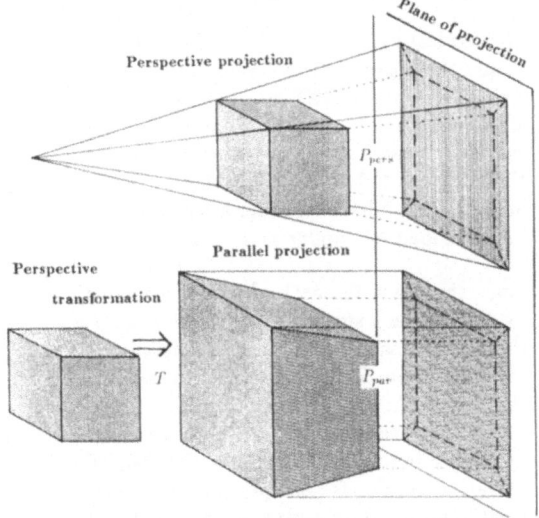

Fig.1 Perspective projection (P_{pers}) is equal to parallel projection (P_{par}) after perspective transformation (T)

$$P_{pers} = P_{par} \quad T, \tag{1}$$

where,

$$P_{pers} = \begin{bmatrix} 1 & 0 & 0 & 0 \\ 0 & 1 & 0 & 0 \\ 0 & 0 & 0 & 0 \\ 0 & 0 & -1/h & 1 \end{bmatrix}, P_{par} = \begin{bmatrix} 1 & 0 & 0 & 0 \\ 0 & 1 & 0 & 0 \\ 0 & 0 & 0 & 0 \\ 0 & 0 & 0 & 1 \end{bmatrix}, T = \begin{bmatrix} 1 & 0 & 0 & 0 \\ 0 & 1 & 0 & 0 \\ 0 & 0 & 1 & 0 \\ 0 & 0 & -1/h & 1 \end{bmatrix} \tag{1a, 1b, 1c}$$

and $(0, 0, h)$ is the projection center.

Making use of this fact, the Vista is directly obtained from the primitives expressed by the quadratic function. Since the problem is reduced to a 4 by 4 matrix representation of a quadratic surface, Vista Ray-tracing can deal with any quadratic primitives in the same way, e.g., spheres, ellipsoids, cones, hyperboloids, paraboloids, cylinders, etc.

First, assuming that the projection plane is $z = 0$ and the projection center is $(0, 0, h)$, quadratic surface A is given in quadratic form as

$$\bar{x}^T \quad A \quad \bar{x} = 0, \tag{2}$$

where

$$\bar{x}^T = [x \quad y \quad z \quad 1]. \tag{2a}$$

Quadratic surface A is converted to B by perspective transformation T as

$$\bar{x}^T \quad B \quad \bar{x} = 0, \tag{3}$$

where
$$B = (T^{-1})^T \quad A \quad T^{-1}. \tag{3a}$$

The contour of the parallel projection of B is obtained as a quadratic curve, which is given by the following equation.

$$\frac{\partial(\bar{x}^T \quad B \quad \bar{x})}{\partial z} = 0 \tag{4}$$

Thus, the Vista is analytically obtained by eliminating z in the simultaneous equations (3) and (4).

2.2.2 Consistent Handling of CSG Model

In practical applications, it is important to obtain the Vista for the CSG model, where AND, OR and MINUS operations are handled in the same way. To simplify the discussion, consider the problem to obtain the Vista for the OR of two ellipsoids as shown in Fig.2. The Vistas for other operations can be developed by similar methods.

Since the Vista for each object is obtained by the method stated in sub-section 2.2.1, the problem is reduced to obtaining the intersecting lines of two objects on the screen, these are shown as thick lines in Fig.2. These intersecting lines are not expressed by simple functions on the two dimensional screen. However, for our purpose, it is sufficient to obtain the crossing points P and Q at each scanline $y = k$, as illustrated in Fig.2. In this figure, S_1 and S_2 denote the start point, and E_1 and E_2 denote the end point of the intersecting lines at each scanline. P and Q are determined as follows.

   1) Draw a line $(S_1 \ E_1)$ with index 1 in the perspective image plane.
   2) Draw a line $(S_2 \ E_2)$ with index 2 in the perspective image plane.
   3) If the two lines overlap, determine P and Q as follows.

Let us consider two ellipsoids given by the following equations,

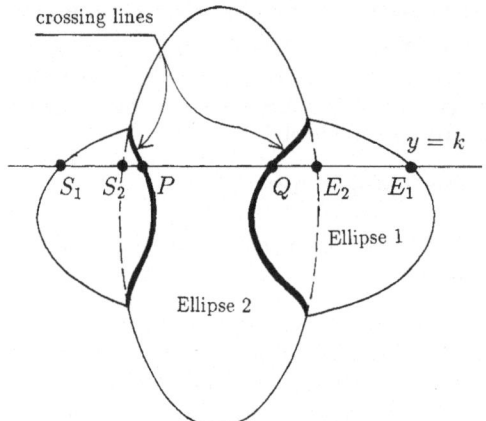

Fig.2 Intersection of Quadratic primitives S_1, E_1, S_2, E_2, P and Q on Scan-line $y = k$

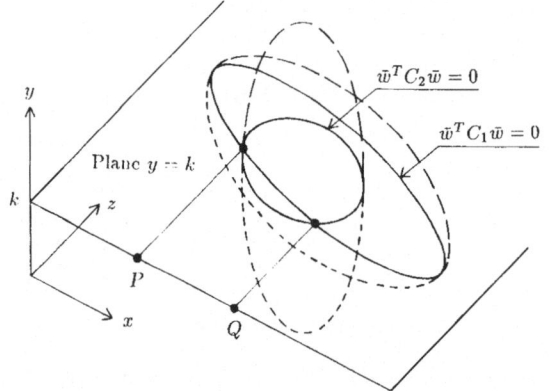

Fig.3 Intersection Figures of Quadratic Primitives

$$\bar{x}^T \quad B_1 \quad \bar{x} = 0 \tag{5}$$

and
$$\bar{x}^T \quad B_2 \quad \bar{x} = 0 \tag{6},$$

where
$$B_1 = \begin{bmatrix} a_{11} & b_{11} & b_{21} & c_{11} \\ b_{11} & a_{21} & b_{31} & c_{21} \\ b_{21} & b_{31} & a_{31} & c_{31} \\ c_{11} & c_{21} & c_{31} & d_1 \end{bmatrix} \qquad B_2 = \begin{bmatrix} a_{12} & b_{12} & b_{22} & c_{12} \\ b_{12} & a_{22} & b_{32} & c_{22} \\ b_{22} & b_{32} & a_{32} & c_{32} \\ c_{12} & c_{22} & c_{32} & d_2 \end{bmatrix} \tag{6a, 6b}$$

Two ellipses formed by cutting the two ellipsoids with a plane $y = k$ (See **Fig.3**) are given by,

$$\bar{w}^T \quad C_1 \quad \bar{w} = 0 \tag{7}$$

and

$$\bar{w}^T \quad C_2 \quad \bar{w} = 0, \tag{8}$$

where

$$\bar{w}^T = [\, x \quad z \quad 1 \,], \tag{8a}$$

and

$$C_1 = \begin{bmatrix} a_{11} & b_{21} & c_{11} + k \times b_{11} \\ b_{21} & a_{31} & c_{31} + k \times b_{31} \\ c_{11} + k \times b_{11} & c_{31} + h \times b_{31} & d_1 + 2 \times k \times c_{21} + k^2 \times a_{21} \end{bmatrix} \tag{8b}$$

and

$$C_2 = \begin{bmatrix} a_{12} & b_{22} & c_{12} + k \times b_{12} \\ b_{22} & a_{32} & c_{32} + k \times b_{32} \\ c_{12} + k \times b_{12} & c_{32} + h \times b_{32} & d_1 + 2 \times k \times c_{22} + k^2 \times a_{22} \end{bmatrix} \tag{8c}$$

We can get P and Q by eliminating z from the simultaneous equations (7) and (8). These simultaneous equations can be rewritten to a fourth order equation of x. Thus, at most four sets of solutions $(x\ z)$ are obtained. Then we can select the correct two sets of solutions which present P or Q by checking the following two conditions.

(1) Both x and z must be real.
(2) Both n_{z1} and n_{z2} must be less than zero, where $((n_{x1}\ n_{z1}),(n_{x2}\ n_{z2}))$ are normal vectors of ellipses 1 and 2.

By replacing x and z in the following equations with the four sets of solutions, we get n_{x1}, n_{x2}, n_{z1} and n_{z2} as follows.

$$n_{x1} = a_{11} \times x + b_{21} \times z + b_{11} \times k + c_{11} \tag{9}$$

$$n_{z1} = a_{31} \times z + b_{21} \times x + b_{31} \times k + c_{31} \tag{10}$$

$$n_{x2} = a_{12} \times x + b_{22} \times z + b_{12} \times k + c_{12} \tag{11}$$

$$n_{z2} = a_{32} \times z + b_{22} \times x + b_{32} \times k + c_{32} \tag{12}$$

Here, P is the point $(x\ z)$ which satisfies $n_{z1} < 0$, $n_{z2} < 0$ and $n_{x1} > n_{x2}$. Q is the point which satisfies $n_{z1} < 0$, $n_{z2} < 0$ and $n_{x2} > n_{x1}$. Thus we can determine Index 1 from S_1 to P, Index 2 from P to Q and again Index 1 from Q to E_1. The above procedure considers the intersection of only two primitives. However, complicated combinations of more than two primitives can be handled by considering only two primitives at a time. AND and MINUS operations are treated in the same way for solving eqs. (9) to (12), except for the judgement on n_{x1}, n_{x2}, n_{z1} and n_{z2}.

2.3.1 Algorithm of Vista Ray-tracing

The algorithm of Vista Ray-tracing is illustrated as follows.

```
[Algorithm VISTA_RAY-TRACING]
VISTA_RAY-TRACING()
{
        Generate Vista ............................. (See Section 2.2)
        Subdivide the screen into squares ........... (See Sub-section 2.3.2)
        for (all squares)
            RENDER_SQUARE();
}

RENDER_SQUARE()
{
        Select ray-tracing pixels using Vista ........ (See Sub-section 2.3.3)
        if (n_r > 2) { ............................... (See Sub-section 2.3.3)
            Subdivide the square into 4
            for (each of 4 squares)
                RENDER_SQUARE();
```

```
    } else {
        Perform ray-tracing and
        smoothness test ........................   (See Sub-section 2.3.4)
        if (smooth)
            Interpolation ......................   (See Sub-section 2.3.5)
        else {
            Subdivide the square into 4
            for (each of 4 squares)
                RENDER_SQUARE();
        }
    }
  }
}
```

2.3.2 Screen Subdivision into Squares

The actual rendering step in Vista Ray-tracing begins with subdividing the screen having $n \times n$ pixels into $m \times m$ squares, where both n and m are powers of 2. Assume that each square consists of $d \times d$ pixels, and d $(= n/m)$ is also a power of 2. Each square is recursively subdivided into smaller ones according to the number of indexed sub-regions (n_r) within the square. An indexed sub-regions is an area of pixels mapping the same object. If a square contains more than two indexed sub-regions $(n_r > 2)$, it is sub-divided into four equal squares. Each smaller square is checked for the number of sub-regions.

2.3.3 Active-pixel Selection

Active pixels are selected according to n_r as follows. (See Figs.4(a)-(e).)
$n_r = 1$: Four active pixels in the corners of the square are selected as shown in Fig.4(b).
$n_r = 2$: Four (sometimes three or two) active pixels in the corner of each indexed sub-region are selected as shown in Fig.4(c) and (d).
$n_r > 2$: The square is subdivided into four as shown in Fig.4(e).
Thus, at most eight active pixels are selected, when $n_r = 2$. Here, the 'corners' mean the four pixels which are placed at the extremities of the indexed sub-region.

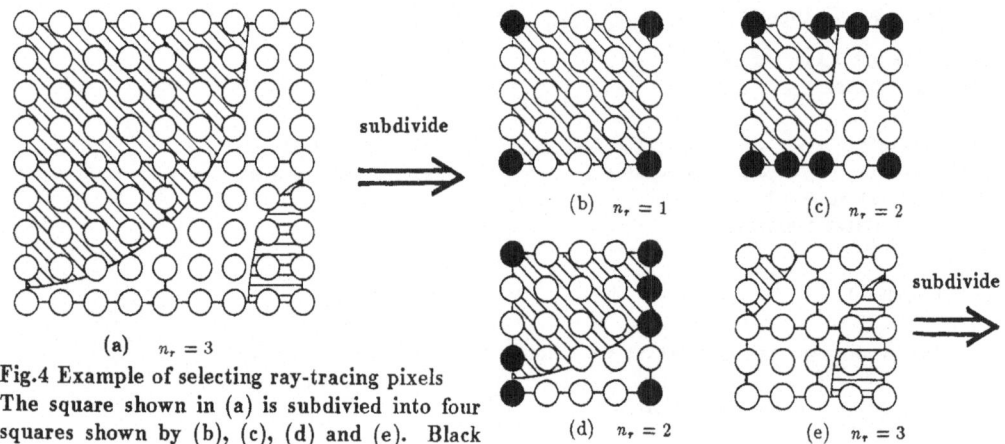

(a) $n_r = 3$

subdivide

(b) $n_r = 1$

(c) $n_r = 2$

(d) $n_r = 2$

(e) $n_r = 3$

subdivide

Fig.4 Example of selecting ray-tracing pixels
The square shown in (a) is subdivied into four squares shown by (b), (c), (d) and (e). Black circles show selected active pixels.

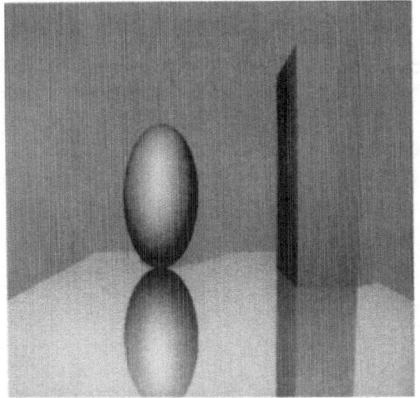

(a) Standard Ray-tracing (628 sec)

(b) Vista Ray-tracing (41 sec)

Fig.5   Image A (number of primitives = 5)

(a) Standard Ray-tracing (2349 sec)

(b) Vista Ray-tracing (303 sec)

Fig.6   Image B (number of primitives = 50)

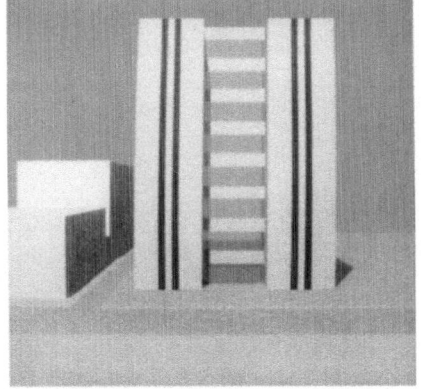
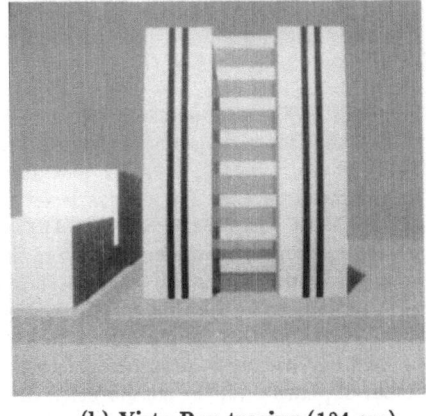

(a) Standard Ray-tracing (6065 sec)

(b) Vista Ray-tracing (184 sec)

Fig.7   Image C (number of primitives = 71)

2.3.4 Area Smoothness Test

For each indexed sub-region, the four active pixels are ray-traced to obtain color intensity and the ray-object intersection history including shadow. In order to test the area smoothness, check the following two conditions.

    1) All four active pixels have the same ray-object intersection history.

    2) The intensity deviation v is less than a predetermined threshold δ, where v is given by

$$v^2 = \sum_{j=1}^{4} (i_j - i_m)^2, \tag{13}$$

where

$$i_j = i_{RED\,j} + i_{GREEN\,j} + i_{BLUE\,j} \qquad (j = 1, 2, 3, 4) \tag{14}$$

and

$$i_m = \frac{1}{4}(i_1 + i_2 + i_3 + i_4). \tag{15}$$

2.3.5 Interpolation

The intensity of the remaining pixels in an indexed sub-region are obtained by interpolation. If all four active pixels are on the corners, interpolation equation (16) is given as

$$P(x,y) = \frac{(d-x)(d-y)P_1 + x(d-y)P_2 + (d-x)yP_3 + xyP_4}{d^2}. \tag{16}$$

If the number of pixels is less than four or some pixels are not on the corners, the intensities of the corner pixels are first determined by extrapolation.

2.4 Experiments

Three kinds of images were rendered by Vista Ray-tracing and by standard ray-tracing for comparison, as shown in Fig.5(a)and(b), Fig.6(a)and(b), and Fig.7(a)and(b). Roughly speaking, these images are rendered by Vista Ray-tracing in "minutes", while it takes "hours" to synthesize them by standard ray-tracing. Image A is a metal ellipsoid and a rectangular solid on a flat mirror. Image B is 49 floating metal balls above a flat mirror. Image C is three buildings on the ground.

Programs were written in C language on a SUN3/260C with a floating point accelerator. In order to estimate the capability of Vista Ray-tracing, no other acceleration method (e.g., space subdivision) was used. All experiments were done under the condition of a threshold level of 16.

The graph in Fig.8 shows the relative computation time for various screens having $n \times n$ pixels, where $n = 128$, 256, 512 and 1024. The computation time for $n = 128$ is set to unity for both Vista Ray-tracing and standard ray-tracing. The broken line shows the computation time of standard ray-tracing and solid line shows the time for Vista Ray-tracing. While the computation time of standard ray-tracing is proportional to the number of pixels $n \times n$, the computation time of Vista Ray-tracing is almost proportional to n. This means the relative speed improvement over standard ray-tracing is almost

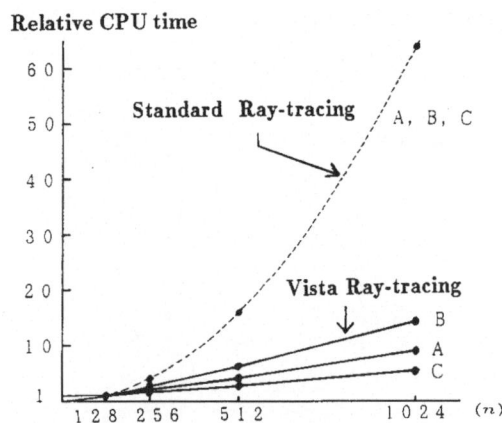

Fig.8   Relative CPU time for Standard Ray-tracing and Vista Ray-tracing

proportional to n, as shown in Fig.9. This ratio is independent of image complexity. Other methods based on ray-tracing calculation at each pixel do not have this favorable feature. The solid line in Fig.9 shows the relative speed of Vista Ray-tracing. Dotted line in Fig.9 shows the relative speed of Pixel Selected Ray-tracing (Akimoto 1986). Fig.10 shows that the Vista generation time occupies only one to five percent of the total processing time for Vista Ray-tracing. For a larger number of quadratic primitives, the relative Vista generation time becomes smaller, as shown in Fig.10, since more complex calculation is needed for each pixel.

3. TEXTURE MAPPING

3.1 Texture Mapping Problem in Vista Ray-tracing

Texture mapping is a very useful technique to express complex scenes in a compact data structure. This chapter describes how to implement the texture mapping in Vista Ray-tracing. The area smoothness test described in sub-section 2.3.4 is usually sufficient for Vista Ray-tracing. However, a serious problem occurs when texture mapping is used. Assume a checkered plane is synthesized by texture mapping in Vista Ray-tracing. When all the active pixels have the same color as shown in Fig.11(a), that color will be given to all other pixels within the square, which causes a lack of texture as shown in Fig.11(b). When the active pixels do not have the same color as shown in Fig.12(a), the square must be subdivided, which causes wasteful ray-tracing computation for all the pixels around the border of the texture pattern as shown in Fig.12(b). Thus, the straightforward application of texture mapping to Vista Ray tracing would not produce good results. The more complex the texture pattern is, the more pixels should be ray-traced, which will decrease the speed of Vista Ray-tracing.

Relative speed improvement
over Standard Ray-tracing

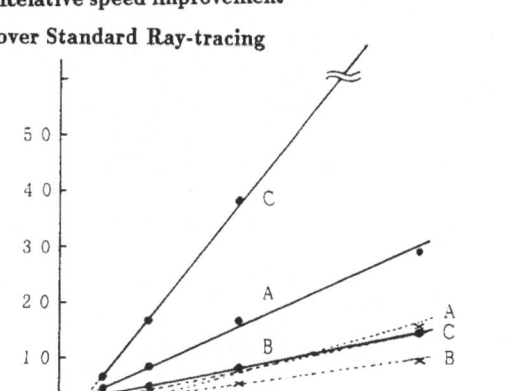

Fig.9   Relative speed of Vista Ray-tracing and Pixel Selected Ray-tracing

—————————   Vista Ray-tracing

- - - - - - - - - -   Pixel Selected Ray-tracing

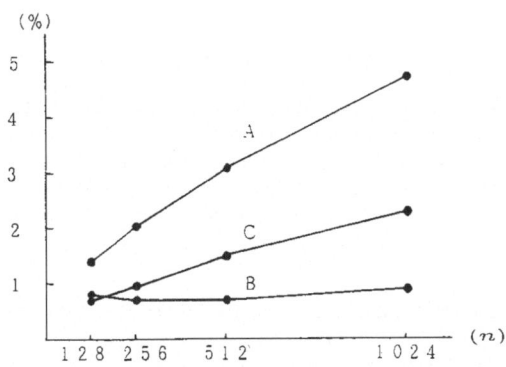

Fig.10   Percentage of Vista generation time in Vista Ray-tracing

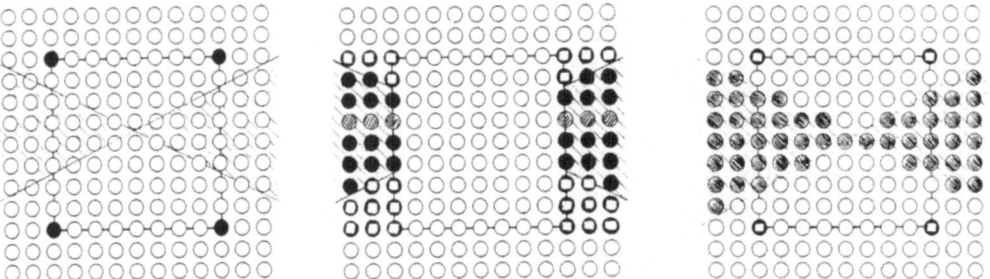

(a) Before processing   (b) Result by usual interpolation   (c) Result by improved interpolation

Fig.11   An example of texture degradation (The lack of texture)

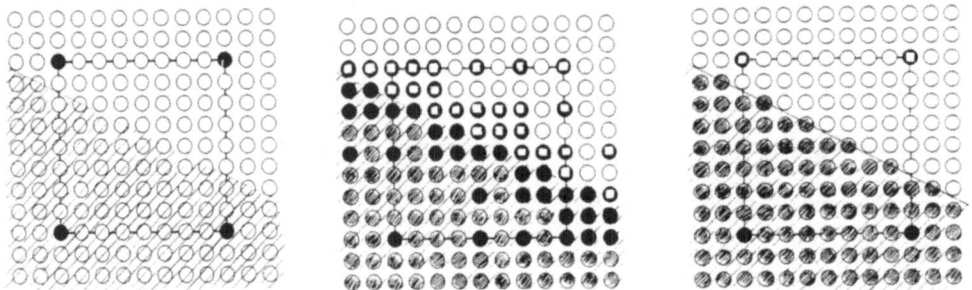

(a) Before processing   (b) Result by usual interpolation   (c) Result by improved interpolation

Fig.12   An example of wasteful subdivision

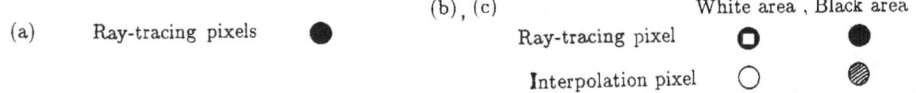

(a)   Ray-tracing pixels   ●

(b), (c)   White area , Black area

Ray-tracing pixel   ○   ●

Interpolation pixel   ○   ◎

3.2 New Interpolation Algorithm for Texture Mapping in Vista Ray-tracing

We propose a new interpolation algorithm for texture mapping in Vista Ray-tracing without doing wasteful ray-tracing calculations at many pixels. First, intensities of active pixels are calculated without texture color information, and the area smoothness test described in sub-section 2.3.4 is applied. It is essential that the texture is ignored at this stage. Then, texture mapping is applied, by interpolation method given below. The intensity i is defined by,

$$i = i_a + k_d * \sum (N, L_i) + k_s * S + k_t * T \tag{17}$$

where i_a is ambient, k_d is a coefficient of diffuse reflection, N is a normal vector, L_i is the i' th light vector, k_s is a coefficient of specular, S is reflection ray vector, k_t is coefficient of transparency, and T is a transparent ray vector. In color texture mapping, only the first and second terms of the right hand side of eq.17 are affected. Equation 17 can be rewritten as, $i = i_{tex} + i_{ntex}$ where $i_{tex} = \{i'_a + k'_d * \sum (N, L_i)\} c_{tex}$, $i_{ntex} = k_s * S + k_t * T$ and c_{tex} is the texture color. Only the intensity i_{ntex} is used in the area smoothness test. The position and direction of each tracing level of the ray must be memorized when a pixel is ray-traced. After the area smoothness test under the conditions described in sub-section 2.3.4, the intensity i_{ntex} is obtained by the interpolation described by eq.16. Then the intensity i_{tex}, depending on color texture, is calculated at each pixel and added to i_{ntex}.

In order to refer to the texture map, ray-object crossing position is obtained by the intersection calculation between the primitive for texture mapping and the ray vector obtained by interpolation using the intersection history. The new interpolation algorithm presented here needs only one ray-object intersection calculation at each pixel for every texture mapped primitive in the intersection history. However the number of ray-object intersection calculations in the standard ray-tracing with shadowing needs $2pq$ for each pixel, where p is the number of primitives, and q is a number of branches in the ray-tracing tree. Thus the calculation time for texture mapping is reduced to $1/(2pq)$ compared with straightforward calculation.

3.3 Experiments

Computer simulation was carried out for the texture mapping in Vista Ray-tracing under the same conditions as described in section 2.4. Ordinary interpolation requires a lot of active pixels as shown in Fig.13(a), and the texture is not correctly mapped onto objects as shown in Fig.13(b). Using the new interpolation algorithm presented here, the number of active pixels is drastically reduced as shown in Fig.14(a), and, the texture is Although Vista Ray-tracing uses under-sampling, it can synthesize images correctly mapped onto objects as shown in Fig.14(b).

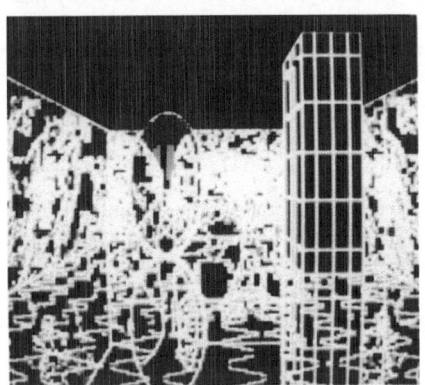

(a) Active pixels   (b)Result

Fig.13   Texture mapping by usual interpolation

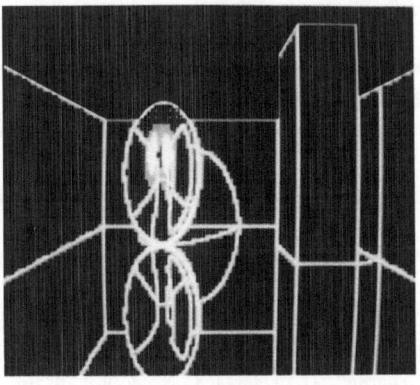

(a) Active pixels   (b)Result

Fig.14   Texture mapping by improved interpolation

4. CONCLUSION

A fast ray-tracing method named Vista Ray-tracing was proposed. faster with less degradation of image quality than other simple under-sampling methods, because small regions among sampling points can be detected in advance by using the Vista. A new efficient method to synthesize Vistas for CSG model of quadratic objects was developed for Vista Ray-tracing. Though this method is very powerful, it cannot synthesize a Vista of reflected or refracted objects. However, this defect is not very serious, since the objects merely lose the guarantee to be synthesized as strictly correct reflection or refraction patterns in rendering, and most of the objects themselves are detected during rendering.

One annoying problem of under-sampling is the rendering of texture mapped objects. An efficient method to accurately render texture mapped objects was developed. It uses discrete intensity calculations and intersection calculations using interpolated rays. This method can be applied not only to Vista Ray-tracing but also to all under-sampling methods. The experiments have shown that the acceleration rate of Vista Ray-tracing is 16 to 75 times faster thsn that of conventional ray-tracing when the image size is 1024 × 1024 pixels. Vista generation time is negligible compared with rendering time. The capacity of Vista Ray-tracing to handle various images and the acceleration rate when mixed with other fast ray-tracing methods (e.g., the space subdivision method) will be clarified by further experiments.
Consequently, Vista Ray-tracing is very promising for intermediate processes in making various images for TV animation, movies, high definition television, printing, etc.

ACKNOWLEDGEMENTS

The authors wish to thank the members of computer graphics groups in the Visual Perception Laboratory and Visual Media Laboratory, NTT Human Interface Laboratories, Nippon Telegraph and Telephone Corporation, for their advice and participation in helpful discussions. The authors would be like to express their thanks to Dr. Kazuaki Komori, the director general of the Visual Perception Laboratory, NTT Human Interface Laboratories, NTT, for his encouragement and promotion of the project.

REFERENCES

Akimoto T. and Mase K. (1986) "Pixel Selected Ray-tracing", Trans. I.E.C.E of Japan, Vol.J-69-D, No.12, pp.1943-1952 (in Japanese)

Atherton P.R. (1983) "A Scan-line Hidden Surface Removal Procedure For Constructive Solid Geometry", Proc. SIGGRAPH, vol.17, No.3, pp.73-82

Cook R.L., Porter T. and Carpenter L. (1984) "Distributed Ray Tracing" Proc. SIGGRAPH 1984, Vol.18, No.3, pp.137-146

Cook R.L. and Robert L. (1986) "Stochastic Sampling in Computer Graphics", ACM Trans. Graphics, Vol.5, No.1

Cook R.L., Carpenter L. and Catmull E. (1987) "The Reyes Image Rendering Architecture", Proc. SIGGRAPH 1987, Vol.21, No.4, pp.95-102

Fujimoto A. and Iwata K. (1985) "Accelerated Ray-Tracing", Proceeding of Computer Graphics Tokyo '85

Glassner A.S. (1984) "Space Subdivision for Fast Ray Tracing", IEEE CG&A, No.4, Vol.10, pp.15-22

Kajiya J.T. (1986) "The Rendering Equations", Computer Graphics, Vol.20, No.4, pp.143-150

Lee M.E., Redner R.A., Uselton S.P. (1985) "Statistically optimized sampling for distributed ray tracing", Proc. SIGGRAPH 1985, Vol.19, No.3, July, pp.61-65

Mitchell D.P. (1987) "Generating Antialiased Images at Low Sampling Densities", Proc. SIG-GRAPH 1987, Vol.21, No.4, pp.65-72

Pueyo X. and Mendoza J.C. (1987) "A New Scanline Algorithm for The Rendering of CSG trees", Proc. EUROGRAPHICS, pp.347-361

Shannon C.E., (1949) "Communication in the presence of noise", Proc. IRE Vol.37, pp.10-21

Shinya M. and Takahashi T. (1987) "Principles and Applications of Pencil Tracing", Proc. SIG-GRAPH 1987, Vol.21, No.4, pp.45-52

Whitted T. (1980) "An Improved Model for Shaded Display", Comm. ACM, 23, 6, pp.343-349

Hashimoto, Akihiko   received a B.S. degree in Mechanical Engineering from Tokyo Institute of Technology, Tokyo, Japan in 1983, and an M.S. degree from the same institute in 1985. He joined NTT Electrical Communications Laboratories of Nippon Telegraph and Telephone Corporation in 1985. His research interests include computer graphics and computer architectures.
Address: Visual Perception Laboratory, NTT Human Interface Laboratories, 1-2356, Take, Yokosuka, Kanagawa, 238-03 Japan

Akimoto, Taka-aki   received a B.S. degree in Information Engineering from Kyushuu Institute of Technology, Kita-Kyushu, Japan in 1982, and an M.S. degree from the same institution in 1984. He joined NTT Electrical Communications Laboratories of Nippon Telegraph and Telephone Corporation in 1984. His research interests include computer graphics and image processing.
Address: Visual Perception Laboratory, NTT Human Interface Laboratories, 1-2356, Take, Yokosuka, Kanagawa, 238-03 Japan

Mase, Kenji   received a B.S. degree in Electrical Engineering and an M.S. degree in Information Engineering from Nagoya University, Nagoya, Japan, in 1979 and 1981. He joined NTT Electrical Communications Laboratories of Nippon Telegraph and Telephone Corporation in 1981. His research interests include image processing, computer graphics, integrated visual communications, and computer vision.
Address: Visual Perception Laboratory, NTT Human Interface Laboratories, 1-2356, Take, Yokosuka, Kanagawa, 238-03 Japan

Suenaga, Yasuhito   received a B.S., M.S., and Ph.D. degrees in Electrical Engineering from Nagoya University, Nagoya, Japan, in 1968, 1970 and 1974. Since joining the Electrical Communications Laboratories, Nippon Telegraph and Telephone Public Corporation in 1973, he has been engaged in research image processing. He currently leads a research group on computer graphics and vision in Human Interface Laboratories, Nippon Telegraph and Telephone Corporation.
Address: Visual Perception Laboratory, NTT Human Interface Laboratories, 1-2356, Take, Yokosuka, Kanagawa, 238-03 Japan

Fast Ray Tracing of Unevaluated Constructive Solid Geometry Models

P. Getto

ABSTRACT

We present a refinement of the ray tracing algorithm, for use with unevaluated constructive solid geometry models. Bounding enclosures around the children of a part are combined into a tree with nearly optimal minimum expected number of extent-ray intersections. An approximate evaluation of the expression represented by the part can be evaluated on the enclosure-ray intersections to find the subset of children that might be hit by a ray. These candidate children are then used to evaluate the expression exactly. Several criteria are suggested which allow early termination of the exact expression evaluation.

1. INTRODUCTION

Unevaluated constructive solid geometry (CSG) is one of a number of popular representations of geometric information. The advantages of the CSG approach are flexibility, generality of the underlying structure, and similarity to the design process. CSG models can be represented by a directed acyclic graph whose arcs correspond to Boolean operations and nodes to operands. Using this representation, internal nodes are denoted as *parts* or *sub-parts*, and leaf nodes are geometric objects, denoted as *primitives*. Alternatively, one can think of a CSG model as a single Boolean expression whose parts are sub-expressions set off by parentheses and whose primitives are literals. It should be clear that our representation is not restricted to a binary tree. Figure 1 shows the CSG graph and the resulting image (with a table top, flame, material properties and lighting added), from the expression,

$$candleHolder = M_1(b) - M_2(c) - M_3(s) - M_4(s) - M_5(s) - M_6(s) - M_7(s) - M_8(s), \qquad (1)$$

where b denotes a block, c a cylinder, s a sphere, and M_i transformation matrices.

Note that the circular nodes, which we denote *pieces*, in the graph are labels for the arcs connecting a part with each of its children. A piece contains the Boolean operation and a transformation matrix. Thus, the six instances of the primitive sphere are not necessarily in the same place.

It is sometimes convenient to think of the CSG model as a tree, with parts at the root and the internal nodes and primitives at the leaves. The directed acyclic graph representation can be converted to a tree by duplicating an object each time it is referenced by an arc. Thus, there would be six distinct copies of the sphere in the tree representation of the candle holder.

A disadvantage of the CSG representation is the relatively large amount of time and computation which is required to evaluate and render a model, especially one involving complex primitives such as superquadrics and bi-parametric tensor-product surfaces. Often systems using the CSG representation will employ a second representation, such as the boundary representation, or will limit the types of geometric primitives available for modeling to those for which the model can be quickly evaluated. This approach suffers because it unnecessarily restricts the user in order to save computation time.

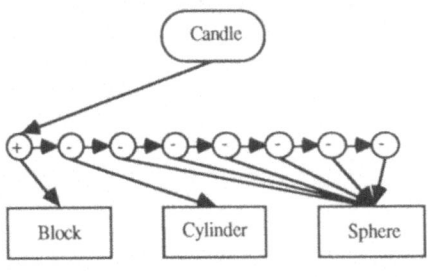

Fig. 1. CSG graph and image of a candle holder

Systems using the boundary representation will typically approximate higher order surfaces by polygons and then evaluate the Boolean expression on the polygons. Unfortunately, the accuracy of this approximation is poor unless a very large number of polygons is used. Further, while it is relatively easy to find the visible polygons, it is not straight forward to produce high quality images from polygonal data.

2. CURRENT METHODS OF CSG EVALUATION BY RAY INTERSECTION

Roth (1982) first proposed the use of ray tracing as a technique to evaluate and render CSG models. Ray tracing has the added advantage of being able to portray complicated effects such as reflections, refractions, and shadows, on a wide variety of geometries. On the other hand, ray tracing is infamous for the copious quantities of computing resources it can absorb. Roth examines several measures of the cost of ray tracing a CSG model and goes on to describe a method using bounding enclosures, boxes, to reduce these costs by about a factor of two. This use of bounding enclosures is a form of sorting which we will characterize as an object-based tree sort. The idea of partially sorting the objects in a model as a preprocessing step was first used by Whitted (1980); he used a sphere as an enclosure for each primitive.

Woodwark and Quinlan (1982) used a second form of sorting to improve the performance of ray casting on CSG models. The model is sorted, during visible surface determination, by subdividing space using a spatially-based tree sort. At each step in their algorithm, the model is subdivided by planes perpendicular to either the XY plane (which is parallel to the image plane) or the Z axis. The XY plane subdivisions form a quad-tree on the image plane and are used to solve for the visible surfaces in a manner similar to Warnock's (1969) visible surface algorithm. When the the cross-section of the front face a sub-space is about the size of a pixel, a ray is generated to evaluate the model for the pixel. Otherwise, the model is, after some pruning, subdivided perpendicular to the XY plane or perpendicular to the Z axis.

Woodwark and Quinlan report results showing performance in one case that is sub-linear in model complexity. However, their technique cannot be directly applied to ray tracing for several reasons; because, in ray tracing the model can be "viewed" by secondary rays coming from any point in any direction. First, subspaces and the surfaces contained therein cannot be discarded once visibility is determined. Since space is divided until sub-spaces are pixel sized, a large amount of memory would be required to store the entire tree. A second difficulty would be following a ray through the sub-space grid as it moves through space.

Bronsvoort, vanWijk and Jansen (1984) propose an alternative to the box enclosures described by Roth. They suggest the use of intervals enclosing each primitive along each scan line. Intervals for parts (composite objects by their terminology) are computed in a manner similar to box enclosures. They claim that the lengths of the intervals will usually be shorter than those of the original boxes and at worst will be the same. They also note that it is possible to simplify the CSG tree when objects pass out of the active interval list.

The fundamental problem with the interval approach, as with other schemes which use extents projected onto the image plane, is that for even moderately complex images far more secondary rays are fired than primary (viewing) rays. Consider a moderately complex image where every pixel is covered by an object and three light sources are used to illuminate the scene. In the simple case of point light sources three rays would be cast to the lights for each viewing ray. In our models with reflective and transparent objects it is common for the number of viewing rays to be less than 10% of the total number of rays fired. Since the intervals only provide help for the viewing rays, in these models we could achieve, at best, only a 10% time reduction.

Fujimoto, Perrot and Iwata (1986) and Wyvill, Kunii and Shirai (1986) have independently proposed similar solutions to the problem of ray tracing CSG models. Wyvill, et. al. use an oct-tree to subdivide space (a spatially-based tree sort), where Fujimoto, et. al. use a grid (spatially-based bucket sort). As a preprocessing step, both attempt to evaluate the CSG expression in as many cells as possible and where not possible, record reduced CSG expressions. During ray tracing, the ray is followed either through the oct-tree or through the grid until a surface of a solid object is found. A drawback to their approaches, as correctly noted by Wyvill, et. al., is the difficulty of determinating *a-priori* the grid size or subdivision level. Both papers show sets of results at various levels which vary by factors of 2 to 4 from their best.

Arnaldi, Priol, and Bouatouch (1987) offer a third method to divide space. They project each primitive's bounding box onto the image plane. Planes perpendicular to the image plane, each passing through one projected edge, are used to partition space into a BSP tree. The primitive bounding boxes are then projected onto the Z axis (perpendicular to the image plane) and the space is divided again. Since this results in an irregular partitioning of space, they use a set of pointers in four corners of each cell to point to adjacent cells. A ray can be followed through the cells by following the appropriate pointer. Their stepping algorithm visits extra cells which are not on the path of the ray, but it seems to be effective nevertheless. The work of Fujimoto, et. al., Wyvill, et. al., and Arnaldi, et. al. can be characterized as three dimensional extensions to the work of Woodwark and Quinlan.

In the remainder of this paper we develop and describe an alternative approach to fast ray tracing of unevaluated CSG models that makes use of nearly optimal object-based tree sorting. We also propose various criteria that allow early termination of CSG expression evaluation.

3.   CSG EVALUATION WITH AUXILIARY EXTENT TREES

Use of the modelling hierarchy to order primitive intersection testing seems to be a reasonable choice. Since the intersections are found in the same order as required for expression evaluation, it is not necessary to store the intervals of intersection for later evaluation. It is also possible to use information in the expression to reduce the amount of work required to evaluate it. Further, since the expressions use operators on objects which overlap in space (the difference and intersection operators) it can be assumed that the objects are close together in space. This assumption tends to be false for computer generated models or for models which have parts with very large numbers of children.

However, it is not necessary that the intersection tests be performed in the same order as the primitives are found in the expression, as long as the resulting intervals of intersection are stored with the primitives. Goldsmith and Salmon (1987) have proposed an algorithm which builds auxiliary trees for evaluated models so that the expected number of extent-ray intersections is minimized. Using their algorithm we can construct an auxiliary extent tree from the extents all of the primitives found in a model, for example see Fig. 2. This tree is then traversed for each ray and the resulting intersections stored with each primitive. Finally, the expression tree is traversed in order and evaluated on the stored results.

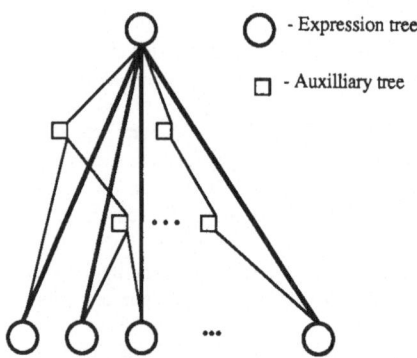

Fig. 2. Example Auxiliary Extent Tree with Expression Tree

Instead of building one large tree containing all of the primitives in a model, a smaller tree can be constructed for each part consisting of only the children of the part. In a sense it is a hybrid of Goldsmith and Salmon's and Roth's work; it uses the model to influence the shape of the intersection tree, but avoids the problem of a large number of children. To evaluate the model, the root part's auxiliary tree is intersected with a ray and the resulting intervals are stored in each primitive child hit by the ray. The algorithm is applied recursively for each non-primitive child hit, following the order in the expression. Results are combined as the recursion unfolds.

It is insightful to note that, in both Roth's method and the method described above, parts and primitives whose enclosures have been hit are tested for intersection with a ray regardless of the role they play in the expression. Further, all possible parts and primitives, whose enclosures have been hit, are tested for intersection, even if the expression degenerates to the "all union" case or in effect an evaluated model. We would like to be able to take advantage of the information in the expression to try to reduce the number of objects which we test for intersection with a ray.

3.1. Approximate Evaluation

We will now examine two further variations to the basic CSG evaluation method with the hope of avoiding some or all of the unnecessary part and primitive intersection tests. The methods proposed are based upon an extended usage of enclosures. First, a breadth first evaluation of the model is made on the enclosures to find an approximate solution. The approximate solution can then be used to exclude children from consideration during exact expression evaluation. Specifically, only those children in the approximate solution need be examined. It is also possible to determine when all of the operations in a part's expression reduce to the union operation, thereby allowing the possibility that only the front-most object needs to be found. (It is not necessarily sufficient to find only the front-most object even if a part's expression reduces to the all union operator case, see Section 3.2 for a full description.)

As in the previous two evaluation schemes, either a single tree can be built from all of the primitives (leaves of the expression tree) or a set of trees can be built, one for each part. In either case, when the traversal reaches a leaf of the extent tree only the enclosure is tested for intersection with the ray, not the primitive. When all of the extent tree leaves have been visited the expression is "evaluated" on the extent-ray intersection intervals, to give an approximate solution. The term evaluation is used loosely here, because the Boolean operators cannot be used directly on the enclosures. Rather, the interval of intersection of a ray and an enclosure is not modified, but is either added to or omitted from a list of output intervals depending on the operator and the position of the interval with respect to those intervals already on the output list.

The modified operators, for approximate evaluation on the enclosures of an expression, are defined as follows. The union (Boolean or) operator will always add a new interval to the output list. The difference operator (Boolean and not) will only add the subtrahend to the output list if it overlaps any other interval on the list. The intersection (Boolean and) operator will add a new interval to the output list if it overlaps any other interval on the list, and will remove any interval which does not overlap the new interval. Figure 3 indicates the results of the modified operators on various pairs of intervals.

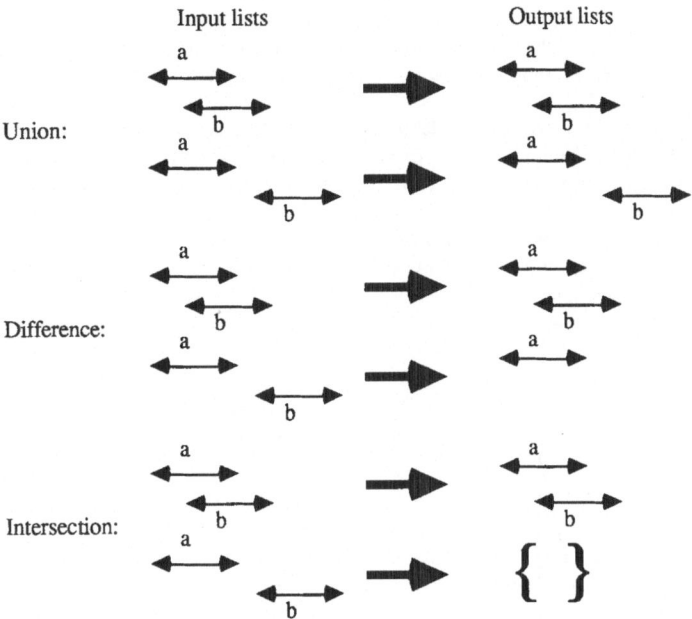

Fig. 3. Modified Boolean Operators

The rationale for the union operator is clear enough, but a comment about the other two operators is probably in order. The extent-ray intersection intervals are not clipped by the modified difference and intersection operators (as they would be by the actual Boolean operators), because the enclosures are only convex hulls around possibly non-convex objects. For example, the object-ray intersection interval of the minuend of a difference expression does not necessarily overlap the subtrahend, even if their enclosures overlap, as depicted in Fig. 4. The same argument holds for the Boolean intersection operator.

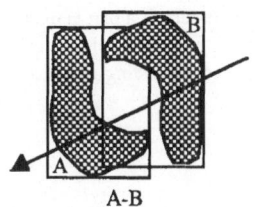

Fig. 4. Overlapping extents of non-overlapping objects

3.2. Stopping Rules

There are two additional rules which can be applied to further limit the number of parts and primitives tested for intersection. First, evaluation of a part can be halted at any point when the resulting set of intervals is empty and all children having the union operator have been processed. This is because, trailing children with the operations intersection and difference need not be considered when the running result becomes is empty. It is not atypical for a model to have these trailing children. The trailing children can be marked as such during preprocessing. Further, if the last child or children have the union operator, then it is possible to generate an equivalent part by creating a new parent whose children are the current part (without the trailing union'd children) and the trailing children. It should be noted that all of the operators in the new part will of the type union. This rule is a direct extension of Roth's "Early Outs" from a binary tree to a n-ary tree.

The second method is based on unevaluated model techniques. If all children of a part use only the union operator and if all children of all parts between the root of the model and the current part use only the union operator, then only the front most object need be found. The requirement for the current part to have all union operators is obvious. The direct ancestors of the part must have all union operators since some difference or intersection operator might affect the current part. For example, the two blocks shown in Fig. 5 are joined together in one part and a hole is removed from an ancestor part. It is clear that more than just the front object is required to accurately evaluate the expression.

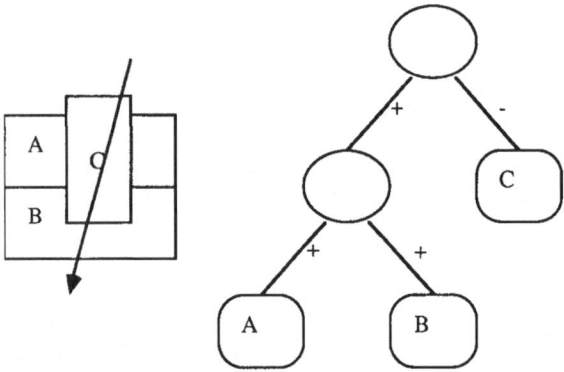

Fig. 5. All union part, (A-B), which needs full evaluation.

We have proposed four new ways to improve the performance of the ray tracing algorithm for CSG models. The first two apply Goldsmith and Salmon's ideas directly to either the entire model or to each part. The auxiliary tree is traversed to find object-ray intersections and then the model tree is traversed to evaluate the model. The second pair use auxiliary trees to find extent-ray intersections for either the entire model or on a part by part basis. An approximate evaluation of either the model or a part is made, and the results are used to guide object-ray intersection testing. Finally, the model or part is evaluated with the object-ray intersections. We have also proposed two rules for terminating the object-ray intersection testing and model (or part) evaluation.

4. RESULTS

We have run our algorithm on several sets of test models of increasing complexity. All results, unless otherwise stated, are for images computed at a resolution of 128 by 128 pixels on DEC VAXStation II running Ultrix 2.0 with nine megabytes of fast memory. Samples are taken at the corners of pixels and a simple box filter is applied to determine pixel colors. All comparisons are made on two algorithms. The first is a Roth style algorithm which has been used and constantly improved for about for about three years. The new algorithm has been implemented on top of the old Roth version. We have added extent trees to each part, approximate evaluation using the extent trees, and two early termination criteria.

4.1. Plate with Holes

The first set of models is composed of a thin plate with an increasing number of randomly placed holes. The holes are generated by subtracting cylinders from the plate. Figure 6 shows the sequence of images generated by varying the number of holes from 100 to 5000. Figure 7 is a graph of the CPU times required by each algorithm to render images of models with an increasing number of holes. Least-squares logarithmic approximations to the times for the initial and new algorithms are given by Equations (2) and (3),

$$t_R = 28.5h^{0.982}, \tag{2}$$

$$t_N = 9.03h^{0.768}, \tag{3}$$

where t_R is the time for the initial algorithm (Roth's), t_N is the time for the new algorithm, and h is the numbers of holes. This yields a speed up, of $S = 3.16h^{0.214}$ as shown in Fig. 8. The time for the new algorithm does not include the time to create the auxiliary trees. However, it is insignificant — it takes about 15 seconds to create the trees for the 5000 hole model, and has been shown by Goldsmith and Salmon to have asymptotic complexity of $O(n \log n)$.

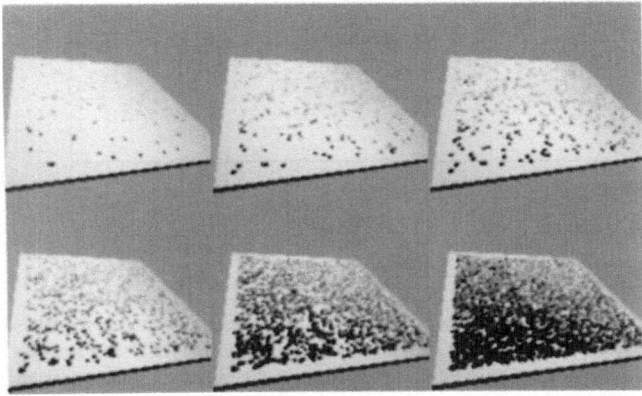

Fig. 6. Images of plate with holes

The other curves in Fig. 8 represent the decrease in extent and primitive intersection tests. Extent intersection tests, in the new algorithm, are decreased by 12 to 20 times from the original. Both algorithms use the same bounding volume — a box. It is probable that other bounding volumes would produce an even greater reduction. Primitive intersections are only slightly reduced, by a factor of 1.5 to 3. The reduction in primitive intersection tests is due to the early termination criteria. When these criteria are disabled the new algorithm test the same number of primitives as the original and runs 1.5 to 3 times slower.

The slight upturn in the t_N curve in Fig. 7 and corresponding dip in the curves in Fig. 8 above 1000 holes is attributable to the density of the subtracting cylinders, see Fig. 6. Because of the overlap of the bounding volumes, the trees generated are not as good. The curves in Fig. 9 are the expected and actual costs (number of bounding volume intersections per ray), for the model set. The decrease in the quality of the trees is evident. However, the

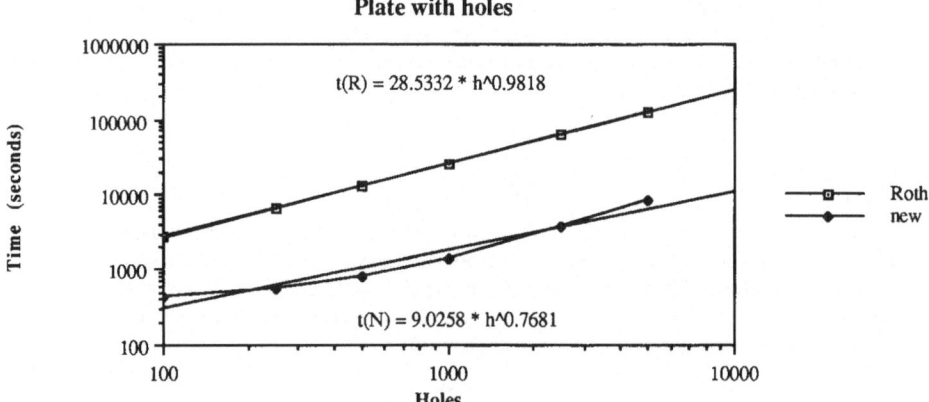

Fig. 7. CPU times for plate with holes

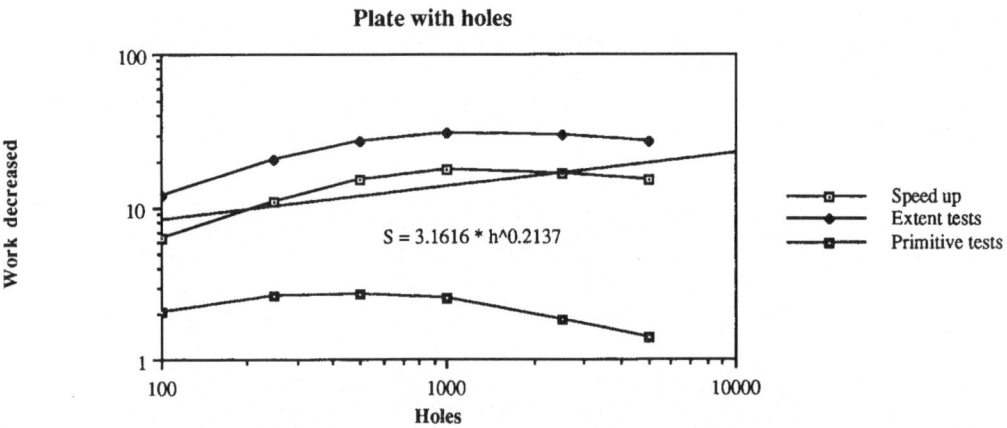

Fig. 8. Work decreased for plate with holes

tree quality can be improved with tighter bounding volumes, such as those proposed by Kay, and by computing several possible trees and choosing the best, as suggested by Goldsmith and Salmon. Yet, it is important to note that the new algorithm is still more than 10 times faster than the initial algorithm when there are over 1000 holes.

Figure 10 compares the number of extents (bounding volumes) tested by each algorithm. The curves are very similar to those for the total computation times seen in Fig. 7. This implies that the bounding volume intersection time dominates the primitive intersection time. Thus, it probably does not make sense to use a more complex bounding volume, unless it results in an overall reduction in the amount of time needed to intersect all bounding volumes in the model.

In Fig. 11, the extent efficiency of the algorithms is graphed as a function of the number of holes in the model. Extent efficiency is the ratio of extent hits to extent tests. The initial algorithm hits about 6% of the extents it tests when there are few holes and gets worse (down to about 2%) as the number of holes increases. Our new algorithm consistently hits about 55% of the extents it tests. This means that most of the work of excluding extent tests is done once as a preprocessing step in the new algorithm, but that original algorithm is doing most of the work for each ray.

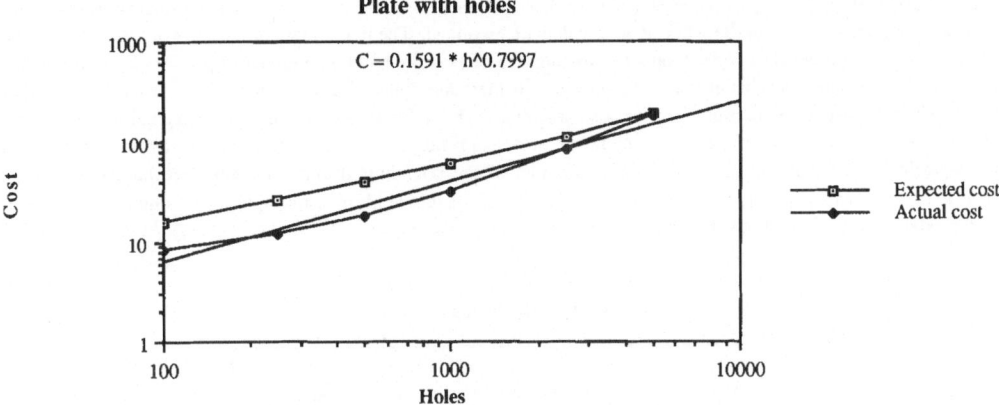

Fig. 9. Costs for plate with holes

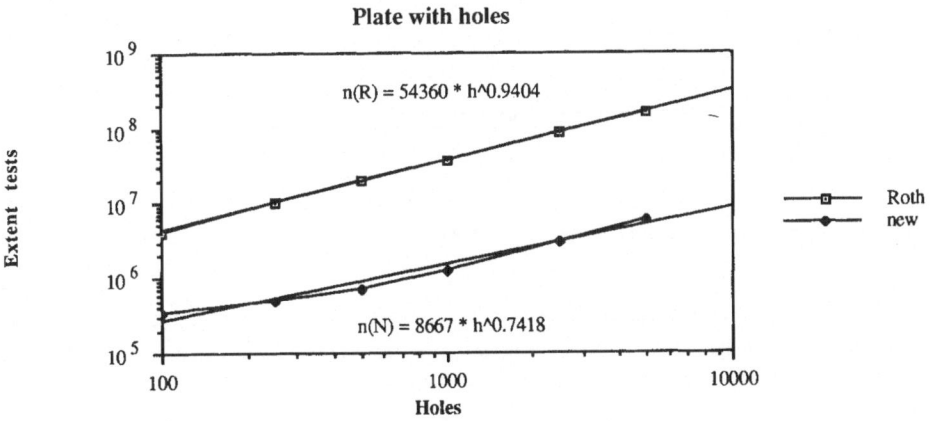

Fig. 10. Extent tests for plate with holes

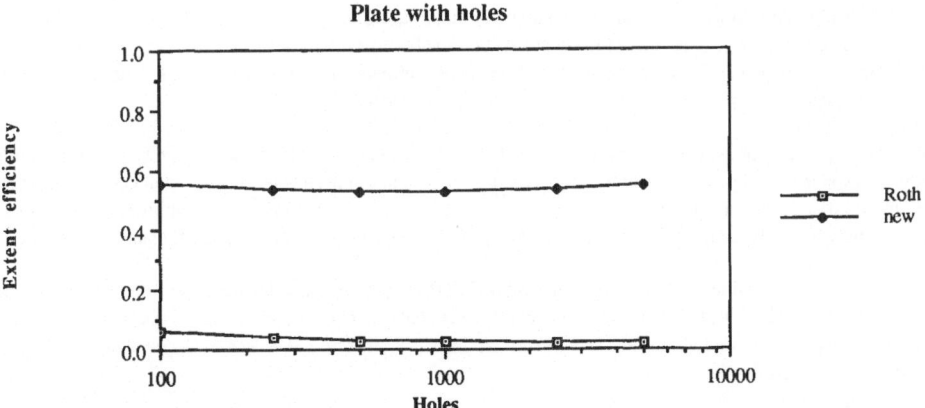

Fig. 11. Extent efficiency for plate with holes

If we assume that the Boolean evaluation does not take too much time, then we can use the number of intersections as an approximate measure of the work done to calculate an image. The maximum amount of work we would hope any algorithm would perform is the product of the number of rays fired and the number of primitives — in practice we would hope to do much better than this; however, if there are many extent-ray intersection tests, an algorithm may use more than the maximum. If we also assume, at least for this set of models, that bounding volume intersection tests require about the same amount of work as primitive intersection tests (boxes and cylinders), then we can calculate the amount of work done as the sum of the bounding volume and primitive intersection tests, because of the number of extent tests! Figure 12 is a graph of this work measure against the number of holes in each model in the set for both the original and new algorithms.

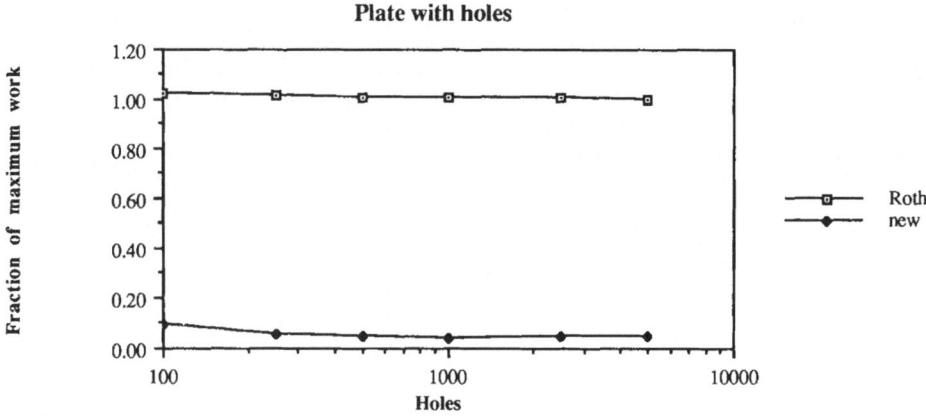

Fig. 12. Fraction of maximum work used for plate with holes

The original algorithm does almost exactly the maximum expected amount of work. The new algorithm performs between 10% and 4% of the maximum work. Thus, neglecting traversal and other computations, the new algorithm does about 10 to 20 times less work. This is consistent with the times presented above.

4.2. Anti-aliased Plate with Holes

The second series of results were taken from the same model, all with 1000 randomly placed holes, but at varying levels of anti-aliasing. Anti-aliasing is done by recursively subdividing pixels with too much intensity variation. Sub-pixels are treated similarly. The maximum depth of pixel subdivision was set to 0, 1, and 2 (a maximum of 4, 9, and 25 samples per pixel) for the three trials. The resulting images are shown in Fig. 13. Figure 14 shows the CPU time needed to compute an image at each of the three subdivision depths.

A performance improvement of about a factor of 15 is found; decreasing from about 17, when the maximum subdivision depth is 0, to about a factor of 12, at a depth of 2. While the performance improvement decreases as the maximum number of samples per pixel increases, based on the least-squares logarithmic approximation shown in Fig. 15, the new algorithm will still be approximately 7 times faster than the original at 200 samples per pixel.

The number of extents examined by the initial algorithm is 20 to 30 times greater than the new algorithm; 20 times at a depth of 0 and 30 times at a maximum depth of 2. The extent efficiency is very similar to the first set of models. It varies between about 2% and 3% in the initial algorithm and is nearly a constant 55% in the new algorithm, as shown in Fig. 16.

Examining the fraction of maximum work (as defined above), shown in Fig. 17, we see the original algorithm does approximately the maximum amount of work, while the new algorithm does between 3% and 7% of the maximum.

Fig. 13. Images of antialiased plate with holes

Antialiased plate with 1000 holes

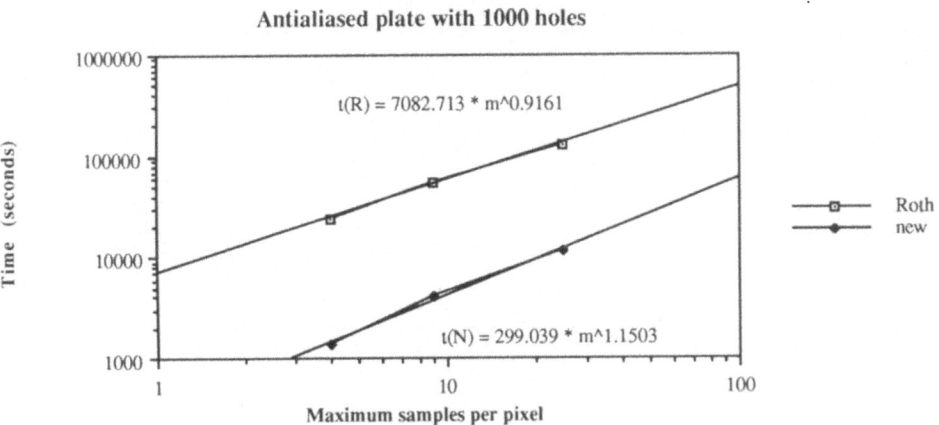

Fig. 14. CPU times for antialiased plate with holes

Antialiased plate with 1000 holes

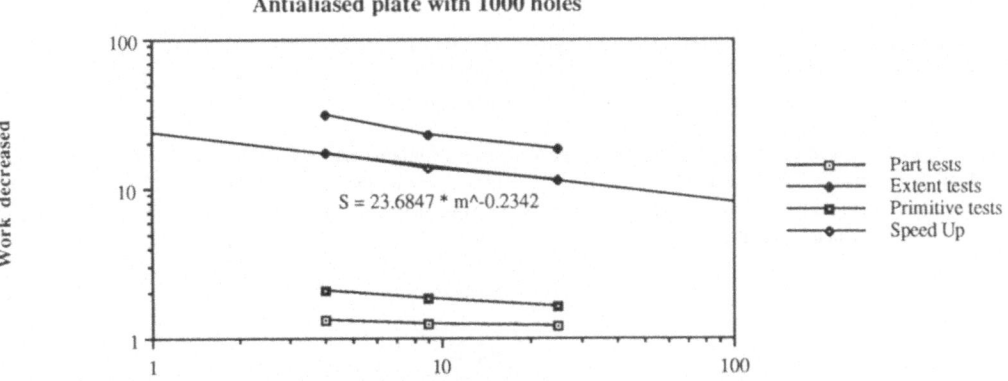

Fig. 15. Work decreased for antialiased plate with holes

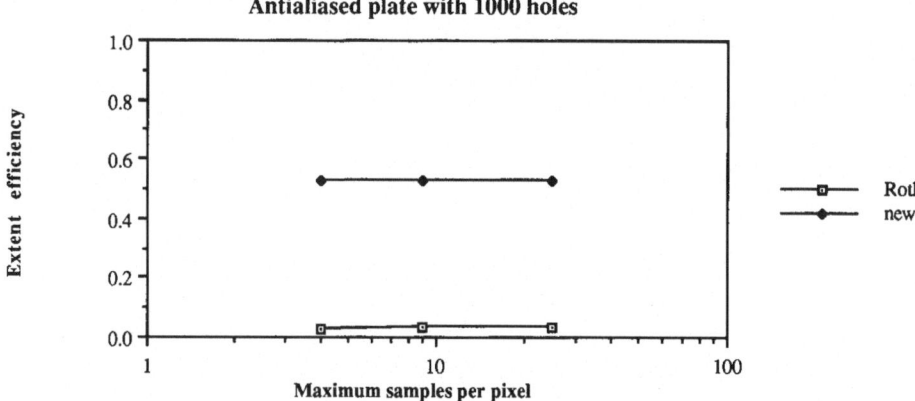

Fig. 16. Extent efficiency for antialiased plate with holes

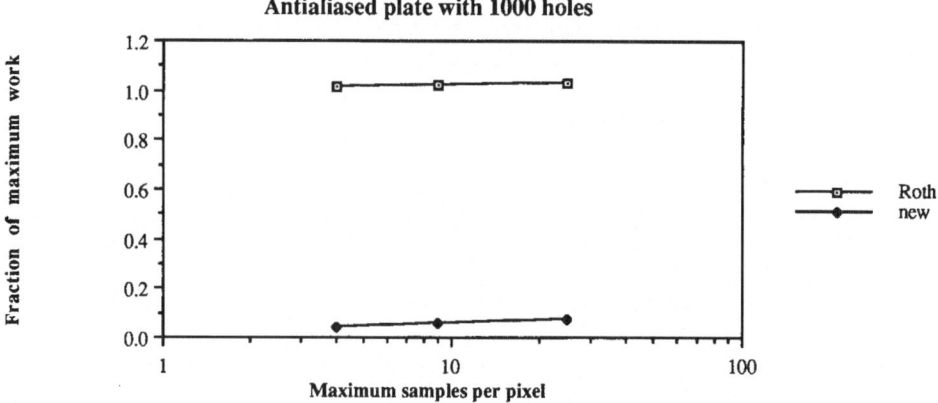

Fig. 17. Fraction of maximum work used for antialiased plate with holes

4.3. Randomly Placed Balls

The third model set consists of an increasing number of randomly placed balls, all combined with the Boolean union operator, see Fig. 18. This is essentially an evaluated model in the sense that no further Boolean evaluation is necessary and the front-most intersection is all that is required.

Figure 19 is a graph of the CPU time used to render the set of models by each algorithm. The curves are nearly identical to those in Fig. 7, especially for the new algorithm. Least-squares logarithmic approximations are given by Equations (4) and (5), where b is the number of balls. Note the exponents in Equations (3) from the first model set and (5) are nearly identical.

$$t_R = 5.16b^{1.14} \tag{4}$$

$$t_N = 6.78b^{0.78} \tag{5}$$

We can conclude that the new algorithm does equally well when there are many subtractions as when there are only unions, in which case the model need not be evaluated and only the front-most intersection is needed.

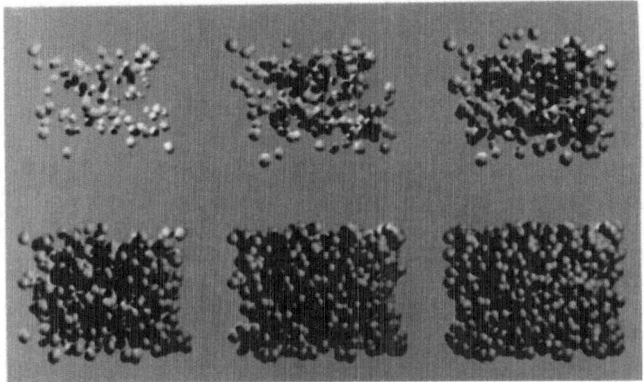

Fig. 18. Images of randomly placed balls

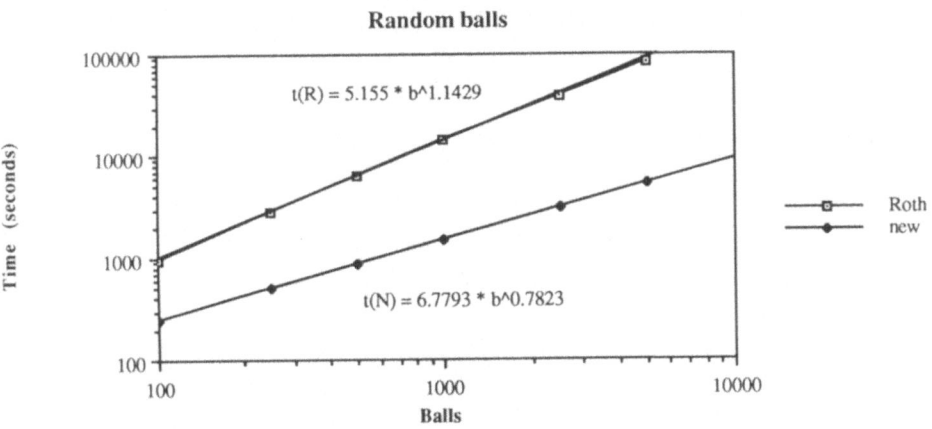

Fig. 19. CPU times for randomly placed balls

Unlike the first set of models, the speed up and decrease in the amount of work performed does not peak at about 1000 objects, as visible in Fig. 20. Rather, the benefit from the new algorithm continues to increase through all test cases. This is because of the early termination criteria; once the front-most object has been found the work stops. In the first set of models, it was necessary to find several or all of the subtractive objects.

The actual cost follows the expected cost quite closely, as shown in Fig. 21. The actual cost is somewhat less than expected because of the early terminations. The results depicted in Figs. 22 and 23 mirror those for the first of models, although the extent efficiency is slightly lower and the fraction of the maximum amount of work done is slightly higher (~35% and falling from ~15% to ~3% respectively).

5. CONCLUSIONS

We have presented a new, fast algorithm to ray trace unevaluated constructive solid geometry models. The algorithm uses auxiliary trees connecting each part to its children to reduce the number of extent-ray intersection tests. The trees are constructed in a fast preprocessing step, by minimizing the expected number of extent-ray intersections.

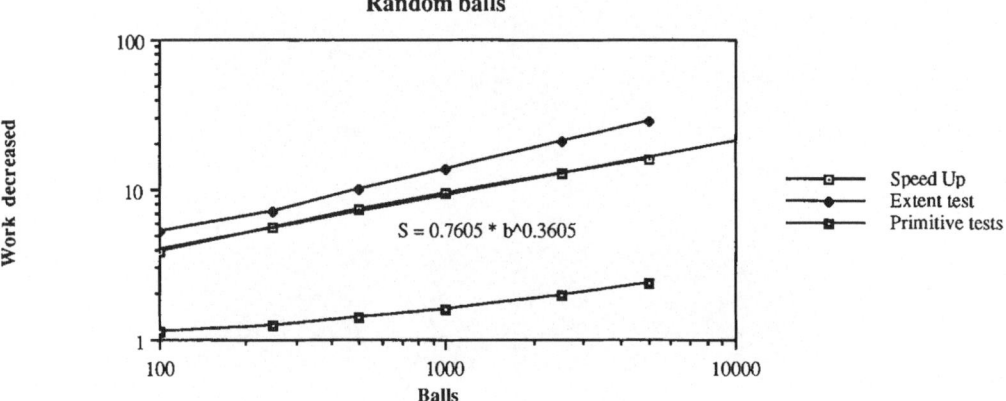

Fig. 20. Work decreased for randomly placed balls

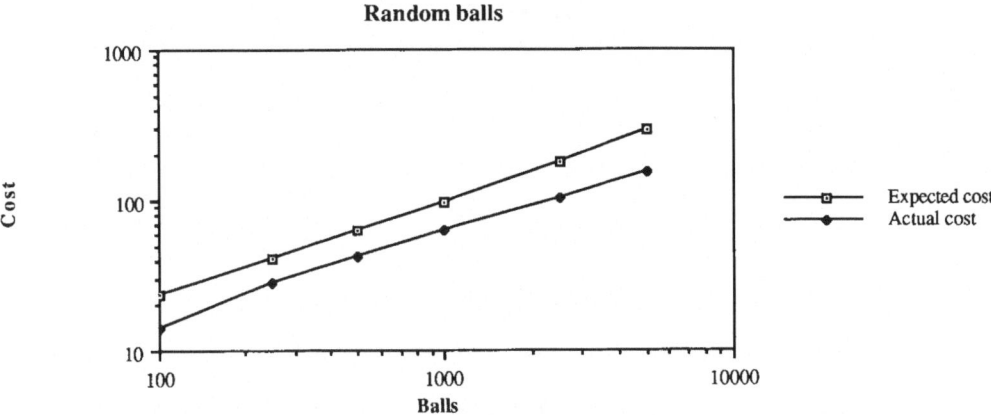

Fig. 21. Costs for randomly placed balls

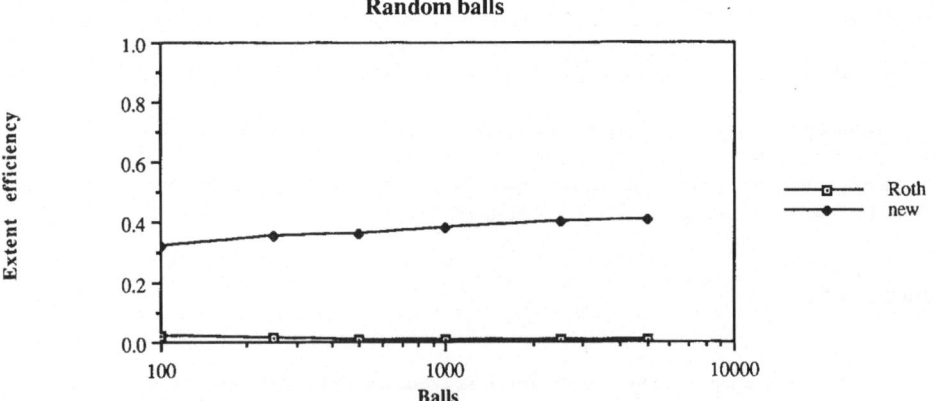

Fig. 22. Extent efficiency for randomly placed balls

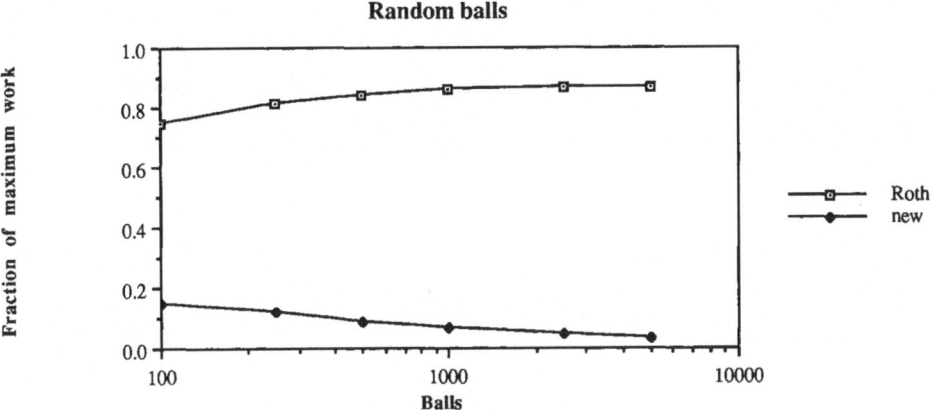

Fig. 23. Fraction of maximum work used for randomly placed balls

We have also presented two rules for stopping the evaluation early, when the result can be determined without evaluating the entire expression.

The new algorithm is approximately 10 times faster than Roth's original algorithm, including his use of bounding volumes. Alternatively, it is a reduction from approximately linear behavior in model complexity to about $x^{0.75}$, where x is the model complexity. This result holds for models which require expression evaluation as well as for models which are evaluated.

The reduction of the number of extents tested is 2 to 3 times greater than the reduction in time, i.e. the new algorithm tests 20 to 30 times less extents than does Roth's algorithm. If we were to use more complex bounding volumes, rather than the simple boxes used, this reduction would be of even greater importance.

The stopping rules reduce the number of primitives tested by a factor 1.5 to 3 from Roth. First, by detecting when the result of an expression will be the null set and stopping. Second, by detecting the degenerate all union operator case, the algorithm need only look for the front-most surface and can stop when it is found, without fully evaluating the expression.

Our results compare favorably with other published work by Fujimoto, et. al., Wyvil, et. al., and Amaldi, et. al.. However, since our algorithm uses object-based sorting rather than space-based sorting, such as grids or oct-trees, we do not have the problem of *a-priori* needing to determine a global subdivision level. Therefore we do not have the wide variation of results for a single model as in algorithms using space based sorting, such as Wyvil, et. al.. Further, while we have not examined it in detail, general consensus holds that space-based sorting data structures, such as grids and oct-trees, use far more storage than object-based structures. Therefore, we feel that object-based techniques work at least as well as space-based techniques and probably enjoy an advantage in the amount of storage required.

REFERENCES

Amaldi B, Priol T, Bouatouch K (1987) A new space subdivision method for ray tracing CSG modelled scenes. Visual Computer 3:98-108.

Bronsvoort W, van Wijk JJ, Jansen FW (1984) Two methods for improving the efficiency of ray casting in solid modelling. CAD 16(1):51-55.

Fujimoto A, Perrot CG, Iwata K (1986) Environment for Fast Elaboration of Constructive Solid Geometry. In: Kunii TL (ed) Advanced Computer Graphics. Springer-Verlag, Tokyo, pp 20-33.

Goldsmith J, Salmon J (1987) Automatic creation of object hierarchies for ray tracing. IEEE CG & A 7(5):14-20.

Kay TL, Kajiya JT (1986) Ray Tracing Complex Scenes. Computer Graphics 20(4):269-278.

Roth SD (1984) Ray Casting for Modeling Solids. CG & IP 18:109-144.

Warnock JE (1969) A Hidden-Surface Algorithm for Computer-Generated Halftone Pictures. Computer Science Department, University of Utah, TR 4-15, UT, 1969.

Watkins JS (1970) A Real-Time Visible Surface Algorithm. Computer Science Department, University of Utah, UTECH-CSC-70-101, 1970.

Weghorst H, Hooper G, Greenberg DP (1984) Improved Computational Methods for Ray Tracing. ACM TOG 3 (1):52-69.

Whitted T (1980) An Improved Illumination Model for Shaded Display. Comm. ACM 23(6):343-349.

Woodwark JR, Quinlan KM (1982) Reducing the effect of complexity on volume model evaluation. CAD 14 (2): 89-95.

Wyvil G, Kunii TL, Shirai Y (1986) Space Division for Ray Tracing in CSG. IEEE CG & A 6(4):28-34.

Philllip H. Getto is a research engineer with the Rensselaer Polytechnic Institute, where he is co-leader of the Visual Simulation Project in the Rensselaer Design Research Center. His research interests focus on realistic image synthesis, computational geometry, object-oriented computer graphics and user interface design. Getto is currently a PhD candidate in the Department of Electrical, Computer and Systems Engineering at Rensselaer. He has recieved a BS and ME in computer and systems engineering from Rensselaer. Getto is a member of the IEEE, IEEE Computer Society, the ACM and ACM Siggraph, and Computer Professionals for Social Responsibility.

The author can be reached at Rensselaer Design Research Center, Rensselaer Polytechnic Institute, G. M. Low Center for Industrial Inovation, Room 7015, Troy, New York, 12180-3590, USA, or by electronic mail at phil@rdrc.rpi.edu.

Fast Antialiasing of Ray Traced Images

G. Wyvill and P. Sharp

Abstract

The best way to antialias an image is by prefiltering. But for many ray traced images, there is no adequate description of the ideal image to filter. The only information you have is the sample points. We present an efficient algorithm for antialiasing in these cases.

Keywords: Antialiasing, CAD, CSG, Geometric modelling, Ray tracing.

Introduction

For the last three years, most of our experimental work in computer graphics at the University of Otago has explored problems associated with solid modelling by constructive solid geometry (CSG). In particular, we have been trying to improve the speed and quality of direct rendering from solid models. In a CSG system, all objects are treated as sets of points in three dimensions. Objects are built by combining simpler objects, and since the objects are sets, the combining operators are the ordinary operations of set theory. Ultimately, the simplest objects are mathematical functions that are represented in the computer by procedures. Our experimental system, Katachi, is structured so that these primitive objects can be written to order and included in the system according to a standard procedure interface (Wyvill 1985, 1986).

Katachi generates high quality images by ray tracing directly from the solid models (Roth 1982). No geometric approximation is needed and Katachi does not support polygon or spline-based surface models at all. Because of the very general nature of our primitives, a ray tracer can be written independently and several have been (Brown 1987).

A ray tracer of this kind has one disadvantage. It has no inherent knowledge of the image it is creating. The only information for building the image is a colour value at each sample point associated with a primary ray from the eye point. Because of this, aliasing is a problem. Until recently, we have been using supersampling to alleviate this problem but this is expensive. Using the algorithm presented here, we generate excellent antialiased pictures at a cost of only fifty percent above the time for unantialiased images.

Aliasing and filtering

The real cause of aliasing is that a pixel image consists of samples of an original image. An original image that contains sharp edges or small repeating patterns is said to exhibit a high frequency of spatial change. If the highest frequency in the picture is comparable with the pixel density, then aliasing artifacts will appear.

From this point of view, the only way to handle the problem properly is to filter the original image to remove these high components of spatial frequency. This is discussed in Fujimoto (1983, 1985, 1986), Catmull(1978) and especially, Lobb (1987).

We can prefilter an image if we have a reasonable, mathematical description of it. We can design the filter to suit the resolution of our screen, and when we sample the filtered image, aliasing cannot occur. Abram (1985) uses an approximate method for polygon filtering where simple cases are handled by a precomputed filter function and more complicated cases are combined using a bit mask. Lobb (1987) tells us how to construct a filtered image from *any* original composed of polygons, by providing an exact decomposition of Abram's 'more complicated' cases. Similarly, by using beam or cone tracing (Heckbert 1984, Amanatides 1984), we can establish an exact description of part of an image and filter that.

The problem with our ray traced images is that the only way we have to generate them is by ray tracing. The samples constitute the whole of our knowledge of the image and we can never be certain that we have eliminated aliasing. For this reason, we must be satisfied with an ad hoc approach that improves the picture and eliminates the most obvious artifacts.

Cone tracing and ray bounding

The technique of cone tracing (Amanatides 1984), provides an estimate of the proportion of each pixel's area that is coloured by a particular object. Where there is only partial coverage, a new cone is generated with an appropriate area and spread angle. The main disadvantage is that the intersection calculations become more complicated. Solutions are described for the case of spheres and polygons. We see no simple way to extend this approach to the very complicated edges produced by our CSG interaction.

Ray bounding is a technique proposed by Ohta (1988). A cone is treated as a bounding volume for a bundle of rays. By performing exact intersections with the cone and primitive objects, he determines that some pixels will definitely not require antialiasing. For other pixels, further cones can be cast. The method is almost ideal, in principle, but as yet it has been demonstrated only with spherical and ellipsoidal primitives.

Supersampling

One popular way to reduce the most obvious effects of aliasing is to increase the sampling frequency. In context, this means that we cast many rays for each pixel and average the results to get a brightness or colour for that pixel. This reduces the effect of jagged lines on straight edges, and in the case of stochastic sampling (Mitchell 1986, Cook 1986), even hides moiré fringes to some extent. Unfortunately, the cost of supersampling is very high. This is true even if we only supersample pixels in the areas of sharp change (Whitted 1980).

One reason for this high cost is that far more rays are needed than at first appears necessary. This is illustrated in Figure 1 where three adjacent pixels are represented with an edge crossing them. Each pixel is divided into nine sub-pixels so there are ten possible ratios of colour available and it would be reasonable to expect a nearly horizontal edge to produce a succession of pixels changing intensity in small steps. But the edge shown causes a jump in covering ratio from three to six, resulting in an overlarge change and a jagged line. Because of this effect, a pixel must be divided into about eight by eight sub-pixels to eliminate jags on some lines.

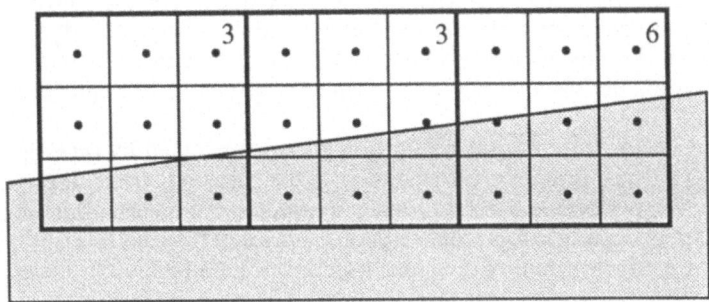

Figure 1: Failure of supersampling. Dots show sample points.

Fujimoto's method

Fujimoto (1985) described a better approach to handling jagged edges by estimating the distance of an edge from the centre of the pixel. First he detects an edge because adjacent pixels have different values. Then he determines whether the edge is more nearly horizontal or vertical. This can require casting an additional ray. Then, by casting extra rays he finds the distance of the edge, vertically or horizontally, from the pixel centre by binary search. This is illustrated in Figure 2 for the case of a near vertical edge.

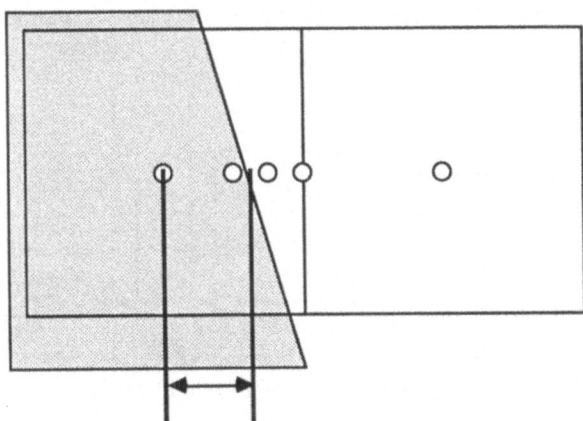

Figure 2: Estimate of distance of an edge from pixel centre.

The distance from the edge, coupled with a rough knowledge of the edge direction, is enough to enable a crude estimate of the area of that pixel inside the edge. The cost is up to four rays per pixel in the vicinity of edges. Fujimoto says nothing about the more complex cases, where several edges meet.

The algorithm

Our algorithm uses two central ideas: Firstly, we assume that the image is coherent in the sense that a region that shows no sudden changes of colour will not require antialiasing. This simplifies the problem but it also makes the solution less general. Ideally, we would prefer to have some better knowledge as to where antialiasing is necessary, but we are dealing with cases where the point samples constitute our whole knowledge of the picture. Secondly, we attach more importance to the removal of jagged edges than to other peculiar effects. We are taking advantage of the fact that most of our pictures are of simple engineering objects and will not contain delicate details like hairs or grassblades.

We define an image with m rows of n pixels to be represented by $(m+1)(n+1)$ primary ray samples. This means that we cast four rays at the corners of each pixel rather than one in the centre. We perform sub-pixel analysis by finding the places where edges cross the border of the rectangle that represents a pixel, and we define the *level* of antialiasing as the maximum number of binary divisions used to locate an edge. So if the *level* is zero, there will be no sub-pixel analysis, and the edge is assumed to pass through the centre of one or more sides of the pixel. Even in this case, the result is better than with no antialiasing.

There is a certain logic to the idea of casting rays at the corners of the pixels. It means that without subdivision, any horizontal or vertical edge will be represented by two brightness changes rather than one. In a conventional unantialiased, ray traced image, diagonal jagged lines are evidence of error. But the error is also present in horizontal and vertical lines. Instead of looking jagged, they are constrained to sit on an exact pixel boundary. In our *level zero* images, the edge sits between two rays and the pixel has an intermediate colour.

If the brightness of two adjacent rays is sufficiently different, we must cast additional rays. A ray is cast halfway between the pair, and this process is repeated recursively to identify where on the pixel boundary an edge crosses. At *level* three, each edge is located to within one eighth of the pixel side. With this information, we can estimate the area of the pixel covered by each colour.

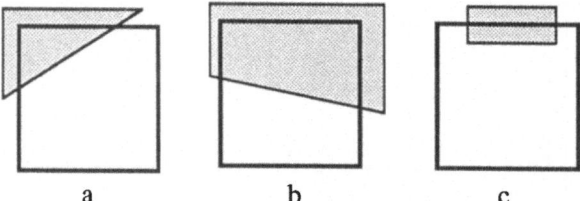

Figure 3: Single edge and pixel.

Consider firstly, the situation where there is a single edge intersecting the pixel. If we assume that the edge is approximately straight within the pixel, we can easily calculate the area of each colour by simple geometry. There are three cases (Figure 3). In case (a), the area of the triangle in the corner of the pixel is used as a weight; in (b), we take the area of the trapezium; and in (c), we regard the shaded area as just grazing the pixel and ignore it.

When the binary search reveals more than one edge in a pixel, the analysis becomes more complicated. Take, for example, the two pixels represented in Figure 4. Examination of the edges of the pixels (thick rectangles) reveals that exactly the same colour information is detected by our binary search, for two very different cases.

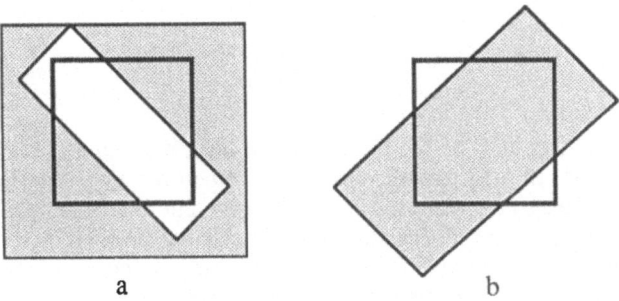

a   b

Figure 4: Ambiguous edges.

This is because we are looking only at the edges of the pixel. To resolve this ambiguity, we would need to examine more rays over the area of the pixel, and the cost would rise again. Cases like this occur in practice when more than two areas of colour meet, or nearly meet, at an isolated point. We contend that, in these cases, the exact colour of the pixel where they meet is unimportant. The eye picks out some sort of an apex and this is good enough.

We require, therefore, a simple rule that will yield the areas of Figure 3 and still give a reasonable result in the more complicated cases. This is shown in Figure 5. From the binary search, we get a number of points on the pixel boundary where the colour changes. Between each pair of adjacent points is a boundary segment all of one colour. We define the point, m, to be the centroid of these points of colour change. That is, for n points: p_1, $p_2 \cdots p_n$

$$m_x = \frac{1}{n}\sum_{i=1}^{n} p_{i_x} \quad \text{and} \quad m_y = \frac{1}{n}\sum_{i=1}^{n} p_{i_y}$$

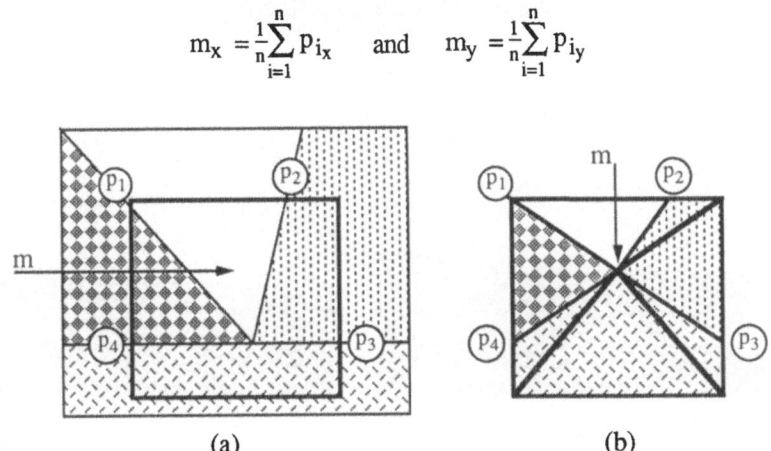

(a)   (b)

Figure 5: Many areas meet in one pixel.

We then treat the pixel as if the various colour areas meet at m. The area of each colour is easily calculated as the sum of up to four triangles. A sample triangulation is shown in Figure 5(b). Of course, this is not the true area covered, but it is a useful approximation. Where only one straight edge intersects the pixel, the centroid of the entry and exit points lies on the edge, so the same process reduces to the simpler case.

Sample results

Figure 6 shows an edge at 4° to the horizontal. In 6(a), it is not antialiased and shows an obvious jagged edge. In 6(b), antialiasing is performed by supersampling, using a 4 x 4 grid. Our ray tracer uses edge-following to reduce the number of rays cast (Wyvill 1987), and because of this, the cost of this supersampling is between eight and twelve rays per pixel rather than sixteen. Figure 6(c) shows the same edge antialiased with the new algorithm at level three. The cost here is three rays per pixel. To show better the difference between 6(b) and 6(c), we have magnified the pixels, artificially, to produce Figure 7. Notice that in 7(c), each successive pixel along the line has a different shade produced by our algorithm. This is as close to ideal as can be achieved with the given pixel density. By contrast, the supersampled edge changes brightness irregularly. This produces a slightly wavy appearance.

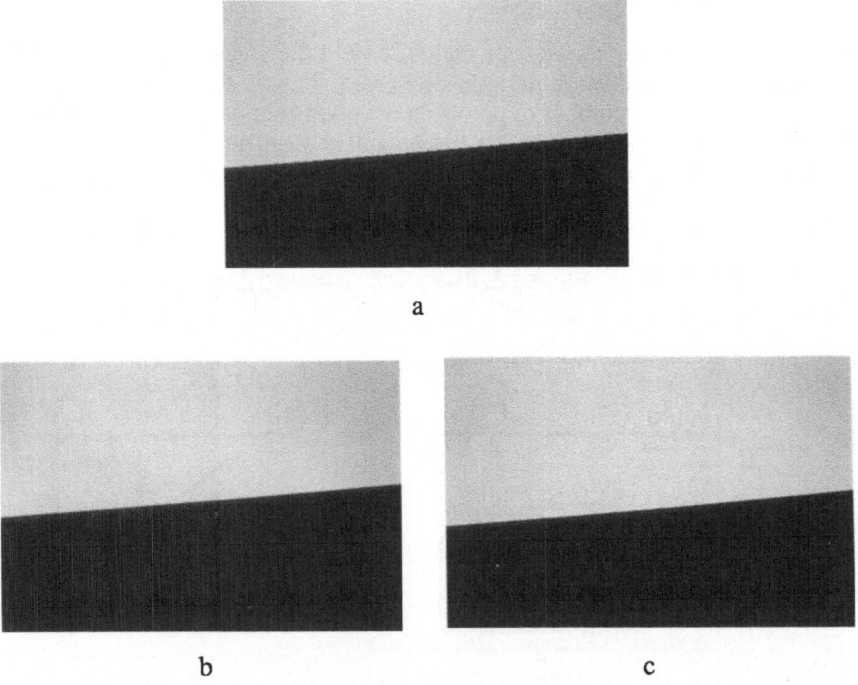

a

b   c

Figure 6:   4° edge, unantialiased (a), supersampled (b), with new algorithm (c).

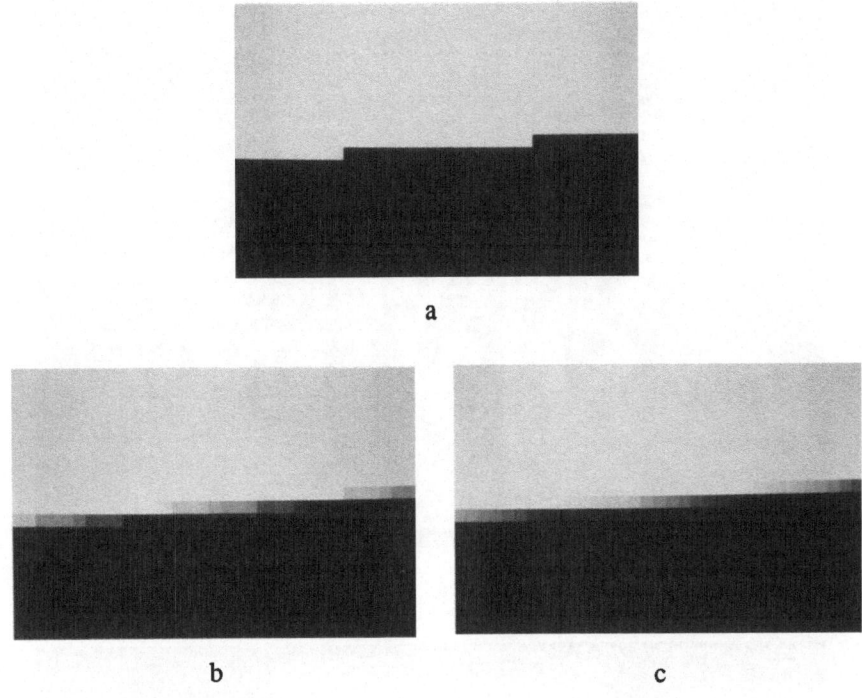

a

b   c

Figure 7:   Magnified 4° edge, unantialiased (a), supersampled (b), with new
            algorithm (c).

Figure 8 shows a frame from a recent animation made with the Katachi system. 8(a) is
supersampled using a 3 x 3 grid and 8(b) uses the new algorithm at level 3. The number of
primary rays cast is 1,274,883 for 8(a) and 426,868 for 8(b).

Conclusion

By locating the places where edges in an image intersect pixel boundaries we can antialias
images produced by ray tracing. Our algorithm is robust and produces results
demonstrably better than those made by supersampling and at a fraction of the cost. This,
together with our edge-following ray tracer (Wyvill 1987), has enabled us to produce
high quality ray traced animation without using supercomputers or specialised parallel
hardware.

The method, as it stands, is not suitable for images containing very small details or certain
textures. It should, however, be possible to handle such textures because a texture function
contains implicit knowledge of its spatial frequencies. We are currently investigating
ways to make fine texture functions self-filtering, so they can be used with this renderer.

a

b

Figure 8: Opening titles of *University Challenge* (courtesy of TVNZ)

Acknowledgements

The computer graphics project at Otago has been jointly funded by Otago University and the University Grants Committee. Our thanks also go to Television New Zealand for loan of equipment and studio time.

References

Abram, G., Westover, L. and Whitted, T. 1985: Efficient Alias-free Rendering using Bit-masks and Look-up Tables, *Computer Graphics* (Proc. SIGGRAPH 1985), Vol. 19, No. 3, 53-59

Amanatides, J. 1984: Ray Tracing With Cones, *Computer Graphics* (Proc. SIGGRAPH 1984), Vol. 18, No. 3, 129-135

Brown, T. 1987: Efficient Ray Tracing of Solid Models, *MSc thesis,* University of Otago

Catmull, E. 1978: A Hidden Surface Algorithm with Anti-aliasing, *Computer Graphics* (Proc. SIGGRAPH 1978) Vol. 12, No. 3, 6-11

Cook, R. L. 1986: Stochastic Sampling in Computer Graphics, *ACM Trans. on Graphics* Vol. 5, No. 1

Fujimoto, A. and Iwata, K. 1983: Jag-Free Images on Raster Displays, *IEEE CG&A,* Vol. 3, No. 9, 26-34

Fujimoto, A. and Iwata, K. 1985: Accelerated Ray Tracing, *Computer Graphics Visual Technology and Art* (Proc. of CG Tokyo '85), 41-65

Fujimoto, A., Tanaka, T. and Iwata, K. 1986: ARTS: Accelerated Ray Tracing System, *IEEE CG&A,* Vol. 6, No. 4, 16-26

Heckbert, P. S. and Hanrahan P. 1984: Beam Tracing Polygonal Objects, *Computer Graphics* (Proc. SIGGRAPH 1984) Vol. 18, No. 3, 119-127

Lobb, R. 1987: Antialiasing of Polygons with a Weighted Filter, *Computer Graphics 1987* (Proc. CG International '87, Karuizawa), 109-127

Mitchell, D.P. 1986: Generating Antialiased Images at Low Sampling Densities, *Computer Graphics* (Proc. SIGGRAPH '86), Vol. 21, No. 4, 65-72

Ohta, M. 1988: Ray Bounding for Perfectly Efficient Antialiasing, (in press)

Roth, S. D. 1982: Ray Casting for Modeling Solids, *Computer Graphics and Image Processing,* Vol. 18, 109-144

Whitted, T. 1980: An Improved Illumination Model for Shaded Display, *Comm. ACM,* Vol. 23, No. 6, 343-349

Wyvill, G. and Kunii, T. L. 1985: A functional model for constructive solid geometry, *The Visual Computer,* Vol. 1, No. 1, 3-14

Wyvill, G., Kunii, T. L. and Shirai, Y. 1986: Space Division for Ray Tracing in CSG, *IEEE CG&A,* Vol. 6, No. 4, 28-34

Wyvill, G., Ward, A. and Brown, T. 1987: Sketches by Ray Tracing, *Computer Graphics 1987* (Proc. CG International '87, Karuizawa), 315-333

Geoff Wyvill graduated in physics from Jesus College, Oxford, and started working with computers as a research technologist with the British Petroleum Company. He gained MSc and PhD degrees in computer science from the University of Bradford where he lectured in computer science from 1969 until 1978. He is currently senior lecturer in computer science at the University of Otago. He is on the editorial board of The Visual Computer and a member of ACM, SIGGRAPH and NZCS.

Address: Department of Computer Science
University of Otago Box 56
Dunedin, New Zealand

Paul Sharp is a graduate student at Otago University. His research interests include constructive solid geometry and computer animation. He received his BSc degree in computer science in 1987, having also completed a degree in architecture at Auckland University in 1985. He is a student member of ACM.

Address: Department of Computer Science
University of Otago Box 56
Dunedin, New Zealand

Chapter 10
Rendering

A Fast Hidden Line Removal Algorithm

J. Zhang

ABSTRACT

A new and fast hidden line removal algorithm is presented, which detects boundary and contour edges for general scenes made of planar faces, and applies an area subdivision technique similar to Franklin's (1980) to obtain the linear time performance. A method for re-ordering edge sequences of faces for general scenes is introduced to define the orientations of face normals for easy detection of contour edges. Only visible and partially visible boundary and contour edges are considered for calculation of intersections with other edges. The algorithm usually runs three or more times faster than the version without boundary and contour edge detection.

Keywords: hidden line removal, boundary and contour edge detection, area subdivision

1. INTRODUCTION

The problem of hidden-line removal is one of the basic problems that have been addressed in three-dimensional computer graphics generation. Many algorithms have been developed to cope with the problem, with continuing attempts to reduce the computing time for image generation (Roberts 1963; Appel 1966; Galimberti and Montanari 1969; Loutrel 1970; Franklin 1980).

Consider a collection of planar faces, possibly with holes, in a scene. The purpose of a general hidden-line removal algorithm is to generate and plot those edge segments of faces visible from a given view point. An easy solution to the problem, developed by Roberts (1963), compares edges to faces. For each edge, it considers all faces to see if they hide it. Hidden portions of the edge are removed gradually, the remaining ones at the final stage are those visible from the view point. This solution is conceptually clear but extremely slow due to its time complexity of $O(n^2)$.

Since for solid objects only contour edges, where two faces meet and one hides the other, can change the visibility of edges, Appel (1966) developed an algorithm which only compares contour edges to each edge, and calculates intersections between them. This method finds the numbers of faces hiding each edge, or edge segment cut by contour edges, by calculating initial ones and then propagating them along the connected edges. This method has a much better time performance, but still suffers from the inefficiency in calculating edge intersections etc. Another drawback is that only solid objects are dealt with in the algorithm.

Franklin (1980) developed a linear time expected approach, based on an area subdivision technique. A grid of cells with the size of the order of an edge in the scene is overlaid on the screen. At each cell the algorithm looks for a covering face (if any) and determines which edges are in front of this face. It then computes the intersections of these edges and determines their visibility. The main advantage of this approach is that edges are handled locally within a cell, which avoids global searching on all the edges in the scene. However, since arbitrary scenes made of planar faces are handled, no attempt is made to detect contour edge and boundary edges (where one or more than two faces meet) for efficient treatment.

This paper presents a new hidden line removal algorithm, which detects boundary and contour edges for general scenes made of planar faces, and applies a picture cell subdivision technique similar to Franklin's to obtain the linear time performance. A method for examining and re-ordering edge sequences of faces for general scenes is introduced to define the orientations of face normals for easy detection of contour edges. Only visible or partially visible boundary and contour edges are considered for calculation of intersections with other edges. The new algorithm usually runs three or more times faster than the version without boundary and contour edge dectection.

2. THE ALGORITHM

The algorithm is designed to eliminate hidden portions of edges for any 3-D objects in a scene made of planar faces. Objects in the scene are not necessarily solid ones, and surfaces made of a number of connected planar faces without forming any solid objects are also dealt with. Faces in the scene are first searched to establish the connectivity information between edges and faces. Boundary edges which connect to one or more than two faces are then detected. For each surface made of planar faces connected to each other through their non-boundary edges, edges within these faces are re-ordered in a consistent way such that edge sequences define orientations of face normals. Contour edges can easily be found by examining normals of two adjacent faces against the view point.

After projecting all the faces onto a picture plane defined by a given view point, the picture plane is divided into a grid of rectangular cells. The number of cells is chosen to be of the order of that of edges in the scene. Faces and boundary/contour edges are then distributed into cells such that $cell_y$ consists of indices of faces and boundary/contour edges whose extents intersect $cell_y$.

Since only visible or partially visible boundary/contour edges can change the visibility of edges, the algorithm first deals with all the boundary/contour edges in the scene to find their visible segments. Those boundary/contour edges which are entirely invisible from the viewer are no longer used to calculate edge intersections when detecting the visibility of the other edges.

When detecting the visibility of an edge, all the boundary/contour edges (excluding those detected to be entirely invisible from the view point) whose extents intersect the cells intersected by the extent of the edge, are considered for the calculation of edge intersections. For each segment of the edge between two subsequent intersections, the algorithm examines all the faces whose extents intersect the cell holding the middle point of the edge segment, to determine its visibility. Since intersections between interior edges (i.e., non-boundary/contour edges) are not calculated, it reduces the computing time greatly for normal scenes where most edges are interior edges. In addition, distribution of faces and boundary/contour edges into cells enables fast access to the data on a cell by cell basis.

The layout of the algorithm is then summarized as follows.

1. Read in the representation of a scene: planar faces, edges, and vertex co-ordinates, etc.
2. Find the connectivity information and determine boundary edges.
3. Re-order edge sequences of faces by using the connectivity and boundary edge information.
4. Calculate normals of faces and determine contour edges.
5. Project the scene onto a picture plane.
6. Distribute faces and boundary/contour edges respectively into cells.
7. Hidden-line elimination for boundary/contour edges.
8. Hidden-line elimination for other edges.

The sub-algorithm to eliminate hidden portions of an edge is then described:

1. For a given edge, determine the cells intersected by the extent of the edge.
2. Find intersections between the edge and the other boundary/contour edges whose extents intersect the cells (if any), excluding those which have been detected to be entirely invisible from the viewer.
3. Determine the visibility of each edge segment between two adjacent intersections (or the entire edge if there is no intersection) by considering all the faces whose extents intersect the cell holding the middle point of the edge segment.

The following sub-sections discuss each step of the algorithm in detail.

2.1 Data Structure

Suppose a scene to be dealt with has *nface* planar faces, *nedge* edges, and *nvertex* vertices. The representation of the scene is first read and then stored into corresponding data structures.

Two arrays *face*[1:*nface*+1] and *face_edge*[1:*mface*] are used to store faces so that the *i*th face has the number of edges = *face*[*i*+1]-*face*[*i*], and the *j*th edge of the face has the edge number *face_edge*[*face*[*i*]+*j*-1], where *mface* is a constant greater than the total occurrences of all the edges in the scene.

An array *edge*[1:*nedge*,1:2] is used to store edges such that *edge*[*i*,1] and *edge*[*i*,2] give indices of the two vertices of edge *i*. In addition, three arrays of *x*[1:*nvertex*], *y*[1:*nvertex*], and *z*[1:nvertex] are used to store x,y and z co-ordinates of vertices respectively.

A planar face may have holes. A face without a hole is a single polygon. A face with holes is expressed as a number of polygons such that the first one is the main polygon and the others are holes inside it. It is only required that the edges of the main polygon are entered in a consistent way (in either counter-clockwise or clockwise sense), whereas the edges of the holes (if any) are entered in its reverse order (i.e., either clockwise or counter-clockwise). By examining closed loops of vertices in a face, one can easily distinguish all the polygons in the face. Figure 2.1 illustrates a face with a hole and its edge sequence.

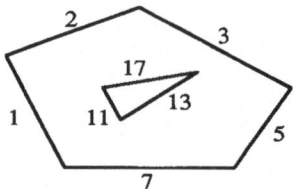

Fig. 2.1.   Edge sequence = {1,2,3,5,7,11,13,17}

The reason why edges within a face are entered in this way is to guarantee that following edge re-ordering process will produce the right edge sequences to define the orientations of face normals for detecting contour edges.

2.2 Finding the Connectivity Information and Determining Boundary Edges

A boundary edge is an edge where only one or more than two faces share it. Clearly, a solid object has no boundary edges at all since each of its edges is shared exactly by two faces. However, an arbitrary scene made of planar faces may have boundary edges. Boundary edges have the same effect on edge visibility as contour edges and thus need to be detected. Figure 2.2 illustrates a surface and its boundary edges.

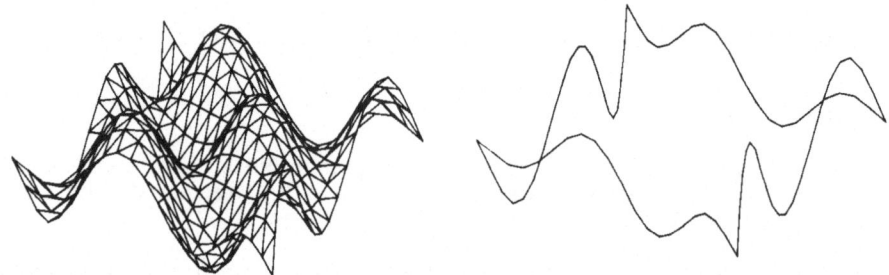

Fig. 2.2.   A surface and its boundary edges

To find boundary edges, the algorithm searches the connectivity information among edges and faces. By looping faces and examining their edges, a connectivity array $connect[1:nedge, 1:2]$ is built up such that for any boundary edge i, $connect[i,1]=-1$; and any other non-boundary edge i, faces $connect[i,1]$ and $connect[i,2]$ share it.

Suppose $connect[i,1]$ and $connect[i,2]$ $(i=1,...,nedge)$ have been initialized to 0. Then the following piece of code simply detects the connectivity and boundary edges.

```
{ Calculate connectivity of faces }
      for i := 1,nface do
         for j := face[i],face[i+1] - 1 do
            begin
               k = face_edge[j];
               if (connect[k,1]=0) then connect[k,1] := i
               else if (connect[k,2]=0) then connect[k,2] := i
               else connect[k,1] := -1
            end

{ Set boundary edges }
      for i := 1,nedge do
         if (connect[i,2]=0) then connect[i,1] := -1
```

2.3 Examining and Re-ordering Edge Sequences of Faces

Once all the boundary edges and the connectivity information has been found, the whole scene can easily be divided into several groups of faces. In each group, faces are connected to each other through their non-boundary edges. Clearly, all the faces within a group form a surface without intersection with other faces in the scene.

It is assumed that such surfaces always have two sides: a front side, and a back side. Cases of Moebus strips are not allowed in the algorithm. With this assumption, the algorithm is able to examine the edge sequences of faces for each group, and re-order them when necessary, such that the edge sequences of faces within a group are consistent, i.e., in either counter-clockwise sense or clockwise sense. Figure 2.3 gives such a surface having only two faces F_1 and F_2.

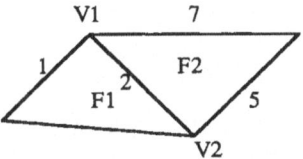

Fig. 2.3.   A surface made of two triangles

If the original edge sequences are $F_1=\{1,2,3\}$ and $F_2=\{2,5,7\}$, then the re-ordered edge sequences are $F_1=\{1,2,3\}$ and $F_2=\{2,7,5\}$ provided that the first face chosen is F_1.

The algorithm always chooses the first face encountered in a face group as the reference face, i.e., its edge sequence is assumed to be correct. By using the connectivity information, all the faces in the group are examined and re-ordered. Letting face j be a new face considered, which connects face i at edge k and the edge sequence of face i has already been re-ordered. The edge sequence of face j is correct if the vertex sequences of face i and face j are reversed at edge k. If the test fails, the edges of face j are then re-ordered. For example, the vertex sequence of F_1 and F_2 at edge 2 are the same, i.e., $\{V_1,V_2\}$, resulting in a re-ordering of the edge sequence of F_2.

Since the normal orientation of a face is determined by its edge sequence, re-ordering edges guarantees normals of faces within each group to have the consistent orientations, i.e., one can travel from one face to another in the same group without changing the normal orientations, although the normal vectors change. Edge re-ordering enables the algorithm to find contour edges by simply examining normals of adjacent faces against the view point.

2.4 Calculation of Normals and Determining Contour Edges.

The method adopted here for calculating normals of faces is suggested by Newell (Harrington 1987) and described as follows: If the n vertices of a face are (x_i, y_i, z_i), then form the sums over all vertices

$$a = \sum_{i=1}^{n} (y_i - y_j)(z_i + z_j) \qquad b = \sum_{i=1}^{n} (z_i - z_j)(x_i + z_j)$$

$$c = \sum_{i=1}^{n} (x_i - x_j)(y_i + y_j)$$

where if $i = n$, then $j = 1$; otherwise, $j = i+1$.

The result $[a\ b\ c]$ is a vector normal to the face. An edge is defined as a contour edge if two faces meet there and one hides the other at the edge. To detect contour edges from non-boundary edges for a given view point, the algorithm first calculates normals of all the faces, and then a dot product Dot_i for each face i by the formula

$$Dot\_i = n_i \cdot v_i$$

where n_i is the vector normal of face i, and v_i the vector from the view point to any vertex of face i. Thus an edge connected by two faces i and j is said to be a contour edge if $Dot\_i * Dot\_j \leq 0$. Once all the contour edges have been detected, an array $contour[1:nedge]$ is used so that $contour[i] > 0$ if edge i is a contour edge. Figure 2.4 illustrate all the contour edges of the scene of Fig. 2.2.

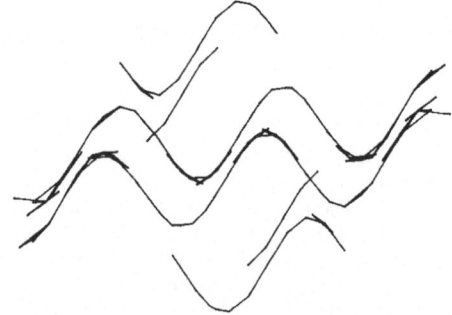

Fig. 2.4.   Contour edges in the scene of Fig. 2.2

2.5 Projection onto Picture Plane

The picture plane is chosen perpendicular to the direction defined by the view point $P=(x0,y0,z0)$ and the origin $O=(0,0,0)$ of the object space. The x' axis of the picture plane is chosen to lie in the x-y plane to preserve the sensation of vertical and horizontal for the viewer (Loutrel 1970).

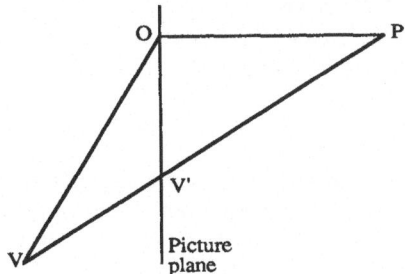

Fig. 2.5.   The projective drawing V' of vertex V

For each vertex V in the scene, its projective drawing on the picture plane is defined by the point V' formed by the vector OV' (Fig. 2.5) which can be calculated by the formulas

$$PV' = PV \frac{PO.PO}{PO.PV} \qquad\qquad OV' = PV' - PO$$

After all vectors $OV'(u,v,w)$ are computed, the 2-D coordinates $V'(x',y')$ on the picture plane are calculated to generate the actual drawing. Let $D = sqrt(x_0^2+y_0^2+z_0^2)$ and $d = sqrt(x_0^2+y_0^2)$, then the transformation is written as

$$
\begin{Vmatrix} x' \\ \\ y' \end{Vmatrix}
=
\begin{Vmatrix} -\dfrac{y0}{d} & \dfrac{x0}{d} & 0 \\ \\ -\dfrac{x0z0}{dD} & \dfrac{y0z0}{dD} & \dfrac{x0^2 + y0^2}{dD} \end{Vmatrix}
\begin{Vmatrix} u \\ \\ v \\ \\ w \end{Vmatrix}
$$

except for the case $x_0=0$, $y_0=0$, for which $x' = u$, $y' = v$.

2.6 Distributing Faces and Boundary/Contour Edges into Cells.

Consider that the picture is divided into rectangular cells. The number of cells $ncell$ is chosen of the order of $nedge$. Let $N_x=N_y=Int[sqrt(nedge)]$, where $Int[x]$ is the integer part of x. The number of cells $ncell$ is given by N_x*N_y.

Find the extent of the projected scene on the picture plane $P_{xmin},P_{xmax},$ $P_{ymin},P_{ymax}.$ Let $dx = (P_{xmax}-P_{xmin})/N_x,$ and $dy = (P_{ymax}-P_{ymin})/N_y.$ Hence $cell_y$ is the set

$$\{(x',y'): (i-1)dx \leq x'-P_{xmin} \leq idx, \ (j-1)dy \leq y'-P_{ymin} \leq jdy\ \}$$

Let $xmin,xmax,ymin,ymax$ be the extent of face k on the picture plane. Compute

$$
\begin{aligned}
I_1 &= Int[(xmin-P_{xmin})/dx]+1;\\
I_2 &= Int[(xmax-P_{xmin})/dx]+1;\\
J_1 &= Int[(ymin-P_{ymin})/dy]+1;\\
J_2 &= Int[(ymax-P_{ymin})/dy]+1;
\end{aligned}
$$

The cells intersecting the extent of face k are given by $\{i,j: I_1 \leq i \leq I_2, \ J_1 \leq j \leq J_2\ \}$.

By looping over all the faces in the scene, the algorithm will set $cell_{ij}$ to index all those faces whose extents intersect the cell. All boundary/ contour edges are similarly distributed into cells. Figure 2.6 illustrates the cell subdivision of the scene in Fig. 2.2.

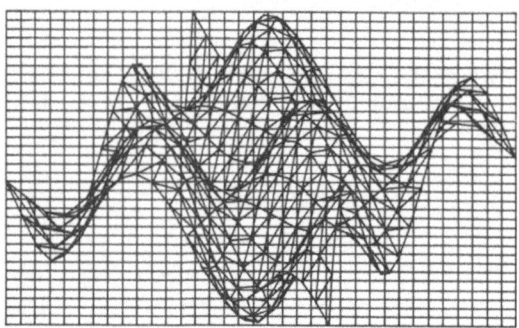

Fig. 2.6. Cell division for the scene in Fig. 2.2

Three arrays $face\_cell[1:N_x,1:N_y]$, $edge\_cell[1:N_x,1:N_y]$, $link[1:nlink,1:2]$ are used to distribute faces and boundary/contour edges into cells. Indices of faces and boundary/contour edges are stored in $link[*,1]$ and linked by $link[*,2]$. Non-zero $face\_cell[i,j]$ and $edge\_cell[i,j]$ point to the first face and boundary/contour edge stored in the $link$ array whose extents intersect $cell_{ij}$ respectively. A zero in $face\_cell[i,j]$, $edge\_cell[i,j]$ or $link[*,2]$ indicates an empty cell without faces or boundary/contour edges, or the end of a sequence of linked faces or boundary/contour edges in a cell.

2.7 Hidden Line Elimination for Each Edge

After faces and boundary/contour edges are distributed into cells, the algorithm is ready to carry out hidden line elimination for each edge. For efficiency, the algorithm first deals with boundary/contour edges to detect their visibility. Only visible and partially visible boundary/contour edges are considered for the calculation of edge intersections in its second step to determine the visibility of interior edges.

The following sections deal with the issues of finding edge intersections and determining the visibility of edge segments.

2.7.1 Determination of Edge Intersections

For each edge i considered, every boundary/contour edge j (excluding those detected to be entirely invisible from the view point) whose extents intersect the cells intersected by that of edge i, is tested to see whether or not they have an apparent intersection It on the picture plane, and if edge j lies in front of edge i as seen from the view point through It.

In the determination of intersection It, the parametric values t_1 and t_2 of intersection It on both the projections of edges i and j are calculated (Foley and Dam 1984; Newman and Sproull 1984). If $0 \leq t_1 \leq 1$ and $0 \leq t_2 \leq 1$, edges i and j have a real intersection in the picture plane. The parametric value of a point V on a line $V_1 V_2$ in the object space does not have the the same value after perspective projection onto a picture plane. Let s be the parametric value of point V on the line $V_1 V_2$ in the object space and t be the parametric value of the same V projected onto a picture plane. Then we have

$$s = \frac{\lambda t}{1 + \lambda t - t} \; ; \qquad \text{where } \lambda = \frac{PV_1 . PV_2'}{PV_1' . PV_2} \qquad \text{Equation 2.7.1}$$

For parallel projection only, $\lambda = 1$ and $s = t$. Fig. 2.7.1 illustrates a projection of line $V_1 V_2$ onto the picture plane.

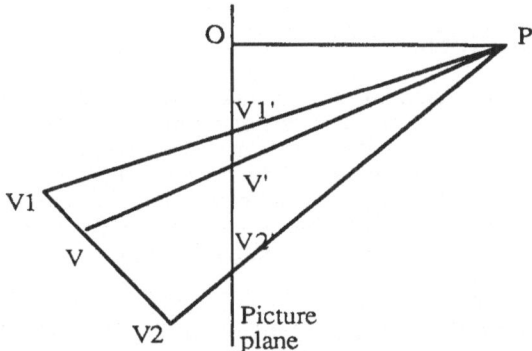

Fig. 2.7.1. Projective of line $V_1 V_2$ onto the picture plane

The parametric values $\{t_1, t_2, ..., t_l\}$ of the intersections on the projection of edge i are then sorted into ascending order. Each edge segment of edge i between two subsequent intersections defined by s_k and s_{k+1} $(1 \leq k \leq l)$ is then dealt with to see whether it is visible or not.

2.7.2 Determination of Visibility of Edge Segments

Let S_0 be an edge segment of edge i defined by parametric values s_k and s_{k+1}, and P_0 the middle point of S_0. Using Equation 2.7.1, the projected point P_0' of P_0 can be obtained. The algorithm searches all the faces whose extents on the picture plane intersect the cell holding P_0'. Only these faces are considered to test the visibility of point P_0, therefore obtaining the same visibility of edge segment S_0. The necessary and sufficient conditions for a face Fp to hide P_0 are:

> *Condition 1*: The plane of Fp must separate the view point P from P_0.
> *Condition 2*: P_0' must lie inside Fp', where Fp' is the projection of Fp in the picture plane.

Every face Fp satisfying Condition 1 is tested for Condition 2. Let n_p be the normal vector of face Fp. Compute the vector PF_p from the view point P to the intersection of line PP_0 and face F_p:

$$PF_p = PP_0 \frac{n_p.n_p}{n_p.PP_0}$$

Condition 1 succeeds if $||PP_0|| < ||PF_p||$. Condition 2 is tested by calculating intersections of the projected edges of Fp and the horizontal line passing P_0' on the picture plane. Thus, condition 2 succeeds if the number of the intersections on the left (or right) hand side of P_0' is even. Special care should be taken to handle intersections at vertices properly (Zhang 1989).

3. TESTS AND DISCUSSIONS

The algorithm has been implemented in FORTRAN 77 and run on a VAX 8700 with several examples. To analyze the efficiency obtained by applying boundary/contour edge techniques, another algorithm, which is similar to the former except that all the edges are considered in the calculation of intersections of each edge, was also coded and run under the same environment. The test results indicate linear expected performances for both the algorithms, but the former is usually three or more times as fast as the latter.

Table. 3.1. The CPU time (*in seconds*) spent in runing two algorithms

Scene size	100	200	400	800	1600	3200	6400	12800
The former	0.08	0.17	0.34	0.63	1.20	2.42	4.80	9.71
The letter	0.15	0.44	0.96	2.13	4.67	10.7	22.6	50.1

The test data are a group of surface meshes defined by a function $z=c*sin(x)*cos(y)$ and their 2-d meshes at the xy plane. Mesh elements are all triangles. Mesh sizes increase from 100 up to 12,800. Figure 3.2 illustrate two line drawings of the surfaces of sizes 400 and 3,200 respectively.

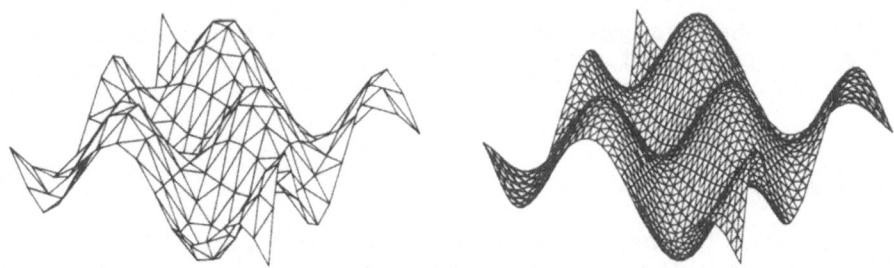

Fig. 3.2.   Two line drawings of surfaces

Further extensions can be made to improve the performance. The algorithm can be extended to detect solid objects in a scene and remove their back faces directly (Loutrel 1970). Solid objects can be found by examining all the faces belonging to each object and making sure there are no boundary edges within these faces. Since the face furthest away from the viewer among the faces of a solid object is a back face, it is possible to find all the back faces by checking their face normals against the view point and comparing them to that of the first back face detected. The major advantage of this method is that solid objects can be efficiently processed no matter whether or not a scene contains non-solid objects.

A face is defined as a 'black' face if there is a boundary/contour edge hiding it as seen from the view point, and is otherwise defined as a 'white' face. Obviously, white faces connected to each other through their interior edges always have the same visibility so that it is only necessary to detect the visibility of one face among them (Loutrel 1970). Once this face is determined visible, all the faces in the group are known visible and their edges are plotted. The algorithm can be extended to detect white and black faces first and then process edges of white faces in the extended approach. Only remaining edges are handled in the same way as the original algorithm.

Two main factors effect the efficiency of the algorithm. The first is the ratio $R_1(S)$ of the boundary/contour edges amongst all the edges in scene S. $R_1(S)$ actually reflects the shape complexity of scene S. If $R_1(S)$ is close to 1.0, the algorithm doesn't reduce the computing time at all. In general, the higher the ratio $R_1(S)$ is, the less the computing time saved. On the other hand, if $R_1(S)$ is very low, the extended algorithm with white face detection will work best in that case. The second is the ratio $R_2(S)$ of the average face size over the cell size. Theoretically, if $R_2(S)$ is around 1.0, the best performance of the algorithm is expected. The algorithm always selects the number of edges as the number of cells, and therefore works best for the scenes having nearly uniform sized faces, such as meshed 3-d objects etc.

Finally, although only the perspective projection is discussed in this paper, any parallel projection can be used, which actually results in a simpler and more efficient algorithm with only a little bit lost in reality.

ACKNOWLEDGMENTS

The author wishes to express his sincere gratitude to D.J. Byrne for his careful reading of the manuscript and helpful suggestions.

REFERENCES

Appel, A, (1966) The Visibility Problem and Machine Rendering of Solids. *IBM Research Paper* RC-16-18, IBM Watson Research Center

Foley, JD, Dam, AV (1984) *Fundamentals of interactive Computer Graphics.* Addision-Wesley, Canada

Franklin, R (1980) A Linear Time Exact Hidden Surface Algorithm. *Computer Graphics* 14(3):117-123

Galimberti, R, Montanari, U (1969) An Algorithm for Hidden-Line Elimination. *Commun. ACM* 12(4):206-211

Harrington, S (1987) *Computer Graphics: A Programming Approach. McGraw-Hill,* Singapore

Loutrel, PE (1970) A Solution to the Hidden-line Problem for Computer-drawn Polyhedra. *IEEE Trans. Comp.* 19:205-213

Newman, WM, Sproull, RF (1984) *Principles of Interactive Computer Graphics.* McGraw-Hill, Japan

Roberts, LG (1963) Machine Perception of Three Dimensional Solids. *Mech. Report 315,* M.I.T. Lincoln Lab., Lexington

Sutherland, IE, Sproull, RF, Schumacker, RA (1974) A Characterization of Ten Hidden Surface Algorithms. *ACM Computing Surveys* 6(1):1-55

Weiler, K, Atherton, P (1977) Hidden Surface Removal Using Polygon Area Sorting. *Computer Graphics* 11(2):214-222

Zhang, J (1989) A Dynamic Span Storing Method for Hidden Surface Removal. *Proc. of ACM 1989 Computer Science Conference*

Jian Zhang was born in 1961 in Shanghai, People's Republic of China. He received the B.Sc. degree in Computer Science from Fudan University, Shanghai, in 1982. He then worked as an assistant lecturer in the Department of Computer Science, Fudan University. In April 1984, he started his Ph.D. research in logic programming and program development methodologies, in the Department of Computer Science, University College of Swansea, U.K. Since September 1987, he has been a research assistant in the Department of Electrical and Electronic Engineering, University College of Swansea, working in the area of computer graphics. A few papers on logic program transformations and computer graphics have been published. His current research interests include logic programming environments, computer graphics, software engineering and AI. The author is expecting to have his Ph.D. degree soon.

Address: Department of Electrical and Electronic Engineering, University College of Swansea, University of Wales, Singleton Park, Swansea, SA2 8PP, Wales, U.K.

Texture Characterization Using Random Sampling

A.J. Maeder

ABSTRACT

Granular textures in digital images have small regions with relatively homogeneous visual properties embedded in a contrasting background. Popular conventional methods for characterizing granular textures measure absolute image properties describing granules and granule inter-relationships. These measurements can be expensive if they require several passes over the image. For approximate characterization a cheaper approach samples subsets of the data to estimate the desired characteristics. This paper presents Monte Carlo random sampling techniques to estimate granule area, perimeter, orientation and separation. Results for several images are presented and compared with those obtained by conventional techniques.

Keywords: texture, granule, characterization, shape, random sampling

1. INTRODUCTION

Analyzing digital images of natural world scenes is often difficult to automate because the data is usually very perturbed and complicated. For this reason, characterizing natural textures offers a challenge to computer science to find efficient computational methods that are general and consistent enough to be widely used. Methods which apply broad principles of information processing directly are preferable to those which rely on the choice of constants (such as threshold values) or heuristics (such as search strategies) governed by the data used.

Many natural textures can be considered **granular** i.e. composed of small regions of fairly homogeneous appearance, embedded in a contrasting background. In digital images this homogeneity may be represented by pixel intensities having a small range of nearby values (smooth shading) or may be a repeating, recognizable intensity pattern (periodicity). Granular textures often occur in fields such as particle analysis, mineralogy, biological and medical image analysis.

Typical characteristics of interest when describing a granular texture are the **area, perimeter, orientation** and **separation** of granules. In many natural granular textures these characteristics are not uniform across space and such textures are thus said to be **irregular.** In characterizing irregular textures, both the distribution of values for a characteristic and the dominant value of the characteristic may be used as descriptors.

Many computational methods have been suggested for analyzing regular or approximately regular textures to determine characteristics such as the above. These methods tend to be expensive as they often require the computation of various first or second order statistics over an entire image or numerous subimages. For instance, determining the separation of granules may require the formation of co-occurrence matrices for pixels at a variety of distances (e.g. Zucker & Terzopoulos 1980). Some other processing such as thresholding, segmentation or clustering (e.g. Leu & Wee 1985) may also be necessary. Other methods, such as Fourier techniques and fractal approximation (e.g. Clark 1986), also tend to be expensive and the transformed data resulting from them can be difficult to analyze automatically.

Methods for regular texture analysis are even more expensive when adapted for use on irregular textures. In these cases further statistics may need to be gathered to estimate the distribution of values for texture characteristics before an average value or suitable range of values can be obtained. This approach requires excessive work to collect detailed information from the image when only approximate characteristic values are desired.

An important occasion when the need for approximate texture characteristic values arises is in the first stage of analyzing an image, when no knowledge of any properties of the image has yet been derived from the data. Often this requires an exhaustive search to determine size and intensity distributions prior to further analysis. Accurate values for these characteristics are seldom necessary at this stage as details will be refined during later processing.

The motivation behind the methods described in this paper is that approximate granular texture characterization can be performed cheaply and effectively by random sampling techniques. This approach of estimating quantities rather than computing them exactly works well because instances of natural textures in images are themselves merely samples from some larger, unknown and considerably variable population. The effect of further uniform subsampling as proposed here is to favour any properties which are pervasive and diminish those which are only local variations in part of an image.

A number of traditional properties used for characterizing granular textures are discussed and typical methods for computing them are described in this paper. In each case an estimator for the same quantity is suggested based on random sampling. The direct 'hit-or-miss' Monte Carlo approach (Rubinstein 1981) has been be adapted to suit the particular property being sought in an image, sometimes by employing several stages of random sampling and sometimes by saving values for later reuse. A related random sampling technique has been used successfully for estimating subimage size for an image segmentation algorithm (Choo et al 1989).

Results generated by applying the above techniques to four different irregular granular textures are presented. For simplicity the techniques are applied to binarized versions of the images. Acceptable approximations to all the texture characteristics mentioned above are obtained. The results are compared with those obtained by more conventional methods and it is thereby demonstrated that the random sampling approach can be significantly cheaper than these.

2. GRANULAR TEXTURE CHARACTERIZATION

Characterization of patterns in natural images is a widely discussed topic in both the computer science and applications literatures (e.g. Tiechgraeber & Philipp 1985). Granular textures may be characterized from two different aspects: properties of the granules as isolated entities and properties of the position of granules within the image.

An approach to granular texture characterization based on the first aspect is called **shape analysis** (Pavlidis 1978). This process involves the measurement of some overall properties of a granule that classify it in broad terms (such as length) or some unique numbers that precisely identify the shape (such as chain codes). Typical broad properties are granule area, perimeter, orientation and position. These broad properties lend themselves to statistical estimation as they are inherently imprecise and variable across an image.

An approach based on the second aspect, termed **texture analysis** (Van Gool et al. 1985), tends to describe the inter-relationship of the granules over the entire image, possibly in terms of shape properties. For example, separation between granules or dominant orientation might be chosen. Usually texture analysis requires the computation of second order statistics for the image. Both the above approaches have been represented in the properties used here to demonstrate the application of random sampling characterization techniques.

2.1 Total Area Occupied by Granules

Counting all pixels which form part of granules in the texture requires one complete image scan, incrementing a counter each time such a pixel is encountered. Pixel testing is trivial in the case of binary images (e.g. black background, white granule) but may require some neighbourhood information to be used in greyscale images (e.g. for adaptive thresholding).

The total granule area is straightforward to estimate using the classical 'hit-or-miss' Monte Carlo technique. A sequence of random number pairs which specify co-ordinate values for pixels is generated. Each pixel in this sequence is inspected and a counter is incremented if it is part of a granule. Again this may need inspection of other pixel values in the neighbourhood if greyscale images are used.

2.2 Area of an Individual Granule

A conventional algorithm for finding the individual granule areas requires each separate granule to be identified. A fast serial method involves scanning the image and assigning a unique number to each runlength of granule pixels on every scanline. Overlapping runlengths on successive lines must belong to the same granule and so an appropriate renumbering can be computed. A subsequent scan of the image thus produces a psuedo-image with a unique number for each granule and with all pixels on the granule represented by this number. The area of each granule can be found by counting the number of pixels corresponding to each unique number in the psuedo-image.

A random sampling method for estimating individual granule areas can be devised by assuming a granule has some ideal shape and using observations to approximate the area for instances of such a shape. In this case a circle was chosen as the ideal shape. Points in the image were randomly chosen until one which fell on a granule was detected. The radius of the circle with centre at this point and perimeter lying approximately on the perimeter of the granule was estimated by making a pair of random observations at stepped distances from the centre. The pair consisted of a separate row and column number with the alternate co-ordinate equal to the current step distance. The radius estimate was

obtained by taking the last case for which at least one of the co-
ordinate pairs was on the granule in all previous cases and computing
its Euclidean distance from the centre.

2.3 Perimeter of an Individual Granule

Detecting the perimeter of a granule can be achieved by scanning the
image in two passes, horizontally and vertically, and preserving only
those pixels values which lie on a transition from background to
granule on either pass. This transition can be found by searching for
adjacent black-white pixel pairs in the binary image. The resulting
psuedo-image will consist entirely of points on the granule perimeters.
The length of each perimeter can then be determined by applying an
area-finding algorithm to this psuedo-image.

A random process which selects pixels uniformly over the entire image
(as used in section 2.1) can be modified to inspect as many neighbours
of the pixel as necessary to deduce whether it lies on an edge. This
will be so if any one of the neighbours belongs to the opposite class
(i.e. granule or background) from the current pixel. The proportion of
these perimeter pixels to the number of pixels in the sample that were
found to lie on granules can be used as an estimate of the proportion
of perimeter to area pixels for the whole image. The number of
perimeter pixels in a granule can be estimated from this proportion and
the individual granule area from section 2.2 using the formula:

```
image perimeter pixels
---------------------- x granule area pixels = granule perimeter pixels
    image area pixels
```

2.4 Orientation of Granules

The usefulness of measuring orientation of granules lies in the
characterizing of overall direction or alignment properties of the
texture. Ideally this characteristic should be determined by
observations made over the whole image. Granule orientation can be
represented crudely but easily by quantizing the range of possible
directions into the 8 compass directions and determining which one of
these best aligns with the longest chord passing through some central
point of the granule. Since a direction and its diametrically opposite
direction yield the same orientation for a granule, only 4 orientations
are possible using this model. Other factors, such as the strength of
orientation and the granule shape, could be approximated using the same
information (e.g. aspect ratio and chord ratio).

A central point for a granule can be found by applying the perimeter
extraction algorithm of section 2.3, then subtracting the perimeter
psuedo-image from the original image and repeating these two steps
until only the innermost point remains. An alternative method which is
usually faster is to skeletonize the image and choose a point on the
skeleton of each granule. For instance, a maximal point on the
distance skeleton of a granule might be selected. It is then an easy
matter to iterate outwards from this centre point along any of the 8
directions as long as granule pixels continue to be found. The final
direction in which granule pixels are still detected when all other
directions have encountered background gives the granule orientation.

A random sampling algorithm based on the above strategy can be derived
by randomly choosing a point on a granule as an assumed centre point

and then testing along the 8 directions radiating out from it. If the distance from the assumed centre point at which pixels are to be tested is incremented for each successive test, and the direction in which the pixel lies is randomly chosen, at least an 8-fold saving in the number of pixels to be inspected should be achieved. When a background pixel is encountered in a particular direction, that direction is excluded from the set of possible directions for future test points. This bias corresponds to the notion of **importance sampling,** a Monte Carlo technique for variance reduction (Rubenstein 1981). Again the final surviving direction gives the granule orientation. Since the chosen point may be quite far from the true centre point, the estimate of the direction using random sampling may be poor unless sufficient trial observations have been made.

2.5 Separation of Granules

The average separation between neighbouring granules can be calculated by using the same centre points as described in section 2.4. By considering all centre points within some row and column distance of a given one, the closest in terms of Euclidean distance can be found. Repeating this operation for all centre points results in O(n*n) comparisons. An alternative method is to construct co-occurrence matrices for different distances and directions, and to observe trends in them that indicate overall orientation and separation of granules. This is also an O(n*n) exercise, potentially even more expensive than the centre point distance method.

To apply random sampling to this problem, the same assumption is made as in section 2.4: that a randomly chosen point in a granule is a suitable centre point substitute. Sets of random pixel pair selections are made and the minimum distance between pairs of pixels which are both on granules is observed for each set. By increasing the number of pixels in each set, the average distance between pairs decreases. The closest pairs in sets with large numbers of observations correspond to pixels inside the same granule. As the number of observations is decreased, these pairs will become less likely and instead pixels in nearest neighbouring granules will dominate the average distance between pairs. Decreasing the number of observations even more will tend to find granules that are quite far apart. The estimated separation of granules can thus be found by constructing a sequence of sets with different numbers of observations in each and observing where the first plateau occurs in the sequence of minimum distances in the sets as the number of observations decreases.

3. RESULTS AND DISCUSSION

Four natural images captured in operational environments were used to demonstrate the effectiveness of the above estimation methods (Fig. 1). Each image was digitized at 480x480 8-bit pixel resolution. A simple adaptive thresholding process previously used for line-removal (Pham & Maeder 1989) was used to construct binarized versions of the images (Fig. 2). NUTS is a view of peanuts after mechanical sorting and alignment during a food production process. OATS and RICE are observations of seeds from certain plant varieties for biological analysis. Each contains granules shaped alike but scattered chaotically and at different orientations. ROCK is a polished geological specimen for identification, with a wide variety of granular inclusions on a matrix of mixed finer particles.

608

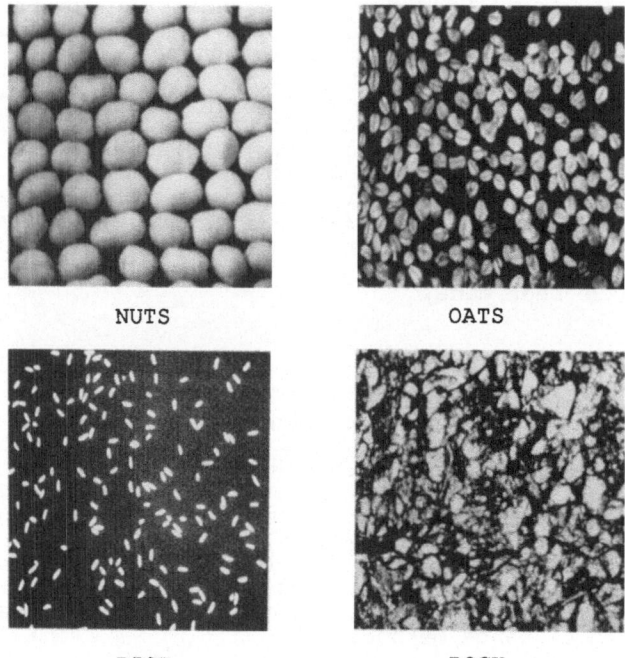

NUTS   OATS

RICE   ROCK

Fig. 1. Original images

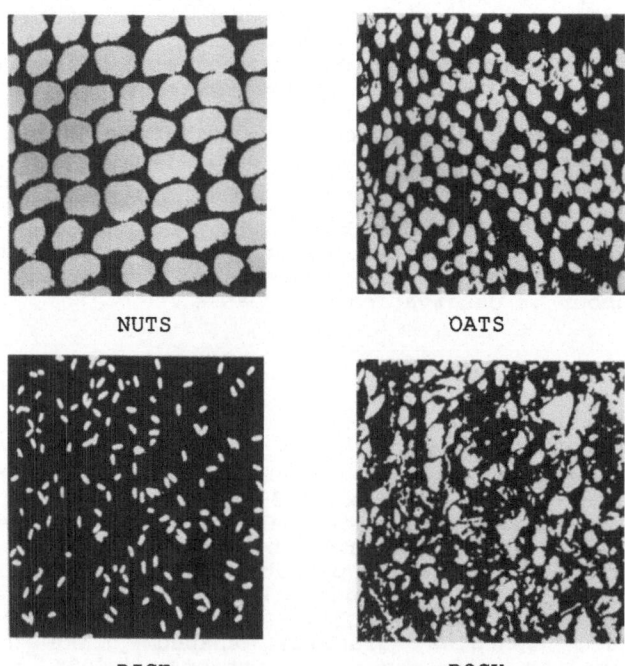

NUTS   OATS

RICE   ROCK

Fig. 2. Binarized images

Table 1: Characteristic texture properties from conventional algorithms

	NUTS	OATS	RICE	ROCK
Total area pixels	141850	88633	15922	80740
Area pixels %image	61.5	38.5	6.9	35.0
Total perimeter pixels	11042	15716	5357	18199
Perimeter pixels %image	4.8	6.8	2.3	7.9
Number of granules	58	165	145	320
Area pixels per granule	2445	537	109	252
Perimeter pixels per granule	181	90	36	57
Orientation pixels % E-W NE-SW N-S NW-SE	27 29 22 22	22 24 28 26	22 24 27 27	22 27 26 25
Separation distance	33.0	23.6	24.4	15.3

Table 2: Characteristic texture properties estimated by random sampling

	Trials	NUTS	OATS	RICE	ROCK
Area pixels %image	10	50.0	40.0	10.0	20.0
	100	61.0	33.0	4.0	32.0
	1000	64.1	38.2	7.6	36.5
	10000	61.8	38.3	7.5	35.7
Perimeter pixels %image	100	7.0	5.0	11.8	7.0
	1000	5.0	6.4	7.1	7.5
	10000	4.6	6.4	7.9	7.8
Area pixels per granule	10	1417	464	201	658
	100	2295	552	138	623
	1000	2310	531	131	565
	10000	2326	534	125	518
Orientation pixels % E-W NE-SW N-S NW-SE	100	30 40 20 10	20 30 30 20	30 30 30 10	30 10 30 30
	1000	37 28 22 13	34 26 23 17	23 31 21 25	30 22 20 28
	10000	29 27 27 17	21 29 24 26	21 38 24 17	30 28 22 20
Separation distance	10	128.3	254.6	−	193.0
	20	78.6	82.2	−	127.0
	40	36.5 *	51.5	49.8	36.5 *
	80	33.4 *	40.1	62.8	30.6 *
	160	21.9	22.1 *	39.2 *	22.8
	320	11.3	14.7 *	38.5 *	15.8
	640	8.7	14.9 *	33.7 *	9.4
	1280	6.2	6.6	13.9	6.6

Table 1 shows the values obtained for various characteristic granular texture properties by the conventional exact algorithms described in section 2. Table 2 shows the estimates of the same quantities computed using the corresponding random sampling methods. These results are averaged over several program runs using different random numbers. In practice, only one run is likely to be used to derive estimates because the cost of several runs may approach the cost of processing the entire image if many observations are made.

Due to the large number of successive random samples needed in some tests, a long-sequence psuedo-random number generator (Wallace 1988) was used to construct the random variates. This generator is based on table-lookup followed by a few arithmetic and bit operations and so is extremely fast. In the assembly language implementation used here, the time taken to generate a single random number was measured as 16 microseconds. By comparison, a single in-memory pixel comparison took 3 microseconds to execute.

The random sample estimates for area and perimeter are reasonable approximations to the exact values in almost all cases. This is true even when the number of trials is quite low, which is consistent with the claim that irregularity in the texture makes very accurate calculation of the values unnecessary. The ROCK image contains the most varied granules and so has the worst estimates e.g. the granule area estimate is about double the anticipated value. The perimeter estimate for RICE is much higher than expected because the granules are rather sparsely distributed in that image so that the number of observations falling on granule edges is too low.

Orientation of granules was strongest in the NUTS image, amounting to 56% in the E-W and NE-SW directions. The random sampling method gave good results for this image, consistently finding dominant orientation in those direction. OATS has orientations spread over 3 of the 4 directions and since granules are quite abundant in the image, the random sampling method was able to detect this property when the number of observations was relatively high. RICE and ROCK suffer from granule area sparsity and highly variable granules respectively, which rendered the estimates for orientation unreliable at all numbers of trial observations. It can be concluded that the random sampling technique for characterizing orientation is suited only to images with definite alignment of granules and fairly consistent and abundant granules. These are precisely the circumstances under which it would be meaningful to characterize orientation.

The results for separation distance are marked with a star to indicate the first discernible plateau in distances once the intra-granule distances are damped out by a decrease in the observation set size. The number of observations and the number of different set sizes needed to observe the plateau depends on the nature of the granules in the image and their layout. In the cases of NUTS and OATS good estimates were obtained due to the similar size and arrangement of the granules. Both RICE and ROCK were over-estimated, more seriously so in the latter case. Once again this was due to the sparsity of data and the chaotic nature of the data rendering the number of observations insufficient. However, this situation could not be improved by making still further observations as the intra-granule region of the observations has already been reached in both cases.

Table 3 shows execution times measured for implementations of the various algorithms in C on a Pyramid 98X superminicomputer. All times were obtained for the OATS image. Times for the other images were found to be within a few percent of these figures due to different image content. For all cases the random sampling algorithms were quicker than the conventional algorithms until fairly large sample sizes were reached. The estimates obtained were accurate to within a few percent before these sample sizes were reached. Random sampling methods can thus be expected to yield good estimates of granular texture properties more cheaply than conventional methods provided the sample size is limited.

All the conventional methods used to calculate texture properties are pixel-based algorithms that require at least one sequential scan through the entire image (Agrawala & Kulkarni 1977). Some are more complex than this: granule area requires a second pass to renumber granule pixels; granule centre location requires several successive passes in the skeletonizing process. Each random sampling algorithm uses only those pixels in the image selected by one or more random processes, so the total number of such pixels is a relevant measure of their efficiency. Since this number can be selected by the user when running the programs, performance can be obtained which is of constant complexity in terms of pixels examined. Naturally this choice will affect the degree of confidence in the answer.

Table 3. Execution times in seconds for implemented algorithms on OATS

	Conventional	100 trials	1000 trials	10000 trials
Total area pixels	0.742	0.007	0.073	0.731
Total perimeter pixels	6.149	0.008	0.084	0.847
Area pixels per granule	4.285	0.130	1.295	12.958
Orientation pixels %	7.415	0.038	0.383	3.816
Separation distance	7.298	0.233	29.251	–

4. CONCLUSION

It has been argued that random sampling is an acceptable substitute for exact methods of granular texture characterization where approximate values are required or computational expense must be constrained. Some measurements for characterizing granular textures were discussed and methods for computing them using both exact and random sampling approaches were presented. Results obtained by applying the methods to four realistic textures have confirmed these claims, with some limitations for data which has widely spaced or small granules, or data which has granules of widely varied sizes in chaotic arrangement.

The ideas described here could be extended in several directions. The most immediate need is to cater for greyscale images where illumination and surface variation become important. The assessment of distribution functions for each characteristic being measured could also be estimated rather than just the mean. Different models could be used for the texture properties being estimated by random sampling (e.g. the shape model used when estimating granule area), allowing better correspondence with the data and possibly further improvements in computational efficiency. Other characteristics of granular textures (e.g. perimeter shape) could also be estimated using random sampling.

REFERENCES

Agrawala AK, Kulkarni AV (1977) A sequential approach to the extraction of shape features. Comput. Graph. Image Process. 6:538-557

Choo AP, Maeder AJ, Pham B (1989) Image segmentation for complex natural scenes. Technical Report, Department of Computer Science, Monash University, Melbourne

Clark NN (1986) Three techniques for implementing digital fractal analysis of particle shape. Powder Technology 46:45-52

Leu J-G, Wee WG (1985) Detecting the spatial structure of natural textures based on shape analysis. Comput. Vision Graph. Image Process. 31:67-88

Pavlidis T (1978) A review of algorithms for shape analysis. Comput. Graph. Image Process. 7:243-258

Pham B, Maeder AJ (1989) Line extraction and removal in greyscale images. Procs. AUSGRAPH 89 Conf., Sydney, July 10-14 1989 (to appear)

Rubinstein RY (1981) Simulation and the Monte Carlo method. John Wiley & Sons, New York

Tiechgraeber M, Philipp B (1985) Pattern analysis of irregularly shaped particles. Ultramicroscopy 17:193-202

Van Gool L, Dewaele P, Oosterlinck A (1985) Texture analysis anno 1983. Comput. Vision Graph. Image Process. 29:336-357

Wallace CS (1988) A long-period psuedo-random generator. Technical Report, Department of Computer Science, Monash University, Melbourne

Wechsler H, Citron T (1980) Feature extraction for texture classification. Pattern Recogn. 12:301-311

Zucker SW, Terzopoulos D (1980) Finding structure in co-occurrence matrices for texture analysis. Comput. Graph. Image Process. 12:286-308

Anthony J. Maeder gained his MSc in Computer Science from Natal University, Durban in 1982 for a thesis on the construction of a MIMD parallel computer system. During 1982-3 he worked as a researcher at Scitec Corporation in Sydney on the design of communications processors. Since 1984 he has held posts as Senior Tutor and Lecturer in the Department of Computer Science at Monash University in Melbourne, where he is concluding a PhD in the area of software for solving ordinary differential equations. His current research interests are computer graphics, image processing, remote sensing, data compression, parallel computing and numerical methods. He is a member of the ACM.

Address: Department of Computer Science, Monash University, Clayton, Victoria 3168, Australia.

Highlighting Rounded Edges

T. Saito, M. Shinya, and T. Takahashi

ABSTRACT

This paper proposes an efficient method for rendering highlights on rounded edges, which is important for photorealism and comprehensibility. The rounded edges are shaded as thin cylinders separately from the planar surfaces. To ensure coherence with the planar surfaces, an edge shading equation is proposed, which derives an appropriate edge shading model from any conventional model. The final image is obtained by drawing edges like wire-frames onto the planar surface image. Using this method, aliasing-free edge highlights can be generated from simple edge data with little increase in computation cost.

Keywords:
photorealistic rendering, comprehensible presentation, anti-aliasing, wire-frame, shading model

1   INTRODUCTION

Photorealistic image synthesis is one of the most important goals in the field of computer graphics. There have been a lot of techniques developed for this purpose. Among them, shading techniques have been investigated, and useful shading models (Phong 1975; Blinn 1977; Cook 1982) have been proposed and improved. Calculation of highlight and shade effects that exhibit physical fidelity has notably contributed to the realistic image generation of many materials, especially shiny surfaces such as metals and plastics.

However, an important phenomenon, *edge highlights*, has been ignored in conventional shading methods. Consequently, unrealistic images without edge highlights are often generated. Most edges are smooth tightly curved surfaces so that they reflect light sources over a wide angle. Thus, real edges are highlighted more often than relatively flat surfaces.

The importance of edge highlights has been already noticed in the field of technical illustration for industrial design. When a designer manually draws an illustration, edges are often shown by emphasized highlights. This is because edges greatly enhance the comprehension of two-dimensional representations of three-dimensional objects. Recognizing this, Kondo *et al.* (1988) developed an interactive rendering system containing various painting tools, which simulated the rendering rules used in technical illustrations. Their system can create effective edge highlights from the designer's commands. The final effect is quite comprehensible, but it requires extensive efforts by the designer to nominate edges and produce highlights. Recently, it has become necessary to generate realistic images automatically from CAD data and given lighting environments.

Conventional shading methods are, of course, theoretically applicable to edge highlighting if rounded edges are defined as thin curved patches. In such an approach, however, it is difficult to avoid aliasing artifacts, and impractical to input patch data for all rounded edges. In reality, edge highlights have been ignored in many applications.

In this paper, a new method for automatically highlighting edges is proposed. The edges are regarded as thin cylinders in shading calculations. The shape of a cylinder is so simple that pixel intensities are easily calculated by integration, and it requires only a rounding radius instead of complete patch data. For accurate edge shading calculation, we propose an *edge shading equation* which derives an appropriate edge shading model from the conventional model used for surfaces. In our method, rounded edges are rendered separately from ordinary surfaces as shaded wire-frames. The final image is obtained by superposing the shaded wire-frames onto the ordinary surface image.

This technique is similar to Miller's rendering method (Miller 1988), where shaded wire-frames are drawn onto surface rendered images. His method, however, was mainly for an object composed of many wire-like components such as animal fur. Thus, his shading model aimed at fast calculation of wire-frames but sacrificed physical fidelity. On the other hand, the main subject of this paper is to create realistic edges which are not separate components. Therefore, our edge shading model is based on the one used for surfaces.

In this paper, conventional methods are reviewed from the view point of edge highlighting, and their limitations and disadvantages are revealed in section 2. The new method for highlighting edges of polyhedra is introduced in section 3. Then, the method is extended to curved surfaces in section 4. In addition, a rendering technique for ordinary high-curvature surfaces is also presented. Finally, evaluations of the method and remaining problems are discussed in section 5.

2 CONVENTIONAL METHODS

Edges on shiny objects often reflect light sources and cause highlight lines (Fig.1), and it is important for realistic or intelligible image generation to describe this phenomenon. In this section, conventional methods are reviewed and their limitations are discussed.

Fig.1 An example of edge highlights. (a real photograph)

Before we begin, let us define the classes of *edges* to make the discussion clear (see Fig.2).

- *sharp edge*:
  The boundary of two surfaces across which the normal vector changes discontinuously. Such ideal edges rarely exist.

- *rounded edge*:
  It means an edge with a very small radius. Even if it looks like a sharp edge in macroscopic view, actually it is not a *line* but a high-curvature *surface* like a thin cylinder. Most *edges* of actual objects belong to this class.

- *others*:
  The word *edge* is sometimes used for a *profile* of a projected curved surface or a *boundary line* of smoothly joined patches. Note that we do not call them edges in this paper.

In conventional rendering systems, surface patch representation of rounded edges makes it possible to create edge highlights. This approach, however, is impractical because of aliasing artifacts and the manipulation cost of surface patches. In the following subsections, each difficulty is detailed.

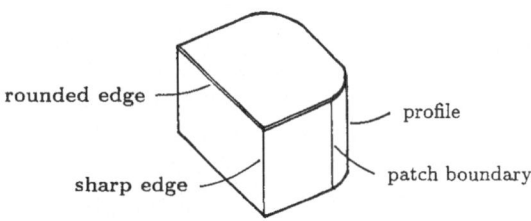

Fig.2 Classes of edges.

2.1 Aliasing Artifacts

Rounded edges have high curvature; thus, the intensity level changes so rapidly that severe aliasing artifacts often occur (Amadatides 1987). One of the simplest anti-aliasing techniques would be super-sampling. If the sub-pixel sampling rate is efficient, the aliasing artifact is eliminated by filtering. However, the width of highlighted area on a rounded edge is usually so thin that a super-sampling method would be too costly.

Consider the situation shown in Fig.3, where the object edges have a $1mm$ radius, and the surfaces are flat and completely specular-reflective. A light source, $30cm$ in diameter, is located $2m$ above the object. When a $30cm \times 30cm$ area including the object is projected onto an screen at a resolution of 512×512 pixels, the highlighted area on the edge is only 0.09 pixel wide on the screen (where the edge itself is 1.7 pixels wide). More than 10×10 sampling points per pixel, therefore, are required for sufficient anti-aliasing, which is prohibitively expensive. Although a stochastic sampling technique (Cook 1986) with a coarser sampling rate could improve image quality, it is not the best solution.

When object surfaces are perfectly specular, reflection mapping techniques are applicable, and anti-aliasing can be performed by pre-filtering maps. Using hierarchical integral tables (Williams 1983) or summed-area tables (Crow 1984), the integrated value for each pixel can be obtained with small computation effort even if the area has high curvature. However, there are also several problems in this approach.

- Such kind of techniques are not applicable to even simple situations where point light sources illuminate partially specular objects.

- The integrated value cannot be obtained correctly when the curvature across a pixel changes quickly. This situation often arises where a rounded edge is lies across in a pixel (Fig.4).

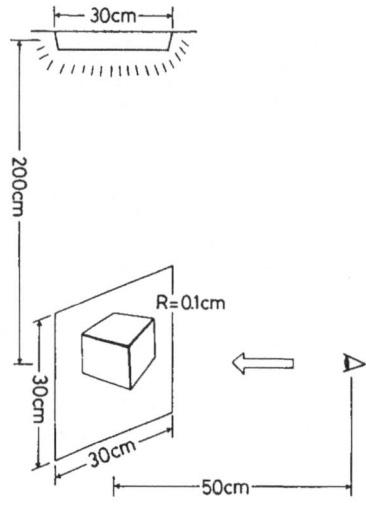

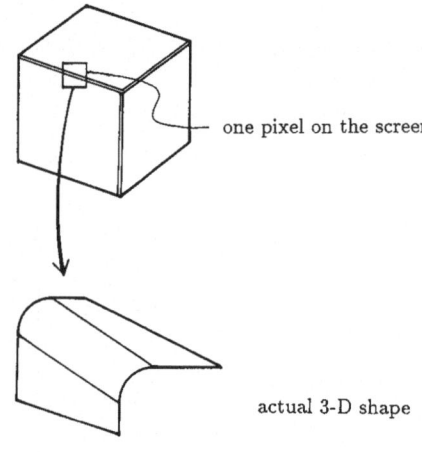

Fig.3 An example situation to evaluate edge highlights.

Fig.4 Quick change of the curvature across a pixel.

2.2 Manipulation Cost of Surface Patches

The cost of manipulating surface patches depends on the modeling tool, but it is usually expensive. It requires even more effort to input them if simple modeling software is used. When a rounded edge is located between two plane polygons, it is defined as a part of a cylinder. Located at the intersection of a cylindrical surface and a plane, a rounded edge is defined as a part of a torus. Generally, rounded edges have to be defined as parametrical surface patches. We must adjust the boundary lines of both neighboring surfaces, and define a new surface between them by a cylindrical axis and a radius, or by control points of a patch, so as to connect the surfaces smoothly.

To reduce the operator's effort, it is necessary to use a more sophisticated modeling system which provides an edge rounding operation; *i.e.* the system can generate surface patch data automatically from a specified rounding radius. Similar functions are used in mechanical CAD systems. However, it is rather complicated to generate appropriate patches in all conditions. Therefore, such functions cannot be supplied in low-cost simple modeling systems.

Actually, it is almost useless to define these patches completely when the edges have small radii. In mechanical design drawings, only the rounding radii are defined for many edges. Except edge highlighting, complete patch data is required only when the edges are being enlarged in computer animation sequences. It is desirable to render rounded edges by inputting simple data, so as not to be the burden to the designer.

3 HIGHLIGHTING EDGES OF POLYHEDRA

In this section, we propose a new method for highlighting rounded edges of polyhedral objects. In our method, rounded edges are regarded as thin cylinders and rendered separately from other surface rendering.

3.1 Effect of Edge Rounding

Before introducing the new method, let us explain how the overall image is enhanced by edge rounding. By analyzing this effect, we can observe what is required to adequately render rounded edges.

Consider two cubes: one has *sharp edges* and the other has *rounded edges*. In the latter, the rounding radius is 1 pixel-length on the screen. If all other properties of the two cubes and the rendering conditions (view angle, lighting environments, *etc.*) are the same, the differences between the two images can be analyzed as follows.

- *geometrical shape*
  The only difference is the silhouette lines; one is sharp and the other is rounded. However, the difference is less than 1 pixel.

- *intensity based on diffuse reflection*
  When one neighboring surface of an edge is illuminated and the other is in the shade, the location of the shade line is changed by edge rounding. The difference is less than 1 pixel. In another case, a rounded edge may have higher intensity than neighboring surfaces. Maximum intensity ratio of the rounded edge to the sharp edge is $\sqrt{2}$.

- *intensity based on specular reflection*
  When a light source is reflected from a rounded edge, the reflection intensity is sometimes extremely high. It depends on the strength of the light source and the reflection parameters. However, the intensity ratio of the rounded edge to the sharp edge can be more than 100 times in bright sunshine.

The above analysis explains that specular reflection is changed most notably by an edge-rounding operation, and that it is the dominant effect on image appearance.

3.2 Outline of the Proposed Method

The outline of the new method is as follows.

1. **shading for surfaces** (Fig.5(a))
   Make a surface image ignoring rounded edges (*i.e.* all edges are processed as sharp edges). Any conventional shading method can be used in this process.

2. **shading for edges** (Fig.5(b))
   Regard a rounded edge as a part of a thin cylinder with a radius R. Integrate the reflected flux from the cylinder within one pixel length. Render the edge as a wire-frame with variable intensity, and make a line-drawing image.

3. **mixing the two images** (Fig.5(c))
   Add the line-drawing image onto the surface image, and then obtain the final image.

The key idea of this rendering technique is to calculate edge specular reflections separately from surface rendering. With this idea, we simultaneously solve the two major problems discussed in section 2 as follows.

- *effective anti-aliasing*
  By drawing edges as lines instead of areas, the drop-out errors in highlighted edges can be avoided. Moreover, it is possible to calculate the intensity efficiently and accurately by considering cylinders, instead of square pixel areas, as the integral sections.

- *using simple data*
  To define a rounded edge as a part of a cylinder, we need:
    - the location of the edge
    - the surface normals of the polygons bounded by the edge
    - the radius R of the edge.
  Since the first two data are generated in the modeling process of surfaces, only the radius R must be input to permit the edge shading operation. This greatly reduces input operations.

Fig.5 Outline of the proposed method.
(a) (*left-top*) a surface image (conventional surface shading)
(b) (*right-top*) a line-drawing image (edge shading)
(c) (*bottom*) a final image ((a)+(b))

3.3   Shading Models for Rounded Edges

Shading models for rounded edges, which derive intensity of shaded wire-frames, are described here. Shading models for wire-frames can be derived independently from conventional surface shading models. For example, Miller (1988) has proposed a pseudo-reflectance map, in which pre-computed intensities of wire-frames are stored. In his method, intensity depends solely on the tangent vector of the wire-frame, and this simple approach enables a lot of wire-frames to be rendered efficiently.

However, rounded edges are not wires but surfaces; edges with large radii have to define as surface patches. Thus, the edge shading model must be consistent with conventional surface shading model employed. Otherwise, the same edge may have different shading properties if its radius changes on the screen. Such inconsistency causes unnatural change of highlights, especially in animation sequences.

Instead of obtaining an edge shading model directly, we propose an *edge shading equation*, which can derive an appropriate edge shading model from any conventional model. As an example, Blinn's shading model (Blinn 1977) is applied to the edge shading equation.

3.3.1   An edge shading equation

A rounded edge is regarded as a part of a thin cylinder, as explained in section 3.2. Consider the relationship between specular reflection from flat surfaces and from thin cylinders. Let the flux from a planer surface per unit area be Φ_s. The flux Φ_e from a thin cylinder per unit length is given by

$$\Phi_e = \int_{\psi_0}^{\psi_1} \Phi_s(R\,d\psi), \tag{1}$$

where R is the radius of the cylinder, ψ is a rotation angle along the circumference, and the boundaries of the rounded edges corresponds to the rotation angle ψ_0 and ψ_1 (see Fig.6). Note that Eq.(1) gives the relationship in world coordinates.

In the next step, the same relationship in screen coordinates is developed. That is, we derive the relationship between the reflected flux s_s and s_e, where s_s is the flux from a planer surface into one pixel-area, and s_e is from a thin cylinder into one pixel-length. Assume 1 pixel-length on the screen corresponds to a length a at the cylinder position. Let N be a unit normal vector at the reflected point of a surface, V be the unit vector directed to the viewer, r be the radius scaled on the screen, and β be the angle between the screen and the cylinder axis. The following relationship is obtained between s_s, s_e, r, and Φ_s, Φ_e, R respectively:

$$s_s = \frac{a^2}{(N \cdot V)}\,\Phi_s, \tag{2}$$

$$s_e = \frac{a}{\cos\beta}\,\Phi_e, \tag{3}$$

$$R = ar. \tag{4}$$

From the foregoing, we can establish the expression:

$$s_e = \frac{r}{\cos\beta} \int_{\psi_0}^{\psi_1} s_s(N \cdot V)\,d\psi. \tag{5}$$

Flux s_s corresponds to the specular reflection component of pixel intensity given by conventional shading models (Phong 1975; Blinn 1977; Cook 1982). Therefore, Eq.(5) is the required edge shading equation.

3.3.2 An example of Blinn's shading model

One widely-used shading model is the one proposed by Blinn (1977). In Fig.7, **L** is the unit vector directed to the light source. **H** is the unit angular bisector between **V** and **L**. Let α, θ be the angles between **N** and **H**, **L** and **H** respectively. In his shading model, the specular reflection component is given by

$$s_s = I \cdot \frac{DGF}{(\mathbf{N} \cdot \mathbf{V})}. \tag{6}$$

Where, I is the strength of the incident light. G, called *geometrical attenuation factor*, is the amount by which the facets shadow and/or mask each other. It is a function of $\mathbf{N} \cdot \mathbf{H}$, $\mathbf{N} \cdot \mathbf{V}$, $\mathbf{N} \cdot \mathbf{L}$, and $\mathbf{H} \cdot \mathbf{V}$. F is the Fresnel reflection ratio which depends on the incident angle θ. D is the distribution function of the normal of micro facets on the surface. Several functions for D have been proposed, such as:

$$D = \cos^k \alpha, \tag{7}$$

$$D = e^{-(c\alpha)^2}. \tag{8}$$

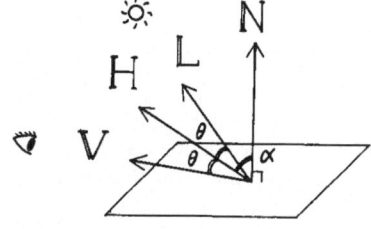

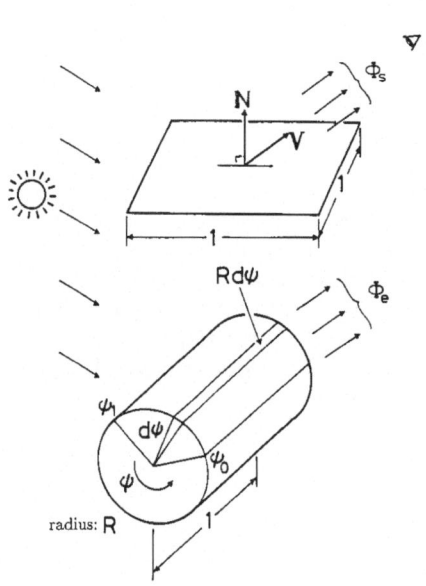

Fig.7 Reflection on a plane.

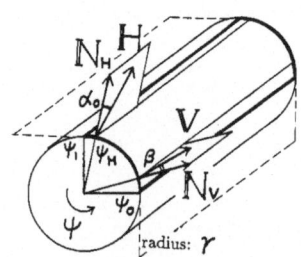

Fig.6 Integral calculation of reflected flux off a thin cylinder.

Fig.8 Reflection on a thin cylinder.

Blinn's shading model can be adapted for rounded edges by the substitution of Eq.(6) into Eq.(5):

$$s_e = \frac{IFr}{\cos \beta} \int_{\psi_0}^{\psi_1} DG \, d\psi. \tag{9}$$

An actual procedure for the integral computation is described below. To simplify the calculations, choose Eq.(7) as the distribution function, and let $G = 1$. Let N_H be the normal vector on the surface including H and a cylinder diameter. Let ψ_H be the rotation angle at N_H. And let α_0 be the angle between H and N_H, as shown in Fig.8. By spherical trigonometry, the following equation is satisfied:

$$\cos \alpha = \cos \alpha_0 \cos(\psi - \psi_H). \tag{10}$$

Substituting Eq.(7) and Eq.(10) into Eq.(9), we have

$$s_e = \frac{IFr \cos^k \alpha_0}{\cos \beta} \int_{\psi_0 - \psi_H}^{\psi_1 - \psi_H} \cos^k \psi \, d\psi. \tag{11}$$

When coefficient k is large enough, such as 10 or 50, it is better to approximate the integral factor in Eq.(11) as a polynomial of ψ. In our implementation, the following polynomial approximation is adapted:

$$\int_0^\psi \cos^k \psi \, d\psi \approx \min(\psi - \frac{k}{6}\psi^3 + (\frac{k^2}{40} - \frac{k}{60})\psi^5, C_k), \tag{12}$$

where

$$C_k = \int_0^{\frac{\pi}{2}} \cos^k \psi \, d\psi \approx \sqrt{\frac{\pi}{2k + 1}}. \tag{13}$$

3.3.3   Usage of the shading model

After calculation of the intensity based on the above procedure, the rounded edges are anti-aliased and drawn onto the frame-buffer as shaded wire-frames. In this step, it is necessary to compensate s_e from the edge slope on the screen, since s_s is not for the square area of a pixel but for the length of 1 pixel.

3.4   Shading Model for Rounded Vertices

Highlights often appear at vertices for the same reason as on rounded edges. These highlights are not so important as those on rounded edges, but are sometimes required for improving the reality of images. They can be also rendered by calculating the specular reflection factor on rounded vertices and by drawing them as points with calculated intensities.

A rounded vertex can be approximated as a part of a sphere in most cases. Therefore, integration of specularly reflected flux from the sphere gives the intensity of the point. Since the integral region is a spherical polygon (Fig.9(a)) and it is difficult to calculate accurately, an approximation method is described in this section.

First of all, 4 unit vectors N, V, L, and H are defined as the same meaning as section 3.3 (see Fig.7). Assume the surface is almost completely specular-reflective; i.e. k in Eq.(7) or c in Eq.(8) is large enough. In these conditions, the integral around the region where $N = H$ is the dominant in the total flux off the spherical polygon. Therefore, to simplify the integral region, we can change the spherical-polygon boundary that is far from the dominant region.

The following simplified model is proposed (Fig.9(b)). To begin with, obtain the integral region P from the shape of vertex, the view point, and the direction of the light source. Next, check the direction of $\mathbf{H}$ as to whether it is inside P or not, and get the nearest large circle c forming the boundary of P. Then split the hemisphere into two regions by large circle c, select one containing P, and let it be the integral region. Let r be the radius of the small sphere scaled on the screen, and let ω_1 be the angle (*i.e.* distance on the unit sphere) between $\mathbf{H}$ and c. The sign of ω_1 is positive if $\mathbf{H}$ is inside of P, and negative if outside. Using the similar idea for rounded edges in section 3.3, the flux from the vertex is given by

$$s_v = \int_{\psi=-\frac{\pi}{2}}^{\frac{\pi}{2}} \int_{\omega=-\frac{\pi}{2}}^{\omega_1} s_s(\mathbf{N}\cdot\mathbf{V})(r\,d\psi)(r\cos\psi\,d\omega)$$

$$= r^2 \int_{\psi=-\frac{\pi}{2}}^{\frac{\pi}{2}} \int_{\omega=-\frac{\pi}{2}}^{\omega_1} s_s(\mathbf{N}\cdot\mathbf{V})\cos\psi\,d\psi\,d\omega. \tag{14}$$

This equation is a vertex shading equation which adapts any convectional surface shading model.

If Blinn's shading model is applied to Eq.(14), the vertex shading model is given by

$$s_v = IFr^2 \int_{\psi=-\frac{\pi}{2}}^{\frac{\pi}{2}} \int_{\omega=-\frac{\pi}{2}}^{\omega_1} DG\cos\psi\,d\psi\,d\omega. \tag{15}$$

Simplifying Eq.(15) with the same technique as section 3.3, we have

$$s_v = IFr^2 \int_{-\frac{\pi}{2}}^{\frac{\pi}{2}} \cos^{k+1}\psi\,d\psi \int_{-\frac{\pi}{2}}^{\omega_1} \cos^k\omega\,d\omega. \tag{16}$$

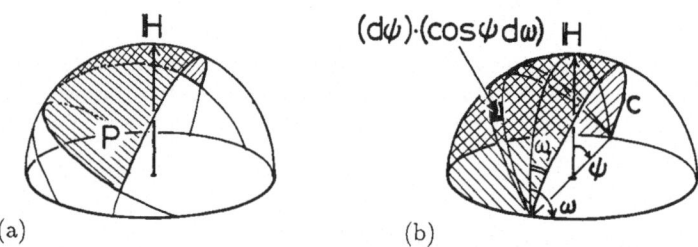

(a) (b)

Fig.9 Integral calculation of reflected flux off a rounded vertex.

3.5 Examples

Example images in Fig.10 and Fig.11 show the improvement in anti-aliasing with the proposed method. In these images, the rounding radius of the object and most viewing parameters are the same as the example in section 2.1 (Fig.3). Four light sources are located at the lower front, above, left side, and back of the object. They are point light sources, which are a little bit different from Fig.3. However, by adjusting the facet distribution function (Eq.(7) is used as $k = 250$ in this case), we can make the highlighted area almost same as in Fig.3.

Images in Fig.10 are generated by a conventional method. All edges are approximated with polygons, and rendered by using Phong's smooth shading (Phong 1975). In the images, (a) was generated by simple sampling (1 sampling-point/pixel). Images (b), (c) and (d) were by super-sampling with 2×2, 4×4, and 8×8 sampling-point/pixel respectively. Under this condition, aliasing artifacts are conspicuous even with 4×4 super-sampling. On the other hand, Fig.11 was generated using the proposed method. The highlighted edges are smoothly displayed even without super-sampling.

Comparing Fig.10 with Fig.11, we find the upper highlight line was dropped in Fig.10. It is because the edge is reversed and thus not rendered by polygon approximation. Such an error cannot occur in the proposed method, which is another advantage.

Another example with many rounded edges is shown in Fig.12. Shiny sticks are rendered with and without edge highlighting. Two light sources are assumed in both images. Comparing the two images, we find that image reality is notably improved by edge highlights.

Fig.10 Anti-aliasing effects
by conventional super-sampling.
(a) (*left-top*) not super-sampled
(b) (*right-top*) 2×2 super-sampled
(c) (*left-bottom*) 4×4 super-sampled
(d) (*right-bottom*) 8×8 super-sampled

Fig.11 Anti-aliasing effects
by the proposed method.
(a) (*left-top*) not super-sampled
(b) (*right-top*) 2×2 super-sampled
(c) (*left-bottom*) 4×4 super-sampled
(d) (*right-bottom*) 8×8 super-sampled

Fig.12 Shiny sticks.
(*reft*) without edge highlights; (*right*) with edge highlights

4   EXTENSION TO CURVED SURFACES

In this section, the proposed method is extended for curved surfaces. The extension contains two subjects. One is highlighting *rounded curved-edges*, *i.e.* edges between curved patches. The other is rendering *general high-curvature surfaces*, *i.e.* rounded edges with comparatively large radii, or high-curvature surface patches which cannot be regarded as edges.

4.1   Highlighting Rounded Curved-Edges

Curved surfaces are often tessellated and approximated as polygon patches in the rendering process. In this case, a rounded curved-edge, which is originally a curved line, is approximated as a broken line. Thus, applying the proposed method to each segment of the broken line, we can effectively render highlights on rounded curved-edges.

When curved surfaces are rendered as polygon patches, an interpolation technique, typically Gouraud's smooth shading (Goutaud 1971) or Phong's smooth shading (Phong 1975), is usually used to maintain smoothness. It is possible to apply similar techniques for rounded curved-edges. For each smooth shading method the following interpolations are recommended for shading edges.

- **for Gouraud's smooth shading:**
  Calculate the intensity value at both ends of an edge segment, and then interpolate the intensity value at each pixel linearly.

- **for Phong's smooth shading:**
  At both ends of an edge segment, get tangent vectors, normal vectors of the neighboring surfaces, and rounding radii on the screen. Interpolating these values, calculate the intensity value at each pixel. To simplify the computation, it is also possible to interpolate the four angles α_0, β, $\psi_0 - \psi_H$, and $\psi_1 - \psi_H$, instead of tangent and normal vectors.

4.2   Rendering General High-Curvature Surfaces

A method for rendering highlights on general high-curvature surfaces is proposed here. Some surfaces must be defined as surface patches, even if the highlighted area on the surfaces is too thin to draw correctly. For example, a rounded edge with the radius of 2–5 pixel-lengths has to be defined as a surface, because its geometrical shape is clearly different from a sharp edge. On this edge, however, the width of the highlight is still thin. A surface patch with partially high curvature is another example. In this case, the patch itself cannot be regarded as a rounded edge.

In the proposed method, the curved surfaces are tessellated to polygons, and then rendered by Phong's smooth shading. Before shading, the size of the highlighted area is estimated for each polygon from its curvature. If the size is large enough, the polygon is rendered as an ordinary surface. If the size is thin or small, on the other hand, specular reflection is calculated separately from the surface rendering, and the intensity is added by wire-frame drawing or point drawing onto the surface image.

The size of highlighted area is estimated as follows. To begin with, compute a curvature (differential of normal vector) along patch boundary lines. Let the curvature be c (angle/pixel). Then, assuming the light source is reflected just in the boundary line, calculate the highlight width d. When Eq.(7) is used as a facet distribution function, d can be given by

$$d = \frac{2}{c} \cos^{-1}(\frac{1}{2})^{\frac{1}{k}}. \tag{17}$$

Using the width d for each boundary, approximate the highlighted area as a rectangle of length d_u and width d_v.

The specular reflection is calculated as follows.

- $(d_u > 1)$ and $(d_v > 1)$:
  — Calculate by point sampling in surface rendering process.
- $(d_u > 1)$ and $(d_v \leq 1)$:
  — Calculate as a rounded curved-edge.
- $(d_u \leq 1)$ and $(d_v \leq 1)$:
  — Calculate as a rounded vertex with radius d_v.

4.3 Examples

An example of an image with curved-edges is shown in Fig.13, where a machine nut is drawn with five light sources. In this figure, image (a) with edge highlights is much more comprehensible than image (b) without edge highlights. Figure 14 is an image of a Japanese style tea cup with green tea. Note that the edge of the water surface is rounded by surface tension, and thus highlights also appear on the concave edge. We can easily recognize this phenomenon when we have something to drink, however, it is ignored in conventional.

In these figures, Phong's smooth shading was applied to both surfaces and rounded edges as proposed before. Using the extended method, smooth highlight lines appear on curved-edges naturally and impressively.

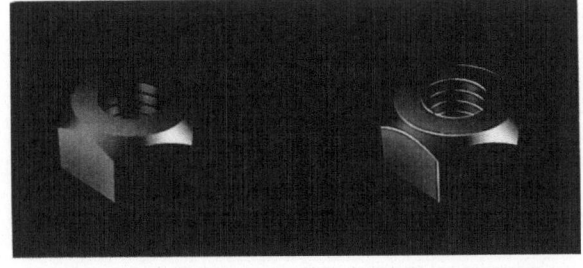

Fig.13 A machine nut.
(a) (*left*) without edge highlights
(b) (*right*) with edge highlights

Fig.14 A Japanese tea cup with green tea.

(a) without edge highlights

(b) with edge highlights

Fig.15 A glass of water

An example of photorealistic image generation is shown in Fig.15. In image (a) (Shinya 1988), a glass of water is rendered by pencil tracing (Shinya 1989). Image (b) was generated by adding edge highlights[1] onto image (a). Though the illuminance pattern of image (a) is realistic enough, some unnatural parts are still remain. Image (b) shows that edge highlights can improve naturalness in photorealistic image generation.

---

[1]These edge highlights were calculated roughly; refraction was ignored and the area light source was not supported exactly.

5   DISCUSSION

5.1   Computation Cost

The computation cost for rendering rounded edges is evaluated here. Using the proposed method, additional calculations for rendering rounded edges are required. Table 1 shows execution times for rendering several figures with and without rounded edges. Z-buffer algorithm, Blinn's shading model, and Phong's smooth shading were used for generating the images. The time depends on the number of rounded edges, however, the increase in calculation time is 11% at most.

A comparison between the proposed method and conventional super-sampling method can be estimated as follows. Suppose the rendering time is in proportion to the total number of sampled points. From Table 1, the ratio of edge-rendering time to surface-rendering time per sampling point is less than 2. Since 3 times as many additional sampling points are required for 2×2 super-sampling, the proposed method is faster than any super-sampling method.

Table 1 Comparison of computation times.

Image	Fig.12	Fig.13	Fig.14
total CPU-time			
(A) surface only	511 sec	239 sec	429 sec
(B) with edge shading	562 sec	254 sec	433 sec
ratio (B)/(A)	1.11	1.06	1.01
average rendering-time for 1 sampling-point			
(C) surface rendering	0.85 msec	3.18 msec	—
(D) edge rendering	1.31 msec	3.11 msec	—
ratio (D)/(C)	1.6	1.0	—

5.2   Hidden Surface/Line Removal Algorithms

In the proposed method, it is necessary to remove both hidden surfaces and hidden lines. Many algorithms on hidden surface or line removal have been proposed. It is possible to apply any hidden surface algorithm and any hidden line algorithm independently. For efficient calculation, however, it is recommended to modify a hidden surface algorithm so as to remove both hidden surfaces and hidden lines simultaneously.

In this case, algorithms should be carefully modified not to eliminate visible edges, because the depth value of an edge is as same as that of the corresponding surface. For area-coherence algorithms and scan-line algorithms, it is easy to maintain connection information between polygons and edges. Therefore, these algorithms are suitable for hidden line elimination. With z-buffer algorithms, on the other hand, the connection information is usually lost. Thus the depth value of a wire-frame is sometimes larger than that of the corresponding pixel on the polygon because of sampling errors. A simple solution is to move the edge wire-frames a little bit nearer to the viewpoint to give a smaller depth value. This method was used for generating the images in this paper, however, it is not a fundamental solution. For ray-tracing algorithms, it is difficult to apply to edges; independent elimination of hidden lines is recommended.

5.3 Discussion on Area Light Sources

Using the proposed method, highlight lines become short when the surfaces are almost completely specular, which is shown in the upper edge of Fig.11. In actual scenes, however, long highlight lines usually appear under similar conditions because of extended area light sources such as windows. This suggests that an extension of the proposed method is required for generating more realistic images under area light sources.

6 CONCLUSION

In this paper, we proposed a new rendering method for highlights appearing on rounded edges, which are important but had been ignored in existing photorealistic rendering methods. By shading edges as thin-cylinders and drawing them as wire-frames, we can simultaneously solve two problems, aliasing artifacts and manipulation cost of surface patches. Using an edge shading equation, surfaces and rounded edges can be consistently shaded and any conventional shading model can be used. Several experiments show that edge highlights can be effectively created by the proposed method, and additional computation cost is less than any super-sampling method.

Highlighting rounded edges provides a new rendering technique not only for photorealistic image generation but also for more comprehensible presentation. Since the additional computation cost is small, our method can be easily utilized in various fields, such as mechanical CAD and computer animation.

ACKNOWLEDGEMENTS

We would like to thank Dr. Hiroshi Yasuda and Kei Takikawa for their continuous support. We also wish to thank Toshimitsu Tanaka, Tadashi Naruse, Masaharu Yoshida, and other colleagues in our section for their advice and encouragement.

References

[Amadatides87] Amanatides J (1987) Realism in Computer Graphics: A Survey. *IEEE Computer Graphics and Applications* **7**(1): 44–56

[Blinn77] Blinn JF (1977) Models of Light Reflection for Computer Synthesized Pictures. *Computer Graphics* **11**(2) (*Proc. SIGGRAPH 77*) pp 192–198

[Cook82] Cook RL, Torrance KE (1982) A Reflectance Model for Computer Graphics. *ACM Trans. Graphics* **1**(1): 7–24

[Cook86] Cook RL (1986) Stochastic Sampling in Computer Graphics. *ACM Trans. Graphics* **5**(1): 51–72

[Crow84] Crow FC (1984) Summed-Area Tables for Texture Mapping. *Computer Graphics* **18**(3) (*Proc. SIGGRAPH 84*) pp 207–212

[Gouraud71] Gouraud H (1971) Continuous Shading of Curved Surfaces. *IEEE Trans. Computers* **C-20**(6): 623–629

[Kondo88] Kondo K, Kimura F, Tajima T (1988) An Interactive Rendering System with Shading. In: Kitagawa T (ed) *Japan Annual Reviews in Electronics, Computers & Telecommunications, Vol.18, Computer Science and Technologies*. Ohbunsha and North-Holland, Tokyo, pp 255–271

[Miller88] Miller GSP (1988) From Wire-frames to Furry Animals. *Proc. Graphics Interface '88*, pp 138–145

[Phong75] Phong BT (1975) Illumination for Computer Generated Pictures. *Comm. ACM* **18**(6): 311–317

[Shinya88] Shinya M (1988) A Glass of Water. In: Brown BE (ed) SIGGRAPH '88 Technical Slide Set Credits. *Computer Graphics* **22**(5): 251

[Shinya89] Shinya M, Saito T, Takahashi T (1989) Rendering Techniques for Transparent Objects. submitted to: *Graphics Interface '89*

[Williams83] Williams L (1983) Pyramidal Parametrics. *Computer Graphics* **17**(3) (*Proc. SIGGRAPH 83*) pp 1–11

Takafumi Saito has been working for Nippon Telegraph and Telephone Corporation (NTT) since 1987. He is currently a research engineer of Visual Media Laboratory. He received the B.E. degree in mathematical engineering and M.E. degree in information engineering at the University of Tokyo, Japan, in 1982 and 1984, respectively. His research interests include computer graphics, geometric modeling, and image processing. He is a member of ACM SIGGRAPH and Information Processing Society of Japan.

Mikio Shinya received the B.E. degree in 1979, and M.E. degree in 1981, in applied physics from Waseda University, Japan. He has been working for Nippon Telegraph and Telephone Corporation (NTT) since 1981, where he is a senior research engineer of Visual Media Laboratory. He has been a visiting scientist of the University of Toronto since 1988. He has been engaged in research on color science, pattern recognition, and computer graphics. His research interests include computer graphics, computer vision, and psychophysics on human vision. He is a member of ACM SIGGRAPH, the Institute of Electronics, Information and Communication Engineerings of Japan, and the Japan Society of Applied Physics.

Tokiichiro Takahashi received the B.E. degree in electronics from Nigata University, Japan, in 1977. He has been working for Nippon Telegraph and Telephone Corporation (NTT) since 1977, where he is a senior research engineer of Visual Media Laboratory. His research interests include computer graphics, computer hologram, use interface, and pattern recognition. He is a member of IEEE Computer Society, the Institute of Electronics, Information and Communication Engineerings of Japan, and NICOGRAPH Association.

Authors' address: NTT Human Interface Laboratories, 1-2356 Take, Yokosuka-shi, Kanagawa, 238-03, JAPAN

Chapter 11
Applications

Reliability of Computer Graphics Images As Visual Assessment Tool

E. Nakamae, K. Kaneda, K. Harada, T. Miwa, T. Nishita, and R. Saiki

ABSTRACT

This paper analyzes the use of computer graphics images as an architectural assessment tool. The characteristics of such images as an architectural simulation tool are discussed and their reliability as an assessment tool is evaluated and compared with that of traditional hand-generated perspective drawings. An example application, architectural simulation of a city renewal plan, is presented.

Key words: reliability, montage image, assessment, architectural simulation, computer graphics system.

1   INTRODUCTION

Assessing the impact of new construction, such as bridges, buildings, and roads, on the local visual environment, is very important and should be considered in conjunction with their physical, chemical, and other environmental impacts. Traditionally, this evaluation has been carried out using hand-generated perspective drawings. However, the method is inevitably artificial, and this obstructs objective assessment of the visual impact of new construction. Moreover, hand drawings are very costly to prepare, and cannot be dynamically altered during the course of the design.

If highly realistic (or photographic) images are able to be created dynamically (from various view points), we can foretell what visual impact is followed due to the new constructions to the environments. The best planning that taking into account of the visual impact might be obtained by using these images. We could call the checking process by using the highly realistic images as the visual assessment of the new constructions to their environments.

The authors have proposed an image montage method to address this problem [Nakamae 86]. In this method, the computer combines a computer generated image of the proposed construction with a scanned in photograph of the visual background to create a composite image suitable for objective visual assessment. This technique produces highly realistic images with relatively short calculation times.

In the case of a large scale city renewal effort, however, little or none of the image area will be filled by a scanned in background. The image will consist almost entirely of computer-generated objects. This implies that long calculation times will be required to generate highly realistic images. In order to take best advantage of computer generated images, it is important to keep the calculation time low so that dynamic alterations of view point or view reference point are practical. Thus, for city planning, the utility for assessment purposes of computer generated images is less than that of montage images.

There has not been a comprehensive discussion of the reliability of drawings (including both hand and computer prepared drawings) as a visual assessment tool. Thus, we will first present an analysis of computer graphic images for assessment. In the following section we discuss the characteristics of computer images as an assessment tool, the possibility of using these images as a highly reliable assessment tool, and compare their reliability to that of traditional hand prepared drawings.

Section 2 describes a computer graphic based assessment method by using a set of images developed by the authors. In Section 3 the relative reliability of assessment using computer images compared to that using hand-drawn images is investigated, and the characteristics of our method are discussed. Section 4 provides an example of assessment using our images, and Section 5 gives a summary of results obtained.

2 VISUAL ASSESSMENT USING COMPUTER GRAPHIC DRAWINGS

As discussed in the previous section, the current application differs from montage images in that most of the image area is computer generated, with very little scanned-in background. Images are composed of many elements, which we will call image segments. We will further classify image segments into natural and artificial objects. In order to make possible objective visual assessment, the overall picture must exhibit a sort of "harmony of realisticness." While one wishes to render each image segment as realistically as possible, there is a competing desire to keep calculation times down in order to create a practical chain of image creation steps for dynamic assessment.

For artificial objects, calculation time can be reduced by reducing the rendering accuracy for objects distant from the viewpoint. Thus, distant objects are rendered with less, and nearby objects are rendered with more accuracy.

Natural objects have previously been displayed by using probabilistic algorithms [Reeves 85], botanical and rule-based methods [Aono 84], and fractals [Smith 84]. However, due to the wide variety of trees used in city planning, none of these methods are suitable for use in the computer image based assessment problem. Our method provides two methods for displaying natural objects. First, natural objects can be very roughly sketched using primitive shapes. Thus natural objects are treated identically with artificial objects. Second, natural objects can be displayed by the montage method. A natural object database is generated by extracting necessary objects from their backgrounds in scanned-in photographs. Each application can reference the most appropriate object from the natural object database. By choosing between the two methods on a case-by-case basis, our method generates highly realistic computer graphic images for visual assessment.

Figure 1 shows a block diagram of our image management system. The total operations are composed of three blocks, the data input step, the image creation step, and the representation step.

2.1 Data Input Step

In the data input step, operations are carried out to handle the input of 3D data, and the step allows the data to be verified using simple wire frame output. This step is implemented on microcomputers with a view to its simultaneous use by many operators.

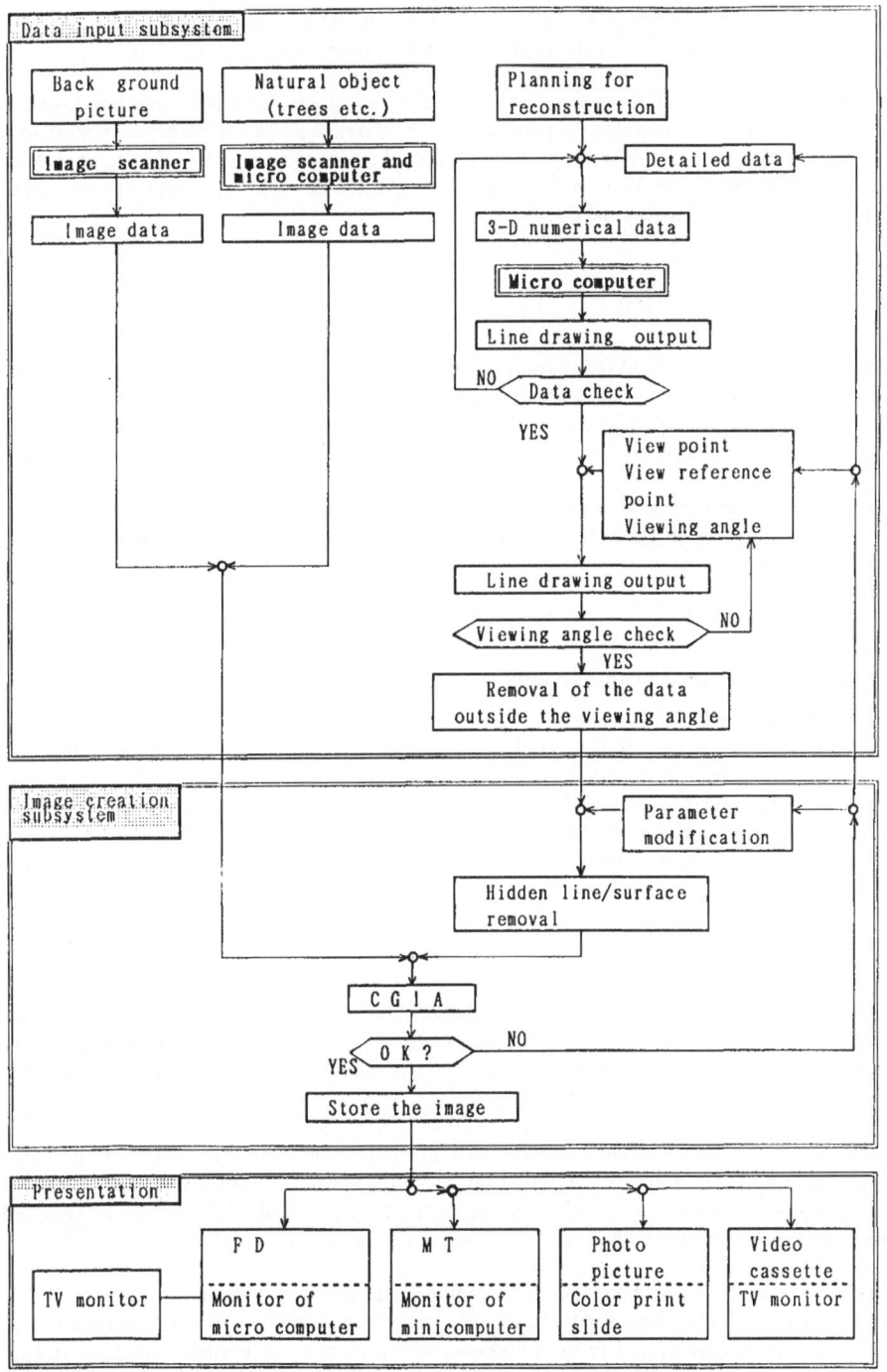

Figure 1: **Block Diagram of our Assessment Image Creation. The total procedures are for creating computer graphic images for assessment (CGIA)**

3D objects are represented as sets of primitives. Each object also has color and texture attributes. When an error is encountered in the input, it can be edited.

When data input and verification are completed, the view point, view reference point, and viewing angle can be set. For a constant view point and view reference point, varying the viewing angle produces very different images. With a wide viewing angle, a wide angle lens effect is produced, while a narrow viewing angle produces a telescopic lens effect. The viewing angle can be dynamically selected based on line drawing output.

2.2 Image Creation Step

The main merit of our method is inherent in the shading process. By properly adjusting the color and texture of each object, a computer image with very nearly photographic appearance can be generated. Data is transferred to the mini-computer based image creation step from the data input step. Here hidden line and surface removal, and shading with illumination maps are performed.

Artificial objects, such as buildings, can be adequately described numerically. However, natural objects, such as low brush thickets and roadside trees, cannot be easily described using geometric primitives. Our empirical work has yielded the following composite method for displaying natural objects.

2.2.1 Displaying low brush thickets

This class of natural objects is displayed using primitives such as parallelepipeds. The color and intensity of each surface of the resulting object are calculated as for artificial objects, based on the light source. The calculated color of each surface is then modulated by a prescribed, semi-random function. This produces realistic appearing low brush thickets. The method may also be applied to artificial objects such as walls of buildings or stone walls to increase the rendering quality.

2.2.2 Displaying tall roadside trees

Two methods are provided for displaying roadside trees. The first is the composite image montage method. A photograph of a real tree is scanned in and a microcomputer is used to extract the tree from its background. The tree image data is composited into the overall image by the image creation step, using intensity and position data.

A major drawback of this method is the difficulty of creating the database. Assembling photographs of a wide variety of trees and assembling them into a database is a formidable task. However, once the database is completed, it provides a very valuable source of realistic tree images, allowing realistic assessment images to be created using many different types of trees.

The second method is approximation with geometric primitives, similar to the method described for brush thickets above. Each roadside tree is approximated with appropriate primitives, and the obtained tree figures are stored in the database. When used, a randomizing function is applied to the surfaces as discussed for the brush thickets. This method is very simple, but unfortunately does not produce highly realistic trees. However, it can be useful as a first approximation for selecting the general shape of tree to be used.

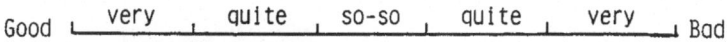

Good ⌊ very │ quite │ so-so │ quite │ very ⌋ Bad

Figure 2: Preference Scale for the Category Method.

As shown in Figure 1, conversion of image data from the image scanner is carried out in the data input step. Our method also supports scanned-in background pictures for montage images, but that is beyond the scope of this paper.

3   COMPUTER GRAPHIC IMAGES FOR VISUAL ASSESSMENT

In actual assessment applications, the style of computer graphics used must be tailored carefully to the assessment purpose. For example, in the initial stages of renewal planning, it is important to keep calculation time low enough to facilitate very dynamic interaction with the required operations. Line drawings (with or without hidden line removal) are thus very valuable at this stage. The main objective here is to verify the basic plan. As planning proceeds, requirements move to more and more realistic images. The process moves through a progression from simple line drawings, through ever more realistic (and computationally expensive) drawings.

In order to ascertain that the computer graphic images are meeting the requirements, it is helpful to do some analysis of the human user's reaction to various images, and subjective preferences. Psychologists have developed the following types of methodology for quantifying a viewer's reaction to an image [Yasuda 77], [Wright 60].

a) Ordering Method.
Each viewer selects r objects out of n total objects, or orders the r objects.

b) Pair Comparison Method.
Pairs of objects selected from the set are shown together to the viewer, who names a preference within each pair.

c) Category Method.
Some number of categories are defined over the preference scale, (Figure 2) and the viewer is asked to put each object into the most suitable category.

d) SD Method.
Pairs of adjectives of opposite meaning are set up, and the viewer rates each object on a linear scale between each pair of adjectives.

In this paper we focus on the use of highly realistic images for assessment, since they provide a basis for a wider range of use. One of the items to be evaluated using such images is the overall color design of the construction. This includes i) determining the basic color of the environment, and ii) comparing monotone colors against other color schemes. Highly realistic images are also very useful for evaluating the appearance from various view points. In the final step, these images are used to select the best of a number of reconstruction plans. Of the above listed psychological evaluation methods, b), c), and d) are useful for visual assessment using computer generated images.

Please observe Figures 3 through 5 for a comparison of hand drawings with computer drawings. Figure 3 shows three hand prepared drawings from a view point 3.5 meters above the ground (a

638

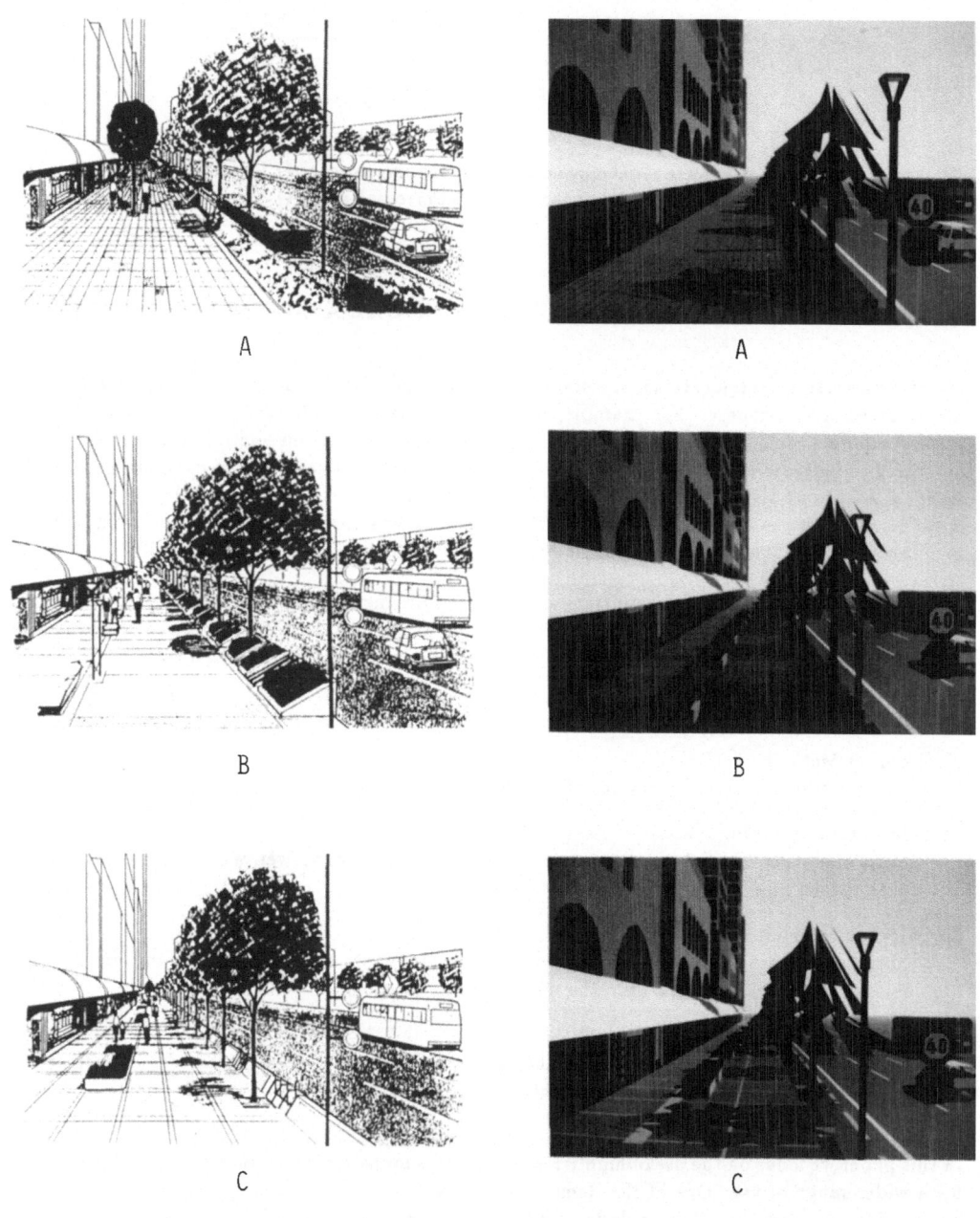

Figure 3: Example of Hand Prepared Perspective Drawing.

Figure 4: Example of Computer Prepared Perspective Drawing. Viewpoint is 3.5m above the ground.

height very commonly used in hand prepared architectural drawings). Figure 4 shows drawings from the same perspective, but prepared by computer. Figure 5 is also computer generated, but with the height now set to 1.6 meters above the sidewalk. This is approximately the eye height of a pedestrian. The trees along the sidewalk in Figures 4 and 5 were generated using the simple approximation by primitives described in 2.2.2. Slides of each of these images were presented to a number of testees. The testees consisted of 34 non-specialists and 31 engineers with responsibility for the reconstruction plan, for a total of 65 testees. The evaluation was carried out as described in the next section.

3.1 Application of Category Method

The testees were questioned on:

1) Total image impression.

2) Showiness.

3) Lightness.

4) Softness.

5) Color and texture of the sidewalk.

6) Flower pots and benches on the sidewalk.

7) Width of the sidewalk.

The testees were asked to place each image in one of five categories on a preference scale (Figure 2). Items 2) through 4) were phrased using adjectives, and thus the category method applied to these items is equivalent to the SD method. Tables 1, 2, and 3 summarize the result of applying the category method to images A, B, and C for Figures 3, 4, and 5. In each table, the first row contains the results for the non-specialists, and the second row for the engineer testees. The third row is the total result, and the number in parentheses is the variance.

We can discuss each image's reliability as a tool for the assessment by using the variance. If an image is presented to a group of people who are supposed to share the same aspect or preference for the plan, lower variance between each person's answer is derived only if the image shows the expected scene faithfully. Therefore, the results obtained from the specialist group in our test serve as the useful source to decide what is the better image for assessment. In the following discussions, we suppose that the variance is closely related to the reliability of the assessment, with small variance indicating that the testees gave largely similar answers. Thus, the media is considered to provide a reliable base for assessment.

The results in Tables 1 through 3 show that the variance was smaller for the engineers than for the non-specialists. This is a natural result, and verifies the accuracy of the image comparing method c).

On the other hand, comparing the hand and computer drawn images (drawn from the same viewpoint) in Figures 3 and 4, the variance is smaller for the hand drawn images in every case except that of B, that is, the hand drawn images are more reliable. This may be due to the fact that the height in Figures 3 and 4 is the standard height for hand prepared perspective drawings, giving a preferential bias to the hand drawings. In A, the viewpoint is set higher, and the test results for the engineers favor the computer drawings. As a final result, computer graphic images are judged to provide a more stable media for assessment (one with less variance), than hand prepared drawings.

Table 1: Category Method Applied to Image A of Figures 3, 4, and 5. First row of each block is the result for non-specialists, and second row is for engineer testees. The third row gives the total result. Variance is given in parentheses. X is results for hand drawings. Y and Z are results for computer drawings of the higher view point and of the lower view point, respectively.

Evalnation items	X	Y	Z
(1) Total evaluation	3.35 (0.96)	2.91 (1.54)	3.82 (1.06)
	3.20 (0.89)	2.27 (0.55)	3.26 (0.80)
	3.28 (0.90)	2.61 (1.16)	3.55 (1.00)
(2) Showiness	3.00 (1.52)	2.53 (1.35)	2.94 (0.91)
	2.97 (0.72)	2.40 (0.59)	2.87 (0.52)
	2.98 (1.13)	2.47 (0.98)	2.91 (0.71)
(3) Lightness	3.44 (1.16)	2.97 (1.12)	3.88 (0.77)
	3.00 (0.55)	2.45 (0.81)	3.55 (0.46)
	3.23 (0.91)	2.73 (1.02)	3.72 (0.64)
(4) Tenderness	3.00 (0.97)	2.24 (0.97)	2.94 (0.66)
	2.70 (0.63)	1.97 (0.52)	2.71 (0.55)
	2.86 (0.82)	2.11 (0.77)	2.83 (0.61)
(5) Color/texture of sidewalk	3.30 (1.18)	3.15 (1.46)	3.68 (0.77)
	2.60 (0.73)	2.30 (0.49)	2.94 (0.80)
	2.97 (1.08)	2.75 (1.18)	3.32 (0.91)
(6) Impression of flower pots and benches	3.06 (1.27)	2.82 (1.24)	3.44 (1.28)
	3.10 (1.06)	2.14 (0.62)	2.80 (0.58)
	3.08 (1.15)	2.51 (1.06)	3.14 (1.04)
(7) Width of sidewalk	4.21 (0.71)	3.71 (0.82)	3.91 (1.23)
	3.93 (0.62)	2.80 (0.86)	3.58 (0.65)
	4.08 (0.68)	3.28 (1.03)	3.75 (0.97)

Table 2: Category Method Applied to Image B of Figures 3, 4, and 5. Contents are as for Table 1.

Evalnation items	X	Y	Z
(1) Total evaluation	3.53 (1.05)	4.09 (0.39)	4.03 (0.82)
	3.60 (0.66)	3.45 (0.72)	3.68 (0.36)
	3.56 (0.85)	3.79 (0.64)	3.86 (0.62)
(2) Showiness	3.71 (0.94)	4.03 (0.45)	4.12 (0.59)
	3.57 (0.53)	3.19 (0.63)	3.71 (0.23)
	3.64 (0.74)	3.63 (0.71)	3.92 (0.45)
(3) Lightness	3.42 (0.56)	3.85 (0.68)	3.88 (0.59)
	3.67 (0.51)	3.36 (0.70)	3.55 (0.32)
	3.54 (0.54)	3.62 (0.74)	3.72 (0.49)
(4) Tenderness	3.03 (0.88)	3.59 (0.67)	3.68 (0.77)
	2.97 (0.65)	3.10 (0.82)	3.48 (0.46)
	3.00 (0.76)	3.35 (0.80)	3.59 (0.62)
(5) Color/texture of sidewalk	3.27 (1.53)	3.56 (0.80)	3.85 (0.61)
	3.12 (0.70)	3.07 (0.73)	3.19 (0.55)
	3.22 (1.13)	3.32 (0.82)	3.54 (0.69)
(6) Impression of flower pots and benches	3.44 (1.28)	3.74 (0.99)	4.00 (0.79)
	3.53 (0.74)	3.13 (1.18)	3.23 (0.91)
	3.48 (1.02)	3.45 (1.16)	3.63 (0.99)
(7) Width of sidewalk	3.85 (1.16)	3.77 (0.67)	3.44 (0.86)
	3.43 (0.74)	3.39 (0.51)	3.13 (0.32)
	3.66 (0.99)	3.59 (0.62)	3.29 (0.62)

Table 3: Category Method Applied to Image C of Figures 3, 4, and 5. Contents are as for Table 1.

Evalnation items	X	Y	Z
(1) Total evaluation	3.09 (1.13)	3.18 (0.88)	2.82 (1.06)
	3.20 (1.06)	2.42 (0.52)	2.55 (0.72)
	3.14 (1.08)	2.82 (0.84)	2.69 (0.90)
(2) Showiness	2.88 (0.83)	3.00 (0.85)	3.06 (0.72)
	2.83 (0.83)	2.65 (0.37)	2.71 (0.41)
	2.86 (0.82)	2.83 (0.64)	2.89 (0.60)
(3) Lightness	3.56 (0.92)	3.50 (0.44)	3.03 (1.09)
	3.30 (0.70)	2.81 (0.63)	2.97 (0.63)
	3.45 (0.82)	3.17 (0.64)	3.00 (0.86)
(4) Tenderness	2.97 (1.00)	2.97 (0.70)	2.44 (0.86)
	3.00 (0.83)	2.65 (0.70)	2.39 (0.51)
	2.98 (0.91)	2.82 (0.72)	2.42 (0.68)
(5) Color/texture of sidewalk	3.18 (1.12)	3.18 (0.70)	2.85 (1.22)
	3.20 (0.58)	2.58 (0.65)	2.97 (0.70)
	3.19 (0.85)	2.89 (0.75)	2.91 (0.96)
(6) Impression of flower pots and benches	3.00 (1.15)	3.09 (1.05)	2.59 (1.10)
	3.07 (1.10)	2.45 (0.66)	2.48 (0.73)
	3.03 (1.11)	2.79 (0.95)	2.54 (0.91)
(7) Width of sidewalk	3.74 (1.11)	3.68 (0.65)	3.29 (1.00)
	3.47 (0.95)	3.03 (0.43)	3.00 (0.53)
	3.61 (1.04)	3.37 (0.64)	3.15 (0.79)

3.2 Application of the Pair Comparison Method

The hand drawings of Figure 3 were compared to the computer drawings (with a lower viewpoint) of Figure 5, by the pair comparison method. Two images (for example, Figure 3A and Figure 3B) are shown to the testees, who are asked to judge which is preferable in some dimension (for instance, "showy"). Testees who answered neither were excluded from the results. The results were summarized using a comparison matrix P, where element P_{ij} (here indices i and j run from 1 to 3) is the normalized count of testees answering that image j is preferable ("showy", for instance) to image i. It is clear then that $P_{ij} + P_{ji} = 1$. The normalized values for the sum of each row of P, namely

$$Ps_i = \frac{1}{N} \sum_{j=1}^{3} P_{ij}$$

are plotted in Figure 6. Here N is the number of testees. Figure 6 gives separate results for engineers and for non-specialists. In both cases the images prepared by computer from the lower viewpoint show a larger range (difference between largest and smallest Ps_i). This indicates that assessment based on computer prepared drawings provides a more stable result than hand prepared drawings.

4   ASSESSMENT WITH COMPUTER GRAPHIC IMAGES

The results of Section 3 indicate that computer graphic drawings allow more stable assessment than hand prepared ones, justifying work to apply computer graphics techniques to architectural simulation. However, Figures 4 and 5 were generated using the artificially simple method for

A

B

C

Figure 5: Example of Computer Prepared Drawing. Viewpoint at 1.6m above the ground.

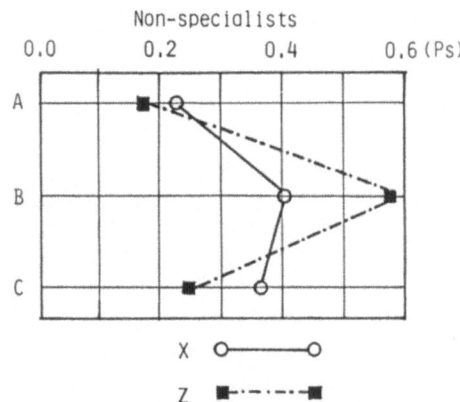

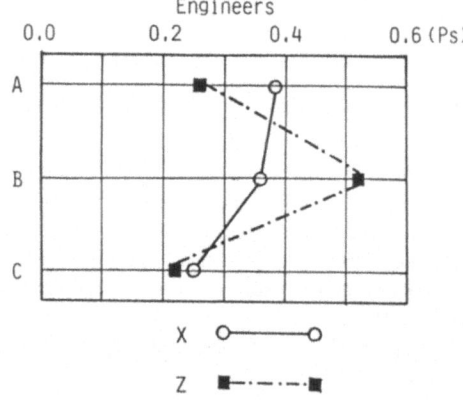

Figure 6: Sum of Rows of Comparison Matrix P. Engineer and non-specialist results are shown separately. X is results for hand drawings, and Z for computer drawings of the lower view point.

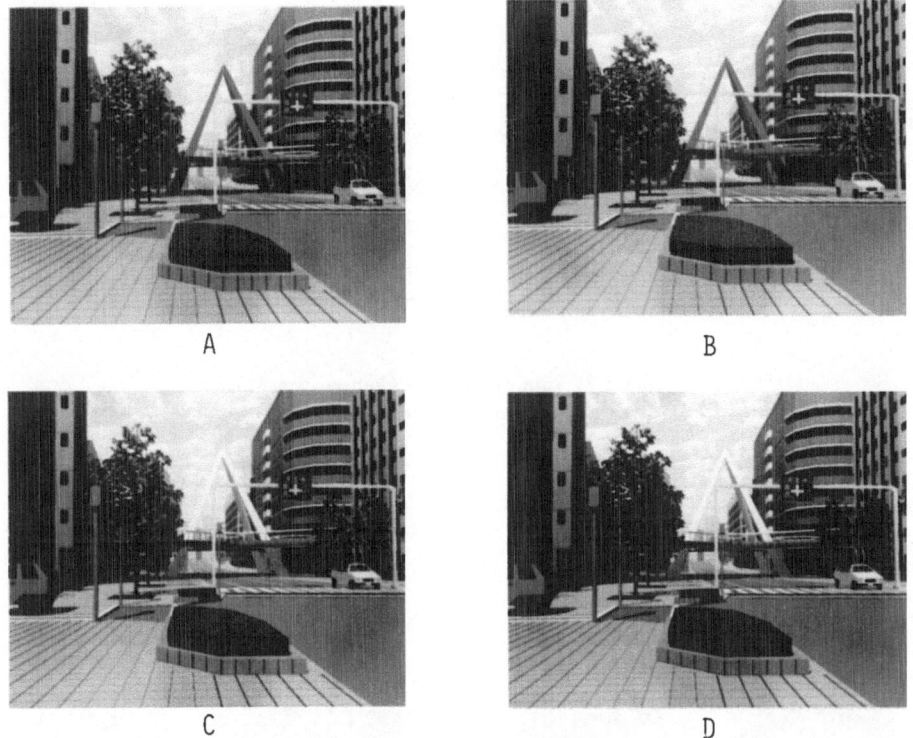

Figure 7: Computer Drawings for Selection of Bridge Color.

natural objects, leading to a fairly low level of realism. This problem was pointed out by many of the testees. The worst problem they pointed out was the representation quality of trees. Thus, we recognized the necessity of displaying trees by the more sophisticated method described in 2.2.2. The resulting, more realistic images were actually used in the further discussions. Since total image assessment is the goal, the pair comparison method was used.

Suppose that the objective of the assessment in the example is to determine the appropriate color and shape of a pedestrian bridge to be constructed near an intersection (a problem from an actual urban reconstruction application). Figure 7 shows a set of images used to select a harmonious color for the bridge. Roadside trees were generated using the cutting and montage method described in 2.2.2. The viewpoint is 1.6 meters above the ground.

The four images of Figure 7 were investigated via the pair comparison method, with the help of 89 testees, including 31 engineers. The results, in Figure 8, show a clear preference for D over the other plans. The next application, in Figure 9, is selection of the color and shape of the bridge. The results, in Figure 10, again show an overwhelming preference for the plan of Figure 7D.

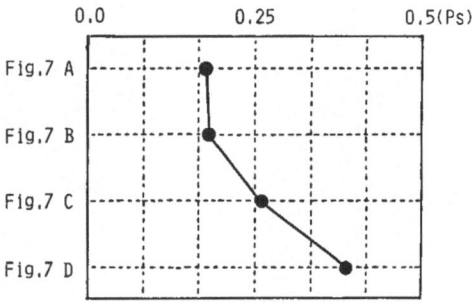

Figure 8: Sum of Rows of Comparison Matrix
P, for Images from Figure 7.

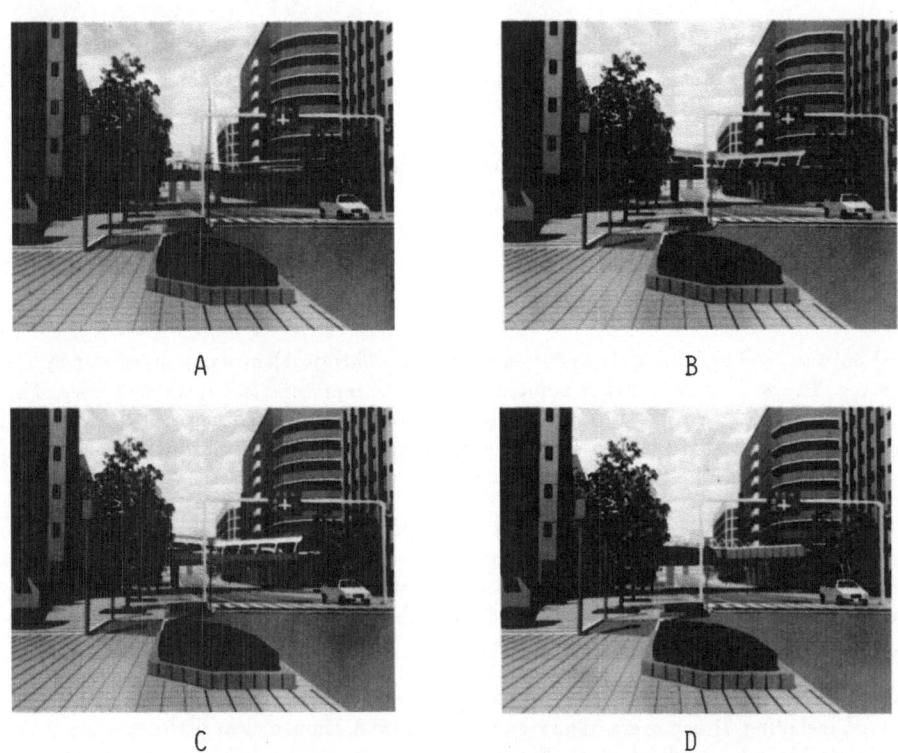

Figure 9: Computer Drawings for Selection of Bridge Color/Shape.

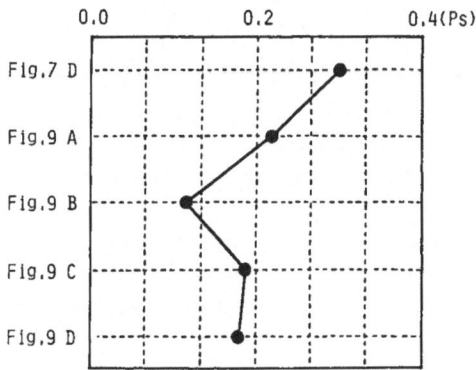

Figure 10: Sum of Rows of Comparison Matrix
P for Images from Figures 9 and 7D.

5 CONCLUSIONS

The value of applying computer graphics techniques to assessment of the visual impact of new construction has already been appreciated, and some applications have been reported. However, no results had been reported with regard to the characteristics of using computer graphics images for architectural simulation, the reliability of the media, or a comparison of its reliability in comparison to traditional techniques. We have investigated these issues using the preference experiment with testees. The principal results of our investigations are:

a) computer drawings, in general, lead to a result with smaller variance. Hence, reliable assessments results are guaranteed.

b) The range of results obtained using computer drawings is larger than that using traditional hand drawings. Thus, more stable assessment results are possible.

c) Selection of the viewpoint is a dominating factor in the assessment results. The fact that the viewpoint may be easily, dynamically altered proved to be one of the greatest merits of using computer drawings.

To sum up, our results show that computer graphic images hold great promise for environmental assessment.

ACKNOWLEDGMENTS

We are grateful to Bonnie G. Sullivan for her discussions and preparing the manuscript. A referee's comments were very useful to clarify the point of the paper. Special thanks to Masahiko Tsuchihashi for his discussions and computer operation for obtaining data of the images.

References

[Aono 84] Aono M and Kunii TL (1984) "Botanical Tree Image Generation," IEEE CG&A 4(5): 10-34

[Nakamae 86] Nakamae E, Harada K, Ishizaki T and Nisita T (1986) "A Montage Method: The Overlaying of the Computer Generated Images onto a Background Photograph," Computer Graphics 20(4): 207-214

[Reeves 85] Reeves WT and Blau R (1985) "Approximate and Probabilistic Algorithms for Shading and Rendering Structured Particle Systems," Computer Graphics 19(3): 313-322

[Smith 84] Smith AR (1984) "Plants, Fractals and Formal Languages," Computer Grapics 18(3): 1-10

[Wright 60] Wright and Swewall (1960) "Path Coefficients and Path Regression: Alternative or Complementary Concepts," Biometrics 16: 189-202

[Yasuda 77] Yasuda and Umino (1977) "Social Statistics," Maruzen, Tokyo

Eihachiro Nakamae is a professor at Hiroshima University where he was appointed as research associate in 1956 and a professor in 1968. He was an associate researcher at Clarkson College of Technology, Potsdam, N. Y., from 1973 to 1974. His research interests include computer graphics and electric machinery.
Nakamae received the BE, ME, and DE degrees in 1954, 1956, and 1967 from Waseda University. He is a member of IEEE, IEE of Japan, IPS of Japan and IEICE of Japan.
Address: Faculty of Engineering, Hiroshima University, Saijo-cho, Higashi-hiroshima, 724 Japan.

Kazufumi Kaneda is a research associate in Faculty of Engineering at Hiroshima University. He worked at the Chugoku Electric Power Company Ltd., Japan from 1984 to 1986. He joined Hiroshima University in 1986. His research interests include computer graphics and image processing.
Kaneda received the BE and ME in 1982 and 1984, respectively, from Hiroshima University. He is a member of IEE of Japan, IPS of Japan and IEICE of Japan.
Address: Faculty of Engineering, Hiroshima University, Saijo-cho, Higashi-hiroshima, 724 Japan.

Koichi Harada is an assistant professor in Faculty of Engineering at Hiroshima University. He worked at Takamatsu Technical College, Japan, in 1978 and studied neural networks. He is with the Faculty of Engineering, Hiroshima University from 1979. His research interests include data interpolation and computer graphics.

Harada received the BE in 1973 from Hiroshima University, and MS and Ph. D in 1975 and 1978, respectively, from Tokyo Institute of Technology. He is a member of ACM, IPS of Japan, IEE of Japan and IEICE of Japan.

Address: Faculty of Engineering, Hiroshima University, Saijo-cho, Higashi-hiroshima, 724 Japan.

Toshihide Miwa is a professor in the department of Civil Engineering at Fukuyama University from 1985. He was an associate researcher at Kyoto University from 1950 to 1953, and he was a planning staff of Osaka Municipal Government from 1955 to 1982. His research interests include landscape design and civil engineering.

Miwa received the B. Eng. and Ph. D. in 1950 and 1981 from Kyoto University. He is a member of JSCE.

Address: Faculty of Engineering, Fukuyama University, Sanzo, Higashimura-cho, Fukuyama, 729-02 Japan.

Tomoyuki Nishita is an associate professor in the department of Electronic and Electrical Engineering at Fukuyama University, Japan. He was on the research staff at Mazda from 1973 to 1979 and worked on design and development of computer-controlled vehicle system. He joined Fukuyama University in 1979. He was a visiting professor and research associate in the Engineering Computer Graphics Laboratory at Brigham Young University from 1988 to the end of March, 1989. His research interests involve computer graphics including lighting model, hidden-surface removal, and antialiasing.

Nishita received his BE, ME and Ph. D in Engineering in 1971, 1973, and 1985, respectively, from Hiroshima University. He is a member of ACM, IPS of Japan and IEE of Japan.

Address: Faculty of Engineering, Fukuyama University, Sanzo, Higashimura-cho, Fukuyama, 729-02 Japan.

Ryoichi Saiki is an administrative official of Osaka Municipal Government. He belongs to the Public Engineering Works Foundation Office. He is charged with civil engineering and city planning as a deputy section chief. His duties include research and development concerning road space, its efficient usage and landscaping.

Saiki received the B. Eng. from Kansai University in 1975.

Address: City of Osaka Public Engineering Works Foundation Office, Umeda UN Building, 5-14-10, Nishi-tenma, Kita-ku, Osaka, 530 Japan.

A Digitisation Algorithm for the Entry of Planar Maps

J.F. Dufourd, C. Gross, and J.C. Spehner

Abstract

In this paper, we present an algorithm for the digitisation of closed polygons, represented by their boundaries. This algorithm is especially well-adapted in cartography to the digitisation of base maps on a graphic tablet. It automatically detects the closure of polygons and checks for planarity whenever the map is modified.

Keywords : 2-D modelling, combinatory maps, topology, planarity, cartography.

INTRODUCTION

A map is a graphical representation of data concerning geographical objects, objects that have spatial reference [Bertin 73]. It is built from a base map, which is the set of information required to localise those objects on the plan. In former times, base maps were drawn on a fixed, concrete paper support; today they are stored in computer files. The advent of computer technology in cartography has led to many research efforts and to developments in many areas, [Peucker 75, Nagy 79, Monmonier 82]. Despite advances, many problems have yet to be solved, especially in the digitisation of base maps, problems related to the nature of the data, their size, and their verification and validation. Also, the amount of data to digitize may be very large, and the digitisation often becomes a tedious task that one wishes to facilitate.

In this context, we present a digitisation algorithm for closed polygons based on the concept of combinatorial topological maps. This concept which was originally developed by mathematicians [Jacques 70, Tutte 84] , has been rapidly adopted into computer science [Michelucci 84, Spenher 86, Dufourd 88, Lienhardt 88]. It leads to a topological representation of regions by their boundaries, and therefore to data structures of a topological nature. The fundamental unit of the data structures is the *dart* : a directed polygonal line, whose end points are called *vertices*.

The algorithm automatically detects the closure of polygons, which constitutes a first validation check on the data. A check on planarity is performed by systematically detecting intersections of edges, except at the vertices, in a highly efficient manner. At the completion of the digitisation process, the base map is complete and does not require any further adjustment. We give the algorithm in the case of a manual digitising on a digital table by an operator, but the chains of points may result from an automatic or semi-automatic digitiser.

After a review of combinatorial topological maps in section 1, section 2 introduces some definitions related to our application domain. Section 3 shows an example of data structures based on the preceding concepts. In section 4 the entry of a planar map is described, and section 5 explains the processing of intersections. The algorithm itself is given in section 6, before our conclusion.

1. REVIEW OF THE CONCEPT OF COMBINATORIAL TOPOLOGICAL MAPS

We shall give here some definitions related with the notion of an *oriented map* [Spehner 86] originally called a *constellation* [Jacques 70] and subsequently generalized to the case of a non-oriented map [Cori 75, Fontet 79, Tutte 84, Guibas 85].

Definition 1.1. A **map** is defined as a triplet $M = (D, \alpha, \sigma)$ where :
- D is a finite set, whose elements are called **darts**, which are directed topological edges.
- α is an involution without fixed points on $D \Leftrightarrow \alpha^2 = 1$ and $\not\exists x / \alpha(x) = x$,
- σ is a permutation on D.

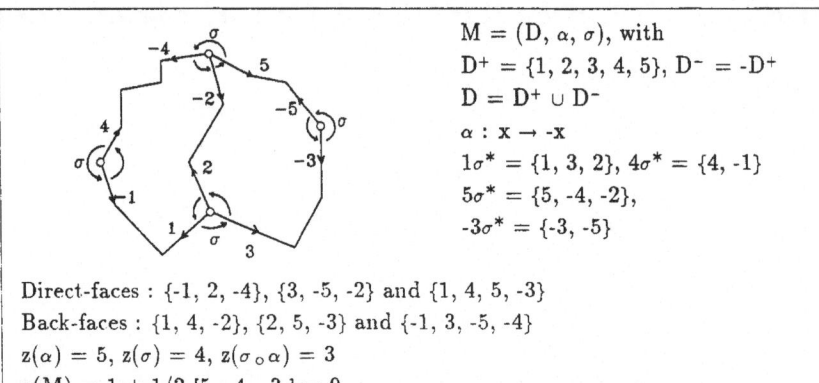

Direct-faces : {-1, 2, -4}, {3, -5, -2} and {1, 4, 5, -3}
Back-faces : {1, 4, -2}, {2, 5, -3} and {-1, 3, -5, -4}
$z(\alpha) = 5$, $z(\sigma) = 4$, $z(\sigma \circ \alpha) = 3$
$g(M) = 1 + 1/2 [5 - 4 - 3] = 0$

Figure 1. An example of a planar map

Definition 1.2. Let $M = (D, \alpha, \sigma)$ be a map; the orbit $d\alpha^* = \{d, \alpha(d)\}$ (where $d \in D$) is called an **edge** of the map M, and darts d and $\alpha(d)$ are said to be **opposits**. For any given dart d, the dart $\alpha(d)$ is denoted -d.

The orbit $d\sigma^* = \{d, \sigma(d), \sigma^2(d), ..., \sigma^{k-1}(d)\}$ such that $\sigma^k(d) = d$ is called a **vertex** of M ; $|d\sigma^*|$ is the **degree** of the vertex $v = d\sigma^*$; darts of the same vertex are said to be **adjacent**.

The set V of all vertices and the set U of all edges define a non directed multigraph G(M), which is said to be **underlying** the map M (fig. 1).

Definition 1.3. Any sequence $c = (d_1, ..., d_n)$ of darts of a map $M = (D, \alpha, \sigma)$, such that $\forall i \in \{2, ..., n\} \; \exists \; k_i \in \mathbf{Z} \; d_i = \sigma^{k_i} \circ \alpha(d_{i-1})$, is called a **path** of M. If $\exists \; k_{n+1} / d_1 = \sigma^{k_{n+1}} \circ \alpha(d_n)$, this path is called a **circuit** of M.

If $c = (d_1, ..., d_n)$ is a circuit, then $\forall \; i \in 1, ..., n$, $(d_{i+1}, ..., d_n, d_1, ..., d_i)$ is identified with c. It is sometimes said that c is a cyclic sequence. It is often the case that c is assimilated to the set of darts $\{d_1, ..., d_n\}$.

Definition 1.4. A **direct-face** (resp. **back-face**) of M is a circuit of M for which :

$$\forall \; i \in \{2, ..., n\}, \; d_i = \sigma^{-1} \circ \alpha(d_{i-1}) \; (\text{resp. } d_i = \sigma \circ \alpha(d_{i-1}))$$

From here on, we shall denote $A\tau^*$ as the orbit $\{\tau^p(b), b \in A, p \geq 0\}$, for any dart subset $A \subset D$ and any permutation τ of D; in other words, it is the set of all darts in D reachable through τ from those of A.

Definition 1.5. The map $M' = (D', \alpha', \sigma')$ is a **submap** of $M = (D, \alpha, \sigma)$ if

    (i) $D' \subseteq D$;
    (ii) $D' = D - (D - D'\sigma^*)\alpha^*$ and $D'\alpha = D'$;
    (iii) $\alpha' = \alpha \; |D'$ and $\sigma' = \sigma \; |D'$
        where σ' is such that $\forall \; d \in D'$, $\sigma'(d) = \sigma^k(d)$ where k is the smallest integer
        such that $\sigma^k(d) \in D'$.

The map M' is obtained by suppressing darts in the map M. The graph G(M') is a subgraph of G(M).

Definition 1.6. $M' = (D', \alpha', \sigma')$ is a **partial map** of $M = (D, \alpha, \sigma)$ if

    (i) $D' \subseteq D$;
    (ii) $D'\sigma^* = D \; (= \{\sigma^p(d) \; ; d \in D', p \geq 0\})$ and $D'\alpha = D'$;
    (iii) $\alpha' = \alpha \; |D'$ and $\sigma' = \sigma \; |D'$.

The map M' is obtained by suppressing edges in the map M but keeping the same vertices. The graph G(M') is a partial graph of G(M).

Definition 1.7. A map M is said to be **connected** if the graph G(M) is connected.

Definition 1.8. Let M = (D, α, σ) be a connected map; the number

$$g(M) = 1 + 1/2 \left[z(\alpha) - z(\sigma) - z(\sigma \circ \alpha) \right]$$

where, for all permutation ω of D, z(ω) is the number of orbits of ω, is called the **genus** of the map M. In this case, z(α), z(σ) and z(σ∘α) are respectively the number of edges, of vertices and of faces. It has been demonstrated that g(M) is a natural [Jacques 68]. The genus of a non-connected map is the sum of the genus of the connected sub-maps which constitute it.

Definition 1.9. A map with a null genus is said **planar**.
A planar map can be drawn on the plan without edges intersecting, except at the vertices.

Definition 1.10. Let M = (D, α, σ) be a planar connected map and d ∈ D ; an edge e = {d, α(d)} of M is called an **isthmus** if, by suppressing it from map M, the submap resulting is not connected. (fig. 2), i.e. the two darts d and α(d) belong to the same face with σ(d) ≠ d and σ∘α(d) ≠ α(d)

Definition 1.11. Let M = (D, α, σ) be a planar map and d ∈ D ; the edge {d, α(d)} is called a **peninsula** if σ(d) = d and σ∘α(d) ≠ α(d) or σ(d) ≠ d and σ∘α(d) = α(d) (fig. 2).

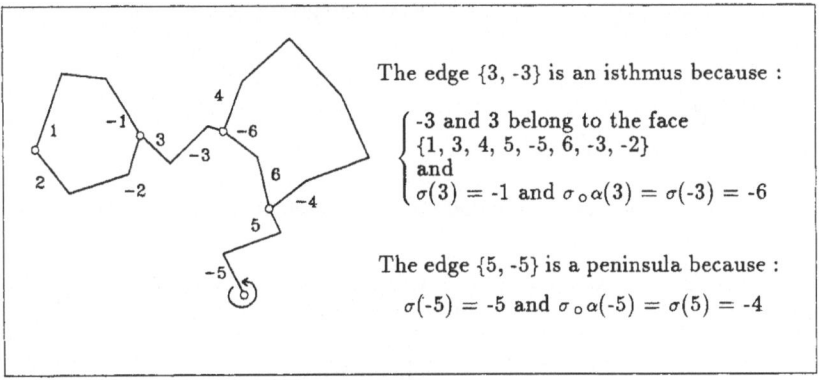

The edge {3, -3} is an isthmus because :

$$\left\{ \begin{array}{l} \text{-3 and 3 belong to the face} \\ \{1, 3, 4, 5, \text{-5}, 6, \text{-3}, \text{-2}\} \\ \text{and} \\ \sigma(3) = \text{-1 and } \sigma \circ \alpha(3) = \sigma(\text{-3}) = \text{-6} \end{array} \right.$$

The edge {5, -5} is a peninsula because :

$$\sigma(\text{-5}) = \text{-5 and } \sigma \circ \alpha(\text{-5}) = \sigma(5) = \text{-4}$$

Figure 2. Isthmuses and peninsulas

2. APPLICATION TO CARTOGRAPHY

The following definitions are specific to the domain of cartography. From now on in this paper, we shall assume an Euclidean plan, and also assume that the permutation σ orientates this plan : for each vertex v, σ permutate incoming darts to s in the conterclockwise direction. Moreover it is assumed that a vertex always has at least one incoming dart; therefore suppressing an edge may lead to the suppression of one or two vertices.

Representation of a map in the plane :

A point P is represented in the plane by its coordinates (x, y).

An edge is represented by a sequence of points (P₁,P₂,..., Pₙ)) with n ≥ 2. P₁ and Pₙ are the vertices of the edge, P₁ is the origin and Pₙ the end. P₂,..., Pₙ₋₁, if they exist, are intermediate points of the edge. Consequently, a face is represented by a cyclic sequence of points.

Definition 2.1. Let M = (D, α, σ) be a planar map and f = {d, σ⁻¹∘α(d),..., (σ⁻¹∘α)ⁿ(d)} a face of M ; we say that f is **open** iff :

$$\forall\, d \in f,\ \alpha^*(d) \subseteq (\sigma^{-1} \circ \alpha)^*(d)$$

This definition can also be expressed by : all edges belonging to an open face are either isthmuses, peninsulas, or isolated edges with distinct vertices.
A face that is not open is said to be **closed**. From a closed face f, a circuit may be extracted that does not use the same edge twice.

Definition 2.2. A closed direct-face f oriented in the conterclockwise direction is said to be **internal**. A face that is not internal is said to be **external** (fig. 3).

A connected component of a planar map is made of one external face, and at least one internal face.

Each edge {d, -d} can be associated to either two internal faces, or one internal face and one external face, or one unique external face.

In figure 3, the external faces f_3 and f_5 are closed, and the external face f_6 is open.

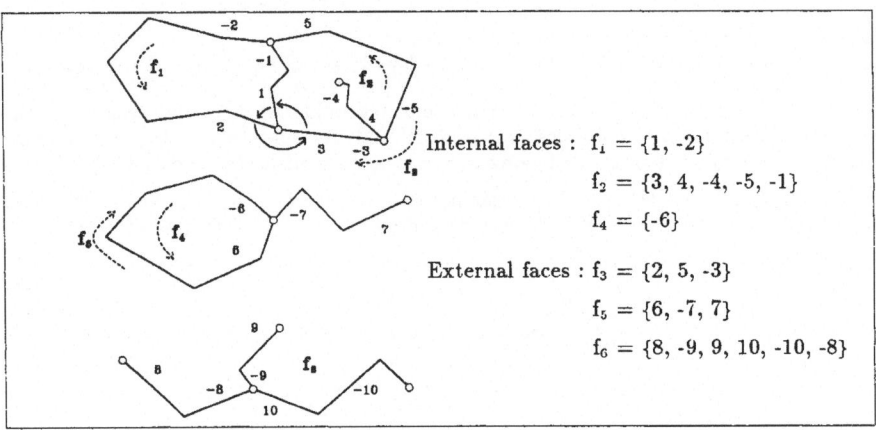

Internal faces : $f_1 = \{1, -2\}$

$f_2 = \{3, 4, -4, -5, -1\}$

$f_4 = \{-6\}$

External faces : $f_3 = \{2, 5, -3\}$

$f_5 = \{6, -7, 7\}$

$f_6 = \{8, -9, 9, 10, -10, -8\}$

Figure 3. Internal faces and external faces

Definition 2.3. Let M be a planar map represented in a plan ; generally M is made out of several *connected components* which may be embedded one into another or not. It is possible to represent the inclusion relationships between those connected components by a labelled tree with root M, as shown on figure 4. In this example, the map M is composed of six connected components C_i, for

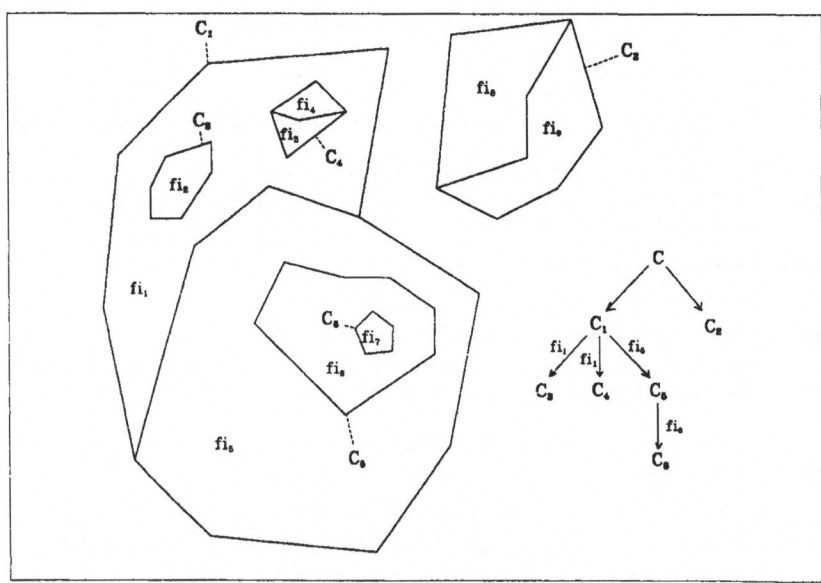

Figure 4. Inclusion tree

$i \in \{1, ..., 6\}$, The component C_1 including C_3, C_4 and C_5, itself including C_6. A link of inclusion between two components C_i and C_j is labelled by the internal face of C_i which contain C_j. Such a tree is called the **inclusion tree** of the map M.

From this can also be defined the **inclusion list** of an internal face, which is extracted from the inclusion tree as the list of all external faces contained in that internal face.

Definition 2.5. Let $e = ((x_1, y_1), ..., (x_n, y_n))$ be an edge; we shall call the **bounding window** of e the rectangle defined by the two points with coordinates

$$(\text{Xmin} = \min_{1 \le i \le n}(x_i), \text{Ymin} = \min_{1 \le i \le n}(y_i)) \text{ and } (\text{Xmax} = \max_{1 \le i \le n}(x_i), \text{Ymax} = \max_{1 \le i \le n}(y_i))$$

The bounding window of a face can be similarly defined.

3. DATA STRUCTURE

We chose the relational model [Codd 70] to implement the notions introduced in the previous chapters. Types of objects are described using a PASCAL-like notation. The formal techniques used to describe relational data bases can be introduced in the standard techniques for type specification and software engineering [Hoare 69, Jones 80, Dufourd 84].

The resulting data structure describes the graphical part of a base map made out of geographical object which are represented with closed polygons. The *geometrical* part, with points and coordinates and the *topological* part with darts and operators α and σ are clearly separated.

We first define the types :

type point = **record**
        x : **real** ; *x coordinate*
        y : **real** ; *y coordinate*
   end ;

type listpoint = **list of** point;

Then the types that allow the description of the various objects in a map are introduced :

type vertex = **record**
        novert :   **integer** > 0 ; *number of the vertex*
        s :   point ;   *coordinates of the vertex*
        nodart :   **integer** ;   *number of the distinguished dart of the vertex*
   end ;

The type *vertex* has four attributes : a positive number, both coordinates and a distinguished dart. This dart allows from a vertex to iterate through all its incoming darts.

type edge = **record**
        noedge : **integer** > 0 ; *number of the edge*
        pmin: **point** ;   *left lower point of the including window*
        pmax: **point** :   *right upper point of the including window*
        novert_1 : **integer** ;   *number of the starting point*
        novert_2 : **integer** ;   *number of the end point*
        lpoints : listpoint ;   *intermediate points*
   end ;

The types *edge* has six attributes : a positive number, the two points defining the including window, the number of the vertices and the *lpoints* attributes.

type tdart = **record**
        nodart : **integer** > 0 ; *number of the dart*
        nodart_1 : **integer** ;   *number of the preceding dart : $\sigma^{-1}(nodart)$*
        nofac_1 : **integer** ;   *number of the face of the dart*
        novert_1 : **integer** ;   *number of the vertex of the dart*
        nodart_2 : **integer** ;   *number of the preceding dart of*
                            the opposite dart : $\sigma^{-1} \circ \alpha(nodart)$
        nofac_2 : **integer** ;   *number of the face of the opposite dart*
        novert_2 : **integer** ;   *number of the vertex of the opposite dart*
   end ;

The type *tdart* combine two darts, a dart and its opposite dart (α permutation). A positive number identifies the dart with the characteristics ($nodart_1$, $nofac_1$, $novert_1$) and a negative number identifies the dart with the charateristics ($nodart_2$, $nofac_2$, $novert_2$). The integer *nodart* is the number *noedge* of the corresponding edge and its sign gives the direction of the edge.

type face = **record**

noface :	**integer** ;	*number of the face*
nobject :	**integer** ;	*number of the object*
nodart :	**integer** ;	*number of the distinguished dart of the face*
noffol :	**integer** ≤ 0 ;	*number of the following face in the including list*
nofprec :	**integer** ;	*number of the preceding face in the including list*
nofwith :	**integer** ≥ 0 ;	*number of an internal face*
pmin :	**point** ;	*left lower point of the including window*
pmax :	**point** ;	*right upper point of the including window*

end ;

The type *face* represents the internal faces (positive numbers) and the external faces (negative numbers). The attribute *nobject* identifies the object represented by this face ; *nodart*, like the type *vertex*, is the number of the distinguished dart and allows the retrieval of the contour of a face from a dart.

The attributes *nofprec*, *noffol* and *nofwith* allow the representation of one object with several faces, i.e. a complex polygon with holes and separated parts. The attributes *nofprec* and *noffol* respectively give the preceding face in the inclusion list which may be internal or external, and the following face which is external. When no corresponding face exists, these attributes are null. For an internal face, the attribute *nofwith* identifies an other internal face which represents the same object (fig. 6);

The following type describes the geographical objects whose contour compose the base map.

type object = **record**

nobject :	**integer** ;	*number of the object*
noface :	**integer** ≥ 0 ;	*number of an internal face*

end ;

Two attributes, *nobject* and *noface*, are sufficient here. We can represent an object with a complex polygon. If an internal face, containing one or more external faces, is assigned to an object, then these external faces will represent holes; moreover, we can assign several internal faces to a unique object by linking the inclusion list of each internal faces assigned to this object. With the map of figure 4, figure 6 gives an example with an object O represented by the internal faces fi_1, fi_6 and fi_8; the faces fe_3, fe_4 and fe_6 are the external faces associated with the connected components C_3, C_4 and C_6.

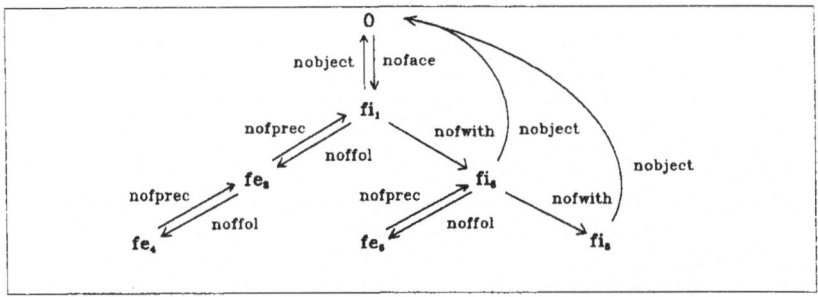

Figure 6. Representation of an object by a complex polygon

We now define the following types of relations, i.e. sets of objects, with the defined types :

type robject = **relation of** *object* ;
type rface = **relation of** *face* ;
type rtdart = **relation of** *tdart* ;

type redge = **relation of** *edge* ;

type rvertex = **relation of** *vertex* ;

Finally, we define the type :

> **type** map = **record**
>> rob : robject ;
>> rfa : rface ;
>> rda : rtdart ;
>> red : redge ;
>> rvx : rvertex
> **end** ;

This relationnal data base schema must be completed with *integrity constraints* or *invariants* [Dufourd 84]. There are, for instance, *referential constraints* such as "the set of values for attribute *noface* in relation *robject* is included in the set of values for attributes *noface* in relation *rface*". Or there are *functional dependencies* which define *identifiers* or *keys*. We may also mention here a geometrical kind of constraint such as the planarity of the map for the relation *redge*.

4. THE ENTRY OF A PLANAR MAP

The addition of a new edge is the elementary operation in the entry of a planar map. Deletion shall not be discussed here because its processing is similar. We distinguish six cases of addition which are described in figure 7. In each case, we shall have addition or deletion of one or more vertices, darts, internal or external faces. All six cases have the addition of two darts in common. Case 6 (fig 7.) is excluded because it includes an intersection of two edges not at a vertex. The five other cases correspond to operations which do not change the genus of the map, i.e. EULER operators [Mäntylä 82, Ansaldi 85].

When we digitise an edge, we can determine the case of addition with :
- the previous existence in the map of the two vertices of the edge;
- the associated faces of the darts which precede the two darts of the edge in the σ permutation;

Each case is processed with a different addition function whose profile is given.

For a given edge {d, -d} we have the following notations :

> - dp_1 (resp. dp_2) is the dart which precedes the dart d (resp. -d) in the σ permutation after the addition;
> - lp, whose type is *listpoint*, represents the list of the intermediate points;
> - v_1 and v_2 whose type is *point*, represent the vertices of the edge which may or may not exist in the map before the addition.

The type of the variables m and m' is *map*.

Case 1 : isolated edge
> in this case, the darts dp_1 and dp_2 do not exist in the map before addition and, after we have : dp_1 = d, dp_2 = -d. There is creation of an external face and of two vertices.

> **function** ADISEDGE : map × listpoint × point × point ⟶ map

> (m, lp, v_1, v_2) ⟶ m'

Case 2 : isolated loop
> this case is similar to the preceding case except that the two ends of the edge are one unique vertex and, after the addition dp_1 = -d and dp_2 = d. One vertex, one internal face and one external face are created.

> **function** ADISLOOP : map × listpoint × point ⟶ map

> (m, lp, v_1) ⟶ m'

Case 3 : peninsula

in this case, one of the end of the edge is a vertex that exists in the map before the addition and the other end is not in the map. We have d = dp$_1$ or -d = dp$_2$, but not both, and no faces are created. To simplify, we chose here the vertex v$_2$ as the existing vertex.

function ADPEN : map × listpoint × point × dbrin ⟶ map

(m, lp, v$_1$, dp$_2$) ⟶ m'

Case 4 : isthmus

in this case, the two ends of the edge exist in the map before the addition and the face of dp$_1$ is different from the face of dp$_2$. An external face is deleted.

function ADISTHM : map × listpoint × tdart × tdart ⟶ map

(m, lp, dp$_1$, dp$_2$) ⟶ m'

Case 5 : false handle

This case is similar to case 4 except that the face of dp$_1$ is the same as the face of dp$_2$. Moreover, this case includes the case "non isolated loop" which is the same as case 2, except that the two ends of the edge form one unique vertex, which exists before addition. An internal face is created.

function ADFHAND : map × listpoint × tdart × tdart ⟶ map

(m, lp, dp$_1$, dp$_2$) ⟶ m'

		Addition/Deletion	Case
1	 d = dp$_1$ / -d = dp$_2$	D^{++}V^{++}Fe$^+$/D^{--}V^{--}Fe$^-$	Isolated edge
2	 d = dp$_2$ / -d = dp$_1$	D^{++}V$^+$FI$^+$Fe$^+$/D^{--}V$^-$FI$^-$Fe$^-$	Isolated loop
3	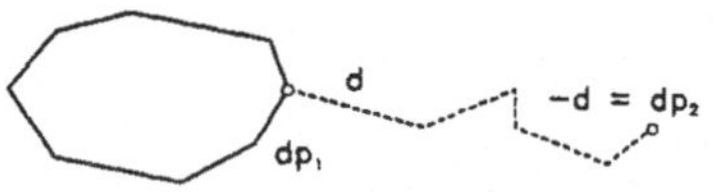 d / -d = dp$_2$, dp$_1$	D^{++}V$^+$/D^{--}V$^-$	peninsula
4	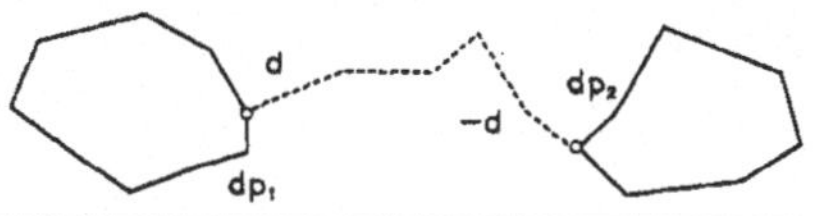 d , -d , dp$_2$, dp$_1$	D^{++}Fe$^-$/D^{--}Fe$^+$	isthmus
5	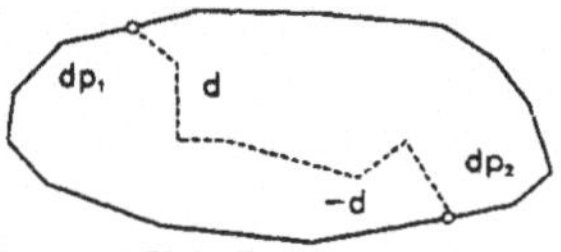 dp$_1$, d , dp$_2$, -d	D^{++}FI$^+$/D^{--}FI$^-$	false handle
6	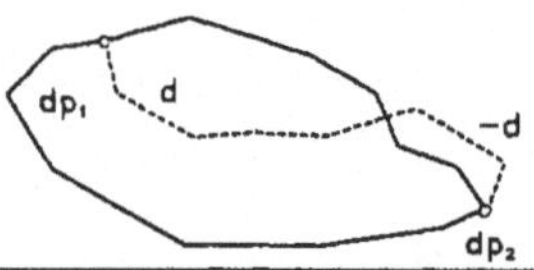 dp$_1$, d , -d , dp$_2$	D^{++}F$^-$/D^{--}F$^+$	true handle

Figure 7. Addition and deletion of an edge

We shall note respectively D⁺, V⁺, Fi⁺ and Fe⁺ the creation of a dart, of a vertex, of an internal face and of an external face; The same letter, suffixed with a minus sign, shall denote deletion. V⁺⁺ means the addition of two vertices. In case 6, for which the notion of internal and external faces is not defined, we shall simply note F⁺ and F⁻ the creation and the suppression of a face.

5. THE CHECK OF PLANARITY

The check of planarity must not be too costly in terms of CPU time. The data structure we propose can minimize this by allowing the selection of edges which may potentially intersect. This selection proceeds as follows :

- if the current edge entered is located within an internal face, then all edges out of this face will not be considered for the test; we shall only consider the edges of this internal face, plus those of the external faces included in this internal face, which we obtain through the inclusion list. If the edge is not in any internal face, selected edges are those from the external faces that are not included in any internal face.

- among the faces selected as described above, and for the entry of each point of the edge, we reject those whose including window is not intersected by this new line segment. For the remaining faces, we apply this process to every edge : we test whether the entered line segment intersects any edge of a selected face, if and only if this line segment intersects the including window of this edge.

The first selection represents a very important benefit from the use of the notion of combinatorial topological map, because although edges are entered in a disorderly manner, automatic construction of faces allows to detect whether an edge is included in one of them.

Figure 8 shows a segment s_1 completely included in the internal face fi, but not intersecting the including window of the external face fe included in fi; the only edges to be considered are those of fi, less edge e_1 whose including window is not intersected by s_1. The final test for intersection will only apply to edge e_2 and e_3. The same process applied to the next segment s_2 will yield a unique edge for the test of intersection.

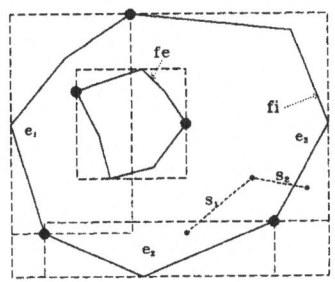

Figure 8.

During the entry, we are in the following state : an edge is being digitised; the last point entered is p_0 and we are about to enter point p_1 :

From here, several cases may occur :

(1) point p_0 and point p_1 are not vertices in the map before entry of this edge;
(2) one of the two points p_0 or p_1 is a vertex in the map before entry of this edge but the other is not;
(3) the two points p_0 and p_1 are vertices in the map before entry of this edge.

These cases shall be taken care off by the following Boolean predicate which shall return *true* if and only if there exists an intersection :

INTERFAC(c, p_0, p_1, f)
This function correspond to case (1) ; f identifies the internal face, if it exists, in which the edge is included;

INTERVER1(c, p, q, dp)

this function correspond to (2) ; p and q are the points p_0 and p_1 and p is the vertex which exists in the map before addition ; dp is the preceding dart of segment pq;

INTERVER2(c, p_1, p_2, dp_1, dp_2)

this function corresponds to case (3); dp_1 is the preceding dart of segment p_0p_1 and dp_2 of segment p_1p_0.

Function INTERI(s, lp, p_1) completes the processing by checking the existence of intersections between the line segment to add to the edge and the other line segments of this edge.

6. EDGE DIGITISATION ALGORITHM

Besides the points to be entered, the operators shall also indicate the end of a series of intermediate points (Boolean READEND), and also whether one of the vertices of the edge entered is already in the map (Booleans EXIST1 and EXIST2). The algorithm decomposes in four phases :

1- *entry of the first vertex* ; if this vertex does not already belong to the map, we check whether it is included in an internal face;

2- *entry of the intermediate points* (if any) with a test on eventual intersections ; if the first vertex already belongs to the map, the entry of the first intermediate point is sufficient to locate the preceding dart incoming to this vertex.

3- *entry of the second vertex* with test on eventual intersections; if this vertex already belongs to the map, we locate the preceding dart incoming to this vertex. If there are no intermediate points and if the first vertex already exists in the map, then we also locate the preceding dart incoming to this vertex.

4- *invocation of the appropriate addition function* after determination of the case of addition with the characteristics of the darts;

We define the following functions :

- LOCAFAC(m, p) returns the internal face of the map m which contains the point p ;
- DARTPREC(m, v, p) gives the dart of the map m which precede the line segment (v, p), v is a vertex and p a point;
- READVER(m) returns a vertex v and a Boolean which indicates if this vertex v belongs to the map m;
- READPOINT returns an intermediate point;
- READEND returns a Boolean which indicates the end of the entry of the intermediate points;

VARIABLES		
	m : map ;	the map concerned
	v_1, v_2 : point ;	vertices of the edge
	dp_1, dp_2 : dart ;	preceding darts incoming to v_1 and v_2
	lp : listpoints ;	list of the intermediate points
	np : integer ;	number of the intermediate points
	f_1, f_2 : face ;	faces of the darts dp_1 and dp_2
	inter : Boolean ;	indicate the existence of an intersection
	exist1 : Boolean ;	indicate if the first vertex already belongs to the map m
	exist2 : Boolean ;	indicate if the second vertex already belongs to the map m
	p : point ;	point to be entered
	pr : point ;	preceding entered point
	f : face ;	the internal face which contains the edge

BEGIN

/* *entry of the first vertex* */

- (v_1, exist1) = READVER(m) /* *reading of the first vertex* */
- IF (NON exist1) THEN
    - f = LOCAFAC(m, v_1))
  /* *we check if v_1 is included in an internal face* */
  ELSE
    - f = nil /* *variable f is undefined* */
  ENDIF
- pr = v_1 /* *pr is the last entered point* */

```
                        /* entry of the intermediate points */


- np = 0
- WHILE (NOT READEND) DO
    - inter = 'true'
    - IF (exist1 AND np = 0) THEN
        /* the 1st vertex belongs to the map and entry of the 1st intermediate point */
        - WHILE (inter) DO /* if there is an intersection, we read an other point */
            - p = READPOINT
            - dp₁ = DARTPREC(m, v₁, p) /* locating of the 1st preceding dart */
            - inter = INTERVER1(m, v₁, p, dp₁) OR INTERI(m, v₁, lp, p)
          ENDDO
        - f = face(dp₁) /* if f is an internal face, then it contains point p */
      ELSE
        - WHILE (inter) DO /* entry of the intermediate points */
            - p = READPOINT
            - inter = INTERFAC(m, pr, p, f) OR INTERI(m, v₁, lp, p)
          ENDDO
      ENDIF
    - pr = p
    - np = np + 1
    - lp(np) = p
  ENDDO


                        /* entry of the second vertex */


- inter = 'true'
- WHILE (inter) DO /* if there is an intersection, we read an other point */
    - (v₂, exist2) = READVER(m) /* reading of the 2nd vertex */
    - IF (exist1 AND np = 0) THEN
        /* the 1st vertex belongs to the map and there are no intermediate points */
        - dp₁ = DARTPREC(m, v₁, v₂) /* locating of the 1st preceding dart */
      ENDIF
    - IF (exist2) THEN /* the vertex belongs to the map */
        - dp₂ = DARTPREC(m, v₂, pr) /* locating of the 2nd preceding dart */
        - IF (exist1 AND np = 0) THEN
            /* the 1st vertex already belongs to the map and there are no intermediate points */
            - inter = INTERVER2(m, v₁, v₂, dp₁, dp₂) OR INTERI(m, v₁, lp, v₂)
          ELSE
            - inter = INTERVER1(m, v₂, pr, dp₂) OR INTERI(m, v₁, lp, v₂)
          ENDIF
      ELSE /* the 2nd vertex does not already belong to the map */
        - IF (exist1 AND np = 0) THEN
            /* the 1st vertex already belongs to the map and there are no intermediate points */
            - inter = INTERVER1(m, v₁, v₂, dp₁) OR INTERI(m, v₁, lp, v₂)
          ELSE
            - inter = INTERFAC(m, v₂, pr, f) OR INTERI(m, v₁, lp, v₂)
          ENDIF
      ENDIF
  ENDDO
```

```
                    /* invocation of the addition functions */
- f₁ = face(dp₁)
- f₂ = face(dp₂)
- IF (exist1 AND exist2) THEN /* the two vertices belong to the map */
    - IF (v₁ = v₂) THEN /* one unique vertex */
        - ADFHAND(m, lp, dp₁, dp₂) /* isolated loop */
    ELSE /* two different vertices */
        - IF f₁ = f₂ THEN
            - ADFHAND(m, lp, dp₁, dp₂) /* false handle */
        ELSE
            - ADISTHM(m, lp, dp₁, dp₂) /* isthmus */
        ENDIF
    ENDIF
ELSE /* one of the vertices does not belong to the map */
    - IF (exist1 AND NOT exist2) THEN
        /* the 1ˢᵗ vertex already belongs to the map */
        - ADPEN(m, lp, v₂, dp₁) /* peninsula */
    ELSE
        - IF (exist2 AND NOT exist1) THEN
            /* the 2ⁿᵈ vertex already belongs to the map */
            - ADPEN(m, -lp, v₁, dp₂) /* peninsula */
        ELSE /* the two vertices do not already belong to the map */
            - IF (v₁ = v₂) THEN /* one unique vertex */
                - ADISLOOP(m, lp, v₁) /* isolated loop */
            ELSE
                - ADISEDGE(m, lp, v₁, v₂) /* isolated edge */
            ENDIF
        ENDIF
    ENDIF
ENDIF
ENDIF
```

END

Example

Figure 9 gives an example of addition of an edge $e = (d, -d)$ in a map M. The edge e is digitized from vertex s_1 to vertex s_2 which is different from s_1. The preceding dart of d is the dart 5 and the preceding dart of -d is the dart 2. These two darts belong to the same external face $fe = \{1, 2, 5, 6, -8\}$. Thus, the case of addition is the case *false handle* and the internal face $fi = \{b, 2, 5\}$ is created with function ADFHAND. The external face fe is modified into $fe = \{-b, 6, -8, 1\}$. Thus, polygons may be created just by the topological overlook on the map, and without processing at the geometrical level.

Complexity

The complexity of the planarity check is discussed below. Let s be a line segment to be entered; we may distinguish two cases :

1st case : s is included in an internal face f; the time complexity is $\mathcal{O}(n_1 + n_2)$, with n_1 is the number of points of the edges of f whose the including window is intersected by s, and n_2 the number of points of the edges of the external faces including in f whose including window is intersected by s;

2nd case : s is not in any internal faces; the time complexity is $\mathcal{O}(n)$, with n is the number of points of the edges of the external faces which are not in any internal faces, and whose including window is intersected by s;

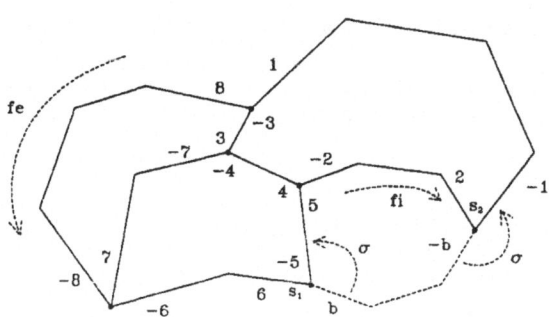

Figure 9. Example of addition of an edge

CONCLUSION

The use of the combinatorial topological maps concept has lead us to the development of an accurate and efficient algorithm for the digitisation of closed polygons. On one hand, it allows the reduction of the amount of information entered by automatically detecting the closure of polygons; on the other hand, it continuously and rapidly checks the planarity of the map.

This model may be implemented in several ways, which do not exhibit any special problems. Such a relational data base has been implemented at the CNRS computer center at Strasbourg, in order to test the validity and the efficiency of the algorithm.

The use of combinatorial topological maps is not only justified by data entry and digitisation, but brings several other benefits. It allows to clearly separate topology and geometry, an important property which has not been fully exploited here. This data structure model may be expanded to richer structures that can completely describe a map : an example of this is adjacency bound to the notion of dart (the *dual* map concept) which leads to the notion of a *neighbourhood* of an object. This approach also has other advantages : it makes specification easier and offers a rigorous mathematical framework, with many results that allows the improvements of the algorithms. Finally, it provides an easy way to represent the notion of *vertex*, *edge*, *dart* and *face* which may be found in numerous applications.

References

[Ansaldi 85] S. ANSALDI   & al. : *Geometric Modelling of Solid Objects by Using a Face Adjacency Graph Representation* ; SIGGRAPH'85 Conf., San Francisco, ACM, 1985, 131-139.

[Bertin 73] J. BERTIN : *Sémiologie Graphique* ; Gauthier-villars (ed.) 1973.

[Codd 70] E. F. CODD : *A relationnal Model of Data for Large Shared Data Banks* ; Comm. ACM, **13**(6), 1970.

[Cori 75] R. CORI : *Un Code pour les Graphes Planaires et ses Applications* ; Astérisque, SMF, 27, Paris, 1975.

[Dufourd 84] J. F. DUFOURD : *Types Abstraits et Bases de Données Relationnelles* ; TSI, 4(4), Dunod, 1984.

[Dufourd 88] J. F. DUFOURD : *Construction Progressive d'une Algèbre pour Manipuler les Cartes Orientées;* PIXIM'88, Paris-La Villette, 1988.

[Fontet 79] M. FONTET : *Connectivité des graphes et automorphismes des cartes : propriétés et algorithmes;* (thèse d'état), Université Paris 7, 1979.

[Guibas 85] L. GUIBAS & J. STOLFI : *Primitives for the Manipulation of General Subdivision and the Computation of Voronoï Diagrams* ; Transactions on Graphics, 4(2), ACM, 1985, 74-123.

[Hoare 69] C. A. R. HOARE : *An Axiomatic Basis for Computer Programming* ; Comm. ACM, **12**(10), 1969, 576-580, 583.

[Jacques 68] A. JACQUES : *Sur le Genre d'une Paire de Substitutions* ; C. R. Acad. Sc. Paris, 1968, t. 267, 625-627.

[Jacques 70] A. JACQUES : *Constellations et Graphes Topologiques* ; in Combinatorial Theory and Applications, Budapest, 1970, 657-673.

[Jones 80] C. B. JONES : *Software Development. A Rigourous Approach* ; C. A. R. HOARE (ed.), Prentice-Hall, 1980.

[Lienhardt 88] P. LIENHARDT : *Extension of the Notion of Map and Subdivision of Three Dimensionnal Space* ; STACC'88, Bordeaux, 1988.

[Mäntylä 82] M. MANTYLA & R. SULONEN : *GWB, A Solid Modeler with Euler Operators;* CG&A, 2(7), IEEE, 1982, p.17-31.

[Michelucci 84] D. MICHELUCCI & M. GANGNET : *Saisie de Plans à Partir de Tracés à Main Levé;* Proceeding of MICAD'84, Paris, 1984, 96-110. Prentice-Hall, 1972, 1-32.

[Nagy 79] G. NAGY & S. WAGLE : *Geographic Data Processing* ; Computing Survey, Vol. 11, n° 2, June 1979, 139-181.

[Peucker 75] T. K. PEUCKER & N. CHRISMAN : *Cartographic Data Structures* ; The American Cartographer, Vol. 2, n° 1, 1975, 55-69.

[Spehner 86] J. C. SPEHNER : *Les Cartes Topologiques* ; DEA graphique-image, Cours polycopié, Strasbourg, 1986.

[Tutte 84] W. T. TUTTE : *Graph Theory* ; in Encyclopedia of Mathematics and its Applications, Addison-Wesley, 1984.

Pr. Jean-François DUFOURD, Ph.D in computer science 1980, is currently chairman of Computer Science Department of Louis-Pasteur University in Strasbourg (France). He leads a research team on specification and programming in the area of computer graphics. Application in cartography, graphical data bases, C.A.D. and remote sensing are also studied by the group.
address : Département d'Informatique, Université Louis-Pasteur, 7 rue René Descartes, 67084 Strasbourg Cedex-France.

Claude GROSS, M.Sc. 1986, researcher of the Louis-Pasteur University in Strasbourg (France). He works actually in the area of graphical data bases.
address : Centre de Calcul du CNRS, 23 rue du loess, 67037 Strasbourg Cedex-France.

Pr. Jean-Claude SPEHNER, Ph.D in computer science 1976, is currently professor of Mulhouse University (France). His research is in the following areas : computer graphics, computational geometry, complexity theory and theory of automata and languages.
address : Département de Mathématique et Informatique, Faculté des Sciences et Techniques, Université de Haute Alsace, 68093 Mulhouse Cedex-France.

Microcomputer Visualization of Molecules

F.T. Marchese and M.R. Tiongson

ABSTRACT

High quality molecular rendering on microcomputers remains a challenge!
We experimented with rendering shaded intersecting sphere models of
molecules on low resolution frame buffers, with high degrees of color
quantization, to determine how well a standard microcomputer can display
representations of molecules. We found that excellent shaded sphere
renderings can be provided, given a microcomputer system based on the
Intel 80286 microprocessor, with either an IBM EGA (640 X 350 X 4) or VGA
(320 X 200 X 8) color graphics adaptor. Moreover, the time required to
generate these images is comparable to that for similar procedures
implemented on a Vax 11/780.

KEY WORDS: molecular graphics, shaded spheres, z-buffer.

INTRODUCTION

In the thirty years since the first molecular graphics system was
designed and implemented, the use of computers as tools for interactive
display and manipulation of molecules consisting of tens to hundreds of
thousands of atoms has become commonplace. The degree of visualization
inherent in such systems is unprecedented, giving insight into molecular
structure and function, from enzyme specificity to the protein coat of the
polio virus. However, such insight remains expensive, with single user
molecular graphics systems easily costing $50000.

Alternatively, many chemists turn to microcomputers for implementation
of molecular graphics software. But high quality rendering remains a
challenge!

We experimented recently with molecular rendering on inexpensive microcomputers with low resolution color frame buffers. Our initial work
resulted in a program called MOPIC (MOlecular PICtures) (Marchese and Reda
1988), an easy to use, menu driven package that displays real-time
animated wireframe models and high quality dot-sphere plots of molecules.
Most recently, we experimented with rendering shaded, intersecting sphere
molecular representations on low resolution frame buffers with high
degrees of color quantization. We present herein our results and a
discussion of the degree of visualization possible on such systems.

BACKGROUND

There are five problems to address when rendering molecules on microcomputers:

1. **Speed of host processor:** Many microcomputers may be too slow to support real-time rendering. For example, the Intel 8088/8087 microprocessors running at 5 MHz provide approximately 1/20th the computational capability of a Vax 11/780.

2. **Memory limitations:** Restrictions on useable memory can be imposed by either the operating system or programming language. MS-DOS, for example, allows access to only 640K of memory and the programming language itself may limit array size to 64K. Hence, implementation of a complete z-buffer for a 640 X 480 X 8 display is impossible because it consumes 900K of memory for the data structures alone.

3. **Inadequate spatial resolution of display:** The IBM VGA graphics adaptor (320 X 200 X 8) aliases severely because of its low pixel density and large pixel size. As a result, adequate display of half-tones might require implementation of smoothing algorithms.

4. **High degree of color quantization:** The IBM CGA (320 X 200 X 2) and EGA (640 X 350 X 4) graphics adaptors provide four and 16 colors, respectively. Will a halftone image, represented in these color spaces, provide adequate visual information about the chemical system?

5. **Rendering algorithms can be time consuming:** For example, each pixel on every surface must be considered in a simple z-buffer algorithm. Thus, for molecules consisting of thousands of atoms, such as a protein, calculation and display could take too much time.

These concerns are not new to the computer graphics literature. However, today they have become progressively less important with current implementation of molecular graphics systems. Computers such as Sun, Vax and Silicon Graphics workstations provide sufficient computer horsepower and memory to accommodate the addition of graphics devices, such as E&S PS300 series or high pixel density graphics displays (typically 1K X 1K X 8), to boost graphic power to render images of excellent quality.

Indeed, it is possible to find remedies for each of these problems by purchasing the appropriate hardware/software solution, but a microcomputer then evolves into another entity - a much more expensive entity. Moreover, software implementation becomes less structured, more proprietary and less maintainable. Hence, we sought to implement some generic algorithms to display molecules on a generic microcomputer system, with the singular purpose of demonstrating the effectiveness of a simple personal computer's ability to render molecular information.

Thus, we selected an Intel 80286/80287 microprocessor with 640K running under MS-DOS with the following graphics adaptors by IBM: CGA (320 X 200

X 2), EGA (640 X 350 X 4) and VGA (320 X 200 X 8); and the VX/PC (672 X 480 X 9) by Vectrix. These microprocessors and IBM graphics adaptors are configured easily for less than $2500 (including hard disk), making them accessible to any laboratory.

The most frequently used algorithm for displaying shaded sphere representations of molecules is based on a z-buffer. Clearly, a complete z-buffer is impractical, but a scanline z-buffer is executed easily. In some applications, spheres are represented by some high order geometrical solid, then disassembled into individual polygons which are scan converted and sent to the z-buffer. However, the method we use is that of Porter, who ingeniously extended Bresenham's algorithm for circle generation into three dimensions, to generate all visible points on the hemisphere facing the observer. Each point corresponds to a pixel position so that no unnecessary points are considered in the hidden surface elimination (Porter 1978).

Lighting models are important for graphical realism; but molecules are not real in the sense of Newtonian physics. A simple light model is as good as any other, probably even better than models which make molecular renderings look like plastic or metallic balls. Thus, we adhere to a simple Lambertian model:

$$I = I_1 N \cdot L$$

excluding an ambient term, where $N \cdot L$ is the cosine of the angle between the light source and the surface normal; I_1 is the intensity of the light source and I is the observed intensity. For simplicity, the light source is placed behind the observer at infinity. Shades for each atom type (e.g. carbon, nitrogen, oxygen) are calculated by multiplying $N \cdot L$ by the maximum number of shades available for a particular color. This number becomes an index to a color look-up table on the graphics card and the color is displayed.

For systems with insufficient colors, such as the CGA or EGA graphics cards, shading is simulated by dithering. The Floyd-Steinberg procedure (Floyd and Steinberg 1975) is useful because it can be used on displays with low pixel densities to represent a wide range of shades; whereas, digital half-toning requires groups of pixels to approximate shades. For example, a 2 X 2 matrix of pixels displays only five different intensity levels; while the Floyd-Steinberg dither matrix juxtaposes high and low intensity pixels to render N^2 intensities, where N is the dimension of the matrix. Thus, for the CGA display, each of three colors is dithered with the background (assumed black) to represent shades of each of these colors. On the EGA display, the 16 colors are paired into two intensities of each color and dithered.

Finally, images produced on the VGA display are expected to alias severely. Consequently, some form of antialiasing is needed to smooth the image. However, the antialiasing method is not at issue, but rather the number of colors available for smoothing. Most molecular graphics systems use from six to eight basic colors to represent atom types (red, blue, white, green, yellow, orange, violet, pink) with at least 16 shades per color. There are $N(N-1)/2$ combinations of basic colors or shades of basic colors. For a system consisting of eight basic colors, there are $8(7)/2$, that is, 28 combinations of basic colors; for a system with 16 shades of each basic color, there are $16(15)/2$, that is, 120 combinations, or blends of shades, for each basic color. So a bare minimum of 120 X 28, 3360 colors, corresponding to a 12 bit color look-up table, are necessary to define an antialiased image. This means that for a standard eight bit look-up table, 128 colors must be used for shading, leaving 128 for blends between base colors for antialiasing. Hence, the problem of sampling the color space for a set of optimal blends presents itself.

A number of authors (Gervautz and Purgathofer 1988; Campbell 1986; Hechbert 1982) have considered filling the color look-up table with a representative set of colors. These authors have approached the problem by using a post-rendering scheme with a color image (usually 24 bits per pixel) that is compressed to eight bits per pixel. Post-rendering analysis is unacceptable in a real-time system. Consequently, the remaining look-up table blends are selected in another way.

Since our software generates the same type of image each time, only the size and position of each sphere changes, the number of blends used for antialiasing form a subset of the 3360 possible two-color blends. By generating a histogram representing all colors calculated and the relative frequency of each, we place the most used blends into the look-up table. At runtime, the entire look-up table is scanned to find the closest color to the blend. This is accomplished by using a cartesian distance metric.

METHOD

All algorithms are implemented in Turbo Pascal 4.0 on a NEC Powermate II microcomputer with 640K of memory running at 10MHz. A Video 7 Vega VGA graphics card is used at both EGA and VGA resolutions and the Vectrix VX/PC is used in the CGA mode and its own 672 X 480 X 9 mode. Images are generated at 200 X 200 (CGA), 640 X 350 (EGA), 480 X 480 (VX/PC) and 200 X 200 and 600 X 600 (VGA) with timing studies performed at EGA and VGA resolutions.

Porter's algorithm for scan-line z-buffer rendering of spheres is employed with the following modifications for the dithered sphere renderings on the EGA adaptor. A large prototype sphere is generated (100 pixel radius) and the three cartesian coordinates of each pixel stored. In addition, 64 levels of intensity are calculated according to the simple Lambertian model, dithered and stored as combinations of zeroes and ones in a corresponding array. The sphere is then scaled according to atom size, with the scale factor used as a counter for selecting array elements. Thus, Bresenham's algorithm is invoked only once during a rendering session. We carried this one step further by saving the prototype sphere on a disk for loading at runtime, eliminating additional invocation of Bresenham's algorithm.

For VGA and VX/PC rendering, the coordinates of the prototype sphere are generated at runtime and stored with the fractional intensities from the illumination model. Shaded spheres are drawn on the VX/PC graphics adaptor with 32 levels of intensity. Thirty-two intensities are sufficient for drawing a shaded sphere with no perceptible contouring. However, on the VGA, 32 levels produce noticeable contouring, even on small spheres. As a remedy, the Floyd-Steinberg dithering technique is used to blend shades of color.

To demonstrate the effect of antialiasing on image quality, images that were to be displayed on the VGA adaptor are created at 600 X 600 resolution and filtered down to 200 X 200 using a Bartlett window. Blended colors are selected from the 256 color look-up table through exhaustive search. Since 32 shades are needed for each of the six base colors only 64 remain for blends. These blends are determined from a histogram representing a cumulative distribution of colors from 12 different molecules of varying size and chemical composition. A minimum of four blends are selected for each of the 15 color combinations.

RESULTS AND DISCUSSION

Ten images are displayed (Figs. 1-10, 5 of BDNA and 5 of Formamide * 10H2O (FH2O)) to depict the loss in image quality as spatial resolution decreases and color quantization increases. The images of BDNA and FH2O from the VX/PC card (Figs. 1 and 4) are clear and show every structural detail; while the molecules rendered on the VGA card (Figs. 2 and 5) show excessive aliasing. This is particularly true for BDNA where aliasing artifacts give the impression of an incomplete, rough image. Smoothing the VGA images (Figs. 3 and 6) result in pictures of quality comparable to those of the VX/PC.

The effects of color quantization are further demonstrated in Figs. 7-10. Here, the same two molecules are rendered on the EGA (Figs. 7 and 9) and CGA (Figs. 8 and 10) graphics adaptors.

The images of BDNA and FH2O appear cartoon-like. Yet, all structural details are clearly visible. For FH2O (Fig. 7), the eight water molecules nearest the observer are well defined with their orientations in space perceived easily. BDNA (Fig.9) clearly shows the phosphate backbone and base pair stacking.

The CGA card makes available only four colors. Hence, different atom types share the same color. Images of FH2O (Fig.8) and BDNA (Fig.10) become difficult to interpret at this resolution. The structural features are discernible, only because of the simplicity or orderliness of the structure.   Representations of proteins, which have highly irregular shapes, would be unintelligible on a CGA display.

Execution times for the z-buffer algorithms are found in Table 1 and Fig.11. The eight test molecules range in size from three to 486 atoms. Times for the EGA algorithm range from .2 to 3.3 minutes. Aliased VGA images require from .25 to 6.7 CPU minutes. These are quite reasonable times and place our results well within the domain of rendering times for images created on a Vax 11/780. For example, Goodsell implemented Porter's algorithm, including shadows, on a Vax 11/780 and GPX workstation and estimated execution times for a range of molecules, including the BDNA dodecamer, from 2 to 15 minutes (Goodsell 1988).

Comparing the relative speed of the EGA and VGA card rendering procedures show that despite the fact that the EGA implementation must process more pixels (nearly 4 times more) it runs twice as fast as the VGA. The difference in performance manifests itself in the VGA's use of floating point calculations for the Floyd-Steinberg dithering and calculation of final intensities. This probably can be alleviated by dithering the prototype sphere and storing the intensities as integers as opposed to reals.

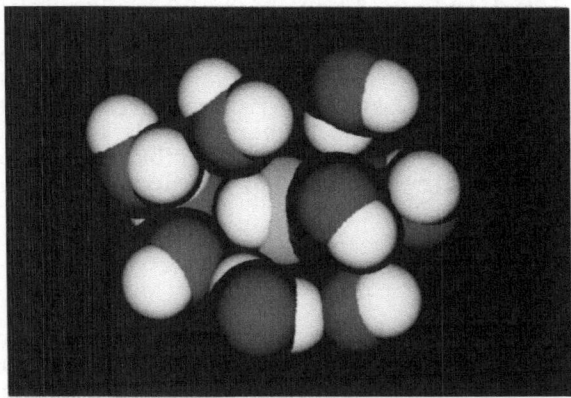

Fig.1. Shaded sphere model of Formamide*10H2O (FH2O) at 480 X 480 X 8 resolution.

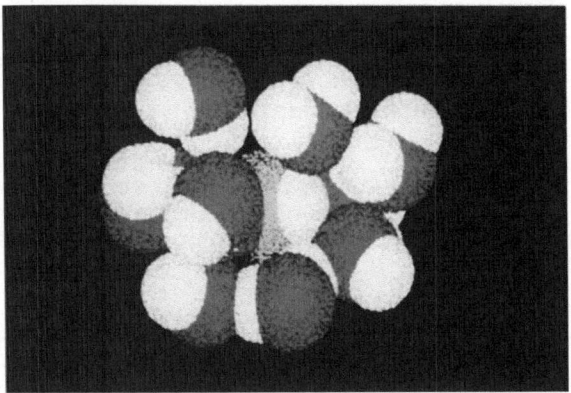

Fig.2. FH2O model on VGA graphics card at 200 X 200 X 8 resolution.

Fig.3. FH2O molecule at 200 X 200 X 8 with antialiasing.

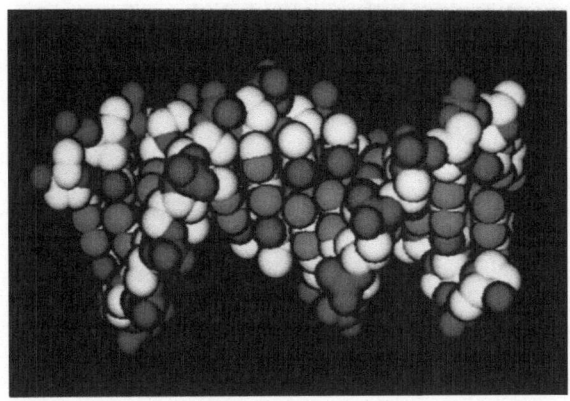

Fig.4. Shaded sphere image of BDNA at 480 X 480 X 8 resolution.

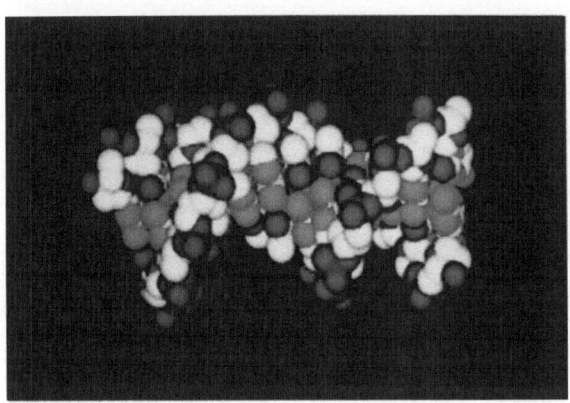

Fig.5. BDNA model on VGA graphics card at 200 X 200 X 8 resolution.

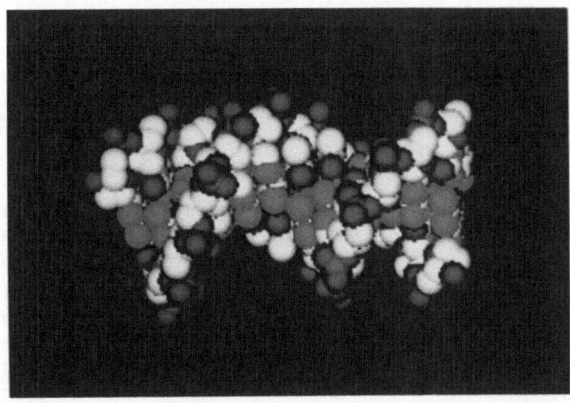

Fig.6. BDNA model on VGA graphics card with antialiasing.

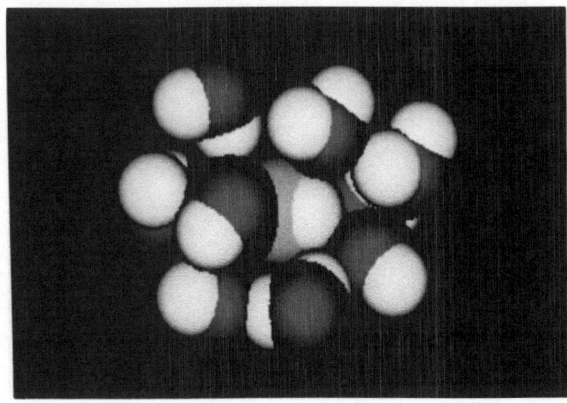

Fig.7. FH2O model rendered on EGA graphics card at 640 X 350 X 4 resolution.

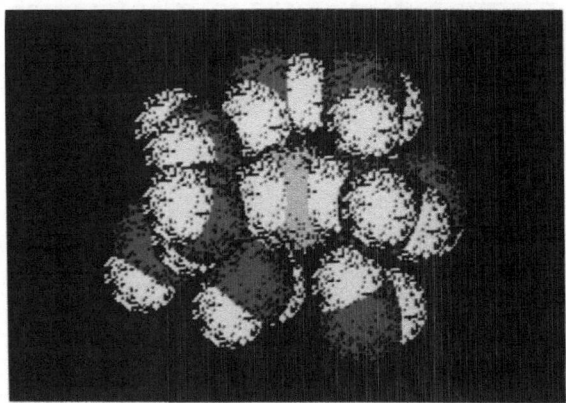

Fig.8. FH2O model rendered on CGA graphics card at 200 X 200 X 2 resolution.

Table 1. Timing Studies for z-buffer algorithms

Molecule	No. of Atoms (N)	Time(Seconds)	
		EGA	VGA
Water	3	11.9	14.4
Dimethylphosphate	13	31.9	52.3
Phenylalanine	23	48.2	84.9
bis-p-nitrophenylphosphate	31	64.5	75.8
Formamide * 10 H2O	36	63.7	107.6
Dodecahedrane	40	71.3	133.6
Chloramphenicol	78	76.5	110.9
DNA (two base pairs)	125	128.3	192.5
BDNA (twelve base pairs)	486	196.2	402.6

Fig.9. BDNA model rendered on EGA graphics card at 640 X 350 X 4
resolution.

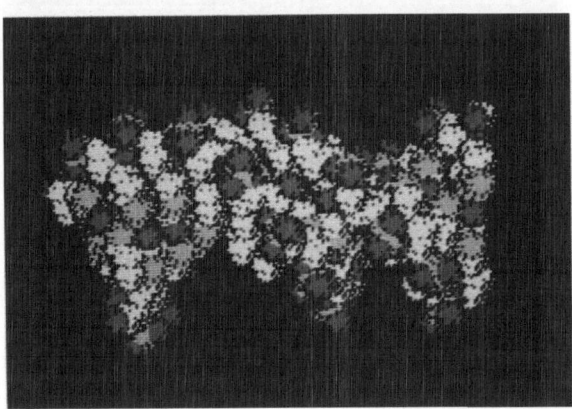

Fig.10. BDNA model rendered on CGA graphics card at 200 X 200 X 2
resolution.

The overall performance of the z-buffer algorithm is shown in Fig. 11,
which displays plots of execution times vs. numbers of atoms for the EGA
and VGA procedures. Least squares fits of these data to powers of N
produce the following equations:

$$\text{Time(EGA)} = 8.06 \ N^{0.55}$$

$$\text{Time(VGA)} = 9.69 \ N^{0.62}$$

The execution time for EGA varies as the square root of the number of
atoms; for VGA, as the 1.5 root. This time dependence is not expected from
z-buffer calculations where time should increase linearly with the number
of spheres. However, in our application, as the molecules increase in
size, they must be scaled to fit within the viewport. Thus, there are
fewer pixels to process for each sphere.

Finally, we can make predictions of the time required to display large molecules such as proteins. For a molecule of 5000 atoms, the EGA algorithm should take approximately 15 minutes while the VGA, about 33 minutes. These times should be considered as worst case projections because the algorithms have not been optimized for speed. It should be possible, therefore, to increase computation speed significantly by implementing spanning scan-line methods.

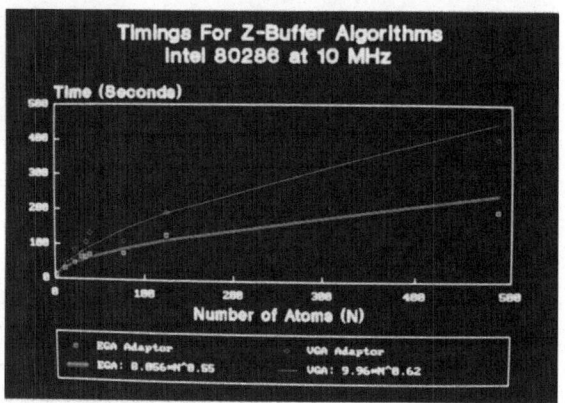

Fig.11. Execution time versus number of atoms for z-buffer algorithms on EGA and VGA (aliased) displays.

SUMMARY AND CONCLUSIONS

We present the results of experiments for rendering shaded sphere representations of molecules on microcomputers with low resolution graphics displays and find:

1.   Overall image quality is very good on an EGA display with only 16 displayable colors. Although the pictures appear cartoon-like, every detail of large or small molecules is easily discernible.

2.   Because of low spatial resolution and very few colors, the CGA display of molecules is difficult to interpret. This is particularly true for a large molecule where spheres are small and the depth information provided by dithering colors is offset by the small number of pixels.

3.   Molecular rendering on the VGA display suffers from severe aliasing. However, we show that image quality is improved significantly by antialiasing, even with a small set of blended colors. The resulting images are comparable in quality to images six times their resolution.

4.   The modified z-buffer procedure displays images of molecules ranging in size from 10 to 500 atoms with execution times from .2 to 7 minutes. These times are in good agreement with those for similar calculations on Vax 11/780.

The results of our z-buffer implementations on a generic microcomputer are strong evidence for the ability of microcomputers to display high quality images of molecules at reasonable computational expense. With some modification of the algorithms and optimization of the code for speed, it should be possible to increase performance for large molecules by a factor of 10. We are currently pursuing this line of research.

REFERENCES

Campbell G, et al. (1986) Two Bit/Pixel Full Color Encoding. Proc. Siggraph '86, Computer Graphics 20(4): pp 215-223.

Floyd R, Steinberg L (1975) An Adaptive Algorithm for Spatial Gray Scale. SID 1975, Int. Symp. Dig. Tech., Pap.: pp 36-37.

Gervautz M, Purgathofer W (1988) A Simple Method for Color Quantization: Octree Quantization. In: New Trends in Computer Graphics: Proceedings of CG International '88, N. Magnenat-Thalmann and D. Thalmann, eds., Springer-Verlag, Heidelberg, pp 219-231.

Goodsell DS (1988) RMS: Programs for Generating Raster Molecular Surfaces J. Molecular Graphics 6: pp 41-44.

Hechbert P (1982) Color Image Quantization For Frame Buffer Display. Proc. Siggraph '82. Computer Graphics 16(3): pp 297-307.

Marchese FT, Reda S (1988) MOPIC: An Advanced Molecule Rendering Program for Microcomputers. In: New Trends in Computer Graphics. Proceedings of CG International '88, N. Magnenat-Thalmann and D.Thalmann, eds.,Springer-Verlag, Heidelberg, pp 519-526.

Porter TK (1978) Spherical Shading. Proc. Siggraph '78. Computer Graphics 12(3): 282-285.

Francis T. Marchese is an Associate Professor of Computer Science at Pace University. He received a B.S. in Natural Science from Niagara University (New York), M. S. in Chemistry from Youngstown State University (Ohio) and Ph.D.. in Theoretical Chemistry from the University of Cincinnati (Ohio). From 1978 to 1983 he was a National Institutes of Health Postdoctoral Research fellow at Hunter College of C.U.N.Y (New York). His research has covered the fields of theoretical spectroscopy, quantum mechanics of intermolecular interactions, statistical mechanics of fluids and statistical pattern recognition for scientific visualization. Presently, Dr. Marchese's research is concerned with microcomputer molecular modeling and graphics, derivation of new lighting models for computer rendering and application of cellular automata to model and simulate physical systems.

Address: Department of Computer Science, Pace University, 1 Pace Plaza, New York, NY 10038 USA.

Mary Rose Tiongson received a M.S. in Computer Science from Pace University in 1988. While at Pace, she was a research assistant with Dr. Frank Marchese where she developed computer graphics applications in molecular modeling.

Tiongson received her B.S. in Industrial Management Engineering with a minor in Chemical Engineering at De la Salle University in Manila, Philippines.

Three-Dimensional Models of Molecular Structures and Chemical Properties

J. Weber, P.-Y. Morgantini, P. Fluekiger, and A. Goursot

ABSTRACT

As three-dimensional models of chemical objects are essential tools for understanding their intimate structure and function, molecular graphics techniques allow nowadays to build, visualize and manipulate complex molecular structures and their related properties. This paper presents several developments recently achieved in this field, namely : (i) the representation of macromolecular structures such as proteins; (ii) the modelization of molecular envelopes as dot surfaces, mesh surfaces and solid models; (iii) the evaluation and visualization of color-coded reactivity indices based on intermolecular interaction energies. This later application is shown to be particularly useful in several applications such as molecular recognition and drug design.

Keywords : Molecular graphics; computational chemistry; molecular recognition; 3D models.

INTRODUCTION

As noted by the French chemist Berthelot (1886) about a century ago, "chemistry creates its own object". Looking today at the evolution of chemistry in the last decades, which have witnessed spectacular progresses both in bench synthesis techniques and computer-assisted molecular design, this statement has the value of an extraordinarily lucid anticipation. Indeed, the language of contemporary chemistry is made of roughly 8 millions of compounds generated from hundreds of elementary building blocks (chains, cycles, functional groups, atoms, etc...) much in the way of a giant molecular lego (Panaye and others 1988), and the range of chemical species yet to be created is probably limited only by the chemist's own imagination. The major characteristic of chemistry as compared with other sciences lies therefore in its extraordinary ability to create new objects with specific properties such as catalysts, drugs, molecular devices, etc... (Lehn 1988). Fortunately, in the conceptual phase of his creative work, the chemist can nowadays rely on computers to perform searches within large data bases of compounds or to simulate the structure and properties of novel, unknown species. Quoted here as examples among many others, these computerized applications have undoubtedly opened the way to significant progresses in the conception of new chemical objects.

Furthermore, as it is essential in chemistry to build, visualize and manipulate 3D molecular structures and their related chemical properties, molecular graphics (MG) has become an indispensable technique (Dubois and others 1985). MG may be defined as the application of computer graphics to study molecular structure, function and interaction, by using microscopic models describing the behaviour of single molecules. In the last few years, MG has known a spectacular development mainly due : (i) to considerable developments in both hardware and software available in computer-assisted chemistry, and (ii) to recent progress in MG applications of increasing popularity such as drug design (Marshall 1987) or protein structure and dynamics (Karplus and McCammon 1986). In these fields, MG techniques have evolved towards a tool complementary to experimental studies and, as such, they have become indispensable in both fundamental and applied research activities (Frühbeis and others 1987).

Molecules are made of atoms linked together by chemical bonds. The very first piece of information concerning a given compound is therefore topological by nature, using a graph-like structure to describe the type of nodes (atoms) and the different connections (bonds). Coded in a compact form within an adequate chemical information system such as DARC (Dubois 1974), this topological pattern is essential as it enables an efficient management of large data bases containing several millions of chemical structures (Rhodes 1985). However, the topological code contains no metric information and it is essential, before doing any further step towards MG modelization, to generate the corresponding 3D architecture either by searching a standard crystallographic data file (Allen and others 1983) or by using a computerized 3D model builder (Weiner and Kollman 1981). Indeed, most chemical properties of a given compound are intimately connected with the spatial arrangement of the atoms, and the 3D representation of its stereochemical characteristics is a important step in molecular modeling. Modern MG facilities enable therefore the chemist to build or retrieve from a data base the 3D architecture of given compounds, i.e. the cartesian coordinates of their constituting atoms, and then to manipulate in real time, by applying simple transformation such as rotations, translations, scale factor, etc..., molecular models made of skeletons or ball-and-stick representations, where vector bonds connect color-coded balls depicting the atoms. Another common model is the space-filling one, which displays a molecule as the union of large intersecting spheres with van der Waals radii, centered on the atoms (Max 1984). By rolling a probe sphere simulating the solvent over the surface defined by the space-filling model, smooth and continuous envelopes such as the solvent-accessible surface or the molecular surface may be generated (Lee and Richards 1971; Richards 1977). These surfaces are actually very useful models as they lead to clear representations of the steric properties of the molecules while depicting the boundary of the volume that may be occupied by the solvent or an incoming reagent around the substrate compound. In addition, these surfaces may be colored according to the value of a local property such as the interaction energy between substrate (S) and reagent (R), which leads to a pseudo 4D representation of the corresponding chemical objects (Weiner and others 1982; Weber, Fluekiger, Ricca, Morgantini 1988). This recent development leads actually to a significant progress in MG techniques, as the visualization of the structural model only can be misleading when simulating the interaction between two molecules such as the docking of a reagent onto a protein

In this paper, we would like to briefly review some MG applications we have recently achieved in our laboratory in the following areas : (i) representation of macromolecular structures such as proteins; (ii) modelization of molecular envelopes as dot surfaces, mesh surfaces and 3D solid models; (iii) development of a new method for the evaluation of interaction energies leading to a color-coded reactivity index represented on dot surfaces or solid models.

MACROMOLECULAR MODELS

Up until recently, macromolecular structure display and modeling was almost totally dependent on the results obtained by X-ray crystallographers. It is only in the last few years that important theoretical developments have been made so as to enable the user to generate accurate structures from empirical energy functions (Weiner and Kollman 1981; Brooks and others 1983). In addition, the corresponding computer programs allow to analyze the structural, equilibrium and dynamic properties of large systems such as proteins or DNA, and to simulate the behaviour of macromolecules in solution, i.e., in a situation which closely mimics the environment conditions of these systems in biology. Limiting ourselves here to the representation and manipulation of macromolecules, the MG techniques used in this field can be compared to those which monitor and trigger a "marionette", according to the vivid expression of Lesk (1977). In particular, a visual presentation of the most important stereochemical parameters and steric properties as well leads to a complete 3D grasp of the structure. This is especially true if depth cueing, zooming and clipping features are provided by the MG equipment in addition to the usual geometric transformations such as 3D rotations and translations.

In our laboratory, molecular models are usually generated using the MANOSK package (Cherfils and others 1988) and displayed on the Evans & Sutherland PS-390 graphics system linked to a VAX-11/780 host computer. As an example, Figure 1

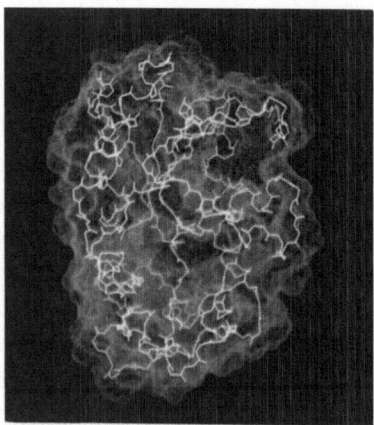

Fig. 1. Bond skeleton model of the diphosphoglyceromutase (DPGM) protein displaying the peptide backbone (yellow) and the various side chains (purple). The protein structure has been taken from the Brookhaven Protein Database.

represents the bond skeleton of the diphosphoglyceromutase protein with the peptide backbone and the various side chains. As the 3D folding of the backbone is a key stereochemical property for understanding the protein function, the Richardson (1981) ribbon model is frequently used to depict such information as secondary structure residue type or temperature factors (Fig. 2). Finally, the molecular surface may be represented using the dot model suggested by Connolly (1983). In this method, dots are scattered across the molecular surface with an approximately

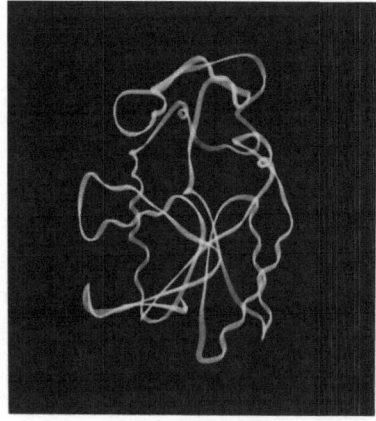

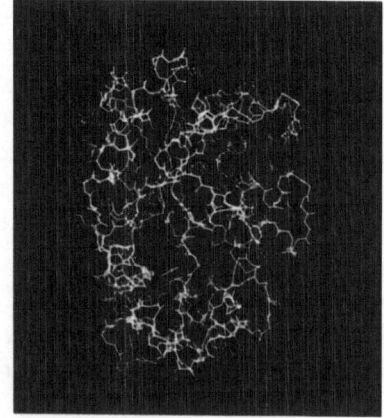

Fig. 2. Ribbon model of the DPGM protein.

Fig. 3. Dot surface generated for the DPGM protein with the protein backbone (yellow).

constant density per unit area. The advantages of the display of such surfaces on a vector or high performance raster system are : (i) the transparency of the envelope, which allows to simultaneously visualize the structural model, and (ii) the small number of points generated, which enables the user to manipulate and clip the model in real time. Most of the molecular modeling packages available today for drug design purposes allow to generate with a very short response time the dot surface of large compounds such as proteins (Fig. 3), which is very useful for localizing and visualizing in detail the active sites, i.e. the regions which are most likely to be attacked and blocked by an incoming reagent.

MOLECULAR SURFACES

In this section, we are going to present some of the most popular models of molecular surfaces used in MG applications, choosing the example of a zeolite fragment made of 126 atoms. Zeolites are inorganic solids with remarkable structural, absorptive and catalytic properties, which explains their importance in industrial chemistry (Breck 1974). The aluminosilicate framework of zeolites is made of corner-sharing SiO_4 and AlO_4 tetrahedra, which tend to form rings giving rise to channels or cages in the material. Because of their porous character, which is at the origin of their unique catalytic properties, zeolites have been often given the name of molecular sponges or sieves. The modelization by MG techniques of several physico-chemical properties of zeolites has been recently reviewed by Ramdas and others (1984) and we would like to concentrate here on the representation of their molecular surfaces using various algorithms. For compounds with intricate shapes such as zeolites, molecular volumes and their associated envelopes generated on a graphics system are undoubtedly very useful and valuable models in structure-activity relationship studies (Van de Waterbeemd and Testa 1987).

Figure 4 presents a 126 atoms (i.e. 24 tetrahedra) fragment of a zeolite of offretite type together with the dot surface calculated for this compound. It is seen that this surface model allows a clear representation of the structural characteristics of this porous material. Another interesting representation of the molecular surface is the mesh or chicken-wire model (Fig. 5), which consists of a mosaic of triangles obtained from a triangulation of the dot surface previously generated. To this end, we have developed a procedure which is described in detail elsewhere (Weber, Fluekiger, Ricca, Morgantini 1988). Suffices to mention here that a connection algorithm has been developed for a unique construction of adjacent triangles from a selected number of dots belonging to the Connolly (1983) surface. In order to generate from 2300 dots the triangulated surface presented in Fig. 5, the CPU time required is about 70 minutes on the IBM 3090/180. As seen in Fig. 5, it is advantageous to represent the skeleton structural model within the molecular surface, which allows to rapidly identify the main features of the molecular envelope with the functional groups they belong to.

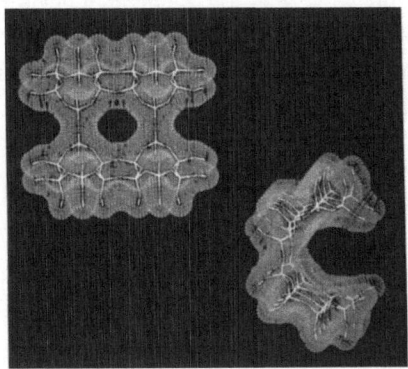 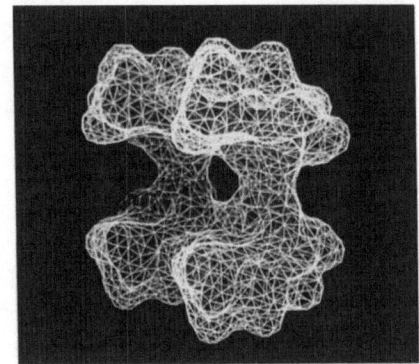

Fig. 4. Two different views of the dot surface generated for the 24 tetrahedron framework of the zeolite of offretite type, with the corresponding bond skeleton model.

Fig. 5. Mesh surface of the zeolite model obtained from triangulation of the dot envelope.

In several applications, it is useful to represent the molecular surface as a 3D solid model with perspective setting, hidden surfaces treatment and Phong or Gouraud shading (Weber and Roch 1986). In addition to the aesthetic aspect of this representation, it may indeed lead to a better perception of the 3D steric features related to the molecular structure, which is important for macromolecules and compounds with intricate shapes. However, the display of these 3D models requires raster systems and real-time manipulation is practically impossible. As the PS-390 system offers various capabilities of shaded image rendering, the generation of solid models from triangulated surfaces is a rather straightforward task, and Figure 6 presents the faceted 3D model corresponding to the triangulated surface of Fig. 5, whereas Fig. 7 displays the smooth model obtained from the faceted surface using the firmware supported Phong rendering capability. For MG applications, however, it is important to visualize the structural model within the molecular envelope, which was possible with both the dot and mesh model previously described. To this end, we have developed a module allowing to display a skeleton structural model within the clipped 3D molecular surface, as shown in Fig. 8.

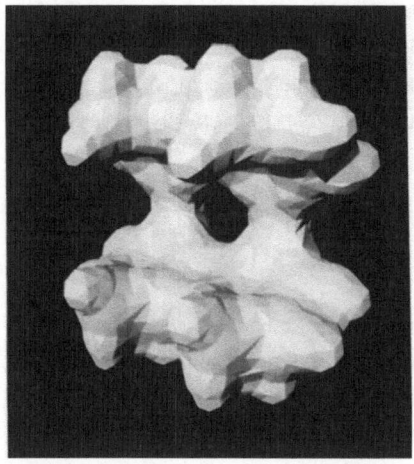

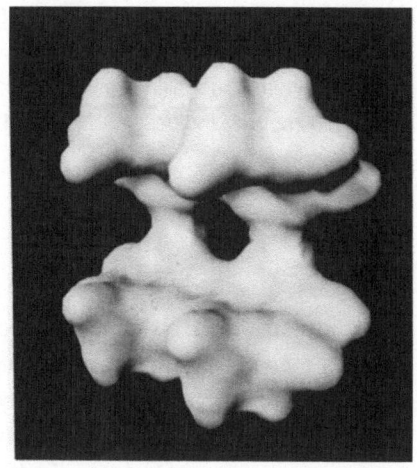

Fig. 6. Faceted model of the molecular surface of the zeolite model obtained from a solid rendering of the triangulated surface.

Fig. 7. Smooth solid model of the molecular surface of the zeolite model.

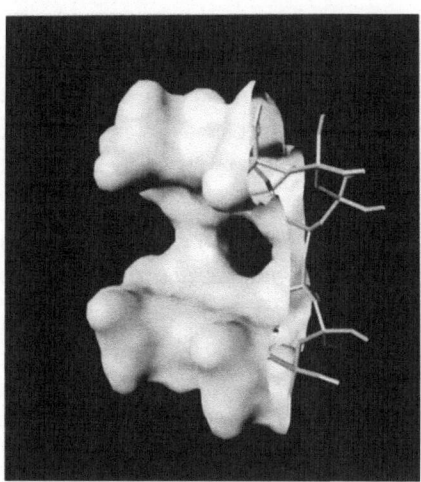

Fig. 8. Solid model of the molecular surface of the offretite zeolite, with side clipping and partial representation of the structure model.

In routine MG applications, the various models of molecular surfaces we have presented here are a very useful tool for the visualization and perception of the 3D structures and shapes of molecules. However, in order to investigate fundamental problems in biology and chemistry such as molecular recognition (Lehn 1988), it is essential to evaluate the most favourable site for the docking of the reagent onto a substrate in terms of geometric fitting and intermolecular interaction energies. To this end, molecular surfaces may be color coded to indicate various physical properties such as electron densities, electrostatic potentials or intermolecular energies to be used as reactivity indices, and this will be illustrated using several examples in the next section.

MOLECULAR PROPERTIES

Interactivity is an important factor in MG applications. Indeed, while it is essential for a chemist to manipulate in real time chemical objects made of molecular structures and properties, the computerized construction of these models should be performed with response times as short as possible, i.e., of the order of a few seconds or, in the worst cases, of a few minutes. To this end, efficient strategies for structure and substructure searching within chemical data bases have been proposed (Hassanaly and Dou 1986) and, for the modelization of novel, unknown compounds, several powerful model builders, based on molecular mechanics techniques (Osawa and Musso 1983), are now available which take full advantage of parallel and vector processing. The calculation of molecular properties, however, generally requires using time-consuming quantum chemical methods and there is no doubt that faster alternatives have to be derived for MG applications. To this end, we have developed recently a fast and reliable procedure for the calculation of the interaction energy between a given substrate S, generally of organometallic nature, and an incoming reagent R characterized by its nucleophilic (i.e. electron donor) or electrophilic (electron acceptor) behaviour (Weber, Morgantini, Leresche, Daul 1988). The purpose of this model is to rationalize and predict organometallic reactivity, enlarging thus the scope of MG applications to : (i) the description of chemical activation of organic ligands by transition metals, and (ii) the design of novel homogeneous catalysts with highly specific properties.

Within our model, the S-R interaction energy $E_{int}(\vec{r})$ is expressed as a sum of several components :

$$E_{int}(\vec{r}) = E_{es}(\vec{r}) + E_{ct}(\vec{r}) + E_{ex}(\vec{r}) \tag{1}$$

where r specifies the position of incoming reagent in the vicinity of the rigid substrate; E_{es}, E_{ct} and E_{ex} being electrostatic, charge transfer and exchange energy components, respectively (Morokuma 1977). The detailed expressions we have developed for E_{es}, E_{ct} and E_{ex} have been reported elsewhere (Weber, Morgantini, Leresche, Daul 1988; Weber, Fluekiger, Morgantini, Schaad, Goursot, Daul 1988). Suffices here to mention that the electrostatic component corresponds to the classical Coulomb energy arising from the interaction of molecular, i.e. electronic and nuclear, charge distributions, whereas the charge transfer component accounts for the energy lowering due to the delocalization of the electrons of one partner onto the other one as a result of their middle-range interaction. In our model, both E_{es} and E_{ct} are evaluated within the fast and reliable extended Hückel (Hoffmann 1963) molecular orbital framework. The exchange term, which describes the short-range repulsion due to the overlap of both S and R electron distributions, is simply chosen to be zero outside the molecular surface of S and infinite on the surface itself (hard sphere approximation), which means that the minima of $E_{es} + E_{ct}$ on this surface are automatically taken as the most reactive sites (Goldblum and Pullman 1978). Indeed, negative (respectively positive) values of E_{int} correspond to S-R attractive (repulsive) interactions, and regions where E_{int} is minimum are the most reactive sites of S towards attack by R. In all cases, the color-coding range from red to yellow to blue extends smoothly over the numerical range of E_{int} from the most negative to zero to most positive values, which means that red zones correspond to preferred sites of attack.

It is important to choose simple, though realistic, models for reagent R as the computer time required to evaluate E_{int} increases rapidly as a function of the complexity of R. In order to have E_{int} values depending only on the position of R with respect to S, and not on its orientation, two standard, spherically symmetric reagents have been chosen : a naked proton as the model of an electron acceptor and a H^- hydride anion as the model of an electron donor. This simple modeling is the same as that used successfully in previous theoretical investigations of reaction mechanisms in organic chemistry (Kahn and others 1986; Shimomura and Kikuchi 1987). In order to display 3D dot surfaces or solid models of E_{int} as a reactivity index, this quantity is evaluated repeatedly at selected points $\vec{r}$ located on the molecular surface of substrate S and generated by the program of Connolly (1981). The number of points depends of course on the size and the complexity of the substrate, and in the cases presented here this number varies between 4'000 and 10'000. In order to generate the color-coded molecular surface within a reasonable response time (typically 1 minute of CPU time on the VAX-11/780), an approximate evaluation of E_{ct}, accounting for a large part of the exact charge transfer energy, is made in most cases (Weber, Fluekiger, Morgantini, Schaad, Goursot, Daul 1988).

Turning back to the zeolite case, it is seen in Fig. 9 that the color-coded molecular surface exhibits large red zones in the vicinity of aluminum tetrahedra, which is in agreement with the experimental finding that the basicity of the zeolite framework increases as measure as the $Al/(Al+Si)$ ratio increases and that aluminum sites are more basic than silicium ones (Goursot and others 1988).

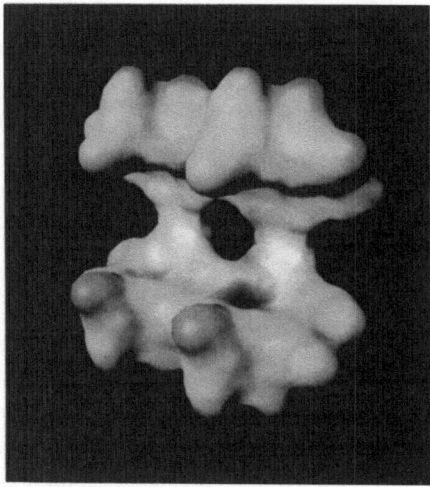

Fig. 9. Solid model of the molecular surface of the offretite zeolite colored according to the E_{int} property. The most reactive site for electrophile attack corresponds to the red zone on the surface.

The structure and reactivity of benzene-chromium tricarbonyl, $(C_6H_6)Cr(CO)_3$ (Scheme I), have been the subject of intensive investigations in organometallic

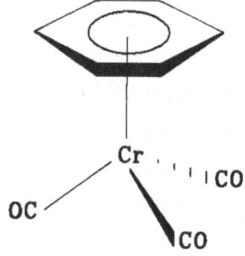

Scheme I. Benzene-chromium tricarbonyl.

chemistry (Solladie-Cavallo 1985). This complex is indeed a prototype of a large series of organometallic compounds exhibiting complexation of an aromatic ring with a tricarbonyl metal species, which leads to a rich and multifaceted chemistry. It is generally accepted that metal-benzene bonding leads to a net intramolecular charge transfer from the ring to the carbonyls, with the result that this compound is easily attacked by an electron donor (nucleophilic attack) on the exo-face of the ring, i.e. on the face opposite to metal. It was therefore interesting to modelize the basic aspects of the chemical reactivity of this compound, by calculating and representing the interaction energy between $(C_6H_6)Cr(CO)_3$ and an incoming nucleophile (Fig. 10). It is seen in this Figure that the most reactive site towards nucleophilic attack is indeed located on the face opposite to metal of complexed benzene, though some regions with considerably less negative values of E_{int} are also observed in the vicinity of metal. The carbonyl (CO) groups, however, are highly unreactive as large repulsive blue zones surround the oxygen ends of the molecule. Another interesting feature which emerges from Fig. 10 is the important change in reactivity which, as expected, accompanies benzene coordination : whereas the uncomplexed ligand, i.e. the C_6H_6 benzene ring, exhibits an uniformly yellow molecular surface, indicating a very small interaction energy, the molecular envelope above the coordinated ring presents deep red color revealing a high reactivity towards the incoming nucleophile. This underlines the important activation of benzene generated by metal coordination. Finally, Figure 11 presents the solid model corresponding to the color-coded molecular dot surface of $(C_6H_6)Cr(CO)_3$. Comparing with Fig. 10, it is seen that both models, though exhibiting the same physico-chemical content, have clearly distinct features : whereas the dot representation presents the advantage of the interactive manipulation and of a rapid visualization of the molecular properties, the solid model leads to a better detailed perception of the 3D characteristics of the chemical object and, ultimately, of the elaborate relations between geometrical structures and molecular properties.

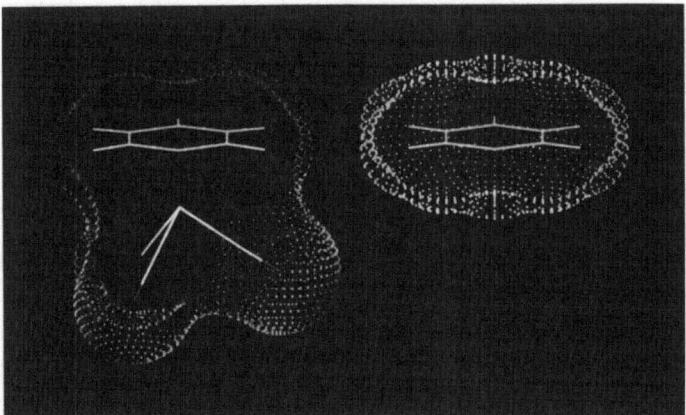

Fig. 10. Color-dot surface of $(C_6H_6)Cr(CO)_3$ (left) and C_6H_6 (right). The color coding of E_{int} for nucleophilic attack is the same for the two compounds, which emphasizes the increase in reactivity of C_6H_6 when coordinated in the complex.

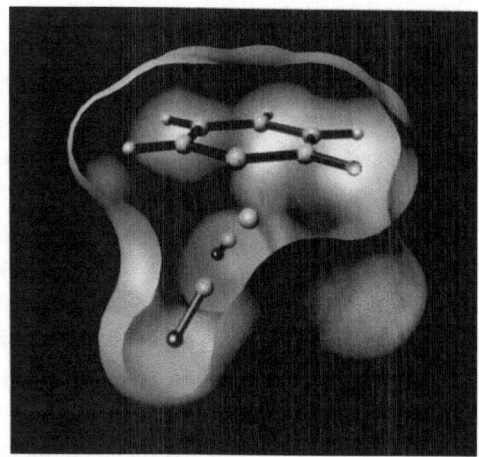

Fig. 11. Solid model of the molecular surface of $(C_6H_6)Cr(CO)_3$ colored according to the E_{int} property for nucleophilic attack.

CONCLUSIONS

In this paper, we have presented several tools which have been recently developed in molecular graphics in order to build, visualize and manipulate 3D models of chemical objects such as molecular structures and their related properties. In particular, we have shown that a simplified description of intermolecular forces and interactions is essential for a rationalization and a reasonable prediction of receptor binding and molecular recognition. To this end, the use of color-coded molecular surfaces is essential for a good perception of the geometrical and stereoelectronic features of the compounds under study.

The recent progresses of molecular graphics and, more generally speaking, computer-assisted chemistry have been so spectacular that we may conceive that these techniques will shape the evolution of disciplines such as chemistry and biotechnology. With the help of computers, the chemist or biologist is indeed free to design new processes or to create novel compounds with yet unknown properties, which could open new horizons in both basic and applied molecular research.

ACKNOWLEDGEMENTS

The authors are grateful to Professors C. Daul, E.P. Kündig and J.P. Mornon for fruitful discussions and to Mr. J. Leresche and Ms. L. Maislisch for their assistance. This work is part of Project 2.806-0.85 of the Swiss National Science Foundation.

REFERENCES

Allen FH, Kennard O, Taylor R (1983) Systematic analysis of structural data as a research technique in organic chemistry. Acc. Chem. Res. **16**:146-153

Berthelot MPE (1886) Science et philosophie. Calmann Levy, Paris

Breck DW (1974) Zeolite molecular sieves. Wiley, New York

Brooks BR, Bruccoleri RE, Olafson BD, States DJ, Swaminathan S, Karplus M (1983) Charm: a program for macromolecular energy, minimization, and dynamics calculations. J. Comput. Chem. **4**:187-217

Cherfils J, Vaney MC, Morize I, Surcouf E, Colloc'h N, Mornon JP (1988) Manosk: a graphics program for analyzing and modeling molecular structure and functions. J. Mol. Graphics **6**:155-160

Connolly ML (1981) Molecular surface calculation. QCPE program 429

Connolly ML (1983) Solvent-accessible surfaces of proteins and nucleic acids. Science **221**:709-713

De Waterbeemd H Van, Testa B (1987) The parametrization of lipophilicity and other structural properties in drug design. Adv. Drug Res. **16**:85-225

Dubois JE (1974) DARC system in chemistry. In: Wipke WT, Heller S, Feldmann R, Hyde E (eds) Computer representation and manipulation of chemical information. Wiley, New York, pp 239-263

Dubois JE, Laurent D, Weber J (1985) Chemical ideograms and molecular computer graphics. Visual Computer **1**:49-63

Frühbeis H, Klein R, Wallmeier H (1987) Computer-assisted molecular design (CAMD) - An overview. Angew. Chem. Int. Ed. Engl. **26**:403-418

Goldblum A, Pullman B (1978) Study of anion binding to protonated nucleic acid bases using electrostatic molecular potentials. Theoret. Chim. Acta **47**:345-347

Goursot A, Fajula F, Daul C, Weber J (1988) Study of the molecular electrostatic potentials of zeolites: the acidity in offretite. J. Phys. Chem. **92**:4456-4461

Hassanaly P, Dou H (1986) Online access to chemical information. In: Vernin G, Chanon M (eds) Computer aids to chemistry. Ellis Horwood, Chichester, pp 334-375

Hoffmann R (1963) An extended Hückel theory. I. Hydrocarbons. J. Chem. Phys. **39**:1397-1412

Kahn SD, Pau CF, Overman LE, Hehre WJ (1986) Modeling chemical reactivity. I. Regioselectivity of Diels-Alder cycloadditions of electron-rich dienes with electron-deficient dienophiles. J. Am. Chem. Soc. **108**:7381-7396

Karplus M, McCammon JA (1986) The dynamics of proteins. Scient. Amer. **254**:30-39

Lee B, Richards FM (1971) The interpretation of protein structures: estimation of static accessibility. J. Mol. Biol. **79**:379-400

Lehn JM (1988) Supramolecular chemistry - Scope and perspectives: molecules, supermolecules, and molecular devices (Nobel lecture). Angew. Chem. Int. Ed. Engl. **27**:89-112

Lesk AM (1977) Macromolecular marionettes. Comput. Biol. Med. **7**:113:129

Marshall GR (1987) Computer-aided drug design. Ann. Rev. Pharmacol. Toxicol. **27**:193-213

Max NL (1984) Computer representation of molecular surfaces. J. Mol. Graphics **2**:8-13

Morokuma K (1977) Why do molecules interact ? The origin of electron donor-acceptor complexes, hydrogen bonding, and proton affinity. Acc. Chem. Res. **10**:294-300

Osawa E, Musso H (1983) Molecular mechanics calculations in organic chemistry: examples of the usefulness of this simple non-quantum mechanical model. Angew. Chem. Int. Ed. Engl. **22**:1-12

Panaye A, Doucet JP, Cayzergues P, Carrier G, Mathieu G (1988) L'élucidation structurale: des données spectrales à la reconnaissance moléculaire. L'Actualité Chimique **4-5**:103-112

Ramdas S, Thomas JM, Betteridge PW, Cheetham AK, Davies EK (1984) Modelling the chemistry of zeolites by computer graphics. Angew. Chem. Int. Ed. Engl. **23**:671-679

Rhodes P (1985) Chemical structures on-line. Chem. Britain **21**:53-58

Richards FM (1977) Areas, volumes, packing and protein structure. Ann. Rev. Biophys. Bioeng. **6**:151-176

Richardson JS (1981) The anatonomy and taxonomy of protein structure. Adv. Protein Chem. **34**:167-339

Shimomura S, Kikuchi O (1987) Reaction potential map analysis of site selectivity of acrylic acid and acrylonitrile. J. Mol. Struct. Theochem **150**:289-295

Solladie-Cavallo A (1985) Arene-chromium tricarbonyl complexes: bonding and behaviour. Polyhedron **4**:901-927

Weber J, Roch M (1986) Computer graphics applications of electron deformation densities and electrostatic potentials in coordination chemistry. J. Mol. Graphics **4**:145-148

Weber J, Fluekiger P, Morgantini PY, Schaad O, Goursot A, Daul C (1988) The modelling of nucleophilic and electrophilic additions to organometallic complexes using molecular graphics techniques. J. Comp. Aid. Mol. Design 2:235-253

Weber J, Fluekiger P, Ricca A, Morgantini PY (1988) Recent developments in molecular graphics. In: Barth H (ed) Visualisierungstechniken und Algorithmen. Springer, Berlin, pp 17-30

Weber J, Morgantini PY, Leresche J, Daul C (1988) Molecular graphics as a tool for modelling nucleophilic and electrophilic reactions in organometallic chemistry. In: Carbo R (ed) Quantum chemistry: basic aspects, actual trends. Elsevier, Amsterdam, in the press

Weiner PK, Langridge R, Blaney JM, Schaefer R, Kollman PK (1982) Electrostatic potential molecular surfaces. Proc. Natl. Acad. Sci. USA 79:3754-3758

Weiner PK, Kollman PA (1981) Amber: assisted model building with energy refinement. A general program for modeling molecules and their interactions. J. Comput. Chem. 2:287-303

Jacques Weber is currently a professor of computer-assisted chemistry at the University of Geneva. After completion of his Ph.D. thesis in chemical physics in Geneva (1969), he spent two years as a post-doc in the USA, working at the Quantum Theory Project of the University of Florida and at the IBM Research Laboratory of San Jose (California). Back at the University of Geneva, he founded in 1975 the Laboratory of Computational Chemistry, which he has headed since then. His research interests include computational quantum chemistry, Monte Carlo and molecular dynamics simulations, and molecular graphics. In his recent research projects, supported by the Swiss Science Foundation, Weber is combining different techniques deriving from these various fields so as to develop interactive molecular graphics tools for the prediction and interpretation of organometallic reaction mechanisms. Weber was the organizer, or a member of the scientific committee, of several international congresses in computational chemistry and molecular graphics; in addition, he has authored and published over 120 refereed scientific papers in a broad range of chemistry and computer science journals.

Address: Laboratory of Computational Chemistry, University of Geneva, 30 quai Ernest Ansermet, 1211 Geneva 4, Switzerland.

Pierre-Yves Morgantini received his Ph.D. in organic chemistry from the University of Geneva in 1986. Since then, he is working as a post-doctoral fellow in the Laboratory of Computational Chemistry of this University. He is particularly interested in several applications of computer-assisted chemistry which are at the present time in development in this Laboratory, namely in designing better molecular graphics tools in organometallic chemistry.

Address: Laboratory of Computational Chemistry, University of Geneva, 30 quai Ernest Ansermet, 1211 Geneva 4, Switzerland.

Peter Fluekiger received his M.Sc. in chemistry from the University of Geneva in 1987. He is now a graduate student in the Laboratory of Computational Chemistry of this University. The main theme of his Ph.D. thesis is closely related to the calculation and representation of molecular properties on high-performance graphics equipments.

Address: Laboratory of Computational Chemistry, University of Geneva, 30 quai Ernest Ansermet, 1211 Geneva 4, Switzerland.

Annick Goursot is a member of the french National Research Council. She received her Ph.D. in chemical physics from the University of Marseille in 1972. After 2 years as a post-doc in the University of Montreal, she spent 10 years in the School of Chemistry of Mulhouse, working in quantum chemistry applied to organometallic compounds. Since 1985, she works in the School of Chemistry of Montpellier, where she began to be interested in catalysis. In her present research projects, computational quantum chemistry and molecular graphics are combined in the order to analyze the acid properties of zeolites and the electronic properties of metallic aggregates used in fine chemistry reactions.

Address: School of Chemistry, 8 rue de l'Ecole Normale, 34075 Montpellier cedex, France.

Drawing Human Hair Using Wisp Model

Y. Watanabe and Y. Suenaga

ABSTRACT

This paper presents a new powerful method for hair image generation. A simplified Computer Graphics (CG) model of human hair is presented to describe and render various kinds of hair images with a small number of parameters. Practical methods for handling hair styles and for generating realistic images are presented. A notable feature of the proposed method is that it is run on the conventional z-buffer algorithm. Experiments proved that the proposed algorithm is very useful for the generation of various human hair images.

Keywords: anisotropic shading, surface modeling, hair, z-buffer, real-time rendering

1. INTRODUCTION

Despite the fact that hair is an essential part of human images, few reports have been published on the generation of hair images by CG technologies. Human hair image generation is not discussed in representative previous reports on human animation (Badler 1987; Thalmann 1987; Platt 1981; Parke 1982; Waters 1987).

The difficulty of handling hair in CG seems to be due to the following two considerations.

(1) The total number of human hairs is too large. This prevents getting results in a reasonably short turnaround time.
(2) A cross section of human hair is round. Enormous number of patches is needed to generate the image of even a single hair in the usual manner.

Yamana & Suenaga (1987) and G. Miller (1988) independently employed anisotropic reflection models to generate hairy and furry images. Both methods require a long computation time. Actually, G. Miller took 2.0 hours with the Celerity 1230 to get an animal fur image. In addition to the above problems, anisotropic reflection based methods by Yamana et al. and G. Miller were devised mainly for giving hair texture on some previously given surface. A CG hair model which allows changing the hair style (outer shape) is needed. J. Weil (1988) presented a technical slide and an animation video to SIGGRAPH'88. However, his algorithm has not yet been published, and the picture quality seems less than satisfactory.

This paper presents a new efficient method of CG human hair generation. A trigonal prism model is employed to present each hair in the human hair area. A hair bundle (wisp) model is also introduced to control the shape of hair easily with a small number of parameters. The proposed hair image generation method fits today's fastest renderer, "z-buffer", which makes it possible to draw an enormous number of hairs within a reasonably short time.

2. HAIR

Usually, there are 50,000 to 100,000 hairs in the hair area on the human head. Without any restrictions, each hair might grow in a random direction. However, usual hair grows in a regular, almost parallel manner due to the effects of adjacent hairs. Moreover, some artificial effects like combing or hair oil make the hair grow in a somewhat orderly direction.

Human hair appearance is characterized by the texture and shape of the hair. Both characteristics must be generated correctly from the CG hair model. The CG hair model should allow us to see each hair from any viewpoint. The hair model does not necessarily need to have the same characteristics as real hair. For example, wigs are not always made from real human hair, and they give a very realistic appearance. The essential factors needed for the CG hair model are (1) simplicity, (2) controllability and (3) practicality.

3. HAIR DRAWING

Yamana & Suenaga (1987) applied an anisotropic reflection model to human hair generation. Regarding hairs as a scratch-like texture on the human head surface, hair images are synthesized by using ray-tracing with an anisotropic reflection table. However, this method was time consuming, and the synthesized hair images had a somewhat "metallic" appearance as shown in Photo-1.

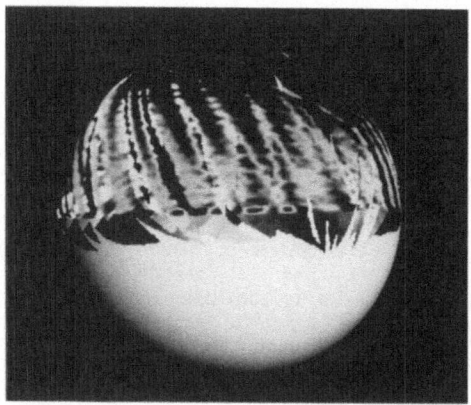

Photo-1. Early work of hair generation using anisotropic reflection by Yamana & Suenaga (May 1987)

In G. Miller's work (1988), the anisotropic shading model was employed to produce furry images. He adopted the anisotropic shading on many hair "sticks" to get a more realistic image of the fur. G.Miller used the efficient method called the "pseudo-reflectance map" to compute the intensity of the anisotropic shaded sticks. His method is suitable for the generation of short, straight, thick (stick-like) hairs, shiny fur, hairy skins or needle leaves. Though he successfully obtained various furry images, he himself pointed out the following problems with his method in his paper.

(1) *The hairs are too thick.*
In order to get drawing result within a reasonable turnaround time, the number of sticks is suppressed⁻ to a far smaller number than that of the hairs of real animals. Moreover, in order to cover the animal body with a smaller number of hairs, the stick must be thicker than real animal hair. Consequently, the furry images appear to have thick hairs.

(2) *The hairs are all straight.*

Since short straight sticks are employed, the resultant furry image has all short, straight hairs.

(3) *The hairs are not attractive and realistic.*

This is a result of problems (1) and (2). The thick and straight hair do not give attractive and realistic images.

(4) *The computation is still expensive.*

The computation cost is expensive even if the number of sticks is suppressed and the pseudo-reflectance map is used for fast anisotropic shading calculation. All intensity computation must be executed by software, because the anisotropic shading is not usually implemented on hardware (firmware).

4. HAIR MODEL

4.1 Representation of a Hair (Trigonal Prism Model)

The CG hair model described in this paper defines each hair as a basic object. This approach is based on the assumption that if each basic object is appropriate, the total set composed of these basic objects would give appropriate images. If each object is controllable, the total set would become controllable.

A straightforward way to approximate a hair is using a series of cylinders. However, each cylinder requires a large number of polygonal patches, and an enormous number of patches is needed for the total hair set. If, for example, we suppose a hair is approximated by 32 cylinders and each cylinder is approximated by 32 triangular patches, and if a person has 100,000 hairs, the total number of triangular patches would become 102,400,000. It is impossible to draw such a big number of triangular patches in a reasonably short time.

In order to solve this problem, we have to reduce the total number of patches. For this purpose, the authors employed a trigonal prism model to approximate cylinders as shown below.

The bending of a hair is represented by a series of short trigonal prisms. A trigonal prism is the most basic primitive to define a hair model as shown in Fig. 1. In the model, a hair is defined by controlling the length (l), angle (a, b and c) and thickness (d) of a trigonal prism. Figure 2 shows a bending hair model which uses the conjunction of many trigonal prisms. This hair has constant thickness. Length, angles and thickness are the parameters defining a trigonal prism. Various kinds of hair (e.g., straight, wavy or curly) are generated by controlling these parameters.

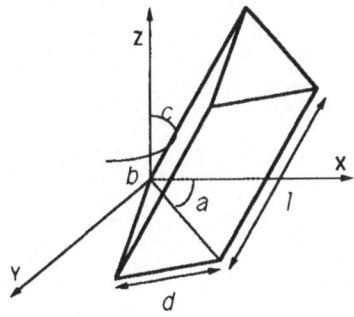

Fig. 1. Trigonal prism

Fig. 2. Bending hair model

A cylinder is approximated by a prism having many flat surfaces (patches). By reducing the number of patches, we finally arrive at a trigonal prism. Needless to say, more patches give a better approximation, and trigonal prisms are a very bad approximation of cylinders. However, the number of flat surfaces can be reduced by employing smooth shading. The dodecagonal and the trigonal prisms are shown in Fig. 3(a) and (b). Figure 3(a) was generated with flat shading, and Fig. 3(b) was generated with smooth shading (Gouraud). When flat shading is used, the difference in appearance between the dodecagonal prism and the trigonal prism is very big as shown if Fig. 3(a). The difference is drastically reduced by employing smooth shading as shown in Fig.3(b).

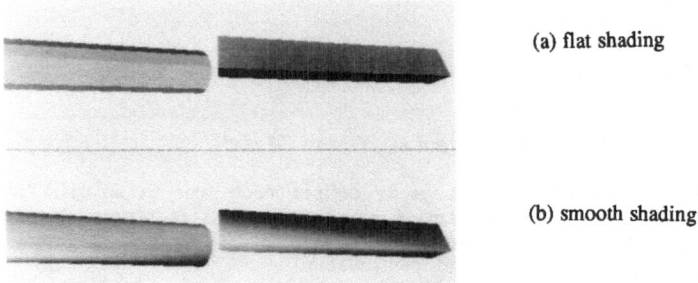

(a) flat shading

(b) smooth shading

Fig. 3. Dodecagonal prism and trigonal prism

4.2 Representation of Hair Bundle ("Wisp" Model)

The authors noticed that there are many bundles in a hair set. If the hair is combed, long bundles are formed in the hair. When hair is waving in the wind, the bundles appear as streams of hair. We make use of bundles, or "wisps" of hairs as units to efficiently draw the total hair set, because most wisps have basically the same shape. By introducing wisps, the number of control parameters to obtain hair images is drastically reduced. Details of wisps are determined by the control parameters of each hair. Figures 4(a) and (b) show wisps of hairs, where each hair is defined as a conjunction of trigonal prisms, as described in section 4.1. Figure 4(a) shows a wisp having hairs in rather random direction, and Fig. 4(b) shows a wisp whose hairs have grown in an almost parallel direction. Each wisp has one hundred hairs.

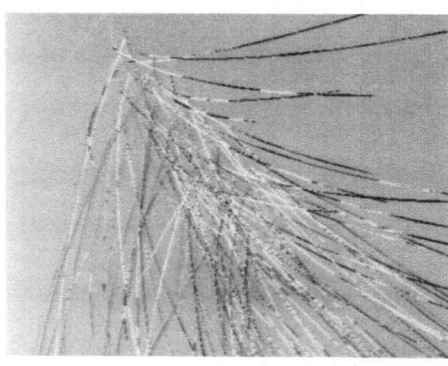 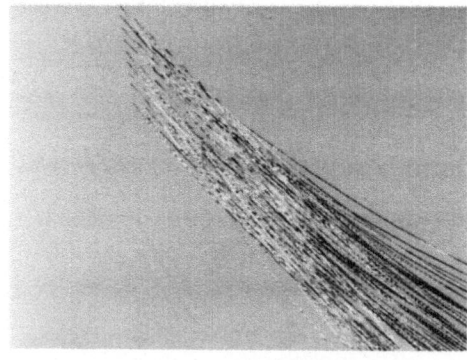

(a) random direction   (b) almost parallel direction

Fig. 4. Wisps of hairs

The images of a single hair and a wisp of hair are shown in Figs. 5 and 6. In both figures, the hair length ratio of (a), (b) and (c) is 1:2:4, respectively. The longer hair is, the more it bends. The (d) figures are close-ups of the (c) figures, showing the details and root(s) of the hairs.

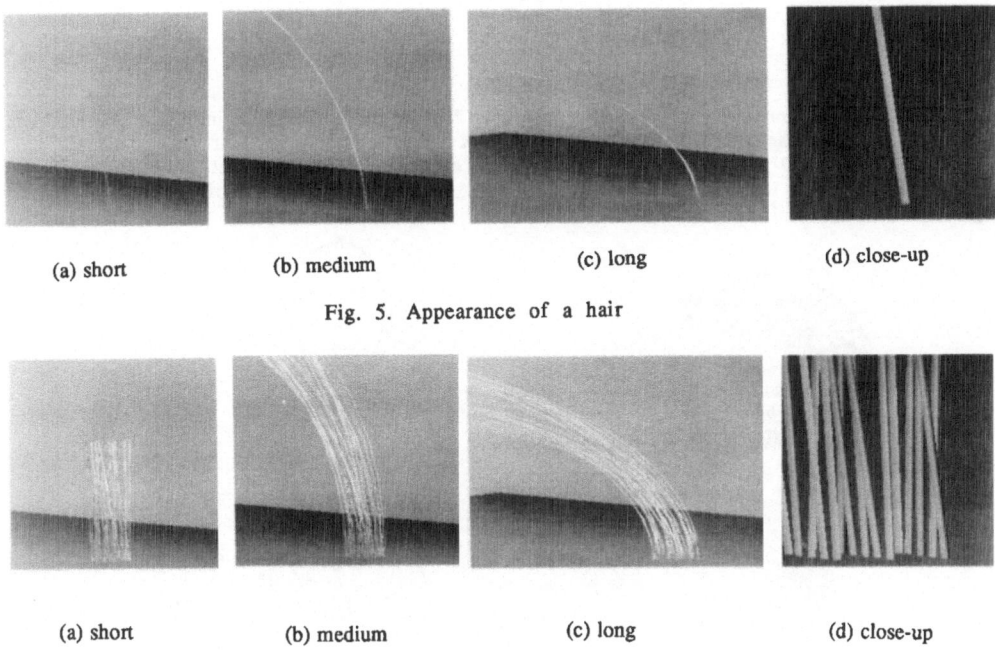

(a) short   (b) medium   (c) long   (d) close-up

Fig. 5. Appearance of a hair

(a) short   (b) medium   (c) long   (d) close-up

Fig. 6. Appearance of a wisp

Various hair images can be obtained by controlling only a small number of parameters, which are the number of wisps, the number of hairs in a wisp, hair length, thickness and color of each hair. More wisps produce thicker hair, and more hairs in a wisp also produce thicker hair. By changing the number of hairs, hair thickness in a wisp is controlled. Figures 7(a), (b) and (c) show wisp images generated for various numbers of hairs in a wisp. All other parameter values are the same as those used in Fig. 4(b).

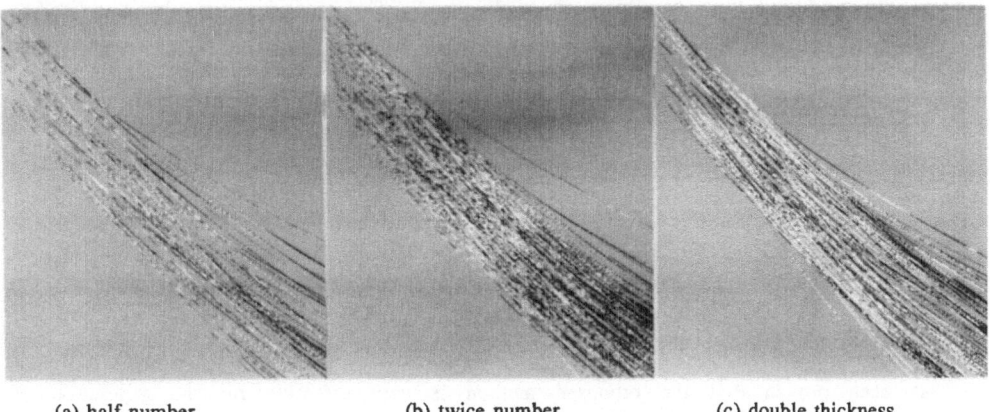

(a) half number   (b) twice number   (c) double thickness

Fig. 7. A wisp of hairs

Hair style is effectively determined by what shape of wisp is used and how many kinds of wisps are used. The possibility of style control based on the wisp might be compared to the way hairdressers style hair. Hairdressers create hair styles not by cutting each individual hair, but by cutting wisps of hairs. Hence, wisp-based control is probably a realistic approach to controlling hair style.

5. EXPERIMENTS

The CG hair was drawn on a 3-D CG model of a human head, as shown in Fig. 8. A total of about 800 triangular patches were used for this model; about 500 for the forehead and face, and about 300 for the hair region, the dark area in Fig. 8. The root directions of hairs are determined by the root directions of wisps. Because of the lack of hair, this picture gives a strong artificial impression.

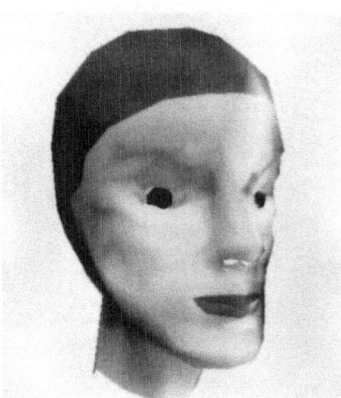

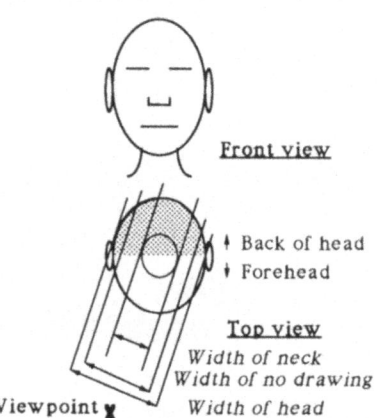

Fig. 8. Human head model   Fig. 9. No hair drawing area

The results of hair drawing on the human head are shown in Figs. 10-14. Some parameters used to obtain these pictures are listed in Table 1. Each hair model to draw Fig. 10 uses 48 triangular patches. The total number of hairs in Fig. 10 is 76,302. Therefore, the number of total triangular patches required to draw this picture was 3,662,496.

Only about one third of the triangular patches of hair were on the front side of the head; two thirds of the hair patches were on the back side of the head. When drawing the front view, the patches which would not be seen from the front can be removed in advance to reduce the rendering time as illustrated in Figure 9. The rendering time by this method with some parameters are listed in Table 2.

Figures 10(a) and (b) show short curly hair, Figs. 11(a) and (b) show medium-length straight hair, and Figs. 12(a) and (b) show the closely-cropped hair. To obtain the effect of combing, Figs. 13(a) and (b) show long hair made with hair wisps whose hairs are aligned in the same direction. An image generated from straight black hair on another 3-D human face model is shown in Fig. 14.

It was necessary to control a lot of wisps and patches to complete Figs. 10-14. Although the number of patches does not seem to be small enough to get the results so quickly, in reality it takes only 1-20 minutes to draw total primitives, and only 20 seconds to 12 minutes to draw the reduced primitives using the IRIS-4D/70GT, as shown in Tables 1 and 2. Therefore, the processing is completed within a realistic turnaround time, even for a large number of drawing primitives.

It has been proven that the proposed method is very effective for the generation of human hair images. By simply controlling the parameters, various styles and textures of hair can be generated by using standard graphics hardware.

697

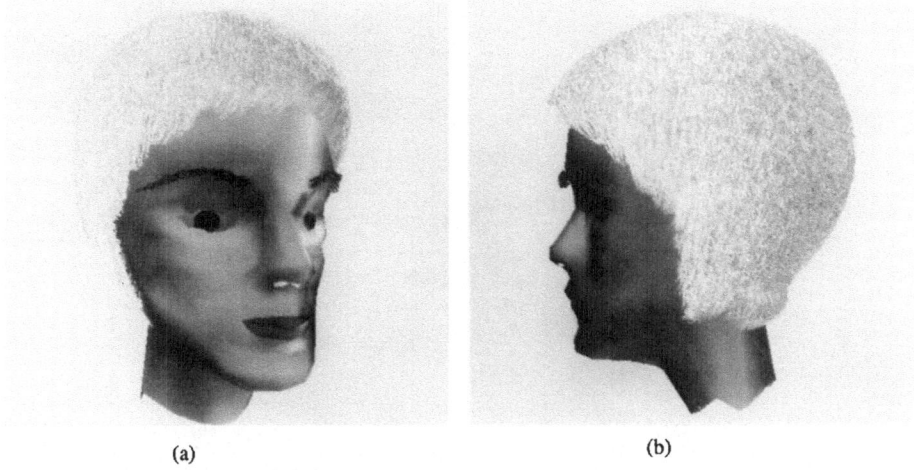

(a)   (b)

Fig. 10. Short curly hair

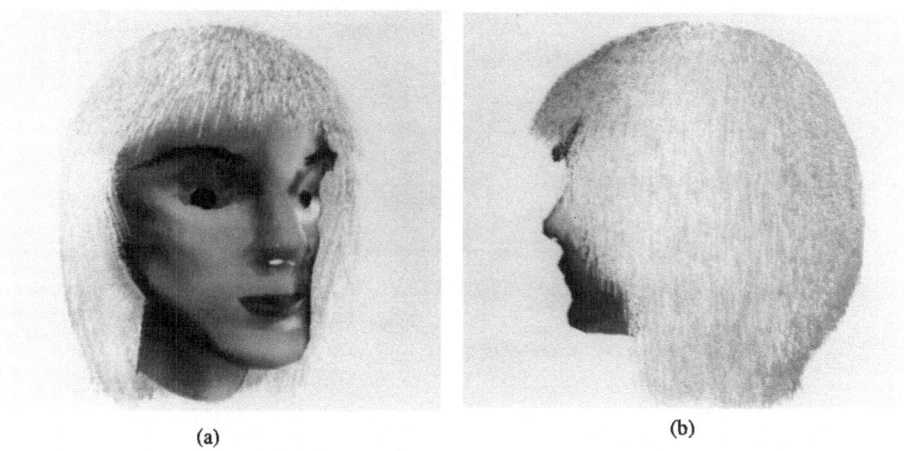

(a)   (b)

Fig. 11 Medium-length hair

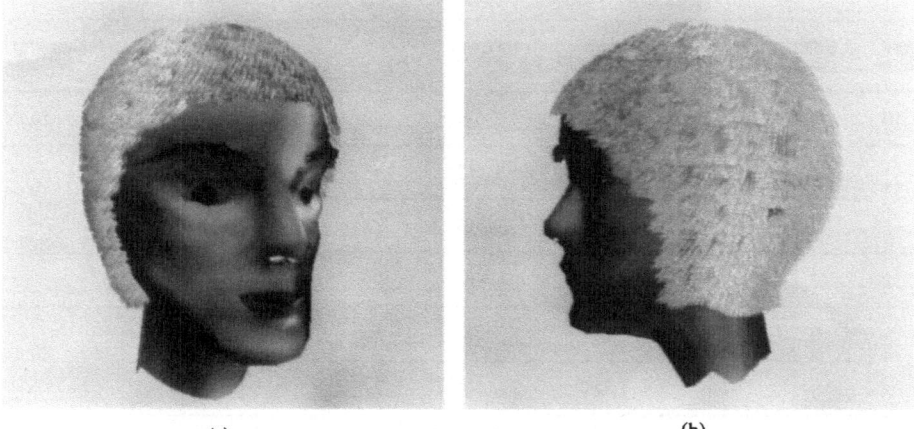

(a)   (b)

Fig. 12. Closely-cropped hair

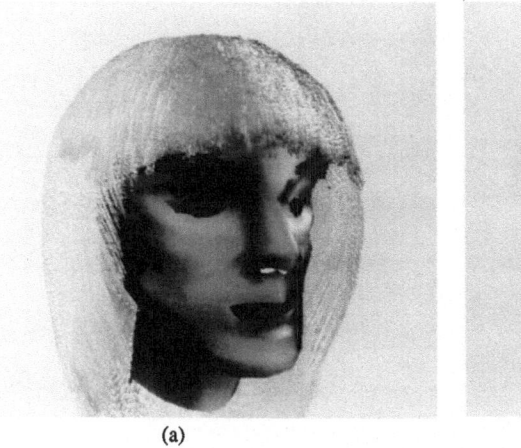
(a)

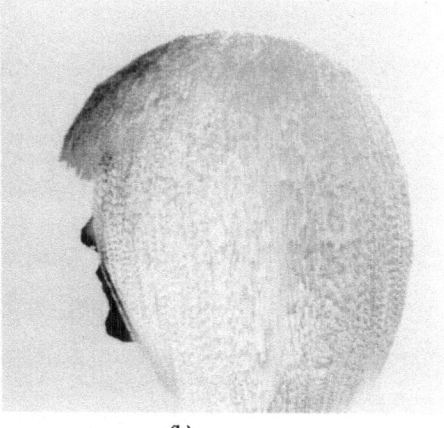
(b)

Fig. 13. Long hair (combed)

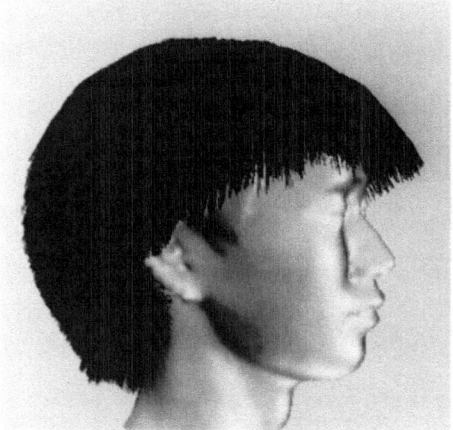

Fig. 14 Black hair

Table 1.   Total count of drawing primitives

Picture number	Hairs / wisp	Thickness	Wisp	Total hair count	Primitives / hair	Total primitives	Rendering time
Fig. 10	9	2	8,478	76,302	48	3,662,496	10 min.
Fig. 11	9	1	648	5,832	48	279,936	19 min.
	9	1	7,830	70,470	72	5,073,840	
Fig. 12	9	8	3,258	19,548	8	156,384	1 min.
Fig. 13	9	1	1,944	17,496	48	839,808	20 min.
	9	1	7,830	70,470	72	5,073,840	
Fig. 14	9	1	8,478	76,302	48	3,662,496	10 min.

Table 2.   Reduced count of drawing primitives

Picture number	Picture kind	Reduced wisp	Reduced hair count	Reduced drawing primitives	Reduced rendering time
Fig. 10	(a)	2,826	25,434	1,220,832	3 min.
	(b)	5,087	45,781	2,197,498	6 min.
Fig. 11	(a)	2,826	25,434	1,784,592	6 min.
	(b)	5,087	45,781	3,212,266	11 min.
Fig. 12	(a)	1,086	6,516	52,128	20 sec.
	(b)	1,955	11,729	93,830	36 sec.
Fig. 13	(a)	3,108	29,322	1,971,216	7 min.
	(b)	5,594	52,779	3,548,189	12 min.
Fig. 14		4,239	38,151	1,831,248	5 min.

6. CONCLUSION

This paper presented a new practical method for CG hair drawing based on a simplified model of hairs and wisps. A practical method to handle the hair style using only a small number of parameters was discussed. The proposed method can be run on ordinary z-buffer hardware. Experiments using a typical CG workstation proved the proposed algorithm is very effective for the generation of various human hair images. A notable feature of the proposed method is that it is suited to the conventional z-buffer algorithm and hardware, which is known as the fastest practical rendering tool.

Some problems still remain for easy generation of truly photorealistic images. For example, drawing based on trigonal prism model causes aliasing. An effective antialiasing method must be introduced. Also, parameters to define wisps and hairs should be given manually to the computer.

Analyzing the effects of adjacent hairs and optical characteristics of hair could be useful to determine the shape of wisp for better image generation. Furthermore, if the control of wisps is fine and precise, a picture of waving hair can also be created by this method. Moreover, in some cases, artificial effects should be taken into account. For example, hair appears to shine when it is placed in front of the light source; backlighting of hair. Hair oil certainly affects the reflectivity and slickness of hairs. Also, hair styles are formed by combing or brushing. All these things must be taken into consideration for truly photorealistic hair image generation.

ACKNOWLEDGEMENT

We thank the members of Visual Perception Lab., NTT HI Lab. for various helps and discussions. Especially, we would like to thank Mr. Takashi Yamana for nice discussion on various aspects of hair image generation. We would also like to thank Mr. Taka-aki Akimoto for good suggestions for computer programming and 3-D drawing object definition format. In addition, we thank Dr. Kazuaki Komori, the Executive Manager, Visual Perception Lab. for his encouragement and advice.

REFERENCES

F. I. Parke (1982) Parameterized Model for Facial Animation, IEEE Computer Graphics and Applications, Vol. 12, No. 9, pp. 61-68

G. S. Miller (1988) FROM WIRE-FRAMES TO FURRY ANIMALS, Graphic Interface '88, pp. 138-145

J. Weil (1988) Technical Slide and Technical Animation Video, SIGGRAPH'88

K. Waters (1987) A Muscle Model for Animating Three-Dimensional Facial Expression, Proc. SIGGRAPH '87, Vol. 21, No.4, pp. 17-24

N. I. Badler, K. H. Manoochehri (1987) Articulated Figure Positioning by Multiple Constraints, IEEE Computer Graphics and Applications, Vol.7, No.6, pp. 28-38

N. Magnenat-Thalmann, E. Primeau, D. Thalmann (1987) Abstract Muscle Action Procedures for Human Face Animation, The Visual Computer, Springer, Vol. 3, No. 4

N. Magnenat-Thalmann, D. Thalmann (1987) The Direction of Synthetic Actors in the film Rendez-vour a Montreal, IEEE Computer Graphics and Applications, Vol. 7, No.12

S. M. Platt, N. I. Badler (1981) Animating Facial Expressions, Proc. SIGGRAPH '81, pp. 245-252

T. Yamana and Y. Suenaga (1987) A Method of Hair Representation Using Anisotropic Reflection, IECEJ Tech. Report, PRU87-3, pp. 15-20 (May 1987) (in Japanese)

Yasuhiko Watanabe is Research Engineer in the Visual Perception Laboratory of the NTT Human Interface Laboratories. He is presently engaged in research on 3-D model based coding systems. Since joining the Electrical Communications Laboratories, NTT, in 1981, he has been working on facsimile communication systems and Videotex communication systems. He received the Bachelor's degree from Niigata University, Niigata, Japan, in 1981. He is a member of the Information Processing Society of Japan.

Address: Visual Perception Laboratory, NTT Human Interface Laboratories, 1-2356, Take, Yokosuka-shi, Kanagawa, 238-03 Japan.

Yasuhito Suenaga is Senior Research Engineer, Supervisor, of Visual Perception Laboratory in NTT Human Interface Laboratories. He leads a research group of computer graphics and vision. Since joining the Electrical Communications Laboratories, NTT, in 1973, he has been engaged in the research of image processing. He received the B.S., M.S., and Ph.D. degrees in electrical engineering from Nagoya University, Nagoya, Japan, in 1968, 1970 and 1974 respectively. He is a member of the Institute of Electronics, Information and Communication Engineers, and the Information Processing Society of Japan.

Address: Visual Perception Laboratory, NTT Human Interface Laboratories, 1-2356, Take, Yokosuka-shi, Kanagawa, 238-03 Japan.

Logarithmic Spirals and Computer Art

K.G. Suffern

ABSTRACT

Interesting geometric patterns are obtained by mapping a rectangular region in one coordinate system onto an annular region in another coordinate system. The mapping involves logarithmic spirals and several examples are presented which involve interlocking spirals, cubes and dragon patterns.

KeyWords : mathematical transformations, logarithmic spirals, interlocking shapes, computer art

INTRODUCTION

Logarithmic spirals occur in several places in nature, for example the nautilus shell, elephant's tusks, and the horns of other animals. Similar spirals also occur in flower heads, the sunflower being the most notable example. Many people find an intrinsic beauty in these spirals, probably because of their simple proportions and elegant winding shapes.

It is therefore of interest to explore ways of creating works of art based on these spirals. Because logarithmic spirals have a simple mathematical representation, they are ideally suited for incorporating into computer art, and this paper examines one way of doing this. The technique involves mapping a rectangular arrangement of interlocking geometrical shapes in one coordinate system onto an annulus in another coordinate system. Some of the resulting patterns are strictly two dimensional, while others create a three dimensional illusion which goes beyond that present in the original pattern.

THE TRANSFORMATION

We consider a mapping between two rectangular coordinate systems (u,v) and (x,y). A logarithmic spiral in the (x,y) plane is given by $r = a e^{b\theta}$ where (r,θ) are the usual polar coordinates related to (x,y) by $x = r \cos \theta$ and $y = r \sin \theta$, and a and b are constants. We can achieve the desired transformation by mapping straight lines $v = $ constant in the (u,v) plane onto the spirals in the (x,y) plane. We relate u to the angle θ by $\theta = \alpha u$ where α is a scaling parameter, and map $v = 0$ onto $r = a e^{b\alpha u}$.

To obtain a family of spirals rotated about the origin we can interpret v as a rotation parameter about the origin of the (x,y) coordinate system. Consequently, the point (u,v) is transformed to the point (x,y) where the two points are related by

$$[x \ y] = a \, e^{b\alpha u} \, [\cos (\alpha u) \ \sin (\alpha u)] \begin{bmatrix} \cos v & \sin v \\ -\sin v & \cos v \end{bmatrix} \qquad (1)$$

and we need only consider values of v in the range $0 \le v \le 2\pi$. Under this transformation, lines u = constant are mapped onto circles in the (x,y) plane with radii $r = a\,e^{b\alpha u}$, and rectangular regions in the (u,v) plane are mapped onto anulli on the (x,y) plane. However, the transformation (1) is not the same as the conformal transformation which maps rectangular regions to anulli, because there, lines v = constant are mapped onto radial lines with θ = constant. The transformation (1) reduces to the conformal transformation in the limit $b \to \infty$.

Line segments with v = constant are mapped onto segments of logarithmic spirals in the (x,y) plane and Fig. 1 shows a series of equally spaced line segments in the (u,v) plane and their images in the (x,y) plane.

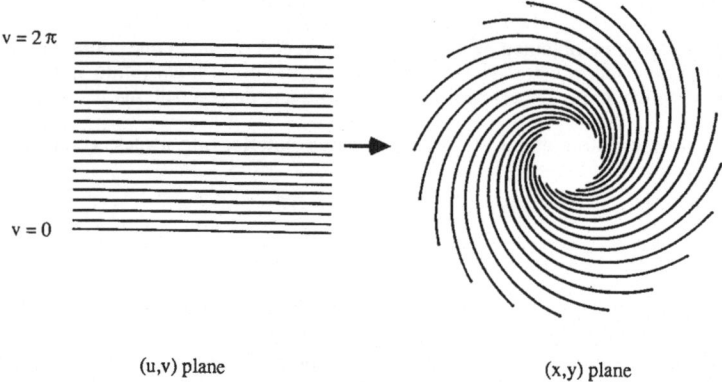

(u,v) plane   (x,y) plane

Fig. 1 Equally spaced lines v = constant in the (u,v) plane and their images in the (x,y) plane under the transformation (1).

The image of an arbitrary curve of the form

$$v = f(u) + c \tag{2}$$

is

$$[x \ y] = a\,e^{b\alpha u}\,[\cos(\alpha u + f(u)) \quad \sin(\alpha u + f(u))]\begin{bmatrix} \cos c & \sin c \\ -\sin c & \cos c \end{bmatrix}, \tag{3}$$

where c acts as a rotation parameter. In the case where eqn. (2) is the straight line

$$v = mu + c,$$

eqn. (3) becomes

$$[x \ y] = a\,e^{b\alpha u}\,[\cos(m + \alpha)u \quad \sin(m + \alpha)u]\begin{bmatrix} \cos c & \sin c \\ -\sin c & \cos c \end{bmatrix} \tag{4}$$

When the above transformation is used to produce computer art, it is convenient to be able to restrict the drawing to an annulus of specified radii r_1 and r_2 on the output device, and to be able to specify the angle $\Delta\theta$ through which each spiral turns as it traverses the annulus. This can be achieved by specifying the minimum value of $u : u_{min}$, of the rectangular region in the (u,v) plane. It then follows that $\Delta\theta = \alpha\,\Delta u$ where $\Delta u = (u_{max} - u_{min})$ and u_{max} is the maximum value of u that is mapped. The quantity u_{min} is always arbitrary, but in most cases u_{max} will depend on the particular pattern of interlocking shapes in the (u,v) plane that is being mapped.

It now follows that the parameters α, a, and b in eqn. (1) are given by

$$\alpha = \Delta\theta\,/\,\Delta u\ ,$$

$$b = \ln\,(r_2\,/\,r_1)\,/\,\Delta\theta\ ,\tag{5}$$

and

$$a = r_1\,e^{-b\alpha u_{min}}\ .$$

EXAMPLES

(a) Spirals

One of the simplest patterns to plot is a series of interlocking logarithmic spirals $r = a\,e^{\pm b\theta}$ rotated in equal increments about the origin, with the spaces between them filled with different colours. To plot these we need to know which line in the (u,v) plane is mapped to the spiral $r = a\,e^{-b\theta}$. It follows from eqn. (4) that this is the straight line with gradient $m = -\alpha$, because its image under the transformation (1) is related to $r = a\,e^{b\theta}$ by a reflection across the x axis.

Fig. 2 (a) shows a pattern of straight line segments in the (u,v) plane that map to a series of 10 clockwise and 10 counter clockwise spiral segments, and Fig. 2 (b) displays the results of applying the transformation (1) to this pattern.

(b) Cubes

An example which appears three dimensional in both coordinate systems is a series of interlocking cubes as shown in Fig. 3 (a). Fig. 3 (b) is the result of applying the transformation to this pattern of cubes. Here the angular increment $\Delta\theta$ is zero and the spiral patterns arise from diagonal lines of cubes in Fig. 3 (a). An example involving cubes where $\Delta\theta = 90^\circ$ appears in Fig. 4. but the angular increment is completely lost in the apparent spirals created by diagonal lines of cubes in the (u,v) plane. The effect of clipping the pattern to a rectangular window is to create the illusion of looking down a cylindrical tube. In both Figs. 3 and 4 the transformation imparts a degree of three dimensionality to the image which is missing from the (u,v) plane patterns. Leavitt (1986) presents the results of other transformations on interlocking cubes.

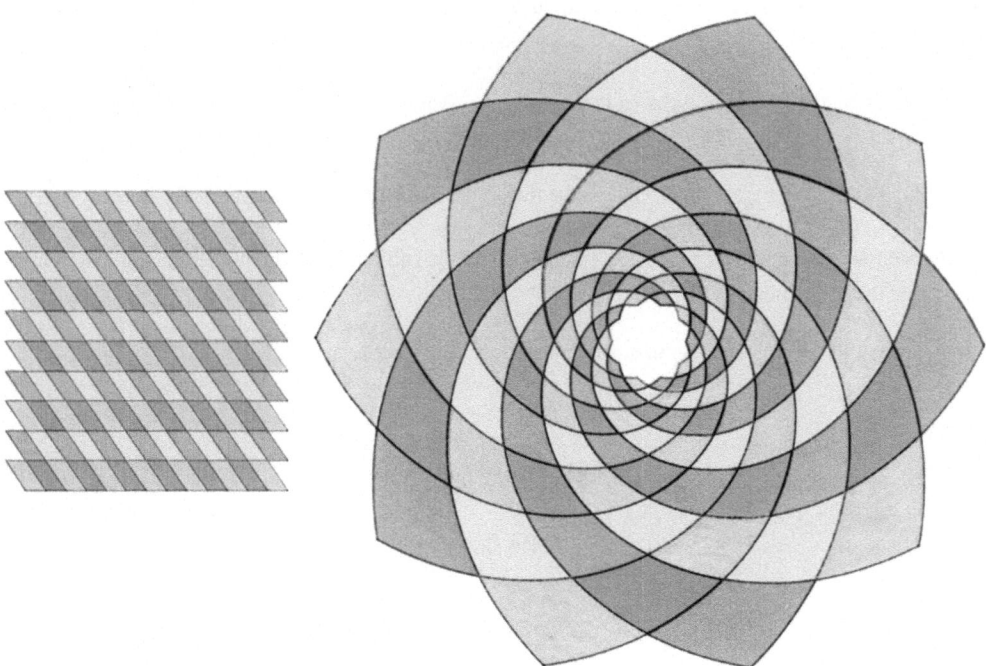

Fig. 2 (a) Pattern in the (u,v) plane formed by straight line segments. Here $u_{min} = 1.0$ and $u_{max} = 2\pi$, both of which are arbitrary. In this case the angle $\Delta\theta = 252°$ which is determined by the number of horizontal lines (14) crossed by each diagonal line.

Fig 2 (b) The image in the (x,y) plane of the pattern in Fig. 2 (a).

Fig. 3 (a) A series 26 rows of interlocking cubes with 12 cubes per row in the (u,v) plane. Here u_{max} is not arbitrary, but is determined by the number of rows of cubes (which determines their physical size in the (u,v) plane), and the number of cubes per row.

Fig 3 (b) The result of applying the transformation to the pattern in Fig. 3 (a) with the angular increment $\Delta\theta$ set to zero.

Fig. 4 Interlocking cubes plotted with $\Delta\theta = 90°$ and clipped to a rectangular boundary.

(c) Dragon patterns

The previous figures could all have been produced, with varying degrees of difficulty, without the use of the transformation because the interlocking shapes being mapped were very simple. The great utility of the transformation is that it can act as filter to any program that produces graphics in a rectangular coordinate system. This means that any series of shapes can be mapped, and Fig. 5 (a) shows a shape which is a configuration of four dragon patterns. The result of applying the mapping with $\Delta\theta = 30^\circ$ to a rectangular arrangement of these configurations appears in Fig. 5 (b).

Fig. 5 (a) A configuration of four 11th order dragon patterns joined at their heads. This configuration can be used to cover the cartesian plane.

Fig 5 (b) The result of mapping a pattern consisting of 11 rows of the configuration in Fig. 5 (a) with 2 configurations per row.

(d) Variations

There are many ways in which the transformation (1) can be varied, and here we discuss a simple technique where the spiral parameter b varies with v. We take

$$b = b_0 + \beta v \tag{6}$$

where β is a constant and b_0 is given by eqn. (5). This breaks the rotational symmetry of the transformation about the origin $(x,y) = (0,0)$, and results in patterns that have some resemblance to shells.

Under this new transformation lines u = constant in the (u,v) plane are mapped onto logarithmic spirals in the (x,y) plane instead of onto circles. If β is large enough, the image of the point $(u_{min}, 2\pi)$ will be further from the origin than the image of $(u_{max}, 0)$ and the pattern in the (x,y) plane will not overlap as v is increased past 2π. . The condition for this is

$$\beta > b_0 \, \Delta u / (2\pi u_{min}),$$

which removes the necessity to restrict v to $0 \le v \le 2\pi$. Fig. 6 shows the results of mapping a pattern of cubes in the (u,v) plane with $\beta = 0.17$.

Fig. 6 The result of applying the modified transformation (6) to 24 rows of cubes with 4 cubes per row. Here $\beta = 0.1$, $\Delta\theta = 45°$ and the maximum value of v is $5\pi/4$.

CONCLUDING REMARKS

The programs were written in Turbo Pascal running under CP/M on an Apple IIe computer, and the plots were produced on an HP 7475 pen plotter. The algorithm could easily be adapted to produce output on raster devices.

REFERENCE

Leavitt R (1986) Transformations of space and design. The Visual Computer **2** : 176 - 177.

Kevin Suffern received an M.Sc. from Cornell University in Astronomy in 1973 and a Ph.D. in Applied Mathematics from the University of Sydney in 1978. From 1979 to 1981 he worked in the School of Mathematics and Physics at Macquarie University in Sydney before joining the School of Computing Sciences at the University of Technology, Sydney, where he is currently a Senior Lecturer. In 1986 he was a Visiting Research Scientist in The Center for Interactive Computer Graphics, Rensselaer Polytechnic Institute. His main research interests are computer graphics, computer aided geometric design, and computer art.

Address : School of Computing Sciences, University of Technolgy, Sydney, PO Box 123, Broadway, NSW 2007, Australia

List of Contributors

Keyword Index

Conference Committees and Co-Sponsors

Conference Co-Chairs:
Rae A. Earnshaw (University of Leeds, UK)
Robert D. Parslow (University of Otago, NZ)
David F. Rogers (US Naval Academy, USA)

International Program Chairman:
Brian Wyvill (University of Calgary, Canada)

International Program Committee:
P. Brunet (Ecole Polytechnique of Barcelona, Spain)
R.A. Earnshaw (University of Leeds, UK)
H. Fuchs (University of North Carolina, USA)
G. Hegron (INRIA/IRISA, France)
T.L. Kunii (University of Tokyo, Japan)
R.J. Lansdown (Middlesex Polytechnic, UK)
T.H. Liebling (Ecole Polytechnique de Lausanne, Switz)
N. Magnenat-Thalmann
    (University of Geneva, Switzerland & HEC Montreal, Canada)
J.F.C. Mortelmaans (University of Leuwen, Belgium)
E. Nakamae (University of Hiroshima, Japan)
D.F. Rogers (US Naval Academy, USA)
D. Thalmann (Ecole Polytechnique de Lausanne, Switz)
G. Toussaint (McGill University, Canada)
J. Weber (University of Geneva, Switzerland)
M.J. Wozny (NSF and RPI, USA)
G. Wyvill (University of Otago, New Zealand)

Conference Secretary:
Frances J. Johnson (University of Leeds, UK)

Keynote Speaker:
Henry Fuchs (Frederico Gil Professor of Computer
    Science, University of North Carolina at Chapel Hill, USA)

Invited Speakers:
James F. Blinn (Jet Propulsion Laboratory, USA)
Tosiyasu L. Kunii (University of Tokyo, Japan)
David F. Rogers (US Naval Academy, USA)
Godfried Toussaint (McGill University, Canada)
John V. Tucker (University of Leeds, UK)
Michael J. Wozny (RPI and NSF, USA)

Co-Sponsors:
Computer Graphics Society
British Computer Society
University of Leeds
Japan Systems Company Ltd
Graphica Computer Corporation
University of Calgary

List of Technical Reviewers

Allan, Jeff (Jade Simulations International Inc, Calgary, Canada)
Brown, John (University of Calgary, Calgary, Canada)
Calvert, Tom (University of British Columbia, British Columbia, Canada)
Chengfu, Yao (University of Calgary, Calgary, Canada)
Chmilar, M. (University of Calgary, Calgary, Canada)
Cleary, John (University of Calgary, Calgary, Canada)
Coulson, M. (University of Calgary, Calgary, Canada)
Crow, Frank (Xerox Parc, Palo Alto, CA, USA)
Earnshaw, Rae (University of Leeds, Leeds, England)
England, Nick (University of North Carolina, North Carolina, USA)
Enomoto, H. (University of Tokyo, Tokyo, Japan)
Fuchs, Henry (University of North Carolina, North Carolina, USA)
Fuller, Norma (University of Saskatchewan, Saskatchewan, Canada)
Green, Mark (University of Alberta, Edmonton, Canada)
Hall, Roy (Cornell University, South Carolina, USA)
Hill, David (University of Calgary, Calgary, Canada)
Jevans, David (University of Calgary, Calgary, Canada)
Kunii, T. (University of Tokyo, Tokyo, Japan)
Kwok, Paul (University of Calgary, Calgary, Canada)
Lansdown, John (Middlesex Polytechnic, London, England)
Lodwick, Graham (University of Calgary, Calgary, Canada)
Magnenat-Thalmann, Nadia (Universite de Montreal, Montreal, Canada)
Maulsby, David (University of Calgary, Calgary, Canada)
Miller, Gavin (Apple Computer Inc., Cupertino, CA, USA)
Mortelmaans, J. (University of Leuven, Leuven, Belgium)
Nakamae, T. (Hiroshima University, Higashi-Hiroshima, Japan)
Pearce, Andrew (Alias Research Inc, Toronto, Canada)
Poicker, Tom (Simon Fraser University, British Columbia, Canada)
Pratt, Michael (Cranfield Institute of Technology, Bedford, England)
Rogers, David (United States Naval Academy, Annapolis, MD, USA)
Rokne, Jon (University of Calgary, Calgary, Canada)

Sherson, Isaac (Princeton University, Princeton, NJ, USA)
Shoemake, Ken (Xerox Parc, CA, USA)
Thalmann, D. (Universite de Montreal, Montreal, Canada)
Toussaint, G. (McGill University, Montreal, Canada)
Weber, Jacques (University of Geneva, Geneva, Switzerland)
Witten, Ian (University of Calgary, Calgary, Canada)
Wozny, Michael (Rensselaer Polytechnic Institute, Troy, NY, USA)
Wyvill, Brian (University of Calgary, Calgary, Canada)
Wyvill, Geoff (University of Otago, Dunedin, New Zealand)